THE WILEY BLACKWELL COMPANION TO SOCIAL MOVEMENTS

WILEY BLACKWELL COMPANIONS TO SOCIOLOGY

The *Wiley Blackwell Companions to Sociology* provide introductions to emerging topics and theoretical orientations in sociology as well as presenting the scope and quality of the discipline as it is currently configured. Essays in the Companions tackle broad themes or central puzzles within the field and are authored by key scholars who have spent considerable time in research and reflection on the questions and controversies that have activated interest in their area. This authoritative series will interest those studying sociology at advanced undergraduate or graduate level as well as scholars in the social sciences and informed readers in applied disciplines.

THE WILEY BLACKWELL COMPANION TO

Social Movements

SECOND EDITION

EDITED BY

DAVID A. SNOW, SARAH A. SOULE, HANSPETER KRIESI, AND HOLLY J. McCAMMON

WILEY Blackwell

Registered Office(s)
John Wiley & Sons, Inc., 111 River Street, Hoboken, NJ 07030, USA
John Wiley & Sons Ltd, The Atrium, Southern Gate, Chichester, West Sussex, PO19 8SQ, UK

Editorial Office
9600 Garsington Road, Oxford, OX4 2DQ, UK

For details of our global editorial offices, customer services, and more information about Wiley products visit us at www.wiley.com.

Library of Congress Cataloging-in-Publication Data

Names: Snow, David A., editor. | Soule, Sarah Anne, 1967– editor. | Kriesi, Hanspeter, editor. | McCammon, Holly J., editor.
Title: The Wiley Blackwell companion to social movements : second edition / edited by David A. Snow, Sarah A. Soule, Hanspeter Kriesi, and Holly J. McCammon.
Other titles: Blackwell companion to social movements
Description: Second Edition. | Hoboken : Wiley, [2019] | Series: Wiley Blackwell companions to sociology | Revised edition of | Includes bibliographical references and index.
Identifiers: LCCN 2018008676 (print) | LCCN 2018012661 (ebook) | ISBN 9781119168607 (pdf) | ISBN 9781119168591 (epub) | ISBN 9781119168553 (cloth)
Subjects: LCSH: Social movements.
Classification: LCC HM881 (ebook) | LCC HM881 .B53 2018 (print) | DDC 303.48/4–dc23
LC record available at https://lccn.loc.gov/2018008676

Cover Design: Wiley
Cover Image: © Shawn Goldberg / Alamy Stock Photo

Set in 10/12.5pt Sabon by SPi Global, Pondicherry, India
Printed in Singapore by C.O.S. Printers Pte Ltd

10 9 8 7 6 5 4 3 2 1

Contents

Notes on Contributors

Paul D. Almeida is the Chair of Sociology at the University of California, Merced. His articles have appeared in the *American Journal of Sociology*, *Social Forces*, *Social Problems*, *Mobilization*, and other scholarly outlets. Almeida's books include: *Mobilizing Democracy: Globalization and Citizen Protest* (Johns Hopkins University Press, 2014); *Waves of Protest: Popular Struggle in El Salvador, 1925–2005* (University of Minnesota Press, 2008); *Handbook of Social Movements across Latin America* (co-edited with Allen Cordero Ulate, Springer, 2016); and *Latin American Social Movements: Globalization, Democratization and Transnational Networks* (co-edited with Hank Johnston, Rowman & Littlefield, 2006). In 2015, he received the Distinguished Scholarship Award from the Pacific Sociological Association. He recently had a Fulbright Fellowship for research on the role of NGOs in local-level social outcomes in Central America.

Edwin Amenta is a Professor of Sociology and Political Science at the University of California, Irvine. He is the author of *Bold Relief: Institutional Politics and the Origins of Modern American Social Policy* (Princeton University Press, 2000), *When Movements Matter: The Townsend Plan and the Rise of Social Security* (Princeton University Press, 2008), *Professor Baseball* (University of Chicago Press, 2008), and is the co-editor of the *Wiley-Blackwell Companion to Political Sociology* (Wiley-Blackwell, 2014). He is working with Neal Caren on book about US movements and the news media tentatively entitled *The First Draft of Movement History*.

Massimiliano Andretta is Associate Professor at the University of Pisa, Italy. Among his recent publications are *Late Neoliberalism and its Discontents in the Economic Crisis* (with Donatella della Porta et al., Palgrave, 2016); "Between Resistance and Resilience, *Partecipazione & Conflitto* (8(2), 2015, with Riccardo Guidi); and "Il Movimento 5 Stelle in Toscana: un movimento post-subculturale?" in Roberto Biorcio (ed.), *Gli attivisti del Movimento a 5 Stelle: dal web al territorio* (Franco Angeli, 2015).

Kenneth T. Andrews is Professor of Sociology at the University of North Carolina at Chapel Hill. His work examines the dynamics of social and political change including the influence of protest, civic associations, and social movements. Current projects examine civil rights campaigns to desegregate public facilities, the adoption of local prohibition laws, and the organization and leadership of contemporary environmental movements.

Colin J. Beck is Associate Professor of Sociology at Pomona College, CA. He is the author of *Radicals, Revolutionaries, and Terrorists* (Polity, 2015) and his work on terrorism and radical social movements has appeared in *Social Forces*, *Mobilization*, *Sociological Forum*, and *Sociology Compass*. His award-winning work on revolutionary waves has been published in *Theory and Society* and *Social Science History*. His current project is a meta-analysis of theories and methods in the comparative study of revolution.

Kraig Beyerlein is an Associate Professor in the Department of Sociology at the University of Notre Dame, IN. He studies social movements, civic engagement, religion, and immigration. Among his current research projects is the National Study of Protest Events (NSPE). Kraig's published work has appeared in the *American Sociological Review*, *Journal for the Scientific Study of Religion*, *Mobilization*, *Sociological Methods and Research*, *Social Problems*, *Social Forces*, *Social Science Research*, and *Sociology of Religion*.

Clifford Bob is Professor of Political Science and Raymond J. Kelley Endowed Chair in International Relations at Duquesne University, Pittsburgh, PA. His books include *The Global Right Wing and the Clash of World Politics* (Cambridge University Press, 2012) and *The Marketing of Rebellion: Insurgents, Media, and International Activism* (Cambridge University Press, 2005).

Steven A. Boutcher is Assistant Professor of Sociology and Public Policy at the University of Massachusetts, Amherst. His work focuses on law and social movements, cause lawyers, access to justice, and the legal profession. He has published on these topics in the *American Sociological Review*, *Mobilization*, *Law & Social Inquiry*, *Research in Social Movements, Conflict & Change*, and *Studies in Law, Politics & Society*.

Megan E. Brooker is a PhD candidate in Sociology at the University of California, Irvine. Her research interests include social movements and political sociology. Her dissertation examines how presidential elections offer institutionalized political opportunities through which social movements gain access to political parties and candidates and their ideas become incorporated into the political agenda.

Neal Caren in an Associate Professor of Sociology at the University of North Carolina, Chapel Hill. His research interests center on the quantitative analysis of protest and social movements. His work has been published in the *American Sociological Review*, *Social Forces*, *Social Problems*, and the *Annual Review of Sociology*. He is also the editor of the social movements journal, *Mobilization*.

Xi Chen is an Associate Professor of Political Science at the Chinese University of Hong Kong. He is the author of *Social Protest and Contentious Authoritarianism in*

China (Cambridge University Press, 2012), and is currently completing another book, *Disempowering Contention: Restructuring, Resistance, and State Domination in China*. He has also published articles in journals such as *Comparative Politics, Comparative Political Studies, Politics and Society*, the *China Quarterly*, and the *Journal of Democracy*.

Catherine Corrigall-Brown is an Associate Professor at the University of British Columbia in Vancouver, Canada. Her research focuses on social movement participation, the mass media, and collective identity. She is the author of *Patterns of Protest* (Stanford University Press, 2011) and articles in journals such as *Social Forces, Mobilization, Sociological Perspectives*, and the *International Journal of Comparative Sociology*.

Alison Dahl Crossley is Associate Director of the Clayman Institute for Gender Research at Stanford University, CA. Her book, *Finding Feminism: Millennial Activists and the Unfinished Gender Revolution*, was recently published by NYU Press. Crossley's research and publications focus on gender, social movements, and feminism. She received her PhD in Sociology with an emphasis in Feminist Studies from the University of California, Santa Barbara.

Nick Crossley is Professor of Sociology at the University of Manchester, UK. He has published widely on social movements. His most recent books are: *Networks of Sound, Style and Subversion: The Punk and Post-Punk Worlds of Manchester, London, Liverpool and Sheffield, 1975–1980* (Manchester University Press, 2015) and *Social Networks and Social Movements* (co-edited with John Krinsky, Routledge, 2015).

David Cunningham is Professor of Sociology at Washington University in St. Louis. His current research focuses on the causes, sequencing, and legacy of racial conflict. His latest book, *Klansville, U.S.A.: The Rise and Fall of the Civil Rights-Era's Largest KKK*, was published by Oxford University Press in 2013 and served as the basis for a PBS *American Experience* documentary of the same name.

Donatella della Porta is Professor of Political Science and Dean of the Institute for Humanities and the Social Sciences at the Scuola Normale Superiore in Florence, Italy, where she directs the Centre on Social Movement Studies (Cosmos). Among her recent publications are: *Social Movements in Times of Austerity* (Polity, 2014); *Methodological Practices in Social Movement Research* (Oxford University Press, 2014); *Clandestine Political Violence* (Cambridge University Press, 2013); *Wiley-Blackwell Encyclopedia on Social and Political Movements* (edited with David A. Snow, Bert Klandermans, and Doug McAdam, Wiley-Blackwell, 2013).

Chares Demetriou, is a Senior Lecturer in the Department of Sociology at Lund University, Sweden. He is a political and historical sociologist focusing on social movement radicalization, legitimization of political violence, and processual sociology. He co-authored *Dynamics of Radicalization: A Relational and Comparative Perspective* (with Eitan Alimi and Lorenzo Bosi, Oxford University Press, 2015) and co-edited *Dynamics of Political Violence: A Process-Oriented Perspective on*

Radicalization and the Escalation of Political Conflict (with Lorenzo Bosi and Stephan Malthaner, Routledge, 2014).

Mario Diani is Professor of Sociology at the University of Trento, Italy. He has also taught at Strathclyde University in Glasgow and Universitat Pompeu Fabra in Barcelona. He has published extensively on social movements and social networks (with Donatella della Porta, *Social Movements*, Blackwell, 1999/2006); *Social Movements and Networks* (co-edited with Doug McAdam, Oxford University Press, 2003); *The Cement of Civil Society* (Cambridge University Press, 2015); and *The Oxford Handbook of Social Movements* (co-edited with Donatella della Porta, Oxford University Press, 2015).

Brian Doherty is Professor of Political Sociology and Head of the School of Politics, Philosophy, International Relations at Keele University, UK. His primary research interest is in the relationship between radical ideas and actions, particularly in environmental movements. His published work includes *Ideas and Actions in the Green Movement* (Routledge, 2002) and *Environmentalism, Resistance and Solidarity: The Politics of Friends of the Earth International* (Palgrave, 2013) and journal articles in *Environmental Politics*, *Political Studies*, *Mobilization*, *Comparative Political Studies*, *Social Movement Studies* and the *European Journal of Political Research*.

Jennifer Earl is Professor of Sociology and (by courtesy) Government and Public Policy at the University of Arizona. Her research focuses on social movements, information technologies, and the sociology of law, with research emphases on Internet activism, social movement repression, and legal change. She is the recipient of a National Science Foundation CAREER Award for research from 2006–2011 on Web activism and is a member of the MacArthur Research Network on Youth and Participatory Politics.

Bob Edwards is Professor and Chair of the Department of Sociology at East Carolina University in Greenville, NC. An enduring research and teaching interest in the social organization of inequalities integrates his published work on social movement organizations and protest, civil society and social capital, and environmental justice. Edwards has published over 50 articles or chapters including in *American Sociological Review*, *Annual Review of Sociology*, *Social Forces*, *Social Problems*, and *Mobilization*.

Barry Eidlin is an Assistant Professor of Sociology at McGill University, Montreal, Canada. He is a comparative historical sociologist studying class, politics, social movements, and institutional change. His book, *Labor and the Class Idea in the United States and Canada* (Cambridge University Press, forthcoming) explains diverging trajectories of working-class organizational power in the United States and Canada. Other research has been published in the *American Sociological Review*, *Politics & Society*, *Sociology Compass*, and *Labor History*.

Cristina Flesher Fominaya is Reader in Social Politics and Media, Department of Politics, History, and International Relations, Loughborough University, Loughborough, UK.

She earned her PhD in Sociology, at the University of California, Berkeley. A founder of the open-access activist/academic *Interface Journal* and co-editor of *Social Movement Studies Journal*, she has published widely on collective identity and social movements, autonomous movements, digital media, and European and Global social movements. Her most recent book is *Social Movements and Globalization: How Protests, Occupations and Uprisings are Changing the World* (Palgrave, 2014).

Robert Futrell is Professor of Sociology and Chair in the University of Nevada, Las Vegas. His research focuses on social movements and social change, environmental sustainability, and urban life. He co-authored *American Swastika: Inside the White Power Movement's Hidden Spaces of Hate* (with Pete Simi, Rowman & Littlefield, 2015).

Marshall Ganz is a Senior Lecturer in Public Policy at the Harvard Kennedy School. He worked on staff of the United Farm Workers for 16 years before becoming a trainer and organizer for political campaigns, unions, and nonprofits. He has published in the *American Journal of Sociology, American Political Science Review*, and elsewhere. His book, *Why David Sometimes Wins: Leadership, Organization, and Strategy in the California Farm Worker Movement* (Oxford University Press, 2010) earned the Michael J. Harrington Book Award.

Amin Ghaziani is an Associate Professor of Sociology at the University of British Columbia, Canada, where he is also a Canada Research Chair in Sexuality and Urban Studies. He is co-editor of *A Decade of HAART* (with José M. Zuniga, Alan Whiteside, and John G. Bartlett, Oxford University Press, 2008), and is the author of three books: *The Dividends of Dissent* (University of Chicago Press, 2008), *There Goes the Gayborhood?* (Princeton University Press, 2015), and *Sex Cultures* (Polity, 2017). His work has appeared in the *American Sociological Review, Annual Review of Sociology, Contexts, International Journal of Urban and Regional Research, Social Problems*, and *Theory and Society*.

Marco Giugni is a Professor in the Department of Political Science and International Relations and Director of the Institute of Citizenship Studies (InCite) at the University of Geneva, Switzerland. His research interests include social movements and collective action, immigration and ethnic relations, unemployment, and social exclusion.

Jack A. Goldstone is the Hazel Professor of Public Policy and Eminent Scholar at the Schar School of Policy and Government, George Mason University, VA. He is the author of *Revolution and Rebellion in the Early Modern World* (25th anniversary edition, Routledge 2016), and *Revolutions: A Very Short Introduction* (Oxford University Press, 2014).

Maria T. Grasso is a Lecturer in Politics and Quantitative Methods in the Department of Politics, University of Sheffield, UK. Her main research interests are in political sociology, social change, political participation, and social movements.

Graeme Hayes is a Reader in Political Sociology at Aston University, Birmingham, UK, co-editor of *Environmental Politics*, and Consulting Editor for *Social Movement*

Studies. His work on social movement activism includes *Environmental Politics and the State in France* (Palgrave, 2002), and *Occupy! A Global Movement. Hope, Tactics and Challenges* (Routledge, 2014), as well as articles in journals including *Comparative Political Studies, Environmental Politics, European Journal of Political Research, Law and Policy, Modern & Contemporary France*, and *Sociology*. He is co-editor of four collections, most recently *Resisting Austerity: Collective Action in Europe in the Wake of the Global* (Routledge, 2018).

Heather McKee Hurwitz is the Post-Doctoral Fellow in the Department of Sociology and the Athena Center for Leadership Studies at Barnard College, Columbia University, New York. She studies gender, social movements, and globalization, using qualitative and quantitative methods, with specialization in urban ethnography. Her research focuses on the Occupy Wall Street Movement, global feminisms, and activism using new social media. She has published chapters and articles on these topics in the journals *Information Communication and Society, Sociology Compass*, and *Financial Crisis*.

Swen Hutter is a postdoctoral research fellow at the European University Institute in Florence, Italy. He holds a PhD in political science from the University of Munich. His research interests involve social movements, party competition, and cleavage structures. Hutter is the author of *Protesting Culture and Economics in Western Europe* (University of Minnesota Press, 2014) and co-editor of *Politicising Europe* (Cambridge University Press, 2016).

James M. Jasper has written a number of books and articles on culture and protest, among them *The Art of Moral Protest* (University of Chicago Press, 1997), *Protest: A Cultural Introduction to Social Movements* (Polity, 2014), *The Animal Rights Crusade* (Free Press, 1992), and "The Emotions of Protest," *Sociological Forum*.

Hank Johnston is Professor of Sociology and Hansen Chair of Peace Studies at San Diego State University. His research broadly focuses on nonviolent protests in different state systems and the cultural analysis of movement processes. He is founding editor of *Mobilization: An International Quarterly*, the leading research journal on protest and social movements, and edits the Mobilization-Routledge Series on Protest and Social Movements. His recent books are *What Is a Social Movement?* (Polity, 2014), *States and Social Movements* (Polity, 2012), and *Culture, Social Movements, and Protest* (Ashgate, 2009).

Jasmine Kerrissey is an Assistant Professor of Sociology at the University of Massachusetts, Amherst, as well as a core faculty member of the UMass Labor Center. She holds a PhD in sociology from the University of California, Irvine. Kerrissey's research focuses on how workers' movements matter. Her work on income inequality, political participation, and safety has recently appeared in the *American Sociological Review* and *Social Forces*.

Pauline Ketelaars is a postdoctoral researcher of the Fonds Wetenschappelijk Onderzoek (FWO), Brussels. She is a member of the M²P (Media, Movements &

Politics) research group in the Department of Political Science of the University of Antwerp. Her main research interests are political communication and street protests.

Brayden G. King is Professor of Management and Organizations and is also affiliated with the Department of Sociology at Kellogg School of Management, Northwestern University. His research focuses on how social movement activists influence corporate social responsibility, organizational change, and legislative policy-making. He also studies the ways in which the reputations and identities of businesses and social movement organizations emerge and transform in response to their institutional environments. More recently, his research has begun to examine social media and its influence on individual and organizational reputations.

Bert Klandermans is Professor in Applied Social Psychology at the Vrije Universiteit, Amsterdam, the Netherlands. He has published extensively on the social psychology of protest. He is the author of the now classic *Social Psychology of Protest* (Blackwell, 1997). He is co-editor and author of *The Future of Social Movement Research. Dynamics, Mechanisms, and Processes* (University of Minnesota Press, 2013) and *Social Movements in Times of Democratic Transition* (Temple University Press, 2015). In 2014, he received the John D. McCarthy Award from Notre Dame University.

Kelsy Kretschmer is an Assistant Professor of Sociology at Oregon State University, where she researches and teaches in social movements, gender, and organizations. She is currently writing a book examining the factionalism, schism, and spinoff processes in the National Organization for Women and the American feminist movement over time. Her work has appeared in *Mobilization: An International Quarterly*, *Sociological Forum*, *Sociological Perspectives*, *Contexts*, and the *American Behavioral Scientist*.

Hanspeter Kriesi holds the Stein Rokkan Chair in Comparative Politics at the European University Institute in Florence, Italy. Previously, he has taught at the universities of Amsterdam, Geneva, and Zurich. He is the prinicipal investigator of the ERC Advanced Grant, Political Conflict in the Shadow of the Great Recession. His most recent co-edited books include *Populism in the Shadow of the Great Recession* (ECPR Press, 2015) and *How Europeans View and Evaluate Democracy* (Oxford University Press, 2016).

Jasmine Lorenzini is a postdoctoral research fellow at the European University Institute in Florence, Italy. She holds a PhD in political science from the University of Geneva. Her thesis analyzes how the lived experience of unemployment contributes to political participation, focusing on mechanisms related to social inclusion and personal well-being. She is currently working on protest in times of crisis, questioning how economic and political grievances, as well as specific events, trigger protest.

Andrew W. Martin is Professor of Sociology at The Ohio State University. His research focuses on the organizational dynamics of social protest. His current work examines how movement actors target corporations. He is also investigating the role of social media in political campaigns. His work appears in the *American Sociological Review*, *Administrative Science Quarterly*, and the *American Journal of Sociology*.

Dane R. Mataic is a doctoral candidate in the Department of Sociology at the Pennsylvania State University. His research explores the intersection of social organizations, religion, and collective action. His two primary streams of research attempt to understand the mobilizing abilities of religious communities as well as the occurrence of religious conflict and religious freedoms.

Lilian Mathieu is a sociologist, Research Director at the Centre national de la recherche scientifique (CNRS) and works at the Centre Max Weber in the École normale supérieure in Lyon, France. His most recent research on social movements includes studies of moral crusades against prostitution and of the biographical consequences of activism among French people who participated in the May 68 revolt.

Doug McAdam is Ray Lyman Wilbur Professor of Sociology at Stanford University and the former Director of the Center for Advanced Study in the Behavioral Sciences. He is the author or co-author of 18 books and some 90 articles in the area of political sociology, with a special emphasis on race in the US, American politics, and the study of social movements. Among his best known works are *Political Process and the Development of Black Insurgency, 1930–1970* (University of Chicago Press, 1999), *Freedom Summer* (Oxford University Press, 1988), which was awarded the 1990 C. Wright Mills Award, and *Dynamics of Contention* (with Sid Tarrow and Charles Tilly, Cambridge University Press, 2001). He is also the co-author of two recent books, *Putting Social Movements in Their Place* (with Hilary Boudet, Cambridge University Press, 2012) and *Divided America: Racial Politics and Social Movements in Post-war America* (with Karina Kloos, Oxford University Press, 2014). He was elected to membership in the American Academy of Arts and Sciences in 2003.

Holly J. McCammon is Cornelius Vanderbilt Professor of Sociology at Vanderbilt University, TN. She studies women's activism and has published articles in the *American Journal of Sociology*, *American Sociological Review*, *Gender & Society*, and *Social Forces*. Her 2012 book, *The U.S. Women's Jury Movement and Strategic Adaptation: A More Just Verdict*, was published by Cambridge University Press. She is past editor of the *American Sociological Review* and is currently editing *100 Years of the Nineteenth Amendment: An Appraisal of Women's Political Activism*.

John D. McCarthy is Distinguished Professor of Sociology at Penn State University. During the last half decade he has worked with many graduate students and faculty colleagues in crafting what has become known as the "Resource Mobilization" approach to account for the emergence and trajectory of social movements, focusing, especially, on social movement organizations. His subsequent research includes extensive attention to protest events in the US during the later years of the twentieth century, explaining media bias in the reporting of those events, and trends in the policing of those protest events. He is currently tracking, with Patrick Rafail, the local activities of the grass roots "Tea Party" movement in the US.

Elizabeth McKenna is a doctoral candidate in sociology at the University of California, Berkeley. She is the co-author of *Groundbreakers: How Obama's 2.2 Million Volunteers Transformed Campaigning in America* (with Hahrie Han, Oxford University Press, 2015). She studies social movements and political organizing in the United States and Brazil.

Rory McVeigh is Professor of Sociology at the University of Notre Dame, IN, Director of the Center for the Study of Social Movements, and co-editor of *American Sociological Review*. His work examines both causes and consequences of conflict and inequality. He is the author of *The Rise of the Ku Klux Klan: Right-Wing Movements and National Politics* (University of Minnesota Press, 2009).

David S. Meyer is Professor of Sociology, Political Science, and Planning and Public Policy at the University of California, Irvine. He has published numerous articles and is the author or editor of eight books, most recently, the second edition of *The Politics of Protest: Social Movements in America* (Oxford University Press, 2014).

Gian-Andrea Monsch is a postdoctoral researcher at FORS, the Swiss Centre of Expertise in the Social Sciences based at the University of Lausanne, Switzerland. His research interests include contentious politics, activism, and commitment in various civic and political areas. His PhD focused on the importance of meanings in the sustainment of protest participation. He is particularly interested in the links between meanings, political participation, and processes of (de-)democratization. He is currently working, with Florence Passy, on a book, *Contentious Minds*, that shows how the activist's mind and social interactions enable commitment in contentious politics, volunteering action, and unionism to be sustained.

Dana M. Moss is an Assistant Professor of Sociology at the University of Pittsburgh, specializing in the study of collective action, authoritarian regimes, repression, diaspora movements, transnationalism, and the Middle Eastern region. Dana's work appears in the *American Sociological Review* (with David A. Snow), *Social Problems, Mobilization: An International Journal*, the *Journal of Immigrant and Refugee Studies*, and the *Blackwell Encyclopedia of Social and Political Movements*.

Peter B. Owens was recently a Postdoctoral Research Associate in the Sociology Department at Washington University in St. Louis. His research focuses on the role of social movements and other contentious efforts in creating and enforcing group inequality, with specific interests in vigilantism and collective violence.

Florence Passy is Associate Professor of Political Science at the University of Lausanne, Switzerland. Her area of research includes contentious politics, activism, altruism, and citizenship. She is particularly interested in the examination of the influence of social networks on various processes of individual commitment. She is the author of *L'action altruiste* (Librarie Droz, 1998); co-author of *Contested Citizenship. Immigration and Cultural Diversity in Europe* (with Ruud Koopmans et al., University of Minnesota Press, 2006); and co-editor of *Political Altruism?*

Solidarity Movements in International Perspective (with Marco Giugni, published by Rowman and Littlefield, 2001), *Dialogues on Migration Policy* (with Marco Giugni, Lexington Books, 2006).

Francesca Polletta is Professor of Sociology at the University of California, Irvine. She studies the culture dimensions of politics, protest, and work, and is the author of *Freedom Is an Endless Meeting: Democracy in American Social Movements* (University of Chicago Press, 2002) and *It Was Like a Fever: Storytelling in Protest and Politics* (University of Chicago Press, 2006).

Daniel P. Ritter is Assistant Professor of Sociology at Stockholm University, Sweden, and a visiting fellow at the Centre for International Studies at the London School of Economics. He is the author of *The Iron Cage of Liberalism: International Politics and Unarmed Revolutions in the Middle East and North Africa* (Oxford University Press, 2015).

Conny Roggeband is a Lecturer in the Department of Political Science of the University of Amsterdam, the Netherlands. Her research interests include gender mainstreaming and equality policies, gender-based violence, social movements and transnational feminist networking. Her most recent books are *The Gender Politics of Domestic Violence: Feminists Engaging the State in Central and Eastern Europe* (co-authored with Andrea Krizsan, Routledge, 2017), and *The Handbook of Social Movements Across Disciplines* (co-edited with Bert Klandermans, Springer, 2017).

Deana A. Rohlinger is a Professor of Sociology at Florida State University, and researches mass media, political participation, and politics in America. She is the author of *Abortion Politics, Mass Media, and Social Movements in America* (Cambridge University Press, 2015), as well as dozens of research articles. Her new book, *New Media and Society*, will be published in 2019 by New York University Press.

Fabio Rojas is Professor of Sociology at Indiana University, Bloomington. He works in the fields of organizational behavior, political sociology, higher education, and health care. He is the author of *From Black Power to Black Studies: How a Radical Social Movement Became an Academic Discipline* (Johns Hopkins University Press, 2007) and *Theory for the Working Sociologist* (Columbia University Press, 2017). Along with Michael T. Heaney, he is the co-author of *Party in the Street: The Antiwar Movement and the Democratic Party after 9/11* (Cambridge University Press, 2015).

Clare Saunders is Professor of Politics in the Environment and Sustainability Institute, University of Exeter, UK. Her recent work is on political participation in comparative perspective, especially protest. She has published in a wide range of journals including *British Journal of Sociology*, *Mobilization* and *Political Research Quarterly*. Her most recent book was *Environmental Networks and Social Movement Theory* (Bloomsbury Academic, 2013).

Kurt Schock is Associate Professor of Sociology and Director of the International Institute for Peace, at Rutgers University, NJ. He is the editor of *Civil Resistance:*

Comparative Perspectives on Nonviolent Struggle (University of Minnesota Press, 2015) and author of *Civil Resistance Today* (Polity, 2015) and *Unarmed Insurrections: People Power Movements in Nondemocracies* (University of Minnesota Press, 2005). *Unarmed Insurrections* was awarded Best Book of the Year by the Comparative Democratization section of the American Political Science Association.

Eric W. Schoon is Assistant Professor of Sociology at The Ohio State University. His research examines the roles of culture and institutions in contentious politics. Central to his research agenda is the study of legitimacy, including how it is defined, how it is invoked, and its variable effects. His interest in classification and boundary dynamics has also informed his work in substantive areas, including social movements, crime, and organizational processes. His recent published work has appeared in journals, including *Social Forces*, *Social Problems*, *International Studies Quarterly*, and *Social Networks*.

Pete Simi is Associate Professor in the Department of Sociology and Director of the Earl Babbie Research Center at Chapman University, California. His research interests include political extremism and violence, developmental and life course criminology, and ethnographic methods.

Jackie Smith is Professor of Sociology at the University of Pittsburgh and editor of the *Journal of World-Systems Research*. Her books include *Social Movements and World-System Transformation* (co-edited with Michael Goodhart, Patrick Manning, and John Markoff, Routledge, 2017) and *Social Movements in the World-System: The Politics of Crisis and Transformation* (with Dawn Wiest, Russell Sage, 2012). She coordinates the Human Rights City Alliance in Pittsburgh and is on the National Human Rights Cities Network steering committee.

David A. Snow is Distinguished Professor of Sociology at the University of California, Irvine. He has authored numerous articles on social movements, religious conversion, framing processes, identity, homelessness, and qualitative field methods in a range of sociological and social science journals, and has co-authored or co-edited a number of books, including *Shakubuku: A Study of the Nichiren Shoshu Buddhist Movement in America, 1960–1975* (Garland, 1993); *The Blackwell Companion to Social Movements* (with Sarah A. Soule and Hanspeter Kriesi, Blackwell, 2014), *Readings on Social Movements* (with Doug McAdam, Oxford University Press, 2010), *A Primer on Social Movements* (with Sarah A. Soule, W.W. Norton, 2010), and the *Wiley-Blackwell Encyclopedia of Social and Political Movements* (with Donatella della Porta, Bert Klandermans, and Doug McAdam, Wiley-Blackwell, 2013).

Sarah A. Soule is the Morgridge Professor of Organizational Behavior at the Graduate School of Business, Stanford University. She studies diffusion processes in social movements, and how movements impact both states and firms. Her recent work has been published in the *American Journal of Sociology*, *American Sociological Review*, *Administrative Science Quarterly*, and *Mobilization*. Her book, *Contention and Corporate Social Responsibility*, was published by Cambridge University Press in 2009.

Erika Summers-Effler is an Associate Professor of Sociology at the University of Notre Dame, IN. Her work focuses on the micro dynamics of persistence and social change. She has published in the areas of social theory, the self, cognitive brain science, philosophy of social science, social movements, religion, classical theory, culture, small groups, and gender in a variety outlets, including: *Sociological Theory*, *Theory and Society*, *Contemporary Ethnography*, and *Philosophy of the Social Sciences*. Her book, *Laughing Saints and Righteous Heroes* (University of Chicago Press, 2010), contributes to the above literatures; additionally, this book develops methods for investigating the rise, transformation, decay, collapse, and the eventual reemergence of social organization.

Anna E. Tan is recent PhD recipient in sociology from the University of California, Irvine. Her research interests include political violence and social movements, with particular emphasis on radicalization and identity processes.

Sidney Tarrow is the Emeritus Maxwell M. Upson Professor of Government at Cornell University. His first book was *Peasant Communism in Southern Italy* (Yale University Press, 1967). In the 1980s, he turned to a reconstruction of the Italian protest cycle of the late 1960s and early 1970s, in *Democracy and Disorder* (Oxford University Press, 1989). His most recent books are *Power in Movement* (third edition, Cambridge University Press, 2011), *Strangers at the Gates* (Cambridge University Press, 2012), *The Language of Contention* (Cambridge University Press, 2013), and *War, States, and Contention* (Cornell University Press, 2015), and a revision of his text with the late Charles Tilly *Contentious Politics* (Oxford University Press, 2015). A Fellow of the American Academy of Arts and Sciences, Tarrow has served as Program co-Chair of the American Political Science Association Annual Convention and as President of the APSA Section on Comparative Politics.

Verta Taylor is Professor of Sociology at the University of California, Santa Barbara. Her research focuses on social movements, gender, and sexuality, and her published work focuses on women's and gay and lesbian movements. In 2008, she received the McCarthy Award for her lifetime contributions to the study of social movements and the John Gagnon Award for her scholarship on sexuality, and, in 2010, she was recipient of the American Sociological Association's Jessie Bernard prize for her research on gender.

Kiyoteru Tsutsui is Associate Professor and Associate Chair of Sociology, Director of the Donia Human Rights Center, and Director of the Center for Japanese Studies at the University of Michigan. His mixed-methods research on the interaction between global human rights and local politics has appeared in *American Journal of Sociology*, *American Sociological Review*, and other journals, and his recent book is *Corporate Social Responsibility in a Globalizing World* (co-edited with Alwyn Lim, Cambridge University Press, 2015).

Nella Van Dyke is Professor of Sociology at the University of California, Merced. Her research focuses on social movements and hate crime, with an emphasis on how characteristics of the social context influence levels of collective action. Her work has been published in leading journals including *Social Forces*, *Social Problems*, and the *American Sociological Review*. Her current research includes a study of the effect of sexual violence awareness campaigns on public opinion.

Justin Van Ness is a PhD candidate at the University of Notre Dame, IN. His areas of specialization include culture, collective behavior and social movements, microsociology, social control, and religion. Using data from in-depth ethnographic observation with an activist religious movement, his dissertation integrates cognitive science with micro-interactionist theories to emphasize how social, cultural, and material dynamics of situations influence meaning-making and information transmission. His work has appeared in venues such as *Sociological Theory*, *Contemporary Ethnography*, and *Classical Sociology*.

Jacquelien Van Stekelenburg holds a Chair on Social Change and Conflict at VU-University-Amsterdam, the Netherlands. She is Teaching Portfolio holder of the Faculty of Social Sciences and vice-dean. Her research interests are in the area of protest participation. She co-authored (with Bert Klandermans and Jojanneke van der Toorn) "Embeddedness and Grievances: Collective Action Participation Among Immigrants" (*American Sociological Review*, 2008). She co-edited *The Future of Social Movement Research: Dynamics, Mechanisms and Processes* (with Conny Roggeband and Bert Klandermans, University of Minnesota Press, 2013).

Rens Vliegenthart is Professor of Media and Society in the Department of Communication Science and at the Amsterdam School of Communication Research (ASCoR), University of Amsterdam (UvA), the Netherlands. He completed his dissertation in 2007 at the Vrije Universiteit Amsterdam. He was a Visiting Fulbright scholar at the University of California, Irvine, and a Visiting Associate Professor at the University of Southern Denmark. His work focuses on the interactions between political actors, including social movements, and mass media, and media effects on public opinion. A project on the causes, content and consequences of economic crisis coverage was recently funded by the Dutch science foundation NWO (VIDI grant). His recent work has appeared in journals such as *Social Forces*, *European Journal of Political Research*, and *Journal of Communication*.

Stefaan Walgrave is Professor of Political Science at the University of Antwerp, Belgium. He is the Head of the Media, Movements and Politics Research Group at Antwerp (www.m2p.be). Walgrave's research deals with elections, individual elites, media and politics, and protest and protesters. With regard to the latter domain, and mainly focusing on individual protest participants, his work has been published widely in a variety of journals such as *American Sociological Review*, *American Journal of Sociology*, *Social Forces*, and *Mobilization*. Together with Bert Klandermans and Jacquelien Van Stekelenburg, Walgrave is leading the CCC consortium that comperatively surveys protest participants.

Edward T. Walker is Associate Professor and Vice Chair in the Department of Sociology at UCLA. He is author of *Grassroots for Hire* (Cambridge University Press, 2014). He is also co-editor of *Democratizing Inequalities* (with Caroline Lee and Michael McQuarrie, NYU Press, 2015). His research has appeared in the *American Sociological Review*, *American Journal of Sociology*, *Social Problems*, and other journals. His current research investigates contentious politics and industry countermobilization around hydraulic fracturing.

Yang Zhang is Assistant Professor in the School of International Service at American University, Washington DC. His research interests include historical sociology, political sociology, contentious politics, and political networks. Employing a relational and ecological perspective, Zhang's book project examines the emergence and development of large-scale religious and ethnic rebellions in the Qing Empire of China during the mid-nineteenth century. He also studies environmental movements in contemporary China.

Dingxin Zhao is Max Palevsky Professor of Sociology at the University of Chicago. He is also the Director of the Center for Advanced Studies in Humanities and Social Sciences of Zhejiang University, China. His research interests are historical sociology, social movements, nationalism, social change, economic development and methodology. His most recent book, *The Confucian-Legalist State: A New Theory of Chinese History* (2015) is published by Oxford University Press.

Introduction: Mapping and Opening Up the Terrain

DAVID A. SNOW, SARAH A. SOULE, HANSPETER KRIESI, AND HOLLY J. MCCAMMON

Social movements are one of the principal social forms through which collectivities give voice to their grievances and concerns about the rights, welfare, and well-being of themselves and others by engaging in various types of collective action, ranging from peaceful protest demonstrations to acts of political violence, from pamphleteering to revolution, and from mass vigils memorializing deceased constituents to boisterous gatherings clamoring for retribution, all of which dramatize those grievances and concerns and demand that something be done about them. Although there are other more institutionalized and publicly less conspicuous venues in which collectivities can express their grievances and concerns, particularly in democratic societies, social movements have long functioned as an important vehicle for articulating and pressing a collectivity's interests and claims. Indeed, it is arguable that an understanding of many of the most significant developments and changes throughout human history – such as the ascendance and spread of Christianity and Islam, the Reformation, and the French, American, Russian and Chinese Communist revolutions – are partly contingent on an understanding of the workings and influence of social movements, and this is especially so during the past several centuries. In this regard, it is interesting to note that *Time* magazine's centennial issue (December 31, 1999) included Mohandas Gandhi, the inspirational leader of one of the more consequential movements of the past century, among its three major candidates for the person of the century. Why Gandhi?

> He stamped his ideas on history, igniting three of the century's great revolutions – against colonialism, racism, violence. His concept of nonviolent resistance liberated one nation and sped the end of colonial empires around the world. His marches and fasts fired the imagination of oppressed people everywhere.
>
> (McGeary 1999: 123)

The Wiley Blackwell Companion to Social Movements, Second Edition. Edited by David A. Snow, Sarah A. Soule, Hanspeter Kriesi, and Holly J. McCammon.
© 2019 John Wiley & Sons Ltd. Published 2019 by John Wiley & Sons Ltd.

And "his strategy of nonviolence has spawned generations of spiritual heirs around the world" (*Time* 1999: 127), including Martin Luther King Jr., Cesar Chavez, Gloria Steinem, Lech Walesa, Benigno Aquino Jr., and Nelson Mandela – all prominent leaders of a major, consequential social movement in their respective homelands. A decade after the turn of the century, *Time* again focused attention on social movement actors, naming as its 2011 Person of the Year "The PROTESTOR from the Arab Spring to Athens, From Occupy Wall Street to Moscow" (December 6, 2011).

While one might quibble with *Time*'s estimation of Gandhi's influence, as well as that of the 2011 protestors, the more important point is that some of the major events and figures of the past century, as well as earlier, are bound up with social movements. And that is particularly true today, as social movements and the activities with which they are associated have become an increasingly conspicuous feature of the social landscape. Indeed, rarely does a day go by in which a major daily newspaper does not refer to social movement activity in relation to one or more of the passionately contested issues of our time: abortion, austerity, civil rights, democratization, environmental protection, family values, gender equality, governmental intrusion and overreach, gun control, human rights, healthcare, immigration, income inequality, LGBTQ rights, labor and management conflict, nuclear weapons, populism, policy brutality, religious freedom, terrorism, war, world poverty, and so on. In fact, it is difficult to think of major national or international social issues in which social movements and related collective action events are not involved on one or both sides of the issues. Of course, not all social movements speak directly to, or play a significant role in, major national or international issues, as some are primarily local in terms of the scope and target of their actions. Examples include petitions against the proposed siting of "big box" stores such as Walmart, home-owners protesting the proximate location of a homeless shelter or refugee center, or the expansion of a local hospital, which would increase traffic through the targeted neighborhood. In addition to being local in terms of their constituents and targets, such movements typically go unnoticed beyond the local context because they operate beneath the radar of the national and international media. Nonetheless, such local movement activity probably occurs much more frequently than the large-scale protest events that are more likely to capture the national media's attention.

Because of such observations and considerations, it might be argued that we live not only in a "movement society" (Meyer and Tarrow 1998; Soule and Earl 2005), but even in a movement world. In the Preface to the reissue of his highly regarded historical account of the people, ideas, and events that shaped the New Left in the 1960s, entitled *Democracy Is in the Streets*, James Miller (1994) ponders the legacy of that period, and concludes that maybe its most enduring contributions were cultural. Perhaps so, but only insofar as the cultural includes models for political participation and action. Why? Because whatever the significant consequences of the 1960s, certainly one of the most important was that the movements of that period pushed open the doors to the streets, arguably wider than for some time, as a major venue for aggrieved citizens to press their claims. And large numbers of citizens have "takin' it to the streets" ever since in the US and elsewhere to express their collective views on all kinds of issues, although often at a decreasing rate of increase with variation across types of political engagement and time (see Dalton 2013; Norris 2002; Quaranta 2016; van Deth 2011).[1] For example, in an assessment of forms of political protest in Western Europe from 1981 to 2009, Quaranta (2016) found that while there has been an expansion of protest in Western Europe, its popularity and diffusion vary by the type of protest, with an increase in the popularity of petitioning, boycotting, and attending demonstrations in contrast to more confrontational forms of protests, such as unofficial strikes and occupations, which have not increased proportionately. Such variation notwithstanding, it is arguable that social movements and the activities they sponsor have become a kind of fifth estate in the world today. If so, then understanding our own societies, as well as the larger social world in which they are embedded, clearly requires some knowledge and understanding of social movements and the activities with which they are associated.

In addition to giving voice and being a conspicuous element in modern society, social movements can also be highly influential, and these impacts can be far-reaching. Not only did the New Left produce a lasting cultural legacy, other movements have done so as well. The women's movement of the 1960s and the 1970s brought profound changes in how women's roles in society were understood (Rosen 2000). The black civil rights movement succeeded in winning not only foundational Supreme Court decisions such as *Brown v. Board of Education*, but the movement spurred the Kennedy administration to initiate steps toward federal legislation addressing racial inequality (Greenberg 2004; Risen 2014). The global environmental movement, a rapidly growing and diverse collection of actors, that simultaneously "reach[es] up to states" and "down to the local communities" to educate the public, monitor environmental degradation, and pressure political leadership, is winning the passage of global pro-environmental treaties and law (Princen and Finger 1994: 11; see also Longhofer, Schofer, Miric, and Frank 2016). Moreover, scholars increasingly examine the biographical impacts of movements. Those participating in movement activism, for instance, experience changes in their worldviews and personal identities, their choices in career and marriage, and their social networks of friends and acquaintances (McAdam 1989). While social movements are certainly not always successful and sometimes the changes they foster are unintended and provoke a backlash, as in the case of the breathtaking movements of the 2011 Arab Spring, their effects can unfold at multiple levels, from the broad political and cultural realms to the everyday lives of movement participants.

Just as social movement activity appears to have become a more ubiquitous social form in the world today, even to the point of becoming a routinized avenue for expressing publicly collective grievances, so too there has been a corresponding proliferation of scholarly research on social movements and related activity throughout much of the world, and particularly within Europe and the US. Taking what are generally regarded as the top four journals in American sociology (*American Sociological Review, American Journal of Sociology, Social Forces*, and *Social Problems*), for example, there has been an increase in the proportion of collective action and social movement articles published in these journals since the middle of the past century: from 2.23% for the 1950s, to 4.13% for the 1970s, to 9.45% for the 1990s and 8.72% for 2006–2015.[2] Also suggestive of growing scholarly interest in the study of social movements is the relatively large number of edited volumes, published since the early 1990s (e.g. Costain and McFarland 1998; Davenport, Johnston, and Mueller 2005; della Porta, Kriesi, and Rucht 1999; Diani and McAdam 2003; Givans, Roberts, and Soule 2010; Goodwin, Jasper, and Polletta 2001; Jenkins and Klandermans 1995; Johnston and Klandermans 1995; Larana, Johnston, and Gusfield 1994; Maney et al. 2012; Mansbridge and Morris 2001; McAdam, McCarthy, and Zald 1996; Meyer and Tarrow 1998; Meyer, Whittier, and Robnett 2002; Morris and Mueller 1992; Reger, Myers, and Einwohner 2008; Smith, Chatfield, and Pagnucco 1997; Stryker, Owens, and White 2000; Van Dyke and McCammon 2010; Van Stekelenburg, Roggeband, and Klandermans 2013). As well, during the past couple of decades scholars have produced a number of social movement texts (Buechler 2000; della Porta and Diani 1999; Garner 1996; Johnston 2014; Meyer 2007; Snow and Soule 2010; Staggenborg 2008; Tarrow 1998), and edited, text-like readers (Buechler and Cylke, Jr. 1997; Darnovsky, Epstein, and Flacks 1995; Goodwin and Jasper 2003; Lyman 1995; McAdam and Snow 2010), as well as a three-volume encyclopedia of social and political movements (Snow, della Porta, Klandermans, and McAdam 2013). The publication of two international journals of research and theory about social movements and related collective actions – *Mobilization* (published in the US) and *Social Movement Studies* (published in the UK) – also points to increasing scholarship in this area.

Clearly there has been a proliferation of research and writing on social movements during the past several decades. Yet, there was no single volume that provided in-depth, synthetic examinations of a comprehensive set of movement-related topics and issues in a fashion that reflected and embodied the growing internationalization of social movement scholarship until the 2004 publication of *The Wiley Blackwell Companion to Social Movements*. A more recent addition to this comprehensive genre of original essays is della Porta and Diani's *The Oxford Handbook of Social Movements* (2015), which also opens up the analysis to other fields, such as communication, geography, and history. The current volume is an extensive and expansive revision of our 2004 volume, one that builds further on this growing comprehensive genre of movement scholarship by covering the major processes and issues generally regarded as relevant to understanding the course and character, indeed the dynamics, of social movements, as well as the major intersections between the study of social movements and other sectors and dimensions of social life, such as gender, social class, race and ethnicity, religion, nationalism, war, and terrorism. And, in doing so, it provides broader coverage, and thus is more comprehensive, than other existing edited volumes and texts on social movements. This topical breadth is afforded without sacrificing focus and detail, as each of the contributions to the volume provides an in-depth, state-of-the-art overview of the topics addressed, whether it be facilitative contexts or conditions, strategies and tactics, or a particular set of outcomes. In addition, the volume attempts to open up social movement research to developments in related areas of study. Thus, the last part of the volume is dedicated to "thematic intersections" between social movement research and related fields and opens up the conversation between major social movement agendas and those in related fields. And, finally, in recognition of the growing internationalization of social movement scholarship, the volume was compiled with the additional objective of reflecting this internationalization in terms of both empirical substance and chapter authorship. Our objective with this volume, then, is to provide in-depth, synthetic examinations of a comprehensive set of movement-related topics, issues, and intersections by a blend of a cross-section of established, internationally recognized scholars with a more recent generation of scholars of increasing recognition.

Before outlining how we have organized the contributions that comprise this volume, we seek to establish a conceptualization of social movements that is sufficiently broad so as not to exclude the various and sundry types of social movements while sufficiently bounded to allow us to distinguish movements from other social phenomena that may bear a resemblance to social movements but yet are quite different.

Conceptualizing Social Movements[3]

Definitions of social movements are not hard to come by. They are readily provided in most text-like treatments of the topic (e.g. della Porta and Diani 1999; Snow and Soule 2010; Tarrow 1998; Turner and Killian 1987), in edited volumes of conference proceedings and previously published articles and scholarly papers (e.g. Goodwin and Jasper 2003; McAdam and Snow 2010; Meyer and Tarrow 1998), and in summary, encyclopedia-like essays (e.g. Benford, Gongaware, and Valadez 2000; McAdam, McCarthy, and Zald 1988, Snow and Tan 2015). Although the various definitions of movements may differ in terms of what is emphasized or accented, most are based on three or more of the following axes: collective or joint action; change-oriented goals or claims; some extra- or non-institutional collective action; some degree of organization; and some degree of temporal continuity. Thus, rather than begin with a straightforward conceptualization, we consider first these conceptual axes.

Social movements as a form of collective action

Social movements are only one of numerous forms of collective action. Other types include much crowd behavior, as when sports and rock fans roar and applaud in unison; some riot behavior, as when looting rioters focus on some stores or products rather than others; some interest group behavior, as when the National Rifle Association mobilizes large numbers of its adherents to write or phone their respective congressional representatives; some "gang" behavior, as when gang members work the streets together; and large-scale revolutions. Since these are only a few examples of the array of behaviors that fall under the collective action umbrella, it is useful to clarify the character of social movements as a type of collective action.

At its most elementary level, collective action consists of any goal-directed activity engaged in jointly by two or more individuals. It entails the pursuit of a common objective through joint action – that is people working together in some fashion for a variety of reasons, often including the belief that doing so enhances the prospect of achieving the objective. Since collective action so defined obviously includes a large number of human behaviors, it is useful to differentiate those collective actions that are social movements from other forms of collective action. Social movements entail actors (and their actions) that collectively challenge authorities, sometimes in an attempt to bring about social change, but in other circumstances to prevent such change from occurring. Social movements often use non-institutionalized means of action, such as appropriating and using public and quasi-public places for purposes other than for which they were designed or intended. But they also sometimes agitate inside institutional settings, including inside the government (Banaszak 2010), schools (McCammon et al. 2017), religious institutions (Katzenstein 1998), and corporations (Soule 2009), challenging and pressuring authorities in these settings. Social movement actors, as David Meyer explains, contest a variety of norms and practices, including law and policy, cultural beliefs and values, and everyday and institutional practices (2007: 10). As Sidney Tarrow notes, collective movement action "takes many forms – brief or sustained, institutionalized or disruptive, humdrum or dramatic" (1998: 3).

Social movements and collective behavior

Parsing collective action into social movements and other forms of collective activity still leaves numerous collective actions within the latter category. Traditionally, most of these non-movement collective actions have been treated as varieties of collective behavior. Broadly conceived, collective behavior refers to group action that tends to be more spontaneous and often emotionally driven, as might occur in mass or diffuse phenomena, such as panics, fads, crazes, and sometimes riots.[4] Thus, social movements differ significantly from most other variants of collective action in that, as we discuss below, social movements are coordinated and planned collective action typically involving articulated grievances and claims.

Social movements and interest groups

Just as social movements overlap to some degree with some forms of collective action, they also overlap with interest groups, which also comprise another set of collective actors that are often equated with social movements. Clearly interest groups, such as Planned Parenthood and the Christian Coalition, and some social movements, such as the pro-choice and pro-life movements, are quite similar in terms of the interests and objectives they share with respect to some aspect of social life. Yet there are also noteworthy differences. First, interest groups are generally defined in relation to the government or polity (Walker 1991), whereas the relevance and interests of social movements extend well beyond the polity to other institutional spheres and authorities. Second, even when social movements are directly oriented to the polity or state, their standing is different. Interest groups are generally embedded within the political arena, as most are regarded as legitimate actors within it, although, depending on the group holding political power, interest groups once considered as legitimate political players may now be deemed outsiders. Social movements, on the other hand, are typically outside of the polity, or overlap with it in a precarious fashion, because they seldom have the same standing or degree of access to or recognition among political authorities. A third difference follows: interest groups pursue their collective objectives mainly through institutionalized means, such as lobbying and soliciting campaign contributions, whereas social movements pursue their collective ends mainly via the use of non-institutional means, such as conducting marches, boycotts, and sit-ins.[5]

Connections and overlaps

To note the distinction among social movements, other varieties of collective behavior, and interest groups is not to assert that they do not overlap at times.

The relationship between non-conventional crowd activity and social movements is illustrative. Although some crowds arise spontaneously and dissipate just as quickly, others are the result of prior planning, organization, and negotiation. In such cases, they often are sponsored and organized by a social movement, and constitute part of its tactical repertoire for dramatizing its grievances and pressing its claims. When this occurs, which is probably the dominant pattern for most protest crowds or demonstrations, neither the crowd phenomena nor the movement can be thoroughly understood without understanding the relationship between them. Thus, while social movements can be distinguished conceptually from other forms of collective action and collective behavior, social movements and some crowd phenomena often are intimately linked. Social movements and interest groups can be closely connected too, as when they form an alliance to press their joint interests together. Moreover, as social movements develop over time, they often become more and more institutionalized, with some of them evolving (at least partially) into interest groups or even political parties.

Social movements as challengers to or defenders of existing authority

There is generalized acknowledgment that social movements are in the business of seeking or halting change, but there is a lack of consensus as to the locus and level of changes sought. Must it be the political institutional level? That is, must the changes or objectives sought be in terms of seeking concessions from or altering political institutions? What about changes at the individual or personal level? Do other kinds of changes count, such as those associated with so-called self-help groups, or animal rights, or life styles? And to what extent should the amount or degree of change be considered in conceptualizing movements?

Whatever the components of various definitions of social moments, all emphasize that movements are in the business of promoting or resisting change with respect to some aspect of the world in which we live. Indeed, fostering or halting change is the *raison d'être* for all social movements. But scholars are not of one mind when it comes to specifying the character of the change sought. Some leave the question open-ended, stating simply that social movements are "collective attempts to promote or resist change in a society or group" (Benford, Gongaware, and Valadez 2000; Turner and Killian 1987: 223), while others narrow the range of targets of change primarily to those within the political arena (McAdam, Tarrow, and Tilly 2001).

Neither the open-ended nor manifestly political conceptual strategies are entirely satisfactory. The open-ended one is too ambiguous, while the emphasis on "collective political struggle" is too institutionally narrow, excluding challenges rooted in other institutional and socio-cultural contexts.[6] Thus, in order to have an understanding of social movements that is both more inclusive in terms of what gets counted as social movement activity, and yet more tightly anchored institutionally and culturally, we argue that movements be considered as challengers to, or defenders of, existing *institutional authority* – whether it is located in the political, corporate, religious, or educational realm – or patterns of *cultural authority*, such as systems of beliefs or practices reflective of those beliefs.[7]

Social movements as organized activity

Earlier it was noted that social movements, as a form of collective action, involve joint action in pursuit of a common objective. Joint action of any kind implies some degree of coordination, and thus organization. Scholars of social movements have long understood the relevance of organization to understanding the course and character of movement activity, but they have rarely agreed about the forms, functions, and consequences of organization with respect to social movements. The seeds of this debate were sown in the early twentieth century – with the juxtaposition of the revolutionary Lenin's (1929) call for organization as the key to stimulating working-class consciousness to Luxemburg's (Waters 1970) and Michels' (1962 [1911]) critique of formal party organization as retarding rather than promoting progressive politics and democracy – and flowered full bloom in the latter quarter of the century. Carrying Luxemburg's banner, for example, Piven and Cloward (1977) have argued that too much emphasis on organization was antithetical to effective mobilization, particularly among the poor. In contrast, McCarthy and Zald (1977), among others (Gamson 1990; Lofland 1996), argued that social movement organizations (SMOs) were fundamental not only for assembling and deploying the resources necessary for effectively mounting movement campaigns, but they were also key to the realization of a movement's objectives. Thus, SMOs were proffered as the orienting, focal unit of analysis for understanding the operation of social movements (Lofland 1996; McCarthy and Zald 1977). But, again, not all scholars agreed. This time it was not because of fear of the constraining effects of formal organization, but because movements, according to della Porta and Diani (1999: 16) "are not organizations, not even of a peculiar kind," but "networks of interaction between different actors which may either include formal organizations or not, depending on shifting circumstances."

Given these contrasting arguments regarding the relationship between organization and social movements, it seems reasonable to ask whether one is more accurate than another, or if we must choose one over another? The answer to both questions is "no!" There is absolutely no question about the fact that social movement activity is organized in some fashion or another (Snow and Soule 2010). Clearly there are different forms of organization (e.g. single SMO vs. multiple, networked SMOs) and degrees of organization (e.g. tightly coupled vs. loosely coupled), and clearly there are differences in the consequences of different forms and degrees of organization. But to note such differences is not grounds for dismissing the significance of organization to social movements.

Tarrow (1998: 123–124) helps clarify these issues when he distinguishes between social movements as formal organizations, the organization of collective action, and social movements as connective structures or networks. Conceptually, the issue concerns neither the form nor consequences of organizations, but the fact that the existence of social movement activity implies some degree of organization. To illustrate, consider the civil rights movement of the 1960s, and some of its leaders, such as Martin Luther King and Stokely Carmichael, as well as various organizational representatives, such as the Southern Christian Leadership Conference (SCLC) and the Student Non-Violent Coordinating Committee (SNCC). Indeed, it is difficult to comprehend the civil rights movement in the absence of the leaders and organizations associated with it. The same can be said also about many other social movements. Take, for example, the student-led pro-democracy movement in Beijing (Zhou 2001). Not only were the actions of demonstrators coordinated, but there were various organizing groups.

Thus, in many movements we see the interests and objectives of a particular constituency being represented and promoted by one or more individuals associated with one or more organizations now routinely referred to in the literature as SMOs. While the organizations associated with these movements may vary in a variety of ways, the point still remains that much of the activity, including the relations between participating organizations, was itself organized. It is because of such observations that a semblance of organization needs to be included as a component of the conceptualization of social movements, but without specifying the character and degree of organization for any specific movement.

Social movements as existing with some temporal continuity

The final axis of conceptualization concerns the extent to which social movements operate with some degree of temporal continuity. Some scholars have suggested that social movements are "episodic" in the sense of not being regularly scheduled events (McAdam, Tarrow, and Tilly 2001: 5), which is certainly true inasmuch as social movements are not routinely on the community or national calendar. To be sure, social movement events and activities get placed on the community calendar from time to time, but such is the result of application and/or negotiation processes with officials rather than routine calendarization of a movement's activities.

Yet, to note that movements are temporally episodic is not to suggest that they are generally fly-by-night fads that are literally here today and gone tomorrow. Clearly there is considerable variability in their careers or life course, as some movements do indeed last for a very short time, as with most neighborhood, NIMBY oppositions; while others endure for decades, as with Heaven's Gate "cult" that was first observed in the US in the 1970s (Balch 1995) and the Soka Gakki/Nichiren Shoshu Buddhist movement that was first introduced into the USA in the early 1960s (Snow 1993); and still others persist across generations, alternating between periods of heightened activism and dormancy, as with the Women's movement (Rupp and Taylor 1987). And for many, and perhaps most movements, they are clustered temporally within "cycles of protest" that wax and wane historically (Tarrow 1998). So clearly there is striking temporal variability in the life span of social movements.

Yet, the kinds of changes movements pursue, whatever their degree or level, typically require some measure of sustained, organized activity. Continuity, like organization, is a matter of degree, of course. But it is difficult to imagine any movement making much progress in pursuing its objectives without fairly persistent, almost nagging, collective action. Accordingly, some degree of sustained collective action, and thus temporal continuity, are essential characteristics of social movements.

A Conceptualization of Social Movements

Having explored the various conceptual axes pertaining to social movements, we are now in position to suggest a working conceptualization of social movements based on the various elements highlighted. Accordingly, social movements can be thought of as:

> Collectivities acting with some degree of organization and continuity outside of institutional or organizational channels for the purpose of challenging or defending extant authority, whether it is institutionally or culturally based, in the group, organization, society, culture, or world order of which they are a part.

The major advantage of this conceptualization over other definitions, and particularly those that link social movements to the polity or government, is that it is more inclusive, thus broadening what gets counted and analyzed as social movements. Thus, from this vantage point, a wide range of collective actions constitute social movements, including the following: the Spring 1989 pro-democracy student protests in China; the broader pro-democracy stirrings in Eastern Europe that contributed to fall of Communist regimes throughout the region in the late 1980s; the wave of world-wide anti-war protests associated with the US-UK/Iraq War (variously framed as an "invasion" and a "liberation") of 2003; the 2011 Arab Spring uprisings; the Occupy movement in the US and the corresponding Indignados and anti-austerity movements in Europe; and the current rise of right-wing and populist enthusiasm throughout sectors of the Western world; local, NIMBY movements; the rebellion among parishioners to the sexual abuse scandal in the Catholic Church; and even erstwhile cultish, escapist movements such as Heaven's Gate and the followers of Jim Jones.[8] In some fashion or another, each of these movements constituted challenges to institutional, organizational or cultural authority, or systems of authority.

Structure of the Volume

Social movements, thus conceptualized, can be examined in terms of various contextual factors, dimensions, and processes from a variety of overlapping perspectives via a number of methods. Most edited volumes on movements are typically organized in terms of a few focal contextual factors, dimensions and/or processes. This volume is arranged in terms of these considerations as well, but consistent with our previously mentioned objective of compiling a comprehensive set of detailed, synthetic discussions of the range of factors associated with the dynamics of social movements, we have organized the volume in terms of a broader array of contextual factors, dimensions, and processes than is customary as well as considering the intersectional connections between the study of social movements and a host of other dimensions of social life.

Contextual factors reference the broader structural and cultural conditions that facilitate and constrain the emergence and operation of social movements. Metaphorically, contextual conditions constitute the soil in which movements grow or languish. Part I of the volume consists of seven chapters that focus on and elaborate the relevance of a variety of contextual factors to the course and character of social movements. These include the political context, the role of threat, and the cultural, resource, ecological, transnational, and media contexts from which movements spring or in which they operate.

Dimensions encompass characteristic aspects of social movements, such as organizational forms, organizational fields, leadership, tactical repertoires, collective action frames, emotion, collective identity, and consequences; whereas *processes* encompass the ways in which dimensions evolve and change temporally over the course of a movement's operation, such as participant mobilization, tactical innovation, diffusion, and framing. Parts II, III, IV, and V of the volume examine a broad range of movement-relevant dimensions and processes. Part II consists of seven chapters that dissect and elaborate various meso- or organizational-level dimensions and processes that together constitute the dynamic field of action in which movements operate. Included here are chapters on social networks and fields, social movement organizations, leadership, interactions between movements and organizations, dissent and insurrection within and between movements, diffusion processes, and coalitions. Part III includes six chapters that cast light on various aspects of movement strategies and tactics, including chapters on tactics and strategic action, the uses of technology and social media, legal tactics, violence vs. non-violence, and the uses and functions of art by and within movements. Part IV includes four chapters that illuminate participation and its key interpretative and social psychological dimensions and processes. It should be understood that the dimensions and processes examined in this section – such as framing, emotions, and collective identity – operate in conjunction with the meso-organizational level factors considered in Part III, but are separated for analytical purposes because of their interactive and social psychological grounding.

In Part V, attention is turned to the outcome dimension or aspect of social movements. Here there are two guiding questions: What are the consequences of social movements? And in what ways or domains do they make a difference? The four chapters in this section provide different answers to these questions by focusing on four different sets or domains of consequences: political, economic, cultural, and biographic or personal.

The final section of the volume, Part VI, is organized in terms of important thematic intersections between social movements and major, generic social categories (social class, gender, race and ethnicity, and religion), salient global processes or trends (globalization, nationalism, political extremism), and pressing events or issues (human rights, authoritarian regimes, war, revolution, and terrorism). The 12 chapters included in this section provide focused, synthetic discussions of the intersection between scholarly research on movements and each of the above-listed categories, processes, and events or issues.

Rarely is a volume that seeks comprehensive coverage of a field of study completely successful in covering all relevant phenomena or issues variously referenced in discussions of the field. This volume is no different. We had planned to have a chapter on the intersection of social movements and environmental issues and hazards, as well as one on populism, but the prospective authors of these chapters were unable to complete them, so we set sail without them. Additionally, we considered a section on the various methodologies used in studying social movements, but space limitations forced to us to forego that consideration in favor of retaining the breadth and depth of the initial set of chapters solicited. Better, we thought, to provide a comprehensive discussion of the array of factors relevant to the operation and dynamics of social movements which may, in turn, provide a basis for evaluating aspects of current synthetic efforts and perhaps contribute to the development of further synthesis.

These omissions notwithstanding, it is our hope that by providing an expanded compilation of original, state-of-the-art essays on a comprehensive set of movement-related contexts, dimensions, processes, and intersections, that this volume will prove to be a useful companion to those interested in social movements in general and, more particularly, in the array of factors relevant to understanding their emergence, dynamics, consequences, and intersections.

Notes

1   We use "the streets" both literally and metaphorically: literally as the site or social space in which much social protest occurs, and metaphorically as a cover term for the array of movement-related tactical actions, many of which now extend beyond the streets. The doors to the street as a literal site for protest had been partially opened well before the 1960s, at least a century or so earlier as Charles Tilly emphasized in his numerous works elaborating his seminal and historically grounded concept of "repertoires of contention" (e.g. Tilly 1986, 1995. See also Tarrow 1998, especially Chapters 2 and 6). Thus, our point is not that the streets constituted a new space for protest, but that the 1960s appear to have provided a template or model for collective action that would be adopted by citizens from all walks of life associated with all kinds of causes, as our foregoing examples suggest.

2   We wish to acknowledge the assistance of Catherine Corrigall-Brown and Minyoung Moon, who conducted the analyses from which these data are derived.

3   Portions of this section are drawn from Snow and McAdam's Introduction to their edited volume consisting of previously published work on social movements (McAdam and Snow 2010: 1–8). This section is also influenced by the conceptual efforts of McAdam, Tarrow, and Tilly (2001), Tarrow (1998), Snow and Soule (2010), and Turner and Killian (1972, 1987). The reader familiar with these works will note that the way in which our conceptualization differs from the conceptualizations provided by these works is more nuanced than discordant.

4   For an examination of collective behavior broadly construed, see Turner and Killian (1972, 1987). For an incisive critical examination of the literature on crowds, as well as of the utility of the crowd concept, see McPhail (1991) and Snow and Owens (2013), and for discussion of the collective behavior/collective action intersect, see Oliver (2013).

5   Burstein (1998, 1999) has questioned the analytic utility of distinguishing between interest groups and social movements, arguing that both concepts should be abandoned in favor of "interest organizations."

6   It is both interesting and important to note that McAdam, Tarrow and Tilly would appear to agree with this charge, as they soften their initial conceptualization by suggesting that "contention involving non-state actors" is not beyond the scope of their approach so long as "at least one member and one challenger [are] actively engaged in contestation over the shape of a given organizational or institutional field" (2001: 342–343).

7   The rationale for expanding the conceptualization of social movements in this fashion is elaborated in Snow (2004).

8   Some students of social movements do not consider escapist or other-worldly cults or sects and communes as social movements per se, but a strong case can be made that they constitute significant challenges, albeit often indirect, to their encompassing cultural and/or political systems. Indeed, we would argue, in the language of Hirschman (1970), that "exit" may sometimes not only constitute a form of "voice," but may even speak louder and be more threatening than the voices associated with more conventional challenges (see Snow 2004; Snow and Soule 2010) for an elaboration of this argument).

References

Balch, Robert W. 1995. "Waiting for the Ships: Disillusionment and the Revitalization of Faith in Bo and Peep's UFO Cult." In *The Gods Have Landed: New Religions from Other Worlds*, edited by James R. Lewis, 137–166 Albany: State University of New York Press.

Banaszak, Lee Ann. 2010. *The Women's Movement Inside and Outside the State*. New York: Cambridge University Press.

Benford, Robert D., Timothy B. Gongaware, and Danny L. Valadez. 2000. "Social Movements." In *Encyclopedia of Sociology*, edited by Edgar F. Borgatta and Rhonda J.V. Montgomery, 2nd edn., vol. 4, 2717–2727. New York: Macmillan.

Buechler, Steven M. 2000. *Social Movements and Advanced Capitalism: The Political Economy and Cultural Construction of Social Activism*. New York: Oxford University Press.

Buechler, Steven M. and F. Kurt Cylke, Jr. 1997. *Social Movements: Perspectives and Issues*. Mountain View, CA: Mayfield Publishing Company.

Burstein, Paul 1998. "Interest Organizations, Political Parties, and the Study of Democratic Politics." In *Social Movements and American Political Institutions: People, Passions, and Power*, edited by Anne N. Costain and Andrew S. McFarland, 39–56. Lanham, MD: Rowman & Littlefield.

Burstein, Paul. 1999. "Social Movements and Public Policy." In *How Social Movements Matter*, edited by Marco Giugni, Doug McAdam, and Charles Tilly, 3–21. Minneapolis: University of Minnesota Press.

Costain, Anne N. and Andrew S. McFarland, eds. 1998. *Social Movements and American Political Institutions: People, Passions, and Power*. Lanham, MD: Rowman & Littlefield.

Dalton, Russell. 2013. *Citizen Politics: Public Opinion and Political Parties in Advanced Industrial Democracies*, 6th edn. Washington, DC: CQ Press.

Darnovsky, Marcy, Barbara Epstein, and Richard Flacks, eds. 1995. *Cultural Politics and Social Movements*. Philadelphia, PA: Temple University Press.

Davenport, Christian, Hank Johnston, and Carol Mueller, eds. 2005. *Repression and Mobilization*. Minneapolis: University Minnesota Press.

della Porta, Donatella and Mario Diani. 1999. *Social Movements: An Introduction*. Oxford: Blackwell Publishers.

della Porta, Donatella and Mario Diani, eds. 2015. *The Oxford Handbook of Social Movements*. Oxford: Oxford University Press.

della Porta, Donatella, Hanspeter Kriesi, and Dieter Rucht, eds. 1999. *Social Movements in a Globalizing World*. London: Macmillan.

Diani, Mario and Doug McAdam, eds. 2003. *Social Movements and Networks*. New York: Oxford University Press.

Gamson, William A. 1990. *The Strategy of Social Protest*, 2nd edn. Belmont, CA: Wadsworth.

Garner, Roberta. 1996. *Contemporary Movements and Ideologies*. New York: McGraw-Hill.

Givans, Rebecca Kolins, Kenneth M. Roberts, and Sarah A. Soule, eds. 2010. *The Diffusion of Social Movements: Actors, Mechanisms, and Political Effects*. New York: Cambridge University Press.

Goodwin, Jeff and James M. Jasper. 2003. *The Social Movements Reader: Cases and Concepts*. Oxford: Blackwell Publishing.

Goodwin, Jeff, James M. Jasper, and Francesca Polletta, eds. 2001. *Passionate Politics: Emotions and Social Movements*. Chicago: University of Chicago Press.

Greenberg, Jack. 2004. *Crusaders in the Courts: Legal Battles of the Civil Rights Movement*. New York: Twelve Tables Press.

Hirschman, Albert O. 1970. *Exit, Voice, and Loyalty: Responses to Declines in Firms, Organizations, and States*. Cambridge, MA: Harvard University Press.

Jenkins, J. Craig and Bert Klandermans, eds. 1995. *The Politics of Social Protest: Comparative Perspectives on States and Social Movements*. Minneapolis: University of Minnesota Press.

Johnston, Hank. 2014. *What Is a Social Movement?* Malden, MA: Polity Press.

Johnston, Hank and Bert Klandermans, eds. 1995. *Social Movements and Culture*. Minneapolis: University of Minnesota Press.

Katzenstein, Mary F. 1998. *Faithful and Fearless: Moving Feminist Protest Inside the Church and the Military*. Princeton, NJ: Princeton University Press.

Larana, Enrique, Hank Johnston, and Joseph. R. Gusfield, eds. 1994. *New Social Movements: From Ideology to Identity*. Philadelphia, PA: Temple University Press.

Lenin, Vladimir I. 1929. *What Is to Be Done? Burning Questions of Our Movements*. New York: International Publishers.

Lofland, John. 1996. *Social Movement Organizations: Guide to Research on Insurgent Realities*. New York: Aldine de Gruyter.

Longhofer, Wesley, Evan Schofer, Natasha Miric, and David John Frank. 2016. "NGOs, INGOs, and Environmental Policy Reform, 1970–2010." *Social Forces* 94: 1743–1768.

Lyman, Stanford M., ed. 1995. *Social Movements: Critiques, Concepts, Case-Studies*. New York: New York University Press.

Maney, Gregory M., Rachel V. Kutz-Flamenbaum, Deana A. Rohlinger, and Jeff Goodwin, eds. 2012. *Strategies for Social Change*. Minneapolis: University of Minnesota Press.

Mansbridge, Jane and Aldon D. Morris, eds. 2001. *Oppositional Consciousness: The Subjective Roots of Social Protest*. Chicago: The University of Chicago Press.

McAdam, Doug. 1989. "The Biographical Consequences of Activism." *American Sociological Review* 54(5): 744–760.

McAdam, Doug, John D. McCarthy, and Mayer N. Zald. 1988. "Social Movements." In *Handbook of Sociology*, edited by Neil Smelser. Beverly Hills, CA: Sage, pp. 695–737.

McAdam, Doug, John D. McCarthy, and Mayer N. Zald, eds. 1996. *Comparative Perspectives on Social Movements: Political Opportunities, Mobilizing Structures, and Cultural Framings*. New York: Cambridge University Press.

McAdam, Doug and David A. Snow, eds. 2010. *Social Movements: Origins, Dynamics, and Outcomes*, 2nd edn. New York: Oxford University Press.

McAdam, Doug, Sidney Tarrow, and Charles Tilly. 2001. *Dynamics of Contention*. New York: Cambridge University Press.

McCammon, Holly J., Allison R. McGrath, Ashley Dixon, and Megan Robinson. 2017. "Targeting Culture: Feminist Legal Activists and Critical Community Tactics." In *Research in Social Movements, Conflicts and Change*, vol. 41, 243–278. Bingley: Emerald Publishing.

McCarthy, John D. and Mayer N. Zald. 1977. "Resource Mobilization and Social Movements: A Partial Theory." *American Journal of Sociology* 82: 1212–1241.

McGeary, Johanna. 1999. "Mohandas Gandhi." *Time*, 154, December 31, pp. 118–123.

McPhail, Clark. 1991. *The Myth of the Madding Crowd*. New York: Aldine de Gruyter.

Meyer, David S. 2007. *The Politics of Protest: Social Movements in America*. New York: Oxford University Press.

Meyer, David S. and Sidney Tarrow, eds. 1998. *The Social Movement Society: Contentious Politics for a New Century*. Boulder, CO: Rowman & Littlefield.

Meyer, David S., Nancy Whittier, and Belinda Robnett, eds. 2002. *Social Movements: Identity, Culture, and the State*. New York: Oxford University Press.

Michels, Robert 1962 [1911]. *Political Parties: A Sociological Study of the Oligarchical Tendencies of Modern Democracy*. New York: The Free Press.

Miller, James. 1994. *Democracy Is in the Streets: From Port Huron to the Siege of Chicago*. Cambridge, MA: Harvard University Press.

Morris, Aldon D. and Carol McClurg Mueller, eds. 1992. *Frontiers in Social Movement Theory*. New Haven, CT: Yale University Press.

Norris, Pippa. 2002. *Democratic Phoenix: Reinventing Political Activism*. Cambridge: Cambridge University Press.

Oliver, Pamela. 2013. "Colective Actopn (Collective Behavior)." In *The Wiley-Blackwell Encyclopedia of Social and Political Movements*, edited by David A. Snow, Donatella della Porta, Bert Klandermans, and Doug McAdam, vol. 1, 210–215. Malden, MA: Wiley-Blackwell.

Piven, Francis Fox and Richard A. Cloward. 1977. *Poor People's Movements*. New York: Vintage Books.

Princen, Thomas and Matthias Finger. 1994. *Environmental NGOs in World Politics: Linking the Local and the Global*. New York: Routledge.

Quaranta, Mario. 2016. "Towards a Western European 'Social Movement Society'? An Assessment, 1981–2009." *Partecipazione e Conflicto: The Open Journal of Sociopolitical Studies* 9: 233–258.

Reger, Jo, Daniel J. Myers, and Rachel L. Einwohner, eds. 2008. *Identity Work in Social Movements*. Minneapolis: University of Minnesota Press.

Risen, Clay. 2014. *The Bill of the Century: The Epic Battle for the Civil Rights Act*. New York: Bloomsbury.

Rosen, Ruth. 2000. *The World Split Open: How the Modern Women's Movement Changed America*. New York: Penguin Books.

Rupp, Leila and Verta Taylor. 1987. *Survival in the Doldrums: The American Women's Rights Movement, 1945 to the 1960s*. Columbus: Ohio State University Press.

Smith, Jackie, Charles Chatfield, and Ron Pagnucco, eds. 1997. *Transnational Social Movements and Global Politics: Solidarity Beyond the State*. Syracuse, NY: Syracuse University Press.

Snow, David A. 1993. *Shakubuku: A Study of the Nichiren Shoshu Buddhist Movement in America, 1960–1975*. New York: Garland Publishing.

Snow, David A. 2004. "Social Movements as Challenges to Authority: Resistance to an Emerging Conceptual Hegemony." In *Authority in Contention: Research in Social Movements, Conflict, and Change*, edited by Daniel J. Meyers and Daniel M. Cress, 3–25. Bingley: Emerald Publishing.

Snow, David A., Donatella della Porta, Bert Klandermans, and Doug McAdam, eds. 2013. *The Wiley-Blackwell Encyclopedia of Social and Political Movements*. Malden, MA: Wiley-Blackwell.

Snow, David A. and Peter B. Owens. 2013. "Crowds (Gatherings) and Collective Behavior (Action)." In *The Wiley-Blackwell Encyclopedia of Social and Political Movements*, edited by David A. Snow, Donatella della Porta, Bert Klandermans, and Doug McAdam, vol. 1, 289–296. Malden, MA: Wiley-Blackwell.

Snow, David A. and Sarah A. Soule. 2010. *A Primer on Social Movements*. New York: W.W. Norton & Company.

Snow, David A. and Anna Tan. 2015. "Social Movements." In *International Encyclopedia of Social and Behavioral Sciences*, 2nd edn., vol. 16, edited by J.D. Wright, 8–12. Oxford: Elsevier.

Soule, Sarah A. 2009. *Contention and Corporate Social Responsibility*. New York: Cambridge University Press.

Soule, Sarah A. and Jennifer Earl. 2005. "A Movement Society Evaluated: Collective Protest in the United States, 1960–1986." *Mobilization: An International Journal* 10(3): 345–364.

Staggenborg, Suzanne. 2008. *Social Movements*. New York: Oxford University Press.

Stryker, Sheldon, Timothy J. Owens, and Robert W. White, eds. 2000. *Self, Identity, and Social Movements*. Minneapolis: University of Minnesota Press.

Tarrow, Sidney. 1998. *Power in Movement: Social Movements, Collective Action and Politics*, 2nd ed. New York: Cambridge University Press.

Tilly, Charles. 1986. *The Contentious French*. Cambridge, MA: Harvard University Press.

Tilly, Charles. 1995. *Popular Contention in Great Britain, 1758–1834*. Cambridge, MA: Harvard University Press.

Turner, Ralph H. and Lewis M. Killian. 1972. *Collective Behavior*. 2nd ed. Englewood Cliffs, NJ: Prentice-Hall.

Turner, Ralph H. and Lewis M. Killian. 1987. *Collective Behavior*. 3rd ed. Englewood Cliffs, NJ: Prentice-Hall.

van Deth. Jan W. 2011. "New Modes of Participation and Norms of Citizenship." In *New Participatory Dimensions in Civil Society: Professionalization and Individualized Collective Action*, edited by Jan W. van Deth and William A. Maloney, 115–138. London: Routledge.

Van Dyke, Nella and Holly J. McCammon, eds. 2010. *Strategic Alliances: Coalition Building and Social Movements*. Minneapolis: University of Minnesota Press.

Van Stekelenburg, Jacquelien, Conny Roggeband, and Bert Klandermans, eds. 2013. *The Future of Social Movement Research: Dynamics, Mechanisms, and Processes*. Minneapolis: University of Minnesota Press.

Walker, Jack L. 1991. *Mobilizing Interest Groups in America: Patrons, Professions, and Social Movements*. Ann Arbor: University of Michigan Press.

Waters, Mary-Alice. 1970. *Rosa Luxemburg Speaks*. New York: Pathfinder Press.

Zhao, Dingxin. 2001. *The Power of Tiananmen: State-Society Relations and the 1989 Beijing Student Movement*. Chicago: University of Chicago Press.

Part I

Facilitative and Constraining Contexts and Conditions

1

The Political Context of Social Movements

Doug McAdam and Sidney Tarrow

Introduction

Social movements are an inherently complex, multifaceted set of phenomena, permitting any number of viable analytic perspectives. The first modern perspective on movements was psychological (Adorno et al. 1950; Hoffer 1951; Kornhauser 1959; Le Bon 1960; Smelser 1962). But the emergence and consolidation of a distinct field of social movement studies after the 1960s brought with it the development of analytic frameworks that emphasized the organizational (McCarthy and Zald 1973, 1977), economic (McAdam 1982; Paige 1975; Piven and Cloward 1977; Schwartz 1976), cultural (Emirbayer and Goodwin 1994; Melucci 1985; Snow et al. 1986; Snow and Benford 1988), demographic (Goldstone 1991), and network (Diani 1995; Diani and McAdam 2003; Gould 1991, 1993, 1995; McAdam 1986; McAdam and Paulsen 1993; Snow, Zurcher, and Eckland-Olson 1980) dimensions of social movements.

In the 1950s and the 1960s, scholars of contentious politics took the relations between social movements and their social and economic contexts seriously: In his classic, *The Making of the English Working Class* (1966), E.P. Thompson charted how industrialization shaped the future class consciousness and forms of collective action of English workers; Eric Hobsbawm and George Rudé, in *Captain Swing* (1975), showed how machine-breaking was a response to technological innovation; and in *The Vendée* (1964), Charles Tilly found that the urbanization in Western France produced a secular middle class that found just what it needed in the French Revolution. Politics, for these early specialists, was part of the transmission belt from socio-economic structure to movements.

The first hints of a more political contextual framework for understanding and analyzing movements can be glimpsed in the work of two political scientists writing in the early 1970s. Michael Lipsky (1970: 14) urged scholars to be skeptical of system characterizations presumably true for all times and places. Lipsky argued

that the ebb and flow of movement activity was responsive to changes that left institutional authorities either vulnerable or receptive to the demands of particular challengers. Three years later, another political scientist, Peter Eisinger (1973: 11)
deployed the concept of *political opportunity structure* to help account for variation
in riot behavior in American cities. But it would remain for a pair of sociologists to
translate the central insights of Lipsky and Eisinger into a more systematic analytic
framework emphasizing the reciprocal relationship between social movements and
systems of institutionalized politics.

In 1978, Tilly elaborated on these conceptual beginnings by devoting a full chapter
of his landmark book, *From Mobilization to Revolution*, to the important facilitating effect of "political opportunity" in emergent collective action. Four years later
the key premise underlying the work of Lipsky, Eisinger, and Tilly was incorporated
as one of the central tenets of a new *political process* model of social movements
(McAdam 1982). Like the other early proponents of the general perspective, both
Tilly and McAdam argued that the timing and ultimate fate of movements were
powerfully shaped by the variable opportunities afforded challengers by changes in
the institutional structure of political systems and shifting policy preferences and
alliances of established "polity members" (Gamson 1990). Soon after, three political
scientists added a cross-sectional specification to the temporal changes in opportunity structure: Kitschelt (1986) compared "new social movements" in four democracies, according to the strength or weakness of the state; Kriesi et al. (1995), working
in four European democracies, and Tarrow (1989), working on "cycles of protest,"
took the political opportunity perspective to Europe.

Since then, countless movement analysts have contributed to the ongoing elaboration of the general political process framework. So thoroughgoing has this elaboration been that we cannot hope to summarize all the extensions and nuances now
associated with the perspective. In our structure for the chapter, however, we have
tried to accommodate at least some of the more recent and, in our view, important
critiques and "friendly amendments" that continue to make the analysis of the
political context of movements a vital and central component of the overall field of
study. More specifically, the chapter is organized into three main sections. The first
deals with the ways in which the more *enduring* features of institutionalized politics
help us understand the different fate of the same movements cross-nationally or
cross-sectionally within the same state. The second section deals with how the *variable and changing* features of institutionalized political systems influence the emergence and subsequent ebb and flow of movement activity. While these two analytic
agendas are the oldest in the political process tradition and continue to structure
much of the work on political context, they hardly exhaust all the work that has
defined the framework over the years. We will bring the chapter to a close with a
section devoted to what we see as: (1) the most important lines of criticism; and (2)
theoretical extensions currently enriching the perspective.

Enduring Opportunities and Their Effects on Contention

The underlying assumption of this section is that *stable* political contexts – both within
and across regimes – condition contentious politics. This is not to assume that the
internal properties of movements – i.e., their organizations, resources, composition,

and demands – or characteristics of the individuals within them are unimportant; only that these properties, which are examined in other contributions to this volume, are channeled through political contexts that shape the directions they take and the relative disposition of actors to follow one or another route to collective action.

There is a general tendency – especially among critics – to characterize the political process model as if political opportunities automatically lead to movement emergence or success. While there may be applications of the model that embrace this stark a view, in McAdam's (1982) original formulation, favorable opportunities were just one of three factors that condition the emergence and impact of a movement. It is the confluence of political opportunities, indigenous organizational capacity, and the emergence of an oppositional consciousness (or "cognitive liberation") that shape the rise of a movement and its prospects for success. And of these, the third was seen as the real catalyst to emergent mobilization. To quote McAdam:

> Expanding political opportunities and indigenous organization do not, in any simple sense, produce a social movement …Together they only offer insurgents a certain "structural potential" for collective political action. Mediating between opportunity and action are people and the subjective meanings they attach to their situation.
>
> (1982: 48)

Moreover, consistent with the focus on effective tactics, McAdam's stress on the crucial role of "tactical innovation" in shaping the pace and impact of the civil rights struggle further reinforces the initial formulation of the political process model. We will turn to the "repertoire of contention" below; here it is sufficient to point out that the ultimate impact of a movement depends on the ongoing interaction of the regime context with the specific goals and strategic decisions of challengers and incumbents alike. We see five properties of a regime that help shape perceptions of political opportunities/ threats, and a sixth that we will elaborate in the second section: (1) the multiplicity of independent centers of power within the regime; (2) its openness to new actors and movements; (3) the instability of current political alignments; (4) the availability of influential allies or supporters; (5) the extent to which the regime suppresses or facilitates collective claims; and (6) changes in these properties.

Multiple centers of power provide challengers with the chance to "venue shop" for the most welcoming part of the regime; the regime's *openness to new actors* enables new groups to make claims on elites; *stable alignments* generally mean that many political actors have no potential allies in power, the *availability of influential allies or supporters* strengthens movements outside the gates of the polity; and *regime suppression or facilitation* discourages or encourages the emergence of movements. Threats vary in different opportunity structures, and over time, as we will show in the second section. Most people who mobilize do so to combat threats and risks, but also to take advantage of enduring opportunities (Goldstone and Tilly 2001).

Movements do not mobilize against "objective" threats or take advantage of "objective" opportunities. Threats and opportunities pass through a process of *social construction and attribution*. "No opportunity, however objectively open, will invite mobilization unless it is a) visible to potential challengers, and b) perceived as an opportunity. The same holds for threats…" (McAdam, Tarrow, and Tilly 2001: 43). "Attribution of opportunity or threat is an activating mechanism responsible in part for the mobilization of previously inert populations" (McAdam et al. 2001).

The perception of opportunities where threats are objectively strong can give movements surprising successes, or expose them to risks they fail to perceive. An example of the first phenomenon was the revolution against Communist rule in East-Central Europe, when the real breakthrough was not the objective collapse of Communism but the attribution of opportunity across the region, when activists saw that the "early riser" – Poland – was able to challenge state power (Lohmann 1993); an example of the second was when, in the Middle East, activists in country after country attempted to follow the successful example of the Tunisian "Arab Spring," but eventually succumbed to repression, as in Egypt (Ketchley 2017).

Scholars have identified a number of enduring factors that converge to produce different combinations of opportunity and threat. One set of factors focuses on the strength of the state and its degree of centralization or dispersion; a second deals with states' prevailing strategies toward challengers and the opportunities it affords them for contention within the system; and a third relates to the choice of contentious performances – how different aspects of a regime affect the forms of collective action that movements employ, especially their practices of repression. We summarize these perspectives in turn.

State strength or dispersion

In its most common form, the state strength argument reasons that centralized states which have effective policy instruments at their command attract collective actors to contest the highest reaches of the state. In contrast, because weak states allow criticism and invite participation, they can deal with most challengers through the institutional political process at every level of the state (Lipsky and Olson 1976). A corollary is that movement actors will gravitate to the sector or level of the state that is most susceptible to their claims (Szymanski 2003).

Different political systems vary in how they process even similar movements. For example, when Kriesi and his collaborators studied "new social movements" in four European states in the 1990s, they found differences in levels of mobilization that corresponded to the strength of the state. Switzerland, which they coded as a "weak" state, had a high level of mobilization and a low level of confrontation; at the other extreme, France, which they coded as a strong state, had a lower level of routine mobilization and a higher level of confrontational protest (Kriesi et al. 1995: 49). The Netherlands and Germany were found to be somewhere in the middle empirically.

Most episodes of contention begin locally, but in systems in which local governments lack autonomy, they gravitate to the summit through processes of scale shift (McAdam and Tarrow 2005). In the mid to late-1960s, student unrest in France gravitated quickly to the national level. In contrast, student protests in the United States remained lodged at the campus level. This meant that while the French student movement eventually attacked the entire system, leading to the dramatic "Events of May" (Touraine 1971), American students targeted university administrators and conservative professors and were unable to form a united student movement until the Vietnam War provided them with a unifying theme.

Opportunities for protest are also structured by regional political cultures and institutions. In his comparison of northern and southern Italy, Tarrow (1967) found that popular movements were channeled into mass parties in the industrial North, while movements remained inchoate and potentially more violent in the South. In the United States, regional political cultures continued to shape contention even after the end of the Civil War. Although there was racism in both regions, it was only in the South that racial laws shaped party politics, violence, and community into a "Jim Crow" system that was not effectively challenged until the post-World War II period (McAdam 1999).

Federalism also shapes contention: As Anne-Marie Syzmanski writes of the American temperance movement, the existence of different state systems allowed the movement to gain leverage at the state level when it was impossible to gain traction in Washington (Szymanski 2003). This channeled the movement to the state level until it was possible – with the passage of the 18th Amendment – to ban alcohol nationally. American federalism segments contention into local, state, and national arenas, where it can be processed, pacified, and resolved through compromise. But not all federal institutions channel contention in peaceful ways; federal systems provide ambitious leaders with institutional resources that they can use to develop independent power bases. For example, it was only in the three federal systems of the Communist world– Czechoslovakia, the USSR, and Yugoslavia – that the downfall of communism led to state breakup and, in the case of Yugoslavia, to civil war (Bunce 1999).

Prevailing state strategies

Researchers have found that different states have different prevailing strategies toward movements. Authoritarian states tend to regard all forms of protest as threats to the regime, while liberal-democratic states tolerate a broad range of peaceful contention and, in fact, often modify their policies in response to protest. But even in authoritarian states, there are important variations, as Chapter 38 in this volume shows. With the fall of the Communist bloc in Eastern Europe and the former Soviet Union, democracy seemed for a time to be "the only game in town." Even authoritarian leaders played the game of electoral competition. This gave rise to a historically new form of governance – "hybrid authoritarianism" – in which strong leaders manipulated electoral machinery to legitimate their rule (Levitsky and Way 2002).

Regimes, repertoires, and contention

We have seen how different types of states and their prevailing strategies condition movement perceptions of opportunities and threats. But once the decision to engage in collective action is made, how do characteristics of the state affect the types of collective action that groups choose to engage in? Before addressing this question, we need to introduce another key concept – *the repertoire of contention* – and two sub-types of that concept. We define contentious repertoires as arrays of performances that are currently known and available to some set of actors. Contained contention takes place within a regime, using its established institutional routines; transgressive contention challenges those routines and threatens the primacy of those they protect (Tilly and Tarrow 2015: 49, 62). In liberal-democratic regimes, we find a great deal of contention, but most of it is contained within institutions that are designed to structure and pacify conflict. Electoral and legislative institutions are the prime examples.

But even in liberal-democratic systems, movements that want to bring about fundamental change are very likely to use transgressive as well as contained forms of action (Gamson 1990). We can illustrate the difference by turning to two American earlier examples: Although the rhetoric of the Tea Party was full of verbal pyrotechnics, most of its actions were familiar and contained, especially once it had settled on an electoral strategy of challenging the "Republican establishment." In contrast, albeit softly, the activists of the Occupy movement transgressed routine politics by camping out in public spaces and refusing to move until they were forced to do so by the police.

In authoritarian regimes, there is much less open contention because of the risk of repression, but when contention does arise, it takes largely transgressive forms because the regime regards most forms of expression as dangerous. (But see Chapter 38 in this volume and Moss 2014, for a nuanced empirically-based discussion of this point.) In particular, authoritarian rulers regard organized contention as especially dangerous because it can spread. For example, the Chinese state has a repertoire of tools designed to absorb popular protest before the groups can form organized movements. In response to these risks, Chinese activists have devised innovative tactics such as "disguised collective action" (Fu 2016).

But if all political opportunities and threats were stable, there would be very little change. Yet we know that this is not the case. Below, we shift the focus from enduring features of political systems to variations in and changes of political opportunity and their effects on the ebb and flow of movements. Because much of the literature revolves around both variation and change, we draw selectively both on our own work and on the work of the numerous scholars whose research grows out of a basic interest in the reciprocal relations between opportunities and threats and political contention.

Changes in Opportunity and the Ebb and Flow of Movements

While many scholars have focused on how the stable features of institutionalized political systems affect movement activity, as we noted above, the earliest work on political context by authors like Lipsky, Eisinger, Tilly, and others, stressed the powerful impact of changes in, and variable aspects of, political opportunity and threat. Indeed, virtually all of the early proponents of what would come to be known as the political process perspective saw the timing and ultimate fate of movements, and/or protest, as powerfully conditioned by the variable opportunities afforded challengers by the shifting alliance structure, ideological disposition, and instrumental calculus of those in power. Reflecting the influence of these early works, changes in opportunity quickly became a staple of social movement theory and were used to account for the emergence and development of movements as diverse at the American women's movement (Costain 1992), liberation theology (Smith 1991), the anti-nuclear movement (Meyer 1993), farm worker mobilization in California (Jenkins 1985), and new social movement activity in Germany (Koopmans 1993, 1995), to name just a few early examples. Moreover, the rate at which new cases are offered in support of the general argument shows no signs of abating. Recent examples of work in this tradition would include: Brockett's (2005) comparative analysis of political movements in Central America, Karapin's (2007) study of "movements on the left and right in Germany since the 1960s," Steil and Vasi's (2014) comparative analysis of local pro-immigrant reform efforts in the USA between 2000 and 2011, and Jenkins, Jacobs, and Agnone's (2003: 277) systematic empirical account of the predictive relationship between political opportunities and "the frequency of African-American protest between 1948 and 1997."

As the emphasis on political context has grown, scholars of contention have offered many creative variations on the original model. For example, while nuancing McAdam's (1982, 1999) account of President Truman's advocacy of civil rights reform, Bloom's (2015) work is consistent with the central thrust of the political opportunity perspective, as is Felix Kolb's (2007) reinterpretation of the great victories of the civil rights struggle in the postwar period. In a string of publications, Amenta and collaborators have developed a compatible, if distinctive, "political mediation" model of the relationship between movements and political context (Amenta 2005; Amenta, Carruthers, and Zylan 1992; Amenta, Dunleavy, and Bernstein 1994; Amenta, Halfmann, and Young 1999). Finally, in his two book-length studies of "protest waves" in El Salvador, Almeida (2003, 2008) stressed the complex interplay of variable opportunities and threats in shaping the dynamics of contention.

Sources of change in political opportunities and threats

If political opportunities (and threats) can expand and contract, what are the principal sources of these fluctuations? Perhaps the two major sources of variable political opportunities and threats are changes in the composition of institutional actors and the force of destabilizing events on political context.

Changes in the Composition or Alignment of Institutional Actors

Earlier, we sketched five enduring sources of political opportunities and threats. Changes in these variables often alter perceptions of opportunities and threats helping to catalyze individual movements or broader cycles of contention.

1. *Openness or closure to new actors*: New actors often enter the polity through changes in class structure or immigration, but more often through the suffrage. In 1911, the Italian electoral law was revised to allow almost all male citizens to vote. When this reform was implemented in 1919, following a war that had been disastrous for the Italian economy and for the legitimacy of the elite, it opened the gates to Benito Mussolini's fascist movement, which was able to come to power a mere two years later (Tarrow 2015: Chapter 4). Conversely, when Mussolini's government closed down the electoral process after 1926 and arrested many of his political enemies, opposition movements were forced underground or into exile, not to return until World War II opened new opportunities for an armed Resistance movement.

2. *Stability or instability of political alignments*: Stable political alignments are unlikely to leave much space for insurgencies against the existing party system, which was the case for most of America's history, with a few notable exceptions. For example, in the 1850s, the decline of the Whigs and the splits among the

Democrats opened space for two movements – the Abolitionists and the Free Soil Party – to come together in a new movement-party, the Republican Party, which elected a little-known mid-western lawyer, Abraham Lincoln, as President in 1860 (Tarrow 2015: Chapter 3). Similarly, in the 1960s the embrace of civil rights reform, first reluctantly under President Kennedy, and later more aggressively by Lyndon Johnson, fractured the New Deal coalition, setting in motion a process of sustained racial and regional realignment that brought to a close the preceding period of Democratic dominance and ushered in the rise of an increasingly influential and conservative GOP (McAdam and Kloos 2014).

3. *Influential allies or supporters:* A polity is often seen as made up of "insiders," who run the system and "outsiders," who hammer at its gates to gain entry. But this leaves out a band of intermediate actors who straddle the boundaries of institutional politics, or who reach out from within the system to challengers whose goals they embrace or hope to advantage (Tarrow 2012; Tilly 1978). This was the case of the liberal wing of the Democratic Party in the 1930s, which passed the Wagner Act to empower previously excluded trade unions. As a result, the AFL and the CIO became part of what came to be called "the New Deal coalition," which governed American national politics until the 1960s. Conversely, the Taft-Hartley Act, passed in 1947 by a newly-elected Republican majority in Congress, prohibited some union activities, such as sympathy strikes, secondary boycotts, and discrimination against non-union members, and required union officers to take an oath that they were not communists. The result was a weakening of the American labor movement from which it has never recovered.

4. *Changes in repression or facilitation:* Repression we define as the attempt by a regime or its agents to end movement challenges through physical control. But repression is only one form on a spectrum of modes of social control, some of which aim to slow down or paralyze protest tactics, while others attempt to demobilize dissent by removing the resources for future action. Jules Boykoff (2007: 36) has studied various forms of social control, ranging from legal prosecution, employment discrimination, hearings. surveillance, infiltration, and other forms of harassment to direct violence against demonstrators. Jennifer Earl (2003) has classified protest control into 12 different forms, based on variations in the links between state agents and national elites, which combine (1) the identity of the actor engaging in protest; (2) the links between state agents and national elites; and (3) the form of protest control, ranging from military coercion to legal and financial pressure. Earl's own work shows that we cannot reduce the potential or actual threats to protesters to the overt use of police violence against them and that even states which have predominantly "soft" prevailing strategies sometimes use violence against those they consider a threat to public order.

As Tilly noted long ago in 1978, repression/facilitation are parts of the prevailing strategies of a regime toward protesters, but they vary across social and political sectors and over time. Regimes' facilitation or repression varies between social and political sectors in response to elites' hopes or fears that groups will either support or undermine their power. The most glaring variation in American history is the manipulation of the electoral machinery to favor some groups – for example, rural voters who are overrepresented in most state legislatures – or disfavor others, for example, African-Americans, both during the Jim Crow era and more recently. Political repression also varies over time, both as a result of which party or ruling group is in power or in response to the changing political climate and to destabilizing events, to which we now turn.

Destabilizing events

What kinds of events tend to destabilize political systems in ways that expand or contract opportunities for, or threats to, movement groups? There is no simple answer to the question. As McAdam noted: "A finite list of specific causes would be impossible to compile … *any* event or broad social process that serves to undermine the calculations and assumptions on which the political establishment is structured occasions a shift in political opportunities" (1982: 41; emphasis in original). He did, however, identify a smaller subset of events that he describes as especially "likely to prove disruptive of the political status quo." We take up what we see as the two most important of those identified by McAdam: *war* and *economic crises*. While wars profoundly close off the opportunities for contention, as governments curtail rights and citizens "rally round the flag," and economic crises remove resources from citizens, both war and economic crises have variable effects on both the formation and the character of social movements.

War and movements

James Madison long ago warned that war curtails rights, and for this reason, counselled against the creation of a standing army against his political opponent, Alexander Hamilton. As Madison warned, "Of all the enemies to public liberty, war is, perhaps, the most to be dreaded, because it comprises and develops the germ of every other" (1985: 491–492). As historian Porter found, "A government at war is a juggernaut of centralization determined to crush any internal opposition that impedes the mobilization of militarily vital resources" (1994: xv). Such warnings led legal theorist Scheppele (2006) to argue that modern warfare creates incentives for states to "put people in their place" – that is, to prevent them from protesting. The American Civil War and the two World Wars led to heavy restrictions of rights – especially of groups that were suspected of disloyalty to the regime (Tarrow 2015).

Yet wars have also triggered episodes of contentious politics, first, against the extraction of taxes and the forced quartering of soldiers, then against the draft and the scarcity of food for the civilian population, then against the regime as a whole, as in the Russian Revolution, and, finally, in movements against war itself and in favor of peace (Cortright 2014; Meyer 1993). Moreover, in war's wake, citizen groups of all kinds have profited from state weakening and from newfound militancy to demand new or expanded rights. It was in response to wartime sacrifices that women were granted the suffrage after World War I, that the GI Bill of Rights was passed at the end of World War II, and that 18-year-olds were given the vote during the Vietnam War (Mettler 2004).

Economic crises

Similarly, economic crises have contradictory effects on contentious politics. On the one hand, during economic crises, there is less demand for labor, leading to layoffs and the weakening of the bargaining power of unions. But as grievances grow and governments respond to the crisis with austerity programs, mobilization often grows among both workers and others, as we have seen during the Great Recession in both Europe and the United States (Bermeo and Bartels 2014). The latest crisis in the western economies, touched off by the collapse of the American financial sector in 2008, created new insurgent movements in Spain, Portugal, Greece, and the United States, both on the radical Left and on the populist Right (della Porta 2015).

Reciprocal effects of opportunities and institutions

Up to this point we have focused exclusively on the ways in which various kinds of facilitative changes or ruptures in systems of institutional politics may stimulate movement emergence or growth. But the relationship between these variables is reciprocal. If changes in political opportunities shape the prospects for movement emergence or success, the reverse is true as well (Tilly 2006). That is, once they are mobilized, movements have the capacity to reshape or modify the systems of institutional power within which they are embedded.

The volume of work on the topic of "movement outcomes" is now so large as to preclude an exhaustive summary. Fortunately, the chapters in this volume (see Part V in this volume) devoted to the topic spare us the need to systematically summarize this body of scholarship. Still, we see a selective review of some of the more influential works in this tradition as appropriate. Two movements in particular show how profound the effects of social movements have been on American political institutions: the civil rights movement and the women's movement.

With respect to civil rights, Andrews (1997, 2001, 2004) has carefully assessed the variable impact of the civil rights movement on a number of institutional outcomes (e.g. voter registration rates, number of black elected officials, size of anti-poverty programs) in Mississippi; Luders (2010) fashions a general "cost-assessment" theory of movement outcomes that looks, not at the decisions of government officials, but at economic actors; and Gillion (2013) goes beyond the usual focus on the signature legislative gains of the civil rights struggle to consider the movement's effect on judicial and presidential outcomes.

With respect to the women's movement, Banaszak (1996) has identified key factors that shaped the variable impact of the US women's suffrage movement over time, showing how this movement affected electoral institutions and outcomes; McCammon et al. (2001) assess the long, protracted, but ultimately successful effort of the women's suffrage movement to secure the franchise; Clemens (1997) demonstrated the impact of innovative women's movement organizing on the structure of interest group politics; and Katzenstein (1998) shows the profound impact of feminism on two unlikely institutions: the armed forces and the Catholic Church.

More generally, McAdam and Kloos (2014) attribute the deep divisions in contemporary American society – political, economic and racial – to the centrifugal force of a series of movements, first, on the left in the 1960s, and since then mostly on the right, in a process of "asymmetric polarization." These movements have fundamentally changed the "racial and regional geography" of American politics and pushed both parties off center and toward their respective ideological margins.

In general, American politics has been shaped throughout its history by an ongoing tug-of-war between movements, parties, and government institutions.

Repertoires of contention are not only shaped by regimes and institutions; over the long run, they shape them as well. For example, the strike, which was at first a transgressive form of collective action, eventually became a contained form of contention guided by legislation, habit, and routine interactions (Tarrow 2011). The same is true for other contained forms, like marching on Washington, a practice which descended from a spontaneous demonstration by the "Bonus Army" demanding bonuses for service in World War I, before being adopted in the civil rights demonstrations of the 1960s (Tilly and Tarrow 2015: 51–52). Eventually, marching on – or in – Washington became a routine way of demonstrating a movement's strength and determination.

But as contained forms of contention continue to dominate within American politics, a "forbidden" form – terrorism – has diffused dangerously around the world (see Chapter 37 in this volume). This has had profound effects on aspects of the American state, ranging from the merely annoying – i.e. security checks at airports – to ones that threaten civil liberties and human rights – e.g. the use of secret courts and the infiltration of privacy. Whether these changes are producing a "Schmittian" involution in the United States (Agamben 2005) or merely a shift in the balance of "infrastructural power" toward the government (Tarrow 2015) remains to be seen. What is certain is that violent contention in the form of terrorism is having a profound effect on institutional politics.

Critiques and Extensions

In his article in the *American Sociological Review*, Bloom wrote that "political opportunity theory has proven extremely generative" (2015: 391) in alerting movement scholars to the importance of political context and the variable vulnerability of regimes to insurgent challenge. That said, the theory has also been "generative" of critiques of various aspects of the perspective as well as a host of extensions and permutations of the general framework. Here we review what we see as the most significant criticisms – structural bias, indifference to non-state targets, and overemphasis on opportunity over threat – before adding one of our own – a "movement-centric bias" – and then turning to some of the theoretical "extensions" we see producing a new and improved conceptual perspective on the political contexts of contention.

Structural bias

The earliest and perhaps most common critique of the political process perspective focused on what was seen as the "structural bias" reflected in much of the work in this tradition (Bloom 2015; Goodwin and Jasper 1999; Joppke 1993; McAdam 1999: xi; Polletta 1999). Too often, according to critics, political opportunities were treated as objective features of political contexts that virtually compel movement action in a kind of deterministic response to environmental stimulus. While agreeing with this critique, it should be clear that the bias is not inherent in the model. As Kriesi (2004: 77–78) noted in his chapter on "political context and opportunity" in the first edition of this *Companion*:

> Nothing in the general approach [is inherently deterministic] ... Thus the earliest version of the political process model—McAdam's (1982: 48–51) account of the civil rights movement—was already very much aware of the subjective elements mediating between opportunity and action ... and he, at the time, criticized the proponents of both the classic and resource mobilization perspectives for ignoring [interpretive processes].

If not inherent in the theory, however, the distinction between objective political conditions and their subjective interpretation was missing from much of the work that the model inspired. Perceived and socially constructed opportunities gave way in later work to "political opportunity structures" (POS) and, with this shift in emphasis, what had originally been conceived of as an interpretive account of movement emergence – albeit with structural stimuli – had morphed into a structurally determinist one. What rightly troubled the critics was the implicit claim that objective shifts in the ruling party, institutional rules, or some other dimension of the "political opportunity structure," virtually *compel* mobilization. This, as they were wont to point out, is a structuralist conceit that fails to grant to collective meaning-making its central role in social life.

The good news is that the structural determinist applications of political process theory have largely given way to more processual, interpretive formulations. With the theory's emphasis on the ongoing interaction of movement and state actors within a shifting and necessarily constructed political context, research in the "political mediation" tradition clearly conforms to the latter framework. More importantly, without invoking any specific theory, the best recent work in the field also suggests adherence to this more interpretive, interactive conception of political context and movement dynamics.

Recent works help to make our point. In her 2012 book, *The U.S. Women's Jury Movement and Strategic Adaptation*, comparing the development and impact of the movement in 15 states over time, McCammon argues that progress was fastest in those states where activists showed the greatest skill at reading and responding to the shifting political and cultural "exigencies" confronting them. Similarly, in their comparative study of variation in the level of "transgressive protest" directed at corporate, educational, and other institutional targets, Walker, Martin, and McCarthy (2008) offer a similarly dynamic, interpretive, account of their findings. Just as the strategic responses of McCammon's activists reflected their evolving understanding of the targets of their actions, Walker et al. see the specific repertoires deployed by the movements as reflecting a sophisticated understanding of each target's vulnerabilities and its capacities – or lack thereof – to respond to movement tactics.

Indifference to non-state targets

A second critique of the political process perspective on context challenges the theory's preoccupation with formal state institutions and actors as the central targets of movement activities. While no doubt germane to many conflicts, contexts other than institutionalized systems of state authority are relevant to an understanding of movements. This was the key point in Snow's (2004) article on movements as challenges to authority. While other authors had voiced this criticism before, no one did so in as much detail as Armstrong and Bernstein in their 2008 article in *Sociological Theory*. Moreover, they deployed their critique in the service of an alternative perspective, what they term "a multi-institutional politics approach to social movements." The central insight of the perspective is straightforward: the wide variety of movements that we encounter in the contemporary world aim at a far more varied set of targets and institutional contexts than suggested by the state-centered version of the political process model.

Armstrong and Bernstein make a good case: By privileging political movements over all others, proponents of the political process perspective unwittingly have marginalized other targets and indeed, other types of movements, within the field of social movement studies. Happily, the impact of this second line of critique is inspiring research on a much broader array of movements and targets. The Walker et al. (2008) article on the determinants of movement tactics against corporate and educational targets is only one example of the broadening of empirical work in the field. But it also fits with what is almost certainly the single most prominent line of new work to emerge in the last decade or so. We refer to research that looks at movements that target corporate or other economic actors.

The list of works in this area includes Ingram, Yue, Rao's (2010) analysis of the dynamics of strategic interaction between company officials and anti-Walmart activists; King's (2008a, 2008b) work on both stakeholder activism and its impact on the factors that shape the way corporations respond to movements that target them; Raeburn's (2004) detailed account of lesbian and gay challenges to corporate workplace practices; Schurman and Munro's (2010) book on the dynamics of contention shaping the growing conflict between agribusiness and their varied movement opponents; and Soule's 2009 book, *Contention and Corporate Social Responsibility*. But as we will argue below, this new strand of work on contention against non-state targets can profit from engagement with the political process perspective.

Threat and opportunity

In *From Mobilization to Revolution*, Tilly (1978) assigned equal weight to threat and opportunity as catalysts of emergent collective action. The other early proponents of the political process approach, however, generally downplayed the causal significance of threat in deference to a singular preoccupation with expanding political opportunities (see Chapter 2 by Almeida in this volume, on the importance of threats). McAdam (1982), for example, made no mention of threat in his formal explication of the model. This led to a third important critique of the political process perspective, the failure to grant any real significance to the role of perceived threats, as opposed to opportunities, in the genesis of emergent collective action. This lacuna made it difficult for the early proponents of the perspective to understand whole categories of movements, from ethnic conflict triggered by fears of economic and political competition from other racial/ethnic groups to the wide array of reactive movements that arise in response to "suddenly imposed grievances" (Walsh and Warland 1983) or other perceived NIMBY-style threats (Snow et al. 1998).

The stress on opportunity also did not square with the inconsistent findings regarding the relationship between repression and collective action. If we think of repression as the contraction of opportunities, then an increase in repression should typically lead to lower levels of protest or other forms of collective action. We know, however, from the extensive empirical literature on repression, that this is not always the case. Even controlling for other factors, repression often presages higher levels of insurgent action (Khawaja 1993; Olivier 1991; Rasler 1996). If we think of repression as a form of threat, the failure to assign equal predictive significance to threat and opportunity becomes all the more apparent. Today scholars of contention are apt to see movements as shaped by a complex mix of perceived threats and opportunities, as would-be insurgents seek to make sense of the political and other contexts in which they are embedded.

Ongoing empirical work on repression continues to yield findings that speak to the significance of both threat and opportunity as catalysts of protest (Earl 2003). Scholars of ethnic conflict and violence continue to adduce evidence consistent with competition theory's emphasis on perceived economic and political threats in the genesis of contention (Olzak 2006). And reactive, NIMBY-style, collective action against all manner of perceived threats, remains perhaps the single most common type of protest world-wide. Adding to this, the large number of recent studies that assign principal causal significance to the role of perceived threat in the origin of a movement affords a sense of how analytically central threat has become to the study of contention. A remarkable example in this regard will serve to make the point: Maher's (2010) study of "threat, resistance, and collective action" in the three Nazi death camps of Sobibor, Treblinka, and Auschwitz. Another is Einwohner's (2006) work on Jewish resistance in the Warsaw ghetto.

A movement-centric bias

To these three critiques of the political process perspective we add one of our own. We worry that, relative to the "early days," the field is now far more "movement-centric" and less focused on the relationship between movement and context, even as the field has grown exponentially since its modest beginnings in the 1970s and the 1980s. The absence of a recognized field of social movement studies, circa 1970, forced those scholars whose works defined the emerging field to read widely and frame their work for much broader audiences. Some situated their work within the literature on political economy (Paige 1975; Piven and Cloward 1977; Schwartz 1976; Skocpol 1979); still others within organizational studies (McCarthy and Zald (1973, 1977); and others in world systems theory (Arrighi, Hopkins, and Wallerstein 1989). For their part, those who shaped the emerging political process perspective were in dialogue with colleagues in political science and political sociology (Eisinger 1973; McAdam 1982; Tarrow 1983; Tilly 1978). These scholars simply did not have the luxury of framing their work in terms of a very specific body of social movement theory and research.

As the field developed, however, it quickly grew sufficiently large as to serve as its own primary audience, allowing it to become increasingly insular and self-referential in the process. As Walder observed in his 2009 critical review of the field, social movement scholarship is now squarely – and narrowly – focused on mobilization, on those who mobilize, and in general, on internal movement dynamics. An examination of the index of the first edition of *The Blackwell Companion to Social Movements* affords a telling reflection of the narrowness that has come to characterize social movement studies. (But note the section entitled "Thematic Intersections in the current edition of this book.)

Consider the following list of index entries that reflect a broader *contextual* understanding of movements:

- Capitalism/capital – 5 pages;
- Economic instability – 2 pages;
- Elections/electoral systems – 6 pages;
- Political parties – 4 pages;
- State(s)/state breakdown – 49 pages;
- World economy – 2 pages;
- World system theory – 8 pages.

With the exception of "state(s)/state breakdown," the listings for these contextual topics are somewhat meager. If, at the outset, the field was substantially concerned with understanding movements in macro-political and economic context, this broader "external" focus has atrophied considerably. Contrast the paltry numbers reported above with the large number of listings for the following set of movement-centric topics:

- Collective identity – 47 pages;
- Emotions – 30 pages;
- Framing/frames – 96 pages;
- Mobilization – 75 pages;
- Social movement organization – 48 pages;
- Tactics/tactical repertoires – 39 pages.

We want to be clear about our argument. There is *nothing* wrong with the focus on internal movement dynamics. Forty years of scholarship on social movements have yielded great gains in our understanding of this most important form of purposive collective action. Our concern is with the balance and interaction between this *internal* focus on movement dynamics and how these movements relate to, engage with, are born of and often modify the *external* political, economic, cultural, and legal contexts in which they are embedded. In the next section we examine two growing areas of interest that connect movements with crucial interlocutors – courts and political parties.

Extensions and combinations

If there have been serious and constructive criticisms of the approach we have just described, there have also been creative extensions and combinations. We illustrate this with two extensions – the relations of movements to courts and parties – and with one major combination – the linkages between economic factors and the political process.

Movements and elections

Elections offer opportunities for contention in both liberal-democratic and authoritarian regimes. As we have argued elsewhere (McAdam and Tarrow 2013), movements can transfer their activism to support friendly parties in elections, as the American trade unions have done since the 1930s. This was the pattern of the Tea Party movement, which arose as a grassroots and "astroturf" movement in 2010 and transferred its activism to the Republican Party (Skocpol and Williamson 2011). Movements can also react to disputed elections that they oppose, sometimes leading to "electoral revolutions," as occurred in the Balkans and in the Caucasus (Bunce and Wolchik 2011). Movements can also bring about changes in parties' electoral fortunes. Think of the election of Lincoln in 1860 and of Roosevelt in 1932, or the impact of the anti-Vietnam War movement on the elections of 1968 and 1972; they were mainly the result of the intrusion of movements into the party system.

Movements can force parties to shift to the extremes in order to satisfy their demands (McAdam and Kloos 2014). They can also become parties themselves, as the Green movement did in Germany in the 1980s, becoming an institutionalized part of the party system. Such transformations often lead to the co-option of movement leaders as they enter parliaments, as Michels (1962) long ago predicted, but often have profound effects on the system as a whole, as the recent appearance of insurgent anti-institutional parties has done in Greece, Italy, and Spain (della Porta 2015).

Movements and the courts

Another set of institutions – legal institutions – have only recently come to the attention of social movement scholars. (See Chapter 17 by Boutcher and McCammon in this volume.) Legal scholars are rapidly coming to appreciate that social movements drive much legal change (Balkin 2011; Cole 2016; Edelman, Leachman, and McAdam 2010; McCann 1994), although the verdict is not unanimous (Rosenberg 2008). But our theoretical understanding of the relationship among law and social movements remains one-sided. In particular, little is known about the dynamics by which changes in law and lawmaking translate into changes in advocacy tactics and about the reciprocal relations between movements and legal institutions in these changes.

Ever since the decision in *Brown v. Board of Education* came down from the United States Supreme Court in 1954, legal scholars have been acutely aware of the impact of court decisions on social change. But what has been less clearly recognized are the complicated relations between social movement organizations and legal change. While it is true that it was a movement organization – the NAACP – that brought the case against the Board of Education of Topeka, Kansas, less clear is the role of movements in the implementation – or *non*-implementation – of that decision. While some scholars have seen the Brown case as revolutionary, others have cast doubt on its long-term impact. One scholar even labeled the aspiration to bring about racial justice through the courts *A Hollow Hope* (Rosenberg 2008), pointing out accurately how effectively the decision was dismantled by state authorities in the white-dominated South.

How then was racial justice achieved in the wake of the *Brown* decision? To understand this outcome, we need to turn from the courts and the legislatures back to social movements. For it was not the original court-centered mobilization by the NAACP that brought about racial justice but the far more transgressive protests of the sit-ins and other forms of direct action in the early 1960s that forced federal officials to intervene in the South and compelled the many instances of school integration that the courts had been unable or unwilling to enforce (Klarman 2004).

In both the relations between movements and parties and in legal mobilization on behalf of civil rights, the movement-centeredness we criticized in the last section would only take us so far; but neither could a sole attention to political institutions: it is in the reciprocal relations between public institutions and social movements that social progress was made in both areas; which takes us to our concluding remarks.

Combinations and permutations

We argued earlier against a "movement-centric" approach to contentious politics, and would be untrue to our expansive approach if we did not recognize that "politics isn't everything." Take the emphasis on protests against non-state targets that we sketched in the last section, drawing on the work of Snow and others. Such an emphasis developed in the context of a critique of political process theory (Armstrong and Bernstein 2008), but it can also usefully be *combined with* that approach. For example, are anti-corporate movements more likely to emerge or be more successful under progressive governments than under corporate-friendly ones? Do non-state-targeting movements grow out of broader cycles of contention that initially target the state? And how do the goals of businesses and movements mesh, as we saw in the current coalition of privacy groups and tech businesses against the government's campaign to force Apple to open its iPhones to surveillance? Linking challenges to non-state actors with changes in the political context may well be the next step in the expansion of the political process approach.

More broadly, how are changes in the economic system processed through contentious politics? Every economy in the West was stricken by the economic crisis that was touched off in the United States in 2008, but they did not all respond in the same ways. Some countries – like Canada – barely saw the rise of anti-austerity movements; some – like the United States – saw the near-simultaneous rise of a leftist and rightist populist movements; some – like Ireland and Iceland – saw immediate, but rapidly declining protests against their governments' financial manipulations; while others – like Greece and Spain – have been profoundly roiled by new leftist movements that have shifted the alignments of their party systems.

Despite the appearance of politically-sensitive comparative accounts of the Great Recession by political scientists and sociologists (Bermeo and Bartels 2014; della Porta 2015), we still lack a comparative analysis of the effects of economic crisis that combines economic variables with the political process. "Bringing capitalism back in" and combining it with the political processing of economic crisis and revival may well be the next important step in the study of the political context of social movements.

Conclusion

We have been charged in this chapter with reviewing work on the "political contexts" of social movements. Our interest in movements has always been, first and foremost, motivated by the conviction that the dynamic, reciprocal relationship between movements and systems of institutionalized politics is among the most consequential forces of social and political change in society. This is true whether we examine enduring institutional sources of opportunity and threat, as we did in the first section, or their changing and variable sources, as we have done in the second section. The critiques and self-critiques in the third section were serious enough to produce revisions and permutations in the original theory and will – we hope – lead future scholars to learn from them in a positive fashion. The extensions of political process theory we have highlighted show that the promise of the study of political contexts of movements lies in examining their reciprocal relations with and within institutions.

We close with a confession and heartfelt celebration of the field of social movement studies. Even as we salute the broad, pioneering works that helped give birth to the field, we would be the first to admit that the best social movement scholarship today is far more sophisticated, both theoretically and methodologically, than the "classic" works in the political process tradition. Even as we decry the movement-centric bias we worry about, we have no trouble pointing to countless recent works that reflect the concern with context and the balance between "internal" and "external" foci that we are advocating here. Still, we would be remiss if, in bringing the chapter to a close, we did not urge the field, as a whole, to be mindful of the movement-centric narrowness that too often characterizes the field and to look for ways to redress the narrowness by taking context – of all kinds – more seriously.

References

Adorno, T., E. Frenkel-Brunswick, D.J. Levinson, and R.N. Sanford. 1950. *The Authoritarian Personality*. New York: Harper & Brothers.

Agamben, Giorgio. 2005. *State of Exception*. Chicago: University of Chicago Press.

Almeida, Paul D. 2003. "Opportunity Organizations and Threat-Induced Contention: Protest Waves in Authoritarian Settings," *American Journal of Sociology* 109: 345–400.

Almeida, Paul D. 2008. *Waves of Protest: Popular Struggle in El Salvador, 1925–2005*. Minneapolis: University of Minnesota Press.

Amenta, Edwin. 2005. "Political Contexts, Challenger Strategies, and Mobilization: Explaining the Impact of the Townsend Plan." In *Routing the Opposition: Social Movements, Public Policy and Democracy*, edited by David S. Meyer, Valerie Jenness, and Helen Ingram. Minneapolis: University of Minnesota Press.

Amenta, Edwin, Bruce Carruthers, and Yvonne Zylan. 1992. "A Hero for the Aged? The Townsend Movement, the Political Mediation Model, and U.S. Old-Age Policy, 1934–1950." *American Journal of Sociology* 98: 308–339.

Amenta, Edwin, Kathleen Dunleavy, and Mary Bernstein. 1994. "Stolen Thunder? Huey Long's 'Share our Wealth,' Political Mediation, and the Second New Deal." *American Sociological Review* 59: 678–702.

Amenta, Edwin, Drew Halfmann, and Michael Young. 1999. "The Strategies and Contexts of Social Protest: Political Mediation and the Impact of the Townsend Movement." *Mobilization* 56: 1–25.

Andrews, Kenneth T. 1997. "The Impacts of Social Movements on the Political Process: The Civil Rights Movement and Black Electoral Politics in Mississippi." *American Sociological Review* 62: 800–819.

Andrews, Kenneth T. 2001. "Social Movements and Policy Implementation: The Mississippi Civil Rights Movement and the War on Poverty, 1965–1971." *American Sociological Review* 66: 21–48.

Andrews, Kenneth T. 2004. *Freedom Is a Constant Struggle*. Chicago: University of Chicago Press.

Armstrong, Elizabeth A. and Mary Bernstein. 2008. "Culture, Power, and Institutions: A Multi-Institutional Politics Approach to Social Movements." *Sociological Theory* 26: 74–99.

Arrighi, Giovanni, Terence K. Hopkins, and Immanuel Wallerstein. 1989. *Antisystemic Movements*. London: Verso.

Balkin, Jack. 2011. *Constitutional Redemption*. Cambridge, MA: Harvard University Press.

Banaszak, Lee Ann. 1996. *Why Movements Succeed or Fail*. Princeton, NJ: Princeton University Press.

Bermeo, Nancy and Larry Bartels. 2014. *Mass Politics in Tough Times: Opinions, Votes, and Protest in the Great Recession*. New York: Oxford University Press.

Bloom, Joshua. 2015. "The Dynamics of Opportunity and Insurgent Practice: How Black Anti-colonialists Compelled Truman to Advocate Civil Rights." *American Sociological Review* 80: 391–415.

Boykoff, Jules. 2007. *Beyond Bullets: The Suppression of Dissent in the United States*. Oakland, CA: AK Press.

Brockett, Charles D. 2005. *Political Movements and Violence in Central America*. Cambridge: Cambridge University Press.

Bunce, Valerie. 1999. *Subversive Institutions: The Design and the Destruction of Socialism and the State*. New York: Cambridge University Press.

Bunce, Valerie and Sharon Wolchik. 2011. *Defeating Authoritarian Leaders in Mixed Regimes: Electoral Struggles, U.S. Democracy Assistance, and International Diffusion in Post-Communist Europe and Eurasia*. New York: Cambridge University Press.

Clemens, Elisabeth S. 1997. *The People's Lobby: Organizational Innovation and the Rise of Interest Group Politics in the United States, 1890–1925*. Chicago: University of Chicago Press.

Cole, David. 2016. *Engines of Liberty: The Power of Citizen Activists to Make Constitutional Law*. New York: Basic Books.

Cortright, David. 2014. "Protest and Politics: How Peace Movements Shape History." In *Handbook of Global Security Policy*, edited by Mary Kaldor and Ivor Rangelov, 482–504. Hoboken, NJ: Wiley-Blackwell.

Costain, Anne W. 1992. *Inviting Women's Rebellion: A Political Process Interpretation of the Women's Movement*. Baltimore, MD: Johns Hopkins University Press.

della Porta, Donatella. 2015. *Social Movements in Times of Austerity: Bringing Capitalism Back In*. Cambridge: Polity.

Diani, Mario. 1995. *Green Networks: A Structural Analysis of the Italian Environmental Movement*. Edinburgh: Edinburgh University Press.

Diani, Mario and Doug McAdam, eds. 2003. *Social Movements and Networks: Relational Approaches to Collective Action*. New York: Oxford University Press.

Earl, Jennifer. 2003. "Tanks, Tear Gas, and Taxes: Toward a Theory of Movement Repression." *Sociological Theory* 21: 44–68.

Edelman, Lauren B., Gwendolyn Leachman, and Doug McAdam. 2010. "On Law, Organizations and Social Movements." *Annual Review of Sociology* 6: 653–685.

Einwohner, Rachel. 2006. "Identity Work and Collective Action in a Repressive Context: Jewish Resistance on the 'Aryan Side' of the Warsaw Ghetto." *Social Problems* 38: 38–56.

Eisinger, Peter K. 1973. "The Conditions of Protest Behavior in American Cities." *American Political Science Reviews* 67: 11–28.

Emirbayer, Mustafa and Jeff Goodwin. 1994. "Network Analysis, Culture, and the Problems of Agency." *American Journal of Sociology* 99: 1411–1454.

Fu, Diana. 2016. "Disguised Collective Action in China." *Comparative Political Studies* doi: 10.1177/0010414015626437.

Gamson, William A. 1990. *The Strategy of Social Protest.* 2nd edn. Belmont, CA: Wadsworth Publishing.

Gillion, Daniel Q. 2013. *The Political Power of Protests: Minority Activism and Shifts in Public Policy.* New York: Cambridge University Press.

Goldstone, Jack A. 1991. *Revolution and Rebellion in the Early Modern World.* Berkeley: University of California Press.

Goldstone, Jack A. and Charles Tilly. 2001. "Threat (and Opportunity): Popular Action and State Response in the Dynamics of Contentious Action." In *Silence and Voice in the Study of Contentious Politics*, edited by Ronald Aminzade, Jack A. Goldstone, Doug McAdam, et al. 179–194. New York: Cambridge University Press.

Goodwin, Jeff and James M. Jasper. 1999. "Caught in a Winding, Snarling Vine: The Structural Bias of Political Process Theory." *Sociological Forum* 14: 27–54.

Gould, Roger V. 1991. "Multiple Networks and Mobilization in the Paris Commune, 1871." *American Sociological Review* 56: 716–729.

Gould, Roger V. 1993. "Collective Action and Network Structure." *American Sociological Review* 58: 182–196.

Gould, Roger V. 1995. *Insurgent Identities: Class, Community, and Protest from Paris to the Commune.* Chicago: University of Chicago Press.

Hobsbawm, Eric and George Rudé. 1975. *Captain Swing.* New York: W.W. Norton.

Hoffer, Eric. 1951. *The True Believers: Thoughts on the Nature of Mass Movements.* New York: New American Library.

Ingram, Paul, Lori Qingyuan Yue, and Hayagreeva Rao. 2010. "Trouble in Store: Probes, Protests, and Store Openings by Wal-Mart, 1998–2007." *American Journal of Sociology* 116: 53–92.

Jenkins, J. Craig. 1985. *The Politics of Insurgency: The Farm Workers Movement in the 1960s.* New York: Columbia University Press.

Jenkins, J. Craig, David Jacobs, and Jon Agnone. 2003. "Political Opportunities and African-America Protest, 1948–1997." *American Journal of Sociology* 109: 277–303.

Joppke, Christian. 1993. *Mobilizing against Nuclear Energy: A Comparison of Germany and the United States.* Berkeley: University of California Press.

Karapin, Roger. 2007. *Protest Politics in Germany: Movements on the Left and Right since the 1960s.* University Park, PA: Pennsylvania State University Press.

Katzenstein, Mary Fainsod. 1998. *Faithful and Fearless: Moving Feminist Politics inside the Church and Military.* Princeton, NJ: Princeton University Press.

Ketchley, Neil. 2017. *Mobilizing Egypt.* New York: Cambridge University Press.

Khawaja, Marwan. 1993. "Repression and Popular Collective Action: Evidence from the West Bank." *Sociological Forum* 8: 47–71.

King, Brayden. 2008a. "A Political Mediation Model of Corporate Response to Social Movement Activism." *Administrative Science Quarterly* 53: 395–421.

King, Brayden. 2008b. "A Social Movement Perspective on Stakeholder Collective Action and Influence." *Business Society* 47: 21–49.

Kitschelt, Herbert. 1986. "Political Opportunity Structures and Political Protest: Anti-Nuclear Movements in Four Democracies." *British Journal of Political Science* 16(1): 57–85.

Klarman, Michael J. 2004. *From Jim Crow to Civil Rights: The Supreme Court and the Struggle for Racial Equality*. New York: Oxford University Press.

Kolb, Felix. 2007. *Protest and Opportunities: The Politics of Outcomes of Social Movements*. Frankfurt: Campus.

Koopmans, Ruud. 1993. "The Dynamics of Protest Waves: West Germany, 1965–1989." *American Sociological Review* 58: 637–658.

Koopmans, Ruud. 1995. *Democracy from Below: New Social Movements and the Political System in West Germany*. Boulder, CO: Westview Press.

Kornhauser, William. 1959. *The Politics of Mass Society*. Glencoe, IL: Free Press.

Kriesi, Hanspeter. 2004. "Political Context and Opportunity." In *The Blackwell Companion to Social Movements*, edited by David A. Snow, Sarah A. Soule, and Hanspeter Kriesi, 67–90. Malden, MA: Blackwell Publishing.

Kriesi, Hanspeter, Ruud Koopmans, Jan Willem Duyvendak, and Marco G. Giugni. 1995. *New Social Movements in Western Europe*. Minneapolis: University of Minnesota Press.

Le Bon, Gustave. 1960. *The Crowd: A Study of the Popular Mind*. New York: Penguin.

Levitsky, Steven and Lucan A. Way. 2002. "The Rise of Competitive Authoritarianism." *Journal of Democracy* 16: 57–85.

Lipsky, Michael. 1970. *Protest in City Politics*. Chicago: Rand McNally.

Lipsky, Michael and David Olson. 1976. "The Processing of Racial Crisis in America." *Politics and Society* 13: 51–65.

Lohmann, Susanne. 1993. "A Signaling Model of Informative and Manipulative Political Action." *American Political Science Review* 87: 319–333.

Luders, Joseph E. 2010. *The Civil Rights Movement and the Logic of Social Change*. New York: Cambridge University Press.

Madison, James. 1985. "Political Observations." *Letters and Other Writings of James Madison*, vol. IV. Philadelphia, PA: Lippincott.

Maher, Thomas V. 2010. "Threat, Resistance, and Collective Action: The Cases of Sobibor, Treblinka, and Auschwitz." *American Sociological Review* 75: 252–272.

McAdam, Doug. 1982. *Political Process and the Development of Black Insurgency, 1930–1970*. Chicago: University of Chicago Press.

McAdam, Doug. 1986. "Recruitment to High-Risk Activism: The Case of Freedom Summer." *American Journal of Sociology* 94: 64–90.

McAdam, Doug. 1999. *Political Process and the Development of Black Insurgency, 1930–1970*. 2nd edn. Chicago: University of Chicago Press.

McAdam, Doug and Karina Kloos. 2014. *Deeply Divided: Racial Politics and Social Movements in Postwar America*. New York: Oxford University Press.

McAdam, Doug and Ronnelle Paulsen. 1993. "Specifying the Relationship between Social Ties and Activism." *American Journal of Sociology* 99: 640–667.

McAdam, Doug and Sidney Tarrow. 2005. "Scale Shift in Transnational Contention." In *Transnational Protest and Global Activism*, edited by Donatella della Porta and Sidney Tarrow, 121–147. Lanham, MD: Rowman & Littlefield Publishers.

McAdam, Doug and Sidney Tarrow. 2013. "Social Movements and Elections: Towards a Better Understanding of the Political Context of Contention." In *The Changing Dynamics of Contention*, edited by Jacquelien Van Stekelenburg, Conny M. Roggevand, and Bert Klandermans, 325–346. Minneapolis: University of Minnesota Press.

McAdam, Doug, Sidney Tarrow, and Charles Tilly. 2001. *Dynamics of Contention*. New York: Cambridge University Press.

McCammon, Holly J. 2012. *The U.S. Women's Jury Movements and Strategic Adaptation: A More Just Verdict*. New York: Cambridge University Press.

McCammon, Holly J., Karen E. Campbell, Ellen M. Granberg, and Christine Mowery. 2001. "How Movements Win: Gendered Opportunity Structures and U.S. Women's Suffrage Movements, 1866–1919." *American Sociological Review* 66: 49–70.

McCann, Michael W. 1994. *Rights at Work: Pay Equity Reform and the Politics of Legal Mobilization*. Chicago: University of Chicago Press.

McCann, Michael W., ed. 2006. *Law and Social Movements*. Burlington, VT: Ashgate.

McCarthy, John D. and Mayer N. Zald. 1973. *The Trend of Social Movements in America: Professionalization and Resource Mobilization*. Morristown, NJ: General Learning Press.

McCarthy, John D. and Mayer N. Zald. 1977. "Resource Mobilization and Social Movements: A Partial Theory." *American Journal of Sociology* 82: 1212–1241.

Melucci, Alberto. 1985. "The Symbolic Challenge of Contemporary Movements." *Social Research* 52: 789–812.

Mettler, Suzanne. 2004. *Soldiers to Citizens: The G.I. Bill and the Making of the Greatest Generation*. New York: Oxford University Press.

Meyer, David. 1993. "Institutionalizing Dissent: The United States Structure of Political Opportunity and the End of the Nuclear Freeze." *Sociological Forum* 8: 157–179.

Michels, Robert. 1962. *Political Parties: A Sociological Study of the Oligarchical Tendencies of Modern Democracy*. New York: Collier.

Moss, Dana. 2014. "Repression, Response, and Contained Escalation under 'Liberalized' Authoritarianism in Jordan." *Mobilization: An International Quarterly* 19(3): 489–514.

Olivier, Johan. 1991. "State Repression and Collective Action in South Africa, 1970–84." *South African Journal of Sociology* 22: 109–117.

Olzak, Susan. 2006. *The Global Dynamics of Racial and Ethnic Mobilization*. Stanford, CA: Stanford University Press.

Paige, Jeffrey M. 1975. *Agrarian Revolution*. New York: Free Press.

Piven, Francis Fox and Richard Cloward. 1977. *Poor People's Movements: Why They Succeed. How They Fail*. New York: Pantheon Books.

Polletta, Francesca. 1999. "Snarls, Quacks, and Quarrels: Culture and Structure in Political Process Theory." *Sociological Forum* 14: 63–70.

Porter, Bruce. 1994. *War and the Rise of the State: The Military Foundations of Modern Politics*. New York: The Free Press.

Raeburn, Nicole. 2004. *Changing Corporate America from Inside Out: Lesbian and Gay Workplace Rights*. Minneapolis: University of Minnesota Press.

Rasler, Karen. 1996. "Concessions, Repression and Political Protest." *American Sociological Review* 61: 132–152.

Rosenberg, Gerry. 2008. *The Hollow Hope: Can Courts Bring About Social Change?* Chicago: University of Chicago Press.

Scheppele, Kim Lane. 2006. "The Migration of Anti-Constitutional Ideas: The Post-9/11 Globalization of Public Law and the International State of Emergency." In *The Migration of Constitutional Ideas*, edited by Sujit Choudry, 347–373. New York: Cambridge University Press.

Schurman, Rachel and William A. Munro. 2010. *Fighting for the Future of Food: Activists Versus Agribusiness in the Struggle over Biotechnology*. Minneapolis: University of Minnesota Press.

Schwartz, Michael. 1976. *Radical Protest and Social Structure*. New York: Academic Press.

Skocpol, Theda. 1979. *States and Social Revolutions*. Cambridge: Cambridge University Press.

Skocpol, Theda and Vanessa Williamson. 2011. *The Tea Party and the Remaking of Republican Conservatism*. New York: Oxford University Press.

Smelser, Neil. 1962. *Theory of Collective Behavior*. New York: Free Press.

Smith, Christian. 1991. *The Emergence of Liberation Theology*. Chicago: University of Chicago Press.

Snow, David A. 2004. "Social Movements as Challenges to Authority: Resistance to an Emerging Conceptual Hegemony." In *Authority in Contention: Research in Social Movements, Conflict, and Change*, edited by Daniel J. Meyers and Daniel M. Cress, 3–25. London: Elsevier.

Snow, David A. and Robert D. Benford. 1988. "Ideology, Frame Resonance, and Participant Mobilization." In *International Social Movement Research, vol. 1, From Structure to Action*, edited by Bert Klandermans, Hanspeter Kriesi, and Sidney Tarrow, 197–218. Greenwich, CT: JAI Press.

Snow, David A., E. Burke Rochford Jr., Steven K. Worden, and Robert D. Benford. 1986. "Frame Alignment Processes, Micromobilization, and Movement Participation." *American Sociological Review* 51: 464–481.

Snow, David A., Daniel Cress, Liam Downey, and Andrew Jones, 1998, "Disrupting the Quotidian: Reconceptualizing the Relationship between Breakdown and the Emergence of Collective Action." *Mobilization: An International Journal* 3: 1–22.

Snow, David A., Lewis A. Zurcher, and Sheldon Ekland-Olson. 1980. "Social Networks and Social Movements: A Mircrostructural Approach to Differential Recruitment." *American Sociological Review* 45: 787–801.

Soule, Sarah A. 2009. *Contention and Corporate Social Responsibility*. New York: Cambridge University Press.

Steil, Justin Peter and Ion Bogdan Vasi. 2014. "The New Immigration Contestation: Social Movements and Local Immigration Policy Making in the United States, 2000–2011." *American Journal of Sociology* 119: 1104–1155.

Szymanski, Anne-Marie. 2003. *Pathways to Prohibition: Radicals, Moderates, and Social Movement Outcomes*. Durham, NC: Duke University Press.

Tarrow, Sidney. 1967. *Peasant Communism in Southern Italy*. New Haven, CT: Yale University Press.

Tarrow, Sidney. 1983. "Struggling to Reform: Social Movements and Policy Change during Cycles of Protest." Center for International Studies, Western Societies Occasional Paper no. 15. Ithaca, NY: Cornell University.

Tarrow, Sidney. 1989. *Democracy and Disorder: Protest and Politics in Italy, 1965–1975*. Oxford: Clarendon Press.

Tarrow, Sidney. 2011. *Power in Movement*. 3rd edn. New York: Cambridge University Press.

Tarrow, Sidney. 2012. *Strangers at the Gates: Movements and States in Contentious Politics*. New York: Cambridge University Press.

Tarrow, Sidney. 2015. *War, States, and Contention*. Ithaca, NY: Cornell University Press.

Thompson, E.P. 1966. *The Making of the English Working Class*. New York: Vintage.

Tilly, Charles. 1964. *The Vendée*. Cambridge, MA: Harvard University Press.

Tilly, Charles. 1978. *From Mobilization to Revolution*. Reading, MA: Addison-Wesley.

Tilly, Charles. 2006. *Regimes and Repertoires*. New York: Cambridge University Press.

Tilly, Charles and Sidney Tarrow. 2015. *Contentious Politics*. 2nd edn. New York: Oxford University Press.

Touraine, Alain. 1971. *The May Movement: Revolt and Reform*. New York: Random House.

Walder, Andrew. 2009. "Political Sociology and Social Movements." *Annual Review of Sociology* 35: 393–412.

Walker, Edward T., Andrew W. Martin, and John D. McCarthy. 2008. "Confronting the State, the Corporation, and the Academy: The Influence of Institutional Targets on Social Movement Repertoires." *American Journal of Sociology* 114: 35–76.

Walsh, Edward J. and Rex H. Warland. 1983. "Social Movement Involvement in the Wake of a Nuclear Accident: Activists and Free-Riders in the Three Mile Island Area." *American Sociological Review* 48: 764–781.

2

The Role of Threat in Collective Action

Paul D. Almeida

Introduction

This chapter highlights the role of threats or negative conditions that stimulate collective action. A wide variety of social movements and popular struggles are driven by threats – from local resistance over state and police repression to the global movement combating climate change. Indeed, the Women's March against the newly inaugurated Trump Administration in early 2017 represented the largest simultaneous mass mobilizations in US history, with the organizers explicitly stating a threat to the protection of rights, health, and safety as the primary motive for the unprecedented demonstrations in the opening of their mission statement.[1] In the early history of political process theory, threats were examined in general terms by scholars such as Charles Tilly (1977: 14–24, 1978: 133–135) and Harold Kerbo (1982). The part played by threats in generating social movement activity offers a second strand of inquiry in addition to political opportunities within the political process tradition. In the 1980s and 1990s, political process scholars emphasized political opportunities more than threats in studies of movement emergence (McAdam 2011: 91; Pinard 2011; Van Dyke 2013; see also Chapter 1 by McAdam and Tarrow, in this volume). Since the late 1990s and early 2000s, beginning with influential works by Jasper (1997), Snow et al. (1998) and Goldstone and Tilly (2001), a growing body of empirical research has accumulated, featuring threats and worsening conditions as primary forces generating attempts at collective mobilization (Almeida 2003; Andrews and Seguin 2015; Dodson 2016; Einwohner and Maher 2011; Inclán 2009; Johnson and Frickel 2011; Maher 2010; Martin 2013; Martin and Dixon 2010; Mora et al. 2017; Shriver, Adams, and Longo 2015; Simmons 2014; Van Dyke and Soule 2002; Zepeda-Millán 2017). In order to specify the conditions under which threats are more likely to activate social movement type activity this chapter discusses their relationship to grievances, the core components of political process theory, and resource

The Wiley Blackwell Companion to Social Movements, Second Edition. Edited by David A. Snow, Sarah A. Soule, Hanspeter Kriesi, and Holly J. McCammon.
© 2019 John Wiley & Sons Ltd. Published 2019 by John Wiley & Sons Ltd.

infrastructures. This review also develops a sensitizing scheme for the principal forms of structural threat in extant studies. The chapter concludes with suggestions for future lines of inquiry on threats with a focus on gaps in current scholarship.

Grievances and Threats

One of the first tasks for social movement scholars centers on defining concepts in a concise manner. Often the terms "grievances" and "threats" are treated as synonymous. More recent scholarship treats them as analytically distinct. Early social movement research prioritized the role of grievances, often viewing them in terms of system strain and breakdown (Buechler 2004; Smelser 1962; Snow et al. 1998). Grievances involve the everyday problems subjectively experienced by communities and social groups. Snow and Soule (2010: 23) define grievances as "troublesome matters or conditions, and the feelings associated with them – such as dissatisfaction, fear, indignation, resentment, and moral shock." These grievances may be long-standing over decades or of recent occurrence. One important pre-existing condition for the emergence of social movement-type activity is that these grievances are felt collectively by a community or a social group and not just experienced at the individual level (Snow 2013). Communities and social groups are more likely to collectively attempt to resolve such problems when opportunities or threats enter the political environment of the aggrieved population. Opportunities provide occasions to address long-standing grievances via social movement-type actions. Political opportunities signal to communities experiencing adversity that if they mobilize in the present, they are more likely to alleviate existing wrongs and "collective bads." Threats tend to have a different impact than opportunities by increasing the intensity of existing grievances or creating new ones (Bergstrand 2014). Indeed, Pinard (2011: 17) states in his extensive theoretical work on grievances that "threats can greatly increase the sense of grievances, as when the anticipation of increased hardships accompanies current ones."

Political Opportunity and Threats

Scholars define opportunities and threats at both the micro and macro levels of social life. At the micro level, empirical and theoretical work emphasizes the motivations of why individuals would engage in collective action with increases in political opportunities or threats (Goldstone and Tilly 2001). Opportunities offer the possibility of gaining new advantages and benefits by engaging in social movement activity (ibid.). Life will be better if the collective effort succeeds (Tarrow 2011: 160–161). Threats drive individuals into collective mobilization by making current conditions worse if defensive action is not undertaken.[2] At this micro level of motivations and incentives, opportunities and threats need to be perceived by the relevant actors (see Chapter 1 by McAdam and Tarrow, in this volume). Social constructionist perspectives assist in linking specific opportunities and threats to encouraging individual level participation in collective action. For example, scholars suggest that activists would need to diagnose particular threats in terms of defining the harms they create and attributing culpability in a convincing fashion before mobilization can take place (Jasper 1997; Snow and Benford 1988; Snow and Corrigall-Brown 2005). In addition, moral economy theories (Auyero 2006; Scott 1976) connect cultural processes to the likelihood of opportunities and threats converting grievances into sustained campaigns of protest by contextualizing the particular hardship within the moral belief systems of the community or society in question (Simmons 2016).

At the structural level, scholars have elaborated more objective measures of opportunities and threats. The basic features of political opportunity structure are well codified in the works of McAdam (1996: 26), Tarrow (2011: 163–167), and Meyer (2004) (see also Chapter 1 by McAdam and Tarrow in this volume). The core dimensions of *elite conflict, institutional access, changing electoral alignments, external allies*, and *declining repression* are highlighted in this literature as the facilitating macro conditions encouraging attempts at collective mobilization. In more recent elaborations of the perspective, a new dimension of "the multiplicity of independent centers of power within the regime" has been introduced as an additional opportunity (see Chapter 1 by McAdam and Tarrow, in this volume). In order to give proper analytical weight to the role of various forms of threat, I move the dimension of "external allies" into the category of resource infrastructure (McCarthy 1996), since achieving links to sympathetic allies is partially related to the agency of would-be collective actors to reach out to others under settings of threat or opportunity.[3] The other primary dimensions of political opportunity are more representative of the positive conditions in the political environment favorable to the emergence of a social movement.

Tilly (1978: 134–135) contended that "a given amount of threat tends to generate more collective action than the 'same' amount of opportunity." More recently, Snow et al. (1998), in developing a related "quotidian disruption" model of movement emergence, also postulate from Prospect Theory that groups experiencing potential losses are more motivated to engage in collective action than groups facing the possibility of new gains. Such propositions encourage analysts to be especially interested in more precisely defining types of structural threats that generate large-scale mobilization to guide empirical investigations.

Structural threats are less well established in the social movement literature. Structural threats act as negative conditions intensifying existing grievances and creating new ones in stimulating collective action. Emerging scholarship identifies at least four structural threats driving social movement activity: (1) economic-related problems; (2) public health/environmental decline; (3) erosion of rights; and (4) state repression. In the following sections the basic resource infrastructure permitting mobilization is discussed and these four structural threats are defined more precisely with empirical examples. Such an exercise seeks to balance the causal universe between political opportunities and threats by illustrating the prominent role of structural forms of threat in promoting collective action.

Resource Infrastructure and Threats

In order to fend off threats, communities require some level of resource infrastructure. This infrastructure includes the human, organizational, material, technical, and experiential stockpiles of capital available to populations under various form of threat, including those stockpiles possessed by sympathetic allies (Edwards and Kane 2014; Ganz 2009; see also Chapter 4 by Edwards, McCarthy, and Mataic, in this volume). Resource infrastructures are unevenly distributed across time and geographic space (Edwards and McCarthy 2004). This in part explains why so many grievances and threats fail to materialize into campaigns of collective action. A minimal resource infrastructure is necessary to launch a collective attempt at reducing ongoing and anticipated threats (Almeida 2003). More specifically, resource infrastructure perspectives predict stronger and longer-lasting threat-based mobilizations in communities with denser populations and communication networks, pre-established civic organizations and institutions (labor associations, neighborhood groups, schools, non-profit organizations, etc.), and past collective action experience than in communities lacking in solidarity and organizational vitality (Almeida 2007b, 2014; Andrews 2004; Cress and Snow 2000; Ganz 2009; Gould 1995; Reese, Giedritis, and Vega 2005).

To illustrate, consider one of the largest mass mobilizations in decades in the United States which occurred between February and May of 2006 over an impending Congressional Bill that heightened the criminalization of undocumented immigrants. The threat of legal repression (Menjívar and Abrego 2012) against millions of working-class immigrants with precarious residency status created a three-month-long campaign with demonstrations in hundreds of cities and towns across the nation, with some rallies reportedly reaching up to one million participants (Zepeda-Millán 2017). Bloemraad, Voss, and Lee (2011) report in their national study of the threat-based immigrant rights mobilizations in 2006 a strong correspondence between the locations of the marches and the locations of the strategic resource of immigrant freedom rides in 2003. In a local-level study of the same movement across four low-income cities in the Central Valley of California, Mora (2016) found that the cities with denser activist organizational infrastructures prior to 2006 were able to sustain mobilization over a much longer period of time in response to anti-immigrant legislation than localities lacking such prior activist networks.

In another study of threat-induced collective action of thousands of local protests against free market reforms in Central America, Almeida (2012, 2014) showed that municipalities with higher levels of state and community infrastructures (administrative offices, highways, universities, labor associations, leftist oppositional parties, and NGOs) were more likely to participate in campaigns of defensive mobilization. Between the 1980s and the early 2000s, Martin and Dixon (2010) also find resistance to the threats of post-Fordist economic restructuring in the United States in the form of labor strikes was much more forceful in states with the organizational resource of labor unions and labor union membership. In their exhaustive event history study predicting the diffusion of Occupy Wall Street encampments protesting increasing wealth inequality across over 900 US cities, Vasi and Suh (2016: 150–151) conclude that:

> Despite the movement's anarchist roots and horizontal organizing structure, it benefited from the presence of universities and a progressive community, which provided organizational resources such as meeting spaces and informal networks between activists. These findings demonstrate that organizational resources matter, even for movements that claim to be decentralized and that rely heavily on cyberbrokerage to connect activists.

The above empirical studies all indicate that excluded social groups enjoy a higher probability of collectively resisting threats when a resource infrastructure is available. These works represent a variety of methodologies, settings, forms of threat, and all incorporate variations in resource infrastructure levels within their cases. Beyond establishing the critical intervening role of resource infrastructures in converting threats into collective action, it is necessary to more precisely define common forms of threat found in existing social movement studies.

Structural Threats

In the past two decades, a series of theoretical and empirical studies have highlighted the primary role of threat in generating sustained mobilization. Four broad dimensions of threat tend to appear as the most prominent: (1) economic-related problems; (2) public health/environmental decline; (3) erosion of rights; and (4) state repression.[4] In this section each form of threat is defined, connected to stimulating joint actions, and supported with empirical examples from the social movement literature. Just as political process scholars have developed core dimensions of political opportunity, a similar set of fundamental threats can be established.

Economic-related problems

Problems related to economic conditions are perhaps one of the most common forces motivating threat-induced collective action throughout modern history. There is an abundance of ways that economic and material circumstances catalyze attempts at defensive mobilization. From general economic crises that raise levels of mass unemployment and sharpen income inequality to issues of government austerity and access to land for rural cultivators, a wide range of economic forces may encourage groups to engage in protest (Caren, Gaby, and Herrold 2017). After ethnic and religious conflict and state repression, economic-related issues are likely driving some of the largest mobilizations of the past few decades (Almeida 2010).

Since the 1980s, the Global South has experienced several waves of protests over economic austerity, privatization, and other economic liberalization measures (Roberts 2008; Silva 2009; Walton and Seddon 1994). In some countries, the massive demonstrations against neoliberal reforms in the 2000s broke national records as the largest documented street marches. These cases include health care privatization in El Salvador, a free trade treaty and utility privatization in Costa Rica, and social security reform and privatization in Panama (Almeida 2014). By the late 1990s and early 2000s, Latin America alone had experienced thousands of individual protest events over free market reforms (Almeida 2007a; Almeida and Cordero 2015; Bellinger and Arce 2011; Ortiz and Béjar 2013; Seoane, Taddei, and Algranati 2006). Similar events responding to neoliberal threats can be found in Africa, Asia, and Eastern Europe (Abouharb and Cingranelli 2007; Almeida 2016; Beissinger and Sasse 2014). In the 2010s, the largest demonstrations reported in the southern European nations of Greece, Portugal, and Spain were also driven by government economic austerity programs (della Porta 2015; Kousis 2014; Rüdig and Karyotis 2014).

Mass unemployment and high concentrations of economic inequality also have led to dramatic campaigns of collective action around the globe (della Porta 2017; Dodson 2016; Kawalerowicz and Biggs 2015). In the 1930s, the economic Depression led to mass mobilization of the unemployed in the United States (Kerbo and Shaffer 1986; Piven and Cloward 1979), Britain, Australia, El Salvador, Chile, and Costa Rica. Declining economic conditions have also stimulated mobilizations by the homeless and their advocates in major US cities (Snow, Soule, and Cress 2005). One of the largest social movements in Latin America in the late 1990s and early 2000s was Argentina's unemployed workers movement that faced similar levels of job losses as the United States in the 1930s (Auyero 2002; Rossi 2017). Even rightist and nativist mobilization has been empirically linked to the explicit threats of unemployment and de-industrialization (DiGrazia 2015; Van Dyke and Soule 2002). Mass unemployment, dismissals, labor flexibility laws, and labor market precariousness have also driven social movement campaigns in Europe over the past two decades (della Porta 2015). Plant closures provide a particularly compelling catalyst to working-class mobilization in regions undergoing economic restructuring throughout the world (Auyero 2002; Moody 1997), and especially in China in recent decades (Chen 2014). Labor unions have played a major role in the movements against austerity and mass unemployment, especially in countries with a large industrial base and public infrastructure (Almeida 2007a, 2016). The Occupy Wall Street movement, with over 1000 reported protest events and encampments across the United States in the Fall of 2011, sought government intervention in wealth distribution in general, and specific local policies such as moratoriums on housing evictions and foreclosures.

Rural struggles over the loss of cultivable land and global "land grabs" are also materially based and have driven collective action campaigns throughout the twentieth and early twenty first centuries in the interior regions of the developing world (Enríquez 2010; Hall et al. 2015; Schock 2015a). The list of potential economic-based threats is profuse, including struggles over labor exploitation, regressive taxation, affordable housing, and consumer protection from price inflation. Especially important in precipitating economic-based movements and livelihood struggles is the level of disruption incurred by communities in their daily subsistence routines (Snow et al. 1998). These "quotidian disruptions" provide particularly potent incentives for groups to seek redress for potential losses in resources in the population under threat (ibid.). Given this ubiquity of economic-based threats across time and place, analysts must also incorporate measures of the resource infrastructure available to would-be movement participants to determine the likelihood of collective mobilization.

Public health/environmental decline

Public health and environmental threats provide strong negative incentives for communities to mount a collective campaign for relief and compensation. The threat is to people's actual physical well-being and long-term health (Szasz 2007). At times, this form of threat creates "a suddenly imposed grievance" (Walsh, Warland, and Smith 1997); interruptions to daily patterns (Snow et al. 1998); or a "moral shock" (Jasper 1997). Johnson and Frickel (2011: 305) define "ecological threat" as the "costs associated with environmental degradation as it disrupts (or is perceived to disrupt) ecosystems, human health, and societal well-being." In the late twentieth and early twenty-first centuries, public health and environmental threats appear to be on the rise as well as campaigns to slow down or reverse these deteriorating conditions (Shriver et al. 2015).

Starting in the 1980s, and continuing through the present, thousands of grass-roots movements mushroomed throughout the United States and the world demanding "environmental justice" over the new types of pollution and public health harms associated with industrial societies and their byproducts (Mohai and Saha 2015; Szasz 1994; Taylor 2014). Most of these challenges are contested at the local level, and therefore do not receive national mass media coverage. Similar trends of community mobilization in reaction to local environmental threats have been documented and analyzed in a variety of global settings, including in urban China (Dong, Kriesi, and Kübler 2015), Japan (Almeida and Stearns 1998; Broadbent 1998; Stearns and Almeida 2004), and El Salvador (Cartagena Cruz 2017). Communities within the environmental justice framework organize over a variety of environmental threats, such as lead and pesticide poisoning, along with pollution associated with incinerators, industrial waste dumps, power plants, chemical leaks, superfund sites, and air contamination from high concentrations of particulate matter. A strong current within the environmental justice movement involves campaigns confronting environmental racism or the disproportionate threats of environmental harms documented in working-class communities of color (Bullard 2000; Bullard and Wright 2012). A related set of grassroots movements have launched campaigns over the local threat of the entry of big box stores eroding environmental quality and social tranquility in smaller towns and communities across the United States and beyond (Halebsky 2009; Rao 2008).

Mining and other extractive industry operations act as another major environmental threat mobilizing localities. Across the developing world, from the Philippines and Guatemala to Nicaragua, Panama, and Peru, indigenous communities have launched fierce campaigns over the perceived threats of mining to the ecological health and sustainability of their ancestral lands (Arce 2014; Camba 2016; Díaz Pinzón 2013; Sánchez González 2016; Yagenova 2015). Not just indigenous peoples, but rural populations throughout the Global South are joining in defensive struggles against the ecological threats associated with resource extraction industries and mega-development projects (Bebbington and Bury 2013; Cordero 2015).

At the other end of production, environmental threats from continued global industrial expansion and carbon output appear to be one of the main promoters of collective action in the twenty-first century. More specifically, the transnational movement for climate justice is responding to the long-term threat of global warming. By 2009, the movement reached the capacity to mobilize events in most countries on the planet, often in simultaneous and coordinated actions. During the United Nations Climate Summit in New York City in September 2014, the mass demonstration reached up to 400 000 participants locally with over 2000 additional events held around the world. Similar to economic-based threats in terms of variety, a whole host of public health and environmental threats may act as the main triggers of collective action.

Erosion of rights

Another threat involves the erosion of rights. When rights have been extended for a substantial period where populations have become accustomed to their benefits, attempts at weakening them will often be met with collective resistance. An erosion of rights represents a relative loss of power (McVeigh 2009; Van Dyke 2013). The taking away of suffrage rights acts as one of the most fundamental offenses, creating defensive mobilization. Such governmental actions instantly place a large segment of the national population under similar circumstances. Elections that are perceived to be fraudulent or the canceling of elections frequently set off campaigns of civil society defiance (McAdam and Tarrow 2010; Norris, Frank, and Martinez I Coma 2015). For example, Kalandadze and Orenstein (2009) documented 17 major electoral fraud mobilizations between 1991 and 2005 in Eurasia, Africa, and Latin America. In a separate study between 1989 and 2011, Brancati (2016: 3–5) identified 310 major protests to "adopt or uphold democratic elections" in 92 countries. Since 2011, electoral mobilizations over perceived fraud have continued throughout the world, as in Cambodia in 2013. The 2009 general elections in Iran unleashed the largest post-Revolution mobilizations witnessed in the country as the "Green Movement" launched weeks of street marches contesting the election results as illegitimate (Kurzman 2011; Parsa 2016). Even the extremely close vote count in the 2006 Mexican presidential elections generated a month of mass street demonstrations and disruptions with claims of fraud by the defeated candidate of the left, Manuel López Obrador.[5] In late 2017 and early 2018, perceived fraud and systematic irregularities in the Honduran presidential elections resulted in multiple street marches of over 100,000 people and hundreds of roadblocks erected by citizens across the country.

Ongoing electoral fraud in multiple and sequential electoral cycles may even alter the *character* of collective action to take on more radical forms with the focus of overthrowing the prevailing regime (especially if combined with the threat of state repression). This follows the pattern of El Salvador in the 1970s. After a period of political liberalization in the 1960s, the military regime held four consecutive national fraudulent elections between 1972 and 1978. After several rounds of massive nonviolent demonstrations against the unfair elections, many sympathizers of the center left opposition parties radicalized their position and eventually threw their support behind insurgent revolutionaries, eventuating in El Salvador's long decade of civil war and violence (Almeida 2003, 2008a). Finally, military coups that interrupt the constitutional order and overthrow popularly elected governments may also generate large-scale collective action. This was the case following the 2009 military coup in Honduras that ousted the democratically elected government of Manuel Zelaya. Immediately following Zelaya's expulsion, an anti-coup mass movement erupted that sustained the largest mobilizations in Honduran history until Zelaya's return in 2011, with street demonstrations reaching up to a reported 400 000 participants (Sosa 2012). A similar, but much more concise, dynamic of an anti-coup mass movement took place following the short-lived military coup in Venezuela in 2002 that attempted to drive out President Hugo Chávez Frías.

Other forms of eroding rights also serve as a primary catalyst to collective action. Often, these perceived rights violations come in the form of policy threats by state officials (Martin 2013; Reese 2011). The threat of weakening reproductive rights laws and welfare services, for example, pushes pro-choice and welfare rights groups into campaigns of defensive action (Meyer and Staggenborg 1996; Reese et al. 2005). Military invasions of other countries also operate as a policy threat leading to anti-war mobilization (Reese, Petit, and Meyer 2010; Heaney and Rojas 2015). Conservative groups in the United States often frame "government overreach" as a threat to rights in order to mobilize on a variety of issues such as over taxation, health care insurance, and gun ownership rights (Almeida and Van Dyke 2014; Lio, Melzer, and Reese 2008). The work on policy threats not only opens up critical questions about the conditions for initial movement emergence, but also leads to the potential for furthering our knowledge of movement-related outcomes (Amenta et al. 2010; Bosi, Giugni, and Uba 2016). The outcomes of threat-induced movements are vastly under-theorized and researched in comparison to mobilization outcomes generated by political opportunities. Policy threats provide one avenue for scholarly advance by constructing precise research designs that examine movement-related processes and their consequences on the final policy results (Almeida 2008b).

State repression

A final major form of threat occurs when states coerce, harass, and repress citizens under their jurisdiction (see also Chapter 12 by Ghaziani and Kretschmer, in this volume). Along with the erosion of rights, the threat of state repression operates in stark contrast to the core political opportunities of a relaxation in state repression and widening institutional access, in that movements are responding to the closing down of political space as opposed to its opening (Goodwin 2001). The state repression literature offers a vast and complex accounting of the dynamics between governmental violence and popular response (Chang 2015; Davenport 2010; Earl 2011; Earl and Soule 2010). At times, state repression quells attempts at collective action because of the heavy risks incurred in the mobilization process (Johnston 2011). This aspect of state repression is more consistent with the political opportunity strand of political process theory. At other times, state and police repression encourages heightened attempts at protest (Brockett 2005). For example, police abuse cases against African American citizens in multiple US cities reached such a threshold by 2014, that activists launched the Black Lives Matter campaign with a reported 37 chapters across the United States by late 2016 (Bell 2016).

In authoritarian states, continued repressive action against nonviolent social movements may change the nature of collective action itself and switch the trajectory of protest onto a much more radical path (Alimi, Demetriou, and Bosi 2015; Almeida 2007b; Trejo 2016).[6] This was clearly the case in the Arab Spring cases of Libya and Syria, and, to a lesser extent, Egypt. These protests began as campaigns of mass non-violence in 2011 and 2012, or what Schock (2005; 2015b) refers to as "unarmed insurrections." When the states of Libya, Syria, and later Egypt violently repressed these nonviolent challenges once they had been sustained for several months, the movements radicalized and began using violent and more military-style tactics (Alimi 2016). In contrast, in countries implementing softer forms of repression, states may "contain escalation" from converting into radicalized mobilization, as in the case of Jordan during the Arab Spring (Moss 2014). Scholars of revolutionary movements find that radicalization appears much more likely under exclusionary types of authoritarian regimes that fail to incorporate the middle and working classes into structures of political participation or distribute the benefits of economic growth (Foran 2005; Goodwin 2001). At the micro level, outrageous acts of state repression also push individuals to take on new roles and identities as revolutionary activists and participants (Viterna 2013).

This unique property of repressive threat, with the potential to radicalize collective action, provides another major distinction from political opportunities and other types of threats (with the exception of fraudulent elections). Promising areas for advancing state repression research in terms of predicting the likelihood of protest escalation or demobilization include the severity and probability of the repressive threat being carried out (Einwohner and Maher 2011; Maher 2010), a cataloging of the coercive tactics used by the state (Moss 2014), and the precise type and level of resource infrastructure necessary to sustain mobilization under high-risk conditions (Loveman 1998; Pilati 2016).

Summary of Structural Forms of Threat

Table 2.1 summarizes the major forms of structural threat examined in the collective action literature and some of the most common types of corresponding movements. Table 2.1 does not offer an exhaustive typology, but a sensitizing scheme of frequently occurring threats. Economic-related threats produce movements struggling over material conditions – from government austerity measures to the loss of cultivable land. Movements responding to public health threats and environmental decline range from local struggles over pollution and contamination to transnational mobilizations attempting to slow down the pace of planetary warming.

The threat of eroding rights pushes two forms of movement type activities. First, when states cancel or hold fraudulent elections, this may lead to a massive round of protests against the loss of citizen voting rights and disenfranchisement. Second, newly impending or implemented governmental policies that are perceived by

Table 2.1   Major forms of threat

Form of threat	Examples of collective responses
Economic-related problems	Austerity protests, Unemployed worker movements, Occupy/Indignados, movements over loss of housing, land, affordable food
Public health/ environmental decline	Local actions related to disease and illness outbreaks attributed to government/Corporate ineptitude (e.g. Love Canal, Flint, Pesticide Poisoning, HIV/AIDS), Environmental Justice movements, Transnational Climate Justice movements, anti-mining and extractive industry movements, other environmental hazards
Erosion of rights	Fraudulent election protests, policy threat protest (reproductive rights, anti-war, welfare rights)
State repression	Protest campaigns against government harassment, arrests, killings, states of emergency, police abuse, and other human rights atrocities. Radicalized movements against authoritarian and repressive regimes.

particular constituencies as a loss of power, status, and/or protection, ranging from welfare and reproductive rights policies to gun ownership rights, are likely to facilitate mobilization (McVeigh 2009). These kinds of government measures often trigger group-wise mobilizations for the subpopulations perceived to be most threatened by the policies (Amenta and Young 1999). Repressive threats at times launch campaigns of mass resistance when governments kill popular civic leaders, commit massacres, or even lesser forms of police abuse and harassment. Under special circumstances, the threat of state repression has the unique property to potentially radicalize the form of collective action, resulting in both revolutionary and terrorist movements (see also Chapter 39 by Goldstone and Ritter on revolutions, and Chapter 40 by Beck and Schoon on terrorist movements, in this volume).[7] Many groups and advocates leading campaigns for human rights are also driven by the threat of state repression.

The Future of Threat Research

This chapter has highlighted fundamental questions in the emerging literature on the primary role of threat in driving social movement activity. Students and scholars must continue to advance in our shared understanding of how negative conditions drive attempts at defensive collective action. Some of the largest mobilizations in the twenty-first century appear to be reacting to economic, ecological/health, and political threats.[8] Beyond relating threats to grievances, political opportunities, resource infrastructures, and developing more precise indicators of structural threats, several other tasks remain.

This review has separated threat environments from opportunity environments in order to provide sustained analytical attention to the often underemphasized role of worsening circumstances in stimulating collective action. In many contexts, communities subject to mobilization may likely face a third *hybrid environment* of opportunities and threats operating simultaneously. One area of further refinement is to better understand these "mixed" or hybrid environments that are driven by opportunities and threats. For example, McAdam et al. (2010) implemented such a design of 11 oil and gas pipeline projects crossing 16 developing countries using fuzzy set qualitative comparative analysis (QCA). They concluded that collective conflicts most often emerged under *both* conditions of threat (e.g. no benefits for the host country, potential for environmental harms) and opportunity (e.g. public consultation with affected local communities).

Another line of inquiry would be to construct even more precise and exhaustive sub-typologies of threat, for economic-based problems, public health/environmental decline, erosion of rights, and state repression. Given that each of these structural conditions provides a diversity of threats within each form, examining the differential impacts of each sub-type of threat would enhance our understanding of the kinds of specific threats that are most likely to encourage movement actions. For example, does a government austerity program trigger similar collective responses as mass unemployment? Will lead poisoning from the municipal water supply mobilize people the same way that local air contamination from polluting industries does? Other properties of threats also need more attention such as the magnitude, severity, and extensiveness of the threat in question.

A final consideration, which this largely structural account underplays, would be to give more sustained focus to the social construction of threat that connects structural conditions to people's actual awareness and preparedness to act collectively (Klandermans 2013). Both framing and moral economy perspectives may be especially useful in addressing this lacuna (Snow et al. 2014), as well as work on the emotions triggered by threats (Collins 2001). Even in cases of sudden threats, communities must perceive the harm as a negative cost incurred and interpret it within prevailing belief systems and norms of justice and be energized with collective emotions (Jasper 1998, 2011). Longer-terms threats or slowly encroaching threats (such as increasing state authoritarianism or creeping pollution) may more likely transform into social movement-type activity when activists, community members, and leaders convincingly demonstrate that the best way to reduce current collective bads involves organizing a sustained campaign of resistance.

Notes

1 Available at: www.womensmarch.com/mission/
2 Tilly (1969) originally described these actions as "reactive." I prefer the term "defensive" (Almeida 2007a), so as to avoid misinterpreting threat-based movements as "reactionary" or ultraconservative in their ideological frameworks.
3 Even if collective actors seek out external allies under conditions of threat or opportunity, the availability of such allies may not be completely under the movement's control.
4 While these four forms of threat may be some of the most prominent found in the existing literature, they only sensitize movement scholarship into analyzing the role of "bad news" (Meyer 2002) systematically in models of the generation of collective action. These forms of threat are not exhaustive, and more work is needed in developing a more comprehensive typology of threat.
5 Protests against government corruption could also be classified as a variant of eroding citizenship rights. Between 2013 and 2017, massive protests have occurred in Brazil, Guatemala, Honduras, Russia, South Korea, and Thailand over corruption scandals in the executive branch or central administration.
6 The radicalization of collective action driven by state repression is similar to how the threat of electoral fraud may also convince activists to escalate their tactics to more violent forms.
7 It should be noted, however, revolutionary and terrorist movements can and do arise because of factors other than just state repression (e.g. ethnic conflict, religious strife, colonial/foreign occupation, etc.) (Beck 2015).
8 Mobilization over human rights represents another major movement in the twenty-first century (Smith and Wiest 2012). Such movements are often reacting to the threats of state repression in the political environment (Johnston 2011).

References

Abouharb, M. Rodwan and David Cingranelli. 2007. *Human Rights and Structural Adjustment*. Cambridge: Cambridge University Press.
Alimi, Eitan. 2016. "Introduction: Popular Contention, Regime, and Transition: A Comparative Perspective." In *Popular Contention, Regime, and Transition: The Arab Revolts in*

Comparative Global Perspective, edited by Eitan Alimi, Avraham Sela, and Mario Sznajder, 1–24. Oxford: Oxford University Press.

Alimi, Eitan, Chares Demetriou, and Lorenzo Bosi. 2015. *The Dynamics of Radicalization: A Relational and Comparative Perspective*. Oxford: Oxford University Press.

Almeida, Paul D. 2003. "Opportunity Organizations and Threat-Induced Contention: Protest Waves in Authoritarian Settings." *American Journal of Sociology* 109(2): 345–400.

Almeida, Paul D. 2007a. "Defensive Mobilization: Popular Movements against Economic Adjustment Policies in Latin America." *Latin American Perspectives* 34(3): 123–139.

Almeida, Paul D. 2007b. "Organizational Expansion, Liberalization Reversals and Radicalized Collective Action." *Research in Political Sociology* 15: 57–99.

Almeida, Paul D. 2008a. *Waves of Protest: Popular Struggle in El Salvador, 1925–2005*. Minneapolis: University of Minnesota Press.

Almeida, Paul D. 2008b. "The Sequencing of Success: Organizing Templates and Neoliberal Policy Outcomes." *Mobilization* 13(2): 165–187.

Almeida, Paul D. 2010. "Globalization and Collective Action." In *Handbook of Politics: State and Society in Global Perspective*, edited by Kevin Leicht and J. Craig Jenkins, 305–326. New York: Springer.

Almeida, Paul D. 2012. "Subnational Opposition to Globalization." *Social Forces* 90(4): 1051–1072.

Almeida, Paul D. 2014. *Mobilizing Democracy: Globalization and Citizen Protest*. Baltimore, MD: Johns Hopkins University Press.

Almeida, Paul D. 2016. "Social Movements and Economic Development." In *The Sociology of Development Handbook*, edited by Greg Hooks, Paul Almeida, David Brown, et al., 528–550. Berkeley: University of California Press.

Almeida, Paul D. and Linda Brewster Stearns. 1998. "Political Opportunities and Local Grassroots Environmental Movements." *Social Problems* 45(1): 37–60.

Almeida, Paul D. and Allen Cordero, eds. 2015. *Handbook of Social Movements across Latin America*. New York: Springer.

Almeida, Paul D. and Nella Van Dyke. 2014. "Social Movement Partyism and the Rapid Mobilization of the Tea Party." In *Understanding the Tea Party Movement*, edited by Nella Van Dyke and David Meyer, 55–72. London: Ashgate.

Amenta, Edwin, Neal Caren, Elizabeth Chiarello, and Yang Su. 2010. "The Political Consequences of Social Movements." *Annual Review of Sociology* 36: 287–307.

Amenta, Edwin and Michael P. Young. 1999. "Making an Impact: The Conceptual and Methodological Implications of the Collective Benefits Criterion." In *How Social Movements Matter: Theoretical and Comparative Studies on the Consequences of Social Movements*, edited by Marco Giugni, Doug McAdam, and Charles Tilly, 22–41. Minneapolis: University of Minnesota Press.

Andrews, Kenneth T. 2004. *Freedom Is a Constant Struggle: The Mississippi Civil Rights Movement and Its Legacy*. Chicago: University of Chicago Press.

Andrews, Kenneth T. and Charles Seguin. 2015. "Group Threat and Policy Change: The Spatial Dynamics of Prohibition Politics, 1890–1919." *American Journal of Sociology* 121(2): 475–510.

Arce, Moises. 2014. *Resource Extraction and Protest in Peru*. Pittsburgh, PA: University of Pittsburgh Press.

Auyero, Javier. 2002. "Los Cambios en el Repertorio de Protesta Social en la Argentina." *Desarrollo Económico* 42(146): 187–210.

Auyero, Javier. 2006. "The Moral Politics of Argentinean Crowds." In *Latin American Social Movements: Globalization and Transnational Networks*, edited by Hank Johnston and Paul D. Almeida, 147–162. Lanham, MD: Rowman & Littlefield.

Bebbington, Anthony and Jeffrey Bury, eds. 2013. *Subterranean Struggles: New Dynamics of Mining, Oil, and Gas in Latin America*. Austin: University of Texas Press.

Beck, Colin. 2015. *Radicals, Revolutionaries, and Terrorists*. London: Polity.

Beissinger, Mark and Gwendolyn Sasse. 2014. "An End to 'Patience'? The Great Recession and Economic Protest in Eastern Europe." In *Mass Politics in Tough Times*, edited by Nancy Bermeo and Larry Bartels, 334–370. Oxford: Oxford University Press.

Bell, Joyce. 2016. "Introduction to the Special Issue on Black Movements." *Sociological Focus* 49: 1–10.

Bellinger, Paul and Moises Arce. 2011. "Protest and Democracy in Latin America's Market Era." *Political Research Quarterly* 64(3): 688–704.

Bergstrand, Kelly. 2014. "The Mobilizing Power of Grievances: Applying Loss Aversion and Omission Bias to Social Movements." *Mobilization* 19(2): 123–142.

Bloemraad, Irene, Kim Voss, and Taeku Lee. 2011. "The Immigration Rallies of 2006: What Were They, How Do We Understand Them, Where Do We Go?" In *Rallying for Immigrant Rights*, edited by Kim Voss and Irene Bloemraad, 3–43. Berkeley: University of California Press.

Bosi, Lorenzo, Marco Giugni, and Katrin Uba, eds. 2016. *The Consequences of Social Movements*. Cambridge: Cambridge University Press.

Brancati, Dawn. 2016. *Democracy Protests: Origins, Features, and Significance*. Cambridge: Cambridge University Press.

Broadbent, Jeffrey. 1998. *Environmental Politics in Japan: Networks of Power and Protest*. New York: Cambridge University Press.

Brockett, Charles. 2005. *Political Movements and Violence in Central America*. Cambridge: Cambridge University Press.

Buechler, Steven. 2004. "The Strange Career of Strain and Breakdown Theories of Collective Action." In *The Blackwell Companion to Social Movements*, edited by David A. Snow, Sarah A. Soule, and Hanspeter Kriesi, 47–66. Oxford: Blackwell.

Bullard, Robert. 2000. *Dumping in Dixie: Race, Class, and Environmental Quality*, 3rd edn. Boulder, CO: Westview Press.

Bullard, Robert and Beverly Wright. 2012. *The Wrong Complexion for Protection: How the Government Response to Disaster Endangers African American Communities*. New York: New York University Press.

Camba, Alvin A. 2016. "Philippine Mining Capitalism: The Changing Terrains of Struggle in the Neoliberal Mining Regime." *ASEAS, Australian Journal of South-East Asian Studies* 9(1): 71–88.

Caren, Neal, Sarah Gaby, and Catherine Herrold. 2017. "Economic Breakdown and Collective Action." *Social Problems* 64(1): 133–155.

Cartagena Cruz, Rafael E. 2017. "Conflictos Ambientales y Movimientos Sociales en El Salvador de Posguerra." In *Movimientos Sociales en América Latina: Perspectivas, Tendencias y Casos*, edited by Paul D. Almeida and Allen Cordero Ulate, 415–446. Buenos Aires: CLACSO.

Chang, Paul. 2015. *Protest Dialectics: State Repression and South Korea's Democracy Movement, 1970–1979*. Stanford, CA: Stanford University Press.

Chen, Xi. 2014. *Social Protest and Contentious Authoritarianism in China*. Cambridge: Cambridge University Press.

Collins, Randall. 2001. "Social Movements and the Focus of Emotional Attention." In *Passionate Politics*, edited by Jeff Goodwin, James M. Jasper, and Francesca Polletta, 27–44. Chicago: University of Chicago Press.

Cordero, Ulate A. 2015. "El Movimiento Social Indígena en Térraba, Costa Rica: La Lucha Contra el Proyecto Diquís," *Revista de Estudos Anti-Utilitaristas e Poscoloniais, REALIS* 5(2): 4–25.

Cress, Daniel M. and David A. Snow. 2000. "The Outcomes of Homeless Mobilization: The Influence of Organization, Disruption, Political Mediation, and Framing." *American Journal of Sociology* 105(4): 1063–1104.

Davenport, Christian. 2010. *State Repression and the Domestic Democratic Peace*. Cambridge: Cambridge University Press.

della Porta, Donatella. 2015. *Social Movements in Times of Austerity: Bringing Capitalism Back into Protest Analysis*. London: Polity.

della Porta, Donatella. 2017. "Late Neoliberalism and Its Discontent: Comparing Crises and Movements in the European Periphery." In *Late Neoliberalism and Its Discontent: Comparing Crises and Movements in the European Periphery*, edited by Donatella della Porta, Massimiliano Andretta, Tiago Fernandes, et al. New York: Springer.

Díaz Pinzón, Florencio. 2013. "El Movimiento Ambiental Panameño frente al Neoliberalismo: Estudio de Caso Cerro Colorado contra la Minería a Cielo Abierto, Referenciado a la Región Centroamericana, Año 1989–2010." Master's thesis, FL ACSO, Costa Rica.

DiGrazia, Joseph. 2015. "Using Internet Search Data to Produce State-level Measures: The Case of Tea Party Mobilization." *Sociological Methods & Research*: doi: 0049124115610348.

Dodson, Kyle. 2016. "Economic Threat and Protest Behavior in Comparative Perspective." *Sociological Perspectives* 59(3): 873–891.

Dong, Lisheng, Hanspeter Kriesi, and Daniel Kübler, eds. 2015. *Urban Mobilizations and New Media in Contemporary China*. New York: Routledge.

Earl, Jennifer. 2011. "Political Repression: Iron Fists, Velvet Gloves, and Diffuse Control." *Annual Review of Sociology* 37: 261–284.

Earl, Jennifer and Sarah A. Soule. 2010. "The Impacts of Repression: The Effect of Police Presence and Action on Subsequent Protest Rates." *Research in Social Movements, Conflicts and Change* 30: 75–113.

Edwards, Bob and Melinda Kane. 2014. "Resource Mobilization and Social and Political Movements." In *Handbook of Political Citizenship and Social Movements*, edited by Hein-Anton van der Heijden, 205–232. Cheltenham: Edward Elgar Publishing.

Edwards, Bob and John D. McCarthy. 2004. "Resources and Social Movement Mobilization." In *The Blackwell Companion to Social Movements*, edited by David A. Snow, Sarah A. Soule, and Hanspeter Kriesi, 116–152. Oxford: Blackwell.

Einwohner, Rachel L. and Thomas Maher. 2011. "Threat Assessments and Collective-Action Emergence: Death Camp and Ghetto Resistance During the Holocaust." *Mobilization* 16(2): 127–146.

Enríquez, Laura. 2010. *Reactions to the Market: Small Farmers in the Economic Reshaping of Nicaragua, Cuba, Russia, and China*. University Park, PA: Pennsylvania State University Press.

Foran, John. 2005. *Taking Power: On the Origins of Third World Revolutions*. Cambridge: Cambridge University Press.

Ganz, Marshall. 2009. *Why David Sometimes Wins: Leadership, Organization, and Strategy in the California Farm Worker Movement*. Oxford: Oxford University Press.

Goldstone, Jack and Charles Tilly. 2001. "Threat (and Opportunity): Popular Action and State Response in the Dynamic of Contentious Action." In *Silence and Voice in the Study of Contentious Politics*, edited by Ronald R. Aminzade, Jack Goldstone, Doug McAdam, et al., 179–194. Cambridge: Cambridge University Press.

Goodwin, Jeff. 2001. *No Other Way Out: States and Revolutionary Movements, 1945–1991*. Cambridge: Cambridge University Press.

Gould, Roger V. 1995. *Insurgent Identities: Class, Community, and Protest in Paris from 1848 to the Commune*. Chicago: University of Chicago Press.

Halebsky, Stephen. 2009. *Small Towns and Big Business: Challenging Wal-Mart Superstores*. Lanham, MD: Lexington Books.

Hall, Ruth, Marc Edelman, Saturnino M. Borras Jr., Ian Scoones, Ben White, and Wendy Wolford. 2015. "Resistance, Acquiescence or Incorporation? An Introduction to Land Grabbing and Political Reactions 'From Below'." *The Journal of Peasant Studies* 42(3–4): 467–488.

Heaney, Michael and Fabio Rojas. 2015. *Party in the Streets: The Antiwar Movement and the Democratic Party after 9/11*. Cambridge: Cambridge University Press.

Inclán, María de la Luz. 2009. "Repressive Threats, Procedural Concessions, and the Zapatista Cycle of Protests 1994–2003." *Journal of Conflict Resolution* 53(5): 794–819.

Jasper, James. 1997. *The Art of Moral Protest: Culture, Biography, and Creativity in Social Movements*. Chicago: University of Chicago Press.

Jasper, James. 1998. "The Emotions of Protest: Affective and Reactive Emotions in and around Social Movements." *Sociological Forum* 13(3): 397–424.

Jasper, James. 2011. "Emotions and Social Movements: Twenty Years of Theory and Research." *Annual Review of Sociology* 37: 285–303.

Johnson, Erik W. and Scott Frickel. 2011. "Ecological Threat and the Founding of U.S. National Environmental Movement Organizations, 1962–1998." *Social Problems*, 58(3): 305–329.

Johnston, Hank. 2011. *States and Social Movements*. London: Polity.

Kalandadze, Katya and Mitchell A. Orenstein. 2009. "Electoral Protests and Democratization: Beyond the Color Revolutions." *Comparative Political Studies* 42(11): 1403–1425.

Kawalerowicz, Juta and Michael Biggs. 2015. "Anarchy in the UK: Economic Deprivation, Social Disorganization, and Political Grievances in the London Riot of 2011." *Social Forces* 94(2): 673–698.

Kerbo, Harold R. 1982. "Movements of 'Crisis' and Movements of 'Affluence': A Critique of Deprivation and Resource Mobilization Theories." *Journal of Conflict Resolution* 26(4): 645–663.

Kerbo, Harold and Richard A. Shaffer. 1986. "Unemployment and Protest in the United States, 1890–1940: A Methodological Critique and Research Note." *Social Forces* 64(4): 1046–1056.

Klandermans, Bert. 2013. "The Dynamics of Demand." In *The Future of Social Movement Research: Dynamics, Mechanisms, and Processes*, edited by Jacquelien Von Stekelenburg, Conny Roggenband, and Bert Klandermans, 3–16. Minneapolis: University of Minnesota Press.

Kousis, Maria. 2014. "The Transnational Dimension of the Greek Protest Campaign against Troika Memoranda and Austerity Policies, 2010–2012." In *Spreading Protest: Social Movements in Times of Crisis*, edited by Donatella della Porta and Alice Mattoni, 137–170. Colchester: ECPR Press.

Kurzman, Charles. 2011. "Cultural Jiu-Jitsu and the Iranian Greens," In *The People Reloaded: The Green Movement and the Struggle for Iran's Future*, edited by Nader Hashemi and Danny Postel, 7–17. New York: Melville House.

Lio, Shoon, Scott Melzer, and Ellen Reese. 2008. "Constructing Threat and Appropriating 'Civil Rights': Rhetorical Strategies of Gun Rights and English Only Leaders." *Symbolic Interaction* 31(1): 5–31.

Loveman, Mara. 1998. "High Risk Collective Action: Defending Human Rights in Chile, Uruguay, and Argentina." *American Journal of Sociology* 104(2): 477–525.

Maher, Thomas V. 2010. "Threat, Resistance, and Mobilization: The Cases of Auschwitz, Sobibór, and Treblinka." *American Sociological Review*, 75(2): 252–272.

Martin, Andrew and Marc Dixon. 2010. "Changing to Win? Resistance, Threat and the Role of Unions in Strikes, 1984–2002." *American Journal of Sociology* 116: 93–129.

Martin, Isaac. 2013. *Rich People's Movements: Grassroots Campaigns to Untax the One Percent*. Oxford: Oxford University Press.

McAdam, Doug. 1996. "Conceptual Origins, Current Problems, Future Directions." In *Comparative Perspectives on Social Movements: Political Opportunities, Mobilizing Structures, and Cultural Framings*, edited by Doug McAdam, John D. McCarthy, and Mayer N. Zald, 23–40. Cambridge: Cambridge University Press.

McAdam, Doug. 2011. "Social Movements and the Growth in Opposition to Global Projects." In *Global Projects: Institutional and Political Challenges*, edited by W. Richard Scott, Raymond E. Levitt, and Ryan J. Orr, 86–110. Cambridge: Cambridge University Press.

McAdam, Doug, Hilary Schaffer Boudet, Jennifer Davis, Ryan J. Orr, W. Richard Scott, and Raymond E. Levitt. 2010. "'Site Fights': Explaining Opposition to Pipeline Projects in the Developing World." *Sociological Forum* 25(3): 401–427.

McAdam, Doug and Sidney Tarrow. 2010. "Ballots and Barricades: On the Reciprocal Relationship between Elections and Social Movements." *Perspectives on Politics* 8(2): 529–542.

McCarthy, John D. 1996. "Constraints and Opportunities in Adopting, Adapting, and Inventing." In *Comparative Perspectives on Social Movements: Political Opportunities, Mobilizing Structures, and Cultural Framings*, edited by Doug McAdam, John D. McCarthy, and Mayer Zald, 141–151. Cambridge: Cambridge University Press.

McVeigh, Rory. 2009. *The Rise of the Ku Klux Klan: Right-Wing Movements and National Politics*. Minneapolis: University of Minnesota Press.

Menjívar, Cecilia and Leisy J. Abrego. 2012. "Legal Violence: Immigration Law and the Lives of Central American Immigrants." *American Journal of Sociology* 117(5): 1380–1421.

Meyer, David. 2002. "Opportunities and Identities: Bridge-building in the Study of Social Movements." In *Social Movements: Identity, Culture, and the State*, edited by David Meyer, Nancy Whittier, and Belinda Robnett, 3–21. New York: Oxford University Press.

Meyer, David. 2004. "Protest and Opportunities." *Annual Review of Sociology* 30: 125–145.

Meyer, David and Suzanne Staggenborg. 1996. "Movements, Countermovements, and the Structure of Political Opportunity." *American Journal of Sociology* 101(6): 1628–1660.

Mohai, Paul and Robin Saha. 2015. "Which Came First, People or Pollution? Assessing the Disparate Siting and Post-Siting Demographic Change Hypotheses of Environmental Injustice." *Environmental Research Letters* 10(115008): 1–17.

Moody, Kim. 1997. *Workers in a Lean World: Unions in the International Economy*. London: Verso.

Mora, Maria de Jesus. 2016. "Local Mobilizations: Explaining the Outcomes of Immigrant Organizing in Four Central Valley Cities in California." Master's Degree Paper, Department of Sociology, University of California, Merced.

Mora, Maria de Jesus, Alejandro Zermeño, Rodolfo Rodriguez, and Paul Almeida. 2017. "Exclusión y Movimientos Sociales en los Estados Unidos." In *Movimientos Sociales en América Latina: Perspectivas, Tendencias y Casos*, edited by Paul Almeida and Allen Cordero, 641–669. Buenos Aires: CLACSO.

Moss, Dana. 2014. "Repression, Response, and Contained Escalation under 'Liberalized' Authoritarianism in Jordan." *Mobilization* 19(3): 489–514.

Norris, Pippa, Richard W. Frank, and Ferran Martinez I Coma. 2015. "Contentious Elections: From Votes to Violence." In *Contentious Elections: From Ballots to Barricades*, edited by

Pippa Norris, Richard W. Frank, and Ferran Martinez I Coma, 1–21. New York: Routledge.

Ortiz, David and Sergio Béjar. 2013. "Participation in IMF-Sponsored Economic Programs and Contentious Collective Action in Latin America, 1980–2007." *Conflict Management and Peace Science* 30(5): 492–515.

Parsa, Misagh. 2016. *Democracy in Iran: Why It Failed and How It Might Succeed.* Cambridge, MA: Harvard University Press.

Pilati, Katia. 2016. "Do Organizational Structures Matter for Protests in Nondemocratic African Countries?" In *Popular Contention, Regime, and Transition: The Arab Revolts in Comparative Global Perspective*, edited by Eitan Alimi, Avraham Sela, and Mario Sznajder, 46–72. Oxford: Oxford University Press.

Pinard, Maurice. 2011. *Motivational Dimensions in Social Movements and Contentious Collective Action.* Montreal: McGill-Queen's University Press.

Piven, Frances Fox and Richard Cloward. 1979. *Poor People's Movements: Why They Succeed, How They Fail.* New York: Vintage.

Rao, Hayagreeva. 2008. *Market Rebels: How Activists Make or Break Radical Innovations.* Princeton, NJ: Princeton University Press.

Reese, Ellen. 2011. *They Say Cut Back, We Say Fight Back! Welfare Activism in an Era of Retrenchment.* New York: Russell Foundation.

Reese, Ellen, Vincent Giedritis, and Eric Vega. 2005. "Mobilization and Threat: Campaigns Against Welfare Privatization in Four Cities." *Sociological Focus* 38(4): 287–307.

Reese, Ellen, Christine Petit, and David Meyer. 2010. "Sudden Mobilization: Movement Crossovers, Threats, and the Surprising Rise of the U.S. Anti-War Movement." In *Strategic Alliances: New Studies of Social Movement Coalitions*, edited by Nella van Dyke and Holly J. McCammon, 266–291. Minneapolis: University of Minnesota Press.

Roberts, Kenneth. 2008. "The Mobilization of Opposition to Economic Liberalization." *Annual Review of Political Science* 11: 327–349.

Rossi, Federico. 2017. *The Poor's Struggle for Political Incorporation: The Piquetero Movement in Argentina.* Cambridge: Cambridge University Press.

Rüdig, Wolfgang and Georgios Karyotis. 2014. "Who Protests in Greece? Mass Opposition to Austerity." *British Journal of Political Science* 44(3): 487–513.

Sánchez González, Mario. 2016. "Los Recursos en Disputa. El Caso del Conflicto Minero en Rancho Grande, Nicaragua." *Anuario de Estudios Centroamericanos* 42: 93–131.

Schock, Kurt. 2005. *Unarmed Insurrections: People Power Movements in Nondemocracies.* Minneapolis: University of Minnesota Press

Schock, Kurt. 2015a. "Rightful Radical Resistance: Mass Mobilization and Land Struggles in India and Brazil." *Mobilization* 20(4): 493–515.

Schock, Kurt. 2015b. *Civil Resistance Today.* London: Polity Press.

Scott, James. 1976. *The Moral Economy of the Peasant: Rebellion and Subsistence in Southeast Asia.* New Haven, CT: Yale University Press.

Seoane, José, Emilio Taddei, and Clara Algranati. 2006. "Las Nuevas Configuraciones de los Movimientos Populares en América Latina." In *Política y Movimientos Sociales en un Mundo Hegemónico. Lecciones desde África, Asia y América Latina*, edited by Atilio A. Boron and Gladys Lechini, 227–250. Buenos Aires: CLACSO.

Shriver, Thomas E., Alison E. Adams, and Stefano B. Longo. 2015. "Environmental Threats and Political Opportunities: Citizen Activism in the North Bohemian Coal Basin." *Social Forces* 94(2): 699–722.

Silva, Eduardo. 2009. *Challenges to Neoliberalism in Latin America.* Cambridge: Cambridge University Press.

Simmons, Erica. 2014. "Grievances Do Matter in Mobilization." *Theory and Society* 43: 513–546.

Simmons, Erica. 2016. *Meaningful Mobilization: Market Reforms and the Roots of Social Protest in Latin America*. Cambridge: Cambridge University Press.

Smelser, Neil. 1962. *Theory of Collective Behavior*. New York: Free Press.

Smith, Jackie and Dawn Wiest. 2012. *Social Movements in the World-System: The Politics of Crisis and Transformation*. New York: Russell Sage Foundation.

Snow, David A. 2013. "Grievances, Individual and Mobilizing." In *The Wiley-Blackwell Encyclopedia of Social and Political Movements*, edited by David A. Snow, Donatella della Porta, Bert Klandermans, and Doug McAdam. Oxford: Blackwell.

Snow, David A. and Robert D. Benford. 1988. "Ideology, Frame Resonance, and Participant Mobilization." *International Social Movement Research* 1(1): 197–217.

Snow, David A., Robert D. Benford, Holly McCammon, Lyndi Hewitt, and Scott Fitzgerald. 2014. "The Emergence, Development, and Future of the Framing Perspective: 25+ Years Since 'Frame Alignment'." *Mobilization* 19(1): 23–46.

Snow, David A. and Catherine Corrigall-Brown. 2005. "Falling on Deaf Ears: Confronting the Prospect of Non-Resonant Frames." In *Rhyming Hope and History: Activism and Social Movement Scholarship*, edited by David Croteau, Charlotte Ryan, and William Hoynes, 222–238. Minneapolis: University of Minnesota Press.

Snow, David A., Daniel Cress, Liam Downey, and Andrew Jones. 1998. "Disrupting the 'Quotidian': Reconceptualizing the Relationship Between Breakdown and the Emergence of Collective Action." *Mobilization* 3(1): 1–22.

Snow, David A. and Sarah A. Soule. 2010. *A Primer on Social Movements*. New York: W.W. Norton.

Snow, David A., Sarah A. Soule, and Daniel M. Cress. 2005. "Identifying the Precipitants of Homeless Protest across 17 US Cities, 1980 to 1990." *Social Forces* 83(3): 1183–1210.

Sosa, Eugenio. 2012. "La Contienda Política tras el Golpe de Estado Oligárquico: De la Resistencia en las Calles hacia la Disputa Político Electoral." *Bajo el Volcán* 11(17): 21–42.

Stearns, Linda Brewster and Paul D. Almeida. 2004. "The Formation of State Actor-Social Movement Coalitions and Favorable Policy Outcomes." *Social Problems* 51(4): 478–504.

Szasz, Andrew. 1994. *Ecopopulism: Toxic Waste and the Movement for Environmental Justice*. Minnesota: University of Minnesota Press.

Szasz, Andrew. 2007. *Shopping Our Way to Safety: How We Changed from Protecting the Environment to Protecting Ourselves*. Minnesota: University of Minnesota Press.

Tarrow, Sidney. 2011. *Power in Movement: Social Movements and Contentious Politics*. Cambridge: Cambridge University Press.

Taylor, Dorceta. 2014. *Toxic Communities: Environmental Racism, Industrial Pollution, and Residential Mobility*. New York: New York University Press.

Tilly, Charles. 1969. "Collective Violence in European Perspective." In *Violence in America: Historical and Comparative Perspectives*, edited by Hugh Davis Graham and Ted Robert Gurr, 4–45. New York: Praeger.

Tilly, Charles. 1977. "Studying Social Movements/Studying Collective Action." CSRO Working Paper #168. Center for Research on Social Organization. University of Michigan.

Tilly, Charles. 1978. *From Mobilization to Revolution*. Reading, MA: Addison-Wesley.

Trejo, Guillermo. 2016. "Why and When Do Peasants Rebel?" In *Oxford Handbook of the Social Science of Poverty*, edited by David Brady and Linda Burton. Oxford: Oxford University Press.

Van Dyke, Nella. 2013. "Threat." In *Blackwell Encyclopedia of Social and Political Movements*, edited by David A. Snow, Donnatella della Porta, Bert Klandermans, and Doug McAdam. Oxford: Wiley-Blackwell.

Van Dyke, Nella and Sarah A. Soule. 2002. "Structural Social Change and the Mobilizing Effect of Threat: Explaining Levels of Patriot and Militia Organizing in the United States." *Social Problems* 49(4): 497–520.

Vasi, Ion Bogdan and Chan S. Suh. 2016. "Online Activities, Spatial Proximity, and the Diffusion of the Occupy Wall Street Movement in the United States." *Mobilization* 21(2): 139–154.

Viterna, Jocelyn, 2013. *Women in War: The Micro-processes of Mobilization in El Salvador*. Oxford: Oxford University Press.

Walsh, Edward, Rex Warland, and Douglas Clayton Smith. 1997. *Don't Burn it Here: Grassroots Challenges to Trash Incinerators*. State College, PA: Penn State University Press.

Walton, John and David Seddon. 1994. "Food Riots Past and Present." In *Free Markets and Food Riots: The Politics of Global Adjustment*, edited by John Walton and David Seddon, 23–54. Oxford: Blackwell.

Yagenova, Simona. 2015. "Guatemalan Social Movements: From the Peace Process to a New Cycle of Popular Struggle (1996–2013)." In *Handbook of Social Movements across Latin America*, edited by Paul D. Almeida and Allen Codero, 327–334. New York: Springer.

Zepeda-Millán, Chris. 2017. *Latino Mass Mobilization: Immigration, Racialization, and Activism*. Cambridge: Cambridge University Press.

3

The Cultural Context of Social Movements

JAMES M. JASPER AND FRANCESCA POLLETTA

Introduction

In the past 30 years, an appreciation for culture has permeated research on social movements, from studies of their emergence to those of their eventual outcomes. This appreciation of culture has helped us rethink structural models, reinvigorated interpretive research techniques, opened the way to the study of emotions, decisions, and identities, and suggested ways to link social movement studies with rich traditions in social psychology (Jasper 2017; van Stekelenburg and Klandermans 2013). In this chapter we examine the role of culture in the emergence of new movements, new collective players and identities, and new tactics (see Williams's (2004) earlier discussion of the cultural context of movements).

Culture has been redefined in the past generation in ways that make it more useful to social movement research. In the days of systemic theories (including Marxism, structural functionalism, and French linguistics), a "society" or a "class structure" was thought to have its corresponding "culture," a fairly unified and coherent body of related beliefs, images, and feelings. The underprivileged might resist the cultural hegemony of elites, but they faced great disadvantages in doing so. If they won, they were prepared to impose their own culture in a revolutionary society. Language was often taken as a model for culture, as its pieces fit together into a coherent whole that was hard to break out of.

Now, we are more likely to view culture as discrete meanings that can be combined in a variety of ways for a variety of strategic (and other) purposes. Cultural constructionism hints at agents behind the creation and spread of cultural meanings and products. Rather than a stable system that changes only slowly or occasionally, we now see even the reproduction of culture as an active process. We define *culture* as "shared mental worlds and their embodiments" (Jasper 1997: 12). Culture is not a realm of social life separate from the economy and state, but the symbolic or meaningful

The Wiley Blackwell Companion to Social Movements, Second Edition. Edited by David A. Snow, Sarah A. Soule, Hanspeter Kriesi, and Holly J. McCammon.
© 2019 John Wiley & Sons Ltd. Published 2019 by John Wiley & Sons Ltd.

dimension of people, things, and actions. It undergirds economic, political, and other practices. It is subjective but cannot easily be ignored. It is shared, but also imposed by some people on others. It constrains people but it also changes – sometimes rapidly.

We can think about the cultural *contexts* of movements in several ways. One is as the widely shared beliefs, assumptions, and practical knowledge that define a kind of cultural common sense and that, when altered, lead to the creation of newly contentious issues and collective actors. The focus here is on culture's role in what Klandermans (2004) calls the "demand side" of protest. A second context is the cultural materials available to collective actors to recruit participants and mobilize support. Culture here figures in what Klandermans calls the "supply side" of protest. And a third context is activists' shared beliefs and feelings about the strategies, tactics, and targets they adopt. This is also part of the supply side of protest, but while culture is treated as constituting interests in the first context and enabling the pursuit of those interests in the second, in the third, the emphasis is on how culture constrains strategies. (A fourth context includes the meanings held by other players – opponents, media, the state – who might block, ignore, or support the protestors; we leave that for other chapters.)

In the following, we rehearse some of the scholarship on each context, but also identify two persistent challenges. One is to recognize both culture's relative autonomy from other kinds of structures and the fact that culture is embedded in structured settings, carried by institutional actors, and evoked by material artifacts. The second challenge is to recognize the role of emotions in culture. In the form of both short-run reactions and relatively permanent moral convictions, emotions are what give symbols, identities, narratives, and other carriers of culture their power to *move* people. More cognitive and more emotional meanings are both built up out of similar, or overlapping, "feeling-thinking processes" (Jasper 2014).

The Cultural Context of Newly Contentious Issues and Actors

The idea that a "context" – cultural or otherwise – must be favorable for a movement to emerge, and the associated question of why movements appear when they do, are associated primarily with political process theory. Changes in the environment, originally in the political environment, may provide openings in which potential participants calculate that they may act with less fear of repression and with greater odds of success. A transformation in beliefs – what McAdam (1982) called cognitive liberation – is required alongside objective changes in political elites and repressive apparatuses. For example, the emergence of a northern black voting bloc supplied an "objective" political opportunity for a postwar southern civil rights movement. Without a compelling sense of urgency, outrage, and threat, however, the movement would have remained small, elite, and probably ineffectual (ibid.).

Political process scholars have moved beyond this early view, to argue that political institutions and developments cannot count as opportunities unless they are recognized as such (Meyer and Gamson 1996). Kurzman (1996, 2005) shows that the Iranian Revolution unfolded in the absence of any of the usual political opportunities, but succeeded in part because participants felt that they had opportunities, which they went on to create through their own efforts.

Koopmans and Olzak (2004) use the term *discursive opportunities* to capture the features of political discourse that make protest seem attractive. They show that the incidence and targets of German right-wing violence were affected by the visibility of violence in the media, and by an accompanying commentary that, in its criticism of immigrants, gave the violence some legitimacy. Giugni et al. (2005) argue that European nations' distinctive models of citizenship created or limited opportunities for extreme right-wing claim-making. Ferree et al. (2002) compare the cultural resources available to contenders in abortion debates in the United States and Germany. While Americans' political suspicion of an active, interventionist state gave an advantage to those promoting individual rights, concerns with the protection of life in post-Nazi Germany benefited those promoting a "Fetal Life" frame.

One can stretch the concept of discursive opportunities to encompass all manner of cultural factors: legal discourse and media coverage, gender expectations (McCammon et al. 2001), broad ideological currents and institutional norms. The term "opportunities," however, implies the existence of a collective actor, an organized group that, even if it is small and operating largely under the radar, is scanning the landscape for chances to mobilize a wider constituency. In many cases, that depiction is accurate. But often, the existence of a collective actor is just what needs to be explained (Armstrong and Bernstein 2008; Polletta and Gardner 2015). Why does an issue become a contentious one? What is the cultural context in which previously settled areas of policy and practice become unsettled? When and why do disparate people come to see themselves as having similar grievances and a stake in protest?

To answer questions like these requires understanding the broad cultural currents that shape people's sense of what their interests and concerns are. Many classic works on movements linked them to the dominant image of injustice characteristic of an epoch (Turner 1969). Some scholars have traced such currents to the structural transformations wrought by capitalism. This is the argument that Haskell (1985) makes in his account of the rise of a humanitarian sensibility in Europe and North America after 1750. That sensibility found expression, most notably, in the abolitionist movement. Its source was in the institution of the market, which encouraged people to think in terms of contractual obligations and responsibility for remote developments, a cognitive style that lent itself to an ethos of responsibility for distant others. Two centuries later, according to Inglehart (1977), conditions of economic and physical security led people to mobilize around "postmaterial" values of individual self-fulfillment, the quality of life, and egalitarianism. Movements that emerged in the 1960s and the 1970s around the environment, peace, and feminism did not reflect the objective severity of the problems they tackled but rather this new cultural sensibility.

In a Marxist and Tourainian version of the argument, Castells (1996, 1997) maintains that increasingly networked societies open the way to the information age, in which individuals have considerable power to shape their own lives. Movements become vehicles for people to develop their capacities for autonomous action. Polletta et al. (2013) argue that new digital media may be changing people's everyday understandings of the boundaries between private ownership and public use – in ways that affect the kinds of causes people see as worth mobilizing around.

In each of these accounts, capitalism plays a role in producing the cultural sensibilities that lead, in turn, to new movements. But its role is different than that posited by traditional Marxist analyses, with their emphasis on class interests in protest – or in preventing protest. Rather, new or changed features of capitalist production – the institution of the market, the new boundary between public and private, the eclipse of the production of material goods by that of information – all these lead people to new understandings of what their interests are.

Institutional logics

Scholars have also turned to institutions other than capitalism to trace the emergence of new lines of contention. Their focus has been less on values, or the rise of new values (whether compassion or self-fulfillment) than on the practical understandings that come to dominate, contend, or combine within a particular institution. An institution here is understood as a set of routinized practices around a culturally defined purpose (Jepperson 1991), for example, medicine, law, science, or mental health services. Culture is understood as the logics or schemas or models with which people operate in a particular institution. There are institutionalized schemas for doing medical diagnosis, for religious worship, for treating abused children, and for waging war (Clemens and Cook 1999; Polletta and Gardner 2015). These schemas are often taken for granted. "This is the way we do things" and "this is the way we *appropriately* do things" are identical. At certain points, however, familiar models may lose their prescriptive force. They may be made obsolete by technical developments or they may come into competition with other models. The result may be new lines of contention and new collective actors.

For example, there would not have been the massive movement against breast cancer that emerged in the 1980s if only women with breast cancer saw themselves as victims of the disease (Klawiter 2008). Changes in the medical diagnosis and treatment of breast cancer dramatically expanded the population of women seen as at risk of breast cancer: asymptomatic women, women with precancerous conditions, women who had been treated for cancer in the past. The result was a new collective identity (women "at risk"), new networks of solidarity (support groups), and a new sense of responsibility to other women similarly at risk.

We can see similar kinds of processes behind the rise of other movements. When a view of homosexuality as an identity rather than a practice gained currency, due partly to its medicalization as a problem, this made possible the homophile movement (D'Emilio 1983). When social workers began to view child abuse in terms taken from the feminist anti-rape movement instead of through the lens of Freudian and family-systems therapies, they made possible the emergence of a collective actor of "adult survivor of child abuse" and survivors' mobilization (Davis 2005).

Sometimes existing institutional logics, and the practices based on them, are delegitimized as a result of their connection to other institutions. Institutions lose credibility by something like symbolic contagion. In her study of radical challenges to science, Moore (2008) shows that organized American science at the beginning of the 1960s enjoyed money, power, and prestige. The fact that science's status after World War II was so harnessed to its mutually supportive relationship with the federal government, however, meant that when the government came under challenge in the 1960s, science was implicated too.

Also looking at several institutions at once, Schudson (2015) describes the rise of a belief that citizens have a "right to know" in politics, markets, and other spheres. That belief led to environmental impact statements and the Freedom of Information Act, to informed consent in science, nutritional labeling in grocery stores, and the *Donahue* show. Innumerable social movements formed out of these concerns for transparency and disclosure, especially in the 1960s and the 1970s. Schudson traces this shift to developments in the news media, public opinion polling, and the field of advocacy, as well as to policy shifts and contingencies such as high-profile environmental disasters and who was president, but also to a new ethos of critical inquiry that was promoted in colleges and universities. Of this latter, he remarks (2015: 26), "A 'spirit' is a very spongy kind of causal force. But its elusiveness is no excuse for ignoring it."

A spirit of critical inquiry, like the "regime of practice" described by Klawiter and the "narrative" described by Davis, offers people a new way of thinking about an issue and themselves in relation to it, but one with identifiable institutional sources. These perspectives thus provide purchase on the pre-history of movements, before collective actors with a political agenda even exist.

The cultural infrastructure of new challenges

Another approach has sought to identify the types of organizations or institutions from which mobilizing ideas spring, a kind of cultural infrastructure of movements.

Sometimes formally non-political organizations are settings for the production of mobilizing ideas. Also described as "critical communities" (Rochon 1998) or "political enclaves" (Chavez 2011), "free spaces" are small-scale settings within a community that are removed from the direct control of dominant groups and generate the cultural challenge that precedes political mobilization (Evans and Boyte 1992; Polletta and Kretschmer 2013). Think of the black church for the southern civil rights movement, literary circles for Eastern European nationalist movements, or music festivals for the White Power movement. Contrary to the notion that such settings produce mobilizing identities because they are free in the sense of empty, scholars increasingly recognize that their power lies in their institutional autonomy from the state. The fact that they supply a non-political idiom with which to formulate opposition is a powerful resource, as people are able to adapt moral schemas to political issues (Gahr and Young 2014; Polletta and Kretschmer 2013).

Some organizations have as their mission identifying new causes and actors and introducing them to new audiences. Bob (2006) shows how the Ogoni and the Zapatistas, through combinations of luck and carefully crafted self-presentation, managed to gain the approval of Amnesty International and, through it, a variety of other international supporters. Light and Cunningham (2016) discuss "cultural clearinghouses" that help redirect schemas and narratives. Not quite media outlets and not quite social movement organizations, these are organizations that nonetheless command wide notice. In their example, the Nobel Peace Prize Committee brings attention to causes and heroes but also to new ways of viewing issues. Whereas the prize was once given to figures linked to Christian and international organizations, since 1975 it has focused more on global poverty and health, the consequences of war and development, armaments, and scientific progress. The elite group that gives the award has been influenced by global developments such as neoliberalism, and it in turn affects the international peace movement's vision of itself.

The Cultural Contexts of Mobilization

Activists do a great deal of strategic cultural work to turn an incipient challenge into a full-fledged movement. We can think about the cultural context of movements in this sense as the beliefs, language, images, artifacts, and emotion rules that are available to activists to mobilize participation and support.

Frames, identities, narratives, and ideologies

Activists must produce frames that catch people's imagination, stories that connect to plausible images of the future, collective identities they feel include them, claims of injustices that make them angry, threatening villains who must be stopped. Scholars of collective action framing have analyzed the processes by which activists engage in frame bridging and frame extension to connect movement messages with the preexisting beliefs of the people they are trying to mobilize (Snow et al. 1986). The frames they use draw from larger "master frames" that are common to a cluster of movements or to a "cycle of protest" (Snow and Benford 1992). They provide the material for resonant claims.

Scholars have examined the role of other cultural forms in spurring participation. Collective identities are images of groups with affective boundaries, largely applied to individuals' identification with their own group, but also relevant to outgroups. Narratives are accounts of events that connect the past to the present and to a desired future, providing rationales for action (Polletta et al. 2011). Ideologies reflect intellectuals' efforts to make a broad "spirit" or vision more systematic and explicit, and to derive political programs from them (Oliver and Johnston 2000). Ideologies typically package together specific artifacts, facts and figures, a grand historical narrative, good and bad characters, and moral principles.

What makes particular frames resonate, identities appeal, or narratives gain traction? Undoubtedly, groups with wide political connections and deep pockets have an advantage in gaining support for the message they promote. Undoubtedly, too, the frames or narratives that succeed in mobilizing people appeal to salient values and seem empirically accurate (Haltom and McCann 2004; Snow and Benford 1988). The danger, though, is that we simply describe success rather than accounting for it: resonant messages are the ones that resonate. One response has been to identify additional features of frames that contribute to their mobilizing power: that they describe the problem in broad terms rather than narrow ones (Gerhards and Rucht 1992), for example, or that they offer concrete evidence for their claims (McCammon 2009).

Another strategy has been to focus on the institutional processes that are responsible for resonance. In his study of Muslim and anti-Muslim groups' framing efforts in the wake of 9/11, Bail (2015) shows that the frames that secured the most media coverage did so not because they appealed to Americans' preexisting hostility to Muslims. To the contrary, anti-Muslim groups that were firmly on the fringe of political discourse and unrepresentative of mainstream opinion gained media coverage on account of their sensationalistic and emotional statements. They were able to parlay their coverage into funding and network connections, and those resources, in turn, into political clout.

Resonance differs across the audiences to which activists' messaging efforts are directed. Messages that appeal to activists may not appeal to the people the movement is trying to recruit (Ferree 2003). Those that persuade the public may not persuade judges or bureaucrats. It is not simply that audiences have different tastes. In the case of judges, bureaucrats, and reporters, their jobs specify the kinds of claims and narratives that are acceptable (Polletta 2012). At the same time, the public may have a taste for different kinds of messages at different times. In their study of public discussion on social media about autism, LGBT rights, and climate change, Bail, Brown, and Mann (2017) found a repeating pattern of increasing rational argumentation followed by more emotional discussion, which increased to a point at which it was replaced once again by more rational talk. Advocacy organizations were most successful in spurring discussion about the messages they released when they did so at the tipping point from one style of public talk to the other.

Activists must "speak" to potential participants and supporters in a literal sense as well as a metaphoric one. Transnational movements especially face this problem, although some national movements do as well (Doerr 2012). In some ways, literal language differences are more obvious and easier to negotiate than differences in more subtle forms of expression, as summed up in the idea of habitus. *How* people talk, for how long, with what turn-taking rules, body language, dress, and other nonverbal cues, with varying uses of humor or anger: all these aid or hinder communication (Flesher Fominaya 2015).

Different communicative styles are not restricted to national groupings, but are also found when people of different genders, races, and social classes talk to each other. Class misunderstandings abound. For the upper middle class, for example, "speech is a central work activity" (Leondar-Wright 2014: 150), whereas working-class participants often value actions over words, and close personal bonds of trust over ideological correctness. These communicative styles form part of the cultural context of activists' recruitment efforts.

Artifacts

While scholars have concentrated on the patterns of meaning that mobilize participation, it is important to recognize also that those meanings are stored in and conveyed through material means, ranging from the qualities of the human voice in face-to-face interactions to films and books preserved by the millions in dusty libraries. These materials consist of both products and the tools to produce them. Modern social movements would not exist without the availability of media that, since the nineteenth century, have become cheaper and cheaper (Tarrow 2011: Chapter 3). Movements have arisen from disputes over the canonical status of particular texts, whether the Gnostic Gospels or the *Diagnostic and Statistical Manual of Mental Disorders* (Snow, Owens, and Tan 2014).

Protestors have used every available art and medium in their efforts, from spray paint and murals to documentaries and fiction films, from short poems to elaborate philosophical treatises, from clever chants to lengthy concerts and music festivals. Sometimes cultural products appear outside the context of a social movement, perhaps crafted by a lone philosopher with an agenda. More often, the creators are already engaged in a movement and intentionally generate products helpful to the movement. Such products typically arise from or alongside social movements, but they in turn can stimulate awareness and mobilization (on the impact of the film *Gasland* on anti-fracking mobilization, see Vasi et al. 2015; on books, see Meyer and Rohlinger 2012). In many cases, a social movement inspires a product that utterly transforms the movement, essentially inspiring a distinct and perhaps more radical movement. The Audubon Society financed Rachel Carson, but *Silent Spring* (1962) helped to create a more self-conscious environmental movement; Peter Singer wrote *Animal Liberation* (1975) under the influence of a tiny network of British philosophers but helped to spark the modern animal rights movement (Jasper and Nelkin 1992).

Because they are physical objects, cultural products can outlast the movements that create them. They can be deprived of their political implications and absorbed into mainstream views. But subsequent movements can rediscover them and recover their political thrust, such as the lyrics in songs (Eyerman and Jamison 1998).

Some cultural objects seem to be politically effective as a result of their form rather than their content. For example, civil rights activists drew some anthems from the folk music of the Old Left. But while Old Leftists produced folk music shows with a performer and audience, music in the civil rights movement erased the distinctions between performer and audience. Music-making *was* activism, and it proved more mobilizing as a result (Roy 2010). Fascist theater in Italy created loyalty not only through its content but also through its style. Staged in open air piazzas and using a disciplined mode of direction and acting, fascist plays embodied in their form fascist values of collectivity, ritual, and order (Berezin 1994).

Emotions

In addition to figures of speech and material artifacts, emotions are a key component in the cultural context of mobilization (see also, Chapter 23 by Van Ness and Summers-Effler, in this volume, on emotions). In part, they help explain cultural resonance: collective identities resonate because we love or hate the group; villains grab our attention by frightening us, victims by arousing our pity; narratives create surprise and suspense.

Emotions weave in and out of all these cultural influences, but we can also address them directly as conditions for mobilization. Although some emotions are quick to arise and subside, such as surprise, joy, and anger, others are almost permanent orientations to the world. These are often called background emotions, in that they shape our short-run reactions to events and information (Nussbaum 2001). Like more cognitive cultural meanings, they tend to change slowly and to be unequally distributed – meaning they are subject to disagreement and conflict.

Moral emotions are one category of background emotions central to the emergence of protest. Compassion is a salient moral emotion, as it helps us stoke moral outrage, define worthy victims, and suggest some form of succor. Compassion seems to have expanded in the modern world, to encompass more and more human groups who are different and distant from us but also to include nonhuman species (Haskell 1985; Singer 2011). It entails a gut-level pain or disgust when we see other beings suffer, as well as cognitive elaboration of our kinship with those beings. Movements from abolition to animal rights have based their appeals on compassion (Cherry 2016). Of course, other movements, such as nationalism, work hard to limit those feelings of kinship and compassion, and even to replace them with resentment or hate (Betz 1994; Greenfeld 1992) (see Chapter 39 by Goldstone and Ritter, in this volume, on terrorism).

Charles Cooley (1902) thought that pride and shame are master emotions that motivate most social action (also Scheff 1990, 1994). Our moral intuitions and principles shape what makes us feel proud or ashamed, and these can entail either actions or group membership. Caste systems, for example, try to impose pride on members of higher castes and an inherent shame on those of lower castes. We also feel proud when we act in ways that live up to or exceed group expectations, and ashamed when we violate a group's basic values.

Extensive research has shown that social movements of oppressed groups work hard to replace shame with pride. Not only is this transformation an end in itself, but it fosters a collective identity that leads to further mobilization and action. Gay pride is the most studied case (and perhaps the most influential one, Gould 2009), but there are many others (Bruce 2016). Britt and Heise (2000) suggest that anger aids the transition from shame to pride, perhaps by shifting the blame from the group itself to its oppressors. Like many other contributors to movement emergence, pride must be created in the early stages of a movement, a form of emotional liberation every bit as important as cognitive liberation.

In addition to moral emotions, a second set of emotions crucial to protest is comprised of our positive and negative feelings about people, places, ideas, and things. Jasper (2011) labels these "affective commitments." The most salient of these are collective identities, but humans develop similar attachments to many places, whether a temple, a mountain range, national park, or more abstract places such as home or nation (Duyvendak 2011). Equally strong convictions form around ideas and ideologies, especially religious ideas, and they come in negative forms (hate or mistrust) as well as positive ones (love or trust).

The Cultural Context of Strategic Action

Activists are strategic actors. Even those who are committed to "prefiguring" within their own personal relations the radically different society they hope to bring into being are almost always also concerned about being politically effective: changing laws or policies, winning political representation, or altering institutional practices (Downey 1986). But activists' very ideas about what is strategic, as well as what is legitimate and appropriate, are cultural. We can think about the cultural context of movements in this sense as the beliefs available to activists about the viability and merits of different strategic options.

Tilly's concept of a repertoire of protest was intended to capture the fact that at any given time, only a limited range of options are considered possible and desirable.

Such "collectively-learned shared understandings," Tilly writes, "greatly constrain the contentious claims political actors make on each other and on agents of the state" (1999: 419). Tilly (1993) argued that a modern repertory – national, modular, and centered on electoral politics – emerged when the state's war-making projects required that it extract substantial resources from its subjects, and established accountable legislatures to do so. Food riots and local skirmishes over taxation yielded to strikes and "demonstrations," in which people massed at seats of formal state power with banners proclaiming their collective identity and interests.

Young (2006) takes issue with Tilly's focus on the nation state as driving the emergence of the national social movement. He makes a more explicitly cultural argument to account for the repertory of protest that animated movements around temperance, abolition, and anti-vice in the United States in the 1830s. Reformers were able to combine two schemas of faith to create a new kind of activism. Mainstream Protestant churches were creating a network of benevolent societies aimed at eradicating national sins like Sabbath-breaking and drinking at the same time as upstart Methodist sects were popularizing a revivalist style that focused on public confession. Reformers joined these schemas of special sins and public confession to create a "confessional mode of protest" in which participants publicly swore off the products of industries connected with the slave trade, gave emotional testimonials to the evils of drink, and fought to outlaw both slavery and alcohol.

Repertories of protest may include identities and emotions as well as strategies and tactics (Tarrow 2013; Taylor et al. 2009). They include conscious know-how but also tacit, preconscious knowledge embodied in action. The language of practices and habitus, both associated with Bourdieu (e.g. 1990), suggest pre-conscious forms of thought, embodied in gestures and stances that we often learn from an early age. There can be an activist habitus, which individuals carry with them as a form of know-how from movement to movement, as part of activist careers (Fillieule 2016; Flesher Fominaya 2015).

There are strategic virtues to the familiarity of forms. For example, women activists in the late nineteenth and early twentieth centuries drew on familiar associational forms such as the club, parlor meeting, and charitable society to become a major force for social reform. As Clemens (1997) explains, these forms were seen as appropriate for women but as nonpolitical. Braunstein (2012) shows that a storytelling strategy came naturally to religious advocacy groups, whose leaders regularly told stories from the pulpit, and did so effectively. The notion of a repertory also alerts us to the constraints that come with familiarity. Options lying outside the repertory are often rejected not because they are likely to be ineffective but because they seem somehow inappropriate (Polletta 2005).

At the same time, repertories are never fixed. Activists modify their strategies – and their ideas about what is strategic – as they interact with opponents, authorities, allies, and each other. After the battle in Seattle in 1999, for example, groups in only some cities adopted the tactics that were showcased there – the use of puppets, street blockades, and jail solidarity. Wood (2012) identifies organizational features that made some clusters of groups more open to discussing new alternatives than others. Blee (2012) portrays groups that are initially open to new possibilities, and then retreat to the realm of the tactically familiar. McCammon (2012) finds that the ideological orientation of groups fighting to get women on juries mattered for whether they chose a radical framing (insisting on women's rights) or a more moderate framing (arguing for the value of women's unique perspective in trials), but so did the presence of women lawmakers in the state, who could be expected to be more sympathetic to a rights framing, and whether activists were radicalized by opponents' charges.

Scholars of digital technologies have argued that a fundamentally new repertory of contention may be in the making (see Chapter 16 by Earl, in this volume, on technology and social media). The Internet has not only made it easier to do the traditional tasks of mobilization, such as recruiting participants, staging demonstrations, communicating with the authorities, and so on. It has changed what protest looks like in more fundamental ways (Earl and Kimport 2011; Juris 2008; Yang 2009). Online mobilizations are sporadic rather than deep-rooted and enduring. Protests flare up, gather huge numbers to the cause, then fade away. People participate because they care passionately about the cause or because they are mildly concerned; because they believe that protest will be effective or because they just want to express themselves. Targets and issues are also diverse. There are few clear dividing lines between politics and, variously, leisure, consumption, and popular culture: people may use the same tactics to protest the war in Iraq and the cancelation of their favorite TV show. And movement organizations are becoming obsolete: protests are often organized by small groups, "lone wolves," or participants who never even meet each other. Bennett and Segerberg (2013) similarly describe a "logic of connective action" that has replaced the earlier "logic of collective action." People used to be recruited to protest by formal organizations with clear frames; today, they mobilize each other by sharing their experiences online and under the banner of broad but personalizable themes like "we are the 99 percent."

Conclusion: Culture in Context

Activists draw on existing cultural meanings, whether these are embodied in physical objects, decision-making arenas such as legislatures, or particular individuals who have come to symbolize ideas to a broad audience. Of special importance are the collective identities that help political players emerge, and then guide them in their choice of goals and tactics. But participants in social movements also try to change all of these meanings, symbols, and practices.

New images of culture cast doubt on the very notion of a "context" for movement emergence. This traditional image suggests that there are structural openings and reasons for a movement to emerge, and cultural or discursive openings for symbols, frames, and so on, to resonate. The movement makes its claims with its repertory of tactics, with or without success depending on its resonance and resources. It may leave a mark on culture, or it may not. With a less systemic vision of culture, we can see that most political conflicts continue for long periods, with gains and losses for various players along the way. When a movement "ends," this usually means that its component sub-players regroup or pursue different tactics in new arenas. Any new effort is built out of the pieces of the old, including personnel and cultural products.

Cultural meanings are indispensable to the emergence of social movements, but that does not make it easy to identify them or trace their consequences. They are inside us as expectations, interpretations, and perceptions, outside us as traces and artifacts. Political players accept some and change others. Or try to: other players resist, reverse, extend, and redirect their cultural efforts. Scholars have made great progress in understanding the role that culture plays in politics, but much remains to be done.

We need to recognize both that lines of contention are often longstanding, even though the people and particular issues in dispute may change, and that they are sometimes new. In the first instance, players use culture creatively; in the second, culture creates new players. Scholars have tended to emphasize culture's enabling or constitutive dimensions depending on their theoretical predilections, but it is likely that culture figures differently in the emergence of specific kinds of movements. We need to figure that out. Our accounts of culture's role in creating new collective actors and issues would be improved by a better grasp of the cultural currents that spread through multiple institutions, unsettling policies and practices that once seemed benign. Our accounts of culture's role in turning incipient challenges into full-fledged movements would benefit from a better understanding of the conditions in which messages resonate, conditions that undoubtedly have to do with the message's content and its context, but also with the emotions it displays and arouses. Finally, with respect to the third cultural context, that of the strategies and tactics activists adopt, we need to better understand how repertoires work to exclude options and how they change. Like the other questions we have identified, these require research and theorizing at both micro and macro levels of interaction.

References

Armstrong, Elizabeth A. and Mary Bernstein. 2008. "Culture, Power, and Institutions: A Multi-Institutional Politics Approach to Social Movements." *Sociological Theory* 26: 74–99. doi: 10.1111/j.1467-9558.2008.00319.

Bail, Christopher A. 2015. *Terrified: How Anti-Muslim Fringe Organizations Became Mainstream*. Princeton, NJ: Princeton University Press.

Bail, Christopher A., Taylor W. Brown, and Marcus Mann. 2017. "Channeling Hearts and Minds: Cognitive-Emotional Currents and Public Deliberation on Social Media." *American Sociological Review* 82 (6): 1188–1213.

Bennett, W. Lance and Alexandra Segerberg. 2013. *The Logic of Connective Action: Digital Media and the Personalization of Contentious Politics*. New York: Cambridge University Press.

Berezin, Mabel. 1994. "Cultural Form and Political Meaning: State-Subsidized Theater, Ideology, and the Language of Style in Fascist Italy." *American Journal of Sociology* 99(5): 1237–1286.

Betz, Hans-Georg. 1994. *Radical Right Wing Populism in Western Europe*. New York: St. Martin's Press.

Blee, Kathleen M. 2012. *Democracy in the Making: How Activist Groups Form*. New York: Oxford University Press.

Bob, Clifford. 2006. *The Marketing of Rebellion*. Cambridge: Cambridge University Press.

Bourdieu, Pierre. 1990. *The Logic of Practice*. Stanford, CA: Stanford University Press.

Braunstein, Ruth. 2012. "Storytelling in Liberal Religious Advocacy." *Journal for the Scientific Study of Religion* 51(1): 110–127.

Britt, Lori and David R. Heise. 2000. "From Shame to Pride in Identity Politics." In *Self, Identity, and Social Movements*, edited by Sheldon Stryker, Timothy J. Owens, and Robert W. White. Minneapolis: University of Minnesota Press.

Bruce, Katherine M. 2016. *Pride Parades*. New York: New York University Press.

Carson, Rachel. 1962. *Silent Spring*. Boston: Houghton Mifflin.

Castells, Manuel. 1996. *The Rise of the Network Society*. Oxford: Blackwell.

Castells, Manuel. 1997. *The Power of Identity*. Oxford: Blackwell.

Chavez, Karma R. 2011. "Counter-Public Enclaves and Understanding the Function of Rhetoric in Social Movement Coalition-Building." *Communication Quarterly* 59: 1–18.

Cherry, Elizabeth. 2016. *Culture and Activism: Animal Rights in France and the United States*. New York: Routledge.

Clemens, Elisabeth. 1997. *The People's Lobby: Organizational Innovation and the Rise of Interest Group Politics in the United States, 1890–1925*. Chicago: University of Chicago Press.

Clemens, Elisabeth S. and James M. Cook. 1999. "Politics and Institutionalism: Explaining Durability and Change." *Annual Review of Sociology* 25: 441–466.

Cooley, Charles. 1902. *Human Nature and the Social Order*. New York: Charles Scribner's Sons.

Davis, Joseph E. 2005. *Accounts of Innocence: Sexual Abuse, Trauma, and the Self*. Chicago: University of Chicago Press.

D'Emilio, John. 1983. *Sexual Politics, Sexual Communities: The Making of a Homosexual Minority in the United States, 1940–1970*. Chicago: University of Chicago Press.

Doerr, Nicole. 2012. "Translating Democracy: How Activists in the European Social Forum Practice Multilingual Deliberation." *European Political Science Review* 4: 361–384.

Downey, Gary L. 1986. "Ideology and the Clamshell Identity: Organizational Dilemmas in the Anti-Nuclear Power Movement." *Social Problems* 33(5): 357–373.

Duyvendak, Jan Willem. 2011. *The Politics of Home*. London: Palgrave Macmillan.

Earl, Jennifer and Katrina Kimport. 2011. *Digitally Enabled Social Change: Activism in the Internet Age*. Cambridge, MA: MIT Press.

Evans, Sara M. and Harry C. Boyte. 1992. *Free Spaces: The Sources of Democratic Change in America*. Chicago: University of Chicago Press.

Eyerman, Ron and Andrew Jamison. 1998. *Music and Social Movements*. Cambridge: Cambridge University Press.

Ferree, Myra Marx. 2003. "Resonance and Radicalism: Feminist Framing in the Abortion Debates of the United States and Germany." *American Journal of Sociology* 109(2): 304–344.

Ferree, Myra Marx, William A. Gamson, Jürgen Gerhards, and Dieter Rucht. 2002. *Shaping Abortion Discourse: Democracy and the Public Sphere in Germany and the United States*. New York: Cambridge University Press.

Fillieule, Olivier. 2016. "Demobilization and Disengagement in a Life Course Perspective." In *Oxford Handbook of Social Movements*, edited by Donatella della Porta and Mario Diani. Oxford: Oxford University Press.

Flesher Fominaya, Christina. 2015. "Cultural Barriers to Activist Networking: Habitus (In) action in Three European Transnational Encounters." *Antipode* 48: 151–171.

Gahr, Joshua and Michael P. Young. 2014. "Evangelicals and Emergent Moral Protest." *Mobilization* 19: 185–208.

Gerhards, Jürgen and Dieter Rucht. 1992. "Mesomobilization: Organizing and Framing in Two Protest Campaigns in West Germany." *American Journal of Sociology* 98(3): 555–596.

Giugni, Marco, Ruud Koopmans, Florence Passy, and Paul Statham. 2005. "Institutional and Discursive Opportunities for Extreme-Right Mobilization in Five Countries." *Mobilization* 10(1): 145–162.

Gould, Deborah B. 2009. *Moving Politics*. Chicago: University of Chicago Press.

Greenfeld, Liah. 1992. *Nationalism*. Cambridge, MA: Harvard University Press.

Haltom, William and Michael McCann. 2009. *Distorting the Law: Politics, Media, and the Litigation Crisis*. Chicago: University of Chicago Press.

Haskell, Thomas L. 1985. "Capitalism and the Origins of the Humanitarian Sensibility." *American Historical Review* 90: 339–361, 547–566.

Inglehart, Ronald. 1977. *The Silent Revolution*. Princeton, NJ: Princeton University Press.

Jasper, James M. 1997. *The Art of Moral Protest*. Chicago: University of Chicago Press.

Jasper, James M. 2011. "Emotions and Social Movements: Twenty Years of Theory and Research." *Annual Review of Sociology* 37: 285–304.

Jasper, James M. 2014. "Feeling-Thinking Processes: Emotions as Central to Culture." In *Conceptualizing Culture in Social Movement Research*, edited by Britta Baumgarten, Priska Daphi, and Peter Ullrich. Basingstoke: Palgrave Macmillan.

Jasper, James M. 2017. "The Doors that Culture Opened: Parallels between Social Psychology and Social Movement Studies." *Group Processes and Social Interaction* 20: 285–302.

Jasper, James M. and Dorothy Nelkin. 1992. *The Animal Rights Crusade*. New York: Free Press.

Jepperson, Ronald L. 1991. "Institutions, Institutional Effects, and Institutionalism." *The New Institutionalism in Organizational Analysis*, edited by Paul J. DiMaggio and Walter W. Powell, 143–163. Chicago: University of Chicago Press.

Juris, Jeffrey S. 2008. *Networking Futures: The Movements Against Corporate Globalization*. Durham, NC: Duke University Press.

Klandermans, Bert. 2004. "The Demand and Supply of Participation: Social-Psychological Correlates of Participation in Social Movements." In *The Blackwell Companion to Social Movements*, edited by David A. Snow, Sarah A. Soule, and Hanspeter Kriesi, 360–379. Oxford: Blackwell.

Klawiter, Maren. 2008. *The Biopolitics of Breast Cancer: Changing Cultures of Disease and Activism*. Minneapolis: University of Minnesota Press.

Koopmans, Ruud and Susan Olzak. 2004. "Discursive Opportunities and the Evolution of Right-Wing Violence in Germany." *American Journal of Sociology* 110: 198–230.

Kurzman, Charles. 1996. "Structural Opportunity and Perceived Opportunity in Social Movement Theory." *American Sociological Review* 61: 151–170.

Kurzman, Charles. 2005. *The Unthinkable Revolution in Iran*. Cambridge, MA: Harvard University Press.

Leondar-Wright, Betsy. 2014. *Missing Class*. Ithaca, NY: Cornell University Press.

Light, Ryna and Jeanine Cunningham. 2016. "Oracles of Peace: Topic Modeling, Cultural Opportunity, and the Nobel Peace Prize, 1902–2012." *Mobilization* 21: 43–64.

McAdam, Doug. 1982. *Political Process and the Development of Black Insurgency, 1930–1970*. Chicago: University of Chicago Press.

McCammon, Holly J. 2009. "Beyond Frame Resonance: The Argumentative Structure and Persuasive Capacity of Twentieth-Century U.S. Women's Jury-Rights Frames." *Mobilization* 14(1): 45–64.

McCammon, Holly J. 2012. "Explaining Frame Variation: More Moderate and Radical Demands for Women's Citizenship in the US Women's Jury Movements." *Social Problems* 59(1): 43–69.

McCammon, Holly J., Karen E. Campbell, Ellen M. Granberg, and Christine Mowery. 2001. "How Movements Win: Gendered Opportunity Structures and the State Women's Suffrage Movements, 1866–1919." *American Sociological Review* 66: 49–70.

Meyer, David S. and William A. Gamson. 1996. "Framing Political Opportunity." In *Comparative Perspectives on Social Movements*, edited by Doug McAdam, John D. McCarthy, and Mayer N. Zald. Cambridge: Cambridge University Press.

Meyer, David S. and Deana A. Rohlinger. 2012. "Big Books and Social Movements: A Myth of Ideas and Social Change." *Social Problems* 59: 136–153.

Moore, Kelly. 2008. *Disrupting Science*. Princeton, NJ: Princeton University Press.

Nussbaum, Martha C. 2001. *Upheavals of Thought*. Cambridge: Cambridge University Press.

Oliver, Pamela E. and Hank Johnston. 2000. "What a Good Idea! Ideologies and Frames in Social Movement Research." *Mobilization* 4: 37–54.

Polletta, Francesca. 2005. "How Participatory Democracy Became White: Culture and Organizational Choice." *Mobilization* 10(2): 271–288.

Polletta, Francesca. 2012. "Three Mechanisms by Which Culture Shapes Movement Strategy: Repertoires, Institutional Norms, and Metonymy." In *Strategies for Social Change*, edited by Gregory Maney, Rachel Kutz-Flamenbaum, Deana Rohlinger, and Jeff Goodwin. Minneapolis: University of Minnesota Press.

Polletta, Francesca, Pang Ching Bobby Chen, Beth Gharrity Gardner, and Alice Motes. 2011. "The Sociology of Storytelling." *Annual Review of Sociology* 37: 109–130.

Polletta, Francesca, Pang Ching Bobby Chen, Beth Gharrity Gardner, and Alice Motes. 2013. "Is the Internet Creating New Reasons to Protest?" In *The Future of Social Movement Research: Dynamics, Mechanisms, and Processes*, edited by Jacquelien van Stekelenburg, Conny Roggeband, and Bert Klandermans. Minneapolis: University of Minnesota Press.

Polletta, Francesca and Beth Gharrity Gardner. 2015. "Culture and Social Movements." In *Emerging Trends in the Social and Behavioral Sciences*, edited by Robert A. Scott and Stephen M. Kosslyn. New York: Wiley.

Polletta, Francesca and Kelsy Kretschmer. 2013. "Free Spaces." In *The Wiley-Blackwell Encyclopedia of Social and Political Movements*, edited by David A. Snow, Donatella della Porta, Bert Klandermans, and Doug McAdam. New York: Blackwell.

Rochon, Thomas R. 1998. *Culture Moves*. Princeton, NJ: Princeton University Press.

Roy, William G. 2010. *Reds, Whites, and Blues: Social Movements, Folk Music, and Race in the United States*. Princeton, NJ: Princeton University Press.

Scheff, Thomas J. 1990. *Microsociology*. Chicago: University of Chicago Press.

Scheff, Thomas J. 1994. *Bloody Revenge*. Boulder, CO: Westview Press.

Schudson, Michael. 2015. *The Rise of the Right to Know*. Cambridge, MA: Harvard University Press.

Singer, Peter. 1975. *Animal Liberation*. New York: New York Review of Books.

Singer, Peter. 2011. *The Expanding Circle*, rev. edn. Princeton, NJ: Princeton University Press.

Snow, David A. and Robert D. Benford. 1988. "Ideology, Frame Resonance, and Participant Mobilization." *International Social Movement Research* 1(1): 197–217.

Snow, David A. and Robert D. Benford. 1992. "Master Frames and Cycles of Protest." In *Frontiers in Social Movement Theory*, edited by Aldon Morris and Carol McClurg Mueller, 133–155. New Haven, CT: Yale University Press.

Snow, David A., Peter B. Owens, and Anna E. Tan. 2014. "Libraries, Social Movements, and Cultural Change: Toward an Alternative Conceptualization of Culture." *Social Currents* 1(1): 35–43.

Snow, David A., E. Burke Rochford Jr., Steven K. Worden, and Robert D. Benford. 1986. "Frame Alignment Processes, Micromobilization, and Movement Participation." *American Sociological Review* 51(4): 464–481.

Tarrow, Sidney. 2011. *Power in Movement*, 3rd edn. Cambridge: Cambridge University Press.

Tarrow, Sidney. 2013. *The Language of Contention: Revolutions in Words, 1688–2012.* Cambridge: Cambridge University Press.

Taylor, Verta, Katrina Kimport, Nella Van Dyke, and Ellen Ann Andersen. 2009. "Culture and Mobilization: Tactical Repertoires, Same-Sex Weddings, and the Impact on Gay Activism." *American Sociological Review* 74(6): 865–890.

Tilly, Charles. 1993. "Contentious Repertoires in Great Britain, 1758–1834." *Social Science History* 17(2): 253–280.

Tilly, Charles. 1999. "Epilogue: Now Where?" In *State/Culture: State-Formation After the Cultural Turn*, edited by George Steinmetz, 407–419. Ithaca, NY: Cornell University Press.

Turner, Ralph. 1969. "The Theme of Contemporary Social Movements." *British Journal of Sociology* 20: 390–405.

van Stekelenburg, Jacquelien and Bert Klandermans. 2013. "The Social Psychology of Protest." *Current Sociology* 61(5–6): 886–905.

Vasi, Ion Bogdan, Edward T. Walker, John S. Johnson, and Hui Fen Tan. 2015. "'No Fracking Way!' Documentary Film, Discursive Opportunity, and Local Opposition against Hydraulic Fracturing in the United States, 2010 to 2013." *American Sociological Review* 80: 934–959.

Williams, Rhys H. 2004. "The Cultural Contexts of Collective Action: Constraints, Opportunities, and the Symbolic Life of Social Movements." In *The Blackwell Companion to Social Movements*, edited by David A. Snow, Sarah A. Soule, and Hanspeter Kriesi. Oxford: Blackwell.

Wood, Lesley J. 2012. *Direct Action, Deliberation, and Diffusion: Collective Action after the WTO Protests in Seattle.* New York: Cambridge University Press.

Yang, Guobin. 2009. *The Power of the Internet in China: Citizen Activism Online.* New York: Columbia University Press.

Young, Michael. 2006. *Bearing Witness against Sin.* Chicago: University of Chicago Press.

4

The Resource Context of Social Movements

Bob Edwards, John D. McCarthy, and Dane R. Mataic

Introduction

Social movement scholarship continued to expand rapidly in the twenty-first century, spreading well beyond its "home front" in sociology across the full spectrum of social science disciplines, and far beyond, even including the life sciences. Contemporary analysts pursue a wide range of research questions about an equally broad range of movements pressing traditionalist, reformist, or radical agendas. The proliferation of organized collective action has resulted in continued efforts to explain the successes and failures of social movements. The burgeoning literature is routinely grouped within three theoretical perspectives: political opportunity, cultural framing, and resource mobilization (RM) (see McAdam, McCarthy, and Zald 1996; and Travaglino 2014, for reviews). Recent, widely noted, reviews have continued to emphasize the importance of the political opportunity and the cultural strands summarizing their ongoing development and refinement (e.g. Amenta et al. 2010; Armstrong and Bernstein 2008). Despite the continuous evolution of each of these perspectives, some scholars have argued that the emphasis has been unbalanced, with greater attention directed to refining and synthesizing extant research on political opportunities and cultural framing (Edwards and Kane 2014). Thus, the substantial recent research literature focused primarily upon the resource mobilization strand has until now remained relatively unexamined and unsynthesized. That the continuing relevance and usefulness of RM concepts and ideas are undiminished and the broader approach contains vital conceptual tools for analyzing the full spectrum of contemporary movements will become clear in the brief review of the recent research we present below, one that emphasizes publications appearing since the beginning of 2004. Before turning to that review, however, we rearticulate what we described as the core ideas of the broader resource mobilization approach in our earlier review (Edwards and McCarthy 2004).

The Wiley Blackwell Companion to Social Movements, Second Edition. Edited by David A. Snow, Sarah A. Soule, Hanspeter Kriesi, and Holly J. McCammon.
© 2019 John Wiley & Sons Ltd. Published 2019 by John Wiley & Sons Ltd.

Resource Types

Despite the obvious importance of resources to the RM approach, analysts who made resources central to their thinking about movements neglected to specify in much detail the concept of resources, and, especially, failed to develop clear specification of resource types, with most analyses focusing on money, people or formal organizations (McCarthy and Zald 2001). Yet, more recently RM analysts have benefitted from broader developments in social science that have better theorized forms of capital (Bourdieu 1986; Coleman 1988; Lin 2001). This enables the specification and differentiation of five distinct resource types: material, human, social-organizational, cultural, and moral, while avoiding the criticism of treating "everything as a resource" (Edwards and McCarthy 2004).

Material resources

The category of material resources combines what economists would call financial and physical capital, including monetary resources, property, office space, equipment, and supplies. The importance of monetary resources for social movements should not be under-estimated. No matter how many other resources a movement mobilizes, it will incur costs and someone has to pay the bills. Material resources have received much analytic attention because they are generally more tangible, more proprietary, and, in the case of money, more fungible than other resource types. In other words, money can be converted into other types of resources (e.g. renting office space, organizing events, hiring of picketers, funding documentaries, even paying for celebrity appearances), while the opposite is less often the case.

Human resources

Similar to material resources, human resources are more tangible and easier to appreciate than the three resource types to be discussed below. This category includes resources like labor, experience, skills, and expertise as well as leadership because it involves a combination of other human resources included here. Human resources are inherent in individuals rather than in social-organizational structures or culture more generally. Thus, a movement's capacity to recruit and deploy personnel is limited by the cooperation of the individuals involved. By deciding whether or not to participate in a movement, event or social movement organization (SMO), individuals exert proprietary control over their labor. This is one reason why voluntary participation on a mass scale, the sheer power of numbers, is an important human resource for movements of all kinds, regardless of any particular skills participants may also possess.

Beyond labor, human resources include value-added components like experience, savvy, skills, or expertise, known also as human capital (Becker 1964). Clearly, not all adherents offer the same mix of capabilities. A savvy and seasoned activist is not directly inter-changeable with an eager undergraduate, no matter how effective the student may become with additional experience. SMOs often require expertise of varying kinds and having access to lawyers, web designers, organizers, or outside experts when the need arises is important. A key issue in whether the availability of skilled individuals enhances movement mobilization hinges on how their expertise fits with what is needed at the time. For example, a prominent climate scientist may have less to offer a climate justice group than a savvy intern if the web page needs restoration after a crash (Oliver and Marwell 1992). Similarly, a celebrated musician offers no additional human resource to blockading the entrance of an investment bank than either the tone-deaf academic or the grocery clerk with whom she has linked arms. Yet, from the standpoint of the moral resource contributed by her presence the evaluation would be quite different.

Social-organizational resources

Researchers have highlighted several forms of social organization, besides formal organizations, that serve as the mobilizing structures for social movements, including infrastructures, social ties and networks, affinity groups, and coalitions (McCarthy 1996). These forms clearly vary in their degree of organizational formalization and bureaucratic structure, and in the extent to which access to them can be controlled, or in other words, how proprietary they are. Infrastructures are non-proprietary, relatively open-access social resources that facilitate the smooth functioning of everyday life (McCarthy 1987). By contrast, access to social networks, including both social media and coalitions, but especially so in face-to-face affinity groups and formal organizations, *can* be limited by insiders through a variety of exclusionary practices, both formal and informal. Thus, resources embedded in them can be hoarded by insiders and denied to outsiders, which often intensifies pre-existing inequalities among groups in their ability to access and utilize crucial resources of other kinds (Tilly 1998). A chief benefit of any form of social organization is to provide access to other resources, which raises the question of how uneven access to social-organizational resources favors some potential social movement constituencies over others. Does differential access create further inequalities in access to crucial resources of other kinds leading to disparities in mobilization capacity across and within movements?

This resource category includes both intentional and appropriable social organization (Coleman 1988). Intentional social organization is created specifically to further social movement goals. The form receiving the most scholarly attention is the variety of social movement organizations founded to pursue movement goals. From named groups of a few activists operating locally with little to no formal structure to fully bureaucratized, formalized organizations deploying hundreds of professional staff across multiple nations (Edwards 1994), SMOs are both reservoirs of movement resources and a crucial movement tool used to mobilize collective actions of all kinds. By contrast, appropriable social organizations are originally created for non-movement purposes, but movement actors are able to gain access to other types of resources through it. Recruiting volunteers or disseminating information through work, congregation, civic, neighborhood, education or recreation-based connections are widely cited examples (McCarthy 1996). The two are further distinguished by the typical means by which movement actors gain access to them. Resources embedded in appropriable social organization must be *co-opted*, while the exchange relationships providing movement access to intentional social organization are presumably more collaborative and potentially less problematic. In either case, the ease of accessing such resources and the viability of relationships through which resources are exchanged will vary according to the goodness of fit between the specific legitimacy, organizational form, goals, and tactics of those groups involved.

Both intentional and appropriable forms of social-organization have proven crucial in explaining patterns of movement mobilization and access to other resource types. Moreover, that dense levels of pre-existing social organization among movement adherents facilitate the emergence, mobilization, varied activities and spatial distribution of social movements is one of the most consistent findings to emerge from nearly four decades of social movement research (Edwards and McCarthy 2004). Social movement researchers seldom discuss these findings in terms of "social capital." However, if one reviews that body of work from the vantage point of recent sociological theorizing, it becomes quite apparent that social capital has long been an important element in the analysis of social movements (Diani 1997; Minkoff 1997). Conceived as networked access to resources, social capital is a relational and structural concept referring to the ability of individuals, groups organizations to utilize their social relations and positions in specific social networks to access a variety of resources, and to accumulate a reservoir of viable exchange relationships by consciously investing in social relations (Bourdieu 1986; Coleman 1988; Lin 2001). Exchange relations are discussed more below.

Cultural resources

Culture is often conceptualized as the tacit and taken-for-granted symbols, beliefs, values, identities, and behavioral norms of a group of people that orient and facilitate their actions in everyday life. Thus, culture is a reserve supply of resources ready for use by the individuals, groups, and organizations able to access them. It can be usefully understood in much the same way as the kinds of structural resources discussed above (Williams 2004). Consistent with Bourdieu's concept of "habitus" as a structural and relational constraint upon access to "cultural capital" and an emphasis on resource stratification, we stress that cultural resources, though widely available in a given society, are neither evenly distributed (socially or spatially), nor universally accessible to potential movement actors. For example, McGurty (2009) argues persuasively that the rapid emergence and national mobilization in the 1980s of the environmental justice movement among African Americans benefited greatly from their ready access to cultural, and other, resources produced by the civil rights movement during the 1950s and 1960s. In contrast, predominantly white, working-class communities confronting similar issues in the same period mobilized much more slowly, in large part, because they lacked the cultural resources of a resonant collective frame rooted in the civil rights struggle against racial discrimination, and by a general unfamiliarity with tactical repertoires they had to learn from scratch (Edwards 1995). This example makes clear that, through decades of sustained resistance to racial injustice, African Americans produced a rich repository of symbols, ideas, rhetorical frames, and behavioral repertoires of protest transferable to the issue of environmental inequality. Over the last 50 years, those cultural resources have entered the public domain and became culturally available and accessible to subsequent social movements.

Cultural resources also include movement- or issue-relevant productions, such as music, literature, blogs, web pages, or film/videos. Cultural products facilitate the recruitment and socialization of new adherents and help movements maintain their readiness and capacity for collective action. For example, Corte and Edwards (2008) show how the production and marketing of White Power Music by racist activists funded extremist mobilizations, helped create and spread a White Power collective identity, and facilitated the recruitment of new participants. Other cultural resources relevant to social movements include the diffusion into the public domain or taken-for-granted templates for how to accomplish specific tasks like enacting a protest event, holding a news conference, maintaining a tree-sit, or snake marching through a field of protest to disrupt the police. For example, prior to the 2011 Occupy Wall Street movement, the suggestion to use "the People's Mic" would have been met with perplexed looks and questions about what is a People's Mic? Yet, because of the widespread use of that face-to-face communication tactic in OWS protest encampments and the attention garnered by the movement, many Americans would now respond, "Okay. Yeah, let's do that." This illustrates that the People's Mic is now a culturally available resource accessible for use by a wide range of individuals and groups.

A key difference between human and cultural resources is that individuals have proprietary control over human resources and can decide who benefits from their labor, skills, knowledge, and talents. By contrast, cultural resources, once they enter the public domain, are more difficult to control by those who created them in the first place. For example, Operation Rescue, a radical and confrontational anti-abortion organization in the USA, widely employed non-violent direct action tactics modeled directly and explicitly upon those used during the heyday of the US civil rights movement. They did so without the blessing, and sometimes with the derision, of civil rights organizations and leaders. Undesirable use of cultural resources can be condemned in an attempt to undermine the moral authority or legitimacy of that use, but it cannot be prevented. Yet, while cultural resources may be more generally available, their relative accessibility continues to be mediated through patterns of social, economic, or spatial stratification, so that some groups and individuals are more able to utilize these resources than others.

Moral resources

Moral resources include legitimacy, authenticity, solidary support, sympathetic support, and celebrity (Cress and Snow 1996). Of these, legitimacy has received the most theoretical attention. Neo-institutional organizational theorists make strong claims about the importance of legitimacy as a link between macro cultural contexts and meso and micro level organizational processes (Suchman 1995). Thus, they claim that collective actors who most closely mimic institutionally legitimated features for their particular kind of endeavor gain an advantage relative to groups that do not reflect that template as well (DiMaggio and Powell 1992; Meyer and Rowan 1977). The neo-institutional emphasis typically looks to the legitimating power of governmental or culturally hegemonic institutions like the US Internal Revenue Service provision of tax-exempt status to non-profit organizations that agree, among other things, to refrain from certain forms of partisan political activity (McCarthy, Britt, and Wolfson 1991). Yet, legitimacy takes several forms (Suchman 1995) and originates from a range of sources (Gillham and Edwards 2011) beneficial to social and political movements. For example, by endorsing a specific issue campaign, or lending their fame to a particular SMO, celebrities can increase media coverage, generate public attention, open doors to influential allies and generally increase the recipient's ability to access other resources. Similarly, winning awards like the Nobel Peace Prize or receiving public endorsements from widely respected public figures, legitimates recipients to the broader public, while similar endorsement by well-respected issue activists authenticates an SMO or campaign among other activists and can facilitate cross-movement or cross-issue participation.

As discussed, moral resources often originate outside of a social movement or SMO and are bestowed by an external source known to possess them. Nevertheless, some movements succeed in the challenging and long-term task of creating and legitimating moral resources from within. This was clearly the case with the US southern civil rights movement of the 1950s and 1960s and more recently by a range of other movements including feminism, environmentalism, LGBT rights, and animal welfare. The moral values and ethical practices represented by concepts like "fair trade," "sustainable," "cruelty-free" or "gay-affirming" have been produced and disseminated by social movements. Moreover, such movement-produced moral resources can be conferred upon specific SMOs by credentialing bodies located within civil society. Moral resources are also produced at the organizational level. For example, Pilny, Atouba, and Riles (2014) examine the creation of moral resources by formal SMOs and find that their acquisition is influenced by the prior acquisition of social-organizational and material resources, and Corte (2013) finds that the informal interpersonal dynamics in a sub-cultural mobilization depended upon a distinct arrangement of moral, material, and context-dependent "locational" resources.

Mechanisms of Resource Access

Table 4.1 cross-classifies the five resource types described above with four mechanisms of resource access to be discussed next. Each of the twenty cells of Table 4.1 represents a distinct type of exchange relationship through which movement actors gain access to the specific mix of resources described above. Table 4.1 provides representative examples to help clarify the conceptual tools of the RM approach and help researchers use them to formulate more specific and analytically useful research questions. Exchange relationships are discussed below.

Self-production

Social movements access resources by producing those resources themselves through the agency of existing organizations, activists, and participants (Edwards and McCarthy 2004). Movements produce social-organizational resources when they form SMOs, cultivate networks of allies, form coalitions, or communication networks with webpages and social media. They produce human resources by socializing their

Table 4.1 Means of social movement and SMO resource access and resource types

Resource types	Self-production	*Means of access*		
		Aggregation	Co-optation	Patronage
Material	– Grassroots fund-raising events – Conducting "reality tours" – Producing and marketing movement music or art – Creating items to sell at events (T-shirts, CDs, coffee mugs, etc.)	– Member contributions – Bundling financial contributions(Emily's List) – Individual donations from non-members	– Office space – Gaining use of equipment (computers, buses, etc.) – WiFi or Internet access	– Start-up grants – Large donations – Foundation grants – Government grants – Service contracts – Corporate sponsorship
Human	– Raising and socializing children – Issue-/movement-oriented summer camps – Mentoring and training leaders – Movement mentors – Teaching of African-American, women's, LGBTQ, and environmental studies programs	– Recruiting constituents – Mobilizing large numbers of participants – Recruiting activists with particular skills	– Networked recruitment – Acquiring a mailing list – Organizational members – Bloc recruitment – Drawing on members of coalition partners	– Providing staff or volunteers – Providing technical assistance
Social-organizational	– Founding SMOs – Starting a task force – Launching web pages – Maintaining Facebook pages – Twitter feeds	– Building networks – Forming coalitions	– Recruiting local affiliates from existing organizations – Gaining access to congregations or civic groups for recruitment – Mesomobilization	– Being loaned the mailing lists and telephone lists of sympathetic individuals

(Continued)

Table 4.1 (Continued)

Resource types	Self-production	Means of access		
		Aggregation	Co-optation	Patronage
Cultural	– Social construction of ideologies – Collective action frames – Producing innovative tactics and repertoires – Issue and movement music – Producing and preserving movement history, oral history	– Social movement schools movement mentoring organizations – Movement-initiated summits and workshops where groups come together to share advice, information, strategy – Working groups	– Providing links on your webpage to materials produced by someone else – Links to someone else's webpage	– Excellence awards aimed at competence or effectiveness – Accreditation of fiscal procedures to enhance confidence of supporters and donors
Moral	– Moral authority from the effective use of non-violence (e.g. King, Gandhi) – Creation of new moral classifications such as cruelty-free, gay-affirming	– Compiling lists of endorsers – Recruiting celebrity endorsers – Listing advisory committee members on letterhead – Soliciting statements of support for specific projects	– Allying yourself with a well-respected group – Hiring grassroots supporters to lobby officeholders – Company unions – Links to well-respected groups on your webpage without permission	– A widely respected person or organization recognizing a group or activist in order to call positive attention to their work – Human rights awards – Nobel Peace Prize – An audience with the Pope

children and others into the values of the movement or mentoring emerging activists and leaders. Movements produce cultural resources when they socially construct ideologies (Williams 1995). Movements like those for civil and human rights produced out of their struggle a powerful moral authority disseminated through movement-specific cultural productions such as music, literature, art, engaged research, and technical expertise. At times, they even bake cakes and cookies, sold to raise money.

Aggregation

Resource aggregation refers to the ways movement actors convert resources held by dispersed individuals or groups into collective resources available for movement purposes. Social movements aggregate privately held resources from a range of supporters in order to pursue collective goals. Movement actors aggregate moral resources by publicizing lists of respected individuals and organizations that endorse the goals and actions of a specific group or event. Monetary or human resources are aggregated through donations from dispersed individuals to fund group activities or by recruiting volunteers to help with an activity (Edwards and McCarthy 2004).

Co-optation

Social movements often exploit relationships they have within existing forms of social organization that were not formed for explicit movement purposes. Co-optation refers to the transparent, permitted borrowing of resources already under the control of such groups. A large proportion of SMOs include other organizations, more or less formally, among their members. In doing this they are able, to some extent, to co-opt resources previously produced or aggregated by those other organizations. Co-optation usually implies some form of subsequent reciprocity with a tacit understanding that the resources will be used for mutually agreeable purposes. Co-optation has been common in many consequential movements including the southern civil rights (McAdam 1982), women's liberation (Freeman 1975), environmental justice (McGurty 2009), and the Tea Party movement in the USA (Skocpol and Williamson 2012).

Patronage

Patronage refers to the bestowal of substantial, often financial, resources by an individual or organization. Patrons typically exercise some degree of proprietary control over how that money can be used and may attempt to influence day-to-day operations and policy decisions.

Government contracts, foundation grants, and large private donations are the common forms of financial patronage. Yet, financial patrons can also be internal sources from within the movement, as when a national SMO funds a local issue campaign or when wealthy individuals, who are themselves civil rights, feminist, or environmental activists, donate money to particular issue campaigns (Edwards and McCarthy 2004). Patronage relationships can also provide some level of human resources, including the loan of personnel for periods of time. Patronage is common when temporary coalitions of SMOs field large and complex events (McCammon and Van Dyke 2010). For example, the Washington, DC, Area AFL-CIO agreed to provide hundreds of unionists to canvass door-to-door in the Washington, DC, area to educate residents about global justice issues and recruit them to participate in upcoming protest events planned by the Mobilization for Global Justice coalition (Gillham and Edwards 2011).

Exchange Relationships and Source Constraints

Early formulations of RM emphasized aggregate patterns of resource availability based on the well-founded expectation that the presence of social-organizational resources in a particular locale would increase the overall likelihood of movement mobilization and action in that setting. Much analysis examined associations between aggregate patterns of resource availability (e.g. monetary wealth, the proportion of college graduates within a community, or the number of religious or civic organizations present) and the likelihood of movement mobilization. Yet, recent RM analysts emphasize more explicitly durable patterns of inequality in the social, economic, and spatial distribution of resources and seek to understand how movement actors alter that distribution by accessing a range of resources in order to direct them into social and political movements.

Exchange relationships

In order for social movements to use resources generally available in a particular social context, two distinct and necessary components must be present. First, individual or collective actors must perceive that a specific resource is present in their social context. Second, they must have an exchange relationship capable of brokering their access to that resource. Exchange relationships exist between two entities when resources of various kinds are made available and accessed (Blau 1964). Social movement actors typically cultivate, maintain, and preserve numerous exchange relationships through which they gain access to the specific mix of resources supporting their endeavors (McAdam 1982). Exchange relationships are not reducible to network ties or position in a strictly structural sense because a tie, per se, only indicates the opportunity for an exchange, and does not carry with it the social, cultural, or ideological meaning of a relationship. Without some knowledge of the content of the exchange relations, and of the specific resources available through them, one cannot assess the import of the exchange relationships movement actors have at their disposal (Gillham and Edwards 2011).

With respect to SMOs, exchange relationships can be internal or external, vary in the value they provide, and are context-dependent. Internal exchange relations refer to those that exist within an organizational body, as when an SMO obtains financial resources through contributions or dues paid by members. External exchange relations refer to those outside of the formal organizational structure, as in receiving foundation grants or patron contributions. Exchange relationships also vary in the value of the resources they make accessible to an SMO. Hence, an SMO wanting to start a campaign that influences a broad base of the American public might seek out as an exchange partner a large national organization with the capacity to provide staff, thousands of members and dollars, rather than a small organization with far fewer resources. Conversely, an organization planning a confrontational and disruptive campaign seeking to divide elites may enter into exchange relations with radical groups known for deploying innovative tactics. Finally, the use-value of exchange relationships is context-dependent varying by both time and place. For example, valuable relationships with individuals who are elected officials, foundation program officers, or leaders in an allied SMO lose substantial use-value when such individuals leave their positions or their party is voted out of office. Similarly, the use-value of relationships with celebrities or morally authoritative public figures evaporates if a public figure is disgraced by scandal.

Source constraints

Two intertwined debates about resources center around whether social movements obtain their support primarily from indigenous or external sources and the extent to which external support causes SMOs to moderate their goals and tactics (see Cress and Snow 1996; McAdam 1982). First, note that this debate depends entirely upon how one defines a "social movement" (Diani 1992). Second, the long-standing debate over source constraints has been cast very narrowly, focusing almost exclusively on a single exchange relationship – financial patronage. Even SMOs benefitting from financial patronage typically engage in other exchange relationships with various sources. In addition, this debate can be reframed in a broader and more analytically useful way. From the perspective advocated here, this debate becomes a researchable question: to what extent do movement actors moderate their goals and activities in order to preserve existing exchange relationships (or attract new ones) with external supporters? Cast more broadly, it asks what is the range of distinct exchange relationships through which specific movement actors access resources and how do those particular exchange relations constrain (or facilitate) goals, actions, or public statements?

Clearly, movement actors simultaneously manage numerous exchange relationships of varying importance and duration with multiple exchange partners. Each exchange relationship brings a reciprocal set of expectations and obligations between the parties, with each relationship having widely varying potential for either social control or facilitation. Thus, the perspective advocated here encourages analysts to consider the varying mix of facilitation and constraint across the full range of exchange relationships through which specific SMOs, coalitions, issue campaigns, or event organizers mobilize resources.

Their impact on movement actors depends in part upon the specific means of resource access and the type of resource accessed (Gillham and Edwards 2011). For example, among the 117 organizations actively involved in planning a series of over 30 inter-related Global Justice Week protests in Washington, DC, in 2001, Global Exchange, Essential Action, and the AFL-CIO were all professionalized SMOs. Yet, they had different financial exchange relations. The AFL-CIO depended upon contributions from its member unions, which in turn relied upon dues paid by individual union members. Essential Action depended upon a large grant from another organization, Public Citizen, for most of its operating expenses, and had no formal members. Global Exchange self-produced much of its operating funds internally from proceeds collected from coordinating and leading socially conscious "travel tours" and selling T-shirts, books, and other merchandise. The AFL-CIO has a much larger and broader base of support, which is in many ways a substantial advantage. Yet, the actions it can take without alienating substantial parts of its base are constrained by the very size and diversity of its base. By contrast, as long as Essential Action preserved its core exchange relationship with Public Citizen, it was free to proceed. Clearly, this patronage relationship imposes some constraints on Essential Action. Yet, it also freed Essential Action from the demands of managing multiple and potentially countervailing exchange relationships. For its part, Public Citizen receives no corporate or government support and forgoes the benefits of tax-exempt status in order to operate free of constraints imposed by the US Internal Revenue Service. This enabled the organization to give more free rein to Essential Action. Lastly, as a self-sufficient SMO, Global Exchange's core financial exchange relationship was internal, and its actions relatively unconstrained by outsiders.

Recent Utilization of Resource Mobilization

As we noted at the outset, RM has been widely deployed, but the dimensions of its use have not been well summarized. We begin to address this gap in what comes next by drawing upon a comprehensive review of research articles published since 2004 focusing upon resource mobilization ideas (Mataic and McCarthy 2017). After describing the details of that review, we will very selectively summarize work that illustrates its main conclusions. First, RM remains vital in two ways: (1) by being taken up across many fields exploring research questions far afield from those originally motivating the perspective; and (2) by providing the basis of ongoing systematic efforts to compare its utility with competing factors nested in political opportunity and cultural framing ideas. Second, recent work also refines RM ideas in two ways: (1) by extending the varying influence of different resource types by specifying the contextual importance of their use with organizational and national level data; and (2) by combining the perspective with other widely explored conceptual frameworks.

Research review methods

The Social Science Citation Index was searched for all references to McCarthy and Zald's (1977) initial formulation and Edwards and McCarthy's (2004) reconstruction and review of resource mobilization appearing since 2004. The search identified 1145 unique journal articles, books or chapters, and conference presentations as of November 2016. The sample of articles was narrowed to only the 885 journal articles, books, and conference presentations that included abstracts. Figure 4.1 displays

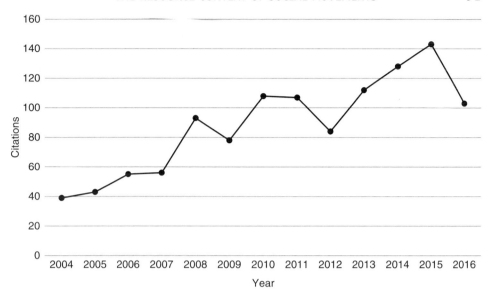

Figure 4.1   Number of unique citations of McCarthy and Zald (1977) or Edwards and McCarthy (2004) by journal articles, books or chapters, and conference presentations, 2004–2016.

the annual citation counts for the years 2004–2016 (where counts are truncated since the search was completed before 2016 was ended).

Vitality seen in disciplinary spread

RM research has spread during the last decade far beyond its origins in the discipline of sociology, so that a majority of the papers referenced in Figure 4.1 were published in fields other than sociology. In contrast to previous years when social movements and RM were relatively neglected by political scientists, RM is now widely cited by them, as well as in work by scholars of business with increased citations in business and management journals. Social psychologists have also increased their attention to social movements and utilization of RM concepts. Further, while the majority of scholarly work utilizing RM applies it to an understanding of social movements, a few scholars have expanded its use beyond collective action to topics such as the development of communal resources in open source software development (O'Mahony and Bechky 2008; Spaeth et al. 2008), the founding of women's and African American studies majors in US institutions of higher education (Olzak and Kangas 2008), or cultural innovation in extreme sport communities (Corte 2013).

Extensive and increasingly rigorous comparison of RM to other perspectives

Widespread work has been accomplished recently comparing the strength of dimensions of resources in explaining social movement mobilization with dimensions of political opportunity and of cultural framing. The comparisons frequently demonstrate that resource dimensions are stronger and more reliable determinants of collective action than variable elements of political opportunities.[1] Systematic measures of cultural framing dimensions are quite rare, but an earlier paper (McCammon 2001) employing a particularly strong measure of framing shows it and resources to be better predictors of suffragette mobilization than multiple measures of political opportunity. Another strong comparative test of resources against political opportunity, that by Snow, Soule, and Cress (2005), demonstrates that certain resource dimensions are good predictors of homeless mobilization in US cities, but that political opportunity variables are not. This paper, as well, shows the central importance of grievances in mobilization, a dimension neglected to a great extent by all three perspectives until recently. As well, Martinez (2008) evaluated the impact of RM and political opportunities dimensions on Latino participation in protests, finding strong evidence for RM, such that education, income, belonging to an organization as well as the presence of Latino organizations in the community significantly increased the likelihood of Latino protest. Contrary to their expectations, their assessment of political opportunities was less conclusive, where the higher concentration of Latino elected officials was associated with a decrease in the likelihood of participation in protests. Clearly, when compared to the other key SM perspectives, resource mobilization remains a strong predictor of collective action and social movement involvement.

Organizational and national contextual dependence of the importance of resources

With the advent of new organizational and international datasets, RM has been widely utilized in the exploration of international activism, organizational change, and organizational responses to activism. Dalton, Van Sicjlke, and Weldon

> demonstrate that the macro-level context – levels of economic and political development – significantly influences the amount of popular protest, suggesting that contemporary protest is expanding not because of increasing dissatisfaction with government, but because economic and political development provide the resources for those who have political demands.
>
> (2010: 51)

Their finding buttresses an original claim of RM theorists about the impact of societal level resources on levels of social movement mobilization. The importance of resource contexts is also seen in cumulating work that shows variation in levels of mobilization among organizations within the same populations, such as congregations, Fortune 500 firms, and restaurants, based upon variable dimensions of organizational structure. Stenger (2005) used RM to explain the limited spread of liberal Christian congregations by demonstrating that networks between churches, i.e. the lack thereof, is the primary reason why liberal congregations are unable to mobilize resources to attract additional members. Others, such as Soule and King (2008), show how RM influences tactical specialization by SMOs with particular emphasis placed on the concentration of SMOs as well as formalization and establishment of organizations.

Integrating RM ideas with other approaches and methods

The vitality of resource mobilization extends beyond its strong comparisons to other SM perspectives and utilization in expanded domains through efforts to build and refine key aspects of RM. Corcoran, Pattinicchio, and Young, for instance, integrating social capital theory with the RM approach,

> find that efficacy increases collective action, that certain political institutions increase efficacy, and that the effect of efficacy on collective action is partly conditional on the inclusiveness of a country's political institutions. These findings suggest the insufficiency of purely structural as well as social psychological explanations of collective action.
>
> (2011: 575)

Recent developments within RM have also provided renewed interest in the leaders of SMs and organizations, emphasizing the leader's ability to mobilize emotions that elicit support for a movement (Reger 2007), an overview of three types of leadership capital (Nepstad and Bob 2006), and how changes in leadership significantly influence action opportunities and resource mobilization (Kretschmer and Meyer 2007). The wide expansion of social network ideas and methods has, not surprisingly, led to extensive recent work quite consistent with our review here (Sanyal 2006; Saunders 2007; Schurman 2004). Moreover, scholars continue to explore the production and mobilization of resources necessary for collective action, with many emphasizing the importance of networks and coalition formations as a way to pool resources (Almeida and Delgado 2008; Mahoney 2007).

Conclusion

Resources and access to them are core defining concepts in RM, argued to be the required link between sentiments for change (i.e., a grievance) and the ability to mobilize around those sentiments (McCarthy and Zald 2001). RM remains a central and salient theory for analyzing and explaining how social groups overcome the differential distribution of and access to the resources needed to pursue social, political, and cultural change. As the review of recent literature sketched above makes clear, an increasingly diverse set of scholars use RM theory to investigate a wide range of empirical questions regarding how access to or the formation of resources influences movement emergence and development, movement outcomes, media coverage, and protest frequency, to name a few. Resource mobilization tenets and concepts are so ingrained in the social movement literature that they have to some extent become taken for granted, and yet, are so fundamental to our understanding of movements that scholars are required to consider them before alternative explanations can be found to be convincing.

Notes

1 There are some exceptions. For instance, Smith and Wiest (2005) found that national economic integration (conceptualized as a form of RM) did not significantly predict membership in transnational social movement organizations while increased political integration (conceptualized within a political opportunity framework) was a significant predictor of participation.

References

Almeida, Paul and Roxana Delgado. 2008. "Gendered Networks and Health Care Privatization." In *Patients, Consumers and Civil Society,* vol. 10, *Advances in Medical Sociology,* edited by Susan M. Chambre, and Melinda Goldner, 273–299. Bingley: Emerald Publishing.

Amenta, Edwin, Neal Caren, Elizabeth Chiarello, and Yang Su. 2010. "The Political Consequences of Social Movements." *Annual Review of Sociology* 36: 287–307.

Armstrong, Elizabeth A. and Mary Bernstein. 2008. "Culture, Power, and Institutions: A Multi-Institutional Politics Approach to Social Movements." *Sociological Theory* 26(1): 74–99.

Becker, Gary. 1964. *Human Capital.* New York: National Bureau of Economic Research, Columbia University Press.

Blau, Peter. 1964. *Exchange and Power in Social Life.* New York: Wiley and Sons.

Bourdieu, Pierre. 1986. "The Forms of Capital." In *Handbook of Theory and Research for the Sociology of Education,* edited by John Richardson, 241–258. New York: Greenwood Press.

Coleman, James S. 1988. "Social Capital in the Creation of Human Capital." *American Journal of Sociology* (Supplement), 94: S95–S120.

Corcoran, Katie E., David Pattinicchio, and Jacob T.N. Young. 2011. "The Context of Control: A Cross-National Investigation of the Link between Political Institutions, Efficacy and Collective Action." *British Journal of Social Psychology* 50: 575–605.

Corte, Ugo. 2013. "A Refinement of Collaborative Circles Theory: Resource Mobilization and Innovation in an Emerging Sport." *Social Psychology Quarterly* 76(1): 25–51.

Corte, Ugo and Bob Edwards. 2008. "White Power Music and the Mobilization of Racist Social Movements." *Music & the Arts in Action* 1(1): 3–20.

Cress, Daniel M. and David A. Snow. 1996. "Mobilization at the Margins: Resources, Benefactors, and the Viability of Homeless Social Movement Organizations." *American Sociological Review* 61(6): 1089–1109.

Dalton, Russel, Alex Van Sicjle, and Steven Weldon. 2010. "The Individual-Institutional Nexus of Protest Behavior." *British Journal of Political Science* 40(1): 51–73.

Diani, Mario. 1992. "The Concept of Social Movement." *Sociological Review* 40: 1–25.

Diani, Mario. 1997. "Social Movements and Social Capital." *Mobilization* 2(2): 129–147.

DiMaggio, Paul J. and Walter Powell, eds. 1992. *The New Institutionalism in Organizational Analysis.* Chicago: University of Chicago Press.

Edwards, Bob. 1994. "Semi-formal Organizational Structure Among Social Movement Organizations: An Analysis of the U.S. Peace Movement." *Nonprofit and Voluntary Sector Quarterly* 23(4): 309–333.

Edwards, Bob. 1995. "With Liberty and Environmental Justice for All: The Emergence and the Challenge of Grassroots Environmentalism in the USA." In *Ecological Resistance*

Movements: The Global Emergence of Radical and Popular Environmentalism, edited by
Bron Taylor, 35–55. Albany, NY: SUNY Press.

Edwards, Bob and Melinda Kane. 2014. "Resource Mobilization Theory and Contemporary
Social and Political Movements." In *Handbook of Political Citizenship and Social
Movements*, edited by Hein-Anton van der Heijdenk, 205–232. Camberley, UK:
Edward Elgar Publishers.

Edwards, Bob and John D. McCarthy. 2004. "Resource Mobilization and Social Movements."
In *The Blackwell Companion to Social Movements*, edited by David A. Snow, Sarah A.
Soule, and Hanspeter Kriesi, 116–152. Oxford: Blackwell.

Freeman, Jo. 1975. *The Politics of Women's Liberation*. New York: McKay.

Gillham, Patrick and Bob Edwards. 2011. "Legitimacy Management, Preservation of Exchange
Relationships, and the Dissolution of the Mobilization for Global Justice Coalition."
Social Problems 58(3): 433–460.

Kretschmer, Kelsy and David S. Meyer. 2007. "Platform Leadership – Cultivating Support for
a Public Profile." *American Behavioral Scientist* 50(10): 1395–1412.

Lin, Nan. 2001. *Social Capital: A Theory of Social Structure and Action*. New York: Cambridge
University Press.

Mahoney, Christine. 2007. "Networking vs. Allying: The Decision of Interest Groups to
Join Coalitions in the US and the EU." *Journal of European Public Policy* 14(3):
366–383.

Martinez, Lisa M. 2008. "The Individual and Contextual Determinants of Protest among
Latinos." *Mobilization* 13(2): 189–204.

Mataic, Dane R. and John D. McCarthy. 2017. "A Survey of Resource Mobilization Research,
2004–2016." Unpublished manuscript. Department of Sociology, Penn State University.

McAdam, Doug. 1982. *Political Process and the Development of Black Insurgency,
1930–1970*. Chicago: University of Chicago Press.

McAdam, Doug, John D. McCarthy and Mayer N. Zald. 1996. "Introduction: Opportunities,
Mobilizing Structures, and Framing Processes." In *Comparative Perspectives on Social
Movements*, edited by Doug McAdam, John D. McCarthy and Mayer N. Zald, 1–22.
New York: Cambridge University Press.

McCammon, Holly J. 2001. "Stirring Up Suffrage Sentiment: The Formation of State Woman
Suffrage Organizations, 1866–1914." *Social Forces* 80(2): 449–480.

McCammon, Holly J. and Nella Van Dyke, eds. 2010. *Strategic Alliances: Coalition Building
and Social Movements*. Minneapolis: University of Minnesota Press.

McCarthy, John D. 1987. "Pro-life and Pro-choice Mobilization: Infrastructure Deficits and
New Technologies." In *Social Movements in an Organizational Society*, edited by Mayer
N. Zald and John D. McCarthy, 49–66. New Brunswick, NJ: Transaction Press.

McCarthy, John D. 1996. "Mobilizing Structures: Constraints and Opportunities in Adopting,
Adapting and Inventing." In *Comparative Perspectives on Social Movements*, edited by
Doug McAdam, John D. McCarthy, and Mayer N. Zald, 141–151. New York: Cambridge
University Press.

McCarthy, John D., David W. Britt, and Mark Wolfson. 1991. "The Institutional Channeling
of Social Movements by the State in the United States." *Research in Social Movements,
Conflict, and Change* 14: 45–76. Bingley: Emerald Publishing.

McCarthy, John D. and Mayer N. Zald. 1977. "Resource Mobilization and Social Movements:
A Partial Theory." *American Journal of Sociology* 82: 1212–1241.

McCarthy, John D. and Mayer N. Zald. 2001. "The Enduring Vitality of the Resource
Mobilization Theory of Social Movements." In *Handbook of Sociological Theory*, edited
by Jonathan H. Turner, 533–565. New York: Kluwer Academic/Plenum Publishers.

McGurty, Eileen M. 2009. *Transforming Environmentalism: Warren County, PCB's, and the Origins of Environmental Justice*. New Brunswick, NJ: Rutgers University Press.

Meyer, John and Brian Rowan. 1977. "Institutionalized Organizations: Formal Structure as Myth Ceremony." *American Journal of Sociology* 83: 340–363.

Minkoff, Debra C. 1997. "Producing Social Capital: National Social Movements and Civil Society." *American Behavioral Scientist* 40(5): 606–619.

Nepstad, Sharon Erickson and Clifford Bob. 2006. "When Do Leaders Matter? Hypotheses on Leadership Dynamics in Social Movements." *Mobilization* 11(1): 1–22.

O'Mahony, Siobhan and Beth A. Bechky. 2008. "Boundary Organizations: Enabling Collaboration among Unexpected Allies." *Administrative Science Quarterly* 53: 422–459.

Oliver, Pamela E. and Gerald Marwell. 1992. "Mobilizing Technologies for Collective Action." In *Frontiers in Social Movement Theory*, edited by Aldon D. Morris and Carol McClurg Mueller, 251–272. New Haven, CT: Yale University Press.

Olzak, Susan and Nicole Kangas. 2008. "Ethnic, Women's, and African American Studies Majors in US Institutions of Higher Education." *Sociology of Education* 81(2): 163–188.

Pilny, Andrew N., Yannick C. Atouba, and Julius M. Riles. 2014. "How Do SMOs Create Moral Resources? The Roles of Media Visibility, Networks, Activism, and Political Capacity." *Western Journal of Communication* 78(3): 358–377.

Reger, Jo. 2007. "Where Are the Leaders? Music, Culture, and Contemporary Feminism." *American Behavioral Scientist* 50(10): 1350–1369.

Sanyal, Paromita. 2006. "Capacity Building through Partnership: Intermediary Nongovernmental Organizations as Local and Global Actors." *Nonprofit and Voluntary Sector Quarterly* 35(1): 66–82.

Saunders, Clare. 2007. "The National and the Local: Relationships among Environmental Movement Organisations in London." *Environmental Politics* 16(5): 742–764.

Schurman, Rachel. 2004. "Fighting 'Frankenfoods': Industry Opportunity Structures and the Efficacy of the Anti-Biotech Movement in Western Europe." *Social Problems* 51(2): 243–268.

Skocpol, Theda and Vanessa Williamson. 2012. *The Tea Party and the Remaking of Republican Conservatism*. New York: Oxford University Press.

Smith, Jackie and Dawn Wiest. 2005. "The Uneven Geography of Global Civil Society: National and Global Influences on Transnational Association." *Social Forces* 84(2): 621–652.

Snow, David A., Sarah A. Soule, and Daniel M. Cress. 2005. "Identifying the Precipitants of Homeless Protest Across 17 U.S. Cities, 1980–1990." *Social Forces* 83(3): 1183–1210.

Soule, Sarah A. and Brayden G. King. 2008. "Competition and Resource Partitioning in Three Social Movement Industries." *American Journal of Sociology* 113(6): 1568–1610.

Spaeth, Sebastian, Stefan Haefliger, Georg von Krogh, and Birgit Renzl. 2008. "Communal Resources in Open Source Software Development." *Information Research: An International Electronic Journal* 13(1).

Stenger, Katherine E. 2005. "The Underrepresentation of Liberal Christians: Mobilization Strategies of Religious Interest Groups." *Social Science Journal* 42(3): 391–403.

Suchman, Mark C. 1995. "Managing Legitimacy: Strategic and Institutional Approaches." *The Academy of Management Review* 20(3): 571–610.

Tilly, Charles. 1998. *Durable Inequality*. Berkeley: University of California Press.

Travaglino, Giovanni A. 2014. "Social Sciences and Social Movements: The Theoretical Context." *Contemporary Social Science: Journal of the Academy of Social Sciences* 9(1): 1–14.

Williams, Rhys. 1995. "Constructing the Public Good: Social Movements and Cultural Resources." *Social Problems* 42(1): 124–144.

Williams, Rhys. 2004. "The Cultural Context of Collective Action: Constraints, Opportunities, and the Symbolic Life of Social Movements." In *The Blackwell Companion to Social Movements*, edited by David A. Snow, Sarah A. Soule, and Hanspeter Kriesi, 91–114. Oxford: Blackwell.

5

The Ecological and Spatial Contexts of Social Movements

Yang Zhang and Dingxin Zhao

Introduction

Within the field of biology, ecology studies the relations of organisms to one another and to their physical surroundings. The nature of the discipline encourages a mode of thinking that is not variable-based but is relational and dialectic. Ecological thinking is also necessarily "historical," because it is more sensitive to mechanisms and patterns that emerge in the interactions between different organisms or between organisms and their environments. Ecological thinking enters sociology and social movement studies in different forms at different times, but this migration more or less maintains these basic precepts: Sociologists employing ecological perspectives are interested in: (1) the nature of "space" and its impact on the patterns of interactions of individuals or social groups in that "space"; and (2) the regularities organizing the interactions of different individuals or social groups. In this chapter, we refer to the first perspective as spatial ecology and to the second as social ecology.

This chapter first reviews the literature bearing the perspectives of spatial and social ecology. It then discusses several works that incorporate both the spatial and social ecological perspectives. We conclude with a discussion of possible directions of ecological perspectives in social movement studies.

Spatial Ecology of Movement Mobilization

Three theoretical traditions are related to the space-oriented analysis of movement mobilization: (1) space as built environment, which takes up the Simmelian tradition (Simmel 1971; see also Spykman 1964); (2) the human ecology of the Chicago School tradition (Park 1936; Park and Burgess 1921; Park, Burgess, and McKenzie 1967; see also Hawley 1950, 1986); and (3) the critical geography of the Marxian

The Wiley Blackwell Companion to Social Movements, Second Edition. Edited by David A. Snow, Sarah A. Soule, Hanspeter Kriesi, and Holly J. McCammon.
© 2018 John Wiley & Sons Ltd. Published 2018 by John Wiley & Sons Ltd.

tradition (Agnew 1987; Harvey 1989).[1] In addition, place is often attributed symbolic meaning that constitutes the basis for the memory, identity, and ideology construction. Despite their huge differences, all the approaches agree on the following spatial/ecological logic: although the spatial form of a community is socially constructed and reflects socioeconomic relations, once it is formed, it can functionally act as a social structure and its impact on social actions cannot always be reduced to socioeconomic relations.

The first approach, i.e. the Simmelian tradition, understands space as a particular social form shaping human relations. In his discussion of mobile/immobile artifacts, Simmel concludes that when an artifact is immobile, certain social relationships must be ordered around it; in this way, the artifact becomes a socially important pivot of human interaction (Spykman 1964: Chapter 4). This Simmelian idea serves as the foundation for several research areas, including urban studies, human geography, small group ecology, and environmental psychology (Zhao 1998). Scholars have shown that design factors of houses and their overall spatial arrangements can encourage or discourage individuals' mutual interaction and communication, which could have considerable impact on movement mobilization (ibid.).

In the human ecology tradition, ecology is defined as "the relation of organisms or groups of organisms to their environment" (Hawley 1950: 3). Human ecologists have been primarily interested in the forces underpinning the spatial order of urban communities, such as land values, logistical requirements of local economies (McKenzie 1924; Park 1936; Warner 1963), or conflicts between peoples with different cultural, ethnic, and class backgrounds (Lofland 1973; Suttles 1968, 1972). These scholars treat spatial relations as expressions of social relations. This idea plays a key role in Gould's seminal works on the relationship between spatial configurations and mobilizational networks during the two Parisian insurrections of the nineteenth century (Gould 1991, 1995).

Finally, critical geography, a discipline emerging in the 1970s, has been deeply concerned with spatially constituted injustice and inequalities (Agnew 1987; Brenner et al. 2008; Castells 1978; Harvey 1985; Smith 1984). Yet it was not until the 1990s that this line of inquiry began entering social movement studies (Kittikhoun 2009; Leitner, Sheppard, and Sziarto 2008; Martin and Miller 2003; Miller 2000; Nicholls, Miller, and Beaumont 2013; Routledge 1993, 1997). Borrowing rich vocabularies and toolkits from critical geography, scholars elaborate how different aspects of spatiality – place, scale, location, mobility – shape social movements.

To further discuss how space and place play a role in social movements, we need better working definitions of "space" and "place," since these concepts have been used in a variety of ways by different scholars. In his enlightening review, Tilly (2000) offers a taxonomy of the types of spatial analysis used in social movement research by categorizing space-centered analysis into "bare space analysis," "textured space analysis," and "place-oriented analysis." Bare space analysis simply uses location and time-distance as proxies for other non-spatial structural effects. Textured space analysis instead introduces location and time-distance as explicit causes and effects, while place-oriented analysis treats the interactions among (1) location; (2) time-distance; and (3) representations of spaces in terms of explicit causes and effects. Tilly labels the latter two kinds of analysis as place-centered. Likewise, Gieryn (2000) defines "place" in three different ways: (1) geographic location; (2) geographical differentiation of the natural or built environment (including streets, railways, canals, public squares, or design factors of architecture) that shapes social interactions; and (3) attributed meaning of a location. In the following reviews, we will emphasize the geographical and environmental aspects of space and place rather than "bare space analysis" or "attributed meanings."

Overall, space has been conceived in different ways in social movement studies: space can facilitate the formation of certain organizations and social networks that hinder or foster social movement mobilization. On the other hand, space itself sometimes becomes an independent mobilization base through spatial processes. In addition to spatial mechanisms operating within individual movement, there are also spatial mechanisms operating in the diffusion of protests across places. The following discussion will elaborate the three themes in turn.

First, spatial arrangements produce certain kinds of organizations and social networks that facilitate movement mobilization. Marx (1978) provides a classical example in the *Communist Manifesto*: spatial concentration of workers in modern factories facilitates the development of class consciousness, organizational power, and mobilization capacity of the workers, thereby catalyzing revolutionary actions. Gould's study of nineteenth-century Paris uprisings (Gould 1991, 1995) is a notable development in this line of reasoning. He shows that Haussmann's urban construction project in Paris (1852–1870) transformed the city's residential structure, and consequently changed the mobilization basis from working-class consciousness during the 1848 insurrection to neighborhood solidarity during the 1871 Paris commune. Likewise, Bayat (1997) analyzes how the active street life of the unemployed and impoverished immigrants in major Iranian cities gave rise to what he calls "passive networks," which greatly facilitated their resistance to state control and their collective fight for both survival and improvement of their living conditions. Stillerman (2003) shows how the characteristics of the built environment and the everyday spatial routines of metal workers and coal miners in Chile influenced the mobilizing structures of strikers.

Second, rather than indirectly affecting movement mobilization via organizations or social networks, space is itself the basis of movement mobilization. To further elaborate on this point, below we will discuss five space-related factors: (1) spatial concentration; (2) spatial proximity; (3) spatial scale and scale shift; (4) symbolic meanings of places; and (5) spontaneity of spatial mobilization.

1. *Spatial concentration.* It is noted in human ecology that, other factors being equal, the higher the population density of a place, the greater the chance of unintentional contacts and active group-making (e.g. Case 1981; Festinger, Schachter, and Back 1950) – especially when the population is homogeneous (e.g. Gans 1967; Newcomb 1961). The impact of spatial concentration on movement mobilization has been demonstrated in community movements (e.g. Delgado 1986; Perry, Gillespie, and Parker 1976) and in riots in American cities. As Feagin and Hahn (1973) and Fogelson (1971) mention, the sudden and massive African-American riots that erupted in some American cities in the early 1970s were possible partly because the African-American communities were so densely populated and the residents in those areas tended to spend a great deal of their leisure time on the street. University students are another

homogeneous population that is densely grouped, so university campuses are frequently hotbeds for student mobilization. It has been observed that the campus environment facilitated student movements during the 1960s in the United States (Berk 1974; Heirich 1971; Lofland 1970), Russia (Kassow 1989), and China (Chow 1967; Zhao 1998, 2009). For example, Heirich (1971: 59–65) describes how changes in the campus layout at Berkeley beginning in the 1950s made Berkeley students more available for political recruitment during the stormy 1960s. Kassow (1989) shows that the dining halls built by Nicholas II for Moscow students to get cheap meals became meeting places where students could trade news, make new contacts, and hold assemblies. Likewise, Chow (1967) notes that the congested living conditions on Chinese campuses facilitated student activism in China during the Republican era.

2. *Spatial proximity*. Spatial proximity to hazardous industrial projects (Dokshin 2016), threatening groups (Andrews and Seguin 2015; Dixon 2006), or protest sites (Beissinger 2003; Zhao 1998) lead to threat-based mobilization (Cunningham and Phillips 2007) or rapid communication and diffusion of contentious actions. One notable example is the NIMBY (Not In My Backyard) Movement, which is ostensibly a reaction against hazardous locations because of spatial proximity (McAdam and Boudet 2012; Wright and Boudet 2012). Notably, a number of studies examine the growing local opposition to hydraulic fracturing ("fracking") in North America in recent years (Boudet 2011; Vasi et al. 2015). Subtle studies have found that the relationship between proximity to the planned project and opposition is not linear but hinges upon the relationship between the perceived economic benefits and risks of the project among different residential communities. For example, in anti-fracking movements in New York, communities that see little economic benefit pass restrictive ordinances, while communities anticipating economic gains from shale gas development have less incentives to ban fracking (Dokshin 2016).

3. *Spatial scales and scale shift*. Geographical scale is traditionally considered a neutral metric of physical space in a vertically ordered hierarchy that proceeds from the local to the regional, national, and global. Since the 1990s, however, scale has been reconceptualized by critical geographers to account for the fluid spatial arrangements that are the site of contention among different social forces (Brenner 1999; Smith 1995). The "politics of scale" is especially salient for social movements, in which protestors often challenge and transform fixed scalar arrangements. Not surprisingly, scholars have enduring interest in "scale-jumping" (Smith 1993) and "scale shift" (Tarrow and McAdam 2005; Tilly and Tarrow 2007) within contentious politics (Leitner et al. 2008: 158). According to Tilly and Tarrow (2007: 94), "Scale shift is a complex process that not only diffuses contention across space or social sectors, but also creates instances for new coordination at a higher level or level than its initiation." In particular, *upward scale shift* involves coordination of collective action at a higher spatial level – regional, national, transnational, and international – extending the movement site beyond its place of origins, and sometimes inspiring transformative momentum through rapid and extensive diffusion (ibid.: 95–96). For instance, through direct

diffusion and mediated brokerage (Tarrow and McAdam 2005), small but spectacular local events such as the arrest of student activists in May 1968 triggered a nation-wide explosion of protest in France and beyond. Likewise, there are also cases of *downward scale shift*, in which transnational and national oppositional forces retreat or downgrade to a local level for more flexible and diffuse forms of struggle, as evidenced by classical guerrilla warfare (Sewell 2001: 68).

4. *Symbolic meaning of places.* Certain historical sites can generate symbolic meanings in ways that facilitate movement mobilization. A place loaded with symbols of repressive power, such as the Bastille (Sewell 1996), can become the target of protest; likewise, a place loaded with revolutionary symbols of the past, such as Tiananmen Square (Hershkovitz 1993; Zhao 2001), is ideal for protest mobilization if the state no longer maintains an authoritative interpretation of those symbols. As these places gradually grew reputations as sites for demonstration, their spatial meanings could be magnified and then institutionalized. Notable examples include Tiananmen Square in Beijing, the People's Park in Berkeley, Hyde Park in London, and capital cities in general (Tilly and Schweitzer 1982; Traugott 1995). Hyde Park, for instance, became a location for mass demonstrations in the middle of the nineteenth century, hosting the Chartist Movement in 1840s, the Universal Suffrage Movement organized by the Reform League in 1866, the Women's Suffrage Movement in 1910s, and the Anti-War Protest in 2003. Because of its association with free speech, Hyde Park's Speakers' Corner has gained an international reputation for inviting demonstrations and protests. For citizen activists, it is always necessary "to go again to Hyde Park" (Mitchell 2003: 13–14).

5. *Spontaneity of spatial mobilization.* Space not only constitutes a structure that shapes movement development but can also give rise to spontaneous mobilization. Referring to Zhao's study of spatial mobilization, Snow and Moss (2014: 15–16) show that ecological factors made possible an array of onset spontaneous student mobilizations during the 1989 Beijing Student Movement: Student activists' marching and shouting around the campus "created an atmosphere of excitement and heightened the pitch of their anger" (Zhao 2001: 261), helping gather thousands of students to join in the march towards Tiananmen Square. In this kind of spatial mobilization, many of their activities represented spontaneous and individualistic responses to events rather than conscious decisions arrived at collectively by their organizations. Particular spatial layouts can also stimulate unplanned responses from the state and sometimes escalate confrontation and violence between the protesters and policing forces (Collins 2009; Snow and Moss 2014).

To illustrate how multiple spatial mechanisms can contribute to a single movement, we refer to Zhao's works (1998, 2001). Zhao has elaborated five different ways that the built environment of Beijing campuses and the associated rhythmic spatial activities of Chinese students facilitated student mobilization during the 1989 Beijing Student Movement: (1) it facilitated the spread of dissident ideas before the movement and the transmission of news about events during the movement; (2) it nurtured dormitory-based student networks and sustained a high rate of student participation; (3) it shaped students' spatial activities on campus, creating centers of student mobilization; (4) the concentration of many universities in one district encouraged mutual imitation and interuniversity competition for activism among students from different universities; and (5) it facilitated the formation of many ecology-dependent strategies of collective action.

Finally, space-related factors also facilitate the diffusion of protests across different movements or regions. Though diffusion does not necessarily require spatial proximity, social movements do have a greater likelihood of spreading to adjacent locations (Biggs 2005; Biggs and Andrews 2015). During the 1960s sit-in protests in the US South, "desegregation in one city raised the probability of desegregation nearby" (Biggs and Andrews 2015: 1). Geographical factors across regions or nations also have a critical influence on national movements, including revolutions. For example, spatial diffusion was central in the 1848 European revolutions (Weyland 2009). Another classic example is the diffusion of communist revolution from the Soviet Union to China, and from China to its Southeast Asia neighbors, including Vietnam, Laos, and Cambodia (Kittikhoun 2009; Skocpol 1979).

The Social Ecology of Movements

In the last section, we treated "space" as a variable of causal impact on social movement mobilization and outcomes. However, as Abbott (2005: 248) argues, ecology should be understood "in terms of interactions between multiple elements that are neither fully constrained nor fully independent." In other words, the key to ecological thinking is not causality, but sensitivity to the regularities emerging out of interactions among multiple social organizations/actors or among social organizations/actors and their environments. This defines the perspective of social ecology.

Social ecology weighed heavily in early works on social movement and collective action. Blumer's (1946) "circular reaction" describes the formation of an "excited" crowd through the interactions among restless individuals. Turner and Killian's (1957) "emergent norm" models the development of an anti-establishment norm in the interactions among anxious individuals. At the center of Kornhauser's (1959) mass society theory is also an ecological idea: Interactions among a rich assembly of intermediate organizations of different natures facilitate the formation of cross-cutting interests and identities, prevent the manipulation of the masses by political elites, and enhance elite decision-making autonomy. He suggests that these are the keys preventing the success of a totalitarian social movement.

Two works from the 1960s defined social ecology perspective in movement studies. Stinchcombe (1965: 169) advocated an ecological approach to studying revolutionary situations:

Rather than explaining the occurrence of revolution, a sociological theory ought to try to explain the occurrence of a "revolutionary situation." Whether or not a change in the ruling powers of a society takes place by means of violence depends both on the predisposing characteristics of the social structure and on concrete military and political situations at given historical times.

About the same time, Zald and Ash (1966) were tackling another touchstone of the ecological theorizing in movement studies, by studying how the relations among movement organizations – including inter-organizational competition – and among individual organizations and the broader environment affect movement growth, decay and change, and influence movement mergers, factions, and schisms. Together, they pioneered an "organizational turn" in studies of social movements that significantly differed from previous works in social ecology.

Although the social ecology perspective has been applied to study a variety of phenomena – notably, the professions (Abbott 1988) and science studies (Gieryn 1983) – in social movement studies, it has largely been shaped by the field of organizational ecology (e.g. Carroll 1984; Freeman and Audia 2006; Hannan and Freeman 1977,1989). This is not surprising given the paradigm shift that occurred in social movement studies in the late 1970s from psychology-centered grievance theories to organization-centered resource mobilization theory (McCarthy and Zald 1973, 1977). It is worth noting that McCarthy and Zald's works contain a significant social ecology angle, because their analysis centers on the expansion of the universities and of the new middle-class population in the post-World War II United States, and they argue that these expansions altered the organizational environment and made available a huge amount of resources previously unavailable to social movement organizers. Yet, the same works also treat resources as a variable and argue that it was the expansion of resources rather than the rise of grievances – which is regarded as another variable – that contributed to the spread of social movements in the 1960s. The popularity of resource mobilization theory and political opportunity structure theory (e.g. Eisinger 1973; McAdam 1982), in conjunction with the rising importance of variable-based statistical analysis, rendered such causal (rather than ecological) thinking the norm in social movement studies after the 1970s.

The direct influence of organizational ecology theory on social movement studies appeared in the 1980s: Zald and McCarthy (1980) examined inter-movement competition within an organizational environment; Langton (1987) offered a conceptual discussion of how niche overlap could influence movement participation; Olzak (1992) found that ethnic conflicts and mobilization in American cities were greatly driven by competition among different ethnic immigrant groups; Finally, Tarrow contended that "competitive mobilization" – including competition for ideological domination, for media attention, or for the achievement of more effective tactics – results in protest diffusion across multiple movement sectors (Tarrow 1989: 19, 221).

Yet it was not until a series of publications by Minkoff (1993, 1994, 1997, 1999) that the population ecology became a prevailing perspective in social movement studies (see also Edwards and Marullo 1995; Sandell 2001; Soule and King 2008; Stern 1999; for reviews, see Clemens and Minkoff 2004; Soule 2013). These works share many commonalities with organizational ecology theory: they study not a single social movement organization, but a set of social movement organizations with significant niche overlap; they examine how competition among these movement organizations has affected member recruitment and resource extraction; they rely heavily on statistical methods, especially event history analysis.

We now examine studies of social movement ecology in terms of the type of the outcome variables, moving from variables within one movement population to those across movement populations: (1) membership recruitment; (2) tactical and ideological repertoires; (3) organizational forms; and (4) population diversity.

1. *Membership recruitment.* Stern (1999) shows that competition between SMOs (modeled according to degree of organizational niches overlap) affects member recruitment of movement organizations. Sandell (2001) studies member recruitment of nearly 30 000 local SMOs in three major social movement sectors – the temperance, free church, and trade union movements – in Sweden between 1881 and 1940. To test the ecological model, Sandell includes information on both the movements' internal features (e.g. initial size) and their environmental features (organizational niches and intra- and inter-movement density). He finds that the remaining variation in aggregate membership has more to do with movement organization density and the overall structure of a movement sector than the strategy and capacity of each movement organization.

2. *Tactics and ideological repertoires.* Drawing upon the theory of density-dependent legitimation and competition (Hannan and Carroll 1992; Hannan and Freeman 1989), Minkoff (1994) examines how these two mechanisms have played a role in the evolution of "organizational repertoire" (Clemens 1993) among women and minority organizations since 1955. She finds that the increase in the number of SMOs employing tactics of conventional *service* or confrontational *protest* facilitated the expansion of *advocacy* organizations as a middle-of-the-road method functioning between service and protest. On the other hand, the increased legitimacy and growing number of advocacy organizations created limitations for the further development of both service and protest organizations after 1970 due to the heightened competition among the three types of SMOs. In a subsequent study, Minkoff (1997) further posits that the organizational density of SMOs is an essential component of protest cycles since it promotes protest diffusion and creates opportunities for other challengers.

   In line with Minkoff's works, Olzak and Uhrig (2001: 710) further suggested that when social movements shared low levels of tactical overlap, they cooperated and emulated each other; in contrast, high levels of tactical overlap resulted in intensified competition, and thus had negative effects on the rate of (women's) movement protest activity. This finding is echoed by a study of ideological competition among Viennese newspapers during the rise of National Socialism: Barnett and Woywode (2004: 1452) finds that "competition is strongest among ideologically adjacent organizations – those too different ideologically to enjoy esprit de corps but similar enough to vie for the same base of support."

3. *Organizational forms.* In other works, Minkoff (1993, 1999) finds that the selection process at the organizational level generally tends to favor older, professional, moderate, and reform-oriented SMOs. Likewise, in a study of peace movement organizations at the end of the Cold War, Edwards and Marullo (1995) find that younger, smaller, and less "legitimate" SMOs had a higher death rate, albeit with variations across movement "domains." These findings all support the expectations of organizational ecology theory: selection

processes largely determine the growth and death of movements within the movement population, or of movement populations within a movement community.

4. *Community-level population diversity.* Scholars have extended ecological theory to community-level population diversity (e.g. Minkoff, Aisenbrey, and Agnone 2008; Olzak and Ryo 2007). Building upon resource mobilization and resource partitioning theories,[2] Soule and King (2008) examine how interorganizational competition and organizational concentration lead to more specialized tactical and goal repertoires in SMOs associated with the peace, women's, and environmental movements. In addition, they find that tactical and goal specialization might decrease organizational survival, unless the industry is highly concentrated.

In sum, studies of social movement ecology have produced a number of valuable works and added considerable insights to single movement-centered studies. However, these studies also share the same weakness of organizational ecology theory (Young 1988). By reducing social *movements* to movement *organizations*, they overlook the fact that the former is also comprised of non-organizational characteristics.[3] It also reduces social ecology to organizational ecology by assuming that social movements – operating like business organizations in an unregulated competitive market – function in an apolitical environment, unaffected by the state.

The Intersection between Spatial and Social Ecologies

Spatial ecology and social ecology have often been treated as if they are separate entities. But in real life, the physical environment is usually the result of human activities; organizations' interactions with other organizations are always located in a particular physical environment; and the physical environment shapes the patterns of organizational interactions (Koopmans 2004: 40). A few studies have thus found answers to their research questions in the intersection between spatial and social ecologies. Working within the organizational ecology tradition, Greve (2002: 80) integrates the two perspectives by examining "how geographically delineated subpopulations grow and interact with neighboring subpopulations." Likewise, Hedstrom (1994) applies the organizational ecology model to capture the spatial diffusion of the Swedish trade union movement between 1890 and 1940. Specifically, he argues that spatially contentious processes were of considerable importance for the growth of union movements.

Gould (1991, 1995) has pushed this line of study to new heights. As mentioned before, Gould found that while the 1848 insurgence was based on class identity, the insurgence during the 1871 Paris Commune was mobilized around neighborhood solidarity. Gould explains this change in organization ecology by the changes of the Paris built environment generated by the Haussmann project. Specifically, he finds that, during the Paris Commune, insurgents in different neighborhoods influenced each other's degrees of commitment to the insurrection through the links created by overlapping militia enlistments across districts. High levels of commitment in one area enhanced commitment elsewhere when enlistment patterns provided a conduit for communication and interaction.[4]

Zhao's (2001) study of student mobilization during the 1989 Beijing Student Movement is also conducted at the intersection between spatial and social ecology. For instance, Zhao has argued that while the campus built environment facilitated student mobilization, the built environment was itself a product of the Chinese state's social engineering project in the 1950s. The built environment became a hotbed for student mobilization only after most Chinese no longer believed in the communist ideology and the systems in place to control students had lost their effectiveness.

Integrating the two ecological perspectives, Zhang (2016) posits that some new, heterodox rebel groups enjoy unique environmental advantages when they are situated in an interstitial place, a place that is both spatially peripheral and politically marginalized. This place gives the rebel group possibilities to accumulate resources and manpower without direct, immediate intervention from the state. Building upon the concept of "interstitial emergence,"[5] Zhang demonstrates that many transformative movements abruptly emerged as *insurgencies in the interstices*.

Conclusion

Social movement scholars have urged a relational turn in studying contentious politics (Fligstein and McAdam 2012; McAdam, Tarrow, and Tilly 2001; Tilly and Tarrow 2007). The ecological perspective, especially the holistic approach of social ecology theory, is an inherently relational way of thinking about the social world (Abbott 2005; Liu and Emirbayer 2016). This chapter provides an up-to-date brief of the social and spatial ecological contexts of social movements. The two subfields – spatial ecology and social ecology – have developed relatively independently and both have produced a number of great works.

We conclude our review with four remarks concerning the future direction of ecological perspectives in social movement studies. First, we urge a rediscovery of the early generation's broader understanding of social ecology as a replacement of the current reference to organizational ecology theory. An expanded understanding of social ecology would bring space, time, organization, and environment together (Hawley 1950), and therefore offer a contextualized understanding of social movements (Koopmans 2004). Second, we expect the emergence of more qualitative and quantitative studies focusing on the interactive effects of spatial and social ecologies. The rapid development of spatial analysis toolkits based upon Geographic Information System (GIS) makes more substantive (rather than merely conceptualized) studies possible. Third, with the increasing importance of social media in movement mobilization, we also expect more Internet-based data collection and analytic methods in studying spatial and social ecology of social movements. For instance, Twitter data with geographical information have been used to examine whether selection or influence mechanisms played a more vital role in the shift of movement identities before, during, and after the protest in the Occupy Gezi movement (Budak and Watts 2015). Finally, we see many possibilities for combining network analysis and ecological theory in social movement studies, a tradition pioneered by Gould's well-known yet less-inherited works. In past decades, social network analysis has become a popular approach in organizational studies and also affects studies on contentious politics (e.g. Braun 2016; Diani and McAdam 2003; Hadden 2015; Heaney and Rojas 2015). Meanwhile, in spatial analysis, "networked space" has been given increasing attention by geographers (Featherstone 2008; Marston, Jones, and Woodward 2005; Nicholls 2009). A dialogue between the two threads would be productive.

Notes

1   See also Cresswell (2004), Entrikin (1991), Gieryn (2000), Gregory and Pred (2007), and Tuan (1977), among others, for the developments and uses of the concepts of space and place in analyzing social processes.
2   A branch of organizational ecology theory, resource partition theory attempts to explain specialization in a population of organizations, especially the relations between generalists and specialists (Carroll 1985).
3   Davis and Powell (1992: 353) have critiqued this problem in organizational ecology studies:

> It is assumed that American labor unions, semiconductor firms, early telephone companies, newspapers, and breweries in various areas of the world and voluntary social service organizations in Toronto all share timeless casual regularities by dint of the fact that we can refer to them as organizations.

4   This specific form of interaction between spatial and social ecologies held true for nineteenth-century Western Europe, when a nascent civil society coexisted with traditional communities. Most social movements occurring in that period, such as Chartism in England and the Paris Commune in Paris, were organized by formal organizations that relied heavily on the infrastructure of traditional community to extend their mobilizing potential (Mann 1993: Chapter 15).
5   "Interstitial emergence" is understood as the (unexpected) rise of new social forces in the crevices of the intersecting principal power networks (Mann 1986: 15–16).

References

Abbott, Andrew. 1988. *The System of Professions: An Essay on the Division of Expert Labor.* Chicago: University of Chicago Press.
Abbott, Andrew. 2005. "Linked Ecologies: States and Universities as Environments for Professions." *Sociological Theory* 23: 245–274.
Agnew, John A. 1987. *Place and Politics: The Geographical Mediation of State and Society.* Boston: Allen & Unwin.
Andrews, Kenneth T. and Charles Seguin. 2015. "Group Threat and Policy Change: The Spatial Dynamics of Prohibition Politics, 1890–1919." *American Journal of Sociology* 121: 475–510.
Barnett, William P. and Michael Woywode. 2004. "From Red Vienna to the Anschluss: Ideological Competition among Viennese Newspapers during the Rise of National Socialism." *American Journal of Sociology* 109: 1452–1499.

Bayat, Asef. 1997. *Street Politics: Poor People's Movements in Iran*. New York: Columbia University Press.

Beissinger, Mark R. 2003. *Nationalist Mobilization and the Collapse of the Soviet State*. Cambridge: Cambridge University Press.

Berk, Richard A. 1974. "A Gaming Approach to Crowd Behavior." *American Sociological Review* 39: 355–373.

Biggs, Michael. 2005. "Strikes as Forest Fires: Chicago and Paris in the Late Nineteenth Century." *American Journal of Sociology* 110: 1684–1714.

Biggs, Michael and Kenneth T. Andrews. 2015. "Protest Campaigns and Movement Success: Desegregating the US South in the Early 1960s." *American Sociological Review* 80: 416–443.

Blumer, Herbert. 1946. "Elementary Collective Groupings." *New Outlines of the Principles of Sociology* 178–198.

Boudet, Hilary. 2011. "From NIMBY to NIABY: Regional Mobilization against Liquefied Natural Gas in the United States." *Environmental Politics* 20: 786–806.

Braun, Robert. 2016. "Religious Minorities and Resistance to Genocide: The Collective Rescue of Jews in the Netherlands during the Holocaust." *American Political Science Review* 110: 127–147.

Brenner, Neil. 1999. "Beyond State-Centrism? Space, Territoriality, and Geographical Scale in Globalization Studies." *Theory and Society* 28: 39–78.

Brenner, Neil, Bob Jessop, Martin Jones, and Gordon Macleod, eds. 2008. *State/Space: A Reader*. New York: John Wiley & Sons, Inc.

Budak, Ceren and Duncan J. Watts. 2015. "Dissecting the Spirit of Gezi: Influence vs. Selection in the Occupy Gezi Movement." *Sociological Science* 2: 370–397.

Carroll, Glenn R. 1984. "Organizational Ecology." *Annual Review of Sociology* 10: 71–93.

Carroll, Glenn R. 1985. "Concentration and Specialization: Dynamics of Niche Width in Populations of Organizations." *American Journal of Sociology* 90: 1262–1283.

Case, F. Duncan. 1981. "Dormitory Architecture Influences." *Environment and Behavior* 13: 23–41.

Castells, Manuel. 1978. *City, Class, and Power*. New York: St. Martin's Press.

Chow, Tse-tsung. 1967. *The May Fourth Movement: Intellectual Revolution in Modern China*. Stanford, CA: Stanford University Press.

Clemens, Elisabeth S. 1993. "Organizational Repertoires and Institutional Change: Women's Groups and the Transformation of US Politics, 1890–1920." *American Journal of Sociology* 98: 755–798.

Clemens, Elisabeth S. and Debra C. Minkoff. 2004. "Beyond the Iron Law: Rethinking the Place of Organizations in Social Movement Research," In *The Blackwell Companion to Social Movements*, edited by David A. Snow, Sarah A. Soule, and Hanspeter Kriesi, 155–170. Oxford: Blackwell.

Collins, Randall. 2009. *Violence: A Micro-Sociological Theory*. New York: Greenwood Publishing Group.

Cresswell, Tim. 2004. *Place: An Introduction*. Chichester: John Wiley & Sons, Ltd.

Cunningham, David and Benjamin T. Phillips. 2007. "Contexts for Mobilization: Spatial Settings and Klan Presence in North Carolina, 1964–1966." *American Journal of Sociology* 113: 781–814.

Davis, Gerald F. and Walter W. Powell. 1992. "Organizations-Environment Relations." In *Handbook of Industrial and Organizational Psychology*, edited by Marvin Dunnette, 315–375. New York: Consulting Psychologist Press.

Delgado, Gary. 1986. *Organizing the Movement: The Roots and Growth of Acorn.* Philadelphia, PA: Temple University Press.

Diani, Mario and Doug McAdam. 2003. *Social Movements and Networks: Relational Approaches to Collective Action.* Oxford: Oxford University Press.

Dixon, Jeffrey C. 2006. "The Ties that Bind and Those that Don't: Toward Reconciling Group Threat and Contact Theories of Prejudice." *Social Forces* 84: 2179–2204.

Dokshin, Fedor A. 2016. "Whose Backyard and What's at Issue? Spatial and Ideological Dynamics of Local Opposition to Fracking in New York State, 2010–2013." *American Sociological Review* 81: 1–28.

Edwards, Bob and Sam Marullo. 1995. "Organizational Mortality in a Declining Social Movement: The Demise of Peace Movement Organizations in the End of the Cold War Era." *American Sociological Review* 70: 908–927.

Eisinger, Peter K. 1973. "The Conditions of Protest Behavior in American Cities." *American Political Science Review* 67: 11–28.

Entrikin, J. Nicholas. 1991. *The Betweenness of Place: Towards a Geography of Modernity.* Baltimore, MD: Johns Hopkins University Press.

Feagin, Joe R. and Harlan Hahn. 1973. *Ghetto Revolts: The Politics of Violence in American Cities.* New York: Macmillan Company.

Featherstone, David. 2008. *Resistance, Space and Political Identities: The Making of Counter-Global Networks.* Chichester: John Wiley & Sons. Ltd.

Festinger, Leon, Stanley Schachter, and Kurt Back. 1950. *Social Pressures in Informal Groups.* Stanford, CA: Stanford University Press.

Fligstein, Neil and Doug McAdam. 2012. *A Theory of Fields.* New York: Oxford University Press.

Fogelson, Robert M. 1971. *Violence as Protest: A Study of Riots and Ghettos.* Garden City, NY: Anchor Book.

Freeman, John H. and Pino G. Audia. 2006. "Community Ecology and the Sociology of Organizations." *Annual Review of Sociology* 32: 145–169.

Gans, Herbert J. 1967. *The Levitowners: Ways of Life and Politics in a New Suburban Community.* New York: Pantheon Books.

Gieryn, Thomas F. 1983. "Boundary-Work and the Demarcation of Science from Non-Science: Strains and Interests in Professional Ideologies of Scientists." *American Sociological Review* 48: 781–795.

Gieryn, Thomas F. 2000. "A Space for Place in Sociology." *Annual Review of Sociology* 26: 463–496.

Gould, Roger V. 1991. "Multiple Networks and Mobilization in the Paris Commune, 1871." *American Sociological Review* 56: 716–729.

Gould, Roger V. 1995. *Insurgent Identities: Class, Community, and Protest in Paris from 1848 to the Commune.* Chicago: University of Chicago Press.

Gregory, Derek and Allan Pred, eds. 2007. *Violent Geographies: Fear, Terror, and Political Violence.* New York: Routledge.

Greve, Henrich R. 2002. "An Ecological Theory of Spatial Evolution: Local Density Dependence in Tokyo Banking, 1894–1936." *Social Forces* 80: 847–879.

Hadden, Jennifer. 2015. *Networks in Contention: The Divisive Politics of Climate Change.* New York: Cambridge University Press.

Hannan, Michael T. and Glenn Carroll. 1992. *Dynamics of Organizational Populations: Density, Legitimation, and Competition.* Oxford: Oxford University Press.

Hannan, Michael T. and John Freeman. 1977. "The Population Ecology of Organizations." *American Journal of Sociology* 82: 929–964.

Hannan, Michael T. and John Freeman. 1989. *Organizational Ecology*. Cambridge, MA: Harvard University Press.

Harvey, David. 1985. *Consciousness and the Urban Experience*. Baltimore, MD: Johns Hopkins University Press.

Harvey, David. 1989. *The Condition of Postmodernity*. Oxford: Blackwell.

Hawley, Amos H. 1950. *Human Ecology: A Theory of Community Structure*. New York: Ronald Press.

Hawley, Amos H. 1986. *Human Ecology: A Theoretical Essay*. Chicago: University of Chicago Press.

Heaney, Michael T. and Fabio Rojas. 2015. *Party in the Street: The Antiwar Movement and the Democratic Party after 9/11*. New York: Cambridge University Press.

Hedstrom, Peter. 1994. "Contagious Collectivities: On the Spatial Diffusion of Swedish Trade Unions, 1890–1940." *American Journal of Sociology* 99: 1157–1179.

Heirich, Max. 1971. *The Spiral of Conflict: Berkeley 1964*. New York: Columbia University Press.

Hershkovitz, Linda. 1993. "Tiananmen Square and the Politics of Place." *Political Geography* 12: 395–420.

Kassow, Samuel D. 1989. *Students, Professors, and the State in Tsarist Russia*. Berkeley: University of California Press.

Kittikhoun, Anoulak. 2009. "Small State, Big Revolution: Geography and the Revolution in Laos." *Theory and Society* 38: 25–55.

Koopmans, Ruud. 2004. "Protest in Time and Space: The Evolution of Waves of Contention." In *The Blackwell Companion to Social Movements*, edited by David A. Snow, Sarah A. Soule, and Hanspeter Kriesi, 19–46. Oxford: Blackwell.

Kornhauser, William. 1959. *The Politics of Mass Society*. New York: Free Press.

Langton, Nancy. 1987. "Niche Theory and Social Movements: A Population Ecology Approach." *Sociological Quarterly* 28: 51–70.

Leitner, Helga, Eric Sheppard, and Kristin M. Sziarto. 2008. "The Spatialities of Contentious Politics." *Transactions of the Institute of British Geographers* 33: 157–172.

Liu, Sida and Mustafa Emirbayer. 2016. "Field and Ecology." *Sociological Theory* 34: 62–79.

Lofland, John. 1970. "The Youth Ghetto." In *The Logic of Social Hierarchies*, edited by Edward Laumann, Paul M. Siegel, and Robert W. Hodge, 756–778. Chicago: Marrham Publishing Company.

Lofland, Lyn H. 1973. *A World of Strangers: Order and Action in Urban Public Space*. New York: Basic Books.

Mann, Michael. 1986. *The Sources of Social Power*, vol. 1. Cambridge: Cambridge University Press.

Mann, Michael. 1993. *The Sources of Social Power*, vol. 2. Cambridge: Cambridge University Press.

Marston, Sallie A., John Paul Jones, and Keith Woodward. 2005. "Human Geography without Scale." *Transactions of the Institute of British Geographers* 30: 416–432.

Martin, Deborah G. and Byron Miller 2003. "Space and Contentious Politics." *Mobilization* 8: 143–156.

Marx, Karl. 1978. *The Marx-Engels Reader*, edited by Robert C. Tucker. New York: WW Norton.

McAdam, Doug. 1982. *Political Process and the Development of Black Insurgency, 1930–1970*. Chicago: University of Chicago Press.

McAdam, Doug and Hilary Boudet. 2012. *Putting Social Movements in Their Place: Explaining Opposition to Energy Projects in the United States, 2000–2005*. New York: Cambridge University Press.

McAdam, Doug, Sidney Tarrow, and Charles Tilly. 2001. *Dynamics of Contention*. Cambridge: Cambridge University Press.

McCarthy, John D. and Mayer N. Zald. 1973. *The Trend of Social Movements in America: Professionalization and Resource Mobilization*. Morristown, NJ: General Learning Corporation.

McCarthy, John D. and Mayer N. Zald. 1977. "Resource Mobilization and Social Movements: A Partial Theory." *American Journal of Sociology* 82: 1212–1241.

McKenzie, Roderick D. 1924. "The Ecological Approach to the Study of the Human Community." *American Journal of Sociology* 30: 287–301.

Miller, Byron A. 2000. *Geography and Social Movements*. Minneapolis: University of Minnesota Press.

Minkoff, Debra C. 1993. "The Organization of Survival: Women's and Racial-Ethnic Voluntarist and Activist Organizations, 1955–1985." *Social Forces* 71: 887–908.

Minkoff, Debra C. 1994. "From Service Provision to Institutional Advocacy: The Shifting Legitimacy of Organizational Forms." *Social Forces* 72: 943–969.

Minkoff, Debra C. 1997. "The Sequencing of Social Movements." *American Sociological Review* 62: 779–799.

Minkoff, Debra C. 1999. "Bending with the Wind: Strategic Change and Adaptation by Women's and Racial Minority Organizations." *American Journal of Sociology* 104: 1666–1703.

Minkoff, Debra C., Silke Aisenbrey, and Jon Agnone. 2008. "Organizational Diversity in the US Advocacy Sector." *Social Problems* 55: 525–548.

Mitchell, Don. 2003. *The Right to the City: Social Justice and the Fight for Public Space*. New York: Guilford Press.

Newcomb, Theodore M. 1961. *Acquaintance Process*. New York: Holt, Rinehart & Winston.

Nicholls, Walter. 2009. "Place, Networks, Space: Theorising the Geographies of Social Movements." *Transactions of the Institute of British Geographers* 34: 78–93.

Nicholls, Walter, Byron Miller, and Justin Beaumont. 2013. *Spaces of Contention: Spatialities and Social Movements*. Farnham: Ashgate.

Olzak, Susan. 1992. *The Dynamics of Ethnic Competition and Conflict*. Stanford, CA: Stanford University Press.

Olzak, Susan and Emily Ryo. 2007. "Organizational Diversity, Vitality and Outcomes in the Civil Rights Movement." *Social Forces* 85: 1561–1591.

Olzak, Susan and S.C. Noah Uhrig. 2001. "The Ecology of Tactical Overlap." *American Sociological Review* 66: 694–717.

Park, Robert E. 1936. "Human Ecology." *American Journal of Sociology* 42: 1–15.

Park, Robert E. and Ernest Watson Burgess. 1921. *Introduction to the Science of Sociology*. Chicago: University of Chicago Press.

Park, Robert E., Ernest Watson Burgess, and Roderick Duncan McKenzie. 1967. *The City*. Chicago: University of Chicago Press.

Perry, Ronald, David F. Gillespie, and Howard A. Parker. 1976. *Social Movements and the Local Community*. Beverly Hills, CA: Sage.

Routledge, Paul. 1993. *Terrains of Resistance: Nonviolent Social Movements and the Contestation of Place in India*. Westport, CT: Praeger Publishers.

Routledge, Paul. 1997. "A Spatiality of Resistances: Theory and Practice in Nepal's Revolution of 1990." In *Geographies of Resistance*, edited by Steve Pile and Michael Keith, 68–86. London: Routledge.

Sandell, Rickard. 2001. "Organizational Growth and Ecological Constraints: The Growth of Social Movements in Sweden, 1881 to 1940." *American Sociological Review* 66: 672–693.

Sewell, William H. Jr. 1996. "Historical Events as Transformations of Structures: Inventing Revolution at the Bastille." *Theory and Society* 25: 841–881.

Sewell, William H. Jr. 2001. "Space in Contentious Politics." In *Silence and Voice in the Study of Contentious Politic*, edited by Ronald R. Aminzade, Jack A. Goldstone, Doug McAdam, and Elizabeth J. Perry, 51–88. Cambridge: Cambridge University Press.

Simmel, Georg. 1971. *Georg Simmel on Individuality and Social Forms*. Edited by Donald N. Levine. Chicago: University of Chicago Press.

Skocpol, Theda. 1979. *States and Social Revolutions: A Comparative Analysis of France, Russia, and China*. Cambridge, New York: Cambridge University Press.

Smith, Neil. 1984. *Uneven Development: Nature, Capital, and the Production of Space*. Athens: University of Georgia Press.

Smith, Neil. 1993. "Homeless/Global: Scaling Places." In *Mapping the Future*, edited by John Bird, Barry Curtis, Tim Putnam, and Lisa Tickner, 87–119. London: Routledge.

Smith, Neil. 1995. "Remaking Scale: Competition and Cooperation in Prenational and Postnational Europe." In *Competitive European Peripheries*, edited by Heikki Eskelinen and Folke Snickars, 59–74. Berlin: Springer.

Snow, David A. and Dana M. Moss. 2014. "Protest on the Fly: Toward a Theory of Spontaneity in the Dynamics of Protest and Social Movements." *American Sociological Review* 79: 1122–1143.

Soule, Sarah A. 2013. "Bringing Organizational Studies Back into Social Movement Scholarship." In *The Future of Social Movement Research: Dynamics, Mechanisms and Processes*, edited by Jacquelien van Stekelenburg, Conny J. Roggeband, and Bert Klandermans, 107–124. Minneapolis: University of Minnesota Press.

Soule, Sarah A. and Brayden G. King. 2008. "Competition and Resource Partitioning in Three Social Movement Industries." *American Journal of Sociology* 113: 1568–1610.

Spykman, Nicholas J. 1964. *The Social Theory of Georg Simmel*. New York: Atherton.

Stern, Charlotta. 1999. "The Evolution of Social-Movement Organizations: Niche Competition in Social Space." *European Sociological Review* 15: 91–105.

Stillerman, Joel. 2003. "Space, Strategies, and Alliances in Mobilization: The 1960 Metalworkers' and Coal Miners' Strikes in Chile." *Mobilization* 8: 65–85.

Stinchcombe, Arthur L. 1965. "Organizations and Social Structure." In *Handbook of Organizations*, edited by James G. March, 153–193. Chicago: University of Chicago Press.

Suttles, Gerald D. 1968. *The Social Order of the Slum*. Chicago: University of Chicago Press.

Suttles, Gerald D. 1972. *Social Construction of Communities*. Chicago: University of Chicago Press.

Tarrow, Sidney G. 1989. *Democracy and Disorder: Politics and Protest in Italy, 1965–1975*. Oxford: Clarendon Press.

Tarrow, Sidney G. and Doug McAdam. 2005. "Scale Shift in Transnational Contention." In *Transnational Protest and Global Activism*, edited by Donatella della Porta and Sidney G. Tarrow, 121–150. Lanham, MD: Rowman & Littlefield.

Tilly, Charles. 2000. "Spaces of Contention." *Mobilization* 5: 135–159.

Tilly, Charles and R. A. Schweitzer. 1982. "How London and its Conflicts Changed Shape: 1758–1834." *Historical Methods* 15: 67–77.

Tilly, Charles and Sidney G. Tarrow. 2007. *Contentious Politics*. Oxford: Oxford University Press.

Traugott, Mark. 1995. "Capital Cities and Revolution." *Social Science History* 19: 147–168.

Tuan, Yi-fu. 1977. *Space and Place: The Perspective of Experience*. Minneapolis: University of Minnesota Press.

Turner, Ralph H. and Lewis M. Killian. 1957. *Collective Behavior*. Englewood Cliffs, NJ: Prentice-Hall.

Vasi, Ion Bogdan, Edward Walker, John Johnson, and Hui Fen Tan. 2015. "'No Fracking Way!' Documentary Film, Discursive Opportunity, and Local Opposition against Hydraulic Fracturing in the United States, 2010 to 2013." *American Sociological Review* 80: 934–959.

Warner, W. Lloyd. 1963. *Yankee City*. New Haven, CT: Yale University Press.

Weyland, Kurt. 2009. "The Diffusion of Revolution: '1848' in Europe and Latin America." *International Organization* 63: 391–423.

Wright, Rachel A. and Hilary Schaffer Boudet. 2012. "To Act or Not to Act: Context, Capability, and Community Response to Environmental Risk." *American Journal of Sociology* 118: 728–777.

Young, Ruth. 1988. "Is Population Ecology a Useful Paradigm for the Study of Organizations?" *American Journal of Sociology* 94: 1–24.

Zald, Mayer N. and Roberta Ash. 1966. "Social Movement Organizations: Growth, Decay, and Change." *Social Forces* 44: 327–341.

Zald, Mayer N. and John D. McCarthy. 1980. "Social Movement Industries: Competition and Conflict Among SMOs" In *Social Movements in an Organizational Society*, edited by Mayer N. Zald and John D. McCarthy, 161–180. New Brunswick, NJ: Transaction Books.

Zhang, Yang. 2016. "Insurgent Dynamics: The Coming of the Chinese Rebellions, 1850–1873." PhD dissertation, University of Chicago.

Zhao, Dingxin. 1998. "Ecologies of Social Movements: Student Mobilization during the 1989 Prodemocracy Movement in Beijing." *American Journal of Sociology* 103: 1493–1529.

Zhao, Dingxin. 2001. *The Power of Tiananmen: State-Society Relations and the 1989 Beijing Student Movement*. Chicago: University of Chicago Press.

Zhao, Dingxin. 2009. "Organization and Place in the Anti-US Chinese Student Protests after the 1999 Belgrade Embassy Bombing." *Mobilization* 14: 107–129.

6

Social Movements and Transnational Context: Institutions, Strategies, and Conflicts

CLIFFORD BOB

Introduction

Social movements around the world have long had ties that cross national boundaries. Nationalist movements of the eighteenth and nineteenth centuries reached out for overseas support. In the American Revolution, the independence movement sought and received aid from European governments. In turn, the ringing words and ideas influenced revolutionary movements in Europe and beyond (Polasky 2015). The British abolitionist movement, working at times with the government of the United Kingdom, worked globally to end the slave trade. As the movement swelled in the early nineteenth century, opponents also formed loose-knit networks that provided ideological support in a quest to preserve slavery (Faust 1981). Decades later, women's suffrage movements in many countries had important cross-border dimensions, with marginal regions often providing the vote earlier and acting as models for more powerful countries (Markoff 2003). Similar nation-spanning activities are common today, bolstered by technological advances making for cheaper, easier, and faster global communication and influence than ever before. Along with longstanding nationalist and ethnic movements, there are today numerous others focusing on such varied issues as human rights, environmentalism, and global justice (della Porta 2007).

This chapter reviews and critiques the burgeoning literature on transnational contexts and conditions for social movements. These, like other movement contexts, can be understood in two ways. First, they include the institutions, actors, and attitudes within which movements arise, mobilize, and strategize. This would include supranational organizations such as the European Union, interstate organizations such as the United Nations or the Association of Southeast Asian Nations, and global conclaves such as the World Economic Forum and the World Social Forum. Although these institutions clearly evolve, often in response to social movement activism, at

The Wiley Blackwell Companion to Social Movements, Second Edition. Edited by David A. Snow, Sarah A. Soule, Hanspeter Kriesi, and Holly J. McCammon.
© 2019 John Wiley & Sons Ltd. Published 2019 by John Wiley & Sons Ltd.

any particular time they can be considered relatively static and stable. Second, however, transnational contexts and conditions may be viewed in dynamic and interactive terms. Movements constantly adjust their approaches to deal with the reactions they provoke from targets, the responses they elicit from third parties, and the progress or regress they encounter in reaching their goals. In this view, strategies and tactics are so closely tied to context that, although the two can be separated for certain analytic purposes, for others, their interactive aspects must come to the fore.

This double conceptualization of transnational contexts and conditions mirrors the ways in which movements understand other political contexts, from the local to the national (McAdam 1999), and this chapter will explore both views. I begin with a genealogy and definition of the term "transnational." In this, I stress the ways that movements extend beyond national borders for ideas, sympathizers, and supporters – and the reciprocal ways in which elements of the transnational context interact with them. Next, I examine some of the most important theorization and research in the area, necessarily a selective enterprise given the large amount of scholarship in recent years. In particular, I consider various institutions that condition transnational activism, as well as the forms and mechanisms of transnationalism arising in relation to that context, highlighting their dynamic aspects. Finally, I probe the under-examined question of effects, asking what impacts, positive or negative, transnational interactions have on national and international policy, on the movements themselves, and on broader transnational conditions. Throughout, I seek to move beyond the dominant focus in the literature, left-wing and nonviolent movements. Although these are clearly important and, for legitimate reasons, have attracted scholarly attention, they represent only an ideologically and tactically narrow slice of movements that act beyond national borders. In addition, I highlight another critical but understudied aspect of transnational context, the ways in which movements contend with rival movements, sometimes violently, not only within national borders but also across them.

The Transnational: Genealogy, Definition, and Limitations

The term "transnational" appears to have been used first by author Ralph Bourne in a 1916 *Atlantic Monthly* article, "Trans-National America." Presciently, Bourne's article probed linkages between new American immigrant communities and their homelands. He highlighted continuing cross-border ties and the effects this might have on the relevant context – an existing American society that had overlooked both its immigrant roots and the continuing power of its predominantly Anglo-Saxon origins. Even if ethnic identity is only one of many sources of transnational interaction, Bourne was right to emphasize its importance. Ethnic movements and organizations, with their ideas, goals, and support structures spanning national borders, continue to exert great influence on national and international institutions, even as their strategies are also shaped by those contexts. The Israel Lobby is perhaps the most powerful example of this in the USA (Mearsheimer and Walt 2008), although it is hardly alone in its efforts to navigate and influence those contexts. In a violent example of religiously-related transnational interactions, the Islamic State movement has inspired young Muslims to become "foreign fighters" in Iraq and Syria – and to engage in terrorism in Europe and North America (Malet, forthcoming). Whether one characterizes this as a religious or nationalist movement, its ability to exploit technological and legal contexts spanning national borders has had important effects on contemporary politics.

Bourne's brief life exemplifies other interactions beyond the ethno-religious, again indicating the dynamic aspects of the transnational. He was an outspoken peace activist who staunchly opposed American involvement in World War I. Like activists who organized transnationally for a nuclear freeze in the 1980s, to ban landmines and control the small arms trade in the 1990s (Erickson 2015), against cluster munitions in the 2000s (Nash 2012), and against drone strikes in the 2010s, the late nineteenth- and early twentieth-century movement against war seized available institutional, legal, and ideational contexts to advance its goals, invoking a "higher cosmopolitan ideal" to organize against militarism (Bourne 1916: 96). It also opposed the transnational movement urging American intervention in World War I. In words similar to those used by members of today's global justice movement, Bourne and the larger peace movement of the time critiqued a "plutocratic" and "undemocratically controlled foreign policy," questioning whether the USA should fight against the "social democracy of the new Russia" (1917: 200, 202). Such social, political, and economic motives are all continuing wellsprings for transnational ties. At any particular time, they provide not only a relatively static context for movement development, but also a basis for interactions that constantly alter both the movement and the larger political landscape.

Accordingly, we must define the "transnational" broadly. One of the most useful starting points is Keohane and Nye's (1971: 333–334) definition of "transnational interactions" as any interaction across borders involving one or more nonstate actors. The definition is useful because the relational component highlights agency, whether or not the movement views the larger context as facilitating or constraining mobilization. It is comprehensive in that it covers a wide variety of transnational interactions, and does not highlight only the rarest, full-scale transnational movements. It, like Tarrow's definition (2005: 25), is inclusive as to the "direction" of relations, inviting an examination of the agency of all members of such interactions. This contrasts with one important approach, the "boomerang model," which highlights transnational advocacy networks (TANs) that form when local movements repressed or stymied by their home states reach out for overseas support (Keck and Sikkink 1998). Certainly, this is an important process, but it is far from the only way in which such ties develop. In other cases, powerful international actors seek out, nurture, or even create "local" interlocutors. Typically, these two processes, one bottom-up, the other top-down, occur simultaneously. For instance, in one of the most consequential transnational interactions of the twenty-first century, Iraqi exile organizations exploited a favorable American political context in the years after 9/11, lobbying a US government dominated by the neoconservative movement for military intervention against Saddam Hussein (Roston 2008). The result, despite opposition from a grassroots peace movement spanning national borders, was the 2003 invasion of Iraq and a continuing, devastating war. Keohane and Nye's definition, like the others noted, is agnostic as to the participants in such cross-border relations, as long as at least one nonstate actor is involved. It thereby encompasses not only the interactions that have been the focus of most scholarship – involving nonviolent, rights-based or environmental networks – but also other ones such as nationalist, traditionalist, or neo-liberal groups (Smith 2008).

Such interactions become possible only with awareness of the transnational context. With the rise of new technologies over the last 30 years, a wide range of overseas events, actors, and institutions are better known and more accessible than ever before. The mass media remains crucial in this, with "old" broadcast media such as newspapers, radio, and television, now joined by Internet-based "narrowcast" media and social media such as Facebook and Twitter. Some believe that these new technologies fundamentally change the transnational prospects of movements (Castells 2015). Such technologies clearly make a difference in the speed and breadth with which information about protest and movements may spread. This increases the possibilities for "scale-shift" (Tarrow 2005), with activists strategically seeking to transfer appeals, frames, and mobilization among local, national, and transnational arenas.

Caution about the prospects for transnationalism remains in order, however. New technologies may make the transnational context more accessible to movements than in prior periods. For two reasons, however, it remains less accessible – and sometimes less worth accessing given many movements' limited resources – than local and national political contexts. First, states remain the dominant actors on the global scene. The most authoritarian can still close off their borders to material and online exchanges, encumbering or halting transnational interactions (Morozov 2012). Even weak states have the capacity to undermine foreign-supported organizing and activism (Dupuy, Ron, and Prakash 2015). And even democratic states monitor and manipulate movements, often using new technologies (Fang and Horn 2016).

Second, geographic and cultural distances complicate transnational interactions. On one hand, the existence of a "global village" – in which events occurring thousands of miles away pose direct challenges or opportunities at home – may be largely a myth (Porter 2015). As with the study of movements more broadly, analysts need to pay greater attention to the many potential transnational ties that fail to develop, rather than dwelling on the relatively few that do (Bob 2005; McAdam and Boudet 2012). On the other hand, the global village myth is powerful, and movement organizations exploit this ideational context. Drawing linkages to events occurring far away, they mobilize constituents out of sympathy, inspiration, or fear. Importantly, distance leaves open the door to strategic manipulation. Consider recent Western campaigns against "honor killings" in Muslim societies, which describe incidents in stark terms and suggest that the problem is of epidemic proportions. Yet as deep anthropological dives into local communities have shown, many of the incidents used in such campaigns are distorted, and the lived realities of women in such societies are more complex than portrayed by activists (Abu-Lughod 2013: 128–136).

Multi-Level Governance and Transnational Activism

If sovereignty and distance limit and distort them, transnational interactions are nonetheless increasingly common (Tarrow 2005: 4). Technological change plays a role in this, but another important reason is changes in the global political context, especially growth in international institutions. Recent decades have seen a marked increase in intergovernmenal agreements, some the result of transnational campaigns involving international NGOs, local activists, and interested states (Posner 2014). From these have sprung new international organizations and institutions to which states transfer limited decision-making powers. The web of new international actors and institutions has created a weak but real system of "multi-level governance" in which enduring institutions located outside a state's borders can affect its politics (Avant, Finnemore, and Sell 2010; Sikkink 2005). This in turn provides both incentives for movement organizations to promote their goals there and forums for transnational organizing – an institutional "coral reef" (Tarrow 2005: 27) around which activists from varied nations may meet and form ties. The European Court of Human Rights and the Council of Europe, for instance, have become venues for litigation and lobbying by rights activists of many kinds. Other institutions such as the World Trade Organization (WTO) and G-8 which symbolically embody global capitalism, have become objects of recurrent protest by the global justice movement. Even when such organizations repress or ignore protest, their meetings or decisions provide opportunities to promote the movement. In some cases, powerful global institutions have adapted to social movement pressure by creating new mechanisms to channel objections and demands by local groups. One important example is the World Bank's Inspection Panel which hears civil society challenges to Bank decisions that allegedly violate its mandate to end poverty and promote sustainable development (Clark, Fox, and Treakle 2003).

The proliferation of global institutions facilitates forum shopping, as movements seek out and work in institutions that are powerful and friendly, avoiding if they can those which are inhospitable (Murphy and Kellow 2013). In cases such as the Inspection Panel and international courts, the institutions' structures and procedures shape the form of activism, with more moderate and professionalized approaches at a premium. Whether this leads movements to reduce more disruptive protest is an important area for future research. There are also deeper questions about whether limited movement resources are best spent on institutions of "global governance" when national governments remain most powerful (Conca 2015). To return to the World Bank case, Inspection Panel decisions favoring local movements have sometimes been ignored by governments such as India, intent on achieving development goals (Randeria 2003).

Forms of Transnational Interaction

Networks

Whether seeking to influence such institutions through professionalized engagement from within or more disruptive actions from without, activists work together through transnational networks and movements. The former come in two broad types, solidarity and policy networks. Solidarity networks, involving outsiders' assistance to local or national movements, have been most thoroughly analyzed in the literature, starting with Keck and Sikkink's seminal work (1998). Solidarity networks are essentially a form of third party involvement in overseas conflicts. As analysts have long known, even local conflicts cannot be viewed in isolation from political contexts within and beyond national borders (Schattschneider 1975).

Contending parties often seek to change the conflict's power balance by rallying out-siders to their side – or tearing them away from their foes. International institutions such as UN bodies can play key roles in such contests. For instance, in Central America, both sides to national conflict over reproductive rights/right to life have reached out for and received overseas support. Transnational women's networks anchored by UN agencies have supported the former, whereas conservative "family values" networks associated with the Catholic Church and conservative Evangelicals have helped the latter (Walsh 2016).

By contrast to solidarity networks, the goals of policy networks are broader than simply empowering or disempowering a particular local movement. Instead, they aim at international law-making, treaty negotiations, or cultural change. Given the scope of their concerns, policy networks have multiple targets, including states, international organizations, and multinational corporations. In recent decades, many such networks have organized, for instance, to fight climate change, improve wom-en's rights, forestall the development of "killer robots," end human trafficking, and much more. As with solidarity networks, policy networks usually come in opposi-tional pairs – ideologically polar regarding the policy issue, but similar to one another in tactics, organization, and membership (Bob 2012).

Whatever their ideologies, a key part of both policy and solidarity networks are nongovernmental organizations (NGOs), which often act as their organizers or anchors. NGOs come in a variety of forms. Most resemble classic social movement organizations (SMOs), relatively small, elite-run groups. Although part of broad social movements such as the environmental or women's rights movements, they typ-ically seek to mobilize mass publics for decentralized and low risk activities, such as fundraising, letter-writing campaigns, or electronic petitions. Even the most "grass-roots" of such activist groups, such as Amnesty International, differ substantially from mass-based social movements, such as national democratization or independence movements with which they sometimes stand in solidarity (Hopgood 2006).

The sociological, political science, and legal literature on such advocacy networks focuses on a number of major issues. For one, there is the question of how and why such networks form. Early work characterized the transnational context, with its NGOs and international organizations, as the "conscience of the world," high-lighting the "principled" reasons that motivated overseas activism (Willetts 1996). In this view, it is most likely to arise in the most egregious cases of bodily harm to indi-viduals, as in the human rights movement, or de jure discrimination against racial groups, as in the anti-Apartheid movement (Keck and Sikkink 1998). Others have questioned whether these factors alone can explain wide variations in support for seemingly similar movements – why in the same transnational context certain move-ments are neglected, whereas other similar ones become global *causes célèbres* (Ron, Ramos, and Rodgers 2005). Bob (2005) has analogized transnational activism to a market, with numerous local movements demanding outside support and a more limited supply of NGO patrons, who pick and choose among possible clients based as much on organizational needs as moral principles. In turn, local groups do not merely appeal for help but actively market themselves, repackaging parochial con-flicts to fit into the larger global context. All of this throws into question the view that transnational activists are primarily moved by "principles." Fine-grained analyses show all sides to conflicts are motivated by a combination of moral and material factors (Sell and Prakash 2004).

A related set of questions concerns power dynamics within networks. In some cases, this is a matter of unequal resources – including money, expertise, credibility, and contacts. Such inequalities often characterize relations between Northern NGOs and Southern movements, creating the potential for dependency. To gain support, relatively weak members must meet the demands of the relatively strong – they must navigate the transnational context with regard to everything from financial accountability to gender balance (Wendoh and Wallace 2005). All of these matters give advantages to local groups or movements led by individuals who are adept in that context and understand global conditions, often those who are urban, connected, and educated in the North. These same activists, however, may have limited linkages to the poorer, rural populations that they sometimes claim to represent. As Herring and Kandlikar (2009) show in their study of contention over genetically modified (GM) seeds in India, urban environmentalists may have little sense of what poor farmers want or need. Such concerns have helped spawn important research on the representation and accountability of NGOs (Grant and Keohane 2005). But more empirical and normative work is needed: whom do transnational actors actually represent – and to what degree are local voices reflected in transnational contexts?

In recent years, scholars have sought to map networks, aiming to provide a comprehensive description of them. More controversially, those who deploy this approach seek to show that characteristics and relationships of networks explain important outcomes, such as the tactical choices of climate change activists (Hadden 2015) or the issue focus of human security organizations (Carpenter 2014). Such approaches hold promise, particularly if there is recognition of their limitations: topology provides at best a static structural picture of dynamic political entities. Applied to the social realm, key concepts of network theory such as "connectedness" and "betweenness" are themselves functions of more important underlying factors such as the power, resources, and credibility of particular organizations (Lake and Wong 2009). On the other hand, network approaches do provide a relatively easy means of producing indicators that can allow scholars to assess the more fundamental forces at work. They also draw attention to lock in effects and highlight an understudied phenomenon: how power relationships within networks can affect member behavior at specific times.

Movements

If transnational networking is common, true transnational movements, involving sustained, large-scale, and high-intensity activism are rare. Domestic movement organizations sometimes develop overseas offshoots, but in alien cultural and political terrain, these often fail to thrive (Nepstad 2008). Internationally oriented movement organizations, such as those focusing on development, human rights, or environmentalism frequently found overseas branches to gather information, implement directives, or spread the organizations' beliefs. Oxfam, Amnesty International, Greenpeace, and Friends of the Earth exemplify such an approach, but they are organizations with multi-state operations not transnational movements.

At a more abstract level, one could argue that the human rights, environmental, and global justice movements are truly transnational. They have numerous component organizations even if these have difficulty coordinating actions globally or even within specific international institutions (Hadden 2015). They have raised consciousness among millions worldwide and spurred widespread behavioral changes, even if underlying concepts such as rights or sustainability are vague and contested (Wapner 1996). In particular countries, national movements that claim to subscribe to such global principles have engaged in large-scale activism, changing policies and even governments. And at particular events, such as international conferences or UN sessions, smaller-scale lobbying and activism have targeted key decision-makers.

On the other hand, the concept of a transnational and especially a global movement may be analytically inapt in current circumstances. Most international institutions are relatively weak and dependent on decisions by state actors. The strongest, such as the European Union, provide rich opportunities for activism, and a host of social movement organizations and interest groups now seek to achieve their goals in part by lobbying European institutions (Ayoub 2013; Coen and Richardson 2009). But even in such contexts, as careful studies show, national institutions remain most influential. Movements target them first, usually exploiting transnational institutions as a supplementary tactic (Imig and Tarrow 2001: 33).

Rival activism

As noted previously, such interactions typically provoke reaction by groups whose interests or values are threatened. Often such reactions cross national borders and constitute full-fledged instances of rival networks or in some cases rival movements. Some of this is opportunistic. For instance, fringe events such as the publication of cartoons said to be of the Prophet Muhammad in Denmark or the burning of a Koran in Florida can be picked up by movements or governments overseas, which use them as resources to set off protest and bloodshed. In turn, such distant events are used as rhetorical fodder by anti-Muslim activists in Europe and America (Klausen 2009). In the USA and European countries, as a result, a nativist movement has moved from the fringe to the mainstream since 9/11. As Bail (2015) shows, efforts to fight this opportunistic scale-shift have only fueled its rise.

Rivalry may also take the form of more sustained transnational contention, usually as an echo of inter-movement conflict in domestic contexts. As shown by the literature on counter-movements, a single movement seldom seeks cultural or political goals unchecked (Meyer and Staggenborg 1996). More commonly, movements are opposed by powerful states and other entities. Transnational forces promoting neo-liberal economic institutions, such as NAFTA, have been met by rival transnational movements involving labor and environmental movements (Kay 2011; Smith 2008). The World Social Forum and various national social forums have brought similar groups together to fight neo-liberal globalization epitomized by the World Economic Forum. Gay rights activists have organized transnationally but have from the start faced opposition from a transnational network of conservative groups spanning various religions (Buss and Herman 2003; Fetner 2008).

Although prolonged conflicts among movements play themselves out primarily within domestic settings, the transnational context often plays a role. Events occurring overseas serve as exemplars, rallying points, or horror stories that rivals can use to mobilize their own forces or attack foes. One important historical example is the American civil rights movement early in the Cold War. It used America's vulnerability to international criticism for Jim Crow discrimination to press for racial equality. As should be clear, this was not a simple matter of a new transnational "climate" directly sparking change. Rather, it involved strategic action by all parties. On one hand, the Soviet Union used the existence of racist violence in the American South to win ideological points with audiences in nonaligned states. Activists in the civil rights movement carefully leveraged this international threat to advance their domestic goals. In the sharp competition of the Cold War, US government officials saw the danger and became more receptive to movement demands (Dudziak 2000). In turn, this loosening helped make change appear possible for mass protesters in the civil rights movement (McAdam 1999). At the same time, however, activists shifted from what many wanted – a UN-backed human rights agenda including social and economic rights – to a narrow civil and political rights agenda. This strategic retreat occurred under withering criticism from a rival movement of White Southerners who portrayed the more expansive goals as Communist-inspired (Anderson 2003).

Effects

Another important, if understudied, set of questions concerns the effects of transnational interactions. These can be difficult to isolate because of the tight interweaving of domestic and transnational contexts. How much, for instance, did the transnational anti-Apartheid movement add to domestic activism by the African National Congress (Klotz 1995)? Does the contemporary Boycott, Divest, and Sanction (BDS) movement contribute to local Palestinian organizing against Israel's occupation? Yet seeking to measure the effects of transnational activism represents an important, policy-relevant issue – one that should attract greater scholarly attention with regard to both desired and unanticipated consequences. Key areas to probe include the effects of transnational interactions on typical targets of activism – states, international organizations and multinational corporations (policy effects); on the transnationally-linked organizations, networks and movements themselves (organizational effects); and on broader aspects of globalization and global culture (systemic effects). It is obvious that there will be no single answer to these questions even within each of these broad categories. Researchers should therefore carefully analyze the conditions under which effects may occur. In this, it is important again to bear in mind that transnationally-related conflicts typically involve oppositional pairs of networks. As a result, the failures of one side to a conflict usually represent successes for the other. Policy change may be the most obvious indicator of success, but "nonpolicy" may represent success as well – for movements opposing change (Crenson 1971; McCright and Dunlap 2003). Close analysis of conflict wholes – of the interactive strategies of opposing networks, rather than only one side to a conflict – provides a fuller understanding of the meanings of success and failure in dynamic political contexts.

With regard to policy effects, transnational interactions may at minimum draw international attention to pressing issues that have previously remained obscure.

Campaigns to raise awareness about human trafficking, female genital mutilation, climate change, and other issues have been successful at least at this level, even if their broader policy impacts are less certain. Awareness raising can sometimes spill over into fear-mongering, but it can also play a key role in convincing others to join the cause. As Ayoub (2016) shows, transnational activism made LGBT populations more visible in European countries, in turn, boosting governmental compliance and societal acceptance of evolving gay rights norms. A more significant and more difficult level of impact involves direct policy outcomes on target entities. The literature on transnational human rights activism has analyzed issues of effects more thoroughly than most others, although substantial controversy remains. Proponents of the "spiral model" argue that sustained interactions between local rights groups and transnational supporters can persuade repressive states to loosen their policies, even if this is a long-term process marked by periods of denial, lip service, and tactical concessions (Risse, Ropp, and Sikkink 2013).

Other scholars are more skeptical of the real policy impacts of transnational activism, however. In the human rights area, some argue that any effects are most likely in states that are relatively less repressive, whereas the most important and difficult cases go unaddressed (Hafner-Burton 2013). Others question more broadly the evidence for human rights improvements or "justice cascades" (Posner 2014). Careful studies of environmental and climate change activism suggest as well that transnational activists opt for institutionalized lobbying rather than extra-institutional protest, limiting their impact although maintaining access (Hadden 2015).

Along these lines, a third strand of research on effects of transnational activism highlights unanticipated negative effects. For one thing, transnational support for local movements can create dependency on overseas funding, sometimes discouraging indigenously based mobilization (Englund 2006). Analysts have shown that overseas activists sometimes misunderstand situations in alien cultures and polities (Chuang 2014). Whether accidentally or strategically, they breathe into distant conflicts their own culturally specific or organizationally advantageous visions of who the parties are, what they want, and how they fit into potential supporters' agendas. Typically, indigenous nuances are replaced at the global level by stark black-and-white images of victim and perpetrator (De Waal 2016). Local activists can sometimes overcome or exploit such misunderstandings to gain transnational support (Hertel 2006). But the result may be distortion and simplification of complex local realities, with sometimes dire consequences at the grassroots (Mamdani 2009). Some have argued that the pursuit of international justice by human rights groups in alliance with international courts can prolong conflicts (Snyder and Vinjamuri 2006). Others show that the possibility of overseas support can create "moral hazard": local movements provoke states into greater violence, hoping (often vainly) that this will spur rights activism and ultimately "humanitarian" intervention – arguably the case in Kosovo in 1999, Libya in 2011, and Syria today (Kuperman 2013; Kuperman and Crawford 2006). At a minimum, it is important to recognize possible linkages between civil society activists and state-based military interventions, with some arguing that the former all too easily pave the way to the latter (Douzinas 2007).

In recent years, it has become clear as well that the presence of transnational linkages provides authoritarian governments with easy arguments for undermining domestic movements – as fifth columnists supported by foreign NGOs and governments.

A recent raft of anti-NGO laws in countries as diverse as Ethiopia, Russia, and Israel has joined earlier efforts by countries such as Singapore, Malaysia, and China in limiting the role of foreign support (Dupuy, Ron, and Prakash 2015; Heller 2016). Meanwhile, in the name of vaguely defined "anti-terror" policies, major democracies have implemented stronger monitoring and control of civil society, particularly NGOs and foundations that operate overseas (Braman 2006). For the moment, the latter initiatives primarily affect interactions involving Muslim communities and organizations, but their logic and mechanisms have worryingly broad effects. They pose strong constraints and challenges on a wide variety of movements and expression itself (PEN America 2015). Yet research has only begun on the problem of "closing space" for civil society (Carothers and Brechenmacher 2014), with much still needed about the causes of restrictions and their effects on transnationally linked domestic movements. Do such movements go into abeyance, or are they completely undermined? If the latter, what alternatives are left to overseas activists who seek to assist like-minded locals in repressive settings?

Beyond examining policy outcomes, scholars have debated whether transnational interactions involve convergence to particular ideological, strategic, or organizational forms. On one hand, there is no doubt that the frames and tactics used by movements are often "modular" – easily taken up, and innovated upon, by movements far from the places they were originally used (Tarrow 1993). Wong (2012) suggests more controversially that there is an archetypal organizational form that allows rights NGOs and their causes to gain salience. In some views, organizational imperatives provide strong incentives for NGOs to act in similar ways, making material concerns a central aspect of all activism (Cooley and Ron 2002).

By contrast, Stroup (2012) shows that national laws and cultures shape organizational structures, fund-raising models, and long-term strategies, even among NGOs from the same sector and sharing similar goals. As Tarrow (2005: 29) argues, transnational activists are best characterized as "rooted cosmopolitans," tied to national social and political contexts but working for goals that may be advanced by cross-border interactions. In this, they naturally carry with them their national experiences and attitudes. This sometimes aids them in navigating distant institutions, especially if those are similar to the ones they know best from their home states or if they have good understanding of the international institutions they seek to penetrate. In other cases, however, it may impede them from achieving their goals, as local rootedness hinders their ability to project or frame their causes in ways that resonate beyond home (Bob 2005; Coy 1997). In any case, the core question of how transnational interactions affect the parties themselves remains an important area of study.

A final area of research connects to broader debates about globalization (see Chapter 34 by Andretta, della Porta, and Saunders, in this volume). Some have argued that NGOs constitute a "global civil society" that serves as a counterweight to state and multinational corporate power (Castells 2008). Others see NGOs and activist networks as partaking in new forms of "global governance," forging international laws and norms that shape state behavior (Avant, Finnemore, and Sell 2010). The "world culture" literature goes further, suggesting that transnational NGOs enact a "set of cultural rules or scripts that specify how institutions around the world should deal with common problems" (Lechner and Boli 2005: 56).

A contrary literature takes a more skeptical view. Some argue that the impact of international law and global norms, as well as the activists who have promoted them, is limited – except in cases where states find it in their interest to follow them (Goldsmith and Posner 2005). Others question the existence of a single "world culture," highlighting sharp cultural and ideological divisions even within particular countries (Bob 2012). If "global civil society" is no more unified than national civil societies, its supposed ability to counter-balance state power seems overdrawn. Some of the most powerful movements of 2016 – Britain's Brexit campaign and the insurgent Presidential candidacies of Bernie Sanders and Donald J. Trump – promoted national interests over international institutions. There are transnational linkages among these populist, nationalist, and nativist movements (Legum 2016), but they have also mobilized support by attacking international institutions and global governance.

Conclusion

In the wake of these momentous events, questions about the systemic effects of transnational contexts and interactions become particularly important for future research. In addition to the important institutional and ideational contexts that movements assess for their facilitating or constraining characteristics, the transnational is a dynamic and conflictive realm which in today's world impinges ever more strongly on national and even local activism. It is a resource that activists may draw on to advance their goals and undermine their foes. In turn, those who provide such resources do so alertly and strategically, with their own goals and interests in mind. For scholars of social movements, the study of transnational relations, with the many debates outlined above, therefore presents a base from which to explore core issues in the field.

References

Abu-Lughod, Lila. 2013. *Do Muslim Women Need Saving?* Cambridge, MA: Harvard University Press.

Anderson, Carol. 2003. *Eyes off the Prize: The United Nations and the African American Struggle for Human Rights, 1944–1955*. Cambridge: Cambridge University Press.

Avant, Deborah D., Martha Finnemore, and Susan K. Sell. 2010. "Who Governs the Globe?" In *Who Governs the Globe?*, edited by Deborah D. Avant, Martha Finnemore, and Susan K. Sell, 1–31. Cambridge: Cambridge University Press.

Ayoub, Phillip M. 2013. "Cooperative Transnationalism in Contemporary Europe: Europeanization and Political Opportunities for LGBT Mobilization in the European Union." *European Political Science Review* 5(2): 279–310.

Ayoub, Phillip M. 2016. *When States Come Out: Europe's Sexual Minorities and the Politics of Visibility*. New York: Cambridge University Press.

Bail, Christopher. 2015. *Terrified: How Anti-Muslim Fringe Organizations Became Mainstream*. Princeton, NJ: Princeton University Press.

Bob, Clifford. 2005. *The Marketing of Rebellion: Insurgents, Media, and International Activism*. Cambridge: Cambridge University Press.

Bob, Clifford. 2012. *The Global Right Wing and the Clash of World Politics*. Cambridge: Cambridge University Press.

Bourne, Randolph S. 1916. "Trans-National America." *Atlantic Monthly*, 118(July): 86–97.

Bourne, Randolph S. 1917. "Twilight of Idols." *Seven Arts*, 11 (1917): 688–702, reprinted in *John Dewey: Critical Assessments*, edited by J.E. Tiles, 199–208. New York: Routledge, 1999.

Braman, Sandra. 2006. *Change of State: Information, Policy, and Power*. Cambridge, MA: MIT Press.

Buss, Doris and Didi Herman. 2003. *Globalizing Family Values: The Christian Right In International Politics*. Minneapolis: University of Minnesota Press.

Carothers, Thomas and Saskia Brechenmacher. 2014. *Closing Space: Democracy and Human Rights Support Under Fire*. Washington, DC: Carnegie Endowment for International Peace.

Carpenter, Charli. 2014. *"Lost" Causes: Agenda Vetting in Global Issue Networks and the Shaping of Human Security*. Ithaca, NY: Cornell University Press.

Castells, Manuel. 2008. "The New Public Sphere: Global Civil Society, Communication Networks, and Global Governance." *The Annals of the American Academy of Political and Social Science* 616(1): 78–93.

Castells, Manuel. 2015. *Networks of Outrage and Hope: Social Movements in the Internet Age*. Cambridge: Polity.

Chuang, Janie A. 2014. "Exploitation Creep and the Unmaking of Human Trafficking Law." *American Journal of International Law* 108(4): 609–649. doi:10.5305/amerjintelaw.108.4.0609.

Clark, Dana, Jonathan Fox, and Kay Treakle, eds. 2003. *Demanding Accountability: Civil-Society Claims and the World Bank Inspection Panel*. Lanham, MD: Rowman & Littlefield.

Coen, David and Jeremy Richardson. 2009. *Lobbying the European Union: Institutions, Actors, and Issues*. Oxford: Oxford University Press.

Conca, Ken. 2015. *An Unfinished Foundation: The United Nations and Global Environmental Governance*. Oxford: Oxford University Press.

Cooley, Alexander and James Ron. 2002. "The NGO Scramble: Organizational Insecurity and the Political Economy of Transnational Action." *International Security* 27(1): 5–39.

Coy, Patrick G. 1997. "Cooperative Accompaniment and Peace Brigades International in Sri Lanka." In *Transnational Social Movements and Global Politics: Solidarity beyond the State*, edited by Jackie Smith, Charles Chatfield, and Ron Pagnucco, 81–100. Syracuse, NY: Syracuse University Press.

Crenson, Mathew. 1971. *The Un-Politics of Air Pollution: A Study of Non-Decisionmaking in the Cities*. Baltimore, MD: Johns Hopkins University Press.

della Porta, Donatella, ed. 2007. *The Global Justice Movement: Cross-National and Transnational Perspectives*. New York: Routledge.

De Waal, Alex. 2016. "Writing Human Rights and Getting it Wrong." *Boston Review*, June 6. Available at: http://bostonreview.nct/world/alex-de-waal-writing-human-rights (accessed December 21, 2017).

Douzinas, Costas. 2007. *Human Rights and Empire: The Political Philosophy of Cosmopolitanism*. New York: Routledge.

Dudziak, Mary L. 2000. *Cold War Civil Rights: Race and the Image of American Democracy*. Princeton, NJ: Princeton University Press.

Dupuy, Kendra E., James Ron, and Aseem Prakash. 2015. "Who Survived? Ethiopia's Regulatory Crackdown on Foreign-Funded NGOs." *Review of International Political Economy* 22: 419–456. doi: 10.1080/09692290.2014.903854.

Englund, Harri. 2006. *Prisoners of Freedom: Human Rights and the African Poor*. Berkeley: University of California Press.

Erickson, Jennifer. 2015. *Dangerous Trade: Arms Exports, Human Rights, and International Reputation*. New York: Columbia University Press.

Fang, Lee and Steve Horn. 2016. "Federal Agents Went Undercover to Spy on Anti-Fracking Movement, Emails Reveal." *The Intercept*, July 19. Available at: https://theintercept.com/2016/07/19/blm-fracking-protests/

Faust, Drew G., ed. 1981.*The Ideology of Slavery: Proslavery Thought in the Antebellum South, 1830–1860*. Baton Rouge, LA: Louisiana State University Press.

Fetner, Tina. 2008. *How the Religious Right Shaped Lesbian and Gay Activism*. Minneapolis: University of Minnesota Press.

Goldsmith, Jack L. and Eric A. Posner. 2005. *The Limits of International Law*. Oxford: Oxford University Press.

Grant, Ruth W. and Robert O. Keohane 2005. "Accountability and Abuses of Power in World Politics." *American Political Science Review* 99(1): 29–43. doi:10.1017.S0003055405051476.

Hadden, Jennifer. 2015. *Networks in Contention: The Divisive Politics of Climate Change*. New York: Cambridge University Press.

Hafner-Burton, Emilie M. 2013. *Making Human Rights a Reality*. Princeton, NJ: Princeton University Press.

Heller, Jeffrey. 2016. "Israel NGO Bill, Seen as Targeting Left-Wing Groups, Becomes Law." *Reuters*, July 11. Available at: http://www.reuters.com/article/us-israel-ngo-idUSKCN0ZR2JB (accessed July 30, 2016).

Herring, Ronald J. and Millind Kandlikar. 2009. "Illicit Seeds: Intellectual Property and the Underground Proliferation of Agricultural Biotechnologies." In *The Politics of Intellectual Property: Contestation over the Ownership, Use, and Control of Knowledge and Information*, edited by Sebastian Haunss and Kenneth C. Shadlen, 56–79. Cheltenham: Edward Elgar.

Hertel, Shareen. 2006. *Unexpected Power: Conflict and Change among Transnational Activists*. Ithaca, NY: Cornell University Press.

Hopgood, Stephen. 2006. *Keepers of the Flame: Understanding Amnesty International*. Ithaca, NY: Cornell University Press.

Imig, Doug and Sidney Tarrow. 2001. "Mapping the Europeanization of Contention: Evidence from a Quantitative Data Analysis." In *Contentious Europeans: Protest and Politics in an Emerging Polity*, edited by Doug Imig and Sidney Tarrow, 27–49. Lanham, MD: Rowman & Littlefield.

Kay, Tamara. 2011. *NAFTA and the Politics of Labor Transnationalism*. Cambridge: Cambridge University Press.

Keck, Margaret E. and Kathryn Sikkink. 1998. *Activists beyond Borders: Advocacy Networks in International Politics*. Ithaca, NY: Cornell University Press.

Keohane, Robert and Joseph Nye. 1971. "Transnational Relations and World Politics." *International Organization* 25(3): 329–349.

Klausen, Jytte. 2009. *The Cartoons That Shook the World*. New Haven, CT: Yale University Press.

Klotz, Audie. 1995. *Norms in International Relations: The Struggle against Apartheid*. Ithaca, NY: Cornell University Press.

Kuperman, Alan J. 2013. "A Model Humanitarian Intervention? Reassessing NATO's Libya Campaign." *International Security*. 38(1): 105–136.

Kuperman, Alan J. and Timothy Crawford. 2006. *Gambling on Humanitarian Intervention*. New York: Routledge.

Lake, David A. and Wendy H. Wong. 2009. "The Politics of Networks: Interests, Power, and Human Rights Norms." In *Networked Politics: Agency, Power, and Governance*, edited by Miles Kahler, 127–150. Ithaca, NY: Cornell University Press.

Lechner, Frank J. and John Boli. 2005. *World Culture: Origins and Consequences*. Malden, MA: Blackwell.

Legum, Gary. 2016. "Joining Forces in Cleveland: European-Style Nationalism Is Poised to Unite with Trump's GOP." *Salon*. July 19. Available at: http://www.salon.com/2016/07/19/joining_forces_in_cleveland_european_style_nationalism_is_poised_to_unite_with_trumps_gop/?source=newsletter (accessed July 30, 2016).

Malet, David. Forthcoming. "Foreign Fighters in the Syrian Civil War." In *Transnational Actors in War and Peace: Militants, Activists, and Corporations in World Politics*, edited by David Malet and Miriam J. Anderson, 124–145. Washington, DC: Georgetown University Press.

Mamdani, Mahmood. 2009. *Saviors and Survivors: Darfur, Politics, and the War on Terror*. New York: Doubleday.

Markoff, John. 2003. "Margins, Centers, and Democracy: The Paradigmatic History of Women's Suffrage." *Signs* 29(1): 85–116.

McAdam, Doug. 1999. *Political Process and the Development of Black Insurgency, 1930–1970*, 2nd edn. Chicago: University of Chicago Press.

McAdam, Doug and Hilary Boudet. 2012. *Putting Social Movements in Their Place: Explaining Opposition to Energy Projects in the United States, 2000–2005*. Cambridge: Cambridge University Press.

McCright, Aaron M. and Riley E. Dunlap. 2003. "Defeating Kyoto: The Conservative Movement's Impact on US Climate Change Policy." *Social Problems* 50(3): 348–373. doi: http://dx.doi.org/10.1525/sp.2003.50.3.348.

Mearsheimer, John J. and Stephen Walt, 2008. *The Israel Lobby and U.S. Foreign Policy*. New York: Farrar, Straus and Giroux.

Meyer, David S. and Suzanne Staggenborg. 1996. "Movements, Countermovements, and the Structure of Political Opportunity." *American Journal of Sociology* 101: 1628–1660.

Morozov, Evgeny. 2012. *The Net Delusion: The Dark Side of Internet Freedom*. New York: Public Affairs.

Murphy, Hannah and Aynsley Kellow. 2013. "Forum Shopping in Global Governance: Understanding States, Business and NGOs in Multiple Arenas." *Global Policy* 4(2): 139–149.

Nash, Thomas. 2012. "Civil Society and Cluster Munitions: Building Blocks of a Global Campaign." In *Global Civil Society 2012*, edited by Mary Kaldor, Henrietta L. Moore, and Sabine Selchow, 124–141. New York: Palgrave Macmillan.

Nepstad, Sharon E. 2008. *Religion and War Resistance in the Plowshares Movement*. Cambridge: Cambridge University Press.

PEN America. 2015. "Global Chilling: The Impact of Mass Surveillance on International Writers." Available at: http://www.pen.org/sites/default/files/globalchilling_2015.pdf (accessed July 30, 2016).

Polasky, Janet. 2015. *Revolutions without Borders: The Call to Liberty in the Atlantic World*. New Haven, CT: Yale University Press.

Porter, Patrick. 2015. *The Global Village Myth: Distance, War, and the Limits of Power*. Washington, DC: Georgetown University Press.

Posner, Eric A. 2014. *The Twilight of Human Rights Law*. New York: Oxford University Press.

Randeria, Shalini. 2003. "Glocalization of Law: Environmental Justice, World Bank, NGOs and the Cunning State in India." *Current Sociology* 51(3–4): 305–328.

Risse, Thomas, Stephen C. Ropp, and Kathryn Sikkink. 2013. *The Persistent Power of Human Rights: From Commitment to Compliance*. Cambridge: Cambridge University Press.

Ron, James, Howard Ramos, and Kathleen Rodgers. 2005. "Transnational Information Politics: NGO Human Rights Reporting, 1986–2000." *International Studies Quarterly* 49(3): 557–588.

Roston, Aram. 2008. *The Man Who Pushed America to War: The Extraordinary Life, Adventures, and Obsessions of Ahmad Chalabi*. New York: Nation Books.

Schattschneider, E.E. 1975. *The Semi-sovereign People: A Realist's View of Democracy in America*. New York: Harcourt Brace.

Sell, Susan K. and Aseem Prakash. 2004. "Using Ideas Strategically: The Contest Between Business and NGO Networks in Intellectual Property Rights." *International Studies Quarterly* 48: 143–175.

Sikkink, Kathryn. 2005. "Patterns of Dynamic Multilevel Governance and the Insider-Outsider Coalition." In *Transnational Protest and Global Activism: People, Passions, and Power*, edited by Donatella della Porta and Sidney Tarrow, 151–173. Lanham, MD: Rowman & Littlefield.

Smith, Jackie. 2008. *Social Movements for Global Democracy*. Baltimore, MD: Johns Hopkins University Press.

Snyder, Jack, and Leslie Vinjamuri. 2006. "Trials and Errors: Principle and Pragmatism in Strategies of International Justice." *International Security* 28(3): 5–44. doi: 10.1162/016228803773100066.

Stroup, Sarah S. 2012. *Borders among Activists: International NGOs in the United States, Britain, and France*. Ithaca, NY: Cornell University Press.

Tarrow, Sidney. 1993. "Modular Collective Action and the Rise of the Social Movement: Why the French Revolution Was Not Enough." *Politics & Society* 21(1): 69–90.

Tarrow, Sidney. 2005. *The New Transnational Activism*. Cambridge: Cambridge University Press.

Walsh, Shannon D. 2016. "Advocacy Networks and Exclusionary Politics: Creating and Dismantling the Violence against Women Law in Nicaragua." Paper prepared for International Studies Association Annual Meeting, March.

Wapner, Paul. 1996. *Environmental Activism and World Civic Politics*. Albany, NY: SUNY Press.

Wendoh, Senorina and Tina Wallace. 2005. "Re-Thinking Gender Mainstreaming in African NGOs and Communities." *Gender & Development* 13(2): 70–79. doi: 10.1080/13552070512331332288.

Willetts, Peter. 1996. *The Conscience of the World: The Influence of Non-Governmental Organizations in the UN System*. Washington, DC: Brookings Institution Press.

Wong, Wendy. 2012. *Internal Affairs: How the Structure of NGOs Transforms Human Rights*. Ithaca, NY: Cornell University Press.

7

Social Movements and Mass Media in a Global Context

DEANA A. ROHLINGER AND CATHERINE CORRIGALL-BROWN

You will not be able to stay home, brother.
You will not be able to plug in, turn on and cop out.
You will not be able to lose yourself on skag
and skip out for beer during commercials,
because the revolution will not be televised.

From the poem and song "The Revolution Will Not Be Televised"
by Gil Scott-Heron, 1970

Introduction

Struck by the dramatic differences in what he saw on television and the protests he witnessed on American college campuses, Gil Scott-Heron used prose to remind activists that media were unfriendly to causes that could not be "brought to you by Xerox in 4 parts without commercial interruptions" ("The Revolution Will Not Be Televised" 1970). Times – and mass media – have changed. In the digital era, the revolution may not be televised, but it probably will be tweeted, blogged, vined, and snapped around the world. Indeed, recent collective actions, such as the Arab Spring, the Occupy movement, the anti-austerity protests, and Never Again, underscore the importance of mass media for social movements.

There are two important limitations in the existing scholarship on social movements and mass media. The first shortcoming is the overemphasis on outcomes. Scholars try to connect strategy, or the link activists make between how they deploy their resources to achieve their goals and their relative success at doing so, to tangible outcomes (Gamson 1990; Ganz 2000). Naturally, this focuses attention on

The Wiley Blackwell Companion to Social Movements, Second Edition. Edited by David A. Snow, Sarah A. Soule, Hanspeter Kriesi, and Holly J. McCammon.
© 2019 John Wiley & Sons Ltd. Published 2019 by John Wiley & Sons Ltd.

the effectiveness of easily measurable outcomes, such as mainstream news coverage (Amenta et al. 2012; Andrews and Caren 2010; Rohlinger 2002; Ryan 1991) or mobilization of individuals in the digital and real worlds (Bennett 2012; Earl and Kimport 2011; Fisher et al. 2005; Mercea 2012; and see Chapter 16 by Earl, in this volume, on technology and social media). The problem is that getting mainstream media attention and mobilizing people to action are not the only reasons activists use mass media. Movement groups also use mass media to communicate with niche (sometimes sympathetic) audiences, develop a collective identity outside the prying eyes of a broader public, and engage in artistic expression (Futrell and Simi 2004; Nip 2004; Roscigno and Danaher 2004). Likewise, activists use mass media to affect cultural change and improve their political legitimacy; the success of which is much more difficult to measure (Rochon 1998). Finally, the focus on outcomes ignores that activists sometimes prioritize authentic communication over media coverage (Sobieraj 2011) and that activists often use very different mediums simultaneously in their social change efforts (Rohlinger 2015).

The second, and more glaring, shortcoming is that sociologists studying movements and mass media rarely consider the applicability of their concepts across political contexts. Most research on the movement-media relationship is country specific. Focusing on one country makes empirical sense as the particulars of a national context shape the relationship between activists and mass media. However, given that social movements increasingly engage in global claims-making (Mattoni 2012), and movements exist in a variety of different national contexts, it is critical that scholars develop conceptual frameworks that transcend the boundaries of the nation-state. For example, the notion that ideas can "cross-over" or move from partisan outlets to mainstream ones is compelling in political contexts such as the US that are relatively open to outsider claims (Berry and Sobieraj 2014; Rohlinger and Brown 2013). Cross-over, however, is virtually irrelevant in authoritarian countries where media are state-controlled and heavily censored. Likewise, "polite protest," or the use of coded language to subtly challenge state positions and actions online, is necessary in China (Yang 2013) but would have little traction in the US media environment, where outlandish rhetoric and creative insults get activists in the news.

This chapter summarizes and extends the existing literature on the movement-media relationship in an attempt to address these two shortcomings. To do so, we offer a strategic choice model which outlines how activists operating in different political contexts use mass media – which includes traditional outlets such as newspapers and television as well as Internet Communication Technologies (ICTs) and social media – to affect change in ways that are (in)visible to a general public. Our model is comprised of two dimensions central to determining how activists use mass media: the *target* of activist communication and the relative openness of a state's *media system*. These two dimensions highlight which mediums activists use in their strategic efforts (and how they use them) as well as the risks associated with these decisions in different political contexts. We use the existing, and increasingly interdisciplinary, literature on social movements and mass media to outline the utility of the strategic choice approach. We conclude the chapter by outlining avenues for future research.

A Strategic Choice Model

Strategy is the lifeblood of social movements. Activists make choices about how to deploy their resources in ways they deem likely to advance their goals (Maney et al. 2012; McCammon 2012). This is no less true of media strategy. Activists craft messages for a particular audience and disseminate their ideas via mediums that they think will help them reach their targets (Rohlinger 2015). As a starting point for understanding how activists use mass media to affect change across space, time, and political contexts, we argue that scholars should consider: (1) the target of communication; and (2) the media context in which activists are operating. Using these two key dimensions, we propose a Strategic Choice Model (see Table 7.1).

Activists use different mass media to talk to different audiences. When activists want to sell their ideas to a broader public and mobilize bystanders to action, they target general interest media outlets such as newspapers and the nightly news to communicate with large swaths of the citizenry (Gamson 1990; Gamson and Meyer 1996; Sobieraj 2010). In contrast, when activists want to update their members about movement activities or get feedback from supporters on movement strategies, they target mediums (and programs) watched, listened to, or navigated to by sympathetic publics (see Chapter 16 by Earl, in this volume, on technology and social media). In Canada and the US, for instance, conservatives have a long history of using radio, rather than general interest media, to reach and mobilize sympathetic publics to action (Fetner and Sanders 2012; Jamieson and Cappella 2010). Likewise, if activists want to engage in creative expression, or cultivate "free spaces" for those interested in movement ideas to engage in dialogue, they use everything from music and newsletters to websites and social media (Earl and Kimport 2011; Eyerman and Jamison 1998, Nip 2004; Wald 1998). Given that activists use different mediums for different purposes, it is important to distinguish the targets of activists' communication and, specifically, whether they are trying to reach *external mass audiences* or *internal and sympathetic audiences*.

It also is necessary to consider how the relationship between the state and mass media affects activists' decision-making regarding which medium to use and to what end. The state's relative control over mass media and which news gets circulated to the citizenry varies dramatically globally.[1] Consequently, some *media systems* are more open to challenger claims than others, which affect the strategic calculations that activists make. In relatively open media systems, such as the US, Canada, the UK, Ireland, France, the Netherlands, and Germany, the state has limited control over what information news outlets circulate to the citizenry. Consequently, challengers looking to raise awareness regarding their efforts to change one or more aspects of the political system and mobilize citizens to action may have an opportunity to use mass media to do so. In relatively closed media systems, such as transitional governments like Egypt during the Arab Spring, Italy, Ukraine, China, and some Latin American countries, the state has a great deal of control over what news is covered and how. State actors in these contexts often use mass media to maintain their authority and control over the citizenry, and, as a result, accurate coverage of movements and movement claims is virtually nonexistent.

Table 7.1 Strategic choice model

		Media target	
		External audiences	Supporters and sympathetic audiences
Relatively open system	Type of media	Broad range of mediums and platforms available to activists including news, op-eds, social media, commercial media (e.g. music and books), and organizational websites.	Broad range of mediums and platforms available to activists including social media, discussion boards, newsletters, email, partisan media, and organizational websites.
	Use of media	Educate the broader public about movement claims, mobilize a public to action, and frame political debates.	Cultivate collective identity, build alternative institutions, and mobilize support or action among sympathizers on movement issues.
	Obstacles and risks	Obstacles include media expertise, the profit focus of mainstream and social media, journalistic routines, and government intervention. Risks include marginalization, censorship, trolling, and covert repression.	Obstacles include organizational resources (time, skill, and connections). Risks include hacking, trolling, and marginalization.
Relatively closed system	Type of media	Limited range of mediums and platforms available to activists who want to avoid repression. Activists who want to attract international attention may try to provoke repression in order to spark international outrage.	Limited range of mediums and platforms available to activists, especially since groups may not be able to create platforms (e.g. websites, newsletters, or discussion forums) that allow them to speak to sympathizers directly.
	Use of media	Educate the broader public, nationally and internationally, through either polite protest or tactics that invite repression, and, hopefully, create international visibility.	Cultivate collective identity and mobilize consensus and support among sympathizers on movement issues.
	Obstacles and risks	Obstacles include state ownership and censorship. Risks include hacking, trolling, overt repression, and death.	Obstacles include state regulation of Internet access and censorship. Risks include hacking, trolling, overt repression, and death.

Again, this model does not focus on media coverage, but on how activists strategically choose venues that allow them to put forward their goals in a political context that may be more or less amenable to their claims. This shift is important because: (1) it considers the various types of mediums, including ICTs, available for challengers' use; (2) it complicates the intent of activists' media use; and (3) it highlights the obstacles and risks challengers face when using mass media in their political projects (see Table 7.1).

Consider the range of options available to activists operating in relatively open media systems. Activists can use news media, music, books, op-eds, political blogs, organizational websites, and social media (among others) to educate the broader public about their cause and their suggested solutions (Isaac 2012; Lievrouw 2011; Theocharis et al. 2015). Challengers who want to communicate with supporters directly can easily target sympathetic media outlets or use ICTs to create virtual spaces for conversation and connection (Earl and Kimport 2011; Rohlinger et al. 2012). As we discuss in detail below, activists face obstacles and risks when they try to connect with a broader public even within relatively open systems. For example, if challengers want their ideas included in mainstream news coverage, they must understand how their media targets operate and the potential biases of those in charge. Even when activists do so, they run the risk of being marginalized in coverage (Gitlin 1980) or, if they engage in illegal activities to draw attention to their issues, of being arrested. However, relying on free social media platforms such as Facebook and Twitter do not remove obstacles and risks. Activists must have the time, skill, and connections to use social media effectively, especially if their issues are likely to attract trolls or hackers.

Activists operating in relatively closed systems, in contrast, have far fewer ways to reach a broader public and face far more risks when the state becomes aware of their efforts to affect political change. Since the state uses mass media to control what (and how) information is disseminated to the citizenry, challengers who want to raise collective consciousness about an issue or mobilize supporters to action must use mediums, such as low-powered radio, art, music, poetry, and traveling political theater, which can fly under the radar of authorities. For instance, the Latin American Boom in the 1960s and 1970s illustrates that activists can use commercial products such as poetry and novels to carefully challenge the political status quo; at least until their work is identified by the state as potentially revolutionary. Of course, using mass media is far more dangerous in countries where the media system is relatively closed. Activists who choose to criticize power holders publicly may find themselves jailed, tortured, or put to death. Despite these risks, some activists will try to use mass media to attract international attention to their causes. As we discuss below, provoking repressive action from the state can be an effective way to both get media attention and mobilize global audiences to pressure a government to change its practices or policies (Keck and Sikkink 1998).

There are three additional points worth making about the strategic choice model. First, media systems should be understood as a continuum along which relatively open and relatively closed represent two general poles. Countries are arrayed along this continuum and there is no ideal model of either pole. Second, media systems are not static. A state's position on the continuum can change over time and in response to political exigencies, such as revolutions and regime changes. Finally, media targets are not mutually exclusive categories. Activists, particularly those operating in relatively closed media systems, have limited opportunities to use media and, consequently, may talk to multiple targets simultaneously, particularly when the risk of repression is high. In short, the strategic choice model is a starting point for understanding how activists' media choices are tied to their political contexts. The remainder of the chapter uses the existing literature on social movement and mass media to highlight the utility of the strategic choice model in different media systems.

Challenging the Status Quo in Open Systems

In countries where the political system is relatively open, social movement actors have access to a broad range of mass media, from traditional news media to social media and organizational websites. The choices activists make regarding how to use media largely depend upon their intended target of communication. However, as we discuss below, activists do not necessarily achieve their desired goals even in a relatively open media system. We outline the obstacles and risks activists' in these systems face.

Using media to target external audiences

Movement actors use mass media to target external audiences in order to spread information about a cause to the broader public, shape political debates and outcomes, and mobilize bystander publics to action. There are a variety of ways that movements can use mass media to disseminate information in an open system. Activists can target general interest media outlets, such as newspapers, radio, and television news, in an effort to get their ideas to large and diverse audiences (Andrews and Caren 2010; Gamson 1990; Ryan 1991). This serves two primary purposes. First, media coverage in general interest outlets can create an opportunity for movement actors to challenge elite power and perspectives as well as shape political debates (Gamson and Meyer 1996; Rojecki 1999). There are a number of examples where movement actors have successfully opened public discourse and affected policy debates around an issue. For example, Sampedro's (1997) work on the anti-military movements in Spain between 1976 and 1993 shows how the movement used media to challenge compulsory military service and pass conscientious objector legislation. Likewise, in 1963, American Civil Rights activists brought the brutality of Southern law enforcement against African Americans into homes worldwide by accessing more sympathetic media in the North (Berger 2011; McAdam 1996). A mere month after Bull Connor had his deputies turn high-pressure fire hoses on black youth, John F. Kennedy publicly promised legislative change.

Second, movement actors use media to mobilize individuals to action (McCarthy and Zald 1977; Snow and Benford 1992). Coverage of the race riots in the USA, for example, helped spread collective protests – and the idea that the riots were a response to racial inequality – within and across cities (Myers 2000), but did not build long-term support for the Black Power Movement (Davenport 2009). Media coverage in mainstream outlets, even if the coverage is negative (Koopmans 2004), can help movements grow their support and membership ranks. Vliegnenthart and his colleagues (2005), for example, found that even just mentioning the name of a movement group in coverage increased its membership.

Activists do not have to rely on mainstream media alone in the digital age. ICTs have dramatically altered how activists communicate with the general public. Movement actors can create websites, open social media accounts, and even construct alternative outlets in an attempt to communicate their issues and goals to a larger audience (Bennett and Segerberg 2012; Earl et al. 2010). These outlets are strategically appealing because activists have more control over how their ideas and issues are presented. For example, activists created Independent Media Centers such as Indymedia to communicate their issues and experiences in their own words when mainstream media were less receptive to their messages (Lievrouw 2011). Websites like Idle No More employs livestreams and webinars to disseminate information about a variety of issues facing Indigenous peoples internationally, and pro-choice activists use the hashtag #ShoutYourAbortion to encourage women to share their stories about how choosing the timing and number of their children is empowering rather than shameful.

Of course, mediums do not operate in isolation. There is evidence that the ideas activists circulate in virtual spaces, given the right conditions, can get picked up by mainstream outlets (Rohlinger and Brown 2013). Organizational websites, online forums, and social media play an important role in mobilization as well (Carty 2015; Earl and Kimport 2011; Fisher et al. 2005, and see Chapter 16 by Earl, in this volume, on technology and social media). ICTs have helped activists mobilize citizens into movements such as Occupy Wall Street and the Tea Party movement (Castells 2012; Gerbaudo 2012; Rohlinger and Bunnage 2015), around causes as diverse as the Vinegar Protests in Brazil, the Indignado protests in Spain (Bastos, Mercea, and Charpentier 2015), and the #soblakaustralia campaign (Dreher, McCallum, and Waller 2016).

Using media to target internal and sympathetic audiences

Activists are not always interested in framing the debate for or mobilizing a general public. When movement actors are testing out new ideas, for instance, they often disseminate their frames in politically like-minded outlets in order to see how members and sympathetic publics respond (Koopmans 2004; Rohlinger 2007). When actors strategically use media aimed at internal and sympathetic audiences, they often do so in order to foster collective identity, or a shared sense of "we-ness" (Polletta and Jasper 2001; Snow and Corrigall-Brown 2015; and Chapter 24 by Cristina Flesher Fominaya, in this volume, on collective identity). Cultivating a collective identity is critical to movements because it predicts member engagement in organizations and helps ensure movement continuity over time (Corrigall-Brown 2011; Hunt and Benford 1994; Klandermans 1997). Mass media have long played a role in collective identity formation. Music, film, books, theater, and poetry can be used to foster a sense of solidarity and collective identity among individuals who share a set of grievances or concerns (Bogad 2016; Eyerman and Jamison 1998; Roy 2010). For example, ex-mill workers wrote anthems of protest. Songs such as Dave McCarn's (1930) "Cotton Mill Colic" sold thousands of copies and were later sung by striking workers across the USA (Roscigno and Danaher 2004). Likewise, books, film, poetry, and online forums have been used to cultivate identities around causes as diverse as labor rights (Isaac 2012), animal rights (Jasper 1997), gay rights (Nip 2004), women's rights (Crossley 2015), and environmental justice (Reed 2005).

Activists across the ideological spectrum use mass media to cultivate collective identity. In fact, online forums may be particularly important for groups that express identities that are not regarded as socially acceptable or that engage in violent activities. Scholars, for instance, find that movement actors have been able to sustain and grow the White Supremacy movement by cultivating collective identity via ICTs (Blee 2002). Online forums such as Stormfront allow supporters to conceal their real-world identities and express their ideology and opinions without censorship (Futrell and Simi 2004; Hier 2000). Additionally, these online forums have both public and "member-only" spaces. This is important because the former allows White Supremacists to maintain a less stigmatized public identity for their regular face-to-face interactions, which can help the movement attract new members (Adams and Roscigno 2005; Caren, Gaby, and Bond 2012), while the latter creates a "free space" for authentic identity expression and action (Douglas et al. 2005).

More obstacles than risks

Movement actors who use legal tactics to affect change face few risks of repression in open media systems. However, that does not mean activists get media attention at will, particularly from mainstream outlets. Much of the literature on movements and media focuses on the obstacles activists face in their attempts to use mainstream media to frame debates and mobilize individuals to action, particularly within the US context. News venues, for instance, have limited "carrying capacities" (Hilgartner and Bosk 1988), which means movements compete with other groups and events for attention. Likewise, journalists do not need activists to comment on their issues and events. They can always ask institutional actors such as politicians, scientists, academics, and law enforcement officers to summarize and interpret movement events and campaigns for the broader public, which may cast movement claims in a negative light (Gamson and Wolfsfeld 1993; Meyer and Gamson 1995). In short, competition for news space and "standing," or voice (Ferree et al. 2002), is a key obstacle that movement actors face in their efforts to frame debates and mobilize outside of sympathetic audiences.

Bias is another obstacle activists face in open media systems. Scholars have identified a number of factors, including the issue, the size of the event, the time of day the event is held, whether the event is staged near a power center, the presence of opponents, and the outbreak of violence that affect whether or not an event is selected for inclusion in the news (McCarthy, McPhail, and Smith 1996; Mueller 1997; Myers and Schaefer Caniglia 2004; Oliver and Myers 1999; Smith et al. 2001). And, when events are covered, there is a wide body of research that illustrates that news media tends to accent the most emotive, violent, and extreme elements of the event (Smith et al. 2001; Sobieraj 2011), thus creating an "illusion of homogeneity" (Turner and Killian 1987). Consequently, activists and their causes often are marginalized in news coverage.

There are risks associated with negative media attention. Movements that are marginalized in mainstream media coverage may experience a loss of public and political support, which makes it more difficult for activists to forward their goals and, in some cases, maintain functioning organizations (Gitlin 1980). Likewise, activists using disruptive or dramatic tactics may find that mass media coverage brings unwanted attention from the state. Even in relatively open media systems, the state may take actions against movements that they regard as a threat to the status quo. The US government, for example, monitored movement communications and used covert methods to disrupt Students for a Democratic Society (SDS) and the Black Panthers in the 1960s and early 1970s (Cunningham 2004; Davenport 2009). In the digital age, activists looking to connect with a broader public may find it difficult to do so if their causes do not fit the guidelines of corporatized social media. Facebook, for instance, continues to come under fire for censoring breast-feeding activist pages under the auspices of indecency while allowing white supremacists to organize without interruption. Trolls also are a risk in the contemporary media environment (Binns 2012). Activists who take their issues online may find that their conversations attract individuals who simply want to disrupt their communication for their own entertainment (Herring et al. 2002).

Engaging from the Shadows: Strategic Media Choices in Closed Systems

In countries where the media system is relatively closed to challengers, using media for political purposes can be quite difficult. This is because the state either owns or controls the media outlets that reach broad swaths of the citizenry and uses its authority to censor challenging ideas and/or determine the flow and content of information. Chinese media, for instance, is largely state-run, and the General Administration of Press and Publication and the State Administration of Radio, Film, and Television monitor media outlets. ICTs, including social media sites, are also under close supervision by state officials. In fact, the Chinese government tries to control citizens' access to information through firewalls (aka "The Great Firewall of China"), which blocks access to certain websites. Journalistic practices in relatively closed systems reinforce state control, making it difficult for activists to get their claims to a broader audience. And, journalists working in relatively closed systems are far more likely to engage in self-censorship, which make it even more difficult for activists to get their ideas to a broader public (Lauk 2009; Whitten-Woodring 2009; Whitten-Woodring and James 2012). As a result, activists in closed systems have limited strategic options because they often must operate below the radar of the state or risk repression (Dong, Kriesi, and Kubler 2015; King, Pan, and Roberts 2013).

In closed media systems, the distinctions between the targets of communication (external audiences and internal and sympathetic publics) are particularly blurred. This is because activists use mass media for consciousness-raising, social analysis, and as a catalyst to political action and social transformation simultaneously. This changes how media are employed to cultivate a collective identity. Sometimes the aim of a film, story, poem, or piece of art is to crystalize a collective identity, often in direct opposition to those with power (Burton 1978; Martin 1997a, 1997b). For example, before the junta of Brazil restricted artistic expression in 1968, filmmakers used the medium to expose the connections among those in the country's ruling class, cultivate dissent, and create a new, more inclusive national identity. After the passage of the junta's Institutional Act Number Five, "obfuscation, double entendre, smoke screening, outlandish and circumvoluted satire" (Burton 1978: 54) were the only way filmmakers could get their political messages past the censors.

The production of media can lead to the formation of a collective identity. During the Pinochet regime, for instance, Chilean women secretly gathered in churches and in homes to make *arpilleras* (small tapestries) documenting the atrocities taking place within the country including the "disappearances" of their husbands and sons. Gathering together in secret to create *arpilleras* provided women a space and medium through which to share their stories and create a narrative of resistance. In this way, the creation of *arpilleras* was important as a goal in and of itself, allowing women to cultivate a shared identity (Moya-Raggio 1984).

International audiences are important external targets in closed media systems. Movement actors who can use mass media to bring international scrutiny to a political problem can create an opportunity to effect political change (Gamson and Meyer 1996; Keck and Sikkink 1998). Getting the attention of international audiences has been made somewhat easier in the digital age. Activists can use websites, discussion boards, email, and social media to expose political problems to a global audience. In Chiapas, Mexico activists associated with the Zapistista movement famously used discussion boards to communicate with journalists and bring their struggles to an international audience (Langman 2005; Rich 1997; Schulz 1998). More recently, activists in Egypt and Tunisia used mobile phones and social media to organize protests, report events, and offer commentary designed to build momentum for democratic change within the countries and attract the attention of the world.

It is important to note that the level of restriction varies across closed media systems. For example, activists operating in Libya, where the government had substantial control over the Internet, and Syria, where governmental officials monitor online communication, had a more difficult time using ICTs, including social media, to their advantage since the states quickly cracked down on communication (Amar and Prashad 2013; Khondker 2011). These cases can be compared to Egypt, which, prior to the Arab Spring, promoted Internet usage among its citizens. By the time the Egyptian government shut down the Internet in January 2011, activists had long established ties online in social media forums such as Facebook and had found other ways to communicate and organize (Cottle 2011; Khamis 2011; Lim 2012). In short, the political outcomes of Arab Spring movements differed, in part, because the media systems, and the resulting strategic options available to activists, varied by country.

More risks than obstacles

The level of restriction in a media system is related to activists' risk of repression. Activists take great risks when they use media to directly challenge elites. They sometimes take these risks in an attempt to frame a debate and draw international media attention to an issue. The Russian punk group Pussy Riot, for instance, protested the "dictatorship" of Russian President Vladimir Putin and his close relationship with the Russian Orthodox Church. Pussy Riot staged unauthorized performances in public spaces, including Moscow's Cathedral of Christ the Savior, and posted them online for the world to view. Three of the group members were arrested, denied bail, and eventually convicted of hooliganism motivated by religious hatred. The trial and sentence sparked international criticism and, months later, the women were released from prison. The band members were credited with bringing international attention to Putin's opposition to gay rights and for reinvigorating feminism in Russia (Gessen 2014).

Even in closed media systems, activists can use media to mobilize public opinion and force the government to act. In China, chat rooms, news groups, and bulletin boards are popular places where activists can carefully question state practices and policies, and sometimes even effect change. For example, the local government covered up a tin mine explosion in Nandan, Guangxi Province, for almost two weeks despite the fact that it had killed 81 people. Once news of the explosion appeared on Internet bulletin boards, a few activists began to ask questions about the incident. A journalist from the state-run *People's Daily* was dispatched to investigate and posted a brief news report regarding the "mysterious" explosion. The report attracted wide attention with tens of thousands of people commenting on the event. Days later, the Chinese Premiere ordered an investigation into the explosion (Yang and Calhoun 2008). Of course, engaging in this type of polite protest is not without risk. Chinese activists who use ICTs to question the state still risk arrest and prosecution for their actions (Yang 2003; Yang and Calhoun 2008).

Conclusion

Activists make choices about how they use media and to what ends. However, they are not free to make these choices without constraint. We identify two key dimensions that shape how activists make these strategic decisions: (1) the target of activist communication; and (2) the relative openness of the media system. By examining these two dimensions, we are able to move beyond simply focusing on types of outlets (traditional outlets or ICTs and social media) as well as media outcomes to understand how activists use media for different goals across political contexts. This framework underscores that conventional media (such as mainstream news), commercial media (such as books and music), and social media (such as Facebook and Twitter) are all shaped by state mandates and, consequently, affect how activists use them in their political projects. Drawing from the existing literature on social movements and mass media, we highlight the utility of this approach and illustrate the obstacles and risks associated with different choices across media systems.

Given the continued evolution of mass media, the movement-media relationship is ripe for research. The rise of social media, for instance, may have important implications for organizations and movement messages. At the organizational level, scholars should consider if social media help organizations to grow or if these social connections online make survival in an increasingly crowded movement environment more difficult. More importantly, scholars need to examine how social media affect individual participation and individual understandings of political change.

At the level of messages, social media may fundamentally change the nature of movement frames and their use in mobilization processes. Social media platforms with character limits encourage less elaborated frames and, possibly, more experimentation with messaging as activists try to keep their ideas trending. Moreover, efforts to keep trending may be helped (or hindered) by the commercial imperatives of popular platforms like Facebook, which actively censor content.

The media-movement relationship is particularly ripe for investigation in closed media systems. Much of the scholarship focuses on open systems and, consequently, much less is known about the strategic choices of activists in closed systems where media are less responsive to (or more repressive of) activists' messages and campaigns. Scholars could examine the conditions that lead to increased (and decreased) repression of activists who use media to challenge elite positions, how knowledge of backdoors to the Internet shape activism, and whether differential access to social media reinforces some types of claims at the expense of others. Scholars also should analyze how international programs, such as those designed to bring ICTs to the developing world, lend themselves to fostering activism in closed media systems. More generally, future research should delineate the dynamic relationships among movements, media, the state, and the public by examining how changing political contexts shape the strategic choices available to activists. Analyzing systems that are becoming more open (or are closing), will allow scholars to assess how activists alter their tactics in response to changing conditions.

Note

1   Communication scholars debate the relationship between the state, citizenry, and mass media in detail. See, for example, the model outlined by Hallin and Mancini (2004) and subsequent debate over its utility (Hallin and Mancini 2012). Communication scholars also consider the influence of media ownership on content (Gans 2003). While these discussions are relevant, they are beyond the scope of the current review.

References

Adams, Josh and Vincent J. Roscigno. 2005. "White Supremacists, Oppositional Culture and the World Wide Web." *Social Forces* 84(2): 759–778. doi: 10.1353/sof.2006.0001.

Amar, Paul Edouard and Vijay Prashad. 2013. *Dispatches from the Arab Spring: Understanding the New Middle East.* Minneapolis: University of Minnesota Press.

Amenta, Edwin, Beth Gharrity Gardner, Amber Celina Tierney, Anaid Yerena, and Thomas Alan Elliott. 2012. "Set in Stories: Standing and Demands in the Newspaper Coverage of SMOs, and the Townsend Plan." *Research on Social Movements, Conflicts and Change* 33.

Andrews, Kenneth and Neal Caren. 2010. "Making the News: Movement Organizations, Media Attention, and the Public Agenda." *American Sociological Review* 75(6): 841–866.

Bastos, Marco, Dan Mercea, and Arthur Charpentier. 2015. "The Interplay Between Ongoing Protests and Social Media." *Journal of Communication* 65: 320–350.

Bennett, Lance. 2012. "The Personalization of Politics: Political Identity, Social Media, and Changing Patterns of Participation." *The Annals of the American Academy of Political and Social Science* 644(1): 20–39.

Bennett, Lance and Alexandra Segerberg. 2012. "The Logic of Connective Action." *Information, Communication & Society* 15(5): 739–768.

Berger, Martin. 2011. *Seeing through Race: A Reinterpretation of Civil Rights Photography*. Los Angeles: University of California Press.

Berry, Jeffrey and Sarah Sobieraj. 2014. *The Outrage Industry: Political Opinion Media and the New Incivility*. New York: Oxford University Press.

Binns, Amy. 2012. "DON'T FEED THE TROLLS!" *Journalism Practice* 6(4): 547–562. doi: 10.1080/17512786.2011.648988.

Blee, Kathleen. 2002. *Inside Organized Racism: Women in the Hate Movement*. Los Angeles: University of California Press.

Bogad, L.M. 2016. *Electoral Guerrilla Theatre: Radical Ridicule and Social Movements*. 2nd edn. New York: Routledge.

Burton, Julianne. 1978. "The Camera as 'Gun': Two Decades of Culture and Resistance in Latin America." *Latin American Perspectives* 5(1): 49–76.

Caren, Neal, Sarah Gaby, and Kay Bond. 2012. "A Social Movement Online Community: Stormfront and the White Nationalist Movement." *Research in Social Movements, Conflicts and Change* 33.

Carty, Victoria. 2015. *Social Movements and New Technology*. Boulder, CO: Westview Press.

Castells, Manuel. 2012. *Networks of Outrage and Hope: Social Movements in the Internet Age*. Malden, MA: Polity Press.

Corrigall-Brown, Catherine. 2011. *Patterns of Protest: Trajectories of Participation in Social Movements*. Redwood City, CA: Stanford University Press.

Cottle, Simon. 2011. "Media and the Arab Uprisings of 2011: Research Notes." *Journalism* 12(5): 647–659. doi: 10.1177/1464884911410017.

Crossley, Alison Dahl. 2015. "Facebook Feminism: Social Media, Blogs, and New Technologies of Contemporary U.S. Feminism." *Mobilization: An International Quarterly* 20(2): 253–268. doi: 10.17813/1086-671X-20-2-253.

Cunningham, David. 2004. *There's Something Happening Here: The New Left, the Klan, and FBI Counterintelligence*. Los Angeles: University of California Press.

Davenport, Christian. 2009. *Media Bias, Perspective, and State Repression: The Black Panther Party*. New York: Cambridge University Press.

Dong, Lisheng, Hanspeter Kriesi, and Daniel Kubler, eds. 2015. *Urban Mobilizations and New Media in Contemporary China*. Burlington, VT: Ashgate.

Douglas, Karen, Craig McGarty, Ana-Maria Bliuc, and Girish Lala. 2005. "Understanding Cyberhate: Social Competition and Social Creativity in Online White Supremacist Groups." *Social Science Computer Review* 23(1): 68–76.

Dreher, Tanja, Kerry McCallum, and Lisa Waller. 2016. "Indigenous Voices and Mediatized Policy-making in the Digital Age." *Information, Communication & Society* 19(1): 23–39. doi: 10.1080/1369118X.2015.1093534.

Earl, Jennifer and Katrina Kimport. 2011. *Digitally Enabled Social Change: Activism in the Internet Age*. Cambridge, MA: MIT Press.

Earl, Jennifer, Katrina Kimport, Greg Prieto, Carly Rush, and Kimberly Reynoso. 2010. "Changing the World, One Webpage at a Time: Conceptualizing and Explaining 'Internet Activism." *Mobilization* 15(4): 425–446.

Eyerman, Ron and Andrew Jamison. 1998. *Music and Social Movements: Mobilizing Traditions in the Twentieth Century*. Cambridge: Cambridge University Press.

Ferree, Myra, William Gamson, Jürgen Gerhards, and Dieter Rucht. 2002. *Shaping Abortion Discourse: Democracy and the Public Sphere in Germany and the United States*. New York: Cambridge University Press.

Fetner, Tina and Carrie Sanders. 2012. "Similar Strategies, Different Outcomes: Institutional Histories of the Christian Right of Canada and of the United States." In *Strategies for Social Change*, edited by Gregory Maney, Rachel Kutz-Flamenbaum, Deana Rohlinger and Jeff Goodwin, 245–262. Minneapolis: University of Minnesota Press.

Fisher, Dana, Kevin Stanley, David Berman, and Gina Neff. 2005. "How Do Organizations Matter? Mobilization and Support for Participants at Five Globalization Protests." *Social Problems* 52(1): 102–121.

Futrell, Robert and Pete Simi. 2004. "Free Spaces, Collective Identity, and the Persistence of U.S. White Power Activism." *Social Problems* 51(1): 16–42.

Gamson, William. 1990. *The Strategy of Social Protest.* 2nd edn. Homewood, IL: Dorsey Press.

Gamson, William and David Meyer. 1996. "Framing Political Opportunity." In *Comparative Perspectives on Social Movements: Political Opportunities, Mobilizing Structures, and Cultural Framings*, edited by Doug McAdam, John D. McCarthy, and Mayer N. Zald, 275–290. Cambridge: Cambridge University Press.

Gamson, William and Gadi Wolfsfeld. 1993. "Movement and Media as Interacting Systems." *The Annals of the American Academy of Political and Social Science* 578: 104–125.

Gans, Herbert. 2003. *Democracy and the News.* New York: Oxford University Press.

Ganz, Marshall. 2000. "Resources and Resourcefulness: Strategic Capacity in the Unionization of California Agriculture, 1959–1966." *American Journal of Sociology* 105(4): 1003–1062.

Gerbaudo, Paolo. 2012. *Tweets and the Streets: Social Media and Contemporary Activism.* London: Pluto Press.

Gessen, Masha. 2014. *Words Will Break Cement: The Passion of Pussy Riot.* New York: Riverhead Books.

Gitlin, Todd. 1980. *The Whole World Is Watching: Mass Media in the Making and Unmaking of the New Left.* Los Angeles: University of California Press.

Hallin, Daniel and Paolo Mancini. 2004. *Comparing Media Systems: Three Models of Media and Politics.* Cambridge: Cambridge University Press.

Hallin, Daniel and Paolo Mancini, eds. 2012. *Comparing Media Systems Beyond the Western World.* Cambridge: Cambridge University Press.

Herring, Susan, Kirk Job-Sluder, Rebecca Scheckler, and Sasha Barab. 2002. "Searching for Safety Online: Managing 'Trolling' in a Feminist Forum." *The Information Society* 18(5): 371–384. doi: 10.1080/01972240290108186.

Hier, Sean P. 2000. "The Contemporary Structure of Canadian Racial Supremacism: Networks, Strategies and New Technologies." *The Canadian Journal of Sociology/Cahiers canadiens de sociologie* 25(4): 471–494. doi: 10.2307/3341609.

Hilgartner, Stephen and Charles Bosk. 1988. "The Rise and Fall of Social Problems: A Public Arenas Model." *American Journal of Sociology* 94: 53–78.

Hunt, Scott, and Robert D. Benford. 1994. "Identity Talk in the Peace and Justice Movement." *Journal of Contemporary Ethnography* 22: 488–517.

Isaac, Larry. 2012. "Literary Activists and Battling Books: The Labor Problem Novel as Contentious Movement Media." *Research on Social Movements, Conflicts and Change* 33.

Jamieson, Kathleen Hall and Joesph Cappella. 2010. *Echo Chamber: Rush Limbaugh and the Conservative Media Establishment.* New York: Oxford University Press.

Jasper, James. 1997. *The Art of Moral Protest: Culture, Biography, and Creativity in Social Movements.* Chicago: University of Chicago Press.

Keck, Margaret and Kathryn Sikkink. 1998. *Activists Beyond Borders: Advocacy Networks in International Politics.* Ithaca, NY: Cornell University Press.

Khamis, Sahar. 2011. "The Transformative Egyptian Media Landscape: Changes, Challenges and Comparative Perspectives." *International Journal of Communication* 5.

Khondker, Habibul Haque. 2011. "Role of the New Media in the Arab Spring." *Globalizations* 8(5): 675–679.

King, Gary, Jennifer Pan, and Margaret E. Roberts. 2013. "How Censorship in China Allows Government Criticism but Silences Collective Expression." *American Political Science Review* 107(2): 326–343. doi: 10.1017/S0003055413000014.

Klandermans, Bert. 1997. *The Social Psychology of Protest.* New York: John Wiley & Sons, Inc.

Koopmans, Ruud. 2004. "Movements and Media: Selection Processes and Evolutionary Dynamics in the Public Sphere." *Theory and Society* 33: 367–391.

Langman, Lauren. 2005. "From Virtual Public Spheres to Global Justice: A Critical Theory of Internetworked Social Movements." *Sociological Theory* 23(1): 42–74.

Lauk, Epp. 2009. "Reflections on Changing Patterns of Journalism in the New EU Countries." *Journalism Studies* 10(1): 69–84. doi: 10.1080/14616700802560542.

Lievrouw, Leah. 2011. *Alternative and Activist New Media: Digital Media and Society.* New York: Polity.

Lim, Merlyna. 2012. "Clicks, Cabs, and Coffee Houses: Social Media and Oppositional Movements in Egypt, 2004–2011." *Journal of Communication* 62(2): 231–248. doi: 10.1111/j.1460-2466.2012.01628.x.

Maney, Gregory, Rachel Kutz-Flamenbaum, Deana Rohlinger, and Jeff Goodwin, eds. 2012. *Strategies for Social Change.* Minneapolis: University of Minnesota Press.

Martin, Michael T. 1997a. *New Latin American Cinema,* vol. 1: "Theories, Practices, and Transcontinental Articulations." Michigan: Wayne State University Press.

Martin, Michael T. 1997b. *New Latin American Cinema.* vol. 2: "Studies of national cinemas." Michigan: Wayne State University Press.

Mattoni, Alice. 2012. *Media Practices and Protest Politics: How Precarious Workers Mobilise.* Burlington, VT: Ashgate Publishing, Ltd.

McAdam, Doug. 1996. "The Framing Function of Movement Tactics: Strategic Dramaturgy in the American Civil Rights Movement." In *Comparative Perspectives of Social Movements: Political Opportunities, Mobilizing Structures, and Cultural Framings,* edited by Doug McAdam, John D. McCarthy and Mayer N. Zald, 338–355. Cambridge: Cambridge University Press.

McCammon, Holly. 2012. *The U.S. Women's Jury Movement and Strategic Adaptation: A More Just Verdict.* Cambridge: Cambridge University Press.

McCarthy, John D., Clark McPhail, and Jackie Smith. 1996. "Images of Protest: Dimensions of Selection Bias in Media Coverage of Washington Demonstrations, 1982 and 1991." *American Sociological Review* 61: 478–499.

McCarthy, John D. and Mayer N. Zald. 1977. "Resource Mobilization and Social Movements: A Partial Theory." *American Journal of Sociology* 82(6): 1212–1241.

Mercea, Dan. 2012. "Digital Prefigurative Participation: The Entwinement of Online Communication and Offline Participation in Protest Events." *New Media & Society* 14(1): 153–169.

Meyer, David and Joshua Gamson. 1995. "The Challenge of Cultural Elites: Celebrities and Social Movements." *Sociological Inquiry* 65: 181–206.

Moya-Raggio, Eliana. 1984. "'Arpilleras': Chilean Culture of Resistance." *Feminist Studies* 49: 277–290.

Mueller, Carol McClurg. 1997. "International Press Coverage of East German Protest Events, 1989." *American Sociological Review* 62(5): 820–832.

Myers, Daniel. 2000. "The Diffusion of Collective Violence: Infectiousness, Susceptibility, and Mass Media Networks." *American Journal of Sociology* 106(1): 173–208.

Myers, Daniel and Beth Schaefer Caniglia. 2004. "All the Rioting That's Fit To Print: Selection Effects in National Newspaper Coverage of Civil Disorders, 1968–1969." *American Sociological Review* 69(4): 519–543.

Nip, Joyce. 2004. "The Queer Sisters and Its Electronic Bulletin Board: A Study of the Internet for Social Movement Mobilization." *Information, Communication & Society* 7(1): 23–49.

Oliver, Pamela and Daniel Myers. 1999. "How Events Enter the Public Sphere: Conflict, Location, and Sponsorship in Local Newspaper Coverage of Events." *American Journal of Sociology* 105: 463–505.

Polletta, Francesca and James Jasper. 2001. "Collective Identity and Social Movements." *Annual Review of Sociology* 27: 283–305.

Reed, Thomas Vernon. 2005. *The Art of Protest: Culture and Activism from the Civil Rights Movement to the Streets of Seattle*. Minneapolis: University of Minnesota Press.

Rich, Paul. 1997. "NAFTA and Chiapas." *Annals of the American Academy of Political and Social Science* 550: 72–84.

Rochon, Thomas. 1998. *Culture Moves: Ideas, Activism, and Changing Values*. Princeton, NJ: Princeton University Press.

Rohlinger, Deana. 2002. "Framing the Abortion Debate: Organizational Resources, Media Strategies, and Movement-Countermovement Dynamics." *The Sociological Quarterly* 43(4): 479–507.

Rohlinger, Deana. 2007. "American Media and Deliberative Democratic Processes." *Sociological Theory* 25(2): 122–148.

Rohlinger, Deana. 2015. *Abortion Politics, Mass Media, and Social Movements in America*. New York: Cambridge University Press.

Rohlinger, Deana and Jordan Brown. 2013. "Mass Media and Institutional Change: Organizational Reputation, Strategy, and Outcomes in the Academic Freedom Movement." *Mobilization: The International Quaterly Review of Social Movement Research* 18(1): 41–64.

Rohlinger, Deana, and Leslie Bunnage. 2015. "Connecting People to Politics Over Time? Internet Communication Technology and Retention in MoveOn.org and the Florida Tea Party Movement." *Information, Communication & Society* 18(5): 539–552.

Rohlinger, Deana, Ben Kail, Miles Taylor, and Sarrah Conn. 2012. "Outside the Mainstream: Analzying Coverage of Social Movement Organizations in Mainstream, Liberal/Left and Conservative News Outlets." *Research on Social Movements, Conflicts and Change* 33: 51–80.

Rojecki, Andrew. 1999. *Silencing the Opposition: Antinuclear Movements and the Media in the Cold War*. Chicago: University of Illinois Press.

Roscigno, Vincent and William Danaher. 2004. *The Voice of Southern Labor: Radio, Music, and Textile Strikes, 1929–1934*. Minneapolis: University of Minnesota Press.

Roy, William G. 2010. *Reds, Whites, and Blues: Social Movements, Folk Music, and Race in the United States*. Princeton, NJ: Princeton University Press.

Ryan, Charlotte. 1991. *Prime Time Activism: Media Strategies for Grassroots Organizing*. Boston: South End Press.

Sampedro, Viktor. 1997. "The Media Politics of Social Protest." *Mobilization* 2(2): 185–205.

Schulz, Markus. 1998. "Collective Action Across Borders: Opportunity Structures, Network Capacities, and Communicative Praxis in the Age of Advanced Globalization." *Sociological Perspectives* 41(3): 587–616.

Smith, Jackie, John D. McCarthy, Clark McPhail, and Boguslaw Augustyn. 2001. "From Protest to Agenda Building: Description Bias in Media Coverage of Protest Events in Washington, D.C." *Social Forces* 79(4): 1397–1423.

Snow, David A. and Robert D. Benford. 1992. "Master Frames and Cycles of Protest." In *Frontiers in Social Movement Theory*, edited by Aldon Morris and Carol McClurg Mueller, 133–155. New Haven, CT: Yale University Press.

Snow, David A. and Catherine Corrigall-Brown. 2015. "Collective Identity." In *International Encyclopedia of the Social and Behavioral Sciences*, edited by Neil Smelser and Paul Baltes, 2212–2219. New York: Elsevier.

Sobieraj, Sarah. 2010. "Reporting Conventions: Activists, Journalists, and the Thorny Struggle for Political Visibility." *Social Problems* 57(4): 505–528.

Sobieraj, Sarah. 2011. *Soundbitten: The Perils of Media-Centered Political Activism*. New York: New York University Press.

Theocharis, Yannis, Will Lowe, Jan W. van Deth, and Gema García-Albacete. 2015. "Using Twitter to Mobilize Protest Action: Online Mobilization Patterns and Action Repertoires in the Occupy Wall Street, Indignados, and Aganaktismenoi Movements." *Information, Communication & Society* 18(2): 202–220. doi: 10.1080/1369118X.2014.948035.

Turner, Ralph and Lewis Killian. 1987. *Collective Behavior*. Englewood Cliffs, NJ: Prentice-Hall, Inc.

Vliegenthart, Rens, Dirk Oegema, and Bert Klandermans. 2005. "Media Coverage and Organizational Support in the Dutch Environmental Movement." *Mobilization* 10(3): 365–381.

Wald, Gayle. 1998. "Just a Girl? Music, Feminism, and the Cultural Construction of Female Youth." *Signs* 23(3): 585–610.

Whitten-Woodring, Jenifer. 2009. "Watchdog or Lapdog? Media Freedom, Regime Type, and Government Respect for Human Rights." *International Studies Quarterly* 53(3): 595–625. doi: 10.1111/j.1468-2478.2009.00548.x.

Whitten-Woodring, Jenifer and Patrick James. 2012. "Fourth Estate or Mouthpiece? A Formal Model of Media, Protest, and Government Repression." *Political Communication* 29(2): 113–136. doi: 10.1080/10584609.2012.671232.

Yang, Guobin. 2003. "The Internet and Civil Society in China: A Preliminary Assessment." *Journal of Contemporary China* 12(36): 453–475.

Yang, Guobin. 2013. *The Power of the Internet in China: Citizen Activism Online*. New York: Columbia University Press.

Yang, Guobin and Craig Calhoun. 2008. "Media, Power, and Protest in China: From the Cultural Revolution to the Internet." *Harvard Asia Pacific Review* 9(2): 9–13.

Part II
Social Movement Organizations, Fields, and Dynamics

8

Networks and Fields

Nick Crossley and Mario Diani

Introduction

The importance of social networks is widely recognized by social movement scholars (Crossley and Krinsky 2015; Diani and McAdam 2003). In some cases, they are preconditions or inhibiting factors of mobilization, and they are often important channels for recruitment or obstacles that recruiters must circumvent. On another level, it is increasingly common, following Diani (1992), to define movements as social networks; that is, networks of individual activists, of groups and organizations, and/ or of protest and other movement events and activities. To speak of movements is to suggest that actors and events that are discrete nevertheless connect, interact, and form a (reticular) structure, which is bigger than any one of them; they combine to form a network.

In this chapter, we review some of the key literature on networks and movements. We look first at the issue of networks and mobilization, asking why and how networks can either facilitate or inhibit mobilization and exploring their importance for the diffusion of movement goods. This is followed by a discussion of the role of networks in recruitment. The second part looks at social movements as a particular network form, usually embedded in larger organizational settings (recently and increasingly referred to as "fields"). First, we chart the development since the 1970s in social movement research of approaches looking at collective action fields or related concepts such as areas, sectors, etc. Then we illustrate the variety of network patterns through which collective action may be coordinated within fields. We conclude with a few remarks on how to bring a time dimension into the analysis of movement networks.

The Wiley Blackwell Companion to Social Movements, Second Edition. Edited by David A. Snow, Sarah A. Soule, Hanspeter Kriesi, and Holly J. McCammon.
© 2019 John Wiley & Sons Ltd. Published 2019 by John Wiley & Sons Ltd.

From Structure to Action: How Networks Facilitate Collective Action

Networks and mobilization

One of the earliest studies of social movements to focus explicitly on social networks was Tilly's (1978) *From Mobilization to Revolution*. Drawing on White's (2008) concept of "catnets," Tilly argued that disadvantaged groups are more likely to mobilize when their members both form a relatively dense network and share a common identity (e.g. social class or ethnicity). Earlier accounts understood mobilization to be a response to social fragmentation and the alienation it causes, but Tilly observed that mobilization requires coordination, which entails communication and thus connection (see also Marwell and Oliver 1993), and often involves the exchange and mobilization of resources, which again presupposes connection and thus networks. A mass of isolated individuals is poorly placed to mobilize (see also Crossley 2015). What "cat" (short for "category") adds to "net" (short for "network") in the catnet concept is a sense of the cultural elements inherent in a common identity and purpose, around which those involved might mobilize. Aggrieved populations are more likely to mobilize where their members are both connected through networks and share a common identity to which organizers can appeal and around which feelings of solidarity can be built. This conjunction of "cat" to "net" is significant because it signals a recognition which runs through much work on movements and networks: we best understand and explain the importance and effects of networks in movements where we grasp their cultural aspects (McLean 2016; Mische 2003).

Beyond coordination and access to resources, Tilly hints at the role of networks in generating incentive structures for collective action. As Olson (1965) famously argued, the value of the public goods typically pursued by social movements may not be a sufficient incentive to motivate mobilization because individuals stand to benefit from them whether or not they directly participate in their procurement, making it "more rational" to "free ride" on the efforts of others, an attitude which inhibits collective action if adopted *en masse*. Some have questioned the model of rationality deployed in this argument, with good reason. Others, including Tilly, explore the possibility of additional incentives which might tip the balance in favor of mobilization, and networks are among the mechanisms considered. In a relatively dense network, where the actions or inactions of individuals can be both easily observed and rewarded or punished, collective decisions to act can be enforced. Furthermore, if we relax the rationality assumptions of Olson's model, then we might expect dense networks or dense ego-nets to serve as a reference group, shaping the way in which individuals perceive activism and respond to their situation. For example, if most of the people whom you know and who share your (disadvantaged) situation elect to mobilize and fight, then fighting is more likely to seem like the appropriate line of action to you.

The importance of network density for collective action has been emphasized and explored in a more theoretical vein by Coleman (1988, 1990). Building upon observations such as those above, Coleman observes that where dense networks are relatively cut off from external influence ("closed"), they can incentivize actions that are deemed highly problematic in the communities they are cut off from and may demand and indeed secure personal sacrifices from their members, which seem irrational to an outsider. Suicide bombers are one example he cites. In this case, reinforcement by network neighbors and the emergent culture of the network persuade the individual to put certain collective goals and values above their own basic individual interest in survival. In addition, Coleman points to the social capital typically generated in dense networks. He argues that life in dense networks is often such that it is beneficial for those involved to cooperate with and support others, and to prove dependable and trustworthy. These are constraints upon the individual in such networks but because the constraints are generalized through the network, there are also opportunities from which participants can benefit. For instance, trust and mutual support within a network facilitate forms of action, both individual and collective, which would not be possible in their absence. Again, this suggests that, other things being equal, mobilization is more likely on the behalf of communities whose members are densely networked. Networks generate social capital upon which movements can draw.

The very tight-knit communities which often form around traditional industries such as mining, steel, and dock work, provide one example of this. Such industries typically manifest high levels of unionism and industrial action. However, important work on the Paris Commune by Gould (1995) suggests that the political efficacy of the class identities that form around such types of work is conditional upon geographical proximity, diminishing when workforces are geographically displaced. Gould argues that the relocation of workers into mixed class neighborhoods in the years prior to the Commune greatly reduced the role of class identity in the French political struggle. Also, class networks and solidarity were replaced by those of neighborhood and it was neighborhood networks, in the end, which mobilized the revolt. Interestingly, Gould (1991, 1993) finds evidence of greater solidarity and self-sacrifice among those communard battalions involving higher concentrations of members from the same neighborhood, reinforcing the above argument that pre-existing networks lend social capital to movement mobilizations. Similar effects of long-term shifts in network structures for mobilization possibilities have been demonstrated by Bearman (1993) in his work on the English Civil War and have been theorized by Diani (2000), who draws on Rokkan's (1970) notion of political cleavages.

Gould's work identifies a number of local neighborhood clubs which provided the crucible for the formation of the networks which, in turn, mobilized the Commune. These clubs were "foci," to use Feld's (1981) term, which drew people with similar interests (in this case, neighbors seeking local entertainment) together, facilitating the formation of ties between them. Other examples of foci might be university campuses (Crossley 2008), or perhaps particular spaces on campus where individuals with specific political interests hang out (Crossley and Ibrahim 2012; Ibrahim and Crossley 2017; Zhao 1998), and churches. A number of early studies of the black civil rights movement in the USA, for example, point to the importance of churches in networking potential participants and thereby facilitating their collective mobilization (McAdam 1982; Morris 1984; but see also Biggs 2006). The black population was able to mobilize, it is argued, because its members were connected and could therefore communicate, coordinate, exchange resources and, where necessary, provide one another with additional incentivization.

If networks can serve as mobilizing structures, however, they can equally inhibit mobilization. McAdam (1982) observes that mobilization in the civil rights struggle was lower in better integrated states, for example, an association that he explains by reference to the social control which whites were able to exert over blacks where better relations existed between them. Borrowing from Coleman, we might argue that black populations were most conducive for mobilization where their members were densely connected to one another but these networks were relatively closed, admitting little positive contact with white communities. And incorporating catnets, we might add that networks were most effective where their members shared a common ethnic identity. In a slight variation on this, Biggs (2006) observes that black churches only contributed to mobilization where the pastor was mobilized and enjoyed links to the wider movement. Where this was not the case, he notes, the likelihood of mobilization was actually reduced. This might point to the positive significance of "brokerage," a further network effect. Pastors who had ties to the movement were able to serve as a bridge (broker) connecting it to its constituency (and them to it). However, Biggs is equally interested in the potentially conservative effects of networks. They can discourage mobilization (e.g. by attaching negative sanctions to participation) as much as they can incentivize it. If the prevailing opinion in any network to which an individual belongs is that respectable people do not become involved in activism, then they themselves are less likely to become involved.

Whichever way their influence works, the evidence suggests that networks do have a clear and sometimes strong influence. Individual decisions to participate in mobilization are not made in isolation because individuals do not exist in isolation. They are always already connected to other people who inform and influence their decision (for a discussion of such effects in parliamentary politics, see Zuckerman 2005), and who may or may not be willing to coordinate with them in collective actions, exchanging relevant resources, etc.

Brokerage and diffusion

The importance of the concept of brokerage should be underlined. Whatever their importance, dense and closed networks have certain shortcomings (Burt 1992, 2005). In some contexts, for example, closure may mean reduced access to important resources and stimuli, and the presence of brokers, who can channel such goods into an otherwise closed network, may be crucial. It is for this reason that McAdam, Tarrow, and Tilly (2001) identify brokerage as a key condition for mobilization in their landmark study, *Dynamics of Contention*.

This leads us to a much wider literature, moreover, on the role of social networks in the diffusion of movement-relevant resources, frames, identities, and even triggers (Edwards 2014; Givan, Soule, and Roberts 2010; Hedstrom 1994; Hedstrom, Sandell, and Stern 2000; Soule 1997). Since the advent of resource mobilization theory, social movement theorists have understood that movement mobilization is often dependent upon the movement, exchange, and diffusion of various goods between its (potential) participants, and thus upon networks. Recent work on this topic has begun to narrow down and explore the various properties of networks and network positions which best enable such flows (for a review, see Edwards 2014). Some network structures and positions are more conducive to diffusion (and thus mobilization) than others. Importantly, moreover, where studies have focused upon cultural goods, there is an increasing recognition of the interaction between such goods and social networks. Networks facilitate the movement of culture from one group to another but the ties which constitute networks are themselves culturally constituted, and processes of diffusion through a network are often dependent upon cultural variables in addition to the raw existence (or not) of ties (Edwards 2014; McLean 2016; see also Chapter 13 by Soule and Roggeband, in this volume). Edwards (2014), for example, argues that cultural identity influenced the susceptibility of certain British suffragettes to adopt more militant tactics which began to diffuse through their networks after 1910.

Recruitment

Network effects are also widely referred to in studies of individual recruitment. Various studies suggest: (1) that activists seek to recruit participants for their actions, movements, and organizations from amongt their non-activist friends (Crossley and Ibrahim 2012); (2) that non-activists often become involved by this route (McAdam and Paulsen 1993; Snow, Zurcher, and Ekland-Olson 1980, 1983), particularly in totalitarian contexts, where open recruitment is forbidden (Opp and Gern 1993); (3) that initial expressions of interest are more likely to be translated into full participation where those considering participation enjoy ties to others who become involved, particularly in cases of "high risk activism," where contemplation of likely negative consequences might otherwise dampen initial enthusiasm (McAdam 1986); and (4) that connection to an activist encourages both a more positive perception of activism and assimilation of an activist identity (Passy 2001, 2003). There is also some evidence that activists are more inclined to leave a social movement when their key contacts do too (Sandel 1999). The importance of ties to recruitment may vary across movements, however (Passy and Monsch 2014). Some studies find little to no influence (Ray et al. 2003) and some suggest that both network position and wider contextual factors make a difference. Analyzing the networks of individuals who followed through on an initial expression of interest in the 1964 Freedom Summer action and comparing them with those who did not, for example, Fernandez and McAdam (1988) found both that positive network effects were stronger in those who were "prominent" in the network (i.e. those who had a relatively high number of ties to others and who were tied to others who were similarly well connected, a variable referred to more widely as "eigenvector centrality"), and that this effect was much greater in contexts (i.e. on university campuses) where mobilization was generally low and other mechanisms could not be counted upon to secure follow-through.

In addition, there is also evidence, akin to that discussed in the population-level studies described above, that network connections can inhibit recruitment and dissuade would-be activists from involvement, effectively serving as a social control mechanism (Kitts 2000; Snow et al. 1980, 1983). In the case of student activism, for example, parents, lecturers, and friends have all been shown to be capable of inhibiting an individual's inclination to activism where they either disagree with the cause for which the individual is inclined to act or anticipate negative consequences for the individual if they participate (McAdam 1986). Whether or not an individual is recruited to a movement or protest, therefore, depends not only upon whether they have positive ties to an activist within their ego-net (which may facilitate recruitment or increase its likelihood) but also upon whether their involvement is resisted by others in their ego-net.

Others may inhibit an individual's recruitment and involvement in less direct ways too. Ties to romantic partners, dependent children, parents, and employers, to name only the most obvious examples, all entail responsibilities, which consume time and energy, making the individual less available for activism. And even where such ties do not prevent activism completely, they may undermine it, as Goodwin's (1997) work on the Huk rebellion in the Philippines illustrates. The decision of rebel leaders to separate activists from their romantic partners and children, Goodwin shows, served to undermine morale, leading to a collapse of solidarity and discipline. Out of sight does not necessarily mean out of mind and connections to others, or in this case enforced separation from them, exerts "action at a distance."

From Action to Structure: How Collective Action Produces Emerging Forms of Social Organization

Fields of collective action

The notion that collective action develops in fields inhabited by a variety of actors and that we need to go beyond studies centered not only on specific organizations, but also on specific movements, is far from new. It has been articulated in different forms since the 1960s. For example, in their exploration of anti-pornography organizations, Curtis and Zurcher (1973) suggested that their variable properties were best understood taking into account their ties to other actors in local community multi-organizational fields. Introducing concepts such as "social movement industries" and "social movement sector," resource mobilization theorists took into account the overall set of organizations engaged in various combinations of cooperative and competitive strategies to pursue collective goals (see Zald and McCarthy 1980).

These approaches broadly supported a pragmatic view of fields consistent with DiMaggio and Powell's definition as "organizations that, in the aggregate, represent a recognized area of institutional life" (DiMaggio and Powell 1983: 64–65), without necessarily buying into the various hypotheses of the neo-institutional approach such as the one about isomorphism. From a different angle, scholars like Melucci referred primarily to fields as the relational settings for the mechanisms that define collective action. Strongly influenced by Gestalt theory, Melucci's research on social movement "areas" in Milan in the early 1980s (Melucci 1984, 1989) focused on the processes through which mutual recognition and shared understandings emerge among actors, and thus on the cultural dimension of fields. Despite being very influential in sociology at large, including some social movement theorists (e.g. Crossley 2002; Swidler 1986), the approach to fields elaborated by Bourdieu (1992) has developed quite separately from the study of networks and has inspired a limited number of movement studies (e.g. Mayrl 2013).

Through the 1990s and the 2000s, a few studies elaborated on the notion of field from an interactionist, non-structuralist perspective. They focused on the definition of field boundaries, the characteristics and strategies of the main actors within a field, and the environmental conditions affecting its emergence and consolidation.

However, this was mostly done without paying attention to how interactions combined in structural patterns. For example, Armstrong (2002, 2005) traced the consolidation of the LGBT movement in San Francisco, seen as: (1) the move from a radical social transformation movement to one based on identity building; (2) the political consolidation and development of a common gay rights agenda supported by the main gay national organizations; and (3) the spread of a subculture with strong commercial implications, mainly oriented towards sex (Armstrong 2005: 161). Field transformation had mainly to do with the change in the rules that dictated criteria for membership and interaction - including uneven distribution of resources among field members.[1]

Qualitative studies like Armstrong's share with those closer to a social networks perspective the notion that "fields do not exist independently of actors' collective perceptions of them" (Armstrong 2005: 164; see also Diani and Pilati 2011; Melucci 1996). Among the latter, the relational approach developed by White and his collaborators at Columbia University (for an overview, see Mische 2011) probably deserves most credit for the idea that ties, and also their combination in collective action fields, reflect both a strategic and a cultural dimension (see also Mische 2003, 2008). In his study of environmental collective action in Milan in the 1980s, Diani (1995) also treated networks patterns as a reflection of the logics through which actors in that particular field built their alliances and defined their identities.

Modes of coordination in collective action fields

Social movements may be seen as a distinct organizational form, a specific type of "emerging social order" (Ahrne and Brunsson 2011; Den Hond, De Bakker, and Smith 2015; Diani 1995, 2015) which is generated through different forms of interaction. Among such forms, inter-organizational alliances and the ties created by activists' multiple commitments have attracted most attention from analysts. The construction of inter-organizational alliances has been looked at from multiple angles, singling out among others the role of shared values, proximity in ideological stances, similarity in goals and agendas, mechanisms of trust often based on previous personal contacts between activists and leaders (Atouba and Shumate 2010, 2015; Diani 1995, 2015: Chapter 3; Di Gregorio 2012; Saunders 2007, 2013). In his analysis of alliance building in the online network of 55 British health campaign groups, Simpson (2015) draws most explicitly on network theory to show how shared multiplex ties to third parties contribute to triadic closure and the activation of alliances. Drawing more or less systematically on the organizational studies literature on alliances (Kenis and Knoke 2002; Shumate and Contractor 2014), these discussions also significantly overlap with analyses of coalition building, so popular in social movement research (McCammon and Moon 2015; Van Dyke and McCammon 2010).

As alliance building is explored elsewhere in this volume (see Chapter 14 by Brooker and Meyer), here we will focus on the role of activists in generating, through their involvement in multiple organizations and activities, an important relational level within collective action fields. Building on Simmel (1955) and his revisiting by Breiger (1974), we can detect both ties between individuals and ties between organizations. In the first case, individuals are linked by the fact of sharing certain activities. They may not be personal acquaintances, especially in the case of membership of large organizations, but at the very minimum, because of their involvement in the same milieus, they may be exposed to similar cultural and political influences. Conversely, individuals may also be regarded as connections between different organizations, facilitating the circulation of information and the creation of shared understandings of reality and shared identities (e.g. Carroll and Ratner 1996; Diani 1995). In their study of the organizational affiliations of 202 leading feminists in New York State between 1840 and 1914, Rosenthal and her associates (Rosenthal et al. 1985; Rosenthal et al. 1997) provided one of the earliest and most systematic treatment of overlapping memberships as inter-organizational links, taking into account both time and territorial variation.

Looking at how individuals link organizations through their memberships generates useful insights into the structure of social movement milieus and how different frames distribute within them. In their exploration of overlapping networks in the social movement sector in Vancouver, Carroll and Ratner (1996) identified three different views of injustice and domination, labeled "political economy/injustice," "liberal," and "identity" and showed how they could be linked with specific positions within inter-movement networks. More recently, Diani (2009) has integrated this literature by differentiating between participation in associations and participation in "protest communities," suggesting that the same functions of political socialization, individual empowerment, and solidarity building that people experience by participating in associations may be experienced through the sustained involvement in protest activities.

Looking at the distribution of different types of ties within a collective action field also enables us to identify various forms through which collective action is coordinated. To this purpose, various forms of structural equivalence analysis have been attempted, aiming at identifying sets of groups occupying similar positions within the broader networks (Ansell 2003; Diani 1995, 2015; Saunders 2011, 2014). One attempt to conceptualize these forms is Diani's "modes of coordination," defined as "the relational processes through which resources are allocated within a certain collectivity, decisions are taken, collective representations elaborated, feelings of solidarity and mutual obligation forged" (Diani 2015: 13–14). Two broad classes of mechanisms (of *resource allocation* and *boundary definition*) are associated with such processes. A "social movement" mode of coordination is defined by the intersection of *dense networks of informal inter-organizational exchanges* and processes of *boundary definition* that operate at the level of broad collectivities rather than specific groups/organizations. Network multiplexity sets a social movement apart from *coalitional*, *subcultural/communitarian*, and *organizational* modes. Within any episode of collective action it is possible to identify several modes of coordination at work (Diani 2012, 2015; Eggert 2014; Saunders 2014).

The spread of computer-mediated communication (CMC) has affected patterns of collective action in a variety of ways. While most studies have primarily looked at how CMC might change styles of activism and organizational forms (Earl and Kimport 2011; Gerbaudo 2012; see also Chapter 16 by Earl, in this volume), systematic analyses of virtual networks have been relatively more rare. Rather than contrasting online and offline networks, it is worth noting how studies of online ties may contribute to our understanding of both resource allocation and boundary definition in collective action fields. Some studies have explored the connections between organizations' websites, showing how they provide information about the coordination of resources as well as about processes of identity (Ackland and O'Neil 2011; Pavan 2012; Van Laer and Van Aelst 2010). Other studies have looked in depth at the distribution of interpersonal messages through tools like Twitter, showing how communication networks including activists as well as the much broader public may contribute to the promotion of specific campaigns (see e.g. Barbera et al. 2015; Gonzalez-Bailon and Wang 2016; Lotan et al. 2011).

Altogether, however, the most distinctive contribution of new media might be to the extension and consolidation of communities of activists held together by virtual communication without a major role of formal organizations (Bennett and Segerberg 2013). Subcultural and communitarian networks have always been channels of both political and cultural innovation. For example, Crossley (2015) shows how social network analysis (SNA) can be applied to the study of cultural movements by reconstructing the emergence of punk in various UK cities from the 1970s on. Earlier, Melucci's (1984) work on "movement areas" very much anticipated many of these themes, despite not using a network analytic perspective. It is likely that this role will be reinforced by new communication technologies.

Time dynamics and network evolution

The temporal dimension of social movements has certainly attracted attention from a multiplicity of angles, including event sequences (Biggs 2002), waves of protest (Tarrow 2011), and organizational growth and decay (Minkoff 1999). However, changes in network structures have been largely overlooked. The lack of proper, easily accessible data has resulted in most network studies offering snapshots of networks at a single point in time. Admittedly, a number of qualitative, in-depth case studies of the emergence and consolidation of specific movement sectors have generated useful insights in the mechanisms behind alliance building and more broadly tie creation and transformation (e.g. Armstrong 2005). However, those studies have not really managed to capture the complexity of the relational patterns that may characterize different phases of social movement activity over time.

Mische's (2008) study of Brazilian youth activist networks from the 1970s to the 1990s dramatically improved on these shortcomings. Her pioneering application of Galois lattices techniques to collective action processes (Mische and Pattison 2000) enabled her to map the variable nature of the coalitions that mobilized to topple the disgraced president Collor. Mische focused in particular on two-mode network data measuring the involvement of activists in a number of public events and organizations. As such involvements changed over time, so did the connections that activists created between different social sectors and different organizational populations. This approach could be framed as "Simmel over time," as it assigns a temporal dimension to a well-known mechanism such as that of the "duality of persons and groups." The trajectory of individuals' affiliations over time may represent a key to reconstructing change in organizational networks; conversely, the evolution of interpersonal networks may also be interpreted in terms of changing combinations of group memberships (Diani and Mische 2015: 320). This logic of analysis has been applied to a number of different cases. For example, Wada (2014) has used survey data on participation in associations to map the evolution of networks between different organizational types in Mexican civil society.

The dualistic logic of two-mode networks has also been applied to other phenomena. For example, events and campaigns may also provide insights into the evolution of networks over time, as relations may form through joint participation in events. Here we are not talking about co-memberships, rather, co-presences. As Diani and Mische (2015: 311) note:

> This is an important kind of tie for understanding social movement mobilization, incorporating attention to the *social settings* in which the projects, strategies and alliances of movements are articulated. What can be said, planned, or imagined depends upon who is present (or just as crucially, *not* present) at the meeting, activity or protest events. Likewise, the intermingling of previously disconnected groups in broad movement publics and protests can lead to the elaboration of new connections, the sharing of discourse and tactics, or the broader integration (or segmentation) of the field.

Looking at decades of protest activity in the USA, Wang and Soule (2012) have looked at the networks created by organizations participating in events to explore mechanisms of tactical diffusion, as well as alliance building. Jung, King, and Soule (2014) have drawn upon the same dataset to explore shifts in the centrality of issues addressed by protest activities (see also Bearman and Everett 1993; von Bülow 2010). Some variations on this theme have looked for connections between events and claims, in which the fact that two or more claims are addressed in the same events creates links between themes, thus allowing the identification of the agendas pursued in mobilizations; while the fact that similar claims are found across different events enables us to make inferences about the structure of campaigns, conceived as networks of events connected by similar claims (Diani and Kousis 2014; Ghaziani and Baldassarri 2011). In some cases, the structure of networks of claims and events has been used to look for the mechanisms facilitating tactical innovation (e.g. Wang and Soule 2016).

Conclusion

In earlier assessments of research on networks and collective action (Crossley and Krinsky 2015; Diani 2004: 350–352; 2011: 229–230), we identified a number of key areas for future deeper investigation, among them, the exploration of duality mechanisms, e.g. in the form of two-mode networks linking individuals to organizations, or organizations to events; the evolution of networks over time; the characteristic of online networks, especially in relation to offline ones; the way in which the social and political context shapes collective action networks. While progress has been made in all these areas, as our review hopefully illustrates, a lot still remains to be done. The availability of data on two-mode networks, mapping the involvement of organizations in events, or claims in events, has certainly facilitated the study of network evolution over time. However, recent studies still show a considerable degree of ambiguity regarding their real focus, as networks of issues and events are sometimes equated to networks of movements mobilizing on those issues (e.g. Jung et al. 2014). Likewise, the availability of massive datasets on online exchanges has prompted a flourishing of studies of online networks, yet sometimes to the cost of equating aggregates of like-minded individuals tweeting on a specific issue to "movements," with a conflation of social movements and crowd behavior that should be carefully avoided (e.g. Lotan et al. 2011). Finally, attempts to link network properties to features of the political context (Diani 1995; Eggert 2014; Eggert and Pilati 2014; Fishman 2004, 2014) have been hampered by the still vague specification of the impact of social and political opportunities on network patterns (and indeed on actors' behavior in general). For example, one might reasonably expect the closing of opportunities to increase the density of movement networks as challengers brace up to face a more hostile environment; but might also reasonably expect the opposite, as the increasing reliance on moral incentives by actors who are losing access to the polity might well encourage ideological fragmentation within movement networks. In conclusion, we do not feel it is simply a matter of "more research is needed," to use the rhetorical sentence that ends so many literature reviews. It is rather a matter of sounder theorizing, of both the objects of the analysis (social movements, fields) and the mechanisms through which networks shape them. That is the biggest challenge for the years to come, which requires a sustained dialogue with social theory at large (Crossley 2002; Emirbayer and Goodwin 1994).

Note

1 Along similar lines, Fligstein and McAdam (2012) reinterpret some of their earlier work on civil rights activism, yet without adding much to what analysts like Armstrong (2002, 2005) have done in terms of empirical analysis of fields.

References

Ackland, Robert and Mathieu O'Neil. 2011. "Online Collective Identity: The Case of the Environmental Movement." *Social Networks* 33: 177–190.

Ahrne, Göran and Nils Brunsson. 2011. "Organization Outside Organizations: The Significance of Partial Organization." *Organization* 18: 83–104.

Ansell, Christopher. 2003. "Community Embeddedness and Collaborative Governance in the San Francisco Bay Area Environmental Movement." In *Social Movements and Networks*, edited by Mario Diani and Doug McAdam, 123–144. Oxford: Oxford University Press.

Armstrong, Elizabeth A. 2002. *Forging Gay Identities: Organizing Sexuality in San Francisco, 1950–1994*. Chicago: University of Chicago Press.

Armstrong, Elizabeth A. 2005. "From Struggle to Settlement: The Crystallization of a Field of Lesbian/Gay Organizations in San Francisco, 1969–1973." In *Social Movements and Organizations*, edited by Gerald F. Davis, Doug McAdam, Richard W. Scott, and Mayer N. Zald, 161–187. New York: Cambridge University Press.

Atouba, Yannick and Michelle Shumate. 2010. "Interorganizational Networking Patterns Among Development Organizations." *Journal of Communication* 60: 293–317.

Atouba, Yannick and Michelle Shumate. 2015. "International Nonprofit Collaboration Examining the Role of Homophily." *Nonprofit and Voluntary Sector Quarterly* 44: 587–608.

Barbera, Pablo, Ning Wang, Richard Bonneau, et al. 2015. "The Critical Periphery in the Growth of Social Protests." *Public Library of Science ONE* 10(11): e0143611.

Bearman, Peter. 1993. *Relations into Rhetorics*. New Brunswick, NJ: Rutgers University Press.

Bearman, Peter and Kevin D. Everett. 1993. "The Structure of Social Protest, 1961–1983." *Social Networks* 15: 171–200.

Bennett, Lance and Alexandra Segerberg. 2013. *The Logic of Connective Action*. Cambridge: Cambridge University Press.

Biggs, Michael. 2002. "Strikes as Sequences of Interaction: The American Strike Wave of 1886." *Social Science History* 26(3): 583–617.

Biggs, Michael. 2006. "Who Joined the Sit Ins and Why?" *Mobilization* 11: 241–256.

Bourdieu, Pierre. 1992. *An Invitation to Reflexive Sociology*. Cambridge: Polity.

Breiger, Ronald L. 1974. "The Duality of Persons and Groups." *Social Forces* 53: 181–190.

Burt, Ronald S. 1992. "The Social Structure of Competition." In *Networks and Organizations*, edited by Nitin Nohria and Robert Eccles, 57–91. Cambridge, MA: Harvard Business School Press.

Burt, Ronald S. 2005. *Brokerage & Closure*. Oxford: Oxford University Press.

Carroll, William K. and Robert S. Ratner. 1996. "Master Framing and Cross-Movement Networking in Contemporary Social Movements." *Sociological Quarterly* 37(4): 601–625.

Coleman, James. 1988. "Free Riders and Zealots: The Role of Social Networks." *Sociological Theory* 6: 52–57.

Coleman, James. 1990. *Foundations of Social Theory*. Cambridge, MA: Belknap Press.

Crossley, Nick. 2002. *Making Sense of Social Movements*. Buckingham: Open University Press.

Crossley, Nick. 2008. "Social Networks and Student Activism: On the Politicising Effect of Campus Connections." *Sociological Review* 56: 18–38.

Crossley, Nick. 2015. *Networks of Sound, Style and Subversion: The Punk and Post–punk Worlds of Manchester, London, Liverpool and Sheffield, 1975–80*. Manchester: Manchester University Press.

Crossley, Nick and Joseph Ibrahim. 2012. "Critical Mass, Social Networks and Collective Action: The Case of Student Political Worlds." *Sociology* 46: 596–612.

Crossley, Nick and John Krinsky, eds. 2015. *Social Networks and Social Movements*. London: Routledge.

Curtis, Russell L. and Louis A. Zurcher. 1973. "Stable Resources of Protest Movements: The Multi-Organizational Field." *Social Forces* 52(1): 53.

Den Hond, Frank, Frank G.A. De Bakker, and Nikolai Smith. 2015. "Social Movements and Organizational Analysis." In *Oxford Handbook of Social Movements*, edited by Donatella della Porta and Mario Diani, 291–305. Oxford: Oxford University Press.

Diani, Mario. 1992. "The Concept of Social Movement." *Sociological Review* 40(1): 1–25.

Diani, Mario. 1995. *Green Networks: A Structural Analysis of the Italian Environmental Movement*. Edinburgh: Edinburgh University Press.

Diani, Mario. 2000. "Simmel to Rokkan and Beyond: Elements for a Network Theory of (New) Social Movements." *European Journal of Social Theory* 3: 387–406.

Diani, Mario. 2004. "Networks and Participation." In *The Blackwell Companion to Social Movements*, edited by David A. Snow, Sarah A. Soule, and Hanspeter Kriesi, 339–359. Oxford: Blackwell.

Diani, Mario. 2009. "The Structural Bases of Protest Events. Multiple Memberships and Networks in the February 15th 2003 Anti-War Demonstrations." *Acta Sociologica* 52: 63–83.

Diani, Mario. 2011. "Social Movements and Collective Action." In *The Sage Handbook of Social Network Analysis*, edited by Peter Carrington and John Scott, 223–235. London: Sage.

Diani, Mario. 2012. "Modes of Coordination of Collective Action: What Actors in Policy Making?" In *Networks in Social Policy Problems*, edited by Marco Scotti and Balazs Vedres, 101–123. Cambridge: Cambridge University Press.

Diani, Mario. 2015. *The Cement of Civil Society: Studying Networks in Localities*. Cambridge: Cambridge University Press.

Diani, Mario and Maria Kousis. 2014. "The Duality of Claims and Events: The Greek Campaign Against the Troika's Memoranda and Austerity, 2010–2012." *Mobilization* 19(4): 387–404.

Diani, Mario and Doug McAdam, eds. 2003. *Social Movements and Networks*. Oxford: Oxford University Press.

Diani, Mario and Ann Mische. 2015. "Network Approaches and Social Movements." In *Oxford Handbook of Social Movements*, edited by Donatella della Porta and Mario Diani, 306–325. Oxford: Oxford University Press.

Diani, Mario and Katia Pilati. 2011. "Interests, Identities, and Relations: Drawing Boundaries in Civic Organizational Fields." *Mobilization* 16: 265–282.

Di Gregorio, Monica. 2012. "Networking in Environmental Movement Organisation Coalitions: Interest, Values or Discourse?" *Environmental Politics* 21(1): 1–25.

DiMaggio, Paul and Walter W. Powell. 1983. "The Iron Cage Revisited: Institutional Isomorphism and Collective Rationality in Organizational Fields." *American Sociological Review* 48: 147–160.

Earl, Jennifer and Kathrin Kimport. 2011. *Digitally Enabled Social Change Activism in the Internet Age*. Cambridge, MA: MIT Press.

Edwards, Gemma. 2014. "Infectious Innovations? The Diffusion of Innovation in Social Movement Networks, the Case of Suffragette Militancy." *Social Movement Studies* 13: 48–69.

Eggert, Nina. 2014. "The Impact of Political Opportunities on Interorganizational Networks: A Comparison of Migrants' Organizational Fields." *Mobilization* 19: 369–386.

Eggert, Nina and Katia Pilati. 2014. "Networks and Political Engagement of Migrant Organisations in Five European Cities." *European Journal of Political Research* 53: 858–875.

Emirbayer, Mustafa and Jeff Goodwin. 1994. "Network Analysis, Culture and the Problem of Agency." *American Journal of Sociology* 99: 1411–1454.

Feld, Scott. 1981. "The Focused Organization of Social Ties." *American Journal of Sociology* 86: 1015–1035.

Fernandez, Roberto and Doug McAdam. 1988. "Social Networks and Social Movements." *Sociological Forum* 3: 357–382.

Fishman, Robert M. 2004. *Democracy's Voices: Social Ties and the Quality of Public Life in Spain*. Ithaca, NY: Cornell University Press.

Fishman, Robert M. 2014. "Networks and Narratives in the Making of Civic Practice. Lessons from Iberia." In *Varieties of Civic Innovation*, edited by Jennifer Girouard, 159–180. Nashville, TN: Vanderbilt University Press.

Fligstein, Neil and Doug McAdam. 2012. *A Theory of Fields*. Oxford: Oxford University Press.

Gerbaudo, Paolo. 2012. *Tweets and the Streets: Social Media and Contemporary Activism*. London: Pluto Press.

Ghaziani, Amin and Delia Baldassarri. 2011. "Cultural Anchors and the Organization of Differences: A Multi-Method Analysis of LGBT Marches on Washington." *American Sociological Review* 76: 179–206.

Givan, Rebecca, Sarah A. Soule, and Kennneth M. Roberts, eds. 2010. *The Diffusion of Social Movements*. Cambridge: Cambridge University Press.

Gonzalez-Bailon, Sandra and Ning Wang. 2016. "Networked Discontent: The Anatomy of Protest Campaigns in Social Media." *Social Networks* 44: 95–104.

Goodwin, Jeff. 1997. "The Libidinal Constitution of a High Risk Social Movement." *American Sociological Review* 62: 53–69.

Gould, Roger V. 1991. "Multiple Networks and Mobilization in the Paris Commune, 1871." *American Sociological Review* 56: 716–729.

Gould, Roger V. 1993. "Trade Cohesion, Class Unity, and Urban Insurrection. Artisanal Activism in the Paris Commune." *American Journal of Sociology* 98: 721–754.

Gould, Roger V. 1995. *Insurgent Identities*. Chicago: Chicago University Press.

Hedstrom, Peter. 1994. "Contagious Collectivities: On the Spatial Diffusion of Swedish Trade-Unions, 1890–1940." *American Journal of Sociology* 99: 1157–1179.

Hedstrom, Peter, Rickard Sandell, and Charlotte Stern. 2000. "Mesolevel Networks and the Diffusion of Social Movements: The Case of the Swedish Social Democratic Party." *American Journal of Sociology* 106: 145–172.

Ibrahim, Joseph and Nick Crossley. 2017. "Network Formation in Student Political Worlds." In *Student Politics and Protest: International Perspectives*, edited by Rachel Brooks, 173–191. London: Routledge.

Jung, Wooseok, Brayden G. King, and Sarah A. Soule. 2014. "Issue Bricolage: Explaining the Configuration of the Social Movement Sector, 1960–1995." *American Journal of Sociology* 120: 187–225.

Kenis, Patrick and David Knoke. 2002. "How Organizational Field Networks Shape Inter-organizational Tie-Formation Rates." *Academy of Management Review* 27: 275–293.

Kitts, James A. 2000. "Mobilizing in Black Boxes: Social Networks and SMO Participation." *Mobilization* 5: 241–257.

Lotan, Gilad, Erhardt Graeff, Mike Ananny, Devin Gaffney, Ian Pearce, and danah boyd. 2011. "The Revolutions Were Tweeted: Information Flows During the 2011 Tunisian and Egyptian Revolutions." *International Journal of Communication* 5: 1375–1405.

Marwell, Gerald and Pamela E. Oliver. 1993. *The Critical Mass in Collective Action: A Micro-Social Theory*. Cambridge: Cambridge University Press.

Mayrl, Damon. 2013. "Fields, Logics, and Social Movements: Prison Abolition and the Social Justice Field." *Sociological Inquiry* 83: 286–309.

McAdam, Doug. 1982. *Political Process and the Development of Black Insurgency*. Chicago: Chicago University Press.

McAdam, Doug. 1986. "Recruitment to High-Risk Activism: The Case of Freedom Summer." *American Journal of Sociology* 92: 64–90.

McAdam, Doug and R. Paulsen. 1993. "Specifying the Relationship Between Social Ties and Activism." *American Journal of Sociology* 99: 640–667.

McAdam, Doug, Sidney Tarrow, and Charles Tilly. 2001. *Dynamics of Contention*. Cambridge: Cambridge University Press.

McCammon, Holly and Minyoung Moon. 2015. "Social Movement Coalitions." In *Oxford Handbook of Social Movements*, edited by Donatella della Porta and Mario Diani, 326–339. Oxford: Oxford University Press.

McLean, Paul. 2016. *Culture in Networks*. Cambridge: Polity.

Melucci, Alberto, ed. 1984. *Altri Codici. Aree di Movimento nella Metropoli*. Bologna: Il Mulino.

Melucci, Alberto. 1989. *Nomads of the Present: Social Movements and Individual Needs in Contemporary Society*. London: Hutchinson.

Melucci, Alberto. 1996. *Challenging Codes*. Cambridge: Cambridge University Press.

Minkoff, Debra. 1999. "Bending with the Wind: Organizational Change in American Women's and Minority Organizations." *American Journal of Sociology* 104: 1666–1703.

Mische, Ann. 2003. "Cross-Talk in Movements: Reconceiving the Culture-Network Link." In *Social Movements and Networks*, edited by Mario Diani and Doug McAdam, 258–280. Oxford: Oxford University Press.

Mische, Ann. 2008. *Partisan Publics*. Princeton, NJ: Princeton University Press.

Mische, Ann. 2011. "Relational Sociology, Culture, and Agency." In *The Sage Handbook of Social Network Analysis*, edited by Peter Carrington and John Scott, 80–97. London: Sage.

Mische, Ann and Philippa Pattison. 2000. "Composing a Civic Arena: Publics, Projects, and Social Settings." *Poetics* 27: 163–194.

Morris, Aldon. 1984. *The Origin of the Civil Rights Movement*. New York: Free Press.

Olson, Mancur. 1965. *The Logic of Collective Action*. Cambridge, MA: Harvard University Press.

Opp, Karl-Dieter and Christiane Gern. 1993. "Dissident Groups, Personal Networks, and Spontaneous Cooperation: The East-German Revolution of 1989." *American Sociological Review* 58: 659–680.

Passy, Florence. 2001. "Socialization, Connection and the Structure/Agency Gap." *Mobilization* 6: 173–192.

Passy, Florence. 2003. "Social Networks Matter. But How?" In *Social Movements and Networks*, edited by Mario Diani and Doug McAdam, 21–48. Oxford: Oxford University Press.

Passy, Florence and Gian-Andrea Monsch. 2014. "Do Social Networks Really Matter in Contentious Politics?" *Social Movement Studies* 13: 22–47.

Pavan, Elena. 2012. *Frames and Connections in the Governance of Global Communications: A Network Study of the Internet Governance Forum*. Lanham, MD: Rowman & Littlefield.

Ray, Kathryn, Mike Savage, Gindo Tampubolon, Alan Warde, Brian Longhurst, and Mark Tomlinson. 2003. "The Exclusiveness of the Political Field: Networks and Political Mobilization." *Social Movement Studies* 2: 37–60.

Rokkan, Stein. 1970. *Citizens, Elections, Parties*. Oslo: Universitetforlaget.

Rosenthal, Naomi, Meryl Fingrutd, Michele Ethier, Roberta Karant, and David McDonald. 1985. "Social Movements and Network Analysis: A Case Study of Nineteenth-Century Women's Reform in New York State." *American Journal of Sociology* 90: 1022–1054.

Rosenthal, Naomi, David McDonald, Michele Ethier, Meryl Fingrutd, and Roberta Karant. 1997. "Structural Tensions in the Nineteenth Century Women's Movement." *Mobilization* 2: 21–46.

Sandel, Rickard. 1999. "Organisational Life Aboard a Moving Bandwagon." *Acta Sociologica* 42: 3–15.

Saunders, Clare. 2007. "Using Social Network Analysis to Explore Social Movements: A Relational Approach." *Social Movement Studies* 6: 227–243.

Saunders, Clare. 2011. "Unblocking the Path to Effective Blockmodeling in Social Movement Research." *Mobilization* 16: 283–302.

Saunders, Clare. 2013. *Environmental Networks and Social Movement Theory*. London: Bloomsbury.

Saunders, Clare. 2014. "Insiders, Thresholders, and Outsiders in West European Global Justice Networks: Network Positions and Modes of Coordination." *European Political Science Review* 6: 167–189.

Shumate, Michelle and Noshir S. Contractor. 2014. "Emergence of Multidimensional Social Networks." In *The Sage Handbook of Organizational Communication*, edited by Linda L. Putnam and Dennis K. Mumby, 449–474. London: Sage.

Simmel, Georg. 1955. "The Web of Group Affiliations." In Georg Simmel, *Conflict and the Web of Group Affiliations*, 125–195. New York: Free Press.

Simpson, Cohen R. 2015. "Multiplexity and Strategic Alliances: The Relational Embeddedness of Coalitions in Social Movement Organisational Fields." *Social Networks* 42: 42–59.

Snow, David A., Louis Zurcher, and Sheldon Ekland-Olson. 1980. "Social Networks and Social Movements: A Microstructural Approach to Differential Recruitment." *American Sociological Review* 45: 787–801.

Snow, David A., Louis Zurcher, and Sheldon Ekland-Olson. 1983. "Further Thoughts on Social Networks and Movement Recruitment." *Sociological Forum* 3: 357–382.

Soule, Sarah A. 1997. "The Student Divestment Movement in the United States and Tactical Diffusion: The Shantytown Protest." *Social Forces* 75: 855–883.

Swidler, Ann. 1986. "Culture in Action: Symbols and Strategies." *American Sociological Review* 51: 273–286.

Tarrow, Sidney. 2011. *Power in Movement*, 3rd edn. New York: Cambridge University Press.

Tilly, Charles. 1978. *From Mobilization to Revolution*. Reading, MA: Addison-Wesley.

Van Dyke, Nella and Holly McCammon, eds. 2010. *Strategic Alliances: New Studies of Social Movement Coalitions*. Minneapolis: University of Minnesota Press.

Van Laer, Jeroen and Peter Van Aelst. 2010. "Internet and Social Movement Action Repertoires." *Information, Communication & Society* 13: 1146–1171.

von Bülow, Marisa. 2010. *Building Transnational Networks: Civil Society Networks and the Politics of Trade in the Americas*. Cambridge: Cambridge University Press.

Wada, Takeshi. 2014. "Who Are the Active and Central Actors in the 'Rising Civil Society' in Mexico?" *Social Movement Studies* 13: 127–157.

Wang, Dan J. and Sarah A. Soule. 2012. "Social Movement Organizational Collaboration: Networks of Learning and the Diffusion of Protest Tactics, 1960–1995." *American Journal of Sociology* 117: 1674–1722.

Wang, Dan J. and Sarah A. Soule. 2016. "Tactical Innovation in Social Movements: The Effects of Peripheral and Multi-Issue Protest." *American Sociological Review* 81: 517–548.

White, Harrison C. 2008. "Notes on the Constituents of Social Structure. Soc. Rel. 10 – Spring'65." *Sociologica* 1: doi: 10.2383/26576.

Zald, Mayer N. and John D. McCarthy. 1980. "Social Movement Industries: Competition and Cooperation among Movement Organizations." *Research in Social Movements, Conflict and Change* 3: 1–20.

Zhao, DingXin. 1998. "Ecologies of Social Movements: Student Mobilisation During the 1989 Prodemocracy Movement in Beijing." *American Journal of Sociology* 103: 1493–1529.

Zuckerman, Alan S. 2005. *The Social Logics of Politics*. Philadelphia, PA: Temple University Press.

9

Social Movement Organizations

EDWARD T. WALKER AND ANDREW W. MARTIN

Introduction

A social movement organization (SMO) is, to borrow from a classic definition (McCarthy and Zald 1973: 1218), a "complex, or formal organization which identifies its preferences with a social movement or a counter-movement and attempts to implement those goals." SMOs, then, are often seen as critical vehicles for realizing the social changes envisioned by movement leaders, activists, and sympathetic broader publics. Even though SMOs are central to many efforts to effect social change, they should not be conflated with movements themselves; social movements are most centrally about *interactions* between authorities and contentious challengers, and the whole of these interactions cannot be reduced to examining the organized groups who voice such claims (Tilly 1993). In their seminal work on this subject, McCarthy and Zald (1977: 1217–1218) define social movements as "a set of opinions and beliefs in a population which represents preferences for changing some elements of the social structure and/or reward distribution of a society." Our focus here, of course, is on the organizational forms that coordinate resources to make these beliefs manifest.

SMOs today continue to be a central topic of research within the broader field of contentious politics, whether in understanding the evolution of political repertoires (Clemens and Minkoff 2004; Walker, Martin, and McCarthy 2008; Wang and Soule 2012), how funding influences the form and content of movement claims-making and the stability of fields (Bartley 2007; Bob 2005; Caniglia and Carmin 2005; Minkoff and Powell 2006; Simpson 2016; Walker and McCarthy 2010), patterns of coalition-building and networking (Diani 2015; Dixon and Martin 2012; Van Dyke and McCammon 2010; Wang and Soule 2012), founding dynamics (Carmichael, Jenkins, and Brulle 2012; Johnson and Frickel 2011; Stretesky et al. 2011), or ultimate political outcomes (Andrews and Biggs 2006; Andrews and Caren 2010; Burstein and Linton 2002; McCammon

The Wiley Blackwell Companion to Social Movements, Second Edition. Edited by David A. Snow, Sarah A. Soule, Hanspeter Kriesi, and Holly J. McCammon.
© 2019 John Wiley & Sons Ltd. Published 2019 by John Wiley & Sons Ltd.

et al. 2001). There also continues to be debate about the most justifiable approach to documenting SMO populations in quantitative studies, with some contending that scholars must move beyond over-reliance on prominent national-level associational directories (Brulle et al. 2007; Soule and King 2008), and others advocating a compromise approach that balances between the need to generate more inclusive databases of organizational populations while maintaining economy of scholarly effort in data collection (Andrews et al. 2016).

The focus on SMOs as topics of investigation in their own right, of course, reflected the turn away from older approaches in the "collective behavior" tradition of sociological theorizing, which saw social movements as fundamentally similar to other forms of disorderly collective behavior (such as riots, fads, and crazes, see Buechler 2000, for a review). With the turn toward the Resource Mobilization Theory (RMT) of McCarthy and Zald (1973, 1977), as we describe below, scholars reoriented the entire subfield toward investigating SMOs as critical to the mobilizing structures used by organizers to engage in recruitment and outreach, fundraising, (often professional) staffing, and eventual mobilization to meet goals (McCarthy 1996). This perspective, importantly, provided a critical counterweight to classic Michels (1959 [1911]) expectations that "organization" is always antithetical to social change because of organizations' inherent tendencies toward the concentration of power in the hands of increasingly conservative top leaders (see Clemens and Minkoff 2004). While studies continue to be haunted by Michels' ghost, at times suggesting (following Piven and Cloward 1977) that disruptive mobilizations outside the purview of SMOs will be most effective, it is most common today to view Michels' concerns as a tendency rather than an inevitability (e.g. Lee 2015; Osterman 2006).

What is becoming less settled today is the very language we use to describe SMOs. There has been a shift in research on contentious politics toward developing less movement-centric approaches (Diani 2015; Fligstein and McAdam 2011, 2012; McAdam and Boudet 2012; Walder 2009), as analysts increasingly recognize the importance of social movements within the particular politics of distinct fields and their interdependence (e.g. politics, business, health, science, education, see Armstrong and Bernstein 2008; Walker et al. 2008). These changes are part of a growing interest to have social movement theory serve in a generative role toward developing more general sociological theories of institutional and political processes. We discuss these shifts in greater depth below.

As analysts de-center movements in their investigations, they have become more sensitive to similarities between SMOs and other types of organized vehicles for political claims-making. Consider not only the SMO concept but related terms including interest group, non-governmental organization (NGO), advocacy group, or citizen organization. These terms often overlap very heavily on both conceptual and substantive grounds, and at times the main difference is not between the observed structures and behaviors but simply reflects the academic discipline of the observer (e.g. a sociologist rather than a scholar in political science, management, nonprofit studies, or communication). The SMO term today has developed a variety of competitors, as there have been important attempts to develop more inclusive concepts such as "advocacy organization" (Andrews and Edwards 2004; Walker 2014) or "civil society organization" (Bail 2012; Diani 2015).

At the same time, fundamental new questions are being raised about the necessity of SMOs at all in an era in which much social movement activity – including but not limited to recruitment, fundraising, discourse and development of claims, coordination of collective actions, and even protest itself – takes place through online formats, including social media, smartphone applications, internet discussion forums and wikis, blogs, and text messaging (see Earl and Kimport 2011; Chapter 16 by Earl, in this volume). A debate has emerged about the extent to which conventional SMOs continue to be necessary in a context where Information and Communications Technologies (ICTs) seem to be lowering the costs of collective action dramatically, even allowing for coordination in the complete absence of conventional SMOs. As we describe below, although it is clear that many of the parameters of organizing are changing significantly along with ICTs, it is also apparent that SMOs continue to be indispensable vehicles for mounting many types of collective action (see Earl and Kimport 2011; Chapter 16 by Earl, in this volume).

We begin by discussing the enduring value of RMT for understanding the dynamics of SMOs, not only in their funding and support but also in features such as resource partitioning, meta-level divisions of labor within social movements, and mobilizing structures. We continue by considering how ICTs are transforming the meaning of contemporary SMOs, while also addressing widespread questions of the enduring necessity of SMOs in light of these changes. Next, we review recent literature that seeks to understand SMOs through the lens of field theory. In a penultimate section, we discuss recent studies that have developed new insights into the cultural processes operating within SMOs. Finally, we conclude by bringing together these threads of research and charting new directions for research on SMOs.

Resource Mobilization: Alive and Well

The development of the resource mobilization perspective was the critical moment that first brought the scholarly discourses of social movements and organizational theory together. In McCarthy and Zald's (1977) formation of a (modestly titled) "partial" theory of resource mobilization, they forcefully argued for an explicitly organization-centric model of collective action. Their main tenet was that in wealthy modern societies, the mobilization of resources is critical for sustained (and successful) protest activity. Because formal bureaucracies are the primary way individuals amass resources, they postulated that such organizations will be central to most social movement challenges today.

Since the inception of RMT, scholars have identified the critical role of formal organizations in social protest (McCarthy and Zald 2001). Some have examined how organizations matter in specific social movements, from highly bureaucratic sectors such as organized labor (Martin 2008) to those with fewer slack resources like homeless activists (Cress and Snow 1996). McCarthy and Zald (1977) borrowed the concepts of "industry" and "sector" from economists to describe social movement actors that are centered around a specific goal (industry, SMI) and the entire range of social movement actors that exist in society at a given moment (sector, SMS). Since their initial typology, scholars have sought to examine changes in both industries and sector over time. For example, Jung, King, and Soule (2014) explore how different social movement issues become linked together via protest activity, paying particular attention to the cultural overlap of distinct claims-makers. Larson and Soule (2009) adopt a sector-level approach to examine the protest cycle of the 1960s in the United States, drawing upon both organizational theories like neo-institutionalism and organizational ecology, as well as the political opportunity and RMT. Scholars have also been interested in tracing the development of specific social movement industries. Carmichael et al. (2012), for example, examine the rise of the environmental SMI. Explanations for the growth of this SMI were eclectic, encompassing traditional organizational ecology predictors, such as organizational density, critical discourse around environmental issues, resources from external allies like foundations, and quantifiable threats (e.g. air pollution).

A major focus when analyzing SMIs is the degree of competition among SMOs. Organizational ecologists have long maintained that competition is the key for driving innovation in the sector, weeding out those organizations that lack the ability to adapt to changing environmental conditions (Hannan and Freeman 1977). This has provided important insights into the shifts in tactics and goals of various SMOs over time (Minkoff 1994, 1999). More recently, scholars have drawn on the resource partitioning approach (Carroll and Hannan 1995) to extend analysis of SMOs' competition across different sectors. Soule and King (2008) find that SMI concentration tends to breed greater specialization, both in terms of tactics and goals. Not surprisingly, scholars interested in movements with economic goals have used this approach with considerable success (Carroll and Swaminathan 2000).

While much of this research suggests that movement actors generally compete with one another over scarce resources, there is a growing body of research on ways in which SMOs cooperate through coalition-building (Van Dyke and McCammon 2010). The mounting empirical evidence suggests that coalition-building is commonly employed by SMOs, even spanning distinct SMIs (Berg 2003). This is not surprising given the potential resources that coalition partners may provide; Jenkins and Perrow's (1977) classic work on the United Farmworkers points very clearly to this. Beyond enhanced resource flows, coalition building can provide new tactical playlists to SMOs (Voss and Sherman 2000; Wang and Soule 2012), and increase protest activity generally (Larson and Soule 2009). Scholarship on the revitalization of American organized labor (Clawson 2003; Voss and Fantasia 2004) has pointed to the mobilization of outside allies as critical for the shift toward a more activist labor movement.

Scholars have also investigated the factors that lead to alliance-building across social movement actors. While some have found that political opportunities encourage coalitions (Kay 2005), threats appear to be a more powerful impetus for outreach. Research on issues from campus activism (Van Dyke 2003), to suffragist campaigns (McCammon and Campbell 2002), to corporate mobilization (Akard 1992; Quadagno 2004) all demonstrate how political threats encourage alliance-formation (Goldstone and Tilly 2001; Van Dyke and Soule 2002). Overall, then, our understanding of coalition-building is consistent with the broader RMT interest in resource flows, both human and material, across SMO boundaries.

Related to both field-level competition and coalition-building, scholars have also studied the division of labor among SMOs. Work on the "radical flank effect" argues that more militant groups tend to generate greater support for centrist organizations, as in the case of Civil Rights (Haines 1984; McCammon, Bergner, and Arch 2015). Recently, scholars have examined the growth of non-membership organizations. In particular, some see the presence of these organizations as having a negative effect on civic participation by average citizens (Putnam 2000; Skocpol 2003). More recently, however, scholars have suggested that the relationship between membership and non-membership SMOs may be more mutually beneficial than previously imagined. Walker, McCarthy, and Baumgartner (2011), examining the peace, women's, and human rights social movement sectors, find that although the populations of non-membership-based organizations have grown since the 1960s, the breakdown of membership versus non-membership organizations in these sectors has remained quite stable. Moreover, as they argue, given the increasingly complex environment within which SMOs operate, both types of organizations accomplish important tasks necessary for the overall success of SMIs.

The rise of non-membership advocacy organizations is in many ways a result of the growing professionalization of SMOs more generally, a phenomenon that was seen by RMT scholars as inevitable, given the growing technical knowledge required to engage in activism today (McCarthy and Zald 1977). Early work on this topic tended to focus primarily on the ways in which SMOs managed the transition away from charismatic leadership, typically toward more formalized, bureaucratic leaders (Staggenborg 1988; Zald and Ash 1966). Other scholars have examined the role of professionalization and formalization in the ability of movements to secure resources (McCarthy and Wolfson 1996) and mobilize support (Martin 2007). Not surprisingly, the bureaucratization of SMOs is not without its critics (most notably, Piven and Cloward 1977), but there is considerable evidence that formalization does not necessarily breed oligarchy (Andrews et al. 2010; Stepan-Norris and Zeitlin 2003; Voss and Sherman 2000).

Beyond the SMO? How ICTs Are Transforming Organizing

Recent social movement campaigns ranging from Occupy Wall Street to the Arab Spring to Black Lives Matter have been relying heavily on communications technologies in order to recruit and mobilize constituents, draw media attention to their causes, and to ultimately effect political change. The rise of new forms of online activism – both short-term mobilization around particular issues (sometimes referred to as clicktivism or, more derisively, slacktivism) and more durable and long-term online organizing – are leading to new ways of conceptualizing participation (Earl et al. 2010; Han 2014; Karpf 2010, 2012; Lewis, Gray, and Meierhenrich 2014; Yang 2016; see also Lee, McQuarrie, and Walker 2015). The use of ICTs in movements, in combination with changes that appear to make SMOs less essential or necessary overall, are causing a rethinking of the place of SMOs in movements more broadly (see Chapter 16 by Earl, in this volume).

As mentioned above, one of the foundational aspects of RMT on SMOs holds that they require the means of overcoming the collective action dilemmas identified long ago by Olson (1965). This leads organizations to deploy selective incentives to lower the costs of participation for those they seek to recruit. And yet with the use of ICTs as organizing tools, which radically lower the costs of taking part in collective action, many are questioning both (1) whether the free rider problem applies to the same extent when ICTs rather than SMOs are the central vehicle for engaging participants, and (2) whether we must now revise our very definition of resources in light of these changes; we are particularly interested in the first point. Bimber and colleagues (2005: 377) maintain that ICTs such as blogs may supplant the "collective action functions in the absence of traditional organization and accumulated resources," a point echoed elsewhere by many studies that expect either a decline or even an outright disappearance of the free rider problem in light of ICT-driven activism (ibid.; Bennett and Segerberg 2012, 2013; Earl et al. 2010; Earl and Schussman 2003).

In perhaps the most influential perspective on the role of ICTs and how they reshape broader social movements and the place of SMOs within them, Bennett and Segerberg (2012, 2013; see also Bennett 2012) further develop the argument that in place of the conventional Olsonian (1965) logic of collective action, we may now be witnessing the rise of forms of participation that rely upon a logic of "connective" action. Of course, Olson's (1965) classic argument held that rational individuals will not contribute to collective goods unless threatened with penalties or offered selective incentives for their contributions, an insight that informed the seminal RMT perspective of McCarthy and Zald (1977). Bennett and Segerberg (2012: 750) argue that although the full extent of Olson's rational choice assumptions have faded in more recent scholarship, assumptions about the place of SMOs, as well as assumptions about the importance of resources, leadership, coalitions, and other factors still reflect many of Olson's fundamental ideas. The logic of "connective" action, they contend, highlights the central role of "digital media as organizing agents" rather than conventional SMOs at the center (ibid.: 752); SMOs may continue to have a role, but it is one that is more flexible and decentralized. With communication and coordination costs reduced dramatically, normal collective action dilemmas may be reduced considerably.

The shift toward peer production and crowdsourced participation, although usually framed as an alternative to organizing through SMOs – in the vein of Shirky's (2008) influential formulation of "organizing without organizations" – nonetheless may have effects on SMOs themselves, which may use crowdsourced methods to facilitate organizational decision-making (e.g. Shaw and Hill 2014). Websites for SMOs, notably, are less-than-ideal venues in practice for directly generating activism (Stein 2009) and run the risk of merely acting as what Earl et al. (2010) call "brochure-ware," in which online content is one-way and informational rather than interactive and designed to facilitate online organizing or mobilization. Nonetheless, other website formats may help with the development of what Caren and colleagues (2012) call Social Movement Online Communities, which allow for activism that is geographically dispersed activism that may grow very rapidly. Still, such sites may suffer from "a tension between openness and anonymity" (ibid.: 165).

Where does this leave the theory and practice of SMOs today? As Earl (2015: 35) argues, even though SMOs are not always necessary for online protest campaigns, we should not expect to find the "extinction" of SMOs for at least three reasons: SMOs often serve purposes that are less rationalistic (for example, the cultural purposes we describe below), SMOs are still incredibly important for facilitating offline engagement, and SMOs might be "important to healthy movement ecologies" similar to the macro-level divisions of labor we describe above. The conclusion that ICTs are both redefining the meaning of SMOs while also not causing their extinction is one that is shared widely: evidence of the mutually supportive integration of online organizing and offline engagement in SMOs is widespread in cases ranging from healthcare and environmental politics (Han 2014) to abortion rights (Kimport 2012) to the U.S. Social Forum (Gervais 2015) to the 15M movement in Spain (Micó and Casero-Ripollés 2014).

SMOs and Field Theory

As described above in the section on RMT, scholars have long been interested in understanding and conceptualizing the relationships between SMOs, typically under the guise of RMT's framework of social movement industries and the broader social movement sector. This interest helped to generate more recent studies that have taken resource competition and SMO specialization as their central object of investigation (e.g. Soule and King 2008), linking these interests to classic organizational ecology questions related to niches and resource partitioning (Carroll and Swaminathan 2000). And, of course, many past studies have examined ecologies of SMOs using the theories and methods of organizational ecology (e.g. see Minkoff and McCarthy 2005). Nonetheless, despite its enduring impact on SMO studies, the inherent affinity between RMT and both organizational ecology and resource dependency theories (e.g. Davis and Cobb 2010; Pfeffer and Salancik 1978) has also meant that neo-institutional theories of SMOs were less common until relatively recently (Davis et al. 2005).

Inspired by increasing integration of social movement studies and organizational theory (particularly in its neo-institutionalist variations; see Walker 2012, for a review), and connected to the move toward making scholarship less movement-centric, a burgeoning area of research is examining both (1) how the relational dynamics of SMOs shape SMO strategies and practices, and (2) how new conceptualizations of the very idea of an SMO are warranted in light of the fact that many SMOs bridge the SMS and other sectors of society, including business, education, healthcare, science, sports, and other fields. We describe each of these processes as we develop our argument in this section.

First, it is worth discussing the similarities and differences between the RMT concepts of social movement industry (SMI) and social movement sector (SMS) versus the more recent understandings of fields. Importantly, both the RMT and field-theoretic models share an attentiveness to the centrality of competition in the endogenous generation of organizational practices; on the other hand, the key difference between them in this right is that RMT highlights, of course, resources as the central object of competition, and field theories tend to include a broader set of sources of the competition, including concerns over status and power, in addition to conventional resource needs (see King and Walker 2014). Proponents of each perspective also expect the outcomes of organizational competition to vary: RMT expects that competition generates specialization in, for instance, tactics and goals (Soule and King 2008), whereas field theoretic approaches – given their more general nature, applying as they do to organizations of all types – anticipate more variable responses to competition, which will be conditional upon the organization's position in relation to other field-level actors (Fligstein 2001; Fligstein and McAdam 2011, 2012). The two theories also differ in their orientation to internal versus external sources of SMO practices: RMT focuses attention most closely on the relationships between SMOs within the same SMI, and secondarily between SMOs across SMIs; field theories stand out, by contrast, for their focus on the key relationships between SMOs as insurgent actors and power-holding authorities as the incumbents. Additionally, field theories emphasize a process that is generally overlooked altogether by RMT: the ways that change or instability in an *adjacent field* (e.g. how changes in the legal profession may affect women's movements, to take an example from McCammon et al. 2007) may have influences upon both insurgent SMO activity and the actions taken by incumbents.

In particular, field theories are drawing new attention to the relations among SMOs, particularly those that extend beyond competition, such as in importing and translating ideas from other fields into the realm of contentious politics (Landy 2015), building from particular configurations of network ties to develop effective advocacy strategies (Diani 2015), shifting along with discourse in society more broadly (Bail 2012; Vasi et al. 2015), engaging in bridging practices that more effectively link together diverse constituencies (Braunstein, Fulton, and Wood 2014; Walker and Stepick 2014), or adopting hybrid approaches that may help an SMO reach a broader audience (Heaney and Rojas 2014).

Among these, field-theoretic approaches have been most fruitful in uncovering how SMOs benefit by linking together contentious political action with ties to established and institutionalized fields of social action. The pioneering study that helped facilitate research in this area is Armstrong (2002a), which found that in helping to crystalize gay identities in San Francisco during the second half of the twentieth century, organizations that she called "Gay plus one [other function or identity]" were critical. These organizations, such as gay and lesbian swim clubs, LGBT media advocacy groups, and queer technology enthusiast collectives, played a key role in the broader movement by creating SMOs that helped to root the movement more deeply in the institutions of society, operating as "contexts of collective creativity" (Armstrong 2002b). In the time since, scholars of social movements and organizations have paid much closer attention to such field-bridging SMOs and other established organizations that link across fields. For instance, Negro, Perretti, and Carroll (2013) found that commercial organizations aligned with social movements (in their case, LGBT-friendly businesses) were significant forces in shaping the passage of local antidiscrimination ordinances. Heaney and Rojas (2014) found that antiwar SMOs that bridged particular fields, such as those that combined a concern with gender with peace issues, were often more effective in recruiting participants to demonstrations. Ghaziani (2011: 99) points out, in a study of an LGBT SMO at a university, that as field-level changes take place in the broader social inclusion of LGBT individuals and issues, "activists today are motivated less by drawing boundaries against members of the dominant group and more by building bridges toward them." Others are also pointing out that socio-demographic diversity within an SMO's constituency forces not only a concern about finding cultural themes that unify participants but requires broader bridging practices that unite these diverse constituencies and the fields, such as religious, economic, and cultural fields (Braunstein et al. 2014; Walker and Stepick 2014).

Relational dynamics within fields have also become a central area of investigation, especially in uncovering the extent to which network approaches add value to accounts of social movements that extend beyond large-N event studies or single-SMO case studies. For instance, Diani (2015; see also Diani and Pilati 2011), in a set of groundbreaking studies, shows that relational factors in the structuring of the broader civic and political networks of which SMOs are a part are consequential in shaping activist identities and engagement, much more so than a standard issue-based or interest-based explanation might have it. Bail (2012) illustrates how relatively extreme SMOs operating at the "fringes" of an organizational field may be effective in shifting broader attention (and the field itself) toward more extreme positions. A number of other studies have investigated how relational ties among SMOs shape their tactical utilization, often with an eye toward the cultural meanings of particular tactics (Ring-Ramirez, Reynolds-Stenson, and Earl 2014; Wang and Soule 2012).

The Cultural Dynamics of Internal SMO Processes

In the previous section we considered how the neo-institutionalists' emphasis on fields shaped scholarship on SMOs. A potential critique of this approach is that it largely ignores the internal dynamics of such organizations, preferring to focus on how SMOs construct relationships with one another and other actors in their field (and beyond). Fortunately, some scholars have turned to ethnographic work on organizational processes more generally as a starting point to understand how activists within organizations interact with one another (e.g. Kellogg 2011; Kutz-Flamenbaum 2016). Of particular interest is the decision-making process in SMOs, and how these organizations balance member participation with the ability to achieve stated goals.

Perhaps the most seminal work in this area of research is Francesca Polletta's (2002) *Freedom Is an Endless Meeting*, which traces efforts by activists to develop participatory democratic SMOs. Her analysis, which focuses primarily on the social movement wave of the 1960s and 1970s, explores the interaction and often conflicting goals between their efforts to shape society while also ensuring widespread rank-and-file participation. More recently, della Porta (2013) extended the social movement emphasis on deliberation and participation to the broader society, arguing that the logic of liberal democracy that was largely taken for granted throughout the twentieth century may be obsolete. She contends that the model for democracy today can be found in diverse global social movements, from Occupy Wall Street to the Arab Spring. Such organizations present an alternative approach to democratic deliberations, one that is based much more heavily on participation and deliberative decision-making.

More recently, scholars have begun to pay greater attention to what Jasper (2004) refers to as the "strategic choices" of social movements, or how activists construct tactics that successfully overcome environmental challenges. Perhaps the most seminal work in this vein is Marshall Ganz's (2010) in-depth account of the United Farmworkers and the resourcefulness of that SMO's leadership. Others have employed a similar lens to examine civil rights activity (Andrews 2001) and the women's movement (McCammon 2012). See also Maney et al.'s (2011) edited volume for an in-depth analysis of the strategic capacity of SMOs.

As noted above, scholars interested in formal organizations have paid particular attention to the transformation of these organizations, especially when the growth of the organization necessitates the adoption of a more bureaucratic form (Staggenborg 1988; Zald and Ash 1966). Blee's (2012) recent case study of SMOs in Pittsburgh examines how these activist groups evolve over their life-course. She finds that decisions made by founders early in the development of the organization have significant consequences for defining the long-term goals and structure of the organization. Moreover, over the life course of the organization, broader and more ambitious goals tend to be redefined more narrowly. Overall, then, these qualitative analyses of the internal dynamics of SMOs provide considerable nuance on the decision-making logic of activist groups. In particular, it is evident that despite efforts by groups to foster large-scale democratic participation by rank-and-file members, exogenous pressures often define what is possible in terms of power relations in these organizations (see Lee 2015, for a review). Nevertheless, this research also suggests that groups can overcome such challenges to ensure members do indeed have a voice.

Scholars working in the "group styles" tradition of cultural sociology (Eliasoph and Lichterman 2003; Lichterman 2006) have also made considerable advances in our understanding of cultural practices within SMOs and broader fields, including how best to conceptualize the role of religious (Lichterman 2008), civic and participatory (Lichterman and Eliasoph 2014), and women's (Polletta and Chen 2013) influences on modes of engagement and participation. In an important recent contribution, Lichterman and Eliasoph (2014) develop the concept of "scene styles" within associational settings, which may be applied readily to SMOs: these include features of the cognitive maps of participants as revealed through ethnographic observation, the bonds observed among participants, and speech norms that prevail in group interactions.

Conclusion: New Directions in the Study of SMOs

SMOs continue to be a vital area of research in the study of contentious politics, with recent moves to simultaneously extend the established and vital RMT perspective, and also, on the other hand, to move somewhat beyond those insights by incorporating findings about the changing role of SMOs in light of a number of significant changes. These changes include the rising use of ICTs, which may make SMOs less essential in certain instances; the growing necessity of understanding the relational dynamics within (and beyond) fields, especially those that involve interactions that are not solely about resource competition among SMOs; and the attempt to enrich our understanding of the cultural processes at work within SMOs. Although varied in their approaches, in many instances these new perspectives reflect the broader meta-analytic motivation to develop less movement-centric understandings of contentious politics, such that we may conceptualize the varieties of target institutions in which movements seek change (Armstrong and Bernstein 2008; Van Dyke, Soule, and Taylor 2004; Walker et al. 2008), the connections between SMOs and other fields of social action (Fligstein and McAdam 2011, 2012), and the role that organizations beyond traditional SMOs – from corporate-sponsored advocacy campaigns and other business-backed mobilizations (Walker 2014; Walker and Rea 2014) to "awkward" movement groups (Polletta 2006) to foundations and staff-driven non-membership groups (Skocpol 2003; Walker et al. 2011) – play in contentious politics.

The variation in types of groups, as well as the social settings in which they are embedded and the strategies they adopt, are each contributing the emerging debate on terminology, with some scholars now favoring more inclusive terms like "advocacy group" (Andrews and Edwards 2004) or "civil society organization" (Bail 2012; Diani 2015). Although this terminological debate is far from settled, the existence of such a debate is itself revealing about the potentials for new research directions in understanding SMOs, such that we may fruitfully incorporate, for instance, ideas from political science on interest groups and lobbying (e.g. Böhm 2015), ideas from international relations and global politics on the importance of transnational SMOs (see e.g. Smith and Wiest 2005), and studies that examine SMOs through the lens of nonprofit social entrepreneurship (e.g. Dacin, Dacin, and Tracey 2011; Vasi 2009).

Although beyond the scope of this review, we would be remiss not to conclude by describing how changing methods of SMO research are also influencing the direction of the subfield. Of course, one of the primary shifts has been associated with the emergence of "Big Data" based around online resources (e.g. social media sites, scraping of websites and online forums) and computational methods. The availability of these new sources has allowed for investigations into how SMOs communicate with their participants and publics (Bail 2012), in an attempt to connect with emerging themes in broader public discourse through social networking sites like Twitter (Vasi et al. 2015), or, as discussed earlier, to organize activism outside the purview of conventional SMOs. We are also seeing relational methods, whether in ethnographic (e.g. Mische 2011) or in quantitative network-analytic form (e.g. Baldassarri and Diani 2007), to make available new insights into both the culture and structure of movements, and the role of SMOs within those domains. In combination, these new methods are unlocking a variety of new research potentials that will help advance SMO research considerably in the years to come.

References

Akard, Patrick J. 1992. "Corporate Mobilization and Political Power: The Transformation of U.S. Economic Policy in the 1970s." *American Sociological Review* 57(5): 597–615.

Andrews, Kenneth T. 2001. "Social Movements and Policy Implementation: The Mississippi Civil Rights Movement and the War on Poverty, 1965–1971." *American Sociological Review* 66: 71–95.

Andrews, Kenneth T. and Michael Biggs. 2006. "The Dynamics of Protest Diffusion: Movement Organizations, Social Networks, and News Media in the 1960 Sit-Ins." *American Sociological Review* 71(5): 752–777.

Andrews, Kenneth T. and Neal Caren. 2010. "Making the News Movement Organizations, Media Attention, and the Public Agenda." *American Sociological Review* 75(6): 841–866.

Andrews, Kenneth T. and Bob Edwards. 2004. "Advocacy Organizations in the U.S. Political Process." *Annual Review of Sociology* 30: 479–506.

Andrews, Kenneth T., Bob Edwards, Akram Al-Turk, and Anne Kristen Hunter. 2016. "Sampling Social Movement Organizations." *Mobilization* 21(2): 231–246.

Andrews, Kenneth T., Marshall Ganz, Matthew Baggetta, Hahrie Han, and Chaeyoon Lim. 2010. "Leadership, Membership, and Voice: Civic Associations That Work." *American Journal of Sociology* 115(4): 1191–1242.

Armstrong, Elizabeth A. 2002a. *Forging Gay Identities*. Chicago: University of Chicago Press.

Armstrong, Elizabeth A. 2002b. "Crisis, Collective Creativity, and the Generation of New Organizational Forms: The Transformation of Lesbian/Gay Organizations in San Francisco." In *Research in the Sociology of Organizations*, edited by Michael Lounsbury and Marc J. Ventresca, vol. 19, 361–395. Oxford: JAI Press.

Armstrong, Elizabeth A. and Mary Bernstein. 2008. "Culture, Power, and Institutions: A Multi-Institutional Politics Approach to Social Movements." *Sociological Theory* 26(1):74–99.

Bail, Christopher A. 2012. "The Fringe Effect Civil Society Organizations and the Evolution of Media Discourse about Islam since the September 11th Attacks." *American Sociological Review* 77(6): 855–879.

Baldassarri, Delia and Mario Diani. 2007. "The Integrative Power of Civic Networks." *American Journal of Sociology* 113(3): 735–780.

Bartley, Tim. 2007. "How Foundations Shape Social Movements: The Construction of an Organizational Field and the Rise of Forest Certification." *Social Problems* 54(3): 229–255.

Bennett, W. Lance. 2012. "The Personalization of Politics Political Identity, Social Media, and Changing Patterns of Participation." *The ANNALS of the American Academy of Political and Social Science* 644(1): 20–39.

Bennett, W. Lance and Alexandra Segerberg. 2012. "The Logic of Connective Action." *Information, Communication and Society* 15(5): 739–768.

Bennett, W. Lance and Alexandra Segerberg. 2013. *The Logic of Connective Action*. Cambridge: Cambridge University Press.

Berg, John C. 2003. *Teamsters and Turtles?* Lanham, MD: Rowman and Littlefield.

Bimber, Bruce, Andrew J. Flanagin, and Cynthia Stohl. 2005. "Reconceptualizing Collective Action in the Contemporary Media Environment." *Communication Theory* 15(4): 365–388.

Blee, Kathleen M. 2012. *Democracy in the Making*. Oxford: Oxford University Press.

Bob, Clifford. 2005. *The Marketing of Rebellion: Insurgents, Media, and International Activism*. New York: Cambridge University Press.

Böhm, Timo. 2015. "Activists in Politics: The Influence of Embedded Activists on the Success of Social Movements." *Social Problems* 62(4): 477–498.

Braunstein, Ruth, Brad R. Fulton, and Richard L. Wood. 2014. "The Role of Bridging Cultural Practices in Racially and Socioeconomically Diverse Civic Organizations." *American Sociological Review* 79(4): 705–725.

Brulle, Robert, Liesel Turner, Jason Carmichael, and J. Jenkins. 2007. "Measuring Social Movement Organization Populations: A Comprehensive Census of U.S. Environmental Movement Organizations." *Mobilization* 12(3): 255–270.

Buechler, Steven M. 2000. *Social Movements in Advanced Capitalism: The Political Economy and Cultural Construction of Social Activism*. New York: Oxford University Press.

Burstein, Paul and April Linton. 2002. "The Impact of Political Parties, Interest Groups, and Social Movement Organizations on Public Policy: Some Recent Evidence and Theoretical Concerns." *Social Forces* 81(2): 380–408.

Caniglia, Beth and JoAnn Carmin. 2005. "Scholarship on Social Movement Organizations: Classic Views and Emerging Trends." *Mobilization* 10(2): 201–212.

Caren, Neal, Kay Jowers, and Sarah Gaby. 2012. "A Social Movement Online Community: Stormfront and the White Nationalist Movement." In *Research in Social Movements, Conflicts and Change*, vol. 33, *Media, Movements, and Political Change*, 163–193. New York: Emerald Press.

Carmichael, Jason T., J. Craig Jenkins, and Robert J. Brulle. 2012. "Building Environmentalism: The Founding of Environmental Movement Organizations in the United States, 1900–2000." *The Sociological Quarterly* 53(3): 422–453.

Carroll, Glenn R. and Michael T. Hannan. 1995. "Resource Partitioning." In *Organizations in Industry*, by Glenn R. Carroll and Michael T. Hannan, 215–221. Oxford: Oxford University Press.

Carroll, Glenn R. and Anand Swaminathan. 2000. "Why the Microbrewery Movement? Organizational Dynamics of Resource Partitioning in the U.S. Brewing Industry." *American Journal of Sociology* 106(3): 715–762.

Clawson, Dan. 2003. *The Next Upsurge*. Ithaca, NY: Cornell University Press.

Clemens, Elisabeth S. and Debra C. Minkoff. 2004. "Beyond the Iron Law: Rethinking the Place of Organizations in Social Movement Research." In *The Blackwell Companion to Social Movements*, edited by David A. Snow, Sarah A. Soule, and Hanspeter Kriesi, 155–170. Oxford: Blackwell.

Cress, Daniel M. and David A. Snow. 1996. "Mobilization at the Margins: Resources, Benefactors, and the Viability of Homeless Social Movement Organizations." *American Sociological Review* 61(6): 1089–1109.

Dacin, M. Tina, Peter A. Dacin, and Paul Tracey. 2011. "Social Entrepreneurship: A Critique and Future Directions." *Organization Science* 22(5): 1203–1213.

Davis, Gerald F. and J. Adam Cobb. 2010. "Resource Dependence Theory: Past and Future." In *Stanford's Organization Theory Renaissance, 1970–2000*, vol. 28, *Research in the Sociology of Organizations*, 21–42. New York: Emerald Publishing.

Davis, Gerald F., Doug McAdam, W. Richard Scott, and Mayer N. Zald. 2005. *Social Movements and Organization Theory*. Cambridge: Cambridge University Press.

della Porta, Donatella. 2013. *Can Democracy Be Saved?* Chichester: Wiley.

Diani, Mario. 2015. *The Cement of Civil Society*. Cambridge: Cambridge University Press.

Diani, Mario and Katia Pilati. 2011. "Interests, Identities, and Relations: Drawing Boundaries in Civic Organizational Fields." *Mobilization* 16(3): 265–282.

Dixon, Marc and Andrew W. Martin. 2012. "We Can't Win This on Our Own: Unions, Firms, and Mobilization of External Allies in Labor Disputes." *American Sociological Review* 77: 946–969.

Earl, Jennifer. 2015. "The Future of Social Movement Organizations: The Waning Dominance of SMOs Online." *American Behavioral Scientist* 59(1): 35–52.

Earl, Jennifer and Katrina Kimport. 2011. *Digitally Enabled Social Change*. Cambridge, MA: MIT Press.

Earl, Jennifer, Katrina Kimport, Greg Prieto, Carly Rush, and Kimberly Reynoso. 2010. "Changing the World One Webpage at a Time: Conceptualizing and Explaining Internet Activism." *Mobilization* 15(4): 425–446.

Earl, Jennifer and Alan Schussman. 2003. "The New Site of Activism: On-Line Organizations, Movement Entrepreneurs, and the Changing Location of Social Movement Decision-Making." *Research in Social Movements, Conflicts and Change* 24: 155–187.

Eliasoph, Nina and Paul Lichterman. 2003. "Culture in Interaction." *American Journal of Sociology* 108(4): 735–794.

Fligstein, Neil. 2001. "Social Skill and the Theory of Fields." *Sociological Theory* 19(2): 105–125.

Fligstein, Neil and Doug McAdam. 2011. "Toward a General Theory of Strategic Action Fields." *Sociological Theory* 29(1): 1–26.

Fligstein, Neil and Doug McAdam. 2012. *A Theory of Fields*. Oxford: Oxford University Press.

Ganz, Marshall. 2010. *Why David Sometimes Wins. Oxford*; Oxford University Press.

Gervais, Elizabeth Anne. 2015. "Social Network Websites as Information Channels for the US Social Forum." *Media, Culture and Society* 37(4): 547–565.

Ghaziani, Amin. 2011. "Post-Gay Collective Identity Construction." *Social Problems* 58(1): 99–125.

Gitlin, Todd. 1980. *The Whole World Is Watching*. Berkeley: University of California Press.

Goldstone, Jack A. and Charles Tilly. 2001. "Threat (and Opportunity): Popular Action and State Response in the Dynamics of Contentious Action." In *Silence and Voice in the Study of Contentious Politics*, edited by Ronald R. Aminzade, Jack A. Goldstone, Doug McAdam, et al., 179–194. Cambridge: Cambridge University Press.

Haines, Herbert H. 1984. "Black Radicalization and the Funding of Civil Rights: 1957–1970." *Social Problems* 32(1): 31–43.

Han, Hahrie. 2014. *How Organizations Develop Activists*. Oxford: Oxford University Press.

Hannan, Michael T. and John Freeman. 1977. "The Population Ecology of Organizations." *American Journal of Sociology* 82(5): 929–964.

Heaney, Michael T. and Fabio Rojas. 2014. "Hybrid Activism: Social Movement Mobilization in a Multimovement Environment." *American Journal of Sociology* 119(4): 1047–1103.

Jasper, James M. 2004. "A Strategic Approach to Collective Action: Looking for Agency in Social Movement Choices." *Mobilization* 9: 1–16.

Jenkins, J. Craig and Charles Perrow. 1977. "Insurgency of the Powerless: Farm Worker Movements (1946–1972)." *American Sociological Review* 42(2): 249–268.

Johnson, Erik W. and Scott Frickel. 2011. "Ecological Threat and the Founding of U.S. National Environmental Movement Organizations, 1962–1998." *Social Problems* 58(3): 305–329.

Jung, Wooseok, Brayden G. King, and Sarah A. Soule. 2014. "Issue Bricolage: Explaining the Configuration of the Social Movement Sector, 1960–1995." *American Journal of Sociology* 120(1): 187–225.

Karpf, David. 2010. "Online Political Mobilization from the Advocacy Group's Perspective: Looking Beyond Clicktivism." *Policy and Internet* 2(4): 7–41.

Karpf, David. 2012. *The Move On Effect*. Oxford: Oxford University Press.

Kay, Tamara. 2005. "Labor Transnationalism and Global Governance: The Impact of NAFTA on Transnational Labor Relationships in North America." *American Journal of Sociology* 111(3): 715–756.

Kellogg, Katherine. 2011. "Making the Cut: Using Status-Based Countertactics to Block Social Movement Implementation and Microinstitutional Change in Surgery." *Organization Science* 23(6): 1546–1570.

Kimport, Katrina. 2012. "Organizational Dominance and Its Consequences in the Online Abortion Rights and Antiabortion Movements." In *Research in Social Movements, Conflicts and Change*, vol. 33, *Media, Movements, and Political Change*, 139–161. New York: Emerald Publishing.

King, Brayden G. and Edward T. Walker. 2014. "Winning Hearts and Minds: Field Theory and the Three Dimensions of Strategy." *Strategic Organization* 12(2): 134–141.

Kutz-Flamenbaum, Rachel V. 2016. "The Importance of Micro-Level Effects on Social Movement Outcomes: MachsomWatch at Israeli Checkpoints." *Sociological Perspectives* 59(2): 441–459.

Landy, David. 2015. "Bringing the Outside In: Field Interaction and Transformation from Below in Political Struggles." *Social Movement Studies* 14(3): 255–269.

Larson, Jeff and Sarah A. Soule. 2009. "Sector-Level Dynamics and Collective Action in the United States, 1965–1975." *Mobilization* 14(3): 293–314.

Lee, Caroline W. 2015. "Participatory Practices in Organizations." *Sociology Compass* 9(4): 272–288.

Lee, Caroline W., Michael McQuarrie, and Edward T. Walker, eds. 2015. *Democratizing Inequalities*. New York: New York University Press.

Lewis, Kevin, Kurt Gray, and Jens Meierhenrich. 2014. "The Structure of Online Activism." *Sociological Science* 45: 1–9.

Lichterman, Paul. 2006. "Social Capital or Group Style? Rescuing Tocqueville's Insights on Civic Engagement." *Theory and Society* 35(5–6): 529–563.

Lichterman, Paul. 2008. "Religion and the Construction of Civic Identity." *American Sociological Review* 73(1): 83–104.

Lichterman, Paul and Nina Eliasoph. 2014. "Civic Action." *American Journal of Sociology* 120(3): 798–863.

Maney, Gregory, Rachel V. Kutz-Flamenbaum, Deanna Rohlinger and Jeff Goodwin, eds. 2011. *Strategy in Action*. Minneapolis: University of Minnesota Press.

Martin, Andrew W. 2007. "Organizational Structure, Authority and Protest: The Case of Union Organizing in the United States, 1990–2001." *Social Forces* 85(3): 1413–1435.

Martin, Andrew W. 2008. "The Institutional Logic of Union Organizing and the Effectiveness of Social Movement Repertoires." *American Journal of Sociology* 113(4): 1067–1103.

McAdam, Doug and Hilary Boudet. 2012. *Putting Social Movements in Their Place*. Cambridge: Cambridge University Press.

McCammon, Holly J. 2012 "Explaining Frame Variation: Moderate and More Radical Demands for Women's Citizenship in the U.S. Women's Jury Movements." *Social Problems* 59: 43–69.

McCammon, Holly J., Erin M. Bergner, and Sandra C. Arch. 2015. "'Are You One of Those Women?': Within-Movement Conflict, Radical Flank Effects, and Social Movement Political Outcomes." *Mobilization* 20(2): 157–178.

McCammon, Holly J. and Karen Campbell. 2002. "Allies On the Road to Victory: Coalition Formation Between the Suffragists and the Woman's Christian Temperance Union." *Mobilization* 7(3): 231–251.

McCammon, Holly J., Karen E. Campbell, Ellen M. Granberg, and Christine Mowery. 2001. "How Movements Win: Gendered Opportunity Structures and U.S. Women's Suffrage Movements, 1866 to 1919." *American Sociological Review* 66(1): 49–70.

McCammon, Holly J., Courtney Sanders Muse, Harmony D. Newman, and Teresa M. Terrell. 2007. "Movement Framing and Discursive Opportunity Structures: The Political Successes of the US Women's Jury Movements." *American Sociological Review* 72(5): 725–749.

McCammon, Holly J. and Nella Van Dyke, eds. 2010. *Strategic Alliances*. Minneapolis: University of Minnesota Press.

McCarthy, John D. 1996. "Constraints and Opportunities in Adopting, Adapting, and Inventing." In *Comparative Perspectives on Social Movements*, edited by Doug McAdam, John D. McCarthy, and Mayer N. Zald, 141–151. Cambridge: Cambridge University Press.

McCarthy, John D. and Mark Wolfson. 1996. "Resource Mobilization by Local Social Movement Organizations: Agency, Strategy, and Organization in the Movement Against Drinking and Driving." *American Sociological Review* 61(6): 1070–1088.

McCarthy, John D. and Mayer N. Zald. 1973. *The Trend of Social Movements in America*. Morristown, NJ: General Learning Press.

McCarthy, John D. and Mayer N. Zald. 1977. "Resource Mobilization and Social Movements: A Partial Theory." *American Journal of Sociology* 82(6): 1212–1241.

McCarthy, John D. and Mayer N. Zald. 2001. "The Enduring Vitality of the Resource Mobilization Theory of Social Movements." In *Handbook of Sociological Theory*, edited by Johnathan H. Turner, 533–565.New York: Springer.

Michels, Robert. 1959 (1911). *Political Parties*. New York: Dover.

Micó, Josep-Lluís and Andreu Casero-Ripollés. 2014. "Political Activism Online: Organization and Media Relations in the Case of 15M in Spain." *Information, Communication and Society* 17(7): 858–871.

Minkoff, Debra C. 1994. "From Service Provision to Institutional Advocacy: The Shifting Legitimacy of Organizational Forms." *Social Forces* 72(4): 943–969.

Minkoff, Debra C. 1999. "Bending with the Wind: Strategic Change and Adaptation by Women's and Racial Minority Organizations." *American Journal of Sociology* 104(6): 1666–1703.

Minkoff, Debra C. and John McCarthy. 2005. "Reinvigorating the Study of Organizational Processes in Social Movements." *Mobilization* 10(2): 289–308.

Minkoff, Debra C. and Walter W. Powell. 2006. "Nonprofit Mission: Constancy, Responsiveness, or Deflection." In *The Nonprofit Sector: A Research Handbook*, edited by Walter W. Powell and Richard Steinberg, vol. 2, 591–611. New Haven, CT: Yale University Press.

Mische, Ann. 2011. "Relational Sociology, Culture, and Agency." In *The Sage Handbook of Social Network Analysis*, edited by John Scott and Peter Carrington, 80–97. London: Sage.

Negro, Giacomo, Fabrizio Perretti, and Glenn R. Carroll. 2013. "Challenger Groups, Commercial Organizations, and Policy Enactment: Local Lesbian/Gay Rights Ordinances in the United States from 1972 to 2008." *American Journal of Sociology* 119(3): 790–832.

Olson, Mancur. 1965. *The Logic of Collective Action*. Cambridge, MA: Harvard University Press.

Osterman, Paul. 2006. "Overcoming Oligarchy: Culture and Agency in Social Movement Organizations." *Administrative Science Quarterly* 51(4): 622–649.

Pfeffer, Jeffrey and Gerald R. Salancik. 1978. *The External Control of Organizations*. New York: Harper and Row.

Piven, Frances Fox and Richard A. Cloward. 1977. *Poor People's Movements*. New York: Pantheon Books.

Polletta, Francesca. 2002. *Freedom Is an Endless Meeting*. Chicago: University of Chicago Press.

Polletta, Francesca. 2006. "Mobilization Forum: Awkward Movements." *Mobilization* 11(4): 475–500.

Polletta, Francesca and Pang Ching Bobby Chen. 2013. "Gender and Public Talk Accounting for Women's Variable Participation in the Public Sphere." *Sociological Theory* 31(4): 291–317.

Putnam, Robert D. 2000. *Bowling Alone*. New York: Simon & Schuster.

Quadagno, Jill. 2004. "Why the United States Has No National Health Insurance: Stakeholder Mobilization against the Welfare State, 1945–1996." *Journal of Health and Social Behavior* 45: 25–44.

Ring-Ramirez, Misty, Heidi Reynolds-Stenson, and Jennifer Earl. 2014. "Culturally Constrained Contention: Mapping the Meaning Structure of the Repertoire of Contention." *Mobilization* 19(4): 405–419.

Shaw, Aaron and Benjamin M. Hill. 2014. "Laboratories of Oligarchy? How the Iron Law Extends to Peer Production." *Journal of Communication* 64(2): 215–238.

Shirky, Clay. 2008. *Here Comes Everybody*. Harmondsworth: Penguin.

Simpson, Cohen R. 2016. "Competition for Foundation Patronage and the Differential Effects of Prestige on the Grant Market Success of Social Movement Organisations." *Social Networks* 46: 29–43.

Skocpol, Theda. 2003. *Diminished Democracy*. Norman: University of Oklahoma Press.

Smith, Jackie and Dawn Wiest. 2005. "The Uneven Geography of Global Civil Society: National and Global Influences on Transnational Association." *Social Forces* 84(2): 621–652.

Soule, Sarah A. and Brayden G. King. 2008. "Competition and Resource Partitioning in Three Social Movement Industries." *American Journal of Sociology* 113(6): 1568–1610.

Staggenborg, Suzanne. 1988. "The Consequences of Professionalization and Formalization in the Pro-Choice Movement." *American Sociological Review* 53(4): 585–605.

Stein, Laura. 2009. "Social Movement Web Use in Theory and Practice: A Content Analysis of US Movement Websites." *New Media and Society* 11(5): 749–771.

Stepan-Norris, Judith and Maurice Zeitlin. 2003. *Left Out*. Cambridge: Cambridge University Press.

Stretesky, Paul B., Sheila Huss, Michael J. Lynch, Sammy Zahran, and Bob Childs. 2011. "The Founding of Environmental Justice Organizations across US Counties during the 1990s and 2000s: Civil Rights and Environmental Cross-Movement Effects." *Social Problems* 58(3): 330–360.

Tilly, Charles. 1993. "Social Movements as Historically Specific Clusters of Political Performances." *Berkeley Journal of Sociology* 38: 1–30.

Van Dyke, Nella. 2003. "Crossing Movement Boundaries: Factors that Facilitate Coalition Protest by American College Students, 1930–1990." *Social Problems* 50(2): 226–250.

Van Dyke, Nella and Holly McCammon. 2010. *Strategic Alliances: Coalition Building and Social Movements*. Minneapolis: University of Minnesota Press.

Van Dyke, Nella and Sarah A. Soule. 2002. "Structural Social Change and the Mobilizing Effect of Threat: Explaining Levels of Patriot and Militia Organizing in the United States." *Social Problems* 49(4): 497–520.

Van Dyke, Nella, Sarah A. Soule, and Verta A. Taylor. 2004. "The Targets of Social Movements: Beyond a Focus on the State." *Research in Social Movements, Conflict and Change* 25: 27–51.

Vasi, Ion Bogdan. 2009. "New Heroes, Old Theories? Toward a Sociological Perspective on Social Entrepreneurship." In *An Introduction to Social Entrepreneurship*, edited by Rafael Ziegler, 155–173. Cheltenham: Edward Elgar.

Vasi, Ion Bogdan, Edward T. Walker, John S. Johnson, and Hui Fen Tan. 2015. "'No Fracking Way!' Documentary Film, Discursive Opportunity, and Local Opposition against Hydraulic Fracturing in the United States, 2010 to 2013." *American Sociological Review* 80(5): 934–959.

Voss, Kim and Rick Fantasia. 2004. "The Future of American Labor: Reinventing Unions." *Contexts* 3(2): 35–41.

Voss, Kim and Rachel Sherman. 2000. "Breaking the Iron Law of Oligarchy: Union Revitalization in the American Labor Movement." *American Journal of Sociology* 106(2): 303–349.

Walder, Andrew G. 2009. "Political Sociology and Social Movements." *Annual Review of Sociology* 35(1): 393–412.

Walker, Edward T. 2012. "Social Movements, Organizations, and Fields: A Decade of Theoretical Integration." *Contemporary Sociology* 41(5): 576–587.

Walker, Edward T. 2014. *Grassroots for Hire*. Cambridge: Cambridge University Press.

Walker, Edward T., Andrew W. Martin, and John D. McCarthy. 2008. "Confronting the State, the Corporation, and the Academy: The Influence of Institutional Targets on Social Movement Repertoires." *American Journal of Sociology* 114(1): 35–76.

Walker, Edward T. and John D. McCarthy. 2010. "Legitimacy, Strategy, and Resources in the Survival of Community-Based Organizations." *Social Problems* 57(3): 315–340.

Walker, Edward T., John D. McCarthy, and Frank Baumgartner. 2011. "Replacing Members with Managers? Mutualism among Membership and Nonmembership Advocacy Organizations in the United States." *American Journal of Sociology* 116(4): 1284–1337.

Walker, Edward T. and Christopher M. Rea. 2014. "The Political Mobilization of Firms and Industries." *Annual Review of Sociology* 40(1): 281–304.

Walker, Edward T. and Lina M. Stepick. 2014. "Strength in Diversity? Group Heterogeneity in the Mobilization of Grassroots Organizations." *Sociology Compass* 8(7): 959–975.

Wang, Dan J. and Sarah A. Soule. 2012. "Social Movement Organizational Collaboration: Networks of Learning and the Diffusion of Protest Tactics, 1960–1995." *American Journal of Sociology* 117(6): 1674–1722.

Yang, Guobin. 2016. "The Commercialization and Digitization of Social Movement Society." *Contemporary Sociology* 45(2): 120–125.

Zald, Mayer N. and Roberta Ash. 1966. "Social Movement Organizations: Growth, Decay and Change." *Social Forces* 44(3): 327–341.

10

Bringing Leadership Back In

Marshall Ganz and Elizabeth McKenna

Introduction

Social movements drive economic, social, political, and cultural change. But who – or what – makes movements? Because social movement effectiveness depends largely on the extent to which participants learn how to turn individual resources into collective power, leadership development is central to movement capacity building. With rare exceptions, however, it remains understudied and under-theorized (Aminzade, Goldstone, and Perry 2001; Barker, Johnson, and Lavalette 2001; Ganz 2010; Morris and Staggenborg 2004).

We begin with the claim that leadership dynamics are key to understanding social movements. Next, we survey existing literature on leadership in adjacent disciplines and in the social movement canon to learn why it remains a relatively marginalized topic in the subfield. We argue that reducing leadership to a contrast between *charismatic*, *prophetic*, or *enthusiastic* attributes and the *administrative*, *bureaucratic*, or *pragmatic* features of movement structures obscures the practice of leadership itself. Our review of the literature suggests that a failure to distinguish among discrete qualities of leaders, authority structures through which leadership is often exercised, and the practice of leadership – that is, what leaders actually do – inhibits our understanding of: (1) the internal dynamics of social movement organizations (Reger and Staggenborg 2006); (2) the differences between *social movement leadership* – outward-facing work that often requires the management of relationships among multiple constituencies – and *social movement organization* (SMO) *leadership* – inward-facing work requiring management of a distinct organizational entity (della Porta and Diani [1999] 2006); and (3) the reasons why some moments of protest become movements for change while others do not (Tilly 1978), particularly with respect to the emergent role of digital technology (Tufekci 2017).

The Wiley Blackwell Companion to Social Movements, Second Edition. Edited by David A. Snow, Sarah A. Soule, Hanspeter Kriesi, and Holly J. McCammon.
© 2019 John Wiley & Sons Ltd. Published 2019 by John Wiley & Sons Ltd.

Throughout our discussion, we highlight recent scholarship that has begun to address these theoretical and empirical challenges by examining social movement leadership in more agentic, processural, and relational terms (e.g. Ganz 2009, McCammon 2012; Reger 2007). In the second half of the chapter, we elaborate an alternative, practice-based framework for the study of social movement leadership. While much existing research asks whether certain types of *leaders* operating in more or less bureaucratic structures contribute to movement outcomes, we argue that a more fruitful line of inquiry is to ask to what extent which different *leadership practices* help explain variation in movement outcomes. We conclude by offering avenues for further research that adopt this theoretical approach.

Leadership Matters

Leadership-rich social movements have anchored political parties (Schlozman 2015), transformed social policy (Amenta 2006), and built power among historically marginalized groups, as in the case of the suffrage movement (McCammon et al. 2001), populist movements (Jansen 2016; McMath and Foner 1992), the labor movement (Voss and Fantasia 2004), the civil rights movement (Andrews 2004; McAdam [1982] 1999; Morris 1984; Robnett 1996), the farmworkers movement (Ganz 2009), the women's movement (Reger and Staggenborg 2006), the conservative movement (Gross, Medvetz, and Russell 2011), the LGBT movement (Ghaziani, Taylor, and Stone 2015), and others (Foner 1999). While these studies offer valuable in-depth examinations of particular movements, their authors rarely treat leadership as a central object of analysis.

By contrast, leadership has been of extensive interest in neighboring disciplines and subfields. Wilson's classic book *Political Organizations* (1973), Burns' paradigm-shifting work on transformational relational leadership (1978), Skworonek's analysis of presidential succession (1993), and more recent work by Miroff (2003) and Han (2014) are examples of the leadership studies tradition in political science. Scholars of union organizing have also long addressed questions of movement leadership (Edelstein and Warner 1976; Ganz et al. 2004; Lipset 1950; McAlevey 2016; Nyden 1985; Voss and Sherman 2000). Ahlquist and Levi (2013) develop a new and compelling theory of organizational leadership to explain why some unions engage in sustained political mobilizations that extend beyond their members' self-interest while others do not. Finally, a more practice-oriented domain in which scholars examine the micro-dynamics of leadership and leadership development is that of community organizing (Christens and Speer 2015; Orr 2007; Schultz and Miller 2015; Walls 2015; Warren 2001).

Research on leadership in goods and service-providing industries and in the military abounds (Avolio, Walumbwa, and Weber 2009; Bennis and Nanus 2007; Day et al. 2014; Haslam, Reicher, and Platow 2011; Snook, Nohria, and Khurana 2012). Several strands of the management literature have examined dimensions of leadership that are more germane to social movements than they are to corporations and troop deployment, including the relational, values-based, motivational, and strategically adaptive characteristics of organizational actors (Bennis [1989] 2009; Eisenmann, Ries, and Dillard 2013; Heifetz 2004; Nohria and Khurana 2010; Senge 1990).[1]

Leadership and Social Movement Studies

In sociology, social movement scholarship has made significant gains in explaining how people mobilize (Saunders et al. 2012; Snow, Zurcher, and Ekland-Olson 1980), hybrid forms of activism (Heaney and Rojas 2014, 2015), network positions (Diani 2011), tactical diffusion (Wang and Soule 2012), target receptivity (McDonnell, King, and Soule 2015; Walker, Martin, and McCarthy 2008), and the ways in which movements can shape institutions and policy change (Amenta et al. 2010). Yet much of this research tends to treat leadership as epiphenomenal, instead emphasizing the external conditions of movement emergence such as the availability of elite allies, the strength of opponents, network positions, historical circumstances, sudden crises, and financial and human resources (Goldstone 1980; Jenkins and Perrow 1977; McCarthy et al. 1988; Tarrow [1994] 2011). Morris and Staggenborg (2004) argued that this structural orientation led scholars to sideline the study of leadership. "Social movement activity," they wrote, "is not a residual activity deducible from political and economic structures" (ibid.: 190).[2] Our critique builds on Morris and Staggenborg's argument that a structural bias in social movement studies continues to orient scholars toward identifying constraining conditions, making outcomes more or less probable, rather than the agentic, resourceful, and hopeful – if risky – dimensions of social movements that contribute to improbable but possible outcomes.

Classic definitions of leadership: charismatic and bureaucratic authority

Social movement leadership is often understood in terms of the distinction between charismatic and bureaucratic authority. We can trace these conceptualizations to Max Weber's specification of three ideal types of "imperative coordination": (1) traditional, culturally-grounded authority; (2) rational-legal bureaucratic authority; and (3) charismatic authority resulting from enthusiastic interactions among leaders and followers (Weber [1887] 1964, [1922] 1978). Influenced by this tradition, scholars tended to categorize those whom they identified as movement leaders as ideologues or pragmatists (Wilson 1973), enthusiasts or bureaucrats (Roche and Sachs 1969), or symbolic leaders or rational decision-makers (Turner and Killian [1957] 1987). These taxonomies linked personality type to authority structure and tended to ignore leader behavior and its effects on movement outcomes.

Staggenborg (1988) began to explore this gap in her analysis of entrepreneurial leadership (associated with movement emergence), and professional leadership (associated with social movement organization stability and continuity). Robnett (1996), too, helpfully identified distinct leadership roles – neither of which were exclusively charismatic or professional – but analyzed in terms of gender, hierarchy, and focus (inward or outward). Yet some recent work, such as Clifford and Nepstad's (2007) study of the consequences of the assassination of prophetic versus administrative leaders, returned to Weber's ideal types. As Nepstad and Clifford argue in a separate article, such descriptive categorizations "provide an overview of leadership types and trajectories, but they do not tell us much about the factors that make people compelling and capable organizers" (2006: 4). In other words, dualistic accounts of social movement leader types that essentialize personas – or identify leaders based on the structures in which they are embedded – reveal little about the role of leadership dynamics in movement efficacy.

Mass society and the "magic man"

Weber's classic formulation also influenced debate as to the role of charismatic leadership in mass psychology and collective action. Writing in the wake of World War II, scholars assigned "charismatic" leaders and their followers prominent explanatory roles in the study of collective behavior (Hoffer 1951; Kornhauser 1959; Smelser 1962). Reacting to this approach, political process theorists argued that far from being an irrational response to extraordinary charismatic appeal, social movements were highly rational attempts to pursue shared collective goals (McAdam [1982] 1999). Social movement scholars' rejection of mass society theory was so absolute that charisma – as well as much of what *else* goes on between leaders and followers – was effectively "banished" from the subfield (Andreas 2007: 435).

At the same time, as research programs shifted from historical investigations to contemporary protest cycles, individuals who had participated in the movements under study began to raise questions about how leadership operates in social movements (Freeman 1999; Ganz 2000; Gitlin 1980).[3] For example, civil rights leader Ella Baker distinguished between Martin Luther King's preacher-congregation leadership style and the more widely shared leadership practice of enabling others to achieve purpose. Baker argued:

> Instead of 'the leader'—a person who was supposed to be a magic man—you would develop individuals who were bound together by a concept that benefited larger numbers of individuals and provided an opportunity for them to grow into being responsible for carrying out a program.
>
> (Ransby 2003: 188)

Baker's insight implies that the practice of leadership within a single organization may be distinct from King's combination of outward-facing interpretive skills, oversight of his own SMO, the Southern Christian Leadership Conference, and management of the complex dynamics among leaders of other civil rights SMOs. These distinctions have yet to be fully explored in the literature.

From the "iron law" to the "tyranny of structurelessness"

Robert Michels extended Weber's analysis of imperative coordination in his study of the bureaucratization of the German Social Democratic Party. He argued that the profound goal and authority shifts that he observed were the result of the party's effort to translate movement objectives into sustained benefits (Michels [1915] 1968). The "iron law of oligarchy," Michels argued, was the necessary result of any large-scale organization, including those whose initial aims were highly subversive. Scholars have since cast doubt on the determinisms of Michels' iron law (Clemens 1993; Lipset 1950; Tolbert 2010; Voss and Sherman 2000), but Francis Fox Piven and Richard Cloward (1977) built influentially on Michels' work, linking movement-stifling effects to any formal organization and its leadership. Recent attention to anti-hierarchical mass mobilizations "unencumbered" by formal leadership has resurrected this debate (Bennett and Segerberg 2013; Bimber, Flanagin, and Stohl 2012; Castells 2013; Sutherland, Land, and Böhm 2013).

A review of this literature suggests that one of the reasons that social movement leadership remains an analytical afterthought is due to a failure to differentiate authority structures (often assumed to be bureaucratic) from the interactions of leaders and followers in the exercise of leadership. Jo Freeman ([1972] 2008) was one of the first scholars to make this crucial distinction, arguing that formal positions of authority and the exercise of leadership are not always covalent. Freeman warned that the absence of formal authority structures does not mean that informal authority structures are inoperative: "Contrary to what we would like to believe, there is no such thing as a structureless group," she wrote ([1972] 2008: 152). Individuals with the money, know-how, and interest can fill organizational vacuums, resulting in what Freeman called the "tyranny of structurelessness." Later work supported her theory. For example, Kathleen Blee's (2013) comparative ethnography of grassroots groups found that implicit discursive rules can legitimate some voices and silence others. Similarly, Ruth Milkman's research on Occupy Wall Street suggests that ostensibly horizontalist movements can reinforce gender, race, and class hierarchies as informal leaders emerge (2017: 18).

Still-unresolved tensions between the "iron law" and the "tyranny of structurelessness" demonstrate why researchers must carefully assess group structure and leadership practices as separate but interdependent dimensions of a social movement. Scholarship that has begun to examine the interaction of structure and action has required theorizing movement leadership in different ways. For example, in their insightful and original study of the evolution of four local chapters of the National Organization for Woman (NOW) over a 40-year period, Reger and Staggenborg (2006) examine leaders' behavior, the strategic choices they make, and who they are – not in terms of personality attributes, but rather how the specifics of their life experience, relationships, and motivations interact with the organizational structures they help create (Ganz 2000). Similarly, in their studies on the Sierra Club, a research team found that organizational leadership practices (Andrews et al. 2010) and team dynamics (Baggetta, Han, and Andrews 2013) mediate the effects of exogenous political factors. In these studies, the role of leadership in movements is best operationalized through attention to who they are, the work that they do, and the structures they create – rather than formal positions they hold or the number of hours they invest in the movement (McCarthy and Wolfson 1996).

Theorizing Leadership Practice: An Alternative Approach

In the following section, we offer an alternative theoretical framework for the study of social movement leadership. It is based on three interdependent propositions.[4] First, we propose that movement leadership can be conceptualized as accepting responsibility to enable others to achieve shared purpose in the face of uncertainty (Ganz 2010). In this view, leadership is conceived of as a set of practices related to one's own part of the work as well as that of a collective. Second, leadership work is most evident in moments of encounter with uncertainty: a new threat, a natural disaster, a critical dilemma, a consequential election, or a sudden opportunity. Third, the capacity to turn such moments of uncertainty – and potential agency – into constructive purpose by *responding* as opposed to *reacting* is rooted in the cultivation of five leadership practices: (1) relationship building; (2) storytelling; (3) strategizing; (4) structuring; and (5) action. We posit that these five practices can serve as analytical dimensions with which to study and carry out the essential work that leadership does in social movements.

The relational dimension of social movement leadership

Movements acquire social reality in the relationships that participants construct with each other (Tarrow 2008; Tilly [2008] 2016). A person joins a movement less by signing a petition or showing up at a protest than by entering into a set of lateral peer relationships. As Munson's research on pro-life activists (2008) and Clemens' historical analysis of interest group politics (1997) demonstrate, although movements involve information diffusion, belief activation, and policy preferences, it is through organizationally-enabled social ties that potential activists acquire the learning, motivation, and resources to exercise collective voice. Relationship building, then, is significant not only for access that may be offered to other resources (Granovetter 1973), but also because it serves as the medium through which the participants construct their movement (Mische 2008).[5]

What is the role of social movement leadership in this process? Because building and maintaining relationships are labor-intensive processes, a key way that social movements scale is through the motivation and capacity of participants to recruit more participants. Community organizers have long recognized how fundamental relationship building is to their leadership work (Christens and Speer 2015; Gecan 2002; McKenna and Han 2014; Warren 2001), which explains why one-on-ones and relational house meetings are often the first steps in building new social movement organizations. Both practices cultivate the social ties that constitute the relational fabric of movements. As Granovetter (1973) observed, strong ties facilitate trust, motivation, and commitment, while weak ties broaden access to salient information, skills, and learning. Successful social movement leaders learn to combine both (Ganz 2000, 2009; Shi et al. 2017). This research suggests that the leadership practice of relationship building is a key mechanism by which individual and collective identities are crafted (Polletta and Jasper 2001; Taylor 1989), understandings of interests are developed (Gecan 2004; de Tocqueville [1835–40] 2000; Warren 2001), and new collective capacity takes root (Putnam, Leonardi, and Nanetti 1994).

The narrative dimension of social movement leadership

Social movement leaders and participants not only form new relationships, they also learn to tell new stories at the individual, communal, and movement level. A turn toward dimensions of meaning and of emotion signaled a welcome shift in the subfield (Benford and Snow 2000; Snow et al. 1986), but attended little to the role of leadership in the production of such meaning. In the framing literature, leaders are concieved of as reproducers of "cultural codes in an effort to sway target audiences to their interpretation of events" (Noakes and Johnston 2005: 4). Social movement "entrepreneurs" assess resonance, tactically frame grievances, and communicate the movement's frame to would-be adherents (Berbrier 1998; Cormier 2004; Haussman 2013; Kubal 1998). By contrast, in the approach we propose here, movement leaders focus on narrative as a source of individual and collective agency rather than a cultural constraint or marketing parameter. Agentic response requires turning a threat to be feared into a challenge to be engaged. In this way, narrative can be drawn upon to inspire the self-efficacy, solidarity, and hopefulness to overcome the fear, isolation, and self-doubt that often inhibit courageous action.[6]

Successful social movement leaders develop narratives that can articulate individual identity, group identity, and the need for action: a story of self, a story of us, and a story of now (Ganz 2010, 2011). In the civil rights movement, for example, modeled on religious "testimony," African Americans constructed stories that linked the pain, hurt, and fear of the status quo to the hope, agency, and solidarity that could enable the courage needed to secure a better future. These stories were self-emancipatory in that they altered how participants thought of themselves, each other, and the change they sought in the world (Couto 1993). Similarly, leaders in the farmworkers movement constructed a narrative rooted in Mexican cultural tradition, Roman Catholic religious practice, and elements of the civil rights and labor movements that linked Mexican immigrants, Mexican Americans, and a broader range of public support (Ganz 2009). The women's movement, too, had leaders who "restoried" their own lives using consciousness-raising as a "radical weapon" (Sarachild 1978). Stories of pain could be shared, but so too could stories of hope (Polletta 2006), weaving individual narrative into a shared narrative within which to ground collective action. Social movement leaders also employ narrative to interpret what can be frequent reverses along the way to success (Beckwith 2015; Voss 1996). As with relationship building, crafting narrative is an empirically observable leadership practice. In contrast to the signifying work that the framing literature typically restricts to strategic messengers, all participants in a robust social movement do the work of translating values into action.[7]

The strategic dimension of social movement leadership

A third practice of social movement leadership is creative and adaptive strategizing (McCammon 2012; Reger and Staggenborg 2006). Just as narrative can enable the emotional capacity to deal with the unexpected, so strategizing draws on one's cognitive capacity to form an agentic response to threat (Ganz 2000). Because social movements often challenge those with superior traditional resources like wealth, status, and expertise, leaders must find ways to compensate with greater resourcefulness: figuring out how to turn resources one has into the power one needs to get what one wants. Strategy is ongoing; it is something you do, not something you have, especially in the uncertain setting of a social movement (Jansen 2016).

Strategizing seems to be most successful when located within a team whose members have experience in the various domains in which the movement is unfolding (Ganz 2000, 2009). Leaders who make up such a team are often deeply motivated and have created an effective venue within which they can combine a view of the whole with deep knowledge of the specific context within which the action unfolds – on the top of the mountain and down in the valley at the same time (McAlevey 2015). At the same time, the more distributed the leadership of a movement, the more important it is for each unit to be able to respond in its own domain – as opposed to a strategy team removed from the rank-and-file implementation. High motivation, access to diverse sources of salient knowledge, and an organizational structure that facilitates learning are key components of this link between leadership practice and movement strategy (Ganz 2000).[8]

The structural dimension of social movement leadership

Many social movements start out as decentralized, self-governed, and voluntary operations. These informal features present leadership challenges because sustained effectiveness depends on crafting structures of coordination, accountability, and decision-making that enable the strategic use of a constituency's resources (Einwohner 2007). Successful movement leadership therefore requires ongoing organizational structuring, often a major challenge confronting movements as they evolve. As Ahlquist and Levi show, leaders make choices about an organization's governance institutions and principles (used to set members' expectations), thus forming a self-reinforcing equilibrium that enables some organizations to take collective action for wider social and political causes (2013: 7–8).

Despite the demonstrated importance of such coordination mechanisms, some movements may reject formal organization entirely because they emerge in reaction to oppressive – often hierarchical and bureaucratic – structures (Sitrin 2014). A focus on freeing oneself "from" the past may overwhelm a need to focus on the freeing oneself "to" create a more desirable future (Berlin [1958] 1969). Horizontalism is not a phenomenon new to the digital age. However, movements without explicit structure may succumb to the tyranny of structurelessness described above (Freeman [1972] 2008), characterized by chaotic meetings, opaque decision-making, lack of follow-through, and an incapacity to turn reaction to threats into a capacity for strategic intentionality.

As Richard Hackman (2002), Ruth Wageman (1995) and others (Mathieu et al. 2008) have established, self-governing groups – like those that make up a SMO – must do three things to improve their odds of effective functioning: (1) define a shared purpose; (2) establish norms of decision-making, accountability, and time management; and (3) decide on roles. Functional teams must also be bounded, stable, and diverse enough to operate interdependently. Although few social movement leadership structures have been evaluated in these terms (Andrews et al. 2010), the benefits of this approach in terms of motivation, accountability, and capacity were the foundation of the 2008 Obama campaign's more than 10,000 leadership teams. A shift from the notoriously hierarchical setting of an electoral campaign to an inclusive, clearly structured, and interdependent team approach proved critical to the successes of that grassroots campaign (McKenna and Han 2014).

Teams are just one example of how to scaffold leadership development throughout a movement. The broader question of how to structure the exercise of leadership is critical for understanding how – and where – strategizing actually occurs, the extent to which leadership development is distributed, and how participants engage in the movement in activities beyond episodic protest.[9] Developing a leadership-rich organization not only requires learning to delegate, it requires a conscious strategy to identify, recruit, develop, and embed leaders in a structure that has staying power (Andrews 2004).

The collective action dimension of social movement leadership

We have argued that building relationships, storytelling, strategizing, and structuring are key practices of social movement leadership. Yet shifts in power relations only result from the mobilization and deployment of resources (Oliver and Marwell 1992). The craft of obtaining, making good on, and deepening commitments over time is often the difference between a movement's success or failure (Abelson 1983; Han 2014). If people converge at a protest, picket line, direct action, or strike but lack the discipline to manage themselves, to keep a strategic focus, and to preempt or respond to opposition and setbacks, the collective capacity that sustained success requires may dissipate and even discourage future actions. McAlevey has referred to the extent to which rank-and-file leaders repeatedly turn out their followers as a "structure tests" (2016: Chapter 2). According to McAlevey, each successive action reveals whether the leadership team truly leads its constituency – and whether the movement is owned by the people who make it up – or not.

Finally, a capacity to learn from each structure test is critical to movement success. It is not enough to deploy novel tactics once; movements must also adapt as contexts change over time (McCammon 2012). Such adaptation requires accurate information as to the results of ongoing actions. As a result, the quality, accuracy, availability, rigor, and appropriateness of metrics that can be used to analyze mobilization events can have a decisive impact on the strategic development of a movement and the breadth and depth of its leadership.

Conclusion: New Directions for Social Movement Leadership Studies

We have argued that neglecting the relational, motivational, strategic, structural, and operational dimensions of leadership practice limits the utility of scholarship intended to illuminate how social movements work. A failure to adequately theorize leadership risks circumscribing our analyses of how social movements function, and more importantly, the possibilities of the movements themselves. Below, we outline a series of research questions that follow from the theoretical framework outlined above.

Longitudinal directions

- What is the role of leadership in the transition from protest to power?
- How do different leadership practices shape participants' understanding of their own agency over time?

Processual directions

- What is the role of leadership in protest instigation, protest management, and protest interpretation?
- Under what circumstances can top-down social movement organizations transform into democratic and leadership-rich movement organizations (and vice versa)?
- How do leaders and participants communicate movement narratives – as distinct from movement frames?
- What are the organizational conditions of social movements that create the space within which strategic leadership can grow?
- Is there a relationship between the source of resources – money, people, political ties – and how leadership is exercised within the movement?

Comparative directions

- How is leadership exercised in social movements around the world? What are the similarities and differences across cases?
- What is the relational fabric from which movements are constructed? To what extent does it vary by values, issues, or national culture?
- What are the conditions that make some groups better than others at leadership interdependence?

Creating the conditions for change: criticality and hope

Leading social movements requires learning to manage the core tension that theologian Walter Brueggemann ([1978] 2001) describes as the heart of the prophetic imagination: criticality (experience of the world's pain) and hope (experience of the world's possibility). In this view, achieving social change not only requires leaders to cultivate practices like the ones outlined above, it also requires finding an equilibrium between numbing despair and optimistic delusion (Wilson 1973: 215–16). The twelfth-century philosopher Maimonides viewed hope as belief in the "plausibility of the possible" as opposed to the "necessity of the probable." Much existing research in the social movement subfield continues to focus on the structures and taxonomies that constrain and predict the probable. It is to the exercise of leadership and agency, however, that we must look to appreciate the power of the possible.

Notes

1 One of the primary ways in which social movements can be distinguished from interest groups is that they not only contest the allocation of goods, but, rather what it is that constitutes a "good" – what is of value – in the first place. Values inform action not as intellectual concepts but as growing out of emotional experience (Cates 2009; Damasio 1994; Nussbaum 2001).
2 For example, Chun's longitudinal study of a movement that organizes Chinese immigrant women working in precarious jobs showed that constituents took on leadership roles regardless of their language ability or socioeconomic status (Chun 2016: 380). The

workers lacked the propitious external and biographical conditions that scholars have theorized to be a precondition to success, yet they still built significant power through collective action.

3 Morris (1984) reasserts a role for charisma, but embeds it institutionally and combines it with an analysis of strategic creativity and organizational discipline.

4 This framework grew out of work by Marshall Ganz and colleagues integrating social movement leadership experience and social science in the development of a pedagogy of practice in online and offline classrooms, workshops, and campaigns in the USA and around the world (Ganz and Lin 2012). Its empirical basis stems from the 2003–2005 research project with the Sierra Club mentioned in the text (Andrews et al. 2010). A follow-up study led by Ganz and Ruth Wageman in 2006 and 2007, developed a series of four workshops carried out over 18 months in four states and with 20 local groups. This approach, in turn, grounded the Obama campaign's grassroots field organization, beginning with an initial "Camp Obama" in Burbank in July 2007 (McKenna and Han 2014). Since then, it has been used in diverse domains in the USA, especially through the New Organizing Institute, including that of immigration reform, climate change, gun control, health care, union organizing, among other efforts. Globally, it has grounded effective adaptations in locations as diverse as Jordan, Serbia, Denmark, Kenya, Australia, Senegal, Nepal, Japan, and China. The five leadership practices have also served as the basis of 448 workshops in which 32,184 people in 25 countries have participated since 2007.

5 While interpersonal relationships are often operationalized as exchanges of interests and resources (Blau 1955) in the context of social movements, it is in the commitments individuals make to one another that they can become more than an exchange, acquire a past, and develop a future. The learning that comes from association and commitment is what enables participants to go beyond narrow concepts of "self-interest" to broader notions of what de Tocqueville called "common interest," or at least "enlightened self-interest" ([1835–40] 2000).

6 A large body of interdisciplinary research has shown how social support, solidarity, and empathy constructed in story can contribute to a sense of individual and collective efficacy (Appadurai 2007; Cohen-Chen et al. 2014; Gamson 1992; Hunt and Benford 1994; Lueck 2007; Niederhoffer and Pennebaker 2009; Seligman and Csikszentmihalyi 2000; Snyder 2000).

7 Elsewhere Ganz (2011) analyzes the way in which leaders use narrative to translate the emotional content of values into a capacity for agentic action.

8 As with social movement strategy, recent literature in new product design argues that who is doing the strategizing and how they do it are particularly critical (Eisenmann et al. 2013).

9 The literature on distributed leadership encourages experimentation, with each team member forming his or her own team and each of their team members, in turn, forming their own as well (Bolden 2011; Gronn 2002). This form of cascaded leadership, which came to be known as the "snowflake" leadership approach, has proven to be effective at supporting the development of leadership deeply within a constituency. Along with public narrative, it is a practice that has been emulated, for example, by the DREAMers movement.

References

Abelson, Robert. 1983. "Whatever Became of Constituency Theory?" *Personality and Social Psychology Bulletin* 9(1): 37–64.

Ahlquist, John and Margaret Levi. 2013. *In the Interest of Others: Organizations and Social Activism.* Princeton, NJ: Princeton University Press.

Amenta, Edwin. 2006. *When Movements Matter*. Princeton, NJ: Princeton University Press.

Amenta, Edwin, Neal Caren, Elizabeth Chiarello, and Yang Su. 2010. "The Political Consequences of Social Movements." *Annual Review of Sociology* 36: 287–307.

Aminzade, Ron, Jack A. Goldstone, and Elizabeth J. Perry. 2001. "Leadership Dynamics and the Dynamics of Contention." In *Silence and Voice in the Study of Contentious Politics*, edited by Ron Aminzade, Jack A. Goldstone, Doug McAdam, Elizabeth J. Perry, William H. Sewell, Sidney Tarrow and Charles Tilly, 126–154. New York: Cambridge University Press.

Andreas, Joel. 2007. "The Structure of Charismatic Mobilization: A Case Study of Rebellion Druing the Chinese Cultural Revolution." *American Sociological Review* 72: 434–458.

Andrews, Kenneth T. 2004. *Freedom Is a Constant Struggle: The Mississippi Civil Rights Movement and Its Legacy*. Chicago: University of Chicago Press.

Andrews, Kenneth, Marshall Ganz, Matthew Baggetta, Hahrie Han, and Chaeyoon Lim. 2010. "Leadership, Membership, and Voice: Civic Associations that Work." *American Journal of Sociology* 115(4): 1191–1242.

Appadurai, Arjun. 2007. "Hope and Democracy." *Public Culture* 19(1): 29–34.

Avolio, Bruce J., Fred O. Walumbwa, and Todd J. Weber. 2009. "Leadership: Current Theories, Research and Future Directions." *Annual Review of Psychology* 60: 421–449.

Baggetta, Matthew, Hahrie Han, and Kenneth Andrews. 2013. "Leading Associations: How Individual Characteristics and Team Dynamics Generate Committed Leaders." *American Sociological Review* 78(4): 544–573.

Barker, Colin, Alan Johnson, and Michael Lavalette. 2001. "Leadership Matters: An Introduction." In *Leadership in Social Movements*, edited by Colin Barker, Alan Johnson and Michael Lavalette, 1–23. Manchester: Manchester University Press.

Beckwith, Karen. 2015. "Narratives of Defeat: Explaining the Effects of Loss in Social Movements." *The Journal of Politics* 77(1): 2–13.

Benford, Robert D. and David A. Snow. 2000. "Framing Processes and Social Movements: An Overview and Assessment." *Annual Review of Sociology* 26: 611–639.

Bennett, Lance W. and Alexandra Segerberg. 2013. *The Logic of Connective Action: Digital Media and the Personalization of Contentious Politics*. New York: Cambridge University Press.

Bennis, Warren. [1989] 2009. *On Becoming a Leader*. New York: Basic Books.

Bennis, Warren and Burt Nanus. 2007. *Leaders: The Strategies for Taking Charge*. New York: HarperCollins.

Berbrier, Mitch. 1998. "'Half the Battle': Cultural Resonance, Framing Processes, and Ethnic Affectations in Contemporary White Supremacists' Rhetoric." *Social Problems* 45: 431–450.

Berlin, Isaiah. [1958] 1969. "Two Concepts of Liberty." In *Four Essays on Liberty*. Oxford: Oxford University Press.

Bimber, Bruce, Andrew Flanagin, and Cynthia Stohl. 2012. *Collective Action in Organizations: Interaction and Engagement in an Era of Technological Change*. New York: Cambridge University Press.

Blau, Peter. 1955. *The Dynamics of Bureaucracy: A Study of Interpersonal Relations in Two Government Agencies*. Chicago: University of Chicago Press.

Blee, Kathleen. 2013. "How Options Disappear: Causality and Emergence in Grassroots Activist Groups." *American Journal of Sociology* 119(3): 655–681.

Bolden, Richard. 2011. "Distributed Leadership in Organizations: A Review of the Research." *International Journal of Management Reviews* 13: 251–269.

Brueggemann, Walter. [1978] 2001. *The Prophetic Imagination*. Minneapolis, MN: Fortress Press.

Burns, James M. 1978. *Leadership*. New York: Harper & Row.

Castells, Manuel. 2013. *Networks of Outrage and Hope: Social Movements and the Internet Age*. Cambridge: Polity.

Cates, Diana Fritz. 2009. "Conceiving Emotions: Martha Nussbaum's 'Upheavals of Thought'." *Journal of Religious Ethics* 32(2): 325–341.

Christens, Brian D. and Paul Speer. 2015. "Community Organizing: Practice, Research, and Policy Implications." *Social Issues and Policy Review* 9(1): 193–222.

Chun, Jennifer Jihye. 2016. "Building Political Agency and Movement Leadership: The Grassroots Organizing Model of Asian Immigrant Women Advocates." *Citizenship Studies* 20(3–4): 379–395.

Clemens, Elisabeth. 1993. "Organizational Repertoires and Institutional Change: Women's Groups and the Transformation of U.S. Politics, 1890–1920." *American Journal of Sociology* 98: 755–798.

Clemens, Elisabeth. 1997. *The People's Lobby: Organizational Innovation and the Rise of Interest Group Politics in the United States, 1890–1925*. Chicago: University of Chicago Press.

Clifford, Bob and Sharon Nepstad. 2007. "Kill a Leader, Murder a Movement? Leadership and Assassination in Social Movements." *American Behavioral Scientist* 50(10): 1370–1394.

Cohen-Chen, Smadar, Eran Halperin, Roni Porat, and Daniel Bar-Tal. 2014. "The Differential Effects of Hope and Fear on Information Processing in Intractable Conflict." *Journal of Social and Political Psychology* 2(1): 11–30.

Cormier, Jeffrey. 2004. *The Canadianization Movement: Emergence, Survival, and Success*. Toronto: University of Toronto Press.

Couto, Richard A. 1993. "Narrative, Free Space, and Political Leadership in Social Movements." *The Journal of Politics* 55(1): 57–79.

Damasio, Antonio. 1994. *Descartes' Error: Emotion, Reason, and the Human Brain*. New York: Avon Books.

Day, David V., John W. Fleenor, Leanne E. Atwater, Rachel E. Strurm, and Rob A. McKee. 2014. "Advances in Leader and Leadership Development: A Review of 25 Years of Research and Theory." *Leadership Quarterly* 25(1): 63–82.

della Porta, Donatella and Mario Diani. [1999] 2006. *Social Movements: An Introduction*, 2nd edn. Malden, MA: Blackwell Publishing.

de Tocqueville, Alexis. [1835–40] 2000. *Democracy in America*. Translated by Stephen Grant. Indianapolis, IN: Hackett Publishing Company, Inc.

Diani, Mario. 2011. "'Leaders' or 'Brokers'? Positions and Influence in Social Movement Networks." In *Social Movements and Networks: Relational Approaches to Collective Action*, edited by Mario Diani and Doug McAdam, 105–122. New York: Oxford University Press.

Edelstein, David J. and Malcolm Warner. 1976. *Comparative Union Democracy: Organisation and Opposition in British and American Unions*. Piscataway, NJ: Transaction Publishers.

Einwohner, Rachel. 2007. "Leadership, Authority, and Collective Action: Jewish Resistance in the Ghettos of Warsaw and Vilna." *American Behavioral Scientist* 50(10): 1306–1326.

Eisenmann, Thomas, Eric Ries, and Sarah Dillard. 2013. *Hypothesis-Driven Entrepreneurship: The Lean Startup*. edited by Harvard Business School. Boston, MA: President and Fellows of Harvard College.

Foner, Eric. 1999. *The Story of American Freedom*. New York: W.W. Norton & Company.

Freeman, Jo. [1972] 2008. "The Tyranny of Structurelessness." *Peacework* 35(389): 6–8.

Freeman, Jo. 1999. "On the Origins of Social Movements." In *Waves of Protest: Social Movements Since the Sixties*, edited by Jo Freeman and Victoria Johnson, 7–24. Lanham, MD: Rowman & Littlefield.

Gamson, William. 1992. *Talking Politics*. Cambridge: Cambridge University Press.

Ganz, Marshall. 2000. "Resources and Resourcefulness: Strategic Capacity in the Unionization of California Agriculture, 1959–1966." *American Journal of Sociology* 105(4): 1003–1062.

Ganz, Marshall. 2009. *Why David Sometimes Wins*. New York: Oxford University Press.

Ganz, Marshall. 2010. "Leading Change: Leadership, Organization, and Social Movements." In *Handbook of Leadership Theory and Practice: A Harvard Business School Centennial Colloquium*, edited by Nitin Nohria and Rakesh Khurana, 527–568. Boston, MA: Harvard Business Press.

Ganz, Marshall. 2011. "Public Narrative, Collective Action, and Power." In *Accountability Through Public Opinion: From Inertia to Public Action*, edited by Sina Odugbemi and Taeku Lee, 273–290. Washington, DC: The International Bank for Reconstruction and Development/The World Bank.

Ganz, Marshall and Emily Lin. 2012. "Learning to Lead: A Pedagogy of Practice." In *The Handbook for Teaching Leadership: Knowing, Doing, and Being*, edited by Scott Snook, Nitin Nohria, and Rakesh Khurana, 353–366. Thousand Oaks, CA: Sage.

Ganz, Marshall, Kim Voss, Teresa Sharpe, Carl Somers, and George Strauss. 2004. "Against the Tide: Projects and Pathways of the New Generation of Union Leaders (1984–2001)." In *Rebuilding Labor*, edited by Ruth Milkman and Kim Voss. Ithaca, NY: Cornell University Press.

Gecan, Michael. 2002. *Going Public: An Organizer's Guide to Citizen Action*. Boston, MA: Beacon Press.

Gecan, Michael. 2004. "Three Public Cultures." In *Going Public: An Organizer's Guide to Citizen Action*, by Michael Gecan, 151–166. New York: Anchor Books.

Ghaziani, Amin, Verta Taylor, and Amy Stone. 2015. "Cycles of Sameness and Difference in LGBT Social Movements." *Annual Review of Sociology* 42: 165–183.

Gitlin, Todd. 1980. "Certifying Leaders and Converting Leadership to Celebrity." In *The Whole World Is Watching: Mass Media in the Making and Unmaking of the New Left*, by Todd Gitlin, 146–179. Berkeley: University of California Press.

Goldstone, Jack. 1980. "The Weakness of Organization: A New Look at Gamson's *The Strategy of Social Protest*." *American Journal of Sociology* 85(5): 1017–1042.

Granovetter, Mark. 1973. "The Strength of Weak Ties." *American Journal of Sociology* 78: 1360–1380.

Gronn, Peter. 2002. "Distributed Leadership as a Unit of Analysis." *Leadership Quarterly* 13(4): 423–451.

Gross, Neil, Thomas Medvetz, and Rupert Russell. 2011. "The Contemporary American Conservative Movement." *Annual Review of Sociology* 37: 325–354.

Hackman, Richard J. 2002. *Leading Teams*. Boston, MA: Harvard Business School Press.

Han, Hahrie. 2014. *How Organizations Develop Activists: Civic Associations and Leadership in the 21st Century*. New York: Oxford University Press.

Haslam, S. Alexander, Stephen D. Reicher, and Michael J. Platow. 2011. *The New Psychology of Leadership: Identity, Influence, and Power*. New York: Psychology Press.

Haussman, Melissa. 2013. *Reproductive Rights and the State: Getting the Birth Control, RU-486, Morning-After Pills, and the Gardasil Vaccine to the U.S. Market*. Santa Barbara, CA: Praeger.

Heaney, Michael T. and Fabio Rojas. 2014. "Hybrid Activism: Social Movement Mobilization in a Multimovement Environment." *American Journal of Sociology* 119(4): 1047–1103.

Heaney, Michael T. and Fabio Rojas. 2015. *Party in the Street: The Antiwar Movement and the Democratic Party after 9/11*. New York: Cambridge University Press.

Heifetz, Ronald. 2004. "Adaptive Learning." In *Encyclopedia of Leadership*, edited by George R. Goethals, Georgia J. Sorenson, and James M. Burns. Thousand Oaks, CA: SAGE.

Hoffer, Eric. 1951. *The True Believer: Thoughts on the Nature of Mass Movements*. New York: New American Library.

Hunt, Scott and Robert D. Benford. 1994. "Identity Talk in Peace and Justice Movements." *Journal of Contemporary Ethnography* 22(4): 488–517.

Jansen, Robert S. 2016. "Situated Political Innovation: Explaining the Historical Emergence of New Modes of Political Practice." *Theory and Society* 45: 319–360.

Jenkins, Craig J. and Charles Perrow. 1977. "Insurgency of the Powerless: Farm Worker Movements (1946–1972)." *American Sociological Review* 42: 249–268.

Kornhauser, William. 1959. *The Politics of Mass Society*. Glencoe, IL: The Free Press.

Kubal, Timothy. 1998. "The Presentation of Political Self: Cultural Resonance and the Construction of Collective Action Frames." *Sociological Quarterly* 39(4): 539–554.

Lipset, Seymour Martin. 1950. *Agrarian Socialism: The Cooperative Commonwealth Federation in Saskatchewan, A Study in Political Sociology*. Berkeley: University of California Press.

Lueck, Michelle A. M. 2007. "Hope for a Cause as Cause for Hope: The Need for Hope in Environmental Sociology." *The American Sociologist* 38: 250–261.

Mathieu, John, Travis Maynard, Tammy Rapp, and Lucy Gilson. 2008. "Team Effectiveness 1997–2007: A Review of Recent Advancements and a Glimpse into the Future." *Journal of Management* 34(3): 410–476.

McAdam, Doug. [1982] 1999. *Political Process and the Development of Black Insurgency, 1930–1970*, 2nd edn. Chicago: University of Chicago Press.

McAlevey, Jane. 2015. "The Crisis of New Labor and Alinsky's Legacy: Revisiting the Role of the Organic Grassroots Leaders in Building Powerful Organizations and Movements." *Politics & Society* 43(3): 415–441.

McAlevey, Jane. 2016. *No Shortcuts: Organizing for Power in the New Gilded Age*. New York: Oxford University Press.

McCammon, Holly J. 2012. *The U.S. Women's Jury Movements and Strategic Adaptation: A More Just Verdict*. Cambridge: Cambridge University Press.

McCammon, Holly J., Karen E. Campbell, Ellen M. Granberg, and Christine Mowery. 2001. "How Movements Win: Gendered Opportunity Structures and U.S. Women's Suffrage Movements, 1866 to 1919." *American Sociological Review* 66(1): 49–70.

McCarthy, John D. and Mark Wolfson. 1996. "Resource Mobilization by Local Social Movement Organizations: Agency, Strategy, and Organization in the Movement Against Drinking and Driving." *American Sociological Review* 61(6): 1070–1088.

McCarthy, John, Mark Wolfson, David P. Barker, and Elaine Mosakowski. 1988. "The Founding of Social Movement Organizations: Local Citizens' Groups Opposing Drunken Driving." In *Ecological Models of Organizations*, edited by Glenn R. Carroll. Cambridge, MA: Ballinger.

McDonnell, Mae Hunter, Brayden G. King, and Sarah A. Soule. 2015. "A Dynamic Process Model of Private Politics: Activist Targeting and Corporate Receptivity to Social Challenges." *American Sociological Review* 80(3): 654–678.

McKenna, Elizabeth and Hahrie Han. 2014. *Groundbreakers: How Obama's 2.2 Million Volunteers Transformed Campaigning in America*. New York: Oxford University Press.

McMath, Robert and Eric Foner. 1992. *Populism: A Social History, 1877–1898*. New York: Hill and Wang.

Michels, Robert. [1915] 1968. *Political Parties: A Sociological Study of the Oligarchical Tendencies of Modern Democracy*. New York: Free Press.

Milkman, Ruth. 2017. "A New Political Generation: Millennials and the Post-2008 Wave of Protest." *American Sociological Review* 82(1): 1–31.

Miroff, Bruce. 2003. "Entrepreneurship and Leadership." *Studies in American Political Development* 17(2): 204–211.

Mische, Ann. 2008. *Partisan Publics: Communication and Contention Across Brazilian Youth Activist Networks*. Princeton, NJ: Princeton University Press.

Morris, Aldon D. 1984. *The Origins of the Civil Rights Movement*. New York: Free Press.

Morris, Aldon D. and Suzanne Staggenborg. 2004. "Leadership in Social Movements." In *The Blackwell Companion to Social Movements*, edited by David A. Snow, Sarah A. Soule, and Hanspeter Kriesi, 171–196. Malden, MA: Blackwell.

Munson, Ziad. 2008. *The Making of Pro-Life Activists*. Chicago: University of Chicago Press.

Nepstad, Sharon and Bob Clifford. 2006. "When Do Leaders Matter? Hypotheses on Leadership Dynamics in Social Movements." *Mobilization* 11(1): 1–22.

Niederhoffer, Kate G. and James W. Pennebaker. 2009. "Sharing One's Story: On the Benefits of Writing or Talking About Emotional Experience." In *The Oxford Handbook of Positive Psychology*, edited by Shane Lopez and C.R. Snyder, 1–23. New York: Oxford University Press.

Noakes, John A. and Hank Johnston. 2005. "Frames of Protest: A Road Map to a Perspective." In *Frames of Protest: Social Movements and the Framing Perspective*, edited by Hank Johnston and John A. Noakes, 1–32. Lanham, MD: Rowman & Littlefield.

Nohria, Nitin and Rakesh Khurana. eds. 2010. *Handbook of Leadership Theory and Practice*. Boston, MA: Harvard Business Press.

Nussbaum, Martha. 2001. *Upheavals of Thought: The Intelligence of Emotions*. Cambridge: Cambridge University Press.

Nyden, Philip W. 1985. "Democratizing Organizations: A Case Study of a Union Reform Movement." *American Journal of Sociology* 90(6): 1179–1203.

Oliver, Pamela and Gerald Marwell. 1992. "Social Movement Theory." In *Frontiers in Social Movement Theory*, edited by Aldon D. Morris and Carol McClurg Mueller, 251–272. New Haven, CT: Yale University Press.

Orr, Marion. 2007. *Transforming the City: Community Organizing and the Challenge of Political Change*. Lawrence, KS: University of Kansas Press.

Piven, Francis Fox and Richard A. Cloward. 1977. *Poor People's Movements: Why They Succeed, How They Fail*. New York: Vintage.

Polletta, Francesca. 2006. *It Was Like a Fever: Storytelling in Protest and Politics*. Chicago: University of Chicago Press.

Polletta, Francesca and James Jasper. 2001. "Collective Identity and Social Movements." *Annual Review of Sociology* 27: 283–305.

Putnam, Robert, Robert Leonardi, and Raffaella Nanetti. 1994. *Making Democracy Work: Civic Traditions in Modern Italy*. Princeton, NJ: Princeton University Press.

Ransby, Barbara. 2003. *Ella Baker and the Black Freedom Movement*. Chapel Hill, NC: University of North Carolina Press.

Reger, Jo. 2007. "New Dimensions in the Study of Social Movement Leadership." *American Behavioral Scientist* 50(10): 1303–1305.

Reger, Jo and Suzanne Staggenborg. 2006. "Patterns of Mobilization in Local Movement Organizations: Leadership and Strategy in Four National Organization for Women Chapters." *Sociological Perspectives* 49(3): 297–323.

Robnett, Belinda. 1996. "African American Women in the Civil Rights Movement, 1954–1965: Gender, Leadership and Micromobilization." *American Journal of Sociology* 101(6): 1661–1693.

Roche, John P. and Stephen Sachs. 1969. "The Bureaucrat and the Enthusiast: An Exploration of the Leadership of Social Movements." In *Studies in Social Movements: A Psychological Perspective*, edited by Barry McLaughlin, 207–222. New York: Free Press.

Sarachild, Kathie. 1978. "Consciousness-Raising: A Radical Weapon." In *Feminist Revolution*, edited by Kathie Sarachild. New York: Random House.

Saunders, Clare, Maria Grasso, Cristiana Olcese, Emily Rainsford, and Christopher Rootes. 2012. "Explaining Differential Protest Participation: Novices, Returners, Repeaters, and Stalwarts." *Mobilization* 17(3): 263–280.

Schlozman, Daniel. 2015. *When Movements Anchor Parties: Electoral Alignments in American History*. Princeton, NJ: Princeton University Press.

Schultz, Aaron, and Mike Miller. 2015. *People Power: The Community Organizing Tradition of Saul Alinsky*. Nashville, TN: Vanderbilt University Press.

Seligman, Martin, and Mihaly Csikszentmihalyi. 2000. "Positive Psychology: An Introduction." *American Psychologist* 55(1): 5–14.

Senge, Peter M. 1990. *The Fifth Discipline: The Art and Practice of the Learning Organization*. New York: Currency Doubleday.

Shi, Yongren, Fedor Dokshin, Michael Genkin, and Matthew Brashears. 2017. "A Member Saved Is a Member Earned? The Recruitment-Retention Trade-Off and Organizational Strategies for Membership Growth." *American Sociological Review* 82(2): 407–434.

Sitrin, Marina. 2014. "Definitions of Horizontalism and Autonomy." *NACLA Report on the Americas* (Fall 2014): 44–45.

Skworonek, Stephen. 1993. *The Politics Presidents Make: Leadership from John Adams to Bill Clinton*. Cambridge, MA: Harvard University Press.

Smelser, Neil. 1962. *Theory of Collective Behavior*. New York: The Free Press.

Snook, Scott A., Nitin N. Nohria, and Rakesh Khurana. 2012. *The Handbook for Teaching Leadership: Knowing, Doing, and Being*. Thousand Oaks, CA: SAGE.

Snow, David A., E. Burke Rochford, Steven Worden, and Robert D. Benford. 1986. "Frame Alignment Processes, Micromobilization, and Movement Participation." *American Sociological Review* 111: 1718–1761.

Snow, David A., Louis A. Zurcher, and Sheldon Ekland-Olson. 1980. "Social Networks and Social Movements: A Microstructural Approach to Differential Recruitment." *American Sociological Review* 45(5): 787–801.

Snyder, C.R. ed. 2000. *Handbook of Hope: Theory, Measures, and Applications*. San Diego, CA: Academic Press.

Staggenborg, Suzanne. 1988. "The Consequences of Professionalization and Formalization in the Pro-Choice Movement." *American Sociological Review* 53(4): 585–605.

Sutherland, Neil, Christopher Land, and Steffen Böhm. 2013. "Anti-leaders(hip) in Social Movement Organizations: The Case of Autonomous Grassroots Groups." *Organization* 21(6): 759–781.

Tarrow, Sidney. [1994] 2011. *Power in Movement: Social Movements and Contentious Politics*. New York: Cambridge University Press.

Tarrow, Sidney. 2008. "Charles Tilly and the Practice of Contentious Politics." *Social Movement Studies* 7(3): 225–246.

Taylor, Charles. 1989. *Sources of the Self: The Making of the Modern Identity*. Cambridge, MA: Harvard University Press.

Tilly, Charles. 1978. *From Mobilization to Revolution*. Reading, MA: Addison-Wesley.

Tilly, Charles. [2008] 2016. *Explaining Social Processes*. New York: Routledge.

Tolbert, Pamela S. 2010. "Robert Michels and the Iron Law of Oligarchy." Available at: digitalcommons.ilr.cornell.edu/cgi/viewcontent.cgi?article=1404& (accessed September 25, 2016).

Tufekci, Zeynep. 2017. *Twitter and Tear Gas: The Power and Fragility of Networked Protest.* New Haven, CT: Yale University Press.

Turner, Ralph and Lewis Killian. [1957] 1987. *Collective Behavior.* 3rd edn. Englewood Cliffs, NJ: Prentice-Hall.

Voss, Kim. 1996. "The Collapse of a Social Movement The Interplay of Mobilizing Structures, Framing, and Political Opportunities in the Knights of Labor." In *Comparative Perspectives on Social Movements: Political Opportunities, Mobilizing Structures, and Cultural Framings*, edited by Doug McAdam, John D. McCarthy, and Mayer N. Zald, 227–258. New York: Cambridge University Press.

Voss, Kim and Rick Fantasia. 2004. *Hard Work: Remaking the American Labor Movement.* Berkeley: University of California Press.

Voss, Kim and Rachel Sherman. 2000. "Breaking the Iron Law of Oligarchy: Union Revitalization in the American Labor Movement." *American Journal of Sociology* 106(2): 303–349.

Wageman, Ruth. 1995. "Interdependence and Group Effectiveness." *Administrative Science Quarterly* 40: 145–180.

Walker, Edward, Andrew Martin, and John McCarthy. 2008. "Confronting the State, the Corporation, and the Academy: The Influence of Institutional Targets on Social Movement Repertoires." *American Journal of Sociology* 114(1): 35–76.

Walls, David. 2015. *Community Organizing.* Malden, MA: Polity Press.

Wang, Dan and Sarah A. Soule. 2012. "Social Movement Organizational Collaboration: Networks of Learning and the Diffusion of Protest Tactics, 1960–1995." *American Journal of Sociology* 17(6): 1674–1722.

Warren, Mark. 2001. *Dry Bones Rattling: Community Building to Revitalize American Democracy.* Princeton, NJ: Princeton University Press.

Weber, Max. [1887] 1964. "The Sociology of Charismatic Authority." In *From Max Weber: Essays in Sociology*, edited by Hans H. Gerth and C. Wright Mills, 245–252. New York: Oxford University Press.

Weber, Max. [1922] 1978. *Economy and Society.* Edited by Guenther Roth and Claus Wittich. Berkeley: University of California Press.

Wilson, James Q. 1973. *Political Organizations.* New York: Basic Books.

11

How Social Movements Interact with Organizations and Fields: Protest, Institutions, and Beyond

Fabio Rojas and Brayden G. King

Introduction

The study of social movements and the study of organizations and institutions have often been viewed as separate matters (Weber and King 2014). Movements are disruptive actors that often eschew the status quo and gravitate toward "contentious politics" (McAdam, Tarrow, and Tilly 2001; Tilly 1978). Organizations, in contrast, induce stability, and are seen as the cornerstones for institutional reproduction. Institutions are stable behavioral patterns that reflect the coordinated behavior of individuals and organizations (DiMaggio and Powell 1983; Rojas 2013; Scott 2001). It should not be surprising that the history of social movement research and organizational analysis have not overlapped much.

In the 1990s, social movement research, organizational analysis, and institutional theory began converging. Each area of research had stumbled into the other and bridges began to form between these scholarly communities. Empirically, scholars of social movements began to appreciate that protest doesn't happen just in "the street." Researchers in fields as diverse as management, education, public policy, and sociology focused on the fact that organizations were frequently targeted by social movements (e.g. Bartley 2007; Binder 2002; King 2008; Rojas 2007). Student activists might demand change in the college curriculum or "fair trade" activists might target corporations or feminists may move inside government as insider activists, reflecting the diversity of movement targets (Banaszak 1996).

Research on the feminist movement illustrates this dynamic well. Feminist organizations developed in ways to address the overall political environment as well as the internal political processes of organizations. Lee Ann Banaszak's (1996) seminal study of women's suffrage in the United States focuses on how differing electoral systems affected the growth and development of women's suffrage groups in the United States and Switzerland. Banaszak found that while resources and political

The Wiley Blackwell Companion to Social Movements, Second Edition. Edited by David A. Snow, Sarah A. Soule, Hanspeter Kriesi, and Holly J. McCammon.

opportunities mattered in both nations, it was the perceptions of each movement that shaped the movement. A second way that the feminist movement was affected by the political system was in terms of abeyance. Scholars have noted that the feminist movement sought collaborations with other movements in between the major phases of the movement (Taylor 1989). In contrast, other scholarship draws attention to the ways that feminists mobilize within organizations to promote equality. For example, Katzenstein's multiple treatments of feminist-led policy reform emphasize the "unobtrusive" nature of activism. By working with allies and out of the view of the public, reformers could institutionalize more women-friendly policies in religious and military institutions (e.g. Katzenstein 1990, 1999).

Social movement research and organizational analysis have pushed each other to revise and expand their theoretical frameworks. For social movement scholars, protest was no longer a simple issue of "call and response" where movements issue a call and wait to see how incumbents respond. Instead, social movement researchers realized that challengers and incumbents each belonged to a larger "organizational field" that created opportunities, permitted some claims while suppressing others, and acted as the environment for social movements (Fligstein and McAdam 2012; Schneiberg and Lounsbury 2008). For corporate organizational scholars, it has become apparent that social movements increase the "cost of doing business" and seek to apply reputational or regulatory pressures on firms to change (King 2008; Luders 2006).

This chapter provides an overview of the new synthesis of social movement research and organizational analysis and to further provoke debate about how organizational research and movement theory should respond to each other. After this introduction, we quickly describe the "pre-history" of movement-organization studies and then explore the wave of scholarship in the 1990s and early 2000s that set the stage for the movement-organizations synthesis. Then, we summarize the current state of organizational theory, with an emphasis on institutionalism, and formulate a series of questions about how institutional theory might change in response to social movement research.

Precursors of the Movement and Organizations Research

An important precursor to the literature on social movements and organizations is Marxist scholarship that focuses on worker mobilization and revolutionary uprisings. Even though the literature on movements and organizations addresses many types of firms, the Marxist analysis of workers in firms provided a number of insights about movements' relationships to economic institutions. A key argument of Marx and Engels was that latent class interests would be transformed into concrete revolutionary activity once workers were concentrated in manufacturing firms. Engels' analysis of strikes, for example, explicitly noted that labor resistance emerged in England once machines were introduced, which encouraged unionism (Engels 1845: Chapter 10). In Marx and Engels' account, actual revolutionary activity required shared beliefs among workers, which could be fostered through constant workplace contact, such as we see in labor-intensive manufacturing. Marxist analysis solidified the view that worker mobilization would precede the institutional transformation of capitalism.

In American sociology, conflict theorists, many of whom were decidedly neo-Marxist, carried on the tradition of studying mobilization and institutional change. Scholars viewed revolt or resistance to organizational authorities as manifestations of this mobilization. The best-known example might be Alvin Gouldner's (1954) *Wildcat Strike: A Study in Worker Management Relationships*, which examined why a gypsum plant experienced a worker revolt. He observed that workers and managers jointly developed a dense web of informal relationships and norms. The daily life of the mining facility is defined both by the formal rules of the organization and the negotiated, informal order. In Gouldner's account, a strike occurred when new managers ignored, or actively violated, the informal order. Thus, the new managers inadvertently triggered a movement within their organization by violating workers' expectations. Michael Burawoy (1979) further developed the organizational conflict perspective by offering a theory of how managers obtain consent from workers. Burawoy's argument is that capitalist firms offer polices that "gamify" work and thus reduce dissent, disruption, and shirking. If workers believe they have opportunities for promotion by performing the game well, they participate in the system rather than challenge it. Scholars of labor unions have continued this tradition, although notably they have observed the decline of unions as a form of activism within companies (e.g. Clawson and Clawson 1999; Rosenfeld 2014). Outside of the Marxist tradition, scholars approached disruption with the tools of social movement research, such as Goldstone and Useem's studies of prison revolts (e.g. Goldstone and Useem 1999; Useem and Goldstone 2002).

Contacts between Movement Theory and Organizational Analysis

From the 1970s to the 1990s, a series of studies made a conscious and overt effort to link social movement research and organizational analysis and go beyond the observation that organizations are sites of worker mobilization. Social movement scholars made the jump into organizational analysis when they observed two processes that required more theoretical and empirical work. First, organizations are ubiquitous in recruiting participation in movements. When scholars examined the way that individuals chose to participate in a social movement, formal advocacy organizations were often the conduit. Snow, Zurcher, and Ekland-Olsen's (1980) early study of college student participation in protest finds that religious groups frequently recruited students for protest. Schussman and Soule (2005) further explore this in a cross-movement context. McAdam and Paulsen (1993) provide evidence that recruitment to high-risk activism was correlated with ties to social movement organizations. Later Munson (2009) shows that involvement in radical "pro-life" movements was initiated as individuals were attracted to organizations that provided social opportunities with friends. Radicalization came as a consequence of participating regularly in a radical organization.

At the same time, other scholars explored the organizations that sponsor and manage activism and in the process developed the influential resource mobilization perspective. McCarthy and Zald (1977) present the view that movements can only emerge and flourish if they have the backing of formal advocacy groups who provide money, legal advice, and logistical support. They analogize social movements to industries in which social movement organizations compete with one another, just as firms would, for resources. The argument is important for two reasons. First, it draws attention to the fact that social movement participation is not merely a matter of intention or grievances. Movements need an infrastructure. Second, McCarthy and Zald draw attention to the vast world of non-profits, interest groups, social clubs, media groups, and legal organizations that constitute the social movement sector.

Since then, scholars have spent considerable amounts of time investigating the organizational field of movement organizations. Early examples include Bearman and Everett's (1993) social network analysis of activist organizations in the Washington, DC, area and Carrol and Ratner's (1996) study of activists who move across organizations. Bearman and Everett use newspaper data to study how organizations were connected to each other and how that changed over time. Using rally sponsorship data to operationalize connections, the analysis showed the ebb and flow of the social movement sector. Carrol and Ratner's study of Vancouver activists showed individuals move from one social movement organization to another during the course of their lives. Some types of organizations, such as unions and peace organizations, were frequently mentioned by participants, serving as the hubs in the larger organizational network. More recently, Soule and King (2006) and Jung, King, and Soule (2014) demonstrate that social movement sectors evolve as a result of competition and collaboration between organizations pursuing similar or related causes. Similarly, there is a tradition of work that examines the ecological contexts of movement organizations, such as how the density of movement fields affects the entry and exit of organizations and the spread of tactics (e.g. Minkoff 1997, see King and Soule 2008, for a review).

Movements in Organizations and Movements Targeting Organizations

This section explains how organizational scholars developed an interest in movements and how that affected theories of organizational and institutional change. Early attempss to import social movement theory to the study of organizations sought to understand how mobilization efforts inside and outside companies may influence certain types of institutional change. Frequently, scholars would use the term "movement-like" to point out the analogical reasoning of this argument, as when we see Strang and Jung (2005) describe collective efforts to lead bank reform. One starting point for seeing the growing interest in social movement theory is a 1994 article by Davis and Thompson about shareholders in publicly traded companies. Stakeholders in firms would often pursue their interests in ways that were highly analogous to what "street protest" movements did – challenge policy, create counter-groups, and recruit allies in the media.

More recently, organizational scholars have adopted a social movement lens to study how other organizational stakeholders, including many traditional movement organizations, have sought to change corporate practices and policies. Environmental, feminist, human rights, and civil rights organizations have always targeted corporations in addition to governments in seeking to institute broader social change (Soule

2009). For example, consider that sit-ins and boycotts in the segregationist South often directly targeted local businesses in an attempt to put economic pressure on cities to change (Luders 2006). Boycotts and protests are core tactics that movements still use when targeting companies (King 2008; King and Soule 2007). Such tactics are effective inasmuch as they create threats against companies' reputations and trigger actions to protect their public images (e.g. Bartley and Child 2014; McDonnell and King 2013; McDonnell, King, and Soule 2015). Moreover, tactics like protests serve as effective information signals that amplify perceptions of risk (Vasi and King 2012). Thus, even if a boycott or protest has no discernible impact on sales revenue or short-term profitability, it may still disrupt a company's ability to acquire and maintain its reputation and status position.

The analogy between political protest and intra-organizational disruption has been extended to many types of groups. Organizational scholars commonly look at educational institutions because they frequently experience internal disruption (Binder 2002; Rojas 2007). Students protest colleges for numerous reasons, including because they want more racial or gender equality or more environmentally friendly policies. Conservative movements also target universities as well, often demanding an end to affirmative action policies. Often, universities reflect broader political trends. When movements arise in society, they frequently find defenders and recruits from within the ranks of universities and many movements try to institutionalize movement demands within universities (Rojas 2012).

Universities are also the site of primarily "internal" movements that are driven by academics. Neil Gross' (2002) analysis of heterodox philosophers is an excellent example. Gross argues that philosophy was dominated and controlled for decades by "analytic" philosophy, a group of philosophers who strive for linguistic precision and the use of symbolic logic and mathematics. "Heterodox" philosophers, who hail from a wide range of schools such as pragmatism, Continental philosophy, feminism, or Marxism, were excluded from positions of leadership and rarely received the same professional rewards as analytic philosophers. Eventually, heterodox philosophy mobilized and challenged the analytic mainstream. Not only did heterodox philosophers develop a grievance and collective identity, they employed many of the same tactics that "street movements" use, such as staging a protest at a meeting of the American Philosophical Association and creating their own movement organizations.

Of course, universities are also frequently targeted by outsiders. Rojas (2007), for example, examines how Black Power activists in the 1960s enrolled in colleges so they could mobilize students and demand reform. Binder (2002) examines a similar process in the 1980s and 1990s, when multiculturalists demanded that K-12 schools include Afrocentric materials in their courses. Binder and Wood's (2013) most recent work shows the ways that national conservative organizations sponsor and promote right-wing activist on campus. Other examples include the targeting of universities by the anti-apartheid activists (Soule 1997) and the spread of recycling programs on campuses (Lounsbury 2001).

Increasingly, management scholars identify movements as the impetus for the origin of innovative practices that subsequently diffuse (e.g. Briscoe and Safford 2008; Soule, Swaminathan, and Tihanyi 2015; Strang and Soule 1998); and the emergence of new markets (Hiatt, Sine, and Tolbert 2009; Sine and Lee 2009).

Inasmuch as disruption is a necessary component to any sort of institutional change (Seo and Creed 2002), "movement-like" collective action frequently underlies such disruptive sparks. Thus, movements aren't "outsiders" in industries. They are often key actors in the development of organizations and markets.

A First Synthesis: Movements as Political Process

These varied studies suggested that there needed to be a more systematic account of how movements and organizations interact to trigger institutional changes. The first attempt might be called a "political process" model. In this view, social movements are one important actor, among many, that constitute an organization's regulatory environment. Thus, movements could affect organizations by changing public opinion, lobbying the state, and shaping the norms and systems of governance that moderate organizations' actions.

A more thorough review of institutional theory can be found in Scott (2001), Rojas (2013), and Greenwood et al. (2008), but we outline the major points here. First, organizations must, in some way, satisfy the demands made by actors in the environment (Meyer and Rowan 1977; Stinchcombe 1965). Some scholarship suggests that organizations do genuinely attempt to satisfy their audiences (DiMaggio and Powell 1983) while others suggest that compliance is ritualistic (Meyer and Rowan 1977). Regardless, institutional scholars tend to agree that organizations must satisfy certain environmental demands to retain their legitimacy. Second, the environment's demands are translated into specific patterns of behavior that are often viewed as the legitimate way for an organization to behave. Thus, a lot of institutional research is not only about organizational environments, but also about how individuals, and larger collectives, develop rules for behavior and how these rules spread throughout various sectors of society (Boxenbaum and Jonsson 2008).

Social movements have a natural place in institutional theory if we consider them as mediators within the institutional environment (Schneiberg and Soule 2005). Social movements spur innovations, some of which might be picked up by organizations and later become institutionalized (Lounsbury 2001). Activists try to change public opinion, which influences organizations (Gamson and Modigliani 1989; Walker 2014). And they spend a great deal of time lobbying the state, which allows them to impose regulations on their targets (Walker and Rea 2014). The net result is that social movements play a role in creating, imposing, and rewriting the regulations, both formal and informal, that govern organizations.

In a series of articles, Schneiberg and collaborators discuss how social movements have shaped the American insurance and agricultural industries (Schneiberg and Soule 2005). They discuss how farmers groups and local constituencies encouraged municipalities to regulate various industries. Political challenges required states, both locally and nationally, to intervene in the economy and create new rules which can be used by both economic incumbents and their challengers. Later, Schneiberg and Soule (2005) offer a "multi-level" model of how movements affect industries. Their model depicts movement challenges as happening at multiple "levels" of society. This is important in the history of insurance and farming regulation because the responses of the Federal government and states varied a great deal and the sequencing of regulation is important to knowing its history. The way the Federal government reacted to these movements depended on how states regulated farming and insurance.

This analysis combines two insights about movements and organizations. First, there is no "single" institutional environment or political order (Rojas 2010; Soule 2009). Organizational environments have "layers" or "segments." Each part of the environment has its own dynamics and we can only understand the impact of a movement after investigating these different sub-environments. Movements vary in how much influence they have in each level, but each level has its own distinct process.

Second, the process is dynamic and results in periodic "resettlements." Movement actors disrupt the existing regulations of industry, which then leads to public attention and a re-articulation of the rules of the game. Movements are actors who trigger cycles of political disruption and reconstruction. Recently, McDonnell et al. (2015) described the "political opportunity structure" of corporations in just this way. Opportunities evolve as organizations initially respond to the demands of movement activists by attempting to placate them with symbolic gestures, which creates new pathways for influence and change within the organizations.

From this perspective, social movements and organizations jointly create their institutional environments, as well as being constrained by them once new practices or systems emerge. Tim Bartley (2007) and others (e.g. Brammer, Jackson, and Matten 2012; Campbell 2007; Vogel 2010) have argued that social movements play a large role in the construction of transnational systems of private regulation, which have in some cases replaced governmental regulation. Businesses and activists have collaborated to set up nongovernmental certification systems, like the Forest Stewardship Council or Fair Trade branding, that brand firms as being pro-environmental or pro-human rights. These systems, scholars argue, institutionalize global norms about good business practice and sanction firms that do not abide by them. Bartley (2007) argues that the path to institutionalizing global norms around corporate social responsibility has been marked by contestation and conflict between social movements and corporations. Social movements, again, are seen as the agitators for the shifts in the institutional environment in which organizations operate.

A Second Synthesis: Fields and Resettlements

This section investigates a related point of view called "field theory" that attempts to present an integrated view of both movements and organizations. Field theory synthesizes various literatures on institutions, states, and organizations, including those cited in this chapter. But unlike political process theory, field theory draws heavily from Bourdieu's (1977) conceptualization of society as stratified by class positions and differential access to capital. Field theory begins with a "meso-level" description of society as layered by fields: populations of organizations and other actors that jockey for positions of control and influence, internal status orders, and rules for interaction. Fields are shapes by periodic disruptions and "resettlements." Those without status or power will come to view the current state of affairs as illegitimate and gather the resources needed to challenge those with power. Successful mobilization can destabilize power holders and can force a "resettlement," which is accompanied by changes in the rules and distribution of resources.

Although the concept of fields has disseminated broadly through Bourdieusian work or institutional theoretical research on organizational fields, the concept entered the social movement literature through *The Dynamics of Contention* by Doug McAdam, Sidney Tarrow and Charles Tilly (2001). The book's principal argument was that the rise and decline of social movements depend on the push and pull of states and their challengers through various mechanisms and processes. The process of challenging states required that actors delegitimize existing policies, acquire the resources for challenge, and then interact with the state through various channels such as voting, lobbying, protest, or even violent revolution. This cycle of delegitimization, framing, mobilization, and resettlement, though critiqued by scholars as being too focused on the state and being too casual in its description of particular mechanisms, suggested that movements instigated new episodes of contention, which ultimately led to the reordering of states.

Fligstein and McAdam (2012) extended these ideas to produce a more general theory of strategic action fields. This text builds on the basic ideas of *The Dynamics of Contention* in three ways. First, and most importantly, the cycle of challenge and resettlement is thought to occur in many fields, not just politics. Strategic framing, resource mobilization, and protest occur in many domains of social life. Second, they draw attention to the multiplicity of fields and their connections. Thus, a disruption in one field could "spill over" into other social domains. Industries are fields, but the organizations that make up an industry are also fields. Struggles over defining the "rules of the game" occur both within and between organizations. Of course, certain fields and organizations merit additional attention. The state, for example, wields disproportionate influence because of its monopoly of violence and its role as a regulator. Within fields, there are accreditors that are influential because they award symbolic capital to ordinary organizations.

Field theory sensitizes scholars to the strategic interactions that take place between movements, organizations, and other actors. Shifts in broader societal norms result from these interactions. Consider, for example, recent research on the strategic interaction of social movements and corporations (Bartley and Child 2014; King 2008; King and McDonnell 2015; McDonnell and King 2013; Soule and King 2006), which emphasizes how field position – status orders and reputation rankings – shapes the dynamics and outcomes of these interactions. Activists often target high status corporations precisely because they know these firms will be susceptible to the reputational threats imposed by negative media attention related to boycotts or protests. Furthermore, high status firms that concede to activists' demands have a broader impact on a field's norms and practices than is true of changes made by less visible companies. Activists are able to turn the strengths of the powerful into vulnerabilities that create ripples of change throughout the entire field. For empirical tests of these ideas, see Wang and Soule (2012, 2016) and Jung et al. (2014).

The synthesis of movement theory and organizational analysis offered by field theory has a number of strengths. First, it recognizes that disruption and challenge are not limited to states; rather, conflict erupts between and within organizations over contestation of informal norms and access to power and resources. It provides a template for the generic social processes that might drive controversy in any social domain. Second, it suggests how social conflict and resettlements might reverberate through societies. Some change may be "top down" and imposed by states, while other change is transmitted from one field to the next. Third, field theory suggests that the structure of the field itself, including actors' relative status position, influences how challenger battle incumbents.

Beyond Field Theory

In this section, we challenge the synthesis of movement theory and organizational analysis represented by political process models and field theory. We do not suggest that such approaches are wrong. Instead, we suggest that field theories and political process theory are incomplete descriptions of how movements and organizations interact because these theories are motivated by very specific historical examples.

Here, we make two arguments. First, field theory is predicated on the view that there is a clear distinction between incumbents and challengers, but, rather, we argue that there are many types of contentious politics and organized social change that do not clearly have incumbents and challengers. In many cases, movements seem to be guided by elites who occupy positions of authority and influence (Duffy, Binder, and Skrentny 2010). Often, they do not represent a marginal or excluded group, nor do they represent elites who are defending their status or position against challengers. There are movements that appear to be organized by elites and do not trigger contention. Thus, movements are not always well described as triggering a cycle of incumbent-challenger conflict. Moreover, many movements – especially "identity movements" – seem to be less oppositional. Field position is likely more varied than the incumbent-challenger dichotomy captures. Consider, for example, Heaney and Rojas's (2014) study of the antiwar movement of the 2000s, which demonstrated that antiwar organizations with more complex, flexible identities were more successful at recruiting protest participants than organizations with "narrow" identities.

To motivate the first claim, we present examples of contentious behavior that do not emerge from a clear dispute between incumbents and challengers. One important example is the rise of Buddhism and meditative practice in American social life (Kucinskas 2014b). Originally, the history of American Buddhism appears to be a classic case of challenger-incumbent interaction. The first Buddhists in America were members of a low-status ethnic group and they created organizations that were designed to promote a religion that was actively rejected by mainstream religions. It was not uncommon for meditation, and related practices, to be framed as un-Christian and heretical. Later, American Buddhism gained prominence in American life, partly through the legitimation efforts of academic elites who reformulated Buddhist ideology so it could co-exist with Western scientific principles. "Mindfulness" is a personal practice that has been featured in mainstream media and has been adopted by major corporations, universities, and even the American military. This change in the status of American Buddhism occurred without the hallmarks of social change. There were no "meditation protests," there was little overt conflict between Christians and Buddhists, and there has been extremely little counter-movement backlash.

Second, both theories focus on the point of contact between movements and the organizations they target. This assumes that there is a direct point of contact between movements and organizations. Instead, there are important cases where movements actively avoid direct conflict with incumbents and choose to work in "parallel" with the mainstream – they "by-pass the state" and thus circumvent conflict (Davis and Robinson 2012; Kucinskas 2014a; Rojas and Byrd 2014). For that reason, it is important to consider how movements may influence organizations not by directly challenging them, or rallying support through the media, but by creating alternatives that expand the "menu of options" available to organizations. Increasingly, we see movements collaborating with incumbents (e.g. Duffy, Binder and Skrentny 2010; Kucinskas 2014a). Many LGBT activists also held prominent positions within the organizations they sought to change, thus tempering their radicalism and aligning their incentives to find "win-win" solutions (Meyerson and Scully 1995). We see this pattern repeated in today's environmental movement, in which many former activists are taking positions in the corporate world and seeking more direct forms of intervention. And, as Mary-Hunter McDonnell (2015) has illustrated, companies might also take activist positions that are highly aligned with the movements that once targeted them, embracing the change-oriented ideals of movements (see also Briscoe, Chin, and Hambrick 2014; McDonnell, King, and Soule 2015).

The example of American Buddhism is a case of elites using their status to effectively avoid confrontation with the mainstream and use their social capital to legitimize new ideas. The case of corporate grassroots lobbying raises different issues (Walker 2014, see also Fisher 2006). Grassroots lobbying, sometimes known as "astroturfing," refers to the practice of hiring a professional staff to mobilize people to protest on your behalf. For example, a firm that wants to build a manufacturing plant might mobilize protesters to signal that people might like the firm because of the jobs it brings. In some cases, astroturfing might be done to overcome opposition to the firm's project. In other cases, it might be done in the absence of opposition as a form of reputation management and to influence people who have power over the firm, such as zoning boards or regulatory agencies.

One of Walker's main findings about "grassroots for hire" organizations is that they tend to crowd out traditional activists and increase political inequality. His research suggests that protest, as understood by social scientists, is not always a tool of the challenger and there is now a form of protest that is sponsored by incumbents that helps incumbents. Traditionally, in social movement research, protest is usually not described as a form of push-back, except by counter-movements that wish to roll back a movement's victories. These two examples illustrate the need to expand movement-organization beyond the model suggests by challenger-incumbent models.

Our second argument is that the dynamics between movements and organizations are not always characterized by the types of behaviors described in political process models or field theory, which show movements as influencing organizations through regulation or media. Here, we provide examples of movements that affect organizational fields not by confronting organizations but by-passing them altogether.

We begin with an example of a movement that has failed to influence the mainstream and has decided to stop directly challenging older, more established organizations – creationism (Oberlin 2014). This movement has decided to develop its own institutions in parallel with its competitors. Throughout the twentieth century, creationists have won some victories, but not enough to displace Darwinian biology in schools and universities. Instead, creationism has, at best, a circumscribed position in American society. In response to this situation, creationists have created their own institutions, such as research institutes and, more importantly, a museum in Kentucky that is supposed to represent the creationist view in the most positive light. This museum not only entertains young people, but has carefully constructed exhibits that explain how fossils and other physical evidence can be made compatible with creationist theory. The museum itself stands as both a critique of mainstream biology and as a "free space" where movement sympathizers can gather and form a collective representation of what they believe in.

The literature on social movements is replete with examples of movements that choose to "by-pass" the state and other dominant organizations and instead build their own organizations that obviate the need to work within these institutions. In other words, activists may decide that working with elected officials, business leaders, and other elites may not be in their best interest and opt to create organizations that promote the social practices and policies that they prefer. Many resemble the creationists who mobilized against the mainstream and failed. Scholars of Black Power have documented multiple cases where black nationalists failed to extract concessions from universities, such as creating Black Studies programs and colleges within predominantly white organizations, and then created their own free-standing Black Studies colleges (Rojas and Byrd 2014). Many religious movements exhibit this pattern as well. Davis and Robinson (2012) survey a range of traditional religious movements, such as Israel's Shas and the Salvation Army, and note that they often establish their own social services, such as schools, hospitals, and poverty support groups. These movements-operated social services not only cultivate support among a target population, but they also allow the movement to grow and spread its ideas outside the state. In this manner, movements can grow and expand without directly challenging the state, which often triggers violent repression.

Perhaps the most interesting example of by-passing is when social movements decide not to even directly challenge incumbents at all and simply operate independently of the mainstream. One interesting example of this is the urban farming movement (White 2011). The black-dominated movement argues that the food produced for urban populations is poor in quality and unreasonably expensive. They also argue that urban regions contain "food deserts" where residents would have to travel to find quality food. Urban farmers urge people to grow their own food and develop their own distribution channels. White (2011) documents the way these movement participants need to completely redevelop the supply chains that are taken for granted by customers. These institutions – food cooperatives – not only embody the ideology of the urban farming movement, but they encourage others to disassociate themselves from the mainstream of food production.

Expanding Field Theory and Political Process Models

The various examples in the previous section show that the incumbent-challenger conflict does not capture the range of how movements and organizations interact.

Table 11.1   Typology of movements in fields with examples

Incumbent challenge	Conflict style	
	Direct	Indirect/Bypassing
Yes	Civil Rights Movement	Separatist Ethnic Movements
No	Intra-corporate conflict/ shareholder activism	American Buddhism

To describe the full spectrum of movement-organization interaction, one might start with the types of examples that motivated the theory of fields, such as the civil rights movement or revolutionary movements that try to topple states (Table 11.1). These movements have two traits: (1) a strong distinction between incumbent and challenger; and (2) clear moments of conflict.

Then, we can think about movements that vary along one or both of these dimensions. Some movements have clear challenger-incumbent distinctions but they do not play as direct conflicts. The movements that "by-pass" states are an example. By establishing rival organizations that have movement adherents as an audience, they can clearly compete with the mainstream while avoiding conflict. Conversely, some movements may have well-defined conflict with an incumbent but it is not clearly a conflict between "insiders" and "challengers." Many disputes in the corporate sector may have this characteristic as coalitions of shareholders build coalitions to assert their positions. Then, some movements interact with organizations without any obvious conflict and without incumbents in the traditional sense of the word. The example of American Buddhism is an excellent example. This elite-driven movement used the resources of the academy to legitimate its ideologies and avoid conflict with religious institutions altogether. There is little sense that American Buddhists have a clear antagonist they were struggling with to disseminate their ideas.

"Insider activism" is a topic that is now more widely recognized by scholars. Briefly, it refers to ways the actors within organizations promote social change without the type of contention traditionally studied in social movement research. This may include leaders instituting new policies or rank and file workers speaking up to promote a specific issue. Perhaps the starting point of this literature is Katzenstein's (1999) work on reform in the Catholic Church and the US military. Her analysis classifies "insider activism" according to whether the protest is disruptive or discursive and whether it is radical, and thus challenges existing values and norms. Wayne A. Santoro and Gail M. McGuire (1997) explain when external movements can help, or facilitate, insiders who can promote their cause, which has been reinforced by more recent studies such as Raeburn's study of LBGT activism in corporate America (2004). Recently, Briscoe and Gupta (2016) review research on insider activism and identify various aspects of insider activism that require more scholarly attention, such as whether "insiders" are completely or only partially inside the organization and whether organizational change is a direct or indirect effect of activism.

The purpose of the typology is to sensitize the reader to the spectrum of movement-organization interactions. The aim is to draw attention to examples of collective action that are not characterized by low-status challengers struggling against high-status incumbents. These movements that exist "off the diagonal" in Table 11.1 require more theorizing. Further research can ask how the protest cycle differs across different types of movements. It can also be hypothesized that moving from one trajectory (direct conflict with challengers) to parallelism might be a normal evolution for unsuccessful movements. Thus, this theoretical exercise suggests that how movements and organizations interact affects the life cycle of movements, the sequencing of which needs to be more fully understood.

Conclusion

The study of movements, organizations, and institutions has gone through multiple phases. The earliest work examined the ways that movements erupt in organizations and used movement theory to provide a vocabulary for intra-organizational conflict. Then, from the 1990s to the 2000s, research on movements and organizations became more systematic. One stream attempted to examine the mechanisms that linked activism to organizational behavior. Another stream, motivated by classical movement studies, tried to generalize the theory that was used to explain cycles of challenger-incumbent conflict. We argued in this chapter that there is much more to be learned about movement-organization interaction by looking at collective action that does not resemble prototypical case studies. Movements and organizations interact in a multitude of ways that both create and reproduce their institutional environments.

References

Banaszak, Lee Ann. 1996. *Why Movements Succeed and Fail: Opportunity, Culture, and the Struggle for Women's Suffrage*. Princeton, NJ: Princeton University Press.

Bartley, Tim. 2007. "Institutional Emergence in an Era of Globalization: The Rise of Transnational Private Regulation of Labor and Environmental Conditions." *American Journal of Sociology* 113(2): 297–351.

Bartley, Tim and Curtis Child. 2014. "Shaming the Corporation: The Social Production of Targets and the Anti-Sweatshop Movement." *American Sociological Review* 79(4): 653–679.

Bearman, Peter S. and Kevin D. Everett. 1993. "The Structure of Social Protest, 1961–1983." *Social Networks* 15(2): 171–200.

Binder, Amy. 2002. *Contentious Curricula: Afrocentrism and Creationism in American Public Schools*. Princeton, NJ: Princeton University Press.

Binder, Amy and Kate Wood. 2013. *Becoming Right: How Campuses Shape Young Conservatives*. Princeton, NJ: Princeton University Press.

Bourdieu, Pierre. 1977. *An Outline of a Theory of Practice*. Chicago: University of Chicago Press.

Boxenbaum, Eva and Stefan Jonsson. 2008. "Isomorphism, Diffusion, and Decoupling." In *The Sage Handbook of Organizational Institutionalism*, edited by Royston Greenwood, Christine Oliver, Thomas B. Lawrence, and Renate E. Meyer, 78–98. London: Sage.

Brammer, Stephen, Gregory Jackson, and Dirk Matten. 2012. "Corporate Social Responsibility and Institutional Theory: New Perspectives on Private Governance." *Socio-Economic Review*, 10(1): 3–28.

Briscoe, Forrest, M.K. Chin, and Donald C. Hambrick. 2014. "CEO Ideology as an Element of the Corporate Opportunity Structure for Social Activists." *Academy of Management Journal* 57(6): 1786–1809.

Briscoe, Forrest and Abhinav Gupta. 2016. "Social Activism in and around Organizations." *Academy of Management Annals* 10(1): 671–727.

Briscoe, Forrest and Sean Safford. 2008. "The Nixon in China Effect: Activism, Imitation, and the Institutionalization of Contentious Practices." *Administrative Science Quarterly* 53: 460–491.

Burawoy, Michael. 1979. *Manufacturing Consent: Changes in the Labor Process under Monopoly Capitalism*. Chicago: University of Chicago Press.

Campbell, John L. 2007. "Why Would Corporations Behave in Socially Responsible Ways? An Institutional Theory of Corporate Social Responsibility." *Academy of Management Review* 32: 946–967.

Carrol, William K. and R. S. Ratner. 1996. "Master Framing and Cross-Movement Networking in Contemporary Social Movements." *The Sociological Quarterly* 37: 701–725.

Clawson, Dan and Mary Ann Clawson. 1999. "What Has Happened to the US Labor Movement? Union Decline and Renewal." *Annual Review of Sociology* 45: 95–119.

Davis, Nancy J. and Robert V. Robinson. 2012. *Claiming Society for God: Religious Movements and Social Welfare*. Bloomington: Indiana University Press.

Davis, Gerald F., and Tracy A. Thompson. 1994. "A Social Movement Perspective on Corporate Control." *Administrative Science Quarterly* 39: 141–173.

DiMaggio, Paul and Walter Powell. 1983. "'The Iron Cage Revisited': Institutional Isomorphism and Collective Rationality in Organizational Fields." *American Sociological Review* 48: 147–160.

Duffy, Meghan, Amy Binder, and John Skrentny. 2010. "Elite Status and Social Change: Using Field Analysis to Explain Policy Formation and Implementation." *Social Problems* 57: 49–73.

Engels, Friedrich. 1845. *Conditions of the Working Class in England*. Marxists Internet Archive. Available at: https://www.marxists.org/archive/marx/works/1845/condition-working-class/ch10.htm (accessed September 16, 2016).

Fisher, Dana R. 2006. *Activism, Inc.* Stanford, CA: Stanford University Press.

Fligstein, Neil and Doug McAdam. 2012. *A Theory of Fields*. Oxford: Oxford University Press.

Gamson, William A. and Andre A. Modigliani. 1989. "Media Discourse and Public Opinion on Nuclear Power: A Constructionist Approach." *American Journal of Sociology* 95(1): 1–37.

Goldstone, Jack A. and Bert Useem. 1999. "Prison Riots as Revolutions: An Extension of State-Centered Theories of Revolution." *American Journal of Sociology* 104: 985–1029.

Gouldner, Alvin. 1954. *Wildcat Strike: A Study in Worker Management Relationships*. New York: Harper.

Greenwood, Royston, Christine Oliver, Roy Suddaby, and Kerstin Sahlin-Andersson. 2008. *The Sage Handbook of Organizational Institutionalism*. London: Sage.

Gross, Neil. 2002. "Becoming a Pragmatist Philosopher: Status, Self-Concept, and Intellectual Choice." *American Sociological Review* 67(1): 52–76.

Heaney, Michael T. and Fabio Rojas. 2014. "Hybrid Activism: Social Movement Mobilization in a Multimovement Environment." *American Journal of Sociology* 119(4): 1047–1103.

Hiatt, Shon Russell, Wesley D. Sine, and Pamela Tolbert. 2009. "From Pabst to Pepsi: The Deinstitutionalization of Social Practices and the Creation of Entrepreneurial Opportunities." *Administrative Science Quarterly* 54: 635–667.

Jung, Wooseok, Brayden G. King, and Sarah A. Soule. 2014. "Issue Bricolage: Explaining the Configuration of the Social Movement Sector, 1960–1995." *American Journal of Sociology* 120(1): 187–225.

Katzenstein, M. 1990. "Feminism within American Institutions: Unobtrusive Mobilization in the 1980s." *Signs* 16(1): 27–54.

Katzenstein, M. 1999. *Faithful and Fearless: Moving Feminist Protest Inside the Church and Military*. Princeton, NJ: Princeton University Press.

King, Brayden G. 2008. "A Political Mediation Model of Corporate Response to Social Movement Activism." *Administrative Science Quarterly* 53: 395–421.

King, Brayden G. and Sarah A. Soule. 2007. "Social Movements as Extra-Institutional Entrepreneurs: The Effect of Protest on Stock Price Returns." *Administrative Science Quarterly* 52: 413–442.

King, Brayden G. and Sarah A. Soule. 2008. "Competition and Resource Partitioning in Three Social Movement Industries." *American Journal of Sociology* 113(6): 1568–1610.

King, Brayden G. and Mary-Hunter McDonnell. 2015. "Good Firms, Good Targets: The Relationship between Corporate Social Responsibility, Reputation, and Activist Targeting." In *Corporate Social Responsibility in a Globalizing World: Toward Effective Global CSR Frameworks*, edited by Kiyoteru Tsutsui and Alwyn Lim, 430–454. Cambridge: Cambridge University Press.

Kucinskas, Jaime. 2014a. "The Unobtrusive Tactics of Religious Movements." *Sociology of Religion* 75(4): 537–550.

Kucinskas, Jaime. 2014b. "Change without Confrontation: The Making of Mainstream Meditation." Dissertation. Department of Sociology, Indiana University, Bloomington.

Lounsbury, Michael. 2001. "Institutional Sources of Practice Variation: Staffing College and University Recycling Programs." *Administrative Science Quarterly* 46: 29–56.

Luders, Joseph. 2006. "The Economics of Movement Success: Business Responses to Civil Rights Mobilization." *American Journal of Sociology* 111(4): 963–998.

McAdam, Doug and Ronnelle Paulsen. 1993. "Specifying the Relationship Between Social Ties and Activism." *American Journal of Sociology* 99: 640–667.

McAdam, Doug, Sidney Tarrow, and Charles Tilly. 2001. *Dynamics of Contention*. Cambridge: Cambridge University Press.

McCarthy, John D. and Mayer N. Zald. 1977. "Resource Mobilization and Social Movements: A Partial Theory." *American Journal of Sociology* 82(6): 1212–1241.

McDonnell, Mary-Hunter. 2015. "Radical Repertoires: The Incidence and Impact of Corporate-Sponsored Social Activism." *Organization Science* 27: 53–71.

McDonnell, Mary-Hunter and Brayden G. King. 2013. "Keeping up Appearances Reputational Threat and Impression Management after Social Movement Boycotts." *Administrative Science Quarterly* 58(3): 387–419.

McDonnell, Mary-Hunter, Brayden G. King and Sarah A Soule. 2015. "A Dynamic Process Model of Private Politics Activist Targeting and Corporate Receptivity to Social Challenges." *American Sociological Review* 80(3): 654–678.

Meyer, John and Brian Rowan. 1977. "Institutionalized Organizations: Formal Structure as Myth and Ceremony." *American Journal of Sociology* 83: 340–363.

Meyerson, Debra and Maureen Scully. 1995. "Crossroads Tempered Radicalism and the Politics of Ambivalence and Change." *Organization Science* 6: 585–600.

Minkoff, Debra. 1997. "The Sequencing of Social Movements." *American Sociological Review* 62(5): 779–799.

Munson, Ziad. 2009. *The Making of Pro-Life Activists: How Social Movement Mobilization Works*. Chicago: University of Chicago Press.

Oberlin, Kathleen C. 2014. "Mobilizing Epistemic Conflict: The Creation Museum and the Creationist Social Movement." Dissertation. Department of Sociology, Indiana University, Bloomington.

Raeburn, Nicole. 2004. *Changing Corporate America from the Inside Out: Lesbian and Gay Workplace Rights*. Minneapolis: University of Minnesota Press.

Rojas, Fabio. 2007. *From Black Power to Black Studies: How a Radical Social Movement Became an Academic Discipline*. Baltimore, MD: Johns Hopkins University Press.

Rojas, Fabio. 2010. "Power Through Institutional Work: Building Academic Authority in the 1968 Third World Strike." *The Academy of Management Journal* 53: 1263–1280.

Rojas, Fabio. 2012. "Social Movements and Universities." In *Organizing Higher Education*, edited by Michael Bastedo, 256–277. Baltimore, MD: Johns Hopkins University Press.

Rojas, Fabio. 2013. "Institutions." In *Oxford Bibliographies in Sociology*, edited by Jeff Manza, Oxford: Oxford University Press. See http://oxfordbibliographies.com

Rojas, Fabio and Carson Byrd. 2014. "The Four Histories of Black Power: The Black Nationalist Sector and its Impact on American Society." *Black Diaspora Review* 4(1): 113–156.

Rosenfeld, Jake. 2014. *What Unions No Longer Do*. Cambridge, MA: Harvard University Press.

Santoro, Wayne A. and Gail M. McGuire. 1997. "Social Movement Insiders: The Impact of Institutional Activists on Affirmative Action and Comparable Worth Policies." *Social Problems* 44(4): 503–519.

Schneiberg, Marc and Michael Lounsbury. 2008. "Social Movements and Institutional Analysis." In *The Handbook of Organizational Institutionalism*, edited by Royston Greenwood, Christine Oliver, Kerstin Sahlin-Andersson and Roy Suddaby, 650–672. London: Sage.

Schneiberg, Marc and Sarah A. Soule. 2005. "Institutionalization as a Contested, Multi-level Process: Politics, Social Movements and Rate Regulation in American Fire Insurance." In *Social Movements and Organizations*, edited by Gerald Davis, Doug McAdam, W. Richard Scott and Mayer N. Zald, 122–160. Cambridge: Cambridge University Press.

Schussman, Alan and Sarah A. Soule. 2005. "Process and Protest: Accounting for Individual Protest Participation." *Social Forces* 84(2): 1083–1108.

Scott, Richard W. 2001. *Institutions and Organizations*, 2nd edn. Thousand Oaks, CA: Sage.

Seo, Myeong-Gu and W. E. Douglas Creed. 2002. "Institutional Contradictions, Praxis, and Institutional Change: A Dialectical Perspective." *The Academy of Management Review* 27(2): 222–247.

Sine, Wesley D. and Brandon H. Lee. 2009. "Tilting at Windmills? The Environmental Movement and the Emergence of the U.S. Wind Energy Sector." *Administrative Science Quarterly* 54: 123–155.

Snow, David A., Louis A. Zurcher, and Sheldon Ekland-Olson. 1980. "Social Networks and Social Movements: A Microstructural Approach to Differential Recruitment." *American Sociological Review* 45(5): 787–801.

Soule, Sarah A. 1997. "The Student Divestment Movement in the United States and the Shantytown: Diffusion of a Protest Tactic." *Social Forces* 75(3): 855–883.

Soule, Sarah A. 2009. *Contention and Corporate Social Responsibility*. Cambridge: Cambridge University Press.

Soule, Sarah A. and Brayden G. King. 2006. "The Stages of the Policy Process and the Equal Rights Amendment, 1972–1982." *American Journal of Sociology* 111(6): 1871–1909.

Soule, Sarah A., Anand Swaminathan, and Laszlo Tihanyi. 2015. "The Diffusion of Foreign Divestment from Burma." *Strategic Management Journal* 7: 1032–1052.

Stinchcombe, Arthur L. 1965. "Social Structure and Organizations." In *Handbook of Organizations*, edited by James G. March, 142–193. Chicago: Rand McNally & Co.

Strang, David and Dong-Il Jung. 2005. "Organizational Change as an Orchestrated Social Movement: Recruitment to a 'Quality Initiative'." In *Social Movements and Organization Theory*, edited by Gerald F. Davis, Doug McAdam, W. Richard Scott, and Mayer N. Zald, 280–309. Cambridge: Cambridge University Press.

Strang, David and Sarah A. Soule. 1998. "Diffusion in Organizations and Social Movements: From Hybrid Corn to Poison Pills." *Annual Review of Sociology* 56: 265–290.

Taylor, Verta. 1989. "Social Movement Continuity: The Women's Movement in Abeyance." *American Sociological Review* 54(5): 761–775.

Tilly, Charles. 1978. *From Mobilization to Revolution*. Reading, MA: Addison-Wesley.

Useem, Bert and Jack A. Goldstone. 2002. "Forging Social Order and Its Breakdown: Riot and Reform in U.S. Prisons." *American Sociological Review* 67: 499–525.

Vasi, Ion Bogdan and Brayden G King. 2012. "Social Movements, Risk Perceptions, and Economic Outcomes: The Effect of Primary and Secondary Stakeholder Activism on Firms' Perceived Environmental Risk and Financial Performance." *American Sociological Review* 77(4): 573–596.

Vogel, David. 2010. "The Private Regulation of Global Corporate Conduct: Achievements and Limitations." *Business & Society* 49: 68–87.

Walker, Edward T. 2014. *Grassroots for Hire: Public Affairs Consultants in American Democracy*. Cambridge: Cambridge University Press.

Walker, Edward T. and Christopher M. Rea. 2014. "The Political Mobilization of Firms and Industries." *Annual Review of Sociology* 40: 281–304.

Wang, Dan and Sarah A. Soule. 2012 "Social Movement Organizational Collaboration: Networks of Learning and the Diffusion of Protest Tactics, 1960–1995." *The American Journal of Sociology* 117(6): 1674–1722.

Wang, Dan and Sarah A. Soule. 2016. "Tactical Innovation in Protest: The Effects of Movement Spillover and Structural Isolation." *American Sociological Review* 81(3): 517–548.

Weber, Klaus and Brayden King. 2014. "Social Movement Theory and Organization Studies." In *Oxford Handbook of Sociology, Social Theory and Organization Studies: Contemporary Currents*, edited by Paul Adler, Paul du Gay, Glenn Morgan, and Mike Reed, 487–509. Oxford: Oxford University Press.

White, Monica M. 2011. "D-Town Farm: African American Resistance to Food Insecurity and the Transformation of Detroit." *Environmental Practice* 13(4): 406–417.

12

Infighting and Insurrection

Amin Ghaziani and Kelsy Kretschmer

Introduction

Research on social movements highlights the centrality of conflict, yet scholars frequently conflate its diverse forms and associated consequences for mobilization. In this chapter, we take a special interest in infighting, a type of conflict that is remarkably pronounced in political organizing (Balser 1997; Levitsky 2007). Early debates between Booker T. Washington and W.E.B. Du Bois about the nature of black political progress are instructive. Washington advocated gradualism and accommodation to white oppression, while Du Bois countered that social change required persistent agitation, direct action, and higher education. The disagreement between them shows how conflict can clarify trajectories of activism. "The black men of America have a duty to perform, a duty stern and delicate—a forward movement to oppose a part of the work of their greatest leader" (Du Bois 1903). Du Bois did not insist that activists had to converge in their viewpoints. Rather, his disagreements with Washington clarified the meanings and material expressions of civil rights, including the importance of agitation, action, and academic education.

The contemporary landscape is also peppered with "horizontal hostility," a term that feminist Florynce Kennedy coined to describe fights among minority group members (Penelope 1992). Consider that Harry Belafonte dismissed Colin Powell as a "house slave" who only serves his "master" (President Bush) and sells out the black community. Belafonte contends that conservative African Americans damage the legacy and future of the civil rights movement. Years earlier, Malcolm X attacked Martin Luther King Jr. for wanting to be part of the white man's world (McAdam 1982; Morris 1984). This argument resembles what DuBois said to Washington and, one hundred years later, the assault that Richard Goldstein launched against "Homocons," or conservative, especially Republican, LGBT people (Goldstein 2003).

The Wiley Blackwell Companion to Social Movements, Second Edition. Edited by David A. Snow, Sarah A. Soule, Hanspeter Kriesi, and Holly J. McCammon.
© 2019 John Wiley & Sons Ltd. Published 2019 by John Wiley & Sons Ltd.

Infighting is the expression of a dissenting opinion, a discrepant view, or a debate among activists that attempts to redefine past struggles, frame the present moment, or shape future trajectories of activism. It is a type of conflict that flares as activists spar over their political ethos (Geertz 1973; Melucci 1996), collective identity (Brown-Saracino and Ghaziani 2009; Taylor and Whittier 1992), perceived moral order (Wuthnow 1987), strategy and tactics (Cohen 1985), or types of leadership (Weber 1958). These battles reflect both pre-existing and emergent differences between groups of activists. In organizing a march on Washington, for example, lesbian and gay activists fought lengthy battles over the inclusion of bisexual and transgender people in the title of their demonstrations (Ghaziani 2008). Should they call the march "The National March on Washington for Lesbian and Gay Rights" or "... for Lesbian, Gay, Bisexual, and Transgender Rights?" This decision had concrete implications for matters like fundraising, formulating demands, and selecting speakers. Similarly, feminists used dissent to find answers to broad concerns like "What is a woman?" and "What are female values?" (Echols 1989; Rich 1980; Taylor and Rupp 1993: 41). Infighting in this instance was a source of "creative disunity" that birthed a distinctly female way of life and worldview (Lorde 1984).

Infighting typically erupts in small-group brainstorming and planning sessions as activists strive for a "precarious equilibrium" between inclusion and group boundaries (Ghaziani and Fine 2008: 65), and the fights have implications for the distribution of power, status, authority, and resources. For students of social movements, infighting provides a "measurement directive" to identify the underlying assumptions that motivate political engagement (Ghaziani 2009: 589). Indeed, "if we emphasize integration and coherence at the expense of dissonance and discontinuity," scholars risk overlooking how participating in protest can "crystalize, objectify, and communicate group experience" (Hebdige 1979: 79).

We argue that infighting is analytically and empirically distinct from other movement outcomes like factions, schisms, and defections, and it does not uniformly or inevitably lead to them. For example, following an auspicious start with a group of well-connected professional founders and great media fanfare, the National Organization for Women (NOW) experienced two schisms during its early days. The first split occurred when a group of conservative Ohio members walked out of a conference in protest of NOW's decision, at the behest of radical East Coast chapters, to support abortion rights. The Ohio faction later formed the Women's Equity Action League, which served as a safe haven for women who were uncomfortable with polarizing social issues like abortion (Kretschmer 2014). The second schism occurred over NOW's decision to support the Equal Rights Amendment (ERA), a Constitutional Amendment mandating women's equality in all areas of the law. American unions had long championed labor protections for working women. Because the ERA would invalidate these policies, many labor-affiliated members chose to stay loyal to their union and exit NOW (Barakso 2004). The conference revealed insurmountable factionalism over what NOW should be, who it should represent, and what it should fight for—so much that one participant wondered if any members would be left by the end of all the organizational defections.[1] These examples show that factions, schisms, and defections are a common class of phenomena in which groups fail at conflict resolution, resulting in "the proper break-up of the group" and a "certain release" (Simmel 1955: 48-49) of the generative potential of conflict. Infighting is the antecedent to factionalism, threatening to separate activists in terms of their instrumental and expressive goals, but such splits are by no means destined from the mere presence of disagreements.

The examples with which we have opened this chapter include civil rights, feminist, and LGBT social movement organizing, yet they all reveal the same core insight: no analysis of social change can ignore the role of conflict (Weber 1949). Early theorists explained how its presence can promote self-conscious action (Park and Burgess 1921). Their work shows that conflict is not uniformly destructive but rather a form of sociation that can also produce unity (Simmel 1955). "Society is sewn together by its inner conflicts," Ross (1920: 164–165) remarked. Three decades later, Coser (1956: 80) echoed that conflict "sews the social system together." Many thinkers noted the ability of conflict to create a deeper engagement with social life, enable members of a group to become aware of the ties that bind them to a shared moral universe, and fashion a sense of cultural commonality and political coherence. Others like Parsons (1949) critiqued conflict for undermining collective norms. A concern with the conservation of social order motivated many structural functionalists to dismiss the generative potential of conflict and define it instead as a social sickness. These scholars favored consensus over conflict because they saw the latter as "destructive of the social organism" (Horowitz 1962: 180).

Whether conflict is productive or pernicious depends on its form. This is why it is theoretically important to recognize the unique properties of infighting. Simmel (1955: 48–49) states, "People who have many common features often do one another worse or 'worser' wrong than complete strangers." Infighting is a special case of conflict that is unlike factions, defections, schisms, or splits. When activists express a dissenting opinion from others in the same organization or across organizations that belong to the same movement, they implicitly define the boundaries of their group without unraveling the network ties that bind them together. Conflict in this situation can promote integration by allowing activists to negotiate the concerns that matter most to them.

Movement scholars have long debated the relationship between infighting and insurrection. In this chapter, we review this vast literature and organize it into three major traditions: (1) classical; (2) conditional; and (3) causal treatments of conflict. Extant research is based on case studies of social movement organizations, and it is primarily concerned with the causes and consequences of conflict. Much of this work treats conflict as an undifferentiated pathogen that infects and eventually destroys mobilization efforts by producing paralyzing factional splits, schisms, defections, or counter-movements. These outcomes are related to infighting yet distinct in theoretical terms from it. Factions, splits, splinters, schisms, and defections ensue when groups mismanage disagreements (Bernstein 1997, 2003), fail to resolve internal conflicts (Gamson 1975), diverge in their perceptions of injustice (McAdam 1982), seek organizational independence (Rochford 1989), and pursue non-overlapping courses of action (Balser 1997; Miller 1983; Mushaben 1989; Stern, Tarrow, and Williams 1971; Zald and McCarthy 1980).

Some caveats are worth mentioning before we proceed. Not all research on infighting can be classified into one of our three traditions, while some work evokes multiple themes, blending aspects of one intellectual tradition with another. We have organized the literature in this way to identify variation in how scholars have conceptualized conflict and illustrate that its effects are neither uniform nor always destructive. We also want to be clear that by grouping research into one tradition, we do not mean to suggest that those respective pieces are the same across the board, but rather that the works are similar only on those aspects of conflict that are of interest to us in this review. The ideal types that we offer enable us to trace how students of social movements have imagined the relationship between infighting and insurrection, and they represent in broad strokes the state of the field. We conclude by outlining the tenets of a sociology of infighting that synthesizes insights from across the three traditions. We also advocate that future researchers should reconceptualize the relationship between infighting and insurrection through a field-theoretic perspective that links micro-level interpersonal instances of infighting with macro-level contentious actions for social change.

The Classical Tradition

Foundational research on the labor movement finds that competition between workers thwarts their ability to organize (Marx and Engels 1978). As they form into a self-conscious class, competition cedes to antagonism against those who own the means of production. Infighting in this analysis is the antecedent of inter-group conflict, which holds the potential for economic transformation through revolution. Inspired by Marx and Engels, movement scholars in the 1960s and 1970s studied social class and organizational cohesion, and their primary concern was to predict infighting using variables like the composition of the mass base, organizational form, and competition for limited resources (Zald and Ash 1966).

Research shows that inclusive organizations require little commitment and have a small initiation period. These groups are harmonious because they have relaxed criteria for joining (members are allowed to affiliate with other groups) and political orthodoxy (members are not subjected to ideological purity). Inclusive organizations are "split-resistant" (ibid.: 337). Exclusive organizations hold new members in an extended trial period and require submission to the group's strict principles and leadership. They demand intense investments of time and energy, and members are discouraged from exploring other interests. Exclusive organizations "spew" forth factions because activists are barred from expressing multiple allegiances; sometimes they prefer to "switch than fight" (ibid.). In later work, Piven and Cloward (1977) identified strategy as a mediator between organizational form and factionalism. Their analysis is consistent with other research that finds recruitment procedures and membership requirements affect the causes and consequences of conflict (Gamson 1975; Stern, Tarrow, and Williams 1971). Finally, internal dissent flares when social movement organizations (SMOs) compete for scarce resources like money, media attention, and new members (Gitlin 1980; Jenkins 1983; McCarthy and Zald 1977; Morris 1984; Oberschall 1973). As they struggle for position in a crowded field and search for stable sources of financing, competition compels leaders to reassess their strategy, resulting in groups that change their views from radical to moderate or vice versa. This causes conflict if activists feel confused or uncertain about the organization's values, goals, and targets of action.

Unlike most scholarship that devoted itself to predicting the causes of conflict, Gamson's (1975) work on 53 protest groups that mobilized over 150 years focused on effects. He argues that groups with inadequate mechanisms for managing conflict will fail. To make this strong claim, he first concedes to the ubiquity of infighting. "Internal division is a misery that few challenging groups escape completely – it is the nature of the beast" (ibid.: 99). Such conflicts arise for a number of reasons, including disagreements over strategy and tactics, the leadership profile, the distribution of power within the group, differences in political priorities, movement goals, and short- and long-term solutions for change. What differentiates successful movements from others is whether activists can resolve their disputes. Poor channels for conflict resolution induce factional splits, and for Gamson, these undermine effective political action. "The sorry reputation of factionalism is a deserved one," he argues. "That factional splits are a concomitant of failure is clear enough" (ibid.). In his study, Gamson uses "formal schism" (ibid.: 101) as his only measure of conflict, although he mentions "internal divisions," "internal disputes," "factions," "factional splits," and "factionalism" throughout his analysis. While the findings introduce new questions about the consequences of infighting, his limited measures prevent theoretical nuance, especially the conditions under which internal disputes are generative. Defections are more detrimental for a movement's longevity than the mere presence of dissent, but this hypothesis about the comparative effects of different forms of conflict remained empirically untested in the classical tradition.

Like Gamson, McAdam (1982) also offered a negative assessment of infighting. He found that infighting caused organizational proliferation (the splintering off of more organizations that compete with one another); persistent disagreements over the core issues and goals of the movement; the escalation of intra-movement conflict (animosity across organizations); and geographic diffusion (infighting was partly responsible for the spread of the civil rights movement from the South to the North). These findings led McAdam to conclude, "Once effective insurgent organizations were rendered impotent by factional disputes that drained them of the unity, energy, and resolve needed to sustain protest activity" (ibid.: 189). Infighting obstructed opportunities for cooperative action between civil rights groups and reduced the political strength and effectiveness of each one.

Gamson and McAdam became the leading voices in social movement scholarship, and their position on infighting defined it as toxic for the next generation of students. Mushaben (1989: 269) summarizes the wisdom that coalesced in the field: "Intramovement or group conflict is viewed as a disruptive, destructive force, with few exceptions." Her review of research leads her to summarize that "factionalization is engraved all too often as the 'cause of death' upon the tombstones of protests past in the graveyard of SMOs."

The Conditional Tradition

Researchers in the mid-1980s and 1990s began to examine the uneven effects of conflict. Findings from the women's movement in its organizational doldrums was among the first to challenge Gamson's and McAdam's conclusions that internal divisions are always destructive (Rupp and Taylor 1987). This work showed that the presence of infighting mattered less than the ability of activists to channel it toward productive purposes. Studies of the West German peace movement show that conflict can be a "destructive or creative force" for social movements (Mushaben 1989: 269). Under certain conditions, it is a mobilization resource for activists who can use it to foster creativity, protect diversity, and promote concilia-tion among contending voices. Like classical researchers, scholars whom we group in the conditional tradition also isolated organizational problems (Downey 1986; Walsh and Cable 1989), but they were less likely to conclude that infighting was "internecine dog fighting" (Gerlach and Hine 1970: 64). The objective for scholars who were writing at this time shifted from predicting infighting to assessing its effects. New research specified the conditions under which infighting creates benefi-cial pressures for accountability and transparency in decision-making.

In his work on frame disputes in the nuclear disarmament movement, Benford (1993: 694) finds that infighting is "detrimental and facilitative" for organizing efforts. It halts the mobilization of some SMOs by depleting their resources while catalyzing others. Although it can cause splits, internal dissent also inspires cohesive-ness. It aids in the division of interpretive labor, a type of culture work that helps activists diversify their articulations of strategy and identity (Cohen 1985). Several other studies contributed to a theoretical diplomacy about infighting. Balser (1997) offers a compelling comparison of its effects across four movement organizations: Students for a Democratic Society (SDS), the Student Nonviolent Coordinating Committee (SNCC), the American Federation of Labor (AFL), and Earth First! (EF!). Her work is exemplary because she carefully distinguishes infighting from factional splits. Like conflict theorists, Balser finds that defection is a variable outcome that requires explanation. It does not follow inevitably from an internal dispute nor is it interchangeable with it. Her findings showcase the role of the external environment on mobilization, including the nature of political opportunities (access to the system, the ability of activists to pass favorable legislation, the presence of allies, and the relative stability of electoral alignments); social control mechanisms like government infiltration, repression, and institutional pressures to espouse moderate views; and resources like money, meeting facilities, and media attention; and power-exchange relationships with other SMOs (see also Eisinger 1973; Glass 2009; King 2008; Kitschelt 1986; McAdam 1982; Romanos 2011; Shriver and Adams 2013).

The Causal Tradition

The classical tradition of infighting assumed that conflict within movements deserved its sorry reputation; it was a form of internecine dog fighting; and it hastened movement collapse by rendering insurgent groups impotent. Highly cited studies from the conditional tradition also documented the capacity of infighting to immo-bilize activists, but they considered its generative potential as well. These trends inspired a new generation of scholars to identify the causal factors that explain why some SMOs become mired in infighting while others avoid it. This work developed in a context when movement scholars were concerned with questions about the ori-gins of social movements (Morris and Herring 1987), while sociology as a discipline was in the midst of a cultural turn (Friedland and Mohr 2004). For these reasons, the

1990s and 2000s comprise what we call a causal tradition that isolated cultural variables in particular – like frames, ideologies, identities, communities, and consciousness – to explain the origins of infighting.

Why does infighting occur in social movements? Research shows that its primary causes are racist attitudes and beliefs among members (Fantasia 1988; Moraga and Anzaldúa 1981), sexist attitudes and beliefs (Chesler 2001; Robnett 1997), and other social divisions that arise from differing structural positions (Cohen 1999, 2000; Gamson 1995, 1997; Goldstein 2003; Waite 2001; Walker and Stepick 2014). Infighting is also a function of coordination and communication problems that activists confront when they are situated at the intersection of multiple oppressions (Cohen 1999; Collins 2000; McCall 2005; Stockdill 2003), the changing generational and cohort profile of activists (Klandermans 1994; Whittier 1997), competing economic interests among individuals (Oliver 1993), failure to mobilize consensus (Klandermans 1988), disagreements over the political logics that drive the selection of strategies and tactics (Armstrong 2002; Wrenn 2012), challenges with participatory democracy as a structure for decision-making (Polletta 2002; Wilde 2004), and the struggle to maintain continuity and coherence across different stages of mobilization (Blee 2012; Ghaziani and Baldassarri 2011; Taylor 1989).

Most research on infighting in this tradition focused on contradictions in movement culture and identity (Bernstein 1997; Jasper 1997; Johnston and Klandermans 1995; Larana, Johnston, and Gusfield 1994; Lichterman 1995; Melucci 1985, 1995; Polletta 1997; Polletta and Jasper 2001; Stryker, Owens, and White 2000); pressures for ideological purity in values, viewpoints about the past and present, and visions for the future (Echols 1983, 1989; Klatch 2004; Ryan 1989; Taylor and Rupp 1993); and disputes over how to identify and define situations that require change most urgently, what to do about those situations, and how to inspire the rank and file to act (Benford 1993; Snow and Benford 1988, 1992). The literature shows the common occurrence of frame disputes in particular, which provide competing answers to questions like who are we (the protagonists), who are they (the antagonists and audience), what are we doing, and why are we doing it (Hunt, Benford, and Snow 1994; Trumpy 2014).

Scholars who published in the causal tradition refrained from taking an evaluative stance on the relationship between infighting and insurrection. Instead, they attributed the causal significance of infighting to single explanatory variables. This happened for several reasons. Avoiding evaluation was a reaction against the provocative language that Gamson, McAdam, and others used in prior years. Neutral language also continued the diplomatic stance that Benford advocated. Finally, many scholars skirted evaluation because they saw infighting as epiphenomenal to other theoretical concerns.

In summary, the classical, conditional, and causal traditions offer distinct insights about infighting in social movements. Table 12.1 summarizes the major themes from each.

Table 12.1 displays an ongoing debate among scholars about infighting. At one end are scholars who conclude that infighting is destructive. It is a form of internecine dog fighting that saps political potency. Infighting deserves its sorry reputation because it hastens movement collapse and renders insurgent groups impotent. It is the cause of death written upon the tombstones of protests past. The imagery here is

Table 12.1   Classical, conditional, and causal traditions in the study of infighting

Dimensions of infighting	Scholarly tradition		
	Classical	Conditional	Causal
Why study it?	To predict its occurrence	To determine its impact	Epiphenomenal
Is it distinct from defection?	No	Sometimes	Yes
Why does it matter?	Spews forth defection	Prompts defection, decline or growth	Highlights diversity
Why does it occur?	Organizational form	Organizational form	Many causal variables
How can it be resolved?	Change organizational form	Allow for articulation of dissent	Remedy causal variable
Is it positive or negative?	Negative	Positive or negative	Negative, but rectifiable
What is its relationship to defection?	Inevitable – always causes defection and decline	Unclear – may or may not cause defection and decline	Unspecified – emphasis of research is elsewhere

powerful, and the language is sharp. In the middle is a space for theoretical diplomacy: infighting can be beneficial or burdensome depending on how activists think about it and manage the challenges that they confront. At the other end are a collection of studies that show the resourceful contributions of infighting. Infighting allows activists to account for and celebrate their internal differences, and it offers moments of reflection as they calculate new directions in a shifting political terrain. This work offers some counterintuitive insights: consensus, rather than conflict, can be dangerous if it allows disputes to fester without careful examination and deliberation. Infighting is painful for those who must endure it, but it recalibrates and rebalances the movement in a way that sustains it over time (Luna 2010; McCammon 2012).

Some studies show that activists can successfully reframe their internal divisions as a source of strength. Hewitt (2011) found that international networks of feminist activists faced significant obstacles in generating a common understanding for what women needed globally, but they used infighting as proof to both insiders and outsiders that they incorporated diversity in ways that made their network stronger. This finding is consistent with the research by Armstrong (2002), Ghaziani (2008, 2009), Stein (2012), and Bernstein and Taylor (2013), all of whom have shown that LGBT activists established a sense of unity through their diversity, not despite it or by ignoring it. Rather than stunting movement growth, dissent can expand options for adherents, create new styles of participation, produce tactical innovation, and generate a wider array of strategies and tactics for achieving a movement's goals (Ferree and Hess 2002; McCammon 2003). This can be true even in the event of a factional split. In their study of the Texas women's movement, McCammon, Bergner, and Arch (2015) find that disagreeing with radical groups in their movement allowed moderates to gain entry into a closed political system. Contrasting their limited proposal with the sweeping Equal Legal Rights Amendment (ELRA), moderate activists leveraged factionalism in the movement to create a positive radical flank effect. The specter of radical feminism worked to win institutional allies for movement moderates in the short run, and it set the stage for Texas legislators to eventually pass the ELRA after feminists had made the necessary inroads.

Conclusion

There is no denying that people fight. Conflict is a constitutional element of social life and social movements, and it is a dynamic process with variable outcomes. As a type of conflict, we believe that infighting ought to be a central category for the analysis of mobilization. Activists express dissenting opinions to define what it means to be involved in a movement, how to strategize their objectives, and how to execute those strategies with the most effective tactics. Infighting can generate multiple perspectives, despite the unease it sometimes evokes among activists who do the hard work of organizing on the ground. The expression of discrepant opinions highlights the fine line between including some while excluding others, and it reveals clues for which actions, cultural worldviews, and collective identities will be effective in the planning and organizing stages in light of volatile and shifting power dynamics (Walker and Stepick 2014). Infighting privileges differences among activists, and it directs scholarly attention away from shared concerns and group building to contested questions of political agency.

Based on insights from our review of research in the classical, conditional, and causal traditions, we advocate a sociology of infighting that frames this type of conflict as a case of cultural skepticism (Swidler 2001). The doubts and challenges activists articulate against each other enable them to concretize abstract ideas of culture and collective identity, the nature of injustice, the operations of inequality, and strategic remedial action. This is why we believe that any analysis of the cultural consequences of mobilization must examine the prevalence, role, and patterns of infighting. Glossing over the conflicts that arise between "us versus thems-inside" (Gamson 1997), conflating it with factions and defections (Balser 1997), or an exclusive emphasis on coherence, consensus, integration, and unity among activists at the expense of "dissonance and discontinuity" (Hebdige 1979: 79) undermines the validity of research findings by denying the negotiation that activists require to objectify, communicate, and act on their visions for social justice.

Our review shows that focusing on infighting can allow scholars to learn about the micro-dynamics that underlie the construction of activist identities and cultures over time. Left unaccounted is how conflict at once shapes and is shaped by the broader political context in which activists are situated. To round out our proposed sociology of infighting, we bring it into conversation with the increasingly prominent field theory in social movements (Barman 2016; Fligstein and McAdam 2012; Pettinicchio 2013). Both approaches treat conflict as a constant feature of social life and a potentially productive aspect of mobilization. Strategic action fields are the meso-level bridge that connects infighting among activists with the political opportunity structure. Like a set of Russian nesting dolls, strategic action fields are nested within one another, and the rules and structures of those that are higher in order (e.g. presidential parties, relationships with elites, the view of municipal authorities) shape those that they surround (e.g. conflicts and collaborations among activists). Every field is comprised of multiple actors, each with varying access to the resources they need to get what they want. In this framework, a single organization is both an actor in the larger field, where it competes and negotiates with other organizations, as well as a field with its own set of internal actors (chapters, regions, and board members, among others) who themselves are competing and collaborating as they struggle to create a culture and collective identity that is consistent with their goals.

Infighting shapes relationships across strategic action fields, including other organizations in the same movement, opposing and allied movements, public organizations, and state agencies (Pearlman 2011). For example, Whittier (2014) finds that feminist infighting over pornography in the 1980s and 1990s kept their organizations on the sidelines during the major policy campaigns around it. The absence of an organized feminist presence gave religious conservatives an advantage in spotlighting their own frames and minimizing feminist critiques of pornography in the policy process. Bringing field theory to a sociology of infighting clarifies how conflicts within a movement affect strategic action fields by expanding, limiting, or shifting how activists and counter-activists are positioned within different parts of a complex, nested political and policy structure. Bringing a sociology of infighting to field theory articulates how shifts in the configuration of the political and policy context affects local struggles over cultural meanings and collective identities (Harrison, Lopez, and Martin 2015).

Our review of the literature suggests some slippage between infighting at the organizational level (or conflicts within a single organization) and that which occurs at the movement level (or inter-organizational conflicts). Existing studies inadequately distinguish these forms of infighting, yet our review shows that the tasks required of members within an organization are unlike those that exist between organizations. A notable exception is Davenport's (2014) research, which shows that repression and infighting interact at the organizational and individual levels to "kill" a movement. His findings raise new questions: How are internal organizational conflicts different from larger-scale fights between movement organizations? And how do these distinctions affect mobilization efforts? Because field theory focuses on the layered nature of political life, researchers can use it to conceptualize the nuances of infighting.

To make this less abstract, we return to an example with which we opened this chapter. NOW's early schisms were the outcome of conflict over strategies, goals, resource distribution, and collective identity. A narrow focus on just the individual organization tells us one story about the effects of conflict. But these disputes also represented flashpoints in a broader, and ultimately productive, struggle to settle the emerging feminist field. Activists and organizations were unsure of which issues and which actors would come to define feminism. Multiple rounds of infighting within and between organizations clarified the boundaries of the movement and shaped the larger field. Despite the controversy of its positions on abortion and the ERA, NOW's prominence in the feminist field helped to institutionalize its preferences as the central tenets of the movement (Kretschmer 2014). In fact, WEAL, which was formed by the faction of Ohio members of NOW who defected, adopted abortion rights as a plank of its own platform just a few years after splitting with NOW over that very same issue.

We use this example to open and close the chapter because it shows that theories of infighting fit well with those of strategic action fields. Together, they provide a comprehensive explanation for the micro-, meso-, and macro-dynamics that interact when activists contend with questions of culture, identity, and strategy. Future research can investigate the conditions under which activists invoke field relationships to shape the outcome of their local conflicts or when those conflicts reconfigure alliances in larger arenas, as well as how fields shape whether infighting produces factionalism or buffers against it.

Note

1   Mary Jean Collins, telephone interview, May 29, 2009.

References

Armstrong, Elizabeth A. 2002. *Forging Gay Identities: Organizing Sexuality in San Francisco, 1950–1994*. Chicago: University of Chicago Press.

Balser, Deborah B. 1997. "The Impact of Environmental Factors on Factionalism and Schism in Social Movement Organizations." *Social Forces* 76: 199–228.

Barakso, Maryann. 2004. *Governing NOW: Grassroots Activism in the National Organization for Women*. Ithaca, NY: Cornell University Press.

Barman, Emily. 2016. "Varieties of Field Theory and the Sociology of the Non-profit Sector." *Sociology Compass* 10: 442–458.

Benford, Robert D. 1993. "Frame Disputes within the Nuclear Disarmament Movement." *Social Forces* 71: 677–701.

Bernstein, Mary. 1997. "Celebration and Suppression: The Strategic Uses of Identity by the Lesbian and Gay Movement." *American Journal of Sociology* 103: 531–565.

Bernstein, Mary. 2003. "Nothing Ventured, Nothing Gained? Conceptualizing Social Movement 'Success' in the Lesbian and Gay Movement." *Sociological Perspectives* 46: 353–379.

Bernstein, Mary and Verta Taylor. 2013. *The Marrying Kind? Debating Same-Sex Marriage within the Lesbian and Gay Movement*. Minneapolis: University of Minnesota Press.

Blee, Kathleen M. 2012. *Democracy in the Making: How Activist Groups Form*. New York: Oxford University Press.

Brown-Saracino, Japonica and Amin Ghaziani. 2009. "The Constraints of Culture: Evidence from the Chicago Dyke March." *Cultural Sociology* 3: 51–75.

Chesler, Phyllis. 2001. *Woman's Inhumanity to Woman*. New York: Nation Books.

Cohen, Cathy J. 1999. *The Boundaries of Blackness: AIDS and the Breakdown of Black Politics*. Chicago: University of Chicago Press.

Cohen, Cathy J. 2000. "Contested Membership: Black Gay Identities and the Politics of AIDS." In *Creating Change: Sexuality, Public Policy, and Civil Rights*, edited by John D'Emilio, William B. Turner, and Urvashi Vaid, 382–406. New York: St. Martin's Press.

Cohen, Jean L. 1985. "Strategy or Identity: New Theoretical Paradigms and Contemporary Social Movements." *Social Research* 52: 663–716.

Collins, Patricia Hill. 2000. *Black Feminist Thought: Knowledge, Consciousness, and the Politics of Empowerment*. New York: Routledge.

Coser, Lewis. 1956. *The Functions of Social Conflict*. New York: The Free Press.

Davenport, Christian. 2014. *How Social Movements Die: Repression and Demobilization of the Republic of New Africa*. Cambridge: Cambridge University Press.

Downey, Gary L. 1986. "Ideology and the Clamshell Identity: Organizational Dilemmas in the Anti-Nuclear Power Movement." *Social Problems* 33: 357–373.

Du Bois, William Edward Burghardt. 1903. *The Souls of Black Folk*. Chicago: A.C. McClurg & Company.

Echols, Alice. 1983. "Cultural Feminism: Feminist Capitalism and the Anti-Pornography Movement." *Social Text* 7: 34–53.

Echols, Alice. 1989. *Daring to Be Bad: Radical Feminism in America 1967–1975*. Minneapolis: University of Minnesota Press.

Eisinger, Peter K. 1973. "The Conditions of Protest Behavior in American Cities." *American Political Science Review* 67: 11–28.

Fantasia, Rick. 1988. *Cultures of Solidarity: Consciousness, Action, and Contemporary American Workers*. Berkeley: University of California Press.

Ferree, Myra Marx and Beth Hess. 2002. *Controversy and Coalition: The New Feminist Movement across Four Decades of Change*. New York: Routledge.

Fligstein, Neil and Doug McAdam. 2012. *A Theory of Fields*. New York: Oxford University Press.

Friedland, Roger and John W. Mohr. 2004. "The Cultural Turn in American Sociology." In *Matters of Culture: Cultural Sociology in Practice*, edited by Roger Friedland and John W. Mohr, 1–70. Cambridge: Cambridge University Press.

Gamson, Joshua. 1995. "Must Identity Movements Self-Destruct? A Queer Dilemma." *Social Problems* 42: 390–407.

Gamson, Joshua. 1997. "Messages of Exclusion: Gender, Movements, and Symbolic Boundaries." *Gender & Society* 11: 178–199.

Gamson, William A. 1975. *The Strategy of Social Protest*. Belmont, CA: Wadsworth Publishing Company.

Geertz, Clifford. 1973. *The Interpretation of Cultures*. New York: Basic Books.

Gerlach, Luther and Virginia Hine. 1970. *People, Power, Change: Movements of Social Transformation*. Indianapolis, IN: Bobbs-Merrill.

Ghaziani, Amin. 2008. *The Dividends of Dissent: How Conflict and Culture Work in Lesbian and Gay Marches on Washington*. Chicago: University of Chicago Press.

Ghaziani, Amin. 2009. "An 'Amorphous Mist'? The Problem of Measurement in the Study of Culture." *Theory and Society* 38: 581–612.

Ghaziani, Amin and Delia Baldassarri. 2011. "Cultural Anchors and the Organization of Differences: A Multi-method Analysis of LGBT Marches on Washington." *American Sociological Review* 76: 179–206.

Ghaziani, Amin and Gary Alan Fine. 2008. "Infighting and Ideology: How Conflict Informs the Local Culture of the Chicago Dyke March." *International Journal of Politics, Culture, and Society* 20: 51–67.

Gitlin, Todd. 1980. *The Whole World Is Watching*. Berkeley: University of California Press.

Glass, Pepper G. 2009. "Unmaking a Movement: Identity Work and the Outcomes of Zapatista Community Centers in Los Angeles." *Journal of Contemporary Ethnography* 38: 523–546.

Goldstein, Richard. 2003. *Homocons: The Rise of the Gay Right*. London: Verso.

Harrison, Jill Ann, Steven H. Lopez, and Andrew W. Martin. 2015. "Rethinking Organizational Decoupling Fields, Power Struggles, and Work Routines." *Social Currents* 2: 341–360.

Hebdige, Dick. 1979. *Subculture: The Meaning of Style*. London: Routledge.

Hewitt, Lyndi. 2011. "Framing across Differences, Building Solidarities: Lessons from Women's Rights Activism in Transnational Spaces." *Interface: A Journal for and about Social Movements* 3: 65–99.

Horowitz, Irving Louis. 1962. "Consensus, Conflict and Cooperation: A Sociological Inventory." *Social Forces* 41: 177–188.

Hunt, Scott A., Robert D. Benford, and David A. Snow. 1994. "Identity Fields: Framing Processes and the Social Construction of Movement Identities." In *New Social Movements: From Ideology to Identity*, edited by Enrique Larana, Hank Johnston, and Joseph R. Gusfield, 185–208. Philadelphia, PA: Temple University Press.

Jasper, James M. 1997. *The Art of Moral Protest: Culture, Biography, and Creativity in Social Movements*. Chicago: University of Chicago Press.

Jenkins, Craig J. 1983. "Resource Mobilization Theory and the Study of Social Movements." *Annual Review of Sociology* 9: 527–553.

Johnston, Hank and Bert Klandermans. 1995. "Social Movements and Culture." In *Social Movements, Protest, and Contention*, vol. 4, edited by Bert Klandermans. Minneapolis: University of Minnesota Press.

King, Leslie. 2008. "Ideology, Strategy and Conflict in a Social Movement Organization: The Sierra Club Immigration Wars." *Mobilization* 13: 45–61.

Kitschelt, Herbert P. 1986. "Political Opportunity Structures and Political Protest: Anti-Nuclear Movements in Four Democracies." *British Journal of Political Science* 16: 57–85.

Klandermans, Bert. 1988. "The Formation and Mobilization of Consensus." *International Social Movement Research* 1: 173–196.

Klandermans, Bert. 1994. "Transient Identities? Membership Patterns in the Dutch Peace Movement." In *New Social Movements: From Ideology to Identity*, edited by Enrique Larana, Hank Johnston, and Joseph R. Gusfield, 168–184. Philadelphia, PA: Temple University Press.

Klatch, Rebecca E. 2004. "The Underside of Social Movements: The Effects of Destructive Affective Ties." *Qualitative Sociology* 27: 487–509.

Kretschmer, Kelsy. 2014. "Shifting Boundaries and Splintering Movements: Abortion Rights in the Feminist and New Right Movements." *Sociological Forum* 29: 893–915.

Larana, Enrique, Hank Johnston, and Joseph R. Gusfield. 1994. *New Social Movements: From Ideology to Identity*. Philadelphia, PA: Temple University Press.

Levitsky, Sandra R. 2007. "Niche Activism: Constructing a Unified Movement Identity in a Heterogeneous Organizational Field." *Mobilization* 12: 271–286.

Lichterman, Paul. 1995. "Piecing Together a Multicultural Community: Cultural Differences in Community Building among Grassroots Environments." *Social Problems* 42: 513–534.

Lorde, Audre. 1984. *Sister Outsider: Essays and Speeches*. Trumansburg, NY: Crossing Press.

Luna, Zakiya T. 2010. "Marching Toward Reproductive Justice: Coalitional (Re)-framing of the March for Women's Lives." *Sociological Inquiry* 80: 554–578.

Marx, Karl and Friedrich Engels. 1978. "Manifesto of the Communist Party." In *The Marx-Engels Reader*, edited by Robert C. Tucker, 469–500. New York: W.W. Norton and Company.

McAdam, Doug. 1982. *Political Process and the Development of Black Insurgency, 1930–1970*. Chicago: University of Chicago Press.

McCall, Leslie. 2005. "The Complexity of Intersectionality." *Signs: Journal of Women in Culture and Society* 30: 1771–1800.

McCammon, Holly J. 2003. "Out of the Parlors and Into the Streets." *Social Forces* 81: 787–818.

McCammon, Holly J. 2012. *The U.S. Women's Jury Movements and Strategic Adaptation: A More Just Verdict*. New York: Cambridge University Press.

McCammon, Holly J., Erin M. Bergner, and Sandra C. Arch. 2015. "'Are You One of Those Women?' Within-Movement Conflict, Radical Flank Effects, and Social Movement Political Outcomes." *Mobilization* 20: 157–178.

McCarthy, John D. and Mayer N. Zald. 1977. "Resource Mobilization and Social Movements: A Partial Theory." *American Journal of Sociology* 82: 1212–1241.

Melucci, Alberto. 1985. "The Symbolic Challenge of Contemporary Movements." *Social Research* 52: 789–816.

Melucci, Alberto.1995. "The Process of Collective Identity." In *Social Movements and Culture*, edited by Hank Johnston and Bert Klandermans, 41–63. Minneapolis: University of Minnesota Press.

Melucci, Alberto. 1996. *Challenging Codes*. Cambridge: Cambridge University Press.

Miller, Frederick D. 1983. "The End of SDS and the Emergence of Weatherman: Demise through Success." In *Social Movements of the Sixties and Seventies*, edited by Jo Freeman, 279–297. New York: Longman.

Moraga, Cherríe and Gloria Anzaldúa. 1981. *This Bridge Called My Back: Writings by Radical Women of Color*. New York: Kitchen Table: Women of Color Press.

Morris, Aldon. 1984. *The Origins of the Civil Rights Movement: Black Communities Organizing for Change*. New York: Free Press.

Morris, Aldon and Cedric Herring. 1987. "Theory and Research in Social Movements: A Critical Review." *Annual Review of Political Science* 2: 137–198.

Mushaben, Joyce Marie. 1989. "The Struggle Within: Conflict, Consensus, and Decision Making among National Coordinators and Grass-Roots Organizers in the West German Peace Movement." *International Social Movement Research* 2: 267–298.

Oberschall, Anthony. 1973. *Social Conflict and Social Movements*. Englewood Cliffs, NJ: Prentice Hall.

Oliver, Pamela E. 1993. "Formal Models of Collective Action." *Annual Review of Sociology* 19: 271–300.

Park, Robert E. and Ernest W. Burgess. 1921. *Introduction to the Science of Society*. Chicago: University of Chicago Press.

Parsons, Talcott. 1949. *The Structure of Social Action*. Glencoe, IL: The Free Press.

Pearlman, Wendy. 2011. *Violence, Nonviolence, and the Palestinian National Movement*. Cambridge: Cambridge University Press.

Penelope, Julia. 1992. *Call Me Lesbian: Lesbian Lives, Lesbian Theory*. Freedom, CA: Crossing Press.

Pettinicchio, David. 2013. "Strategic Action Fields and the Context of Political Entrepreneurship: How Disability Rights Became Part of the Policy Agenda." *Research in Social Movement Conflict and Change* 36: 79–106.

Piven, Frances Fox and Richard Cloward. 1977. *Poor People's Movements: Why They Succeed, How They Fail*. New York: Vintage.

Polletta, Francesca. 1997. "Culture and Its Discontents: Recent Theorizing on the Cultural Dimensions of Protest." *Sociological Inquiry* 67: 431–450.

Polletta, Francesca. 2002. *Freedom Is an Endless Meeting: Democracy in American Social Movements*. Chicago: University of Chicago Press.

Polletta, Francesca and James M. Jasper. 2001. "Collective Identity and Social Movements." *Annual Review of Sociology* 27: 283–305.

Rich, Adrienne. 1980. "Compulsory Heterosexuality and Lesbian Existence." *Signs: Journal of Women in Culture and Society* 5: 631–660.

Robnett, Belinda. 1997. *How Long? How Long? African-American Women in the Struggle for Civil Rights*. New York: Oxford University Press.

Rochford, E. Burke, Jr. 1989. "Factionalism, Group Defection, and Schism in the Hare Krishna Movement." *Journal for the Scientific Study of Religion* 28: 162–179.

Romanos, Eduardo. 2011. "Factionalism in Transition: A Comparison of Ruptures in the Spanish Anarchist Movement." *Journal of Historical Sociology* 24: 355–380.

Ross, Edward Alsworth. 1920. *The Principles of Society*. New York: The Century Company.

Rupp, Leila J. and Verta Taylor. 1987. *Survival in the Doldrums: The American Women's Rights Movement, 1945 to the 1960s*. New York: Oxford University Press.

Ryan, Barbara. 1989. "Ideological Purity and Feminism: The U.S. Women's Movement from 1966 to 1975." *Gender & Society* 3: 239–257.

Shriver, Thomas and Alison Adams. 2013. "Collective Identity and the Subjective Terrain of Political Opportunities: Movement Dissension Over Participation in Party Politics." *Mobilization* 18: 65–82.

Simmel, Georg. 1955. *Conflict and the Web of Group-Affiliations*. Translated by Kurt H. Wolff and Reinhard Bendix. New York: Free Press.

Snow, David A. and Robert D. Benford. 1988. "Ideology, Frame Resonance, and Participant Mobilzation." *International Social Movement Research* 1: 197–217.

Snow, David A. and Robert D. Benford. 1992. "Master Frames and Cycles of Protest." In *Frontiers in Social Movement Theory*, edited by Aldon D. Morris and Carol M. Mueller, 133–155. New Haven, CT: Yale University Press.

Stein, Marc. 2012. *Rethinking the Gay and Lesbian Movement*. New York: Routledge.

Stern, A. J., Sidney Tarrow, and M. F. Williams. 1971. "Factions and Opinion Groups in European Mass Parties. Some Evidence from a Study of Italian Socialist Activists." *Comparative Politics* 3: 529–559.

Stockdill, Brett C. 2003. *Activism Against AIDS: At the Intersections of Sexuality, Race, Gender, and Class*. Boulder, CO: Lynne Rienner.

Stryker, Sheldon, Timothy J. Owens, and Robert W. White. 2000. *Self, Identity, and Social Movements*. Minneapolis: University of Minnesota Press.

Swidler, Ann. 2001. *Talk of Love: How Culture Matters*. Chicago: University of Chicago Press.

Taylor, Verta. 1989. "Social Movement Continuity: The Women's Movement in Abeyance." *American Sociological Review* 54: 761–775.

Taylor, Verta and Leila J. Rupp. 1993. "Women's Culture and Lesbian Feminist Activism: A Reconsideration of Cultural Feminism." *Signs: Journal of Women in Culture and Society* 19: 33–61.

Taylor, Verta and Nancy E. Whittier. 1992. "Collective Identity in Social Movement Communities." In *Frontiers in Social Movement Theory*, edited by Aldon D. Morris and Carol McClurg, 104–129. New Haven, CT: Yale University Press.

Trumpy, Alexa J. 2014. "Woman vs. Fetus: Frame Transformation and Intramovement Dynamics in the Pro-life Movement." *Sociological Spectrum* 34: 163–184.

Waite, Lori G. 2001. "Divided Consciousness: The Impact of Black Elite Consciousness on the 1966 Chicago Freedom Movement." In *Oppositional Consciousness: The Subjective Roots of Social Protest*, edited by Jane Mansbridge and Aldon H. Morris, 170–203. Chicago: University of Chicago Press.

Walker, Edward T. and Lina M. Stepick. 2014. "Strength in Diversity? Group Heterogeneity in the Mobilization of Grassroots Organizations." *Sociology Compass* 8: 959–975.

Walsh, Edward and Sherry Cable. 1989. "Realities, Images, and Management Dilemmas in Social Movement Organizations: The Three Mile Island Experience." *International Social Movement Research* 2: 199–211.

Weber, Max. 1949. *The Methodology of the Social Sciences*. Translated by Edward A. Shils and Henry A. Finch. Glencoe, IL: Free Press.

Weber, Max. 1958. "The Three Types of Legitimate Rule." *Berkeley Publications in Society and Institutions* 4: 1–11.

Whittier, Nancy. 1997. "Political Generations, Micro-Cohorts, and the Transformation of Social Movements." *American Sociological Review* 62: 760–778.

Whittier, Nancy. 2014. "Rethinking Coalitions: Anti-Pornography Feminists, Conservatives, and Relationships between Collaborative Adversarial Movements." *Social Problems* 61: 175–193.

Wilde, Melissa J. 2004. "How Culture Mattered at Vatican II: Collegiality Trumps Authority in the Council's Social Movement Organizations." *American Sociological Review* 69: 576–602.

Wrenn, Corey Lee. 2012. "Applying Social Movement Theory to Nonhuman Rights Mobilization and the Importance of Faction Hierarchies." *Peace Studies Journal* 5: 27–44.

Wuthnow, Robert. 1987. *Meaning and Moral Order: Explorations in Cultural Analysis.* Berkeley: University of California Press.

Zald, Mayer N. and Roberta Ash. 1966. "Social Movement Organizations: Growth, Decline, and Change." *Social Forces* 44: 327–340.

Zald, Mayer N. and John D. McCarthy. 1980. "Social Movement Industries: Competition and Cooperation among Movement Organizations." *Research in Social Movements, Conflict, and Change* 3: 1–20.

13

Diffusion Processes Within and Across Movements

Sarah A. Soule and Conny Roggeband

Introduction

Over the past decade or so, scholarly and public attention alike has been drawn to the numerous examples of the apparent diffusion of social movement activity within, and across, national boundaries.[1] Dramatic waves of protest, such as the Arab Spring protests, the precarity demonstrations in Southern Europe, the 15-M Movement in Spain, the Black Lives Matter protests, and the protests and encampments associated with the Occupy Wall Street movement, have all been heralded as examples of diffusing social movements. While these movements developed in different national contexts, and engaged different publics, the connective tissue between the movements facilitated their spread (e.g. della Porta and Mattoni 2014; Romanos 2015, 2016). Activists operating in different contexts took inspiration and learned from the successes and failures of other movements. Their ideas and tactics traveled between national contexts, facilitated by the use of new social media like Twitter and Facebook, but also by classic media forms, such as television and print media. In some instances, direct personal contacts between protesters facilitated the exchange of information and ideas, as has been shown to be the case between the Spanish Indignados and the Occupy Wall Street protesters (Romanos 2015).

While these notable cases have captivated our collective attention, it is important to remember that the topic of diffusion of social movements and collective action has been of interest to social movement scholars for years. Early on, LeBon (1897), Tarde (1903), and Blumer (1939) described (and warned of the potential ill effects of) the contagion of collective aggression. A similar negative view of the spread of collective behavior was taken by scholars of race riots, lynching, Nazism, Fascism, Stalinism, and McCarthyism (see reviews in Garner 1997 and Morris 1981). More recent scholarship has worried less about the contagion of maladaptive impulses and

The Wiley Blackwell Companion to Social Movements, Second Edition. Edited by David A. Snow, Sarah A. Soule, Hanspeter Kriesi, and Holly J. McCammon.
© 2019 John Wiley & Sons Ltd. Published 2019 by John Wiley & Sons Ltd.

aggression among individuals, and instead examines the diffusion of innovative tactics, frames, and organizing structures between social movements, and articulates the mechanisms by which this happens (see reviews in Givan et al. 2010; Soule 2004, 2013; and Strang and Soule 1998).

Specifically, the recent literature on social movements and diffusion focuses on a number of related topics. First, researchers focus on what is diffused between movements, with some studies considering the flow of practices and tactics, while others examining frames and ideology. Second, scholars focus on the various mechanisms or channels of diffusion, such as direct contact between activists or information through media. Third, researchers examine the factors that seem to catalyze the diffusion process. Fourth, social movement scholars have related diffusion processes to protest cycles or waves, arguing that intra- and inter-movement diffusion and movement spillover are the central mechanisms that lead to cycles of protest and changes in the repertoire of contention. Finally, some researchers of the diffusion of social movements have been curious about the impact of diffusion on other social phenomena.

What Is Diffused?

A fundamental question of all diffusion research is the question of what, precisely, spreads between actors. At some basic level, scholars are interested in the spread of something *innovative*, however, there is not much consensus on how to define innovation in a social movement context (Wang and Soule 2016). Some scholars consider innovation to happen when a movement or movement organization adopts a tactic or a frame that it has not previously used (e.g. McCammon 2003; Wang and Soule 2016), while others insist on innovation being something that is truly novel, having never been seen in a social system previously (e.g. Tilly 2004), and still others consider the novel pairing of frames or tactics to be innovation (e.g. Morris 1984; Wang and Soule 2016).

Beyond broadly considering what constitutes innovation, it is also useful to parse innovation (however defined) into three categories: (1) behaviors; (2) ideas; and (3) organizational forms or structures. *Behavioral diffusion* includes the spread of tactics such as strikes (e.g. Biggs 2005; Conell and Cohn 1995; Jansen, Sluiter, and Akkerman 2016), riots (e.g. Myers 2000), or sit-ins (e.g. Andrews and Biggs 2006; Morris 1981). For example, Morris (1981) studies the diffusion of the sit-in protests in the late 1950s and early 1960s during the US civil rights movement, and Soule (1997) studies the diffusion of an innovative protest tactic, the shantytown, which was used to protest apartheid in South Africa in the United States in the 1980s. More recently, Edwards (2014) explores the diffusion of a tactical innovation within the British Suffrage movement; the "militancy" strategy of intentional arrest and imprisonment was devised, and then disseminated by, a new organization whose members acted as "innovation champions," bringing news and information about this new tactic to local areas.

Ideational diffusion, or the spread of new ideas and collective action frames, is also a central topic in the study of social movements. Collective action frames are key to mobilization in that they are developed and deployed to recruit new members, mobilize adherents, define opponents, and find resources. Because they are shaped by concrete social struggles in specific contexts, frames are continuously refined and changed to fit new contexts so as to ensure resonance among (potential) adherents. For example, Jenness and Broad (1994) demonstrate how the LGBT movement strategically selected and adapted the "sexual terrorism" frame from the women's movement in order to define violence against LGBT people as a social problem. And Stern (2005) studies the diffusion of the international women's rights frame to the female inheritance movement in Hong Kong, showing the spectrum of alteration and modification such that the frame would "fit" into this new context.

In addition to behavior and ideational diffusion, scholars point to the transfer of *organizational forms and structures*. Clemens's (1997) comparison of labor, agrarian, and women's associations of the late nineteenth century makes clear that the creative transposition of familiar, but apolitical, forms of association facilitated the diffusion of these new organizational forms across the country. O'Connor (1980) shows how the structure of NAACP's legal branch (NAACP Legal Defense Fund) spread to women (NOW's Legal Defense and Education Fund), and O'Connor and Epstein (1984) describe the spread of this organizational structure to the Mexican American Legal Defense and Educational Fund. And, finally, Meyer and Whittier (1994) discuss the diffusion of non-hierarchical organizational structures created by feminists to the nuclear freeze movement.

What Are the Mechanisms of Diffusion?

There are several pathways or channels along which behavioral and/or ideational diffusion may occur. Social movement scholars distinguish between *relational* (or *direct*), *non-relational* (or *indirect*), and *mediated* models of diffusion. Most attention is given to *relational* forms of diffusion in which actors have pre-existing relationships or social networks that facilitate exchange of ideas and/or behaviors (Lee and Strang 2006; Oliver and Myers 2000). A classic example of work in this area is Rude's (1964) examination of the diffusion of collective action through interpersonal communication between travelers along transportation routes in England and France between 1730 and 1848. Interpersonal networks or relational ties between individuals also facilitated the diffusion of mobilization of the Swedish Social Democratic Party and Swedish trade unions in the late 1800s (Hedström 1994; Hedström, Sandell, and Stern 2000), Marxist ideology and political rebellion in Chile (Petras and Zeitlin 1967), civil rights ideology and Freedom Summer mobilization (Morris 1984), and resistance to the Versailles army (Gould 1991). Finally, Meyer and Whittier (1994) show that social movement ideas and tactics "spilled over" the boundaries of one movement to influence other social movements via interpersonal connections.

While these studies focus on the spread of ideas via relationships, direct ties between actors also facilitate the diffusion of tactics. For example, Bohstedt and Williams (1988) analyze the spread of rioting in Devonshire in the late eighteenth century, arguing that food riots spread through dense networks formed through market transactions, and Morris (1981) studies the diffusion of the sit-in protests during the civil rights movement, arguing that network ties facilitated their spread, and others have argued that network ties facilitated the spread of urban riots in the latter part of the same movement (Feagin and Hahn 1973; Singer 1970; Wilson and Orum 1976). In more recent work, Wang and Soule (2012) use an organizational learning perspective and sophisticated network analytic techniques to model the diffusion of protest tactics between organizations participating at the same protest event. Additionally, Àlvarez de Andrés, Zapata, and Zapata Campos (2015) show how the Spanish Mortgage Victims movement in Spain created internal and external communication networks to facilitate the replication of its tactics, ideas and organizational form in other cities. Finally, Hadden (2014) argues that similar processes were at work during more recent climate change mobilization, and that the emergence of more transgressive and confrontational activism during the Copenhagen Climate Summit in 2009 was a result of inter-movement diffusion between the global justice movement and the climate change movement.

Relational diffusion of ideas and behaviors can also occur across national boundaries, as when transatlantic contacts between German and American students were forged through travel in the 1960s, and served to facilitate the spread of activism (McAdam and Rucht 1993). Rupp's (1997) analysis of early twentieth-century transnational women's peace organizations makes clear how women leaders from different continents developed close and family-like relations that were key to the construction of a shared international understanding of the relationship between war, peace, and gender. Finally, Chabot (2010) argues that strong interpersonal networks between intellectuals in India and the United States facilitated the spread of the Ghandian repertoire of action to the United States, while Romanos (2015) argues that the spread of information and tactics from the Egyptian Tahrir Square Protests to the Spanish 15-M Movement, and eventually to the Occupy Wall Street movement required direct connections between activists (ibid.: 116).

While direct or relational network ties are often studied, researchers also emphasize the importance of the identification of adopters with the organization they imitate and how this might create indirect network ties that facilitate *nonrelational* diffusion (e.g. Pitcher, Hamblin, and Miller 1978; Soule 1997; Strang and Meyer 1993). For instance, research has demonstrated the importance of news media (e.g. newspaper, radio, and television) to the diffusion of protest tactics since the 1960s (Andrews and Biggs 2006; Braun 2011; Koopmans and Olzak 2004; Myers 2000). In a well-known series of studies on race riots, Spilerman (1970, 1971, 1976) hypothesized that riots diffused throughout urban areas in the United States because they were televised, which created "black solidarity that transcended boundaries of communities" and familiarized individuals all over the country with the "details of rioting and with the motivations of rioters" (1976: 790). Relatedly, Singer's (1970) work on the Detroit riot of 1967 points to the media (as well as interpersonal or direct communication) as a leading source of information on the riot in their city (see also Myers 2000).

More recently, the increased importance of new social media plays a central role in the spread of protest (Earl 2013), as the Internet has increased both the intensity and speed of diffusion processes (Earl and Kimport 2010). A case in point are the 2011 protests in Tunisia and Egypt, which featured prominent use of social media, both by activists organizing the demonstrations, and by those disseminating or discussing the events locally and globally. Twitter emerged as a key instrument, especially in Tunisia, where (at that time) few mainstream media organizations had a formal presence or staff (Lotan et al. 2011). In contrast, Rane and Salem (2012) point out that in Egypt, mainstream media were still an important additional source of information about the uprisings in the Middle Eastern and North African region. Among Egyptians, 81% relied on Egyptian state television as their main source of information about the uprising, while another 63% relied on Al Jazeera. Only 8% relied on social media (Rane and Salem 2012: 101). Important here is Oliver and Myers's (2000) observation that *communication* should not be confused with *influence*. While both types of media may convey information, media communication overall is less likely to change opinions than is more direct person-to-person influence, and influence likely requires some degree of deeper interpersonal connection.

A third and final pathway for diffusion is *mediated*, wherein actors with no preexisting ties are connected through third parties who maintain relations with both the initiator and the adopter (Tarrow 2010). McAdam, Tarrow, and Tilly (2001) mention the central role of "brokers" in connecting two or more previously disparate sites. This is illustrated in the work of Herring (2010) who points to the role of epistemic brokers in organizing and spreading opposition to biotechnology. Romanos (2016) argues that Spanish residents in New York City acted as brokers between the Spanish Indignados associated with the 15-M Movement, and the Occupy Wall Street protesters. As brokers, they served as conduits of information about organizational inclusiveness, which spread from Spain to the United States. Finally, Vasi (2011) delineates different types of brokers in the spread of innovation in his study of peace and civil liberties movements.

Catalysts to the Diffusion Process

Beyond identifying an innovative behavior, idea or organizational form that diffuses from one group to another, and the mechanisms or pathways by which it may diffuse, research on the diffusion of social movements has also tried to identify the factors that catalyze the diffusion of innovation. Some of these focus on the innovation itself, while others focus on the character of the relationship between the adopter and the transmitter, and others focus on the more or less facilitative environments in which an adopter is embedded.

First, some research focuses on the particular attributes of an innovation that make it more likely to be taken up by others. The perception of such new tactics as catchy, useful, or effective facilitates the adoption of similar tactics in different contexts (Soule 1999). Clemens suggests that models are more likely to be adopted "to the extent that the proposed model of organization is believed to work, involves practices and organizational relations that are already familiar, and is consonant with the organization of the rest of those individuals' social worlds" (1996: 211). For example, the innovative shelter model for battered women developed in London was perceived by Dutch activists as a "powerful concept" and they almost immediately adopted after their visit to the shelter. In contrast, Spanish feminists thought the original model did not fit the Spanish context, and started searching for adaptations of the model elsewhere in Europe in order to find a model that was more compatible with their own context and resources (Roggeband 2004). Flexibility and "trialability" of innovations are additional important attributes that make diffusion easier (Chabot 2000; McCurdy, Feigenbaum, and Frenzel 2016; Rogers 1983; Soule 2004).

Second, social movement scholars also examine the organizational conditions for diffusion. Staggenborg (1989) finds that nonhierarchical and decentralized movement organizations are more likely to adopt new tactics, compared to organizations with more rigid, bureaucratic organizations. McCammon (2003) shows that movements that are organizationally diverse, and that are constituted by less formally structured movement organizations, are more likely to adopt innovative tactics. Also, movements need to have the necessary resources to adopt an innovation (Beissinger 2007; McCammon 2003).

Third, there is an assumption in much research on the diffusion of social movements that higher levels of homogeneity between the transmitter and adopter facilitate the diffusion of tactics and ideas. For example, cultural and structural similarity between transmitters and adopters has been shown to be a precondition of diffusion (Soule 1997; Strang and Meyer 1993). Similarly, Edwards's (2014) study of the diffusion of the risky and controversial tactic of militancy shows that this particular tactical innovation required "symbolic legitimization" that had to be established through discussion and consensus, which was easier to achieve in more homogeneous networks. This idea is also emphasized by Vasi (2011), who argues that ideological compatibility of transmitters and adopters is an important precondition for diffusion.

When adopters and transmitters are less homogeneous, diffusion may be more difficult, as Chabot (2000) argues in the case of the diffusion of the Ghandian repertoire to the United States. Despite the fact that African Americans felt inspired by the anticolonial movement in India, there was an intensive debate about the extent to which the Ghandian repertoire could be used within the US context because of the lack of homogeneity between the adopters and the transmitters (Chabot 2000). Similarly, many European feminists felt unsure about whether sexual harassment should be seen as a specific cultural problem that prevailed in the USA or whether it also was also a common problem in the European context (Roggeband 2010).

Fourth, it is clear that agency in the diffusion process is an important catalyst in the spread of social movement ideas and tactics (Snow and Benford 1999). Tactics and frames are not simply transplanted from one site to another, but are often adapted and modified as they diffuse across movements and borders. In some instances, the transmitter of an innovation actively tailors the innovation to the needs of a potential adopter, while in other instances, the adopter is agentic, and strategically selects an innovation from a transmitter, and alters it so that it fits into a new context (ibid.). Diffusion thus does not imply that the objects of diffusion are clear-cut and fixed packages that are transplanted in whole cloth from one site to another, but rather that creative borrowing, adaptation, and learning are central to diffusion processes (Givan et al. 2010). Adopters do not always passively receive innovations; rather, they play an active role in interpreting, selecting, and adapting elements from elsewhere. Therefore, it has become commonplace to refer to the process of diffusion as adaptation (Snow and Benford 1999), bricolage (Clemens 1996), or reinvention (Chabot 2000).

These ideas have been taken up by several authors who examine the role of adopter movements in adapting ideas and models developed by other movements (Chabot 2000, 2010; Roggeband 2007, 2010; Scalmer 2002). Scalmer (2002: 269), for instance, conceptualizes diffusion as the "sustained labor of cultural, intellectual, and practical translation" and thus emphasizes the work done by adopters to overcome existing boundaries and differences between contexts of invention and adoption. Chabot (2000) shows that American civil rights activists who tried to transplant the Ghandian repertoire from India to the United States started processes of collective experimentation and learning to relocate the repertoire. By paying more attention to the agentic and processual character of diffusion processes, social movement scholarship has moved beyond the initial mechanistic accounts of diffusion (Givan et al. 2010; Schneiberg and Soule 2005).

Fifth, some argue that the broader political and/or economic contexts are important to diffusion. For example, della Porta and Mattoni (2014) show how in the 2011 transnational protest wave that included the Occupy Movement and the 15-M/ Indignados protests, the tactic of building protest camps (despite its global success) notoriously failed to diffuse to some locales. They argue that the tactic did not spread to countries where the economic crisis was less severe. For instance, the tactic of "*acampados*" that originated in the Spanish Indignados movement spread to places like Brussels, London, Amsterdam, and Berlin, but had a limited capacity to mobilize in these cities. In a similar vein, Bunce and Wolchik (2011) show how the ideas of the Orange Revolution[2] traveled to other countries, but had limited capacity to produce successful mobilization. della Porta and Mattoni (2014) contend that structural differences (e.g. differences in resources or contextual factors) provide an important explanation as to why innovations often do not successfully travel, despite their innovative or effective qualities. Wood (2015) argues that for diffusion to be successful, the political context is crucial. She claims that the identity and strategy of the Porto Alegre Youth Camp with its emphasis on direct democracy and consensus did not diffuse successfully to the new site in Caracas, Venezuela, because of the centralization and polarization of the political field in Caracas.

Cycles of Protest and Repertoires of Contention

Diffusion is a key mechanism explaining both the rise of *protest cycles* (Tarrow 2011) and changes to the *repertoire of contention* (Soule 1997; Tilly 1978). A cycle of protest is a period of increased conflict that extends across many sectors of a social system. During such periods, new forms of action and frames are produced, which diffuse to other sectors and organizations that test and refine these innovations in new contexts. The most successful and transferable innovations are modularized, which means that they can be used in many different places under very different socio-political circumstances (e.g. Tarrow 2011) and become part of a new repertoire of contention (Tilly 1978). The repertoire of contention is the complete set of protest tactics available to a social movement at any given time (ibid.). Social movement actors frequently employ a flexible repertoire of contention that allows for the observation of other groups' tactics and for the adoption of tactics believed to be effective. Imitation of protest tactics leads to their diffusion and to "waves" of certain forms of protest (ibid.).

An empirical illustration of the role of diffusion for the emergence of a protest wave is Beissinger's (2007) study of the interrelated wave of "color revolutions" that spread from Serbia to Georgia to Ukraine to Kyrgyzstan. Key to this wave was the modular form of nonviolent electoral challenge developed by the dissident student group Otpor (Resistance), which played a central role in the protests to overthrow Serbian leader Milošević in 2000. Otpor activists traveled to neighboring countries to spread this model, and train local groups in how to organize a democratic revolution.

McAdam (1995) further develops the link between diffusion and the wave-like structure of popular contention. He points to the central role of initiator movements that set in motion a protest wave and are followed by "spin-off" movements that "draw their impetus and inspiration from the original initiator movement" (ibid.: 219). Diffusion plays an important role in the rise of spin-off movements, as spin-offs follow the lead of initiators. Closely akin to this observation is Snow and Benford's (1992) discussion of the way in which innovative "master frames" are developed early on in the cycle of protest and diffuse to later movements within the cycle.

What Is the Impact of Diffusion?

A nascent area of research examines the impact of diffusion on some other social process. For example, scholars have studied the impact of diffusion on the founding and growth of new movement organizations. In this research, there are different effects of diffusion, depending on the context. While Biggs and Andrews (2010) show that the diffusion of the sit-in tactic had no effect on the founding rate of movement organizations, Moravec (2012) finds that the diffusion of tactics used by a women's artist group did result in the rapid growth of new movement organizations.

Other studies have pointed to the wider social, institutional and political effects of diffusion. For example, Rasler (1996) demonstrates a strong positive effect of spatial diffusion of protest on government concessions in Iran. Or, others argue that the diffusion of an innovative tactic among student groups eventually caused the electoral defeats of authoritarian leaders in the post-Communist region between 1996 to 2005 (Beissinger 2007; Bunce and Wolchik 2006, 2011). Finally, Bakke (2014) shows that transnational movements may boost a national movement by providing ideas, tactics, and resources, yet they can also jeopardize a domestic movement's strength because domestic populations may resist radical transnational frames and tactics.

Some have argued that diffusion often leads to shifts in scope and/or scale of protest. Vertical diffusion from local social movements to transnational movements is labeled "scale shift" (McAdam, Tarrow, and Tilly 2001; Soule 2013). Scale shift implies "a change in the number and level of coordinated contentious actions to a different focal point, involving a new range of actors, different objects, and broadened claims" (McAdam, Tarrow, and Tilly 2001: 331). When French and Dutch feminist activists found that the issue of sexual harassment was not given priority at the national level, they decided to coordinate collective action at a higher level and started to target the European Commission (Roggeband 2010). Such processes may move both upward, from local protest to the transnational level and downward, from transnational movements to local organizations. Tarrow identifies a number of mechanisms that steer such processes. Scaling up requires *coordination* to create "instances of cross-spatial collaboration" (2005: 122), which is helped by brokerage and theorization. For scaling down, certification, which validates actors, their performances, and their claims to authorities, is a crucial precondition (ibid.: 194). Scale shift often results in the creation of transnational advocacy networks or other forms of coordinated action. For example, in Europe, transnational advocacy networks strategically reframed the issue of sexual harassment, which diffused from the US context, to make it fit the European context (Roggeband 2010). By framing harassment as the violation of dignity, activists managed to theorize the issue and create a new European understanding of sexual harassment. The certification of this frame by the EU created the necessary legitimation to further diffuse the issue.

Critical to understanding the effect of diffusion of a particular ideology or behavior on other social processes is disentangling the effect of the idea or behavior itself, from the effect of the fact that it has diffused. While there is a growing literature on the impact of social movement tactics and frames on various outcomes, it is important to specify what, if any, additional impact arises from the fact that the idea or behavior has diffused.

Outlook and Future Directions

The recent international wave of protest and the apparent diffusion of tactics and ideas from movement to movement and across national boundaries have stimulated a new wave of research on diffusion of social movements. The spread of social movements in recent years has been facilitated by new, fairly readily available, and inexpensive modes of communication, and research has been facilitated by the footprint (e.g. tweets, Facebook posts, Instagram photos) that these new modes of communication leave (e.g. Lotan et al. 2011). This recent work has been a welcome addition to the extant body of research, and has enhanced what we know about innovation in social movements, as well as how innovations diffuse. Nonetheless, it makes sense to conclude this chapter with some suggestions for future research.

First, much of the empirical work on diffusion has not adequately conceptualized which actors are truly at risk for adopting an innovation. While all people and organizations may *technically* be at risk of adopting a new protest tactic or frame, in actuality, many of these would not really be at risk because they may not have the resources to deploy the new tactic or because their own particular identity may preclude adopting a given frame or because their political context may prevent adoption. This point has been made in research on policy diffusion, and in particular on the diffusion of divestment policy (e.g. Soule 2009; Soule, Swaminathan, and Tihanyi 2014), however, it has yet to be incorporated into empirical research on the diffusion of protest tactics and frames.

Second, scholarship on diffusion should move away from the imagery of mechanical transfer of some innovation across different social actors and consider the way in which diffusion is a creative, agentic, and strategic process (Chabot 2000; Snow and Benford 1999). The diffusion process frequently is uneven and contested, and people and groups experiment with innovations, which are then adopted in a piecemeal and variegated fashion (Givan et al. 2010; Schneiberg and Soule 2005).

Similarly, scholars should recognize, and model, the multidirectional nature of the diffusion process, whereby information and influence come from multiple sources (Wang and Soule 2012). This is even more important, given the growth of transnational advocacy networks, which are mutual and fluid, and involve the flow of ideas and information in different directions (Matsuzawa 2011). Ideas and models often come from multiple sources, different actors are involved in transmitting ideas, and the adaptation of ideas and models by receivers often results in the creation of new objects that are subsequently diffused within the network (Van Eerdewijk and Roggeband 2014).

Fourth, most of the research focuses on the behavior of adopters and how practices spread rather than on innovators and exporters of ideas and standards. Little is known, for example, about if and how activists actively promote and format ideas and practices to facilitate their travel to new contexts. Edwards's (2014) study of "innovator champions" in the British Suffrage movement suggests that movements can actively promote their ideas, as does the work of Àlvarez de Andrés et al. (2015), who argue that the founders of Spanish Mortgage Victims Group created the organization with the explicit strategy of reproducing itself throughout Spain via forging tactics and organizational forms that were generic and transferable: "practices, procedures, forms, and documents were standardized and uploaded as files that can be downloaded freely from PAH websites" and the design of the webpage was "easy to understand, decode, and translate into new local contexts" (ibid.: 257). Nonetheless, more research is needed to further analyze the strategies of actors who try to pass on innovative ideas and practices to potential adopters.

Fifth, research should begin to compare and contrast innovations that diffuse with those that fail to diffuse (for an example, see Wang and Soule 2012). To date, work on diffusion in social movements has focused mostly on charting the process of diffusion of tactics or frames, with some recent attention to defining innovation (Wang and Soule 2016) and establishing why a given tactic diffuses to some, but not other, contexts (della Porta and Mattoni 2014). However, we need to better theorize which innovations will be chosen, by whom, and under what conditions.

Conclusion

Social movement scholars have recognized the central importance of diffusion processes for the expansion of contestation and the emergence of waves of contention. In this chapter we discussed the insights yielded by studies that look closer into inter- and intra-movement diffusion. We categorized the empirical work based on factors that are diffused and the different diffusion channels that help spread tactical and ideational innovations. We discussed how social movement scholars have theorized the relation between cycles of protest and diffusion. Next, we have looked into the few studies that try to understand the impact of diffusion on the spread and development of protest and movements. An important insight of this growing body of research is that diffusion processes are interactive processes that involve a range of different actors, networks and mechanisms. Social movement scholars have drawn considerable attention to the role of agency in translating, transforming, and adapting innovations invented by others. This makes clear how diffusion is a process conditioned by political agency (Givan et al. 2010). While we have come quite a distance since some of the original work in this area that conceived of diffusion as a pathological and disturbing phenomenon, there are still questions that might be addressed by those interested in diffusion of social movements. The complexity and multidimensionality of diffusion processes require more research to arrive at a more comprehensive understanding of how and why diffusion occurs and with what effects for the further development of movements and protests cycles.

In particular, this review has suggested that scholars need to examine more carefully the content of the innovation being diffused and whether or not the mechanisms and processes of diffusion are the same in cases of ideational and behavioral diffusion. Also, still little is known about why some ideas or practices travel successfully, while others fail and which audiences are more at risk of diffusion. It would be useful to look more into failed cases of diffusion (where attempts to introduce an innovation were made either by innovators, brokers or activists interested in adopting), or unsuccessful innovations that diffuse nonetheless. Also, we need a better understanding of the role of different agents involved in diffusion processes and how their role, position, status, and strategies affect the processes and outcomes.

Notes

1 Social movement scholars have used the concept of diffusion to refer to the spread of some innovation through either direct or indirect channels of communication (Givan, Roberts, and Soule, 2010).
2 The Orange Revolution was a series of protests and political events that took place in Ukraine from late November 2004 to January 2005.

References

Àlvarez de Andrés, Eva, Patrik Zapata, and María José Zapata Campos. 2015. "Stop the Evictions! The Diffusion of Networked Social Movements and the Emergence of a Hybrid Space: The Case of the Spanish Mortgage Victims Group." *Habitat International* 46: 252–259.

Andrews, Kenneth T. and Michael Biggs. 2006. "The Dynamics of Protest Diffusion: Movement Organizations, Social Networks, and News Media in the 1960 Sit-Ins." *American Sociological Review* 71(5): 752–777.

Bakke, Kristin M. 2014. "Help Wanted? The Mixed Record of Foreign Fighters in Domestic Insurgencies." *International Security* 38(4): 150–187.

Beissinger, Mark R. 2007. "Structure and Example in Modular Political Phenomena: The Diffusion of Bulldozer/Rose/Orange/Tulip Revolutions." *Perspectives on Politics* 5(2): 259–276.

Biggs, Michael. 2005. "Strikes as Forest Fires: Chicago and Paris in the Late Nineteenth Century." *American Journal of Sociology* 110(6): 1684–1714.

Biggs, Michael and Kenneth T. Andrews. 2010. "From Protest to Organization: The Impact of the 1960 Sit-ins on Movement Organizations in the American South." In *The Diffusion of Social Movements: Actors, Frames, and Political Effects*, edited by Rebecca Kolins Givan, Kenneth M. Roberts, and Sarah A. Soule, 187–203. Cambridge: Cambridge University Press.

Blumer, Herbert. 1939. "Collective Behavior." In *Principles of Sociology*, edited by Robert E. Park, 219–288. New York: Barnes & Noble.

Bohstedt, John and Dale Williams. 1988. "The Diffusion of Riots: The Patterns of 1766, 1795, and 1801 in Devonshire." *Journal of Interdisciplinary History* 19: 1–24.

Braun, Robert. 2011. "The Diffusion of Racist Violence in the Netherlands: Discourse and Distance." *Journal of Peace Research* 48(6): 753–766.

Bunce, Valerie J. and Sharon L. Wolchik. 2006. "International Diffusion and Postcommunist Electoral Revolutions." *Communist and Post–Communist Studies* 39(3): 283–304.

Bunce, Valerie J. and Sharon L. Wolchik. 2011. "International Diffusion and Democratic Change." In *The Dynamics of Democratization: Dictatorship, Development and Diffusion*, edited by Nathan J. Brown, 283–310. Baltimore, MD: Johns Hopkins University Press.

Chabot, Sean. 2000. "Transnational Diffusion and the African American Reinvention of Gandhian Repertoire." *Mobilization: An International Quarterly* 5(2): 201–216.

Chabot, Sean. 2010. "Dialogue Matters: Beyond the Transmission Model of Transnational Diffusion between Social Movements." In *The Diffusion of Social Movements: Actors, Mechanisms, and Political Effects*, edited by Rebecca Kolins Givan, Kenneth M. Roberts, and Sarah A. Soule, 99–124. New York: Cambridge University Press.

Clemens, Elisabeth S. 1996. "Organizational Form as Frame: Collective Identity and Political Strategy in the American Labor Movement, 1880–1920." In *Comparative Perspectives on Social Movements: Political Opportunities, Mobilizing Structures, and Cultural Framings*, edited by Doug McAdam, John D. McCarthy, and Mayer N. Zald, 205–226. New York: Cambridge University Press.

Clemens, Elisabeth S. 1997. *The People's Lobby: Organizational Innovation and the Rise of Interest Group Politics in the United States, 1890–1925*. Chicago: University of Chicago Press.

Conell, Carol and Samuel Cohn. 1995. "Learning from Other People's Actions: Environmental Variation and Diffusion in French Coal Mining Strikes, 1890–1935." *American Journal of Sociology* 101: 366–403.

della Porta, Donatella and Alice Mattoni. 2014. *Spreading Protest: Social Movements in Times of Crisis*. Colchester: ECPR Press.

Earl, Jennifer. 2013. "Spreading the Word or Shaping the Conversation: 'Prosumption' in Protest Websites." *Research in Social Movements, Conflicts, and Change* 36: 3–38.

Earl, Jennifer and Katrina Kimport. 2010. "The Diffusion of Different Types of Internet Activism: Suggestive Patterns in Website Adoption of Innovations." In *The Diffusion of Social Movements: Actors, Mechanisms, and Political Effects*, edited by Rebecca Kolins Givan, Kenneth M. Roberts, and Sarah A. Soule, 125–139. Cambridge: Cambridge University Press.

Edwards, Gemma. 2014. "Infectious Innovations? The Diffusion of Tactical Innovation in Social Movement Networks, the Case of Suffragette Militancy." *Social Movement Studies* 13(1): 48–69.

Feagin, Joe R. and Harlan Hahn. 1973. *Ghetto Revolts: The Politics of Violence in American Cities*. New York: Macmillan.

Garner, Roberta. 1997. "Fifty Years of Social Movement Theory." In *Social Movement Theory and Research*, edited by Roberta Garner and John Tenuto, 1–60. Lanham, MD: Scarecrow Press.

Givan, Rebecca Kolins, Kenneth M. Roberts, and Sarah A. Soule. 2010. "Introduction: The Dimensions of Diffusion." In *The Diffusion of Social Movements: Actors, Mechanisms, and Political Effects*, edited by Rebecca Kolins Givan, Kenneth M. Roberts, and Sarah A. Soule, 1–18. Cambridge: Cambridge University Press.

Gould, Roger. 1991. "Multiple Networks and Mobilization in the Paris Commune, 1871." *American Sociological Review* 56: 716–729.

Hadden, Jennifer. 2014. "Explaining Variation in Transnational Climate Change Activism." *Global Environmental Politics* 14(2): 7–25.

Hedström, Peter. 1994. "Contagious Collectivities: On the Spatial Diffusion of Swedish Trade Unions, 1890–1940." *American Journal of Sociology* 99: 1157–1179.

Hedström, Peter, Rickard Sandell, and Charlotta Stern. 2000. "Mesolevel Networks and the Diffusion of Social Movements: The Case of the Swedish Social Democratic Party." *American Journal of Sociology* 106(1): 145–172.

Herring, Ronald J. 2010. "Framing the GMO: Epistemic Brokers, Authoritative Knowledge and Diffusion of Opposition to Biotechnology." In *The Diffusion of Social Movements: Actors, Mechanisms, and Political Effects*, edited by Rebecca Kolins Givan, Kenneth M. Roberts, and Sarah A. Soule, 78–96. Cambridge: Cambridge University Press.

Jansen, Giedo, Roderick Sluiter, and Agnes Akkerman. 2016. "The Diffusion of Strikes: A Dyadic Analysis of Economic Sectors in the Netherlands, 1995–2007." *American Journal of Sociology* 121(6): 1885–1918.

Jenness, Valerie and Kendall Broad. 1994. "Antiviolence Activism and the (In)visibility of Gender in the Gay/Lesbian and Women's Movements." *Gender & Society* 8(3): 402–423.

Koopmans, Ruud and Olzak, Susan. 2004. "Discursive Opportunities and the Evolution of Right-Wing Violence in Germany." *American Journal of Sociology* 110(1): 198–230.

Lotan, Gilad, Erhardt Graeff, Mike Ananny, Devin Gaffney, Ian Pearce, and danah boyd. 2011. "The Arab Spring Revolutions Were Tweeted: Information Flows During the 2011 Tunisian and Egyptian Revolutions." *International Journal of Communication* 5(31): 1375–1404.

LeBon, Gustave. 1897. *The Crowd*. London: Unwin.

Lee, Chang Kil and David Strang. 2006. "The International Diffusion of Public-Sector Downsizing: Network Emulation and Theory-Driven Learning." *International Organization* 60(4): 883–909.

Matsuzawa, Setsuko. 2011. "Horizontal Dynamics in Transnational Activism: The Case of Nu River Anti-Dam Activism in China." *Mobilization: An International Quarterly* 16(3): 369–387.

McAdam, Doug. 1995. "'Initiator' and 'Spin-off' Movements: Diffusion Processes in Protest Cycles." In *Repertoires and Cycles of Collective Action*, edited by Mark Traugott, 217–239. Durham, NC: Duke University Press.

McAdam, Doug and Dieter Rucht. 1993. "The Cross National Diffusion of Movement Ideas." *Annals of the American Academy of Political and Social Science* 528: 36–59.

McAdam, Doug, Sidney Tarrow, and Charles Tilly. 2001. *Dynamics of Contention*. Cambridge: Cambridge University Press.

McCammon, Holly J. 2003. "'Out of the Parlors and into the Streets': The Changing Tactical Repertoire of the US Women's Suffrage Movements." *Social Forces* 81(3): 787–818.

McCurdy, Patrick, Anna Feigenbaum, and Fabian Frenzel. 2016. "Protest Camps and Repertoires of Contention." *Social Movement Studies* 15(1): 97–104.

Meyer, David S. and Nancy Whittier. 1994. "Social Movement Spillover." *Social Problems* 41: 277–298.

Moravec, Michelle. 2012. "Toward a History of Feminism, Art, and Social Movements in the United States." *Frontiers: A Journal of Women Studies* 33(2): 22–54.

Morris, Aldon. 1981. "Black Southern Sit-in Movement: An Analysis of Internal Organization." *American Sociological Review* 46: 744–767.

Morris, Aldon. 1984. *The Origins of the Civil Rights Movement: Black Communities Organizing for Change.* New York: Free Press.

Myers, Daniel J. 2000. "The Diffusion of Collective Violence: Infectiousness, Susceptibility, and Mass Media Networks." *American Journal of Sociology* 106(1): 173–208.

O'Connor, Karen. 1980. *Women's Organizations' Use of the Courts.* Lexington, MA: Lexington Books.

O'Connor, Karen and Lee Epstein. 1984. "A Legal Voice for the Chicano Community: The Activities of the Mexican American Legal Defense and Educational Fund, 1968–1982." *Social Science Quarterly* 65(2): 245–256.

Oliver, Pamela E. and Daniel J. Myers. 2000. "Networks, Diffusion, and Cycles of Collective Action." Paper presented at the Workshop for Social Movement Analysis: The Network Perspective, Scotland, June.

Petras, James and Maurice Zeitlin. 1967. "Miners and Agrarian Radicalism." *American Sociological Review* 32: 578–586.

Pitcher, Brian, Robert Hamblin, and Jerry Miller. 1978. "The Diffusion of Collective Violence." *American Sociological Review* 43(1): 23–35.

Rane, Halim and Sumra Salem. 2012. "Social Media, Social Movements and the Diffusion of Ideas in the Arab Uprisings." *Journal of International Communication* 18(1): 97–111.

Rasler, Karen. 1996. "Concessions, Repression, and Political Protest in the Iranian Revolution." *American Sociological Review* 61(1): 132–152.

Rogers, Everett M. 1983. *Diffusion of Innovations.* New York: John Wiley.

Roggeband, Conny. 2004. "'Immediately I Thought We Should Do the Same Thing.' International Inspiration and Exchange in Feminist Action against Sexual Violence." *European Journal of Women's Studies* 11(2): 159–175.

Roggeband, Conny. 2007. "Translators and Transformers: International Inspiration and Exchange in Social Movements." *Social Movement Studies* 6(3): 245–259.

Roggeband, Conny. 2010. "Transnational Networks and Institutions: How Diffusion Shaped the Politicization of Sexual Harassment in Europe." In *The Diffusion of Social Movements: Actors, Mechanisms, and Political Effects,* edited by Rebecca Kolins Givan, Kenneth M. Roberts, and Sarah A. Soule, 19–33. Cambridge: Cambridge University Press.

Romanos, Eduardo. 2015. "Immigrants as Brokers: Dialogical Diffusion from Spanish Indignados to Occupy Wall Street." *Social Movement Studies* 15(3): 247–262.

Romanos, Eduardo. 2016. "From Tahrir to Puerta del Sol to Wall Street: The Transnational Diffusion of Social Movements in Comparative Perspective." *Revista Española de Investigaciones Sociológicas* 154: 103–118.

Rude, George. 1964. *The Crowd in History, 1730–1848.* New York: John Wiley & Sons, Inc.

Rupp, Leila J. 1997. *Worlds of Women: The Making of an International Women's Movement.* Princeton, NJ: Princeton University Press.

Scalmer, Sean. 2002. "The Labor of Diffusion: The Peace Pledge Union and the Adaptation of the Gandhian Repertoire." *Mobilization: An International Quarterly* 7(3): 269–286.

Schneiberg, Marc and Sarah A. Soule. 2005. "Institutionalization as a Contested, Multi-level Process: Politics, Social Movements and Rate Regulation in American Fire Insurance." In *Social Movements and Organizations,* edited by Gerald Davis, Doug McAdam, W. Richard Scott and Mayer N. Zald, 122–160. Cambridge: Cambridge University Press.

Singer, Benjamin D. 1970. "Mass Media and Communication Processes in the Detroit Riot of 1967." *Public Opinion Quarterly* 34(2): 236–245.

Snow, David A. and Robert D. Benford. 1992. "Master Frames and Cycles of Protest." In *Frontiers in Social Movement Theory*, edited by Aldon D. Morris and Carol McClurg Mueller, 133–155. New Haven, CT: Yale University Press.

Snow, David A. and Robert D. Benford. 1999. "Alternative Types of Cross-National Diffusion in the Social Movement Arena." In *Social Movements in a Globalizing World*, edited by Donatella della Porta, Hanspeter Kreisi, and Dieter Rucht, 23–39. London: Macmillan.

Soule, Sarah A. 1997. "The Student Divestment Movement in the United States and Tactical Diffusion: The Shantytown Protest." *Social Forces* 75: 855–883.

Soule, Sarah A. 1999. "The Diffusion of an Unsuccessful Innovation." *Annals of the American Academy of Political and Social Sciences* 566: 120–131.

Soule, Sarah A. 2004. "Diffusion Processes Within and Across Movements." In *The Blackwell Companion to Social Movements*, edited by David A. Snow, Sarah A. Soule, and Hanspeter Kreisi, 294–310. Oxford: Blackwell.

Soule, Sarah A. 2009. *Contention and Corporate Social Responsibility*. Cambridge: Cambridge University Press.

Soule, Sarah A. 2013. "Diffusion and Scale Shift." In *The Wiley-Blackwell Encyclopedia of Social and Political Movements*, edited by David A. Snow, Donatella della Porta, Bert Klandermans, and Doug McAdam. Oxford: Wiley-Blackwell.

Soule, Sarah A., Anand Swaminathan, and Laszlo Tihanyi. 2014. "The Diffusion of Foreign Divestment from Burma." *Strategic Management Journal* 35(7): 1032–1052.

Spilerman, Seymour. 1970. "The Causes of Racial Disturbances: A Comparison of Alternate Explanations." *American Sociological Review* 35: 627–649.

Spilerman, Seymour. 1971. "The Causes of Racial Disturbances: A Test of Alternate Explanations." *American Sociological Review* 36: 427–442.

Spilerman, Seymour. 1976. "Structural Characteristics of Cities and the Severity of Racial Disorders." *American Sociological Review* 41: 771–793.

Staggenborg, Suzanne. 1989. "Stability and Innovation in the Women's Movement: A Comparison of Two Movement Organizations." *Social Problems* 36(1): 75–92.

Stern, Rachel. 2005. "Unpacking Adaptation: The Female Inheritance Movement in Hong Kong." *Mobilization: An International Quarterly* 10(3): 421–439.

Strang, David and John W. Meyer.1993. "Institutional Conditions for Diffusion." *Theory and Society* 22: 487–511.

Strang, David and Sarah A. Soule.1998. "Diffusion in Organizations and Social Movements: From Hybrid Corn to Poison Pills." *Annual Review of Sociology* 24: 265–290.

Tarde, Gabriel. 1903. *The Laws of Imitation*. New York: Holt.

Tarrow, Sidney. 2005. *The New Transnational Activism*. Cambridge: Cambridge University Press.

Tarrow, Sidney. 2010. "Dynamics of Diffusion: Mechanisms, Institutions, and Scale Shift." In *The Diffusion of Social Movements: Actors, Mechanisms, and Political Effects*, edited by Rebecca Kolins Givan, Kenneth M. Roberts, and Sarah A. Soule, 204–219 Cambridge: Cambridge University Press.

Tarrow, Sidney. 2011. *Power in Movement*, 3rd edn. Cambridge: Cambridge University Press.

Tilly, Charles. 1978. *From Mobilization to Revolution*. Reading, MA: Addison-Wesley.

Tilly, Charles. 2004. *Contention and Democracy in Europe, 1650–2000*. Cambridge: Cambridge University Press.

Van Eerdewijk, Anouka and Conny Roggeband. 2014. "Gender Equality Norm Diffusion and Actor Constellations: A First Exploration." In *Gender Equality Norms in Regional*

Governance, edited by Anna Van der Vleuten, Anouka van Eerdewijk, and Conny Roggeband, 42–64. Basingstoke: Palgrave Macmillan.

Vasi, Ion. 2011. "Brokerage, Miscibility, and the Spread of Contention." *Mobilization: An International Quarterly* 16(1): 11–24.

Wang, Dan J. and Sarah A. Soule. 2012. "Social Movement Organizational Collaboration: Networks of Learning and the Diffusion of Protest Tactics, 1960–1995." *American Journal of Sociology* 117(6): 1674–1722.

Wang, Dan J. and Sarah A. Soule. 2016. "Tactical Innovation in Social Movements: The Effects of Peripheral and Multi-Issue Protest." *American Sociological Review* 81(3): 517–548.

Wilson, Kenneth, and Anthony M. Orum. 1976. "Mobilizing People for Collective Political Action." *Journal of Political and Military Sociology* 4: 187–202.

Wood, Lesley J. 2015. "Horizontalist Youth Camps and the Bolivarian Revolution: A Story of Blocked Diffusion." *Journal of World-Systems Research* 16(1): 48–62.

14

Coalitions and the Organization of Collective Action

MEGAN E. BROOKER AND DAVID S. MEYER

Introduction

In the fall of 2016, thousands of people assembled near the Standing Rock Indian Reservation, where just over 8000 Sioux people live. They were demonstrating against the construction of the Dakota Access Pipeline, planned to carry 450,000 barrels of crude oil each day from North Dakota to Southern Illinois. Because the pipeline would cross under the Missouri River, not far from the reservation, the Sioux argued that the pipeline was an environmental threat to its water supply, and a desecration of some of their sacred sites (Plummer 2016). Their campaign had commenced months earlier, and the Sioux were joined by thousands of Native Americans from other tribes, concerned more directly about the denigration of tribal rights than the local environmental threat. They were also joined by environmental activists who expressed concerns about fossil fuels and climate change, clergy from a range of faiths who supported religious freedom, and civil liberties activists concerned with press freedom and aggressive policing (Sammon 2016). The protesters agreed on opposition to the proposed route for the pipeline, but beyond that their priorities diverged. Some demonstrated at a distance, and issued statements, while others sought to occupy the construction site to stop the pipeline, facing arrest and police violence. The Sioux filed a federal lawsuit, while a minor party presidential candidate visited to announce her support for the demonstrators, and 1.7 million Facebook friends "checked in" to announce their support.

The Dakota Access Pipeline protests illustrate the importance of coalitions to contemporary protest politics. Groups and individuals may agree on a specific campaign, but for a variety of reasons. To the campaign, each group brings a specific set of larger concerns and resources, as well as a particular menu of tactics. When these groups can work together, their diversity can make them more powerful. But the diversity of a movement coalition also presents vulnerabilities. Disruptive tactics

The Wiley Blackwell Companion to Social Movements, Second Edition. Edited by David A. Snow, Sarah A. Soule, Hanspeter Kriesi, and Holly J. McCammon.
© 2019 John Wiley & Sons Ltd. Published 2019 by John Wiley & Sons Ltd.

may discredit groups that seek more mainstream support. Authorities can accede to the demands of one faction and undermine cooperation within the coalition. Rerouting the pipeline, for example, might be enough to satisfy concerns about local pollution and tribal sovereignty, but not to assuage the concerns about fossil fuels and climate change that animate environmentalists' opposition. Can a coalition survive as circumstances change?

To understand the development, dynamics, and potential influence of protest movements, we need to understand the forms coalitions can take and the factors influencing them. Successful and sustained mobilization is contingent upon organizing, engaging, and coordinating at least somewhat disparate interests. The nature of those challenging coalitions affects the responses that authorities craft, often intended to make subsequent coalitions' cooperation and mobilization more difficult (Meyer 1993). Here, we review some of the developing literature on social movement coalitions, outlining key issues for further inquiry. We begin by offering a usable definition for the range of social movement coalitions that emerge and we identify key characteristics that vary across them. We then address coalition dynamics, considering the external circumstances and internal dynamics that promote coalition formation. Finally, we examine coalition survival and outcomes and propose future directions for coalition research.

Defining and Differentiating Coalitions

Coalitions are organizations of social movement organizations (SMOs) and/or networks that animate social movements and collective action more generally. Although scholars have long recognized the phenomenon, further inquiry is required in order to attain a fuller understanding of both their internal dynamics and the contexts in which they operate. In the taxonomy of political formations, coalitions sit somewhere between the interest group (or social movement organization) and the social movement. As an ideal type, the former is defined by relative stability marked by coherent and purposeful structure, while the latter is characterized by temporal and structural volatility. *Social movement coalitions* are structuring mechanisms that bridge political organizations and the looser, more permeable, social movements. Movements are at least partly defined by the more or less coordinated activities of multiple organizations, sympathetic individuals, and their interactions with supporters, authorities, and opponents. Indeed, in liberal polities, coalitions often animate and define social movements, coordinating events, claims, and strategies targeted toward social change. Despite their importance, however, social movement coalitions have received only episodic attention.

Long ago, Gamson (1961: 374) defined coalitions as "temporary, means oriented, alliances among individuals or groups which differ in goals." Gamson's definition of coalitions assumed clear and distinct membership (in or out) and discrete payoffs to participants. But social movement coalitions vary in terms of their longevity, their shared activities, the costs and risks individual organizations face, the nature of the goals they pursue, and the political outcomes they achieve. Recognizing this diversity, McCammon and Moon (2015: 327) state simply that social movement coalitions "occur when distinct activist groups mutually agree to cooperate and work together toward a common goal."

As a striking variety of arrangements operate under the banner of coalition, it is helpful to identify the dimensions along which they vary. Here, we identify four: (1) type; (2) geographic boundaries; (3) duration; and (4) organizational form. These stylized types are neither exhaustive nor mutually exclusive, but provide a useful heuristic for making sense of coalition dynamics.

Coalition type

Type encompasses both the composition of a coalition's membership and the scope of its aims. *Within-movement coalitions* form through the alliance of multiple organizations within the same movement family. In the civil rights movement, for example, the "Big Four" – the Southern Christian Leadership Conference, the Student Nonviolent Coordinating Committee, the Congress of Racial Equality, and the National Association for the Advancement of Colored People – were loosely allied and each contributed resources to the sit-in and freedom ride campaigns (McAdam 1982). Scholars have documented the dynamics of within-movement coalitions in an array of movements, including the labor (Cornfield and McCammon 2010; Dixon, Danaher, and Kail 2013), environmental (Grossman 2001; Lichterman 1995; Murphy 2005; Shaffer 2000), women's and pro-choice (Borland 2008, 2010; Ferree and Hess 1994; Kretschmer 2014; McCammon and Campbell 2002; Reger 2002; Staggenborg 1986), gay and lesbian rights (Ghaziani 2008; Van Dyke and Cress 2006), and nuclear freeze (Hathaway and Meyer 1993; Rochon and Meyer 1997) movements.[1]

Cross-movement coalitions unite members of two or more movements in pursuit of a common goal (e.g. Beamish and Luebbers 2009; Krinsky and Reese 2006; Rose 2000; Van Dyke 2003). The Win Without War coalition, for instance, assembled 41 member groups in opposition to the second Gulf War. Only about a quarter of these focused strictly on issues of war and peace while the others identified primarily with a diverse array of causes including religious, identity, environmental, international policy, and social justice groups (Corrigall-Brown and Meyer 2010; Meyer and Corrigall-Brown 2005). They united in response to a common threat of imminent war in Iraq.

Organizers work to forge other cross-movement coalitions that link discrete movements—like the Standing Rock effort described at the outset. Prime contemporary examples include "blue-green" coalitions between organized labor and environmentalists. Two large forces on the political left, these well-resourced movements envision strong potential for political influence when they join forces (Obach 2004). Translating promise to influence is difficult. Cooperation between "Teamsters and Turtles" during the 1999 World Trade Organization protests, for example, dissipated by 2001 when Teamsters fought directly against the environmental lobby to support the Bush administration's plan to drill for oil in the Arctic National Wildlife Refuge (Gould, Lewis, and Roberts 2004).

Identity group coalitions, such as interracial, panethnic, and intersectional coalitions, broker cooperation across two or more identity groups. Interracial, or cross-ethnic, coalitions foster alliances across racial or ethnic groups. The "Rainbow Coalition," a community organizing association active in Chicago in the 1960s and 1970s, offers an example. Coordinated by Fred Hampton and Bob Lee, leaders of the Illinois Black Panther Party, the coalition brought together ethnically diverse constituencies under the banner of class struggle. Other members included the Young Patriots, a left-wing organization of young, white migrants from Appalachia; the Young Lords, a Puerto Rican nationalist group; and Rising Up Angry, a group of radical young greasers (Williams 2013). Jesse Jackson resurrected, moderated, and extended this Rainbow Coalition as part of his presidential campaign in 1984.

Panethnic coalitions bring together two or more ethnic or national origin groups within the same racial category. Threat is a common impetus for panethnic coalitions. Racially motivated attacks against Asian Americans and residential segregation provoked panethnic coalitions in the 1970s to 1990s (Okamoto 2010). Proposed changes to immigration law motivated a wave of Latino panethnic mobilization in 2006 (Barreto et al. 2009), promoted through advantageous structural conditions such as access to ethnic media (Rim 2009).

Intersectional coalitions unite across different identity groups including gender, race, class, and sexuality. Race, for example, can be understood both as "a coalition between men and women of color" as well as "a coalition of straight and gay people of color" (Crenshaw 1991: 1299). Proponents of intersectionality see it "not only a tool for understanding difference, but also a way to illuminate less obvious similarities" (Cole 2008: 444). The National Organization for Women (NOW), for example, overcame early fears of the "lavender menace" of lesbian members to embrace an intersectional approach, helping to organize the inaugural March on Washington for Lesbian and Gay Rights in 1979 and supporting LGBT organizations campaigning for same-sex marriage (Gilmore and Kaminski 2007).

Other coalitions extend their membership beyond movement communities. A *state actor-social movement coalition* "comes into existence when state actors agree to apply their organizational resources and influence in ways that further the general aims of a social movement" (Stearns and Almeida 2004: 479). Such alliances can aid the advancement of movement goals, including policy change. Japanese anti-pollution movements, for example, partnered with state agencies, opposition parties, local governments, and the courts to effect policy reforms (ibid.).

Movement alliances with and within political parties are critical to policy reform. Recent scholarship in political science conceptualizes parties as "coalitions of politicians, activists, and interest groups" (Karol 2016). Movements sometimes establish long-term influence within parties, becoming anchoring groups who hold veto power over partisan priorities (Schlozman 2015). The Christian Right, for example, not only used access to Republican legislators to lobby for adoption of state laws banning same-sex marriage, but was often directly involved in drafting the bills (Haider-Markel 2001). More often, the relationship between movements and parties is more contingent. Although the anti-Iraq War movement worked closely with the Democratic Party when the president was a Republican, the election of a Democrat to office compromised that coalition (Heaney and Rojas 2015). In Latin America as well, opposition parties are the most likely to ally with movements, adopting both their causes and tactical repertoires through a process of "social movement partyism" (Almeida 2010).

Geographic boundaries

Coalitions may recruit organizational members and direct their activities on a local, national, or transnational scale. *Local coalitions* draw members from a narrow region, such as a city or state, and focus on issues of local significance. Local coalitions show considerable disparity in terms of their division of labor, however, with some models more capable of successful mobilization than others (Jones et al. 2001). *National coalitions* focus on nationwide mobilization on issues of broad importance, but may draw membership from both national and local organizations. Political threats generate particularly fertile ground for the emergence of national coalitions.

Transnational coalitions draw members from multiple countries and concentrate on causes that transcend national boundaries. Analysis of transnational coalitions is an ever-growing focus of social movement scholarship and a product of ever-increasing globalization in the modern world (Bandy and Smith 2005). Regional cooperation can foster transnational alliance across countries in specific geographic areas (Wiest 2010), while other transnational activism targets international organizations and draws a global base.

Duration

Some coalitions are enduring and others ephemeral. *Event-based coalitions* are temporary alliances of organizations uniting for a single protest (Levi and Murphy 2006; Wang and Soule 2012). *Issue-based* coalitions exhibit longer-term cooperation due to the presence of a unifying cause or threat (Meyer and Corrigall-Brown 2005) or to advance a reasonably defined set of interests through lobbying over an extended period of time (Hula 1999). Limited duration alliances sometimes extend into more formal, longstanding arrangements. As plans progressed for what would become the 1963 March on Washington for Jobs and Freedom, six prominent civil rights organizations agreed to form the Council for United Civil Rights Leadership (CUCRL) to centralize fundraising efforts (Kirk 2013). Although plagued by conflict from its inception, the CUCRL persisted for several years after the march.

A coalition formed to stage a distinct event offers different coordination costs and risks than one designed to endure. The former requires intensive investment in public promotion of political goals and mass mobilization; the latter requires negotiated goals, but little in the way of a public profile. The debates about a one-time relationship are likely to be more heated and difficult than discussions that coordinate what is intended to be a sustained relationship. Organizers, often representing different organizations, argue about how much can and should be articulated within a particular event, and what issues are really most urgent or promising (Ghaziani 2008). Even more complicated are the movement coalitions that form around a set of issues without a narrowly defined strategy or political endpoint, and groups renegotiate their boundaries and terms to fit new contexts (Levi and Murphy 2006).

Organizational form

Often, organizations work together to coordinate and promote events without ever negotiating a formal alliance. *Formal coalitions*, on the other hand, develop a centralized coordinating organization and officially declared member groups. Organizational form dictates the degree of cooperation between coalition members. Contingent upon coalition formality, organizational members may actively negotiate strategy and share resources, or offer little more than endorsement to the cause (Meyer and Corrigall-Brown 2005).

We need to understand how coalition type, geographic boundaries, duration, and organizational form affect one another. Coalitions seeking to outlast one event, for example, must build the infrastructure necessary to sustain themselves (Staggenborg 1988). We think that there is a parabolic relationship between the geographic bounds of a coalition and its duration and organizational form. National coalitions, at the peak at the parabola, require greater homogeneity in goals but offer a higher likelihood of formalization and long-term sustenance. In contrast, local and transnational coalitions, at opposite tails of the parabola, consist of looser and more short-lived alliances, but offer greater possibility to organize across causes. We turn next to determinants of coalition formation, as placing coalition dynamics at the center of real political struggles complicates both modeling and prediction.

Coalition Emergence and Dynamics

We now look at the coalition as a structuring form of dissent and protest. In this section, we first examine the benefits and risks of coalition participation, before discussing determinants of coalition formation.

A social movement organization operates in the service of at least three distinct, but inter-related goals: (1) to pressure government to effect the policy changes it wants; (2) to educate the public and persuade people of the urgency of the problems it addresses and the wisdom of its position; and (3) to sustain a flow of resources that allow it to maintain its existence and efforts (Wilson [1973] 1995; Zald and McCarthy 1987). Coalition work can upset the difficult balancing act of coordinating these distinct missions. What is useful in achieving one objective isn't always helpful in working toward another. Lobbying legislators requires moderation, credibility, and restraint (e.g. Berry 1999; Schlozman and Tierney 1986), for example, but those very qualities are anathema to maintaining a high public profile, and thus publicizing ideas. In contrast, a politics of polemic, characterized by dramatic action and polarizing speech, helps in maintaining visibility, but the actions may alienate the less engaged and more moderate constituencies, including potential supporters. Speaking or acting upon an unvarnished version of *truth* may satisfy supporters, but do more to provoke and mobilize the opposition than reach new partisans (Meyer and Staggenborg 1996). Organizations must develop a profile that contains some mix of these three functions, mindful of maintaining a balance that works for them. Every choice of issue, tactic, and alliance should be seen as something that offers advantages and risks along these three dimensions.

Accordingly, any group's decision to join with other groups carries with it potential costs and benefits. On the one hand, cooperation among groups increases the visibility of the movement, increasing its chances at political efficacy. Additionally, because organizations have distinct audiences, a broad coalition affords the prospects of mobilizing a wider range of people, expanding tactics, and gaining entry into a greater number of institutional niches (Staggenborg 1986). Tactical diversity and multiple constituencies are an asset for a movement in many ways. For instance, radical action can enhance the visibility and credibility of moderates – although it can also discredit them (Haines 1988). At the same time, participation carries risks. By cooperating with groups that may appeal to the same funders or members, an organization may obscure its own identity in the service of the larger movement, hurting its well-being. Alliances can compromise identities, and can put organizations in league with unreliable or tainted allies.

Another set of factors that alter the costs and opportunities for coalitions are external circumstances, which are critical in facilitating or undermining the process of building movement coalitions. These circumstances reflect the interests the coalitions and their participating organizations represent, the populations they seek to mobilize, and the institutions and venues in which they operate (Meyer and Staggenborg 2012). Four sets of conditions contribute to coalition emergence: (1) the political environment; (2) ideological alignment; (3) social ties; and (4) organizational structures and resources (McCammon and Moon 2015; McCammon and Van Dyke 2010; Van Dyke and Amos 2017).

The political environment

Political threats play an important role in coalition formation (see Chapter 2 by Almeida, in this volume, on threats). A shared sense of threat stemming from the broader political environment can motivate groups to form coalitions. Corrigall-Brown and Meyer (2010) show that opposition to an imminent war diminished the salience of political differences and established a consensual priority. Once the prospect of actually stopping the war evaporated, however, antiwar coalitions frayed as other interests and more complicated and contested ideas came to the fore. Once Barack Obama, an explicit opponent of the war, won the presidency, protests in the streets declined in number and size, and committed Democrats were largely absent (Heaney and Rojas 2015).

Similarly, the Republican Party found the Tea Party a more welcome force when its opponents controlled both houses of Congress as well as the presidency. They shared the work of opposing President Obama's initiatives, employing diverse tactics and rhetoric in the service of common goals. That they could not agree on a common agenda or even shared incremental steps was not a problem until such steps were possible (Meyer 2015). Allies in opposition became problematic when there were negotiations about matters of policy to manage (Van Dyke and Meyer 2014).

Political openings, as opposed to threats, are less likely to promote coalition work. Allies in government can facilitate communication between movements and institutional actors (della Porta and Rucht 1995; Stearns and Almeida 2004), they can also dampen mobilization, making coalition more difficult (Heaney and Rojas 2015). For the pro-choice movement, chances to effect state-level legislative victories encouraged coalition formation, but threats, such as countermovement attempts to repeal *Roe v. Wade,* were more powerful (Staggenborg 1986).

In general, the empirical literature on coalitions shows the importance of political threats in facilitating coalition organizing because it is easier to unite against a common enemy (McCammon and Van Dyke 2010). McCammon and Campbell (2002) find that cooperation between suffragists and the Women's Christian Temperance Union emerged in response to threats of legislative defeat or organized opponents, while coalition work was unlikely during periods of political opportunity.

Van Dyke (2003) differentiates the role of threat for within- and cross-movement coalitions of college student activists. Within-movement coalitions responded primarily to local threats, such as unsupportive college administrators or counter-protesters while cross-movement coalitions required a broader threat, such as an elite antagonist in the White House. Similarly, the local threat to abortion clinics united previously fragmented chapters of the National Organization for Women in Cleveland (Reger 2002). Effective coalition work across ethnic groups and immigrant organizations in California arose in response to policy threats from proposed federal welfare reform legislation (Reese 2005). Cooperation between gay men and lesbians increased in the 1980s in response to common threats from the Christian Right and the HIV crisis (Fetner 2008; Van Dyke and Cress 2006). Economic threats also promote coalition activity. For example, threat of neoliberal policy promoted an alliance between movements and oppositional political parties across Latin America (Almeida 2010), while Argentina's 2001 economic crisis fostered cooperation among women's groups that had previously faced deep class-based and generational cleavages (Borland 2010).

Ideological alignment

Ideological alignment, often via framing (see Chapter 22 by Snow, Vliegenthart, and Ketelaars, in this volume), is routinely described as a precursor to coalition emergence. Cohesion of organizational ideologies and frames can thwart potential conflict and ease coalition work (Bandy and Smith 2005; Gerhards and Rucht 1992; McCammon and Campbell 2002). Cornfield and McCammon (2010), for example, emphasize how ideological convergence regarding public policy goals enabled the merger of the American Federation of Labor (AFL) and the Congress of Industrial Organizations (CIO).

Lack of ideological alignment fosters conflict and stifles successful within-movement cooperation. Divergent positions on abortion led to splintering within the feminist movement (Kretschmer 2014). Debates over the need for external support from the federal government and white liberals created hostility between civil rights groups (Barkan 1986). Cross-movement coalitions are also prone to ideological conflicts (Bell and Delaney 2001: Roth 2010).

Social ties

Prior cooperation enhances the likelihood of subsequent cooperation, partly through *social ties*. In analyzing social ties, scholars emphasize the labor required to negotiate coalition building. Most coalition recruitment takes place *en bloc*, that is, by connecting and engaging the already organized through their existing affiliations. Individuals connected to more than one organization or movement often play an integral role in coalition development. Corrigall-Brown and Meyer (2010), for example, demonstrate how overlapping ties between key organizers of Win Without War provided a foundation for coalition recruitment and established trust among members. Rose (2000) accents the role of "bridge builders," showing how they facilitated communication between environmental, labor, and peace organizations, helping them overcome differences. Obach (2004), Grossman (2001), and Levi and Murphy (2006) also accent the bridging function of brokers, key leaders, and entrepreneurs. Finally,

Reese, Petit, and Meyer (2010) identify four types of "movement crossovers" and explain how their social positions allowed them to rapidly mobilize personnel and resources from multiple movements around opposition to the Iraq War.

Organizational structures and resources

Organizational characteristics, including goals, formalization, and resources, affect coalition formation. Groups that embrace broad goals and identities that span across two or more issues or movements are more likely to join coalitions. Van Dyke (2003) concludes that these multi-issue groups help build coalitions by establishing ties across ostensibly distinct movements. Similarly, Heaney and Rojas (2014) describe the central position of US Labor Against the War in national antiwar coalitions and its role as a bridge between peace organizations and labor unions. Organizations with nonhierarchical structures and participatory democratic decision-making face more difficulty in negotiating coalition participation (Arnold 1995), while a clearly defined division of labor makes coalition work easier (Borland 2008). Professional organizers are more likely to see the value of alliances, and to have the skills and resources to negotiate them (Bob 2005; Shaffer 2000).

Coalitions, like their member organizations, require *resources* to sustain themselves. Groups with limited resources are more likely to join coalitions as doing so offers the potential to expand their activities (Staggenborg 1986) and amplify their impact (Bickel 2001). But the groups that contribute more substantial resources tend to dominate the alliances (Hathaway and Meyer 1993). Coalitions are most enduring when resources are plentiful, and resources are more abundant in response to threats (Staggenborg 1986). In contrast, when the availability of resources declines, organizations are prone to competition and conflict (Zald and McCarthy 1987). Competition over resources, for example, led to intense rivalries amongst major civil rights organizations (Barkan 1986). Because organizations in the same movement sector are more likely to compete for support (Minkoff 1997), ample resources are likely more important for forming within-movement coalitions than those across movements (Van Dyke 2003).

Both external and internal factors may also work together to expedite or undermine alliances. Scholars have started to take conjectural causality into account when examining coalition formation. McCammon and Van Dyke (2010) perform qualitative comparative analysis (QCA) on a dataset of 24 empirical studies related to coalition emergence. Though no single factor was necessary for a coalition to emerge, ideological alignment and threat were the most common contributors, and each was sometimes sufficient for alliance. Ideological alignment and plentiful resources were the most likely conditions to co-occur in support of coalition efforts.

Coalition Outcomes

While coalition emergence has received considerable attention, coalition outcomes remain understudied in social movements literature. Coalition dynamics influence coalition survival and dissipation, and may also generate movement and organizational changes and political outcomes (McCammon and Moon 2015; Van Dyke and Amos 2017).

Coalition survival and dissipation

Although both theorists and activists often imagine themes that can unify diverse groups, many divisions and differences have bedeviled the dream of a grand coalition, for instance, class, race, gender, industry, religion, and region. Holding together a large and diverse coalition requires compromise and successful balancing of member organizations' competing ideologies and interests. The dilemma for activists is that deploying diversity, that is, showing a range of interests and constituencies in support of a common cause, is newsworthy and suggests potential political power. But managing diversity, that is, serving the range of interests and groups within a coalition to maintain engagement, is an ongoing and often frustrating struggle. Conflict may arise within coalitions over competition for resources (Barkan 1986; Staggenborg 1986), frame disputes (Benford 1993), or an incompatibility between coalition structure and organizational collective identity (Arnold 1995). Internal disagreements may be insurmountable obstacles to coalition work, especially absent external conditions to unify members.

Although the dynamics of coming together and growing apart are mediated by personal relationships and political skill, the relationship of the coalition to external political circumstances is critical. The peak of mobilization always passes, at least partly because political leaders respond. Although unambiguous victories and defeats are relatively rare, the time during which a movement can maintain a very broad and engaged coalition of organizations is limited. Changes in policy, political alignments, or even rhetoric, alter the political environment for each organization, leading to a reconsideration of previous political choices and alliances (Meyer 2004).

The nuclear freeze movement illustrates this process. Uniting to oppose the Reagan administration's arms control and nuclear weapons policies during the early 1980s, a broad coalition united behind a "nuclear freeze" proposal that participating groups defined differently (Meyer 1990; Rochon and Meyer 1997). At the height of mobilization, it comprised groups that opposed nuclear weapons altogether and advocated unilateral action and others that saw the freeze as a vehicle to use in forcing the Reagan administration to return to the previous US policies of bilateral arms control negotiations and managed technical modernization. As the administration responded to movement pressures, by moderating rhetoric, cutting the growth in military spending, and re-establishing arms control negotiations with the Soviet Union, the freeze coalition dissipated. Differences among the various organizations became more prominent as institutionally-oriented politics consumed more activist efforts. Groups that had enlisted in the freeze because they faced closed doors on Capitol Hill left the coalition when those doors opened. The movement's more institutional wing saw the prospect of progress, while the disarmament wing saw a sellout on the horizon (Meyer 1990, 1993).

Alliances that form in response to political threats are susceptible to decline as those conditions pass and groups no longer have an impetus to set aside conflicting ideologies and preferences (Staggenborg 1986). Without a catalyst or common enemy, ideological disputes and resource competition become more salient. We contend that coalition dynamics roughly approximate similar decisions about mobilization for individuals. Groups join coalition efforts when they see a particular set of issues and efforts as urgent and potentially efficacious (Meyer and Corrigall-Brown 2005).

When external circumstances change, altering either the perceived urgency or efficacy of mobilization, they will return to core activities that sustain the organization.

Coalition participation is often murkier than it appears in the literature. While it may be analytically useful to treat coalition participation as dichotomous, with members either in a coalition or not, the empirical reality is far more ambiguous. Organizations are likely to vary their commitment to a coalition over time, without making formal announcements about being in or out. Involvement varies across groups and across time as members continually reassess their priorities. Often groups do not formally exit a coalition, but instead limit contributions of labor and resources. The anti-Iraq War coalition United for Peace and Justice, for example, continued to claim a "network of hundreds of peace and justice organizations" (UFPJ 2017), long after the movement demobilized and many of its member organizations reduced their contributions or ceased to exist. Organizations remain "members" so long as they do not officially request removal of their name. While paper coalitions continue, the commitment to coordinated collective action dissipates. Coalitions rarely end in a bang, but rather slowly fade away as member organizations redirect their attention elsewhere.

Movement and organizational changes

Coalition involvement affects mobilization for the movement and for participating groups. Coalition work often bolsters movement mobilization, by drawing a wider array of participants (Gerhards and Rucht 1992; Luna 2010). Jones et al. (2001) find that specific coalition forms, namely those where a single organization holds primary decision-making and planning authority, are most successful at mobilizing participants in local coalition events. Organizations flourish when coalition participation provides members access to resources and networks not previously available to them (Lee 2011; Mix 2011). Organizations may make strategic adaptations when they alter their frames to align with those of coalition partners (Croteau and Hicks 2003; Luna 2010) or adopt new tactics (Wang and Soule 2012). Coalitions may also affect the broader organizational field, either by encouraging (Lee 2011) or discouraging (Murphy 2005) the formation of new organizations.

Political outcomes

While political outcomes, such as policy or legislative change, are a common goal of coalition work, further empirical data is necessary to determine whether coalitions tend to achieve their desired results. Studies of state actor-social movement coalitions indicate that these coalitions have successfully contributed to legislative change. Using the case of environmental coalitions in Japan, Stearns and Almeida (2004: 497) conclude that "the existence of multiple coalitions between state actors and social movements greatly raises the probability that favorable policy implementation occurs." Feminist coalitions in the United States (Banaszak 2010) and transnational campaigns against child labor (Brooks 2005) have also been successful in achieving favorable policy outcomes. Coalitions may also generate more localized outcomes. Gelb and Shogan (2005) describe how coalitions successfully prevented mergers of Catholic hospitals with secular ones, thereby ensuring access to reproductive healthcare services that were threatened. Nonetheless, coalitions may not always achieve their political goals. Joyner (1982) describes how, despite organizing a strong coalition, women's groups were unsuccessful in passing the Equal Rights Amendment in Illinois. Additional research is needed, then, to ascertain the conditions under which coalitions are likely to be successful in achieving political gains.

Future Directions

Increasingly, social movement scholars recognize that movement politics is conditioned by coalition dynamics. We've outlined some of the achievements of prior research, but also underscored areas where substantial progress is possible. First, the growing library of case studies skews heavily to the left. New work should redress the imbalance by paying close attention to movements of the right, including contemporary populist mobilizations. Second, it is important to distinguish how coalition dynamics vary in relation to different coalition characteristics. The factors that drive or challenge short-term alliances are likely to differ from those that encourage longer-term arrangements. Importantly, we can see that all of these coalition forms are influenced by both factors inherent in the particular coalition (including the history, skill, and orientation of key actors) and those of the context (including policy, political alignments, and institutional arrangements). In short, the coalition is a place where we can see the interplay between structure and agency, and this focus should animate subsequent research.

Third, although activist enthusiasm for coalition efforts remains unabated (e.g. Enriquez 2014; Kadivar 2013; Tattersall 2010; von Bülow 2011), scholars need to investigate whether it is justified. In particular, it is critical to examine coalition outcomes and the extent to which coalition work enhances the prospects for political influence. It is also important to investigate the potential detrimental outcomes resulting from coalition work including clouding political messages and the risks of tainted allies or blocking the creation of new groups (Murphy 2005). Finally, we need to understand that the boundaries of coalitions extend across the institutions of governance; subsequent research should apply a more inclusive approach that looks at institutional allies. This is a great deal of work, of course, but academics are hardly strangers to the division of labor that coordinated efforts can inspire.

Note

1   See Table 1 in Van Dyke and Amos (2017: 2) for a more extensive list of coalition studies by movement.

References

Almeida, Paul D. 2010. "Social Movement Partyism: Collective Action and Oppositional Political Parties." In *Strategic Alliances: Coalition Building and Social Movements*, edited by Nella Van Dyke and Holly J. McCammon, 170–196. Minneapolis: University of Minnesota Press.

Arnold, Gretchen. 1995. "Dilemmas of Feminist Coalitions: Collective Identity and Strategic Effectiveness in the Battered Women's Movement." In *Feminist Organizations: Harvest of the New Women's Movement*, edited by Myra Marx Ferree and Patricia Yancey Martin, 276–290. Philadelphia, PA: Temple University Press.

Banaszak, Lee Ann. 2010. *The Women's Movement Inside and Outside the State*. New York: Cambridge University Press.

Bandy, Joe and Jackie Smith, eds. 2005. *Coalitions across Borders: Transnational Protest and the Neoliberal Order*. Lanham, MD: Rowman & Littlefield.

Barkan, Steven E. 1986. "Interorganizational Conflict in the Southern Civil Rights Movement." *Sociological Inquiry* 56: 190–209.

Barreto, Matt A., Sylvia Manzano, Ricardo Ramírez, and Kathy Rim. 2009. "Mobilization, Participation, and *Solidaridad*: Latino Participation in the 2006 Immigration Protest Rallies." *Urban Affairs Review* 44: 736–764.

Beamish, Thomas D. and Amy J. Luebbers. 2009. "Alliance Building across Social Movements: Bridging Difference in a Peace and Justice Coalition." *Social Problems* 56: 647–676.

Bell, Sandra J. and Mary E. Delaney. 2001. "Collaborating across Difference: From Theory and Rhetoric to the Hard Reality of Building Coalitions." In *Forging Radical Alliances across Difference: Coalition Politics for the New Millennium*, edited by Jill M. Bystydzienski and Steven P. Schacht, 63–76. Lanham, MD: Rowman & Littlefield.

Benford, Robert D. 1993. "Frame Disputes within the Nuclear Disarmament Movement." *Social Forces* 71: 677–701.

Berry, Jeffrey M. 1999. *The New Liberalism*. Washington, DC: Brookings Institution.

Bickel, Christopher. 2001. "Reasons to Resist: Coalition Building at Indiana University." In *Forging Radical Alliances across Difference: Coalition Politics for the New Millennium*, edited by Jill M. Bystydzienski and Steven P. Schacht, 207–219. Lanham, MD: Rowman & Littlefield.

Bob, Clifford. 2005. *The Marketing of Rebellion: Insurgents, Media, and International Activism*. New York: Cambridge University Press.

Borland, Elizabeth. 2008. "Social Movement Organizations and Coalitions: Comparisons from the Women's Movement in Buenos Aires, Argentina." *Research in Social Movements, Conflicts and Change* 28: 83–112.

Borland, Elizabeth. 2010. "Crisis as Catalyst for Cooperation? Women's Organizing in Buenos Aires." In *Strategic Alliances: Coalition Building and Social Movements*, edited by Nella Van Dyke and Holly J. McCammon, 241–265. Minneapolis: University of Minnesota Press.

Brooks, Ethel. 2005. "Transnational Campaigns against Child Labor: The Garment Industry in Bangladesh." In *Coalitions across Borders: Transnational Protest and the Neoliberal Order*, edited by Joe Bandy and Jackie Smith, 121–139. Lanham, MD: Rowman & Littlefield.

Cole, Elizabeth R. 2008. "Coalitions as a Model for Intersectionality: From Practice to Theory." *Sex Roles* 59: 443–453.

Cornfield, Daniel B. and Holly J. McCammon. 2010. "Approaching Merger: The Converging Public Policy Agendas of the AFL and CIO, 1938–1955." In *Strategic Alliances: Coalition Building and Social Movements*, edited by Nella Van Dyke and Holly J. McCammon, 79–98. Minneapolis: University of Minnesota Press.

Corrigall-Brown, Catherine and David S. Meyer. 2010. "The Prehistory of a Coalition: The Role of Social Ties in Win Without War." In *Strategic Alliances: Coalition Building and Social Movements*, edited by Nella Van Dyke and Holly J. McCammon, 3–21. Minneapolis: University of Minnesota Press.

Crenshaw, Kimberle. 1991. "Mapping the Margins: Intersectionality, Identity Politics, and Violence against Women of Color." *Stanford Law Review* 43: 1241–1299.

Croteau, David and Lyndsi Hicks. 2003. "Coalition Framing and the Challenge of a Consonant Frame Pyramid: The Case of a Collaborative Response to Homelessness." *Social Problems* 50: 251–272.

della Porta, Donatella and Dieter Rucht. 1995. "Left-Libertarian Movements in Context: A Comparison of Italy and West Germany, 1965–1990." In *The Politics of Social Protest: Comparative Perspectives on States and Social Movements*, edited by J. Craig Jenkins, 229–227. Minneapolis: University of Minnesota Press.

Dixon, Marc, William F. Danaher, and Ben Lennox Kail. 2013. "Allies, Targets, and the Effectiveness of Coalition Protest: A Comparative Analysis of Labor Unrest in the U.S. South." *Mobilization* 18: 331–350.

Enriquez, Laura E. 2014. "Undocumented and Citizen Students Unite: Building a Cross-Status Coalition through Shared Ideology." *Social Problems* 61: 155–174.

Ferree, Myra Marx and Beth B. Hess. 1994. *Controversy and Coalition: The New Feminist Movement across Three Decades of Change*. New York: Routledge.

Fetner, Tina. 2008. *How the Religious Right Shaped Lesbian and Gay Activism*. Minneapolis: University of Minnesota Press.

Gamson, William A. 1961. "A Theory of Coalition Formation." *American Sociological Review* 26: 373–382.

Gelb, Joyce and Colleen J. Shogan. 2005. "Community Activism in the USA: Catholic Hospital Mergers and Reproductive Access." *Social Movement Studies* 4: 209–229.

Gerhards, Jürgen and Dieter Rucht. 1992. "Mesomobilization: Organizing and Framing in Two Protest Campaigns in West Germany." *American Journal of Sociology* 98: 555–596.

Ghaziani, Amin. 2008. *The Dividends of Dissent: How Conflict and Culture Work in Lesbian and Gay Marches on Washington*. Chicago: University of Chicago Press.

Gilmore, Stephanie and Elizabeth Kaminski. 2007. "A Part and Apart: Lesbian and Straight Feminist Activists Negotiate Identity in a Second-Wave Organization." *Journal of the History of Sexuality* 16: 95–113.

Gould, Kenneth A., Tammy L. Lewis, and J. Timmons Roberts. 2004. "Blue-Green Coalitions: Constraints and Possibilities in the Post 9-11 Political Environment." *Journal of World-Systems Research* 10: 91–116.

Grossman, Zoltan. 2001. "'Let's Not Create Evilness for This River': Interethnic Environmental Alliances of Native Americans and Rural Whites in Northern Wisconsin." In *Forging Radical Alliances across Difference: Coalition Politics for the New Millennium*, edited by Jill M. Bystydzienski and Steven P. Schacht, 146–162. Lanham, MD: Rowman & Littlefield.

Haider-Markel, Donald P. 2001. "Policy Diffusion as a Geographical Expansion of the Scope of Political Conflict: Same-Sex Marriage Bans in the 1990s." *State Politics and Policy Quarterly* 1: 5–26.

Haines, Herbert H. 1988. *Black Radicals and the Civil Rights Mainstream, 1954–1970*. Knoxville: University of Tennessee Press.

Hathaway, Will and David S. Meyer. 1993. "Competition and Cooperation in Social Movement Coalitions: Lobbying for Peace in the 1980s." *Berkeley Journal of Sociology* 38: 157–183.

Heaney, Michael T. and Fabio Rojas. 2014. "Hybrid Activism: Social Movement Mobilization in a Multimovement Environment." *American Journal of Sociology* 119: 1047–1103.

Heaney, Michael T. and Fabio Rojas. 2015. *The Party in the Street: The Antiwar Movement and the Democratic Party after 9/11*. New York: Cambridge University Press.

Hula, Kevin W. 1999. *Lobbying Together*. Washington, DC: Georgetown University Press.

Jones, Andrew W., Richard N. Hutchinson, Nella Van Dyke, Leslie Gates, and Michele Companion. 2001. "Coalition Form and Mobilization Effectiveness in Local Social Movements." *Sociological Spectrum* 21: 207–231.

Joyner, Nancy Douglas. 1982. "Coalition Politics: A Case Study of an Organization's Approach to a Single Issue." *Women & Politics* 2: 57–70.

Kadivar, Mohammad Ali. 2013. "Alliances and Perception Profiles in the Iranian Reform Movement, 1997 to 2005." *American Sociological Review* 78: 1063–1086.

Karol, David. 2016. "Political Parties in American Political Development." In *The Oxford Handbook of American Political Development*, edited by Richard M. Valelly, Suzanne Mettler, and Robert C. Lieberman, 473–491. Oxford: Oxford University Press.

Kirk, John A. 2013. *Martin Luther King, Jr. and the Civil Rights Movement*. New York: Routledge.

Kretschmer, Kelsy. 2014. "Shifting Boundaries and Splintering Movements: Abortion Rights in the Feminist and New Right Movements." *Sociological Forum* 29: 893–915.

Krinsky, John and Ellen Reese. 2006. "Forging and Sustaining Labor-Community Coalitions: The Workfare Justice Movement in Three Cities." *Sociological Forum* 21: 623–658.

Lee, Jung-eun. 2011. "Insularity or Solidarity? The Impacts of Political Opportunity Structure and Social Movement Sector on Alliance Formation." *Mobilization* 16: 303–324.

Levi, Margaret and Gillian H. Murphy. 2006. "Coalitions of Contention: The Case of the WTO Protests in Seattle." *Political Studies* 54: 651–670.

Lichterman, Paul. 1995. "Piecing Together Multicultural Community: Cultural Differences in Community Building among Grass-Roots Environmentalists." *Social Problems* 42: 513–534.

Luna, Zakiya T. 2010. "Marching Toward Reproductive Justice: Coalitional (Re)Framing of the March for Women's Lives." *Sociological Inquiry* 80: 554–578.

McAdam, Doug. 1982. *Political Process and the Development of Black Insurgency, 1930–1970*. Chicago: University of Chicago Press.

McCammon, Holly J. and Karen Campbell. 2002. "Allies on the Road to Victory: Coalition Formation Between the Suffragists and the Woman's Christian Temperance Union." *Mobilization* 7: 231–251.

McCammon, Holly J. and Minyoung Moon. 2015. "Social Movement Coalitions." In *The Oxford Handbook of Social Movements*, edited by Donatella della Porta and Mario Diani, 326–339. New York: Oxford University Press.

McCammon, Holly J. and Nella Van Dyke. 2010. "Applying Qualitative Comparative Analysis to Empirical Studies of Social Movement Coalition Formation." In *Strategic Alliances: Coalition Building and Social Movements*, edited by Nella Van Dyke and Holly J. McCammon, 292–315. Minneapolis: University of Minnesota Press.

Meyer, David S. 1990. *A Winter of Discontent: The Nuclear Freeze and American Politics*. New York: Praeger.

Meyer, David S. 1993. "Institutionalizing Dissent: The United States Structure of Political Opportunity and the End of the Nuclear Freeze." *Sociological Forum* 8: 157–179.

Meyer, David S. 2004. "Protest and Political Opportunities." *Annual Review of Sociology* 30: 125–145.

Meyer, David S. 2015. "Social Movement Politics IS Coalition Politics." *Mobilizing Ideas*, November 3. Available at: https://mobilizingideas.wordpress.com/2015/11/03/social-movement-politics-is-coalition-politics/

Meyer, David S. and Catherine Corrigall-Brown. 2005. "Coalitions and Political Context: U.S. Movements against Wars in Iraq." *Mobilization* 10: 327–344.

Meyer, David S. and Suzanne Staggenborg. 1996. "Movements, Countermovements, and the Structure of Political Opportunity." *American Journal of Sociology* 101: 1628–1660.

Meyer, David S. and Suzanne Staggenborg. 2012. "Thinking about Strategy." In *Strategies for Social Change*, edited by Gregory M. Maney, Rachel V. Kutz-Flamenbaum, Deana A. Rohlinger, and Jeff Goodwin, 3–21. Minneapolis: University of Minnesota Press.

Minkoff, Debra C. 1997. "The Sequencing of Social Movements." *American Sociological Review* 62: 779–799.

Mix, Tamara L. 2011. "Rally the People: Building Local-Environmental Justice Grassroots Coalitions and Enhancing Social Capital." *Sociological Inquiry* 81: 174–194.

Murphy, Gillian. 2005. "Coalitions and the Development of the Global Environmental Movement: A Double-Edged Sword." *Mobilization* 10: 235–250.

Obach, Brian K. 2004. *Labor and the Environmental Movement: The Quest for Common Ground*. Cambridge, MA: The MIT Press.

Okamoto, Dina G. 2010. "Organizing across Ethnic Boundaries in the Post-Civil Rights Era: Asian American Panethnic Coalitions." In *Strategic Alliances: Coalition Building and Social Movements*, edited by Nella Van Dyke and Holly J. McCammon, 143–169. Minneapolis: University of Minnesota Press.

Plummer, Brad. 2016. "The Battle over the Dakota Access Pipeline, Explained." *Vox*. November 29. Available at: http://www.vox.com/2016/9/9/12862958/dakota-access-pipeline-fight (accessed July 7, 2017).

Reger, Jo. 2002. "Organizational Dynamics and Construction of Multiple Feminist Identities in the National Organization for Women." *Gender & Society* 16: 710–727.

Reese, Ellen. 2005. "Policy Threats and Social Movement Coalitions: California's Campaign to Restore Legal Immigrants' Rights to Welfare." In *Routing the Opposition: Social Movements, Public Policy, and Democracy*, edited by David S. Meyer, Valerie Jenness, and Helen Ingram, 259–287. Minneapolis: University of Minnesota Press.

Reese, Ellen, Christine Petit, and David S. Meyer. 2010. "Sudden Mobilization: Movement Crossovers, Threats, and the Surprising Rise of the U.S. Antiwar Movement." In *Strategic Alliances: Coalition Building and Social Movements*, edited by Nella Van Dyke and Holly J. McCammon, 266–291. Minneapolis: University of Minnesota Press.

Rim, Kathy H. 2009. "Latino and Asian American Mobilization in the 2006 Immigration Protests." *Social Science Quarterly* 90: 703–721.

Rochon, Thomas R. and David S. Meyer, eds. 1997. *Coalitions & Political Movements: The Lessons of the Nuclear Freeze*. Boulder, CO: Lynne Rienner Publishers.

Rose, Fred. 2000. *Coalitions across the Class Divide: Lessons from the Labor, Peace, and Environmental Movements*. Ithaca, NY: Cornell University Press.

Roth, Benita. 2010. "'Organizing One's Own' as Good Politics: Second Wave Feminists and the Meaning of Coalition." In *Strategic Alliances: Coalition Building and Social Movements*, edited by Nella Van Dyke and Holly J. McCammon, 99–118. Minneapolis: University of Minnesota Press.

Sammon, Alexander. 2016. "A History of Native Americans Protesting the Dakota Access Pipeline." *Mother Jones*, September 9. Available at: http://www.motherjones.com/environment/2016/09/dakota-access-pipeline-protest-timeline-sioux-standing-rock-jill-stein (accessed July 7, 2017).

Schlozman, Daniel. 2015. *When Movements Anchor Parties: Electoral Alignments in American History*. Princeton, NJ: Princeton University Press.

Schlozman, Kay Lehman and John T. Tierney. 1986. *Organized Interests and American Democracy*. New York: Little, Brown.

Shaffer, Martin B. 2000. "Coalition Work among Environmental Groups." *Research in Social Movements, Conflicts and Change* 22: 111–126.

Staggenborg, Suzanne. 1986. "Coalition Work in the Pro-Choice Movement: Organizational and Environmental Opportunities and Obstacles." *Social Problems* 33: 374–390.

Staggenborg, Suzanne. 1988. "The Consequences of Professionalization and Formalization in the Pro-Choice Movement." *American Sociological Review* 53: 585–605.

Stearns, Linda Brewster and Paul D. Almeida. 2004. "The Formation of State Actor-Social Movement Coalitions and Favorable Policy Outcomes." *Social Problems* 51: 478–504.

Tattersall, Amanda. 2010. *Power in Coalition: Strategies for Strong Unions and Social Change.* Ithaca, NY: Cornell University Press.

United for Peace and Justice. (UFPJ). 2017. "Member Groups." Available at: http://www.unitedforpeace.org/member-groups/ (accessed July 4, 2017).

Van Dyke, Nella. 2003. "Crossing Movement Boundaries: Factors that Facilitate Coalition Protest by American College Students, 1930–1990." *Social Problems* 50: 226–250.

Van Dyke, Nella and Bryan Amos. 2017. "Social Movement Coalitions: Formation, Longevity, and Success." *Sociology Compass* 11: 1–17.

Van Dyke, Nella and Ronda Cress. 2006. "Political Opportunities and Collective Identity in Ohio's Gay and Lesbian Movement, 1970 to 2000." *Sociological Perspectives* 49: 503–526.

Van Dyke, Nella and David S. Meyer, eds., 2014. *Understanding the Tea Party Movement.* New York: Routledge.

von Bülow, Marisa. 2011. "Brokers in Action: Transnational Coalitions and Trade Agreements in the Americas." *Mobilization* 16: 165–180.

Wang, Dan J. and Sarah A. Soule. 2012. "Social Movement Organizational Collaboration: Networks of Learning and the Diffusion of Protest Tactics, 1960–1995." *American Journal of Sociology* 117: 1674–1722.

Wiest, Dawn. 2010. "Interstate Dynamics and Transnational Social Movement Coalitions: A Comparison of Northeast and Southeast Asia." In *Strategic Alliances: Coalition Building and Social Movements*, edited by Nella Van Dyke and Holly J. McCammon, 50–76. Minneapolis: University of Minnesota Press.

Williams, Jakobi. 2013. *From the Bullet to the Ballot: The Illinois Chapter of the Black Panther Party and Racial Coalition Politics in Chicago.* Chapel Hill: University of North Carolina Press.

Wilson, James Q. [1973] 1995. *Political Organizations.* 2nd ed. Princeton, NJ: Princeton University Press.

Zald, Mayer N. and John D. McCarthy. 1987. *Social Movements in an Organizational Society: Collected Essays.* New Brunswick, NJ: Transaction Publishers.

Part III
Social Movement Strategies and Tactics

15

Tactics and Strategic Action

Brian Doherty and Graeme Hayes

Introduction

In this chapter, we discuss the dominant approaches to the analysis of social movement tactics and strategies. If there is broad agreement among scholars about their importance to the performance and understanding of collective action, there is considerably less consensus on how best to explain the decisions over tactics and strategy that social movements make, the extent to which decisions reflect individual or group preferences, or the importance that should be accorded to the micro and macro levels of analysis. The debates concerning these questions provide the main focus of our discussion, from contentious politics to actor-centered and interactionist approaches.

Repertoires of Contention

The dominant approach to the study of social movement tactics remains Tilly's "repertoires of contention." Tilly adopted the term to denote the "established ways in which pairs of actors make and receive claims bearing on each other's interests" (1993a: 265). In so doing, he emphasized the extent to which episodes of public claims-making are sets of interactions that constitute a public performance. Perhaps his primary insight was to identify how limited and regularly repeated these performances are. When social movements engage in public displays of worthiness, unity, numbers, and commitment (and for Tilly 2008, these displays *are* the social movement), they do so following scenarios, or approximate scenarios, whose staging is analogous to the performance of a piece of jazz, improvisational theatre, or dance. As Traugott (2010: 20) stresses, repertoires are structured around routines: though

The Wiley Blackwell Companion to Social Movements, Second Edition. Edited by David A. Snow, Sarah A. Soule, Hanspeter Kriesi, and Holly J. McCammon.
© 2019 John Wiley & Sons Ltd. Published 2019 by John Wiley & Sons Ltd.

formally unscripted, participants collaborate in a joint production, adopting stock roles and prescribed behaviors.

Tactical forms are therefore constrained, culturally saturated, relatively stable sets of potential ways of acting; the "repertoire" is the "set of performances available to any given actor within a regime" (Tilly 2003: 45). At the macro level, these forms reveal the wider structural patterns at play within a polity during a given period, underscoring the role that the "protest histories of individual populations" play within national political cultures (Imig and Tarrow 2001a: 5). At the micro level, collective actors choose tactical forms on the basis that they *already know how to perform them*. For Tarrow, the repertoire is "at once a structural and cultural concept, involving not only what people do when they are engaged in conflict with others but what they know how to do and what others expect them to do" (1998: 30). As such, they become routinized and institutionalized (Tilly 1978: 158). This codification process reduces uncertainty for participants and observers alike, enabling both mobilization and the communication of the significance of any given mobilization (Conell and Cohn 1995: 367).

As such, the repertoire is a historicized concept. Studying the development of repertoires in France (1986) and Great Britain (1993a, 1993b), Tilly identified a "hinge moment" between the late eighteenth and mid-nineteenth centuries. A series of profound social structural transformations (the industrial revolution, urbanization, the rapid expansion of state institutions, the nationalization of markets and of electoral politics) generated new social and political demands, expressed in new tactical forms: petitions, demonstrations, national associations, strikes, rallies, public meetings. These new tactics replaced localized and typically violent protest as the central forms of claims-making. Early modern protest was concentrated in a single local community, targeted offenders directly, and was characterized by detailed routines which varied greatly by issue and locality; that is, in Tarrow's (1998) analysis, it was *parochial*, *segmented*, and *particular*. In contrast, modern forms establish relationships between claimants and nationally significant centers of power, often refer to interests and issues spanning multiple localities, and are readily transferable from setting to setting; that is, they are *autonomous*, *cosmopolitan*, and *modular*.

Modularity

In this reading, protest tactics are produced by the organization of the modern state, which enables their rapid diffusion between and within similar polities. Modularity, of course, does not mean uniformity: tactics are open to adaptation as they move across political cultures (indeed, it is because of their adaptability that modular forms are so prevalent, though how they are adopted will depend on the local conditions of reception (Chabot and Duyvendak 2002; Wood 2012)). Once particular protest tactics become recognized parts of public life, they can be taken up by other movements in different ways, and with different aims: demonstrations, boycotts, petitions, and the like can all be used by a given movement, but also by its opponents in a counter-movement.

This capacity for "tactical travel" can in large measure be explained by the fact that tactics are not only historically conditioned, but are already interactively co-produced by social movements and public authorities: they do not therefore "belong" to any one group. Hayat (2006), in his reading of the development of the street demonstration in France, underlines that its evolution into a legitimate form of public claims-making in the late nineteenth and early twentieth centuries was the result of a double movement: on the one hand, the definition by the Republican regime and its coercive apparatus of acceptable forms of conduct; on the other, the emergence of social agents – unions, political parties – that could police and maintain the boundaries of permissible and prohibited conducts. This double movement also served to legitimize the role of leaders within these organizations, conferring on them the authority to represent and negotiate. In other words, the demonstration as an action form is produced by the intersection of strategic rationalities: of the regime, on the one hand, and social movements, on the other. While apparently in competition, these rationalities are in fact mutually constitutive, each recognizing and dependent upon the legitimacy and ordering power of the other.

Contentious politics

The birth of the social movement and its associated tactical forms thus presented a further epochal shift: from direct to indirect forms of action. In the "contentious politics" model (McAdam, Tilly, and Tarrow 2001; Tilly and Tarrow 2007), social movements are quintessentially organized around indirect tactical forms, designed to force public authorities to intervene. The modern state is therefore central to the contentious politics approach: precisely because it is the primary target of social representation, the state can channel protest toward forms it recognizes as legitimate. Major strategic decisions for social movements are most likely to be shaped by the political opportunities available to them, whether as a result of short-run variations in the configuration of power within a given polity (particularly in North American scholarship's conceptualization of political process theory, e.g. McAdam 1982), or of long-run institutional differences between states (particularly in comparative analysis and European scholarship, e.g. Kitschelt 1986; Kriesi et al. 1995).

The contentious politics approach thus holds that dominant forms of public claims-making develop in limited clusters, produced through and by the political and institutional arrangements of state power. As such, work on tactics in this vein has predominantly analysed repertoires at the aggregate level. Methodologically, though some studies aim to do this through qualitative interview data (e.g. Kriesi, Tresch, and Jochum 2007), most have been based upon large n data sets, drawn from general population questionnaires and surveys of political participation (Barnes et al. 1979; Caren, Ghoshal, and Ribas 2011; Dalton, van Sickle, and Weldon 2010; Painter-Main 2014), and surveys of NGOs and interest groups (Binderkrantz and Krøyer 2012; Dalton, Recchia, and Rohrschneider 2003), or via protest event analysis (PEA), whether drawn from activist media (Doherty, Plows, and Wall 2007; Wood 2004) or national mainstream media reports (Evans 2016; Imig and Tarrow 2001b; Johnson, Agnone, and McCarthy 2010; Kriesi et al. 1995; McAdam and Su 2002; Ratliff and Hall 2014; Ring-Ramirez, Reynolds-Stenson, and Earl 2014; Rootes 2003; Soule and Earl 2005; Walker, Martin, and McCarthy 2009).[1]

Tactics as Particular Events

This approach has a series of consequences for how we understand tactics as analytical constructs. Leaving aside potential problems of selection and description bias when using data derived from mainstream media reporting (Earl et al. 2004; Hutter 2014), large n comparative work inescapably involves a coding and aggregation process. Coding involves two operations: the prior definition of types of action (such as demonstrations, marches, blockades), refined during data collection as a result of experience; and the identification of events as particular instances of these categories. This process enables the development of external validity across cases, and thus comparative analysis (over time, across issues, between polities, between targets).

However, coding also inevitably reduces complex events to categories, and flattens the variety of actions that can occur even within familiar categories. It necessarily leaves out non-protest electoral and institutional tactics (della Porta et al. 2016; Goldstone 2003; Heaney and Rojas 2015; Kriesi et al. 2012; McAdam and Tarrow 2013). Most importantly, it cannot answer the question of how social movements make tactical choices, or imbue them with meanings. Of course, there are epistemological difficulties here: if we understand tactics to be intentional, the result of deliberate choices made by social movement actors (Taylor and Van Dyke 2004), it is often difficult to ascertain who makes choices and how; activists may be more interested in articulating narratives of self-justification or developing popular legitimacy than in giving accurate accounts of how decisions emerged, or why specific tactics were adopted, while post-hoc qualitative data collection may inevitably be influenced by problems of recall or attribution. Decisions by groups on how to act are collective and, in informal, non-bureaucratized (dis)organizations, it is often unclear who decided what and when. Yet if we are to develop understandings of protest tactics which have internal analytical validity, we need an ontology which focuses on how social actors enact, appropriate, and construct the meanings of their tactics. This inescapably involves the detailed study of particular interactions.

Tilly consistently stresses that tactics are the result of *inter*action: the repertoire does not belong to any one set of actors, but is produced through the encounter between different sets of actors. But this is a curious form of interaction, because – setting aside the archival descriptions of individual episodes of contention which punctuate and give life to his accounts – it is an interaction without particular actors, or rather where particular actors are analytically inconsequential in explaining the tactic. The repertoire is an aggregate construct, structurally produced through the relationships between historicized social forces. As such, the relationships between individual performances and specific interests and identities are (at best) of secondary importance (Tilly 1993a: 267–268); particular stagings of say, a demonstration, are of interest only in so far as they weigh upon the general rule. As Offerlé (2006) points out, there is a tension in this position: it is precisely because repertoires are produced in interaction that the development of legitimized tactical forms cannot be separated from the social agents that construct them (discursively and operationally), from the meanings that they ascribe to them, or from the attendant processes of delegitimization of alternative and competing action forms that accompany them. Crucially, "every performance is the object of multiple investments" (Offerlé 2008: 189). Thus, even though action forms may appear similar, the significations given to them, the understandings by actors of them, the public and political spaces occupied by them, may be highly divergent.

Claiming space

A tactic is not just a form, therefore. A given demonstration is not just one more example of a contentious gathering in a chain of contentious gatherings: each iteration enjoys a separate and specific symbolic power, drawn from its context, design, enactment, reception. A demonstration has symbolic power because it integrates the individual into the group, enacts collective forward movement through urban space (the onward march of history), and has obvious metonymic potential ("class unity," "social transformation," "revolution"). This generic power also opens up a given demonstration for all manner of conversions, diversions, and subversions: such as when groups stage die-ins or sit-ins, or break away to graffiti buildings, or assert alternative narratives and identities within an action (as when global justice protesters organized themselves into different colors according to political identity, strategy, and repertoire in protests against the IMF/World Banks summit in Prague in 2000; see Chesters and Welsh 2004). These are what Goffman (1981: 133–134) would call "subordinate communications": the actions and interactions that routinely pepper demonstrations and are seldom reported per se (save perhaps where they involve disorder, arrests, bodily violence, property destruction); and yet are central to the character and experience of the event. Equally, the symbolic power of a demonstration is specific to the particular conditions of its staging. It is not simply a display of unity, or a vehicle for carrying demands: it invests, appropriates, and configures urban space, drawing meanings from and applying new meanings to it.

This type of dynamic was apparent during the demonstration organized by climate justice networks for the final Saturday of the COP21 climate conference, in Paris in December 2015. This "red lines" action, undertaken by about 5000 activists, was co-produced by the state of emergency declared by the French government following terrorist attacks four weeks previously. Under these circumstances, a highly complex plan to carry out a mass civil disobedience action at Le Bourget airport (where the conference was being held) was effectively rendered impossible.[2]

Further, any action would be undertaken and received under a climate of tension, where gatherings of more than two people were considered a political mobilization and were banned, and where police had reacted repressively toward a peaceful demonstration two weeks previously. Plan B was to stage a demonstration on the west side of the Arc de Triomphe. In briefings the day before the action, activists were repeatedly advised to be non-violent, to avoid property destruction, to arrive in pairs, to memorize contact numbers of lawyers, and so on; those who did not respect the "consensus of action," would "no longer be part of the action." Only at the last minute did the authorities permit the demonstration; on the morning of the action, many activists we spoke to were still uncertain how the police would react, and were prepared for police violence. In the event, although riot police mobilized in large numbers in side streets, they did not intervene.

In such circumstances, the capacity of activists to "own" their choice of tactic is highly circumscribed. In a state of emergency, and lacking the resources to bargain with the authorities and the central organizational capacity to regulate action, organizers enjoyed little strategic power. Wahlström and de Moor (2017), indeed, note that the public authorities were able in two ways to forestall the ambitions of activists to stage a civilly disobedient direct action: by forcing them to abandon their initial Le Bourget plan, and by finally permitting the alternate action, rendering it formally non-disobedient.

Yet the relocation of the action into the "space of national sovereignty" (Tartakowsky 2010) around the Arc de Triomphe also enabled activists to occupy a space which lay, according to one of the French organizers, between the "expression of military power and the expression of the financial power of multinational corporations [at La Défense]." As a prominent British activist put it:

> The Arc de Triomphe is a monument to war and empire. La Défense is also an arch which represents war and empire, but this empire is the empire of corporate fossil fuels. We will create a red line between these two empires!

Organizers were in this way able to create a movement narrative of action, establishing it as a collective and counter-hegemonic appropriation of an ideologically determined space, that of military and corporate power. Moreover, the prohibition of the demonstration in the days preceding it enabled organizers to already define the action as "doing disobedience," and place it within a movement tradition of action, drawing on both shared ideological positions and shared understandings of how activists within climate justice networks *act*, "making red lines with our disobedient bodies." Claiming the protest as civil disobedience was important for participants, irrespective of whether it fitted the normative category of civil disobedience, because doing so was seen as appropriate to the type of action one takes as a climate justice activist.

An Actor-Centered Approach

In an actor-centered approach, the choice of tactics, and, crucially, how movements stage and pursue them, the roles they play in the development and expression of collective identity at the group level, the meanings they appropriate and give to them, must be accounted for with reference to movement ideas, cultures, and traditions (Doherty and Hayes 2012, 2014). In aggregate, tactical forms may appear similar, belonging to a single category of collective action. But for each particular action or set of actions, if they differ according to their precise circumstances, they also differ according to the way participants give rein to their creative instincts, not just through banners, placards, chants, and so on, but through their comportments, clothing, movements. Of course, in seeing all actions as displays of worthiness, unity, numbers, and commitment (WUNC), Tilly places the expressive qualities of action at the center of his analysis. But for Tilly, expression is defined by values: worthiness, unity, representativity, commitment. These values are transferable, are not the property of any one group, and are power-oriented; in other words, the expressive nature of action is recognized only in so far as it has instrumental value, despite the fact that the instrumental purpose of protest can sometimes be hard to discern.

Precisely because tactics are always negotiated through interaction, the relationship between actor and action must be central to our understanding of the contours and meanings of any particular event. As Jasper underlines, "Tactics are rarely, if ever, neutral means about which protestors do not care. Tactics represent important routines, emotionally and morally salient in these people's lives. Just as their ideologies do, their activities express protestors' political identities and moral visions" (1997: 237). Tactics are thus always expressive of identity claims (Rupp and Taylor 2003; Smithey 2009; Taylor and Van Dyke 2004). The analysis of protest events and repertoires uncovers the incidence and range of tactics that gain most public attention; but this focus needs to be complemented by analysis encompassing how claims-making incorporates and reveals the collective identities, emotions, and ideas of activists. This involves detailed attention to the conducts of activists, to the way they appropriate spaces, narrate actions, maintain subordinate communications, and express preferences.

Regime-challenging protests in Chile and Argentina provide an illustrative example. In Santiago, in December 1971, in *La Marcha de las cacerolas vacias*, 5000 women took to the streets, banging empty pots and pans in protest at the lack of basic foodstuffs. The March was a pivotal moment in the development of opposition to Salvador Allende's socialist regime, as the *cacerolas vacias* became an important symbol of failing economic governance. Thirty years later, in December 2001, as Argentina's President de la Rúa declared a state of emergency in the face of imminent economic collapse, the balconies of Buenos Aires similarly rang with the beating of pots and pans, to be followed by over 2000 further *cacerolazo* protests across the country by the end of March 2002 (Villalón 2007).

In both cases, the protests had a strong middle-class composition. But what is most striking about them is their gendered character. In Chile, the *cacerolas vacias* were a crucial way for women to express domestic grievances within the public spaces of street and politics, enabling them to "assert their autonomy from the political parties and even to articulate an incipient vision of feminist identity" (Baldez 2002: 82). In Argentina, *cacerolazos* spoke similarly to the gendering of the routines of daily life, and the divisions between public and private spheres. Eltantawy argues that the key aspect of these actions was performative, as the banging of pots and pans publicly displayed a militant motherhood, which worked precisely because it relied on traditional gender roles. These actions thus constituted a radical affirmation of women's access to public space:

> [They] allowed women to access the public sphere and shame policymakers for their suffering; they endowed women with a new identity – namely, a powerful, autonomous, and fearless identity – that enabled them to take over where the government fell short; and they also allowed women to experience the power of collective action.
>
> (Eltantawy 2008: 55)

Tactical continuity and innovation

Actor-centered approaches to tactics accordingly stress the social-psychological and ideological significance to collective actors of detail and nuance in tactical choice, emphasizing the importance of the precise contours of public conducts for the group's moral vision and its internal cohesion. Not only is tactical choice important to the group, but, equally, it is important to the individual activist, disposed to adopt behaviors they feel comfortable with. In Jasper's parlance, this is a question of "taste in tactics"; to explain tactical choice, "we must first explain the available repertory, the selection of tactics from within that repertory, and the subtle choices made in applying those tactics. All three are affected by internal movement culture as well as external constraints and opportunities" (Jasper 1997: 250).

Given the intimate relationship between tactical choice and collective identity (for a fuller discussion of collective identity, see Chapter 24 by Cristina Flesher Fominaya, in this volume), this approach accordingly stresses tactical consistency over the lifespan of a constituted group or defined collective. At the meso-level, it is not easy for groups to change their tactics, because they reflect moral commitments and shared histories; tactics are thus subject to a collective rationality, and are inherently stable at the group level. Thus where repertoire approaches explain consistency through structures of cultural availability – actors do what they already know how to do, from a pre-constituted and limited range of available of means – actor-centered approaches explain consistency through collective agency, as actors choose means which express, consolidate, and sustain their personal and collective identities and group reputations.

Actor-centered approaches therefore assume preferences for specific ways of acting to be an expression of identity, and a prior condition of group affiliation (Melucci 1989). The dynamic properties of this approach center on the capacity for agency that it ascribes to collective actors: tactical creativity is central to interaction, because collective actors are able to strategically "deploy" their identities in multiple forms in order to further their political goals (Bernstein 1997; Einwohner 2006). Tactical evolution is therefore possible despite the path dependency of initial choices; indeed, it is likely at the micro-level of action, as groups seek to modify and renegotiate the precise contours of their conduct, as a result of a normative valuing of creativity, an instrumental need to resist predictability, and a situational drive to flexibility. Tactical change thus takes place over the course of repeated encounters, with emphasis on the various abilities to harness collective agency, surprise one's opponent, and adopt contextual conducts, but to do so within an overall framework of moral or ideological consistency.

Of course, the capacity for innovation is also central to the repertoire model; but there are key differences. Repertoire theorizing pays little attention to the relationship between identity and change, privileging instead reflective learning based on "what works." McAdam, in his discussion of innovation in the US civil rights movement, argues that it proceeds by a "chesslike" process of mutual offsetting, such that actors consciously evaluate and adapt to each other's tactical developments (1983: 736). The emphasis is therefore on rational, instrumental thinking, rather than on expressivity and identity. Otherwise, the pace of innovation is usually slow, not least because performances involve other participants, who also learn what to expect. Although theorizing in this tradition therefore allows for the micro-level processes of choice and expression, its principal concern is with the wider structural patterns at play within regimes.

Long(er) histories

In the repertoire approach, new forms can emerge, evolve, and stabilize in times of crisis ("moments of madness"; Tarrow 1993), but major tactical transformations are epochal, as in the separation between pre-modern and modern action forms. This emphasis on epochal shifts privileges analysis of forms over meanings; it also privileges historical discontinuities, rather than connections across time. If the repertoire approach has had surprisingly little purchase among social historians, this may be because, as Navickas suggests, most have rejected the "quantifying approach … of 'repertoires of protest' that first unsatisfactorily separated types of action that may have been connected, and second implicitly denigrated 'pre-industrial' collective action as disorganized and unsophisticated" (2011: 197).

Borman's discussion of the boycott is intriguing in this respect. The boycott is a quintessentially "modern" repertoire form, taking its name from community resistance to an absentee landlord's agent in late nineteenth-century Ireland, where it marked "a decisive step in the development from rough, violent social intimidation to nonviolent but politically more effective [protest] practices" (te Velde 2005: 212), and correspondingly "a crucial step forwards in the efforts on the part of the state to monopolize the physical use of force" (Taatgen 1992: 167). Through multiple acts of diffusion, adoption, and adaptation (Chabot 2000; Mansour 2014), the boycott has since developed into a key practice in consumer and labor movement action (Balsiger 2010; Seidman 2007), and is closely associated with what McAdam and Sewell (2001) identify as the "master template" of modern tactics, as developed by the US civil rights movement (Morris 1984).

Rather than historicizing the boycott in terms of its particular forms, however, Borman places it within a "long social tradition of intolerance," alongside forms as ostensibly diverse as rough music, the general strike, and electronic denial-of-service attacks. What connects these tactics is that they aim to enforce the norms of a community's "moral economy": for Borman, "to boycott is to refuse passive acceptance of, or complicity with, parasitism" (2015: 14). Consequently, he argues, the key task for movements such as Occupy, and the global justice and environmental movements, is "to identify and regenerate the appropriate level of community on which their opponents depend, within which they are vulnerable, and to refuse to tolerate that dependence or parasitism" (ibid.: 15).

In this light, we can see *cacelorazos* in Latin America, the *búsáhaldabyltingin* which culminated in January 2009 in the resignation of the Icelandic government (Bernburg 2016), and the *manifs casseroles* of student protests against increased tuition fees in Quebec in 2011–2012 (Spiegel 2015) not simply as an epiphenomenal resurgence of pre-modern forms. Rather, they point to continuities, placing the expression of community identity at the heart of resistance to neo-liberalism, and appropriating and reclaiming privatized space as public space. Other tactical forms that emerged in Europe following the 2008/2009 economic crisis similarly challenge the division between private and public spheres of action. In Spain, activists carried out *escraches*, holding demonstrations outside the headquarters of the banks and the homes of the politicians held responsible for housing evictions (Romanos 2014; Flesher Fominaya 2015a); in France, workers threatened with factory closures forcibly detained company CEOs, HR directors, and plant managers for periods of up to 48 hours in a series of "bossnappings" (Hayes 2012). Beyond their distinct instrumental aims and cultural histories, these actions share common purpose and symbolism: the desire to confront the liquidity of capital with the bonds of social relations, forcing corporate and political decision-makers to participate in a counter-hegemonic public theatre (Hayes 2017).

Strategic Action

If strategy denotes longer-term thinking connecting action with overall goals, while tactics are the particular means chosen to advance them (Popovic 2015: 191–192; Rucht 1990: 161, 174 n5), how we understand each will depend on our interpretation of the scope for movement agency. North American scholars in particular have paid increasing attention to the concept of strategy in recent years, partly in response to disagreements about explanations of action that relied on structural categories. Early formulations of political opportunity were sometimes defined as structures (Tarrow 1994), and some defined the approach as structural because of the focus on state institutions to explain movement strategies (Kitschelt 1986; Kriesi et al. 1995). Culture can also be seen as structural when it is viewed as an external constraint on movements. Yet when both institutions and culture are used to explain movement strategies, little room is left for agency (Goodwin and Jasper 1999).

As a consequence, in recent years there has been more interest in relational approaches, focusing on strategic interaction between social movements and other actors, as in Fligstein and McAdam's account of *strategic action fields*. In their formulation, strategic action is "the attempt by social actors to create and maintain stable social worlds by securing the cooperation of others" (2011: 7), and is most often located in specific sub-fields (the religious field, the political field, and so on). Accordingly, interaction "is best analysed as an ongoing game where incumbents and challengers and members of political coalitions make moves and countermoves" (ibid.: 14).

The metaphor of players and games has also been used by critics of the structuralism of contentious politics. Rather than taking place in fields, which rely on rules that all players know, Jasper and collaborators locate *strategic interaction* within arenas. Unlike fields, and other abstract categories such as structures and institutions, arenas are real physical places, such as parliaments, courts, and marketplaces, where actual events can be observed (Jasper 2015: 17–18). At issue here is the relationship between reason and action: Jasper seeks to move explanations of strategy away from structural categories, which he sees as reducing the agency of activists, toward an approach that assumes that action is rational in the broadest sense, explicable by feelings as well as by cognitive reasoning about interests. Movements are diverse, and individuals carry multiple and sometimes incompatible goals. Accordingly, he argues for an empirical focus on studying what activists do, and the reasons they give for their actions – a perspective which accords with the fluidity of action and diversity of experience found in social movements (Duyvendak and Fillieule 2015: 303; Jasper 2015).

Consequently, analysis focuses on the processes by which groups decide what to do, which always involve dilemmas and trade-offs, and accepts that other players (the police, counter-movements, bureaucrats, editors, judges) also make their own choices, and are not simply the "structural context." This interest in understanding the motivations and reasons activists give for their actions separates Jasper's "cultural" approach from Tilly's, who argued that – given the impossibility of getting inside the heads of the subjects of study – it was better to focus on the observable relations of interaction between different groups (Mische and Tilly 2003).

Because structure and agency are at issue in these different approaches, it is perhaps inevitable that they are seen as overemphasizing one at the expense of the other.

For example, if we concentrate on identifying the dilemmas that actors face, we might be led to ask why the same dilemmas tend to recur systematically, if not because of structures. A second area of debate concerns whether game-based approaches can explain how strategy changes, without falling into the trap of privileging an instrumental logic based on winning. In game-based analysis, the focus is on explaining the rationality of the moves and interaction of various players, given the goals they seek (Goffman 1970); but missing from this approach is how movements might learn, and even gain some control over, the conditions of the game (Hay 2002: 133). For example, in contentious politics approaches, movements might gain access to the state, but are incorporated within it, rather than transforming it.

To move beyond the limits of strategy (understood as goal-oriented action) requires a different sense of what movement strategy is. An alternative way of viewing strategy sees movements as simultaneously engaged in interpreting and changing the social world through action, and makes reflexive learning about structures an element of strategic action. A central achievement of many social movements is to make us see the social and political world in a different way, to reveal as constructed what is considered "natural," such as in the way that LGBTQ activism challenges sexual and gender norms. If movements are searching for an understanding of the potentials and limits of social change in the worlds they live in, then "the investigation of the strategies and goals of movements are opportunities for insights into the nature of domination in contemporary societies" (Armstrong and Bernstein 2008: 82). Strategy is then understood as part of the process through which social movement actors define their world, including asymmetries of power and the potential means to change them.

Strategic action is thus not merely the action that takes place when collective actors plan protests, or choose tactics; it is also present in intuitive form, when their ways of doing things become routinized, as habits, repertoires, traditions. This intuitive aspect of strategic action also helps explain the apparently "spontaneous" decisions made in the heat of the moment by movement actors. For Snow and Moss (2014), even though they take place in compressed time, spontaneous actions are still decisions, often best explained by the combination of cultural priming, ambiguity about the script for an event, and lack of hierarchy within movements; Flesher Fominaya (2015b) argues that claims to spontaneity fulfill a narrative function in mobilization, conveying novelty and creativity, but often without acknowledging their debt to previous action forms. Even though they are intuitive, these ways of acting have developed because they are seen as appropriate conduct for shared aims, in shared contexts. This does not mean that they are not also open to change based on reflexive analysis.

This approach is implicit in some work on lifestyle movements, or movements that aim to make material interventions in everyday life struggles (de Moor 2016; Haenfler, Johnson, and Jones 2012). Lifestyle movements are not necessarily even social movements in the terms of contentious politics, if they do not engage in public campaigns; and even in more cultural approaches, they have been seen mainly as an abeyance between bigger public mobilizations (Taylor 1989) or as a base from which protest can be organized (Maeckelbergh 2011; Polletta 2002). But since the 1960s, many movements have experimented with less-hierarchical ways of living, and less-consumerist forms of consumption. While such practices have been acknowledged as part of the lifeworld of movements, as subcultures, or as expressive modes of action, they have not usually been seen as strategic (with the important exception of Melucci 1989). In his analysis of the movement practices of social centres in Barcelona in the early 2000s, Yates shows that they can be seen as pre-figurative actions, in the sense that they are experimental forms, which intervene materially in society, enable reflexive debate about their meaning, and communicate "messages of dissent, collective force and the existence of political alternatives" (2014: 12).

Analysis of strategic adaptation by left-libertarian movements in Sweden illustrates the process of reflexive learning (Jacobsson and Sörbom 2015). After riots at the June 2001 European Council meeting in Gothenburg, activists undertook a process of strategic adaptation (Koopmans 2005; McCammon 2012), away from confrontational mass protests and toward more concrete micro-projects. This was not simply a cyclical process following the tailing off of a major and polarizing series of protests, but a deliberate decision to change strategy. Activists saw the global justice movement as having provided greater coherence than the more single-issue politics of the 1980s and the 1990s, but importantly their move toward local, community-based material struggles was based on deliberation and debate within the activist community and an attempt to learn lessons from the past (in Italy, Zamponi and Daphi 2014 note a similar process). Analysis of this kind of reflexive learning process within movements is difficult, as it tends to rely on intensive observation and interview techniques that are costly and challenging. However, analysing movements from the "inside out" (Flesher Fominaya 2015a) is important because it takes the agency of movements as interpreters of social worlds seriously.

Conclusion

Protest is firmly entrenched as a familiar feature of political participation in liberal democracies and many semi-democratic states, while in recent decades it has been a vehicle for regime change in many authoritarian states (Chernoweth and Stephan 2011). Yet, in an age where protest seems to be ubiquitous, our understanding of the decisions that activists make about tactics and strategy remains underdeveloped and disputed. Given the centrality of these concepts to all major theories of social movements (Mueller 1999), it is perhaps unsurprising that there is still uncertainty about so many key questions.

In this chapter we have argued that the dominant model of explanation, repertoires of contention, has limitations. Its strength is in the quantitative aggregation of large numbers of events, demonstrating important changes in form over time. But this process of aggregation necessarily reduces events to instances of particular types, and takes us away from examining the meanings that actors invest in particular tactics. Decisions over tactics reflect not only collective identities and tastes in tactics, but also a strategic sense of how the social world works, which differs substantially in different movements, even within the same polity. In this sense, internal movement cultures and external macro-structures are linked through strategic analysis.

We have argued that qualitative analysis is essential to an adequate understanding of decision-making within movements. Qualitative studies are also necessary to unpicking the intuitive, or taken-for-granted, features of strategic action within movements and its outcomes; this is perhaps one of the reasons why case studies of particular events and campaigns remain prevalent in social movement research, though they bring with them the attendant problem of systematization across cases, and the difficulty of developing comparative analysis. The application of fuzzy-set methods to movement tactics is one potential response to this problem (Ragin and Sedziaka 2013). In making the case for qualitative analysis, we are not arguing that movements are expressive rather than instrumental: just as structure and agency are inseparable elements of explanation in social science, movements and their tactics cannot be reduced to the purely instrumental or purely expressive. Movements vary in the specificity of their goals, but even those most concentrated on campaigning for particular goals, such as changes in the law, also presuppose an understanding of what is legitimate and appropriate conduct that reflects ideological and moral positions.

This accumulates in movements as traditions and cultures that allow action to be taken in ways that are intuitive as well as explicitly planned. Thus areas for further study include the interrelations between goal-oriented decision-making and legitimated conduct, and more longitudinal analysis of strategic change on issues which spill over between movements, or across different movement generations, such as confrontation with opponents or pre-figurative institution-building. Finally, as this chapter also reflects, the study of protest tactics and strategies remains resolutely centered on the Global North, even while movements proliferate in the Global South: future analysis is likely to be much less Northern-dominated.

Notes

1 While PEA is conducted using various media sources, the *Dynamics of Collective Protest in the U.S. 1960–1995* dataset of protest events reported by the *New York Times* has been particularly influential. For a summary of and links to key activism datasets, see the Digital Activism Research Project, available at: http://digital-activism.org/resources/open-access-activism-data-sets/

2 These and subsequent data are derived from fieldnotes taken at activist briefings in Paris on Friday, December 11, 2015, at "Le 104" social center (English) and La Bourse du Travail (French).

References

Armstrong, Elizabeth A. and Mary Bernstein. 2008. "Culture, Power, and Institutions: A Multi-Institutional Politics Approach to Social Movements." *Sociological Theory* 26: 74–99.

Baldez, Lisa. 2002. *Why Women Protest: Women's Movements in Chile*. New York: Cambridge University Press.

Balsiger, Philip. 2010. "Making Political Consumers: The Tactical Action Repertoire of a Campaign for Clean Clothes." *Social Movement Studies* 9: 311–329.

Barnes, Samuel H., Max Kaase et al. 1979. *Political Action: Mass Participation in Five Western Democracies*. Beverly Hills, CA: Sage.

Bernburg, Jón Gunnar. 2016. *Economic Crisis and Mass Protest: The Pots and Pans Revolution in Iceland*. London: Routledge.

Bernstein, Mary. 1997. "Celebration and Suppression: The Strategic Uses of Identity by the Lesbian and Gay Movement." *American Journal of Sociology* 103: 531–565.

Binderkrantz, Anne Skorkjær, and Simon Krøyer. 2012. "Customizing Strategy: Policy Goals and Interest Group Strategies." *Interest Groups & Advocacy* 1: 115–138.

Borman, David A. 2015. "Protest, Parasitism, and Community: Reflections on the Boycott." *Social Philosophy Today* 31: 7–22.

Caren, Neal, Ghoshal, Raj Andrew, and Vanesa Ribas. 2011. "A Social Movement Generation: Cohort and Period Trends in Protest Attendance and Petition Signing." *American Sociological Review* 76: 125–151.

Chabot, Sean 2000. "Transnational Diffusion and the African American Reinvention of Gandhian Repertoire." *Mobilization* 5: 201–216.

Chabot, Sean and Jan Willem Duyvendak. 2002. "Globalization and Transnational Diffusion between Social Movements: Reconceptualizing the Dissemination of the Gandhian Repertoire and the 'Coming Out' Routine." *Theory and Society* 31: 697–740.

Chernoweth, Erica and Maria Stephan. 2011. *Why Civil Resistance Works: The Strategic Logic of Nonviolent Conflict*. New York: Columbia University Press.

Chesters, Graeme and Ian Welsh. 2004. "Rebel Colours: 'Framing' in Global Social Movements." *The Sociological Review* 52: 314–335.

Conell, Carol and Samuel Cohn. 1995. "Learning from Other People's Actions: Environmental Variation and Diffusion in French Coal Mining Strikes, 1890–1935." *American Journal of Sociology* 101: 366–403.

Dalton, Russell J., Steve Recchia, and Robert Rohrschneider. 2003. "The Environmental Movement and the Modes of Political Action." *Comparative Political Studies* 36: 743–771.

Dalton, Russell, Alex van Sickle, and Steven Weldon. 2010. "The Individual–Institutional Nexus of Protest Behaviour." *British Journal of Political Science* 40: 51–73.

della Porta Donatella, Joseba Fernández, Hara Kouki, and Lorenzo Mosca. 2016. *Movement Parties Against Austerity*. Cambridge: Polity.

de Moor, Joost. 2016. "Lifestyle Politics and the Concept of Political Participation." *Acta Politica*. doi:10.1057/ap.2015.27.

Doherty, Brian and Graeme Hayes. 2012. "Tactics, Traditions, and Opportunities: British and French Crop-Trashing Actions in Comparative Perspective." *European Journal of Political Research* 51: 540–562.

Doherty, Brian and Graeme Hayes. 2014. "Having Your Day in Court: Judicial Opportunity and Tactical Choice in Anti-GMO Campaigns in France and the United Kingdom." *Comparative Political Studies* 47: 3–29.

Doherty, Brian, Alex Plows, and David Wall. 2007. "Environmental Direct Action in Manchester, Oxford and North Wales: A Protest Event Analysis." *Environmental Politics* 16: 805–825.

Duyvendak, Jan Willem and Olivier Fillieule. 2015. "Patterned Fluidity: An Interactionist Perspective as a Tool for Exploring Contentious Politics." In *Players and Arenas: The Interactive Dynamics of Protest*, edited by James M. Jasper and Jan W. Duyvendak, 295–318. Amsterdam: Amsterdam University Press.

Earl, Jennifer, Andrew W. Martin, John D. McCarthy, and Sarah A. Soule. 2004. "The Use of Newspaper Data in the Study of Collective Action." *Annual Review of Sociology* 30: 65–80.

Einwohner, Rachel L. 2006. "Identity Work and Collective Action in a Repressive Context: Jewish Resistance on the 'Aryan Side' of the Warsaw Ghetto." *Social Problems* 53: 38–56.

Eltantawy, Nahed. 2008. "Pots, Pans, & Protests: Women's Strategies for Resisting Globalization in Argentina." *Communication and Critical/Cultural Studies* 5: 46–63.

Evans, Erin M. 2016. "Bearing Witness: How Controversial Organizations Get the Media Coverage They Want." *Social Movement Studies* 15: 41–59.

Flesher Fominaya, Cristina. 2015a. "Redefining the Crisis/Redefining Democracy: Mobilising for the Right to Housing in Spain's PAH Movement." *South European Society and Politics* 20: 465–485.

Flesher Fominaya, Cristina. 2015b. "Debunking Spontaneity: Spain's 15-M/Indignados as Autonomous Movement." *Social Movement Studies* 14: 142–163.

Fligstein, Neil and Doug McAdam. 2011. "Toward a General Theory of Strategic Action Fields." *Sociological Theory* 29: 1–26.

Goffman, Erving. 1970. *Strategic Interaction*. Oxford: Basil Blackwell.

Goffman, Erving. 1981. *Forms of Talk*. Oxford: Basil Blackwell.

Goldstone, Jack A., ed. 2003. *States, Parties, and Social Movements*. Cambridge: Cambridge University Press.

Goodwin, Jeff and James M. Jasper. 1999. "Caught in a Winding, Snarling Vine: The Structural Bias of Political Process Theory." *Sociological Forum* 14: 27–54.

Haenfler, Ross, Brett Johnson, and Ellis Jones. 2012. "Lifestyle Movements: Exploring the Intersection of Lifestyle and Social Movements." *Social Movement Studies* 11: 1–20.

Hay, Colin. 2002. *Political Analysis*. Basingstoke: Palgrave.

Hayat, Samuel. 2006. "La République, la rue et l'urne." *Pouvoirs* 116: 31–44.

Hayes, Graeme. 2012. "Bossnapping: Situating Repertoires of Industrial Action in National and Global Contexts." *Modern & Contemporary France*, 20: 185–201.

Hayes, Graeme. 2017. "Regimes of Austerity." *Social Movement Studies*, 16: 21–35.

Heaney, Michael T. and Fabio Rojas. 2015. *Party in the Street: The Antiwar Movement and the Democratic Party after 9/11*. Cambridge: Cambridge University Press.

Hutter, Swen. 2014. "Protest Event Analysis and its Offspring." In *Methodological Practices in Social Movement Research*, edited by Donatella della Porta, 335–367. Oxford: Oxford University Press.

Imig, Doug and Sidney Tarrow. 2001a. "Studying Contention in an Emerging Polity." In *Contentious Europeans: Protest and Politics in an Emerging Polity*, edited by Doug Imig and Sidney Tarrow, 3–26. Oxford: Rowman & Littlefield.

Imig, Doug and Sidney Tarrow. 2001b. "Mapping the Europeanization of Contention: Evidence from Quantitative Data Analysis." In *Contentious Europeans: Protest and Politics in an Emerging Polity*, edited by Doug Imig and Sidney Tarrow, 27–49. Oxford: Rowman & Littlefield.

Jacobsson, Kerstin and Adrienne Sörbom. 2015. "After a Cycle of Contention: Post-Gothenburg Strategies of Left-Libertarian Activists in Sweden." *Social Movement Studies* 14: 713–732.

Jasper, James M. 1997. *The Art of Moral Protest: Culture, Biography, and Creativity in Social Movements*. Chicago: University of Chicago Press.

Jasper, James M. 2015. "Playing the Game." In *Players and Arenas: The Interactive Dynamics of Protest*, edited by James M. Jasper and Jan Willem Duyvendak, 9–32. Amsterdam: Amsterdam University Press.

Johnson, Erik W., Jon Agnone, and John D. McCarthy. 2010. "Movement Organizations, Synergistic Tactics and Environmental Public Policy." *Social Forces* 88: 2267–2292.

Kitschelt, Herbert P. 1986. "Political Opportunity Structures and Political Protest: Anti-Nuclear Movements in Four Democracies." *British Journal of Political Science* 16: 57–85.

Koopmans, Ruud. 2005. "The Missing Link Between Structure and Agency: Outline of an Evolutionary Approach to Social Movements." *Mobilization* 10: 19–33.

Kriesi, Hanspeter, Edgar Grande, Martin Dolezal, et al. 2012. *Political Conflict in Western Europe*. Cambridge: Cambridge University Press.

Kriesi, Hanspeter, Ruud Koopmans, Jan Willem Duyvendak, and Marco Giugni. 1995. *New Social Movements in Western Europe: A Comparative Analysis*. London: UCL Press.

Kriesi, Hanspeter, Anke Tresch, and Margit Jochum. 2007. "Going Public in the European Union." *Comparative Political Studies* 40: 48–73.

Maeckelbergh, Marianne. 2011. "Doing is Believing: Prefiguration as Strategic Practice in the Alterglobalization Movement." *Social Movement Studies* 10: 1–20.

Mansour, Claire. 2014. "The Cross-National Diffusion of the American Civil Rights Movement: The Example of the Bristol Bus Boycott of 1963." *Miranda* 10.

McAdam, Doug. 1982. *Political Process and the Development of Black Insurgency, 1930–1970*. Chicago: University of Chicago Press.

McAdam, Doug. 1983. "Tactical Innovation and the Pace of Insurgency." *American Sociological Review* 48: 735–754.

McAdam, Doug and William Sewell Jr. 2001. "It's About Time: Temporality in the Study of Social Movements and Revolutions." In *Silence and Voice in the Study of Contentious Politics*, edited by Ron Aminzade, Jack A. Goldstone, Doug McAdam, et al., 89–125. Cambridge: Cambridge University Press.

McAdam, Doug and Yang Su. 2002. "The War at Home: Antiwar Protests and Congressional Voting, 1965 to 1973." *American Sociological Review* 67: 696–721.

McAdam, Doug and Sidney Tarrow. 2013. "Social Movements and Elections: Toward a Broader Understanding of the Political Context of Contention." In *The Future of Social Movement Research: Dynamics, Mechanisms, and Processes*, edited by Jacquelien Van Stekelenburg, Conny Roggeband, and Bert Klandermans, 325–346. Minneapolis: University of Minnesota Press.

McAdam, Doug, Charles Tilly, and Sidney Tarrow. 2001. *Dynamics of Contention*. Cambridge: Cambridge University Press.

McCammon, Holly J. 2012. *The U.S. Women's Jury Movements and Strategic Adaptation: A More Just Verdict*. Cambridge: Cambridge University Press.

Melucci, Alberto. 1989. *Nomads of the Present: Social Movements and Individual Needs in Contemporary Society*. London: Hutchinson.

Mische, Anne and Charles Tilly. 2003. "Conversation with Charles Tilly about His Recently Published Book, *Dynamics of Contention*." *Social Movement Studies* 2: 85–96.

Morris, Aldon D. 1984. *The Origins of the Civil Rights Movement: Black Communities Organizing for Change*. New York: The Free Press.

Mueller, Carol. 1999. "Escape from the GDR, 1961–1989: Hybrid Exit Repertoires in a Disintegrating Leninist Regime." *American Journal of Sociology* 105: 697–735.

Navickas, Katrina. 2011. "What Happened to Class? New Histories of Labour and Collective Action in Britain." *Social History* 36: 192–204.

Offerlé, Michel. 2006. "Périmètres du politique et coproduction de la radicalité à la fin du XIXe siècle." In *La démocratie aux extrêmes. Sur la radicalisation politique*, edited by Annie Collovald and Brigitte Gaïti, 247–268. Paris: La Dispute.

Offerlé, Michel. 2008. "Retour critique sur les répertoires de l'action collective (XVIIIe–XXIe siècles)." *Politix* 81: 181–202.

Painter-Main, Michael A. 2014. "Repertoire-Building or Elite-Challenging? Understanding Political Engagement in Canada." In *Canadian Democracy from the Ground Up:*

Perceptions and Performance, edited by Elisabeth Gidengil and Heather Bastedo, 62–82. Vancouver: University of British Columbia Press.

Polletta, Francesca. 2002. *Freedom Is an Endless Meeting: Democracy in American Social Movements*. Chicago: University of Chicago Press.

Popovic, Srdja. 2015. *Blueprint for Revolution: How to Use Rice Pudding, Lego Men, and Other Non-Violent Techniques to Galvanise Communities, Overthrow Dictators, or Simply Change the World*. London: Scribe.

Ragin, Charles C. and Alesia Alexandrovna Sedziaka. 2013. "QCA and Fuzzy Set Applications to Social Movement Research." In *The Wiley-Blackwell Encyclopedia of Social and Political Movements*, edited by David A. Snow, Donatella della Porta, Bert Klandermans, and Doug McAdam. Oxford: Wiley-Blackwell.

Ratliff, Thomas N. and Lori L. Hall. 2014. "Practicing the Art of Dissent: Toward a Typology of Protest Activity in the United States." *Humanity & Society* 38: 268–294.

Ring-Ramirez, Misty, Heidi Reynolds-Stenson, and Jennifer Earl. 2014. "Culturally Constrained Contention: Mapping the Meaning Structure of the Repertoire of Contention." *Mobilization* 19: 405–419.

Romanos, Eduardo. 2014. "Evictions, Petitions and *Escraches*: Contentious Housing in Austerity Spain." *Social Movement Studies* 13: 296–302.

Rootes, Christopher, ed. 2003. *Environmental Protest in Western Europe*. Oxford: Oxford University Press.

Rucht, Dieter. 1990. "The Strategies and Action Repertoires of New Movements." In *Challenging the Political Order: New Social and Political Movements in Western Democracies*, edited by Russell J. Dalton and Manfred Kuechler, 156–175. Cambridge: Polity.

Rupp, Leila J. and Verta Taylor. 2003. *Drag Queens at the 801 Cabaret*. Chicago: University of Chicago Press.

Seidman, Gay W. 2007. *Beyond the Boycott: Labor Rights, Human Rights, and Transnational Activism*. New York: Russell Sage Foundation.

Smithey, Lee A. 2009. "Social Movement Strategy, Tactics, and Collective Identity." *Sociology Compass* 3: 658–671.

Snow, David A. and Dana M. Moss. 2014 "Protest on the Fly: Toward a Theory of Spontaneity in the Dynamics of Protest and Social Movement." *American Sociological Review* 79: 1122–1143.

Soule, Sarah A. and Jennifer Earl. 2005. "A Movement Society Evaluated: Collective Protest in the United States, 1960–1986." *Mobilization* 10: 345–364.

Spiegel, Jennifer B. 2015. "*Rêve Général Illimité*? The Role of Creative Protest in Transforming the Dynamics of Space and Time during the 2012 Quebec Student Strike." *Antipode* 47: 770–791.

Taatgen, H. A. 1992. "The Boycott in the Irish Civilizing Process." *Anthropological Quarterly* 65: 163–176.

Tarrow, Sidney. 1993. "Cycles of Collective Action: Between Moments of Madness and the Repertoire of Contention." *Social Science History* 17: 281–307.

Tarrow, Sidney. 1994. *Power in Movement: Social Movements, Collective Action and Politics*. Cambridge: Cambridge University Press.

Tarrow, Sidney. 1998. *Power in Movement: Social Movements and Contentious Politics*, 2nd edn. Cambridge: Cambridge University Press.

Tartakowsky, Danielle. 2010. *Manifester à Paris 1880–2010*. Seyssel: Champ Vallon.

Taylor, Verta. 1989. "Social Movement Continuity: The Women's Movement in Abeyance." *American Sociological Review* 54: 761–775.

Taylor, Verta and Nella Van Dyke. 2004. "'Get Up, Stand Up': Tactical Repertoires of Social Movements." In *The Blackwell Companion to Social Movements*, edited by David A. Snow, Sarah A. Soule, and Hanspeter Kriesi, 262–293. Malden, MA: Blackwell.

te Velde, Henk. 2005. "Political Transfer: An Introduction." *European Review of History/ Revue européenne d'histoire* 12: 205–221.

Tilly, Charles. 1978. *From Mobilization to Revolution*. Reading, MA: Addison-Wesley.

Tilly, Charles. 1986. *The Contentious French*. Cambridge, MA: Harvard University Press.

Tilly, Charles. 1993a. "Contentious Repertoires in Great Britain, 1758–1834." *Social Science History* 17: 253–280.

Tilly, Charles. 1993b. "Social Movements as Historically Specific Clusters of Political Performances." *Berkeley Journal of Sociology* 38: 1–30.

Tilly, Charles. 2003. *The Politics of Collective Violence*. Cambridge: Cambridge University Press.

Tilly, Charles. 2008. *Contentious Performances*. Cambridge: Cambridge University Press.

Tilly, Charles and Sidney Tarrow. 2007. *Contentious Politics*. New York: Paradigm.

Traugott, Mark. 2010. *The Insurgent Barricade*. Berkeley: University of California Press.

Villalón, Roberta. 2007. "Neoliberalism, Corruption, and Legacies of Contention: Argentina's Social Movements, 1993–2006." *Latin American Perspectives* 34: 139–156.

Wahlström, Mattias and Joost de Moor. 2017. "Governing Dissent in a State of Emergency: Police and Protester Interactions in the Global Space of the COP." In *Climate Action in a Globalizing World: Comparative Perspectives on Social Movements in the Global North*, edited by Carl Cassegård, Linda Soneryd, Hakan Thörn, and Åsa Wettergren. London: Routledge.

Walker, Edward T., Andrew W. Martin, and John D. McCarthy. 2009. "Confronting the State, the Corporation, and the Academy: The Influence of Institutional Targets on Social Movement Repertoires." *American Journal of Sociology* 114: 35–76.

Wood, Lesley J. 2004. "Breaking the Bank and Taking to the Streets: How Protesters Target Neoliberalism." *Journal of World Systems Research* 10: 69–89.

Wood, Lesley J. 2012. *Direct Action, Deliberation, and Diffusion*. Cambridge: Cambridge University Press.

Yates, Luke. 2014. "Rethinking Prefiguration: Alternatives, Micropolitics and Goals in Social Movements." *Social Movement Studies* 14: 1–21.

Zamponi, Lorenzo and Priska Daphi. 2014. "Breaks and Continuities in and Between Cycles of Protest: Memories and Legacies of the Global Justice Movement in the Context of Anti-Austerity Mobilizations." In *Spreading Protest: Social Movements in Times of Crisis*, edited by Donatella della Porta and Alice Mattoni, 193–226. Colchester: ECPR Press.

16

Technology and Social Media

Jennifer Earl

Introduction

Although the origins of the Internet date back to the 1960s and the basic elements of the Web were put in place around 1990, Internet use by the wider US public did not take off until the turn of the century. Indeed, PEW polling suggests that August 2000 was the month in which 50% of Americans were going online and 50% were not (PEW Internet & American Life Project 2016). It is not surprising, then, that there was only a little research published on digital technologies and social movements before the turn of the century. Over the last decade and half, though, this area of research has mushroomed, moving from a specialty niche to a major issue that is incrementally becoming integrated into contemporary social movement research. This review introduces readers to the historical growth of the field and contemporary research findings. It begins by tracing the initial skepticism expressed about information communication technologies (ICTs) and disciplinary trajectories in the study of digital media and social movements. It continues by reviewing early and then current contributions to the field as well as debates that are increasingly important to the continuing study of digital media and social movements. The argument across this review is that social movement scholars, whether generally concerned with ICTs or not, should begin to consider the relationship between ICTs and their research topics, if doing contemporary research, and that research would benefit from the broad, extant literature on ICTs and social and political life, that already exists.

The Wiley Blackwell Companion to Social Movements, Second Edition. Edited by David A. Snow, Sarah A. Soule, Hanspeter Kriesi, and Holly J. McCammon.
© 2019 John Wiley & Sons Ltd. Published 2019 by John Wiley & Sons Ltd.

It's Here, It's Digital, Get Used to It

As research and public discussion about Internet activism began to rise around the turn of the century, a wider debate over whether ICTs (e.g. the Internet) could support meaningful social connections or were socially isolating was brewing (Hampton, Sessions, and Her 2011; Nie and Erbring 2000). Although there were certainly some utopian predictions about the importance of ICTs to democratic expression (Rheingold 1993; Shirky 2008), initial scholarship by many senior social movement scholars was skeptical of the likely impact of Internet usage on activism. Researchers argued that since the Internet was presumed to be unable to sustain strong social ties, or facilitate the development of new ties, which these scholars saw as essential to micro-mobilization, Internet usage would have little impact (Diani 2000; Tarrow 1998). While subsequent research has largely borne out the social capital-enhancing qualities of ICT usage (Rainie and Wellman 2012) and shown that ICT usage can help movements emerge and mobilize, this early skepticism was nonetheless deep.

As ICTs became more ubiquitous, skepticism among social movement scholars grew. For instance, would the digital divide limit access to the Internet to the most well-off, such that online movements would increasingly be composed of, and attentive to, the interests of the most privileged activists (Tilly 2004)? Alternatively, others argued that the utility of ICTs to protesters was outweighed by the surveillance capacity it provided states (Morozov 2011a, 2011b). Current research has subsequently called both concerns into question. As discussed further below, research on micro-mobilization shows no continuing notable impacts of the digital divide on protest engagement in the USA (although this may be different around the world; Elliott and Earl 2018; Lee, Chen, and Huang 2014; Stalker and Wood 2013). Instead, it is possible that ICTs are compensatory technologies that help otherwise more marginalized individuals gain voice and national attention (Cohen et al. 2012; Enjolras, Steen-Johnsen, and Wollebæk 2013). Likewise, although it is clear that ICTs can be used to surveil and repress protest, repression does not always deter future protest participation and sometimes even increases subsequent engagement (Earl and Beyer 2014; Zuckerman 2008).

The Arab Spring changed what scholars were skeptical about once more. The Arab Spring spotlighted the importance of ICTs to mobilization (Tufekci and Wilson 2012) and the diffusion of protest (Castells 2012), among other topics (Howard and Hussain 2013). As such, it became difficult for even the most critical of social movement scholars to entirely dismiss the likely continuing relevance and importance of ICTs to protest and social movements, even if there were still debates over how ICT usage affected the Arab Spring exactly (Wolfsfeld, Segev, and Sheafer 2013).

After the Arab Spring, skepticism shifted to concerns about the efficacy of online activism (sometimes dubbed "slacktivism"). While social movement consequences are discussed at greater length later, it is worth noting that like other earlier criticisms, this concern not only may be empirically problematic but it also reduces the importance of ICTs to questions of tactical alternatives and their effectiveness. However, it is arguable that ICTs have potential impacts on the entire life-cycle of a social movement and potential impacts on individual participants from recruitment to sustaining engagement, making such a reduction problematic. In sum, a number of social movement scholars have surfaced skepticism about the role and importance of ICTs to protest, but world events and data have continued to challenge each reservation in turn.

Disciplinary Differences in Studying Digital Technologies and Protest

While researchers who self-identify as social movement scholars have been slow, and often only skeptically attentive to ICTs, scholars in other fields, particularly communication and the interdisciplinary field of political communication, have been eagerly studying digital protest for some time. It is important to note that since many social movement scholars are trained as sociologists, reluctance to broadly study new media and its effects is not literature-specific but rather reflects a disciplinary difference in interest in questions about media and media effects that is more than 50 years old (Earl 2015). Sociologists in general, including social movement scholars (with notable exceptions in both areas, of course; see, for example, Chapter 7 by Rohlinger and Corrigall-Brown, in this volume), have simply been slower and less aggressive as a field than communication and other allied interdisciplinary fields in examining the relationship between ICTs and social life.

Over time, this difference in the perceived importance or centrality of research on ICTs and activism has resulted in a dramatically different publishing environment between self-identified social movements journals and leading interdisciplinary and communication journals. To demonstrate this difference, my research team looked at publications from 2010–2015 in the three major social movement journals and three interdisciplinary journals that are popular in communication and the interdisciplinary Internet studies fields (see Table 16.1 for journal titles), counting the total number of articles (i.e. book reviews are excluded) and the number of articles that dealt with digital media and social movements (this was broadly construed such that articles, for instance, about the Internet and elections that also discussed social movements would be counted in the affirmative). While not meant to be an exhaustive analysis, the results, presented in Table 16.1, clearly show that communication and interdisciplinary Internet studies journals publish far more articles on ICTs and social movements. Each of the three social movement journals published eight relevant articles across the 2010–2015 period, which made up between 5–10% of all their articles in the period, depending on the journal. By contrast, *Information, Communication & Society* (iCS, as it is known) published 59 articles on ICTs and social movements in the same period, representing 15% of the total articles published in that journal. *Policy & Internet* alone published 21 relevant articles in this period, which means it published only three fewer articles on its own than all three social movement journals published together on the topic!

Put in coarse terms, this publishing trajectory should give social movement scholars pause. Communication and allied interdisciplinary areas such as political communication and Internet studies are publishing on this topic at a breakneck pace because this research is seen as imminently important in those fields and is not met with the same kind of skepticism that has dogged research on ICTs within social movement studies. If these publishing trends continue, it would be reasonable for scholars in those fields to claim in 5–10 years that they have a better collective

Table 16.1   Percentage of articles on ICTs and protest in leading journals

Journal title	2010 (%)	2011 (%)	2012 (%)	2013 (%)	2014 (%)	2015 (%)	Total n	Total (%)
Research in Social Movements, Conflicts, and Change	6	11	19	12	10	0	8	10
Mobilization	9	4	0	9	5	8	8	6
Social Movement Studies	0	6	6	5	12	4	8	5
Policy & Internet	15	22	9	32	12	9	21	17
Information, Communication, & Society	21	15	16	9	13	15	59	15
Journal of Information Technology & Politics	0	17	4	11	17	10	14	10

understanding of this aspect of contemporary social movements than the self-identified field of social movement scholarship. This situation represents both a professional opportunity and a danger for social movement studies as a field.

What communication and other fields may have to offer

I argue there are at least three advantages to taking scholarship on digital protest from other areas seriously. First, communication and allied fields have established track records for thinking about how different ICTs impact social interactions and social life that social movement scholars can draw upon. That cross-fertilization can help prevent more sociologically-trained social movement scholars from repeating well-known "mistakes" from other fields. For instance, it is not uncommon to read sociological or social movement arguments that suggest the Internet did X or was responsible for Y. In communication or Internet studies, such an argument would be viewed as unacceptable because it is technologically deterministic in that it argues that a technology inherently leads to some outcome. Virtually all contemporary research on ICTs would argue that it is how technologies are used (since how they are used varies and can vary from their intended or expected uses) or the different context for action that pervasive technology use and/or ICT availability creates that matters in terms of creating social impacts, not the inherent existence of the technology itself.

This is not to suggest that the materiality of ICTs is ignored. One common way of acknowledging both uses and features of a technology is to discuss the "technological affordances" that are leveraged or ignored by users. For example, Earl and Kimport's (2011) discussion of online activism centers on the social implications of uses that leverage two key affordances of the Internet: (1) the ability to radically reduce coordination and action costs; and (2) the ability to act together without physically being together. Broader awareness of the risk of technological determinism, and common concepts such as affordances, would advance social movements theorizing and research on ICTs and protest.

A second key opportunity exists in what social movement scholars might learn from the interdisciplinary field of political communication, which is interested in how media, including ICTs and new media, are used politically. Earl and Garrett

(2017) outline, for instance, the opportunities that exist for social movement scholars who draw on political communication research to better understand social movement audiences and the reception of social movement communications. They note traps that social movement scholarship can fall into by not considering this research, such as assuming that newspapers have a larger audience share than they actually do, or assuming that radicalizing language is equally mobilizing for current adherents as opposed to potential adherents. They also discuss new questions about audience reception and the contextual effects of information reception that could be important to social movement scholarship.

Finally, attention to the broader literature on ICTs and social life could powerfully inform social movement research related to ICTs. This broader literature investigates many of the concerns that social movement scholars have had about ICTs: Do ICTs lead to social isolation or support and/or expand social capital? Does activity online substitute for offline behavior? To what extent and in what ways do digital divides impact social behavior and opportunities? In many of these cases, the results of research on ICTs and social life broadly contradict assumptions that social movement scholars carry around about these topics. Sustained connection with this broader literature would certainly improve social movement research involving ICT usage.

Potential downsides of differential attention to ICTs and activism across fields

While I have noted three ways that social movement scholarship could be improved, there is also a real professional danger in ignoring or treating scholarship connected to ICTs as a research niche. Put bluntly, social movement studies becomes better and better at understanding important historical periods such as the 1960s and 1970s every day. Our historical understanding of protest is commendable and constantly improving. While this is critical, so too is ensuring the field's relevance to understanding contemporary protest. If most of the research on ICTs and social movements is being published outside of social movement journals and it is not central to how social movement scholars understand our field, who will policy-makers, the media, and other researchers rely on to understand online activism in 10 years?

From Exotic to Mainstream: Major Findings

My goal thus far has been to highlight the skepticism that research on the intersection of ICTs and protest has faced within, but not outside of, social movement studies. I now turn to what research has been done, without respect to disciplinary area. Given that several literature reviews of this topic already exist (e.g. Earl, Hunt, and Garrett 2014; Earl et al. 2015; Garrett 2006), my focus is on larger animating questions, recent theoretical trends, and contemporary research debates.

I argue that over time, research is slowly shifting from casting ICT usage by social movements as exotic to routine; this shift has been accompanied by changes in the larger animating debates, which have moved from being about larger theoretical shifts to more specific questions about the impacts of ICTs on specific social movements' processes. In many ways, this mirrors the general development of the field of social movement studies. Social movement studies, as we know it today, was formed around contention over broad theoretical paradigms to explain movement emergence that moved from collective behavior and grievance-based models to models such as resource mobilization, political process, and framing. Having developed general explanations, the majority of contemporary research has since shifted to more specific questions, such as the factors that drive micro-mobilization, and the causes and consequences of repression. Likewise, scholarship on ICTs has shifted from major animating debates to more focused specialty questions.

Initial major debates over ICTs and social movements

Scholars in the early 2000s who considered digital protest to be important argued for potential large-scale changes in social movement processes (Earl and Schussman 2003), involving new forms of activity (Vegh 2003), the migration of classic forms of activism into an online environment (Earl 2006), changes to the internal infrastructure of movements (Benkler 2006; Shirky 2008), and the development of entirely new movements around information freedom and access (Eschenfelder and Desai 2004; Eschenfelder, Howard, and Desai 2005; Postigo 2012).

Earl and Kimport (2011) crystalized the issues at stake in this debate, arguing that a central animating question in this area was whether existing social movement theory was prepared to explain the use and consequences of digital media for social movements, activism, and protest. They suggested that three schools existed: (1) senior skeptics, introduced above, populated one school and argued that ICT usage would not lead to lasting changes in social movement processes; (2) another school, which Earl and Kimport refer to as the "scale change" school, argued that existing theory could be adapted to account for unique issues that might arise from ICT usage (e.g. Peckham 1998); and (3) a final school argued that fundamental assumptions of current social movement theorizing could be up-ended by innovative uses of ICTs, requiring some elements of explanations that had been historically constant to be treated as variables. Scholars from this last camp argued that the impact of new-found variability needed to be traced through causal processes. For instance, Earl and Kimport (2011) argue that protest has been historically costly but that ICT usage could dramatically reduce the costliness of some forms of protest for both organizers and participants. Their book traces the theoretical and empirical consequences of these radically lower costs, as well as the consequences of using technologies to allow people to act together without being physically together. They claim that basic social movement processes operate differently in this context and they outlined many of these differences.

Earl et al. (2010) furthered this argument, showing that these three camps tended to study very different kinds of activism. The first camp was primarily focused on long-term and high-risk activism. The second camp tended to focus on how ICTs could be used to mobilize individuals to attend offline events. The third camp tended to focus on protest activity that could be organized and/or participated in while online (e.g. online petitioning, hacktivism). Thus, although there were three camps, there was little chance of resolving disagreements among them because they rarely studied similar cases. In terms of empirical frequency, however, Earl et al. (2010) were able to show that the forms of activism studied by the third camp were much more common online, suggesting that scholars from the first two camps should be careful not to overgeneralize from their research.

As the Arab Spring substantially increased the amount of research being done on ICTs and social movements, new researchers in this area have moved away from these major theoretical debates and migrated toward more specific questions. Much like general social movement research began to do in the late 1980s and early 1990s, recent research often avoids these larger theoretical debates, even implicitly, and focuses instead on understanding how digital media impacts specific areas. I review five areas of research here.

Movement emergence

Much of the research on movement emergence and ICTs focuses on the rise of movements organized primarily online, such as strategic voting (Earl and Schussman 2003) or the digital rights movement (Postigo 2012), or on specific campaigns that appear to be organized online, such as campaigns by Anonymous (Beyer 2014) or other early skirmishes around digital rights (Eschenfelder and Desai 2004; Eschenfelder, Howard, and Desai 2005). Research in this area also traces out the theoretical implications of a movement emerging online, such as differences in internal decision-making (Earl and Schussman 2003), reactions to repression (Eschenfelder and Desai 2004), and the kinds of topics on which people organize around (Earl and Kimport 2009).

Less research has examined how online technologies can create favorable contexts for movement emergence. For instance, it is possible that Black Lives Matter would not exist as such a robust movement were it not for the ability to easily film and share videos online. Many African-American communities have long faced disproportionate police scrutiny and intervention, and yet it has been hard to sustain a wide-scale movement against police misconduct. The ability to document police misconduct through videos and for people to easily access those videos online has changed both the level of media coverage about police misconduct and, potentially, White Americans' understanding of the difficulties that people of color face when interacting with police officers. Likewise, there is clear evidence suggesting that Internet usage can drive political interest and/or engagement (Boulianne 2009, 2011) and other research tying political interest to protest participation (Schussman and Soule 2005), but few researchers have examined whether the size of the "mobilization potential" (Klandermans and Oegema 1987) is enlarged by wide-scale ICT usage. Another understudied topic involves the role of celebrity in driving the emergence and growth of online campaigns. Some campaigns, such as the #OscarsSoWhite campaign, may emerge more easily in a networked environment that makes celebrities so publicly accessible. While scholars have long considered bloc-recruitment important to mobilization (Gerhards and Rucht 1992), it may be that actors other than social movement organizations (SMOs) can drive that bloc recruitment through massive follower lists (Bird and Maher 2018).

Micro-mobilization

Researchers have also examined the use of ICTs in micro-mobilization and recruitment processes, particularly focusing on explaining offline participation in protest events such as rallies and demonstrations. Evidence is largely supportive of ICTs playing a positive role in micro-mobilization (e.g. Bennett and Segerberg 2013; Crossley 2015). For instance, Fisher and Boekkooi (2010) find that ICTs can be used to reach individuals who lack organizational or network ties to movements. Digital media can also help activists manage a larger number of engagements than they could otherwise, which drives greater mobilization and greater potential for spillover between movements (Walgrave et al. 2011). The positive effects have been documented outside of the USA as well, for instance, Seongyi and Woo-Young (2011) find that ICTs can be used to mobilize young South Koreans into activism. However, it is important to note that not all research is supportive. For instance, Vissers et al. (2012) argue that contacts are medium-dependent, such that online contacts drive online participation while offline contacts drive offline participation. However, whether their experimental research has external validity requires future research.

Discussions of micro-mobilization should also include evaluations of the equality of mobilization. As discussed above, there have been some concerns about ICTs creating greater inequality in who participates in social movements (Tilly 2004). For instance, Van Laer (2010) argues that the Internet largely benefits "super-activists," driving greater inequalities in participation. However, as discussed above, there is growing evidence against the impacts of the digital divide where protest is concerned (Elliott and Earl 2018; Lee et al. 2014; Stalker and Wood 2013), as well as growing evidence against this claim where other kinds of political participation are concerned (Cohen et al. 2012). Indeed, evidence is mounting that ICTs are compensatory technologies that help otherwise more disadvantaged individuals engage in protest (Enjolras et al. 2013). Research also suggests that online groups may allow people to persist in activism who would otherwise withdraw when they become temporarily biographically unavailable (Anduiza, Cristancho, and Sabucedo 2014; Rohlinger and Bunnage 2015).

Continuity and Internal movement dynamics

The two largest areas of research focus on: (1) the changing necessity and role of SMOs; and (2) ICTs and diffusion. The former – debates over the necessity and role of SMOs – has been a very substantial area of concern. Indeed, at least one review of protest and ICTs frames this issue as one of the most important infrastructural changes in social movements and one of the most important effects of ICT usage (Earl et al. 2014). Scholars have argued that ICT usage can decenter and/or destabilize traditional organizations, in part, as Shirky (2008) notes, because organizations require considerable resources and may return less value when start-up and/or coordination costs are very low. Earl and collaborators have pushed this argument the farthest, empirically demonstrating that a great deal of organizing happens online without SMOs (Earl and Kimport 2011). While not arguing that SMOs are on their way out or that SMOs return no value, this line of research does challenge the synecdoche between social movements and SMOs that has developed over time.

For instance, research critiques the study of online protest through the exclusive study of organizational websites (Earl 2013) and argues social movement theory needs to adjust to explain under what conditions SMOs will be important and/or what the consequences of routing around SMOs may be (Earl and Kimport 2011). While Earl and collaborators are strongly associated with this line of research, it is consistent with theoretical positions taken by others, who challenge the importance of organizations because of declining costs (Benkler 2006; Shirky 2008), the ability to rely on more informal networks to organize instead (Bennett and Segerberg 2013; Beyer 2014; Castells 2012; Howard and Hussain 2011), and the relative unimportance of the free rider dilemma online (Bimber, Flanagin, and Stohl 2005), among other reasons.

The primary challenge to this scholarship argues that although it is possible to organize without SMOs, SMOs are still important because they drive popularity. In other words, this challenge, represented best by Karpf (2012), argues that while protest can happen without SMOs, continuity and popularity cannot (or cannot with any frequency). Thus, Karpf argues, it is important to focus on major, popular SMOs online, such as MoveOn, to understand how their activity is changing the advocacy landscape. Others have argued that whether or not SMOs are strictly necessary, they are still commonplace and it is therefore important to understand how SMOs are adapting to an ICT-rich environment (Bimber, Flanagin, and Stohl 2012). It is likely more appropriate to see both of these lines of research as having merit: it is likely that SMOs are less necessary for organizing in some circumstances and that existing SMOs are changing to adapt to an ICT-rich environment (Earl et al. 2014).

Beyond this debate about the necessity and role of organizations, researchers have also been interested in diffusion and ICTs. Many scholars have argued that ICTs are critical because online networks help to diffuse information and contention (Ayres 1999; Myers 1994). Indeed, the power of ICTs to diffuse ideas, tactics, and a sense of opportunity is at the heart of Castells' (2012) work on ICTs and social movements, and has been important in discussing the role of ICTs in the Arab Spring (Tufekci and Wilson 2012). However, Earl (2010) argues that researchers need to be clearer about exactly what is diffusing, since information, specific tactics, or a more general interest in protest can diffuse and the dynamics of diffusion likely vary by what is diffusing (see Chapter 13 by Soule and Roggeband, in this volume, on diffusion).

External dynamics

ICT usage can also impact how external actors interact with social movements and/ or the consequences of those encounters. The two chief areas of research in this area have been social movement repression and the relationship between social movements, the media, and digital media. I discuss media hybridity within the final section on continuing debates, and so limit my remarks to research related to repression in this section. In that vein, some scholars have worried that as states gain such powerful tools for surveillance and repression (King, Pan, and Roberts 2013), social movements may ultimately be in a worse position now than before the development of digital technologies (Lynch 2011), with Morozov (2011a, 2011b) being the most ardent critic of ICTs.

However, there are two problems with this argument. First, just because a technology affords a capacity to do something does not mean that users will take advantage or maximize its usage. Zuckerman (2008), for instance, introduced the cute cat theory of repression, which argues that when governments repress online, it often takes the form of censorship and is overbroad in what it limits access to. As such, online repression may limit access to socially favored uses of ICTs, such as viewing cute cats online, and therefore face substantial resistance from the wider population. Research modeling the relationship between offline and online repression also shows that just because a government is a large repressor offline does not imply it will be highly repressive online, or vice versa (Maher, Reynolds-Stenson, and Earl 2016), or as effective at engaging in online repression as it is at offline repression (Alexanyan et al. 2012). Online repression can be difficult for regimes from a technical perspective, partly because of the decentralized nature of online protest (Etling, Faris, and Palfrey 2010). Protesters can also use technological tools to try to circumvent repression (Roberts et al. 2010).

Second, even if repression does occur, that does not have an automatic set of consequences for movements. Although research shows substantial agreement about the predictors of repression, the effects of repression are very inconsistent (see Earl 2011, for a review of the literature on repression). That is, even if surveillance or repression is more probable, its application will likely vary and its effects will certainly vary, making it unlikely that all democratizing effects of ICTs are automatically washed away. In fact, early research on online repression demonstrates the same broad range of reactions to repression as have been found for decades in research on offline repression (Earl and Schussman 2004), and some researchers argue that backfire may be even more likely online than offline when it involves digital rights or information freedom (Earl and Beyer 2014). Even research on the Arab Spring, which Morozov was concerned with, argues backfire occurred (Mourtada and Salem 2011).

Movement consequences

As discussed earlier, a popular contemporary objection to online protest is to presume that it is likely to be ineffective. Indeed, a wide range of public intellectuals nostalgically compare traditional street activism to what they presume to be ineffective online activism (e.g. Gladwell 2010). Earl (2016) comprehensively evaluates existing scholarship on the consequences of online activism and she finds that critics such as Gladwell paint with much too broad a brush.

First, critics typically assume that online tactics such as online petitions operate on a traditional model of social movement influence in which persistent struggle creates change. Instead, many online tactics rely on a model of power more akin to the power of a flash flood – sudden and overwhelming surges of activity can lead to influence by "flash activism" (Bennett and Fielding 1999). For instance, major banks such as Bank of America have reversed policies after major online protest, cities such as New York have removed proposed regulations that were heavily opposed online, and SOPA/PIPA was derailed. This model of power can be exceptionally effective at gaining political or corporate concessions or impacting political or corporate decisions and the theoretical importance of this changing model of power cannot be understated in understanding the consequences of online activism (Earl et al. 2015).

Second, critics often forget or fail to acknowledge that social movement scholars often struggle to show that traditional street protest leads to specific changes, whether that is at the general movement level or when looking at a specific protest (e.g. a specific rally). In other words, many scholars assume an effectiveness of traditional protest that is still being debated and ignore the conditional or contextual nature of offline successes. It is imperative that studies assessing offline, online, and hybrid (discussed below) forms of activism are examined and that scholars look to the actual empirical findings regarding the consequences of these modes of activism in resolving these debates. Just as the current fashion is to ask under what conditions offline protest can be successful (since it is empirically sometimes successful but often not), researchers should ask the same question of online protest as the success of online protest is also likely conditional and contextual.

Continuing Debates and Theoretical Shifts

Having reviewed this growing area of research, I close by highlighting two issues that represent current controversies among scholars who study online activism.

What kinds of cases are studied and impacts on findings

One of the most important, if implicit, controversies in this area concerns the kinds of cases that we should be studying. For instance, some have argued that social movement research gets the largest return by studying exemplary cases such as MoveOn, in part, because these cases are so popular (Karpf 2012). Indeed, a veritable cottage industry has developed around studying MoveOn (Bennett and Fielding 1999; Carty 2010, 2011, 2015; Rohlinger and Bunnage 2015). Other research implicitly or explicitly argues for studying specific platforms, such as Facebook (e.g. Gaby and Caren 2012; Harlow 2012; Mercea 2013; Vissers and Stolle 2014), YouTube (e.g. McBeth et al. 2012; Thorson et al. 2010; Thorson et al. 2013), or Twitter (e.g. Merry 2013; Penncy and Dadas 2014; Theocharis et al. 2015; Wojcieszak and Smith 2014). Still others argue for studying movements whose emergence is seen as heavily digitally enabled (Costanza-Chock 2012; Thorson et al. 2013; Tremayne 2014), or for studying the migration of extant SMOs online (e.g. Stein 2009). Still other research is event-centered, focusing on how ICTs are used broadly to turn individuals out to large-scale offline protest events (Bennett and Segerberg 2013; Fisher et al. 2005; Fisher and Boekkooi 2010).

All these approaches have merit, but also implications for findings; after all, case selection has been shown to influence likely findings in this area (Earl et al. 2010; Earl 2013). This has led Earl and collaborators to champion a sampling-based approach that looks at "reachable" web-addressable spaces to try to generalize (Earl and Kimport 2011), and has prompted others to use survey data on usage (e.g. the PEW Internet & American Life project). What is clear is that: (1) there is little consensus on how to best select cases to study in this area; and (2) case selection shapes the likely findings of research. I urge further debate on this topic in the literature.

Hybridity in action and media

A second major issue was raised by Bennett and Segerberg (2013), among others: activism often blends offline and online elements, making it more accurate to think of the field as consisting increasingly of hybrid forms of activity. This implies that it is artificial to divide online and offline spaces, given the fluidity with which people move between physical and screen worlds and the extent to which ICTs are embedded in everyday action and relationships.

A similar argument about hybridity has been made about the Internet as a media platform. Chadwick (2011, 2013) argues that news stories can emerge through new media and then move into traditional media or vice versa. This research shows that considering media crossover and tracking stories across multiple media and platforms are essential.

Conclusion

Research on ICTs and protest has been a growing area, particularly over the last decade, although growth in communication, Internet studies, and political communication has outpaced the publication of articles within social movement studies. As the area has grown, researchers have had to address morphing skepticism about online activism and shift questions from large theoretical debates to more focused specific theoretical debates. Findings across a range of areas – from movement emergence to outcomes – were reviewed. Within those areas, there are several animating debates, including those about the necessity and role of SMOs, the likely impact of repression on online protesters and movements, and shifting models of power, represented online through "flash activism." More recent shifts – including continuing debates over the most appropriate cases to study and the importance of hybridity – were also noted. In reviewing and summarizing current scholarship on the intersection of ICTs and social movements, the aim of the chapter has been not only to provide a snapshot of the current status of scholarship on this intersection, but also to stimulate further inquiry which will provide greater understanding and accent the increasing relevance of ICTs for understanding the dynamics of contemporary social movements. Hopefully the chapter will achieve some success in realizing these objectives.

References

Alexanyan, Karina, Vladimir Barash, Bruce Etling, et al. 2012. *Exploring Russian Cyberspace: Digitally-Mediated Collective Action and the Networked Public Sphere*. Cambridge, MA: Berkman Center for Internet & Society at Harvard University.

Anduiza, Eva, Camilo Cristancho, and José M. Sabucedo. 2014. "Mobilization through Online Social Networks: The Political Protest of the Indignados in Spain." *Information, Communication & Society* 17(6): 750–764. doi: 10.1080/1369118x.2013.808360.

Ayres, Jeffrey M. 1999. "From the Streets to the Internet: The Cyber-Diffusion of Contention." *The Annals of the American Academy of Political and Social Science* 566(1): 132–143.

Benkler, Yochai. 2006. *The Wealth of Networks: How Social Production Transforms Markets and Freedom*. New Haven, CT: Yale University Press.

Bennett, Daniel and Pam Fielding. 1999. *The Net Effect: How Cyberadvocacy Is Changing the Political Landscape*. Merrifield, VA: e-advocates Press.

Bennett, W. Lance and Alexandra Segerberg. 2013. *The Logic of Connective Action: Digital Media and the Personalization of Contentious Politics*. Cambridge: Cambridge University Press.

Beyer, Jessica L. 2014. *Expect Us: Online Communities and Political Mobilization*. New York: Oxford University Press.

Bimber, Bruce, Andrew J. Flanagin, and Cynthia Stohl. 2005. "Reconceptualizing Collective Action in the Contemporary Media Environment." *Communication Theory* 15(4): 365–388.

Bimber, Bruce, Andrew J. Flanagin, and Cynthia Stohl. 2012. *Collective Action in Organizations: Interaction and Engagement in an Era of Technological Change*. Cambridge: Cambridge University Press.

Bird, Jackson and Thomas V. Maher. 2018. "Turning Fans Into Heroes: How the Harry Potter Alliance Uses the Power of Story to Facilitate Fan Activism and Bloc Recruitment." *Studies in Media and Communications* 14: 23–54.

Boulianne, Shelley. 2009. "Does Internet Use Affect Engagement? A Meta-Analysis of Research." *Political Communication* 26(2): 193–211.

Boulianne, Shelley. 2011. "Stimulating or Reinforcing Political Interest: Using Panel Data to Examine Reciprocal Effects Between News Media and Political Interest." *Political Communication* 28(2): 147–162. doi: 10.1080/10584609.2010.540305.

Carty, Victoria. 2010. "Bridging Contentious and Electoral Politics: MoveOn and the Digital Revolution." In *Research in Social Movements, Conflicts and Change*, edited by Patrick G. Coy, 171–196. Bingley: Emerald Group.

Carty, Victoria. 2011. "Multi-Issue, Internet-Mediated Interest Organizations and their Implications for US Politics: A Case of MoveOn.org." *Social Movement Studies* 10(3): 265–282. doi: 10.1080/14742837.2011.590029.

Carty, Victoria. 2015. *Social Movements and New Technology*. Boulder, CO: Westview Press.

Castells, Manuel. 2012. *Networks of Outrage and Hope: Social Movements in the Internet Age*. Malden, MA: Polity Press.

Chadwick, Andrew. 2011. "Britain's First Live Televised Party Leader's Debate: From the News Cycle to the Political Information Cycle." *Parliamentary Affairs* 64(1): 24–44.

Chadwick, Andrew. 2013. *The Hybrid Media System: Politics and Power*. Oxford: Oxford University Press.

Cohen, Cathy J., Joseph Kahne, Benjamin Bowyer, Ellen Middaugh, and Jon Rogowski. 2012. *Participatory Politics: New Media and Youth Political Action*. Chicago: MacArthur.

Costanza-Chock, Sasha. 2012. "Mic Check! Media Cultures and the Occupy Movement." *Social Movement Studies* 11(3–4): 375–385. doi: 10.1080/14742837.2012.710746.

Crossley, Alison Dahl. 2015. "Facebook Feminism: Social Media, Blogs, and New Technologies of Contemporary U.S. Feminism." *Mobilization* 20(2): 253–268. doi: 10.17813/1086 671X-20-2-253.

Diani, Mario. 2000. "Social Movement Networks: Virtual and Real." *Information, Communication and Society* 3(3): 386–401.

Earl, Jennifer. 2006. "Pursuing Social Change Online: The Use of Four Protest Tactics on the Internet." *Social Science Computer Review* 24(3): 362–377. doi: 10.1177/0894439305284627.

Earl, Jennifer. 2010. "The Dynamics of Protest-Related Diffusion on the Web." *Information, Communication & Society* 13(2): 209–225.

Earl, Jennifer. 2011. "Political Repression: Iron Fists, Velvet Gloves, and Diffuse Control." *Annual Review of Sociology* 37: 261–284.

Earl, Jennifer. 2013. "Studying Online Activism: The Effects of Sampling Design on Findings." *Mobilization* 18(4): 389–406.

Earl, Jennifer. 2015. "CITASA: Intellectual Past and Future." *Information, Communication & Society* 18(5): 478–491. doi: 10.1080/1369118x.2015.1008544.

Earl, Jennifer. 2016. "Protest Online: Theorizing the Consequences of Online Engagement." In *The Consequences of Social Movements*, edited by Lorenzo Bosi, Marco Giugni, and Katrin Uba, 363–400. Cambridge: Cambridge University Press.

Earl, Jennifer and Jessica L. Beyer. 2014. "The Dynamics of Backlash Online: Anonymous and the Battle for WikiLeaks." *Research in Social Movements, Conflicts and Change* 37: 207–233.

Earl, Jennifer and R. Kelly Garrett. 2017. "The New Information Frontier: Toward a More Nuanced View of Social Movement Communication." *Social Movement Studies* 16(4): 479–493. doi: http://dx.doi.org/10.1080/14742837.2016.1192028.

Earl, Jennifer, Jayson Hunt, and R. Kelly Garrett. 2014. "Social Movements and the ICT Revolution." In *Handbook of Political Citizenship and Social Movements*, edited by Hein-Anton van der Heijden, 359–383. Cheltenham: Edward Elgar Publishing.

Earl, Jennifer, Jayson Hunt, R. Kelly Garrett, and Aysenur Dal. 2015. "New Technologies and Social Movements." In *Oxford Handbook of Social Movements*, edited by Donatella della Porta and Mario Diani, 355–366. Oxford: Oxford University Press.

Earl, Jennifer and Katrina Kimport. 2009. "Movement Societies and Digital Protest: Fan Activism and Other Non-Political Protest Online." *Sociological Theory* 23(3): 220–243.

Earl, Jennifer and Katrina Kimport. 2011. *Digitally Enabled Social Change: Activism in the Internet Age*. Cambridge, MA: MIT Press.

Earl, Jennifer, Katrina Kimport, Greg Prieto, Carly Rush, and Kimberly Reynoso. 2010. "Changing the World One Webpage at a Time: Conceptualizing and Explaining 'Internet Activism.'" *Mobilization* 15(4): 425–446.

Earl, Jennifer and Alan Schussman. 2003. "The New Site of Activism: On-Line Organizations, Movement Entrepreneurs, and the Changing Location of Social Movement Decision-Making." *Research in Social Movements, Conflicts, and Change* 24: 155–187. doi: 10.1016/S0163-786X(03)80024-1.

Earl, Jennifer and Alan Schussman. 2004. "Cease and Desist: Repression, Strategic Voting and the 2000 Presidential Election." *Mobilization* 9(2): 181–202.

Elliott, Thomas, and Jennifer Earl. 2018. "Online Protest Participation and the Digital Divide: Modeling the Effect of the Digital Divide on Online Petition Signing." *New Media & Society* 20(2): 698–719. http://journals.sagepub.com/doi/full/10.1177/1461444816669159.

Enjolras, Bernard, Kari Steen-Johnsen, and Dag Wollebæk. 2013. "Socia Media and Mobilization to Offline Demonstrations: Transcending Participatory Divides?" *New Media & Society* 15(6): 890–908. doi: 10.1177/1461444812462844.

Eschenfelder, Kristin R. and Anuj C. Desai. 2004. "Software as Protest: The Unexpected Resiliency of U.S.-Based DeCSS Posting and Linking." *The Information Society* 20(2): 101–116.

Eschenfelder, Kristen R., Robert Glenn Howard, and Anuj C. Desai. 2005. "Who Posts DeCSS and Why? A Content Analysis of Web Sites Posting DVD Circumvention Software." *Journal for the American Society for Information Science and Technology* 56(13): 1405–1418.

Etling, Bruce, Robert Faris, and John Palfrey. 2010. "Political Change in the Digital Age: The Fragility and Promise of Online Organizing." *SAIS Review* Summer–Fall: 37–49.

Fisher, Dana and Marjie Boekkooi. 2010. "Mobilizing Friends and Strangers." *Information, Communication and Society* 13(2): 193–2008.

Fisher, Dana, Kevin Stanley, David Berman, and Gina Neff. 2005. "How Do Organizations Matter? Mobilization and Support for Participants at Five Globalization Protests." *Social Problems* 52: 102–121.

Gaby, Sarah, and Neal Caren. 2012. "Occupy Online: How Cute Old Men and Malcolm X Recruited 400,000 US Users to OWS on Facebook." *Social Movement Studies* 11(3–4): 367–374. doi: 10.1080/14742837.2012.708858.

Garrett, R. Kelly. 2006. "Protest in an Information Society: A Review of the Literature on Social Movement and New ICTs." *Information, Communication, and Society* 9(2): 202–224.

Gerhards, Jürgen and Dieter Rucht. 1992. "Mesomobilization: Organizing and Framing in Two Protest Campaigns in West Germany." *American Journal of Sociology* 98(3): 555–595.

Gladwell, Malcolm. 2010. "Small Change: Why the Revolution Will Not Be Tweeted." *New Yorker*, October 4.

Hampton, Keith N., Lauren F. Sessions, and Eun Ja Her. 2011. "Core Networks, Social Isolation, and New Media: How Internet and Mobile Phone Use Is Related to Network Size and Diversity." *Information, Comunication & Society* 14(1): 130–155. doi: 10.1080/1369118X.2010.513417.

Harlow, Summer. 2012. "Social Media and Social Movements: Facebook and an Online Guatemalan Justice Movement that Moved Offline." *New Media & Society* 14(2): 225–243. doi: 10.1177/1461444811410408.

Howard, Philip N. and Muzammil M. Hussain. 2011. "The Role of Digital Media." *Journal of Democracy* 22(3): 35–48.

Howard, Philip N. and Muzammil M. Hussain. 2013. *Democracy's Fourth Wave: Digital Media and the Arab Spring*. New York: Oxford University Press.

Karpf, David. 2012. *The MoveOn Effect: The Unexpected Transformation of American Political Advocacy*. New York: Oxford University Press.

King, Gary, Jennifer Pan, and Margaret E. Roberts. 2013. "How Censorship in China Allows Government Criticism but Silences Collective Expression." *American Political Science Review* 107(2): 326–343. doi: 10.1017/s0003055413000014.

Klandermans, Bert and Dirk Oegema. 1987. "Potentials, Networks, Motivations, and Barriers: Steps Towards Participation in Social Movements." *American Sociological Review* 52: 519–531.

Lee, Chung-pin, Don-yun Chen, and Tong-yi Huang. 2014. "The Interplay Between Digital and Political Divides: The Case of e-Petitioning in Taiwan." *Social Science Computer Review* 32(1): 37–55. doi: 10.1177/0894439313497470.

Lynch, Marc. 2011. "After Egypt: The Limits and Promise of Online Challenges to the Authoritarian Arab State." *Perspectives on Politics* 9(2): 301–310.

Maher, Thomas V., Heidi Reynolds-Stenson, and Jennifer Earl. 2016. "From Boots to Bytes: Understanding Offline and Online Political Repression" Paper presented at Four Corners Conflict Network Meeting, Phoenix, AZ.

McBeth, Mark K., Elizabeth A. Shanahan, Molly C. Arrandale Anderson, and Barbara Rose. 2012. "Policy Story or Gory Story? Narrative Policy Framework Analysis of Buffalo Field Campaign's YouTube Videos." *Policy & Internet* 4(3–4): 159–183. doi: 10.1002/poi3.15.

Mercea, Dan. 2013. "Probing the Implications of Facebook Use for the Organizational Form of Social Movement Organizations." *Information, Communication & Society* 16(8): 1306–1327. doi: 10.1080/1369118X.2013.770050.

Merry, Melissa K. 2013. "Tweeting for a Cause: Microblogging and Environmental Advocacy." *Policy & Internet* 5(3): 304–327. doi: 10.1002/1944-2866.POI335.

Morozov, Evgeny. 2011a. *The Net Delusion: The Dark Side of Internet Freedom*. New York: Public Affairs.

Morozov, Evgeny. 2011b. Caught in the Net. *The Economist*. Available at: http://www. economist.com/node/17848401.

Mourtada, Racha and Fadi Salem. 2011. *Civil Movements: The Impact of Facebook and Twitter*. Dubai: Dubai School of Government.

Myers, Daniel J. 1994. "Communication Technology and Social Movements: Contributions of Computer Networks to Activism." *Social Science Computer Review* 12(2): 251–260.

Nie, Norman H. and Lutz Erbring. 2000. *Internet and Society: A Preliminary Report*. SIQSS.

Peckham, Michael H. 1998. "New Dimensions of Social Movement/Countermovement Interaction: The Case of Scientology and Its Internet Critics." *Canadian Journal of Sociology* 23(4): 317–347.

Penney, Joel and Caroline Dadas. 2014. "(Re)Tweeting in the Service of Protest: Digital Composition and Circulation in the Occupy Wall Street Movement." *New Media & Society* 16(1): 74–90. doi: 10.1177/1461444813479593.

PEW Internet & American Life Project. 2016. "Internet Use Over Time." Available at: http:// www.pewinternet.org/data-trend/internet-use/internet-use-over-time/ (accessed October 13, 2016).

Postigo, Hector. 2012. *The Digital Rights Movement*. Cambridge, MA: MIT Press.

Rainie, Lee and Barry Wellman. 2012. *Networked: The New Social Operating System*. Cambridge, MA: MIT Press.

Rheingold, Howard. 1993. *The Virtual Community: Homesteading on the Electronic Frontier*. Reading, MA: Addison-Wesley.

Roberts, Hal, Ethan Zuckerman, Robert Faris, and John Palfrey. 2010. *2010 Circumvention Tool Usage Report*. Cambridge, MA: Berkman Center for Internet & Society at Harvard University.

Rohlinger, Deana and Leslie Bunnage. 2015. "Connecting People to Politics over Time? Internet Communication Technology and Retention in MoveOn.org and the Florida Tea Party Movement." *Information, Communication & Society* 18(5): 539–552.

Schussman, Alan, and Sarah A. Soule. 2005. "Process and Protest: Accounting for Individual Protest Participation." *Social Forces* 84(2): 1083–1108.

Seongyi, Yun and Chang Woo-Young. 2011. "Political Participation of Teenagers in the Information Era." *Social Science Computer Review* 29(2): 242–249. doi: 10.1177/ 0894439310363255.

Shirky, Clay. 2008. *Here Comes Everybody: The Power of Organizing Without Organizations*. New York: Penguin Press.

Stalker, Glenn J. and Lesley J. Wood. 2013. "Reaching Beyond the Net: Political Circuits and Participation in Toronto's G20 Protests." *Social Movement Studies* 12(2): 178–198. doi: 10.1080/14742837.2012.701054.

Stein, Laura. 2009. "Social Movement Web Use in Theory and Practice: A Content Analysis of US Movement Websites." *New Media and Society* 11(5): 749–771. doi: 10.1177/1461444809105350.

Tarrow, Sidney. 1998. "Fishnets, Internets, and Catnets: Globalization and Transnational Collective Action." In *Challenging Authority: The Historical Study of Contentious Politics*, edited by Michael P. Hanaganm, Leslie Page Moch, and Wayne te Brake, 228–244. Minneapolis: University of Minnesota Press.

Theocharis, Yannis, Will Lowe, Jan W. van Deth, and Gema García-Albacete. 2015. "Using Twitter to Mobilize Protest Action: Online Mobilization Patterns and Action Repertoires in the Occupy Wall Street, Indignados, and Aganaktismenoi Movements." *Information, Communication & Society* 18(2): 202–220. doi: 10.1080/1369118X.2014.948035.

Thorson, Kjerstin, Kevin Driscoll, Brian Ekdale, et al. 2013. "YouTube, Twitter and the Occupy Movement." *Information, Communication & Society* 16(3): 421–451. doi: 10.1080/1369118X.2012.756051.

Thorson, Kjerstin, Brian Ekdale, Porismita Borah, Kang Namkoong, and Chirag Shah. 2010. "YouTube and Proposition 8." *Information, Communication & Society* 13(3): 325–349. doi: 10.1080/13691180903497060.

Tilly, Charles. 2004. *Social Movements, 1768–2004*. Boulder, CO: Paradigm Publishers.

Tremayne, Mark. 2014. "Anatomy of Protest in the Digital Era: A Network Analysis of Twitter and Occupy Wall Street." *Social Movement Studies* 13(1): 110–126. doi: 10.1080/14742837.2013.830969.

Tufekci, Zeynep, and Christopher Wilson. 2012. "Social Media and the Decision to Participate in Political Protest: Observations from Tahrir Square." *Journal of Communication* 62(2): 363–379. doi: 10.1111/j.1460-2466.2012.01629.x.

Van Laer, Jeroen. 2010. "Activists 'Online' and 'Offline': Internet as an Information Channel for Protest Demonstrations." *Mobilization* 15(3): 405–421.

Vegh, Sandor. 2003. "Classifying Forms of Online Activism: The Case of Cyberprotests against the World Bank." In *Cyberactivism: Online Activism and Theory and Practice*, edited by Martha McCaughey and Michael D. Ayers, 71–95. New York: Routledge.

Vissers, Sara, Marc Hooghe, Dietlind Stolle, and Valérie-Anne Mahéo. 2012. "The Impact of Mobilization Media on Off-Line and Online Participation: Are Mobilization Effects Medium-Specific?" *Social Science Computer Review* 30(2): 152–169. doi: 10.1177/0894439310396485.

Vissers, Sara and Dietlind Stolle. 2014. "Spill-Over Effects Between Facebook and On/Offline Political Participation? Evidence from a Two-Wave Panel Study." *Journal of Information Technology & Politics* 11(3): 259–275. doi: 10.1080/19331681.2014.888383.

Walgrave, Stefaan, W. Lance Bennett, Jeroen Van Laer, and Christian Breunig. 2011. "Multiple Engagements and Network Bridging in Contentious Politics: Digital Media Use of Protest Participants." *Mobilization* 16(3): 325–349. doi: 10.17813/maiq.16.3.b0780274322458wk.

Wojcieszak, Magdalena and Briar Smith. 2014. "Will Politics Be Tweeted? New Media Use by Iranian Youth in 2011." *New Media & Society* 16(1): 91–109. doi: 10.1177/1461444813479594.

Wolfsfeld, Gadi, Elad Segev, and Tamir Sheafer. 2013. "Social Media and the Arab Spring: Politics Comes First." *The International Journal of Press/Politics* 18(2): 115–137. doi: 10.1177/1940161212471716.

Zuckerman, Ethan. 2008. "The Cute Cat Theory Talk at ETech." Available at: http://www.ethanzuckerman.com/blog/2008/03/08/the-cute-cat-theory-talk-at-etech/ (accessed October 18, 2016).

17

Social Movements and Litigation

STEVEN A. BOUTCHER AND HOLLY J. MCCAMMON[1]

Introduction

Reliance on litigation in the courts as a social movement strategy receives substantially less attention in the sociological movement literature than use of other movement-strategic approaches. While legal scholars and political scientists have "decentered" their analyses by moving away from a focus on the courts and the law specifically to consider also the influence of social movements on judicial decision-making, only a small number of sociologists have taken the step of examining social movement activism in the judicial realm (for recent reviews, see Boutcher and Stobaugh 2013; Levitsky 2015; McCammon and McGrath 2015). Yet, historical and contemporary social movement efforts reveal considerable use of legal activism by collective actors, with many movements pursuing claims via the courts (Chen and Cummings 2013; Handler 1978; O'Connor 1980; Sarat and Scheingold 2001). In fact, a notable trend beginning in the latter half of the twentieth century is the increasing deployment of legal strategies by social movement actors (Chen and Cummings 2013). This chapter begins by briefly defining social movement legal mobilization and examines the use of social movement litigation strategy by a variety of social movements. We then turn to two critical questions in legal mobilization scholarship: (1) under what circumstances do activists pursue litigation strategies?; and (2) what is the impact, for social movements and in terms of broader gains, of utilizing the law in this manner?

What Is Social Movement Litigation?

Social movement litigation typically begins when a movement group articulates a particular claim in terms of rights and then files legal action in the court system. Many scholars use the term "legal mobilization" to refer to a wide range of efforts

The Wiley Blackwell Companion to Social Movements, Second Edition. Edited by David A. Snow, Sarah A. Soule, Hanspeter Kriesi, and Holly J. McCammon.

by activists to challenge the current state of law, from putting pressure on legislative leaders to courtroom litigation to invoking the law as a discursive and symbolic tool (Burstein 1991; McCann 2008; Zemans 1983). The focus of this chapter is particularly on legal mobilization as a litigation strategy, centering the discussion on movement actors' pursuit of social change via judicial avenues, what some scholars refer to as "impact litigation." When pursuing litigation, activists seek to persuade judges, and in some cases juries, to support the movement group's legally-defined goals. Targeting state actors in this way allows social movement groups to invoke the power of law as they make legal claims, demands that are often couched in the language of rights.

The primary carriers of social movement litigation are public interest law organizations. These legal groups are a particular kind of movement organization in that they primarily draw on law and litigation in their attempts to achieve social change (Cummings and Rhode 2009). Social movement scholarship has traditionally treated these groups as non-movement organizations due to the legal groups' reliance on institutionalized tactics and routinized relationship with the state. Yet, as some advocacy-organization scholars (Andrews and Edwards 2004; Burstein 1998) argue, these distinctions break down in practice; within any particular movement, there is a division of labor among the types of tactics and strategies that orient action, with some groups specializing in legal work and others, for example, focusing on grassroots organizing.

Important cases like *Brown v. Board of Education*, *Roe v. Wade*, and *Obergefell v. Hodges* (the latter is the Supreme Court's recent decision on same-sex marriage) are pivotal examples of the promise of social movement litigation. Yet, despite the publicity and appeal of impact litigation, it is only one type of legal mobilization that activists pursue, and it may not be the most common form of social movement legal action. In their study of lawyers in the Southern civil rights movement, Andrews and Jowers (2012) find that impact litigation represented only a small portion of the legal work that movement lawyers pursued. Other actions, including criminal representation of detained activists, were more pronounced. This finding may have to do with the fact that impact litigation requires substantial resources and many organizations cannot pursue a robust docket without the assistance of allied lawyers sometimes working elsewhere in the profession (e.g. pro bono lawyers in large law firms, Boutcher 2013; and funding from foundation and government grants, Albiston and Nielsen 2014).

How Have Social Movements Deployed Litigation Strategy?

Social movements have long relied on litigation strategies. By examining research on a handful of movements and their legal mobilizations, we can discern a variety of approaches to movement litigation. In the USA, the history of movement legal activism begins very early. Wiecek (1977) describes the judicial strategy of late-eighteenth- and early-nineteenth-century abolitionists, explaining that abolitionist lawyers worked closely with abolitionists, such as the Pennsylvania Abolitionist Society, offering legal representation to African Americans seeking freedom from slavery. O'Connor (1980) documents the litigation campaign of the US women suffragists beginning in the late 1860s, as a growing movement initiated a series of test cases to challenge claims that the Fourteenth Amendment did not provide voting rights for women. In neither of these movements was a litigation strategy highly successful. For instance, a number of woman-suffrage cases were heard, including two decided by the US Supreme Court against the suffragists, which made the litigation strategy short-lived for the suffragists.

Other movements have pursued long-term litigation strategies. The US labor movement has a substantial history of taking its battles into the courts and other adjudicative bodies (Garden 2013; McCammon 2001). Legal historians and practitioners (e.g. Greenberg 1994; Tushnet 1994) trace the highly strategic litigation efforts of the NAACP Legal Defense Fund (LDF), especially from the 1930s to the pivotal 1954 *Brown v. Board of Education* decision. The legal work of LDF continued after *Brown*, as the organization, along with a number of other emerging civil rights litigation groups, such as the National Lawyers Guild, defended civil rights activists, fought employment and housing discrimination, and counseled in death penalty cases. Hilbink (2006) explores reasons why lawyers associated with different civil rights advocacy groups brought different legal consciousnesses (or understandings of how the law and legal system could be utilized) and thus different strategic approaches to bear on their work for racial justice.

Meyer and Boutcher (2007) call the *Brown* case a "watershed" event. The case is critical, of course, because of the court's ruling to end racial segregation in public schools. But other circumstances add to the importance of LDF's influence. LDF's successful and strategic litigation in *Brown* invited other movement groups to pursue legal claims. As Yeazell (2004: 1977) states, "*Brown* gave us a model for social change through litigation." Others (e.g. Wasby 1984), however, point out that strategic movement litigation also faces many contingencies as well as resource constraints, which can impede litigator control of a strategic plan.

In time, other social movement groups began to adopt the LDF model, and Meyer and Boutcher point to social movement "spillover," as activists working on other causes began to develop legal organizations and litigation tactics following in LDF's footsteps. Mexican American lawyers founded the Mexican American Legal Defense and Educational Fund in 1968 explicitly modeling the group on LDF (O'Connor and Epstein 1984). Additionally, feminists at the National Organization for Women (NOW) formed the Legal Defense and Education Fund also in the late 1960s, although the group's organizational structure was different than that of LDF in that NOW had limited funds to hire its own attorneys (O'Connor 1980). The women's movement's legal arm also differed in that it was dispersed across multiple organizations. For instance, Ruth Bader Ginsburg at the ACLU's Women's Rights Project in the 1970s spearheaded a series of legal cases seeking Fourteenth Amendment protection against sex discrimination. Her work at the ACLU, like that of LDF, showed other legal activists how to develop a long-term strategy of incremental legal change (Campbell 2003).

While both the civil rights and women's movements focused their legal efforts on a range of issues,[2] the US environmental movement's judicial strategies have tended to center on particular goals in litigation. For instance, the Sierra Club in 1971 coordinated the Environmental Defense Fund specifically to gain legal standing to file claims in court for environmental protections (Turner and Clifton 1990). The title of

Christopher Stone's 1972 book sums up the movement's focused legal goal during this period, *Should Trees Have Standing?* The environmental movement also combined its judicial work with a legislative agenda, and the movement was legislatively highly successful in the 1970s. New statutes then provided a legal platform for later judicial action, suggesting a strategic sequence for movements: legislative tactics followed by judicial tactics. Coglianese (2001) indicates a limit to such an approach, describing the post-1970s environmental movement as conservative and institutionalized in its litigation practices because of its reliance on (and often defense of) its past legislative successes. Environmental litigation strategy today continues to center heavily on enforcing existing laws (largely as a response to legislative resistance to new law), including using the Clean Air Act to confront the challenge of climate change (Gerrard 2014). New legal arguments based on public trust doctrine that expand older notions of standing, however, are a recent innovation in contemporary climate-change litigation (Chemerinsky 2016).

Today, movement legal efforts occur even more broadly in the USA in a multitude of social movements and around the world in diverse national settings and global arenas. In the USA, the LGBT movement recently succeeded in utilizing a litigation strategy to win recognition of same-sex marriage from the US Supreme Court, following a long effort to gain legal rights for gays and lesbians and using finely-honed legal arguments to make its case (Andersen 2005; Cummings and NeJaime 2009; Goldberg 2015). Additionally, ongoing skirmishes in the courts (and legislatures) occur between the pro-choice and pro-life movements, with, as some have argued, increasing sophistication on the part of conservative, anti-abortion legal activists (Teles 2008). In fact, a number of scholars (Den Dulk 2006; Hacker 2005; Southworth 2009) note the rise of a conservative network of movement lawyers who model their legal strategies on that of earlier, progressive legal advocacy.

Scholars are expanding our understanding of trends in social movement legal mobilization by investigating the use of legal approaches in a variety of national and transnational legal and political settings (Dezalay and Garth 2012; Santos and Rodríguez-Garavito 2005; Sarat and Scheingold 2001). Globally, activists use the law to confront neoliberalism, human rights violations, and environmental degradation, among other challenges, and scholars are beginning to pursue comparative analyses to make sense of how legal, political, and social contexts influence movement legal action (Dotan 2015; Fuchs 2013; Pierceson 2005; Vanhala 2011a). They provide in-depth case studies to understand how legal-advocacy groups navigate non-democratic political regimes (Chua 2012; Currier 2009; Lui and Halliday 2011; Meili 2005; Michalowski 1998). And researchers explore the implications of participation in transnational human rights networks (Dezalay and Garth 2001; Meili 2001).

Our review of the social movement litigation literature suggests that two general questions animate much of this research, and we explore both of these in the following discussions.

The Turn to Law: Why Do Social Movement Groups Litigate?

The decision to litigate is a complex one, and some scholars explore the decision at the individual level, considering, for instance, how one's resources or legal consciousness informs choices about whether and how one engages the legal system (Ewick and Silbey 1998; Galanter 1974; Merry 1990). The relationship between individual legal action and social movements poses a number of questions. Some challenges initiated by individuals in court may align with social movement goals but the legal action spearheaded by the individual is not a calculated social movement tactic. NeJaime (2012), for instance, discusses gay and lesbian couples in the USA pursuing the right to marry in court as individual litigants rather than as a strategic social movement tactic. As NeJaime points out, such individual legal actions introduce questions about the boundaries of social movements and who is and is not a participant. Additionally, individual legal actions can help launch a movement. For example, Baker's (2008) research shows that various plaintiffs, many of them African-American women, filed the earliest workplace sexual-harassment suits in the USA, and these suits then helped mobilize a broader women's movement against sexual harassment. Scholars also recognize that it may well be individuals who bring legal cases to the attention of advocacy groups. For instance, Vanhala (2011a: 255) indicates that public-interest law groups may start by helping "anyone who comes through the door" and over time begin to "prioritize issues and proactively seek cases for test case litigation," developing long-term organizational strategies like those used by the NAACP LDF and the ACLU's Women's Rights Project.

Legal mobilization researchers, however, often pose questions about movement litigation in terms of internal movement-organizational dynamics; that is, which movement actors and processes influence a collective-action group's decision to litigate? Barclay and Chomsky (2014) center their discussion of decisions about use of the court on cause lawyers, lawyers who identify as movement members but who also have professional skills, specifically the legal expertise to recognize and pursue issues with legal merit on behalf of the movement. McCann (2004) explains that cause lawyers can help activists develop a legal rights consciousness and make rights claims using the law. Cole and Foster's (2001) account shows that lawyers working with the US environmental justice movement often work closely with community residents and environmental justice organizers and are able to identify matters that qualify as legal complaints. A resource mobilization perspective (McCarthy and Zald 1977) suggests that a movement with active legal professionals is more likely than a movement without the presence of lawyers to turn to the courts. Epp (1998) develops this argument in detail, showing that the "rights revolution" in Britain, Canada, India and the USA, with high courts in each country increasingly ruling in favor of individual rights, can be traced to rights advocacy organizations and the lawyers leading the effort

Yet rank-and-file movement members do not always welcome a litigation strategy.[3] Various researchers (Morag-Levine 2003; Solberg and Waltenburg 2006) demonstrate that internal-movement-group dynamics influence decision-making on the use of the court system. Vanhala's (2011a) investigation of the disability rights movements in Britain and Canada explores how leaders in organizations in both countries work to "sell" a litigation strategy to grassroots members using a public education campaign. Various researchers point to within-movement tensions that emerge over strategic decision-making when some activists view litigation as a fruitful activity while others do not (Levitsky 2006; NeJaime 2012). Cable, Hastings, and Mix (2002) describe difficulties in communication between activists and lawyers (and researchers) in the environmental movement, given differences in language and assumptions about evidence. Vanhala (2009) argues that a group's collective-action framing plays a significant role in whether or not the organization will choose a litigation strategy. She explores how the adoption of a rights-based, anti-discrimination collective-action frame by some groups in the UK's LGBT and disability movements made advocates more receptive to a litigation strategy than the resources possessed by the groups or the broader political and legal opportunities they confronted.

In explaining why some groups pursue litigation, numerous researchers focus less on processes internal to movements and more on the broader context, often using a legal- or political-opportunity perspective approach. Political opportunities, such as receptive political leaders or state structures providing points of access for collective actors, have long been considered by social movement scholars as influencing mobilization by activists (Kitschelt 1986; McAdam 1982). Building on this, Hilson (2002) develops the concept of legal opportunity by pointing to both its structural and contingent dimensions, indicating that movement actors will be more likely to pursue litigation when legal opportunities occur. Similar to political opportunities, legal opportunity structures are largely rooted in state structures that offer access for politicized groups to make their claims before adjudicative bodies, including judicial and administrative agencies, as well as laws and legal doctrine granting standing. Contingent legal opportunity, according to Hilson, occurs when judicial elites are sympathetic to movement claims and thus may decide in their favor.

Substantial empirical evidence supports the claim that groups pursue legal strategies when legal and political opportunities exist (Barclay and Fisher 2006; De Fazio 2012). For example, Andersen (2005) traces the US LGBT movement's legal actions from the 1970s and pinpoints judicial elite receptivity as well as a legal platform from which to make claims as key legal opportunities inviting movement litigation. Hilson (2002) finds that when legal opportunities are closed, activists may shift strategy to public protests. Numerous scholars consider specifically access to a judicial system as an important prerequisite for legal mobilization. Repressive governmental regimes often limit access to adjudicative channels, producing a closed legal opportunity structure (Lemaitre and Sandvik 2015). Van der Vet (2014) reports, for instance, that human rights advocates in Russia confront resistance by the government to activist attempts to litigate in the European Court of Human Rights. Wilson and Cordero (2006) explain that legal mobilization among a variety of Costa Rican marginalized groups was prompted more by changes in legal rules that reduced the costs of accessing the courts than by the establishment of the court system itself. Chua (2012) complicates the role of judicial access further using interview data from the gay and lesbian movement in Singapore, showing that at least some activists view litigation as a less confrontational strategy than street protest, and when confronting a repressive regime, activists may choose to engage in "pragmatic resistance," using a legal rather than direct-action strategy because such a strategy is less likely to provoke authoritarian leaders.

A growing body of investigation suggests that the relationship between opportunity structures and movement litigation is a complex one, for a number of reasons. First, as Gamson and Meyer (1996) tell us, movement actors do not always simply react to external opportunities; they can also create opportunities. NeJaime (2012) echoes this assertion saying that successful social movement legal mobilization begets further legal mobilization as courtroom victories and legal precedents open the legal opportunity structure further for activists. Moreover, African Americans in the early twentieth-century US South confronted a violent regime of white supremacy. The NAACP LDF successfully challenged the regime moving the battle into the federal court system, winning a critical Supreme Court decision removing legal barriers to NAACP legal advocacy, and showing that a movement can open up legal opportunities (Tushnet 1994).[4]

Second, McCann's (1994) early examination of US women's pay-equity movement illustrates a case in which activists continued to pursue a court-based strategy even when confronted with significant losses, given that litigation can benefit the movement in terms of mobilization, press coverage, and public opinion. Similarly, Boutcher's (2011) analysis of LGBT legal mobilization surrounding the issue of anti-sodomy law repeal after the defeat in *Bowers v. Hardwick* shows that significant legal setbacks can be turned into opportunities for further legal mobilization. Both of these studies show that closed opportunities do not always prevent legal activism (see also NeJaime 2011). Vanhala (2012) considers activist agency and argues that an inhospitable political and legal context may not dissuade movement activists from litigation when the group is intent on pressing the cause in court. Behrmann and Yorke (2013), in their recent study of anti-death penalty activism in the European Union, point to litigation decisions made on a case-by-case basis, so that cases are chosen to develop a specific strategy of litigation. Eskridge (2001) explores how exclusionary law that discriminates against social groups aids groups in developing a collective identity and providing a target for resisting subordinate treatment.

Finally, studies increasingly point to an interplay between political and legal opportunities, which also complicates our understanding of both. Alter and Vargas (2000) and Hilson (2002) find that a closed political-opportunity structure encourages activists to turn to the court to pursue their claims. In their study of the US civil rights movement, Jenkins and Peck (2013) identify a long string of failures to enact racial civil rights legislation in the US Congress as the primary reason why civil rights leaders turned to the courts to gain anti-racist policy. Similarly, Kane and Elliott (2014) find that US LGBT activists are likely to pursue court challenges where state legislatures have been largely unresponsive to the movement, suggesting that considering only a legal opportunity structure is too narrow and that a broader field of opportunities and constraints needs to be taken into account. Fuchs (2013) tells us that the media today are an important institutional actor that can shape strategy decisions by advocates. She points out that movement groups will factor into their decision to litigate whether the media (and thus the public) are likely to view litigation as a legitimate strategy (see Dorf and Tarrow 2014, for research bringing counter-movements into the equation). As Cummings and NeJaime (2009) suggest, the multiple institutional layers of opportunity (and constraint), including both legal and political, and the complex field of organizations and actors in which movement litigation strategy occurs must be taken into account in studies of the external constraints and facilitators of legal mobilization.

What Impacts Does Movement Litigation Strategy Have?

Socio-legal scholars debate whether use of litigation to secure rights can achieve substantive social reform. Early scholarship in law and society argued that relying on courts to secure rights was limited. Scholars analyzed the many ways that law, as a formal political institution, maintains the status quo, reinforcing social hierarchies and producing inequality in legal outcomes across different actors using the courts (Galanter 1974). In this view, when challengers rely centrally on litigation and rights-based strategies, any chance of meaningful social change is significantly constrained (Abel 1985).

Early movement studies were equally critical about litigation as a strategy for achieving broad-based social change. The seminal works of Scheingold (1974) and Handler (1978) were highly skeptical about the effectiveness of litigation. These scholars argued that litigation was a conservative strategy dominated by elites that saps the energy from more political and broad-based grassroots organizing. In his critique of social reform litigation, Rosenberg (1991) maintains that the courts cannot produce significant social change due to institutional constraints placed on them as a political institution. Taking the influential case of *Brown v. Board of Education*, Rosenberg concludes that the court had no significant effect on increasing rates of integration in public schools. Instead, *Brown* spurred local opposition to enforcement, and not until after Congress passed the Civil Rights Act of 1964 was there much movement on the issue of desegregation. Rosenberg concludes that courts are limited in their enforcement powers, and their constrained ability to achieve social change only exists when other political institutions are willing to enforce the decision. In fact, scholars (Levinson and Balkin 2005; Rosenberg 2006; Schacter 2009) find that movement court victories can spur a backlash against movements.

Levitsky (2015) points out, however, that others take a more expansive view of legal mobilization outcomes, not solely examining the instrumental value of litigation but the "radiating" (Galanter 1983) and indirect effects that it can have on social movements. McCann (1994) develops a constitutive approach to law and social movements, decentering the courts as the primary actor responsible for social change and placing the movement at the center of analysis. He asks: under what conditions can law be either productive or limiting for ongoing movement struggles? Researchers working under the constitutive approach to legal mobilization have documented the different ways that litigation can positively affect movement constituencies, by leveraging power from opponents, raising expectations among movement constituents, legitimating a movement's goals through publicity, building organizational resources, and mobilizing constituents (McCann 1994; O'Connor 1980; Schneider 1986). Returning to the example of *Brown*, for instance, scholars have highlighted the indirect effects that the decision had on blacks. McAdam (1982) argues that the decision provided a sense of cognitive liberation resulting in increased mobilization and organizational founding. Morris (1984) describes the symbolic power that the decision had on blacks. Quoting one interviewee, Morris (1984: 81) writes "we all underestimated the impact of the 1954 decision ... people literally got out and danced in the streets ... The Negro was jubilant." Moreover, others argue that the backlash thesis is overstated, particularly concerning the *Roe v. Wade* decision (Greenhouse and Siegel 2011) and perhaps for marriage equality as well (Eskridge 2013).

The positive indirect effects of law on social movements are not just limited to successful court victories but can also occur following significant defeats. In his analysis of the LGBT movement following the defeat in *Bowers v. Hardwick* in the

Supreme Court, Boutcher (2011) shows that the movement responded affirmatively through public appeals, mobilizing protests, fund raising, and the creation of new organizations. In response, the movement also shifted policy venues to state courts and legislatures and created new alliances with other groups. Of course, as NeJaime (2011) points out, not all losses will contain positive mobilizing effects for movements. Indeed, despite the political mobilization following the *Bowers* defeat, Dunlap (1994) argues that the decision legitimated further discrimination against gays and lesbians.

Movement litigation strategies can also affect other social movements through "spillover" effects. Meyer and Boutcher (2007), focusing on the example of the NAACP's desegregation campaign, highlight three mechanisms of spillover that affected subsequent movements:[5] (1) shared personnel; (2) political opportunity structures; and (3) emulation of organizational structures and strategies. The spillover argument highlights the important fact that most movements are seldom unitary, neatly bounded phenomena. Rather, their boundaries are highly porous; activists frequently move in and out of movement groups, altering the organization's identity and strategic priorities in fundamental ways. Further, movement litigation and its outcomes can alter the broader political context for other movements, opening and constraining the potential likelihood that other movements can have similar legal outcomes. Finally, movements emulate each other, adopting perceived successful legal arguments from other movements (Mayeri 2011; McCammon et al. 2018).

Early scholarship was skeptical about whether reliance on the courts would yield positive movement outcomes. In part, this critique stems from the concern that lawyers would come to control and dictate the direction of the movement, channeling the movement toward legal ends over political ends. The role that lawyers play within movement campaigns is one of strategic choice: lawyers can prioritize litigation and the courts as the central venue for social change or they can deploy litigation as part of a broader political campaign that also includes other forms of political mobilization, including lobbying and demonstrations (Cummings and Eagly 2001). Within particular movement fields, legal campaigns can heighten tensions between legal and non-legal activists (Levitsky 2006; Vanhala 2011b). In her study of the Chicago LGBT movement, for instance, Levitsky (2006) found that although legal advocates were often asked to assist non-legal groups, they never reciprocated by asking for input on their legal strategies. This unequal relationship has profound implications for the trajectory of the movement because well-resourced legal advocacy organizations can shape the political agenda of the movement.

Conclusion

The study of law and social movements is a vibrant, growing area of scholarly focus, but much of its development has been in law, legal studies, and socio-legal research, and not in social movement scholarship. Contemporary researchers are beginning to bridge these fields, but there remains more to be done. There are a variety of ways social movement scholars can consider the law. Law is not only a target for social movements, but it is a valuable resource that can be mobilized for social change. Law is also an important source of cultural meaning that shapes the terrain that activists navigate in their ongoing struggles and that can be strategically framed by activists. Incorporating law into social movement analyses can reinvigorate longstanding questions in the field, including the role of elites in movement processes, mobilization and its outcomes, the difficult balance between institutional tactics and broader movement building, and the relationship between strategy and tactical choices. Recent research has expanded upon these insights, and we hope that scholars continue to incorporate law and legal institutions into existing social movement theories.

Research could develop around the basic questions that have motivated much research on law and social movements: why do groups decide to turn to the law, and what is the impact of a litigation strategy? For instance, one direction for future studies is to further consider the influence of public opinion on judicial decision-making. Some scholars (Baumgartner, DeBoef, and Boydstun 2008; Egan, Persily, and Wallsten 2008) are beginning to investigate the matter, but more work is needed. We know little about how legal activists can seize moments when public views are shifting to further social movement legal causes. Another promising direction is to further analyze the relationship between activist lawyers and the larger movement. Under what conditions do activist lawyers tend to dominate movement strategy, and how best can they be held accountable by their intended constituencies? Relatedly, what roles do non-activist lawyers from across the profession play for social movements?

Moreover, researchers would do well to augment their exploration in cross-movement and cross-national, comparative directions. Only a small number of researchers offer explicit cross-national comparisons (for examples, see Epp 1998; Fuchs 2013; Kawar 2011; Pierceson 2005). Furthermore, scholars have only begun to consider the influence of international law and transnational governing structures on movements' legal mobilization (Cichowki 2004; Lutz and Sikkink 2001; Van der Vet 2014). For example, studies (e.g. Kay 2011) of the North American Agreement of Labor Cooperation have begun to chart a course, but additional exploration of the impact of such international legal policies is needed.

Examining activists' use of litigation as a movement strategy provides substantial opportunity for additional research for social movement scholars. As we have briefly outlined here, both the basic questions long motivating movement research and those that move our thinking in more comparative and international directions need further consideration.

Notes

1   Authors contributed equally and list their names in alphabetical order.
2   Both movements focused on a variety of forms of discrimination, in employment and education, for instance. The women's movement also considered reproductive rights, while the civil rights movement in this era fought staunchly for voting rights.
3   Below we discuss possible negative consequences of pursuing grievances via the courts.
4   In the Supreme Court's 1963 *NAACP v. Button* decision, the court set aside Virginia statutes barring legal-advocacy groups from pursuing cases in court. The Virginia laws were established to prevent the NAACP from taking legal steps against racist practices in that state.

5 Although Meyer and Boutcher focus on the particular case of the NAACP and the desegregation litigation campaign, the mechanisms identified undoubtedly matter for other examples as well. For example, movements regularly share personnel between each other, alter the political opportunity structure that other movements must work within, and emulate strategies and organizational structures that they think work in a given time and place.

References

Abel, Richard L. 1985. "Lawyers and the Power to Change." *Law & Policy* 7: 5–18.

Albiston, Catherine R. and Laura Beth Nielsen. 2014. "Funding the Cause: How Public Interest Law Organizations Fund Their Activities and Why It Matters for Social Change." *Law & Social Inquiry* 39: 62–95.

Alter, Karen J. and Jeannette Vargas. 2000. "Explaining Variation in the Use of European Litigation Strategies: European Community Law and British Gender Equality Policy." *Comparative Political Studies* 33: 452–82.

Andersen, Ellen. 2005. *Out of the Closets and into the Courts: Legal Opportunity Structure and Gay Rights Litigation*. Ann Arbor: The University of Michigan Press.

Andrews, Kenneth T. and Bob Edwards. 2004. "Advocacy Organizations in the Political Process." *Annual Review of Sociology* 30: 479–506.

Andrews, Kenneth T. and Kay Jowers. 2012. "Lawyers and Litigation in the Southern Civil Rights Movement." Paper presented at the annual meeting of the Law & Society Association, Honolulu, HI.

Baker, Carrie N. 2008. *The Women's Movement against Sexual Harassment*. New York: Cambridge University Press.

Barclay, Scott and Daniel Chomsky. 2014. "How Do Cause Layers Decide When and Where to Litigate on Behalf of Their Cause?" *Law & Society Review* 48: 595–620.

Barclay, Scott and Shauna Fisher. 2006. "Cause Lawyers in the First Wave of Same Sex Marriage Litigation." In *Cause Lawyers and Social Movements*, edited by Austin Sarat and Stuart A. Scheingold, 84–100. Stanford, CA: Stanford University Press.

Baumgartner, Frank R., Suzanna L. DeBoef, and Amber E. Boydstun. 2008. *The Decline of the Death Penalty and the Discovery of Innocence*. New York: Cambridge University Press.

Behrmann, Christian and Jon Yorke. 2013. "The European Union and the Abolition of the Death Penalty." *Pace International Law Review Online Companion* 4: 1–78.

Boutcher, Steven A. 2011. "Mobilizing in the Shadow of the Law: Lesbian and Gay Rights in the Aftermath of *Bowers v. Hardwick*." *Research in Social Movements, Conflict and Change* 31: 175–205.

Boutcher, Steven A. 2013. "Lawyering for Social Change: Pro Bono Publico, Cause Lawyering, and the Social Movement Society." *Mobilization* 18: 179–196.

Boutcher, Steven A. and James E. Stobaugh. 2013. "Law and Social Movements." In *The Wiley-Blackwell Encyclopedia of Social and Political Movements*, edited by David A. Snow, Donatella della Porta, Bert Klandermans, and Doug McAdam. Malden, MA: Blackwell Publishing.

Burstein, Paul. 1991. "Legal Mobilization as a Social Movement Tactic: The Struggle for Equal Employment Opportunity." *American Journal of Sociology* 96: 1201–1225.

Burstein, Paul. 1998. "Interest Organizations, Political Parties, and the Study of Democratic Politics." In *Social Movements and American Political Institutions*, edited by Anne N. Costain and Andrew S. McFarland, 39–56. Lanham, MD: Rowman & Littlefield.

Cable, Sherry, Donald W. Hastings, and Tamara Mix. 2002. "Different Voices, Different Venues: Environmental Racism Claims by Activists, Researchers, and Lawyers." *Human Ecology Review* 9: 26–42.

Campbell, Amy Leigh. 2003. *Raising the Bar: Ruth Bader Ginsburg and the ACLU Women's Rights Project*. Lexington, KY: Xlibris.

Chemerinsky, Erwin. 2016. "Citizens Have a Right to Sue for Climate Change Action." *New York Times* May 23.

Chen, Alan K. and Scott L. Cummings. 2013. *Public Interest Lawyering: A Contemporary Perspective*. New York: Wolters Kluwer Law & Business.

Chua, Lynette J. 2012. "Pragmatic Resistance, Law, and Social Movements in Authoritarian States: The Case of Gay Collective Action in Singapore." *Law & Society Review* 46: 713–748.

Cichowski, Rachel A. 2004. "Women's Rights, the European Court and Supranational Constitutionalism." *Law & Society Review* 38: 489–512.

Coglianese, Cary. 2001. "Social Movements, Law, and Society: The Institutionalization of the Environmental Movement." *University of Pennsylvania Law Review* 150: 85–118.

Cole, Luke W. and Sheila R. Foster. 2001. *From the Ground Up: Environmental Racism and the Rise of the Environmental Justice Movement*. New York: New York University Press.

Cummings, Scott L. and Ingrid Eagly. 2001. "A Critical Reflection on Law and Organizing." *UCLA Law Review* 48: 443–517.

Cummings, Scott L. and Douglas NeJaime. 2009. "Lawyering for Marriage Equality." *UCLA Law Review* 57: 1235–1331.

Cummings, Scott L. and Deborah L. Rhode. 2009. "Public Interest Litigation: Insights from Theory and Practice." *Fordham Urban Law Journal* 36: 604–651.

Currier, Ashley. 2009. "Deferral of Legal Tactics: A Global LGBT Social Movement Organizational Perspective." In *Queer Mobilizations: LGBT Activists Confront the Law*, edited by Scott Barclay, Mary Bernstein, and Anna-Maria Marshall, 21–37. New York: New York University Press.

De Fazio, Gianluca. 2012. "Legal Opportunity Structure and Social Movement Strategy in Northern Ireland and the Southern United States." *International Journal of Comparative Sociology* 53: 3–22.

Den Dulk, Kevin R. 2006. "In Legal Culture, But Not of It: The Role of Cause Lawyers in Evangelical Legal Mobilization." In *Cause Lawyers and Social Movements*, edited by Austin Sarat and Stuart A. Scheingold, 197–219. Stanford, CA: Stanford University Press.

Dezalay, Yves and Bryant G. Garth. 2001. "Constructing Law Out of Power: Investing in Human Rights as an Alternative Political Strategy." In *Cause Lawyering and the State in a Global Era*, edited by Austin Sarat and Stuart A. Scheingold, 354–381. New York: Oxford University Press.

Dezalay, Yves and Bryant G. Garth, eds. 2012. *Lawyers and the Construction of Transnational Justice*. New York: Routledge.

Dorf, Michael C. and Sidney Tarrow. 2014. "Strange Bedfellows: How an Anticipatory Countermovment Brought Same-Sex Marriage into the Public Arena." *Law & Social Inquiry* 39: 449–473.

Dotan, Yoav. 2015. "The Boundaries of Social Transformation through Litigation: Women's and LGBT Rights in Israel, 1970–2010." *Israel Law Review* 48: 3–38.

Dunlap, Mary C. 1994. "Gay Men and Lesbians Down by Law in the 1990s USA: The Continuing Toll of *Bowers v. Hardwick*." *Golden Gate University Law Review* 24: 1–39.

Egen, Patrick J., Nathaniel Persily, and Kevin Wallsten. 2008. "Gay Rights." In *Public Opinion and Constitutional Controversy*, edited by Patrick J. Egan, Jack Citrin, and Nathaniel Persily. New York: Oxford University Press.

Epp, Charles R. 1998. *The Rights Revolution: Lawyers, Activists, and Supreme Courts in Comparative Perspective*. Chicago: University of Chicago Press.

Eskridge, William N. 2001. "Channeling: Identity-based Social Movements and Public Law." *University of Pennsylvania Law Review* 150: 419–525.

Eskridge, William N. 2013. "Backlash Politics: How Constitutional Litigation Has Advanced Marriage Equality in the United States." *Boston University Law Review* 93: 275–323.

Ewick, Patricia and Susan Silbey. 1998. *The Common Place of Law: Stories from Everyday Life*. Chicago: Chicago University Press.

Fuchs, Gesine. 2013. "Strategic Litigation for Gender Equality in the Workplace and Legal Opportunity Structure in Four European Countries." *Canadian Journal of Law and Society* 28: 189–208.

Galanter, Marc. 1974. "Why the 'Haves' Come Out Ahead: Speculations on the Limits of Legal Change." *Law and Society Review* 9: 95–160.

Galanter, Marc. 1983. "The Radiating Effects of Courts." In *Empirical Theories about Courts*, edited by Keith O. Boyum and Lynn Mather, 117–142. New York: Longman.

Gamson, William A. and David S. Meyer. 1996. "Framing Political Opportunity." In *Comparative Perspectives on Social Movements: Political Opportunities, Mobilizing Structures, and Cultural Framings*, edited by Doug McAdam, John D. McCarthy, and Mayer N. Zald, 275–290. New York: Cambridge University Press.

Garden, Charlotte. 2013. "Union Made: Labor's Litigation for Social Change." *Tulane Law Review* 88: 193–256.

Gerrard, Michael B. 2014. "Introduction and Overview." In *Global Climate Change and U.S. Law*, edited by Michael B. Gerrard and Jody Freeman, 2nd edn, 3–34. Chicago: American Bar Association.

Goldberg, Suzanne B. 2015. "Obergefell at the Intersection of Civil Rights and Social Movements." *California Law Review* 6: 157–165.

Greenberg, Jack. 1994. *Crusaders in the Courts: How a Dedicated Band of Lawyers Fought for the Civil Rights Revolution*. New York: Basic Books.

Greenhouse, Linda and Reva B. Siegel. 2011. "Before (and After) *Roe v. Wade*: New Questions about Backlash." *Yale Law Journal* 120: 2028–2087.

Hacker, Hans J. 2005. *The Culture of Conservative Christian Litigation*. Lanham, MD: Rowman & Littlefield.

Handler, Joel F. 1978. *Social Movements and the Legal System: A Theory of Law Reform and Social Change*. New York: Academic Press.

Hilbink, Thomas. 2006. "The Profession, the Grassroots and the Elite: Cause Lawyering for Civil Rights and Freedom in the Direct Action Era." In *Cause Lawyers and Social Movements*, edited by Austin Sarat and Stuart A. Scheingold, 145–163. Stanford, CA: Stanford University Press.

Hilson, Chris. 2002. "New Social Movements: The Role of Legal Opportunity." *Journal of European Public Policy* 9: 238–255.

Jenkins, Jeffery A. and Justin Peck. 2013. "Building toward Major Policy Change: Congressional Action on Civil Rights, 1941–1950." *Law and History Review* 31: 139–198.

Kane, Melinda and Thomas Alan Elliott. 2014. "Turning to the Courts: A Quantitative Analysis of the Gay and Lesbian Movement's Use of Legal Mobilization." *Sociological Focus* 47: 219–237.

Kawar, Leila. 2011. "Legal Mobilization on the Terrain of the State: Creating a Field of Immigrant Rights Lawyering in France and the United States." *Law & Social Inquiry* 36: 354–387.

Kay, Tamara. 2011. "Legal Transnationalism: The Relationship between Transnational Social Movement Building and International Law." *Law & Social Inquiry* 36: 419–454.

Kitschelt, Herbert. 1986. "Political Opportunity Structures and Political Protests: Anti-Nuclear Movements in Four Democracies." *British Journal of Political Science* 16: 57–85.

Lemaitre, Julieta and Kristin Bergtora Sandvik. 2015. "Shifting Frames, Vanishing Resources, and Dangerous Political Opportunities: Legal Mobilization among Displaced Women in Colombia." *Law & Society Review* 49: 5–38.

Levinson, Sanford and Jack M. Balkin. 2005. "Should Liberals Stop Defending Roe?" *Legal Affairs* Nov. 28. Available at: http://www.legalaffairs.org/webexclusive/debateclub_ayotte1205.msp (accessed July 5, 2016).

Levitsky, Sandra R. 2006. "To Lead with Law: Reassessing the Influence of Legal Advocacy Organizations in Social Movement." In *Cause Lawyers and Social Movements*, edited by Austin Sarat and Stuart A. Scheingold, 145–163. Stanford, CA: Stanford University Press.

Levitsky, Sandra R. 2015. "Law and Social Movements: Old Debates and New Directions." In *The Handbook of Law and Society*, edited by Austin Sarat and Patricia Ewick, 382–398. Hoboken, NJ: Wiley.

Lui, Sida and Terence D. Halliday. 2011. "Political Liberalism and Political Embeddedness: Understanding Politics in the Work of Chinese Criminal Defense Lawyers." *Law & Society Review* 45: 831–865.

Lutz, Ellen and Kathryn Sikkink. 2001. "The Justice Cascade: The Evolution and Impact of Foreign Human Rights Trials in Latin America." *Chicago Journal of International Law* 2: 1–33.

Mayeri, Serena. 2011. *Reasoning from Race: Feminism, Law, and the Civil Rights Revolution.* Cambridge, MA: Harvard University Press.

McAdam, Doug. 1982. *Political Process and the Development of Black Insurgency, 1930–1970.* Chicago: University of Chicago Press.

McCammon, Holly J. 2001. "Labor's Legal Mobilization: Why and When Do Workers File Unfair Labor Practices?" *Work and Occupations* 28: 143–175.

McCammon, Holly J., Brittany N. Hearne, Allison R. McGrath, and Minyoung Moon. 2018. "Legal Mobilization and Analogical Legal Framing: Feminist Litigators' Use of Race-Gender Analogies." *Law & Policy* 40: 57–78.

McCammon, Holly J. and Allison R. McGrath. 2015. "Litigating Change? Social Movements and the Court System." *Sociology Compass* 9: 128–139.

McCann, Michael W. 1994. *Rights at Work: Pay Equity Reform and the Politics of Legal Mobilization.* Chicago: University of Chicago Press.

McCann, Michael W. 2004. "Law and Social Movements." In *The Blackwell Companion to Law and Society*, edited by Austin Sarat, 506–522. Oxford: Blackwell.

McCann, Michael W. 2008. "Litigation and Legal Mobilization." In *The Oxford Handbook of Law and Politics*, edited by Gregory A. Caldeira, R. Daniel Kelemen, and Keith E. Whittington, 522–540. New York: Oxford University Press.

McCarthy, John D. and Mayer N. Zald. 1977. "Resource Mobilization and Social Movements: A Partial Theory." *American Journal of Sociology* 82: 1212–1241.

Meili, Stephen. 2001. "Latin American Cause-Lawyering Networks." In *Cause Lawyering and the State in a Global Era*, edited by Austin Sarat and Stuart A. Scheingold, 307–333. New York: Oxford University Press.

Meili, Stephen. 2005. "Cause Lawyering for Collective Justice: A Case Study of the Amparo Colectivo in Argentina." In *The Worlds Cause Lawyers Make: Structure and Agency in Legal Practice*, edited by Austin Sarat and Stuart A. Scheingold, 383–409. Stanford, CA: Stanford University Press.

Merry, Sally Engle. 1990. *Getting Justice and Getting Even: Legal Consciousness among Working-Class Americans.* Chicago: University of Chicago Press.

Meyer, David S. and Steven A. Boutcher. 2007. "Signals and Spillover: *Brown v. Board of Education* and Other Social Movements." *Perspectives on Politics* 5: 81–93.

Michalowski, Raymond. 1998. "All or Nothing: An Inquiry into the (Im)Possibility of Cause Lawyering under Cuban Socialism." In *Cause Lawyering: Political Commitments and Professional Responsibility*, edited by Austin Sarat and Stuart Scheingold, 523–545. New York: Oxford University Press.

Morag-Levine, Noga. 2003. "Partners No More: Relational Transformation and the Turn to Litigation in Two Conservationist Organizations." *Law & Society Review* 37: 457–509.

Morris, Aldon. 1984. *The Origins of the Civil Rights Movement: Black Communities Organizing for Change*. New York: Free Press.

NeJaime, Douglas. 2011. "Winning through Losing." *Iowa Law Review* 96: 941–1012.

NeJaime, Douglas. 2012. "The Legal Mobilization Dilemma." *Emory Law Journal* 61: 663–736.

O'Connor, Karen. 1980. *Women's Organizations' Use of the Courts*. Lexington, MA: Lexington Books.

O'Connor, Karen and Lee Epstein. 1984. "A Legal Voice for the Chicano Community: The Activities of the Mexican American Legal Defense and Educational Fund, 1968–82." *Social Science Quarterly* 65: 245–256.

Pierceson, Jason. 2005. *Court, Liberalism, and Rights: Gay Law and Politics in the United States and Canada*. Philadelphia, PA: Temple University Press.

Rosenberg, Gerald N. 1991. *The Hollow Hope: Can Courts Bring about Social Change?* Chicago: University of Chicago Press.

Rosenberg, Gerald N. 2006. "Courting Disaster: Looking for Change in All the Wrong Places." *Drake Law Review* 54: 795–815.

Santos, Boaventura de Sousa and César A. Rodríguez-Garavito. 2005. *Law and Globalization from Below: Towards a Cosmopolitan Legality*. New York: Cambridge University Press.

Sarat, Austin and Stuart A. Scheingold, eds. 2001. *Cause Lawyering and the State in a Global Era*. New York: Oxford University Press.

Schacter, Jane S. 2009. "Courts and the Politics of Backlash: Marriage Equality Litigation, Then and Now." *Southern California Law Review* 82: 1153–1223.

Scheingold, Stuart A. 1974. *The Politics of Rights: Lawyers, Public Policy, and Political Change*. New Haven, CT: Yale University Press.

Schneider, Elizabeth M. 1986. "The Dialectic of Rights and Politics: Perspectives from the Women's Movement." *New York University Law Review* 61: 589–652.

Solberg, Rorie Spill and Eric N. Waltenburg. 2006. "Why Do Interest Groups Engage the Judiciary? Policy Wishes and Structural Needs." *Social Science Quarterly* 87: 558–572.

Southworth, Ann. 2009. *Lawyers of the Right: Professionalizing the Conservative Coalition*. Chicago: University of Chicago Press.

Stone, Christopher. 1972. *Should Trees Have Standing? Law, Morality, and the Environment*. New York: Oxford University Press.

Teles, Steven M. 2008. *The Rise of the Conservative Legal Movement: The Battle for Control of the Law*. Princeton, NJ: Princeton University Press.

Turner, Tom and Carr Clifton. 1990. *Wild by Law: The Sierra Club Legal Defense Fund and the Places It Has Saved*. San Francisco, CA: Sierra Club Legal Defense Fund.

Tushnet, Mark V. 1994. *Making Civil Rights Law: Thurgood Marshall and the Supreme Court, 1936–1961*. New York: Oxford University Press.

Van der Vet, Freek. 2014. "Holding on to Legalism: The Politics of Russian Litigation on Torture and Discrimination before the European Court of Human Rights." *Social & Legal Studies* 23: 361–381.

Vanhala, Lisa. 2009. "Anti-discrimination Policy Actors and Their Use of Litigation Strategies: The Influence of Identity Politics." *Journal of European Public Policy* 16: 738–754.

Vanhala, Lisa. 2011a. *Making Rights a Reality? Disability Rights Activists and Legal Mobilization*. New York: Cambridge University Press.

Vanhala, Lisa. 2011b. "Social Movements Lashing Back: Law, Social Change, and Intra-Social Movement Backlash in Canada." *Studies in Law, Politics, and Society* 54: 113–140.

Vanhala, Lisa. 2012. "Legal Opportunity Structures and the Paradox of Legal Mobilization by the Environmental Movement in the UK." *Law & Society Review* 46: 523–556.

Wasby, Stephen L. 1984. "How Planned Is 'Planned Litigation'?" *American Bar Foundation Research Journal* 1984: 83–138.

Wiecek, William M. 1977. *The Sources of Antislavery Constitutionalism in American, 1760–1848*. Ithaca, NY: Cornell University Press.

Wilson, Bruce M. and Juan Carlos Rodríguez Cordero. 2006. "Legal Opportunity Structures and Social Movements: The Effects of Institutional Change on Costa Rican Politics." *Comparative Political Studies* 39: 325–351.

Yeazell, Stephen C. 2004. "*Brown*, the Civil Rights Movement, and the Silent Litigation Revolution." *Vanderbilt Law Review* 57: 1975–2003.

Zemans, Frances Kahn. 1983. "Legal Mobilization: The Neglected Role of the Law in the Political System." *American Political Science Review* 77: 690–703.

18

Social Movements in Interaction with Political Parties

SWEN HUTTER, HANSPETER KRIESI, AND
JASMINE LORENZINI

Introduction

Social movements and political parties play vital and often complementary roles for democratic representation (e.g. Kitschelt 1993). At the same time, social movement and party scholars often fail to engage in a fruitful dialogue in order to understand large-scale processes of social and political change. However, new attempts have been made to revitalize this discussion. Among others, McAdam and Tarrow (2010, 2013) have outlined a research agenda on social movements and electoral politics based on the "contentious politics approach." Moreover, recent research has brought back the cleavage concept to social movement studies (Hutter 2014; Kriesi et al. 2012). Finally, the rise of new hybrid political forces has revived interest in concepts like Kitschelt's (2006: 280) "movement parties" (defined as coalitions of activists who emanate from social movements and try to apply the organizational and strategic practices of social movements in the electoral arena) or Almeida's (2010, 2014) "social movement partyism" (defined as opposition parties that align with civil society organizations and use their organizational resources to heavily engage in street protests).

In this chapter, we take up these recent attempts and sketch a research agenda that conceptualizes and empirically studies how movement-party interactions might vary both quantitatively and qualitatively under conditions of functioning representative linkages, on the one hand, and a "crisis of representation" (Mainwaring 2006), on the other. A "crisis of representation" is characterized by unstable patterns of representation and citizens who believe that they are not well represented. Telling examples come from Latin America in the 1990s and early 2000s (e.g. Lupu 2014; Mainwaring, Bejarano and Pizarro Leongomez 2006; Roberts 2013) but also, more recently, from Southern Europe in the early 2010s. In Southern Europe, new political actors have entered the scene after the onset of the Great Recession in late 2008. In a

The Wiley Blackwell Companion to Social Movements, Second Edition. Edited by David A. Snow, Sarah A. Soule, Hanspeter Kriesi, and Holly J. McCammon.
© 2019 John Wiley & Sons Ltd. Published 2019 by John Wiley & Sons Ltd.

first phase, social movements have taken to the streets to oppose not only austerity policies, but also the way representative democracy currently works (e.g. Ancelovici, Dufour, and Nez 2016; Giugni and Grasso 2016). They occupied the squares and encouraged political deliberation to give voice to those whose demands remained unanswered. In a second phase, new parties have been created to bring these demands to the institutional arena (e.g. della Porta et al. 2017). Thus, we have seen sustained, accelerated, and complex interactions and fusion of movements and parties. These developments have been linked to declining political trust and dissatisfaction with democracy and have resulted in some of the highest electoral volatility levels ever recorded in the post-war period in Europe (e.g. Hernandez and Kriesi 2016).

To develop our ideas on how movement-party interactions play out in "normal" and "crisis" periods, we proceed in four steps. First, we briefly introduce political parties and social movements as key actors for democratic representation and highlight the various functions that they perform. Second, we present four selected research fields that treat political parties and social movements as separate entities and attempt to understand the various linkages and interactions at work. Third, we bring in the idea of a "crisis of representation" and how this might influence party-movement relations. Finally, we conclude with a discussion on how well our ideas might travel to non-democratic settings.

Movements and Parties: Two Key Actors for Democratic Representation

We begin by defining the two actors that we are discussing in this chapter: social movements and political parties. Political parties are organizations that represent and aggregate citizens' interests so that electoral majorities can be built to govern a country (Mudge and Chen 2014). They compete with other political parties through electoral contests to gain votes and access to power. Social movements, by contrast, are "networks of informal interaction between a plurality of individuals, groups and/ or organizations, engaged in a political and/or cultural conflict, on the basis of a shared collective identity" (Diani 1992: 3). The key features of social movements relate to informal interactions, shared beliefs and solidarity, and contentious participation through collective non-institutional political action.

Tilly (1978) proposed a distinction between social movements and polity members, the former being challengers who seek access to the institutionalized realm of politics, the latter having routinized access to decision-making. However, as Goldstone (2003) noted, the boundaries between these two realms of politics are fuzzy and permeable. In a similar vein, Kriesi (2015) argues that social movement and parties are linked in different ways that go beyond alliances between the two. In general terms, parties can become social movements in as much as they are based on strong social movements and use the social movements' mobilization strategies, while social movements can choose to become political parties in order to defend and represent their interests directly in the electoral channel. Moreover, we have recently seen the emergence of a rather contradictory political actor, the anti-party as an organization competing for election through attacks against the mainstream parties (for examples, see below).

In democracies, political parties and social movements fulfill similar functions in that they both are key actors in the process of democratic representation (e.g. Kitschelt 1993, 2003). They both contribute to articulating citizens' demands and preferences, as well as to decision-making by aggregating preferences and by providing information. In a well-functioning democracy, they may play complementary roles in the representation of interests. Political parties offer political programs and participate in elections in order to gain access to government and to implement them. Social movements seize new demands that remain unanswered by institutional actors and articulate them in the non-electoral channels of the public sphere. Together with interest groups which we do not address in the present chapter, both parties and movements constitute the backbone of citizens' representation.[1]

Historically, parties emerged as the "political creatures of social groups" (Mudge and Chen 2014: 311), but they moved away from their representative function – aggregating demands and preferences – and increasingly sought to gain office by shaping policy preferences of voters and complying with interest groups' demands. We witnessed the transformation of parties into catch-all parties which recruit their voters from all walks of life, the withdrawal and transfer of the leadership of the mainstream (cartel-)parties into the government institutions, and the de-politicization and convergence of mainstream parties on the major policy issues. Mair (2013) attributed this erosion of the mainstream parties' representative function to the increasing tension between "responsibility" and "responsiveness," i.e. the tension between the parties' role as representatives of the national citizen publics and their role as governments being responsible to a wide range of domestic, inter- and supranational stakeholders. This process opened a "window of opportunity" for new challenger parties and social movements which constitute alternatives to political parties when they are not delivering on their representative functions. Indeed, social movements advance demands that are unheard or unaddressed by political parties. They relate to conflicts in society that are not (yet) articulated in institutional politics. Contrary to political parties, social movements are not always at the forefront of political conflict, however. Nevertheless, social movements remain active in other fields, such as the cultural one, when they are less visible in the political arena (Diani 1992; Taylor 1989). During periods of intense political conflict they may regain visibility and play a key role in shaping and transforming political parties and systems.

Movement Versus Parties: Mutual Influence and Interdependence

We identified four strands in the literature that study the relations between social movements and political parties but keep them analytically apart. All four strands emphasize the dynamic nature of the interactions at play, but they differ in terms of how they conceptualize the interactions and the time frame studied. More specifically, we introduce: (1) the idea of parties as allies in the political process approach; (2) parties and movements as key actors involved in the articulation of new societal cleavages; (3) research on the agenda-setting power of protest; and (4) the contentious politics approach to movements and elections.

In the political process approach, political parties mainly enter the stage as part of the political context of social movements and protest politics (see Chapter 1 by

McAdam and Tarrow, in this volume). That is, political parties are part of the alliance and conflict structure in which social movements are embedded. The party system, in turn, is seen as shaped by the institutional structure, most importantly, by the electoral system, which determines to a large extent the number and orientation of the parties available as possible allies of the social movements. It is this idea of parties as potential allies that has been most important in this strand of the literature (but see Van Dyke 2003, on the role of threats). Ideally, social movements expand a given issue-specific conflict in the general public, i.e. they create public controversy where there was none before, they draw the public's attention to the issue in question and frame it in line with their own demands, and, by doing so, they strengthen the hand of their allies, particularly political parties within the parliamentary arena. To put it differently, the expansion of conflict in the public sphere is seen as the general "weapon of the weak" that allows social movements to create political opportunities for elites, not only in the negative sense of repression, as Tarrow (1994: 98) has observed, but also in the positive sense that politicians seize the opportunity created by the challengers and defend their cause within the political system. Parties and their representatives may pick up the cause of the challengers for opportunistic reasons, as is the case when political entrepreneurs seize the opportunity created by the challengers to proclaim themselves tribunes of the people. They may also do so for more substantive or ideological reasons. Telling examples of both dynamics can be found in partisan reactions to the nuclear incident in Fukushima and the anti-nuclear protests that it spurred (see Müller and Thurner 2017). Viewed from the party's perspective, the challenger's outside mobilization may be a welcome support for the party's long-term agenda in a given policy subsystem, which may help the party to undermine the established policy monopoly in the subsystem in question.

In line with the idea of parties as allies, work in the tradition of the political process approach has emphasized the role of ideologically close parties. In the European context, this was mainly about the role of radical and mainstream parties from the left as movement allies (e.g. della Porta and Rucht 1995; Kriesi et al. 1995; Maguire 1995). Moreover, government participation of these parties was identified as a crucial condition for the facilitation of movement activities. In opposition, the left-wing parties were more likely to act as allies of ideologically close movements, such as the new social movements in the 1970s and early 1980s.

A second and related strand of the literature deals with the rise of new cleavages and the interplay between movement and party politics. Here, the starting point of the analysis is newly emerging social divisions and how they are politically articulated and organized. While the cleavage concept figured still prominently in the literature on the "new social movements," it has only recently been brought back to the analysis of social movements (see della Porta 2015; Hutter 2014; Kriesi et al. 2012). The aim of the approach is to study the long-term development and relations of political conflict in different arenas. The question of who is being organized into politics by whom is a key subject of cleavage models, which not only focus on the perpetuation of established cleavages but also on the emergence of new divides (see Bartolini 2000; Rokkan 2000).

In this spirit, Kriesi and colleagues (2008, 2012) have shown that two major waves of political change have fundamentally altered the structure of political conflict in Western Europe since the 1980s, giving rise to what they call a new "integration-demarcation" cleavage that divides the "losers" and "winners" of globalization. In party politics, the new populist right, rather than simply articulating a populist challenge to the mainstream parties which habitually govern, has given voice to this new structural conflict by successfully mobilizing the cultural anxieties of those social strata that feel threatened by increasing economic, cultural, and political globalization. By contrast, the Greens and other new left parties constitute their most clear-cut opponents in this new structural conflict.

Based on the idea of how social divides are politically articulated, Kriesi and his colleagues have taken into account a broader view on movement-party relations (see, especially, Hutter 2012, 2014). They have also started from the most common assumption of the political process tradition, i.e. "a simple, positive relationship between openings in the political structure [electoral politics, in our case] and protest mobilization" (Meyer and Minkoff 2004: 1484). However, as Goldstone (2003: 9) suggested, they have also taken into account that protest politics might be "both an alternative and a valuable supplement" to electoral politics. More specifically, their empirical analysis on the way new conflicts are articulated in protest and movement politics in Western Europe shows that the relationship between the two arenas depends on the political actors involved. In Western Europe, the political left and right follow different logics with respect to the relationship between electoral and protest mobilization. The left waxes and wanes at the same time in both arenas, while the right alternatively turns to one arena or the other, but not to both at the same time. The differences in the way protest and electoral politics are used to mobilize the adherents are rooted in differing ideological and strategic orientations.

Other empirical research indicates that the idea of "different logics" tends to hold in the Western European context only. When summarizing the development of US politics in the last decades, McAdam and Tarrow (2013) highlight positive relations between protest and electoral politics for both the political right and the left. In line with the dominant view in the political process approach, they argue that while the dominance of the left in electoral politics triggered left-libertarian movements, the hegemony of right-wing forces came with strong right-wing and conservative movements. By contrast, in Central and Eastern Europe, Cisar and his colleagues (Cisar and Navratil 2015; Cisar and Vrablíkova 2016) observe negative relations between movement and party politics for all ideological camps in the years since 1989. Thus, the *more* certain collective actors and their claims are represented in party politics, the *less* visible they are on the streets in the Czech Republic, Hungary, Poland, and Slovakia.

A third approach to movement-party relations focuses on the agenda-setting power of social movements and protest activities (for an overview, see Walgrave and Vliegenthart 2012). This research area also builds on the general insights of the political process approach, but it presents a specific and more short-term view of the processes at stake. More precisely, it adopts the agenda-setting literature's emphasis on issue attention as the main mechanism of how to study linkages across different arenas or sites. If different actors, in our case, movements and parties, emphasize an issue in a sequential way, one can assume some kind of interdependence at play. Such a view on movement-party relations allows for "standardizing" the measures of protest and party politics. The unit of analyses is the attention devoted to a given issue during a specific time period, which introduces the possibility of comparing the effect of protest across issue areas, over time, and across countries.

Most of the existing agenda-setting studies indicate that protest matters in terms of which issues are emphasized by other actors. Political elites start giving more attention to an issue when protests over this issue increase. This finding raises the question of why other actors (in our case, political parties) should care about the signals sent by protesters. Vliegenthart et al. (2016) argue that protests can be seen as a particular type of information about urgent societal problems communicated to elites. The protest signal seems particularly attractive because "it is public and accessible, negative, most of the time unambiguous, with a clear evaluative slant, applicable to one's task, and (for some elites) compatible with existing predispositions" (ibid.: 8). Moreover, involvement in protest allows participants to raise issue-specific concerns, and it shows their commitment implied by the fairly high "costs" involved in this form of political participation. Thus, protest – and especially protest that gets into the news – is a strong signal sent by a mobilized part of the population. Depending on the strength of the signal, political parties might ultimately interpret it even as an electoral threat (e.g. Burstein 1999; Lohmann 1993; Uba 2016).

Based on the idea that protest is an informative signal and that its effects depend on both the characteristics of the signal and the recipient, previous studies have shown that, for example, protest size matters more than protest frequency (e.g. McAdam and Su 2002), and that protests related to certain issues matter more than others (e.g. Walgrave and Vliegenthart 2012). Regarding the recipients, the existing literature usually compares different political agendas (like the parliamentary or governmental agenda). Studies in the US context indicate that protest is especially effective early on in the policy cycle (e.g. King, Cornwall, and Dahlin 2005; Soule and King 2006). In the case of Belgium, the government seems to react more than parliament, however (Walgrave and Vliegenthart 2012). A recent study by Hutter and Vliegenthart (2016) on four West European countries does not treat the parties in parliament as a unitary actor but focuses on the responses of single parties. Overall, their results indicate that parties are more likely to respond if they are in opposition and if their competitors have reacted to the issue previously. Once opposition status is controlled for, left-right orientations no longer significantly affect parties' reactions to social movement activities.

Overall, agenda-setting presents a highly instructive and systematic way to study the political consequences of movements, i.e. the translation of movement claims into political decisions. At the same time, the broader literature on political movement outcomes (for recent reviews, see Chapter 25 by Amenta, Andrews, and Caren, in this volume; Bosi, Giugni, and Uba 2016) stresses even more the crucial role played by incumbent parties in government. Incumbent parties have the key resources at their disposal to repress or make concessions to social movements, and such concessional responses go beyond agenda-setting and include policy change and cooptation into government. In line with the argument that we propose here, Bosi et al. (2016: 14ff.) emphasize that research on the political consequences of movements could profit from an even closer attention to the "targets" of protests and the mechanisms linking social movement activities and the reactions of (party) political decision-makers.

Finally, McAdam and Tarrow (2010, 2013), drawing on the contentious politics approach, have introduced a set of mechanisms that link elections, parties, and social movements. In part, the mechanisms build on earlier work in the political process approach. However, they move beyond it and hint at the fuzzy boundaries between electoral and movement politics. More precisely, McAdam and Tarrow (2013: 328) introduce five types of what they call "electoral contention" – defined as a "set of recurring links between elections and movements that powerfully shapes movement dynamics and electoral outcomes." These processes include elections as movement tactics, proactive and reactive electoral mobilization by social movements, the long-term impact of changes in electoral outcomes on patterns of movement mobilization (similar to what we have discussed in view of changing cleavage structures) and, finally, movement-induced party polarization.

Let us briefly turn to McAdam and Tarrow's last process as it presents a sequential view of movement-party interactions. In a nutshell, this process refers to the possibility that the victory of movement allies in party politics may trigger reactive mobilizations on the part of the movement after the electoral contest. While such mobilizations in the streets by close movement allies may strengthen the governing party, they can also backfire as they might increase the tensions between the "logics of movement and electoral politics," as McAdam and Tarrow (2013: 333) suggest – or in the terms used by Mair (2013), such mobilizations may foster the tension between "responsibility and responsiveness." That is, political parties may be keener to collaborate with social movements before elections when they seek their support to show commitment to specific issues or their help to bring out the votes in the campaign. Once in government, the party ally has to take into account various stakeholders and appeal to the median voter, and might therefore shy away from a strong commitment to single issues and the radical solutions promoted by the social movement. By contrast, the movement that has been closely aligned with the new incumbent party tends to stick to its more radical solutions on the issue it pursues. McAdam and Tarrow (2010, 2013) argue that the movement activists will challenge the compromise-seeking solutions of their party allies and even attempt to take control of the party organization. If they are successful in this effort, the party in office may adopt policy solutions that may encourage "defections by moderate voters who now regard the party as too extreme in its views" (McAdam and Tarrow 2013: 333). In other words, too close relations between movements and parties can lead to the capture of parties by movement activists and polarization that might not be electorally beneficial for the party in the mid to long term.

In the USA, social movements from the left and right – i.e. from the civil rights movement in the 1950 and 1960s to the Tea Party movement in more recent years – have pushed both major US parties (the Republicans and Democrats) toward the fringes of the political spectrum. McAdam and Tarrow (2010) nicely illustrate this process with the example of the antiwar movement and its influence on the American party system after 9/11 (see also Heaney and Rojas 2007, 2015). Similarly, McAdam and Kloos (2014) show how social movements contribute to the radicalization of party stances and to the polarization of institutional politics more generally. Their study is important in offering an in-depth analysis of parties on the right of the political spectrum. It shows that although social movements of the right do not often occupy the public space or resort to protest activities, they do have a strong influence on party positions and agendas by other means. In the UK, the British Labour Party under Michael Foot and Jeremy Corbyn offers ample illustrations of these kinds of processes as well.

Overall, the four research fields indicate the complexity and dynamic nature of the interactions between social movements and political parties. They highlight that alliance building is a core type of interaction, but that there are other potential ways for parties and movements to influence each other, and that parties' strategic considerations are key to understanding the processes at work. At the same time, they do not systematically discuss the way a more profound crisis of representation might affect the interplay of movements and parties.

Crises of Representation and the Emergence of New Parties

As stated in the Introduction, a crisis of representation refers to unstable patterns of representation and citizens who believe that they are not well represented by the political elites (Mainwaring 2006). Thus, the functioning of the representative linkages between parties and popular preferences is put into question. According to Mainwaring et al. (2006), both attitudinal and behavioral indicators signal such a situation. More specifically, a crisis of representation is related not only to attitudinal factors such as suddenly increasing political distrust and dissatisfaction with how democracy works, but also to behavioral factors such as lower turnout at the polls, increasing electoral volatility, and protest behavior. Overall, these factors might render movement-party interactions more frequent, conflictive, and complex. Moreover, these short-term interaction dynamics blur the boundaries between movement and electoral politics and they may result in prominent outcomes such as policy changes or the rise of new political forces. In this section, we briefly sketch how a crisis of representation opens opportunities for the emergence of specific types of social movements and the creation of new parties. We discuss first how movements transform parties, then we introduce the idea of new parties created by social movements, and, lastly, we discuss some social movements that take up the form of hybrid political parties.

The first notable instance of transformed relationships between social movements and parties in times of a crisis of representation relates to the capacity of social movements to transform existing political parties. Notably, in two-party systems, social movements choose to gain influence through intra-party mobilization since they have very little or no chance of winning any electoral contest. In particular, research shows that the introduction of primaries and the selection of candidates by members of the parties contributed to the growing influence of social movements over established political parties (McAdam and Kloos 2014). This finding is based on a thorough historical research on the links between the Tea Party and the Republican Party in the USA. This example illustrates the transformative capacity of a social movement and, in particular, the radicalization of the Republican Party under the growing influence of the Tea Party. In Austria and Switzerland, radical populist right parties resulted from the transformation or adaptation of liberal-conservative and agrarian parties to the emergence of new issues (anti-immigration) and to new social cleavages (opposing winners and losers of globalization) (Kriesi et al. 2008). Hence, the transformation of existing political parties can also happen in the absence of a strong and highly visible social movement external to the party system. These two examples illustrate the transformations of political parties in multiparty systems.

Another illustration of the transformation of political parties by social movements comes from the social movements of the 1970s and 1980s in Western European countries. These social movements reflected changes in the class structure and the cultural preferences of the middle class in Western democracies. The left libertarians demanded new rights related to cultural liberalism and individual freedom. In this context, contestation on the streets often resulted in an alliance between existing parties on the left and these social movements (Kitschelt 1988, 1989). In particular, in countries where the social democrats were not threatened on their left by a communist party, they responded to the demands of the new social movements by including cultural liberalism and environmental concerns in their programmatic stances (Kriesi et al. 1995). In other words, social movements and parties can make alliances that build on respective strengths – bringing to the institutional arena the issues defended by social movements and reinforcing the popular support of parties (Heaney and Rojas 2015; Schwartz 2010). However, as this example also illustrates, such close alliances are not without consequences for the parties involved: as a result of their alliance with the new social movements, the social democrats have become middle-class parties in almost all countries of Western Europe (Gingrich and Häusermann 2015; Kitschelt 1994).

Second, some movements create opportunities for the emergence of new parties or they themselves enter the electoral contest and, therefore, constitute a political party. The creation of a party is a strategic choice made by social movement actors to innovate when confronted with the failure of other mobilization tactics (Cowell-Meyers 2014). The creation of new parties is more likely in proportional systems, as these offer more chances of electoral success. Therefore, running for election is a potential strategy to advance issues neglected by the mainstream parties (Kitschelt 2006; Kriesi 2015). The history behind the creation of the Green Parties in many European countries illustrates the social movements' adoption of an electoral strategy. The Green Parties were first founded in the 1980s once the social movement actors who had mobilized against nuclear power plants realized that their alliance with the parties on the left did not bring about the expected change in terms of energy policies (Kitschelt 1989; Poguntke 1993).

Another illustration comes from Latin America, where social movements supported the emergence of indigenous political parties. The social movements of the late 1990s emerged as a response to neoliberal reforms and brought about revolutions in the political landscape of many Latin American countries (Almeida 2007; Johnston and Almeida 2006; Shefner, Pasdirtz and Blad 2006). Research on Latin America shows that the failure of existing parties to address the grievances of their constituencies led to a class alliance between the poor and the middle class who joined forces to oppose neoliberal measures (Walton and Ragin 1990). As mainstream parties converged towards austerity measures and neoliberal reforms, parties lost their brand and their distinctive appeal to their constituencies (Lupu 2014). In a process described by multiple studies (see, for instance, Bellinger and Arce 2011; Lupu 2014; Roberts 2013; Weyland 2003), the adoption of austerity measures across the political spectrum, the broad dissatisfaction among the population, the rising violence in the streets, and ultimately the alliance between social classes weakened political parties and created opportunities for the emergence of indigenous-based parties. It is interesting to note here that "brand dilution" and the loss of electoral appeal were stronger among the left-wing parties which, as incumbents, were forced to embrace neoliberal ideologies. As mainstream parties from the left lost votes, new parties with a strong indigenous base gained power. These parties were deeply connected to social networks promoting the rights of indigenous groups (Rice and Van Cott 2006). Similar processes can be observed when studying party competition in Southern Europe since 2010. The most extreme example is PASOK, the incumbent social-democratic party in Greece when the euro-crisis struck in early 2010. The electorate punished the party heavily, much more than the mainstream parties from the right. Moreover, the most dramatic change in the Greek party system was the rise of a challenger party (Syriza) from the left of the political spectrum (see della Porta et al. 2017; Hutter, Kriesi, and Vidal 2018).

Third, some social movements form hybrid political parties, as recent examples illustrate. Kriesi (2015) refers to some of these hybrid organizations as "anti-party," which is a contradiction in terms, but nevertheless an empirical reality: it is a political organization that mobilizes against the established party system as a whole by competing with the established parties in the electoral channel. For instance, in Italy, the Movimento Cinque Stelle (M5S) represents an example of a social movement that evolved into an anti-party. The M5S started as a social movement during the V-tour in 2007 (Bordignon and Ceccarini 2013). In this event, taking place across Italian cities, the activists collected signatures for an initiative demanding to reform the law on political candidates and the criteria for eligibility. In this first phase, the movement opposed corruption in Italian politics. Only a year later, the movement decided to enter the electoral contest through "civic lists" supported by Beppe Grillo, the movement's leader, and, in 2010, some candidates emerged more directly from the M5S to run for elections at the local level. From there, M5S moved on to participate in regional (2012) and national (2013) elections. Although the M5S increasingly entered the electoral competition, it retained an anti-party character, as the militants of the movement continued to defend direct democracy and deliberation, denounced politicians as being corrupt, and dissuaded party leaders from running for election (e.g. Baldini 2013; Biorcio 2013).

In part, our discussion on the way movement-party interactions work in times of a crisis of representation differs from the four lines of research presented above because it questions the neat separation of movement and party politics, points to accelerated interaction dynamics, and the rise of what can be called anti-parties, i.e. organizations competing in elections through attacks against the mainstream parties at large. This calls for research that is more process-oriented, integrates long-term and short-term interaction dynamics, and focuses on hybrid actors.

Broadening the Perspective: Transformations in Context

Most studies presented so far are theoretical accounts of processes that took place in Europe and the United States, with a small incursion into Latin America. We have presented four research fields on how parties and social movements interact in "normal" political times and we have sketched ideas of a changing relationship in times of a crisis of representation. Yet, we have not touched upon the idea of party-movement interactions in non-democratic contexts. This question is interesting for it paves the way to research that is less western-centered and that systematically compares stages of party-movement relationships in consolidated democracies, in troubled democracies, and during transitions to democracy. In concluding this chapter, we want to broaden the discussion to two specific cases of such interactions in authoritarian regimes. Research shows that protests in non-democratic settings emerge in times of economic turmoil because citizens are no longer ready to comply with corrupt, anti-democratic elites when they do not supply economic welfare (Brancati 2014). Furthermore events play a crucial role in triggering protest, thanks to their transformative potential (Berezin 2012). Moreover, both our examples highlight the accelerated and more contingent interactions of movements and parties in such contexts and how these interactions may shape the outcome of the transition processes.

The Arab Spring seems a perfect illustration of a protest wave in a non-democratic setting where the weakness of social movements and the quasi-absence of political parties played a considerable role in the emergence of the protest and its aftermath. The Arab Spring came as a surprise to many observers in the light of the weakness of civil society and the strength of the state (Dupont and Passy 2011). Nonetheless, widespread dissent brought down authoritarian regimes first, in Tunisia, then in Egypt, and next in Libya. These movements built on broad dissatisfaction among the population, in particular among young people who benefitted from access to higher education but could not enter the labor market. Yet, grievances alone did not bring about these revolutions (Bennani-Chraïbi and Fillieule 2003; Gamson 2011). In the case of Tunisia, a strong labor movement sustained a series of strikes and the dissidents of the 1980s (union activists and Islamist militants) were at the core of the mobilization (Anderson 2011). In Egypt, family ties, as well as neighborhood and mosques relations contributed to spreading information and sustaining mobilization (Diani 2011). In addition to civil society organizations and private networks, it is interesting to analyze the specific role of parties in Tunisia and Egypt where opposition parties existed in spite of their ban from public life (Lesch 2014). In Egypt, the Muslim Brotherhood endorsed Tahrir Square mobilizations quite rapidly and, thanks to their experience in campaigning for votes, they obtained more than 40% of the votes at the first elections. Similarly, in Tunisia, Ennahda obtained electoral success at the first elections. Yet, the two countries' fate was quite different subsequently. In Egypt, a strong polarization emerged when the pro-Morsi/Muslim Brotherhood camp confronted the party that endorsed the legacy of Mubarak, the SCAF (Supreme Council of the Armed Forces), whereas, in Tunisia, political elites tried to build a broad consensus by involving all parties and political tendencies to write the Constitution (Lesch 2014). Note that multiple organizations played a critical role in bringing about socio-political transformations. But when these other organizations are weak, the transition to a new (democratic) regime is rendered more difficult. More generally, the limited political experience of political parties and other political organizations in a context of authoritarianism hinders the capacity of such organizations to effectively govern.

A last illustrative example of the dynamic interactions between social movements and public authorities in times of transition to democracy is provided by Beissinger's (2002) study of nationalist mobilization and the collapse of the Soviet Union. In his impressive study, Beissinger argues that the sweeping institutional change obtained by nationalist mobilization in the streets was far from predetermined by structural factors but can only be understood by a close analysis of the processes that unfolded in the period 1987–1991. Based on a combination of qualitative process-tracing with various kinds of quantitative techniques that take time seriously, such as event history and cross-sectional time series analysis, he shows how the wave of nationalist mobilization emerged, how it was related to other struggles, and how it ultimately contributed to the fall of the Soviet State. The pace of the events outstripped the reaction capacity of the institutions and the understanding of the leaders (to say nothing of outside observers). The tidal force of nationalism produced enormous confusion and division within Soviet institutions, making it even more difficult to find institutional solutions. The nationalist mobilizations developed their own self-reinforcing dynamics as recursive and emulative processes multiplied. While structural factors such as the prevailing ethnic composition and the degree of urbanization of a given territory facilitated early mobilizations, their effect weakened over time as the mobilization shifted to groups with less propitious initial conditions who emulated the early risers.

For the present purpose, it is most interesting to point out that during such critical junctures interactions between challengers in the streets and the party in power are contracted in time and their outcomes are far more contingent than during "normal periods." To put it differently, Beissinger highlights the dynamic role that protest events have in challenging those in power but also in shaping the agency of those involved in the struggle and their future actions. Thus, protest events have the potential to become a causal variable in the chain of subsequent actions:

> As the constraints of order weaken, the clustering and linkage of contentious events themselves can provide a structure-like patterning of action that can gain a particular weight and alter expectations about the possibilities for future action, thereby facilitating further agency. In this way, events can come to act as part of their own causal structure.
>
> (Beissinger 2002: 17)

Once such a dynamic development is set in motion, party-movement interactions take place under far less predictable conditions than in "normal" periods of more stable interaction patterns and incremental change. In such context, protest activities might lead to more profound (and often unintended) changes in the alliance and conflict structure in which social movements are embedded.

Acknowledgments

The authors gratefully acknowledge funding from the ERC Project 'Political Conflict in Europe in the Shadow of the Great Recession' (Project ID: 338875).

Note

1   As ideal types, interest groups operate mainly through pressure politics in and through institutions, and they have heavily invested in organization-building (see Kitschelt 2003).

References

Almeida, Paul. 2007. "Defensive Mobilization: Popular Movements Against Economic Adjustment Policies in Latin America." *Latin American Perspectives* 34(3): 123–139.

Almeida, Paul. 2010. "Social Movement Partyism: Collective Action and Political Parties." In *Strategic Alliances: Coalition Building and Social Movements*, edited by Nella Van Dyke and Holly J. McCammon, 170–196. Minneapolis: University of Minnesota Press.

Almeida, Paul. 2014. *Mobilizing Democracy: Globalization and Citizen Protest*. Baltimore, MD: Johns Hopkins University Press.

Ancelovici, Marcos, Pascale Dufour, and Héloïse Nez. eds. 2016. *Street Politics in the Age of Austerity: From Indignados to Occupy. Amsterdam*; Amsterdam University Press.

Anderson, Lisa. 2011. "Demystifying the Arab Spring: Parsing the Difference Between Tunisia, Egypt, and Libya." *Foreign Affairs* 90(3): 2–7.

Baldini, Gianfranco. 2013. "Don't Count Your Chickens Before They're Hatched: The 2013 Italian Parliamentary and Presidential Elections." *South European Society and Politics* 18(4): 473–497.

Bartolini, Stefano. 2000. *The Political Mobilization of the European Left, 1860–1980: The Class Cleavage*. Cambridge: Cambridge University Press.

Beissinger, Mark. 2002. *Nationalist Mobilization and the Collapse of the Soviet State.* Cambridge: Cambridge University Press.

Bellinger, Paul T. and Moisés Arce. 2011. "Protest and Democracy in Latin America's Market Era." *Political Research Quarterly* 64(3): 688–704.

Bennani-Chraïbi, Mounia and Olivier Fillieule. 2003. *Résistances et protestations dans les sociétés musulmanes*. Paris: Les Presses de Sciences Po.

Berezin, Mabel. 2012. "Events as Templates of Possibility: An Analytic Typology of Political Facts." In *The Oxford Handbook of Cultural Sociology*, edited by Jeffrey C. Alexander, Ronald Jacobs, and Philip Smith, 613–635. Oxford: Oxford University Press.

Biorcio, Roberto. 2013. *Politica a 5 Stelle. Idee, Storia e Strategie del Movimento di Grillo.* Milan: Feltrinelli.

Bordignon, Fabio and Luigi Ceccarini. 2013. "Five Stars and a Cricket. Beppe Grillo Shakes Italian Politics." *South European Society and Politics* 18(4): 427–449.

Bosi, Lorenzo, Marco Giugni, and Katrin Uba, eds. 2016. *The Consequences of Social Movements*. Cambridge: Cambridge University Press.

Brancati, Dawn. 2014. "Pocketbook Protests: Explaining the Emergence of Pro-Democracy Protests Worldwide." *Comparative Political Studies* 47(11): 1503–1530.

Burstein, Paul. 1999. "Social Movements and Public Policy." In *How Social Movements Matter*, edited by Marco Giugni, Doug McAdam, and Charles Tilly, 3–21. Minneapolis: University of Minnesota Press.

Cisar, Ondrej and Jiri Navratil. 2015. "At the Ballot Boxes or in the Streets and Factories: Economic Contention in the Visegrad Group." In *Austerity and Protest: Popular Contention in Times of Economic Crisis*, edited by Marco Giugni and Maria Grasso, 35–53. London: Routledge.

Cisar, Ondrej and Katerina Vrablíkova. 2016. "At the Parliament or in the Streets? Issue Composition of Contentious Politics in the Visegrad Countries." Unpublished manuscript.

Cowell-Meyers, Kimberly B. 2014. "The Social Movement as Political Party: The Northern Ireland Women's Coalition and the Campaign for Inclusion." *Perspectives on Politics*, 12(01): 61–80.

della Porta, Donatella. 2015. *Social Movements in Times of Austerity*. Cambridge: Polity Press.

della Porta, Donatella, Joseba Fernandez, Hara Kouki, and Lorenzo Mosca. 2017. *Movement Parties against Austerity*. Cambridge: Polity Press.

della Porta, Donatella and Dieter Rucht. 1995. "Left-Libertarian Movements in Context: A Comparison of Italy and West Germany, 1965–1990." In *The Politics of Social Protest: Comparative Perspectives on States and Social Movements*, edited by J. Craig Jenkins and Bert Klandermans, 113–133. Minneapolis: University of Minnesota Press.

Diani, Mario. 1992. "The Concept of Social Movement." *The Sociological Review* 40(1): 1–25.

Diani, Mario. 2011. "Networks and Internet into Perspective." *Swiss Political Science Review* 17(4): 469–474.

Dupont, Cédric and Florence Passy. 2011. "The Arab Spring or How to Explain those Revolutionary Episodes?" *Swiss Political Science Review* 17(4): 447–451.

Gamson, William A. 2011. "Arab Spring, Israeli Summer, and the Process of Cognitive Liberation." *Swiss Political Science Review* 17(4): 463–468.

Gingrich, Jane and Silja Häusermann. 2015. "The Decline of the Working-Class Vote, the Reconfiguration of the Welfare Support Coalition and Consequences for the Welfare State." *Journal of European Social Policy* 25(1): 50–75.

Giugni, Marco and Maria Grasso. eds. 2016. *Austerity and Protest: Citizens' Reactions to the Economic Crisis and Policy Responses to It*. Farnham: Ashgate.

Goldstone, Jack A. 2003. "Introduction: Bridging Institutionalized and Noninstitutionalized Politics." In *States, Parties, and Social Movements*, edited by Jack A. Goldstone, 1–24. Cambridge: Cambridge University Press.

Heaney, Michael T. and Fabio Rojas. 2007. "Partisans, Nonpartisans, and the Antiwar Movement in the United States." *American Politics Research* 35(4): 431–464.

Heaney, Michael T. and Fabio Rojas. 2015. *Party in the Street: The Antiwar Movement and the Democratic Party after 9/11*. Cambridge: Cambridge University Press.

Hernandez, Enrique and Hanspeter Kriesi. 2016. "The Electoral Consequences of the Financial and Economic Crisis in Europe." *European Journal of Political Research* 55(2): 203–224.

Hutter, Swen. 2012. "Congruence, Counterweight or Different Logics? Comparing Electoral and Protest Politics." In *Political Conflict in Western Europe*, edited by Hanspeter Kriesi et al., 182–203. Cambridge: Cambridge University Press.

Hutter, Swen. 2014. *Protesting Economics and Culture in Western Europe: New Cleavages in Left and Right Politics*. Minneapolis, MN: University of Minnesota Press.

Hutter, Swen, Hanspeter Kriesi, and Guillem Vidal. 2018. "Old Versus New Politics: The Political Spaces in Southern Europe in Times of Crises." *Party Politics* 24(1): 10–22.

Hutter, Swen and Rens Vliegenthart. 2016. "Who Responds to Protest? Protest Politics and Party Responsiveness in Western Europe." *Party Politics* OnlineFirst. doi: 10.1177/1354068816657375.

Johnston, Hank and Paul D. Almeida, eds. 2006. *Latin American Social Movements: Globalization, Democratization, and Transnational Networks*. Lanham, MD: Rowman & Littlefield.

King, Brayden G., Marie Cornwall, and Eric C. Dahlin. 2005. "Winning Woman Suffrage One Step at a Time: Social Movements and the Logic of the Legislative Process." *Social Forces* 83(3): 1211–1234.

Kitschelt, Herbert. 1988. "Left-Libertarian Parties: Explaining Innovation in Competitive Party Systems." *World Politics* 40(2): 194–234.

Kitschelt, Herbert. 1989. *The Logics of Party Formation: Ecological Politics in Belgium and West Germany*. Ithaca, NY: Cornell University Press.

Kitschelt, Herbert. 1993. "Social Movements, Political Parties, and Democratic Theory." *The Annals of the American Academy of Political and Social Science* 528: 13–29.

Kitschelt, Herbert. 1994. *The Transformation of European Social Democracy*. Cambridge: Cambridge University Press.

Kitschelt, Herbert. 2003. "Landscapes of Political Interest Intermediation. Social Movements, Interest Groups, and Parties in the Early Twenty-First Century." In *Social Movements and Democracy*, edited by Pedro Ibarra, 83–103. New York: Palgrave Macmillan.

Kitschelt, Herbert. 2006. "Movement Parties." In *Handbook of Party Politics*, edited by Richard S. Katz and William Crotty, 278–290. London: Sage.

Kriesi, Hanspeter. 2015. "Party Systems, Electoral Systems, and Social Movements." In *The Oxford Handbook of Social Movements*, edited by Donatella della Porta and Mario Diani, 667–680. Oxford: Oxford University Press.

Kriesi, Hanspeter, Edgar Grande, Martin Dolezal, et al. 2012. *Political Conflict in Western Europe*. Cambridge: Cambridge University Press.

Kriesi, Hanspeter, Edgar Grande, Romain Lachat, Martin Dolezal, Simon Bornschier, and Timotheos Frey. 2008. *West European Politics in the Age of Globalization*. Cambridge: Cambridge University Press.

Kriesi, Hanspeter, Ruud Koopmans, Jan Willem Duyvendak, and Marco Giugni. 1995. *New Social Movements in Western Europe: A Comparative Analysis*. Minneapolis: University of Minnesota Press.

Lesch, Anne M. 2014. "Troubled Political Transitions: Tunisia, Egypt, and Libya." *Middle East Policy* 21(1): 62–74.

Lohmann, Susanne. 1993. "A Signalling Model of Informative and Manipulative Political Action." *American Political Science Review* 87(2): 319–333.

Lupu, Noam. 2014. "Brand Dilution and the Breakdown of Political Parties in Latin America." *World Politics* 66(4): 561–602.

Maguire, Diarmuid. 1995. "Opposition Movements and Opposition Parties: Equal Partners or Dependent Relations in the Struggle for Power and Reform?" In *The Politics of Social Protest: Comparative Perspectives on States and Social Movements*, edited by J. Craig Jenkins and Bert Klandermans, 99–112. Minneapolis: University of Minnesota Press.

Mainwaring, Scott. 2006. "The Crisis of Representation in the Andes." *Journal of Democracy* 17(3): 13–27.

Mainwaring, Scott, Anna Maria Bejarano, and Eduardo Pizarro Leongomez. 2006. *The Crisis of Democratic Representation in the Andes*. Stanford, CA: Stanford University Press.

Mair, Peter. 2013. *Ruling the Void*. London: Verso.

McAdam, Doug and Karina Kloos. 2014. *Deeply Divided: Racial Politics and Social Movements in Postwar America*. Oxford: Oxford University Press.

McAdam, Doug and Yang Su. 2002. "The War at Home: Antiwar Protests and Congressional Voting, 1965 to 1973." *American Sociological Review* 67(5): 696–721.

McAdam, Doug and Sidney Tarrow. 2010. "Ballots and Barricades: On the Reciprocal Relationship Between Elections and Social Movements." *Perspectives on Politics* 8(2): 529–542.

McAdam, Doug and Sidney Tarrow. 2013. "Social Movements and Elections: Toward a Broader Understanding of the Political Context of Contention." In *The Future of Social Movement Research: Dynamics, Mechanisms, and Processes*, edited by Jacquelien Van Stekelenburg, Conny Roggeband, and Bert Klandermans, 325–346. Minneapolis: University of Minnesota Press.

Meyer, David S. and Debra C. Minkoff. 2004. "Conceptualizing Political Opportunity." *Social Force* 82(4): 1457–1492.

Mudge, Stephanie L. and Anthony S. Chen. 2014. "Political Parties and the Sociological Imagination: Past, Present, and Future Directions." *Annual Review of Sociology* 40: 305–330.

Müller, Wolfgang C. and Paul W. Thurner, eds. 2017. *The Politics of Nuclear Energy in Western Europe*. Oxford: Oxford University Press.

Poguntke, Thomas. 1993. *Alternative Politics: The German Green Party*. Edinburgh: Edinburgh University Press.

Rice, Roberta and Donna Lee Van Cott. 2006. "The Emergence and Performance of Indigenous Peoples' Parties in South America: A Subnational Statistical Analysis." *Comparative Political Studies* 39(6): 709–732.

Roberts, Kenneth M. 2013. "Market Reform, Programmatic (De)alignment, and Party System Stability in Latin America." *Comparative Political Studies* 46(11): 1422–1452.

Rokkan, Stein. 2000. *Staat, Nation und Demokratie in Europa. Die Theorie Stein Rokkans aus seinen gesammelten Werken rekonstruiert und eingeleitet von Peter Flora*. Frankfurt: Suhrkamp.

Schwartz, Mildred A. 2010. "Interactions Between Social Movements and US Political Parties." *Party Politics* 16(5): 587–607.

Shefner, Jon, George Pasdirtz, and Cory Blad. 2006. "Austerity Protests and Immiserating Growth in Mexico and Argentina." In *Latin American Social Movements: Globalization, Democratization, and Transnational Networks*, edited by Hank Johnston and Paul D. Almeida, 19–42. Lanham, MD: Rowman & Littlefield.

Soule, Sarah A. and Brayden G. King. 2006. "The Stages of the Policy Process and the Equal Rights Amendment, 1972–1982." *American Journal of Sociology* 111(6): 1871–1909.

Tarrow, Sidney. 1994. *Power in Movement*. Cambridge: Cambridge University Press.

Taylor, Verta. 1989. "Social Movement Continuity: The Women's Movement in Abeyance." *American Sociological Review* 54(5): 761–775.

Tilly, Charles 1978. *From Mobilization to Revolution*. Reading, MA: Addison-Wesley.

Uba, Katrin. 2016. "Protest against School Closures in Sweden: Accepted by Politicians?" In *The Consequences of Social Movements*, edited by Lorenzo Bosi, Marco Giugni, and Katrin Uba, 159–168. Cambridge: Cambridge University Press.

Van Dyke, Nella. 2003. "Protest Cycles and Party Politics. The Effects of Elite Allies and Antagonists on the Student Protest in the United States, 1930–1990." In *States, Parties, and Social Movements*, edited by Jack A. Goldstone, 226–245. Cambridge: Cambridge University Press.

Vliegenthart, Rens, Stefaan Walgrave, Ruud Wouters, et al. 2016. "The Media as a Dual Mediator of the Political Agenda Setting Effect of Protest: A Longitudinal Study in Six West-European Countries." *Social Forces* 95(2): 837–859.

Walgrave, Stefaan and Rens Vliegenthart. 2012. "The Complex Agenda-Setting Power of Protest. Demonstrations, Media, Parliament, Government, and Legislation in Belgium, 1993–2000." *Mobilization* 17(2): 129–156.

Walton, John and Charles Ragin. 1990. "Global and National Sources of Political Protest: Third World Responses to the Debt Crisis." *American Sociological Review* 55(6): 876–890.

Weyland, Kurt. 2003. "Economic Voting Reconsidered: Crisis and Charisma in the Election of Hugo Chávez." *Comparative Political Studies* 36(7): 822–848.

19

Nonviolent and Violent Trajectories in Social Movements

Kurt Schock and Chares Demetriou

Introduction[1]

Violent and nonviolent resistance are analyzed by scholars of social movements as well as by scholars in other disciplines and sub-disciplines who study civil resistance, political violence, international security, and conflict resolution. However, there is relatively little recognition of each other's research. Our aim is to identify main lines of research across disciplinary divides with regard to: (1) processes of radicalization, whereby nonviolent contention becomes violent; (2) processes of demilitarization, whereby there is a decisive strategy shift from armed to unarmed contention; and (3) the impact of armed actors on the likelihood of success of unarmed actors in contemporaneous struggles.

We recognize that although observers may make distinctions between violent and nonviolent action, participants in struggles do not necessarily make these distinctions. We also recognize that a mix of violent and nonviolent action is often implemented in highly charged struggles. We regard violent resistance as threatened or actual use of arms or physical force to produce bodily harm or death to opponents, bystanders, and in some cases the general public, and we regard nonviolent resistance as overt unarmed methods of protest waged outside routine and institutional political channels.[2] However, we also recognize that distinctions between violent and nonviolent action are often fuzzy. For example, there are unarmed acts that are not nonviolent, such as the destruction of property and physical altercations between opposing parties. We recognize that actual violence against the state, the threat of violence against the state, and nonviolent contention all exist under the long shadow of state coercion and violence; and we recognize that in some instances nonviolent action may be implemented to provoke the intervention of the state, an institution based on violence. We also recognize that strategies and actions may have expressive as well as strategic motivations. Expressive considerations "are those involving the gratifications that come with the exercise and display of power" and strategic

The Wiley Blackwell Companion to Social Movements, Second Edition. Edited by David A. Snow, Sarah A. Soule, Hanspeter Kriesi, and Holly J. McCammon.
© 2019 John Wiley & Sons Ltd. Published 2019 by John Wiley & Sons Ltd.

considerations "are those having to do with the judgment of which strategy is likely to contribute toward the attainment of the movement goals" (Turner 1970: 154).

A fundamental analytical distinction between various approaches to strategy concerns the assumption about the degree to which actors have choice. That is, do actors have complete knowledge of various forms of resistance and make instrumental calculations in their selection of strategies and actions? Or is choice of strategy and actions severely constrained or entirely absent due to incomplete information, group dynamics, or structural or cultural context? Civil resistance and security theories, and some social movement literature based on rational choice assumptions tend to emphasize strategic choice, whereas more structural theories of social movements and revolution tend to emphasize the determining impact of context through the elimination of choice. A problem cutting through both approaches is the assumption of coherent actors – an untenable assumption in many instances.

At the extremes, context may determine strategy. For example, unarmed resistance may be the only option in a totalitarian regime where the state monopolizes arms and security forces are cohesive; and armed violence may be necessary in self-defense to prevent a group from being completely exterminated through violence. In most contexts, however, there is some degree of latitude available to challengers – which may vary from minimal to maximum choice – and the choices made are shaped by culture, history, and learning. In his analysis of democratizing Britain and France in the eighteenth and nineteenth centuries, Tilly (1986, 1995) identified repertoires of contention that tended to characterize specific times, places, and conflict dyads. He defined contentious repertoires as:

> a limited set of routines that are learned, shared, and acted out through a relatively deliberate process of choice. Repertoires are learned cultural creations, but they do not descend from abstract philosophy or take shape as a result of political propaganda; they emerge from struggle. People learn to break windows in protest, attack pilloried prisoners, tear down dishonored houses, stage public marches, petition, hold formal meetings, organize special-interest associations. At any particular point in history, however, they learn only a rather small number of alternative ways to act collectively.
>
> (1986: 42)

At the extremes, *no repertoires* exist when previous strategies and actions have no impact on subsequent strategies and actions; and *rigid repertoires* exist when strategies and actions persist despite changes in context, reactions of opponents, and likelihood of success. Tilly argued that *strong repertoires* are most common. That is, the choice of protest methods is relatively limited and results from interactions between challengers and authorities over time as well as the broader structural context in which these interactions occur, with regime type and state capacity being most important (Tilly 2006, 2008).

Although we concur with Tilly that strong repertoires are most common, we are concerned here with *strategy shift*, i.e. a decisive change in the predominant forms of action by challengers engaged in struggle, such as from nonviolent to violent resistance (e.g. radicalization) or vice versa (e.g. demilitarization). Mechanisms that contribute to radicalization and demilitarization in a variety of contexts are identified in the following two sections. In the third section we examine potential consequences of contemporaneous armed resistance for groups engaged in unarmed struggle.

Radicalization: Towards Strategies and Methods of Violent Contention

The adoption by non-state actors of strategies of violent contention is often termed radicalization. Although we adhere to this terminology, we recognize that coupling the term radicalization to violence is not always accepted in the literature. Some authors, rather, define radicalization as the deployment of tactics of contention that are high risk or illegal but not necessarily violent (Cross and Snow 2011; Moskalenko and McCauley 2009), while other authors do not define radicalization through the tactics of contention at all; among the latter, are conceptualizations of radicalization based on ideology or extent of change sought (Demetriou 2012; Juergensmeyer 2005; Sprinzak 1998). Explanations of the use of strategies or methods of violence by non-state actors vary according to the specific phenomena to be explained, on the one hand, and to the explanatory logic, on the other. The focus of explanation and the logic of explanation often interrelate, as, for example, when aggregate phenomena across episodes are explained by macro-level factors; but in principle the focus and the logic of explanation are distinct from each other, and many analysts heed the distinction. Below, while some disciplinary distinctions are drawn, the guiding distinctions are epistemological and cut across disciplines. One of these distinctions regards the type of inquiries on political violence, particularly whether "why" or "how" questions are posed. Another distinction regards the level of analysis and explanation, particularly whether it is the macro-, meso-, or micro-level. Of course, these distinctions are not firm in the literature, with many works traversing them; they are taken here as mapping guidelines.

At the macro-level, studies typically ask why political violence occurs, without being particularly concerned about how strategies of violence develop. They seek to identify root causes or permissive factors setting the stage for political violence. But the "violence-prone stage" is often taken to concern the group or population from which militants emerge. This is the case most particularly in the security studies literature, which is interested in developing predictors for the emergence of violence as well as explanations for past violence. Accordingly, this literature often makes reference to "groups at risk" and employs environmental conditions to explain or identify groups' violence-prone attributes and other relevant dispositional characteristics (Gurr 2000; Piazza 2006; Stern 2003). Thus, for example, factors regarding the international political system may explain dominated and therefore indignant populations; ideology and political culture may explain revolutionary goals and therefore belligerent populations; socio-economic factors may explain economic deprivation and therefore populations with grievances; and so on. Of course, combinations or interactions of different sorts of environmental factors can enter the analysis, such as the interaction of inequalities and political opportunities (Schock 1996).

It is worth adding that analyses at the aggregate level are often forced to conceptualize with broad strokes, which has repercussions for theory building. More specifically, how to operationalize violence as the dependent variable is both crucial and contested. While an inclusive conceptualization and operationalization add cases and confidence in the analysis, some scholars are uneasy at grouping together phenomena that, to them, do not belong together. Perhaps nowhere is this uneasiness and tension more palpable than when the concept of terrorism is involved. This is an exceptionally stretched concept, as over one hundred different definitions of terrorism are in use (Schmid and Jongman 1988; Weinberg, Pedahzur, and Hirsch-Hoefler 2004). Given this, the concept may denote a range of different phenomena. Based on their preferred definition, some scholars argue that the strategy of terror is *sui generis* and must therefore not be considered akin to other strategies of violence, such as those aiming at military or material targets. Bergesen (2007), for example, who effectively holds terrorism to be the exercise of categorical violence, maintains that the willingness to harm civilians implies a disconnect between perpetrator and victim that must be treated as foundational in research. By contrast, Tilly (2004, 2005), while recognizing the existence of strategies of terror, argues that the factors precipitating them are not exclusive, and so the study of this strategy must not be divorced from the study of other strategies of violence or even strategies of transgressive but nonviolent contention.

Studies at the micro-level, too, tend to focus on "why" questions (Lichbach 1995; Moghaddam 2005; Pape 2005), seeking to explain motivations of those participating in political violence. The identified motivations may vary, ranging from ones relating to grievances and other material conditions to ones relating to emotions, such as hatred or resentment of the opponent, sense of belongingness with a militant group, and a search for identity. Micro-level works connected to social psychology may treat political violence as psychopathology, but this is not true of all micro-level works. Most particularly, those stemming from security studies often operate on rational choice theory presuppositions, in which case the motivation of greed as well as rationality are employed to account for individuals' trajectories towards militancy and violence – trajectories often referred to as "radicalization." The tendency is to use statistical or qualitative methods, including interviewing, in order to extrapolate the "mindset" of militants.

However, there is also a line of micro-level works that leaves the window open for "how" questions. These works focus on the reconstruction of individuals' pathways to radicalization (Bosi and della Porta 2012; McCauley and Moskalenko 2011; Viterna 2013). As they examine life trajectories, these works produce predominantly "how accounts" – accounts of how individuals take turns in their lives down the path to violent activism. Often these works – and especially those stemming from the social movement studies tradition – follow constructivist epistemologies, building on activists' own narratives. For example, studying the recruitment of women into the guerrilla insurgency in El Salvador, Viterna (2013) develops accounts of micro-level mobilization. Using hundreds of interviews and combining constructivist and relational sociology, she delineates various paths to mobilization and to the advancing engagement with activism, violence, and the guerillas' quotidian activities – most notably romance and reproduction. Furthermore, taking up the issue conceptually, Cross and Snow (2011) argue that individuals' pathways to radicalism – here taken to mean the adoption of direct and high risk action which may not necessarily be violent – vary depending on whether or not the activists believe they are persecuted by the state and whether or not they are trusted by their grassroots peers. Four types of radicals emerge from this account, one of them being the "militant radical." It is this type of radical, trusted by peers and seemingly persecuted by the state who most typically adopts violence.

The analysis by Cross and Snow bridges the micro- and meso-levels. But other pertinent studies exist firmly at the meso-level. In fact, this is the level of analysis championed most particularly by the many social movement studies emphasizing organizational factors. These are not uniform studies, of course, but it is fair to suggest that in general they focus on "how" questions in addition to, or in lieu of "why" questions. Accordingly, they consider strategies of violence to be gradual and interactive developments, which must then be explained in terms of social interaction. When they bring root causes or other underlying factors in the analysis – as they often do via ideologies and cultural templates – they still keep the focus on the interactions that activate those causes and factors. After all, these studies start from the assumption that social movements develop strategies of violence typically after they have pursued strategies of nonviolent contention;[3] from this perspective, an exclusive focus on root causes is inadequate, since the same causes would be invoked to explain both the nonviolent and the violent phase of social movements.

A branch of such meso-level studies follows what may be labeled the strategic interaction approach, which includes works from both security studies and social movement studies (Brym and Bader 2006; Crenshaw 1995; Weinstein 2006). The disciplinary distinction produces differences in preferred concepts and theories as well as a tacit division of labor. Works in the social movement studies tradition tend to focus on the emergence and persistence of violence, while works in the security studies tradition tend to focus on the "escalation" of violence after its onset; among the works in the latter line – studying how authorities and the challengers end up outbidding each other – one often finds rational actor or game-theory explanations of strategy. In general, however, the two lines converge in using units of analysis that tend to be discrete and pre-given, such as individuals or groups. Weinstein (2006), for example, through a comparison of several historical instances of insurgency, identifies three broad rebel group strategies, one leaning toward governance, the second toward violence, and the third toward resilience. Combining strategic interaction with the analysis of environmental conditions, his approach holds mobilization into the insurgency to be crucial and shaped by factors that raise or lower the barriers to insurgency organization. In general, he argues, resource-rich environments create strategies and pathways pursuing high levels of indiscriminate violence, while resource-poor environments are conducive to more selective violence.

A second branch of meso-level studies evolved from the "political process" approach in the study of social movements (see Chapter 1 by McAdam and Tarrow, in this volume). Its key characteristics are the comprehensive analysis of the context of strategizing and the analysis of strategizing as a dynamic and contingent phenomenon emerging out of that context. So, while many studies related to approaches reviewed above tend to focus on the violent group or its immediate milieu, this approach examines various environmental and organizational factors and explains turns toward violence based on those factors. Thus, for example, the turn to violence by groups that splinter from other groups – a recurring pattern in the development of strategies of violence – is explained not only by the dynamics regarding the groups in question but also by broader dynamics in their environment (e.g. Pearlman 2011).

Furthermore, the work of McAdam, Tarrow, and Tilly (2001) in particular, argues for a mechanism-based epistemology and explains emergent dynamics in terms of social, cognitive, and environmental mechanisms – though the explicit use of mechanisms is not universal in this branch of studies. This approach generally heeds the demarcation of "contentious politics" as wide ranging but comparable forms of activism, including activism that employs strategies of violence and activism that does not. At the same time, it must be added that the comparison of violent to nonviolent strategies of contention has yet to build up steam in the related scholarship, despite the fact that Tilly and Tarrow (2015) discuss together violent and nonviolent activism, showing, for example, similar patterns of mobilization in nonviolent social movements and lethal conflicts.

della Porta (2013) is an exemplar of this branch of meso-level studies. She employs the concept of mechanism to capture the dynamism in phenomena of violent activism, but she does not cover the whole range of contentious politics. She is concerned only with "clandestine political violence," i.e. phenomena of political violence in which the perpetrators act from underground and therefore are organized in relatively small groups with limited military capacity and little or no control of territory. She identifies seven main mechanisms accounting for the emergence of clandestine political violence. Three of these mechanisms work to produce processes of polarization: "escalating protest policing," "competitive escalation during process cycles," and "activation of militant networks." Another three mechanisms contribute more particularly to the development of the clandestine organizations: "organizational compartmentalization," "action militarization," and "ideological encapsulation." The seventh mechanism, pertaining to the groups' later-stage reconfiguration, is labeled "militant enclosure." While della Porta's focus is not on strategizing per se, she makes important contributions in the analysis of the contexts in which strategizing takes place.

Alimi, Demetriou, and Bosi (2015), working in the same tradition at the meso-level, pay closer attention to strategizing. They seek to analyze the emergence of strategies of violence by social movement organizations (a process they call "radicalization") out of five arenas of interaction: (1) the arena between the movement and its political environment; (2) the arena between the movement and the state security forces; (3) the intra-movement arena; (4) the arena between the movement and a counter-movement; and (5) the arena between the movement and its constituencies. In these arenas, they argue, there tend to operate five respective mechanisms conducive to radicalization: (1) "upward spirals of political opportunities and threats"; (2) "outbidding"; (3) "competition for power"; (4) "object shift;" and (5) "dissociation." They maintain that these mechanisms (the first three more than the last two) recur in a wide range of episodes of radicalization, from those featuring social movements where only fringe organizations turned to violence, to those (such as many ethno-nationalist ones) where violence is embraced by most of the movement, to transnational ones featuring organizational spread and pluralism. But they also expect that these mechanisms have roles in the production of radicalization that differ across episodes. For example, they find that the mechanism "outbidding" – referring to the action-counteraction dynamics between social movement organizations, on the one hand, and the state security forces, on the other, that raise the stakes for the two sides – had a particularly important role in the early stage of both the radicalization of the Red Brigades, connected to the Extra-Parliamentary Left movement in the 1960s and 1970s Italy, and the radicalization of al-Qaeda, connected to the Salafi Transnational Jihad movement. By contrast, it had a lesser role in the later stage of these radicalization processes, despite increases in violence; in those later stages, rather, the mechanism of "upward spirals of political opportunities" gained particular salience in the Red Brigades episode, and the mechanism "competition for power" in the al-Qaeda episode (ibid.: 187–192). The authors expect, too, that the five mechanisms they identify are constituted by sub-mechanisms differentially. Thus, for example, in the episode of the Red Brigades, "outbidding" was constituted principally by the sub-mechanisms "provocation," "repression by proxy," and "de-legitimization," whereas in the episode of al-Qaeda, it was constituted principally by the sub-mechanisms "boundary control" and "threat attribution" (ibid.: 175–182). Through analysis of mechanism emergence and interaction, therefore, the authors purport to explain strategic choices about not only the resort to violence but also its progression, including the type of violence pursued.[4]

In short, explanations of the shift to violent contention vary according to the level of analysis and to whether "why" or "how" questions are posed. As a result of this plurality of explanations there has been little academic agreement on how to delineate and typify the various strategies pursued. While the contours of these strategies, and of the various repertoires of contention more broadly, are known to academics, just as activists know them, the details of these strategies and repertoires have not been put under systematic academic scrutiny and so authoritative generalizations about them have yet to be produced. Turner's observations decades ago still sound preliminary: one could therefore adopt his classification of strategies of contention as persuasion, bargaining, and coercion; and one could accept with him that coercive strategies – aiming to manipulate those with the power to make decisions into making decisions they dislike – are particularly, but not necessarily, prone to the adoption of violent means of contention, but one would still have difficulty making fine distinctions among coercive strategies (Turner 1970). The problem is that "what is explained" – in this case, the adoption and development of strategies of violence – cannot be divorced from the explanation.

Demilitarization: From Armed to Unarmed Strategies and Methods

As discussed above, processes of conflict escalation and radicalization have received substantial attention by scholars of social movements and security. Similarly, processes of conflict "de-escalation" and "resolution," such as individual disengagement from terrorist groups (e.g. Horgan 2009) and collective shifts from armed resistance to negotiation, demobilization, or institutional politics (e.g. Zartman 1996) have received substantial attention in the security and conflict resolution literatures. However, decisive strategy shifts from violent to nonviolent resistance have received scant scholarly attention. This is due in part to a common assumption in the social movement literature that nonviolent resistance is situated on an ordinal continuum between conventional politics and violence and that there is a natural escalation from nonviolent to violent resistance when nonviolent action is repressed or deemed ineffective (Schock 2013, 2015). Nevertheless, nonviolent resistance may be a powerful method of struggle in repressive contexts and may even succeed where violence has failed (Chenoweth and Stephan 2011; Nepstad 2011; Schock 2005).[5] Moreover security studies, based on realist assumptions, often glorify the power of violence and dismiss the power of nonviolent resistance; and conflict resolution studies are often merely concerned with cessation of armed conflict, i.e. the attainment of "negative peace."

Dudouet (2013, 2015) and her collaborators have done the most systematic work on demilitarization, i.e. a decisive strategy shift from armed to unarmed contention. They incorporate a mechanism-based epistemology and identify factors at the micro- (leadership) and meso-levels (interrelations between movements and constituents or other parties) that contribute to shifts from predominantly armed to predominantly unarmed strategies in resistance and liberation movements.

At the micro-level, changes in leadership may contribute to demilitarization. This may occur through a generational change in leadership whereby a younger cohort of leaders prefers unarmed over armed resistance. Generational leadership change contributed to a shift from armed to unarmed resistance in the Western Saharan national liberation movement in recent years. The belief system of leaders may also change, which occurred in the Egyptian *Jama'a Islamiya* movement in 1997 as a result of the reinterpretation of doctrinal texts by Islamist scholars leading the movement. Movement leadership may also shift strategy as a result of cost-benefit analysis, which contributed to a shift from guerrilla resistance to unarmed struggle by Maoists in Nepal in 2006 (Dudouet 2013, 2015).

Meso-level organizational factors, such as pressure from a movement's constituency or from within a movement's organizational structure may contribute to demilitarization. Leaders of the violent Egyptian *Jama'a Islamiya* movement, for example, felt responsibility toward their supporters who were subject to mass imprisonment and torture, which contributed to its demilitarization. Similarly, the Zapatista movement in Mexico, which originally engaged in armed action, subsequently shifted to unarmed methods of struggle due to preferences of many of its indigenous constituents who opposed armed struggle (Dudouet 2013, 2015).

Meso-level inter-group and contextual factors may also contribute to demilitarization. Armed challengers often operate in societies composed of multiple civil society actors who cooperate or compete with each other in their attempt to influence or topple the state. In such contexts, demilitarization mechanisms may include reverse outbidding, emulation, and coalition building. Similar to what occurs during processes of radicalization whereby groups competing for support and resources radicalize their goals and strategies in an attempt to "outbid" each other (Alimi, Demetriou, and Bosi 2015; Bloom 2004), a "reverse outbidding" process may occur whereby armed actors shift to unarmed methods and strategies to differentiate themselves from armed actors in order to broaden their domestic or international legitimacy and support. Emulation occurs when groups adopt strategies or tactics that have been effectively implemented by others (McAdam, Tarrow, and Tilly 2001). Effective nonviolent resistance implemented by grassroots Palestinian groups along the separation wall in the West Bank, for example, convinced the leadership of *Fatah* to embrace nonviolent resistance in a more systematic manner. The desire to build coalitions may also contribute to demilitarization. The ETA, part of the Basque independence movement, for example, realized that a shift to nonviolent resistance would contribute to broad-based coalition building across Basque political groups (Dudouet 2013, 2015).

In their work on processes of radicalization, Alimi, Demetriou, and Bosi (2015) maintain that such processes entail potentials for demilitarization as well. According to their analytical framework, this can happen when any or all of the mechanisms that they hold to be conducive to radicalization cease to operate. Indeed, it can happen more decisively when any or all of these mechanisms reverse. Such reverse mechanisms are made up of operations conducive to nonviolent activism and can be thought as mirror images of the identified radicalization-conducive mechanisms. Thus "underbidding" in the arena between the movement and the state security forces is the reverse of "outbidding," "downward spirals of political opportunities" in the arena between the movement and its political environment are the reverse of "upwards spirals of political opportunities," "consensus mobilization" in the intra-movement arena is the reverse of "competition for power," and so on.

Other scholars of political violence have proposed a "substitution model" of conflict that is also cast at the meso-level and focuses on interactions between challengers and authorities. The substitution model maintains that challengers rationally choose between nonviolent and violent strategies and tactics and shift away from methods that are repressed by authorities (Lichbach 1987; Moore 1998). When armed resistance is ineffective in the face of repression, challengers shift to unarmed methods. With regard to the civil rights struggle in Northern Ireland from 1963 to 1976, for example, Cunningham and Beaulieu (2010) argue that the consistent use of repression against violent action promoted shifts to nonviolent action. Inconsistent responses by authorities are hypothesized to encourage further violent action.

The causal chain between macro-level factors and demilitarization is longer and more complex, however, a number of factors can be considered that may be conducive to strategy shifts to nonviolent resistance in recent decades. These include an increasing disparity in the means of violence between civilians and the state in most contexts, development of effective state counter-insurgency techniques, an increasing global concern with human rights, advances in information and communication technologies that publicize human rights violations and promote transnational networking among civil society groups, cross-national diffusion of methods of nonviolent action, cross-national transfer of generic knowledge about nonviolent resistance, an increasing recognition of the effectiveness of nonviolent resistance, and a recognition of the relationship between means and ends (Schock 2005, 2015). In an examination of maximalist challenges that were predominantly armed or unarmed, Chenoweth and Stephan (2011) found that the likelihood of unarmed maximalist challenges became more frequent and more effective as the twentieth century progressed.

Interaction of Violent and Nonviolent Contention

Scholars of radicalization and demilitarization address the questions "How and/or why is there a decisive shift between violent and nonviolent strategies and actions during episodes of contention?" A related question is "What are the consequences for nonviolent struggle when some challenging groups call for or implement violent resistance?" The dynamics and outcomes of the interaction of violent and nonviolent contention among challengers in contemporaneous struggles are complex and understudied.

Scholars of social movements in democratic contexts have *partially* addressed this question through the study of "radical flank" effects. A *positive radical flank* effect occurs when the leverage of moderate challengers is strengthened by the presence of radical challengers. A *negative radical flank* effect occurs when the activities of a radical wing weaken the leverage of moderates (Haines 1988). In the social movement literature, the most common criteria used to differentiate "moderates" and "radicals" are methods of action, extent of change sought, ideology, rhetoric, and compromising stance. The call for or use of violence is considered to be more radical than nonviolent action; revolutionary demands are considered to be more radical than reformist demands; and violent rhetoric, exclusive ideology, and an uncompromising stance are considered to be more radical than rhetoric that is not violent, ideologies that are inclusive, and the willingness to compromise.

Concerning positive radical flank mechanisms, radicals (including violent actors) may make moderate challengers (including nonviolent actors) seem less threatening to elite interests, contribute to public or third party support for moderates, or create a political crisis that is resolved in favor of the moderates (Anner 2009; Braithwaite 2013, 2014; Haines 1988; Jenkins and Eckert 1986; Koopmans 1995; McCammon, Bergner, and Arch 2015). The diffusion of oppositional culture from radical to moderate actors may facilitate nonviolent mobilization of the latter (Isaac, McDonald, and Lukasik 2006). Some have argued that limited uses of armed violence (e.g. for self-defense) by some groups have protected activists from worsening regime or communal violence (Cobb 2014; Wendt 2010), therefore increasing the likelihood of a successful nonviolent challenge.

Concerning negative radical flank mechanisms, radicals (including violent actors) discredit all regime opponents (whether violent or nonviolent) (Haines 1988; Sharp 1973), provoke widespread repression against all challengers (Barrell 1993; Pearlman 2011), reduce popular participation in unarmed campaigns (Chenoweth and Stephan 2011; Chenoweth and Schock 2015), and alienate potential third-party supporters thereby decreasing the possibility that repression backfires (Martin 2015; Wasow 2015).

Scholars of US social movements, while recognizing that radical flank effects may be positive or negative, almost always identify positive radical flank effects. For the US civil rights movement, scholars maintain that the emergence of militant Black Power activists helped increase the public's acceptance of methods of nonviolent action and integrationist goals supported by Martin Luther King, Jr. and the Southern Christian Leadership Conference (Killian 1972; Oberschall 1973: 230) and that the more militant ideology of Black Power and the outbreak of urban riots resulted in increased support and funding for moderate civil rights organizations (Haines 1988; Jenkins and Eckert 1986).

Furthermore, Freeman (1975) found evidence for a positive radical flank effect in the US women's rights movement, maintaining that radical women's groups such as lesbian and socialist feminists increased the bargaining power of mainstream reform organizations such as the National Organization for Women. McCammon, Bergner, and Arch (2015) found that conflict within the Texas women's movement generated a positive radical flank effect by allowing moderate factions to publicly distance themselves from radicals, thereby creating opportunities to appeal to political elites in ways that helped moderates achieve their goals. Similarly, only after the mobilization of more radical socialist labor organizations in the early twentieth century did US labor movement demands for collective bargaining and an eight-hour workday became negotiable issues (Ramirez 1978; Rayback 1966). For the pro-life movement, Rohlinger (2006) found that moderate organizations may benefit from the more extreme rhetoric of more ideologically rigid organizations, but when the extreme organizations use violence, the moderate ones must distance themselves in order to avoid a negative radical flank effect.

Collectively the social movement scholarship on radical flank effects is biased by a reliance on single case studies. The few studies that employ cross-sectional or longer-term longitudinal analysis find less support for a positive radical flank effect. In his study of a random sample of 53 cases from a population of challenges in the USA from 1800 to 1945, Gamson (1990) found that with regard to challenging groups pursing the same general interests, factionalism decreased the likelihood of success of challenging groups. Moreover, evaluating data from thousands of US counties in the 1960s and 1970s, Wasow (2015) demonstrated that proximity to violent protest led to higher proportions of votes for Republican candidates. Conversely, he found that higher frequencies of nonviolent protest led voters to support Democratic candidates. Similarly, at the national level, he found that higher incidences of violent protest led survey respondents to identify "law and order" as the country's greatest priority, while higher incidences of nonviolent protest led voters to identify civil rights as the most important issue.

Moreover, the existing literature often conflates short-term tactical goals (e.g. process goals) with long-term outcomes (e.g. strategic goals) (see Chenoweth and Schock 2015). Haines (1988), for example, concluded that violence had a positive overall impact on the US civil rights movement by drawing funding and support to the movement. Funding, support, and increased attention are important process goals for social movements; however, studies that evaluate the long-term political effects (e.g. Wasow 2015) suggest that radical flanks (in this case violent flanks) may have important strategic costs in terms of the campaign's ability to succeed in the long run.

More specifically, with regard to violent flank effects – rather than the much broader "radical" flanks, which may or may not include violence – the civil resistance literature advances the view that simultaneous violent challenges are likely to undermine the leverage of unarmed struggles. This literature assumes that violent and nonviolent resistance are typically antithetical and that the combination of these strategies is problematic given their diametrically opposed logics and dynamics. It is assumed that in most contexts civilians have the strategic advantage with regard to nonviolent resistance, while the strategic advantage of authorities is with violence. Once challengers take up arms against the state, then they are fighting the state where it is strongest and any restraints on repression that may have existed are removed (Sharp 1973). Moreover, the degree of participation is likely to be less in armed campaigns, as barriers to participation are higher for armed resistance compared to nonviolent resistance (Chenoweth and Stephan 2011).[6]

The civil resistance literature also suggests that under certain conditions violent suppression of unarmed protest may backfire and lead to increased support for the challengers and decreased support for authorities (Martin 2015). However, nonviolent discipline may be important requirement for backfire, since repression of violent challengers is more likely to be perceived as legitimate by the public. In fact, states may attempt to label nonviolent challenges as "violent" or as "terrorists" or use agents provocateurs to spark violence, which enables the state to more easily justify violent repression. Thus, the optimal situation for an unarmed resistance movement, according to assumptions of the civil resistance literature, is strict adherence to nonviolent discipline by all challenging groups.[7] A major problem with maintaining nonviolent discipline, however, is the fragmentation of a challenge into competing groups with diverging goals and methods (Pearlman 2011).

In a quantitative cross-national analysis that focused on *armed* flank effects across up to 106 cases of maximalist unarmed challenges,[8] Chenoweth and Schock (2015) found no systematic evidence for the existence of positive armed flank effects across a wide variety of polities. They did, however, find evidence for an indirect negative armed flank effect whereby the existence of armed challenges decreases the level of participation and therefore the likelihood of success of unarmed challenges. However, they maintain that armed flanks may have varied impacts across a population of cases. For example, if armed flanks help an unarmed campaign to succeed in country *A* but undermine an unarmed campaign in country *B*, then the net cross-national impact might be zero. The complexity of the dynamic is revealed in the qualitative case study part of their analysis, where they found the existence of both positive and negative armed flank effect mechanisms in two of their four cases. Thus, for example, if armed flanks protect activists from state violence but also decrease the number of participants in the unarmed campaign at the same time, the simultaneous positive and negative effects might also have a net impact of zero. Clearly much more research, especially comparative and longitudinal, and analyses of data that is disaggregated from the campaign level, are needed to untangle the complexity of radical, violent and armed flank effects.

Conclusion

Much work still needs to be done to understand processes of radicalization and demilitarization, as well as the dynamics of coeval armed and unarmed challenges. For radicalization and demilitarization, meso-level approaches that identify mechanisms of strategy shift based on analyses of iterative interactions among multiple actors and the context in which these occur seem to be the most fruitful line of sociological research. An even clearer picture of strategy shift emerges when these studies are supplemented by micro-level analyses of life trajectories of activists and social psychological and within-group dynamics, as well as macro-level analyses of relevant structural and cultural changes in national and global contexts.

For dynamics of violent or armed flank effects (as well as broader radical flank effects) more comparative and longitudinal analysis and disaggregate data are needed to untangle the complexity of the phenomena. We must also examine the role of unarmed violence, such as riots on this dynamic; and we must identify various mechanisms through which positive and negative (radical, violent or armed) flank effects occur, recognize the possibility that both positive and negative flank effects may be operating within specific campaigns, and distinguish between short-term tactical goals and long-term strategic goals.

Notes

1 We thank Erica Chenoweth and David A. Snow for their comments.
2 Some take a broader view and regard property as well as people as targets of violence (e.g. Martin, McCarthy, and McPhail 2009), whereas others take a narrower view of violence as acts targeted at human bodies rather than physical objects (e.g. Keane 2004).
3 For a contrasting assumption on this point from the civil resistance literature, see Schock (2013, 2015).
4 The authors single out four types of violence, anchored on the characteristic of the victims: (1) against specific individuals (selective violence); (2) against members of a category of individuals (categorical violence); (3) against victims indiscriminately (indiscriminate violence); and (4) against victims more or less unintentionally (collateral violence). They suggest that these types are common in the literature, even though they do not amount to an exhaustive or even mutually exclusive typology (Alimi, Demetriou, and Bosi 2015: 209–217).
5 For overviews of the literature, see Nepstad (2015) and Schock (2015).
6 Of course, barriers to participation in violent campaigns may decrease under some conditions (Weinstein 2006).
7 It is also possible that under some conditions, violent repression of *violent* challengers may also backfire, however this dynamic has received less scholarly attention.
8 The number of cases varies across models in the logistic regression. Maximalist challenges have goals of regime change, liberation from foreign occupation, or secession.

References

Alimi, Eitan, Chares Demetriou, and Lorenzo Bosi. 2015. *The Dynamics of Radicalization: A Relational and Comparative Perspective*. New York: Oxford University Press.

Anner, Mark. 2009. "Two Logics of Labor Organizing in the Global Apparel Industry." *International Studies Quarterly* 53: 545–570.

Barrell, Howard. 1993. "Conscripts to Their Age: African National Congress Operational Strategy, 1976–1986." PhD dissertation, St. Antony's College, Oxford University.

Bergesen, Albert. 2007. "A Three-Step Model of Terrorist Violence," *Mobilization* 12: 111–118.

Bloom, Mia M. 2004. "Palestinian Suicide Bombing: Public Support, Market Share, and Outbidding." *Political Science Quarterly* 119: 61–88.

Bosi, Lorenzo and Donatella della Porta. 2012. "Micro-Mobilization into Armed Groups: The Ideological, Instrumental and Solidary Paths." *Qualitative Sociology* 35: 361–383.

Braithwaite, John. 2013. "Rethinking Radical Flank Theory: South Africa." RegNet Research Paper No. 2014/23. Canberra: Australian National University.

Braithwaite, John. 2014. "Limits on Violence; Limits on Responsive Regulatory Theory." *Law & Policy*. [Published online August 2014.]

Brym, Robert and Araj Bader. 2006. "Suicide Bombing as Strategy and Interaction." *Social Forces* 84: 1969–1986.

Chenoweth, Erica and Kurt Schock. 2015. "Do Contemporaneous Armed Challenges Affect the Outcomes of Mass Nonviolent Campaigns?" *Mobilization* 20: 427–451.

Chenoweth, Erica and Maria J. Stephan. 2011. *Why Civil Resistance Works: The Strategic Logic of Nonviolent Conflict*. New York: Columbia University Press.

Cobb, Raymond. 2014. *This Nonviolent Stuff'll Get You Killed: How Guns Made the Civil Rights Movement Possible*. New York: Basic Books.

Crenshaw, Martha, ed. 1995. *Terrorism in Context*. University Park, PA: Pennsylvania State University Press.

Cross, Remy and David A. Snow. 2011. "Radicalism within the Context of Social Movements: Processes and Types." *Journal of Strategic Security* 4: 115–130.

Cunningham, Kathleen Gallagher and Emily Beaulieu. 2010. "Dissent, Repression, and Inconsistency." In *Rethinking Violence: States and Non-State Actors in Conflict*, edited by Erica Chenoweth and Adria Lawrence, 173–195. Cambridge, MA: MIT Press.

Demetriou, Chares. 2012. "Political Radicalization and Political Violence in Palestine (1920–1948), Ireland (1859–1921), and Cyprus (1914–1959)." *Journal of Social Science History* 36: 391–420.

della Porta, Donatella. 2013. *Clandestine Political Violence*. Cambridge: Cambridge University Press.

Dudouet, Véronique. 2013. "Dynamics and Factors of Transition from Armed Struggle to Nonviolent Resistance." *Journal of Peace Research* 50: 401–413.

Dudouet, Véronique, ed. 2015. *Civil Resistance and Conflict Transformation: Transitions from Armed to Nonviolent Struggle*. New York: Routledge.

Freeman, Jo. 1975. *The Politics of Women's Liberation*. New York: Longman.

Gamson, William A. 1990. *The Strategy of Social Protest*. Belmont, CA: Wadsworth.

Gurr, Ted. 2000. *Peoples versus States: Minorities at Risk in the New Century*. Washington, DC: United States Institute of Peace.

Haines, Herbert H. 1988. *Black Radicals and the Civil Rights Mainstream, 1954–1970*. Knoxville: University of Tennessee Press.

Horgan, John. 2009. *Walking Away from Terrorism: Accounts of Disengagement from Radical and Extremist Movements*. New York: Taylor & Francis.

Isaac, Larry, Steve McDonald, and Greg Lukasik. 2006. "Takin' It from the Streets: How the Sixties Mass Movement Revitalized Unionization." *American Journal of Sociology* 112: 46–96.

Jenkins, J. Craig and Craig Eckert. 1986. "Channeling Black Insurgency: Elite Patronage and Professional Social Movement Organizations in the Development of the Black Movement." *American Sociological Review* 51: 812–829.

Juergensmeyer, Mark. 2005. *Terror in the Mind of God: The Global Rise of Religious Terrorism*. Berkeley: University of California Press.

Keane, John. 2004. *Violence and Democracy*. Cambridge: Cambridge University Press.

Killian, Lewis M. 1972. "The Significance of Extremism in the Black Revolution." *Social Problems* 45: 41–48.

Koopmans, Ruud. 1995. *Democracy from Below: New Social Movements and the Political System in West Germany*. Boulder, CO: Westview.

Lichbach, Mark Irving. 1987. "Deterrence or Escalation? The Puzzle of Aggregate Studies of Repression and Dissent." *Journal of Conflict Resolution* 31: 266–297.

Lichbach, Mark Irving. 1995. *The Rebel's Dilemma*. Ann Arbor: University of Michigan Press.

Martin, Andrew W., John D. McCarthy, and Clark McPhail. 2009. "Why Targets Matter: Toward a More Inclusive Model of Collective Violence." *American Sociological Review* 74: 821–841.

Martin, Brian. 2015. "From Political Jiu-Jitsu to the Backfire Dynamic: How Repression Can Promote Mobilization." In *Civil Resistance: Comparative Perspectives on Nonviolent Struggle*, edited by Kurt Schock, 145–167. Minneapolis: University of Minnesota Press.

McAdam, Doug, Sidney Tarrow, and Charles Tilly. 2001. *Dynamics of Contention*. Cambridge: Cambridge University Press.

McCammon, Holly J., Erin M. Bergner, and Sandra C. Arch. 2015. "'Are You One of Those Women?' Within-Movement Conflict, Radical Flank Effects, and Social Movement Political Outcomes." *Mobilization* 20: 157–178.

McCauley, Clark and Sophia Moskalenko. 2011. *Friction: How Radicalization Happens to Them and Us*. New York: Oxford University Press.

Moghaddam, Fathali. 2005. "The Staircase to Terrorism: A Psychological Exploration." *American Psychologist* 60: 161–169.

Moore, Will H. 1998. "Repression and Dissent: Substitution, Context, and Timing." *American Journal of Political Science* 42: 851–873.

Moskalenko, Sophia and Clark McCauley. 2009. "Measuring Political Mobilization: The Distinction Between Activism and Radicalism." *Terrorism and Political Violence* 21: 239–260.

Nepstad, Sharon Erickson. 2011. *Nonviolent Revolutions: Civil Resistance in the Late 20th Century*. New York: Oxford University Press.

Nepstad, Sharon Erickson. 2015. *Nonviolent Struggle: Theories, Strategies, & Dynamics*. New York: Oxford University Press.

Oberschall, Anthony. 1973. *Social Conflict and Social Movements*. Englewood Cliffs, NJ: Prentice Hall.

Pape, Robert. 2005. *Dying to Win: The Strategic Logic of Suicide Terrorism*. New York: Random House.

Pearlman, Wendy. 2011. *Violence, Nonviolence, and the Palestinian National Movement*. Cambridge: Cambridge University Press.

Piazza, James. 2006. "Rooted in Poverty?: Terrorism, Poor Economic Development, and Social Cleavages." *Terrorism and Political Violence* 18: 159–177.

Ramirez, Bruno. 1978. *When Workers Fight: The Politics of Industrial Relations in the Progressive Era, 1989–1916*. Westport, CT: Greenwood.

Rayback, Joseph G. 1966. *A History of American Labor*. New York: Free Press.

Rohlinger, Deana A. 2006. "Friends and Foes: Media, Politics, and Tactics in the Abortion War." *Social Problems* 53: 537–561.

Schmid, Alex and Albert Jongman. 1988. *Political Terrorism*. New Brunswick, NJ: Transactions Books.

Schock, Kurt. 1996. "A Conjunctural Model of Political Conflict: The Impact of Political Opportunities on the Relationship between Economic Inequality and Violent Political Conflict." *Journal of Conflict Resolution* 40: 98–133.

Schock, Kurt. 2005. *Unarmed Insurrections: People Power Movements in Nondemocracies*. Minneapolis: University of Minnesota Press.

Schock, Kurt. 2013. "The Practice and Study of Civil Resistance." *Journal of Peace Research* 50: 277–290.

Schock, Kurt. 2015. *Civil Resistance Today*. Cambridge: Polity.

Sharp, Gene. 1973. *The Politics of Nonviolent Action*. Boston: Porter Sargent Publishers.

Sprinzak, Ehud. 1998. "The Psychological Formation of Extreme Left Terrorism in a Democracy: The Case of the Weathermen." In *Origins of Terrorism*, edited by Walter Reich, 65–85. Washington, DC: Woodrow Wilson Center.

Stern, Jessica. 2003. *Terror in the Name of God: Why Religious Militants Kill*. New York: HarperCollins.

Tilly, Charles. 1986. *The Contentious French*. Cambridge, MA: Harvard University Press.

Tilly, Charles. 1995. *Popular Contention in Great Britain, 1758–1834*. Cambridge, MA: Harvard University Press.

Tilly, Charles. 2004. "Terror, Terrorism, Terrorists." *Sociological Theory* 22: 5–13.

Tilly, Charles. 2005. "Terror as Strategy and Relational Process." *International Journal of Comparative Sociology* 46: 11–32.

Tilly, Charles. 2006. *Regimes and Repertoires*. Chicago: University of Chicago Press.

Tilly, Charles. 2008. *Contentious Performances*. Cambridge: Cambridge University Press.

Tilly, Charles and Sidney Tarrow. 2015. *Contentious Politics*. 2nd edn. New York: Oxford University Press.

Turner, Ralph H. 1970. "Determinants of Social Movement Strategies." In *Human Nature and Collective Behavior: Papers in Honor of Herbert Blumer*, edited by Tamotsu Shibutani, 145–164. Englewood, NJ: Prentice-Hall.

Viterna, Jocelyn. 2013. *Women in War: The Micro-Processes of Mobilization in El Salvador*. New York: Oxford University Press.

Wasow, Omar. 2015. "Nonviolence, Violence, and Voting: The Effects of the 1960s Black Protest Movements and White Voting Behavior." Unpublished manuscript, Princeton University.

Weinberg, Leonard, Ami Pedahzur, and Sivan Hirsch-Hoefler. 2004. "The Challenges of Conceptualizing Terrorism." *Terrorism and Political Violence* 16: 777–794.

Weinstein, Jeremy. 2006. *Insight Rebellion: The Politics of Insurgent Violence*. New York: Cambridge University Press.

Wendt, Simon. 2010. *The Spirit and the Shotgun: Armed Resistance and the Struggle for Civil Rights*. Gainesville: University Press of Florida.

Zartman, I. William, ed. 1996. *Elusive Peace: Negotiating an End to Civil Wars*. Washington DC: Brookings Institution.

20

Art and Social Movements

Lilian Mathieu

Introduction

Art and protest are distinct activities, but they share many similarities and often intersect. These similarities and intersections have proven stimulating for social movement analysis, as some of its main concepts are based on artistic metaphors. Tilly's (2004) seminal concept of the repertoire of collective action refers to Commedia dell'arte and to jazz in order to stress that there is always some improvisation in the way challengers mobilize conventional ways of protesting, and he defined contentious actions as *performances* – a word that also designates happenings (often with a scandalous or disruptive dimension) that are widely used in modern arts. References to art in describing protest have also been used in Jasper's book, *The Art of Moral Protest* (1997), in which he insists on creativity and culture in contention.[1]

Although they have much in common, art and protest refer to and belong to different social spheres.[2] In his book on cultural expressions in social movements, Reed (2005: 303) refers to Pierre Bourdieu's theory of fields to stress that the "logic of politics and the logic of aesthetic objects seldom, if ever, perfectly coincide," and that "the field of power never exhausts the meaning of the work of art, and political meanings are always also in excess of aesthetic ones on their own terms." Recognizing that the art world and the social movement sector form two different fields helps to understand the complex relations between art and contention (Balasinski and Mathieu 2006). These include contention within artistic fields, artists' commitment to movements, the aestheticization of protest, and the mobilization of art as a resource for movements.

The Wiley Blackwell Companion to Social Movements, Second Edition. Edited by David A. Snow, Sarah A. Soule, Hanspeter Kriesi, and Holly J. McCammon.
© 2019 John Wiley & Sons Ltd. Published 2019 by John Wiley & Sons Ltd.

Contention within Art Worlds

Becker's analysis of art worlds (1982) has stressed that producing art is not a solitary activity performed by an isolated and gifted individual, but a collective process in which people considered as "artists" or "creators" work along with "support personnel" or "cultural intermediaries." Being a collective activity, art can itself be the setting of various forms of collective action, including contentious ones.

First, aesthetic movements within art worlds can be very similar, in their forms or dynamics, to political and social movements, and can benefit from being analyzed as such. One of the most paradigmatic examples of such movements is Surrealism (Bandier 1999). It appeared in the early 1920s as a gathering of various artists (poets, painters, filmmakers, carvers, photographers) who shared the same aesthetic principles. Those principles were expressed in *manifestos* that had been written by a charismatic leader, André Breton, whose authoritative methods led to repeated internal challenges, exclusions, and secessions. Like protesters who seek change to the social or political structure, the Surrealists fought for a regeneration of the aesthetic norms of their time. Posing as an artistic *vanguard*, they violently challenged the dominant artistic forms of academism using provocation, scandal, and disruption. But the Surrealists did not restrict their criticism to the world of aesthetics; they also set out to challenge the political order by joining the Communist movement and by participating in various mobilizations, for example, against colonial wars. Other artistic movements, such as the Situationists, headed by Guy Debord (Brun 2014), have duplicated the same form of a collective vanguard that provocatively intends to challenge both the aesthetic values and the political order.

Artists also have to collectively mobilize and protest in order to gain or to protect their creative freedom which, according to Bourdieu (1996), is a condition for the autonomy of the artistic field. This is especially the case when creative freedom is constrained by a state censorship that controls artistic production and has the means to prohibit the circulation of books, songs, or movies that challenge existing power relations. Artists who live in authoritarian regimes face many constraints and risks when they produce artworks that do not fit with the state's definition of art. Many studies have stressed the various tactics these artists have to invent in order to perform or circulate their works without incurring state coercion or censure (e.g. Balasinski 2006; Szemere 1992; Wicke 1992). One is to set parallel and clandestine circulation channels that enable artists to reach their audience but reduce it to a limited group of insiders who face the same risks if identified by the authorities. In East European Communist countries, for example, samizdat literature was clandestinely reproduced and circulated from hand to hand, and rock concerts and drama plays were performed in safe places such as private apartments, whose addresses were communicated to small numbers of trusted people. Amar (2015) shows that independent Chinese moviemakers who are banned from official distribution circuits rely heavily on the clandestine circulation of illegal DVD copies of their films. Even if this uncontrolled distribution is detrimental to them from an economic point of view, it represents one of the only ways to reach an audience. Another way to skirt censorship can be labeled "contraband" and consists in using official channels to publicly express double meaning stances. The term was coined during World War II by French writers whose poems could be interpreted either as celebrations of a loved woman or as a glorification of France's spirit of resistance against the enemy (Sapiro 2014). In Cuba, where it is difficult to openly challenge the political order, contentious artists use the rare accessible collective practices, such as religious pilgrimages, poetry performances and music festivals, in order to deflect their official meaning and insert a political message (Geoffray 2011).

State power is not the only one artists have to face. Economic interests also shape and limit creative freedom by imposing mainstream aesthetic forms while rejecting less profitable others. Politics and economics often join in constraining art diffusion, as when local radios stopped broadcasting oppositional hillbilly songs after the mill workers strike in North Carolina in 1934. Here, corporate interests (the alliance of big corporate radio networks with the recording industry for the promotion of a nationalized music) melded with political retaliation to produce a decline in local radio autonomy, which left "little room and little market for music explicitly dealing with worker grievances and the concern of local populations" (Roscigno and Danaher 2004: 135). Artworks that defy censorship are often shaped by their rebellious intentions. Being excluded from mainstream artistic institutions and cultural industries, they suffer from poor production conditions. Chinese moviemakers who cannot obtain an official permit, for example, are excluded from studio facilities and have to shoot their films very quickly, in natural settings and with unknown or amateur actors (Amar 2015). Artworks submitted to such constraints are often recognizable as such; skirting censorship gives them a particular *style* where aesthetics are indivisible from politics.

Censorship threatens the autonomy of the artistic field as it challenges artists' claim to exert a monopoly over the definition of what constitutes art. When this autonomy is threatened or non-existent, artists can decide to retreat from creation or deliberately refuse to collaborate with official cultural institutions, as some French writers did during the authoritative Vichy regime (Sapiro 2014). They were imitated by some famous Polish comedians who stopped appearing in TV programs in the early 1980s, and whose absence was interpreted by the Communist state authorities and by the public as a boycott that had a clear political meaning (Balasinski 2006). The autonomy of art worlds is particularly at stake when provocative art is censored by authorities for not being art but pornography, as in the USA when Robert Mapplethorpe's photographs of male nude black bodies were stigmatized as obscene and museums that displayed his works were threatened with state funding cuts. Another exemplary case is the French film *Baise-moi* whose commercial exploitation was stopped because it included sexually explicit images, although it posed as an auteur film. Social movements played a major role in this case as the demand for censorship emanated from an extreme right moral crusade organization that successfully claimed in court that the film should be considered pornographic and consequently banned from ordinary movie theaters. In a classic movement-counter-movement interaction, the court decision provoked a mobilization of the field of cinema in defense of creative freedom; some independent movie theaters used illegal means as they defied the ban by continuing to show the film (Mathieu 2003).

As in this case, mobilizations against artworks that are considered outrageous often come from conservative or religious movements; they rely on a repertoire of protest that mixes legal (e.g. appealing to courts to have the artwork prohibited) and disruptive (e.g. picketing in front of a museum) or even violent (e.g. destroying artworks, burning down cinemas or theaters, assaulting artists) strategies. "Degenerate" book burnings by the Nazis and contemporary destructions of modern installations mistaken for rubbish rather than sculptures (Gamboni 1997) put the same emphasis on disputes about what should be considered as art and who has the authority to define it as such. Historical forms of iconoclasm (such as the Protestant destruction of Catholic representations during the sixteenth century) are more ambiguous phenomena, as what we nowadays consider art was not always defined as such, but rather as religious or political symbols, at the time it was attacked.

Becker's definition of art worlds also reminds us that art is a professional activity. As professionals, artists and support personnel have to protect their collective interests. They can join social movement organizations such as unions, and sometimes have to mobilize in order to obtain better working conditions or wages. This was the case when hundreds of US film, television, and radio writers joined in the 2007 strike, forcing some TV shows and series to stop. It was also the case in France when the government and employers' representatives decided in 2003 to reform the insurance system that grants entertainment professionals protection during unemployment periods. The reform project resulted in a prominent, though unsuccessful, mobilization of artists (mostly musicians and comedians) and support personnel, and led to the cancellation of major cultural events. However, the mobilization was stirred by an internal tension between art and work. Some protesters defined their cause as a strictly professional one that should be defended by unions, whereas others promoted the artist's condition as a prefiguration of future workers' status, and tried to expand the movement to other groups suffering from intermittent employment and economic insecurity. The tension shaped the movement repertoire as well, as the former group privileged traditional ways of protest, such as street demonstrations and strikes, whereas the latter promoted more innovative and spectacular actions, such as invading TV studios during newscasts or personally shaming the Minister of Culture during a film awards ceremony (Proust 2010; Sinigaglia 2007).

Contention within the art world is also able to challenge internal power relations and transform the way art is produced, taught, perceived, or experienced. Hanna (1990: 342) observes that "the turn-of-the-century modern dance was in part a rebellion against male domination in both dance and society." Female dancers' esthetic innovations – dancing braless, corsetless and barefoot along with new composition techniques, themes or grammars – were at the same time artistic revolutions and contentious stances that joined emerging feminist concerns about sexual freedom, body pleasure, and emancipation from patriarchy. More recently, the Guerrilla Girls activists provocatively denounced the exclusion of female artists from the main museums and galleries, whereas Act Up stigmatized the de-politicization of the AIDS issue as it was evoked by major art institutions (Reed 2005). Major political crises, for their part, have repercussions on the internal dynamics of artistic fields as they open opportunities for aesthetic vanguards to promote their positions against existing artistic hierarchies. The May 1968 events, for example, were the setting for a confrontation between the different French literary vanguards of the time, during which they competed expressing such radical views as the promotion of anonymity in order to abolish domination based on authorship or the recognition of a worker status detached from any publishing activity. The event was shaped by the former structure of the literary field, and especially by the preexisting competition between literary groups, but it also helped to transform its internal hierarchy by giving new legitimacy or audience to groups that appeared consonant with the student revolt (such as the formerly declining Surrealists) while discrediting formerly dominant ones that seemed at odds with it (such as the Communist-friendly *Tel Quel*) (Gobille 2005).

Artistic fields are also affected by social protest when it becomes a source of inspiration. Merging a sociology of culture analysis with an analysis of social movement outcomes, Isaac (2009) shows that a literary innovation, such as the labor problem novel subgenre at the end of the nineteenth century, results from the combination of different factors. Some were endogenous to the literary field, like the emergence of the realist aesthetic in American fiction-writing, but an exogenous process such as the growth of collective contention surrounding the rise of the labor movement was also preponderant. Acknowledging that artistic creation is shaped by a political and social context does not mean that it is a direct or faithful reflection of it. The *translation process* from the social movement sector to the artistic field necessarily involves some distortion, if not bias. This is shown in Reed's comparative study of three fiction movies inspired by the American Indian Movement's (AIM) actions: "AIM members made various attempts to influence a movie-making process that was in the hand of mostly sympathetic but culturally and politically limited outsiders who were *translating* movements ideas and values, sometimes well, more often poorly" (Reed 2005: 130, original emphasis). Isaac's and Reed's analyses also stress the influence of a third field, along with the social movement sector and the art world, which is the economic field, namely, the publishing market in the case of the labor problem novel and the film industry in the case of cinema, that exert its own influence over the content of books and movies.

The Figure of the Committed Artist

Meyer and Gamson (1995: 181) have noted that a "celebrity without a cause has become almost anomalous" and that many contemporary social movements benefit from the support or participation of famous comedians, musicians, or sportspeople. This kind of involvement in protest is different from the situations discussed so far, as celebrities mobilize not as members of a collective, but as individuals whose exceptional talents and fame allow them to express a public position about a given issue that, often, does not concern them directly.

Bourdieu's analysis of the emergence of the figure of the intellectual helps to identify what allows celebrities, and especially artists, to take side for a cause not of their concern. First a derogative term, the word "intellectual" appeared in France at the end of the nineteenth century when several writers, journalists, and academics denounced the anti-Semitism surrounding the slanderous campaign against a Jewish officer, Alfred Dreyfus, who was accused of being a spy. It is the recent achievement of the autonomicization of the literary field that legitimated a novelist like Émile Zola to engage in the political debate. Henceforth emancipated from political and economic pressure, the now autonomous artistic field entitled its members to express their independent point of view as disinterested representatives of universal values such as justice, truth, and freedom. In other words, it is their independence from the political field and its specific concerns or interests that legitimates intellectuals to intervene in the political debate (Bourdieu 1996).

Celebrities' support offers many assets to movements. In societies that celebrate individual success, fame promises some kind of respectability that movements may try to secure via an endorsement (seeking a strategy that Snow (1979) calls "celebrity ingratiation," which can be especially important for movements with poor legitimacy). Celebrities offer visibility as they can bring media and public attention to a cause that would otherwise be neglected, and help to reach and mobilize an extended constituency. They can also provide critical financial help to social movement organizations, first by directly and publicly giving them money (encouraging others to do so as well) but also by organizing or participating in fundraising events (such as the "mega-events" we will talk about below). They can also stand as suitable spokespersons for a cause, when journalists or policy-makers would otherwise avoid unknown movement representatives. It is not only their fame that artists mobilize in their support, but sometimes their talent as well, when singers, writers, painters or movie-makers produce artwork that translates movement grievances in an aesthetic language. Bob Dylan's song "The Lonesome Death of Hattie Carol," for example, expressed his commitment to the civil rights movement, while Michael Moore's *Fahrenheit 9/11* is a cinematographic demonstration of the illegitimacy of the war against Iraq.

On the other hand, Meyer and Gamson (1995) stress that celebrity participation is not without risks or costs for a social movement. A well-known artist's participation can help attract media attention, but it carries the risk of overshadowing the movement s/he supports, causing it to lose control of its self-definition and of its framing of the issue. Celebrity support can produce a "softening effect" on the movement and speed the process of institutionalizing and domesticating dissent. For example, in order to avoid disapprobation from an audience that does not necessarily share his or her political interests, an artist may choose to support consensual claims rather than more disruptive grievances. An artist's commitment can also be viewed as superficial and insincere, mainly designed to maintain personal fame and celebrity at the movement's expense, but unable to raise complex issues and detailed political analysis.

For their part, celebrities know they run a risk when they participate in causes whose legitimacy is debatable. The memory of McCarthyism, during which actors, scriptwriters, and directors were excluded from the Hollywood film industry for their sympathies for Communism, is still a reference that informs artists' relation to activism, as shown by Roussel (2007). She observes, in her study of the mobilization of professionals from the American film and entertainment industries against the 2003 US War in Iraq, that the occupational configuration of these industries structured the mobilization and the form it took, as some committed artists convinced their colleagues to join the movement and to publicly object to the war. Her study mostly stresses that the possible mobilization costs were anticipated differently according to artists' previous activist experience and position within the art world. Risks did not appear very meaningful for very politicized artists who have always associated politics and art; totally unknown artists who have very little to lose from being stigmatized as political, and very big figures who are somewhat out of reach, also felt authorized to adopt public stances against the war. On the contrary, up-and-coming artists saw many dangers and obstacles, such as losing the support of their co-workers, being stigmatized as a person one should not be working with, or cutting off a part of their audience. As a consequence, they had to frame their political commitment so that it remained acceptable within the art field, for example, by detaching their "personal" political preferences from their professional activity.

According to Roussel, a new public role for the artist is currently emerging, one that significantly differs from the traditional figure of the artist devoted to a party or a social movement. Contemporary committed artists both acknowledge and perform the differentiation between the artistic and the political spheres, as

> they demand simultaneously a double role: they define themselves as the new figures of citizenship in the public sphere, but they keep at the same time their artistic practices, especially in the film industry, separate from the first identity that they endorse.
>
> (2007: 387)

Presenting themselves as "ordinary people with an extraordinary power" (ibid.), celebrities like Sean Penn or George Clooney claim a specific public legitimacy that challenges politicians' pretensions to represent the opinion of the people.

Taking into account the differentiation between the artistic and political or social movement fields leads to the hypothesis that coalitions between artists and causes are facilitated when they occupy homologous positions in their sphere of reference. This hypothesis is borrowed from Bourdieu's theory of fields that presupposes that most fields share a homologous structure. Agents who belong to different fields, but who occupy a structurally similar position within it, have greater chances of sharing similar worldviews that predispose them to coalesce. As a consequence, well-known artists are more likely to feel an affinity with consensual causes or mainstream movements, while less famous artists, or marginal aesthetic styles, will be rather inclined to adopt less legitimate political causes. In other words, the position that is occupied by the artist within the artistic field determines the kind of position s/he will take in the political debate: those who are dominant in the art world are structurally prone to adopt consensual or conservative positions whereas those who are dominated or marginal are inclined to embrace heretical issues. This hypothesis has been confirmed by Sapiro (2014) in her study of French writers' attitudes during World War II: dominated within the literary field, vanguard poets were prone to challenge the political state of things by joining the Resistance movement, whereas dominant famous novelists were rather inclined to adopt conservative positions and to support the Vichy regime.

Art as a Contentious Practice

Art and contention meld in *practice* when protesters mobilize artistic means, devices, or works in their repertoire of collective action. Street demonstrators parody traditional songs, slogans are chanted in verses, posters are illustrated with drawings or photographs, picketings are staged with a specific dress code, and so on. This *aestheticization of protest* goes along with a *politicization of art* when artwork that was not meant to be political by its creator is given a new meaning by challengers. Art, and most widely culture, are part of a more global "tool kit" on which protesters draw to encode symbols and elaborate new political meanings (Swidler 1986).

The politicization of art is often but not necessarily a deliberate process by movement entrepreneurs. As shown by Bourdieu (2010), aesthetic tastes are distinctive properties related to various statuses and identities such as class, education, gender, race, or age. Asserting one's aesthetic taste can therefore be considered political when it is associated with a contentious identity, even when the art is not political in itself. Frith cautiously reminds that "music is not in itself revolutionary or reactionary" (quoted in Steinberg 2004: 8), but it can become either depending on the context and on its possible mobilization by revolutionary or reactionary forces. This is clearly demonstrated by Steinberg's study (2004: 22) of the politicization of rock music in Serbia: although it has no political or social essence, rock was circumstantially and temporally given a contentious meaning when it became a powerful aesthetic technology "through which student protesters constructed a collective identity and a discourse of opposition that demarcated them not only from the regime but from other oppositional forces." For these protesters, rock was not only a shared musical taste on which their collective identity was built, but a contentious practice in itself, as dancing, drumming, and singing became part of their repertoire.

The political meaning of a given genre being defined relationally and in a situated way evolves through space and time. Rock music, for example, has lost its sulfurous reputation in Western societies because it is part of the mainstream culture, but it is still marginal, and viewed with suspicion if not coerced, in countries like China or Iran. Pornography was repressed during the eighteenth century because it attacked political and religious powers (Hunt 1993), it was promoted as a vehicle of sexual emancipation in the 1970s, but it is nowadays a target for feminists who stigmatize it as promoting sexual violence against women. The artistic field's own logics, coupled with the progressive institutionalization of former vanguards, contribute to explaining how some artistic forms that first appeared as transgressive become acceptable, if not new academicism, as their promoters become older and integrated into the field.

The political meaning of art is also dependent on the direct situation in which the artistic practice takes place, which determines its reception and interpretation by its audience. As Roussel and Banerji (2017) note:

> The same song performed during a protest or a concert, the same photograph exhibited in a museum or printed in a newspaper, for instance, do not give rise to identical uses, interpretations, and social effects. In other words, the formation of political meanings and consequences depends on active interpretation practices instead of deriving from some inherent property of the artwork itself.

Displays or performances of contentious artworks in institutions may have the effect of valorizing their aesthetic dimension at the expense of their political relevance. Act Up activists, for example, protested against an exhibit of protest graphics at the Museum of Modern Art in New York because they considered it "perpetuated a sense of art as above the political fray by emphasizing formal elements of the protest graphics on display, and by embalming art objects while excluding living activist-artists" (Reed 2005: 191). They had no choice but to organize a counter-exhibition in a less institutionalized place that intended to break the distinction between art as a representation and art as action.

If displayed or performed in different places, artworks are received by different audiences that might have an unequal capacity to decode their political intentions. Artists who use contraband know that what will clearly be interpreted as a political message by insiders will appear as a pure aesthetic, and innocuous, choice by others. French neo-fascist rock bands that play bagpipes, for example, not only give an original tone to their songs but make reference to a regional folklore rooted in the nostalgia of the *Ancien Régime* that has long been valorized among the counter-revolutionary extreme-right (Mathieu 2017). Cuban artists who walk backwards in one of Havana's main streets play on the multiple meanings of their parades, which can be interpreted either as carnivalesque performances or as a transgression of the urban order that defies the authorities (Geoffray 2011).

Most of the politicization of art processes studied so far is based on the division between (professional) artists and activists; it is art created by artists that is given a political meaning by protesters. The reciprocal process of aestheticization of protest rather entails an erasure, or even a subversion, of this division as it gives more place to an amateur practice of art. As observed by Lahire (2015), in Western societies, the respect due to art duplicates the religious opposition between the sacred and the profane, and its translation in aesthetics entertains hierarchical divisions, such as between creator and spectator, or performer and audience. It is this hierarchy between active and passive roles that is challenged by movements when they appropriate art and confer on its practice a contentious tone. Punk's "do-it-yourself" ethic is a good example of such an attitude. Refusing the professionalization and the commercialization of art, the do-it-yourself ethic

> states that punks should not be content with being consumers and spectators, but instead should become active participants in creating culture by starting their own fan magazines (commonly known as "zines"), creating their own record labels, starting their own bands, and creating a network of venues for live performance. The idea has been that these media should, as much as possible, be autonomous from the culture industry and the "mainstream" media to serve as an alternative form of cultural production that can facilitate artistic experimentation by minimizing the impact of commercialization.
>
> (Moore and Roberts 2009: 275, see also Fornäs 1993 and Amar 2015)

Endorsing this ethic was all the more significant for female punks who formed "Riot Grrrl" bands regarding the traditional sexism that pervades in rock milieus and that overshadows young women's experiences and grievances (Moore and Roberts 2009).

Roy's (2010) comparison of how two American movements – the Old Left/Communist-led movement of the 1930s and 1940s and the civil rights movement of the 1950s and 1960s – mobilized folk music in two different cultural projects is also informative.[3] The American Left adopted folk music in the 1930s not only for its populist connotations but because it could be racially inclusive. It transformed it from an esoteric preoccupation of academic musicologists into a genre of popular music, but in a way that reproduced the conventional division and hierarchy between performer and audience, and for that reason failed to reach its target audience, which was the working class. On the contrary, the civil rights movement had a more inclusive approach to music, making it not entertainment for protesters or propaganda to recruit new members, but one of its central activities that would strengthen the sense of community among activists: "music was embedded in the collective action itself, in meetings, picketing, riding on buses, sitting in, and passing the time in jail ... Music was the ideal medium for reinforcing and empowering these forms of collective action" (Roy 2010: 246). Freedom songs were more contentious in practice than in content – in fact, most of them had little obvious political message – as they bound participants together in solidarity. That does not mean that the musical form was indifferent, as freedom songs privileged the leader-and-response format familiar to African American people, but, contrary to the Old Left approach, the lyrics did not retain their mobilizing force (ibid.: 185).

The integrative role of artistic practices in collective action is highlighted in many studies. Roscigno and Danaher (2004) insist that hillbilly songs familiar to mill workers were easily mobilized during their strikes, and that singing and dancing enlivened collective solidarity and reinvigorated picket lines. During Pinochet's dictatorship in Chile, *arpilleras* (appliqué pictures of cloth, usually depicting the difficult situation of poor families under political repression) workshops mobilized shantytown women in a collective artistic practice. During the workshops, women could talk about their own situations and share their grievances, while learning to express them in artworks that would be sold abroad and provide them with an income (Adams 2002). In the 1920s, Nigerian women performed traditional dances in order to resist a colonial administration that restricted their economic autonomy and reinforced male dominance. First using ridicule and satire against male and colonial powers, their dancing mobilization turned into riot and was severely repressed, causing many deaths (Hanna 1990).

That repertoires of collective action frequently adopt a humoresque or carnivalesque tone was already stressed in Tilly's early works on charivari as a form of protest (Tilly 1985). Parody and irony often stand at the core of protest performances as a way to ridicule adversaries but also to make the action a pleasurable moment for participants or bystanders. The dramatization of protest action can take various forms and degrees, and produce various effects – not always under the movement's control. Particularly elaborated forms can be found in movements like Reverend Billy and the Church of Stop Shopping (that denounces excessive consumerism and multinational corporations) and Billionaires for Bush (that ironically pretends to endorse US government decisions in favor of the wealthiest groups) that were studied by Lechaux (2010). Both produce theatrical performances in the streets of New York City that diffuse critical messages using speech forms like anaphora, hyperbole or antiphrasis (as when richly dressed people joyfully assert, about George W. Bush, that "never before has one man done so much for so few at the expense of so many"). But if the aim of these performances is to provoke reactions and actions on the part of the spectators and even to convert them to militancy, the question remains of "their ability to build awareness outside of a relatively circumscribed microcosm ..., as irony and access to the codes needed to appreciate its impact are without doubt socially situated and generated" (ibid.: 186). Ambiguity also pervaded the Black Panthers' public displays of armed force that theatrically challenged the state monopoly over the use of violence. Not only were the Panthers' performances not perceived, nor treated, as pure imagery by the state that severely coerced them, but they ended in crossing the line between symbolic and effective violence and precipitated the movement's decline (Reed 2005).

Art as a Contentious Resource

Last but not least, art itself is one of the various resources movements use to mobilize; many movements use art, and some even produce artworks themselves, as a strategy in its own right. First, movements often rely on artistic works or performances as a way to gather material resources. The selling of artworks that artists have produced specifically for the cause is a typical way to raise funds. Mathieu (2017) shows, for example, that a competition emerged within the French pro-immigrant movement when members of the rock band La Tordue said they would donate the benefits of their new antiracist song; the coordinator of a campaign against the deportation of former delinquent foreigners had to convince the band to donate the song to his own cause but not to the defense of undocumented migrants, as La Tordue first intended.

"Band Aid" and "We are the World" concerts and records, which gathered many pop stars in the mid-1980s in a mobilization against famine in Africa, are also good examples of such popular fundraising operations. Garofalo (1992), Lahusen (2001) and Reed (2005) have stressed their many ambiguities, however. They argue, for example, that since such fundraising operations emanate from the mainstream entertainment industry, they reflect the predominant position white US artists occupy within it, while leaving little place, if any, to African artists and symbolically reinforcing the passivity and dependency associated with African people. Their ecumenical tone is said to have encouraged a depoliticization of the issue, mainly coding it as a natural disaster rather than defining it as an economic and political problem. Depoliticization was reinforced by the events' dependence on big corporate sponsors, raising doubts about their possible misappropriation as a marketing strategy in a search for new consumers. Doubts were also expressed about their real effects, as the funds raised were relatively low compared to the needs of starving African people and as uncertainty prevailed about their use.

Such "agit pop" events (Reed 2005) also claim to have a consciousness-raising effect on their audience, but one that is difficult to estimate. Following Olson's classic approach (1965) to collective action, they can be analyzed as offering *aesthetic selective incentives* to an audience that can be motivated less by the cause that stands at the core of the event than by the opportunity to have a good time by attending a good show for a low price. As this self-interest is what incites the gathering of many people, movements have to make sure they offer a high quality of aesthetic benefits, i.e. the fame and talent of the artists they have hired. Artistic performances themselves create an atmosphere that is in favor of the expression of support. In having a good time together and applauding artists they like, audience members may become more receptive to political messages, or at least become more prone to expressing immediate approval and taking a public stance. However, although the high-energy atmosphere may make people more sensitive to the messages being put out, it does not mean that their receptiveness will be long-lasting. In all likelihood, only a few will become new recruits for the cause, most likely those who already have a political sensibility and share an interest in the given issue. As observed by Rosenthal and Flacks (2012), there can be a discrepancy between an artist's intent and the audience reception, as the context can strongly influence the transmission of a political message between them.

Even with these limitations in mind, art should be considered a powerful vehicle for movement framing as it expresses grievances and appeals for mobilization in a symbolic and emotional language that may be more sensitizing and convincing than pure activist rhetoric. Polletta (2006), for example, has insisted that storytelling – that can be aestheticized in novels, movies or plays – is a powerful tool to mobilize people in social movements, especially for some disadvantaged groups that are reluctant to be subject to complex and abstract political analysis. More widely, as stressed by Adams (2002: 27):

> It is not just at a cognitive, intellectual level that art mobilizes protest ... Song and other art forms help to recruit individuals into a specific movement because they provide reassuring emotional messages ... tap into the spirituality of potential recruits and activists ... reinforce the value structure of individuals who are active supporters of social movements ... and provide a renewed feeling that social and political change is possible.

Mobilizing art as a framing resource can, however, raise doubts about its authenticity and sincerity. It is especially the case when art is used as a rationalized strategy to contact, sensitize, and recruit non-politicized bystanders, in a way similar to what Snow and his colleagues call *frame extension*, i.e. the attempt by a movement "to enlarge its pool by portraying its objectives and activities as attending to or being congruent with the values or interests of potential adherents" (Snow et al. 1986: 472). Such a strategy is adopted by French neo-fascist groups that consider their own music – "RIF" for *rock identitaire français* ("French identity rock") – as an ideological vector intended to sensitize and recruit new members among the youth. As young people appreciate different musical styles, movement leaders insist that all styles should be covered and have a dedicated RIF band (Mathieu 2017).[4]

Both the stigma attached to neo-fascist ideologies and the RIF musicians' low musical skills have led this strategy to failure. But the fact that RIF records and concerts are unable to reach an outside public does not mean that they are politically irrelevant as they are efficient in strengthening internal cohesion among activists. Studying the US White Power movement's music scene, Futrell, Simi and Gottschalk (2006: 286) stress that for a semi-clandestine movement that mostly relies on the Internet, "concerts and music festivals are the scene's primary face-to-face opportunities for participants to experience a level of camaraderie and fellowhip that virtual participation alone cannot provide." Movement-sponsored events like concerts and festivals can thus be analyzed as gatherings of like-minded people who appreciate the same music, and collectively and proudly affirm their feelings of forming a cohesive community with its own sub- or counter-culture. They are identity affirmation rituals, where group membership is mutually recognized, prized, and consolidated. As such, they play a political role, as they contribute to the group's cohesion and mobilization capacity (Rosenthal and Flacks 2012). Neo-fascist organizations are not unique in this way, as many other movements, past or present, conservative or progressive, rely on art and culture to affirm their collective identity and strengthen their sense of belonging.

The same mechanism is described by Staggenborg, Eder, and Sudderth in their study of an American feminist festival. They conclude that "feminist cultural events create social networks and strengthen communities, which can be drawn upon as the organizational basis for movement actions" (1993–1994: 44). It's the identity of both the movement and its members that is exhibited through its use of art, and these performances are at the same time a vector of tradition and one of cultural and social change.

This idea that social movements produce not only political but also cultural change has been further developed by Eyerman and Jamison (1998). They argue for an enlarged perspective on social movements, and do not restrict their analysis to ideologies, strategies, and organizations. On the contrary, they consider social movements as clusters for cultural renewal when they create their own cultural tradition that can itself have a major impact on larger popular culture and inspire further mobilizations. Eyerman and Jamison cite as their main example the US civil rights movement, which rejuvenated the traditional songs of slaves and workers into protest anthems. Indeed, its music is what remained after the movement faded away as a political force. Snow, Tan, and Owens (2013) call *cultural revitalization* and *cultural fabrication* the double process by which, in a *bricolage* fashion, movements rework cultural legacies, give new meanings to older cultural elements and transform cultural reservoirs.

Whether it is lowbrow or highbrow, art is a major component of protest: it provides material and symbolic resources, contributes to movement framing, mobilizes constituencies, sensitizes the broader public, and produces social change by renewing cultural traditions. By bringing culture back into the analysis, the study of the role of art in social movements contributes to enriching the knowledge of collective protest.

Notes

1 On the more global issue of culture in social movements, see Darnovsky, Epstein, and Flacks (1995), Johnston and Klandermans (1995), and Chapter 3 by Jasper and Polletta, Chapter 27 by Van Dyke and Taylor, and Chapter 34 by Andretta, della Porta, and Saunders, in this volume.
2 That can either be labeled "fields," "worlds," or "sectors," the difference being of little relevance here.
3 Roy defines a cultural project as "a self conscious attempt to use music, art, drama, dance, poetry, or other cultural materials, to recruit new members, to enhance the solidarity of members, or to persuade outsiders to adopt the movement's program" (2010: 7).
4 Corte and Edwards (2008) identify a similar strategy among American White Power groups.

References

Adams, Jacqueline. 2002. "Art in Social Movements: Shantytown Women's Protest in Pinochet's Chile." *Sociological Forum* 17(1): 21–56.
Amar, Nathanael. 2015. "Scream for Life. Usages politiques de la culture en Chine: échanges et résistance au sein de communautés alternatives. Le cas des punks et des cinéastes indépendants." PhD dissertation, IEP de Paris.
Balasinski, Justyne. 2006. "Boycott: Les comédiens face à l'État de guerre de 1981 en Pologne." In *Art et contestation*, edited by Justyne Balasinski and Lilian Mathieu, 87–101. Rennes: PUR.

Balasinski, Justyne and Lilian Mathieu, eds. 2006. *Art et contestation*. Rennes: PUR.

Bandier, Norbert. 1999. *Sociologie du surréalisme (1924–1929)*. Paris: La Dispute.

Becker, Howard S. 1982. *Art Worlds*. Berkeley: University of California Press.

Bourdieu, Pierre. 1996. *The Rules of the Art: Genesis and Structure of the Literary Field*. New York: Polity Press.

Bourdieu, Pierre. 2010. *Distinction: A Social Critique of the Judgement of Taste*. London: Routledge.

Brun, Éric. 2014. *Les Situationnistes. Une avant-garde totale*. Paris: éditions du CNRS.

Corte, Ugo and Bob Edwards. 2008. "White Power Music and the Mobilization of Racist Social Movements." *Music & Arts in Action* 1(1): 4–20.

Darnovsky, Marcy, Barbara Epstein, and Richard Flacks, eds. 1995. *Cultural Politics and Social Movements*. Philadelphia, PA: Temple University Press.

Eyerman, Ron and Andrew Jamison. 1998. *Music and Social Movements: Mobilizing Traditions in the Twentieth Century*. Cambridge: Cambridge University Press.

Fornäs, Johan. 1993. "'Play It Yourself': Swedish Music in Movement." *Social Science Information* 32(1): 39–65.

Futrell, Robert, Pete Simi, and Simon Gottschalk. 2006. "Understanding Music in Movements: The White Power Music Scene." *The Sociological Quarterly* 47: 275–304.

Gamboni, Dario. 1997. *The Destruction of Art: Iconoclasm and Vandalism since the French Revolution*. London: Reaktion Books.

Garofalo, Reebee, ed. 1992. *Rockin' the Boat: Mass Music and Mass Movements*. Boston: South End Press.

Geoffray Marie-Laure. 2011. "Étudier la contestation en contexte autoritaire: le cas cubain." *Politix* 93: 29–45.

Gobille, Boris. 2005. "Les mobilisations de l'avant-garde littéraire française en mai 1968." *Actes de la recherche en sciences sociales* 158: 30–53.

Hanna, Judith Lynne. 1990. "Dance, Protest, and Women's 'Wars': Cases from Nigeria and the United States." In *Women and Social Protest*, edited by Guida West and Rhoda Lois Blumberg, 333–345. Oxford: Oxford University Press.

Hunt, Lynn, ed. 1993. *The Invention of Pornography*. New York: Zone Books.

Isaac, Larry. 2009. "Movements, Aesthetics, and Market in Literary Change: Making the American Labor Problem Novel." *American Sociological Review* 74: 938–965.

Jasper, James M. 1997. *The Art of Moral Protest*. Chicago: University of Chicago Press.

Johnston, Hank and Bert Klandermans, eds. 1995. *Social Movements and Culture*. Minneapolis: University of Minnesota Press.

Lahire, Bernard. 2015. *Ceci n'est pas qu'un tableau: Essai sur l'art, la domination, la magie et le sacré*. Paris: La Découverte.

Lahusen, Christian. 2001. "Mobilizing for International Solidarity: Mega-Events and Moral Cursades." In *Political Altruism: The Solidarity Movement in International Perspective*, edited by Marco Giugni and Florence Passy, 177–195. Lanham, MD: Rowman & Littlefield.

Lechaux, Bleuwenn. 2010. "Non-Preaching Activism in New York: The Theatrical Militancy of Billionaires for Bush and Reverend Billy." *International Journal of Politics, Culture, and Society* 23(2/3): 175–190.

Mathieu, Lilian. 2003. "L'art menacé par le droit? Retour sur 'l'affaire *Baise-moi*.'" *Mouvements* 29: 60–65.

Mathieu, Lilian. 2017. "'Singing for a Cause': Music and Political Mobilizations in Contemporary France." In *How to Do Politics with Art?*, edited by Violaine Roussel and Anurima Banerji, 44–64. New York: Routledge.

Meyer, David S. and Joshua Gamson. 1995. "The Challenge of Cultural Elites: Celebrities and Social Movements." *Sociological Inquiry* 65(2): 181–206.

Moore, Ryan and Michael Roberts. 2009. "Do-It-Yourself Mobilization: Punk and Social Movements." *Mobilization* 14(3): 273–291.

Olson, Mancur. 1965. *The Logic of Collective Action*, Cambridge, MA: Harvard University Press.

Polletta, Francesca. 2006. *It Was Like a Fever: Storytelling in Protest and Politics*, Chicago: University of Chicago Press.

Proust, Serge. 2010. "Mobilization of Artists and Understanding of the Political Field: Struggles Around the Contract Work System." *International Journal of Politics, Culture, and Society* 23(2/3): 113–126.

Reed, T.V. 2005. *The Art of Protest: Culture and Activism from the Civil Rights Movement to the Streets of Seattle*. Minneapolis: University of Minnesota Press.

Roscigno, Vincent J. and William F. Danaher. 2004. *The Voice of Southern Labor: Radio, Music, and Textile Strikes, 1929–1934*. Minneapolis: University of Minnesota Press.

Rosenthal Rob and Richard Flacks. 2012. *Playing for Change: Music and Musicians in the Service of Social Movements*. Boulder, CO: Paradigm.

Roussel, Violaine. 2007. "Occupational Logics and Political Commitment: American Artists against the Iraq War." *International Political Sociology* 1(4): 373–390.

Roussel, Violaine and Anurima Banerji. 2017. "Introduction." In *How to Do Politics with Art?*, edited by Violaine Roussel and Anurima Banerji, 1–21. New York: Routledge.

Roy, William. 2010. *Reds, Whites, and Blues: Social Movements, Folk Music, and Race in the United States*. Princeton, NJ: Princeton University Press.

Sapiro, Gisèle. 2014. *The French Writers' War, 1940–1953*. Durham, NC: Duke University Press.

Sinigaglia, Jérémy. 2007. "The Intermittent Workers' Movement: Between a Demobilizing Precarity and Mobilizing Precarious Workers." *Sociétés contemporaines* 65: 27–53.

Snow, David A. 1979. "A Dramaturgical Analysis of Movement Accommodation: Building Idiosyncrasy Credit as a Movement Mobilization Strategy." *Symbolic Interaction* 2(2): 23–44.

Snow, David A., E. Burke Rochford, Jr, Steven K. Worden and Robert D. Benford. 1986. "Frame Alignment Processes, Micromobilization, and Movement Participation." *American Sociological Review* 51(4): 464–481.

Snow, David A., Anna E. Tan, and Peter B. Owens. 2013. "Social Movements, Framing Processes, and Cultural Revitalization and Fabrication." *Mobilization* 18(3): 225–242.

Staggenborg, Suzanne, Donna Eder, and Lori Sudderth. 1993–1994. "Women's Culture and Social Change: Evidence from the National Women's Music Festival." *Berkeley Journal of Sociology* 38: 31–56.

Steinberg, Marc W. 2004. "When Politics Goes Pop: On the Intersections of Popular and Political Culture and the Case of Serbian Student Protests." *Social Movement Studies* 3(1): 3–29.

Swidler, Ann. 1986. "Culture in Action: Symbols and Strategies." *American Sociological Review* 51: 273–286.

Szemere, Anna. 1992. "The Politics of Marginality. A Rock Musical Subculture in Socialist Hungary in the Early 1980s." In *Rockin' the Boat: Mass Music and Mass Movements*, edited by Reebee Garofalo, 93–114. Boston: South End Press.

Tilly, Charles. 1985. *The Contentious French*. Cambridge, MA: Harvard University Press.

Tilly, Charles. 2004. *Social Movements, 1768–2004*, Boulder, CO: Paradigm.

Wicke, Peter. 1992. "The Times They Are A-Changin': Rock Music and Political Change in East Germany." In *Rockin' the Boat: Mass Music and Mass Movements*, edited by Reebee Garofalo, 81–92. Boston: South End Press.

Part IV

Microstructural and Social-Psychological Dimensions

21

Individual Participation in Street Demonstrations

Jacquelien Van Stekelenburg, Bert Klandermans, and Stefaan Walgrave

Introduction

Protest participation has been surging throughout the world. In most countries, political protest has become the modal repertoire citizens employ to demand political changes or to express indignation (Meyer and Tarrow 1998). Protest participation has become normalized and all sorts of people resort to protest to demand social and political change (Meyer and Tarrow 1998; Norris, Walgrave, and van Aelst 2005; van Aelst and Walgrave 2001). This is empirically confirmed by Granberg (2013), who argues that contention is even resurging. Granberg analyzed data from the Cross-National Time-Series (CNTS) on general strikes, riots, anti-government demonstrations, and revolts spanning the 1919–2012 period in 18 western democracies (Figure 21.1). These data not only show that, since 2009, contention spiked to the level of the 1960s, but also that the type of contention has changed in recent years. While in the 1960s rioting was prevalent, (anti-government) demonstrations are at present by far the most employed repertoire of contention.

People can undertake a whole variety of different kinds of political activities ranging from signing a petition, to taking part in a strike or a demonstration, or more violent political activities. Contention is a multifaceted phenomenon. Although the underlying motivational dynamics may differ considerably (Saunders 2014), these distinct political activities are often lumped together. In this chapter, rather than lumping different forms of participation together, we choose to zoom in on one particular type of protest, namely, street demonstrations. Participation in street demonstrations is *the* prototypical protest activity of citizens today, at least, in Western societies. However, demonstrations come in different forms and sizes and, for

The Wiley Blackwell Companion to Social Movements, Second Edition. Edited by David A. Snow, Sarah A. Soule, Hanspeter Kriesi, and Holly J. McCammon.

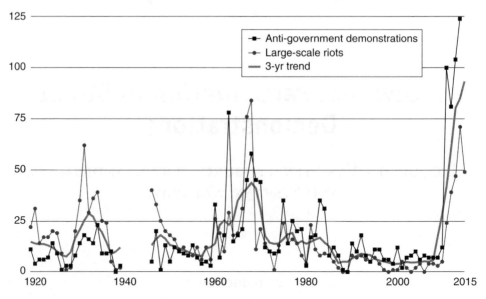

Figure 21.1   Anti-government demonstrations, revolts, riots, and general strikes in 18 western democracies from 1919–2012.

example, the costs and risks involved are dissimilar and highly context-dependent. Compare, for instance, demonstrating LGBTs in Amsterdam or Moscow. Whereas demonstrators in Amsterdam come across as a cheerful party (van Leeuwen, van Stekelenburg, and Klandermans 2015), LGBT demonstrators in Moscow have been known to be beaten by antigay demonstrators and arrested by the police. As a consequence of these differences, there is no uniform, "generalized demonstrator" but rather many types of demonstrators. Verhulst (2011: 213) criticizes the social movement literature for treating demonstrators indiscriminately: "Should we just assume that a routinized peace protester and a worried factory worker have a lot in common, just because they are both protesters?" he rhetorically asks. "Of course not," he replies. A variety of types of people demonstrate, but this is hidden from view because studies of movement participation tend to compare participants with non-participants instead of considering differences among protesters. Consequently, we know relatively little about how demonstrators differ within and between demonstrations.

In this chapter, we first define and conceptualize the phenomenon of a street demonstration; what is a street demonstration and how can it be distinguished from other collective gatherings, such as riots and hooliganism? Next, we shift our focus to the individual demonstrator: who is s/he, why does s/he participate, and how is s/he mobilized? We will use the model of Klandermans (2004) regarding the demand, supply, and mobilization of participation in demonstrations. Then we turn to the question how to investigate participation in street demonstrations. In doing so, we distinguish between methods that focus on the study of protest events, and methods that focus on participants. In the conclusion we raise some methodological issues and challenge how scholars have studied the motives and recruitment techniques that bring individuals to a demonstration.

Defining and Conceptualizing Street Demonstrations[1]

Pierre Favre (1990) – among the first to systematically study street demonstrations – describes how demonstrations, their composition, their participants' motives and mobilization trajectories are social phenomena that develop in multiple interactions between different actors. These different actors are either directly present or involved at a distance in the *moment manifestant* (ibid. see also Fillieule 1997; Fillieule and Tartakowsky 2013). Continuing Favre's pioneering work, Olivier Fillieule compared street demonstrations in various French cities. He defined street demonstrations as "any temporary occupation by a number of people of an open space, public or private, which directly or indirectly includes the expression of political opinions" (1997: 44; our translation). Nine years later, Casquete (2006: 47) defined street demonstrations as "collective gatherings in a public space whose aim it is to exert political, social and/or cultural influence on authorities, public opinion and participants through the disciplined and peaceful expression of an opinion or demand."

Street demonstrations are vehicles for expressing political opinions, ideas, and beliefs; they aim their political communication at authorities, the media, and the public. Casquete (2006) and Eyerman (2006) argue that demonstrations are ritual performances. Eyerman (ibid.: 209) argues that street demonstrations are ritual political street theatre. In the expressive dramatization, he argues, the values, images, and desires of the movement are revealed and membership solidified. The ritual practices help to "frame" understanding by linking present events and practices to those of the past and the future.

To understand how street demonstrations are different from other crowds, gatherings, and riots, we turn to the work of McPhail and Wohlstein (1983). These authors argue that the traditional term "crowd" frequently conveys an "illusion of unanimity," instead, they use the term "gathering" to refer to two or more persons present at one time in a public place, e.g. on sidewalks. If these gatherings protest, it is a demonstration, if it is a festivity or celebration, it is called a parade (e.g. May Day Parade). The term "riots," finally, they describe as gatherings consisting of individual or collective violence against persons or property. Note that gatherings may turn into demonstrations (on spontaneity, see Snow and Moss 2014) and demonstrations may turn into riots (McPhail and McCarthy 2005). To complicate issues even further, hooliganism – violence committed by sport fans – may be very close to riots. This is because hooligans not only use violence in their attempts to humiliate competing gangs who support other club teams, but also to attract attention to their social background and to express grievances related to their social position (Dunning, Murphy, and Waddington 2002, cited by Vliegenthart 2013).

Street demonstrations are the same and different every time they occur. The late Charles Tilly would have seconded that. Street demonstrations, according to Tilly, are examples of contentious performances (2008) obeying the rules of what Tilly called "strong repertoires." Participants are "enacting existing scripts within which they innovate, mostly only in small ways" (ibid.: 17). Wright's (1978) fieldwork observations of crowds, including demonstrations and riots, are of interest here. He differentiates between two broad categories of crowd behaviors: crowd activities and task activities. "Crowd activities" refer to the redundant behavior seemingly common to all incidents of crowds, such as assembling, milling, and departure. McPhail and Wohlstein drill down even deeper, identifying collective locomotion, collective orientation, collective gesticulation, and collective vocalization among the types of crowd behaviors "repeatedly observed across a variety of gatherings, demonstrations, and some riots" (1983: 595). To get at the variation in types of crowds, attention must be turned to what Wright conceptualized as "task activities." These refer to joint activities that are particular to and necessary for the attainment of a specific goal or the resolution of a specific problem. Examples of task activities include mass assembly with speechmaking, picketing, temporary occupations of premises, lynching, taunting and harassment, property destruction, looting, and sniping (Snow and Owens 2013). It is the similarity of crowd activities and the variation in task activities that make that street demonstrations the same and different every time they occur.

Demonstrations may have different functions. Casquete (2006) mentions three functions: (1) demonstrations are staged to *persuade* authorities, e.g. politicians, employers or CEOs, directors, and to acquire and exert influence for social or political change by influencing decision-making processes; (2) demonstrations also allow actors to *vent* frustration. Participants benefit from demonstrating by publicly voicing their anger, indignation, or moral discontent; and (3) demonstrations also serve to *consolidate* participants. Ritual behavior such as protest demonstrations serves to build, convey, and conserve a sense of "we" and fosters sustained commitment among participants in a social movement. Most demonstrations fulfill all three functions, but some functions will likely prevail under specific circumstances. For example, if targeted government actors are ready to make concessions, the persuasive function will probably dominate.

All in all, there is both similarity and variation in how street demonstrations look and feel in their atmosphere (e.g. Eyerman 2006; van Leeuwen et al. 2015), how they are organized (Boekkooi, Klandermans, and Stekelenberg 2011; Boekkooi 2012; Klandermans, Kriesi, and Tarrow 1988), the composition of the crowd (Walgrave and Rucht 2010), their crowd and task activities (McPhail and Wohlstein 1983; Wright 1978) and who they are targeting (Verhulst 2011). Also, protest venues and even weather conditions lead to variance across demonstrations, as does media coverage of the issue at stake. Moreover, demonstrations can be ritualized, peaceful, or violent, with or without a permit, and with or without peaceful interactions with the police. Demonstrations are usually staged by a coalition of organizers, but the composition of the coalition varies and the composition of the crowd on the streets varies with the coalition (Boekkooi 2012). For example, in Spain, the coalition that organized the demonstrations against the war in Iraq in 2003 consisted of major political and social organizations (Walgrave and Rucht 2010), while the coalition staging the same events in the Netherlands consisted of small radical left organizations. As a consequence, the composition of the crowds demonstrating in the two countries differed significantly (Boekkooi et al. 2011).

Demand, Supply, and Mobilization

Individual participation in demonstrations is the consequence of an interaction between individuals and collective actors such as parties, interest groups, and movement organizations. The more individuals are embedded in such organizations and networks, the more they get involved in their activities. The interaction is shaped by the wider political and socioeconomic conditions prevailing in a country, such as the maturity of a democracy and the current economic circumstances. In Figure 21.2, the process is displayed in a schematic fashion.

Klandermans (2004) decomposes the dynamics of participation in demonstrations into the dynamics of demand, supply, and mobilization. Figure 21.2 visualizes the roadmap of our theoretical exercise. *Demand* refers to the potential of participation in a given society for a certain demonstration on a certain issue; it relates to grievances, efficacy, identity, emotions, and social embeddedness of individuals who may be more or less willing to demonstrate for a given issue or problem. Yet, even if many people are willing to demonstrate, this does not mean that there will be demonstrations. There must be demonstration opportunities. This is where the *supply* side of the equation comes in. It refers mostly to social movements staging demonstrations and, thereby, generating opportunities for individuals to demonstrate. Supply relates to the characteristics of the movement. What issues do the organizers mobilize for? Is the movement strong, is there a densely organized multiorganizational field? Are many people identifying with the staging organizations? Demand and supply do not automatically come together. *Mobilization* is the process that links demand and supply. It is the marketing mechanism of social movements. The mobilizing structure that organizers assemble is the connecting tissue between supply and demand. Mobilization refers to the techniques and mechanisms that organizers

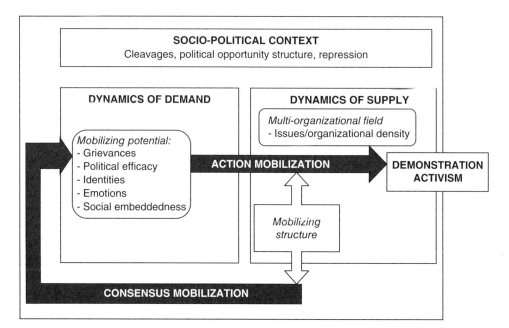

Figure 21.2   Demand, supply, and mobilization.

use to build a mobilizing structure that links a demand for protest to a supply of protest (Boekkooi 2012; Klandermans, Kriesi, and Tarrow 1988; van Stekelenburg and Boekkooi 2013). This makes it highly dynamic. For example, a fit – or misfit – between motives and appeals can make for success or failure (van Stekelenburg and Klandermans 2014; Walgrave and Rucht 2010).

Dynamics of demand

Little is known about how demand is formed. A few decades ago, Klandermans introduced the distinction between *consensus mobilization* and *consensus formation* (1984, 1988). While consensus mobilization concerns "the deliberate attempts to spread the view of a social actor among parts of the population," consensus formation concerns "the unplanned convergence of meaning in social networks and subcultures" (Klandermans, 1988: 175). Both these processes can come about via the use of several information and persuasion channels (Gamson 1992). Nowadays, it can be expected that the Internet and social media will play a crucial role in consensus mobilization and formation (Earl and Kimport, 2011; van Stekelenburg and Boekkooi, 2013) (on the role of the media and the Internet in relation to social movements, see Chapter 7 by Rohlinger and Corrigall-Brown, and Chapter 16 by Earl, in this volume). For example, employing time-series analysis, Vliegenthart (2007) demonstrated regarding the issues of immigration and integration in the Netherlands that, in a complex interplay between real-life events, media attention, debates in the parliament, and debates between politicians, public opinion was formed and converted into anti-immigrant party support.

The social-psychological core of the demand-side of protest consists of grievances, efficacy perceptions, identification, emotions, and social embeddedness (van Stekelenburg and Klandermans 2013).

- *Grievances*. At the heart of every protest lie grievances, be it the experience of illegitimate inequality, feelings of relative deprivation, feelings of injustice, moral indignation about some state of affairs, or a suddenly imposed grievance (Klandermans 1997). Illegitimate inequality is what relative deprivation and social justice theories are about. Suddenly imposed grievances refer to an unexpected threat or inroad upon people's rights or circumstances (Walsh 1981). Feelings of relative deprivation result from comparison of one's situation with a standard, be it one's past, someone else's situation, or a cognitive standard such as equity or justice (Folger 1986; Klandermans 2015). If the comparison results in the conclusion that one is not receiving what one deserves, a person experiences relative deprivation. Runciman (1966) referred to relative deprivation based on personal comparisons as egoistic deprivation and to relative deprivation based on group comparisons as fraternalistic deprivation. Research suggests that fraternalistic deprivation is particularly important for engagement in protest (Major 1994; Martin 1986). On the basis of a meta-analysis, van Zomeren and colleagues (2008) conclude that the cognitive component of relative deprivation (as reflected in the observation that one receives less than the standard of comparison) has less influence on participation than the affective component (as expressed by such feelings as dissatisfaction, indignation, and discontent about these outcomes). In thinking about the importance of grievances to participation in street demonstrations, it is analytically useful to distinguish between *individual* and *mobilizing* grievances (Snow and Soule 2010). Individual grievances are experienced individually rather than collectively. Mobilizing grievances, however, are grievances that are shared, and that are felt to be sufficiently serious to warrant not only collective complaint but also some kind of corrective collective action. Thus, it is mobilizing grievances, rather than individual grievances, that provide the primary motivational impetus for participation in street demonstrations (ibid.).

- *Efficacy perceptions.* Efficacy refers to an individual's perception that conditions or policies can be altered through protest (Gamson 1992). For the perception of the possibility of change to take hold, people need to perceive the group as being able to unite and fight and they must perceive the political context as receptive to their claims. The former refers to *group* efficacy – the belief that group-related problems can be solved by collective efforts (Bandura 1997) while the latter refers to *political* efficacy – the feeling that political actions of citizens can impact the political process (Campbell, Gurin, and Miller 1954).

- *Identification.* Sociologists were among the first to emphasize the importance of collective identity in protest participation. They argued that the production of a collective identity is crucial for a movement to emerge (Melucci 1989; Taylor and Whittier 1992). Similarly, social psychological studies consistently report that the more people identify with a group, the more they are inclined to protest on behalf of that group (e.g. Reicher 1984; Simon et al. 1998; Stryker, Owens, and White 2000; van Zomeren, Postmes, and Spears 2008). Why is group identification such a powerful push to protest? First, identification with others is accompanied by an awareness of similarity and shared fate with those who belong to the same category. Furthermore, the "strength" of an identity comes from its affective component (see Ellemers 1993, for a similar argument); the more "the group is in me," the more "I feel for us" (Yzerbyt et al. 2003) and the stronger "I am motivated to act on behalf of the group." Collective identification, especially the more politicized forms of it, also intensifies perceptions of efficacy (see Simon et al., 1998, van Zomeren et al., 2008). Identification with involved others also generates a felt inner social obligation to behave as a "good" group member (Stürmer et al. 2003). The more one identifies with the group, the more weight the group norm will carry and the more it will result in an "inner felt obligation" to act on behalf of the group. Typically, politicization of identities begins with the awareness of shared grievances. Next, an external enemy is blamed for the group's predicament, and claims for compensation are leveled against this enemy. Unless appropriate compensation is granted, the power struggle continues and gradually the group's relationship to its social environment transforms. If in the course of this struggle the group seeks to win the support of third parties such as more powerful authorities (e.g. the national government) or the general public, identities further politicize (Simon and Klandermans 2001).

- *Emotions.* The study of emotions has become a popular research area in the social psychology of protest. That was not always the case. Emotions were often regarded as some peripheral "error term" in motivational theories. For those of us who have observed protest events or watched reports on protest events in the news media, this is hard to believe. Indeed, it is difficult to conceive of protest detached from emotions. Anger is seen as *the* prototypical protest emotion (van Stekelenburg and Klandermans 2007). van Zomeren et al. (2008) show that group-based anger is an important motivator of protest participation. There exists a relation to efficacy: people who perceive the ingroup as strong are more likely to feel angry and willing to fight; people who perceive the ingroup as weak are more likely to feel fearful and wish flight (Devos, Silver, and Mackie 2002; Klandermans, van der Toorn, and van Stekelenburg 2008). (See Chapter 23 by Van Ness and Summers-Effler, in this volume, for a discussion of emotions.)
- *Social embeddedness.* Social embeddedness, whether it is based on formal, informal, or virtual networks, plays a pivotal role in the context of protest (van Stekelenburg, Klandermans, and Akkerman 2016). Apart from the fact that networks play a pivotal role in action mobilization (see below), it is within these networks that consensus formation and consensus mobilization take place (Klandermans and Stekelenburg 2013). Taylor (2013) proposes the concept of discursive communities to indicate settings in which consensus formation takes place. It is within these networks that processes such as grievance formation, empowerment, identification, and group-based emotions all synthesize into a motivational constellation preparing people for action and building mobilization potential. In fact, the effect of interaction in networks on the propensity to participate in politics is contingent on the amount of political discussion that occurs in social networks and the information that people are able to gather about politics as a result (McClurg 2003). Klandermans et al. (2008) provide evidence for such mechanisms: immigrants who felt efficacious were more likely to participate in protest provided that they were embedded in social networks, especially ethnic networks, which offer an opportunity to discuss and learn about politics. (See Chapter 8 by Crossley and Diani, in this volume, for further discussion of networks.)

Dynamics of supply

The supply side of protest is affected by the characteristics of the social movement sector in a country, its strength, its diversity, and its contentiousness. The social movement sector is often conceived of as a conglomerate of movement organizations (McAdam, McCarthy, and Zald 1996) providing the infrastructure on which protest is built (Diani and McAdam 2003). Increasingly, people seem to avoid long-term engagements and instead opt for loose engagements in informal, often ephemeral, networks embedded in liquid communities (Roggeband and Duyvendak 2013; van Stekelenburg and Boekkooi 2013). This decreases the role of social movement organizations in producing protest supply. At the same time, we witness the emergence of a "global social movement sector" (Smith and Fetner 2007), implying that organizations still play a role in creating a supply of protest events.

Movement organizations work hard to turn grievances into claims, to point out addressable targets, to create moral outrage and anger, and to stage events where all this can be vented. They weave together a moral, cognitive, ideological, and emotional framework communicating their appraisal of the situation to the movement's constituency. In doing so, movement organizations play a significant role in the construction and reconstruction of collective beliefs and in the transformation of individual discontent into collective action. Grievances can be framed in terms of *emotional connections* or violated *interests* and violated *principles*. Organizers try to build collective identities, a shared sense of "we-ness" and "collective agency." In fact, in their review of collective identity, Polletta and Jasper (2001: 284) define collective identity as an individual's cognitive, moral, and emotional connections. It is these connections that organizers try to emphasize. Organizers can frame grievances in terms of emotional connections, I feel for us, which most likely resonates with identity motives. In addition to trying to mobilize people by emphasizing emotional connections, organizers also attempt to promote a sense of outrage about violated interests and principles. Campaigns that emphasize the violation of interests more likely resonate with instrumental motives, i.e. in order to accomplish social change, while campaigns that emphasize the violation of principles more likely resonate with expressive motives, i.e. in order to express one's views (van Stekelenburg, Klandermans, and van Dijk 2009).

- *Issue.* The most prominent supply factor is, obviously, the issue of the demonstration chosen by the organizing organizations (Verhulst 2011). Verhulst defines issues as "subjects, processes or situations that affect particular groups in society and which, through these groups' shared interpretations of these problems and the grievances they evoke, have the potential to mobilize these groups into action" (ibid.: 20). He proposes a two-dimensional distinction between old, new, and consensual issues, on the one hand, and particularistic and universalistic issues, on the other. Old and new issues differ on the survival vs. self-expression value cleavage (Inglehart and Welzel 2005). Many old issues are related to material, socioeconomic factors, such as inequality, social security, and industrial relations while newer issues often deal with moral, cultural, and lifestyle issues, such as sexual orientation, abortion, animal rights, and peace and war issues. But often it is the direction of an issue (pro or against abortion, or pro or against environmental measures) as defined by the organizers which really matters and which allows them to be placed in the "old" or the "new" category. Consensual issues are in essence "cleavageless," they are valence issues, such as opposition to drunk driving or random violence. Nobody is in favor of drunken driving or random violence; these issues do not imply opposing political positions and there is no counter-movement on these issues. Issues differ in the way and degree to which they appeal to, and potentially activate, relevant publics. Universalistic issues are those that, at least in theory, concern the entire population, such as global warming, while particularistic issues concern a specific group. Taking action on an issue like global warming requires different motivations and mobilization techniques than does taking action on a particular issue, for example, protesting against a factory closure. Different people are affected by different issues leading to different motivations and often also to different ways in which they end up demonstrating (e.g. van Stekelenburg and Klandermans 2014).

- *Organizational density*. A second supply factor, next to the issue of the demonstration, is the density of the relevant organizational field (Walgrave and Klandermans 2010). In densely organized fields, more individuals are embedded in the organizer's social network, and this makes establishing a collective identity more likely, which suggests that participants embedded in densely organized fields are more likely to identify with the organizers and the other participants than those embedded in low density fields (Klandermans et al. 2014; Walgrave and Klandermans 2010; Walgrave and Wouters 2014).

Mobilization dynamics

Mobilization is the process that links a specific demand for protest on a certain issue to a protest opportunity around that same issue offered by a social movement organization. Organizers have to build mobilizing structures. *Mobilizing structures* are defined as "those collective vehicles, informal as well as formal, through which people mobilize and engage in collective action" (McAdam et al. 1996: 3). This includes all formal and informal networks that exist both inside and outside a social movement sector. At any time, all kinds of groups, organizations, and networks that exist in a society can become part of a mobilizing structure. However, none can be assumed to automatically become part of it. Networks need to be adapted, appropriated, assembled, and activated by organizers in order to function as mobilizing structures (Boekkooi et al. 2011).

Assembling a mobilizing structure is an important step in the process of micromobilization. Which organizations join the mobilizing coalition is an important predictor of who will participate in protest (e.g. Heaney and Rojas 2008). Most studies show that organizations predominantly mobilize their own members. Similarly, networks tend to reach those who are embedded in their structures. Thus, organizers who assemble different mobilizing structures reach different subsets of a movement's mobilization potential (Boekkooi et al. 2011). Demonstrators who are affiliated with the organizers are mobilized in different manners than unaffiliated demonstrators; moreover, patterns of identification differ, as do the strength and nature of their motivation (Klandermans et al. 2014).

Social networks are indispensable in the mobilization process. Many studies have shown that networks are important in explaining differential participation (e.g. Klandermans and Oegema 1987; Snow, Zurcher, and Ekland-Olson 1980; Walgrave and Klandermans 2010). For instance, Walgrave and Klandermans (2010) demonstrate how open and closed communication channels and weak and strong ties weave a web of connections to a movement's mobilization potential. It is important to distinguish between formal, informal and virtual networks, as it is interpersonal networks in particular that play an important role in mobilization (Walgrave and Wouters 2014).

Yet, sometimes, the demand for protest can be so overwhelming that very little in terms of mobilization is needed to bring large numbers onto the streets. The mobilization process happens then bottom-up and hardly any organization is necessary. For example, in the context of the massive indignation regarding the kidnapping and serial killing of children by Dutroux and judicial errors in Belgium, television and newspapers sufficed as mobilizing actors without the presence of formal organizers (Walgrave and Manssens 2000). Similarly, Walgrave and Klandermans (2010) report findings from a demonstration against the Iraq War revealing that appeals via mass media were more effective in countries with high levels of opposition to the war. Mobilization with minimal or no organization has become more effective with the appearance of virtual networks and social media (Klandermans et al. 2014).

Polletta and colleagues (2013) suggest that the Internet plays an important role in mobilization (see Chapter 16 by Earl, in this volume). Mobilization for so-called connective action (cf. Bennett and Segerberg 2012) moves from one person to another individually, as part of a larger email list, a listserv, or a social network such as Facebook or Twitter. In a process that continues to reproduce itself, the message is copied and redistributed. This matches van Stekelenburg and Klandermans' (2017) observation that technologies such as mobile phones, the Internet, and Facebook played a crucial role in the mobilization of high school students in the Netherlands in a protest campaign against educational policy (van Stekelenburg and Boekkooi 2013; van Stekelenburg and Klandermans 2017). However, empirical analyses reveal that organizational channels are still important (Klandermans et al. 2014). Thus, the organized character of mobilization remains a continuing topic of debate among social movement scholars.

Mobilization is a complicated process that can be broken down into several conceptually distinct steps. Klandermans (1988) proposes breaking the process of mobilization down into consensus and action mobilization. *Consensus mobilization*, as we have discussed, refers to dissemination of the views of the movement organization, while *action mobilization* refers to the transformation of sympathizers into participants. The more successful consensus mobilization is, the larger the pool of sympathizers a mobilizing movement organization can draw upon for action mobilization. In their frame alignment approach to mobilization, Snow, Benford, and their colleagues elaborate consensus mobilization much further (see Benford, 1997, for a critical review; and Snow, 2004, for an overview). In turn, Klandermans and Oegema (1987) detail the process of action mobilization further into four separate steps: (1) people need to *sympathize* with the cause; (2) people need to *know* about the upcoming event; (3) people must be *willing* to participate; and (4) people must be *able* to participate (see Figure 21.3).

Each step brings the supply and demand of protest closer together until an individual eventually takes the final step to participate in a demonstration. The first step accounts for the results of consensus mobilization. It divides the general public into those who sympathize with the cause and those who do not (see Figure 21.3). A large pool of sympathizers is of strategic importance, because many a sympathizer never turns into a demonstrator. The second step is crucial as well; it divides the sympathizers into those who have been the target of mobilization attempts and those who have not. The third step concerns the social psychological core of the process. It divides the sympathizers who have been targeted into those who are motivated to

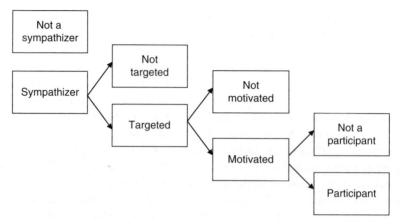

Figure 21.3   Four steps toward participation.

participate and those who are not. Finally, the fourth step differentiates the people who are motivated into those who end up participating and those who do not. With each step, a number of potential participants drop out, but the better the fit between demand and supply, the smaller the number of dropouts.

How to Study Participation in Demonstrations?

Few areas in political behavior research are plagued by such methodological difficulties as the study of participation in political protest (Finkel and Muller 1998). For instance, protest participation usually happens quite spontaneously or at least on short notice, so that researchers cannot plan a well-thought-out study in advance. Moreover, scholars have to come up with creative solutions to avoid problems of reliability and validity. Much of what we know about protest participation comes from studies that roughly can be divided into those that take the protest event as the unit of analysis and those that take the individual as the unit of analysis. In short, there are: (1) studies of *protest events*; and (2) studies of *protest participants*.

Studying protest events

Protest event analysis has been developed to systematically map, analyze, and interpret the occurrence and characteristics of large numbers of protests by means of content analysis, using sources such as newspaper reports, news agencies, police archives, and/or television (e.g. Earl et al. 2004; Koopmans 1993; Wouters 2013). Protest event studies have considerably advanced our understanding of protest waves (Koopmans 1993), social movement outcomes (e.g. see King and Soule 2007; McAdam and Su 2002; Soule and Olzak 2004), and state-opponent interactions (e.g. see Davenport, Soule, and Armstrong 2011; Earl et al. 2004).

  Over the years, two main concerns have been raised about studying protest events based upon newspaper coverage and police records (e.g. Beyerlein et al, 2016; Earl et al. 2004). The first focuses on *selection bias*. Studies show that media coverage captures only a small subset of the universe of protests, for instance, in Belgium, only

11% of protests recorded in police records make it onto the television screen (Wouters 2013). Newspapers, on the other hand, disproportionately select events deemed to be "newsworthy," such as those larger in size or involving conflicts (e.g. see Earl et al. 2004). But police archives miss events as well, namely, those that do not require permits or demonstrations for which activists refuse to file one (McCarthy, McPhail, and Smith 1996). The second concern deals with *description bias*. As far as objective characteristics of events are concerned (e.g. when or where they occurred), the problem seems to be with the lack of information collected rather than its accuracy (Earl et al. 2004). Police and journalists report only a limited number of all the possible event characteristics. Roughly half or more of police records and journalists' coverage of protests in the USA fail to report such important characteristics as date and size (e.g. McCarthy et al. 1996). Moreover, newspaper articles do not delve into protesters' identities, motivations, and emotions. Date and place of a demonstration can be reported accurately and reliable, yet motivations, emotions, and identities are much more difficult to "read" by journalists/policemen.

Due to these biases, Beyerlein and colleagues (2016) argue that the field of contentious politics and social movements lacks a nationally representative sample of street demonstrations with thorough data on event characteristics. Consequently, we do not have good answers to questions such as: How many people, on average, turn out to protests across countries? What types of organizations typically sponsor them? Which issues draw the most protest? Are peaceful or disruptive tactics the norm? Beyerlein and colleagues (2016) employ a novel methodology of hypernetwork sampling. The core idea behind hypernetwork sampling is that a representative sample of protest events can be arrived at by randomly sampling protesters and then having them nominate and describe the protests they attended. Respondents are asked questions about the protests that took place, their protesters, causes, targets, tactics, organizers, speeches and police actions. In doing so, nearly complete information about various event characteristics was collected from protests across the United States in 2010 to 2011 (Beyerlein et al. 2016).

Studying participants

Studies on protest participants tended to be limited to population surveys (e.g. Dalton, Van Sickle, and Weldon 2010; Norris 2003; van der Meer and van Ingen 2009; van Deth, Montero, and Westholm 2007), such as the World Value Survey (WVS) or the European Social Survey (ESS) (cf. Inglehart and Catterber 2002; Norris 2003; Welzel, Inglehart, and Deutsch 2004). General population surveys have the advantage of sampling people, both those who did and did not participate in protest. Consequently, studies relying on population surveys are, most of the time, comparisons of participants with non-participants. Consequently, we now know a lot about how participants differ from non-participants, but we know much less about how demonstrators differ within and between demonstrations. Moreover, while such studies based on general surveys have taught us a lot about general features of protesters (cf. Dalton et al. 2010), they provide little information on the demonstrations protesters participated in, the protesters' specific motivations, and their recruitment. Presumably, motivation and mobilization differ from demonstration to demonstration, but general surveys fail to tell us how and why.

General population surveys do not address specific protests for specific issues, i.e. comparisons between protests are impossible, therefore they are less suited to answering questions such as: Why do people protest? What are the issue-specific attitudes, motives, and beliefs that drive them? How were they mobilized, through what channels and by which techniques? And, especially, how and why does this vary across demonstrations? Collecting such information requires a different methodological approach than protest-event analysis, hypernetworked sampling, or general population surveys. In fact, answers to these seemingly simple questions require a specific type of data. Such questions not only call for comparative data on the who, the why and the how of people who took part in different protests combined with information about the issue they protested against, their mobilizing channels and their motives for taking part in this specific protest event. Until recently, such data were not available. Recently, however, a growing number of studies rely on the so-called protest-survey method (e.g. Klandermans et al. 2010; van Aelst and Walgrave 2001; van Stekelenburg et al. 2012). The protest-survey method, a comparative approach, involves surveying a large number of protesters during a protest while at the same time recording characteristics of the context, police, and mobilizing actors (Walgrave and Verhulst 2011; Walgrave, Wouters, and Ketelaars, 2016).

If one wants to know who participates in a specific protest event and why and how they were recruited, one can ask participants themselves using a take-home questionairre distributed among protesters at protest events. This kind of fieldwork is often conducted in a crowded, unpredictable and erratic environment. A demonstration is a living thing and it can be tricky to sample from a demonstrating crowd. Walgrave and colleagues proposed two techniques to increase the representativity of the sample. In order to control for non-response bias, two types of data collection are employed: a smaller number (e.g. 200) short face-to-face interviews during the demonstration is combined with a larger number (e.g. 800) postal survey questionnaires completed after the demonstration. This is done by a so-called "tear-off system," which implies that demonstrators are approached for a short face-to-face interview (including socio-demographics, most important independent variables, and the dependent variables of the postal survey). After the face-to-face interview is finished the *same* protester is asked to fill out a postal survey questionnaire at home. Hence, survey questionnaires are always filled in at home not *during* the event, again for matters of comparison. The refusal rate for the face-to-face interviews is low (10%). Thus, provided proper sampling is done, by comparing the face-to-face interviews with the postal survey questionnaires, biases due to non-response can be assessed and controlled for.

As for sampling participants, a sampling strategy is designed such that each participant has the same chance of being selected. A demonstration is covered by a team consisting of "pointers" and "interviewers." Pointers count the rows and select a person to be interviewed in that row – alternating between the left, the right, and the middle part. Then, an interviewer is sent in to approach the selected interviewee. Separating these two roles is crucial in minimizing sampling biases. For instance, experiments where interviewers could select their own respondents indicate that they are more inclined to approach the more approachable (those who look like them) (Walgrave and Verhulst 2011).

Although the protest survey method has been refined over the years and enables researchers to answer questions related to protests and their protesters, it is not a perfect methodology. Because the protest survey method focuses only on those people who are actually participating, it samples on the dependent variable. Studies based on protest surveys cannot compare participants to non-participants. Therefore, they are ill-suited to test the determinants of activism. To overcome this problem, case-control designs – widely used in epidemiology – were proposed recently (Vráblíková and Traunmüller 2015). With a case-control design, protest survey data are merged with population survey data. The case-control design thus expands the data to include both protest participants (from protest survey data) and non-participants (from the population surveys). Consequently, case-control designs allow investigation of the determinants of activism.

Conclusion

Taking part in a street demonstration is not just a matter of people who are pushed to act by some internal psychological state (the demand-side of participation), nor is it only a matter of movement organizations pulling people into action (the supply-side of participation). Demand, supply, *and* mobilization account for instances of participation in street demonstrations. For example, the reason why often no demonstration takes place despite widespread discontent, is that there is no viable movement organization to stage any demonstration. At the same time, when present, a movement organization does not get very far if there are no people who are concerned about the issue the organization tries to address. Finally, without effective mobilization campaigns, supply and demand may never meet. There is an intriguing interplay of demand and supply. That is to say, the better the fit between demand and supply – i.e. the more organizers' appeals resonate with people's grumbles – the larger a demonstration.

In terms of methods, research on street demonstrations has been refined over the years and this has enabled researchers to answer many questions related to protests and their protesters; however, it still faces some challenges. Probably the most important challenge is to overcome the problem of sampling on the dependent variable by getting a grip on participants and non-participants. One way to do so would, for instance, be a longitudinal pre-post protest design which follows a group of citizens before, during, and after the demonstration. Such designs enhance the prospect of differentiating between participants and non-participants for a specific event. Another thorny issue is the interaction of demand and supply over the course of a campaign. Indeed, how do grievances, identification, efficacy, and emotions change over the course of a campaign or the lifecycle of a movement? Do they evolve because organizers have changed their frames? Or by the fact that counter-movements appeared on the scene? Or, because of critical incidents? As mobilization is a process, it would be worthwhile examining how demand and supply come together in a dynamic fashion or, at least as interesting, do *not* come together. In fact, especially the case where supply and demand do not come together is poorly understood. Because researchers focus on protest events and their participants, failed mobilizations tend to be overlooked. However, a focus on failed mobilizations in addition to succesful ones, may teach us a lot about the demand and supply of street demonstrations and how they interact.

Note

1   This section builds on a paper by Klandermans and van Stekelenburg (under review).

References

Bandura, Albert. 1997. *Self-Efficacy: The Exercise of Control*. New York: Freeman.

Benford, Robert. 1997. "An Insider's Critique of the Social Movement Framing Perspective." *Sociological Inquiry* 67(4): 409–430.

Bennett, Lance, and Alexandra Segerberg. 2012. "The Logic of Connective Action. Digital Media and the Personalization of Collective Action." *Information, Communication & Society* 15(5): 739–768.

Beyerlein, Kraig, Peter Barwis, Bryant Crubaugh, and Cole Carnesecca. 2016. "A New Picture of Protest: The National Study of Protest Events." *Sociological Methods & Research*. doi: doi.org/10.1177/0049124116661574.

Boekkooi, Marije. 2012. "Mobilizing Protest: The Influence of Organizers on Who Participates and Why." In *Sociology*. Amsterdam: VU University.

Boekkooi, Marije, Bert Klandermans, and Jacquelien van Stekelenburg. 2011. "Quarrelling and Protesting: How Organizers Shape a Demonstration." *Mobilization* 16(2): 223–241.

Campbell, Angus, Gerald Gurin, and Warren E. Miller. 1954. *The Voter Decides*. Evanston, IL: Row, Peterson.

Casquete, Jesus. 2006. "The Power of Demonstrations." *Social Movement Studies* 5(1): 45–60.

Dalton, Russell J., Alix Van Sickle, and Steven Weldon. 2010. "The Individual/Institutional Nexus of Protest Behaviour." *British Journal of Political Science* 40(01): 51–73.

Davenport, Christian, Sarah A. Soule, and David A. Armstrong. 2011. "Protesting While Black? The Differential Policing of American Activism, 1960 to 1990." *American Sociological Review* 76(1): 152–178.

Devos, Thiery, Lisa A. Silver, and Diane M. Mackie. 2002. "Experiencing Intergroup Emotions." In *From Prejudice to Intergroup Emotions: Differentiated Reactions to Social Groups*, edited by Diane M. Mackie and Eliot R. Smith, 111–134. Philadelphia, PA: Psychology Press.

Diani, Mario and Doug McAdam. 2003. *Social Movements and Networks, Relational Approaches to Collective Action*. Oxford: Oxford University Press.

Earl, Jennifer and Katrina Kimport. 2011. *Digitally Enabled Social Change: Activism in the Internet Age*. Cambridge, MA: MIT Press.

Earl, Jennifer, Andrew Martin, John D. McCarthy, and Sarah A. Soule. 2004. "The Use of Newspaper Data in the Study of Collective Action." *Annual Review of Sociology* 30: 65–80.

Ellemers, N. 1993. "The Influence of Socio-Structural Variables on Identity Management Strategies." In *European Review of Social Psychology*, edited by Wolfgang Stroebe and Miles Hewston, 27–58. Chichester: John Wiley & Sons, Ltd.

Eyerman, Ron. 2006. "Performing Opposition or, How Social Movements Move." In *Social Performance: Symbolic Action, Cultural Pragmatics, and Ritual*, edited by Jeffrey C.

Alexander, Bernhard Giesen, and Jason L. Mast, 193–217. Cambridge: Cambridge University Press.

Favre, Pierre. 1990. *La manifestation*. Paris: Presses de la Fondation nationale des Sciences politiques.

Fillieule, Olivier. 1997. *Stratégies de la rue*. Paris: Presses de Sciences Po.

Fillieule, Olivier and Danielle Tartakowsky. 2013. *Demonstrations*. Translated by Phyllis Aronoff and Howard Scott. Halifax: Fernwood.

Finkel, Steven E. and Edward N Muller. 1998. "Rational Choice and the Dynamics of Collective Political Action: Evaluating Alternative Models with Panel Data." *American Political Science Review* 92(01): 37–49.

Folger, Robert. 1986. "Rethinking Equity Theory: A Referent Cognitions Model." In *Justice in Social Relations*, edited by Bierhoff, Hans W., Cohen, Ronald L., and Jerald, Greenberg, 145–162. New York: Plenum.

Gamson, William A. 1992. *Talking Politics*. New York: Cambridge University Press.

Granberg, Magnus. 2013. "The Resurgence of Contention and the Enduring Significance of Labour Militancy." Paper presented at Conference of the European Sociological Association, Torino, Italy, August 28–31.

Heaney, Michael T. and Fabio Rojas. 2008. "Coalition Dissolution, Mobilization and Network Dynamics in the US Antiwar Movement." In *Research in Social Movements, Conflicts and Change* edited by P. G. Coy, 39–82. Bingley: Emerald Group.

Inglehart, Ronald and Gabriela Catterberg. 2002. "Trends in Political Action: The Developmental Trend and the Post-Honeymoon Decline." *International Journal of Comparative Sociology* 43(3–5): 300–316.

Inglehart, Ronald F. and Christian Welzel. 2005. *Modernization, Cultural Change, and Democracy: The Human Development Sequence*. New York: Cambridge University Press.

King, Brayden G. and Sarah A Soule. 2007. "Social Movements as Extra-Institutional Entrepreneurs: The Effect of Protests on Stock Price Returns." *Administrative Science Quarterly* 52(3): 413–442.

Klandermans, Bert. 1984. "Mobilization and Participation: Social-Psychological Expansions of Resource Mobilization Theory." *American Sociological Review* 49(5): 583–600.

Klandermans, Bert. 1988. "The Formation and Mobilization of Consensus." In *From Structure to Action: Comparing Social Movement Research across Cultures*, edited by Bert Klandermans, Hanspeter Kriesi, and Sidney Tarrow, 173–196. Greenwich, CT: JAI Press.

Klandermans, Bert. 1997. *The Social Psychology of Protest*. Oxford: Blackwell.

Klandermans, Bert. 2004. "The Demand and Supply of Participation: Social-Psychological Correlates of Participation in Social Movements." In *The Blackwell Companion to Social Movements*, edited by David A. Snow, Sarah A. Soule, and Hanspeter Kriesi, 360–379. Oxford: Blackwell.

Klandermans, Bert. 2015. "Grievance Formation in Times of Transition: South Africa 1994–2000." *Social Justice Research* 28: 123–142.

Klandermans, Bert, Hanspeter Kriesi, and Sidney Tarrow, eds. 1988. *From Structure to Action: Comparing Social Movement Research across Cultures*. Greenwich, CT: JAI Press.

Klandermans, Bert and Dirk Oegema. 1987. "Potentials, Networks, Motivations, and Barriers: Steps Toward Participation in Social Movements." *American Sociological Review* 52: 519–531.

Klandermans, Bert, Jojanneke van der Toorn, and Jacquelien van Stekelenburg. 2008. "Embeddedness and Grievances: How Immigrants Turn Grievances into Action." *American Sociological Review* 73(6): 992–1012.

Klandermans, Bert and Jacquelien van Stekelenburg. 2013. "Social Movements and the Dynamics of Collective Action." In *Oxford Handbook of Political Psychology*, 2nd edn, edited by Leonie Huddy, David O. Sears, and Jack S. Levy, 850–900. Oxford: Oxford University Press.

Klandermans, Bert, Jacquelien van Stekelenburg, Marie-Louise Damen, Dunya van Troost, and Anouk van Leeuwen. 2014. "Mobilization Without Organization: The Case of Unaffiliated Demonstrators." *European Sociological Review* 30(6): 702–716.

Klandermans, Bert, Jacquelien van Stekelenburg, Dunya van Troost, et al. 2010. "Manual for Data Collection on Protest Demonstrations. Caught in the Act of Protest: Contextualizing Contestation (CCC-Project)." VU University/Antwerpen University.

Koopmans, Ruud. 1993. "The Dynamics of Protest Waves: West Germany, 1965 to 1989." *American Sociological Review* 58(5): 637–658.

Major, Brendy. 1994. "From Social Inequality to Personal Entitlement: The Role of Social Comparisons, Legitimacy Appraisals, and Group Memberships." *Advances in Experimental Social Psychology* 26: 293–355.

Martin, Joanne. 1986. "The Tolerance of Injustice." In *Relative Deprivation and Social Comparison: The Ontario Symposium*, vol. 4, edited by James M. Olson, C. Peter Herman, and Mark P. Zanna, 217–242. Hillsdale, NJ: Lawrence Erlbaum.

McAdam, Doug, John D. McCarthy, and Mayer N. Zald. 1996. *Comparative Perspectives on Social Movements*. New York: Cambridge University Press.

McAdam, Doug and Yang Su. 2002. "The War at Home: Antiwar Protests and Congressional Voting, 1965 to 1973." *American Sociological Review* 67(5) :696–721.

McCarthy, John D, Clark McPhail, and Jackie Smith. 1996. "Images of Protest: Dimensions of Selection Bias in Media Coverage of Washington Demonstrations, 1982 and 1991." *American Sociological Review* 61: 478–499.

McClurg, Scott D. 2003. "Social Networks and Political Participation: The Role of Social Interaction in Explaining Political Participation." *Political Research Quarterly* 56: 448–464.

McPhail, Clark and John D. McCarthy. 2005. "Protest Mobilization, Protest Repression, and Their Interaction." In *Repression and Mobilization*, edited by Christian Davenport, Hank Johnston, and Carol Mueller, 3–32. Minneapolis: University of Minnesota Press.

McPhail, Clark and Ronald T. Wohlstein. 1983. "Individual and Collective Behaviors Within Gatherings, Demonstrations, and Riots." *Annual Review of Sociology* 9(1): 579–600.

Melucci, Alberto. 1989. *Nomads of the Present: Social Movements and Individual Needs in Contemporary Society*. London: Hutchinson Radius.

Meyer, David S. and Sidney Tarrow. 1998. *The Social Movement Society: Contentious Politics for a New Century*. Lanham, MD: Rowman & Littlefield.

Norris, Pippa. 2003. *Democratic Phoenix*. New York: Cambridge University Press.

Norris, Pippa, Stefaan Walgrave, and Peter van Aelst. 2005. "Who Demonstrates? Antistate Rebels, Conventional Participants, or Everyone?" *Comparative Politics* 37(2): 189–205.

Polletta, Francesca, Pang Ching Bobby Chen, Beth Gharrity Gardner, and Alice Motes. 2013. "Is the Internet Creating New Reasons to Protest?" In *The Future of Social Movement Research: Dynamics, Mechanisms, and Processes*, edited by Jacquelien van Stekelenburg, Conny Roggeband, and Bert Klandermans, 17–36. Minneapolis: University of Minnesota Press.

Polletta, Francesca and James M. Jasper. 2001. "Collective Identity and Social Movements." *Annual Review of Sociology* 27(1): 283–305.

Reicher, Steve. 1984. "The St. Paul's Riot: An Explanation of the Limits of Crowd Action in Terms of a Social Identity Model." *European Journal of Social Psychology* 14: 1–21.

Roggeband, Conny M. and Jan Willem Duyvendak. 2013. "The Changing Supply Side of Mobilization: Questions for Discussion." In *The Changing Dynamics of Contention*, edited by Jacquelien van Stekelenburg, Conny M. Roggeband, and Bert Klandermans. Minneapolis: University of Minnesota Press.

Runciman, Walter G. 1966. *Relative Deprivation and Social Justice*. London: Routledge.

Saunders, Clare. 2014. "Anti-politics in Action? Measurement Dilemmas in the Study of Unconventional Political Participation." *Political Research Quarterly* 67(3): 574–588.

Simon, Bernd and Bert Klandermans. 2001. "Towards a Social Psychological Analysis of Politicized Collective Identity: Conceptualization, Antecedents, and Consequences." *American Psychologist* 56(4): 319–331.

Simon, Bernd, Michael Loewy, Stefan Sturmer, Ulrike Weber, Peter Freytag, Corinna Habig, Claudia Kampmeier, and Peter Spahlinger. 1998. "Collective Identification and Social Movement Participation." *Journal of Personality and Social Psychology* 74(3): 646–658.

Smith, Jackie and Tina Fetner. 2007. "Structural Approaches in the Sociology of Social Movements." In *Handbook of Movements: Social Movements Across Disciplines*, edited by Bert Klandermans and Conny M. Roggeband, 13–58. New York: Springer.

Snow, David A. 2004. "Framing Processes, Ideology and Discursive Fields." In *The Blackwell Companion to Social Movements*, edited by David A. Snow, Sarah A. Soule, and Hanspeter Kriesi, 380–412. Oxford: Blackwell.

Snow, David A. and Dana M. Moss. 2014. "Protest on the Fly: Toward a Theory of Spontaneity in the Dynamics of Protest and Social Movements." *American Sociological Review* doi: 0003122414554081.

Snow, David A. and Peter B. Owens. 2013. "Crowds (Gatherings) and Collective Behavior (Action)." In *The Wiley-Blackwell Encyclopedia of Social and Political Movements*, edited by David A. Snow, Donatella della Porta, Bert Klandermans, and Doug McAdam. San Francisco: Wiley-Blackwell.

Snow, David A. and Sarah A. Soule. 2010. *A Primer on Social Movements*. New York: WW Norton.

Snow, David A., Louise A. Zurcher, and Sheldon Ekland-Olson. 1980. "Social Networks and Social Movements: A Microstructural Approach to Differential Recruitment." *American Sociological Review* 45(5): 787–801.

Soule, Sarah A, and Susan Olzak. 2004. "When Do Movements Matter? The Politics of Contingency and the Equal Rights Amendment." *American Sociological Review* 69(4): 473–497.

Stryker, Sheldon, Timothy J. Owens, and Robert W. White, eds. 2000. *Self, Identity, and Social Movements*. Minneapolis: University of Minnesota Press.

Stürmer, S., B. Simon, M. Loewy, and H. Jörger. 2003. "The Dual-Pathway Model of Social Movement Participation: The Case of the Fat Acceptance Movement." *Social Psychology Quarterly* 66(1): 71–82.

Taylor, Verta. 2013. "Social movement participation in the Global Society: Identity, networks and emotions." In *The future of social movement research: dynamics, mechanisms and processes*, eds. Jacquelien van Stekelenburg, Conny M. Roggeband, & Bert Klandermans. Minnesota: University of Minnesota Press.

Taylor, Verta and Nancy E. Whittier. 1992. "Collective Identity in Social Movement Communities: Lesbian Feminist Mobilization." In *Frontiers of Social Movement Theory*, edited by Aldon Morris and Carol Mueller, 104–129. New Haven, CT: Yale University Press.

Tilly, Charles. 2008. *Contentious Performances*. Cambridge: Cambridge University Press.

van Aelst, Peter and Stefaan Walgrave. 2001. "Who Is That (Wo)Man in the Street? From the Normalisation of Protest to the Normalisation of the Protester." *European Journal of Political Research* 39: 461–486.

van der Meer, Tom W.G. and Erik J. Van Ingen. 2009. "Schools of Democracy? Disentangling the Relationship Between Civic Participation and Political Action in 17 European Countries." *European Journal of Political Research* 48(2): 281–308.

van Deth, Jan W., José R. Montero, and Anders Westholm, eds. 2007. *Citizenship and Involvement in European Democracies: A Comparative Analysis*. London: Routledge.

van Leeuwen, Anouk, Jacquelien van Stekelenburg, and Bert Klandermans. 2015. "The Phenomenology of Protest Atmosphere: A Demonstrator Perspective." *European Journal of Social Psychology* 46(1): 44–62.

van Stekelenburg, Jacquelien and Marije Boekkooi. 2013. "Mobilizing for Change in a Changing Society." In *The Future of Social Movement Research: Dynamics, Mechanisms, and Processes*, edited by Jacquelien van Stekelenburg, Conny M. Roggeband, and Bert Klandermans. Minnesota: University of Minnesota Press.

van Stekelenburg, Jacquelien and Bert Klandermans. 2007. "Individuals in Movements: A Social Psychology of Contention." In *The Handbook of Social Movements Across Disciplines*, edited by Conny M. Roggeband and Bert Klandermans, 157–204. New York: Springer.

van Stekelenburg, Jacquelien and Bert Klandermans. 2013. "The Social Psychology of Protest." *Current Sociology* 61: 886–905.

van Stekelenburg, Jacquelien and Bert Klandermans. 2014. "Fitting Demand and Supply: How Identification Brings Appeals and Motives Together." *Social Movement Studies* 13(2): 179–203.

van Stekelenburg, Jacquelien and Bert Klandermans. 2017. "Protesting Youth. Collective and Connective Action Participation Compared." *Zeitschrift für Psychologie* 225: 336–346.

van Stekelenburg, Jacquelien, Bert Klandermans, and Agnes Akkerman. 2016. "Does Civic Participation Stimulate Political Activity?" *Journal of Social Issues* 72(2): 286–314.

van Stekelenburg, Jacquelien, Bert Klandermans, and Wilco W. van Dijk. 2009. "Context Matters: Explaining How and Why Mobilizing Context Influences Motivational Dynamics." *Journal of Social Issues* 65(4): 815–838.

van Stekelenburg, Jacquelien, Stefaan Walgrave, Bert Klandermans, and Joris Verhulst. 2012. "Contextualizing Contestation. Framework, Design and Data." *Mobilization* 17(3): 249–262.

van Zomeren, Martijn, Tom Postmes, and Russell Spears. 2008. "Toward an Integrative Social Identity Model of Collective Action: A Quantitative Research Synthesis of Three Socio-Psychological Perspectives." *Psychological Bulletin* 134: 504–535.

Verhulst, Joris. 2011. "Mobilizing Issues and the Unity and Diversity of Protest Events." Doctoral thesis, Antwerp University.

Vliegenthart, Rens. 2007. *Framing Immigration and Integration: Facts, Parliament, Media and Anti-Immigrant Party Support in the Netherlands*. Amsterdam: Vrije Universiteit.

Vliegenthart, Rens. 2013. "Hooliganism." In *The Wiley-Blackwell Encyclopedia of Social and Political Movements*, edited by David A. Snow, Donatella della Porta, Bert Klandermans, and Doug McAdam, 568–570. San Francisco: Wiley-Blackwell.

Vráblíková, Kateřina and Richard Traunmüller. 2015. "Zero the Hero: Upgrading Targeted Surveys to Case-Control Designs." Paper presented at ECPR Conference, Montreal, August 26.

Walgrave, Stefaan and Bert Klandermans. 2010. "Open and Closed Mobilization Patterns: The Role of Channels and Ties." In *The World Says No to the War*, edited by Stefaan Walgrave and Dieter Rucht, 169–192. Minneapolis: University of Minnesota Press.

Walgrave, Stefan and Manssens, Jan. 2000. "The making of the white march: the mass media as a mobilizing alternative to movement organisations." *Mobilization*, 5(2), 217–1239.

Walgrave, Stefaan and Dieter Rucht, eds. 2010. *The World Says No to the War: Demonstrations Against the War on Iraq*. Minneapolis: University of Minnesota Press.

Walgrave, Stefaan and Joris Verhulst. 2011. "Selection and Response Bias in Protest Surveys." *Mobilization: An International Quarterly* 16(2): 203–222.

Walgrave, Stefaan and Ruud Wouters. 2014. "The Missing Link in the Diffusion of Protest: Asking Others 1." *American Journal of Sociology* 119(6): 1670–1709.

Walgrave, Stefaan, Ruud Wouters, and Pauline Ketelaars. 2016. "Response Problems in the Protest Survey Design: Evidence from Fifty-One Protest Events in Seven Countries." *Mobilization: An International Journal* 21(1): 83–104.

Walsh, Edward J. 1981. "Resource Mobilization and Citizen Protest in Communities Around Three Mile Island." *Social Problems* 29(1): 1–21.

Welzel, Christain, Inglehart, Ronald F. and Deutsch, Franziska. 2004. "Social Capital, Civil Society, and Collective Action: What Makes Some Publics More 'Civic' than Others?" Paper presented at the WVS conference, Budapest, 6–9 September 2004.

Wouters, Ruud. 2013. "From the Street to the Screen: Characteristics of Protest Events as Determinants of Television News Coverage." *Mobilization: An International Quarterly* 18(1): 83–105.

Wright, Sam. 1978. *Crowds and Riots: A Study in Social Organization*. Beverly Hills, CA: Sage.

Yzerbyt, Vincent, Muriel Dumont, Daniel Wigboldus, and Ernestine Gordijn. 2003. "I Feel for Us: The Impact of Categorization and Identification on Emotions and Action Tendencies." *British Journal of Social Psychology* 42(4): 533–549.

22

The Framing Perspective on Social Movements: Its Conceptual Roots and Architecture

David A. Snow, Rens Vliegenthart, and Pauline Ketelaars

Introduction

A two-pronged tenet of social constructionism, and particularly the symbolic inter-actionist variant, is that human behavior, whether individual or collective, is partly contingent on what the object of orientation means, and that the meanings that objects or events have for us are not intrinsic to them but are formed through interpretive processes that arise in the course of interaction between humans. This does not mean that knowing or establishing the meaning of an object or situation is a continuously problematic issue for social actors, and that we therefore are continuously engaged in the interpretive work of constructing and negotiating meaning de novo. To presume otherwise is to underestimate the extent to which meaning is often scripted and thus embedded in and reflective of existing cultural and organizational arrangements and contexts. Yet social life can be laden with ambiguities that beg for interpretive clarification and may thus give rise to interpretive debates, especially when daily routines or taken-for-granted practices are disrupted. In addition, there are moments in social life in which the relevance of existing structures of meaning seem especially fragile, contestable, and open to challenge and transformation. And it is at such moments, or in such situations, that social movements seem especially likely to flourish as agents of interpretation, a view that was concretized in Lofland's (1996: 3) conceptualization of the study of social movements and movement organizations as "a special case of the study of contention among deeply conflicting realities." Thus, it is arguable that social movements, and collective action more generally on the one hand, and the interpretive work of meaning construction on the other hand are closely linked, almost as if there is an elective affinity between them.

The Wiley Blackwell Companion to Social Movements, Second Edition. Edited by David A. Snow, Sarah A. Soule, Hanspeter Kriesi, and Holly J. McCammon.
© 2019 John Wiley & Sons Ltd. Published 2019 by John Wiley & Sons Ltd.

During the past quarter of a century, interest in interpretive meaning construction has gained considerable traction within the social sciences and humanities. In this chapter, we focus on the verbal discursive expression of meaning as manifested primarily in framing processes within the context of social movements. There are, of course, other discursive modalities that are just as important as frames as conveyors of meanings in relation to social movements. Narratives, which are storied accounts of happenings that connect the past to the present and to an anticipated future (Polletta et al. 2011), comprise one such alternative discursive modality. However, we give short shrift to narratives because they have received recent elaboration by scholars more familiar with the construction and character of narratives than we are (e.g. Polletta and Gardner 2015) and because of limitations on textual space.

Conceptualizing Framing

The concept of framing in relation to social and object interaction is borrowed from Erving Goffman's *Frame Analysis* (1974), which is beholden in part to the earlier work of Gregory Bateson (1972) and is rooted in the symbolic interactionist and constructionist principle that meanings, as noted above, arise through interpretive processes mediated by culture. For Bateson and Goffman, as well as for other scholars who use the concept analytically, frames provide answers to such questions as: What is going on here? What is being said? What does this mean? And how should I (or we) act or respond?

Frames contribute to this interpretive work by performing a number of core functions. As explained elsewhere (Snow 2004), they function like picture frames, *focusing attention* by bracketing what in our sensual field is "in-frame" and what is "out-of-frame." They also function as *articulation mechanisms* in the sense of tying together the various punctuated elements of the scene so that one coherent set of meanings rather than another is conveyed. And finally, frames often perform a *transformative function* by reconstituting the way in which some objects of attention are seen or understood as relating to each other or to the actor. Given the focusing, articulation, and transformative functions of frames, it is arguable that how we see, what we make of, and how we act toward the various objects of orientation that populate our daily lives depend, in no small part, on how they are framed.

Development of a framing perspective on social movements

Applied to social movements, the idea of framing problematizes the meanings associated with relevant events, activities, places, and actors, suggesting that those meanings are typically contestable and negotiable and thus open to debate and differential interpretation. From this vantage point, mobilizing grievances are seen neither as naturally occurring sentiments nor as arising automatically from specifiable material conditions, but as the result of interactively-based interpretation or signifying work. Framing conceptualizes this signifying work, which is one of the activities that social movement leaders and participants, as well as their adversaries and the media, do on a regular basis.

Although the link between framing and social movements was foreshadowed in a number of works accenting the importance of symbolic transformations in what is seen as just and unjust (Moore 1978; Piven and Cloward 1979; Turner 1969), framing was not used conceptually in a substantial fashion until Gitlin's (1980) examination of the media's framing of the new left (see Chapter 7 by Rohlinger and Corrigall-Brown, in this volume, for discussion of media and movements). A few years later Gamson, Fireman, and Rytina (1982) used the framing concept analytically in their experimental study of the conditions under which authority is defined as unjust and challenged. In their conceptualization, frames consist of "interpretative packages" in which an "organizing idea," or a frame, is central. However, it was not until Snow, Rochford, Worden, and Benford's (1986) elaboration of "frame alignment processes" and a number of subsequent conceptual extensions (Snow and Benford 1988, 1992) that framing began to secure a foothold as a useful theorized concept for empirically examining the interpretative process through which extant meanings are debated and challenged and new ones are articulated within the context of social movements. Since these initial works, there has been an almost meteoric rise in research on framing and social movements, with most of the work congealing into what is now called the framing perspective on social movements (for overviews, see Benford and Snow 2000; Snow 2004; Snow et al. 2014).

The analytic appeal and utility of this perspective are based largely on the conjunction of three factors. The first is the neglect of the relationship between meaning and mobilization, and the role of interpretative processes in mediating that relationship, by the dominant perspectives on social movements that emerged in the 1970s, namely, the resource mobilization and political process/opportunity perspectives. The second is the rediscovery of culture in conjunction with the so-called discursive turn that occurred during the 1980s and remains prominent today. The third contributing factor is the development of a framing conceptual architecture or scaffolding which has facilitated more systematic theorization and empirical assessment of framing processes and effects, as illustrated by the now common practice of examining framing processes and the resultant frames in terms of variable analyses. Although dimensions of that conceptual architecture were previously outlined (Snow 2013), it has not been fully elaborated in a single essay. We do so in the remainder of the chapter, illustrating and elaborating its analytic utility via reference to a host of relevant works.

Conceptual Architecture

Among the interconnected concepts and processes that have surfaced as the framing literature has expanded, there are at least nine that can be thought of as cornerstone concepts and processes. They build on each other and they provide a conceptual architecture that has stimulated much of the research exploring the relevance of framing to mobilization, both empirically and theoretically. These key concepts or processes include: (1) collective action frames; (2) master frames; (3) core framing tasks; (4) discursive mechanisms/processes; (5) discursive opportunity structures and fields; (6) frame crystallization; (7) frame alignment processes; (8) frame resonance; and (9) framing hazards.

Collective action frames

Collective action frames are the resultant products of framing activity within the social movement arena. They are relatively coherent sets of action-oriented beliefs and meanings that legitimize and inspire social movement campaigns and activities. Like everyday interpretive frames, collective action frames focus attention, articulate, and elaborate the elements within the frame, and often transform the meanings associated with the objects of attention. But collective action frames differ from everyday interactional frames in terms of their primary mobilization functions: to mobilize or activate movement adherents so that they move, metaphorically, from the balcony to the barricades (action mobilization); to convert bystanders into adherents, thus broadening the movement's base (consensus mobilization); and to neutralize or demobilize adversaries (counter-mobilization). Much of the initial research on framing and social movements focused on the identification and naming of collective action frames and specification of their functions with respect to the movements in question, exhibiting what Benford called a "descriptive bias" (1997: 414–415). While the identification of collective action frames contributes to a fuller descriptive understanding of a movement, that focus alone deflects attention from broader questions about movement framings' dynamics and processes, including the ways in which frames can function as both dependent and independent variables (see Snow 2004: 391–393; Snow et al. 2014: 33–35) and the factors that account for frame variation, topics which are among the more recent foci of research on collective action frames.

Master frames

Although most collective action frames are context- and movement-specific, those that emerge early in a cycle of protest (Tarrow 1994) sometimes come to function like master algorithms in the sense that they color and constrain the orientations and activities of other movements within the cycle, such that subsequent collective action frames within the cycle are derivative or reflective (Benford and Snow 2000; Snow and Benford 1992). When the ideational and interpretive scope and influence of a collective action frame expand in this way, such that it is sufficiently elastic, flexible, and inclusive that other movements might employ it in their own campaigns, it can be thought of as a master frame. Examples of master frames in recent history include the civil rights frame, with its emphasis on equal rights and opportunities, in relation to the resurgence of the women's movement and the flowering of movements accenting the rights of the aged, the disabled, indigenous populations, and ethnic groups; the nuclear freeze frame in relation to the peace movement of the 1980s; and the environmental justice frame in relation to various environmental movements.

Caution needs to be exercised, however, in assuming that a master frame previously resonant with some groups will be resonant with all groups who may be targeted with respect to the same issue. For example, as Bloemraad, Silva, and Voss (2016: 1665–1666) found in their innovative experimental survey study of the effectiveness of different frames in influencing Californians' views about immigrant legislation and access to public benefits, the human rights frame, which proved successful for comparable issues previously, was only marginally effective.

Core framing tasks

The relative success of collective action frames in performing their mobilization functions is partly contingent on the extent to which they attend to the three core framing tasks or challenges of "diagnostic framing," "prognostic framing," and "motivational framing" (Snow and Benford 1988).

Diagnostic framing entails two aspects: a diagnosis of some event or aspect of social life or system of government as problematic and in need of repair or change; and the attribution of blame or responsibility for the problematized state of affairs. Diagnostic framing provides answers to the questions of "What is or went wrong?" and "Who or what is to blame?" Much research examining the substance of collective action frames suggests that diagnostic framing typically defines or redefines an event or situation as an "injustice" (Benford and Snow 2000: 615; Gamson 1992). Although the word "injustice" may not be directly invoked, it is typically implied, as clearly evident – as are the problematization and attribution components of diagnostic frames – in what is arguably one of the more robust and consequential diagnostic frames articulated over the past half century:

> For over seven years the United States has been occupying the lands of Islam in the holiest of places, the Arabian Peninsula, plundering its riches, dictating to its rulers, humiliating its people, terrorizing its neighbors, and turning its bases in the Peninsula into a spearhead through which to fight the neighboring Muslim peoples ... Despite the great devastation inflicted on the Iraqi people by the crusader-Zionist alliance ... the Americans are once again trying to repeat the horrific massacres ....
>
> (Osama bin Laden 1998)

Prognostic framing involves the articulation of a proposed solution to the problem, including a plan of attack and the frame-consistent tactics for carrying it out, and often a refutation of the opponent's current or proposed solutions. The extent to which correspondence between a movement's diagnostic and prognostic framing exists might differ across contexts, but sometimes the flow of events in the world yields compelling confirmatory evidence of such correspondence. Graphically illustrative is bin Laden's prognostic framing of what should be done in response to his diagnosis of the problems plaguing the Arabian Peninsula and its neighboring Muslims, chillingly articulated roughly a year prior to the September 11, 2001, terrorist attack on NYC's World Trade Center:

> We – with God's help – call on every Muslim ... to kill the Americans and plunder their money wherever and whenever they find it. We also call on Muslim ulema, leaders, youths, and soldiers to launch the raid on Satan's U.S. troops and the devil's supporters allying with them ....
>
> (ibid.)

The final core framing task, motivational framing, involves elaboration of a call to arms or rationale for action that goes beyond the diagnosis and prognosis. In doing such, it can be understood as the "agency" component of collective action frames (Gamson 1992). Motivational framing entails the construction of "vocabularies of motive" that provide prods to action by, among other things, overcoming both the fear of risks often associated with collective action and the so-called "free-rider" problem (i.e. why contribute to the attainment of some large goal when that goal constitutes a "public good" in the sense of being an indivisible and nonexcludable benefit?). Motivational framing attends to these impediments to action by accenting the severity of the problem, the urgency of taking action now rather than later, the probable efficacy of joining others in the cause, the moral priority of doing so, and the enhancement or elevation of one's status (Benford 1993a), as when suicide bombers – whether piloting aircraft, driving vehicles loaded with explosives, or wearing explosive vests – are promised various divine favors for their "righteous" deeds (Snow and Byrd 2007). As a Hamas member noted in relation to the recruitment and training of such "martyrs":

> We focus attention on Paradise, on being in the presence of Allah, on meeting the Prophet Muhammad, on interceding for his loved ones so that they, too can be saved from the agonies of Hell … and on fighting the Israeli occupation and removing it from the Islamic trust that is Palestine.
>
> (Hassan 2001: 40)

Although the link between framing and emotions has not received the attention it warrants (see Goodwin, Jasper, and Polletta 2004, on this neglect), the appeal to or use of emotion appears to be a central feature of motivational framing. Graphically illustrative is Marx and Engel's famous rallying cry – "Workers of the world, unite! You have nothing to lose but your chains!" – which has embedded within it the appeals to severity, urgency, efficacy, moral propriety and status enhancement. Although few motivational framings are so famously "hot," there is increasing empirical illustration of the link between motivational framing and emotion, both as an independent (see Schrock, Holden and Reid 2004) and dependent variable (see Cadena-Roa 2002).

As suggested earlier, all three core framing tasks are essential for participant mobilization. Much like Klandermans (1984) found that consensus mobilization (shared grievances and goals) does not guarantee action mobilization (actual participation), it follows that potent diagnostic framing guarantees neither effective prognostic nor motivational framings. As Sedgwick (2010) found in his research on al-Qaeda's framing activities, many Muslims may share al-Qaeda's diagnosis (see above bin Laden's diagnostic frame), but relatively few are moved by the group's prognostic and motivational framings.

Discursive processes, framing mechanisms

Snow and several colleagues have suggested two discursive mechanisms through which the generation and modification of collective action frames occur: frame articulation and elaboration (Snow 2004; Snow, Tan, and Owens 2013). Frame articulation involves the connection, or splicing together, and coordination of issues, events, experiences, and cultural items, including strands of one or more ideologies, so that they hang together in a relatively integrated and meaningful fashion. It constitutes a kind of collective packaging device that assembles and collates slices of appropriated, observed, experienced, and/or recorded "reality" so that a particular event, trend, or issue is framed one way instead of another. The topics that constitute slices of reality can assume various and sundry forms. They may include actual events or happenings – such as disasters, legislative decisions, or auto accidents – and contrived or "pseudo-events" (Boorstin 1961) or what today may be called "fake news" (Tavernise 2016). Topics may also include religious, political, or procedural principles and/or discursive matters or issues – that is, topics or issues brought up for discussion among two or more people or groups. Articulation links topics together in a meaningful fashion.

In contrast, frame elaboration involves accenting and highlighting some events, issues, and beliefs or ideas more than others, such that they become more salient in an array or hierarchy of movement-relevant topics or issues. Elaboration is illustrated by the practice of emphasizing and focusing on some topics or issues, rather than others, so that in time some topics rarely get mentioned. One way to get an empirical handle on elaboration is to operationalize it in terms of the amount of discursive space (the total volume of spoken or written discourse in an interactional encounter or some written forum bounded in time and space, like the total amount of column space in a newspaper) consumed or devoted to a topic, issue or frame (Snow, Tan, and Owens 2013).

Examples of both the articulation and elaboration processes are clearly exhibited in the framings of historically prominent movement leaders, such as Gandhi and Martin Luther King, as well as in the rhetoric of contemporary populist figures such as Erdogan of Turkey, Le Pen in France, and Trump in the US. Further illustration of the interplay of the articulation and elaboration mechanisms are provided in Zuo and Benford's (1995) analysis of the mobilization processes in relation to the Beijing Spring student democracy movement, and Snow, Tan and Owens' (2013) examination of the online, discursive chatter and exchanges of adherents of white racialist movements.

Discursive fields and opportunity structures

Framing processes occur during the course of conversations, meetings, and written communications among movement leaders and members within broader enveloping cultural and structural contexts called discursive fields (Snow 2008; Spillman 1995; Steinberg 1999) and discursive opportunity structures, both of which have been found to facilitate and constrain framing efforts (Ferree 2003; Ferree et al. 2002; Koopmans and Statham 1999; McCammon et al. 2007). Discursive fields evolve during the course of debate about contested issues and events, and encompass cultural materials (e.g. beliefs, values, ideologies, myths) of potential relevance and various sets of actors (e.g. targeted authorities, social control agents, countermovements, media), whose interests are aligned, albeit differently, with the contested issues or events, and who thus have a stake in what is done or not done about those events and issues.

Existing in relation to and hypothetically within discursive fields is the kindred concept of discursive opportunity structures (DOS), which encompass various salient ideas and values that have currency within the ambient political culture and thus make it more or less receptive to some collective action framings over others. In their comparative study of abortion discourse in Germany and the US, for example,

Ferree et al. (2002) found that differences in the abortion frames in the two countries can be explained in part by differences in the beliefs and values associated with their respective discursive opportunity structures. Moreover, they found an institutional component to the DOS that also had to be navigated – namely, the media, which function as gatekeepers by shaping discourse within the discursive field (see also Koopmans and Olzak 2004). More recently, research has identified an array of factors that may affect discursive opportunity structures and thus framing processes. Some of these intervening factors include the existence of multiple public discourses (McCammon et al. 2007) and the salience of emotion or various emotional themes (Bröer and Duyvendak 2009).

Whether one focuses on discursive fields or discursive opportunity structures, both direct attention to the cultural contexts in which movements are embedded and the extent to which a movement's messages, mobilizing frames, and/or narratives are linked to and constrained by dominant cultural schemas or themes, particularly those of contemporary currency.

The previously discussed discursive mechanisms of frame articulation and elaboration draw selectively upon these cultural materials and are conducted in relation to the various sets of actors that constitute the discursive field. This suggests that the development of collective action frames is facilitated and/or constrained by the cultural and structural elements of the discursive field and discursive opportunity structure in which the evolving frame is embedded. This further suggests that collective action frames "constitute innovative articulations and elaborations of existing ideologies or sets of beliefs and ideas, and thus function as extensions of or antidotes to them" (Snow 2004: 401). From this vantage point, social movements are viewed not as carriers of pre-configured, tightly-coupled beliefs and meanings, traditionally conceptualized as ideologies, but as signifying agents actively engaged in the production and maintenance of meanings that are intended to mobilize adherents and constituents, garner bystander support, and demobilize antagonists within their fields of operation. Thus, framing is a dynamic process that can differ across time, context, and targeted audience, which is evidenced even further when we consider frame crystallization.

Frame crystallization

For many publicly experienced or media-accessible events that are not taken for granted or readily explicable in terms of some consensually shared cultural script or narrative, we are likely to find the occurrence of alternative, competing diagnostic, prognostic and/or motivational framings (van der Meer et al. 2014), and this is especially so given that most framings are embedded in a discursive field. Examples of competing and contested framings of events, issues, or persons abound almost daily in the media, especially today with the varied and sharpened political alignments of the numerous media outlets (Berry and Sobieraj 2014) and the proliferation of "fake news" (Tavernise 2016). But as the object of the contested framings becomes less novel or newsworthy and/or there is an increase in the weight of "evidence" marshalled in support of one contested frame over another, there is likely to be a convergence of sentiment around some framings over others. Based on their study of the framing of the 2005 French riots, Snow, Vliegenthart, and Corrigall-Brown

(2007) call this ascendance of one or more frames over competitors "frame crystallization." As they found with respect to diagnostic framing across a three-week time period, from the inception of the riots on October 27th to their cessation on November 19th, there was a general decline in framing the problem in terms of social categories or groups, such as criminally-oriented youth and over-reactive control agents, and a corresponding increase in framing the problem in terms of structural factors, like the failure of minority incorporation and/or the economy and the public education system.

There has been a good deal of research on frame variation regarding particular events and issues and across time. Applying the idea of frame variation to the context of the women's jury movement in the US, for example, McCammon (2012) demonstrates how a single movement can shift its framing to a considerable extent over time, and that those shifts can be explained in large part by looking at the broader context in which movements operate. But there has been little comparable research on the factors that account for the crystallization of some frames and the corresponding decline of other frames over time.

Frame alignment processes

Frame alignment processes encompass the strategic efforts of social movement actors and organizations to link their interests and goals with those of prospective adherents and resource providers so that they will contribute in some fashion to movement campaigns and activities. Snow et al. (1986) identified four such basic strategic alignment processes: frame bridging, amplification, extension, and transformation.

Frame bridging involves the linkage of two or more ideologically congruent but structurally disconnected frames regarding a particular issue. Bridging can occur between a movement and individuals, through the linkage of a movement organization with an unmobilized sentiment pool or public opinion cluster, or across social movements. Illustrative of such bridging is the mobilization of West German activists against the World Bank and the International Monetary Fund by successfully bridging their frames with those of peace, ecology, women's, neighborhood, and labor movement groups (Gerhards and Rucht 1992). Many instances of coalition formation (see Chapter 14, by Brooker and Meyer, in this volume, on coalitions) are based, at least in part, on frame bridging, as with the 1999 "Battle of Seattle" in which thousands of activists massed to protest the World Trade Organization Ministerial Conference. Frame bridging can be considered a specific form of frame articulation, with the specific aim of connecting the movement's main frame with one which has a wider resonance in society.

Frame amplification entails the embellishment, crystallization, and invigoration of selected values, beliefs, and understandings so that they are more salient and dominant than other existing values. It is arguable that this is the most potentially resonant alignment strategy in that it builds on existing values and beliefs, attempting to elevate them in importance, rather than seeking to extend or change them. Thus, for "rights movements," the accent is on the value of equal opportunities whereas for movements skewed toward the political right, there may be greater emphasis placed on individualism unconstrained by the rights of others. In the case of American values, it is likely that both kinds of values will be in the value hierarchy of most citizens, but that one kind or subset of values will have greater salience than the other. The previously discussed discursive mechanism of frame elaboration is a central mechanism through which amplification is affected.

Frame extension depicts movement interests and framings as extending beyond the movement's initial constituency to include issues thought to be of relevance to bystander groups or potential adherents, which often happens in the case of coalition formation. A well-known example is the extension of the environmental movement (Rootes 2004) to groups impacted most heavily by environmental hazards, and the evolution of the environmental justice movement (Taylor 2000).

Frame transformation involves changing prior understandings and perspectives, among individuals or collectivities, so that things are seen differently than before. While such transformations are commonly associated with religious conversions, they also occur readily in more political contexts as shown in Berbrier's (1998) analysis of the reversal and equivalence framing strategies of the New Racist White Separatist Movement and reflected in the goals of the so-called alt-right movement's National Policy Institute to protect the "heritage, identity, and future of people of European descent in the United States, and around the world" (Taub 2016).

Frame resonance

The ultimate measure of the effectiveness of proffered collective action frames and the corresponding alignment strategies is whether they resonate with targeted audiences. Although the occurrence of organized protest mobilization implies some degree of resonance with corresponding problem diagnosis, attribution of blame and/or calls for action, there are a number of unresolved issues that plague the resonance proposition. The first issue, which is primarily conceptual, concerns the difference between frame alignment and resonance (Ketelaars 2016; Ketelaars, Walgrave, and Wouters 2014; Opp 2009). Ketelaars (2016: 344) suggests that "[t]he difference … is that frame resonance is a frame attribute, as in some frames resonating more than others, while frame alignment can be attributed to" individuals, "as in someone aligning with a certain frame or not." If we conceptualize resonance as a frame attribute in this way, then we are also conceiving of resonance as an indicator of alignment, or even as an outcome of frame alignment processes. This constitutes a kind of conceptual fine-tuning, but in doing so caution needs to be exercised in order not to gloss over the strategic dimension of the four types of frame alignment from an organizational vantage point.

A second issue relates to the charge that resonance inferences are subject to circular-reasoning in the sense that resonance may be automatically conflated with the occurrence of a protest event. It is therefore important to problematize resonance by attempting to identify, theoretically and/or empirically, the factors that account for its occurrence or non-occurrence. This is the direction the literature has been moving in for some time. Benford and Snow (2000: 621), for example, posed nonresonance as an analytic problem by asking "why some framings seem to be effective or 'resonate' while others do not" and suggesting "two sets of interacting factors [that] account for variation in degree of frame resonance: credibility of the proffered frame and its relative salience." In another piece, it is noted that "framing efforts often fail to inspire or direct collective action because audience resonance was never established or because it withered." In either case, the framing effort is confronted with the problem of nonresonance (Snow and Corrigall-Brown 2005: 223).

The potential problem of circular reasoning notwithstanding, it appears that it is not as troubling as sometimes presumed, as a growing number of empirical studies have shown the importance of resonance and identified various factors that affect its occurrence. For example, in Ketelaars' (2016: 341) survey-based study of the extent to which protest participants' problem diagnoses, as well as their attributions of blame and assessment of what should be done, matched the platform frames of the sponsoring organizations, she found that:

> [F]rames that appeal to people's everyday experiences resonate more than abstract or technical frames … [and that] resonance is higher when blame for the issue is put on a specific person or organization than when intangible forces or causes are held responsible.

Hewitt and McCammon (2004) and Morrell (2015) have also identified a number of other factors, such as professional expertise, which can affect the prospect of frame resonance.

Other studies have shown that establishing resonance is a dynamic and even sometimes fickle process, especially since the associated framing often occurs within a field of relevant actors. McCammon (2001), for instance, finds a positive relationship between "separate spheres" culturally resonant framing and the emergence of women suffrage organizations. While the use of the 'expediency' frame – contending that women should be able to vote because they have special skills and because it would enable them to protect the domestic sphere – had a positive effect on the presence of suffrage associations and the demand for voting rights, the 'justice' frame – stating that women are citizens just like men – did not. The latter frame resonated less as it challenged traditional beliefs regarding separate spheres at the turn of the twentieth century. In another study of resonance showing the importance of anchoring frames in current cultural beliefs and patterns, Wooten (2010) examined the framing efforts of the United Negro College Fund (UNCF) to elicit financial support from wealthy constituents between 1944 and 1954. She found that framing mattered, but not quite in the way we might expect: UNCF stressed that increasing the number of college-educated blacks would help facilitate the "functioning of the black community" but would have few consequences outside the black community. Although this framing risked alienating black targets, it did resonate with potential white donors, largely because of the temper of the times and the discursive opportunity context in which the solicitation efforts were embedded. Oselin and Corrigall-Brown (2010) provide further illustration of the importance of temporality and context in relation to resonance.

These studies also direct attention to another challenge confronting movements seeking to establish resonance with actual or potential adherents: since framing generally occurs within a discursive field consisting of various audiences, both internal and external, framing messages in hopes of resonating with one audience run the risk of undermining the prospect of resonance with another audience (see McVeigh, Meyers, and Sikkink 2004, and Lindekilde 2008, for empirical examples). Taken together, these studies of frame resonance advance our understanding of its character as a frame attribute, of the various factors that facilitate or constrain its occurrence, and of the sometimes unwanted or unanticipated consequences of trying to develop resonant frames within a contested discursive field.

The third issue identified as confronting the resonance thesis concerns the role of emotion in increasing or decreasing the prospect of resonance. The "moral shock" argument (Jasper and Poulsen 1995), with its emphasis on the mobilizing impact of a sudden and deeply emotional stimulus, constitutes, in effect, a resonance hypothesis. Moral shocks may arise because of quotidian disruptions (Borland 2013) or suddenly imposed grievances (Walsh 1981), or frequently because of highly strategic framing. Emotion, then, is at the core of "shock" framing, since its presumed aim is to activate "reflex emotions," such as fear, anger, and disgust (Goodwin, Jasper, and Polletta 2004: 416). In addition to the link between frame-based moral/emotional shocks and resonance, Bail (2012), in his study of the framing efforts of US Muslim and anti-Muslim groups in the post-9/11 era, highlights the importance of the emotional tenor of some framing efforts with the finding that the frames that secured the greatest media coverage were those that were in keeping with the media's penchant for sensationalistic and emotional narratives or frames (see Vliegenthart and Roggeband's (2007) similar findings, regarding the Dutch immigration debate; see also McDonnell, Bail, and Tavory's (2017) more general theorization of cultural resonance, which also accents the role of emotion).

Just as we have seen that collective action frames targeting the mobilization of one audience may unintentionally counter or neutralize the mobilization of another set of potential adherents, the same processes may be at work when playing with emotion in the framing process. Illustrative is Mika's (2006) examination of the frames used by the animal rights movement to recruit new members. Via focus groups with non-activists, she finds that the campaign ads of the PETA animal rights group were actually not an effective recruiting tool, as many of the frames – supposed to produce moral shocks – were met with strong negative reactions.

Framing hazards

Affecting the credibility and salience of proffered frames are various framing hazards that undermine the prospect of resonance and/or processes of frame alignment. There are at least four sets of such framing hazards: (1) *ambiguous events or ailments*, as when there is uncertainty about the correct application of two alternative framings (Goffman 1974); (2) *framing errors or misframings*, as when a diagnostic frame is inappropriately applied or just wrong, or when a frame is overextended (Snow and Corrigall-Brown 2005); (3) *frame disputes*, as when "parties with opposing versions of events may openly dispute with each other over how to define what has been happening" (Goffman 1974: 322; see also Benford 1993b); and (4) *frame shifts* involving the displacement of one frame by another due to a change in the grounds on which the displaced frame was based. In the context of social movements, such frame shifts or displacements are generally preceded by new, often unanticipated, events or the confluence of a number of events (see Ellingson 1995; Noonan 1995; Rothman and Oliver 1999; Snow and Moss 2014).

All four sets of hazards occur in relation to social problems discourse and framing (see, for example, Saguy 2013, on corpulence, and Snow and Lessor 2010), but frame disputes have received the most attention in the context of social movements, because "frame disputes are a pervasive dynamic within social movements" occurring both intra-organizationally and inter-organizationally among two or more movements within a movement coalition or family (Benford 1993b: 468). These disputes, as Benford (ibid.) found in his study of the Texas branch of the nuclear disarmament movement of the 1980s, are generally over disagreement and debate about diagnostic, prognostic, and motivational framings.

It would be reasonable to assume that intra-movement frame disputes are counterproductive in that they are likely to lead to dissension and fictionalization, but a number of studies suggest that this is not necessarily the case (Jessup 1997; Resnick 2009; see Chapter 12 by Ghaziani and Kretschmer, in this volume, on infighting and factionalism within movements). As Benford (1993b: 694) observed, frame disputes can be both "detrimental and facilitative" for mobilization, leading to factionalization in some situations and helping to enable collective action in other situations. (For examples of both, see Balser 1997; Ghaziani 2008; Hewitt 2011; McCammon, Bergner, and Arch 2015.)

Inasmuch as concerted problem-solving is contingent, in part, on some degree of interpretive alignment regarding the diagnosis and prognosis of some problem, then framing hazards constitute potential impediments to concerted collective action. However, since work on framing within the context of social movements has focused principally on frame disputes, we know comparatively little about the degree to which frame ambiguities, errors, and shifts function as mobilization impediments.

Conclusion

Although the connection between framing and social movements has generated considerable theorization and empirical research, there are a number of issues that have not been adequately addressed. One cluster concerns issues specific to conducting frame analysis in relation to movement processes and dynamics. Much research has identified movement-specific collective action frames and how they function as independent variables, but comparatively little research has examined systematically the discursive processes through which frames evolve, develop, and change. The conceptual cluster of frame articulation and elaboration and the theorized discussion of the discursive fields in which these processes are embedded provide a conceptual edifice for research on frame discursive processes, but to date the actual occurrence of systematic, methods-based research on framing processes, particularly in relation to discourse analysis, has not kept pace with calls for more detailed specification of doing such analyses (e.g. Johnston 2002; Lindekilde 2014; Snow 2004; Steinberg 1999).

A second cluster of issues that have not been sufficiently explored concerns the relationship between collective action frames and framing processes and relevant cultural and social psychological factors, such as narrative, ideology, collective identity, and emotion. Clearly, these are overlapping concepts that interact in ways not yet fully understood.

When it comes to frame resonance and the effects of frames, an interesting avenue for further research is the fact that the same framing can have different effects on varying groups. Some of the research cited earlier clearly shows that frames that persuade some people to become active can be counter-productive for winning the support of others. More research is needed to get a better grip on why and how frames have contingent effects. Also the effects of framing efforts by social movements on authorities and indirectly on political decision-making and policy changes deserve more attention. The question whether movements matter politically has become one of the most prominent ones in our field (see Chapter 25 by Amenta, Andrews, and Caren, in this volume) and studies have demonstrated the agenda-setting power of protest (Vliegenthart et al. 2016). Given the centrality of framing in most aspects of the movement's existence, it is likely that effects are not limited to *what* movements protest about, but also *how* they communicate about those issues, which cuts to the heart of framing.

And, finally, our understanding of social movements will be advanced if more attention is devoted, both theoretically and empirically, to how framing intersects with the issues and processes examined via the theoretical lens of resource mobilization, political opportunity, and cultural perspectives. These perspectives should be seen not so much as competing but as addressing different aspects of the character and dynamics of social movements. The framing perspective emerged not as an alternative to other perspectives on social movements, but to investigate and illuminate what these other perspectives have glossed over, namely, the matter of the production of mobilizing and counter-mobilizing meanings and ideas.

References

Bail, Christopher A. 2012. "The Fringe Effect: Civil Society Organizations and the Evolution of Media Discourse about Islam Since the September 11th Attacks." *American Sociological Review* 77: 855–879.

Balser, Deborah B. 1997. "The Impact of Environmental Factors on Factionalism and Schism in Social Movement Organizations." *Social Forces* 76: 199–228.

Bateson, Gregory. 1972. *Steps to an Ecology of the Mind*. Chicago: University of Chicago Press.

Benford, Robert D. 1993a. "Frame Disputes within the Nuclear Disarmament Movement." *Social Forces* 71: 677–701.

Benford, Robert D. 1993b. "'You Could be the Hundredth Monkey': Collective Action Frames and Vocabularies of Motive Within the Nuclear Disarmament Movement." *The Sociological Quarterly* 34: 195–216.

Benford, Robert D. 1997. "An Insider's Critique of the Social Movement Framing Perspective." *Sociological Inquiry* 67: 409–430.

Benford, Robert D. and David A Snow. 2000. "Framing Processes and Social Movements: An Overview and Assessment." *Annual Review of Sociology* 26: 611–639.

Berbrier, Mitch. 1998. "'Half the Battle': Cultural Resonance, Framing Processes, and Ethnic Affectations in Contemporary White Separatist Rhetoric." *Social Problems* 45: 431–450.

Berry, Jeffrey M. and Sarah Sobieraj. 2014. *The Outrage Industry: Political Opinion, Media and the New Incivility*. New York: Oxford University Press.

bin Laden, Osama. 1998. "Osama bin Laden's World Islamic Front Statement Against Jews and Crusaders." February 23. Available at: http://www.fas.org/irp/wprld/para/docs/980223-fatwa.htm

Bloemraad, Irene, Fabiana Silva, and Kim Voss. 2016. "Rights, Economics, or Family? Frame Resonance, Political Ideology, and the Immigrant Rights Movement." *Social Forces* 94: 1647–1674.

Boorstin, Daniel J. 1961. *The Image: A Guide to Pseudo-Events in America*. New York: Harper & Row.

Borland, Elizabeth. 2013. "Quotidian Disruption." In *The Wiley-Blackwell Encyclopedia of Social and Political Movements*, edited by David A. Snow, Donatella della Porta, Bert Klandermans, and Doug McAdam, 1038–1041. Oxford: Wiley-Blackwell

Bröer, Christian and Jan Duyvendak. 2009. "Discursive Opportunities, Feeling Rules, and the Rise of Protests against Aircraft Noise." *Mobilization: An International Quarterly* 14: 337–356.

Cadena-Roa, Jorge. 2002. "Strategic Framing, Emotions, and Superbarrio: Mexico City's Masked Crusader." *Mobilization: An International Quarterly* 7: 201–216.

Ellingson, Stephen. 1995. "Understanding the Dialectic of Discourse and Collective Action: Public Debate and Rioting in Antebellum Cincinnati." *American Journal of Sociology* 101: 100–144.

Ferree, Myra M. 2003. "Resonance and Radicalism: Feminist Framing in the Abortion Debates of the United States and Germany." *American Journal of Sociology* 109: 304–344.

Ferree, Myra M., William A. Gamson, Jürgen Gerhards, and Dieter Rucht. 2002. *Shaping Abortion Discourse: Democracy and the Public Sphere in Germany and the United States*. New York: Cambridge University Press.

Gamson, William A. 1992. *Talking Politics*. New York: Cambridge University Press.

Gamson, William A., Bruce Fireman, and Steven Rytina. 1982. *Encounters with Unjust Authority*. Homewood, IL: Dorsey.

Gerhards, Jürgen and Dieter Rucht. 1992. "Mesomobilization: Organizing and Framing in Two Protest Campaigns in West Germany." *American Journal of Sociology* 98: 555–595.

Ghaziani, Amin. 2008. *The Dividends of Dissent: How Conflict and Culture Work in Lesbian and Gay Marches on Washington*. Chicago: University of Chicago Press.

Gitlin, Todd. 1980. *The Whole World Is Watching: Mass Media and the Making and Unmaking of the New Left*. Berkeley: University of California Press.

Goffman, Erving. 1974. *Frame Analysis: An Essay on the Organization of Experience*. New York: Harper Colophon Books.

Goodwin, Jeff, James M. Jasper, and Francesca Polletta. 2004. "Emotional Dimensions of Social Movements." In *The Blackwell Companion to Social Movements*, edited by David A. Snow, Sarah A. Soule, and Hanspeter Kriesi, 413–432. Oxford: Blackwell.

Hassan, Nasra. 2001. "An Arsenal of Believers: Talking to Human Bombs." *The New Yorker* November 19, pp. 36–41.

Hewitt, Lyndi. 2011. "Framing across Differences, Building Solidarities: Lessons from Women's Rights Activism in Transnational Spaces." *Interface: A Journal for and about Social Movements* 3: 65–99.

Hewitt, Lyndi and Holly J. McCammon. 2004. "Explaining Suffrage Mobilization: Balance, Neutralization, and Range in Collective Action Frames, 1892–1919." *Mobilization: An International Quarterly* 9: 149–166.

Jasper, James M. and Jane D. Poulsen. 1995. "Recruiting Strangers and Friends: Moral Shocks and Social Networks in Animal Rights and Animal Protest." *Social Problems* 42: 497–512.

Jessup, Michael M. 1997. "Legitimacy and the Decline of the 1920s Ku Klux Klan." *Research in Social Movements, Conflict and Change* 20: 177–221.

Johnston, Hank. 2002. "Verification and Proof in Frame and Discourse Analysis." In *Methods of Social Movements Research*, edited by Bert Klandermans and Susanne Staggenborg, 62–91. Minneapolis: University of Minnesota Press.

Ketelaars, Pauline. 2016. "What Strikes the Responsive Chord? The Effects of Framing Qualities on Frame Resonance amongst Protest Participants." *Mobilization: An International Quarterly* 21: 341–360.

Ketelaars, Pauline, Stefaan Walgrave, and Ruud Wouters. 2014. "Degrees of Frame Alignment: Comparing Organizers' and Participants' Frames in 29 Demonstrations in Three Countries." *International Sociology* 29: 504–524.

Klandermans, Bert. 1984. "Mobilization and Participation: Social-Psychological Expansions of Resource Mobilization Theory." *American Sociological Review* 49: 583–600.

Koopmans, Ruud and Susan Olzak. 2004. "Discursive Opportunities and the Evolution of Right-Wing Violence in Germany." *American Journal of Sociology* 110: 198–230.

Koopmans, Ruud and Paul Statham.1999. "Political Claims Analysis: Integrating Protest Event and Political Discourse Approaches." *Mobilization: An International Quarterly* 4: 203–221.

Lindekilde, Lasse. 2008. "Mobilizing in the Name of the Prophet? The Mobilization/Demobilization of Danish Muslims during the Muhammad Caricatures Controversy." *Mobilization: An International Quarterly* 13: 219–232.

Lindekilde, Lasse. 2014. "Discourse and Frame Analysis: In-depth Analysis of Qualitative Data in Social Movement Studies." In *Methodological Practices in Social Movement Research*, edited by Donatella della Porta, 195–228. Oxford: Oxford University Press.

Lofland, John. 1996. *Social Movement Organizations: Guided to Research on Insurgent Realities*. New York: Aldine de Gruyter.

McCammon, Holly J. 2001. "Stirring up Suffrage Sentiment: The Formation of the State Woman Suffrage Organizations, 1866–1914." *Social Forces* 80: 449–480.

McCammon, Holly J. 2012. "Explaining Frame Variation: More Moderate and Radical Demands for Women's Citizenship in the US Women's Jury Movements." *Social Problems* 59: 43–69.

McCammon, Holly J., Erin M. Bergner, and Sandra C. Arch. 2015. "'Are You One of Those Women?' Within-Movement Conflict, Radical Flank Effects, and Social Movement Political Outcomes." *Mobilization: An International Quarterly* 20: 157–178.

McCammon, Holly J., Harmony D. Newman, Courtney Sanders Muse, and Teresa M. Terrell. 2007. "Movement Framing and Discursive Opportunity Structures: The Political Successes of the U.S. Women's Jury Movements." *American Sociological Review* 72: 725–749.

McDonnell, Terence, Christopher Bail, and Iddo Tavory. 2017. "A Theory of Cultural Resonance." *Sociological Theory* 35: 1–14.

McVeigh, Rory, Daniel J. Myers, and David Sikkink. 2004. "Corn, Klansmen, and Coolidge: Structure and Framing in Social Movements." *Social Forces* 83: 653–690.

Mika, Marie. 2006. "Framing the Issue: Religion, Secular Ethics and the Case of Animal Rights Mobilization." *Social Forces* 85: 915–994.

Moore, Barrington. 1978. *Injustice: The Social Bases of Obedience and Revolt.* White Plains, NY: M.E. Sharpe.

Morrell, Erica. 2015. "Unpacking Frame Resonance: Professional and Experiential Expertise in Intellectual Property Rights Construction." *Mobilization: An International Quarterly* 20: 361–378.

Noonan, Rita K. 1995. "Women Against the State: Political Opportunities and Collective Action Frames in Chile's Transition to Democracy." *Sociological Forum* 19: 81–111.

Opp, Karl-Dieter. 2009. *Theories of Political Protest and Social Movements.* London: Routledge.

Oselin, Sharon and Catherine Corrigall-Brown. 2010. "A Battle for Authenticity: An Examination of the Constraints on Anti-Iraq War and Pro-Invasion Tactics." *Mobilization: An International Quarterly* 15: 511–533.

Piven, Francis Fox and Richard Cloward. 1979. *Poor People's Movements.* New York: Vintage Books.

Polletta, Francesca, Pang Ching Bobby Chen, Beth Gardner, and Alice Motes. 2011. "The Sociology of Storytelling." *Annual Review of Sociology* 37: 109–130.

Polletta, Francesca and Beth Gardner. 2015. "Narrative and Social Movements." In *The Oxford Handbook of Social Movements*, edited by Donatella della Porta and Mario Diani, 534–538. New York: Oxford University Press.

Resnick, Danielle. 2009. "The Benefits of Frame Resonance Disputes for Transnational Movements: The Case of Botswana's Central Kalahari Game Preserve." *Social Movement Studies* 8: 55–72.

Rootes, Christopher. 2004. "Environmental Movements." In *The Blackwell Companion to Social Movements*, edited by David A. Snow, Sarah A. Soule, and Hanspeter Kriesi, 608–640. Oxford: Blackwell.

Rothman, Franklin Daniel and Pamela E. Oliver. 1999. "From Local to Global: The Anti-Dam Movement in Southern Brazil, 1979–1992." *Mobilization: An International Quarterly* 4: 41–58.

Saguy, Abigail C. 2013. *What's Wrong with Fat?* New York: Oxford University Press.

Schrock, Douglas, Daphne Holden, and Lore Reid. 2004. "Creating Emotional Resonance: Interpersonal Emotion Work and Motivational Framing in a Transgender Community." *Social Problems* 51: 61–81.

Sedgwick, Mark. 2010. "The Concept of Radicalization as a Source of Confusion." *Terrorism and Political Violence* 22: 479–494.

Snow, David A. 2004. "Framing Processes, Ideology, and Discursive Fields." In *The Blackwell Companion to Social Movements*, edited by David A. Snow, Sarah A. Soule, and Hanspeter Kriesi, 380–412. Oxford: Blackwell.

Snow, David A. 2008. "Elaborating the Discursive Contexts of Framing: Discursive Fields and Spaces." *Studies in Symbolic Interaction* 30: 3–28.

Snow, David A. 2013. "Framing and Social Movements." In *The Wiley-Blackwell Encyclopedia of Social and Political Movements*, edited by David A. Snow, Donatella della Porta, Bert Klandermans, and Doug McAdam, 470–475. Oxford: Wiley-Blackwell.

Snow, David A. and Robert D. Benford. 1988. "Ideology, Frame Resonance, and Participant Mobilization." *International Social Movement Research* 1: 197–217.

Snow, David A. and Robert D. Benford. 1992. "Master Frames and Cycles of Protest." In *Frontiers in Social Movement Theory*, edited by Aldon D. Morris, and Carol M. Mueller, 133–155. New Haven, CT: Yale University Press.

Snow, David A., Robert D. Benford, Holly J. McCammon, Lyndi Hewitt, and Scott Fitzgerald. 2014. "The Emergence, Development, and Future of the Framing Perspective: 25+ Years Since 'Frame Alignment.'" *Mobilization: An International Quarterly* 19: 489–512.

Snow, David A. and Scott C. Byrd. 2007. "Ideology, Framing Processes, and Islamic Terrorist Movements." *Mobilization: An International Journal* 12: 119–136.

Snow, David A. and Catherine Corrigall-Brown. 2005. "Falling on Deaf Ears: Confronting the Prospect of Non-Resonant Frames." In *Rhyming Hope and History: Activism and Social Movement Scholarship*, edited by David Croteau, William Hoynes, and Charlotte Ryan, 222–238. Minneapolis: University of Minnesota Press.

Snow, David A. and Roberta G. Lessor. 2010. "Framing Hazards in the Health Arena: The Cases of Obesity, Work Related Illnesses, and Human Egg Donation." In *Social Movements and the Transformation of U.S. Health Care*, edited by Jane Banaszak-Holl, Mayer N. Zald, and Sandra Levitsky, 284–299. New York: Oxford University Press.

Snow, David A. and Dana Moss. 2014. "Protest on the Fly: Toward a Theory of Spontaneity in the Dynamics of Protest and Social Movements." *American Sociological Review* 79: 1122–1143.

Snow, David A., E. Burke Rochford, Jr., Steven K. Worden, and Robert D. Benford. 1986. "Frame Alignment Processes, Micromobilization, and Movement Participation." *American Sociological Review* 51: 464–481.

Snow, David A., Anna Tan, and Peter Owens. 2013. "Social Movements, Framing Processes, and Cultural Revitalization and Fabrication." *Mobilization: An International Quarterly* 18: 225–242.

Snow, David A., Rens Vliegenthart, and Catherine Corrigall-Brown. 2007. "Framing the 'French Riots': A Comparative Study of Frame Variation." *Social Forces* 86: 385–415.

Spillman, Lyn. 1995. "Culture, Social Structures and Discursive Fields." *Current Perspectives in Social Theory* 15: 129–154.

Steinberg, Marc W. 1999. "The Talk and Back Talk of Collective Action: A Dialogic Analysis of Repertoires of Discourse among Nineteenth-Century English Cotton-Spinners." *American Journal of Sociology* 105: 736–780.

Tarrow, Sidney. 1994. *Power in Movement: Social Movements, Collective Action and Politics*. New York: Cambridge University Press.

Taub, Amanda. 2016. "White Nationalism, Explained." *The New York Times*, November 21. Available at: http://nyti.ms/2ffJlnF

Tavernise, Sabrina. 2016. "As Fake News Spreads Lies, More Readers Shrug at the Truth." *The New York Times*, https://www.nytimes.com/2016/12/06/us/fake-news-partisan-republican-democrat.html.

Taylor, Dorcetta E. 2000. "The Rise of the Environmental Justice Paradigm: Injustice Framing and the Social Construction of Environmental Discourses." *American Behavioral Scientist* 43: 508–580.

Turner, Ralph H. 1969. "The Theme of Contemporary Social Movements." *British Journal of Sociology* 20: 390–405.

van der Meer, Toni, Piet Verhoeven, Hans Beentjes, and Rens Vliegenthart. 2014. "When Frames Align: The Interplay Between PR, News Media and the Public in Times of Crisis." *Public Relations Review* 40: 751–761.

Vliegenthart, Rens and Conny Roggeband. 2007. "Framing Immigration and Integration: Relationships between Press and Parliament in the Netherlands." *International Communication Gazette* 69: 295–319.

Vliegenthart, Rens, Stefaan Walgrave, Ruud Wouters, et al. 2016. "The Media as a Dual Mediator of the Political Agenda-Setting Effect of Protest: A Longitudinal Study in Six Western European Countries." *Social Forces* 95: 837–859.

Walsh, Edward J. 1981. "Resource Mobilization and Citizen Protest in Communities around Three Mile Island." *Social Problems* 29: 1–21.

Wooten, Melissa. 2010. "Soliciting Elites: The Framing Activities of the United Negro College Fund." *Mobilization* 15: 369–391.

Zuo, Jiping and Robert D. Benford, 1995. "Mobilization Processes and the 1989 Chinese Democracy Movement." *Sociological Quarterly* 36: 131–156.

23

Emotions in Social Movements

Justin Van Ness and Erika Summers-Effler

Introduction

Social movement scholars who emphasize emotions in analyses routinely argue that earlier scholars have ignored or short-changed the role of emotions in the literature (e.g. Goodwin 1997; Goodwin, Jasper, and Polletta 2001; Gould 2009; Jasper 1998), thus attending to them was a needed contribution. At this point, social movement scholars attend to emotions fairly regularly and the literature has developed in important ways. In this chapter, we review the development of the field, particularly the last 20 years of contributions to the study of emotions and social movements, and argue for a fresh way forward for the study of emotions in social movements. Specifically, we suggest turning to the interdisciplinary field of Cognitive Social Science to extend the field's understanding of both cognitive and emotive processes. We conclude the chapter with suggestions for future development.

We can find the history of the social movement field in a variety of places (see Goodwin and Jasper 2006; Jasper 2011; Moss and Snow 2016). Early collective behavior theorists focused on the emotional dynamics of crowd situations and social change. Many were interested in what they perceived as processes of unconscious manipulation, hysteria, panic, and tended to interpret emotionality as a sign of irrationality (for a review, see Van Ness and Summers-Effler 2016). Those interested in more structural explanations of collective behavior also argued that various forms of tension and emotional distress could motivate action (e.g. Gurr 1970; Smelser 1962). In the 1960s, activists who had become academics turned to existing literature and found difficulty in explaining personal experiences with existing theoretical frameworks. In light of these deficits, these scholars ushered in the emergence of the social movement field and all but did away with discussions of emotionality to privilege imagery of the rational actor, while also shifting away from theoretical explanations of *why* and toward the analytical questions of *how* (Morris and Herring 1987). As a result, much of the literature focused on meso organization units of analysis, resource flows, and structural explanations, rather than co-presence and processes shaping interactions. Decades of research followed until the 1990s brought the return of emotion in social movement theory and analysis. Ironically, when emotional approaches to social movements were on the margins of social movement theory, the field of sociology more broadly sustained a lineage of scholars interested in emotions and even developed a distinct sociology of emotions sub-field, which we briefly address below.

This subfield of emotions has followed strains of theorizing emotion that hark back to the beginning of the field. Works by Durkheim, Marx, and Weber contain detailed theory about the role of emotions in social life. Durkheim (1912) argues in his theory of collective effervescence, that co-presence in collective behavior environments combined with synchronized ritual can generate emergent properties, particularly emotions. Marx's (1978) theory of estrangement and alienation are emotional processes which arise as capitalism creates contradictions between our human "existence" and "essence." Weber's (1968) typology of social action (falsely) distinguished between instrumental, value-rational, traditional, and *affectual*. During the early twentieth century, the pragmatists retained an attention to emotions (e.g. James 1902). Cooley (1902) explained motivational and social roots of pride and shame. Much later, Goffman (1959, 1963) vividly described the performative processes during the management of emotions and appearances.

As a subfield, the sociology of emotions began to crystallize in the late 1970s and into the 1980s. Hochschild (1979, 1983) explained how culturally anchored "feeling rules" lead to the management of emotional expressions. Kemper (1978) described how one's position in a stratification hierarchy influences the experience and expression of emotions. Collins' (1975, 2004) interaction ritual theory integrates Durkheim and Goffman to explain the competition for emotional energy and attention in situations. Scheff (1988, 1990) draws from Cooley and argues shame threatens social bonds and unacknowledged shame can lead to anger which may erupt in aggression (also see Scheff 1994). Others have continued to theorize emotion at varying analytic levels, including structural (Barbalet 2001), organizational (Summers-Effler 2010), identity (Stryker and Burke 2000), and motivational (Abrutyn and Mueller 2014; Summers-Effler 2004b).

Students of social movements credit the return of emotions in the field of collective behavior and social movements to the cultural turn in the 1980s, which returned analytical interest back to the micro level. Much of this work focused on framing (Snow et al. 1986), collective identity (Taylor and Whittier 1991), codes (Melucci 1996), and narratives (Polletta 2006a). Many who focus on emotions critique the culture turn for being overly cognitive (e.g. Goodwin, Jasper and Polletta 2001; Jasper 1997). More recently, scholars drawing from Cognitive Social Science argue that the field's understanding of cognition as amodal symbol processing is limited in ways we will discuss (see also Van Ness and Summers-Effler 2016; Wood et al. forthcoming).

This chapter continues in four main sections. The next section reviews the ways scholars have studied emotions in social movements. Then, we provide a typology of approaches to studying emotions, while arguing for the need for more situated and embodied theories of emotions. Next, we draw from recent literature in Cognitive

Social Science on emotions and embodiment to provide theoretical scaffolding for new theories of emotions in protest situations. Finally, we close by suggesting fruitful directions for the field.

Emotions in Social Movements

Over the past 20 years of research, social movement scholars have analyzed emotions in wide-ranging areas of social movement campaigns and protest events. Scholars have theorized how emotions play pivotal roles in enabling or inhibiting mobilization and providing the resources that sustain commitment through various endogenous and exogenous changes. While some scholars explicitly theorize emotions, others tend to allude to their role or leave them implicit all together, often warranting greater explication. In this section, we review major contributions from those who have made explicit and left them implicit, while also explaining more recent directions in the field.

Participation

Much of the literature on participation emphasizes the power of social networks and organizations for recruitment, activation, and commitment (e.g. Gould 1991; Oberschall 1973; Morris 1981; Snow, Zurcher Jr, and Ekland-Olson 1980). Actors can be "pushed" and "pulled" in and out of participation, but without attention to emotions, explanations remain underspecified in regards to what affords one tie influence over others. Indeed, the impact of emotions was central to research on participation in religious movements and conversion (e.g. Lofland and Stark 1965). Snow and Philips' (1980) reassessment of the Lofland and Stark conversion model argues that affective bonds bridge information gaps, increase credibility, and intensify pressure for conformity. More recently, Jasper and Owens (2014) continue to argue that the *emotional valence* of social ties makes networks efficacious for activation and mobilization. That is, the mere existence of ties is not enough to explain how and why motivation and commitment arise while the other is of little influence. When we consider the emotions which run through the networks, as well as the ways in which interactions and situations afford particular emotional experiences, we reveal why some actors mobilize, while others remain unmoved.

Other scholars analyzing networks and participation vary in the degree to which emotions are made explicit in explanations. Chong (1991) argues that some may become involved because of "reputational concerns," although he does not fully pursue how being proud or ashamed of one's social standing is an inherently emotional process. Gould (1993) describes "norms of fairness" as influencing decisions for participation, yet he also does not explicate the ways in which emotions signal what is just or unjust. Beyerlein and Andrews (2008) are more explicit, arguing anger, which arose from the perception of both violent and non-violent repression, influenced civil rights electoral participation. Beyerlein and Sikkink (2008) argue that sorrow motivated participation in 9/11 commemoration events. These events tended to increase empathy and identification with victims, while also exposing participants to more opportunities for volunteering.

Motivation for mobilization can also take place without pre-existing network ties. Jasper and Poulsen (1995) argue *moral shocks* can motivate participation when an unexpected event or information generates a sense of outrage. Nepstad and Smith's (2001) research on the Central America peace movement explains how exposure to torture, disappearances, assassinations of civilians, and a lying government generated indignation which motivated mobilization. Young (2001) explains how evangelicals' emotional culture afforded a dramatic conversion into abolitionists. Halfmann and Young (2010) describe how exposure to grotesque imagery can produce strong emotions which may motivate, but also potentially inhibit, mobilization. Luker (1984) finds anger, outrage, and indignation motivate pro-life protestors after *Roe v. Wade*. Oliver (1984) describes how pessimism and frustration can inspire action if one determines they cannot count on others to participate.

Social movement organizations and protest situations also afford opportunities to generate and experience pleasurable emotions. In this regard, it is worth analyzing *emotional affordances* of situations, as some may create opportunities for novelty, thrill, and risk which may be sought when juxtaposed to day-to-day mundanity. Jasper (1997) argues some look for protests because of the *pleasures of protest*, such as fun, opportunities for creativity, flirting, and prospects for sex. Similarly, Wood (2001) also argues that protest situations are unique spaces where one can experience the thrill of agency. Gould's (2009) research on ACT UP describes how satire and humor afforded opportunities for psychic relief and joyful camaraderie. Collins (2001) argues protest situations provide opportunities for rhythmic entrainment and ritual which can generate satisfying emotions, collective identity, and solidarity.

Many have alluded to the power of collective identity in social movements (e.g. Bernstein 1997; Taylor and Whittier 1991) but, similar to the research on social networks, attention to the emotional processes which give rise to the shared identity explains how and why collective identity becomes efficacious for mobilization. Collins (2004) explicates the micro-ritual process, which enables shared identities to be mobilized and passionately defended. Successful interaction rituals require co-presence, barriers to outsiders, a mutual focus of attention, and a shared mood. The rituals generate feelings of collective effervescence, which creates group solidarity, individual emotional energy, symbols of group membership, and standards of morality. Shared symbols may consist of visual icons, words, ideology, gestures, and other representations. Members imbue these symbols with a sense of righteousness and morality, passionately defending them against impropriety and violations.

Many study situations conducive to evoking emotions of morality and righteousness. Einwohner's (2003) research on the Warsaw Ghetto describes how even in the face of anticipated defeat, actors can be activated to defend a community's dignity and honor. Brym (2007) finds anger, hate, and opportunities for revenge motivate Palestinian bombers into action. Stein's (2001) research on Christian anti-gay crusaders illustrates how an organization can generate pride by projecting the experience of shame onto others.[1] Nepstad (2004) describes how Christian rituals were incorporated into protest events to revive and intensify emotions, identity, and commitment. Many others have also captured how emotional experiences of one's identity can be transformed internally through collective emotion work (e.g. Taylor 1996; Whittier 2009). During protest situations, bystanders can be activated and recruited through the evocation of emotions *in situ*, particularly during moments of repression. Perceived injustice over the treatment of activists can incite emotions which may activate and mobilize sympathetic bystanders (e.g. Brockett 2005). For instance, volatility, ambiguity, or inconsistency in interactions between activists and control agents can generate moral outrage, which may energize and mobilize previously uninvolved actors (Koopmans 1997) or relatively spontaneous actions in unanticipated directions (Snow and Moss 2014). In this regard, it is about the perceived violations of expectations for appropriate behaviors as defined by the situation which incites emotions leading to involvement (cf. Moss 2014). The presence and actions of repression agents during protest situations can violate expectations.

Increasingly, US police agencies are becoming militarized culturally and materially as military grade equipment becomes funneled through to local law enforcement (Balko 2014). Protest situations which are otherwise calm and peaceful can quickly become tense when control agents present themselves in battle regalia and give off information which can be threatening. Unfortunately, and a bit ironically, bystanders' presence during situations with activist and control agent engagements can encourage violence by heightening tensions and fears which may promote one group into a forward panic (Collins 2009). At the same time, heightened emotions and general "drama" whether stemming from activists, control agents, bystanders, or relations between any of the three, can increase the probability of having a protest event make the news (Oliver and Meyer 1999).

Commitment

Research on emotions in social movements has also revealed processes sustaining engagement. Just as Jasper and Poulsen (1995) argued that moral shocks can motivate involvement, so too can moral shocks intensify commitment by renewing enthusiasm for a cause, increasing identification with a community, and making perceived threats feel "physiologically real" (e.g. Halfmann and Young 2010). When shocks generate a heightened sense of threat, identification with one's in-group may increase and create unification against enemies or targets. When activists have an identifiable target to blame, feelings of camaraderie and solidarity can grow (see Nepstad 2004: 139–156). Providing a target for blame can unify attention and provide a constructive outlet for negative emotions such as contempt, anger, and hate.

The emotional bonds which tie together activists can also generate emotional rewards for continued participation, as well as potential emotional costs for exiting. The emotions which bind also underlie abeyance structures which can sustain engagement and affiliation even during moments of limited opportunities, resources, or recruiting potential (Taylor 1989). Groups which generate unusually strong emotional cultures can also provide resources for enduring moments of harsh repression (e.g. Khwaja 1993).

Munson (2009) finds that participation in a social movement can function as a conversion process which generates new ideology; activism can also provide situations which create the emotional conditions for a "renewal of faith." Smith (1996) argues protest can create opportunities for both self-sacrifice and the moral witnessing of one's religious convictions. Williamson's (2011) study of a new religious movement reveals how organizations can craft emotional journeys through the patterning of emotions and fluctuations in emotional intensity, which influence one's willingness to return to group events. Gupta (2009) argues that small incremental victories can generate feelings of hope which keep activists oriented to the future with anticipation for more victories. Activists can also develop emotional ties to places which provide continuity through changes in social network structures. Environmentalists might sustain commitment to a cause because of emotional attachments to particular locations, rather than social others. Spaces can also inspire specific types of emotion work which lead to the development of denser ties and increased ideological commitment (e.g. Feigenbaum, McCurdy, and Frenzel 2013).

Demobilization

Previous research also covers emotional processes during the demobilization stages. Pre-existing emotional ties tend to take time and energy to maintain, both of which are scarce resources. Emotional commitments to partners, family, kinship, or even the self may inhibit a movement's solidarity by creating competing loyalties and motivating exit (e.g. Goodwin 1997). In other words, that which pulls one into participation and sustains commitment can also be a source of failure.

Jasper (2004) describes the "Band of Brothers Dilemma" where affective ties that draw one into participation, or develop during participation, can lead to fractured sources of solidarity. In this case, divisions within the collective arise which can threaten a movement by developing competing factions or diffuse centers of attention. Echols (1989) finds affective sources which generated feelings of "sisterhood" were also threatening to group solidarity by creating a sense of alienation. When a movement has factions with emotional states in tension, group rituals are less likely to succeed and shared collective identity is undermined (Collins 2004). Further, when emotional ties between dyads become stronger than ties to the collective, organizations are threatened with dyadic withdrawal. Research on new religious movements reveals how leaders often encourage abstinence or sexual promiscuity to attempt to prevent this type of exit from happening (e.g. Coser 1974; Goldman 1999; Kanter 1968).

The pleasures of protest can also develop into fatigue and burnout. Experiencing sustained fatigue without the emotional intensity of thrill, risk, or hope may eventually lead to frustration at the movement or leader (see Summers-Effler 2010). Movements which are in particularly draining cycles may find it difficult to come up with creative solutions to problems, which may further exacerbate tensions. Debates over tactics can also generate strong negative emotions which threaten solidarity and affective ties (Owens 2009). Fear and paranoia may also develop during moments of state repression which may erode trust within activist networks (Davenport 2005). Comfort and complacency threaten movements (Brown and Pickerill 2009), as can overconfidence (Jasper 2011).

Leaders can also breed failure from an inability to attract, generate the right emotions, or direct them in a constructive direction (see Chapter 10 by Ganz and McKenna, in this volume, on leadership). Charismatic performances offer emotional incentives which may draw in potential adherents. A skillful leader can work crowds into a rhythm, producing feelings of community and emotional intensity. By doing so, they can charge attendees up with feelings of righteousness, which helps to fire mobilization. Absent charisma, however, a movement may lack the emotional incentives which sustain commitment and also find it difficult to attract new adherents. Without emotional incentives and a hopeful vision of the future, it may be difficult to motivate activists to partake in the necessary mundane and at times grueling day-to-day work. Without a target to blame, negative emotions may develop into anxiety rather than a more constructive and targeted outlet for anger. Taken together, leaders who are not charismatic, hopeful, or effective in making blame stick are likely to undermine rather than fire-up a movement.

Analyzing Emotions

In this section, we review some of the ways emotions have become analytically distinguished. Clarifying emotions is particularly important for analyses and theory building because of the tendency to conflate a catch-all traditional understanding of emotions with those theorizing within more specified analytical distinctions. That is, greater analytic clarity prevents the danger of endless theoretical debates about one finding versus another because of a lay understanding of emotion. Thus, we describe some of the distinctions made in the previous literature which may provide useful for theorizing emotions in the study of social movements and collective behavior.

Differentiating

A critical distinction made within the sociology of emotions is between basic and social emotions, or what Turner and Stets (2005) refers to as *primary* and *secondary emotions*. Primary emotions, such as fear, anger, happiness, and sadness, are universal and form the basis for more complex and culturally-defined emotions. Ekman (1977) extends this primary list to include surprise, disgust, and contempt. Secondary emotions, such as shame, disappointment, pride, alienation, hate, anxiety, indignation, and awe, just to name a few, are the more socially constructed emotions and are often combinations of primary emotions with varying valences.[2] Turner and Stets (2005) argue that humans are responsive to the expression of primary emotions during social interaction (e.g. face-to-face involvements during a protest situation). Also, Jasper (1998) argues that secondary emotions, such as outrage and pride, may be more influential for ongoing political involvement (e.g. sustaining commitment to an organization and ideology). Social movement researchers can use this distinction to clarify the foundations of the emotions being theorized. One could also analyze the social and situational conditions which give rise to particular combinations of emotions.

Turner (2000) argues the intensity of emotions (high, medium, low) shapes emotional experiences. For instance, low-happiness might feel like contentment while high-happiness feels like exhilaration. Jasper (1998) distinguishes between shared and reciprocal emotions. Shared emotions can strengthen group affiliation as activists experience similar emotional responses to objects or events. Reciprocal emotions refer to the emotional ties which bind together activists. Collins (2004) argues the self is motivated to maximize emotional energy, which feels like confidence and enthusiasm. It is also motivated to prevent a loss of emotional energy, which feels like depression. Shott (1979) points out that the arousal of guilt, shame, and embarrassment signals that the self has violated social norms, thus motivating corrective actions. In conditions where negative emotions and the loss of emotional energy are difficult to prevent, Summers-Effler (2004a) shows that the self develops various defensive strategies to minimize the consequences; analyzing research on women in abusive relationships, she argues that defensive strategies (e.g. developing an internal locus of control) are both more durable and draining than proactive strategies. Taken together, an analyst can differentiate between the origins of the emotions (primary, secondary), the degree of intensity (high, medium, low), attributions (shared, reactive), and various corrective processes.

Coupling

Some researchers study patterns and combinations of emotions. Jasper (2011) describes *moral batteries* as a coupling between positive and negative emotions, where one is motivated to avoid one emotion while being attracted to the other. The most well-researched example of a moral battery consists of shame and pride (e.g. Castells 2012; Gould 2009). Lively and Heise (2004) theorize *emotional segues* as correlation pathways through which emotions transition from one into another. For instance, movements with stigmatized identities may transition from shame, to fear, to anger, and then into pride. Similarly, Williamson (2011) theorizes *emotion chains* which are groups of emotions produced when one emotion leads directly into another via transformative processes. In this regard, a movement might chain together a series of emotions to create a distinct "emotional journey." Summers-Effler (2010) describes *emotional slingshotting* as the process of transmuting dangerous negative emotions into negative emotions which a group can more directly remedy, a process that indirectly, but ultimately, leads to intense positive emotion.

Temporality

Emotions can be analytically distinguished by how long they persist. Collins (2004) makes a distinction between transient emotions and emotional energy which endures across situations. Jasper (2011) differentiates bodily urges (e.g. lust, hunger), reflex emotions (e.g. surprise, fear), and longer-lasting moods (e.g. love, trust, morality). Summers-Effler (2010) theorizes the rhythm of social movement organizations through her comparative study of an anti-death penalty movement and a Catholic Worker house. She argues shifts in attention influenced the speed and rhythm of involvement within each group. How the speed and rhythm operated influenced whether movements were able to synchronize activity both *within* a group as well as *between* groups, consequently affecting opportunities to take advantage of resources and political openings. Summers-Effler also theorizes the patterning of emotions as they unfold through time. She finds risk followed by success generated feelings of thrilling expansion. Negative experiences, such as grief and horror, served as emotional warning signals, which groups can harness to stabilize themselves.

Data

Social movement scholars can capture emotion through forms of text, surveys, interviews, participation, and observation. One could analyze text from flyers, transcripts of speeches, leaflets, newsletters, protest signs, or stories (e.g. Gould 2009; Polletta 2006a). Surveys could ask about emotional experiences, biographical data, and histories of protest participation (e.g. Beyerlein and Sikkink 2008). Interviews can record how one recalls the emotions of past events, their emotions in anticipation for a projected future, as well as expressed emotion during interviews as an interlocutor remembers the past or imagines the future (e.g. Nepstad 2004).

Observationally, one could use audio-video recordings to analyze the micro-situational details to reveal the factors which give rise to emotions, as well as the micro displays of emotions (e.g. Collins 2009). One could also participate and use the self as a resource to provide experiential depth to analyses, in addition to recording observational data *in situ* (e.g. Blee 2002; Summers-Effler, Van Ness, and Hausmann 2015).

Social movement theory has mostly relied on the use of rhetorical devices to theorize emotional processes. This reliance is in part true because the field as a whole has tended to use forms of text, such as newspaper articles. We argue that the field is most in need of more situated and embodied theories of emotion. Protest events are particularly fruitful places to study the interactional and situational conditions structuring emotions. In the next section, we briefly review recent cognitive science literature on grounded cognition to introduce social movement scholars to research which we believe is particularly useful for recording and theorizing both cognition and emotions *in situ*.

Cognitive Social Science and Emotion

Some critique the cultural turn for an overly "cognitive bias" and the virtual neglect of emotions (Benford 1997; Goodwin and Jasper 2006). This evaluation led to the field's emotions turn which has now developed a rich literature. Now that scholars focus on the importance of both cognitive and emotive processes at the micro level, we argue that the field would benefit from attuning to the interdisciplinary field of Cognitive Social Science to challenge, extend, and deepen our understanding of cognitive and emotive processes in social movements. Cognitive Social Science is an interdisciplinary "inter-field" (Darden and Maull 1977), which emerged in the 1970s as a variety of fields, such as psychology, anthropology, neuroscience, and linguistics arrived at common concerns and theoretical interests. Many sociological concepts actively used by scholars of social movements find shared roots from contributions in this inter-field, such as schemas, scripts, and frames. More fully embracing and integrating Cognitive Social Science literature will benefit the field of social movements by providing a tenable micro foundation for more explicit theorizing about emotions in social movements; this integration is particularly warranted considering social movement theories are increasingly tending towards theories of action (Jasper 2010).

In this section, we briefly review the literature on grounded cognition to modernize the field's conception of cognition and emotion. Grounded cognition research emphasizes the body and bodily states (e.g. Lakoff and Johnson 1980), situated simulations (e.g. Barsalou 2008; Rizzolatti and Sinigaglia 2007), and the relations between perception, action, the body, the environment, and social interaction (e.g. Barsalou et al. 2003; Gibson 1966). In this perspective, links tie the internal cognitive and emotive structures with external structures from the environment, body, and situations. Thus, proper analyses of cognition and emotion need to focus attention on the ways in which the external influences the internal. We briefly provide a few findings that have implications for the field of social movements.

Dual process

Research on dual process models reveals that humans have two memory systems which operate under different situational conditions (see Kahneman 2011; Lizardo et al. 2016; Smith and DeCoster 2000). Mundane, routine, and habitual situations invoke "associative" memory systems, while atypical, surprising, and novel situations invoke "rule-based" memory systems. Research finds that the emotional tone of situations can also affect which memory system is in use (Smith and DeCoster 2000). A situation with positive emotions is likely to encourage associative memory systems, while situations with negative emotions can invoke rule-based memory systems. Rule-based systems afford the opportunity to construct novel lines of action in ways which are more difficult with associative systems. Van Ness and Summers-Effler (2016) draw from this literature and integrate the dual process framework with early collective behavior theories. Given the situated nature of cognition and emotion, they argue for the need to compare within types of situations. We extend this suggestion to situated analyses and argue that one could specify the social, cultural, and material properties in order to further theorize how each aspect of situations structure cognition, emotion, and communication processes.

Memory

The emotional conditions of situations also influence memory coding and recall. Reisberg and Hertel (2005) find that subjects remember emotional situations with greater accuracy and vividness than less emotionally intense events. The activity of the amygdala enhances memory; amygdala activity influences both encoding and consolidation of memories (Phelps 2006). Negative emotional memories are particularly likely to be recalled, as witnessed in those with various pathologies or traumas. Research also finds the embodied mood state during memory recall can influence which memories are retrieved. Scholars describe these as *mood-dependent* and *mood-congruent* memories (Bower and Forgas 2000; Buchanan 2007). Mood-dependent memory recall is when the emotional state of the respondent *in situ* aligns with the emotional conditions which were present when learning is coded. Mood-congruent recall is when triggered emotions during recall align with the emotional status of the retrieved memory. Integrating these findings suggests the need to take into account the emotional conditions of situations, even during interviews which rely on future-projection or memory recall. Additionally, these biases toward the emotionally intense also suggest that much of the mundane fluctuations and emotional rhythms may go unnoticed when one relies only on memory recall.

The body can both reflect and be used to evoke emotional states (Barsalou et al. 2003; Barsalou et al. 2005). An analyst can attune to body posturing, voice inflections, rhythms of speech, the direction of one's gaze, the speed of movement, and facial expressions. Indeed, many of these sources of data are used in microsociological analyses (e.g. Collins 2004; Goffman 1967; Katz 1999). Additionally, positioning the body *into* these various states can create emotional conditions which skew memory recall. Riskind (1983) finds memory recall is more likely to bias toward negative life events, especially when the body forms positions which evoke negative emotions. These findings suggest the need to attune to embodiment *in situ* because bodily states intimately connect cognitive and emotive processes.

There is a litany of literature on emotions within Cognitive Social Science which can inform and be informed by sociological analyses. Consistent with much of the findings is the need for a situational unit of analyses. Social movement scholars should pursue situated studies which attune to the ways in which the environment, body, and social interaction influence emotive and cognitive processes (e.g. Hochschild 2016; Pagis 2009; Tavory 2009; Winchester 2016).

Future Directions

Considering activists often have an explicit desire to influence, persuade, manipulate, recruit, and sustain commitment, we believe protest events and social movement organizations are optimal sites for creating general theories of emotion. In this section, we comment on fruitful ways forward for the study of emotions in social movements.

Cognitive Social Science

Though we only briefly discussed some recent findings above, we suggest that scholars engage the interdisciplinary field of Cognitive Social Science. This literature will not only benefit social movement studies by informing about much of the "hidden" cognitive and emotive processes, but the field will also benefit from uniquely sociological insights. By remaining on the sidelines, sociologists leave other disciplines to fill in the voids with their misconceptions of social processes (Cerulo 2010). Thus, we invite social movement scholars to engage Cognitive Social Science to further pursue a situated study of emotion in social movement contexts in order to advance our understanding of social movements and to use protest events as a *field site* for theorizing sociological processes of emotion more broadly.

Emotional staging

In the section above, we briefly stressed the importance of situated analyses. Building on this argument, we believe one fruitful path forward is to study the way activists construct situations to evoke particular cognitions and emotions in fellow activists, bystanders, and social control agents. In this sense, an analyst can attune to both social and material arrangements of protest events as activists attempt to set the

422   JUSTIN VAN NESS AND ERIKA SUMMERS-EFFLER

stage for desired emotional conditions. Theorizing emotions at a situational level can also reveal the ways activists can benefit from, or be constrained by, habits of perception or ruptured expectations.

One could also explicitly study the staging of protest objects to theorize the variation in emotional outcomes in diverse audiences. For example, Nepstad (2008) describes how the Plowshares movement used blood as a powerful symbol to evoke emotional reactions. Christians could see the blood and recall Christ's decision to give his life, rather than shedding the blood of others. Other audiences may see blood as a symbol of an impending threat of destruction. One could further pursue analyses on the multivocality of objects by revealing how an object can invoke emotional reactions. Such analyses could also explain how intended or unintended emotional conditions skew protest outcomes.

Case selection

Social movement case selection is biased toward leftist, reformist, and progressive movements (Blee 2017; Polletta 2006b; Snow 2006). This lopsided focus skews our understanding of emotions in social movements. We argue that the field is particularly in need of qualitative studies within organizations and protest events which are outside of one's comfort zone. Right-wing movements (see Chapter 35 by Futtrell, Simi, and Tan, in this volume) and religious movements (see Chapter 32 by Snow and Beyerlein, in this volume) provide two arenas which remain understudied although they may yield fruitful empirical and theoretical contributions, particularly about emotional dynamics.

Conclusion

In this chapter, we have reviewed the study of emotions in social movements. We began by situating the absence of emotions in social movement studies in relation to sociology as a field more broadly. Then we reviewed how scholars have theorized emotions in relation to social movement mobilization, commitment, and demobilization. Following that, we drew from studies within the field of social movements and the field of sociology of emotions to provide some useful ways to distinguish emotions analytically. Next, we drew from Cognitive Social Science, particularly the literature on grounded cognition, to emphasize the need for situated analyses of emotion. Finally, we closed with a few fruitful paths forward. All said, given the past developments and prospects for future theorizing, the future of the intersection of the study of emotions and social movement studies looks promising.

Notes

1   Turner (2002) argues when individuals repress negative emotions, they are more likely to make external attributions and blame others, the situation, or structures which may lead to the severance of social bonds and commitments. Stein (2001) provides an example which complements this theory, although at a collective level rather than individual.
2   For a more extensive review of secondary emotions, see Turner and Stets (2005: 11–21).

References

Abrutyn, Seth and Anna S. Mueller. 2014. "The Socioemotional Foundations of Suicide: A Microsociological View of Durkheim's Suicide." *Sociological Theory* 32(4): 327–351. doi: 10.1177/0735275114558633.

Balko, Radley. 2014. *Rise of the Warrior Cop: The Militarization of America's Police Forces.* New York: Public Affairs.

Barbalet, Jack M. 2001. *Emotion, Social Theory, and Social Structure: A Macrosociological Approach.* Cambridge: Cambridge University Press.

Barsalou, Lawrence W. 2008. "Grounded Cognition." *Annual Review of Psychology* 59: 617–645. doi: 10.1146/annurev.psych.59.103006.093639.

Barsalou, Lawrence W., Aron K. Barbey, W. Kyle Simmons, and Ava Santos. 2005. "Embodiment in Religious Knowledge." *Journal of Cognition and Culture* 5(1): 14–57.

Barsalou, Lawrence, Paula M. Niedenthal, Aron K. Barbey, and Jennifer A. Ruppert. 2003. "Social Embodiment." In *The Psychology of Learning and Motivation*, edited by Brian H. Ross, vol. 43, 43–92. San Diego, CA: Academic Press.

Benford, Robert D. 1997. "An Insider's Critique of the Social Movement Framing Perspective." *Sociological Inquiry* 67: 409–430.

Bernstein, Mary. 1997. "Celebration and Supression: The Strategic Uses of Identity by the Lesbain and Gay Movement." *American Journal of Sociology* 103(3): 531–565.

Beyerlein, Kraig and Kenneth T. Andrews. 2008. "Black Voting During the Civil Rights Movement: A Micro-Level Analysis." *Social Forces* 87(1): 65–93.

Beyerlein, Kraig and David Sikkink. 2008. "Sorrow and Solidarity: Why Americans Volunteered for 9/11 Relief Efforts." *Social Problems* 55(2): 190–215. doi: 10.1525/sp.2008.55.2.190.

Blee, Kathleen M. 2002. *Inside Organized Racism: Women in the Hate Movement.* Los Angeles: University of California Press.

Blee, Kathleen M. 2017. "How the Study of White Supremacism Is Helped and Hindered by Social Movement Research." *Mobilization: An International Quarterly* 22(1): 1–15. doi: 10.17813/1086-671x-22-1-1.

Bower, Gordon H. and Joseph P. Forgas. 2000. "Affect, Memory, and Social Cognition." In *Cognition and Emotion*, edited by Eric Eich, John F. Kihlstrom, Gordon H. Bower, Joseph Paul Forgas, and Paula M. Niedenthal. New York: Oxford University Press.

Brockett, Charles D. 2005. *Political Movements and Violence in Central America.* Cambridge: Cambridge University Press.

Brown, Gavin and Jenny Pickerill. 2009. "Spaces for Emotions in the Spaces of Activism." *Emotion, Space and Society* 2: 24–35.

Brym, Robert J. 2007. "Six Lessons of Suicide Bombers." *Contexts* 6(4): 40–45.

Buchanan, Tony W. 2007. "Retireval of Emotional Memories." *Psychological Bulletin* 133(5): 761–799.

Castells, Manuel. 2012. *Networks of Outrage and Hope: Social Movements in the Internet Age.* Cambridge: Polity.

Cerulo, Karen A. 2010. "Mining the Intersections of Cognitive Sociology and Neuroscience." *Poetics* 38: 115–132.

Chong, Dennis. 1991. "Selective Social Incentives and Reputational Concerns." In *Collective Action and the Civil Rights Movement*, by Dennis Chong, 31–72. Chicago: University of Chicago Press.

Collins, Randall. 1975. *Conflict Sociology.* New York: Academic. Press

Collins, Randall. 2001. "Social Movements and the Focus of Emotional Attention." In *Passionate Politics: Emotions and Social Movements*, edited by Jeff Goodwin, James M. Jasper and Francesca Polletta. Chicago: University of Chicago Press.

Collins, Randall. 2004. *Interaction Ritual Chains*. Princeton, NJ: Princeton University Press.

Collins, Randall. 2009. *Violence: A Micro-Sociological Theory*. Princeton, NJ: Princeton University Press.

Cooley, Charles Horton. 1902. *Human Nature and Social Order*. New York: Scribner's and Sons.

Coser, Lewis A. 1974. *Greedy Institutions: Patterns of Undivided Commitment*. New York: Free Press.

Darden, Lindley and Nancy Maull. 1977. "Interfield Theories." *Philosophy of Science* 44(1): 43–64.

Davenport, Christian. 2005. "Repression and Mobilization: Insights from Political Science and Sociology." In *Repression and Mobilization*, edited by Christian Davenport, Hank Johnston, and Carol Mueller. Minneapolis: University of Minnesota Press.

Durkheim, Emile. 1912. *The Elementary Forms of Religious Life*. Oxford: Oxford University Press.

Echols, Alice. 1989. *Daring to Be Bad*. Minneapolis: University of Minnesota Press.

Einwohner, Rachel L. 2003. "Opportunity, Honor, and Action in the Warsaw Ghetto Uprising of 1943." *American Journal of Sociology* 109(3): 199–237.

Ekman, Paul. 1977. "Facial Expression." In *Nonverbal Behavior and Communication*, edited by Aron Siegman and Stanley Feldstein, 97–116. Hillsdale, NJ: Lawrence Erlbaum.

Feigenbaum, Anna, Patrick McCurdy, and Fabian Frenzel. 2013. "Towards a Method for Studying Affect in (Micro) Politics: The Campfire Chats Project and the Occupy Movement." *Parallax* 19: 21–37.

Gibson, James J. 1966. *The Senses Considered as Perceptual Systems*. Boston: Houghton Mifflin Company.

Goffman, Erving. 1959. *Presentation of Self in Everyday Life*. Garden City, NY: Doubleday Anchor.

Goffman, Erving. 1963. *Behavior in Public Places*. New York: The Free Press.

Goffman, Erving. 1967. *Interaction Ritual: Essays on Face-to-Face Behavior*. Garden City, NY: Anchor Books.

Goldman, Marion S. 1999. *Passionate Journeys: Why Successful Women Joined a Cult*. Ann Arbor: University of Michigan Press.

Goodwin, Jeff. 1997. "The Libidinal Constitution of a High-Risk Social Movement: Affectual Ties and Solidarity in the Huk Rebellion, 1946 to 1954." *American Sociological Review* 62(1): 53–69.

Goodwin, Jeff and James M. Jasper. 2006. "Emotions and Social Movements." In *Handbook of the Sociology of Emotions*, edited by Jan E. Stets and Jonathan H. Turner, 611–635. New York: Springer.

Goodwin, Jeff, James M. Jasper, and Francesca Polletta. 2001. "Why Emotions Matter." In *Passionate Politics*, edited by Jeff Goodwin, James M. Jasper and Francesca Polletta, 1–24. Chicago: University of Chicago Press.

Gould, Deborah B. 2009. *Moving Politics: Emotion and Act Up's Fight against AIDS*. Chicago: University of Chicago Press.

Gould, Roger V. 1991. "Multiple Networks and Mobilization in the Paris Commune, 1871." *American Sociological Review* 56(6): 716–729.

Gould, Roger V. 1993. "Collective Action and Network Structure." *American Sociological Review* 58(2): 182–196.

Gupta, Devashree. 2009. "The Power of Incremental Outcomes: How Small Victories and Defeats Affect Social Movement Organizations." *Mobilization: An International Journal* 14: 417–432.

Gurr, Ted Robert. 1970. *Why Men Rebel*. Princeton, NJ: Princeton University Press.

Halfmann, Drew and Michael P. Young. 2010. "War Pictures: The Grotesque as a Mobilizing Tactic." *Mobilization* 15(1): 1–24.

Hochschild, Arlie R. 1979. "Emotion Work, Feeling Rules and Social Structure." *American Journal of Sociology* 85: 551–575.

Hochschild, Arlie R. 1983. *The Managed Heart: The Commercialization of Human Feeling*. Berkeley: University of California Press.

Hochschild, Arlie R. 2016. *Strangers in Their Own Land: Anger and Mourning on the American Right*. New York: The New Press.

James, William. 1902. *The Varieties of Religious Experience: A Study in Human Nature*. London: Longmans, Green and Co.

Jasper, James M. 1997. *The Art of Moral Protest*, vol. 60. Chicago: University of Chicago Press.

Jasper, James M. 1998. "The Emotions of Protest: Affective and Reactive Emotions in and around Social Movements." *Sociological Forum* 13(3): 397–424.

Jasper, James M. 2004. "A Strategic Approach to Collective Action: Looking for Agency in Social-Movement Choices." *Mobilization* 9(1): 1–16.

Jasper, James M. 2010. "Social Movement Theory Today: Toward a Theory of Action?" *Sociology Compass* 4(11): 965–976. doi: 10.1111/j.1751-9020.2010.00329.x.

Jasper, James M. 2011. "Emotions and Social Movements: Twenty Years of Theory and Research." *Annual Review of Sociology* 37(1): 285–303. doi: 10.1146/annurev-soc-081309-150015.

Jasper, James M. and Lynn Owens. 2014. "Social Movements and Emotions." In *Handbook of the Sociology of Emotions*, edited by Jan E. Stets and Jonathan H. Turner, vol. II, 529–548. New York: Springer.

Jasper, James M. and Jane D. Poulsen. 1995. "Recruiting Strangers and Friends: Moral Shocks and Social Networks in Animal Rights and Anti-Nuclear Protests." *Social Problems* 42(4): 493–512.

Kahneman, Daniel. 2011. *Thinking, Fast and Slow*. New York: Farrar, Strauss, Giroux.

Kanter, Rosabeth M. 1968. "Commitment and Social Organization: A Study of Commitment Mechanisms in Utopian Communities." *American Sociological Review* 33(4): 499–517.

Katz, Jack. 1999. *How Emotions Work*. Chicago: University of Chicago Press.

Kemper, Theodore D. 1978. *A Social Interactional Theory of Emotions*. New York: Wiley.

Khwaja, Marwan. 1993. "Repression and Popular Collective Action: Evidence from the West Bank." *Sociological Forum* 8(1): 47–71.

Koopmans, Ruud. 1997. "Dynamics of Repression and Mobilization: The German Extreme Right in the 1990s." *Mobilization: An International Journal* 2(2): 149–164.

Lakoff, George and Mark Johnson. 1980. "The Metaphorical Structure of the Human Conceptual System." *Cognitive Science* 4(2): 195–208.

Lively, Kathryn J. and David R. Heise. 2004. "Sociological Realms of Emotional Experience." *American Journal of Sociology* 109(5): 1109–1136.

Lizardo, Omar, Robert Mowry, Brandon Sepulvado, et al. 2016. "What Are Dual Process Models? Implications for Cultural Analysis in Sociology." *Sociological Theory* 34(4): 287–310. doi: 10.1177/0735275116675900.

Lofland, John and Rodney Stark. 1965. "Becoming a World-Saver: A Theory of Conversion to a Deviant Perspective." *American Sociological Review* 30(6): 862–875.

Luker, Kristin. 1984. *Abortion and the Politics of Motherhood*. Berkeley: University of California Press.

Marx, Karl. 1978. *The Marx-Engels Reader*. New York: W. W. Norton.

Melucci, Alberto. 1996. *Challenging Codes: Collective Action in the Information Age*. New York: Cambridge University Press.

Morris, Aldon. 1981. "Black Southern Student Sit-in Movement: An Analysis of Internal Organization." *American Journal of Sociology* 46(6): 744–767.

Morris, Aldon and Cedric Herring. 1987. "Theory and Research in Social Movements: A Critical Review." *Annual Review of Political Science* 2: 137–198.

Moss, Dana M. 2014. "Repression, Response, and Contained Escalation under 'Liberalized' Authoritarianism in Jordan." *Mobilization: An International Journal* 19(3): 261–286.

Moss, Dana M. and David A. Snow. 2016. "Theorizing Social Movements." In *Handbook of Contemporary Sociological Theory*, edited by Seth Abrutyn. 547–569. New York: Springer.

Munson, Ziad W. 2009. *The Making of Pro-Life Activists: How Social Movement Mobilization Works*. Chicago: University of Chicago Press.

Nepstad, Sharon Erickson. 2004. *Convictions of the Soul: Religion, Culture, and Agency in the Central America Solidarity Movement*. Oxford: Oxford University Press.

Nepstad, Sharon Erickson. 2008. *Religion and War Resistance in the Plowshares Movement*. Cambridge: Cambridge University Press.

Nepstad, Sharon Erickson and Chris Smith. 2001. "The Social Structure of Moral Outrage in Recruitment to the U.S. Central America Peace Movement." In *Passionate Politics: Emotions and Social Movements*, edited by Jeff Goodwin, James M. Jasper and Francesca Polletta, 158–175. Chicago: University of Chicago Press.

Oberschall, Anthony. 1973. *Social Conflict and Social Movements*. Englewood Cliffs, NJ: Prentice-Hall.

Oliver, Pamela. 1984. "'If You Don't Do It, Nobody Else Will': Active and Token Contributors to Local Collective Action." *American Sociological Review* 49(5): 601–610.

Oliver, Pamela E. and Daniel J. Meyer. 1999. "How Events Enter the Public Sphere: Conflict, Location, and Sponsorship in Local Newspaper Coverage of Public Events." *American Journal of Sociology* 105(1): 38–87.

Owens, Lynn. 2009. *Cracking under Pressure*. University Park, PA: Pennsylvania State University Press.

Pagis, Michal. 2009. "Embodied Self-Reflexivity." *Social Psychology Quarterly* 72(3): 265–283.

Phelps, Elizabeth A. 2006. "Emotion and Cognition: Insights from Studies of the Human Amygdala." *Annual Review of Psychology* 57: 27–53.

Polletta, Francesca. 2006a. *It Was Like a Fever: Storytelling in Protest and Politics*. Chicago: University of Chicago Press.

Polletta, Francesca. 2006b. "Mobilization Forum: Awkward Movements." 11(4): 475–478.

Reisberg, Daniel and Paula Hertel. 2005. *Memory and Emotion*. New York: Oxford University Press.

Riskind, John H. 1983. "Nonverbal Expressions and the Accessibility of Life Experience Memories: A Congruence Hypothesis." *Social Cognition* 2: 62–86.

Rizzolatti, Giacomo and Corrado Sinigaglia. 2007. "Mirror Neurons and Motor Intentionality." *Functional Neurology* 22(4): 205–210.

Scheff, Thomas J. 1988. "Shame and Conformity: The Deference-Emotion System." *American Sociological Review* 53(3): 395–406. doi: 10.2307/2095647.

Scheff, Thomas J. 1990. *Microsociology: Discourse, Emotion, and Social Structure*. Chicago: University of Chicago Press.

Scheff, Thomas J. 1994. *Bloody Revenge: Emotions, Nationalism, and War*. Boulder, CO: Westview Press.

Shott, Susan. 1979. "Emotion and Social Life: A Symbolic Interactionist Analysis." *American Journal of Sociology* 84(6): 1317–1334.

Smelser, Neil J. 1962. *Theory of Collective Behavior*. New York: Free Press.

Smith, Christian. 1996. *Resisting Reagan: The U.S. Central American Peace Movement*. Chicago: University of Chicago Press.

Smith, Eliot R. and James DeCoster. 2000. "Dual-Process Models in Social and Cognitive Psychology: Conceptual Integration and Links to Underlying Memory Systems." *Personality and Social Psychological Review* 4(2): 108–131.

Snow, David A. 2006. "Are There Really Awkward Movements or Only Awkard Research Relationships?" *Mobilization* 11(4): 475–478.

Snow, David A. and Dana M. Moss. 2014. "Protest on the Fly: Toward a Theory of Spontaneity in the Dynamics of Protest and Social Movements." *American Sociological Review* 79(6): 1122–1143.

Snow, David A. and Cynthia L. Phillips. 1980. "The Lofland-Stark Conversion Model: A Critical Reassessment." *Social Problems* 27(4): 430–447.

Snow, David A., E. Burke Rochford, Steven K. Worden, and Robert D. Benford. 1986. "Frame Alignment Processes, Micromobilization, and Movement Participation." *American Sociological Review* 51(4): 464–481.

Snow, David A., Louis A. Zurcher Jr and Sheldon Ekland-Olson. 1980. "Social Networks and Social Movements: A Microstructural Approach to Differential Recruitment." *American Sociological Review* 45(5): 787–801.

Stein, Arlene. 2001. *The Stranger Next Door*. Boston: Beacon.

Stryker, Sheldon and Peter J. Burke. 2000. "The Past, Present, and Future of an Identity Theory." *Social Psychology Quarterly* 63(4): 284–297.

Summers-Effler, Erika. 2004a. "Defensive Strategies: The Formation and Social Implications of Patterned Self-Destructive Behavior." *Advances in Group Processes* 21: 309–326.

Summers-Effler, Erika. 2004b. "A Theory of the Self, Emotion, and Culture." *Advances in Group Processes* 21: 273–308.

Summers-Effler, Erika. 2010. *Laughing Saints and Righteous Heroes: Emotional Rhythms in Social Movement Groups*. Chicago: University of Chicago Press.

Summers-Effler, Erika, Justin Van Ness, and Christopher Hausmann. 2015. "Peeking in the Black Box: Studying, Theorizing, and Representing the Micro-Foundations of Day-to-Day Interactions." *Journal of Contemporary Ethnography* 44(4):450–479. doi: 10.1177/0891241614545880.

Tavory, Iddo. 2009. "Of Yarmulkes and Categories: Delegating Boundaries and the Phenomenology of Interactional Expectation." *Theory and Society* 39(1): 49–68. doi: 10.1007/s11186-009-9100-x.

Taylor, Verta. 1989. "Social Movement Continuity: The Women's Movement in Abeyance." *American Sociological Review* 54(5): 761–775.

Taylor, Verta. 1996. *Rock-a-Bye Baby: Feminism, Self-Help and Postpartum Depression*. London: Routledge.

Taylor, Verta and Nancy E. Whittier. 1991. "Collective Identity in Social Movement Communities: Lesbian Feminist Mobilization." In *Frontiers in Social Movement Theory*, edited by Aldon D. Morris and Carol M. Mueller. New Haven, CT: Yale University Press.

Turner, Jonathan H. 2000. *On the Origins of Human Emotions: A Sociological Inquiry into the Evolution of Human Affect*. Stanford, CA: Stanford University Press.

Turner, Jonathan H. 2002. *Face-to-Face: Toward a Sociological Theory of Interpersonal Behavior*. Stanford, CA: Stanford University Press.

Turner, Jonathan H. and Jan E. Stets. 2005. *The Sociology of Emotions*. Cambridge: Cambridge University Press.

Van Ness, Justin and Erika Summers-Effler. 2016. "Reimagining Collective Behavior." In *Handbook of Contemporary Sociological Theory*, edited by Seth Abrutyn. New York: Springer.

Weber, Max. 1968. *Max Weber on Charisma and Institution Building: Selected Papers*. Chicago: University of Chicago Press.

Whittier, Nancy E. 2009. *The Politics of Child Sexual Abuse*. Oxford: Oxford University Press.

Williamson, Elizabeth. 2011. "The Magic of Multiple Emotions: An Examination of Shifts in Emotional Intensity During the Reclaiming Movement's Recruiting/Training Events and Event Reattendance." *Sociological Forum* 26(1): 45–70. doi: 10.1111/j.1573-7861.2010.01224.x.

Winchester, Daniel. 2016. "A Hunger for God: Embodied Metaphor as Cultural Cognition in Action." *Social Forces*. doi: 10.1093/sf/sow065.

Wood, Elizabeth Jean. 2001. "The Emotional Benefits of Insurgency in El Salvador." In *Passionate Politics*, edited by Jeff Goodwin, James M. Jasper, and Francesca Polletta. 267–281. Chicago: University of Chicago Press.

Wood, Michael, Dustin S. Stoltz, Justin Van Ness, and Marshall Taylor. forthcoming. "Schemas and Frames." *Sociological Theory*.

Young, Michael P. 2001. "A Revolution of the Soul: Transformative Experiences and Immediate Abolition." In *Passionate Politics: Emotions and Social Movements*, edited by Jeff Goodwin, James M. Jasper, and Francesca Polletta, 99–114. Chicago: University of Chicago Press.

24

Collective Identity in Social Movements: Assessing the Limits of a Theoretical Framework

CRISTINA FLESHER FOMINAYA

Introduction

The concept of collective identity has been used to analyze social movements of all kinds, and has made important contributions to our understanding of social movements. The existing literature is vast and has been effectively reviewed (e.g. Flesher Fominaya 2010a; Hunt, Benford, and Snow 1994; Polletta and Jasper 2001; Snow and Corrigall-Brown 2015). Yet recent changes in forms of social mobilization call into question its continuing relevance to all varieties of movements. In the face of the proliferation of non-hierarchically organized social movements with diffuse identity markers, such as the autonomous wing of the Global Justice Movement or the recent global wave of Occupy Movements, it can be tempting to dispense with analysis of the process of collective identity formation. When we turn our gaze to movements that organize exclusively or primarily online, where communication and data are often anonymous, ephemeral, highly mutable and mobile (Coleman 2010), finding the analytic boundaries that define movements, let alone movement collective identities, can become extremely challenging.

In this chapter I will do two key things. First, I will provide clarity for a concept that is extremely useful although analytically and methodologically tricky to use. I will do so by drawing on a series of central debates in the existing literature, using empirical examples to help illuminate the analytical components of the concept. Next, I will test the robustness of the concept in the context of two arenas that pose particular challenges to its analytical applicability: (1) autonomous social movements, which reject shared identity markers for ideological and strategic reasons; and (2) online movements, where collective identity formation (and research into it) face a number of challenges due to the mediated nature of communication

The Wiley Blackwell Companion to Social Movements, Second Edition. Edited by David A. Snow, Sarah A. Soule, Hanspeter Kriesi, and Holly J. McCammon.
© 2019 John Wiley & Sons Ltd. Published 2019 by John Wiley & Sons Ltd.

What Is Collective Identity and Why Should
Social Movement Scholars Care?

The concept of collective identity has been of particular interest to social movement scholars who believe that more structural, rationalistic, and goal-driven explanations for the emergence and persistence of movements – such as resource mobilization theory (Gamson 1975; McCarthy and Zald 1977), political process models (McAdam 1982; Tarrow 1989), rational choice models (cost-benefit analysis) (Granovetter 1978), and ideologically based explanations (Oberschall 1995; Zald 2000) – leave out important social psychological, emotional, and cultural factors. In order for movements to emerge and/or persist over time, there must be some form of shared sense of purpose and reciprocal identification and mutual recognition among movement participants. In short, sustained social movements are not possible in the absence of a collective identity, and the inability to maintain some form of collective identity will lead to movement decline and disintegration. Therefore, collective identity processes are particularly important in understanding movement dynamics over time (Gamson 1991; Taylor and Whittier 1992). Most definitions of "social movement" in the literature include the concept of collective identity as a key component (Flesher Fominaya 2014).

The concept of collective identity is often difficult for people studying social movement studies to grasp, not least because there is no consensual definition (Snow and Corrigall-Brown 2015). The first problem lies in a "how will I know it when I see it?" conundrum. People unfamiliar with how collective identity actually works in social movements often assume it is something visible, given, and/or fixed, in short, that a collective identity is simply the same thing as a shared primary or "given" identity based on social location (e.g. being a woman or working class), or else a sort of identifying "product" of movements, a symbol or label that will serve for people to identify the movement (e.g. the raised black fist for the Black Power Movement; the smiling sun of the anti-nuclear movement). Self-identification with and display of identity markers can serve as a means of mutual recognition of shared movement belonging, can have a role in recruitment processes, and can identify the movement to outsiders. But as I will show in this chapter, this limited understanding of collective identity, while useful as a starting point, does not help us fully explore the relationship between collective identity and collective action in social movements. How best to conceptualize and apply the concept of collective identity has been the subject of debates in the literature, some of which I discuss below.

Is Collective Identity Found in Individuals,
in the Collective, or Both?

One key problem related to the "how will I know it when I see it" conundrum is determining where collective identity is located. Is it something people carry around in their heads (part of their self-conceptions) or is it generative and emergent from social movement interactions? Whereas Polletta and Jasper (2001: 285) locate collective identity within the individual, defining it as "an individual's cognitive, moral and emotional connection with a broader community, category, practice, or institution," Whittier (1995: 16) argues that "collective identity [is] located in action and interaction-observable phenomena-rather than in individual self-conceptions, attitudes, or beliefs."

I argue that collective identity is both; it cannot exist unless individuals hold it within their self-conceptions. But unless it is expressed through action and interaction, it cannot be generated in the first place, nor can it be constructed, maintained or developed over time (Flesher Fominaya 2010a; see also Gamson 1991; Snow and McAdam 2000). The danger with *only* locating it in individual self-conceptions is multifold. First, if individual beliefs are not linked to collective action, the concept of collective identity fails the test of being applicable to social movements. Without collective agency, there is no movement to speak of. The second problem is that the specific substantive conceptions and definitions held by any given individual do not have to be shared across different individuals in their totality, nor do they need to be fixed over time. In other words, individuals can claim and recognize in others a shared belonging to a specific movement or movement group or community, without sharing the same *definition* of the movement. This will become immediately apparent if you ask any ten people to define a given movement (although in movements with strong orthodoxies or sect-like tendencies, you may indeed get the same answer!).

Likewise, movement identity markers can be tied to symbolic representations or forms of action that change, sometimes considerably, over time. For example, the now iconic Guy Fawkes mask that is seen as *the* symbol of "Anonymous"[1] was originally used to represent "epic fail guy," a meme that represented not a "we are legion awesomeness" but rather the guy who was doomed to failure (Firer-Blaess 2016). Knowing what the symbol meant (at either point in time) was a way of knowing whether in fact one was a member of that movement community, even if the specific meaning of the symbol shifted dramatically over time, and even if what that symbol meant or *should* mean was contested within the movement community. Indeed, deliberately confusing outsiders about the meanings of memes or symbols used by Anonymous insiders is a favorite pastime of "Anons" and serves to further strengthen collective identity within the movement. It is therefore not an explicit fixed meaning of the meme that matters but whether activists know its current meaning and its past history that marks them as insiders.

Another example of how collective identity elements change over time comes from "Youth without a Future" (*Juventud Sin Futuro*), one of the groups involved in Spain's Indignados/15-M movement.[2] Initially, they subscribed to confrontational direct action as an important component of their movement collective identity. After the groups' experience in the 15-M movement, they shifted their understanding of the role of confrontation, and this new conceptualization became an important component of their shared collective identity. So we need to link individual conceptions to a wider movement group or community and recognize that the specifics of those conceptions can change over time for the concept to be meaningful and useful. Trying to fix collective identity in content, location, and time will not capture how it actually works in social movements. It is never given, never fixed completely, but always renegotiated and reconfigured through a social movement's exposure to new environmental challenges, influences, and experiences. This is true even of identity-based or "identitarian" movements (Flesher Fominaya 2015a). What it means to be "queer," for example, is a shifting, contested category whose very interrogation lies at the heart of subscribing to a queer identity and identifying with queer movements.

Are Collective Identities Given or Constructed?

Goodwin and Jasper (2003: 103) argue that some collective identities, such as African-Americans facing discrimination in the USA in 1955, are widely accepted and activists can take them for granted as a basis for shared action and shared reciprocal identification. Gamson (1991) distinguishes between given identities that are ascribed by social location and those that are reflexively constructed through social interaction in movement settings. Gamson (ibid.) highlights that collective identity formation is a crucial task for movements hoping to sustain commitment over time. Gamson shows that sometimes pre-existing movement identities can be drawn on by actors in subsequent waves of mobilization, at other times no such ready-made identity is available and rather the identity needs to be built up through repeated interactions. He sees organizational, movement, and solidary identities as three embedded layers of collective identity.

The relation between given or primary identities and collective identities has been conceptualized in various ways with most scholars recognizing the active reflexive construction involved in generating movement collective identities (Buechler 2000; Hunt, Benford, and Snow 1994; Rupp and Taylor 1999).[3] Bernstein (1997) highlights the ways lesbian and gay rights campaigners strategically deployed identities as a result of interactions with the state and opposition groups. Snow and McAdam (2000) highlight the importance of constructionist processes in understanding the link between individual identities and movement participation, arguing that the need for confirmation and expression of salient individual identity can just as easily find expression in ways that have nothing to do with movement activism (e.g. church attendance). Crucial here is the recognition that "given" identities or interests do not automatically or necessarily provide the required basis for collection *action* in social movements. A collective identity oriented toward shared action and at least some common goals needs to develop for collective action to take place. The degree to which that collective identity is constructed reflexively or strategically varies across movement settings and is likely to be greater in identitarian movements (where an identity itself is central to movement demands and mobilization, e.g. Black Lives Matter, LGBTQI movements).

While many social movement theorists have focused on different aspects of collective identity, few have offered as comprehensive a theoretical framework for the concept as Alberto Melucci, whose seminal formulation I now turn to.

Melucci's Comprehensive Framework

Alberto Melucci (1995) developed the most systematic, comprehensive, and influential theory of collective identity in social movements. His work was crucial in bringing the concept to the fore of social movement scholarship and continues to be relevant today. I will summarize the key elements of his formulation below.

Melucci's point of departure was that: "The empirical unity of a social movement should be considered as a result rather than a starting point" (ibid.: 43). Therefore, "to understand how a movement succeeds or fails in becoming a collective actor is [...] a fundamental task for sociologists" (ibid.: 55). Melucci rejected the idea that collective identity was given. Drawing on insights from social psychology, he bridged the gap between individual beliefs and meanings and collective action by exploring the dynamic *process* through which actors negotiate, understand, and construct their action through shared repeated interaction. Collective identity as a process involves cognitive *definitions* about ends, means, and the field of action; this process is given voice through a common language, and enacted through a set of rituals, practices, and cultural artifacts. This *cognitive framework* is not necessarily unified or coherent but is shaped through interaction and comprises different and even contradictory definitions.

Anonymous provides a good example of Melucci's assertion that participants do not have to agree on what "Anonymous" should mean, believe, or do, in order to share a sense of collective belonging to the community. Debates over the relative importance of ethical political action versus trickster shenanigans "for the lulz" in defining Anonymous have been at the heart of the community (Firer-Blaess 2016), and how those debates have evolved over time also serve to shape and reshape the community itself. It is precisely contests over self-definition that often form a crucial process of collective identity formation.

This point is important because it means that actors do not necessarily have to be in complete agreement on ideologies, beliefs, interests, or goals in order to come together and generate collective action, an assertion that counters more structural understandings of what brings and keeps movement actors together (e.g. the concept of class consciousness in the Marxist tradition). For Melucci, collective identity refers to a *network of active relationships*, and he stresses the importance of the *emotional involvement* of activists (1995: 45), a central component of collective identity which I will discuss below.

Collective identity involves the ability to distinguish the (collective) self from the "other," and to be recognized by those "others." For Melucci, a social movement recognizes itself through reflexivity about its relation to others in the context or environment in which it acts, including an awareness of the opportunities and constraints it faces in a given field of action (ibid.: 47). Rather than seeing common interests as the basis for cohesion, he argues that *conflict* provides the basis for the consolidation of group identity and for solidarity (ibid.: 48). Understanding conflict rather than consensus or agreement as being crucial to collective identity processes is an important and initially counter-intuitive idea that is connected to the emphasis on its constructed reflexive nature. Collective identity establishes the boundaries of the actor in relation to the field: it regulates membership of individuals, and defines the requisites for joining the movement (ibid.: 49). It is also tied to issues of legitimacy and representation (i.e. what determines the legitimacy of a decision, actor or participant, who can represent and speak for the movement).

Collective Identity: Product, Process or Both?

One of the most coherent arguments against Melucci's "process-"based formulation is that of Snow and Corrigall-Brown (2015), who argue that while process is important, "it is questionable and unnecessary to contend that the process is more fundamental than the product to understanding the character and functionality of collective identity." For Snow and Corrigall-Brown, the *product* is "generative of a sense of agency that can be a powerful impetus to collective action, but it functions as well as the constructed social object to which the movement's protagonists, adversaries, and audience(s) respond." Scholars emphasizing the "product" aspect of collective identity understand it as a sort of public good produced by movements and available to everyone, a "public pronouncement of status," which they see as an important aspect of recruitment or incentives that motivate participation (Friedman and McAdam 1992).

Melucci and others drawing on his framework (e.g. Flesher Fominaya 2010a; Rupp and Taylor 1999; Taylor and Whittier 1992), however, would argue that a full understanding of collective identities in social movements, particularly one that helps understand the processes that sustain movement communities over time, must include attention to process.

Movement Logics and "Ways of Doing"

Why privilege movement cultural practices, shared experiences, and shared "logics of action" (rationales for certain forms of action that rest on the legitimacy and ideological preference for those forms of action and organization) over primary or "given" identities and issue salience in conceptualizing the role of collective identity in social movements? The reasons become clear when one examines what it is that keeps activists not only working together but also feeling a reciprocal recognition with others as having a shared belonging to a movement or movement community. New members of movements need to be effectively socialized into movement cultural practices, they need to learn the codes in operation, and they need to feel affectively integrated into the group or community.

Let's take the example of "Carlos," a previously unpoliticized 72-year-old who became politically active through his contact with the Indignados/15-M movement during their month-long occupation of the Puerta del Sol in Madrid, Spain in 2011. Carlos went down to the plaza one day, drawn to the tarps and activity there. Once there, he was surprised and excited to see people asking for signatures on a whole host of petitions and asking for his input on a series of proposals. He signed against the privatization of water and hospitals, he signed against austerity cuts. But he was not familiar with the participatory assembly-style practices used in the camp, nor was he immediately comfortable expressing his views in public. He felt welcome there, however, and the camp made him also feel useful and that he had something to contribute. Over time, he became socialized into movement practices. He learned what it meant to participate in an assembly and what the rules of engagement were. He learned about the different values that fueled the movement, including inclusivity, horizontality, feminism, reciprocal solidarity, and mutual respect. After the camp decamped, he began to take part in the neighborhood assemblies. He eventually became a leading figure and founder of a number of collectives, managing their communication strategies, and serving as a spokesperson and core organizer. He also defended staunchly the movement "way of doing things" as being "15-M" and the only legitimate way to do politics when in 15-M spaces.

What he (and many others) called the "15-M" way of doing things, earlier generations (much younger than he is) would refer to simply as *asamblearismo* or autonomous practice.[4]

What defined his feeling of belonging, his collective identity as a member of 15-M? Certainly a commitment to anti-austerity issues was an initial draw and still a crucial component of what the movement stands for. But what kept him in the movement, what socialized him into its ways, meanings, and philosophies came through his repeated interactions with other movement participants. In 15-M, the way of "doing politics" was also crucial to the movement's collective identity, and defined the markers of legitimacy and representation of political practice (everything that is "15-M" is OK, anything that isn't is not OK). If a participant of an assembly tried to override or violate the assembly practices, for example, he or someone else would point out that it was "not 15-M" (even if the other person were calling it 15-M) and therefore not acceptable. Many other people drawn to the square who may have signed a petition about issues they cared about, or even participated in an assembly, did not remain identified with the movement in the way Carlos did. For Carlos and many other activists in the movement, who embraced the 15-M identity label, that "product" marker in fact reflected a process of collective identity formation that encompassed a "whole way of doing" politics.

The importance of the relationship between logics of action and collective identity is further borne out by survey data on Spain's 15-M movement: One year after the original 2011 protest and occupations of the squares, over 80% of Spaniards agreed or sympathized with the central *demands* of the movement, but not necessarily with their forms of practice. Sympathy with a movement's goals does not necessarily translate into identification with a movement, nor to a sense of belonging to that movement (*pace* McCarthy and Zald's 1977 definition of social movement; see also Oegema and Klandermans 1994).

While social movement scholars have debated many aspects of collective identity, two components whose importance is widely accepted are boundary work and emotions.

Boundary work: a crucial component of collective identity

Just as collective identities are not given but need to be continually reaffirmed and renegotiated, the ability to distinguish the (collective) self from the "other," and to be recognized by those "others" also requires some kind of *boundary work*, which involves creating a reciprocal identification between group members that simultaneously expresses commonalities with and differences from reference groups. Studies analyzing how this boundary work takes place and its implications for sustaining or impeding commitment and movements include Flesher Fominaya (2007b, 2010b, 2016b), William Gamson (1991), Joshua Gamson (1997), Hunt and Benford (2004), Rupp and Taylor (1999), and Taylor and Whittier (1992). Boundary work can take place between movements and their opponents but also between groups within a social movement network (Gamson 1997; Hunt et al. 1994; Saunders 2008). It also takes place *within* movement groups in the process of consolidation (e.g. between more radical or reformist activists in a given group).

Drawing on his participation in anti-Vietnam War activism, Gamson (1991: 42) shows that boundary work and hence collective identity processes do *not* rely on shared issues or a clearly defined movement identity:

> We made sharp distinctions between ... those who were part of the broader movement and those who were not. This was not a distinction based on support vs. opposition to Vietnam policies ...; a collective identity is more cultural than cognitive, demonstrated both by language and symbols, and by other forms of participation in movement actions and culture.

The importance of emotions in collective identity processes

The importance of *emotions and affective ties* in collective identity formation has been noted by numerous scholars (Goodwin, Jasper, and Polletta 2009; Hunt and Benford 2004). My work on collective identity associated with the Global Justice Movement also reveals the importance of positive emotions in maintaining group cohesion and negative emotions in undermining group cohesion, independently of such factors as agreement on movement goals or evaluations by group members of success in meeting those goals (Flesher Fominaya 2007a, 2010b).

Weathering emotionally charged experiences together, such as police brutality or repression (Fantasia 1988; Gamson 1991; Gamson, Fireman, and Rytina 1982), can foster collective identity, increasing solidarity and the willingness to engage in high-risk activism. Affective ties and reciprocal solidarity are also developed through positive shared experiences and emotions (Flesher Fominaya 2007b; Hirsch 1990; Taylor 1989; Whittier 1995), which can build up narratives, memories, and myths that become part of shared movement community lore. Being "in on the joke" can be an important element of collective identity aiding in cohesion but also potentially alienating newcomers who "don't get it" (Flesher Fominaya 2007b). Effectively integrating newcomers paradoxically becomes harder the more cohesive and strong the group identification becomes (Flesher Fominaya 2007b; Saunders 2008).

Assessing the Conceptual Limits of the Concept of Collective Identity

Having established some of the core issues and components of collective identity, I now turn to the issue of whether it is robust enough to stand up to two particularly challenging research areas: (1) autonomous social movements; and (2) the online arena.

Collective identity in autonomous movements

Viewing collective identity through the lens of autonomous movements enables us to test the robustness of the theory in a challenging analytical context, and to highlight how only through adopting a process approach to collective identity can we recognize autonomous movement groups as collective actors.

Unlike movements that are organized clearly around a strong central issue (i.e. nuclear energy) or a strong identity (i.e. Black Power), autonomous movements are characterized by their ideological heterogeneity,[5] commitment to plurality and diversity, and issue and identity multiplicity, posing a challenge for locating the basis of their collective identity. Autonomous activists see the political subject as having multiple overlapping identities. The ideological base of autonomous politics is heterogeneous and frequently not explicit. Ideologies and orthodoxies are seen as rigid and prescriptive, and also tend to divide and exclude, rather than include and increase diversity. In addition, autonomous activists reject formal organizational structures, so an organizational identity (identified by Gamson 1991 as one of three embedded layers of collective identity) may not provide the "glue" that helps explains reciprocal identification. This poses the puzzle of how collective actors can be constituted from a membership base that is ideologically heterogeneous and does not have any other obvious basis for common identification. How can they create cohesion through such diversity?

The second challenge autonomous movements pose is their strong tendency to reject fixed identities or identity markers and labels, which leads to what I have termed the paradox of anti-identitarian collective identity (Flesher Fominaya 2015a). How can you forge a collective identity if you are anti-identitarian?

Finally, the tendency of autonomous groups to reject labeling and clear identity symbols (product identity markers) leads to a form of deliberate "auto-invisibility," which makes it difficult for outside observers to recognize that they are in fact *collective actors*, even in visible mobilizations such as protest events.

Creating cohesion through diversity

A "product" understanding of social movement collective identity runs into limitations when confronted with autonomous movements, such as groups in the Global Justice Movement that had a very diverse ideological and organizational base, leading some scholars to abandon the concept of collective identity entirely (McDonald 2002). Such a "solution," however, contributes little to our understanding of social movements. Instead, the challenge is to understand how it is that social movement actors reciprocally identify with each other as part of a "we" *across* ideological and organizational differences (Flesher Fominaya 2010b; Hunt, Benford, and Snow 1994). Within the autonomous wings of the European Global Justice network, or in the British anti-roads movement, for example, collective identity was forged between actors with heterogeneous identities (biographically given, ideological, and issue-driven) through a common adherence to a series of often non-explicit autonomous principles that underpinned their political spaces, including commitment to diversity and horizontality, consensus decision-making, maintaining autonomy from institutional left actors, and eschewing formal representations (Flesher Fominaya 2010b). Reciprocal identification of shared belonging came about through a *whole way of doing* politics, located in the movement subcultural milieu, rather than common interests, ideologies, or given identities.

The paradox of anti-identitarian collective identity

Although this seems antithetical to what we would expect from the literature on social movements that highlights the strategic orientation of social movement actors who seek recognition from their targets, opponents, or potential supporters (e.g. Bernstein 1997; Gamson 1975), in general, autonomous activists, such as those in the recent Occupy movements around the world, refuse to define and identify themselves organizationally and to establish a visible "product" collective identity. This is reflected in their strong rejection of acronyms, flags, or organizational names appearing in manifestos and protests, a position that reflects ideological principles of non-hierarchy, a rejection of representation and leadership, and autonomy from established institutional actors, such as parties and unions, as well as a strategic desire to avoid creating identifiable targets for repression or co-optation (Flesher Fominaya 2007a, 2010b, 2014; Katsiaficas 1997).

Yet this very refusal *is* in fact a central defining characteristic of autonomous collective identity; it is the key way that autonomous activists recognize each other and establish boundaries of exclusion (and most importantly self-exclusion) from institutional left groups. These boundaries are not established passively but through a great deal of "invisible" hard work: negotiating in assemblies, refusing to participate in assemblies or platforms that are not based on autonomous principles, rectifying minutes and Internet reports, and even stopping high-profile politicians from joining the front of protest marches (Flesher Fominaya 2015a). This anti-identitarian stance has both ideological and strategic roots, and is behind the self-presentation of many Occupy-style movements as movements of "ordinary citizens" rather than organized activists.

Process collective identity renders autonomous movements visible

Melucci argued that the submerged networks of some movements acquire a life of their own, and their impact or importance cannot be reduced to visible mobilization events.

Moving beyond the "myopia of the visible" and viewing collective identity through the lens of autonomous movements offers insights we would not gain if we conflate given and collective identities or see them as necessarily linked, or if we limit our focus to the product or most visible collective identity markers. In short, it highlights that paradoxically, collective identity can be based on a *refusal* to define a collective identity, and on a political approach that systematically refuses to apply identity labels or to organize around primary or organizational identities. Yet these refusals are an active affirmation of an autonomous collective identity, hard as it is to "see," which encompasses "a whole way of doing politics" (Flesher Fominaya 2015a).

Recognizing collective identity at work in autonomous movements, and indeed recognizing autonomous movement groups as collective actors, relies on a process understanding of collective identity formation based on autonomous logics of action that are rarely clearly or explicitly laid out. This also helps explain the relative lack of attention to autonomous social movements in the literature. In the absence of product identity markers and symbols (e.g. A No Nukes Badge, the acronym, name or symbol of an organization or movement, the rainbow flag), it is difficult to identify autonomous collective actors in protest events. Autonomous activists deliberately play with anonymity, and even the rare "product" markers like the Guy Fawkes mask used by Anonymous represent *anonymity*, and the idea that the person wearing the mask could be anybody. Similarly Occupy's "we are the 99%" slogan establishes the broadest possible category for belonging, but does not privilege or identify any particular representative or organization as movement interlocutor. Only through accessing submerged networks and movement cultures can we recognize the way collective identity works to constitute an autonomous collective political actor.

New frontiers in social movement research: collective identity online

If it is difficult to explore collective identity processes in social movements in face-to-face settings, the challenge becomes even greater when we explore collective identity online and its connection to offline and online mobilization and social movement emergence and continuity. As Coleman (2010: 494) notes in relation to digital ethnography, researchers need to contend with "how to collect and represent forms of digital data whose social and material life are often infused with elements of anonymity, modalities of hybermobility, ephemerality, and mutability" (see Chapter 16 by Earl, in this volume, on social media).

The first question that arises is whether or not online "communities" can even be created. Early formulations considered that virtual communication hindered the ability to develop the strong bonds necessary for "real" communities due to factors such as the deception involved in anonymity, lack of self-disclosure, lower levels of intimacy, the "dehumanizing nature" of computers, and the social isolation fostered by impersonal and likely fleeting communication mediated through computers across space and time (e.g. Beniger 1987; Etzioni and Etzioni 1999). Recent research, in contrast, has validated Rheingold's (2000) conception of virtual communities online as spaces in which a wide range of interactions that are emotionally meaningful and that create significant ties are developed (Firer-Blaess 2016; Milan 2015; Treré 2015). Virtual communities therefore can enable the creation of collective identities online.

The second question is whether or not collective identity formed online is meaningful or sufficient as a precondition for *mobilization* online or offline. Understanding the ways the virtual sphere shapes and contributes to collective identities formed online and their relation to political mobilization on and offline requires recognizing that the online/offline are entwined in complex reciprocal feedback processes that integrate multiple forms of communication (internal and external) and media (digital, mass, alternative, citizen, social, and analogue). Various studies have shown how social media use and online discussion groups fostered a strong sense of collective identity that then correlates to offline mobilization (Hara 2008; Harlow 2012; Wojcieszak 2009).

The rise of social media has led to debates over whether this fundamentally changes collective identity formation online in social movements. Milan (2015) argues that social media amplifies the interactive and shared elements of collective identity, generating a politics of visibility in what she terms "cloud protesting." She explicitly contests the arguments set forth by others (e.g. Bennet and Segerberg 2013) that social media have made collective identity processes largely redundant.

Dey's (2016) work on the India Nirbhaya rape mobilizations suggests that social media was crucial in providing an arena where women could come forward with their stories of rape, and that this possibility to be "silent no more" formed a master frame for mobilization that rested on a shared collective identity. These "digital comfort zones" were also noted in the Mexican youth student movement #YoSoy132 (Treré 2015). Drawing on structural and dynamic network analysis of the 15-M movement, Monterde et al. (2015) have demonstrated that complex network systems can be mapped to help understand online movement collective identity processes.

A recognition that digital media use in the virtual sphere is not power-neutral is also crucial, and the important role of moderators and account administrators as power holders, who can work to fragment and exclude as well as coordinate and include, has long been recognized by activists (who debate fiercely over protocols and access) and by scholars (Pickerill 2004) and has implications for collective identity formation, potentially causing group fragmentation, conflict, and exodus (Flesher Fominaya 2016a; Kavada 2009).

Understanding how participants view and emotionally interpret their own experiences of media use and its relation to collective identity is also a crucial arena of study, still in its infancy. In my own work on the impact of email in autonomous groups (Flesher Fominaya 2016a), I showed that despite an explicit commitment to "horizontalism," the use of email in these groups increased existing informal hierarchies, hindered consensus, decreased participation, and worked toward the marginalization of group members, debilitating collective identity.

In reviewing the literature on online collective identity formation and social movements, what is striking is how central and relevant Melucci's (1995) original framework is for contemporary scholarship, from studies of Anonymous (Firer-Blaess 2016) to numerous studies of social media using a range of methodologies (Kavada 2015; Milan 2015; Monterde et al. 2015, Treré 2015). Far from becoming redundant, a new generation of scholars studying the relationship between online and offline mobilization processes have continued to draw on the theoretically rich framework he devised and subsequent work in that tradition.

Conclusion

Collective identity is not a simple concept to apply to social movement analysis. Complex social processes require clear definitions and robust theoretical frameworks that provide analytical clarity.

Understanding how collective identity works in social movements requires reflexivity about theory and method. The insights the application of the concept can yield, however, have important implications for understanding social movement dynamics far beyond identity processes, helping to explain what sustains movements over time, and the crucial role of emotions, affective ties, and solidarity in maintaining commitment.

Most movements provide some clear "product" identity markers that serve as a sort of shorthand with which to easily identify the movement to insiders and outsiders. This is important, as it enables identities to be strategically deployed by activists and recognized by outsiders. However, in order to fully understand the relation between collective identity and social movement processes, a process model is necessary.

Moving away from a presumption that collective identity is necessarily based on commonalities (i.e. shared interests, ideologies, issue salience, etc.) and adopting a process approach allows us to grasp how it is possible for collective identities to be formed across difference and through conflict and offers insights into how and why social movement actors work together, and why they sometimes won't (Flesher Fominaya 2016b). This can help explain alliance structures within networks that might at first glance be counter-intuitive (i.e. why similar issue groups sometimes work together and sometimes compete, or conversely why dissimilar groups form lasting connections across their differences). This does *not* mean that important differences in such things as issue salience, strategy, or ideology cannot lead to fragmentation and excision; they often do. However, collective identity can be generated across significant differences in these and other areas.

The empirical examples in this chapter show that, in order to capture the way collective identity works to define insiders and outsiders and to sustain cohesion in social movements, paying attention to history and culture is important. Collective identity cannot be captured in the meaning of a given symbol, icon, form of action or even slogan, because their meanings can shift, sometimes dramatically, over time. These meanings are subject to debate and contestation within movements, and this very process of reflexivity and contestation through repeated interaction over time can build up a shared history and knowledge that mark insiders from outsiders. New members (like "Carlos" in 15-M) need to be socialized into that history and those meanings in order to truly belong (see also Flesher Fominaya 2007b). History can also be drawn upon strategically to mark insiders from outsiders (Hunt, Benford, and Snow 1994).

A process approach can also reveal the presence of actors who might otherwise be invisible in the absence of clear representatives, organizations, or "product" markers of collective identity. This is because often the factors that constitute reciprocal identification between actors is not clearly visible or explicit. While I have illustrated this point using the "extreme" case of autonomous movements, which provide few of the factors commonly drawn to explain shared membership in a movement (shared issues, identities, ideologies, organizations), these insights echo work done elsewhere. Gamson (1991: 42), for instance, reflects that often, activists are *not* highly reflexive about what makes a "we" a "we" or might not necessarily embrace a clear movement identity, but nevertheless have a shared sense of belonging and a clear recognition of who "we" are and who "they" are. Attention to cultural "logics of action" and whole ways of doing politics can reveal collective identity formation processes that might not be evident if we restrict our gaze to explicitly articulated ideational and identity frames.

Researchers studying movements that draw on a more fluid, elastic, multiple, and porous understanding of identity, and/or that organize in ways that cross space and time in complex mediated environments, can find the attempt to define the boundaries between "us and them," or to recognize collective identity when they see it, *if* they can see it, difficult. Yet, despite some calls to dispense with the concept in the face of these complexities and evolutions (Bennett and Segerberg 2013; McDonald 2002), the rich and expanding body of work on collective identity in social movements by scholars working in even the most challenging research contexts demonstrates the continuing applicability of a theoretical framework robust enough to yield important insights into social movement processes.

Notes

1 Anonymous is a hacktivist movement that organizes primarily online. For more on collective identity formation in Anonymous, see Firer-Blaess (2016).
2 Spain's 15-M movement, known outside Spain as the Indignados movement, was a key actor in the recent global wave of Occupy-style protests against austerity and bank bailouts in the wake of the financial crisis. Demanding "Real Democracy Now" is at the heart of the movement. For more, see Flesher Fominaya (2014, 2015b).
3 Social psychological approaches emphasize the degree to which individuals identify with groups, and how the strength of group identification increases willingness to protest on behalf of that group, see van Stekelenburg (2013).
4 From the author's field research conducted between 2013–2015 in Madrid on Spain's 15-M movement.
5 An example of ideological heterogeneity in autonomous movements would be the Global Justice Movement. In Madrid's autonomous global justice network, groups encompassed individuals holding anarchist, communist, environmentalist, feminist, and lay Christian ideologies, among others. For more on ideological heterogeneity in autonomous movements, see Flesher Fominaya (2010b).

References

Beniger, James. 1987. "Personalization of Mass Media and the Growth of Pseudo-community." *Communication Research* 14: 352–371.

Bennett, W. Lance and Alexandra Segerberg. 2013. *The Logic of Connective Action: Digital Media and the Personalization of Contentious Politics*. Cambridge: Cambridge University Press.

Bernstein, Mary. 1997. "Celebration and Suppression: The Strategic Uses of Identity by the Lesbian and Gay Movement." *American Journal of Sociology* 103(3): 531–565.

Buechler, Stephen. 2000. *Social Movements in Advanced Capitalism*. Oxford: Oxford University Press.

Coleman, Gabriella. 2010. "Ethnographic Approaches to Digital Media." *Annual Review of Anthropology* 39: 487–505.

Dey, Adrija. 2016. "'Silence No More': An In-Depth Cyberconflict Analysis of the Nirbhaya Rape Case and Digital Gender Activism in India." Unpublished PhD dissertation, University of Hull.

Etzioni, Amitai and Oren Etzioni. 1999. "Face-to-face and Computer-mediated Communities: A Comparative Analysis." *The Information Society* 15: 241–248.

Fantasia, Rick. 1988. *Cultures of Solidarity*. Berkeley: University of California Press.

Firer-Blaess, Sylvain. 2016. *The Collective Identity of Anonymous: Web of Meanings in a Digitally Enabled Movement*. Uppsala Studies in Media and Communication, 12. Uppsala: Acta Universitatis Upsaliensis.

Flesher Fominaya, Cristina. 2007a. "Autonomous Movement and the Institutional Left: Two Approaches in Tension in Madrid's Anti-Globalization Network." *South European Society & Politics* 12(3): 335–358.

Flesher Fominaya, Cristina. 2007b. "The Role of Humour in the Process of Collective Identity Formation in Autonomous Social Movement Groups in Contemporary Madrid." *International Review of Social History* 52(15): 243–258.

Flesher Fominaya, Cristina. 2010a. "Collective Identity in Social Movements: Central Concepts and Debates." *Sociology Compass* 4(6): 393–404.

Flesher Fominaya, Cristina. 2010b. "Creating Cohesion from Diversity: The Challenge of Collective Identity Formation in the Global Justice Movement." *Sociological Inquiry* 80(3). 377–404.

Flesher Fominaya, Cristina. 2014. *Social Movements and Globalization: How Protests, Occupations and Uprisings Are Changing the World*. Basingstoke: Palgrave Macmillan.

Flesher Fominaya, Cristina. 2015a. "Autonomous Social Movements and the Paradox of Anti-Identitarian Collective Identity." In *The Identity Dilemma*, edited by Aidan McGarry and James M. Jasper, 65–84. Philadelphia, PA: Temple University Press.

Flesher Fominaya, Cristina. 2015b. "Debunking Spontaneity: Spain's 15-M/Indignados as Autonomous Movement." *Social Movement Studies* 14(2): 142–163.

Flesher Fominaya, Cristina. 2016a. "Unintended Consequences: The Negative Impact of E-Mail Use on Participation and Collective Identity in Two 'Horizontal' Social Movement Groups." *European Political Science Review* 8(01): 95–122.

Flesher Fominaya, Cristina. 2016b. "Cultural Barriers to Activist Networking: Habitus (In) action in Three European Transnational Encounters." *Antipode* 48(1): 151–171.

Friedman, Debra and Doug McAdam. 1992. "Collective Identity and Activism: Networks, Choices, and the Life of a Social Movement." In *Frontiers in Social Movement Theory*, edited by Aldon Morris and Carol Mueller, 273–297. New Haven, CT: Yale University Press.

Gamson, Joshua. 1997. "Messages of Exclusion: Gender, Movements, and Symbolic Boundaries." *Gender and Society* 11(2): 178–199.

Gamson, William. 1975. *The Strategy of Social Protest*. Belmont, CA: Wadsworth Publishing.

Gamson, William. 1991. "Commitment and Agency in Social Movements." *Sociological Forum* 6(1): 27–50.

Gamson, William A., Bruce Fireman, and Steven Rytina. 1982. *Encounters with Unjust Authority*. Homewood IL: Dorsey Press.

Goodwin, Jeff and James M. Jasper. 2003. *The Social Movements Reader: Cases and Concepts*. Malden, MA: Blackwell.

Goodwin, Jeff, James M. Jasper, and Francesca Polletta, eds. 2009. *Passionate Politics: Emotions and Social Movements*. Chicago: University of Chicago Press.

Granovetter, Mark. 1978. "Threshold Models of Collective Behavior." *American Journal of Sociology* 1: 1420–1443.

Hara, Noriko. 2008. "Internet Use for Political Mobilization: Voices of Participants." *First Monday* 13(7).

Harlow, Summer. 2012. "Social Media and Social Movements: Facebook and an Online Guatemalan Justice Movement that Moved Offline." *New Media & Society* 14(2): 225–243.

Hirsch, Eric. 1990. "Sacrifice for the Cause: Group Processes, Recruitment, and Commitment in a Student Social Movement." *American Sociological Review* 55(2): 243–254.

Hunt, Stephen and Robert D. Benford. 2004. "Collective Identity, Solidarity, and Commitment." In *The Blackwell Companion to Social Movements*, edited by David A. Snow, Sarah A. Soule, and Hanspeter Kriesi, 433–460. Oxford: Blackwell.

Hunt, Stephen, Robert D. Benford, and David A. Snow. 1994. "Identity Fields: Framing Processes and the Social Construction of Movement Identities." In *New Social Movements: From Ideology to Identity*, edited by Enrique Laraña, Hank Johnston, and Joseph R. Gusfield, 185–208. Philadelphia, PA: Temple University Press.

Katsiaficas, George. 1997. *The Subversion of Politics: European Autonomous Movements and the Decolonization of Everyday Life*. Atlantic Highlands, NJ: Humanities Press.

Kavada, Anastasia. 2009. "Email Lists and the Construction of an Open and Multifaceted Identity: The Case of the London 2004 European Social Forum." *Information, Communication & Society* 12: 817–839.

Kavada, Anastasia. 2015. "Creating the Collective: Social Media, The Occupy Movement and its Constitution as a Collective Actor." *Information, Communication & Society* 18(8): 872–886.

McAdam, Doug. 1982. *Political Process and the Development of Black Insurgency, 1930–1970*. Chicago: University of Chicago Press.

McCarthy, John D. and Mayer N. Zald. 1977. "Resource Mobilization and Social Movements: A Partial Theory." *American Journal of Sociology* 82(6): 1212–1241.

McDonald, Kevin. 2002. "From Solidarity to Fluidarity: Social Movements Beyond Collective Identity: The Case of Globalization Conflicts." *Social Movement Studies* 1(2): 109–128.

Melucci, Alberto. 1995. "The Process of Collective Identity." In *Social Movements and Culture*, edited by Hank Johnston and Bert Klandermans, 41–63. Minneapolis: University of Minnesota Press.

Milan, Stephania. 2015. "From Social Movements to Cloud Protesting: The Evolution of Collective Identity." *Information, Communication & Society* 18(8): 887–900.

Monterde, Arnau, Antonio Calleja-López, Miguel Aguilera, Xavier Barandiaran, and John Postill. 2015. "Multitudinous Identities: A Qualitative and Network Analysis of the 15M Collective Identity." *Information, Communication & Society* 18(8): 930–950.

Oberschall, Anthony. 1995. *Social Movements: Ideologies, Interests, and Identities*. New Brunswick, NJ: Transaction Publishers.

Oegema, Dirk and Bert Klandermans. 1994. "Why Social Movement Sympathizers Don't Participate: Erosion and Nonconversion of Support." *American Sociological Review* 59(5): 703–722.

Pickerill, Jenny. 2004. "Rethinking Political Participation: Experiments in Internet Activism in Britain and Australia." In *Electronic Democracy: Mobilisation, Organisation and Participation Via New ICTs*, edited by Rachel Gibson, Andrea Rommele, and Steven Ward, 170–193. London: Routledge.

Polletta, Francesca and James M. Jasper. 2001. "Collective Identity and Social Movements." *Annual Review of Sociology* 27: 283–305.

Rheingold, Howard. 2000. *The Virtual Community: Homesteading on the Electronic Frontier*. Cambridge, MA: MIT Press.

Rupp, Leila and Verta Taylor. 1999. "Feminist Identity in an International Movement: A Collective Identity Approach to 20th-Century Feminism." *Signs* 24: 363–386.

Saunders, Clare. 2008. "Double-edged Swords? Collective Identity and Solidarity in the Environment Movement." *British Journal of Sociology* 59(2): 227–253.

Snow, David A. and Catherine Corrigall-Brown. 2015. "Collective Identity." In *International Encyclopedia of Social and Behavioral Sciences*, 2nd edn, edited by James Wright, 174–179. Oxford: Elsevier.

Snow, David A. and Doug McAdam. 2000. "Identity Work Processes in the Context of Social Movements: Clarifying the Identity/Movement Nexus." In *Self, Identity, and Social Movements*, edited by Sheldon Stryker, Timothy Owens, and Robert White, 41–67. Minneapolis: University of Minnesota Press.

Tarrow, Sidney. 1989. *Struggle, Politics, and Reform: Collective Action, Social Movements and Cycles of Protest*. Ithaca, NY: Center for International Studies, Cornell University.

Taylor, Verta. 1989. "Social Movement Continuity: The Women's Movement in Abeyance." *American Sociological Review* 54(5): 761–775.

Taylor, Verta and Nancy Whittier. 1992. "Collective Identity in Social Movement Communities: Lesbian Feminist Mobilization." In *Frontiers in Social Movement Theory*, edited by Aldon Morris and Carol Mueller, 104–129. New Haven, CT: Yale University Press.

Treré, Emilianio. 2015. "Reclaiming, Proclaiming, and Maintaining Collective Identity in the #Yosoy132 Movement in Mexico: An Examination of Digital Frontstage and Backstage Activism through Social Media and Instant Messaging Platforms." *Information, Communication & Society* 18(8): 901–915.

van Stekelenburg, Jacquelien. 2013. 'Collective Identity.' In *The Blackwell Encyclopedia of Social and Political Movements*, edited by David A. Snow, Donatella della Porta, Bert Klandermans, and Doug McAdam, 219–226. Oxford: Blackwell.

Whittier, Nancy. 1995. *Feminist Generations: The Persistence of the Radical Women's Movement*. Philadelphia, PA: Temple University Press.

Wojcieszak, Magdalena. 2009. "Carrying Online Participation Offline: Mobilization by Radical Online Groups and Politically Dissimilar Offline Ties." *Journal of Communication* 59: 564–586.

Zald, Mayer N. 2000. "Ideologically Structured Action: An Enlarged Agenda for Social Movement Research." *Mobilization* 5(1): 1–16.

Part V
Consequences and Outcomes

25

The Political Institutions, Processes, and Outcomes Movements Seek to Influence

Edwin Amenta, Kenneth T. Andrews, and Neal Caren

Introduction

People participate in social movements and scholars study them at least in part because they think movements may effect social and political change, by influencing institutions like states, economies, families, universities, or religious organizations. Many movements seek to influence political institutions, processes, and outcomes – which is our subject here – but political institutions, like the others, are external to movements and shape movements in many important ways (Amenta 2014; Snow and Soule 2010). Unlike some chapters in this volume, movement mobilization, strategies, and action are potential causal forces in this one, rather than phenomena to be explained. However, because movements typically represent those lacking in power, they are not likely to be dominant causal forces. This is especially true in contexts in which very powerful actors are contending, as is usually the case with states and politics.

Prominent scholars such as Skocpol (2003) and Giugni (2009) argue that movements do not typically matter much in politics. In the extensive literatures on democratization, bureaucratization, political parties, elections, court decision-making, and legislative processes and public policy-making, movements receive limited consideration. And although some scholars, including Gilens and Page (2014) and Hacker and Pierson (2010), argue that organizations matter in US political decision-making, they highlight business-oriented ones, not public-interested advocacy organizations or social movement ones. Also, historically the largest and most influential US movement, the labor movement, has been routed, is on the run elsewhere, and has not been replaced by anything comparable (Sano and Williamson 2008).

The Wiley Blackwell Companion to Social Movements, Second Edition. Edited by David A. Snow, Sarah A. Soule, Hanspeter Kriesi, and Holly J. McCammon.
© 2019 John Wiley & Sons Ltd. Published 2019 by John Wiley & Sons Ltd.

All the same, other scholars, such as Piven (2006) and Baumgartner and Mahoney (2005), argue that movements and related advocacy organizations have mattered quite a bit in politics. Specific movements have been found to be highly influential in some important political processes and policy outcomes (review in Amenta et al. 2010), and provided a necessary motive force behind crucial policy advances as varied as Social Security and civil rights. The case for strong movement influence is aided by the finding that policies and other political changes once enacted are often self-perpetuating, and so even a short-term influence by movements may have a long-run effect (Pierson 2000). In some countries, moreover, labor movements created political parties, took political power, and enacted policies in favor of their constituents (e.g. Huber and Stephens 2001). Even in the United States, where no labor or socialist party ever formed, the labor movement became a key player in the Democratic Party (Amenta 1998; Schickler 2016; Schlozman 2015).

The literature on the political influence of movements has grown tremendously since the previous edition of this handbook (Amenta et al. 2010; Uba 2009). In this chapter, we review key arguments and findings, highlight promising new developments, and connect scholarship on movement influence over political institutions, processes, and outcomes with the academic literatures surrounding them. We limit our attention to movements and politics in democracies and partial democracies, bypassing revolutions and protest in autocracies (but see Chapter 38 by Chen and Moss, and Chapter 39 by Goldstone and Ritter, in this volume) – partly because most of the research is on democracies, but mainly because the determinants of movement influence likely differ between democracies and autocracies. Also, although movements target many other institutions than political ones, our focus here is on movements that target states. We first examine what it means for movements to be influential in politics, including such processes and outcomes as democratization, elections, public opinion, and policy-making and in venues such as legislative bodies, political parties, administrative bureaucracies, and courts. We then discuss where scholarship has advanced. From there we review theoretical pathways to influence for challengers. We conclude with a suggested agenda for research that seeks greater connection between the literatures on social movements and on political institutions.

The Political Institutions, Processes, and Outcomes Movements Seek to Influence

We focus on all movements that are politically oriented in some fashion. We define such movements as actors and organizations seeking to alter power deficits and to effect social transformations through states and governments by mobilizing regular citizens for sustained political action (Amenta and Young 1999; Amenta et al. 2010). The definition focuses on McCarthy and Zald's (1977) social movement organizations and related advocacy organizations (Andrews and Edwards 2004) that can be combined into movements or movement families. We include all the political collective action of movements, both extra-institutional action and institutional action, like lobbying, lawsuits, and press conferences. Our definition excludes "interest groups" based on businesses and professionals, such as the Chamber of

Commerce and the American Medical Association, whose constituents are not facing political power deficits and are seen as members of the polity (Amenta and Young 1999; Hojnacki et al. 2012).

In initial discussions of the political influence of movements, scholars focused broadly on "concessions," "success" and "failure," and "collective benefits." Concessions, as discussed by Lipsky (1968) and Piven and Cloward (1977), include anything granted by a target to a challenger. In Gamson's formulation, success involves whether targets provided "new advantages" to organized challengers by acting on their goals or by "accepting" them as legitimate, with failure meaning not achieving new advantages or acceptance (Gamson 1990). As advanced by Amenta and Young (1999), collective benefits are group-wise advantages or disadvantages for movement constituencies from which non-participants cannot easily be excluded. Although most of the demands of movement actors include such collective benefits, the collective benefit standard takes into account that a challenger can have considerable impact even when it fails to achieve its goals, that successful challengers could have negligible consequences, and that their actions might cause "collective bads" (Agnone 2007; Amenta and Young 1999; Andrews 2004), such as repression (Piven and Cloward 1977), electoral losses (McAdam and Kloos 2014), or policy setbacks (Pierson 2000). In addition, there are many political outcomes that are relevant to movements' goals and constituents, but to which movement actors have paid little attention, given their limited power and resources.

These definitions are valuable for analyzing the influence of movements in politics, but are best applied in confronting the specific features and standard determinants of the institutions they seek to change. That means removing movements from the center of analysis, as McAdam and Boudet (2012) have recently suggested, and focusing on three basic possibilities for movement influence identified by Giugni (2009): (1) movements can influence the main determinants of political institutions and outcomes; (2) movements change the relationship between these determinants and both political institutions and outcomes; or (3) movements provide separate pathways to influence over these institutions and outcomes. To take the example of policy change: Movements might influence public opinion in favor of policy changes or influence elections, each of which in turn might effect a change in policy. Alternatively, movement action may influence the positive relationship between partisan governments and policy enactments, by moving an issue higher on the political agenda. Finally, movements might bypass standard institutional actors, for instance, by way of initiatives or referendums and enact laws, or simply induce political actors to grant concessions due to protest. Included among the political institutions, processes, and outcomes of interest to movements are democratization, political parties, elections and candidates, legislative processes and policy, courts, and bureaucracies. None of these should be called the political consequences or outcomes of movements, given that there are so many other causal influences on them, but are important aspects of politics that movements often target and may influence.

The greatest potential political influences for movements are at the structural or system level and center on democratization (Amenta et al. 2010), which provides challengers continuous leverage over political processes and increases the political returns to their collective action, as Tilly indicated (1999). It is no surprise that the right to vote has been sought by workers, women, African Americans, and others denied it (Andrews 1997; Banaszak 1996; McAdam 1982; McCammon et al. 2001; Rueschemeyer, Stephens, and Stephens 1992). Even once a polity is democratized, these struggles typically continue, as, for instance, in the United States, with battles over felon disfranchisement (Manza and Uggen 2008). However, some important systemic features of democratic polities are less susceptible to change and are rarely targeted, including whether the system is presidential or parliamentarian and its division of authority across functions or territories. Notably, polities with many "veto points" (Immergut 2010) provide difficult terrain for movements and others seeking political change.

Another structural transformation that can provide enduring influence is for a movement to create its own political party, as Goldstone (2003) and Schwartz (2006) among others have argued. For example, labor, green, new left, and anti-immigration parties have appeared in democratic polities (Kitschelt 1986; Kriesi et al. 1995), though in the US polity there have been no permanent movement parties. A movement can also establish an alliance to a catchall party, such as those between the US labor, civil rights, feminist, and abortion rights movements and the Democratic Party or the Christian right, anti-abortion, anti-tax, and the gun rights movements and the Republican Party (Amenta 1998; Fetner 2008; Halfmann 2011; Schickler 2016; Schlozman 2015). Movements can also influence party programs and platforms (Schickler 2016), though not all parties are as susceptible to such influence as US parties (Halfmann 2011). Because policies are typically made by elected officials, or by courts or government bureaucrats, movements also frequently attempt to intervene in elections (McAdam and Tarrow 2010). Movement actors who do not ally with parties may also target individual candidates according to their voting records or campaign promises (Amenta 2006; McVeigh 2009).

These structural and electoral circumstances in turn influence policy-making, which is at the center of politics, of key interest to social movement actors, and the subject of most studies of the political influence of movements (Amenta et al. 2010; Uba 2009). Policies are authoritative lines of action in which states provide goods, protections, and freedoms recurrently to specified groups in a routine fashion to all those meeting specified requirements (Htun and Weldon 2012; Skocpol and Amenta 1986). Such policies then can also regulate and legitimate social actors. Policies can include everything from symbolic gestures to more fundamental changes, such as the right to marry whom one chooses or not to be discriminated against in the workplace and the extensive benefits in programs like Social Security or Medicare. Through policy, states can also ratify or attempt to undermine identity claims (Amenta and Young 1999), ranging from gaining more respectful labels in governmental representations to defining racial categories.

A movement's influence over policy may happen in the short run, but can have long-term consequences, because policies can become self-perpetuating by way of positive feedback effects (Pierson 2000). Moreover, movements and other actors seeking to prevent the adoption of new policies, such as NIMBY movements, have an easier task than those seeking positive changes. Regulatory bureaucracies may make policy decisions without new legislation, and they often also propose legislation (Amenta 1998; Skrentny 2006), and so movement actors can gain influence by staffing or influencing these agencies (Banaszak 2010). In some divided polities, like the US polity, courts can both make and veto policy, and so movement actors can engage in litigation to uphold or overturn laws, as in abortion rights (Halfmann 2011) or in recent marriage equality battles (see also Chapter 17 by Boutcher and McCammon, in this volume).

However, most policy-making happens through legislative processes, which can be divided into parts, including agenda-setting, legislative content, passage, and implementation (Amenta and Young 1999; Andrews and Edwards 2004) and movements have sought to influence each. Much scholarship has shown that protest is most influential at earlier stages such as agenda-setting (Andrews 2001; Johnson 2008; King, Cornwall, and Dahlin 2005; Olzak and Soule 2009; Soule and King 2006). But movement actors can work to make the content of legislation more favorable (Amenta 2006; Bernstein 2001), influence individual legislators to vote for it (Amenta, Caren, and Olasky 2005; Heaney and Rojas 2015), and help to secure its implementation (Andrews and Edwards 2004). We assess research on movement influence on these different institutions and processes below.

Under Which Conditions Do Movements Matter in Politics?

It is not possible to answer whether movements have been highly or mainly influential in politics. That would require an examination of all political outcomes of importance to movements, arraying them in a priority order, and then assessing movement influence over them – an impossible task. The literature on the political consequences of movements, extensive as it is, has been far more modest. It has focused on case studies of the influence of prominent individual movements or organizations on specific policies and policy processes, typically involving the US case. Scholars have generally found movements to be influential in such research, but selection issues make it difficult to generalize. These studies are typically of larger movements, often at their peak of mobilization, focusing on issues they are explicitly contesting (Amenta et al. 2010; Uba 2009). However, there are many relevant political issues and outcomes for which there is mobilization but little political change or simply little mobilization at all (Burstein and Sausner 2005). In addition, journals rarely publish studies about the influence of movements if they show no influence. In perhaps most studies of democratization, political party formation, and policy-making, scholars do not address movements at all or only in a minor way.

The initial question that scholars studying the political consequences of movements must consider is whether movements matter and the forms and strategies of movement actors that might increase the likelihood of influence. The earliest debates in the field considered whether movements were influential at all and whether organization (Gamson 1990) or disruption (Piven and Cloward 1977) was more likely to yield results. Since then scholars have developed stronger explanations by engaging alternative theoretical perspectives that account for the broader range of actors and influences on politics. Moreover, scholars have paid increasing attention to the specific conditions under which movements matter and the interactions between movements, various other interested actors, the characteristics of targets and political institutions, and the contexts in which they engage (Amenta et al. 2010; Uba 2009).

Organization, protest, collective action and strategy

We begin by considering movement forms and strategies that may improve the chances of movements being influential. The main factors hypothesized to increase the likelihood of impact are the amount and forms of mobilization and the various strategies movements may employ. The best work in this tradition has specified the theoretical mechanisms by which movements can matter, engaged relevant alternative explanations, and considered the conditions under which movements are more or less consequential.

Many scholars point to formal organization as critical for providing movement's leverage in politics. The most typical theoretical argument is that formal organization facilitates political influence by concentrating resources, institutionalizing movement claims, and participating in routine bargaining processes. Thus, as Andrews argues, access and negotiation are two of the critical mechanisms of movement influence in politics (Andrews 2001; Andrews and Edwards 2004). For example, some movement organizations come to occupy prominent positions in the interest group sector, form or become central to political parties, or participate in broader political coalitions. Many studies point to the significance of movement organizations. Johnson, Agnone, and McCarthy (2010) show that the growth of environmental movement organizations increased the number of Congressional hearings from 1961 to 1990. Best's (2012) study of advocacy on behalf of disease and medical research shows that advocates secured greater federal funds on behalf of their cause and had a systemic effect by shifting the criteria from scientific ones to those linked to advocates' criteria of worthiness (e.g. dollars per death). Most often, scholars have measured movement organization in terms of organizational resources (e.g. members, funds) or organizational density.

Scholars also focus on collective action, especially protest, as a potential source of influence, with disruption as the main mechanism of movement influence (Piven and Cloward 1977). For example, Luders (2010) indicates ways that civil rights activists sought to impose disruption costs on targets. Andrews and Gaby (2015) find that federal attention to civil rights protest was concerned primarily with disruption. Santoro (2002, 2008) shows a positive impact of black protest on the comprehensiveness of fair employment and voting rights policy. However, Olzak and Soule (2009) find that environmental protest had little impact on congressional attention, although the number of environmental organizations did. Movement protest and activity may matter for reasons beyond disruption. Much protest is not very disruptive and focuses on signaling a broad base of support for a set of claims. The political significance of this kind of collective action may depend on its ability to capture public attention, make persuasive claims, and facilitate organization building. For example, Madestam et al. (2013) show that Tea Party protests spurred local organization building and support for Tea Party candidates in congressional elections.

Some scholars focus on routes to influence through activists holding elected office or as state bureaucrats. For example, Santoro and McGuire (1997) show that "institutional activists" – state officials who are part of a broader social movement – were critical to the passage of US state-level comparable worth policies. Similarly, Böhm (2015) examines the German antinuclear movement showing that activists were able to influence the closing of nuclear power plants by electoral successes at the regional and federal level. Banaszak (2010) traces the ways that feminists inside federal agencies played a critical role in institutionalizing and extending the gains of second-wave feminism by working "inside" the state and lending support to advocacy "outside" the state as well.

These debates are connected to larger questions about the influence of movement strategy (Ganz 2000; Jasper 2004). Because movements operate in complex and changing contexts, some scholars argue that greater attention should be paid to movement leadership and the conditions under which leaders are better able to develop effective strategies (Andrews et al. 2010; Ganz 2000; McCammon 2012). Instead of the amount of organizational resources or the number of protest events, work in this tradition focuses more closely on why some movements are able to devise strategies that are appropriate for particular targets or political settings. Strategy may be enhanced by greater diversity at the movement level with organizations that can deploy multiple tactics (Andrews 2004; Olzak and Ryo 2007). Ganz (2000) argues that organizations with more diverse leaders and deliberative leadership practices may outperform more established organizations. Similarly, McCammon (2012) argues that women's jury rights movements that adapted to political circumstances (including setbacks) secured political victories earlier. Along these lines, scholars have also considered the influence of framing strategies. In their study of 15 homeless social movement organizations, Cress and Snow (2000) point to resonant diagnostic and prognostic frames as critical for multiple outcomes. McCammon (2009) argues that women's jury activists were better able to persuade legislators with frames that emphasized the breadth of the problem, provided a rationale for supporting the movement, and offered credible evidence to support the frame.

Political contexts and political mediation

Other scholars focus on the causal importance of the political contexts in which movements engage. The earliest such claims hold that, once movements were mobilized, their influence depended on a favorable political context, notably "open" states with "strong" administrative capacities (Kitschelt 1986; Kriesi et al. 1995). But within any country, movement influence varies over time (Amenta et al. 2002) and a state's bureaucratic capacities to grant policy demands vary by issue (Giugni 2004). Instead, others focus on more short-term influences, such as partisanship within the government (Meyer and Minkoff 2004) or changes in public opinion (Giugni 2007). Some scholars warn, however, that the sorts of political contexts that spurred mobilization, such as the rise to power of left-wing regime for a left-wing movement (Amenta and Caren 2004) or a change in public opinion (Burstein and Linton 2002), might be responsible for political outcomes erroneously attributed to the influence of movements. Yet others (Cornwall et al. 2007) find that political contexts that aid mobilization do not promote movement influence.

This concern with political contexts led to scholars formulating models that specify the mediated or joint effects of movements' mobilization and collective action and political contexts on policies and other political outcomes (Amenta 2006). These arguments include Piven and Cloward's (1977) claim that mass disruption works best in situations of electoral volatility and Skocpol's (1992) claim that, to be politically influential in the divided US polity, movement and advocacy organizations needed to mobilize across the country.

Political mediation models take mobilization and plausible framing as necessary conditions to influence, but also hold that challengers' action is more likely to produce results when institutional political actors see a benefit in aiding the group the challenger represents (Almeida and Stearns 1998; Kane 2003). To secure political benefits, challengers will typically need to engage in collective action that influences the thinking and action of state actors. For a movement to be influential, state actors need to see it as potentially facilitating or disrupting their own goals – augmenting or cementing new electoral coalitions, gaining in public opinion, increasing the support for the missions of governmental bureaus. More generally, the political mediation argument holds that challengers need to alter strategies and forms to address specific political contexts (Amenta 2006; Amenta, Caren, and Olasky 2005).

Political mediation models tend to focus on "assertive" political strategies, which involve sanctions beyond disruptive or symbolic protest (Lipsky 1968) or providing information about policy preferences (Lohmann 1993). The political collective action of challengers works by demonstrating that a significant segment of the electorate cares strongly about an issue, usually with a policy preference outside the mainstream of political discussion. These assertive strategies include electioneering (seeking to punish political opponents and aid friends, or influencing party platforms), litigating in the courts, legislating new laws, and demanding the implementation of existing laws through direct action (Amenta 2006). Achieving changes in public policy using assertive means is likely to be more difficult, however, without a supportive political regime or administrative authority.

Several lines of research support these claims (see review in Amenta et al. 2010). Martin (2013) finds that anti-tax campaigns had greater impacts when the US political system was dominated by conservatives. Andrews (2004) finds that local movements had much greater influence over federal civil rights policies that provided institutional mechanisms for movement input (e.g. poverty programs) than those that did not (e.g. school desegregation). Research findings that a diversity of tactics or organizational types at the movement level produce political gains are consistent with these claims (Johnson 2008; Olzak and Ryo 2007). Some research that finds little effect of movements on policy also supports joint-effects models. Skrentny (2006) finds that white ethnic groups sought to gain affirmative action benefits, but failed because policy-makers rejected their claims. Moreover, in structurally unfavorable political contexts, where a group's democratic rights are greatly restricted (Amenta 2006), influence over progressive policy may be extremely difficult to achieve, even when groups are mobilized. More generally, certain issues and policies may be very difficult for movements to influence, including policies closely tied to the national cleavage structure, for which high levels of political or material resources are at stake, for instance, regarding military matters, or on which public opinion is very strong (Burstein and Sausner 2005; Giugni 2004; Kriesi et al. 1995).

Some "joint effects" political mediation arguments hold that several factors must coincide to effect extensive change (Amenta 2006; Amenta, Caren, and Olasky 2005; Giugni 2007; McAdam and Su 2002). In the US setting, a national challenger with far-reaching goals is likely to need a favorable partisan context, its issue already on the agenda, high challenger organization and mobilization, credible claims-making directed at elites and the general public, and assertive action (Amenta 2006; Amenta, Caren and Olasky 2005). McAdam and Boudet (2012) find that a lack of mobilization against fracking projects in a community was sufficient to explain approval of the projects, but project rejection depended on a series of jointly occurring conditions, including other political opposition and intergovernmental conflict. The same is likely to be true for bids to transform the structural position of groups, such as through voting or civil rights. Luders (2010) argues that key civil rights legislation depended on several coinciding conditions: events by the movement that focused national attention on civil rights and brought sympathy for their demands, the electoral leverage of African Americans on northern legislators, as well as no counter-mobilization in the North from businesses or the grassroots. Others argue that public opinion must also be favorable (Giugni 2007; Olzak and Soule 2009).

What Is Studied and How

As these examples indicate, most research has been about policy, and there are reasons for this focus, aside from the fact that policies matter. Policies benefit from extensive documentation, can be divided into several processes, including introduction, votes for enactment, and implementation, and policies can be analyzed according to how many people benefit and how much is spent on them. Most of all, policies are also advantageous for study because of a well-established causal literature. The literature on the political consequences of movements has largely taken advantage of this fact, making claims about the influence of movements at various parts of the process and theorizing joint effects of movement influence with known determinants of policy outcomes. However, because most work has focused on policy change, we have less developed theories regarding the possible influence of movements on other state-related consequences.

This policy focus is particularly prominent at the subnational level. At the local level, scholars typically examine the role of movements in influencing municipalities to adopt favorable policies. For example, Vasi et al. (2015) found that showing an anti-fracking documentary as part of an environmental campaign increased the probability of subsequent mobilizations, which has a statistically significant effect on the likelihood that a city passes anti-fracking legislation. Looking beyond movement organizations, Negro, Perretti, and Carroll (2013) examined the relationship between the size and diversity of gay-friendly business and anti-discrimination legislation. In a notable exception to focusing on a policy outcome, Coe (2013) explored the determinants of subnational bureaucrats' attitudes toward feminist issues in Peru. One significant limitation for scholars interested in municipal research is the limited nature of good political contextual variables, such as partisan control, and the overall paucity of information about municipal policies. Social movement scholars examining local politics should engage the broader scholarship on city politics and urban sociology.

Research at the US state level has also primarily explored the determinants of policy adoption. This work generally looks across states to explain the relative success of a single movement. Parris and Scheuerman (2015), for example, used hazard models to explore the impact of movement presence on hate crime legislation.

Amenta, Caren, and Olasky (2005) examined the movement and other influences on the generosity of old-age programs.

In contrast to the local and state-level research, national-level work has explored a much richer variety of political consequences, from structural transformation of the state (Trevizo 2011) to executive action (Bloom 2015), to policy funding (Best 2012), to legislative attention (King, Bentele, and Soule 2007), and to the fate of individual bills (Burstein 2014). Work at the national level is also much more likely to study the impact of movements on intermediate processes for state influence, such as public opinion (Banaszak and Ondercin 2016), voter choice (Arzheimer 2009), and partisan alignments (McVeigh, Cunningham, and Farrell 2014). As noted, much research focuses on the influence of movements early in the policy process. For example, Johnson, Agnone, and McCarthy (2010) found that while any type of US environmental movement activity is associated with an increase in hearings, law passage is the result of complex interactions between movements and political actors. Likewise, Walgrave and Vliegenthart (2012) found that protest influence in Belgium on legislative action varied by not only protest characteristics, but also by media coverage and issue type.

All the same, this literature faces several methodological challenges that can hinder cumulative knowledge. The first is that analyses are typically case studies of a single movement in one country, leading to a lack of comparability across contexts. It is difficult to gain relevant information on movements comparatively, and scholars have to resort to relatively thin measures of movement characteristics when examining a large number of countries. A second challenge is that some designs are better equipped to test alternative explanations, including the possibility of mediated or joint effects. Data availability is an important consideration here as well. At the national level and in some countries, there are rich and systematic data sources for quantitative analysis and extensive archival materials available to scholars, but data to gauge relevant causal factors is much sparser in historical, cross-national, and some sub-national political units. A third challenge is that when movements seek influence over policy, their opponents can vary greatly in their capacity and form, including in terms of counter-movements, political parties, and state actors. This makes identifying the causal influence of movement factors difficult.

We see several promising methodological directions developing in the literature, however. First, several recent studies have developed much stronger quantitative tests of movement influence, such as the use of fixed effect and instrumental variable models and attention to temporal heterogeneity of movement influence (Biggs and Andrews 2015; Madestam et al. 2013; McVeigh, Cunningham, and Farrell 2014). Second, although most research remains focused on agenda-setting and policy adoption, there is an increasing number of studies that examine a broader range of outcomes related to policy and other political consequences, such as policy implementation or systemic effects in policy domains (Andrews 2001; Best 2012). Third, the field has moved toward greater attention to causal mechanisms, such as the relative importance of disruption or persuasion (Andrews 2001; Luders 2010). Fourth, we have also seen some expansion in the range of movements under investigation, including conservative social movements (Johnson, Scheitle, and Ecklund 2016; McVeigh, Cunningham, and Farrell 2014; McVeigh, Myers, and Sikkink 2004; Steil and Vasi 2014), and extending this breadth further is much needed.

Finally, there are also a handful of cross-national studies (Halfmann 2011; Htun and Weldon 2012; Kadivar and Caren 2016; Schofer and Hironaka 2005) that provide potential models for scholars.

Conclusion

Much progress has been made in the study of the political consequences of social movements, probably more so than in other areas surrounding the influence of movements, such as biographical, cultural, or other institutional consequences (Bosi, Giugni, and Uba 2016). But there is also much room for further work. We take off from our point that there are many political institutions, processes, and outcomes that movements seek to influence or that are of interest to the constituency of movements and make suggestions for the future.

On the methodological side, scholarship in this area has done well to apply a wide variety of techniques, ranging from standard quantitative ones to small-N comparisons and qualitative comparative analyses. All the same, most analyses have been case studies of the largest movements. It would be valuable to have more cross-movement analyses, as well as cross-national ones. But given that much future research is likely to be case studies, there can be utility added to these studies in other ways. For example, having more deep historical analyses to address major institutional changes and to appraise the mechanisms and time-order aspects of theoretical arguments holds promise for a more thorough understanding of how movements influence political outcomes or fail to do so. These sorts of analysis can range across different political processes, including all parts of the policy process. Given the variety of movements and contexts, it is critical for theory development that scholars clarify the population of similar cases.

Most existing work on the political consequences of movements concerns policy, especially establishing the connection between protest and agenda setting. Another direction for future research then is that more work is needed to address other aspects of the political process. These include changes in policy content, voting for policy changes, and the implementation of policy. Even in the area of agenda setting it would be valuable to address further the connection between different sorts of protest, media coverage, and policy agendas. In addition, scholars addressing movement influence should be aware that not all policies are the same. It is much easier to prevent the retrenchment of a long-standing policy in a movement constituency's favor or stop a new policy initiative that a movement opposes than it is to create a new policy involving new rights or funding for movement constituencies, especially when there are better funded groups opposing them (Amenta 2006; Pierson 2000). More difficult still is for movement actors to influence long-standing policies already working against the interests of their constituents and that have established policy networks surrounding them (Baumgartner and Jones 1993; Laumann and Knoke 1987). Scholars attempting to understand movement influence should keep these distinctions in mind when making arguments about which movement forms or strategies may work best.

Scholars also need to move beyond policy to include addressing further the influence of movements on elections, political parties, administrative agencies, and courts and legal systems. The greatest progress will be made if scholars take a similar approach to those studying policy: following closely the academic debates and findings surrounding the determinants of the outcome in question and theorizing movement influence as either affecting these determinants, mediating their influence, or providing separate routes to influence. Following this suggestion would also mean becoming expert in the literature on the outcome in question and employing its concepts and theories, while working what we know about the influence of movements into them. In this way, what we know about movement influence can be theorized and analyzed further, alongside and in conjunction with the other determinants of political processes and outcomes.

References

Agnone, Jon. 2007. "Amplifying Public Opinion: The Political Impact of the U.S. Environmental Movement." *Social Forces* 85(4): 1593–1620.

Almeida, Paul and Linda Brewster Stearns. 1998. "Political Opportunities and Local Grassroots Environmental Movements: The Case of Minamata." *Social Problems* 45: 37–60.

Amenta, Edwin. 1998. *Bold Relief: Institutional Politics and the Origins of Modern American Social Policy*. Princeton, NJ: Princeton University Press.

Amenta, Edwin. 2006. *When Movements Matter: The Townsend Plan and the Rise of Social Security*. Princeton, NJ: Princeton University Press.

Amenta, Edwin. 2014. "How to Analyze the Influence of Movements." *Contemporary Sociology: A Journal of Reviews* 43(1): 16–29.

Amenta, Edwin and Neal Caren. 2004. "The Legislative, Organizational, and Beneficiary Consequences of State-Oriented Challengers." In *The Blackwell Companion to Social Movements*, edited by David A. Snow, Sarah A. Soule and Hanspeter Kriesi. 461–488. Oxford: Blackwell.

Amenta, Edwin, Neal Caren, Elizabeth Chiarello, and Yang Su. 2010. "The Political Consequences of Social Movements." *Annual Review of Sociology* 36: 287–307.

Amenta, Edwin, Neal Caren, Tina Fetner, and Michael P. Young. 2002. "Challengers and States: Toward a Political Sociology of Social Movements." *Research in Political Sociology* 10: 47–83.

Amenta, Edwin, Neal Caren and Sheera Joy Olasky. 2005. "Age for Leisure? Political Mediation and the Impact of the Pension Movement on U.S. Old-Age Policy." *American Sociological Review* 70: 516–538.

Amenta, Edwin and Michael P. Young. 1999. "Making an Impact: Conceptual and Methodological Implications of the Collective Goods Criterion." In *How Social Movements Matter*, edited by Marco Giugni, Doug McAdam, and Charles Tilly. Minneapolis: University of Minnesota Press.

Andrews, Kenneth T. 1997. "The Impacts of Social Movements on the Political Process: The Civil Rights Movement and Black Electoral Politics in Mississippi." *American Sociological Review* 62: 800–819.

Andrews, Kenneth T. 2001. "Social Movements and Policy Implementation: The Mississippi Civil Rights Movement and the War on Poverty, 1965–1971." *American Sociological Review* 66: 71–95.

Andrews, Kenneth T. 2004. *Freedom Is a Constant Struggle: The Mississippi Civil Rights Movement and Its Legacy*. Chicago: University of Chicago Press.

Andrews, Kenneth T. and Bob Edwards. 2004. "Advocacy Organizations in the U.S. Political Process." *Annual Review of Sociology* 30: 479–506.

Andrews, Kenneth T. and Sarah Gaby. 2015. "Local Protest and Federal Policy: The Impact of the Civil Rights Movement on the 1964 Civil Rights Act." *Sociological Forum* 30: 509–527.

Andrews, Kenneth T., Marshall Ganz, Matthew Baggetta, Hahrie Han, and Chaeyoon Lim. 2010. "Leadership, Membership, and Voice: Civic Associations That Work." *American Journal of Sociology* 115(4): 1191–1242.

Arzheimer, Kai. 2009. "Contextual Factors and the Extreme Right Vote in Western Europe, 1980–2002." *American Journal of Political Science* 53(2): 259–275.

Banaszak, Lee Ann. 1996. *Why Movements Succeed or Fail: Opportunity, Culture and the Struggle for Woman Suffrage*. Princeton, NJ: Princeton University Press.

Banaszak, Lee Ann. 2010. *The Women's Movement Inside and Outside the State*. Cambridge: Cambridge University Press.

Banaszak, Lee Ann and Heather L. Ondercin. 2016. "Public Opinion as a Movement Outcome: The Case of the US Women's Movement." *Mobilization: An International Quarterly* 21(3): 361–378.

Baumgartner, Frank R. and Bryan D. Jones. 1993. *Agendas and Instability in American Politics*. Chicago: University of Chicago Press.

Baumgartner, Frank R. and Christine Mahoney. 2005. "Social Movements, the Rise of New Issues, and the Public Agenda." In *Routing the Opposition: Social Movements, Public Policy, and Democracy*, edited by David S. Meyer, Valerie Jenness, and Helen Ingram, 65–86. Minneapolis: University of Minnesota Press.

Bernstein, Anya E. 2001. *The Moderation Dilemma: Legislative Coalitions and the Politics of Family and Medical Leave*. PIttsburgh, PA: University of Pittsburgh Press.

Best, Rachel Kahn. 2012. "Disease Politics and Medical Research Funding: Three Ways Advocacy Shapes Policy." *American Sociological Review* 77(5): 780–803.

Biggs, Michael and Kenneth T. Andrews. 2015. "Protest Campaigns and Movement Success Desegregating the US South in the Early 1960s." *American Sociological Review* 80(2): 416–443.

Bloom, Joshua. 2015. "The Dynamics of Opportunity and Insurgent Practice How Black Anti-Colonialists Compelled Truman to Advocate Civil Rights." *American Sociological Review* 80(2): 391–415.

Böhm, Timo. 2015. "Activists in Politics: The Influence of Embedded Activists on the Success of Social Movements." *Social Problems* 62(4): 477–498.

Bosi, Lorenzo, Marco Giugni, and Katrin Uba. 2016. *The Consequences of Social Movements*. Cambridge: Cambridge University Press.

Burstein, Paul. 2014. *American Public Opinion, Advocacy, and Policy in Congress*. New York: Cambridge University Press.

Burstein, Paul and April Linton. 2002. "The Impact of Political Parties, Interest Groups, and Social Movement Organizations on Public Policy: Some Recent Evidence and Theoretical Concerns." *Social Forces* 81(2): 381–408.

Burstein, Paul and Sarah Sausner. 2005. "The Incidence and Impact of Policy-Oriented Collective Action: Competing Views." *Sociological Forum* 20(3): 403–419.

Coe, Anna-Britt. 2013. "Inconsistency in Policy Elites' Support for Movement Claims: Feminist Advocacy in Two Regions of Peru." *Research in Social Movements, Conflicts and Change* 36: 107–132.

Cornwall, Marie, Brayden G. King, Elizabeth Legerski, Eric Dahlin, and Kendra Schiffman. 2007. "Signals or Mixed Signals: Why Opportunities for Mobilization Are Not Opportunities for Policy Reform." *Mobilization: An International Quarterly* 12(3): 239–254.

Cress, Daniel M. and David A. Snow. 2000. "The Outcomes of Homeless Mobilization: The Influence of Organization, Disruption, Political Mediation, and Framing." *American Journal of Sociology* 105(4):1063–1104.

Fetner, Tina. 2008. *How the Religious Right Shaped Lesbian and Gay Activism*. Minneapolis: University of Minnesota Press.

Gamson, William. 1990. *The Strategy of Social Protest*. Belmont, CA: Wadsworth.

Ganz, Marshall. 2000. "Resources and Resourcefulness: Strategic Capacity in the Unionization of California Agriculture, 1959–1966." *American Journal of Sociology* 105: 1003–1062.

Gilens, Martin and Benjamin I. Page. 2014. "Testing Theories of American Politics: Elites, Interest Groups, and Average Citizens." *Perspectives on Politics* 12(3): 564–581.

Giugni, Marco. 2004. *Social Protest and Policy Change: Ecology, Antinuclear, and Peace Movements in Comparative Perspective*. Lanham, MD: Rowman & Littlefield.

Giugni, Marco G. 2007. "Useless Protest? A Time-Series Analysis of the Policy Outcomes of Ecology, Antinuclear, and Peace Movements in the United States, 1977–1995." *Mobilization* 12(1): 53–77.

Giugni, Marco G. 2009. "Protest and Opportunities: The Political Outcomes of Social Movements." *Mobilization* 14(4): 505–506.

Goldstone, Jack A. 2003. "Bridging Institutionalized and Non-Institutionalized Politics." In *States, Parties, and Social Movements*, edited by Jack A. Goldstone, 1–26. New York: Cambridge University Press.

Hacker, Jacob and Paul Pierson. 2010. "Winner-Take-All Politics: Public Policy, Political Organization, and the Precipitous Rise of Top Incomes in the United States." *Politics and Society* 38(2): 152–204.

Halfmann, Drew. 2011. *Doctors and Demonstrators: How Political Institutions Shape Abortion Law in the United States, Britain, and Canada*. Chicago: University of Chicago Press.

Heaney, Michael T. and Fabio Rojas. 2015. *Party in the Street: The Antiwar Movement and the Democratic Party after 9/11*: Cambridge: Cambridge University Press.

Hojnacki, Marie, David C. Kimball, Frank R. Baumgartner, Jeffrey M. Berry and Beth L. Leech. 2012. "Studying Organizational Advocacy and Influence: Reexamining Interest Group Research." *Annual Review of Political Science* 15: 379–399.

Htun, Mala and S. Laurel Weldon. 2012. "The Civic Origins of Progressive Policy Change: Combating Violence against Women in Global Perspective, 1975–2005." *American Political Science Review* 106(03): 548–569.

Huber, Evelyne and John D. Stephens. 2001. *Development and Crisis of the Welfare State: Parties and Policies in Global Markets*. Chicago: University of Chicago Press.

Immergut, Ellen M. 2010. "Political Institutions." In *The Oxford Handbook of the Welfare State*, edited by Francis. G. Castles, Stephan Liebfried, Jane Lewis, Herbert Obinger, and Christopher Pierson. New York: Oxford University Press.

Jasper, James M. 2004. "A Strategic Approach to Collective Action: Looking for Agency in Social Movement Choices." *Mobilization* 9(1): 1–16.

Johnson, David R., Christopher P. Scheitle and Elaine Howard Ecklund. 2016. "Conservative Protestantism and Anti-Evolution Curricular Challenges across States." *Social Science Quarterly* 97(5): 1227–1244.

Johnson, Erik W. 2008. "Social Movement Size, Organizational Diversity and the Making of Federal Law." *Social Forces* 86(3): 967–994.

Johnson, Erik W., Jon Agnone, and John D. McCarthy. 2010. "Movement Organizations, Synergistic Tactics and Environmental Public Policy." *Social Forces* 88(5): 2267–2292.

Kadivar, Mohammad Ali and Neal Caren. 2016. "Disruptive Democratization: Contentious Events and Liberalizing Outcomes Globally, 1990–2004." *Social Forces* 94(3): 975–996.

Kane, Melinda D. 2003. "Social Movement Policy Success: Decriminalizing State Sodomy Laws, 1969–1998." *Mobilization* 8(3): 313–334.

King, Brayden, Keith Gunnar Bentele, and Sarah A. Soule. 2007. "Congressional Agenda-Setting and Fluctuating Attention to Civil and Political Rights, 1960–1987." *Social Forces* 86(1): 137–163.

King, Brayden G., Marie Cornwall, and Eric C. Dahlin. 2005. "Winning Woman Suffrage One Step at a Time: Social Movements and the Logic of the Legislative Process." *Social Forces* 83(3): 1211–1234.

Kitschelt, Herbert P. 1986. "Political Opportunity Structures and Political Protest: Anti-Nuclear Movements in Four Democracies." *British Journal of Political Science* 16: 57–85.

Kriesi, Hanspeter, Ruud Koopmans, Jan Willem Duyvendak, and Marco Giugni. 1995. *New Social Movements in Western Europe: A Comparative Analysis*, vol. 5. Minneapolis: University of Minnesota Press.

Laumann, Edward O. and David Knoke. 1987. *The Organizational State: Social Choice in National Policy Domains*. Madison: University of Wisconsin Press.

Lipsky, Michael. 1968. "Protest as a Political Resource." *American Political Science Review* 62: 1144–1158.

Lohmann, Susanne. 1993. "A Signalling Model of Informative and Manipulative Political Action." *American Political Science Review* 87(2): 319–333.

Luders, Joseph E. 2010. *The Civil Rights Movement and the Logic of Social Change*. New York: Cambridge University Press.

Madestam, Andreas, Daniel Shoag, Stan Veuger, and David Yanagizawa-Drott. 2013. "Do Political Protests Matter? Evidence from the Tea Party Movement." *The Quarterly Journal of Economics* 128(4): 1633–1685.

Manza, Jeff and Christopher Uggen. 2008. *Locked Out: Felon Disenfranchisement and American Democracy*: Oxford: Oxford University Press.

Martin, Isaac William. 2013. *Rich People's Movements: Grassroots Campaigns to Untax the One Percent*. New York: Oxford University Press.

McAdam, Doug. 1982. *Political Process and the Development of Black Insurgency, 1930–1970*. Chicago: University of Chicago Press.

McAdam, Doug and Hilary Boudet. 2012. *Putting Social Movements in Their Place: Explaining Opposition to Energy Projects in the United States, 2000–2005*. New York: Cambridge University Press.

McAdam, Doug and Karina Kloos. 2014. *Deeply Divided: Racial Politics and Social Movements in Post-War America*: Oxford: Oxford University Press.

McAdam, Doug and Yang Su. 2002. "The War at Home: Antiwar Protests and Congressional Voting, 1965 to 1973." *American Sociological Review* 67(5): 696–721.

McAdam, Doug and Sidney Tarrow. 2010. "Ballots and Barricades: On the Reciprocal Relationship between Elections and Social Movements." *Perspectives on Politics* 8(02): 529–542.

McCammon, Holly J. 2009. "Beyond Frame Resonance: The Argumentative Structure and Persuasive Capacity of Twentieth-Century US Women's Jury-Rights Frames." *Mobilization* 14(1): 45–64.

McCammon, Holly J. 2012. *The US Women's Jury Movements and Strategic Adaptation: A More Just Verdict*: Cambridge: Cambridge University Press.

McCammon, Holly J., Kelly E. Campbell, Ellen M. Granberg, and Christine Mowery. 2001. "How Movements Win: Gendered Opportunity Structures and US Women's Suffrage Movements, 1866 to 1919." *American Sociological Review* 66(1): 49–70.

McCarthy, John D. and Mayer N. Zald. 1977. "Resource Mobilization and Social Movements: A Partial Theory." *American Journal of Sociology* 82: 1212–1241.

McVeigh, Rory. 2009. *The Rise of the Ku Klux Klan: Right-Wing Movements and National Politics*. Minneapolis: University of Minnesota Press.

McVeigh, Rory, David Cunningham, and Justin Farrell. 2014. "Political Polarization as a Social Movement Outcome: 1960s Klan Activism and Its Enduring Impact on Political Realignment in Southern Counties, 1960 to 2000." *American Sociological Review* 79(6): 1144–1171.

McVeigh, Rory, Daniel J. Myers and David Sikkink. 2004. "Corn, Klansmen, and Coolidge: Structure and Framing in Social Movements." *Social Forces* 83(2): 653–690.

Meyer, David S. and Debra C. Minkoff. 2004. "Conceptualizing Political Opportunity." *Social Forces* 82(4): 1457–1492.

Negro, Giacomo, Fabrizio Perretti, and Glenn R. Carroll. 2013. "Challenger Groups, Commercial Organizations, and Policy Enactment: Local Lesbian/Gay Rights Ordinances in the United States from 1972 to 2008." *American Journal of Sociology* 119(3): 790–832.

Olzak, Susan and Emily Ryo. 2007. "Organizational Diversity, Vitality and Outcomes in the Civil Rights Movement." *Social Forces* 85(4): 1561–1591.

Olzak, Susan and Sarah A. Soule. 2009. "Cross-Cutting Influences of Environmental Protest and Legislation." *Social Forces* 88(1): 201–225.

Parris, Christie L. and Heather L. Scheuerman. 2015. "How Social Movements Matter: Including Sexual Orientation in State-Level Hate Crime Legislation." *Research in Social Movements, Conflicts and Change* 38: 229–257.

Pierson, Paul. 2000. "Not Just What, but When: Timing and Sequence in Political Processes." *Studies in American Political Development* 14(01): 72–92.

Piven, Frances Fox. 2006. *Challenging Authority: How Ordinary People Change America*. Lanham, MD: Rowman & Littlefield.

Piven, Frances Fox and Richard Cloward. 1977. *Poor People's Movements*. New York: Pantheon Books.

Rueschemeyer, Dietrich, Evelyne Huber Stephens, and John D. Stephens. 1992. *Capitalist Development and Democracy*. Chicago: University of Chicago Press.

Sano, Joelle and John B. Williamson. 2008. "Factors Affecting Union Decline in 18 OECD Countries and Their Implications for Labor Movement Reform." *International Journal of Comparative Sociology* 49(6): 479–500.

Santoro, Wayne A. 2002. "The Civil Rights Movement's Struggle for Fair Employment: A 'Dramatic Events-Conventional Politics' Model." *Social Forces* 81(1): 177–206.

Santoro, Wayne A. 2008. "The Civil Rights Movement and the Right to Vote: Black Protest, Segregationist Violence and the Audience." *Social Forces* 86(4): 1391–1414.

Santoro, Wayne A. and Gail M. McGuire. 1997. "Social Movement Insiders: The Impact of Institutional Activists on Affirmative Action and Comparable Worth Policies." *Social Problems* 44(4): 503–519.

Schickler, Eric. 2016. *Racial Realignment: The Transformation of American Liberalism, 1932–1965*. Princeton, NJ: Princeton University Press.

Schlozman, Daniel. 2015. *When Movements Anchor Parties: Electoral Alignments in American History*. Princeton, NJ: Princeton University Press.

Schofer, Evan and Ann Hironaka. 2005. "The Effects of World Society on Environmental Protection Outcomes." *Social Forces* 84(1): 25–47.

Schwartz, Mildred A. 2006. *Party Movements in the United States and Canada: Strategies of Persistence*. New York: Rowman & Littlefield.

Skocpol, Theda. 1992. *Protecting Soldiers and Mothers: The Political Origins of Social Policy in the United States*. Cambridge, MA: Harvard University Press.

Skocpol, Theda. 2003. *Diminished Democracy: From Membership to Management*. Norman, OK: University of Oklahoma.

Skocpol, Theda and Edwin Amenta. 1986. "States and Social Policies." *Annual Review of Sociology* 12: 131–157.

Skrentny, John D. 2006. "Policy-Elite Perceptions and Social Movement Success: Understanding Variations in Group Inclusion in Affirmative Action." *American Journal of Sociology* 111(6): 1762–1815.

Snow, David A. and Sarah A. Soule. 2010. *A Primer on Social Movements*. New York: W. W. Norton.

Soule, Sarah A. and Brayden G. King. 2006. "The Stages of the Policy Process and the Equal Rights Amendment, 1972–1982." *American Journal of Sociology* 111(6): 1871–1909.

Steil, Justin Peter and Ion Bogdan Vasi. 2014. "The New Immigration Contestation: Social Movements and Local Immigration Policy Making in the United States, 2000–2011." *American Journal of Sociology* 119(4): 1104–1155.

Tilly, Charles. 1999. "From Interactions to Outcomes in Social Movements." In *How Social Movements Matter*, edited by Marco Giugni, Doug McAdam, and Charles Tilly, vol. 10, 253–270. Minneapolis: University of Minnesota Press.

Trevizo, Dolores. 2011. *Rural Protest and the Making of Democracy in Mexico, 1968–2000*. University Park, PA: Pennsylvania State University Press.

Uba, Katrin. 2009. "The Contextual Dependence of Movement Outcomes: A Simplified Meta-Analysis." *Mobilization* 14(4): 433–448.

Vasi, Ion Bogdan, Edward T. Walker, John S. Johnson and Hui Fen Tan. 2015. "'No Fracking Way!' Documentary Film, Discursive Opportunity, and Local Opposition against Hydraulic Fracturing in the United States, 2010 to 2013." *American Sociological Review* 80(5): 934–959.

Walgrave, Stefaan and Rens Vliegenthart. 2012. "The Complex Agenda-Setting Power of Protest: Demonstrations, Media, Parliament, Government, and Legislation in Belgium, 1993–2000." *Mobilization: An International Quarterly* 17(2): 129–156.

26

Economic Outcomes of Social Movements

Marco Giugni and Maria T. Grasso

Economic Outcomes of Social Movements Between State, Market, and Society

In his theory of the state as expressed in the *Philosophy of Right*, Hegel relegated the market to the sphere of civil society – or "the system of needs" – as separate from both the family, as a private institution, and the state, as politics and the site of "ethical life." He regarded civil society and the market as forming a sphere of social life where individuals were set against each other in egoistic terms, each searching to fulfill their own needs and desires. An initial theoretical problem in discussing the economic outcomes of social movements is thus: To what extent and in what sense can social movement action in the sphere of politics change or impact the economic sphere?

Recent scholarship looks at how social movements bring contentiousness to the market and how they might bring about market change (Davis et al. 2005, 2008; de Bakker et al. 2013; King and Pearce 2010; Rao 2009; Soule 2009; Soule and King 2014; Walker 2012). As a system that generates and reproduces inequality, market capitalism centralizes power in the hands of a few. In turn, this spurs contestation in the attempt to change these negative economic conditions. Historically, the transcendence of the market and the overall transition to a socialist economic system have traditionally been the major economic goal of the Marxist-imprint labor movement. Today, on the other hand, economic outcomes are more likely to be linked to reformist trends such as corporate responsibility, ethical business, sustainable development, social enterprise, the green economy, and so forth, posing what is normally a moral critique against some of the more pernicious aspects of the market, but rarely posing a challenge to the system as a whole itself.

The Wiley Blackwell Companion to Social Movements, Second Edition. Edited by David A. Snow, Sarah A. Soule, Hanspeter Kriesi, and Holly J. McCammon.
© 2019 John Wiley & Sons Ltd. Published 2019 by John Wiley & Sons Ltd.

Reformist new social movements have campaigned for market changes and economic outcomes in relation to issues pertaining, for instance, to global warming, child labor, and health care inequalities (King and Pearce 2010). Social movement theorists have shown how contentiousness from the political sphere may spill over into the economic sphere of the market (Armstrong and Bernstein 2008; Snow 2004; Soule 2009; Van Dyke, Soule, and Taylor 2004; Vogel 1978). Given all this, a discussion of economic outcomes of social movements in the current historical juncture will tend to focus on various aspects of change related to the market itself, market behavior, or regulation of markets.

King and Pearce (2010) in their review identify three pathways that movements take: (1) challenging corporations directly; (2) creating transnational systems of private regulation; and (3) creating market alternatives through institutional entrepreneurship. These three pathways suggest that movements may either intervene directly in markets or attempt indirectly to involve the state to attain more regulation. Social movement research has traditionally looked at the latter, but recent research on social movements in markets focuses on the former (King and Pearce 2010). The three pathways also underline that movements may be successful in terms of getting responses from market actors – procedural or substantive – or may succeed in altering markets, and that these impacts are not mutually exclusive.

By economic outcomes we mean impacts achieved by social movements that pertain to the economic sphere either by calling for government actions to regulate the economy or impose redistribution, for reforming the practices of companies and corporations, or by changing social practices and individual behaviors with respect to consumption. Economic outcomes are one type among a wide range of consequences that movement activities may have. In their broadest meaning, most social movements may produce economic outcomes. In a narrower sense, however, economic outcomes refer to changes in market rules, discourses, and practices due, at least in part, to movement activities.

Our review takes into account previous reviews, most notably the one by King and Pearce (2010), but at the same time it reflects the above definition, according to which economic outcomes of social movements may affect not only the market, but also the political and social spheres. We focus our review on research that examines explicitly and empirically the economic impact of movements, as well as research that deals with movements and protests that have economic implications in a broader sense.

Attaining Government Regulation

Much of the activity of social movements in modernity is geared toward the state, to implement or block new legislation and policy (Tilly 1986, 1995). Market-oriented movements are no exception to this rule. Given the state's regulatory functions concerning markets, changing market rules and practices necessitates challenging the state.

Although much of the new research on social movements in markets focuses on their direct intervention (King and Pearce 2010), scholars have also addressed movements' attempts to attain government regulation and the ways in which they attempt to reach economic goals by means of challenges to the state. In the broadest sense, movements aiming to subvert a given political regime, if successful, lead to economic outcomes, for example, the establishment of a new economic system as a result of the Bolshevik Revolution in 1917.

A number of historical and contemporary movements can be seen as aiming to produce economic outcomes. Labor movements, for example, whether reformist or Marxist, make economic claims and, if successful, can have important economic impacts. Work on the impact of strikes on government responsiveness provides some insight on economic outcomes (Cohn 1993). It should be noted that attempting to secure government regulation is only one way through which labor movements have traditionally sought to meet their goals, including through strike activity. They also target corporate actors directly, especially in countries characterized by decentralized collective bargaining in industrial relations (Katz 1993).

Anti-tax movements and fiscal protests are another case in point. Neither markets nor the economy are their primary target. However, if successful, fiscal protests may impact the economy more generally. The anti-globalization and global justice movements have also fought for economic outcomes (Epstein and Schnietz 2002). Their claims have dealt most often with notions of justice and equity on the world scale and of participatory democracy within nations (della Porta 2007). The struggle against neoliberalism as an economic ideology and its practices was certainly a core aspect of these movements, and much of their mobilization was geared towards having states intervene so as to rebalance global (economic) injustices and, more generally, change the current logic of capitalism. However, there were also more radicalized wings of the movement which saw these aims as expressions of a more generalized anti-capitalism. Similarly, anti-austerity movements and protests call for economic outcomes in terms of halting budget cuts, particularly for key public services (Ancelovici, Dufour, and Nez 2016; Giugni and Grasso 2015). By contesting the austerity policies implemented by nation states during the economic crisis under the leadership of the so-called "Troika" of the European Commission, the Central European Bank, and the International Monetary Fund, anti-austerity movements challenged the economic policies of the governments and demanded economic outcomes in the form of changes in state policies.

Reviewing the literature on revolutions as well as that on other movements for socio-economic equality mentioned above is beyond the scope of this chapter. We focus more specifically on movements and protests that attempt to attain greater government regulation in markets. Indeed, market-oriented movements have often sought state intervention. This occurs because of the centrality of the state in policy regulation in modern societies. In this way, movements hope that the state's capacity to regulate the market can curb the more devastating social and moral repercussions of market growth (Dobbin 1994).

Seeking more government regulation in markets goes back a long way. Religion played an important role in this regard (King and Pearce 2010), as seen, for example, in the symbolic crusade to curb alcohol consumption by the American temperance movement of the nineteenth century (Gusfield 1986). More generally, a great deal of the social and environmental regulation introduced in the second half of the twentieth century was influenced by social movement activism (Vogel 1995).

Scholars have stressed the role of disruption as well as other endogenous charac-teristics for policy outcomes concerning the economic domain. This has been shown, for example, for anti-privatization protests in India (Uba 2005). Studying whether and how social movements can be successful by addressing the state in order to gain greater government regulation of markets calls for further investigation of state responsiveness to movement mobilization as well as of the factors leading to it. We explore this question further below.

Direct Interventions in Markets

King and Pearce (2010) note that most new research on markets tends to focus on movements' direct interventions in the market rather than their attempt to get gov-ernments to regulate markets (Bartley 2003; Ingram and Rao 2004). Frequently, social movements attempt to bypass the state and target non-state actors, including corporate actors and businesses (Soule 2009; Van Dyke, Soule, and Taylor 2004; Walker, Martin, and McCarthy 2008). In the absence of state-mandated collective bargaining agreements, labor movements have also targeted businesses directly (Ganz 2000; Jenkins and Perrow 1977).

At the same time, markets can provide alternative opportunities when the state is seen to be closed or unresponsive to movements' demands or when it is seen to defend the rich to the detriment of those more disadvantaged (Chasin 2000). Soule (2009) shows that protest targeting firms is less likely to be policed, which might drive protesters to target firms rather than the state. When states tend to favor the elites and exclude disadvantaged groups, one alternative entry point for some groups and movements can be the market. King and Pearce (2010: 252) note in this regard how "owing to reputational concerns and stakeholder commitments, corporations are often more responsive to new types of social activism than is the government." They cite the example of the US gay rights movement being more successful in securing domestic partnership benefits for employees of Fortune 500 companies than for employees of the federal government (Briscoe and Safford 2008; Raeburn 2004). In this way, companies existing in the market are increasingly seen as rele-vant political targets for social movement activism since their reforms can have influence on multiple individuals.

While regulation of markets via the state has historically been the primary means for disadvantaged groups to lobby for change (Schneiberg and Bartley 2008), more recently, it has been argued, globalization and neoliberalism mean that the market escapes state regulation since trade is transnational (Campbell and Pedersen 2001). In this context, corporations can settle where regulations are the most advantageous for their purposes, and this means that states competing for foreign capital investment become even less likely to regulate markets (Seidman 2007). While social movements have attempted to fight these tendencies (Fourcade-Gourinchas and Babb 2002; Prasad 2006), they face an uphill struggle. Moreover, even where states increase regulations, firms attempt to challenge these developments by claiming that they undermine global competitiveness (Braithwaite and Drahos 2000; Murphy 2004). These issues, in turn, have meant that state regulation itself becomes increasingly transnational (Drezner 2007). As a result, international institutions have themselves become the targets of social movements aiming to address these issues (Smith 2001). Indeed, the rise of transnational movements and contention has meant that local concerns have been brought to global forums, but they have had a difficult time finding influence in international governance arenas that are seen as more able to coerce market actors to their rules (Evans 2005), as well as to challenge the powerful cartels of international corporations (Bowman 1996).

It is no surprise that corporations are rich and powerful and exert a great deal of influence on setting the rules of the market (Fligstein 1996; Perrow 2002). This, in turn, has meant that they receive much attention from activists (Fleming and Spicer 2007; Manheim 2001). Generally speaking, corporations do not have outward political visions or ideology, yet in virtue of being capitalist actors they have interests in maintaining the *status quo* system or improving their own conditions of competition. Moreover, corporations often form cartels and commission research to fight for their positions and deter challengers from fighting them. Activists have nonetheless found ways to be effective in eroding corporations' power (Soule 2009). This may include influencing firms' divestment decisions (Soule, Swaminathan, Tihanyi 2014). At the same time, corporations may or may not concede, depending on a variety of factors. Ingram, Yue, and Rao (2010), for example, have stressed the role of uncertainty over protest occurrence and have pointed to the fact that corporations look more like the strategic actors of game theory than the state.

Social movements typically adopt a wide range of tactics and forms of action. Thus, there are different types of tactics that social movements can apply, as insiders or outsiders, to produce economic outcomes. Balsiger (2016), for example, distinguishes between three different roles movements may play in market change: (1) contention (insider and outsider tactics, public campaigns, boycotts); (2) collaboration (labels, certification); and (3) alternative niches (creation of new markets and categories, movements-as-market-actors).

Insider tactics have been adopted, sometimes successfully, by intra-organizational challengers (Briscoe and Gupta 2016). McDonnell, King, and Soule (2015), for example, show that firms that are targeted by shareholder resolutions adopt "social management devices," that is, structures or practices meant to demonstrate a commitment to social responsibility and aid in the management of social performance, such as enhanced disclosure, externally enforced commitments, or new internal structures for managing corporate social policy. However, movements within market organizations or corporations cannot be as politicized and aggressive as movements in the political realm, and they must seek collaboration in order to achieve their economic outcomes (King and Pearce 2010). As such, they may seek to tone down their language and reframe their objectives so that they emphasize the positive aspects flowing to all stakeholders, including investors, consumers, and organizational players (Creed, Scully, and Austin 2002; Lounsbury, Ventresca, and Hirsch 2003). For example, activists, regulators, and corporate representatives collaborated in changing the perception of environmental responsibility as corporate liability in the 1960s to a sustainable proactive strategy (Hoffman 2001). Similarly, primary stakeholder activism against a firm was shown to affect its perceived environmental risk and its financial performance (Vasi and King 2012). Furthermore, gay rights activists in the USA were able to change corporate practices and win domestic partner benefits by mobilizing LGBT employee networks (Raeburn 2004).

Since there are few conventional access channels to enact economic outcomes within corporations, disruptive tactics are often the only means available to push for change (Weber, Rao, and Thomas 2009). Disruption can be a very effective means of influencing corporate actors and more generally of producing market change. Disruptive practices such as boycotts or protests by social movements can impose very significant costs on their targets (Luders 2006) and generate significant economic impacts, such as a loss of profits, forcing corporations to change their more negatively evaluated practices. Therefore, corporations have developed strategies to try to deal with the negative consequences of protest (Ingram, Yue, and Rao 2010). Such costs assessments by economic actors have, for example, been examined in earlier research on employer responses to strikes and unions organizing (Griffin, Wallace, and Rubin 1986; Korpi and Shalev 1980).

Scholars have repeatedly shown the importance of the larger context – social, political, cultural – for the consequences of social movements. Economic outcomes are no exception. Thus, research on movements in markets has stressed the role played by the characteristics of corporations and industries regarding the impact of movements on markets (King 2008; Schurman 2004; Wahlström and Peterson 2006). Similarly, the cultural context is important for a movement's economic outcomes (Lounsbury, Ventresca, and Hirsch 2003; Schurman and Munro 2009). Movements must adapt to their contexts so as to improve their chances of having an impact (McCammon 2012). For example, Balsiger (2014) shows how tactics by Clean Clothes campaigners were adapted to market contexts in order to have retailers adopt and monitor codes of conduct. Indeed, the transformation of markets depends as well on their structural and cultural characteristics (Carroll and Swaminathan 2000; Sikavica and Pozner 2013).

The media are a particularly important aspect of the broader context for movements in markets. Outsiders often rely on the media to gain public support to their cause (Koopmans 2004). The media can be very useful in translating movement frames for consumption by the larger public. They can help movements when "shaming the corporation" (Bartley and Child 2014) and for conveying a negative image of a given target to damage its public image and reputation (O'Rourke 2005; Schurman 2004). Such a "naming and shaming strategy," under certain circumstances, can be effective, shaping both the market and the field that firms inhabit (Bartley and Child 2011). Negative media exposure of corporations can become particularly damaging as certain companies come to be associated with shady consumer practices and distrust on the part of consumers. In this vein, King (2008) found support for the political mediation model of social movement outcomes, showing that corporate targets of boycotts were more likely to make concessions when the boycott received a great deal of media attention.

Finally, the creation of alternative market practices and niches can be another important pathway through which market-oriented movements may produce economic outcomes. Alternative niches consist in new markets created by social movements that rise outside of established market actors (Balsiger 2016). As such, activists may become market entrepreneurs or provide resources for entrepreneurs (Hiatt, Sine, and Tolbert 2009; McInerney 2014; Weber, Heinze, and DeSoucey 2008). These types of alternatives forms of resilience generally bypass both the market and the state and are dealt with in more detail below.

Changing Market Rules and Practices in the Social Sphere

Identity movements are especially common in postindustrial society, and consumer politics as an expression of these alternative identities has become widespread (Micheletti and Stolle 2013). Political consumerism – the "consumer choice of producers and products with the goal of changing objectionable institutional or market practices" (Micheletti, Follesdal, and Stolle 2004: xiv) – has become part of the action repertoire of contention today, and social movements often exploit this form of political engagement to reach their goals. Political consumerism mostly takes the form of buying (buycott) or refusing to buy (boycott) specific products for ethical or political reasons. In its contemporary forms, it is mainly adopted by young, urban, postmaterialist women who aim to defend, among other things, global justice, international solidarity, and environmental protection (Stolle and Micheletti 2013). In addition to challenging principles, practices, and policies, consumer movements also aim to fundamentally change the ideology and culture of consumerism, raising consciousness about consumption and economic behavior to mold responsible citizens aware of the environmental and other social repercussions of their consumption choices (Kozinets and Handelman 2004).

Individuals coming together to challenge the practices of corporations have been shown to have real economic impacts on corporations and market processes, for example, by causing a company's stock price to fall (King and Soule 2007). However, while demonstrations matter since they can open up the space and media attention for a news story and apply political pressure, individuals can also persuade others to change their consumer behavior and engage in boycotts and other types of consumer action which can challenge economic practices (Friedman 1999; Garrett 1987). Research on movements' challenges to corporations has shown the effectiveness of boycotts via their reputational threats, especially when the challenges attract media attention (Friedman 1985; King 2008, 2011, 2016). Boycotts work because they damage reputation much in the same way that companies will often introduce green policies to project a socially responsible image to stakeholders (Baron 2001; Baron and Diermeier 2007). Furthermore, King (2011) showed that firms with high reputational standing are more likely to attract public attention when they are the targets of activist attacks.

The creation of alternative markets outside hegemonic practices – "alternative niches," as they have been called (Balsiger 2016) – is another pathway for economic outcomes of social movements. Studies show that new organizational activities are legitimized through activism and the development of an alternative culture (Hargrave and Van de Ven 2006; Haveman, Rao, and Paruchuri 2007; Rao, Morrill, and Zald 2000; Schneiberg, King, and Smith 2008). Normally, these efforts are underpinned by groups or communities of like-minded individuals committed to social change for the good of society as a whole (Carroll 1997; Carroll and Swaminathan 2000; Dobrev, Kim, and Hannan 2001; Sine and Lee 2009; Swaminathan 2001; Swaminathan and Carroll 1995; Swaminathan and Wade 2001).

King and Pearce (2010) note the establishment of actual alternatives is often preceded by movements advocating alternative conceptions, for example, with the emergence of cooperatives and developmental associations (Berk and Schneiberg

2005; Schneiberg 2002). All these alternative set-ups are greatly aided by the work of social movements to break down cognitive barriers (Lounsbury and Glynn 2001; Ruef 2000; Sine and Lee 2009; Sine, Haveman, and Tolbert 2005; Weber, Heinze, and DeSoucey 2008). In this way, movements can have both direct and indirect economic impacts in terms of creating economic alternatives, including the creation of new markets (Hiatt, Sine, and Tolbert 2009) and the creation of innovative practices (Lounsbury and Crumley 2007; Munir and Phillips 2005; Pinch and Bijker 1984).

Economic outcomes of social movements can also be seen in what have come to be known as the social economy, the solidarity – or solidary – economy, or, more recently and particularly with respect to the economic crisis, alternative forms of resilience. These terms refer broadly to alternative economic practices initiated by citizen groups and networks. Similarly, in recent years, students of social movements have become increasingly interested in "sustainable community movement organizations" (Forno and Graziano 2014), new collective initiatives which empower consumer and producer networks on a smaller scale, thereby pointing to economic outcomes of those organizations.

Kousis and Paschou (2017) note scholars have focused on a wide range of actions which can be subsumed under the heading of the solidarity economy (Laville 2010), including solidary bartering (Fernández Mayo, 2009), local exchange trading schemes (Granger, Wringe, and Andrews 2010), local and alternative currencies (North 2007), ethical banks (Tischer 2013), local market cooperatives (Phillips 2012), cooperatives for the supply of social services, such as in health and education (Costa et al. 2012), alternative forms of production (Corrado 2010), critical consumption (Fonte 2013), spontaneous actions of resistance and reclaim (Dalakoglou 2012), and the reproduction of cultural knowledge via oral and artistic expression (Lamont, Welburn, and Fleming 2013).

Social innovation (Moulaert et al. 2010) is a particularly important aspect when examining economic impacts of alternative economic practices. When successful, these attempts can restructure existing practices and ultimately change power structures toward greater inclusivity (González, Moulaert, and Martinelli 2010). This latter aspect is emphasized, for example, by Vaillancourt (2009), who notes how the social economy can contribute to the democratization of the state through co-production and co-construction. The argument here is that a solidarity-based model with an open governance state leads to both social innovation and a more just and fit-for-people social policy.

Conclusion

Scholarship on the consequences of social movements has traditionally focused on three main types of outcomes: political, biographical, and cultural (Giugni 2008). The former clearly has been the main focus of extant research, with a specific stress on policy outcomes. Recently, scholars have started to examine other types of movement outcomes, such as those that consist in influencing economic actors and/or altering the structure and functioning of the economic sphere. Economic outcomes have long been neglected by students of social movements, but this gap has been closing in recent years as scholars have become increasingly interested in understanding how movements may bring about changes in the "contentiousness of markets" (King and Pearce 2010).

Our review reveals that social movements and protest activities can have important effects both for markets and for the structuring and functioning of the economy. We have outlined in particular outcomes located in three substantially interrelated and partly overlapping but analytically distinct spheres: (1) effects attained by addressing the state in order to secure greater government regulation on markets; (2) effects stemming from movements' direct interventions in markets, which may take the form of collaboration or contention; and (3) effects consisting in changing market rules and practices in the social sphere, in particular by means of consumerist actions, the creation of alternative market niches, and involvement in the solidarity economy.

Research on the economic outcomes of social movements also allows for important cross-fertilizations among different disciplines and sub-disciplines. As we have tried to show, economic outcomes cross-cut the social, the political, and obviously the economic spheres. Studying them is a way to overcome the tendency endemic in social science to limit attention to a given field and, instead, opens up interdisciplinary avenues for research that may bring together sociologists, political scientists, and economists as well as organizational and consumer researchers and still other specialists interested in discovering how contentious politics may affect the economy and wider society at large.

Future research should continue to investigate the economic outcomes and consequences of social movements. Scholars embarking on such an endeavor should perhaps operate a distinction, rarely if ever applied, between economic-oriented movements – that is, movements that address primarily economic actors or seek, as their primary goal, to challenge markets or the economy at large – and movements that may produce economic outcomes, as a by-product, or indirectly, even if they have other targets and goals. This might help to identify more clearly the mechanisms through which social movements engender economic outcomes through direct and indirect means, which is something which we encourage scholars to pursue systematically.

Finally, scholars might also profit from broadening the definition of economic outcomes. A great deal of the existing literature looks at economic outcomes within markets, thus accepting capitalism as the background condition for these effects. Yet a more radical move would be to start thinking about how social movements could achieve the restructuring or even transcendence of the market and capitalism to put an end to inequalities between rich and poor and the Global North and the Global South, for example, and bring about ready social transformation rather than taking the "band aid approach" of making capitalism less devastating or pursuing escapism into "alternative markets" for the lucky few. In other words, in addition to institutional change in markets due, at least in part, to social movements, we should also tackle how movements may bring about a more profound transformation of the very underpinnings of market economy for greater social justice. This would be in line with recent calls for more attention to capitalism in social movement theory (della Porta 2015; Hetland and Goodwin 2013), as we witness ever-growing inequality across the globe.

References

Ancelovici, Marcos, Pascale Dufour, and Héloïse Nez, eds. 2016. *Street Politics in the Age of Austerity: From the Indignados to Occupy*. Amsterdam: Amsterdam University Press.

Armstrong, Elizabeth A. and Mary Bernstein. 2008. "Culture, Power, and Institutions: A Multi-institutional Politics Approach to Social Movements." *Sociological Theory* 26: 74–99.

Balsiger, Philip. 2014. *The Fight for Ethical Fashion: The Origins and Strategic Interactions of the Clean Clothes Campaign*. Farnham: Ashgate.

Balsiger, Philip. 2016. "Tactical Competition and Movement Outcomes on Markets." In *The Consequences of Social Movements*, edited by Lorenzo Bosi, Marco Giugni, and Katrin Uba, 237–260. Cambridge: Cambridge University Press.

Baron, David P. 2001. "Private Politics, Corporate Social Responsibility, and Integrated Strategy." *Journal of Economics & Management Strategy* 10: 7–45.

Baron, David P. and Daniel Diermeier. 2007. "Strategic Activism and Nonmarket Strategy." *Journal of Economics & Management Strategy* 16: 599–634.

Bartley, Tim. 2003. "Certifying Forests and Factories: States, Social Movements, and the Rise of Private Regulation in the Apparel and Forest Products Fields." *Politics & Society* 31: 433–464.

Bartley, Tim and Curtis Child. 2011. "Movements, Markets, and Fields: The Effects of Anti-Sweatshop Campaigns on U.S Firms." *Social Forces* 90: 425–451.

Bartley, Tim and Curtis Child. 2014. "Shaming the Corporation: The Social Production of Targets and the Anti-Sweatshop Movement." *American Sociological Review* 79: 653–678.

Berk, Gerald, and Marc Schneiberg. 2005. "Varieties in Capitalism, Varieties of Association: Collaborative Learning in American Industry, 1900 to 1925." *Politics & Society* 33: 46–87.

Bowman, Scott R. 1996. *The Modern Corporation and American Political Thought: Law, Power, and Ideology*. University Park, PA: Penn State University Press.

Braithwaite, John and Drahos, Peter. 2000. *Global Business Regulation*. Cambridge: Cambridge University Press.

Briscoe, Forrest and Abhinav Gupta. 2016. "Social Activism in and Around Organizations." *The Academy of Management Annals* 10: 671–727.

Briscoe, Forrest and Sean Safford. 2008. "The Nixon-in-China Effect: Activism, Imitation, and the Institutionalization of Contentious Practices." *Administrative Science Quarterly* 53: 460–491.

Campbell, John L. and Ove K. Pedersen, eds. 2001. *The Rise of Neoliberalism and Institutional Analysis*. Princeton, NJ: Princeton University Press.

Carroll, Glenn R. 1997. "Long-Term Evolutionary Change in Organizational Populations: Theory, Models, and Empirical Findings from Industrial Demography." *Industrial and Corporate Change* 6: 119–145.

Carroll, Glenn R. and Anand Swaminathan. 2000. "Why the Microbrewery Movement? Organizational Dynamics of Resource Partitioning in the American Brewing Industry after Prohibition." *American Journal of Sociology* 106: 715–762.

Chasin, Alexandra. 2000. *Selling Out: The Gay and Lesbian Movement Goes to Market*. New York: Palgrave.

Cohn, Samuel. 1993. *When Strikes Make Sense – and Why: Lessons from Third Republic French Coal Miners*. New York: Plenum Publishing.

Corrado, Alessandra. 2010. "New Peasantries and Alternative Agro-Food Networks: The Case of Réseau Semences Paysannes." In *From Community to Consumption: New and Classical Themes in Rural Sociological Research*, Research in Rural Sociology and Development, vol. 16, edited by Alessandro Bonanno, Hans Bakker, Raymond Jussaume, Yoshio Kawamura, and Mark Shucksmith, 17–30. Bingley: Emerald Group Publishing Limited.

Costa, Ericka, Michele Andreaus, Chiara Carini, and Maurizio Carpita. 2012. "Exploring the Efficiency of Italian Social Cooperatives by Descriptive and Principal Component Analysis." *Service Business* 6: 117–136.

Creed, W. E. Douglas, Maureen A. Scully, and John R. Austin. 2002. "Clothes Make the Person? The Tailoring of Legitimating Accounts and the Social Construction of Identity." *Organization Science* 13: 475–496.

Dalakoglou, Dimitris. 2012. "Beyond Spontaneity: Crisis, Violence and Collective Action in Athens." *City* 16: 535–545.

Davis, Gerald F., Doug McAdam, W. Richard Scott, and Mayer N. Zald. 2005. *Social Movements and Organizational Theory*. Cambridge: Cambridge University Press.

Davis, Gerald F., Calvin Morrill, Hayagreeva Rao, and Sarah A Soule. 2008. "Introduction: Social Movements in Organizations and Markets." *Administrative Science Quarterly* 53: 389–394.

de Bakker, Frank, Frank den Hond, Brayden G. King, and Klaus Weber. 2013. "Social Movements, Civil Society, and Corporations: Taking Stock and Looking Ahead." *Organization Studies* 34: 573–593.

della Porta, Donatella, ed. 2007. *The Global Justice Movement: Cross-National and Transnational Perspectives*. Boulder, CO: Paradigm.

della Porta, Donatella. 2015. *Social Movements in Times of Austerity: Bringing Capitalism Back into Protest Analysis*. Cambridge: Polity.

Dobbin, Frank. 1994. *Forging Industrial Policy: The United States, Britain, and France in the Railway Age*. Cambridge: Cambridge University Press.

Dobrev, Stanislav D., Tai-Young Kim, and Michael T. Hannan. 2001. "Dynamics of Niche Width and Resource Partitioning." *American Journal of Sociology* 106: 1299–1337.

Drezner, Daniel W. 2007. *All Politics Is Global: Explaining International Regulatory Regimes*. Princeton, NJ: Princeton University Press.

Epstein, Marc J. and Karen E. Schnietz. 2002. "Measuring the Cost of Environmental and Labor Protests to Globalization: An Event Study of the Failed 1999 Seattle WTO Talks." The International Trade Journal 16: 129–160.

Evans, Peter. 2005. "Counterhegemonic Globalization: Transnational Social Movements in the Contemporary Global Political Economy." In *The Handbook of Political Sociology*, edited by Thomas Janoski, Robert R. Alford, Alexander M. Hicks, and Mildred A. Schwartz, 655–670. New York: Cambridge University Press.

Fernández Mayo, Manuela. 2009. "El trueque solidario: Una estrategía de supervivencia ante la crisis argentina de 2001". *Revista Pueblos y Fronteras Digital* 4: 5–29.

Fleming, Peter and André Spicer. 2007. *Contesting the Corporation: Struggle, Power, and Resistance in Organizations*. Cambridge: Cambridge University Press.

Fligstein, Neil. 1996. "Markets as Politics: A Political-Cultural Approach to Market Institutions." *American Sociological Review* 61: 656–673.

Fonte, Maria. 2013. "Food Consumption as Social Practice: Solidarity Purchasing Groups in Rome, Italy." *Journal of Rural Studies* 32: 230–239.

Forno, Francesca and Paolo R. Graziano. 2014. "Sustainable Community Movement Organisations." *Journal of Consumer Culture* 14: 139–157.

Fourcade-Gourinchas, Marion, and Sarah L. Babb. 2002. "The Rebirth of the Liberal Creed: Paths to Neoliberalism in Four Countries." *American Journal of Sociology* 108: 533–579.

Friedman, Monroe. 1985. "Consumer Boycotts in the United States, 1970–1980: Contemporary Events in Historical Perspective." *Journal of Consumer Affairs* 19: 96–117.

Friedman, Monroe. 1999. *Consumer Boycotts: Effecting Change Through the Marketplace and Media*. New York: Routledge.

Ganz, Marshall. 2000. "Resources and Resourcefulness: Strategic Capacity in the Unionization of California Agriculture, 1959–1966." *American Journal of Sociology* 105: 1003–1062.

Garrett, Dennis E. 1987. "The Effectiveness of Marketing Policy Boycotts: Environmental Opposition to Marketing." *Journal of Marketing* 52: 46–57.

Giugni, Marco. 2008. "Political, Biographical, and Cultural Consequences of Social Movements." *Sociology Compass* 2: 1582–1600.

Giugni, Marco and Maria T. Grasso, eds. 2015. *Austerity and Protest: Popular Contention in Times of Economic Crisis*. London: Routledge.

González, Sara, Frank Moulaert, and Flavia Martinelli, eds. 2010. "ALMOIN: How to Analyse Social Innovation at the Local Level?" In *Can Neighbourhoods Save the City? Community Development and Social Innovation*, edited by Frank Moulaert, Flavia Martinelli, Erik Swyngedouw, and Sara González, 49–67. London: Routledge.

Granger, Rachel C., Jonathan Wringe, and Peter Andrews. 2010. "LETS as Alternative, Post-capitalist Economic Spaces? Learning Lessons from the Totnes 'Acorn.'" *Local Economy* 25: 573–585.

Griffin, Larry J., Michael Wallace, and Beth A. Rubin. 1986. "Capitalist Resistance to the Organization of Labor before the New Deal: Why? How? Success?" *American Sociological Review* 51: 147–167.

Gusfield, Joseph R. 1986. *Symbolic Crusade: Status Politics and the American Temperance Movement*, 2nd edn. Champaign: University of Illinois Press.

Hargrave, Timothy J. and Andrew H. Van de Ven. 2006. "A Collective Action Model of Institutional Innovation." *Academy of Management Review* 31: 864–888.

Haveman, Heather A., Hayagreeva Rao, and Srikanth Paruchuri. 2007. "The Winds of Change: The Progressive Movement and the Bureaucratization of Thrift." *American Sociological Review* 72: 114–142.

Hetland, Gabriel and Jeff Goodwin. 2013. "The Strange Disappearance of Capitalism from Social Movement Studies." In *Marxism and Social Movements*, edited by Colin Barker, Laurence Cox, John Krinsky, and Alf Gunvald Nilsen, 83–102. Leiden: Brill.

Hiatt, Shon R., Wesley Sine, and Pamela Tolbert. 2009. "From Pabst to Pepsi: the Deinstitutionalization of Social Practices and the Emergence of Entrepreneurial Opportunities." *Administrative Science Quarterly* 54: 635–667.

Hoffman, Andrew J. 2001. *From Heresy to Dogma: An Institutional History of Corporate Environmentalism*. Stanford, CA: Stanford University Press.

Ingram, Paul and Hayagreeva Rao. 2004. "Store Wars: The Enactment and Repeal of Antichain Store Legislation in America." *American Journal of Sociology* 110: 446–487.

Ingram, Paul, Lori Qingyuan Yue, and Hayagreeva Rao. 2010. "Trouble in Store: Probes, Protests, and Store Openings by Wal-Mart, 1998–2007." *American Journal of Sociology* 116: 53–92.

Jenkins, J. Craig and Charles Perrow. 1977. "Insurgency of the Powerless: Farm Worker Movements (1946–1972)." *American Sociological Review* 42: 249–268.

Katz, Harry C. 1993. "The Decentralization of Collective Bargaining: A Literature Review and Comparative Analysis." *Industrial and Labor Relations Review* 47: 3–23.

King, Brayden G. 2008. "A Political Mediation Model of Corporate Response to Social Movement Activism." *Administrative Science Quarterly* 53: 395–421.

King, Brayden G. 2011. "The Tactical Disruptiveness of Social Movements: Sources of Market and Mediated Disruption in Corporate Boycotts." *Social Problems* 58: 491–517.

King, Brayden G. 2016. "Reputation, Risk, and Anti-Corporate Activism: How Social Movements Influence Corporate Outcomes." In *The Consequences of Social Movements*, edited by Lorenzo Bosi, Marco Giugni, and Katrin Uba, 215–236. Cambridge: Cambridge University Press.

King, Brayden G. and Nicholas A. Pearce 2010. "The Contentiousness of Markets: Politics, Social Movements, and Institutional Change in Markets." *Annual Review of Sociology* 36: 249–267.

King, Brayden G. and Sarah A. Soule. 2007. "Social Movements as Extrainstitutional Entrepreneurs: The Effect of Protests on Stock Price Returns." *Administrative Science Quarterly* 52: 413–442.

Koopmans, Ruud. 2004. "Movements and Media: Selection Processes and Evolutionary Dynamics in the Public Sphere." *Theory and Society* 33: 367–391.

Korpi, Walter and Michael Shalev. 1980. "Strikes, Power, and Politics in Western Nations, 1900–1976." *Political Power and Social Theory* 1: 301–334.

Kousis, Maria and Maria Paschou. 2017. "Alternative Forms of Resilience: A Typology of Approaches for the Study of Citizen Collective Responses in Hard Economic Times." *Partecipazione e Conflitto* 10: 136–168.

Kozinets, Robert V. and Jay M. Handelman. 2004. "Adversaries of Consumption: Consumer Movements, Activism, and Ideology." *Journal of Consumer Research* 31: 691–704.

Lamont, Michèle, Jessica S. Welburn, and Crystal M. Fleming. 2013. "Responses to Discrimination and Social Resilience Under Neoliberalism: The United States Compared." *Social Resilience in the Neoliberal Age*, edited by Peter A. Hall and Michèle Lamont, 129–157. Cambridge: Cambridge University Press.

Laville, Jean-Louis. 2010. "Solidarity Economy." In *The Human Economy*, edited by Keith Hart, Jean-Louis Laville, and Antonio David Cattani, 225–235. Cambridge: Polity Press.

Lounsbury, Michael and Ellen T. Crumley. 2007. "New Practice Creation: An Institutional Approach to Innovation." *Organization Studies* 28: 993–1012.

Lounsbury, Michael and Mary Ann Glynn. 2001. "Cultural Entrepreneurship: Stories, Legitimacy, and the Acquisition of Resources." *Strategic Management Journal* 22: 545–564.

Lounsbury, Michael, Marc Ventresca, and Paul M. Hirsch. 2003. "Social Movements, Field Frames, and Industry Emergence: A Cultural-Political Perspective on U.S. Recycling." *Socio-Economic Review* 1: 71–104.

Luders, Joseph. 2006. "The Economics of Movement Success: Business Responses to Civil Rights Mobilization." *American Journal of Sociology* 111: 963–998.

Manheim, Jarol B. 2001. *The Death of a Thousand Cuts: Corporate Campaigns and the Attack on the Corporation*. Mahwah, NJ: Lawrence Erlbaum.

McCammon, Holly J. 2012. *The US. Women's Jury Movements and Strategic Adaptation: A More Just Verdict*. Cambridge: Cambridge University Press.

McDonnell, Mary-Hunter, Brayden G. King, and Sarah A. Soule. 2015. "A Dynamic Process Model of Private Politics Activist Targeting and Corporate Receptivity to Social Challenge." *American Sociological Review* 80: 654–678.

McInerney, Paul-Brian. 2014. *From Social Movement to Moral Market: How the Circuit Riders Sparked an IT Revolution and Created a Technology Market*. Stanford, CA: Stanford University Press.

Micheletti, Michele and Dietlind Stolle. 2013. *Political Consumerism: Global Responsibility in Action*. Cambridge: Cambridge University Press.

Micheletti, Michele, Andreas Follesdal, and Dietlind Stolle. 2004. "Introduction." In *Politics, Products, and Markets: Exploring Political Consumerism Past and Present*, edited by Michele Micheletti, Andreas Follesdal, and Dietlind Stolle, iv–xxvi. New Brunswick, NJ: Transaction Publishers.

Moulaert, Frank, Flavia Martinelli, Erik Swyngedouw, and Sara González, eds. 2010. *Can Neighbourhoods Save the City? Community Development and Social Innovation*. London: Routledge.

Munir, Kamal A. and Nelson Phillips. 2005. "The Birth of the Kodak Moment: Institutional Entrepreneurship and the Adoption of New Technologies." *Organization Studies* 26: 1665–1687.

Murphy, Dale D. 2004. *The Structure of Regulatory Competition: Corporations and Public Policies in a Global Economy*. Oxford: Oxford University Press.

North, Paul. 2007. *Money and Liberation: The Micropolitics of Alternative Currency Movements*. Minneapolis, MN: University of Minnesota Press.

O'Rourke, Dara. 2005. "Market Movements: Nongovernmental Organization Strategies to Influence Global Production and Consumption." *Journal of Industrial Ecology* 9: 115–128.

Perrow, Charles. 2002. *Organizing America: Wealth, Power, and the Origins of American Capitalism*. Princeton, NJ: Princeton University Press.

Phillips, Rhonda. 2012. "Food Cooperatives as Community-Level Self-Help and Development." *International Journal of Self Help and Self Care* 6: 189–203.

Pinch, Trevor J. and Wiebe E. Bijker. 1984. "The Social Construction of Facts and Artifacts: Or How the Sociology of Science and the Sociology of Technology Might Benefit Each Other." *Social Studies of Science* 14: 399–441.

Prasad, Monica. 2006. *The Politics of Free Markets: The Rise of Neoliberal Economic Policies in Britain, France, Germany, and the United States*. Chicago: University of Chicago Press.

Raeburn, Nicole C. 2004. *Changing Corporate America from Inside Out: Lesbian and Gay Workplace Rights*. Minneapolis: University of Minnesota Press.

Rao, Hayagreeva. 2009. *Market Rebels: How Activists Make or Break Radical Innovations*. Princeton, NJ: Princeton University Press.

Rao, Hayagreeva, Philippe Monin, and Rodolphe Durand. 2003. "Institutional Change in Toque Ville: Nouvelle Cuisine as an Identity Movement in French Gastronomy." *American Journal of Sociology* 108: 795–843.

Rao, Hayagreeva, Calvin Morrill, and Mayer N. Zald. 2000. "Power Plays: How Social Movements and Collective Action Create New Organizational Forms." In *Research in Organizational Behavior*, edited by Barry M. Staw and Robert I. Sutton, 237–281. New York: Elsevier/JAI.

Ruef, Martin. 2000. "The Emergence of Organizational Forms: A Community Ecology Approach." *American Journal of Sociology* 106: 658–714.

Schneiberg, Marc. 2002. "Organizational Heterogeneity and the Production of New Forms: Politics, Social Movements, and Mutual Companies in American Fire Insurance, 1900–1930." In *Social Structure and Organizations Revisited (Research in the Sociology of Organizations*, Vol. 19), edited by Michael Lounsbury and Marc J. Ventresca, 39–89. Bingley: Emerald Group Publishing Limited.

Schneiberg, Marc and Tim Bartley. 2008. "Organizations, Regulation, and Economic Behavior: Regulatory Dynamics and Forms from the Nineteenth to Twenty-First Century." *Annual Review of Law and Social Science* 4: 31–61.

Schneiberg, Marc, Marissa King, and Thomas Smith. 2008. "Social Movements and Organizational Form: Cooperative Alternatives to Corporations in the American Insurance, Dairy, and Grain Industries." *American Sociological Review* 73: 635–667.

Schurman, Rachel. 2004. "Fighting 'Frankenfoods': Industry Opportunity Structures and the Efficacy of the Antibiotech Movement in Western Europe." *Social Problems* 51: 243–268.

Schurman Rachel and William Munro. 2009. "Targeting Capital: A Cultural Economy Approach to Understanding the Efficacy of Two Antigenetic Engineering Movements." *American Journal of Sociology* 115: 155–202.

Seidman, Gay W. 2007. *Beyond the Boycott: Labor Rights, Human Rights, and Transnational Activism*. Ithaca, NY: Cornell University Press.

Sikavica, Katarina and Jo-Ellen Pozner. 2013. "Paradise Sold: Resource Partitioning and the Organic Movement in the US Farming Industry." *Organization Studies* 34: 623–651.

Sine, Wesley D. and Brandon H. Lee. 2009. "Tilting at Windmills? The Environmental Movement and the Emergence of the U.S. Wind Energy Sector." *Administrative Science Quarterly* 54: 123–155.

Sine, Wesley D., Heather A. Haveman, and Pamela S. Tolbert. 2005. "Risky Business? Entrepreneurship in the New Independent-Power Sector." *Administrative Science Quarterly* 50: 200–232.

Smith, Jackie. 2001. "Globalizing Resistance: The Battle of Seattle and the Future of Social Movements." *Mobilization* 6: 1–20.

Snow, David A. 2004. "Social Movements as Challenges to Authority: Resistance to an Emerging Conceptual Hegemony." In *Authority in Contention, Research in Social Movements, Conflict, and Change*, vol. 25, edited by Daniel J. Myers and Daniel M. Cress, 3–25. Bingley: Emerald Publishing.

Soule, Sarah A. 2009. *Contentious and Private Politics and Corporate Social Responsibility*. Cambridge: Cambridge University Press.

Soule, Sarah A. and Brayden G. King. 2014. "Markets, Business, and Social Movements." In *The Oxford Handbook of Social Movements*, edited by Donatella della Porta and Mario Diani. Oxford: Oxford University Press.

Soule, Sarah A., Anand Swaminathan, and Laszlo Tihanyi. 2014. "The Diffusion of Foreign Divestment from Burma." *Strategic Management Journal* 35, 1032–1052.

Stolle, Dietlind and Michele Micheletti. 2013. *Political Consumerism: Global Responsibility in Action*. Cambridge: Cambridge University Press.

Swaminathan, Anand. 2001. "Resource-Partitioning and the Evolution of Specialist Organizations: The Role of Location and Identity in the U.S. Wine Industry." *Academy of Management Journal* 44: 1169–1185.

Swaminathan, Anand and Glenn R. Carroll. 1995. "Beer Brewers." In *Organizations in Industry: Strategy, Structure, and Selection*, edited by Glenn R. Carroll and Michael T. Hannan, 223–243. New York: Oxford University Press.

Swaminathan, Anand and James B. Wade. 2001. "Social Movement Theory and the Evolution of New Organizational Forms." In *The Entrepreneurship Dynamic in Population Evolution*, edited by Claudia Bird Schoonhoven and Elaine Romanelli, 286–313. Stanford, CA: Stanford University Press.

Tilly, Charles. 1986. *The Contentious French*. Cambridge, MA: Harvard University Press.

Tilly, Charles. 1995. *Popular Contention in Great Britain 1758–1834*. Cambridge, MA: Harvard University Press.

Tischer, Daniel. 2013. "Swimming against the Tide: Ethical Banks as Countermovement." *Journal of Sustainable Finance and Investment* 3: 314–332.

Uba, Katrin. 2005. "Political Protest and Policy Change: The Direct Impacts of Indian Anti Privatization Mobilizations, 1990–2003." *Mobilization* 10: 383–396.

Vaillancourt, Yves. 2009. "Social Economy in the Co-Construction of Public Policy." *Annals of Public and Cooperative Economics*, 80: 275–313.

Van Dyke, Nella, Sarah A. Soule, and Verta A. Taylor. 2004. "The Targets of Social Movements: Beyond a Focus on the State." In *Authority in Contention, Research in Social Movements, Conflict, and Change*, vol. 25, edited by Daniel J. Myers and Daniel M. Cress, 27–51. Bingley: Emerald Publishing.

Vasi, Ion Bogdan and Brayden G. King. 2012. "Social Movements, Risk Perceptions, and Economic Outcomes: The Effect of Primary and Secondary Stakeholder Activism on Firms' Perceived Environmental Risk and Financial Performance." *American Sociological Review* 77: 573–596.

Vogel, David. 1978. *Lobbying the Corporation: Citizen Challenges to Business Authority*. New York: Basic Books.

Vogel David. 1995. *Trading Up: Consumer and Environmental Regulation in a Global Economy*. Cambridge, MA: Harvard University Press.

Wahlström, Mattias and Abby Peterson. 2006. "Between the State and the Market: Expanding the Concept of 'Political Opportunity Structure.'" *Acta Sociologica* 49: 363–377.

Walker, Edward. 2012. "Social Movements, Organizations, and Fields: A Decade of Theoretical Integration." *Contemporary Sociology* 41: 576–587.

Walker, Edward T., Andrew W. Martin, and John D. McCarthy. 2008. "Confronting the State, the Corporation, and the Academy: The Influence of Institutional Targets on Social Movement Repertoires." *American Journal of Sociology* 114: 35–76.

Weber, Klaus, Kathryn L. Heinze, and Michaela DeSoucey. 2008. "Forage for Thought: Mobilizing Codes in the Movement for Grass-fed Meat and Dairy Products." *Administrative Science Quarterly* 53: 529–567.

Weber, Klaus, Hayagreeva Rao, and L.G. Thomas. 2009. "From Streets to Suites: How the Antibiotech Movement Affected German Pharmaceutical Firms." *American Sociological Review* 74: 106–127.

27

The Cultural Outcomes
of Social Movements

Nella Van Dyke and Verta Taylor

Social Movements as Producers of Culture

Public opinion on same-sex marriage shifted so dramatically between 1996 and 2015 that many observers considered it the fastest civil rights victory in US history. In 1996, a Gallup poll found a mere 27% of Americans supporting same-sex marriage. But that percentage more than doubled in the 20 years that followed, with 60% of Americans in favor by 2015 (McCarthy 2015), the year that a Supreme Court ruling legalized same-sex marriage in the United States. The victory stunned lesbian and gay activists, who proclaimed that they never thought they would see same-sex marriage legalized in their lifetimes. Winning the right to marry, after decades of opposition to gay rights spearheaded by the Religious Right, represented a cultural change so fundamental that it was almost unimaginable (Fetner 2008). While undoubtedly the result of multiple factors, including generational turnover, there is no question that this victory, at least in part, came about as the result of concerted efforts of lesbian, gay, and bisexual activists and their allies to change the hearts and minds of the general public to win legal recognition of their relationships (Ghaziani, Taylor, and Stone 2016). The dramatic shift in public opinion and social policy on same-sex marriage is a clear illustration of the ways that social movements can bring about cultural change at the individual, institutional, and macro-social levels.

The overwhelming body of research on social movement consequences focuses primarily on their policy outcomes (Amenta et al. 2010; Giugni, McAdam, and Tilly 1999). Yet for many social movements, cultural changes are often their most significant and lasting effects, especially when we take into account that most movements ultimately fail to achieve their stated policy objectives. For example, throughout the mid-2010s, the Black Lives Matter movement brought institutional racism and police violence against African Americans to the public's attention by circulating

The Wiley Blackwell Companion to Social Movements, Second Edition. Edited by David A. Snow, Sarah A. Soule, Hanspeter Kriesi, and Holly J. McCammon.
© 2019 John Wiley & Sons Ltd. Published 2019 by John Wiley & Sons Ltd.

videos of police officers shooting and killing unarmed Black men. From 2013 to 2015, the number of Americans who believed that relations between Blacks and whites in the USA were good dropped from 70% to 47% (Newport 2016). The disturbing images of violence circulated by activists affected public perceptions, even if they have not yet resulted in significant changes in policing, the law, and racial differences in the criminal justice system.

Social movements typically generate a range of cultural outcomes. They influence individual beliefs, practices, and identities; create new networks, organizations, and communities; and transform aspects of the broader culture (Earl 2004). Analyzing the cultural politics of the Montreal feminist women's community, Staggenborg and Lecomte (2009:163) suggest that social movement campaigns "generate public consciousness, put issues on the public agenda, create new frames and discourse, forge connections to new constituents, and leave behind new networks, coalition organizations, leaders, and activists." Similarly, Cable and Degutis (1997) find that collective efforts to prevent the opening of a new landfill reconfigured individuals' social networks, inspired the creation of a new community organization, raised the community's political consciousness, and resulted in passage of more stringent landfill regulations. While some of these outcomes can be thought of as political, some as structural in the sense of forging durable networks and coalitions, and some as cultural, it is difficult to separate the political and structural from the cultural because individuals' understanding of political processes and social structures requires the use of symbols and meaning making.

While most social science theory generally treats culture, structure, and politics as distinct spheres of social life, we view them as closely intertwined. Consider the example of same-sex marriage law in the USA. Was the Supreme Court decision legalizing same-sex marriage a political or cultural outcome for the LGBT rights movement? Research suggests that it was both. Powell and his colleagues (2015: 5) demonstrate that marital status "shapes individuals' perceptions of the legitimacy and authenticity of a couple," the rights they are accorded, and whether they are considered a family. These authors and others highlight the constitutive power of the law (McCann 1994), or "the idea that law shapes societal norms and values, along with individual determinations of right and wrong" (Powell, Quadlin, and Pizmony-Levi 2015: 5). Laws regarding marriage are especially powerful culturally. As Moscowitz (2013: 5) explains: "Because marriage is irrevocably tied to citizenship and nationhood, the gay marriage debate is not only about homosexuals' bid for marriage rights but also about how we define ourselves as a culture and a nation." As this example illustrates, the difference between political and cultural outcomes can be a false distinction. Political rhetoric imparts meaning that influences individual beliefs and opinions; and the law and other social policies direct people's behavior in ways that often become part of the broader habitus.

The dearth of research on the non-political cultural outcomes of social movements is glaring in light of the fact that many social movements do not target the state, but other institutional arenas, such as education, the mass media, religion, and the health care industry (Van Dyke, Soule, and Taylor 2004). In addition, movements that seek changes in the law and public policy frequently deploy tactics to influence hearts and minds and sway public opinion. Bernstein (2003) documents how gay and lesbian activists, shocked by the Supreme Court's 1986 ruling upholding sodomy laws, viewed the decision as a signal that they lacked basic rights of citizenship and personhood. LGBT movement organizations made the conscious decision to shift their attention to identity deployment strategies aimed at changing public opinion, and have succeeded in doing so (Bernstein and Taylor 2013; Ghaziani, Taylor, and Stone 2016).

Pointing to the limitations of current research on movement outcomes, a small but growing body of literature has recently turned attention to the cultural outcomes of social movements. In this chapter, we take stock of this research to address two questions: (1) What kinds of cultural consequences have been documented in the social movement scholarship?; and (2) Which factors have been found to be associated with successful cultural outcomes? Research on social movement outcomes has been plagued by lack of agreement on how to define success (Amenta et al. 2010; Cress and Snow 2000), and scholars studying the cultural impact of social movements face additional challenges. There is significant debate among sociologists over how to conceptualize culture (Alexander and Seidman 1990; Baldwin et al. 2006). Snow and colleagues (2014: 35) state the problem well when they describe culture as "a kind of kitchen-sink soup that is difficult to configure because it contains almost everything."

One reason for the lack of research on cultural outcomes is that, until recently, theories of culture emphasized the stability and continuity of cultural systems. However, social movement scholars have embraced more agentic approaches that acknowledge the role of social movements in cultural innovation and change (Earl 2004; Johnston and Klandermans 1995; Swidler 1986). Swidler's (1986) culture as toolkit approach, which has been influential among social movement scholars, focuses on the ways that actors develop strategies of action that combine familiar and established cultural patterns in novel ways to produce cultural innovation. Our analysis relies on a conception of culture proposed by social movement scholars that parses it into three basic categories (Johnston 2009; Snow, Owens, and Tan 2014): (1) performances (protest events, individual behavior, organizational practices); (2) ideations (values, beliefs, ideologies, frames, identities, stories); and (3) artifacts or products (music, art, texts, language, signs and symbols). These are key cultural resources and products of social movements and are also the source of a movement's cultural impact.

All social movements produce culture (Johnston and Klandermans 1995; Taylor and Whittier 1995). Culture is about meaning making, and in order to mobilize participants, social movements must generate resonant interpretive frames and forge a collective identity. Movements create new cultural meanings through protest performances and other collective actions, and protest gives rise to new oppositional communities or subcultures. A movement's cultural products do not always influence the broader culture beyond their effects on individual activists. But at times the culture generated by a social movement diffuses beyond the movement, producing widespread changes in individual identities and practices, organizations and institutions, and the wider society. Thus, the cultural outcomes of social movements are both internal, affecting primarily movement participants – for example, the construction of new collective identities such as feminist, queer, student radical, environmentalist, black power activist – and external, resulting in shifts in the broader culture (Earl 2004). And sometimes they are unintentional, as when Freedom Summer activists popularized wearing denim jeans (McAdam 1988).

Existing research on the cultural consequences of social movements uses varying conceptions of culture and frequently is not cast as cultural outcomes research, which makes it difficult to develop causal explanations of why and how movements succeed in changing the cultural fabric (Earl 2004). We hope to resolve this conceptual confusion by shedding light on the state of cultural outcomes scholarship, suggesting a consistent set of concepts to analyze the cultural impact of movements, and outlining a framework for understanding the conditions under which they occur.

Cultural Analysis of Movement Outcomes: Performance, Ideation, and Artifact

Our analysis of the cultural outcomes literature is organized around three basic cultural factors: performance, ideations, and artifacts. It is important to emphasize that these cultural dimensions are interrelated and recursive, making it difficult to analyze one without invoking the others.

Performances and repertoires

A defining feature of social movements is the use of public performances to express grievances and make claims (Johnston 2009; Tilly 2008). Protest in the form of demonstrations, marches, strikes, stories, debates, violent confrontations, and other change-oriented performances is a fundamental means by which social movements seek to influence authorities, opponents, the media, and the public. Oppositional performances make up the tactical repertoire of a social movement and are major sites where culture is accomplished (Taylor and Van Dyke 2004). Through performances, movement actors forge solidarity, construct collective identity, create collective memories, and generate collective action frames. Movements generally derive their repertoires from prior movements, but they also create new oppositional performances and repertoires by borrowing traditional cultural beliefs and practices, adapting them, and changing their meaning (Snow, Tan, and Owens 2013). The LGBT marriage equality movement's 2004 marriage protests at county clerk's offices across the USA illustrate how cultural rituals, in this case, wedding ceremonies, can be reconfigured as tactical repertoires (Taylor et al. 2009).

While social movement performances are generally collective, social movements also embrace personalized tactics to achieve cultural change. For example, HIV-AIDs activists used "kiss-ins" to promote LGBT visibility. Similarly, feminists frequently have adopted distinct styles of dress and gender presentations to contest sexist beauty standards (Reger 2012), and environmental activists have politicized practices such as recycling and veganism to promote sustainability.

Social movement performances sometimes generate new organizational logics and practices through their efforts to structure their activities. The New Left and radical branches of the civil rights and feminist movements advocated participatory democracy, adopting non-hierarchical organizational structures that emphasize collective decision-making (Polletta 2002). This new organizational logic is an important cultural outcome that has had enduring impact. The New Left's collectivist organizational logic spilled over to other progressive movements

(Meyer and Whittier 1994), most recently the Occupy movement (Hurwitz and Taylor forthcoming).

Social movement performances have influenced individual and institutional practices within a range of social institutions, including education (Arthur 2011; Binder 2002; Rojas 2007; Yamane 2004), environmental management (Freudenberg and Steinsapir 1991; Lounsbury, Ventresca, and Hirsch 2003), the economic market-place and corporations (King 2011; Sine and Lee 2009; Soule 2009), the military (Katzenstein 1998), politics (Clemens 1993), and healthcare (Epstein 1996; Taylor 1996, 2000). Lounsbury (2001) found that student environmental activism has influenced college and university recycling practices. Katzenstein (1998) traces changes in the doctrine and practices of the Catholic Church to feminist activism by women inside the church. Protestors with dual identities as scientists and antiwar activists have been persuasive in changing the core institutional practices of science, including its close ties to the military and government (Moore 2008). Clemens (1993) suggests that woman suffrage activists were instrumental in establishing lobbying as a tactic for influencing political elites. Epstein (1996) traced the impact of AIDS activism on patient access to clinical trials and treatment protocols, and Taylor (1996, 2000) similarly found that self-help activists were influential in defining postpartum psychiatric illness as a medical condition, raising public awareness, and establishing treatment protocols. Social movement performances are both an important cultural outcome in and of themselves, and they also produce other societal outcomes.

Ideations

Scholars have long recognized that ideations are both facilitators and products of social movements. Social movements create and influence a range of ideations, including values and beliefs, opinions, frames, language, stories, public discourse, and collective identities. Ideations are both social psychological, expressed in individuals' cognitions, identities, and emotions, and they also exist in the broader culture in the form of values, codes, institutional logics, social identities, practices, and public discourse. The overwhelming body of work on movement cultural consequences focuses on social movement-instigated changes in ideations.

Social movements influence the beliefs and values of movement participants and sometimes the broader public as well. Several studies find that participation in the New Left, civil rights, and women's movements had lasting effects on individuals' beliefs and political consciousness, shifting them to the left (McAdam 1988; Whalen and Flacks 1989). Research also shows that movement participation can change the value individuals place on activism and their commitment to continued action (Hirsch 1990; Van Dyke and Dixon 2013). Individual outcomes can also produce broader cultural changes by affecting the beliefs, identities, and practices of entire political generations, as Whittier suggests with respect to the women's movement (Whittier 1997). In one of the earliest systematic studies of cultural outcomes, Rochon (1998) traces large-scale shifts in opinions about racial and gender issues to new ideas incubated in "critical communities" that then spread to wider audiences through social movement-inspired diffusion. Illustrating how social movements often have cultural consequences even when they fail to achieve their policy goals, d'Anjou (1996) found that the first campaign of the British abolitionist movement, although not successful in prohibiting slavery, succeeded in changing public discourse by defining slavery and the slave trade as immoral. Several studies suggest that social movement activity influences public opinion by elevating the perceived importance of issues (Gamson and Modigliani 1989; Lee 2002; McAdam 1999).

New framings of issues, discourse, and stories are other important cultural outcomes of social movements. Numerous studies demonstrate that movements must generate frames and interpretive frameworks to mobilize participants (Benford and Snow 2000; Snow 2004). Sometimes the influence of a frame is limited to the beliefs of movement participants, but at other times frames endure and diffuse across social groups or locations, such as the civil rights frame, which was adopted by the Chicano, American Indian, Right to Life, and LGBT movements.

Scholars have also shown that social movements influence public discourse by changing the issues that are discussed, the language used, and the stories that are told. Tsutsui (2006) demonstrates that social movements have influenced international law to include attention to human rights. Exploring shifting terminologies of race, class, gender, and citizenship in the USA, Tarrow (2013) demonstrates that contentious politics has frequently produced new language. For example, the term "male chauvinist pig" was originally used by second-wave feminists to criticize men who considered themselves superior to women, but as use of the term declined among feminists, it diffused into ordinary speech (Mansbridge and Flaster 2007). In addition, social movement actors often mobilize through reclaiming negative labels previously used against their members, as in the case of contemporary anti-sexual violence activists who name their protests "slutwalks." Movements also tell stories or engage in narrative performances to expose concrete instances of bias and injustice and evoke sympathy for victims (Polletta 2006; Tilly 2008; Whittier 2009). Stories also get told about movements (Armstrong and Crage 2006; Meyer and Rohlinger 2012). Popular narrative suggests that Rachel Carson's book *Silent Spring* incited the modern environmental movement; however, the credit really belongs to the movement's political allies. Long before the book's publication, Congress had begun to hold hearings on pollution, and President Kennedy had appointed an environmental crusader as Secretary of Interior (Meyer and Rohlinger 2012).

A large body of work focuses on how social movements influence the production of new collective identities that gain recognition and increase the status of disadvantaged and stigmatized groups (Polletta and Jasper 2001; Taylor 1996; Taylor and Whittier 1992; Whittier 1997; see also Chapter 24 by Flesher Fominaya, in this volume). Researchers have documented collective identity outcomes at the individual, organization, and societal levels. A recent study by Rupp, Taylor, and Miller (2016) of college students' adoption of "queer" as a sexual identity demonstrates how the collective identities promulgated by social movements influence participants' individual identities. Sometimes through strategic action, these redefined identities alter the status and conceptions of stigmatized social groups. Moscowitz (2013) provides convincing evidence that LGBT activists used the campaign for marriage equality to successfully transform media depictions of gays and lesbians by replacing negative representations of LGBT people as criminals, victims, and sex radicals with positive images and mainstream identities as newly-weds and families.

Artifacts

All social movements produce cultural objects that provide representations of the movement's shared injustices and main ideas. Social movements scholars have generally been interested in artifacts as cultural resources for building solidarity (Roscigno and Danaher 2001; Rupp and Taylor 2003), but a movement's cultural artifacts can have lasting effects on individual beliefs and practices, organizations, and the larger culture (Vasi et al. 2015). Social movements invent and leave behind many different kinds of artifacts, such as music (Eyerman and Jamison 1998; Rosenthal and Flacks 2012; Roy 2010), films (Andits 2013; Vasi et al. 2015), books, literature and other print media (Isaac 2009; Meyer and Rohlinger 2012; Pescosolida, Grauerholz, and Milkie 1997), art (Reed 2005), styles of fashion (McAdam 1988; Taylor and Whittier 1992); and theatrical performances (Glenn 1999; Rupp and Taylor 2003; see also Chapter 20 by Mathieu, in this volume, on art and social movements).

Music is the most widely studied social movement artifact, and studies show that music played a fundamental role in mobilizing solidarity and collective identity in the labor, civil rights, women's, LGBT, and ethnic and nationalist movements (Eyerman and Jamison 1998; Rosenthal and Flacks 2012; Roy 2010; Staggenborg, Eder, and Sudderth 1993). The influence of protest music is often experienced by the larger society in a song that comes to symbolize the movement for both supporters and opponents (Eyerman and Jamison 1998). The civil rights movement's anthem, "We Shall Overcome," has been widely sung and coopted by many subsequent movements, even by Gulf War protesters embracing its message of hope (Rosenthal and Flacks 2012). Kaminski and Taylor (2008) find that the gay anthems and other songs performed by drag queens to educate audiences about gay life succeed in forging solidarity between gay and heterosexual audience members and have lasting effects on their audiences.

Researchers demonstrate that film, images, and texts are also important movement outcomes (Bail 2012; Vasi et al. 2015). Social movements texts, as Snow and colleagues (2014) have shown, often produce cultural change through their discovery by subsequent networks of activists who link them to current episodes of contention.

Social Movements and Cultural Change: Conditions of Influence

Existing research (Williams 2004) suggests four factors that influence a social movement's ability to effect cultural change: (1) the cultural symbol or object itself; (2) the movement's organization and actions; (3) non-movement actors, including allies, elites, and opponents; and (4) the institutional, political, and cultural context. Qualities of the cultural content produced by a movement, including its resonance and modularity, influence the movement's wider cultural impact (Tarrow 2013). Characteristics of movement organizations as the producers of ideations, performances, and artifacts also make a difference. Cultural products are frequently contested and debated by actors representing a range of interests, including counter-movements, authorities, the media, and the public, and these all affect the resulting cultural outcomes. Finally, a social movement's ability to achieve cultural

change is determined by the institutional context or cultural field in which contention takes place.

These factors that we have identified are consistent with research on the political
outcomes of social movements (Amenta et al. 2010). Since political and cultural
outcomes frequently overlap, we would expect this congruence.

Qualities of the cultural content

Qualities of the cultural symbols, rhetoric, frames, and performances deployed by a
movement influence whether the movement has an enduring impact. Existing
research suggests two main characteristics of movements' cultural products that are
associated with cultural change: symbolic resonance and modularity (Tarrow 2013).
Framing scholars have long argued that one of the factors that makes a particular
movement frame successful is the extent to which it resonates with the target audience (Benford and Snow 2000; Snow and Benford 1988; Tarrow 2013). Resonance
has partially to do with the legitimacy of the actor(s) articulating the claim; however,
the characteristics of the frame itself also matter. A frame must be logically coherent,
consistent with what people have observed and experienced, and address issues seen
as important (Benford and Snow 2000). d'Anjou and Van Male (1998) suggest that
the resonance of a movement's interpretive package is determined by its connection
to both culturally acceptable values and oppositional themes gaining in popularity.

A second factor that research suggests influences the lasting impact of a movement's interpretive frames, repertoires, and practices is their modularity. Modularity
refers to the extent to which the cultural performance can be employed by various
actors in different locations through diffusion. Tilly (1978) suggests that protest
tactics that are modular are more likely to end up becoming part of a movement's
repertoire. Celebratory or protest parades are illustrative. For example, Armstrong
and Crage (2006) argue that commemoration of the Stonewall Riot as the event that
sparked the gay rights movement was due in part to the portability of Pride parades,
a type of performance that can easily be enacted in different locations (Bruce forthcoming). Ambiguity can allow cultural acts to be modular and can facilitate cultural
diffusion (Polletta 2006). Stories that are ambiguous allow new actors in different
localities to insert themselves into the story and adapt it to fit their circumstances.

Non-movement actors

The cultural consequences of movements also result from interactions among multiple actors situated in various locations. These include not only social movement
participants, but also allies, counter-movements, authorities, the media, and the
broader public. Gamson (1990 [1975]) suggests that the media facilitate positive
cultural outcomes by providing standing to movement actors through interviews
that quote activists and convey movement frames. Counter-movements or other
opponents can also affect a movement's cultural influence by swaying public opinion
against the movement. Gamson and Modigliani (1989) demonstrate how competition between pro- and anti-nuclear power proponents over framing left the public
with ambivalent attitudes regarding nuclear power. Fetner (2008) suggests that the
New Right's vitriolic campaign against gay rights and same-sex marriage in the late

1980s and 1990s, while it had positive effects by bringing discussion of LGBT identity into mainstream discourse, was also successful in passing over 200 anti-gay ballot initiatives at the state and local levels.

Several studies suggest that insider activists, or individuals sympathetic to a social movement working within the target organization, facilitate cultural change (Epstein 1996; Katzenstein 1998; Moore 2008; Raeburn 2004). San Francisco's mayor Gavin Newsom provided support to the LGBT movement in 2004 by ordering the city to issue marriage licenses to same-sex couples, and President Barack Obama's stated support of marriage equality in 2012 signaled an opening of opportunities for the LGBT movement (Ghaziani, Taylor, and Stone 2016).

Movement actors: mobilization, organization, action

The structure and actions of the social movement itself also affect its ability to achieve successful cultural outcomes (Roy 2010). Multiple studies show that, in the USA, the presence of student movement organizations applying pressure to their administrations has been critical for the establishment of new curricular programs (Arthur 2011; Binder 2002; Rojas 2007; Yamane 2004). College campuses that had Black student organizations such as Du Bois Clubs, Student Nonviolent Coordinating Committees, Black Panther or NAACP chapters, or Black Student Unions were more likely to initiate Black Studies programs (Rojas 2007). McCammon and colleagues (2016) find that feminist law students and faculty formed a critical community to bring about feminist cultural change in the structure of law schools.

There is evidence that certain movement organizational structures are better suited for effecting cultural change than others. Studies of the women's movement demonstrate that non-hierarchical collectively structured organizations can have significant cultural impacts for members through consciousness raising and promoting solidarity (Van Dyke 2017; Whittier 1995). The practice of sharing personal stories that occurred within feminist groups in the 1970s allowed women to develop a consciousness of shared oppression that motivated their continued activism (Ferree and Hess 1994). Informal and collectivist organizational structures are also associated with tactical innovations, as well as leader and activist training and development (Polletta 2002; Staggenborg 1988).

Social movement communities (Staggenborg 2013; Taylor and Whittier 1992), consisting of multiple organizations, loosely networked individuals, and social, commercial and cultural organizations connected to a social movement, have been particularly effective in generating cultural outcomes. Ghaziani and colleagues (2016) suggest that the dense local networks of the LGBT social movement community were more successful than the Christian Right's thin networks at influencing public opinion, which helps explain their success in legalizing same sex marriage. Social movement communities foster the development of collective identity and generate other forms of movement culture that can impact the wider culture.

The political, institutional, and cultural context

The political and cultural context can constrain or facilitate a movement's ability to produce cultural change. The receptivity of elites and other actors in institutions targeted for change matters, as do the characteristics and organizational logic of the institutions themselves. Linders (2004) provides evidence that institutional, cultural, and political environments influenced public opinion and abortion practices following the decriminalization of abortion in the USA and Sweden. Ferree and colleagues (2002) report that social movements were able to make significant and enduring changes to abortion discourse in the USA and Germany, but the resulting discourses were very different due to fundamental differences in the two democracies' political and legal institutions, the role of religion in the two countries, and the openness of the mass media. Numerous studies also demonstrate that globalization has created discursive opportunities for movement cultural production and outcomes across nations (Barrett and Kurzman 2004; Paxton, Hughes, and Green 2006; Tsutsui 2006).

The success or failure of a movement's interpretive frames and discourse is conditioned by what scholars call the discursive opportunity structure, which refers to cultural institutions, including the media, that channel and organize discourse in a society (Ferree et al. 2002: 62; Koopmans 2004). Koopmans (2004: 367) suggests that a movement's visibility, resonance, and legitimacy increase its discursive opportunities. Prior research demonstrates the importance of legal discursive opportunities (Ferree 2003) and gender discursive opportunity structures for successful cultural outcomes (McCammon et al. 2001, 2007), but other institutions also provide discursive opportunities (Katzenstein 1998).

The media play a powerful role in determining which movements are able to take advantage of discursive opportunities. The media operates according to its own logic, with attention cycles, concern over advertisers and audiences, preference for professional sources, and geographic preferences taking priority (Andrews and Caren 2010; Oliver and Myers 1999). As a result, the media can alter a movement's message, describe movement performances in a particular way, or emphasize a counter-movement's frames more often. Moscowitz (2013) links the success of the LGBT movement's media campaign to depict gay and lesbian couples as deserving of marriage to the media's use of "poster couples" who conformed to normative definitions of marriage and the family.

Institutions all have their own logic and interests that affect a movement's ability to achieve cultural outcomes. Characteristics of public schools and colleges were a factor in whether proponents of multi-cultural education and women's, LGBT, and ethnic studies programs were able to successfully influence the adoption of new curricula (Arthur 2011; Binder 2002). Arthur (2011: 137) suggests two aspects of the organizational context that promoted adoption of new curricula: the consistency of the proposed changes with an organization's mission and its administrative openness and flexibility. Comparing the outcomes of feminist activism within the military and the Catholic Church, Katzenstein (1998) found that the extent to which an institution is bound to follow particular legal prescriptions affects its permeability, receptivity to challenging groups, and successful movement outcomes. Finally, it is important to note that the cultural performances and products of movements, such as music, art, styles of dress, and theatrical performances, are often reconfigured by cultural production industries that have their organizational logics (Peterson and Anand 2004).

Conclusion

Although research on the consequences of social movements has emphasized political outcomes, our review draws attention to the growing body of literature concerned with cultural outcomes. As Earl (2004) noted over a decade ago, in surveying the literature on cultural outcomes, scholars have not reached consensus about how to define culture or how to identify potential movement outcomes. Our aim has been to propose a theoretical framework for the empirical study of cultural outcomes that will allow scholars to identify cultural change linked to movement efforts over broad areas of cultural life. Summarizing research findings on the conditions that influence culture, we have identified four factors that make a difference: (1) qualities of the cultural content produced by movements; (2) characteristics of social movement communities and organizations; (3) actions of non-movement actors, including counter-movements, authorities, the media, and the public; and (4) institutional and cultural context. An examination of the variety of channels through which movement culture diffuses throughout the wider culture is beyond the scope of this chapter. But it is worth noting that a movement's cultural content is both created and diffused to the larger society through its collective performances, social networks, and other forms of interaction and communication, including new social media.

Our review has shown that there are increasingly more studies concerned with the cultural consequences of movements, but many questions remain for future researchers. The majority of research on movement-instigated cultural change has largely focused on ideations and relied upon framing as the primary explanatory approach. While further research in this tradition is clearly worthwhile, cultural performances and artifacts have received far less attention. We know very little about the broad cultural impact of the art and images produced by social movements. The Guy Fawkes mask, for example, has become a widely recognized anti-government/anti-establishment symbol. Why did that visual artifact, popularized by a comic book hero, become a global symbol of the hactivist group Anonymous and of anti-establishment protests around the world? To what extent do different movements produce cultural artifacts, and how do they matter? For example, what role do images of melting polar ice caps and other effects of climate change play in generating what Jasper (1997) calls "moral shocks" that change beliefs and sometimes inspire activism? Why are some movements able to produce documentaries that capture widespread attention that triggers shifts in public opinion while others are not? The paucity of research on movement cultural performances and artifacts relative to studies on ideations suggests the need for further research on these topics.

Scholars argue that cultural outcomes are especially difficult to study because the wide range of actors and contextual factors that matter in their production make it difficult to determine their relative impact (e.g. Earl 2004). The research reviewed in this chapter nevertheless makes clear that careful research can produce convincing explanations. Our review highlights the variety of cultural products that movements generate as they mobilize participants and seek changes in the broader culture. Often cultural change, via public opinion and discourse, is necessary for political change. When we consider research findings on the political outcomes of movements, it is important to keep in mind that these also generate new beliefs and practices. While much remains to be discovered about the significance of social movements as architects of cultural change, we know more about the cultural outcomes of movements than we think.

References

Alexander, Jeffrey C. and Steven Seidman, eds. 1990. *Culture and Society: Contemporary Debates*. Cambridge: Cambridge University Press.

Amenta, Edwin, Neal Caren, Elizabeth Chiarello, and Yang Su. 2010. "The Political Consequences of Social Movements." *Annual Review of Sociology* 36(1): 287–307.

Andits, Petra. 2013. "Movies and Movements." In *The Wiley-Blackwell Encyclopedia of Social and Political Movements*, edited by David A. Snow, Donnatella della Porta, Bert Klandermans, and Doug McAdam, 1–2. Oxford: Blackwell.

Andrews, Kenneth and Neal Caren. 2010. "Making the News: Movement Organizations, Media Attention, and the Public Agenda." *American Sociological Review* 75(6): 841–866.

Armstrong, Elizabeth A. and Suzanna M. Crage. 2006. "Movements and Memory: The Making of the Stonewall Myth." *American Sociological Review* 71(5): 724–751.

Arthur, Mikaila Mariel Lemonik. 2011. *Student Activism and Curricular Change in Higher Education*. Burlington, VT: Ashgate.

Bail, Christopher A. 2012. "The Fringe Effect: Civil Society Organizations and the Evolution of Media Discourse about Islam since the September 11th Attacks." *American Sociological Review* 77(6): 855–879.

Baldwin, John R., Sandra L. Faulkner, Michael L. Hecht, and Sheryl L. Lindsley, eds. 2006. *Redefining Culture: Perspectives Across the Disciplines*. London: Routledge.

Barrett, Deborah and Charles Kurzman. 2004. "Globalizing Social Movement Theory: The Case of Eugenics." *Theory and Society* 33(5): 487–527.

Benford, Robert D. and David A. Snow. 2000. "Framing Processes and Social Movements: An Overview and Assessment." *Annual Review of Sociology* 26: 611–639.

Bernstein, Mary. 2003. "Nothing Ventured, Nothing Gained? Conceptualizing Social Movement 'Success' in the Lesbian and Gay Movement." *Sociological Perspectives* 46: 353–379.

Bernstein, Mary and Verta Taylor, eds. 2013. *The Marrying Kind? Debating Same-Sex Marriage Within the Gay and Lesbian Movement*. Minneapolis: University of Minnesota Press.

Binder, Amy. 2002. *Contentious Curricula: Afrocentrism and Creationism in American Public Schools*. Princeton, NJ: Princeton University Press.

Bruce, Katherine McFarland. Forthcoming. *Pride Parades: How a Parade Changed the World*. New York: New York University Press.

Cable, Sherry and Beth Degutis. 1997. "Movement Outcomes and Dimensions of Social Change: The Multiple Effects of Local Mobilizations." *Current Sociology/La Sociologie Contemporaine* 45(3): 121–135.

Clemens, Elisabeth S. 1993. "Organizational Repertoires and Institutional Change: Women's Groups and the Transformation of American Politics, 1890–1920." *American Journal of Sociology* 98(4): 755–798.

Cress, Daniel and David A. Snow. 2000. "The Outcomes of Homeless Mobilization: The Influence of Organization, Disruption, Political Mediation, and Framing." *American Journal of Sociology* 105(4): 1063–1104.

d'Anjou, Leo. 1996. *Social Movements and Cultural Change: The First Abolition Campaign Revisited*. Hawthorne, NY: Aldine de Gruyter.

d'Anjou, Leo and John Van Male. 1998. "Between Old and New: Social Movements and Cultural Change." *Mobilization: An International Journal* 3(2): 141–161.

Earl, Jennifer. 2004. "The Cultural Consequences of Social Movements." In *The Blackwell Companion to Social Movements*, edited by David A. Snow, Sarah A. Soule, and Hanspeter Kriesi, 508–530. Oxford: Blackwell.

Epstein, Steven. 1996. *Impure Science: AIDS, Activism, and the Politics of Knowledge*. Berkeley: University of California Press.

Eyerman, Ron and Andrew Jamison. 1998. *Music and Social Movements*. Cambridge: Cambridge University Press.

Ferree, Myra Marx. 2003. "Resonance and Radicalism: Feminist Framing in the Abortion Debates of the United States and Germany." *American Journal of Sociology* 109: 304–344.

Ferree, Myra Marx, William A. Gamson, Jürgen Gerhards, and Dieter Rucht. 2002. *Shaping Abortion Discourse: Democracy and the Public Sphere in Germany and the United States*. Cambridge: Cambridge University Press.

Ferree, Myra Marx and Beth B. Hess. 1994. *Controversy and Coalition: The New Feminist Movement across Three Decades of Change*, rev. edn. New York: Twayne Publishers.

Fetner, Tina. 2008. *How the Religious Right Shaped Lesbian and Gay Activism*. Minneapolis: University of Minneapolis Press.

Freudenberg, Nicholas and Carol Steinsapir. 1991. "Not In Our Backyards: The Grassroots Environmental Movement." *Society & Natural Resources: An International Journal* 4(3): 235–245.

Gamson, William A. 1990 [1975]. *The Strategy of Social Protest*. Homewood, IL: Dorsey.

Gamson, William A. and Andre Modigliani. 1989. "Media Discourse and Public Opinion on Nuclear Power: A Constructionist Approach." *American Journal of Sociology* 95(1): 1–37.

Ghaziani, Amin, Verta Taylor, and Amy Stone. 2016. "Cycles of Sameness and Difference in LGBT Social Movements." *Annual Review of Sociology* 42: 165–183.

Giugni, Marco, Doug McAdam, and Charles Tilly, eds. 1999. *How Social Movements Matter*. Minneapolis: University of Minnesota Press.

Glenn, John K. 1999. "Competing Challengers and Contested Outcomes to State Breakdown: The Velvet Revolution in Czechoslovakia." *Social Forces* 78(1): 187–211.

Hirsch, Eric L. 1990. "Sacrifice for the Cause: Group Processes, Recruitment and Commitment in a Student Social Movement." *American Sociological Review* 55(2): 243–255.

Hurwitz, Heather McKee and Verta Taylor. Forthcoming. "Women Occupying Wall Street: Gender Conflict and Feminist Mobilization." In *100 Years of the Nineteenth Amendment: An Appraisal of Women's Activism*. Oxford University Press.

Isaac, Larry. 2009. "Movements, Aesthetics, and Markets in Literary Change: Making the American Labor Problem Novel." *American Sociological Review* 74(6): 938–965.

Jasper, James. 1997. *The Art of Moral Protest: Culture, Biography and Creativity in Social Movements*. Chicago: University of Chicago Press.

Johnston, Hank. 2009. "Protest Cultures: Performance, Artifacts, and Ideations." In *Culture, Social Movements, and Protest*, edited by Hank Johnston, 3–29. Farnham: Ashgate.

Johnston, Hank and Bert Klandermans. 1995. "The Cultural Analysis of Social Movements." In *Social Movements and Culture*, edited by Hank Johnston and Bert Klandermans, 3–24. Minneapolis: University of Minnesota Press.

Kaminski, Elizabeth, and Verta Taylor. 2008. "'We're Not Just Lip-Synching Up Here': Music and Collective Identity in Drag Performances." In *Identity Work: Negotiating Sameness and Difference in Activist Environments*, edited by Rachel Einwohner, Dan Myers, and Jo Reger, 47–75. Minneapolis: University of Minnesota Press.

Katzenstein, Mary Fainsod. 1998. *Faithful and Fearless: Moving Feminist Protest inside the Church and Military*. Princeton, NJ: Princeton University Press.

King, Brayden G. 2011. "The Tactical Disruptiveness of Social Movements: Sources of Market and Mediated Disruption in Corporate Boycotts." *Social Problems* 58: 491–517.

Koopmans, Ruud. 2004. "Movements and Media: Selection Processes and Evolutionary Dynamics in the Public Sphere," *Theory and Society* 33(3–4): 367–391.

Lee, Taeku. 2002. *Mobilizing Public Opinion: Black Insurgency and Racial Attitudes in the Civil Rights Era*. Chicago: University of Chicago Press.

Linders, Annulla. 2004. "Victory and Beyond: A Historical Comparative Analysis of the Outcomes of the Abortion Movements in Sweden and the United States." *Sociological Forum* 19(3): 371–404.

Lounsbury, Michael. 2001. "Institutional Sources of Practice Variation: Staffing College and University Recycling Programs." *Administrative Science Quarterly* 46(1): 29–56.

Lounsbury, Michael, Marc Ventresca, and Paul M. Hirsch. 2003. "Social Movements, Field Frames and Industry Emergence: A Cultural–political Perspective on US Recycling." *Socio-Economic Review* 1(1): 71–104.

Mansbridge, Jane and Katherine Flaster. 2007. "The Cultural Politics of Everyday Discourse: The Case of 'Male Chauvinist.'" *Critical Sociology* 33(4): 627–660.

McAdam, Doug. 1988. *Freedom Summer*. Oxford: Oxford University Press.

McAdam, Doug. 1999. *Political Process and the Development of Black Insurgency, 1930–1970*, 2nd edn. Chicago: University of Chicago Press.

McCammon, Holly J., Karen E. Campbell, Ellen M. Granberg, and Christine Mowery. 2001. "How Movements Win: Gendered Opportunity Structures and U.S. Women's Suffrage Movements, 1866 to 1919." *American Sociological Review* 66(1): 49–70.

McCammon, Holly J., Allison McGrath, Ashley Dixon, and Megan Robinson. 2016. "Targeting Culture: Feminist Legal Activists and Critical Community Tactics." Unpublished manuscript, Vanderbilt University.

McCammon, Holly J., Courtney Sanders Muse, Harmony D. Newman, and Teresa M. Terrell. 2007. "Movement Framing and Discursive Opportunity Structures: The Political Successes of the U.S. Women's Jury Movements," *American Sociological Review* 72(5): 725–749.

McCann, Michael W. 1994. *Rights at Work: Pay Equity Reform and the Politics of Legal Mobilization*. Chicago: University of Chicago Press.

McCarthy, Jason. 2015. "Record-High 60% of Americans Support Same-Sex Marriage." Washington, DC: Gallup. Available at: http://www.gallup.com/poll/183272/record-high-americans-support-sex-marriage.apx (accessed July 28, 2016).

Meyer, David S. and Deana A. Rohlinger. 2012. "Big Books and Social Movements: A Myth of Ideas and Social Change." *Social Problems* 59(1): 136–153.

Meyer, David S. and Nancy Whittier. 1994. "Social Movement Spillover," *Social Problems* 41(2): 277–298.

Moore, Kelly. 2008. *Disrupting Science: Social Movements, American Scientists, and the Politics of the Military, 1945–75*. Princeton, NJ: Princeton University Press.

Moscowitz, Leigh. 2013. *The Battle over Marriage: Gay Rights Activism through the Media*. Urbana: University of Illinois Press.

Newport, Frank. 2016. "Majority in U.S. Still Hopeful for Solution to Race Problems." Washington, DC: Gallup Organization. Available at: http://www.gallup.com/poll/193682/majority-hopeful-solution-race-problems.aspx (accessed July 28, 2016).

Oliver, Pamela E. and Daniel J. Myers. 1999. "How Events Enter the Public Sphere: Conflict, Location, and Sponsorship in Local Newspaper Coverage of Public Events," *American Journal of Sociology* 105(1): 38–87.

Paxton, Pamela, Melanie M. Hughes, and Jennifer L. Green. 2006. "The International Women's Movement and Women's Political Representation, 1893–2003," *American Sociological Review* 71(6): 898–920.

Pescosolida, Bernice A., Elizabeth Grauerholz, and Melissa A. Milkie. 1997. "Culture and Conflict: The Portrayal of Blacks in U.S. Children's Picture Books through the Mid- and Late-Twentieth Century," *American Sociological Review* 62: 443–464.

Peterson, Richard A, and N. Anand. 2004. "The Production of Culture Perspective." *Annual Review of Sociology* 30: 311–334.

Polletta, Francesca. 2002. *Freedom Is an Endless Meeting: Democracy in American Social Movements*. Chicago: University of Chicago Press.

Polletta, Francesca. 2006. *It Was Like a Fever: Storytelling in Protest and Politics*. Chicago: University of Chicago Press.

Polletta, Francesca and James M. Jasper. 2001. "Collective Identity and Social Movements." *Annual Review of Sociology* 27: 283–305.

Powell, Brian, Natasha Yurk Quadlin, and Oren Pizmony-Levy. 2015. "Public Opinion, The Courts, and Same-Sex Marriage: Four Lessons Learned." *Social Currents* 2: 1–10.

Raeburn, Nicole. 2004. *Changing Corporate America from Inside Out: Lesbian and Gay Workplace Rights*. Minneapolis: University of Minnesota Press.

Reed, T.V. 2005. *The Art of Protest: Culture and Activism from the Civil Rights Movement to the Streets of Seattle*. Minneapolis: University of Minnesota Press.

Reger, Jo. 2012. *Everywhere & Nowhere: Contemporary Feminism in the United States*. New York: Oxford University Press.

Rochon, Thomas. 1998. *Culture Moves: Ideas, Activism, and Changing Values*. Princeton, NJ: Princeton University Press.

Rojas, Fabio. 2007. *From Black Power to Black Studies: How a Radical Social Movement Became an Academic Discipline*. Baltimore, MD: Johns Hopkins University Press.

Roscigno, Vincent J. and William F. Danaher. 2001. "Media and Mobilization: The Case of Radio and Southern Textile Worker Insurgency, 1929 to 1934." *American Sociological Review* 66(1): 21–48.

Rosenthal, Rob and Richard Flacks. 2012. *Playing for Change: Music and Musicians in the Service of Social Movements*. Boulder, CO: Paradigm Publishers.

Roy, William. 2010. *Reds, Whites, and Blues: Social Movements, Folk Music and Race in the United States*. Princeton, NJ: Princeton University Press.

Rupp, Leila J. and Verta Taylor. 2003. *Drag Queens at the 801 Cabaret*. Chicago: University of Chicago Press.

Rupp, Leila J., Verta Taylor, and Shaeleya D. Miller. 2016. "Queer Women on Campus: Learning to Be Queer." In *Introducing the New Sexuality Studies*, edited by Steven Seidman and Nancy Fisher. New York: Routledge.

Sine, Wesley D. and Brandon H. Lee. 2009. "Tilting at Windmills? The Environmental Movement and the Emergence of the U.S. Wind Energy Sector." *Administrative Science Quarterly* 54: 123–155.

Snow, David A. 2004. "Framing Processes, Ideology and Discursive Fields." In *The Blackwell Companion to Social Movements*, edited by David A. Snow, Sarah A. Soule, and Hanspeter Kriesi, 380–412. Oxford: Blackwell.

Snow, David A. and Robert D. Benford. 1988. "Ideology, Frame Resonance, and Participant Mobilization." *International Social Movements Research* 1: 197–218.

Snow, David A., Peter B. Owens, and Anna E. Tan. 2014. "Libraries, Social Movements, and Cultural Change: Toward an Alternative Conceptualization of Culture." *Social Currents* 1(1): 35–43.

Snow, David A., Anna Tan, and Peter Owens. 2013. "Social Movements, Framing Processes, and Cultural Revitalization and Fabrication." *Mobilization: An International Quarterly* 18(3): 225–242.

Soule, Sarah A. 2009. *Contention and Corporate Social Responsibility.* Cambridge: Cambridge University Press.

Staggenborg, Suzanne. 1988. "Consequences of Professionalization and Formalization in the Pro-Choice Movement." *American Sociological Review* 53: 585–606.

Staggenborg, Suzanne. 2013. "Organization and Community in Social Movements." In *The Future of Social Movement Research*, edited by Jacquelien van Stekelenburg, Conny Roggeband, and Bert Klandermans, 125–144. Minneapolis: University of Minnesota Press.

Staggenborg, Suzanne, Donna Eder, and Lori Sudderth. 1993. "Women's Culture and Social Change: Evidence from the National Women's Music Festival." *Berkeley Journal of Sociology* 38: 31–56.

Staggenborg, Suzanne and Josée Lecomte. 2009. "Social Movement Campaigns: Mobilization and Outcomes in the Montreal Women's Movement Community." *Mobilization: An International Journal* 14(2): 163–180.

Swidler, Ann. 1986. "Culture in Action: Symbols and Strategies." *American Sociological Review* 51: 273–286.

Tarrow, Sidney. 2013. *The Language of Contention: Revolutions in Words, 1688–2012.* Cambridge: Cambridge University Press.

Taylor, Verta. 1996. *Rock-a-bye Baby: Feminism, Self-Help, and Postpartum Depression.* New York: Routledge.

Taylor, Verta. 2000. "Mobilizing for Change in a Social Movement Society." *Contemporary Sociology* 29: 219–230.

Taylor, Verta, Katrina Kimport, Nella Van Dyke, and Ellen Andersen. 2009. "Culture and Mobilization: Tactical Repertoires, Same-Sex Weddings, and the Impact on Gay Activism." *American Sociological Review* 74: 865–890.

Taylor, Verta and Nella Van Dyke. 2004. "'Get Up, Stand Up': Tactical Repertoires of Social Movements." In *The Blackwell Companion to Social Movements*, edited by David A. Snow, Sarah A. Soule, and Hanspeter Kriesi, 262–293. Oxford: Blackwell.

Taylor, Verta and Nancy Whittier. 1992. "Collective Identity in Social Movement Communities: Lesbian Feminist Mobilization." In *Frontiers in Social Movement Theory*, edited by Aldon D. Morris and Carol McClurg Mueller, 104–129. New Haven, CT: Yale University Press.

Taylor, Verta and Nancy Whittier. 1995. "Analytical Approaches to Social Movement Culture: The Culture of the Women's Movement." In *Social Movements and Culture*, edited by Hank Johnston, 163–187. Minneapolis: University of Minnesota Press.

Tilly, Charles. 1978. *From Mobilization to Revolution.* Reading, MA: Addison-Wesley.

Tilly, Charles. 2008. *Contentious Performances.* Cambridge: Cambridge University Press.

Tsutsui, Kiyoteru. 2006. "Redressing Past Human Rights Violations: Global Dimensions of Contemporary Social Movements." *Social Forces* 85(1): 331–354.

Van Dyke, Nella. 2017. "Movement Emergence and Resource Mobilization: Organizations, Leaders, and Coalition Work." In *The Oxford Handbook of US Women's Social Movement Activism*, edited by Holly J. McCammon, Verta Taylor, and Jo Reger, 354–375. Oxford: Oxford University Press.

Van Dyke, Nella and Marc Dixon. 2013. "Activist Human Capital: Skills Acquisition and the Development of a Commitment to Social Movement Activism." *Mobilization* 18(2): 197–212.

Van Dyke, Nella, Sarah A. Soule, and Verta Taylor. 2004. "The Targets of Social Movements: Beyond a Focus on the State." *Research in Social Movements, Conflict and Change* 25: 27–51.

Vasi, Ion Bogdan, Edward T. Walker, John S. Johnson, and Hui Fen Tan. 2015. "'No Fracking Way!' Documentary Film, Discursive Opportunity, and Local Opposition against Hydraulic Fracturing in the United States, 2010 to 2013." *American Sociological Review* 80(5): 934–959.

Whalen, Jack and Richard Flacks. 1989. *Beyond the Barricades: The Sixties Generation Grows Up*. Philadelphia, PA: Temple University Press.

Whittier, Nancy. 1995. *Feminist Generations: The Persistence of the Radical Women's Movement*. Philadelphia, PA: Temple University Press.

Whittier, Nancy. 1997. "Political Generations, Micro-Cohorts, and the Transformation of Social Movements." *American Sociological Review* 62(5): 760–778.

Whittier, Nancy. 2009. *The Politics of Child Sexual Abuse: Emotion, Social Movements, and the State*. Oxford: Oxford University Press.

Williams, Rhys H. 2004. "The Cultural Contexts of Collective Action: Constraints, Opportunities, and the Symbolic Life of Social Movements." In *The Blackwell Companion to Social Movements*, edited by David A. Snow, Sarah A. Soule, and Hanspeter Kriesi, 91–115. Oxford: Blackwell.

Yamane, David. 2004. *Student Movements for Multiculturalism: Challenging the Curricular Color Line in Higher Education*. Baltimore, MD: Johns Hopkins University Press.

28

Biographical Consequences of Activism

Florence Passy and Gian-Andrea Monsch

Introduction

The legacy of social movements is a central concern for scholars. We all wonder if contentious politics actually leads to social change. For some, biographical consequences of activism seem somehow less important; after all, the argument goes, biographical outcomes are merely changes in an individual's life. We claim that biographical consequences are indeed relevant and offer two main reasons for their importance in the study of social movements. First, scrutinizing personal outcomes entails investigating *socialization processes*. Participating in contentious groups socializes and re-socializes activists, as their worldviews and behaviors can be subject to transformation. Examining the biographical consequences of activism therefore enables social movement scholars to contribute to sociological research more broadly by supplementing theoretical and empirical knowledge of these socializing processes. A second reason for the study of biographical consequences is that personal outcomes can affect society as a whole, as activists interact with non-activists and through influences on the beneficiaries of a given movement. In these ways, biographical consequences extend beyond the impact on the activist's personal life to include effects on the broader culture.

In this chapter, we review research on the biographical consequences of activism. We begin our discussion, however, with four general remarks. First, although we currently possess better knowledge about biographical consequences than in previous decades (Giugni 2004, 2013, for an overview), studies on the matter remain sparse. Knowledge of biographical outcomes is mainly gleaned from studies that do not specifically investigate the biographical consequences of activism. Indeed, we can safely say that the analysis of biographical consequences is certainly not a research terrain privileged by scholars of social movements.

Second, many research findings lack robustness due to *methodological drawbacks*. Past reviews have already singled out this problem (Giugni 2004; McAdam 1999), but

The Wiley Blackwell Companion to Social Movements, Second Edition. Edited by David A. Snow, Sarah A. Soule, Hanspeter Kriesi, and Holly J. McCammon.
© 2019 John Wiley & Sons Ltd. Published 2019 by John Wiley & Sons Ltd.

it remains relevant to current research. We should acknowledge that assessing biographical outcomes of activism is by no means an easy task. To assess the impact of social movements on an activist's biography, studies require both a before/after research design and a control group. These are core methodological conditions required to establish causality and to provide robust findings. Despite this, many studies rely on retrospective data and/or have no control group. Methodological difficulty in establishing causality is thus a prevailing problem in studies of biographical outcomes.[1]

Our third remark pertains to conceptual problems. We face an *ambiguous conceptualization* of what we mean by biographical impacts. Many studies are interested in the legacy of social movements and therefore conceive of biographical outcomes as long-lasting consequences. That is to say, they examine durable outcomes once activists have left collective action. However, short-term personal outcomes also occur during collective action, but this short-term focus on consequences is usually not integrated into the literature on biographical impacts. Short-term consequences need to be accounted for if we want to fully assess the impact of activism on the activist's life. Therefore, the conceptualization of short-term personal consequences should be improved to refine our understanding of the plurality and diversity of outcomes, and to highlight the range of biographical consequences of activism.

Finally, scholars have paid little attention to the *social mechanisms* that produce biographical outcomes. Many scholars acknowledge effects of commitment on activists' life-spheres by highlighting correlations between activism and individual change, but such studies are limited in their ability to explain how those effects occur. Scholars who investigate biographical consequences in volunteering face a similar problem (Wilson and Musick 2000). We often fall short of knowing how and why commitment to movement activism affects the activist's worldviews and behavior.

We review current knowledge on biographical consequences of social movement participation to advance our understanding in two particular ways. First, we offer a conceptualization of this body of research to understand more particularly what the biographical consequences of activism actually are, including their inherent plurality. To do this, we distinguish short-term from long-lasting outcomes. We also map the diversity of biographical consequences, be it at the individual level as played out in activists' lives, or at the collective level, through a broader impact on culture. Mapping the field of biographical consequences also allows us to emphasize how interwoven these outcomes are with other impacts of social movements, notably cultural changes and to a lesser extent policy outcomes. Second, the chapter highlights several social mechanisms that explain how activism impacts an individual's life and the culture more broadly. We begin with a review of current knowledge about the personal impacts of activism. We rely not only on the social movement literature but also on knowledge provided by the study of other forms of activism such as volunteering and unionism.

Short-term Impacts

Individuals participating in contentious politics are embedded in a social network that can significantly re-socialize them, inviting them to adopt new worldviews and social practices. Recent research stresses that socialization is a life-long process and demonstrates that individuals' understandings and practices are shaped throughout one's life (Sigel 1995). This means that an activist's involvement in contentious politics can substantially impact their biography. However, social movement scholars have paid little attention to what happens during involvement in a movement while this learning process occurs, even though it is precisely during movement action that the impact on an activist's beliefs and practices takes place.

Activism can have multiple impacts on individuals' lives. Involvement in activism can shape the activist's mind; alter activists' social environments, notably their interpersonal networks; and modify activists' practices. One's mind, environment, and behavior may therefore change through participation. Furthermore, we know that activism has an impact on the individual's various life-spheres (Passy and Giugni 2000).[2] Not only does engagement in protest action shape an activist's political life-sphere by influencing their political understandings and behavior, involvement in activism also has an impact on other life-spheres, including family, work, and friendships. But do some of these impacts occur specifically during activists' involvement in collective action?

Several studies indicate that activism impacts the participant's mind, and their *worldviews* in particular. In a comparative study of pro-life activists and non-activists, Munson (2009) highlights that the activists' initial involvement in pro-life groups occurs when they hold ambivalent beliefs on abortion and that some even hold pro-choice positions. Munson shows that once activists join pro-life groups, their views on abortion change as initial ambivalence and pro-choice beliefs turn into pro-life sentiments. Newcomers are partly re-socialized once they become involved in pro-life networks. Further studies show similar results (e.g. Passy and Monsch 2016). Activists who participate in a specific movement community align their worldviews, notably about common good and politics, with those of other participants. During movement involvement, activists undergo a process of mind synchronization that alters their initial perceptions. Other studies that analyze either contentious politics or volunteering show how commitment influences the activists' worldviews and therefore re-socializes them at least to a certain extent (e.g. Beyerlein, Trinitapoli, and Adler 2011; Blee 2002; Flanagan 2004; Galais 2014; Haski-Leventhal and Bargal 2008; McFarland and Thomas 2006; Nepstad 2004).

Movement participation also shapes the *activist's identity*. Identity is an essential component in mobilization (Polletta and Jasper 2001), and the shaping of activists' identities is often a primary goal of a movement. The women's movement offers a case in point: feminist groups work hard to change a woman's understanding of herself (Rupp and Taylor 1987; Whittier 1995). As Whittier emphasizes: "Participating in consciousness-raising groups … gave women a new interpretation of themselves and the events around them" (1995: 93). An activist she interviewed well illustrates her statement:

> Everything that happens in the world, I have a framework for understanding it. And that framework comes from the consciousness raising first … If I didn't have a feminist framework to look at the world, I'd be, like most people, kind of adrift.
>
> (ibid.: 93)

Mobilization has an impact on the activist's identity and this also holds true for contentions where consciousness-raising does not constitute the movement's central task. Studying mobilization in British miners' strikes, Beckwith (2016) underlines how commitment affects the identities of women unionists, despite this not being the primary aim of the unions. Nevertheless, in joining the miners' strike, a political and feminist identity takes shape in the mind of female unionists. In line with other studies (e.g. Drury and Reicher 2000; Gould 1995; McAdam 1988; Rupp and Taylor 1987), the work of Whittier and Beckwith shows that the activist's identity is constructed during participation.

Participation in a social movement may also influence *personal skills*. Beckwith's study further emphasizes that involvement also transforms the personal competencies of the female unionists. Having to organize protest meetings and perform public speeches led women in the union to acquire substantial knowledge and organizational skills. Van Dyke and Dixon (2013) find similar results in their study on unionism. Studies that stress a positive link between activism and personal skills show that a gain in individual competence actually increases activists' sense of empowerment (Beckwith 2016; Drury et al. 2005; Van Dyke and Dixon 2013). Personal skills hence reinforce perceived self-efficiency and activists feel better equipped to bring about social change.[3] Whether we consider worldviews, identities or personal skills, movement participation has an effect on the activist's mind.

Research also shows that commitment in collective action bears on the activist's *relational environment*. By joining contention, participants meet other activists, which often enlarges and can substantially reshape their interpersonal network (e.g. Blee 2016; McAdam 1988; Passy and Monsch 2016; Rupp and Taylor 1987; Whittier 1995). Change in the relational environment has considerable consequences. Blee (2016) finds that women who joined far-right organizations went through a major cognitive and identity change due to a radical shift in their interpersonal network. As stated by one of her interviewees who did not hold racist views before joining the Ku Klux Klan: "I made new friends and started to become obsessed with race ... I thought about race 24/7" (ibid.: 79). Our study of activism in contentious politics, volunteering, and unionism has yielded similar results: conversational interactions that occur during participation shape the activist's mind (Passy and Monsch 2016).

Finally, mobilization in contentious politics affects the *participant's behavior*. The social ties acquired during activism can expand an activist's willingness to join in new mobilization opportunities (e.g. Diani 2011), and can also lead to action in the electoral sphere, so that, on average, movement activists' electoral participation levels are higher than those for other citizens (Fisher 2012). Studies on volunteering confirm these findings (e.g. Fennema and Tillie 2001; Sivesind, Pospíšilová, and Frič 2013; Stolle and Rochon 1998). However, these studies do not rely on a before/after research design. Therefore, the consequence of contentious activism and volunteering on electoral participation remains uncertain, as activists may have been frequent voters prior to joining contentious politics. Indeed, McAdam (1988) finds that civil rights contenders were already highly involved in politics before joining the movement.

Contentious politics also impacts the activist's *behavior in private life*. Contenders can be found to voice their values in other spheres of life, and often they adopt, and adapt, cultural models acquired during activism in their private life. For instance, they align other life-spheres with the political one by selecting specific job positions or making particular choices in their marital and parental sphere (McAdam 1989; Passy 1998; Rupp and Taylor 1987; Whittier 1995). In fact, research on New Left activists shows that the politicization of the activist's daily life seems to be a fairly common occurrence.

Major biographical consequences of activism occur during action, but the question that remains to be addressed is whether these impacts are long-lasting in nature or merely ephemeral outcomes, vanishing once participants leave their commitment communities.

Durable Consequences

Numerous studies of the durability of biographical consequences have been conducted, and these studies tend to show that biographical impacts of commitment are long-lasting consequences (see Giugni 2004, 2013, for a review). These studies emphasize that the contentious wave of social movement mobilization in the 1960s durably marked the lives of those who participated in the mobilizations. Recent studies on New Left activists who mobilized in the 1980s and after reveal similar findings (Giugni and Grasso 2016).

For instance, studies highlight that mobilization has durable impacts on the *political life-sphere* of New Left activists. Participation has a persistent impact on activists' worldviews, with participants remaining oriented to the left and continuing to hold core values of egalitarianism, libertarianism, autonomy, and diversity when compared to their non-activists counterparts (e.g. Abramowitz and Nassi 1981; Dunham and Bengtson 1992; Marwell, Aiken, and Demerath 1987; McAdam 1989, 1999; Sherkat and Blocker 1997; Whalen and Flacks 1989). Moreover, activists sustained the identity of a highly committed activist throughout their lives (Braungart and Braungart 1991). This body of research shows that the activist's mind was durably impacted by participation in the New Left. Consequently, these effects on their cognitive map and identity continue to influence their political behavior, leading to ongoing commitment to movement activism, with most emphasis on New Left mobilizations (McAdam 1989; Whalen and Flacks 1989). In general, New Left activists tend to be more politically active and are more likely to vote (e.g. Abramowitz and Nassi 1981; Braungart and Braungart 1991; Fendrich 1993; Giugni and Grasso 2016; McAdam 1989; Pagis 2014; Sherkat and Blocker 1997).

Studies of other social movements echo these results. The work of Shirlow et al. (2010) highlights that former activists in the Irish Republican Army continue to espouse strong Republican attitudes and identity, and participants remain politically active in the preservation of Irish autonomy. Research on volunteering also highlights durable outcomes on participant's political life-sphere. People who volunteer tend to be more socially and politically active (e.g. Astin, Sax, and Avalos 1999; Flanagan 2004; Hart et al. 2007; McFarland and Thomas 2006; Terriquez 2015; Wilson and Musick 2000). However, it seems as though only activism with an explicit civic and political content impacts volunteers' political life-sphere (e.g. Stolle and Rochon 1998; Van Deth 2006). Similarly, only a positive volunteering experience has a durable consequence on activists' political life-sphere (Finkelstein 2010; McAdam and Brandt 2009). Nevertheless, scholars emphasize that involvement in social movements or in volunteering does have durable effects on the participant's political life.

Durable consequences of activism reach beyond politics. Research underscores that participation in social movements has long-lasting consequences on the activist's private life, notably on family and work life-spheres (Braungart and Braungart 1991; Fendrich and Lovoy 1988; McAdam 1989, 1999; Pagis 2014; Sherkat and Blocker 1997; Taylor and Raeburn 1995; Whittier 1995; Wilhelm 1998). Regarding the *family life-sphere*, scholars show how the experience of activism in the 1960s changed the way activists conceive of the domestic sphere. Fewer of them got married and, when they did so, they married later in life. Divorces were also more frequent among movement members and having children was less likely. Furthermore, these studies emphasize durable consequences on activists' *work life-sphere*. The 1960s contentious experience had a profound effect on activists' work choices: many contenders selected teaching and helping professions; often experienced a non-traditional work life-course; and received lower incomes than the members of the same generation who were not involved in collective action.

Scholars have consistently observed enduring consequences in the activist's mind and behavior both in their political and private life. Unfortunately such studies focus mainly on New Left activism, and we possess little knowledge on other types of movements. A second limitation to our understanding of durable biographical changes pertains to the activist's relational environment. To our knowledge, no study has examined the stability of activists' interpersonal network acquired during commitment. This is quite unfortunate as it could serve to explain how worldviews and practices acquired during action endure over time. We will return to this issue later, when we discuss social mechanisms that explain biographical consequences.

Cultural Change

The existing literature not only offers empirical evidence on the consequences of activism for the activist's life, it also highlights broader cultural changes. Shifting the focus of their analysis from individuals to groups of people enables scholars to seize the diffusion of biographical consequences to a larger population.

A first set of studies examines how activism impacts *age cohorts*. This research investigates aggregate-level changes in life-course patterns to assess if an activist's cohort has a distinct biography compared to a cohort of the same age who did not participate in activism. McAdam's study (1999) on the activists of the 1960s provides some compelling findings. In a first step, he shows that involvement in those movements altered the biography of a whole generation of activists. Their political, domestic, and work life-spheres were significantly distinct from people of the same age who did not participate in social movements. In a second step, McAdam reveals that these biographical disparities between activist and non-activist cohorts vanish over time due to the importation of alternative life-course patterns from activists to non-activists of the same age. That is, the biographical consequences of activism spread via the adoption of certain political and life-models developed by participants in the movements of the 1960s to a cohort of non-participants of the same age group. Findings by Wilhelm (1998) and Jennings (2002) provide further evidence of this same process. Evidence shows that individuals' involvement in the 1960s contentious movements led to broader cultural changes in US society.

Recent studies have also examined *intergenerational transmission*, whereby worldviews, identities, and practices acquired by activists during their commitment in the 1960s movements have been conveyed to their children (Masclet 2016; Pagis 2014, Quéniart, Charpentier, and Chanez 2008). For example, Masclet's (2016) work on feminist activists in France emphasizes overlaps in the way activist mothers and their adult children conceive of gender politics and behave in their political and private spheres. However, Masclet shows that there is neither an automatic nor a complete transmission from one generation to the next. First, the degree to which children appropriate their parents' worldviews and behaviors varies. Second, intergenerational transmission is an interactive and dynamic process. Adult children activate their inherited dispositions in specific moments of their lives by combining them with their own experience. Integration of activist parents' values and practices is therefore not a straightforward transmission, but one that relies on adaptations from one generation to the next.

Finally, a third and more recent research path is that of Whittier (2016), who examines change in the life-course of *movement beneficiaries*, the group on whose behalf the movement advocates. Many movements seek to ameliorate the rights and living conditions of their beneficiaries. Whittier's study of an LGBT movement shows that the biography of movement beneficiaries changes. In particular, their private life changes through the adoption of new identities (e.g. by acquiring the pride discourse) but also by embracing new life-models developed in the movement, such as same-sex parenthood and equal marriage rights. These biographical outcomes are consequences of identities and life-models developed and endorsed by activists who then diffuse them to the movement's beneficiaries. "By producing, redefining, and promulgating collective identities, activists changed the self-definitions available more broadly," as Whittier argues (ibid.: 136), and the same logic applies to the production and diffusion of life-models from the activists to the movement's beneficiaries. These biographical outcomes are also consequences of policy changes brought by the social movement itself. As shown by Whittier, policies championed by the LGBT networks and implemented by the state substantially impacted the movement beneficiaries.

Involvement in movements can therefore indirectly shape the lives of non-activists as biographical consequences of activism are diffused to an entire age cohort; to later generations; and to the movement's beneficiaries. Collective consequences of activism are cultural outcomes, whereby the society at large is affected by the changes that occur in activists' lives. While such impacts are important to understand a movement's legacy, they have received little attention from social movement scholars. In addition, research that examines these impacts has, until recently, focused essentially on the New Left. We certainly need further research to assess the cultural impacts of contentious politics.

Mapping the Field

This review shows that personal outcomes occur in multiple ways, yet this plurality is often neglected due to the scant amount of studies on this research topic. In this section, we map this diversity. This assessment aims to offer a better overall conceptualization of the biographical consequences of activism as a research object and our understanding of what personal outcomes actually are. Finally, this conceptual map also seeks to highlight how biographical consequences of activism are interwoven with other impacts of social movements, notably cultural change and policy outcomes.

Figure 28.1 shows what biographical consequences are in their plurality. We distinguish between individual and collective impacts: to begin with consequences for individuals, we observe two types of outcome located at two distinct moments in the activist's life. First, scholars investigate consequences that occur *during collective action*. This short-term focus on personal outcomes assesses whether the world-views, identities, relational environment, and behavior of participants change during their involvement in contentious politics, and the extent to which they do. Second, researchers investigate biographical change *after an activist's commitment*, once they have left contentious politics. This long-term focus on personal consequences examines durable impacts of participation in contention.

Impacts at the collective level are also multiple and we distinguish three types of consequences. First, scholars focus on *intra-generational impacts*, with the aim of investigating aggregate-level change in life-course patterns to assess whether a cohort of activists possesses a distinct biography compared to a cohort of non-activists of the same age. Researchers also analyze if the same age cohort adopts worldviews and practices in their own lives, and the extent to which they do so. In the latter case, they examine the diffusion of worldviews and lifestyles to a whole generation. A second way to conceptualize generational outcomes is to consider *inter-generational*

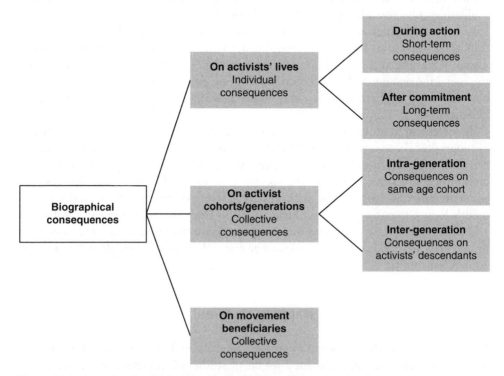

Figure 28.1 Mapping the field of biographical consequences.

impacts. Here, scholars highlight transmission of worldviews, identities, and behaviors from activist parents to their (adult) children. Finally, biographical outcomes of activism also mean *change in the life-course of movement beneficiaries*. Like scholars who examine consequences for generations, here researchers focus on collective consequences but seek to assess biographical changes for a specific group of people, those on whose behalf the movement pursues change.

The biographical consequences of social movements are thus pronounced in that they affect the activist's life and also those of people in other groups, particularly, research shows, generations, kin, and the beneficiaries of the movement. In addition, as Figure 28.2 demonstrates, the various types of biographical consequences are differentially associated with movement outcomes. Social movements scholars distinguish among three types of movement outcomes. First, contentious politics can have a social impact by bringing about political change. Second, movements can affect collective understandings and lifestyles and thus lead to cultural change. Finally, movement activism may also bring about biographical changes in an individual's life. As Figure 28.2 suggests, biographical outcomes and social movement outcomes are highly interwoven.

First, involvement in movement produces biographical outcomes by affecting activists' lives. Second, biographical consequences can have an impact on society more broadly by diffusing worldviews, identities, and behaviors to non-activists. Biographical outcomes, when they occur on a widespread scale, are cultural outcomes, as the personal consequences extend beyond the impact on an activist's personal life to the broader society. Third, changes in the life-course of movement beneficiaries are directly related to policy outcomes of social movements. Changes in policy that result from social movement action are directly beneficial to the group the activists support. As Whittier (2016) shows, antidiscrimination policies championed by the US LGBT movement have successfully impacted the lives of queer

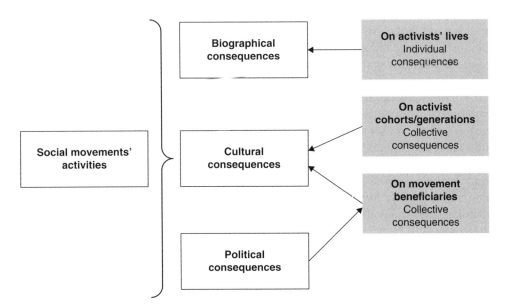

Figure 28.2   Interwoven outcomes.

people, beyond those who participated in the movement. Biographical consequences are therefore intimately interwoven to other social movement outcomes: They are closely tied to both cultural and political change.

Social Mechanisms at Play

Activism impacts the lives of social movement participants, broader age cohorts, and movement beneficiaries. But how do these impacts occur? Understanding how impacts occur requires exploring the causal mechanisms at play, in particular, the socializing process at work. Here, we discuss several socializing mechanisms gleaned from the current literature to understand how participation shapes activists' lives, to explain both short-term and durable impacts. We then turn to a discussion of how socialization mechanisms explain how biographical consequences impact societal culture more broadly.

Crossley's (2003) research provides a starting point for developing an understanding of how an individual's cognitions and practices are altered by contentious politics. During involvement, activists acquire what Crossley calls "a radical habitus." That is, participants gain specific schemas allowing them to question and criticize the social world around them, and they come to possess political know-how that allows them, in turn, to translate ideas into action. This radical habitus affects the activist's life deeply and durably for two reasons. First, habitus structures and orients the activist's actions in most of their life-spheres. Second, the stability of the habitus leads to long-lasting biographical consequences. Yet the process Crossley exposes seems to apply more fruitfully to explain biographical consequences of activists committed in radical political commitment, as in the 1960s contentious wave. It is probable that not all forms of commitment develop such radical habitus.

Crossley, however, leaves the question of how radical habitus specifically impacts the activist self unanswered. To account for this missing element in the puzzle, a number of scholars stress the importance of social interactions in altering cognition and practice (e.g. Blumer 1969; Collins 2004). The interplay between cognitions and social interactions shapes the activist's worldviews, and this influence, in turn, affects practices, in a process we term a *cognitive-relational process* (Passy and Monsch 2016). McAdam (1988) illustrates this process with the example of Freedom Summer volunteers who underwent an identity change during their mobilization. They acquired Crossley's radical habitus but did so through constant interactions with other Freedom Summer volunteers. We find a similar process at work when trying to explain why activists involved in a specific movement community rely on shared understandings about politics and common good (Passy and Monsch 2016). Activists undergo a process in which they come to share similar worldviews as a result of ongoing interactions among activists. Other studies highlight a similar process (e.g. Blee 2002; Corrigall-Brown 2012; Drury and Reicher 2000; Munson 2009; Nepstad 2004; Rupp and Taylor 1987). Social interactions during movement participation hence play an important part in socialization in that they shape an activist's mind and behaviors. This explains how activism can have short-term impacts on participants.

Scholars underline another social mechanism explaining biographical consequences on activists' life, which we name the *experiential process*. This process emphasizes the way individuals experience activism and how this influences their biography and especially their political behavior. McAdam and Brandt (2009), for instance, show that a disappointing experience of participating in volunteering alters an activist's future commitments. Disillusionment explains why volunteers do not continue with political and civic commitments once they have left their initial involvement. Beckwith (2016) also highlights an experiential process. Contrary to volunteers studied by McAdam and Brandt, women committed in the 1984–1985 miners' strike in Yorkshire experimented their first mobilization as a positive experience. Even though it was actually a cruel defeat, they lived their first unionist experience as a highly positive one that substantially enriched their lives, which in turn encouraged them to commit in the next nation-wide miners strike a decade later. The way activists experience their commitment differently impacts their life, specifically, it enables them to maintain their political commitment or to discourage it.

The cognitive-relational and experiential processes explain how activism can impact the individual participant's life. But what do we know about the social mechanisms influencing the collective impacts of contentious politics? Social movement analysts underline that diffusion is a key process. McAdam (1999) develops important elements of this thinking by highlighting a three-stage process to explain the diffusion of worldviews and lifestyles from 1960s activists to non-activists. Participants first rejected traditional life-course norms in favor of more liberal ones. These alternative norms were then embedded in subcultural networks, and in counterculture networks most notably, before finally becoming available for people who did not take part in the New Left contention. Whittier (2016) also emphasizes diffusion mechanisms to explain how members of the broader public, and movement beneficiaries in particular, experience biographical consequences. Activists produce, redefine, and promulgate collective identities and life-models that are then available to non-activists. Diffusion is a pivotal process to explain how biographical consequences of activism impact broader culture (see also Brown and Rohlinger 2015; Sherkat and Blocker 1997; Wilhelm 1998).

What Next?

To conclude, we suggest a few directions for further research on the biographical impacts of social movements. We have selected four research avenues that are particularly crucial to expanding our knowledge of the consequences of social movements on individual lives and societal culture more broadly.

First, we need to broaden our knowledge about *social mechanisms*. Existing research identifies cognitive-relational, experiential, and diffusion processes. We nevertheless require more empirical evidence to consolidate and validate these three social mechanisms. Furthermore, further research is necessary to shed light on other possible causal mechanisms, as these three processes likely do not exhaust all the mechanisms at play in explaining how activism shapes activists' lives and the broader culture. Finally, we should identify social mechanisms explaining long-lasting consequences of activism. How could participation in a movement durably impact activists' life even years after having left commitment? This question still remains unanswered. We urge analysts to scrutinize activists' conversational interactions once they have left commitment. If activists who have left commitment keep friends who remain in the activist group in their interpersonal network, we can assume that continuity in conversational interactions stabilizes their worldviews and behaviors, and therefore explains, at least to a certain extent, how biographical consequences of activism could endure over time.

Second, a more thorough consideration of short-term impacts is needed. Activists' lives change, sometimes substantially, during participation in collective action. Understanding such short-term consequences in more detail will allow us to more precisely specify what actually occurs during collective action and to identify short-term biographical consequences with more accuracy.

Third, we need to apprehend variation in biographical impacts in more detail. Many research findings stem from study of activists committed in the New Left. We therefore know little about biographical consequences stemming from other movements. Similarly, many results derive from the study of active participants and we therefore know too little about passive members, who support protest only financially yet who constitute the largest group of activists in most movements (Passy and Monsch 2016). Finally, research treats activists as an entity without examining variation among participants. Groups of activists may experience activism differently, as can be the case for women and men in the same movement (e.g. Van Dyke, McAdam, and Wilhelm 2000). Investigating activism in movements other than the New Left and inspecting variation among differing groups of activists are crucial to broadening our knowledge about the biographical consequences of protest politics. The study of variation is epistemologically crucial as it highlights that similar action in distinct contexts or for distinct groups can lead to different consequences. The study of variation therefore provides essential knowledge about the processes at stake. Here, for the study of biographical impact, scrutinizing variation would allow scholars to grasp why participation in contentious politics brings different personal outcomes once activists are mobilized in one movement rather than another, and why commitment affect differently various types of activists.

Finally, studies of biographical consequences need to bolster and diversify their *methodological frameworks*. We can improve our research designs in these following ways. First, as highlighted in the Introduction, some studies cannot assess causality because they do not include control groups and do not consider activists before and after movement participation. Scholars need to rely on before/after research designs and control groups of non-activists to provide more robust results. Second, few studies compare participation in distinct social movements. Such comparisons would allow us to move toward generalizing our findings regarding biographical outcomes to diverse types of activism. Such studies would also highlight variation in personal consequences on activists' lives and in the broader cultural impacts. Finally, many studies of biographical outcomes rely on quantitative data and these studies improve our knowledge of personal consequences. However, our knowledge would also be broadened by mobilizing qualitative data. Qualitative data may allow us to learn more about the social mechanisms at play in producing biographical outcomes. Strengthening and diversifying our methodological frameworks will help provide better knowledge of the legacy of participation for both participants' lives and the broader culture.

Notes

1   Studies of volunteering face a similar shortcoming (see Wilson 2012).
2   The life of each of us is composed of life-spheres, which can be defined as distinct though interrelated "regions" in the life of an individual, each one with its own borders, logic, and dynamic. Family, work, friends, politics, and spirituality/religion are examples of spheres that constitute the life of an individual. For more details about life-spheres, see Passy and Giugni (2000).
3   Studies on volunteering present similar findings (e.g. Flanagan 2004).

References

Abramowitz, Stephen I. and Alberta J. Nassi. 1981. "Keeping the Faith: Psychosocial Correlates of Activism Persistence into Middle Adulthood." *Journal of Youth and Adolescence* 10(6): 507–523.

Astin, Alexander W., Linda J. Sax, and Juan Avalos. 1999. "Long-Term Effects of Volunteerism During the Undergraduate Years." *The Review of Higher Education* 22(2): 187–202.

Beckwith, Karen. 2016. "All Is Not Lost: : The 1984–85 British Miners' Strike and Mobilization after Defeat." In *The Consequences of Social Movements*, edited by Lorenzo Bosi, Marco Giugni, and Katrin Uba, 41–65. Cambridge: Cambridge University Press.

Beyerlein, Kraig, Jenny Trinitapoli, and Gary Adler. 2011. "The Effect of Religious Short-Term Mission Trips on Youth Civic Engagement." *Journal for the Scientific Study of Religion* 50(4): 780–795.

Blee, Kathleen M. 2002. *Inside Organized Racism: Women in the Hate Movement*. Berkeley: University of California Press.

Blee, Kathleen M. 2016. "Personal Effects from Far-Right Activism." In *The Consequences of Social Movements*, edited by Lorenzo Bosi, Marco Giugni, and Katrin Uba, 66–84. Cambridge: Cambridge University Press.

Blumer, Herbert. 1969. *Symbolic Interactionism: Perspective and Method*. Englewood Cliffs, NJ: Prentice-Hall.

Braungart, Margaret M. and Richard G. Braungart. 1991. "The Effects of the 1960s Political Generation on Former Left- and Right-Wing Youth Activist Leaders." *Social Problems* 38(3): 297–315.

Brown, Robyn Lewis and Deana A. Rohlinger. 2015. "The Effect of Political Generation on Identity and Social Change: Age Cohort Consequences." *Journal of Women & Aging* November: 1–16.

Collins, Randall. 2004. *Interaction Ritual Chains*. Princeton, NJ: Princeton University Press.

Corrigall-Brown, Catherine. 2012. *Patterns of Protest: Trajectories of Participation in Social Movements*. Stanford, CA: Stanford University Press.

Crossley, Nick. 2003. "From Reproduction to Transformation: Social Movement Fields and the Radical Habitus." *Theory, Culture & Society* 20(6): 43–68.

Diani, Mario. 2011. "Social Movements and Collective Action." In *The Sage Handbook of Social Network Analysis*, edited by Peter Carrington and John Scott, 223–235. London: Sage.

Drury, John, Christopher Cocking, Joseph Beale, Charlotte Hanson, and Faye Rapley. 2005. "The Phenomenology of Empowerment in Collective Action." *British Journal of Social Psychology* 44: 309–328.

Drury, John and Steve Reicher. 2000. "Collective Action and Psychological Change: The Emergence of New Social Identities." *British Journal of Social Psychology* 39(4): 579–604.

Dunham, Charlotte Chorn and Vern L. Bengtson. 1992. "The Long-Term Effects of Political Activism on Intergenerational Relations." *Youth & Society* 24(1): 31–51.

Fendrich, James M. 1993. *Ideal Citizens: The Legacy of the Civil Rights Movement*. Albany, NY: State University of New York Press.

Fendrich, James M. and Kenneth L. Lovoy. 1988. "Back to the Future: Adult Political. Behavior of Former Political Activists." *American Sociological Review* 53(5): 780–784.

Fennema, Meindert and Jean Tillie. 2001. "Civic Community, Political Participation and Political Trust of Ethnic Groups." *Connections* 24(1): 26–41.

Finkelstein, Marcia A. 2010. "Individualism/Collectivism: Implications for the Volunteer Process." *Social Behavior and Personality* 38(4): 445–452.

Fisher, Dana R. 2012. "Youth Political Participation: Bridging Activism and Electoral Politics." *Annual Review of Sociology* 38: 119–137.

Flanagan, Constance A. 2004. "Volunteerism, Leadership, Political Socialization, and Civic Engagement." In *Handbook of Adolescent Psychology*, edited by Richard M. Lerner and Laurence Steinberg, 721–745. Hoboken, NJ: John Wiley & Sons Inc.

Galais, Carol. 2014. "Don't Vote for Them: The Effects of the Spanish Indignant Movement on Attitudes about Voting." *Journal of Elections, Public Opinion and Parties* 24(3): 334–350.

Giugni, Marco. 2004. "Personal and Biographical Consequences." In *The Blackwell Companion to Social Movements*, edited by David A. Snow, Sarah A. Soule, and Hanspeter Kriesi. Oxford: Blackwell.

Giugni, Marco. 2013. "Biographical Consequences of Activism." In *The Wiley-Blackwell Encyclopedia of Social and Political Movements*, edited by David A. Snow, Donatella della Porta, Bert Klandermans, and Doug McAdam, 138–144. Oxford: Blackwell.

Giugni, Marco and Maria T. Grasso. 2016. "The Biographical Impact of Participation in Social Movement Activities: Beyond Highly Committed New Left Activism." In *The Consequences of Social Movements*, edited by Lorenzo Bosi, Marco Giugni, and Katrin Uba, 85–105. Cambridge: Cambridge University Press.

Gould, Roger V. 1995. *Insurgent Identities: Class, Community, and Protest in Paris from 1848 to the Commune*. Chicago: University of Chicago Press.

Hart, Daniel, Thomas M. Donnelly, James Youniss, and Robert Atkins. 2007. "High School Community Service as a Predictor of Adult Voting and Volunteering." *American Educational Research Journal* 44(1): 197–219.

Haski-Leventhal, Debbie and David Bargal. 2008. "The Volunteer Stages and Transitions Model: Organizational Socialization of Volunteers." *Human Relations* 61(1): 67–102.

Jennings, M. Kent. 2002. "Generation Units and the Student Protest Movement in the United States: An Intra- and Intergenerational Analysis." *Political Psychology* 23(2): 303–324.

Marwell, Gerald, Michael T. Aiken, and N.J. Demerath. 1987. "The Persistence of Political Attitudes among 1960s Civil Rights Activists." *Public Opinion Quarterly* 51(3): 359–375.

Masclet, Camille. 2016. "Examining the Intergenerational Outcomes of Social Movements: The Case of Feminist Activists and Their Children." In *The Consequences of Social Movements*, edited by Lorenzo Bosi, Marco Giugni, and Katrin Uba, 106–129. Cambridge: Cambridge University Press.

McAdam, Doug. 1988. *Freedom Summer*. Oxford: Oxford University Press.

McAdam, Doug. 1989. "The Biographical Consequences of Activism." *American Sociological Review* 54(5): 744.

McAdam, Doug. 1999. "The Biographical Impact of Activism." In *How Social Movement Matter*, edited by Marco Giugni, Doug McAdam, and Charles Tilly, 119–146. Minneapolis: University of Minnesota Press.

McAdam, Doug and Cynthia Brandt. 2009. "Assessing the Effects of Voluntary Youth Service: The Case of Teach for America." *Social Forces* 88(2): 945–969.

McFarland, Daniel A. and Reuben J. Thomas. 2006. "Bowling Young: How Youth Voluntary Associations Influence Adult Political Participation." *American Sociological Review* 71(3): 401–425.

Munson, Ziad W. 2009. *The Making of Pro-Life Activists. How Social Movement Mobilization Works*. Chicago: University of Chicago Press.

Nepstad, Sharon Erickson. 2004. "Persistent Resistance: Commitment and Community in the Plowshares Movement." *Social Problems* 51(1): 43–60.

Pagis, Julie. 2014. *Mai 68, un pavé dans leur histoire. Evénements et socialisation politique*. Paris: Presses de Sciences Po.

Passy, Florence. 1998. *L'action altruiste*. Genève: Droz.

Passy, Florence and Marco Giugni. 2000. "Life-Spheres, Networks, and Sustained Participation in Social Movements: A Phenomenological Approach to Political Commitment." *Sociological Forum* 15(1): 117–144.

Passy, Florence and Gian-Andrea Monsch. 2016. "Contentious Minds. How Ties and Talks Sustain Activism." Unpublished.

Polletta, Francesca and James M. Jasper. 2001. "Collective Identity and Social Movements." *Annual Review of Sociology* 27: 283–305.

Quéniart, Anne, Michèle Charpentier, and Amélie Chanez. 2008. "La transmission des valeurs d'engagement des aînées à leur descendance: une étude de cas de deux lignées familiales." *Recherches féministes* 21(2): 143–168.

Rupp, Leila J. and Verta Taylor. 1987. *Survival in the Doldrums: The American Women's Rights Movement, 1945 to the 1960s*. New York: Oxford University Press.

Sherkat, Darren E. and T. Jean Blocker. 1997. "Explaining the Political and Personal Consequences of Protest." *Social Forces* 75(3): 1049–1070.

Shirlow, Peter, Jon Tonge, James McAuley, and Catherine McGlynn. 2010. *Abandoning Historical Conflict? Former Political Prisoners and Reconciliation in Northern Ireland*. Manchester: Manchester University Press.

Sigel, Roberta S. 1995. "New Directions for Political Socialization Research: Thoughts and Suggestions." *Perspectives on Political Science* 24(1): 17–22.

Sivesind, Karl Henrik, Tereza Pospíšilová, and Pavol Frič. 2013. "Does Volunteering Cause Trust?" *European Societies* 15(1): 106–130.

Stolle, Dietlind and Thomas R. Rochon. 1998. "Are All Associations Alike? Member Diversity, Associational Type, and the Creation of Social Capital." *American Behavioral Scientist* 42(1): 47–65.

Taylor, Verta and Nicole C. Raeburn. 1995. "Identity Politics as High-Risk Activism: Career Consequences for Lesbian, Gay, and Bisexual Sociologists." *Social Problems* 42(2): 252–273.

Terriquez, Veronica. 2015. "Training Young Activists: Grassroots Organizing and Youths' Civic and Political Trajectories." *Sociological Perspectives* 58(2): 223–242.

Van Deth, Jan W. 2006. "Democracy and Involvement: The Benevolent Aspects of Social Participation." In *Political Disaffection in Contemporary Democracies: Social Capital, Institutions, and Politics*, edited by Mario Torcal and José Ramon Montero, 101–129. London: Routledge.

Van Dyke, Nella and Marc Dixon. 2013. "Activist Human Capital: Skills Acquisition and the Development of Commitment to Social Movement Activism." *Mobilization* 18(2): 197–212.

Van Dyke, Nella, Doug McAdam, and Brenda Wilhelm. 2000. "Gendered Outcomes: Gender Differences in the Biographical Consequences of Activism." *Mobilization* 5(2): 161–177.

Whalen, Jack and Richard Flacks. 1989. *Beyond the Barricades: The Sixties Generation Grows Up*. Philadelphia, PA: Temple University Press.

Whittier, Nancy. 1995. *Feminist Generations: The Persistence of the Radical Women's Movement*. Philadelphia, PA: Temple University Press.

Whittier, Nancy. 2016. "Aggregate-Level Biographical Outcomes for Gay and Lesbian Movements." In *The Consequences of Social Movements*, edited by Lorenzo Bosi, Marco Giugni, and Katrin Uba, 130–156. Cambridge: Cambridge University Press.

Wilhelm, Brenda. 1998. "Changes in Cohabitation across Cohorts: The Influence of Political Activism." *Social Forces* 77(1): 289–313.

Wilson, John. 2012. "Volunteerism Research: A Review Essay." *Nonprofit and Voluntary Sector Quarterly* 41(2): 1–37.

Wilson, John and Marc Musick. 2000. "The Effects of Volunteering on the Volunteer." *Law and Contemporary Problems* 62: 141–168.

Part VI
Thematic Intersections

29

Social Class and Social Movements

Barry Eidlin and Jasmine Kerrissey

Introduction

Social class has traditionally been one of the fundamental bases for social mobilization. Whether it was slaves revolting against their masters, peasants rising up against their lords, or workers battling capitalists, class hierarchies have often provided both the reason for protesting, as well as the group identities around which people mobilized.

Likewise, for scholars interested in understanding processes of social change, class concepts have provided the crucial analytical building blocks for understanding social conflict and change. This was certainly the case for the founders of sociology, such as Marx, Weber, and Du Bois, even Durkheim, and this persisted for much of the twentieth century.

This seemed to change in the latter part of the twentieth century. In industrialized countries, movements emerged around seemingly non-class issues, including peace, environmental destruction, and oppression based on race, gender, sexual identity, physical ability, and more. In the developing world, decolonization was the order of the day, making race and nation the key dividing lines.

Observing these changes, some argued that postwar economic growth had made class divisions less socially and politically relevant (Bell 1973; Clark and Lipset 1991; Nisbet 1959). Instead, they argued, individuals organized to address "post-materialist" concerns, based on lifestyle and identity-based issues (Inglehart and Rabier 1986).

Around the same time as class came under scrutiny, other groups of researchers sought to develop more sociological understandings of social mobilization in the "post-material" world. Dissatisfied with existing theories that viewed protest as a form of deviance, they sought instead to understand it as a form of politics by other means (Oberschall 1973). They analyzed social mobilization by looking at actors'

The Wiley Blackwell Companion to Social Movements, Second Edition. Edited by David A. Snow, Sarah A. Soule, Hanspeter Kriesi, and Holly J. McCammon.

strategic interests, the structural environment surrounding them, their access to resources, and their ability to define issues and agendas, as opposed to delving into psychology (Benford and Snow 2000; McAdam 1982; McAdam, Tarrow, and Tilly 2001; McCarthy and Zald 1977; Tarrow 1994). To the extent that they continued to focus on psychological aspects of mobilization, it was to understand the role of emotions and collective identities in fostering and sustaining social movements (della Porta and Diani 2006; Goodwin, Jasper, and Polletta 2009; Polletta and Jasper 2001). Rather than being a symptom of social pathology, social movements were now understood as a source of meaning and social cohesion, as well as a mechanism for social change.

This analytical shift entailed a disciplinary shift from the sociology of deviance toward political sociology. Social movement theory sought to carve out a distinctive niche for itself within political sociology, focused on the "contentious politics" of protest, demands, and disruption, rather than the "normal politics" of legislation, negotiation, and administration.

Reinterpreting social mobilization as contentious action informed by strategy, structure, resources, and meaning-making allowed social movement theory to develop sophisticated analytical tools to understand why and under what conditions movements do (or do not) emerge, why and how they win or lose (and how wins and losses are defined), why and under what conditions people do (or do not) resort to contentious politics to express grievances, and other core questions of social mobilization.

In line with scholarship that was rethinking the relevance of social class more generally, this new sociology of social movements also saw a shift in the role of class as a basis for grievances and social mobilization, as well as the type of class most likely to engage in contentious politics. Whereas the "old social movements," such as labor unions and socialist parties largely organized around economic issues and had their base in the working class, the "new social movements" (NSMs) being studied focused on post-materialist concerns of individual autonomy, and were often rooted in a "new middle class" of "social and cultural specialists." They argued that the political class divide had shifted: rather than the traditional opposition between the working class and the bourgeoisie, social conflict now cut across the new middle class, opposing the social-cultural professionals to the technocrats-managers (Buechler 1995; Kriesi 1989; Kriesi et al. 1995). Meanwhile, the study of the modern, more bureaucratized incarnations of "old social movements" was largely left to scholars of "normal politics" and separate groups of labor sociologists.

However, the division between "old" and "new" social movements has not gone unchallenged. Some pointed out that the issues around which "old" and "new" social movements organized were more similar than NSM theorists claimed (Calhoun 1993). Others challenged the old/new counter-position in the Global North, arguing that the working class – including the "precariat" – remains a key actor in social mobilization, and economic grievances remain key drivers of social protest, even in a supposedly post-material age (della Porta 2015). Corroborating this, we present data showing that protest over class grievances, in the form of strikes, was a major part of overall social protest at the time that NSM theories developed. Meanwhile, drawing from movements around the world, scholars have shown that class divisions remained a powerful source of grievances and base for mobilizing identities, even as they intertwine with gender, nation, race, and other cleavages (Chun 2009; della Porta 2015; Eggert and Guigni 2012). The recent surge in mobilization around economic issues in the twenty-first century, including Occupy movements, austerity protests, strikes, and the growth of worker centers and labor NGOs, appears to be bringing class conflict and economic grievances back into the analytical spotlight. While workers' organizations dominate these class movements, scholars also note that, at times, elites also lead movements around their class interests (Martin 2013).

This chapter explores the complex relationship between social class and social mobilization. Starting with a historical account of how the two concepts have been intertwined, we then discuss how the concepts changed as theories of social mobilization became more systematized. We then examine more recent shifts in understanding the relation between social class and social mobilization, and conclude with an assessment of key questions and unresolved debates around the study of social class and social movements.

Class Grievances and Class Identities

If Marx and Engels' (1969) polemical assertion that "the history of all hitherto existing society is the history of class struggles" was overblown, it was not so by much. Human settlement around agricultural production allowed for surplus accumulation, which in turn led to conflicts over the distribution of that surplus. As societies became more complex, these conflicts become more organized (Morehart and de Lucia 2015; Weber 2013). In this, class divisions have long been key drivers of social conflict and social mobilization. This has happened on two levels. Hierarchies and inequalities based on class divisions have provided both a basis for grievances, as well as the basis for collective identities, around which people have mobilized for social change.

As a basis for grievances, it is important to recognize that although class divisions have a core economic component, they have not been limited to economic relations. Rather, they have intersected with and been reinforced by other systems of hierarchy and division. For example, agrarian slave societies created economic divisions between exploited, surplus-producing slaves and an exploiting, non-productive ruling class. But the economic division was reinforced by various traditions, beliefs, and rituals that justified the unequal class relation between slave and master/citizen. Similarly, under feudalism, peasants generated surpluses for their lords, creating a relation of economic exploitation, but this economic class division was buttressed by political hierarchies and religious ideas, which justified the existing social hierarchy (Anderson 1974; Mann 1986).

A key aspect of the transition from feudalism to capitalism involved challenging the ideologies justifying existing social class hierarchies. Class conflicts in this period were also anti-aristocratic and/or anti-clerical, often favoring a new idea of "the nation" (Mann 1993). The formal legal, political, and social inequalities of feudalism were replaced by formal legal, political, and social equality for all citizens of democratic nation-states under capitalism (Marshall and Bottomore 1992; Marx and Engels 1969; Wood 2002). What remained, albeit in radically different form, were unequal economic relations of exploitation, combined with informal but no less real social inequalities based on race, gender, language, ethnicity, region, and more, along with continued formal inequalities based on criteria such as citizenship. The contradiction between formal legal and political equality and economic exploitation and inequality generated conflicts that sparked titanic social mobilizations in the nineteenth and twentieth centuries (Hobsbawm 1989; Mann 1993). The political problem was compounded by the social and economic problem, simply referred to as "the labor problem," of coercing and convincing former peasants, artisans, apprentices, and small merchants to accept the discipline and authority of the industrial workplace (Bendix 1974; Braverman 1998). Simultaneously, the rise of democracy and capitalism in Europe was accompanied by the intensification of colonialism and slavery in the Americas, Africa, and much of Asia, creating social divisions that continue to generate grievances and social mobilization to this day (Cooper 2009; Hobsbawm 1989; Migdal 1974).

The discussion thus far has only addressed how class divisions have provided a material basis for grievances. But as social movement theory shows, grievances alone are insufficient for social mobilization (Jenkins and Perrow 1977; McAdam 1982; McCarthy and Zald 1977). Grievances must be defined, and visions of how those grievances might be addressed must be articulated for social mobilization to happen (Piven and Cloward 1977). Key to this process is the formation of frames and collective identities. These define the issues and actors involved and shape the arena of conflict (Benford and Snow 2000; Eidlin 2014; Polletta and Jasper 2001).

Here again, class identities have historically served as a powerful mobilizing force. While we know very little as to their motivations and organizing tactics, we do know that not all slaves in Antiquity passively accepted their lot. Some organized slave armies to revolt against their masters, and worries about such revolts preoccupied ruling elites (Peterson 2013; Urbaincyzk 2008). Similarly, feudal historical records are full of references to rebellions by peasants, artisans, laborers, small merchants, and others (Cohn 2009; Hilton 2004). Central to their organizing were what we would now recognize as class identities, which they defined both solidaristically, as exploited groups, and oppositionally, against their landlords and masters.

As capitalism revolutionized production and upended social relations, it also gave birth to new identities and axes of conflict. Layers of feudal-era merchants, masters, landlords, and artisans became the manufacturing and financial bourgeoisie under capitalism, while groups of former peasants, merchants, and artisans found common identities as part of a "working class" based on their common experiences of workplace exploitation. But this was in no way an automatic process. As discussed below, the "problem of class formation" has remained a thorny issue of debate.

Theorizing Class and Social Change

While class has long served as a basis for social mobilization, the relation between the two has been a point of scholarly contention. The founders of sociology all understood class as a central concept for analyzing social organization. This was clearest for Marx and his collaborator, Friedrich Engels (1969), although Weber's theory also included a narrower conception of class as determined by "market position," which was mediated by status distinctions based on social hierarchies, as well as distinctions of rank within political orders (Weber 1978). Du Bois was deeply influenced by Marx, which led him to focus on the class dimensions of US racial and political conflict (Du Bois 1896, 1935). Even Durkheim, generally not considered a theorist of class, analyzed how work-based groups structure social relations (Durkheim 1984).

The founders differed, however, in how they conceptualized the role that class played in social organization. Marx, and later Du Bois, focused on the conflictual relationship between exploiting and exploited classes, theorizing that this conflict served as a core driver of social transformation. For his part, Weber studied the relationships of domination that resulted from different distributions of power based on market position, social honor, and political rank, but did not offer an account as to why or how those distributions might change. Against Marx's conflictual view of class, Durkheim saw occupation-based "corporate groups" as key mechanisms for ensuring social cohesion in increasingly complex societies.

It was primarily Marx, then, who sketched the initial outlines of a theory relating social class and social change. He identified the working class as the key revolutionary subject, the collective actor which, by virtue of its structural position within capitalist production, was both best equipped to bring about the change necessary for a more equitable society and stood to gain the most from such a transformation.

A central concern for Marx was the process that led to the formation of new classes as social actors. He theorized that the organization of economic production created not only relations of exploitation, but social bonds among groups of individuals that gave rise to classes in an objective sense. He called this class "in itself." But he recognized that the existence of classes in this objective sense did not guarantee that classes in a subjective sense – class "for itself" – would follow. However, he did not specify the conditions under which class "for itself" could emerge out of class "in itself" (Marx 1973).

It was not clear at the time just how problematic this translation between class position and class identity was. Amidst the social ferment of the nineteenth century, it appeared that members of the working class would naturally recognize their common bond and organize as a class to fight their capitalist enemy. Across Europe and North America, millions of workers united to form trade unions, political parties, and other mutual associations based on a common class identity (Hobsbawm 1989; Kautsky 1910).

However, against nineteenth-century socialists' predictions of capitalism's impending demise, capitalism proved quite resilient. And against theories that workers would naturally bond with each other based on a common working-class identity, workers instead often divided along competing national, religious, craft, or racial lines. By the early twentieth century, the disjuncture between the objective and subjective dimensions of class was obvious: class unity was not automatic, nor was its translation into the political sphere. The question of how to create a unified and mobilized class subject – what became known as the "problem of class formation" – became a central problem for Marxism (Bernstein 1911; Gramsci 1972, 1978; Kautsky 1910; Lenin 1961; Luxemburg 1971; Michels 1915; Sorel 1999).

Out of these early twentieth-century debates emerged some of the key questions at the heart of continued attempts to understand the relation between social class,

522   BARRY EIDLIN AND JASMINE KERRISSEY

collective identity, and social mobilization. Even if analysts agreed that the working class was the key revolutionary subject – itself a major point of contention – what exactly did it mean to be part of something called "the working class"? How and why did people come to identify as members of such a group?

The answer for some was ideas and organization. Ideas could provide an interpretive framework linking material conditions and collective identity, and organization could translate ideas into action. This led these theorists to focus on the central role of parties and intellectuals in mobilizing political identities, particularly those based on class (Gramsci 1978; Lenin 1961).

From Classes to Masses

The crises and conflicts of the early twentieth century culminated in the carnage of World War II. In its aftermath, as Europe and North America transitioned to a postwar economy, class relations began to shift as well. In Western Europe and North America, militant labor unions and socialist parties were replaced by institutionalized and officially recognized bureaucratic organizations, who often engaged in highly formalized "corporatist" bargaining among "peak associations" of labor and employer federations (Hall and Soskice 2001; Schmitter 1974). Many spoke of a supposed "settlement" between labor and capital, wherein each side acknowledged its counterpart's legitimacy, and engaged in regulated, carefully circumscribed collective bargaining (Nissen 1990; Thelen 1994). In Eastern Europe, unions and parties were either crushed or incorporated into bureaucratic Stalinist states (Windmuller 1971).

Around the world, the political and military constraints of the Cold War profoundly shaped relations between parties, unions, and states, and limited the range of acceptable political discourse. Decolonization movements exploded across the Third World. Many of these explicitly organized along class lines, based on Marxist understandings of exploitation. These movements were caught up in the geopolitical struggle between the USA and the USSR over "spheres of influence" (Westad 2005). In "the West," class-based mobilization was inextricably linked to the specter of Communism, leading to intra-class conflict in many countries between socialists and communists and their affiliated parties and labor unions over questions of loyalty and militancy. In "the East," class mobilization became integrated into state ideology, stifling rank-and-file activity. These conflicts constrained union militancy and created pressure for unions to become "responsible" social bargaining partners – although some steadfastly resisted these pressures. As a result, with some notable exceptions, few major parties or labor unions in the West or East resembled anything close to contentious social movement organizations (Cherny, Issel, and Taylor 2004; Kaldor 1990; Sturmthal 1983).

This organizational shift, driven in part by unprecedented postwar economic growth, led some to contend that class was no longer as politically relevant as it once was (Dahrendorf 1959; Nisbet 1959). Class divisions would be managed in the workplace through a system of "industrial pluralism," while political demands would be channeled into a "democratic class struggle" between competing parties (Kerr et al. 1960; Lipset 1963).[1]

As economic growth and well-managed bureaucracies softened class divisions and reduced their political relevance, these theorists argued, class differences were being replaced by more individualized differences based on consumption and lifestyle choices (Bell 1960; Inglehart and Rabier 1986; Riesman, Denney, and Glazer 1950).

Although class conflict was largely contained according to these theorists, they recognized that other social conflicts remained. Some worried that industrial pluralism, while weakening class divisions, risked creating a more alienated, atomized "mass society," increasingly disconnected from bureaucratic elites, be they in business, labor, politics, or the military (Marcuse 2002; Mills 1959). Even those who challenged such dire assessments contended that tendencies towards social "massification" and alienation posed significant challenges to pluralist democracy (Kornhauser 1959).

Operating within such a framework, there was little room for considering social mobilization based on class, or any other identity for that matter, as a *political* phenomenon. Pluralism and bureaucracy supposedly allowed for the expression and processing of political demands through the appropriate channels. Any protest or mobilization outside that framework could only be understood either as a symptom of social strain or systemic disequilibrium. It was more a problem of social psychology than of politics (Gurr 1970; Smelser 2011).

This framework left social analysts ill-equipped to explain the social upheavals that convulsed much of Europe and North America in the 1960s. The mass movements for civil rights, against military intervention and nuclear weapons, and more that challenged the political, social, and economic status quo did not fit existing categories of social protest. The protesters clearly felt that the "appropriate channels" for handling political grievances were insufficient, but they could not be dismissed as social deviants. Moreover, counter to what some theories of collective behavior held, the participants were not merely engaged in forms of collective therapy. Rather, they were making demands on – and changing – the political system (see McAdam 1982, for a critique).

Social Movement Theory and the Retreat from Class

It is in this context that contemporary social movement theory began to emerge. Rather than understand social mobilization as a psychological problem, some saw it as an extension of "normal" politics (Oberschall 1973; von Eschen, Pinard, and Kirk 1971). From this initial insight came the concepts that now form the core of social movement theory: political process, resource mobilization, framing, and collective identity (Benford and Snow 2000; McAdam 1982; McCarthy and Zald 1977; Polletta and Jasper 2001).

Without delving into the theories, what is crucial to understand is the historical and intellectual context in which they took shape. Although social movement theory is meant to be abstract and generalizable, it is also very much the product of a particular time and place: the United States and parts of Western Europe in the late 1970s and 1980s. The pioneers of social movement theory were working in the aftermath of the largest social upheaval of their lifetimes: the movements of the 1960s.

Additionally, the discipline of sociology itself was changing. A new generation of scholars shaped by, and often active in, the movements of the 1960s swelled the ranks of sociology graduate programs in the 1970s, injecting the discipline with a leftward political bent and a suspicion of traditional institutions of power (Buechler 2011; McAdam 2008). Perhaps unsurprisingly, many of the key early pieces in the social movements literature examined the movements in which this new generation of sociologists had been active (Jenkins and Perrow 1977; McAdam 1982, 1988, 1995; Morris 1984).

This context shaped not only the empirical content, but the theoretical conception of what constituted a social movement. And that conception was one that largely excluded class-based movements. For the 1960s New Left, particularly in the USA, there was a stark divide between the social movements in which they were active and traditional vehicles of class-based mobilization. Purged of their left wing and fully incorporated into the Cold War liberal consensus, the once-contentious unions of the pre-war era now seemed like stodgy, bureaucratic behemoths, more tied into the power structure against which the New Left was rebelling than part of their movement (Cherny et al. 2004; Eidlin 2018; Gitlin 1987). While some unions supported aspects of the civil rights movement (Honey 2007; Jones 2013), the New Left's experience of "Big Labor" was framed much more by pro-war hawk and AFL-CIO President George Meany, or the overhyped but symbolically important "hard hats" attacking antiwar protesters (Lewis 2013).

As such, labor and the working class were largely left out of the empirical scope of social movement scholarship. Just as New Leftists distinguished themselves from the class-based politics of the "Old Left," so too did social movement scholars distinguish between "old" and "new" social movements. In this typology, "old" movements were those, like unions, based in the working class and organized around economic issues, while "new" movements were those based among strata of the "new middle class," and organized around "post-materialist" issues of identity, environment, and individual rights (Buechler 1995; Kriesi 1989; Offe 1985).

This empirical separation between labor and social movement studies was occurring at the same time as social theorists were hypothesizing about the "death of class" as a socially and politically relevant category (Bell 1973; Clark, Lipset, and Rempel 1993; Gorz 1982; Pakulski and Waters 1996). Frustration with what were perceived as overly reductionist class-based models of social action led to academic "turns" towards exploring the roles of culture and institutions in creating meaning and guiding individual and group behavior (Bonnell and Hunt 1999; Powell and DiMaggio 1991). While some continued to argue for the relevance of class (Evans 2000; Hout, Brooks, and Manza 1993; Wright 1997), the general trend in social science was away from class. Social movement theory was not immune to this trend, as discussion of class and capitalism faded from view (Hetland and Goodwin 2012).

Counting Contention: From Protests to Strikes

Despite this academic turn, in practice, workers and workers' organizations continued to inform social mobilization. We present two figures to better understand

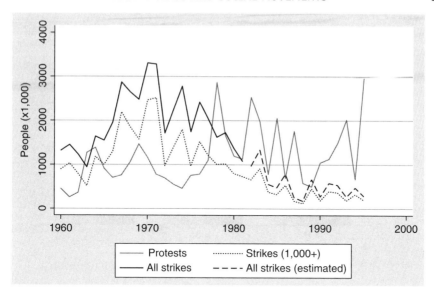

Figure 29.1 Numbers of people involved in protests and strikes, 1960–1995.

"old" and "new" social movements in the United States at the time that social movement theory was developing.

Figure 29.1 compares the participation levels of people involved with strikes and "protests," which include all forms of public collective action except for strikes. This approach builds on Biggs (2015), who finds that strikes account for a large portion of contentious activity in Great Britain. Protest data comes from the *Dynamics of Collective Action* dataset, which uses newspaper accounts to report the number of protest events and participants from 1960 to 1995.[2]

Protest events exclude strikes, but do include events that are union-led and focus on work issues, such as protesting layoffs.[3] Strike data comes from the Bureau of Labor Statistics (BLS), which records workers involved in large strikes and lockouts, classified as over 1000 people lasting over 8 hours. Prior to 1981, the BLS also reported smaller strikes. Including these strikes increases the average yearly strike size by 32%. We approximate participation after 1981 by adding 32% to the large strike measure.

Figure 29.1 shows that for most of the 1960s and 1970s, strikes accounted for more participation than all other protests combined. In 1971, for instance, over 3 million workers went on strike – roughly triple the amount of people who participated in other forms of protests. By the 1980s, a hostile political and legal climate, combined with union decline, had eroded strike participation both in the USA and Europe (Biggs 2015; Richards 2013).

Class mobilization, however, is not limited to strikes. Workers' organizations politicize members, develop leaders, and build cross-movement coalitions, which spills over into broader movement activism, including activism considered to be in the realm of new movements (Kerrissey and Schofer 2013; Terriquez 2011; Vachon and Brecher 2016).

To illustrate union members' engagement in "other" protest activities, we use the *Roper Social and Political Trends Data*. This survey asks nearly 6,000 people whether

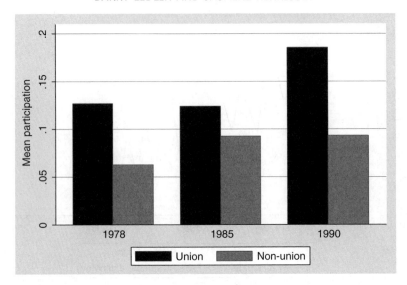

Figure 29.2   Participation in union and non-union protests.

they had participated in a "protest march or sit-in," excluding strikes. Figure 29.2 shows that union members were far more likely to have participated than non-union members.

We can draw two lessons from these figures. First, strikes accounted for a major portion of contentious activity in the late twentieth century in the USA. The strike data suggest that class continued to generate social mobilization, even at the height of the "new" social movements. When strikes are included as a form of contentious politics, it becomes clear that class remained a primary axis of contention. Second, drawing from Figure 29.2, we observe that union members were more likely than average to protest in non-strike marches and sit-ins. Social movement scholars have often focused on the mobilization of the "new middle class" and post-materialist concerns (Kriesi 1989). These figures, however, suggest that class mobilization (in the form of strikes) and protest by working-class actors (in the form of union members) were also major drivers of contentious activity and worthy of scholarly attention.

The "Death of Class" and Labor Movement Scholarship

In spite of their powerful mobilizing role, by the end of the twentieth century, unions were in crisis, particularly in industrialized nations, which experienced plummeting strike rates and union density (Richards 2013). To some, these trends reaffirmed the notion that class no longer served as an important catalyst. As the twentieth century came to a close, however, the "death of class" thesis seemed premature. Moves within the US labor movement suggested possible revitalization: reform candidate John Sweeney won the AFL-CIO presidency in 1995 and began focusing on organizing; for the first time, the AFL-CIO took a public stance against a war; and new campaigns including janitors, students against sweatshops, and worker centers redefined the labor movement. Labor scholars began to discuss the (re-)emergence of what some called "social movement" unionism, which stood in contrast to the "business" unionism of the mid- and late-twentieth century (Fraser and Freeman 1997; Milkman and Voss 2004).

In this context, scholars increasingly turned their attention to class-based movements. For instance, in 2000, US labor sociologists formed the "Labor and Labor Movements" section of the American Sociological Association (ASA). With their own specialty journals and ASA section, labor scholarship developed, largely in parallel to social movement scholarship. Its primary questions have focused on the causes and consequences of union growth and decline, as well as *how* workers have organized collectively in different political, economic, and national contexts around the world (e.g. Agarwala 2013; Anner 2011; Chun 2009; McCallum 2013; Silver 2003; Zhang 2014).

Underlying this scholarship is the argument that class-based continues to be an empirically and theoretically important axis of social mobilization. It challenges the "death of class" thesis in two ways. First, scholars contend that class movements continue to be a primary source of social mobilization, but not always in the same place and form (Evans 2010; Silver 2003). Classes are continuously "made, unmade, and remade" (Silver 2013). This makes it important to analyze class movements with a global and long-term perspective, and to focus not only on traditional labor unions (Agarwala 2013; Milkman and Ott 2014).

Second, others note that the decline in union density in many industrialized nations is not from lack of interest. Rather, workers' movements have been at the losing end of decades-long struggles between capital and labor, which have shaped unions' strength, tactics, and politics (Bronfenbrenner and Juravich 2002; Dixon 2010; Dixon and Martin 2012; Fantasia and Stepan-Norris 2004). This decline in unions has spurred a large literature that examines macro outcomes of workers' movements, including the distribution of resources, politics, and working conditions (Brady 2009; Harris and Scully 2015; Jacobs and Myers 2014; Kerrissey 2015; Kerrissey and Schuhrke 2016; Kristal 2010; Rosenfeld 2014; Western and Rosenfeld 2011).

Some of these movements for class interests involve mobilization led by elites. Demonstrating that class movements erupt not only from workers and their organizations, Martin (2013) reminds us that "rich people's movements" aim to shape policies to consolidate wealth at the top. Others trace the formation of business associations and how they collectively work to maintain power (e.g. Griffin, Wallace, and Rubin 1986).

In recent years, there has been a sharp uptick in mobilization over class grievances, including anti-austerity protests, occupy movements, struggles to increase minimum wages, and high-profile strikes. While traditional unions have played a role in these struggles, other organizational forms have often led these movements, including worker centers, labor NGOs, and left political parties. For example, in the USA, there has been an explosive rise of community-based worker centers, from only a handful in the 1990s to hundreds today (Fine 2006; Milkman and Ott 2014). These worker centers have focused on workers who have been left largely unorganized by unions – immigrants and precarious workers – and use strategies to leverage power that do not focus on collective bargaining. This uptick in labor activity has drawn in a new generation of scholars, many of whom draw on intersectional understandings of oppression, especially how worker exploitation is deeply intertwined with race, gender, sexual identity, and nationality.

Bridging Labor Scholarship and Social Movement Theory

Although labor and social movement scholarship developed largely in their own academic silos, this separation is beginning to break down. Increasingly, social movement scholars are conceptualizing labor struggles as part of the social movement field. For instance, Amenta and colleagues (2009) analyzed newspaper coverage of all social movements over the twentieth century, including labor struggles. Their findings underscore the prominent role of working-class movements: labor struggles account for over a third of all articles – far more than any other social movement.

At the same time, the recent surge in class movements – from Occupy to anti-austerity protests – has attracted the attention of social movement scholars. della Porta (2015) argues that "mainstream" social movement studies do not adequately explain these recent protest waves, which are dominated by the "losers" of globalization. She calls for bringing "capitalism back into protest analysis" and for a conceptualization of class cleavage and protest that includes the precariat – the unemployed, the underemployed, and those who have lost social and civil rights.

Scholars of class movements are also increasingly drawing on theories developed in the social movement literature. Applying social movement theories to class movements has tested and expanded the scope of social movement theories, while deepening our understanding of class movements (Almeida 2008; Ganz 2000). This synthesis has been particularly fruitful in analyses of two realms: counter-movements and political structures.

Social movement scholars insist that movements cannot be understood without analyzing movement opposition and threat. Unions' weak position in the contemporary era offers an important venue for analyzing such dynamics. A small but vibrant scholarship explores how opposition and threat shape legislation, union strategy, and new membership (Dixon 2010; Martin and Dixon 2010).

Scholars of class movements, particularly in the Global South, have also used theories of political opportunities both to explain labor movement outcomes and to expand the empirical and theoretical scope of social movement theory. Examining less democratic contexts, this scholarship informs key social movement theories that were developed by analyzing movements of the comparatively more democratic Global North. Almeida (2008), for instance, examines the relationship between authoritarian regimes and protest in El Salvador. He finds when authoritarian regimes allow for some liberalization, oppositional groups (such as unions) are better able to organize. When the state subsequently increases repression, these groups radicalize and form the basis of oppositional movements. Similarly, Anner's (2011) comparative study of Central and South America traces how political conditions shape unions' strategies. In addition, a series of case studies examine how class mobilization shapes political structures, particularly democratization, decolonization, and policies of redistribution (Buhlungu and Tshoaedi 2013; Collier and Mahoney 1997; Huber and Stevens 2012; Kraus 2007).

In its current form, however, social movement theory is unable to fully capture the dynamics of working-class movements. Social movement scholars have rooted their analyses in theories of identity, politics, resources, framing, and the like. Workers, however, differ from many other groups of social movement actors because of their structural position within capitalist production and their potential ability to stop production. A central question among labor scholars is how structural power influences which workers organize, the strategies unions pursue, and the outcomes of labor struggles (Brookes 2013; Chun 2009; Kimeldorf 2013; Silver 2003; Wright 2000). These types of questions are not easily addressed by existing social movement theories, indicating a continued chasm between the literatures.

Conclusion

Social movement theory developed at a time when "new" social upheavals had recently rocked the United States. These movements of the 1960s and 1970s were "new" in that they focused primarily on issues of identity, ethics, and lifestyle, including movements around civil rights, peace, feminism, and the environment. In contrast, "old" social movements revolved around class and economic issues – divisions that had patterned much of the social mobilization driving the founding of sociology a century prior. In the same historical moment that social movement theory was developing, the purge of left-wing unions and union leaders, along with the rise of the so-called "social contract," meant that unions had become more bureaucratized and conservative – a far cry from the other movements of the day. Unions were also at the start of their decades-long drop in density. Reacting to these trends, some speculated that the "death of class" was imminent, and asked whether class was still relevant to understanding social and political organization. In this context, social movement theorists embraced analyses of "new" social movements, which, at the time, were understood to be driven by the "new middle class."

Separate from this research, labor sociologists continued their interest in class movements. Far from acceding to the death of class argument, labor scholars emphasized class divisions, examining how workers' movements shape and are shaped by the broader social, political, and economic context. This line of scholarship has located workers not only as central to strikes, but also as important contributors to a range of protest activities and social movements (Isaac and Christiansen 2002; Kerrissey and Schofer 2013; Norris 2002; Terriquez 2011; Vachon and Brecher 2016).

Although scholars of labor and social movements focused on similar questions of political identity, mobilization, and political structures, the two literatures developed separately. However, we see signs that these lines of scholarship are in increasing conversation with each other. Notably, recent scholarship conceptualizes labor struggles as part of the broader social movement field (Amenta et al. 2009) and class grievances as a driving force behind the wave of contemporary protest (della Porta 2015). In addition, a stream of research has applied social movement theories to better understand the relationship between class mobilization, counter-movements, and political structures. In so doing, this research expands the empirical and theoretical scope of social movement theory. However, divisions still remain, particularly around how workers' structural position within capitalist production might shape mobilization, strategies, and outcomes.

Looking ahead, we contend that the conceptual distinction between "old" and "new" movements has run its course. Arguing that this separation was always troubled, Calhoun (1993) traces how in the late nineteenth century and early twentieth century, old movements (unions) were steeped with characteristics of "new" movements. We argue that this is just as true today, with working-class organizations fighting for a range of material and non-material issues. While our focus in this chapter has been on where the bulk of class-based social movement activities are located – workers' movements – it is also important to remember that, at times, elites also engage in social mobilization to pursue their interests (Martin 2013).

Figures 29.1 and 29.2 showing strike and protest participation suggest that excluding tactics of "old" movements – strikes – dramatically alters our understanding of protest trends over time. Additionally, working-class organizations remain central sites of mobilization, not only for strikes, but also for the politicization, leadership development, and networks that lead people to broader social movement activity. To better understand social mobilization, we should both recognize strikes and other forms of class-based mobilization as part of the larger field of contentious politics.

Notes

1   In the case of the Eastern Bloc, the solution was to subsume class conflict under a state apparatus that decreed the existence of a classless society.
2   See http://web.stanford.edu/group/collectiveaction
3   About half of the newspaper events report qualitative descriptions of event size. The dataset categorizes these descriptions into six sizes. We take the average of each range (e.g. if the gathering was coded as between 50 and 99 people, we designate it as 75; for the upper category of 10 000 or more participants, we estimate 15 000 people). Analyses of outliers led us to identify two coding errors in 1981, which we omit.

References

Agarwala, Rina. 2013. *Informal Labor, Formal Politics, and Dignified Discontent in India.* Cambridge: Cambridge University Press.

Almeida, Paul D. 2008. *Waves of Protest: Popular Struggle in El Salvador, 1925–2005.* Minneapolis: University of Minnesota Press.

Amenta, Edwin, Neal Caren, Sheera Olasky, and James Stobaugh. 2009. "All the Movements Fit to Print: Who, What, When, Where, and Why SMO Families Appeared in the *New York Times* in the Twentieth Century." *American Sociological Review* 74(4): 636–656.

Anderson, Perry. 1974. *Lineages of the Absolutist State.* London: NLB.

Anner, Mark S. 2011. *Solidarity Transformed: Labor Responses to Globalization and Crisis in Latin America.* Ithaca, NY: Cornell University Press.

Bell, Daniel. 1960. *The End of Ideology: On the Exhaustion of Political Ideas in the Fifties.* Glencoe, IL: Free Press.

Bell, Daniel. 1973. *The Coming of Post-Industrial Society: A Venture in Social Forecasting.* New York: Basic Books.

Bendix, Reinhard. 1974. *Work and Authority in Industry: Ideologies of Management in the Course of Industrialization.* Berkeley: University of California Press.

Benford, Robert D. and David A. Snow. 2000. "Framing Processes and Social Movements: An Overview and Assessment." *Annual Review of Sociology* 26(1): 611–639.

Bernstein, Eduard. 1911. *Evolutionary Socialism: A Criticism and Affirmation [Die Voraussetzungen des Sozialismus und die Aufgaben der Sozialdemokratie].* New York: B. W. Huebsch.

Biggs, Michael. 2015. "Has Protest Increased since the 1970s? How a Survey Question Can Construct a Spurious Trend." *The British Journal of Sociology* 66(1):141–162.

Bonnell, Victoria E. and Lynn Hunt, eds. 1999. *Beyond the Cultural Turn: New Directions in the Study of Society and Culture.* Berkeley: University of California Press.

Brady, David. 2009. *Rich Democracies, Poor People: How Politics Explain Poverty.* Oxford: Oxford University Press.

Braverman, Harry. 1998. *Labor and Monopoly Capital: The Degradation of Work in the Twentieth Century.* New York: Monthly Review Press.

Bronfenbrenner, Kate and Tom Juravich. 2002. "It Takes More than House Calls." *Industrial Relations: Labour Markets, Labour Process and Trade Unionism* 2: 400.

Brookes, Marissa. 2013. "Varieties of Power in Transnational Labor Alliances: An Analysis of Workers' Structural, Institutional, and Coalitional Power in the Global Economy." *Labor Studies Journal* 38(3): 181–200.

Buechler, Steven M. 1995. "New Social Movement Theories." *The Sociological Quarterly* 36(3): 441–464.

Buechler, Steven M. 2011. *Understanding Social Movements: Theories from the Classical Era to the Present.* Boulder, CO: Paradigm.

Buhlungu, Sakhela and Malehoko Tshoaedi. 2013. *COSATU's Contested Legacy: South African Trade Unions in the Second Decade of Democracy.* Leiden: Brill.

Calhoun, Craig. 1993. "'New Social Movements' of the Early Nineteenth Century." *Social Science History* 17(3): 385–427.

Cherny, Robert W., William Issel, and Kieran W. Taylor, eds. 2004. *American Labor and the Cold War: Grassroots Politics and Postwar Political Culture.* New Brunswick, NJ: Rutgers University Press.

Chun, Jennifer J. 2009. *Organizing at the Margins: The Symbolic Politics of Labor in South Korea and the United States.* Ithaca, NY: Cornell University Press.

Clark, Terry N. and Seymour M. Lipset. 1991. "Are Social Classes Dying?" *International Sociology* 6(4): 397–410.

Clark, Terry N., Seymour M. Lipset, and Michael Rempel. 1993. "The Declining Political Significance of Social Class." *International Sociology* 8(3): 293–316.

Cohn, Samuel K. 2009. *Lust for Liberty: The Politics of Social Revolt in Medieval Europe, 1200–1425.* Cambridge, MA: Harvard University Press.

Collier, Ruth B. and James Mahoney. 1997. "Adding Collective Actors to Collective Outcomes: Labor and Recent Democratization in South America and Southern Europe." *Comparative Politics* 29(3): 285–303.

Cooper, Frederick. 2009. *Africa Since 1940.* Cambridge: Cambridge University Press.

Dahrendorf, Ralf. 1959. *Class and Class Conflict in Industrial Society.* Stanford, CA: Stanford University Press.

della Porta, Donatella. 2015. *Social Movements in Times of Austerity: Bringing Capitalism back into Protest Analysis.* Chichester: Wiley.

della Porta, Donatella and Mario Diani. 2006. "Collective Action and Identity." In *Social Movements: An Introduction*, edited by Donatella della Porta and Mario Diani, 1–52. Oxford: Blackwell.

Dixon, Marc. 2010. "Union Threat, Countermovement Organization, and Labor Policy in the States, 1944–1960." *Social Problems* 57(2): 157–174.

Dixon, Marc and Andrew W. Martin. 2012. "We Can't Win This on Our Own: Unions, Firms, and Mobilization of External Allies in Labor Disputes." *American Sociological Review* 77(6): 946–969.

Du Bois, W.E.B. 1896. *The Suppression of the African Slave Trade to the United States of America 1638–1870*. New York: Longmans, Green, and Co.

Du Bois, W.E.B. 1935. *Black Reconstruction in America*. New York: Harcourt Brace.

Durkheim, Émile. 1984. *The Division of Labor in Society*. London: Macmillan.

Eggert, Nina and Marco Giugni. 2012. "Homogenizing 'Old' and 'New' Social Movements: A Comparison of Participants in May Day and Climate Change Demonstrations." *Mobilization: An International Quarterly* 17(3): 335–348.

Eidlin, Barry. 2014. "Class Formation and Class Identity: Birth, Death, and Possibilities for Renewal." *Sociology Compass* 8(8): 1045–1062.

Eidlin, Barry. 2018. *Labor and the Class Idea in the United States and Canada*. Cambridge: Cambridge University Press.

Evans, Geoffrey. 2000. "The Continued Significance of Class Voting." *Annual Review of Political Science* 3: 401–417.

Evans, Peter. 2010. "Is It Labor's Turn to Globalize? Twenty-First Century Opportunities and Strategic Responses." *Global Labour Journal* 1(3).

Fantasia, Rick and Judith Stepan-Norris. 2004. "The Labor Movement in Motion." In *The Blackwell Companion to Social Movements*, edited by David A. Snow, Sarah A. Soule and Hanspeter Kriesi, 555–575. Oxford: Blackwell.

Fine, Janice R. 2006. *Worker Centers: Organizing Communities at the Edge of the Dream*. Ithaca, NY: Cornell University Press.

Fraser, Steve and Joshua B. Freeman. 1997. *Audacious Democracy: Labor, Intellectuals, and the Social Reconstruction of America*. Boston: Houghton Mifflin.

Ganz, Marshall. 2000. "Resources and Resourcefulness: Strategic Capacity in the Unionization of California Agriculture, 1959–1966." *American Journal of Sociology* 105(4): 1003–1062.

Gitlin, Todd. 1987. *The Sixties: Years of Hope, Days of Rage*. New York: Bantam.

Goodwin, Jeff, James M. Jasper, and Francesca Polletta. 2009. *Passionate Politics: Emotions and Social Movements*. Chicago: University of Chicago Press.

Gorz, André. 1982. *Farewell to the Working Class: An Essay on Post-Industrial Socialism*. London: Pluto Press.

Gramsci, Antonio. 1972. *Selections from the Prison Notebooks*. New York: International Publishers.

Gramsci, Antonio. 1978. *Selections from Political Writings (1921–1926)*, edited by Quentin Hoare. London: Lawrence and Wishart.

Griffin, Larry J., Michael E. Wallace, and Beth A. Rubin. 1986. "Capitalist Resistance to the Organization of Labor before the New Deal: Why? How? Success?" *American Sociological Review* 51: 147–167.

Gurr, Ted R. 1970. *Why Men Rebel*. Princeton, NJ: Princeton University Press.

Hall, Peter A. and David W. Soskice. 2001. *Varieties of Capitalism: The Institutional Foundations of Comparative Advantage*. New York: Oxford University Press.

Harris, Kevan and Ben Scully. 2015. "A Hidden Counter-Movement? Precarity, Politics, and Social Protection before and Beyond the Neoliberal Era." *Theory and Society* 44(5): 415–444.

Hetland, Gabriel and Jeff Goodwin. 2012. "The Strange Disappearance of Capitalism From Social Movement Studies." In *Marxism and Social Movements*, edited by Colin Barker, Laurence Cox, John Krinsky, and Alf G. Nilsen. Leiden: Brill.

Hilton, Rodney. 2004. *Bond Men Made Free*. London: Taylor & Francis.

Hobsbawm, Eric J. 1989. *The Age of Empire, 1875–1914*. New York: Vintage.

Honey, Michael K. 2007. *Going Down Jericho Road: The Memphis Strike, Martin Luther King's Last Campaign*. New York: W. W. Norton & Company.

Hout, Michael, Clem Brooks, and Jeff Manza. 1993. "The Persistence of Classes in Post-Industrial Societies." *International Sociology* 8(3): 259–277.

Huber, Evelyne and John D. Stephens. 2012. *Democracy and the Left: Social Policy and Inequality in Latin America*. Chicago: University of Chicago Press.

Inglehart, Ronald and Jacques-René Rabier. 1986. "Political Realignment in Advanced Industrial Society: From Class-Based Politics to Quality-of-Life Politics." *Government and Opposition* 21(4): 456–479.

Isaac, Larry and Lars Christiansen. 2002. "How the Civil Rights Movement Revitalized Labor Militancy." *American Sociological Review* 67(5): 722–746.

Jacobs, David and Lindsey Myers. 2014. "Union Strength, Neoliberalism, and Inequality: Contingent Political Analyses of US Income Differences Since 1950." *American Sociological Review* 79(4): 752–774.

Jenkins, J. Craig. and Charles Perrow. 1977. "Insurgency of the Powerless: Farm Worker Movements (1946–1972)." *American Sociological Review* 42(2): 249.

Jones, William P. 2013. *The March on Washington: Jobs, Freedom, and the Forgotten History of Civil Rights*. New York: W. W. Norton & Company.

Kaldor, Mary. 1990. "After the Cold War." *New Left Review* I/180(Mar.–Apr.): 25–40.

Kautsky, Karl. 1910. *The Class Struggle (Erfurt Program)*. Chicago: Charles H. Kerr & Company Co-operative.

Kerr, Clark, John T. Dunlop, Frederick H. Harbison, and Charles A. Myers. 1960. *Industrialism and Industrial Man: The Problems of Labor and Management in Economic Growth*. Cambridge, MA: Harvard University Press.

Kerrissey, Jasmine. 2015. "Collective Labor Rights and Income Inequality." *American Sociological Review* 80(3): 626–653.

Kerrissey, Jasmine and Evan Schofer. 2013. "Union Membership and Political Participation in the United States." *Social Forces* 91(3): 895–892.

Kerrissey, Jasmine and Jeff Schuhrke. 2016. "Life Chances: Labor Rights, International Institutions, and Worker Fatalities in the Global South." *Social Forces* 95(1): 191–216.

Kimeldorf, Howard. 2013. "Worker Replacement Costs and Unionization Origins of the US Labor Movement." *American Sociological Review* 78(6): 1033–1062.

Kornhauser, William. 1959. *The Politics of Mass Society*. Glencoe, IL: Free Press.

Kraus, Jon. 2007. "Trade Unions in Africa's Democratic Renewal and Transitions: An Introduction." In *Trade Unions and the Coming of Democracy in Africa*, edited by Jon Kraus, 1–33. Basingstoke: Palgrave.

Kriesi, Hanspeter. 1989. "New Social Movements and the New Class in the Netherlands." *American Journal of Sociology* 94(5): 1078–1116.

Kriesi, Hanspeter, Ruud Koopmans, Jan W. Duyvendak, and Marco G. Giugni, eds. 1995. *New Social Movements in Western Europe: A Comparative Analysis*. London: Routledge.

Kristal, Tali. 2010. "Good Times, Bad Times: Postwar Labor's Share of National Income in Capitalist Democracies." *American Sociological Review* 75(5): 729–763.

Lenin, Vladimir I. 1961. "What Is to Be Done? Burning Questions of Our Movement." In *Collected Works*, by Vladimir I. Lenin, vol. 5, 347–530. Moscow: Foreign Languages Publishing House.

Lewis, Penny W. 2013. *Hardhats, Hippies, and Hawks: The Vietnam Antiwar Movement as Myth and Memory*. Ithaca, NY: Cornell University Press.

Lipset, Seymour M. 1963. *Political Man: The Social Bases of Politics*. Garden City, NY: Doubleday.

Luxemburg, Rosa. 1971. *The Mass Strike: The Political Party and the Trade Unions, and the Junius Pamphlet*. New York: Harper & Row.

Mann, Michael. 1986. *The Sources of Social Power, vol. 1: A History of Power from the Beginning to AD 1760*. Cambridge: Cambridge University Press.

Mann, Michael. 1993. *The Sources of Social Power, vol. 2: The Rise of Classes and Nation-States, 1760–1914*. Cambridge: Cambridge University Press.

Marcuse, Herbert. 2002. *One-Dimensional Man*. London: Routledge.

Marshall, T.H. and Tom Bottomore. 1992. *Citizenship and Social Class*, edited by Robert Moore. London: Pluto Press.

Martin, Andrew W. and Marc Dixon. 2010. "Changing to Win? Threat, Resistance, and the Role of Unions in Strikes, 1984–2002." *American Journal of Sociology* 116(1): 93–129.

Martin, Isaac. 2013. *Rich People's Movements: Grassroots Campaigns to Untax the One Percent*. Oxford: Oxford University Press.

Marx, Karl. 1973. *The Poverty of Philosophy: Answer to the 'Philosophy of Poverty.'* Moscow: Foreign Languages Publishing House.

Marx, Karl and Friedrich Engels. 1969. "Manifesto of the Communist Party." In *Marx/Engels Selected Works*, vol. I, 98–137. Moscow: Progress Publishers.

McAdam, Doug. 1982. *Political Process and the Development of Black Insurgency, 1930–1970*. Chicago: University of Chicago Press.

McAdam, Doug. 1988. *Freedom Summer*. New York: Oxford University Press.

McAdam, Doug. 1995. "Initiator and Spin-Off Movements." In *Wiley-Blackwell Encyclopedia of Social and Political Movements*, edited by David A. Snow, Donatella della Porta, Bert Klandermans, and Doug McAdam. Oxford: Blackwell.

McAdam, Doug. 2008. "From Relevance to Irrelevance: The Curious Impact of the Sixties on Public Sociology." In *Sociology in America: A History*, edited by Craig J. Calhoun, 411–426. Chicago: University of Chicago Press.

McAdam, Doug, Sidney G. Tarrow, and Charles Tilly. 2001. *Dynamics of Contention*. New York: Cambridge University Press.

McCallum, Jamie K. 2013. *Global Unions, Local Power: The New Spirit of Transnational Labor Organizing*. Ithaca, NY: Cornell University Press.

McCarthy, John D. and Mayer N. Zald. 1977. "Resource Mobilization and Social Movements: A Partial Theory." *American Journal of Sociology* 82(6): 1212–1241.

Michels, Robert. 1915. *Political Parties: A Sociological Study of the Oligarchical Tendencies of Modern Democracy*. New York: Hearst's International Library.

Migdal, Joel S. 1974. *Peasants, Politics and Revolution: Pressures Toward Political and Social Change in the Third World*. Princeton, NJ: Princeton University Press.

Milkman, Ruth, and Ed Ott, eds. 2014. *New Labor in New York: Precarious Workers and the Future of the Labor Movement*. Ithaca, NY: Cornell University Press.

Milkman, Ruth and Kim Voss. 2004. *Rebuilding Labor: Organizing and Organizers in the New Union Movement*. Ithaca, NY: Cornell University Press.

Mills, C. Wright. 1959. *The Power Elite*. New York: Oxford University Press.

Morehart, Christopher T. and Kristin de Lucia. 2015. *Surplus: The Politics of Production and the Strategies of Everyday Life*, edited by Christopher T. Morehart and Kristin de Lucia. Boulder, CO: University Press of Colorado.

Morris, Aldon D. 1984. *The Origins of the Civil Rights Movement*. New York: Free Press.

Nisbet, Robert A. 1959. "The Decline and Fall of Social Class." *The Pacific Sociological Review* 2(1): 11–17.

Nissen, Bruce. 1990. "A Post-World War II 'Social Accord'?" In *US Labor Relations, 1945–1989: Accommodation and Conflict*, edited by Bruce Nissen. 173–208. London: Garland Publishing, Inc.

Norris, Pippa. 2002. *Democratic Phoenix: Reinventing Political Activism*. Cambridge: Cambridge University Press.

Oberschall, Anthony. 1973. *Social Conflict and Social Movements*. Englewood Cliffs, NJ: Prentice-Hall.

Offe, Claus. 1985. "New Social Movements: Challenging the Boundaries of Institutional Politics." *Social Research* 52(4): 818–868.

Pakulski, Jan and Malcolm Waters. 1996. *The Death of Class*. London: SAGE.

Peterson, David K. 2013. "Slave Rebellions." In *Wiley-Blackwell Encyclopedia of Social and Political Movements*, edited by David A. Snow, Donatella della Porta, Bert Klandermans, and Doug McAdam. Hoboken, NJ: Wiley.

Piven, Frances F. and Richard A. Cloward. 1977. *Poor People's Movements: Why They Succeed, How They Fail*. New York: Vintage Books.

Polletta, Francesca and James M. Jasper. 2001. "Collective Identity and Social Movements." *Annual Review of Sociology* 27: 283–305.

Powell, Walter W. and Paul J. DiMaggio. 1991. *The New Institutionalism in Organizational Analysis*. Chicago: University of Chicago Press.

Richards, Andrew J. 2013. "Strikes within the European Context." In *Wiley-Blackwell Encyclopedia of Social and Political Movements*, edited by David A. Snow, Donatella della Porta, Bert Klandermans, and Doug McAdam. Hoboken, NJ: Wiley.

Riesman, David, Reuel Denney, and Nathan Glazer. 1950. *The Lonely Crowd: A Study of the Changing American Character*. New Haven, CT: Yale University Press.

Rosenfeld, Jake. 2014. *What Unions No Longer Do*. Cambridge, MA: Harvard University Press.

Schmitter, Philippe C. 1974. "Still the Century of Corporatism?" *The Review of Politics* 36(1): 85–131.

Silver, Beverly. 2003. *Forces of Labor: Workers' Movements and Globalization since 1870*. Cambridge: Cambridge University Press.

Silver, Beverly. 2013. "Theorising the Working Class in Twenty-first-century Global Capitalism." In *Workers and Labour in a Globalised Capitalism: Contemporary Themes and Theoretical Issues*, edited by Maurizio Atzeni, 46–69. Basingstoke: Palgrave Macmillan.

Smelser, Neil J. 2011. *Theory of Collective Behavior*. New Orleans, LA: Quid Pro Books.

Sorel, Georges. 1999. *Reflections on Violence*. Cambridge: Cambridge University Press.

Sturmthal, Adolf F. 1983. *Left of Center: European Labor Since World War II*. Urbana: University of Illinois Press.

Tarrow, Sidney. 1994. *Power in Movement: Social Movements, Collective Action, and Mass Politics in the Modern State*. Cambridge: Cambridge University Press.

Terriquez, Veronica. 2011. "Schools for Democracy: Labor Union Participation and Latino Immigrant Parents' School-Based Civic Engagement." *American Sociological Review* 76(4): 581–601.

Thelen, Kathleen. 1994. "Review: Beyond Corporatism: Toward a New Framework for the Study of Labor in Advanced Capitalism." *Comparative Politics* 27(1): 107–124.

Urbaincyzk, Theresa. 2008. *Slave Revolts in Antiquity*. Berkeley: University of California Press.

Vachon, Todd E. and Jeremy Brecher. 2016. "Are Union Members More or Less Likely to Be Environmentalists? Some Evidence from Two National Surveys." *Labor Studies Journal* 41(2): 185–203.

von Eschen, Donald, Maurice Pinard, and Jerome Kirk. 1971. "The Organizational Substructure of Disorderly Politics." *Social Forces* 49(4): 529–544.

Weber, Max. 1978. "The Distribution of Power Within the Political Community: Class, Status, Party." In *Economy and Society: An Outline of Interpretive Sociology*, edited by Guenther Roth and Claus Wittich, vol. II, 926–940. Berkeley: University of California Press.

Weber, Max. 2013. *The Agrarian Sociology of Ancient Civilizations*. London: Verso.

Westad, Odd A. 2005. *The Global Cold War: Third World Interventions and the Making of our Times*. Cambridge: Cambridge University Press.

Western, Bruce and Jake Rosenfeld. 2011. "Unions, Norms, and the Rise in US Wage Inequality." *American Sociological Review* 76(4): 513–537.

Windmuller, John P. 1971. "Czechoslovakia and the Communist Union Model." *British Journal of Industrial Relations* 9(1): 33–54.

Wood, Ellen M. 2002. *The Origin of Capitalism: A Longer View*. London: Verso.

Wright, Erik O. 1997. *Class Counts: Comparative Studies in Class Analysis*. Cambridge: Cambridge University Press.

Wright, Erik O. 2000. "Working-Class Power, Capitalist-Class Interests, and Class Compromise." *American Journal of Sociology*: 105(4): 957–1002.

Zhang, Lu. 2014. *Inside China's Automobile Factories*. Cambridge: Cambridge University Press.

30

Gender and Social Movements

HEATHER MCKEE HURWITZ AND
ALISON DAHL CROSSLEY

Introduction

Gender is "central to the emergence, nature and outcomes of social movements" (Taylor 1996: 166). Social movement scholarship about gender emerged in the 1970s alongside mass feminist activism, and today, this scholarship is expanding and diversifying. A growing body of research poses questions about gender and other identities, uses intersectional approaches to examine women's mobilization, and employs feminist methodologies to contribute simultaneously to the creation of knowledge and social change (Taylor 1998). Using a variety of theoretical approaches, gender and social movement scholars reveal how gender identities, gendered interactions, and structures of gender inequality within social movements shape grievances, tactics, framing, and indeed all aspects of mobilization (see, e.g. Blee 2002; Einwohner, Hollander, and Olson 2000; Ferree and Merrill 2003; Ling and Monteith 1999; Robnett 1997; Taylor 1999). Contemporary gender and social movement scholarship explores how activists advocate for women and transgender persons' rights. This scholarship also explains gender dynamics and gender inequalities within a wide variety of social movement industries and institutional contexts, even those not focused principally on gender issues.

Bringing a gendered lens to social movement scholarship allows for an examination of social movement dynamics at the "intersection" (Crenshaw 1991) of gender, race, class, and sexuality. Intersectional approaches demonstrate how participants shape social movements by either falling back on or challenging identity-based hierarchies and inequalities (Choo and Ferree 2010; Collins 1990; Naples and Desai 2002; Reger, Myers, and Einwohner 2008; Roth 2004). Gender, sexuality, and race scholars extend intersectional approaches by analyzing how identity work in the midst of collective action continuously constructs both identities and mobilization

The Wiley Blackwell Companion to Social Movements, Second Edition. Edited by David A. Snow, Sarah A. Soule, Hanspeter Kriesi, and Holly J. McCammon.

(Butler 2011; Reger, Myers, and Einwohner 2008; Roth 2004; Rupp and Taylor 2003; Rupp, Taylor, and Shapiro 2010).

In this chapter, we focus on the social movement activity of women, feminists, and transgender persons, in addition to the gender dynamics of sex-segregated and mixed-gender social movements. In each section, we examine the social movement theories and concepts that become more comprehensive and precise by evaluating gender processes. We argue that gender and intersectional analyses of social movements explain aspects of mobilization that we would not otherwise under-stand, including cultural dynamics, abeyance structures, women and gender variant persons' participation, and cohesion or conflicts within movements. We argue that research about how activists reproduce or challenge hegemonic gender dynamics and stereotypes helps us to understand how gender inequality has persisted for so long, so deeply, and in so many forms.

For the remainder of the chapter, we address each argument in four general areas of social movement inquiry: (1) tactics and strategies; (2) organizations; (3) collective identity; and (4) opportunities and constraints. We review gender and social movement research in each area, including examples from social movements outside the United States and Europe. In the conclusion, we synthesize the value and significance of gender and social movement research and suggest directions for future research.

Tactics and Strategies

Gender and social movement scholarship highlights the breadth and depth of social movement activity performed by women and transgender persons, despite their history of subordination within formal politics and activism. Although half of the population worldwide, women's participation in formal politics has been limited: the right to vote has been gender- and race-segregated and women hold dispropor-tionately few leadership positions in institutionalized politics (Paxton and Hughes 2015; Ridgeway 2011). Traditionally protest has been considered a masculine activity and "activism" a term from which women and girls have shied away (Bobel 2007; Taft 2006). Women's disproportionate responsibility for the majority of household labor and childcare, along with their participation in the paid labor force, have been barriers to women's availability to act politically (Dalton 2002; McAdam 1992). For example, Beyerlein and Hipp (2006) find that married women in the United States remain much less willing or likely to protest; they argue that women's burden of household labor and responsibilities to the marriage outweigh the time and risks of political participation. Furthermore, transgender persons are largely underrepresented as political leaders, and research rarely addresses transgender per-sons' political activity (exceptions include Currah, Juang, and Minter 2006; Taylor and Haider-Markel 2014). Mirroring their marginalization in the political sphere, mainstream media has devalued and ignored both women and genderqueer persons' political views and activism (Hurwitz 2017). In response to gender inequalities in politics, women and gender minorities advocate for their goals, form oppositional cultures, and generate collective action in social movements. Despite a history of gender disparities in politics, recent studies suggest there is no significant gendered "digital divide" between men and women's participation in online activism (Schradie 2015) or desire to or accomplishment of protest offline in the United States (Schussman and Soule 2005).

Gender and social movement scholars have extended research about protest tactics by studying women's movements. Feminist movements have been particularly successful and longstanding due to participants' use of broad, diverse, and strategic tactical repertoires (Crossley and Taylor 2015; McCammon 2012; Taylor 1989). These range from contentious actions such as petitioning for voting rights and organizing and participating in Take Back the Night anti-rape marches, to high risk mobilization like escorting patients through anti-choice protesters at abortion clinics, to cultural tactics like performing drag or challenging sexist discourse in everyday life (Banaszak 1996; Crossley 2017a; Rupp, Taylor, and Shapiro 2010; Whittier 1995). While the diffusion or disappearance of protest tactics is shaped by activists' ability to adopt tactics easily, garner attention on social media, and/or evade police repression (Galli 2016), contemporary feminist tactical repertoires persist because activists involve an increasingly broad range of participants in tactics updated for modern contexts. For example, consciousness-raising groups were a hallmark of feminism in the 1970s and this tactic has continued through "circles" today in workplaces, friendship groups, and in online communities in the form of blogs, listservs, and Facebook groups (Keller 2012). Today, feminists use online and social media tactics including blogging, email campaigns, and Facebook events that facilitate online and offline organizing, as well as virtual marches, Twitter hashtags, and by developing online communities (Crossley 2015).

Studying global feminism uncovers both the replicability of tactical repertoires and how women of the Global South and feminists in transnational spaces innovate new strategies and tactics to promote gender equality. For example, migrant Thai women garment workers organize for labor rights and protest against global capitalist companies by convening study groups that teach leadership development (Mills 2005). Young women active in participatory democracy and global justice movements in North, South, and Central America critique male-dominated organizations by maintaining non-hierarchical structures that emphasize group consensus and collaboration (Taft 2011). While these tactics are similar to western approaches to feminist change, activists in the Global South often use strategies particular to their socioeconomic context, such as creating small loans through transnational activist networks in order for women's local businesses to thrive in the shadow of dominant global corporations (Naples and Desai 2002). In the Global South, women's movement participants create new opportunities for change when they set quotas for women's representation in newly democratizing governments, or when participants in global feminist movements work inside and outside of the United Nations to improve transnational human rights standards (Grey and Sawer 2008). Over the course of history, as women have come to recognize the subordination of their ideas, bodies, rituals, and emotions in cultures broadly, they have created a variety of protest performances for social change that have redefined and reshaped what it means to be a woman and what it means to protest.

Using a gender lens to examine tactical repertoires reveals the gendered strategies and risks involved in democratic uprisings. For example, Rizzo, Price, and Meyer (2012) find that for a decade before the Arab Spring, even under the Mubarak regime, the Egyptian Center for Women's Rights had been advocating routinely for the enforcement of sexual harassment laws. This was a key strategy for the inclusion of women in high risk public protests during the Arab Spring, which simultaneously advocated gender equality and democratic change. Representative of the power of women's femininity in opposition to authoritarianism is a woman activist who performed civil disobedience and became known in the media as "the girl in the blue bra" when the lingerie beneath her gallibaya was revealed as she was dragged through the streets by military police (Hafez 2014). For the movement and the public, she represented the extreme anti-democratic nature of the regime, but also how women who participate in high risk activism face a threat of sexualized violence. Furthermore, during the mobilization cycle in Morocco, local grassroots women's activism for democracy went beyond street protests and also took the forms of campaigns for community water supplies and women's health, and citizen journalism using Facebook and YouTube videos, which educated women about politics (Salime 2012). Scholars using a gender lens to understand the tactical repertoire of the Arab Spring reveal simultaneously how women's tactics and strategies target the state, gender inequalities, sexual harassment, and women's marginalization within street protests.

While we tend to conceive of social movement activity as occurring outside of and in opposition to established institutions, contemporary feminist research also reveals the dynamics of activists working from within. Political insiders contribute to movements by interpreting activists' messages, helping activists navigate strategic choices for how to pressure the state, and diversifying movements (McCammon 2012). These tactics can lead to broader support for movement goals and successful outcomes as demonstrated by women's movements that desegregated US juries in the early to mid-1900s (ibid.). Feminist government employees have found great success within "the system" using their connections with politicians and other government staff to create policy changes, such as pressuring the Equal Employment Opportunity Commission to desegregate help wanted ads in the 1960s (Banaszak 2010). Since mass feminism declined in the USA after the 1970s, women have continued to use insider tactics: they desegregate workplaces by joining them, change male-dominated cultures, increase women's labor force participation, and reform institutional policy to create family-friendly workplace environments (Staggenborg and Taylor 2005). To provide another example, a critical mass of highly skilled and competent women employees in the military became key protesters from within the military when they demanded modifications to gendered combat exclusions in order to further their careers (Katzenstein 1998). A key strategy for ensuring the continuation of women's movements has been targeting gender inequality in a variety of institutions beyond the state, including schools, workplaces, healthcare organizations, cultural institutions, and communities (Armstrong and Bernstein 2008; Crossley 2017b; Van Dyke, Soule, and Taylor 2004). Research on feminist tactics and strategies in opposition to and within a variety of institutions extends how we understand activists' relationships with the state, and suggests that boundaries between social movement participants and the state are more complicated and connected than scholars have previously conceived.

Gender and social movement scholars have found that gender hierarchies, as well as cultural meanings and practices of masculinity and femininity tend to give rise to distinctive protest performances within social movements (such as Hurwitz and Taylor 2012; Reger 2005; Taylor 1999; Taylor and Whittier 1992). Continued examination of tactics and strategies employed by women, feminists, and other participants targeting gender change contributes to understanding the range of tactics that activists use beyond street protest. For example, LGBTQ activists reduced transphobia and increased support for a law protecting transgender rights in South Florida using door-to-door canvassing and transformative conversations when they defined and explained the term "transgender" and encouraged participants to empathize with the discrimination faced by transgender persons (Broockman and Kalla 2016). Gender and social movements research not only identifies the extent of targets for mobilization, but demonstrates that social movement successes can occur outside of the mainstream political arena. Considering that women and men broadly participate in similar levels but different kinds of activism, we turn to organizational and structural explanations to distinguish how men and women participate in different causes and use different tactics within organizations.

Organizations

Activists, leaders, and movement bystanders coordinate social movement activity within a variety of structures, including social movement organizations, interest groups, and non-governmental organizations. These contexts can be exemplars of equality or they may reflect dominant patterns of gender hierarchies common in most mixed-sex institutions (Acker 1990; Ridgeway 2011). By studying gender processes and social movement organizational structures, scholars uncover how gender inequalities and hierarchies influence the emergence, development, and outcomes of social movements.

Historically and contemporarily, mixed-gender social movement organizations have been sites for the perpetuation of gender inequality. Women in the American New Left gained status mainly if their husbands or boyfriends were leaders (Evans 1979; Morris and Staggenborg 2004). Women and men were not only recruited to Freedom Summer according to gendered criteria, but were for the most part assigned sex-stratified jobs that led to gender differences in their participation in civil rights mobilizations and subsequent activist biographies (McAdam 1992; Robnett 1997). Women in the civil rights movement supported the formal leadership of black men while women participated mainly as "bridge leaders" or grassroots leaders who connected local community organizations to national civil rights organizations (Robnett 1997). "Bridge leaders" rarely appeared in front of the media but often sent press releases and organized interviews for Black men who held formal spokesperson positions in movement organizations (ibid.). This inaccurately conveyed the idea that women played a minor role, even though they were organizing and sustaining many critical aspects of the civil rights movement and the Black Panther Party (ibid.; Farmer 2017).

In a more recent example, Black women's experiences of police murder, brutality, and harassment have been overlooked by activists and news media, as have women's critical contributions to the Black Lives Matter movement (Lindsey 2015). As a result, the African American Policy Forum (AAPF) and the Center for Intersectionality and Social Policy Studies at Columbia Law School (CISPS), directed by Kimberlé

Crenshaw, created a report on Black women and police brutality, a social media guide with images and statistics, and the #SayHerName campaign and organization to advocate for Black women's inclusion in Black Lives Matter (http://www.aapf.org/sayhernamereport/). #SayHerName exemplifies Black feminists' innovative online organizing, new forms of leadership beyond social movement organizations, and the vital interplay between online and offline protest performances.

In addition to explaining the persistence of gender inequality and gendered hierarchies in mixed-gender social movement organizations, scholars also reveal how social movement actors form organizational structures to align with their goals and to prefigure the social change they would like to achieve broadly. The work of feminists to form organizational structures that mirror their ideologies and goals for gender equality is well documented (Whittier 1995). To subvert male-dominated leadership and sexism, women's and feminist movements have used strategies of separatism to create women's organizations (Freedman 1979). Early feminist mobilizing structures included women's study groups and salons, women's colleges, and women-only professional organizations. Stemming from these early single-sex institutions and the suffrage movement in the early 1900s in the United States, feminist organizations have been central to the longevity of the movement and, as a result, have been the subject of much academic study about movement maintenance or abeyance processes (Crossley and Taylor 2015; Taylor 1989). Ferree and Martin (1995) attribute the survival and effectiveness of feminism to the continued existence of feminist organizations. For example, after the fall of state socialism in Eastern Europe and the reunification of Germany, feminists sustained their activism in local organizations each with unique "emotion cultures," which allowed organizations to access distinct resources and meet different goals (Guenther 2010).

Gender and social movement scholarship also reveals the conditions under which activists develop new organizational boundaries and forms. For example, in order to embrace their own strategies, protest performances, and leadership styles, women's movement participants as well as racial and ethnic minorities and LGBTQ activists create "free spaces" that set them apart (geographically, discursively, and organizationally) from social movement organizations dominated by white heterosexual men (Polletta 1999; Roth 2004; Taylor and Whittier 1992). This includes the non-hierarchical consciousness-raising groups in second-wave feminist efforts (Evans 1979). In the fall of 2011, feminists, women, and sexual minorities developed feminist free spaces within the Occupy Wall Street Movement in response to gender conflict and white male dominance. The free spaces took the forms of sex-segregated tents and sections of the park, feminist organizations, and feminist Facebook pages. Ultimately, these free spaces became opportunities for feminists to generate solidarity, promote feminist consciousness, practice feminist politics, and develop leadership among women of many races and sexualities who were otherwise marginalized in the main movement spaces (Hurwitz and Taylor 2018).

Although gender inequalities in movement organizations do persist, organizational change toward gender parity has begun to include men and women in all aspects of social movement organizations and communities. In the case of feminist student organizations in the United States, college campuses' institutional contexts and cultures influence the character and development of feminist collective identities, tactical repertoires, and organizations, including feminist mobilization in a range of social justice organizations not explicitly related to advancing gender equality (Crossley 2017a). Men have also created organizations in alliance with feminists to stop violence against women, often by organizing other men to stop rape and harassment on college campuses and in the military (Messner, Greenberg, and Peretz 2015). Even though they continue to enjoy gender and sexual privilege and typically ignore and leave unchanged gender inequalities and hierarchies, many straight men in the USA form social movement organizations to reject hegemonic masculinity in favor of hybrid, feminist, or gay masculinities (Bridges 2014; Messner, Greenberg, and Peretz 2015). Studying feminist and women's organizations illuminates the increasingly diverse cultures of social movement organizations that contribute to the persistence of feminism (Katzenstein 1998; Meyer and Wittier 1994; Reger 2012; Staggenborg and Taylor 2005; Taylor and Zald 2010).

Collective Identities

The "glue" that holds groups of individuals together in movements and organizations is collective identity, which is shaped by a wide range of gender expressions within social movements (Reger, Myers, and Einwohner 2008). Taylor and Whittier (1992) identified three key processes for how groups construct collective identity: (1) developing group consciousness; (2) constructing group boundaries; and (3) negotiating group practices. Gender shapes collective identity in critical ways, and is central to how groups accomplish each of these processes. In Taylor and Whittier's (1992) research, lesbian feminists emphasized gender differences between men and women when they created a collective identity that celebrated women's particular emotion cultures of caring and their embodied experiences as women who love other women. Additionally, in their study of international feminist solidarity, Rupp and Taylor (1999) distinguish three levels of collective identity that work together to affirm a movement's boundaries and group consciousness. Solidary collective identity includes gender, race/ethnicity, sexual, and class identities, which are distinct from organizational or movement collective identities. Furthermore, individual gender identities and gender inequality within social movement organizations influence how participants develop their group identities.

While participants may share commonalities along gender, race, class, or sexual minority status, gender inequalities may become a source of conflict that limits the boundaries of collective identity. In addition to hierarchies around sexual identity such as between homosexuals and bisexuals, infighting in LGBTQ movements often revolves around gender inequalities such as tension between transgender participants, gay men, and lesbian women (Ghaziani 2008). For example, the Michigan Womyn's Music Festival excluded men and transwomen by creating a boundary between "womyn-born womyn," who were allowed to participate in the annual cultural protest event, and everyone else (Gamson 1997). Within movements centered on masculinity (Schwalbe 1995), right-wing fatherhood movements limit their inclusion of men because of their narrow definitions of modern fatherhood (Dragiewicz 2011). As these examples illustrate, a gender lens on social movements demonstrates how tension around gender inequality limits solidarity and potentially reproduces hegemonic gender hierarchies.

Conflicts about gender affect the formation of collective identities as well as a movement's goals and tactics. One of the three main areas of infighting in the movement for marriage equality has been the concern that, "[Same-sex] marriage will reproduce traditional gender roles and hierarchy within marriage and continue to privilege monogamy" (Bernstein and Taylor 2013: 18). Although the movement has been primarily concerned with sexual minorities' right to marry, debate about whether the institution of marriage is too heteronormative and overly based on the ideology of the traditional gender division of labor contributes to how participants form a boundary between who has been included or excluded. For movement communities in Vermont, conflict about whether the movement's strategies and outcomes recognize queer interpretations of marriage, or whether the right to marry only extends civil rights to LGBTQ persons when they assimilate to the traditional model of the nuclear family, has influenced collective identity among participants as well as the movement's legal tactics (Bernstein and Burke 2013). In San Francisco, the majority of gay and lesbian couples who wed in the 2004 "Winter of Love" created solidarity by challenging normative sexualities and marrying in protest (Taylor et al. 2009), but some also tended to exercise the "heteronormative wedding narrative," when they wore white dresses and dark suits in their wedding photographs (Kimport 2012). In Vermont, San Francisco, and beyond, gender conflict among LGBTQ groups has been a crucial dynamic limiting movement solidarity and sparking infighting over goals and tactics. This research illuminates how a gendered lens allows us to understand more comprehensively the dynamics that influence the same-sex marriage movement's conflicts, cohesion, tactics, and goals.

While gender differences and inequalities may limit collective identity, shared gender identity can become a foundation from which participants generate collective consciousness and solidarity. For example, women's highly gendered, emotional, and embodied experiences of motherhood have motivated collective identity and creative protest actions (Rich 1995). Naples (1998) developed the concept "activist mothering" to recognize how mothers develop distinct collective identities around motherhood in order to better their communities. Mothers create collective identity by separating themselves from men, including from police, government officials, and fathers. For example, in Appalachia, mothers promote environmental justice as an extension of being caretakers for their families and nature in opposition to men in the coal industry (Bell and Braun 2010). In Liberia, mothers excluded men from the movement to end the Second Liberian Civil War and reframed their collective identity as mothers in opposition to African politicians' hyper-masculinity. Their mobilization eventually led to the war's end in 2003 and the awarding of the Nobel Peace Prize to Leymah Gbowee and Ellen Johnson Sirleaf (Prasch 2015). Despite violent police threat, activist mothers in the Brazilian *favela* of Caranguejo create explicitly feminine strategies and tactics, managing their identities as mothers by deploying non-violent tactics (Neuhouser 2008). Likewise, in Latin America, Mothers of the Disappeared were seen as peaceful and feminine, and their protest performances allowed them to avoid police repression and unleash a moral critique against the authoritarian regime (Brysk 1994). Activist mothers often perform successful high risk protests that evade police repression by drawing on both the stereotype of mothers as gentle and nurturing and their resilient collective identities forged through their shared experiences of motherhood.

Analyses of transgender movement collective identities further extend gender and collective identity research. Scholars examine how activists include or exclude genderqueer persons who do not identify as men or women. Davidson (2007) expands the fields of gender research and social movement studies by considering the complex identity negotiations among transsexual, intersex, transmen, transwomen, gender variant individuals, gays, lesbians, and allies in multiple gender non-conforming collective identities. Broad (2002) poses a new direction for collective identity research by questioning whether participants in transgender movements are claiming collective identity or are deconstructing gender and collective identities altogether.

The concept of collective identity emerged out of gender and social movement literature and remains tied to gender processes. Collective identity allows us to fully understand how participants form the cohesion and/or conflicts in movements that allow for the development of tactics, strategies, organizations, and social movement outcomes.

Opportunities and Constraints

Gender expressions and hierarchies shape the opportunities available to movement participants. The gender dynamics in any particular institutional context, for instance, may facilitate or impede who participates in activism and whether activists achieve their goals. Analyzing the gendered dimensions of political and social contexts can explain the persistence of inequalities, as well as how likely movements are to succeed or fail.

A gender regime, or the structural and cultural configuration of gender inequality within a particular institutional or historical context, may facilitate activism or limit social movement activity. McCammon and her collaborators (2001) build on the concept of political opportunity structures by developing the idea of "gendered opportunity structures" (see also Soule and Olzak 2004). They argue that existing laws that limit or advance women's legal rights, as well as organized women's connections to political elites and the relative cultural openness of the field of contention, mattered in women's movements to gain the right to vote. Legislation that circumscribed women's citizenship, such as limits on women's control of property, constrained women's activism, but at the same time, collective outrage unified women to fight for gender equality (McCammon 2012; McCammon, Bergner, and Arch 2015). In another example, globally, the success of mobilization by sex workers and their allies is shaped by whether a country has legalized prostitution, the relative availability of reproductive health services and health care, and the presence of feminist mobilizing structures and sex-positive feminism (Bernstein 2010; Kempadoo, Sanghera, and Pattanaik 2015). Gender regimes within religious contexts also provide relatively more or fewer opportunities for activists, such as for Muslim women in Indonesia who advocate for human rights by critiquing fundamentalist Islamists (Wieringa 2005). Each political context has particular legal, cultural, and sexual expectations for women, which matter immensely for social movements that seek to change gender inequality and gender regimes (Weldon 2002).

Gendered opportunity structures shape the dynamics, organizations, and outcomes of social movements (McCammon et al. 2001). For example, German and US women's movements have chosen distinct strategies over time and have had differing levels of success, largely shaped by their divergent political opportunities for making change in their unique national contexts (Ferree 2012). Even in the relatively similar political contexts in Canada, the United States, and Britain, legal and cultural struggles for reproductive rights have depended not only on organizational goals and resources but also each country's unique political parties and government policies about women (Halfmann 2011). In another example, in Russia, during the 1990s, an ideology of traditional domesticity flourished alongside the rise of semi-authoritarianism. As a result of these gendered constraints, crisis pregnancy centers became government-run, lost their feminist orientation, and focused on women's health rather than violence against women (Johnson and Saarinen 2013). Also, Tripp and her collaborators (2009) explain that the highly contentious recent histories of nationalization within each African country produced distinct constraints and opportunities for African women's activism around nation-building and democratization. For example, after transitioning out of war and genocide in the 1990s, women in Rwanda have grown to hold the most political representation in government of any country, a political opportunity created by international pressure on elites to recognize women as political leaders (Berry 2015). A growing body of research shows that the gender dimensions of political opportunities condition whether activists' claims receive hostility or acceptance.

Scholars also examine more forceful constraints on social movements, typically focusing on the use of repressive and/or violent tactics against movement activists (Davenport, Johnston, and Mueller 2005). Police repression either "frustrates" or "enables" how participants mobilize participation, leadership, and resources, and influences status hierarchies within social movement organizations (McCarthy and Zald 1977: 1222). For example, police threatened the Occupy Wall Street movement's goals to mobilize and occupy space, which generated a gendered response: men in Occupy protest encampments asserted masculinity by competing with the police, while women generally performed femininity when they were submitted to police harassment and neglect (Hurwitz 2016). Furthermore, movement adherents, bystanders, members, or opponents may engage in rape, harassment, or assault to constrain women's and gender-variant activists' participation or goals (Evans 1979; Ferree 2005; McGuire 2011). Using a gender lens, scholars have expanded our understandings of how gendered repression influences activism.

Conclusion

Gender and social movement research exposes underexplored dimensions of mobilization. A gender lens on social movements has advanced the field in critical ways, including demonstrating how gender shapes every facet of movement dynamics and outcomes. Gender and social movement approaches benefit our understandings of the dynamics of all movements, not only those focused on gender. This includes a thorough examination of cultural and institutional targets of social movements using a wide variety of tactics, organizational structures, collective identities, and political opportunities and constraints. This scholarship also illuminates the ways in which mobilized participants transform the gender order and challenge gender and other hierarchies internal and external to movements.

Building upon the arguments in this chapter, we suggest four directions for additional research: (1) the intersectional nature of grievances and protest; (2) new and emerging forms of feminism; (3) transgender activism; and (4) gender and violence in social movements. First, as a growing body of social movement participants utilize and apply intersectional analyses to form their goals and strategies, social movement scholars must also continue to ask questions about how different identity categories intersect and the implications for mobilization. Areas of inquiry include how the interconnectedness of race, class, gender, and sexuality shapes movement emergence, grievances, tactics, framing, persistence, and outcomes. As scholars develop trans-gender and trans-inclusive theories, it would behoove gender and social movement scholars to be in conversation with this body of literature, building on the historical connections between feminist scholarship, gender scholarship, and queer theory.

Second, to understand the persistence of feminism, even when it appears to be taking new forms (Staggenborg and Taylor 2005), future research should pay close attention to debates about gender and feminism in a wide variety of movements that purportedly are not about gender. This is particularly relevant as organizations and individuals debate intersectional approaches to inclusion and justice, such as a part of contemporary feminism (Reger 2012, Crossley 2017a) and #BlackLivesMatter (Lindsey 2015).

Third, while genderqueer populations have participated in activist movements for decades (Stryker 2008), we know little about their rates of participation because most demographic research includes statistics only about men and women. Future research needs to address the contributions of transgender and genderqueer activists in mixed-gender social movement organizations, and how they target changes to culture and the formal political system. We must also focus on understanding the extraordinary collaborations formed between LGBTQ, feminist, civil liberties, and civil rights activists for the shared goal of transgender rights.

Finally, studies of violence and social movements, including violence experienced by mobilized actors and violence as a social movement tactic, have focused predominately on men's lives and have overlooked the gendered dimensions of violence. Far too rare are gender analyses of terrorism, pro-gun movements, the conflicts between men's movements and homophobia, and sexual harassment within social movements. Expanding this body of knowledge will strengthen understandings of threat, repression, and participation in social movements more broadly. While a robust foundation has been laid for the examination of gender and social movements, there is much work to be done to advance the field. Further development of gender and social movement scholarship will not only continue to broaden social movement studies, but will contribute to ending gender inequalities.

References

Acker, Joan. 1990. "Hierarchies, Jobs, Bodies: A Theory of Gendered Organizations." *Gender & Society* 4: 139–158.

Armstrong, Elizabeth A. and Mary Bernstein. 2008. "Culture, Power, and Institutions: A Multi-Institutional Politics Approach to Social Movements." *Sociological Theory* 26: 74–99.

Banaszak, Lee Ann. 1996. *Why Movements Succeed or Fail: Opportunity, Culture, and the Struggle for Woman Suffrage*. Princeton, NJ: Princeton University Press.

Banaszak, Lee Ann. 2010. *The Women's Movement Inside and Outside the State*. New York: Cambridge University Press.

Bell, Shannon Elizabeth and Yvonne A. Braun. 2010. "Coal, Identity, and the Gendering of Environmental Justice Activism in Central Appalachia." *Gender & Society* 24: 794–813.

Bernstein, Elizabeth. 2010. *Temporarily Yours: Intimacy, Authenticity, and the Commerce of Sex*. Chicago: University of Chicago Press.

Bernstein, Mary and Mary C. Burke. 2013. "Normalization, Queer Discourse, and the Marriage-Equality Movement in Vermont." In *The Marrying Kind? Debating Same-Sex Marriage Within the Lesbian and Gay Movement*, edited by Mary Bernstein and Verta Taylor, 319–343. Minneapolis: University of Minnesota Press.

Bernstein, Mary and Verta Taylor. 2013. "Introduction: Marital Discord: Understanding the Contested Place of Marriage in the Lesbian and Gay Movement." In *The Marrying Kind? Debating Same-Sex Marriage Within the Lesbian and Gay Movement*, edited by Mary Bernstein and Verta Taylor, 1–35. Minneapolis: University of Minnesota Press.

Berry, Marie E. 2015. "From Violence to Mobilization: Women, War, and Threat in Rwanda." *Mobilization* 20: 135–156.

Beyerlein, Kraig and John Hipp. 2006. "A Two-Stage Model for a Two-Stage Process: How Biographical Availability Matters for Social Movement Mobilization." *Mobilization* 11: 299–320.

Blee, Kathleen M. 2002. *Inside Organized Racism: Women in the Hate Movement*. Berkeley: University of California Press.

Bobel, Chris. 2007. "'I'm Not an Activist, Though I've Done a Lot of It': Doing Activism, Being Activist and the 'Perfect Standard' in a Contemporary Movement." *Social Movement Studies* 6: 147–159.

Bridges, Tristan. 2014. "A Very 'Gay' Straight?: Hybrid Masculinities, Sexual Aesthetics, and the Changing Relationship between Masculinity and Homophobia." *Gender & Society* 28: 58–82.

Broad, Kendal L. 2002. "GLB+ T?: Gender/Sexuality Movements and Transgender Collective Identity (De) Constructions." *International Journal of Sexuality and Gender Studies* 7: 241–264.

Broockman, David and Joshua Kalla. 2016. "Durably Reducing Transphobia: A Field Experiment on Door-to-Door Canvassing." *Science* 352(6282): 220–224.

Brysk, Alison. 1994. *The Politics of Human Rights in Argentina: Protest, Change, and Democratization*. Redwood City, CA: Stanford University Press.

Butler, Judith. 2011. *Gender Trouble: Feminism and the Subversion of Identity*. New York: Routledge.

Choo, Hae Yeon and Myra Marx Ferree. 2010. "Practicing Intersectionality in Sociological Research: A Critical Analysis of Inclusions, Interactions, and Institutions in the Study of Inequalities." *Sociological Theory* 28: 129–150.

Collins, Patricia Hill. 1990. *Black Feminist Thought: Knowledge, Consciousness, and the Politics of Empowerment*. New York: Routledge.

Crenshaw, Kimberlé. 1991. "Mapping the Margins: Intersectionality, Identity Politics, and Violence Against Women of Color." *Stanford Law Review* 43(6): 1241–1299.

Crossley, Alison Dahl. 2015. "Facebook Feminism: Facebook, Blogs, and New Technologies of Contemporary U.S. Feminism." *Mobilization* 20: 253–269.

Crossley, Alison Dahl. 2017a. *Finding Feminism: Millennial Activists and the Unfinished Gender Revolution*. New York: New York University Press.

Crossley, Alison Dahl. 2017b. "Women's Activism and Educational Institutions." In *The Oxford Handbook of U.S. Women's Social Movement Activism*, edited by Holly J. McCammon, Lee Ann Banaszak, Verta Taylor, and Jo Reger, 582–601. Oxford: Oxford University Press.

Crossley, Alison Dahl and Verta Taylor. 2015. "Abeyance Cycles in Social Movements." In *Movements in Times of Democratic Transition*, edited by Bert Klandermans and Cornelius van Stralen, 64–87. Philadelphia, PA: Temple University Press.

Currah, Paisley, Richard M. Juang, and Shannon Minter, eds. 2006. *Transgender Rights*. Minneapolis: University of Minnesota Press.

Dalton, Russell. 2002. *Citizen Politics: Public Opinion and Political Parties in Advanced Industrial Democracies*. London: Chatham House.

Davenport, Christian, Hank Johnston, and Carol Mueller, eds. 2005. *Repression and Mobilization*. Minneapolis: University of Minnesota Press.

Davidson, Megan. 2007. "Seeking Refuge Under the Umbrella: Inclusion, Exclusion, and Organizing Within the Category Transgender." *Sexuality Research & Social Policy* 4: 60–80.

Dragiewicz, Molly. 2011. *Equality with a Vengeance: Men's Rights Groups, Battered Women, and Antifeminist Backlash*. Boston: Northeastern University Press.

Einwohner, Rachel L., Jocelyn A. Hollander, and Toska Olson. 2000. "Engendering Social Movements: Cultural Images and Movement Dynamics." *Gender & Society* 14: 679–699.

Evans, Sara Margaret. 1979. *Personal Politics: The Roots of Women's Liberation in the Civil Rights Movement and the New Left*. New York: Vintage.

Farmer, Ashley. 2017. *Remaking Black Power: How Black Women Transformed an Era*. Chapel Hill: University of North Carolina Press.

Ferree, Myra Marx. 2005. "Soft Repression: Ridicule, Stigma, and Silencing in Gender-Based Movements." In *Social Movements, Protest, and Contention: Repression and Mobilization*, edited by Christian Davenport, Hank Johnston, and Carol Mueller, 138–155. Minneapolis: University of Minnesota Press.

Ferree, Myra Marx. 2012. *Varieties of Feminism: German Gender Politics in Global Perspective*. Redwood City, CA: Stanford University Press.

Ferree, Myra Marx and Patricia Yancey Martin, eds. 1995. *Feminist Organizations: Harvest of the New Women's Movement*. Philadelphia, PA: Temple University Press.

Ferree, Myra Marx and David A. Merrill. 2003. "Hot Movements, Cold Cognition: Thinking About Social Movements in Gendered Frames." In *Rethinking Social Movements*, edited by Jeff Goodwin and James M. Jasper, 247–262. Lanham, MD: Rowman & Littlefield.

Freedman, Estelle. 1979. "Separatism as Strategy: Female Institution Building and American Feminism, 1870–1930." *Feminist Studies*, 5: 512–529.

Galli, Anya M. 2016. "How Glitter Bombing Lost its Sparkle: The Emergence and Decline of a Novel Social Movement Tactic." *Mobilization* 21(3): 259–282.

Gamson, Joshua. 1997. "Messages of Exclusion: Gender, Movements, and Symbolic Boundaries." *Gender & Society* 11: 178–199.

Ghaziani, Amin. 2008. *The Dividends of Dissent: How Conflict and Culture Work in Lesbian and Gay Marches on Washington*. Chicago: University of Chicago Press.

Grey, Sandra and Marian Sawer, eds. 2008. *Women's Movements: Flourishing or in Abeyance?* London: Routledge.

Guenther, Katja. 2010. *Making Their Place: Feminism After Socialism in Eastern Germany*. Redwood City, CA: Stanford University Press.

Hafez, Sherine. 2014. "Bodies That Protest: The Girl in the Blue Bra, Sexuality, and State Violence in Revolutionary Egypt." *Signs* 40: 20–28.

Halfmann, Drew. 2011. *Doctors and Demonstrators: How Political Institutions Shape Abortion Law in the United States, Britain, and Canada*. Chicago: University of Chicago Press.

Hurwitz, Heather McKee. 2016. "Gender, Leadership and Police Repression in the Occupy Wall Street Movement." Unpublished manuscript. Barnard College.

Hurwitz, Heather McKee. 2017. "From Ink to Web and Beyond: U.S. Women's Activism Using Traditional and New Social Media." In *The Oxford Handbook of U.S. Women's Social Movement Activism*, edited by Holly J. McCammon, Lee Ann Banaszak, Verta Taylor, and Jo Reger, 462–483. Oxford: Oxford University Press.

Hurwitz, Heather McKee and Verta Taylor. 2012. "Women's Cultures and Social Movements in Global Contexts." *Sociological Compass* 6: 808–822.

Hurwitz, Heather McKee and Verta Taylor. 2018. "Women Occupying Wall Street: Gender Conflict and Feminist Mobilization." In *100 Years of the Nineteenth Amendment: An Appraisal of Women's Political Activism*, edited by Lee Ann Banaszak and Holly J. McCammon. New York: Oxford University Press.

Johnson, Janet Elise and Aino Saarinen. 2013. "Twenty-First-Century Feminisms Under Repression: Gender Regime Change and the Women's Crisis Center Movement in Russia." *Signs* 38: 543–567.

Katzenstein, Mary Fainsod. 1998. *Faithful and Fearless: Moving Feminist Protest Inside the Church and Military*, Princeton, NJ: Princeton University Press.

Keller, Jessalynn Marie. 2012. "Virtual Feminisms: Girls' Blogging Communities, Feminist Activism, and Participatory Politics." *Information, Communication, and Society*, 15: 429–447.

Kempadoo, Kamala, Jyoti Sanghera, and Bandana Pattanaik. 2015. *Trafficking and Prostitution Reconsidered: New Perspectives on Migration, Sex Work, and Human Rights*. New York: Routledge.

Kimport, Katrina. 2012. "Remaking the White Wedding? Same-Sex Wedding Photographs' Challenge to Symbolic Heteronormativity." *Gender & Society* 26: 874–899.

Lindsey, Treva B. 2015. "Post-Ferguson: A 'Herstorical' Approach to Black Violability." *Feminist Studies* 41: 232–237.

Ling, Peter J. and Sharon Monteith. 1999. *Gender in the Civil Rights Movement*. New York: Routledge.

McAdam, Doug. 1992. "Gender as Mediator of the Activist Experience: The Case of Freedom Summer." *American Journal of Sociology* 97: 1211–1240.

McCammon, Holly J. 2012. *The U.S. Women's Jury Movements and Strategic Adaptation: A More Just Verdict*. Cambridge: Cambridge University Press.

McCammon, Holly J., Erin M. Bergner, and Sandra C. Arch. 2015. "'Are You One of Those Women?' Within-Movement Conflict, Radical Flank Effects, and Social Movement Political Outcomes." *Mobilization* 20: 157–178.

McCammon, Holly J., Karen E. Campbell, Ellen M. Granberg, and Christine Mowery. 2001. "How Movements Win: Gendered Opportunity Structures and US Women's Suffrage Movements, 1866 to 1919." *American Sociological Review* 66: 49–70.

McCarthy, John D. and Mayer N. Zald. 1977. "Resource Mobilization and Social Movements: A Partial Theory." *American Journal of Sociology* 82(6): 1212–1241.

McGuire, Danielle L. 2011. *At the Dark End of the Street: Black Women, Rape, and Resistance. A New History of the Civil Rights Movement from Rosa Parks to the Rise of Black Power*. New York: Vintage.

Messner, Michael A., Max A. Greenberg, and Tal Peretz. 2015. *Some Men: Feminist Allies and the Movement to End Violence Against Women*. New York: Oxford University Press.

Meyer, David S. and Nancy Whittier. 1994. "Social Movement Spillover." *Social Problems* 41: 277–298.

Mills, Mary. 2005. "From Nimble Fingers to Raised Fists: Women and Labor Activism in Globalizing Thailand." *Signs* 31: 117–144.

Morris, Aldon and Suzanne Staggenborg. 2004. "Leadership in Social Movements." In *The Blackwell Companion to Social Movements*, edited by David A. Snow, Sarah A. Soule and Hanspeter Kriesi, 171–196. Oxford: Blackwell.

Naples, Nancy. 1998. *Grassroots Warriors: Activist Mothering, Community Work, and the War on Poverty*. New York, Routledge.

Naples, Nancy A. and Manisha Desai, eds. 2002. *Women's Activism and Globalization: Linking Local Struggles and Transnational Politics*. New York: Routledge.

Neuhouser, Kevin. 2008. "I Am the Man and the Woman in This House:" Brazilian *Jieto* and the Strategic Framing of Motherhood in a Poor, Urban Community." In *Identity Work in Social Movements*, edited by Jo Reger, Daniel J. Myers, and Rachel L. Einwohner, 141–166. Minneapolis: University of Minnesota Press.

Paxton, Pamela and Melanie M. Hughes. 2015. "The Increasing Effectiveness of National Gender Quotas, 1990–2010." *Legislative Studies Quarterly* 40: 331–362.

Polletta, Francesca. 1999. "'Free Spaces' in Collective Action." *Theory and Society* 28: 1–38.

Prasch, Allison M. 2015. "Maternal Bodies in Militant Protest: Leymah Gbowee and the Rhetorical Agency of African Motherhood." *Women's Studies in Communication* 38(2): 187–205.

Reger, Jo. 2005. *Different Wavelengths: Studies of the Contemporary Women's Movement*. New York: Routledge.

Reger, Jo. 2012. *Everywhere and Nowhere: Contemporary Feminism in the United States*. New York: Oxford University Press.

Reger, Jo, Daniel J. Myers, and Rachel L. Einwohner, eds. 2008. *Identity Work in Social Movements*. Minneapolis: University of Minnesota Press.

Rich, Adrienne. 1995. *Of Woman Born: Motherhood as Experience and Institution*. New York: WW Norton & Company.

Ridgeway, Cecilia L. 2011. *Framed by Gender: How Gender Inequality Persists in the Modern World*. New York: Oxford University Press.

Rizzo, Helen, Anne Price, and Katherine Meyer. 2012. "Anti-Sexual Harassment Campaign in Egypt." *Mobilization* 17: 457–475.

Robnett, Belinda. 1997. *How Long? How Long?: African-American Women in the Struggle for Civil Rights*. Oxford: Oxford University Press.

Roth, Benita. 2004. *Separate Roads to Feminism: Black, Chicana, and White in America's Second Wave*. Cambridge: Cambridge University Press.

Rupp, Leila J. and Verta Taylor. 1999. "Forging Feminist Identity in an International Movement: A Collective Identity Approach to Twentieth-Century Feminism." *Signs* 24: 363.

Rupp, Leila J. and Verta Taylor. 2003. *Drag at the 801 Cabaret*. Chicago: University of Chicago Press.

Rupp, Leila J., Verta Taylor, and Eve Ilana Shapiro. 2010. "Drag Queens and Drag Kings: The Difference Gender Makes." *Sexualities* 13: 275–294.

Salime, Zakia. 2012. "A New Feminism? Gender Dynamics in Morocco's February 20th Movement." *Journal of International Women's Studies* 13: 101.

Schradie, Jen. 2015. "The Gendered Digital Production Gap: Inequalities of Affluence." In *Communication and Information Technologies Annual* (Studies in Media and Communications, vol. 9), edited by Laura Robinson, Shelia R. Cotten, and Jeremy Schulz, 185–213. Bingley: Emerald Group Publishing.

Schussman, Alan and Sarah A Soule. 2005. "Process and Protest: Accounting for Individual Protest Participation." *Social Forces* 84: 1083–1108.

Schwalbe, Michael. 1995. *Unlocking the Iron Cage: The Men's Movement, Gender Politics, and American Culture*. Oxford: Oxford University Press.

Soule, Sarah A. and Susan Olzak. 2004. "When Do Movements Matter? The Politics of Contingency and the Equal Rights Amendment." *American Sociological Review* 69(4): 473–497.

Staggenborg, Suzanne and Verta Taylor. 2005. "Whatever Happened to the Women's Movement?" *Mobilization* 10: 37–52.

Stryker, Susan. 2008. *Transgender History*. Berkeley, CA: Seal Press.

Taft, Jessica. 2006. "'I'm Not a Politics Person': Teenage Girls, Oppositional Consciousness, and the Meaning of Politics." *Politics and Gender* 2: 329–352.

Taft, Jessica 2011. *Rebel Girls: Youth Activism and Social Change Across the Americas*. New York: New York UniversityPress.

Taylor, Jami Kathleen and Donald P. Haider-Markel, eds. 2014. *Transgender Rights and Politics: Groups, Issue Framing, and Policy Adoption*. Ann Arbor: University of Michigan Press.

Taylor, Verta. 1989. "Social Movement Continuity: The Women's Movement in Abeyance." *American Sociological Review* 54: 761–775.

Taylor, Verta. 1996. *Rock-a-Bye Baby: Feminism, Self-Help, and Postpartum Depression*. New York: Routledge.

Taylor, Verta. 1998. "Feminist Methodology in Social Movements Research." *Qualitative Sociology* 21(4): 357–379.

Taylor, Verta. 1999. "Gender and Social Movements: Gender Processes in Women's Self-Help Movements." *Gender & Society* 13: 8–33.

Taylor, Verta, Katrina Kimport, Nella Van Dyke, and Ellen Andersen. 2009. "Culture and Mobilization: Tactical Repertoires, Same-Sex Weddings, and the Impact on Gay Activism." *American Sociological Review* 74: 865–890.

Taylor, Verta and Nancy Whittier. 1992. "Collective Identity in Social Movement Communities: Lesbian Feminist Mobilization." In *Frontiers in Social Movement Theory*, edited by Aldon D. Morris and Carol McClurg Mueller, 104–129. New Haven, CT: Yale University Press.

Taylor, Verta and Mayer N. Zald. 2010. "Conclusion: The Shape of Collective Action in the U.S. Health Sector." In *Social Movements and the Transformation of American Health Care*, eds. Jane Banaszak-Holl, Sandra Levitsky, and Mayer N. Zald, 504–534. New York: Oxford University Press.

Tripp, Aili Mari, Isabel Casimiro, Joy Kwesiga, and Alice Mungwa. 2009. *African Women's Movements: Changing Political Landscapes*. New York: Cambridge University Press.

Van Dyke, Nella, Sarah A. Soule, and Verta A. Taylor. 2004. "The Targets of Social Movements: Beyond a Focus on the State." *Research in Social Movements, Conflicts, and Change* 25: 27–51.

Weldon, S. Laurel. 2002. *Protest, Policy and the Problem of Violence against Women: A Cross-National Comparison*. Pittsburgh: University of Pittsburgh Press.

Whittier, Nancy. 1995. *Feminist Generations: The Persistence of the Radical Women's Movement*. Philadelphia, PA: Temple University Press.

Wieringa, Saskia Eleonora. 2005. "Comparative Perspectives Symposium: Islamization." *Signs* 32: 1–8.

31

Race, Ethnicity, and Social Movements

PETER B. OWENS, RORY MCVEIGH, AND
DAVID CUNNINGHAM

Introduction

Systems of racial and ethnic inequality, and collective efforts to variously create, defend, or dismantle them, have powerfully influenced scholarship on contentious politics and social movements. Much of the scholarship on progressive social movements from the 1970s onward has been strongly, but often relatively implicitly, influenced by the American civil rights movement, which directed scholarly attention to various mobilizing mechanisms, resources, and opportunities that were arguably necessary for insurgent activists to counter the oppressive and stifling environment of Jim Crow segregation and engage in collective action. In contrast, the study of racist and reactionary collective action has focused more centrally on the puzzle of what motivates individuals who are the (relative) beneficiaries of systems of ethnic and racial stratification to collectively maintain or defend such systems from perceived challengers. As such, the study of these movements has focused more centrally on the mobilizing effects of perceived threats to existing systems of stratification, emphasizing structural and ecological factors and the influence of ideologies that render such shifts in resources and privileges as threatening.

Here we engage with both exemplars of and exceptions to these general trends in social movement research, focusing on the determinants of individual and collective participation, identity work and related collective boundary processes, tactical choices, the differential role of state and non-state repression, and the outcomes of social movements. In our review, we focus largely on racial and ethnic social movements in America, since we feel that scholarship on these movements has had the broadest influence on the field. We close by drawing together the insights developed in the above sections to argue for a more thoroughly interactive approach to the relationship between broader structural environments and the varying mobilization of contentious efforts by both challengers to and beneficiaries of racial and ethnic inequality.

The Wiley Blackwell Companion to Social Movements, Second Edition. Edited by David A. Snow, Sarah A. Soule, Hanspeter Kriesi, and Holly J. McCammon.

Race, Ethnicity, and Social Movement Theory

In many ways the historical trajectory of social movement theorizing has run parallel to similar developments in studies of race and ethnic relations. Indeed, it could be said that students of race relations were a step or two ahead in moving toward more contemporary understandings of collective mobilization. Scholars of race relations, like early social movement scholars, initially approached their subject by focusing on individual psychological attributes. As Hirschman (1983) points out, early assimilation theorists placed a great deal of faith in what they perceived to be rational economic and political institutions (i.e. capitalism and democracy) as engines of change that would ultimately undermine what they viewed as misguided and irrational prejudices. Yet even before the mass mobilization phase of the civil rights movement gained steam, some scholars, most notably Herbert Blalock (1960), began thinking of interracial conflict in terms of organizational capacity and as reactions to threats to white privilege. According to this line of thought, the larger size of an oppressed group requires greater organizational capacity and concerted effort among members of the privileged group to protect resources and opportunities that they monopolize.

This key insight was refined and incorporated into theories of racial and ethnic conflict such as split-labor market theory (Bonacich 1972) and ethnic competition theory (Nielsen 1985; Olzak 1992). Bonacich drew inspiration from Marxist scholarship and emphasized how in-migration can influence the bargaining relationship between capitalists and extant labor pools in local settings. Ethnic competition theory, on the other hand, draws primary inspiration from theories of organizational ecology. It focuses on how intergroup conflict is most likely to emerge when previously subordinated ethnic or racial groups enhance their capacity to compete with members of dominant groups for scarce resources. While ethnic antagonisms resulting from group competition may be rooted in labor force dynamics, political and social forms of competition matter as well. Explanatory models, therefore, diverge with split-labor market explanations in their emphasis on racial/ethnic, rather than class, identities as primary drivers of contention.

Importantly, these theories of racial and ethnic conflict anticipated contemporary structural understandings of race (Bonilla-Silva 1997; Omi and Winant 1994). Race is structural in the sense that socially constructed racial boundaries are used to sort individuals into different roles and positions in society based on stereotypes and imagined understandings of group members' characteristics and suitability for particular roles. In the United States, for example, certain rights and privileges (such as voting, sitting at a lunch counter, and seeking employment in particular occupations) were commonly reserved for white people and denied to black people. And while expressions of overt racism have declined in the United States, racial identity continues to play a role in the assignment of individuals to positions and the way in which members of different groups engage (or fail to engage) with each other (Bonilla-Silva 1997; Embrick and Henricks 2013; McVeigh 2004; Pager 2003).

Likewise, it is difficult to overstate the extent to which the American civil rights movement contributed to a parallel shift in the way in which social movement theory has evolved. Given the blatant discrimination and oppression faced by African Americans, social movement scholars could easily recognize that the emergence of the civil rights movement represented a response to collective oppression rather than individuals "acting-out" based on irrational frustration or anxiety. While sociologists studying race relations recognized the collective response of the privileged majority to threats to their privilege, social movement scholars began to recognize the importance of organizational capacity among the oppressed (McAdam 1982; McCarthy and Zald 1977; Morris 1984; Oberschall 1973; Tilly 1978).

Because of gains made through prolonged challenge to systems of racial oppression, the civil rights movement also became a model for other forms of ethnic mobilization in the USA, such as the Chicano movement and the American Indian Movement (e.g. Deloria 1981; Ganz 2000, 2009; Nagel 1996). In each case, shared ethnic identity facilitated recognition of collective oppression and contributed to the solidarity needed to overcome freeriding tendencies. These groups sought to capitalize on their own organizational capacities and to make claims for just treatment during a period when such claims were gaining broader acceptance and legitimacy in society at large (Jenkins and Perrow 1977).

White Racist Mobilization

Although research on race and social movements has long centered on mobilization among oppressed minority groups, a substantial parallel literature has developed to analyze white racist (or separatist) organizations. Ethnographic research has been vitally important to this larger body of work. While many social movement scholars have had extensive contact with activists on the left (and many scholars maintain such an activist identity themselves), very few have had significant exposure to activists on the extreme right. Without such familiarity, it is too easy to resort to the same kinds of stereotypes that were once applied to all activists and to attribute participation to some form of psychological malfunction.

Fortunately, despite this predominant social distance from the research community, foundational theories of racist mobilization have benefited from close interrogation of activist understandings of their own participation. For instance, Blee's (1991) groundbreaking study of the women who participated in the Ku Klux Klan of the 1920s highlights the strong social incentives for their participation. Through Blee's interviews, we can see that the former Klanswomen were attracted to activism by many of the same things that appeal to progressive activists. The women spoke of the excitement of witnessing or actively engaging in the marches and rallies, while also enjoying the camaraderie of the numerous social events organized by the movement (also see McVeigh 1999).

In this work, and also in her later research on women in contemporary racist movements, Blee (2002) shows that unlike what some may expect, most participants were not drawn into the movement based on their strong ideological commitments to the goals of racist organizations. Instead, as is the case in many (if not most) social movements, participants tended to be drawn into movement activity through social ties to people who already were involved. Once exposed to the movement, some would stay and, over time, become more familiar with the organization's teaching, while others would not be drawn into the movement. Even among those who stay, however, Blee (2002) emphasizes that members and participants tend not to have a firm and cohesive grasp of movement ideology; adherents remain connected to the movement for a variety of reasons. Similarly, Simi and Futrell (2015) emphasize the role of close ties in such movements, demonstrating how parents in racist organizations take steps to isolate their children from connections to people outside of the movement in order to manage the stigma associated with the movement's heterodox beliefs.

These kinds of insights drawn from scholars courageous enough to do ethnographic fieldwork among racist activists have provided a foundation for researchers interested in identifying broader patterns in racist mobilization. Core tasks confronting scholars interested in patterns of mobilization involve, first, understanding the range of beliefs and values articulated by movement leaders as well as by rank-and-file members and supporters, and then identifying the historical and geographic contexts that allow individuals to acquire and maintain those beliefs, often in the face of opposition (McVeigh 2004). The most common approach taken thus far is to focus on the ways in which various forms of structurally-induced threats can compel organized racism (McVeigh 1999; Van Dyke and Soule 2002).

The focus on threat as a primary factor contributing to racist collective action flips the logic that underlies dominant theoretical approaches to the mobilization of progressive activism. Conventional resource mobilization and political opportunity models rest on an assumption that individuals who are disadvantaged or who hold grievances often do not act collectively because they lack an organizational infrastructure and/or fail to perceive favorable political circumstances to launch an effective challenge to the status quo. Within this familiar framework, collective action is predicted to emerge when new resources or organizational structures become available or when the political context becomes more favorable to activism. Scholars studying racist mobilization, on the other hand, have pointed out that activism on behalf of the beneficiaries of racial privilege is more likely to be prompted by perceived threats to pre-existing privileges, since the collective action to be explained is not emerging among oppressed groups previously stymied by lack of organizational resources or by fear of political repression.

Recent scholarship in this vein has sought to further specify the nature of threat while also focusing attention on the linkages between threat and action. Cunningham (2012, 2013), for example, has offered a "mediated competition model" as an attempt to bridge scholarship on social movements and racial and ethnic conflict. The theory asserts that racist activism should be most likely to form when members of the racial majority group perceive a threat to their status, when mainstream outlets for addressing the threat are lacking or are ineffective, and when state repression is absent or insufficient to hinder organizing efforts (Cunningham 2013: 7).

Similarly, McVeigh's (1999, 2009) "power devaluation model" seeks to specify the nature of the threats that can give rise to conservative collective action (including those that act to preserve racial privilege). His theory develops a relational approach focusing on the nature of exchange in regard to economics, politics, and status. Power within exchange is depreciated (or undergoes devaluation) by increases in the supply of others who offer the same commodity within an exchange relationship (e.g. goods, labor, wages, votes, campaign contributions, political representation, political patronage, modes of behavior, and esteem), or by a declining demand for those commodities. These "objective" losses in bargaining power can become racialized when groups experiencing devaluation share a common racial identity. This allows for the possibility of framing a broad range of grievances as threats to racial privilege, and can provide incentives to activate organizational resources at the group's disposal and to exploit political opportunities available to the group to contest the threat. Initially applied to explain the phenomenal rise of the Ku Klux Klan in the 1920s, its general logic has been extended to studies of the consequences of conservative or racist activism (McVeigh and Cunningham 2012; McVeigh, Cunningham, and Ferrell 2014).

Racial Oppression and Participation in Social Movements

Early collective behavior scholars tended to view protest and social movement participation as either a product of irrational appeals and crowd dynamics or of structural strains and breakdowns in the fabric of social relations, but such perspectives were eventually supplanted by a host of studies focusing on the social structures and mechanisms that enable individual participation, or "micromobilization" (e.g. McCarthy and Zald 1977; Snow et al. 1986; Snow, Zurcher, and Ekland-Olson 1980). As noted above, this focus on micromobilization was enabled, in part, through the recognition among scholars that individuals involved in racially progressive change efforts possessed legitimate and meaningful grievances but often did not possess the resources or capacities to overcome severe social sanctioning for engaging in protest.

Identification of the mechanisms that helped individuals to overcome systemic racial oppression and engage in contentious action have thus helped to clarify the importance of factors such as organizational linkages between Southern black churches and civil rights organizations (Calhoun-Brown 1996; McAdam 1982; Morris 1984) or the social capital and efficacy benefits of membership in racial justice organizations (Beyerlein and Andrews 2008; Ginwright 2007). Elaborating on the former, McAdam (1982) and Morris (1984) note how the black church promoted solidarity among parishioners that facilitated collective resistance against a powerful foe. At the same time, ministers of the churches were acquainted with other ministers throughout the South, allowing for communication and coordinated action beyond the local level. Pattillo-McCoy (1999) has noted that racial identity and shared cultural traditions nurtured within black churches continue to infuse political mobilization in the modern era.

Martinez (2005) identifies similar processes with regards to organizational and interpersonal support for Latino protest participants. Using nationally representative data, she finds that Latinos who were members of pre-existing political organizations or churches were much more likely to engage in protest activity (see also Heredia 2011; Martinez 2011). Nagel (1996) notes how shifts in American Indian protest actions in the 1960s from the tribal to the pan-tribal level were facilitated by the informational and network linkage of urban indigenous residents and organizations, including churches, community centers, and charitable groups, with reservation-based activists. Robnett (1996) adopts an intersectional approach to participation and leadership within movement organizations, demonstrating how African-American women who often lacked access to formal leadership positions within many civil rights groups instead occupied bridge leadership roles pivotal for recruitment and micromobilization within movement organizations. Within these various studies, mobilizing mechanisms interact with various political and interpersonal opportunities that can be leveraged against the collective disadvantages created by oppressive systems of ethno-racial domination, and their attendant means of repressing activism.

In contrast, and as noted above, participation in racist and white supremacist movements has been largely theorized as a more or less direct result of perceived threats to existing systems of ethno-racial stratification (e.g. Blalock 1967; Bonacich 1972). Much of the scholarship in this area has thus focused on the identification of causal linkages between perceived challenges to existing demographic, economic, and political conditions (Olzak 1992; Van Dyke and Soule 2002), and the mobilization of collective efforts to reduce or eliminate these challenges. Some scholars of repressive ethnic and racial contention have sought to clarify the relationship between such environments and mobilization outcomes by theorizing the ways in which structural shifts can enable ethnic and racial identities and boundaries to become a salient basis for collective action (e.g. McVeigh 2004, 2009; Nielsen 1985). Despite this focus, many such inquiries have generally not shared progressive movement scholars' focus on identification and measurement of the mobilizing structures that enable structural circumstances to be appraised as threatening, or that allow such individual perceptions to translate into contentious action (Cunningham 2012).

In response to this relative oversight, Owens and his colleagues (2015) demonstrate how leadership and organizational presence were particularly important in mobilizing aggrieved (but relatively disorganized) rural whites into joining the Ku Klux Klan in 1960s North Carolina. In areas where state and national KKK leaders were not often present at rallies and events, or in areas where the Klan had not developed an extensive network of meeting places, Klan membership and activities were often much less pronounced. Simi and Futrell (2015) focus on narrower interactive settings to demonstrate the importance of online and offline "free spaces," such as web forums, White Power music concerts, the homes of committed activists, and even the creation of entire White Power communities, in both drawing individuals into the movement and maintaining their commitment to it. Without such spaces, given that open expressions of racism and bigotry are stigmatized in contemporary American society, the movement would likely have much greater difficulty in developing and maintaining commitment and support among adherents. Blee's (2002) research on contemporary racial hate groups similarly highlights the complex pathways to becoming a movement participant by noting that social bonding, solidary incentives, and the desire "to be somebody," rather than pre-existing ideological beliefs, are the main drivers of initial involvement for many contemporary racist activists.

Identity Processes, Race, and Social Movements

Collective change efforts often require individuals to take an oppositional stance to existing social, political, and cultural arrangements – to set themselves apart from the existing status quo in some fashion. Frameworks highlighting how personal understandings of self can be multiple and fragmentary, and thus subject to constant negotiation and maintenance (e.g. Bernstein 1997; Snow and McAdam 2000), direct attention to "identity work" processes: the ways in which social movement participants construct and manage senses of who they are relative to others within a broader political and cultural context (Reger, Myers, and Einwohner 2008; see also Chapter 24, by Flesher Fominaya, in this volume, on collective identity).

Because movements often deploy notions of collective "difference" and "sameness" in strategic ways (Bernstein 1997), important similarities and differences in identity work processes are likely to exist across progressive and repressive ethno-racial movement cases. For instance, those seeking to establish or defend existing systems of inequality often must strategically de-emphasize their dominant social status to identify themselves as "victims," rather than benefactors, of existing social arrangements. Berbrier (1998), for instance, demonstrates that, in order to develop a mobilizing sense of injustice among the beneficiaries of racial inequality, white supremacist activists must both discursively realign themselves as being "just another ethnic minority," and accordingly argue that their rights to protection from defamation and disrespect are equivalent to those of nonwhite minorities. Simi and Futrell's (2009) research on the negotiation of White Power activist stigma also demonstrates the importance of social context in the negotiation of an oppositional identity. Their work demonstrates how White Power activists must strategically conceal their supremacist beliefs in public arenas, and develop movement "free spaces" such as White Power web forums, to share their beliefs with like-minded whites out of the public eye. Historically, in contrast, racist movements such as the Ku Klux Klan (Cunningham 2013; McVeigh 2009), enabled and emboldened by far more permissive social and political contexts, could make conspicuous identity claims through public rallies and other terroristic spectacles.

Movements on the progressive end of this spectrum also frequently clash with dominant models of personal and collective identification. These identity work processes have ranged from the Black Power movement's reformulation of "Black is Beautiful" (Van Deburg 1992), to contemporary movements for the recognition of American Indians as politically sovereign groups rather than domestic minorities (Steinman 2012), and the recognition of novel, multi-racial categories of identification. Addressing the latter issue, Bernstein and De La Cruz (2009) analyze efforts by Hawaiian activists to deconstruct existing racial and ethnic categories and to secure cultural recognition for the explicitly multi-racial "Hapa" identity. In contrast to strategic uses of identity that mobilize or draw attention to conditions for members of already-recognized identity categories, Hapa activists focused their challenges on confronting more diffuse cultural systems of difference, knowledge, and power.

As the above studies variously emphasize, the ways in which activists use and/or transform existing categories of identification are heavily influenced by the broader systems of power and meaning that such attempts occur within, and the various opportunities and constraints they present. For instance, Einwohner's (2006) historical research on Jewish resistance to the Nazi genocide in the Warsaw ghetto demonstrates how certain Jewish resisters had to strategically downplay their personal Jewish identities to "pass" as non-Jewish, while maintaining a personal and confidential Jewish identity to bolster commitment to their stigmatized comrades. Yukich's (2013) ethnographic research on an American immigrant rights organization similarly details how activists selectively deployed a framework of "deserving" versus "undeserving" migrants. These categories, while intended to support greater rights for undocumented migrants, in effect, reified existing "model minority" stereotypes.

Race and Social Movement Strategy and Tactics

Activism oriented toward reducing racial or ethnic inequalities has been extraordinarily influential in shaping scholars' views about the role that social movement tactics play in securing social change. The politics of protest, involving the capacity to disrupt the status quo, can provide the leverage needed to force beneficiaries of the status quo to change their behavior and practices.

Civil rights leaders of the 1960s made a strategic choice to be disruptive while simultaneously practicing nonviolent resistance. This strategic choice reflected an awareness of a severe power imbalance, as representatives of the state could use the state's monopoly over the "legitimate" use of violence to quell riots and other forms of disorder. Violent resistance from African Americans also could potentially generate widespread backlash among the white population. Yet the nonviolent tactics deployed by the civil rights movement would have been ineffective if acts of disruption did not impose costs on powerful actors who had the capacity to grant concessions to the movement and its constituents (Luders 2003; McAdam 1982; Morris 1984).

The civil rights movement's creative and strategic deployment of tactics provided scholars with opportunities to study and theorize ways in which social movements, in general, engage in action to generate solidarity and support, but also to win concessions from the state or from other powerful actors who were either opponents of the movement or potential allies that could be prompted to take action. In his study of the pacing of insurgency during the civil rights movement, McAdam (1983) highlighted the way in which the movement's deployment of new and innovative tactics helped to stimulate movement activity throughout the country. His research, however, also focused on the way in which civil rights opponents developed counter-tactics in an effort to stall the movement's momentum, leading to a chess-like tactical interaction. Ganz's (2000, 2009) explanation for the success of the relatively resource-poor United Farm Workers (UFW) movement, when compared with the AFL-CIO's Agricultural Worker's Organizing Committee, focuses on complex interactions between leadership, organizational structure, and movement strategy. Ganz demonstrates that the UFW's strategic capacity, rooted in organizers' motivation and engagement with available information, enabled a degree of "resourcefulness" that enhanced the group's responsiveness and accountability to a broader constituency of workers. In his analysis of the American Indian sovereignty movement, Steinman (2012) also draws important attention to the ways in which structures of domination influence social movement strategy. Noting the specifically decolonizing objectives of the movement, Steinman emphasizes the unique ways that American Indian activists engaged in pragmatic political relations with state and federal institutions, while also working to create recognition for their sovereign national statuses in broader cultural and international arenas.

Like many social movements, those that have sought to address racial or ethnic inequality have had to grapple with the choice of using nonviolent tactics or resorting to violence (see Chapter 19 by Schock and Demetriou, in this volume, for a fuller discussion of violence vs. non-violence as strategic alternatives). Commonly, there are disagreements over the question within movement ranks. Violent tactics appear to be most likely to appeal to activists frustrated with a lack of progress associated with other forms of action. As McAdam (1982) has argued, nonviolent tactics used by the civil rights movement to challenge Jim Crow segregation in the South were largely effective as they struck at vulnerabilities in systems of overt oppression and garnered support from sympathetic white liberals, particularly in northern states. Yet more militant resistance was advocated by younger activists (e.g. from the Student Nonviolent Coordinating Committee), whose commitment to nonviolence was tested by prolonged exposure to the realities of racial oppression in the South (Carson 1981; McAdam 1986). Militant stances by groups such as the Black Panther Party (Bloom and Martin 2014) or the Nation of Islam also resonated strongly among African Americans in northern cities who were faced with debilitating poverty resulting from racism that was, perhaps, less visibly enacted but brutal in its consequences.

A similar challenge faces activists today in the Black Lives Matter movement, as they seek to challenge inequities in the criminal justice system and, most directly, the frequent police shootings of young African American men. While civil rights activists of the 1960s confronted blatant discrimination encoded into law, Black Lives Matter activists must generate support for their very real grievances in an era of "colorblind racism" (Bonilla-Silva 2006), where many white Americans believe that racism is a thing of the past and tend to view police killings as justifiable in spite of video evidence to the contrary. These conditions produce a context in which violent tactics could surely generate a backlash from the white population, providing government leaders with the cover needed to violently repress the movement. Yet lack of progress obtained through peaceful demonstrations can make it difficult for activists to maintain consensus on the use of nonviolent tactics.

In contrast, common perceptions of racist collective action carry with them images of violent tactics. There is good reason for this association: historically, racist organizations in the United States have played a role not unlike terrorist organizations, using violence and intimidation in an effort to maintain white privilege. Yet, to better understand the nature of racist organizations it is important to recognize that the use of violent tactics has varied across time and across space.

The contours of this variation are rooted in two primary sources. The first involves the extent to which racist activists perceive that violence will be tolerated by legal authorities (Cunningham 2013; Owens et al., 2015). Violence perpetrated by the civil rights-era KKK, for example, was often carried out with the acquiescence of, and sometimes collaboration with, local law enforcement agents. Relatedly, Tolnay and Beck (1995) show that declines in the southern lynching rate were influenced, to a great extent, by a shift in the willingness of southern elites to intervene and discourage the violence. A second primary factor involves the extent to which racist movements feel that their goals can be achieved by influencing mainstream political processes. Klan members of the 1920s, for example, made a deliberate attempt to curtail the violence of its supporters when they perceived that violence would harm their chances of influencing the political process (McVeigh 2009). Even in more recent time periods, racist leaders have, at times, attempted to frame movement goals in a way that downplays violent intent and instead attempts to portray movement goals as consistent with patriotism, Christianity, and mainstream American values (Berbrier 1998).

Indeed, beyond the important question of violent tactics, we should not overlook the ways in which racist organizations utilize nonviolent tactics to advance their goals. Scholars have emphasized how movement-sponsored activities such as rallies, picnics, and music events help to attract supporters (Blee 1991, 2002; Cunningham 2013; McVeigh 2009; Simi and Futrell 2015). In many instances, promotion of these types of events can also be viewed as efforts to assert rights of public assembly and to ward off government surveillance and repression. McVeigh (2009), for example, emphasizes the way in which the Klan sought to broadly publicize charitable acts sponsored by the movement in order to generate public support and hence make it more difficult for the Federal Government to crack down on the movement. In the contemporary context, the Internet and social media have provided racist organizations with an opportunity to present different faces to different audiences. In public, movement leaders can attempt to present a softer side of the movement that aligns with values held by many white Americans. Yet the existence of chat rooms and restricted access websites provides members with opportunities to spew vitriolic rhetoric, appealing to deep-seated prejudices of potential recruits (Caren, Jowers, and Gaby 2012; Simi and Futrell 2015).

State Repression and Social Movement Outcomes: The Racialized Consequences of Contention

The preceding sections have demonstrated that social movement scholarship has predominantly engaged race implicitly, through cases such as the US civil rights movement, where race-based claims-making has motivated and defined contentious campaigns. A more explicit interrogation of how race informs and operates within such campaigns, however, has been more elusive. Indeed, issues associated with the construction of racial boundaries and grievances have been ceded largely to work in the ethnic conflict tradition. As a strength of social movement theory resides in its ability to consider interactive dimensions of contention, we argue that models that integrate these perspectives can offer particularly fertile approaches to engage how race shapes the manner in which state and elite actors react to mobilized challenges, and – by extension – the broader impacts and consequences of contention.

Research on historical patterns of lynching and organized racial violence provide one productive touchstone to inform such approaches. Classic work in this vein orients broadly to issues of race and social control. In their foundational studies of the wave of lynchings occurring between 1880–1930 in the USA, for instance, Tolnay, Beck, and their colleagues rooted the phenomenon in economic, political, and social threat, which "poison[ed] the social environment" (1995: 3) and thereby made racially-motivated violence significantly more likely (Beck and Tolnay 1990; Tolnay and Beck 1995; Tolnay, Deane, and Beck 1996). As a product of threat, vigilante racial violence served as a mode of social control, intended to repress challenges to the racial order, ranging from protest to out-migration to legislative reform.

Social movement scholars' somewhat narrower focus on mobilized collective challenges has provided a basis to understand instances of repression that unfold through tactical exchanges between challengers and power-holders. McAdam (1983), for instance, uses the civil rights movement case to demonstrate the chess-like interplay between civil rights forces and their state opponents, showing that challengers can accelerate the pace of insurgency through successful tactical innovation, with the pace then slowing as authorities learn how to engage and contain the tactic in question. Luders (2003) complicates such dichotomous interactions, arguing that state authorities can enable or hinder protestors' ability to act not only through their direct orientation to those targets but through their suppression, toleration, or encouragement of third-party counter-movements as well.

Such models productively intersect with a large literature on the interactive dynamics of protest policing, much of which centers on the "nexus" of protest and repression, i.e. the impact of policing on the likelihood and scale of subsequent protest activity. While divergent findings along these lines have sparked a robust effort to contextualize flat baseline conceptualizations of policing and protest (Earl 2011), race is rarely treated as a key contingent factor affecting state action. Welcome exceptions include Earl and Soule (2006), who argue that racial and ethnic minorities comprise one of several categories that may be policed aggressively based on their assumed vulnerability, and Davenport and his colleagues (2011), who find that protest events associated with African Americans were more likely to draw police presence than similar "white" actions. While this core association varies over time and across settings, their study importantly uncovers a systematic relationship between race and the policing of protest.

Such findings demonstrate how race can shape police practices both through the assumptions and actions of individual officers and agents as well as through systemic policy enacted by state agencies writ large. Focusing on the latter, Irons' (2010) study of the Mississippi State Sovereignty Commission demonstrates how the racist worldviews of authorities can shape the imposition of state repression, and how such processes can shift over time, as state agents deploy evolving rationales to accomplish the same ends in response to broader shifts in the racial landscape. Treading similar ground, Cunningham's (2003, 2004) study of the Federal Bureau of Investigation (FBI) focuses on how such racist worldviews interact with bureaucratic process to differentially impact protest targets based on racial status. His textual analysis of FBI memos uncovers a clear pattern of racist assumptions that generated strong incentives for agents to formulate and carry out proposals that more intensively and harshly targeted African-American activists. In contrast, "COINTELPRO-White Hate Group" targets such as the Ku Klux Klan were viewed as something to be controlled rather than eliminated.

While these kinds of findings are intended to point to generalizable processes, their tight focus on 1960s activism in the USA risks under-emphasizing or altogether ignoring the changing character of both race and contention over time and under differing regimes (McAdam et al. 2005). As a partial corrective, Simi and Futrell's (2015) study of contemporary racist hate groups demonstrates how white supremacists also work to manage the more quotidian sense of stigma associated with the open expression of their political beliefs, developing a range of strategies to selectively disclose those beliefs as well as insulate themselves and their family members from an inundation of competing (i.e. non-racist) social and political influences. Oliver (2008) offers another important effort to broaden conceptions of the intersection between race and state repression. Paralleling the underexplored synergies between the social movements and ethnic conflict literatures that we emphasize here, she focuses on how massive repression instituted in the wake of widespread urban unrest in the late 1960s related directly to the subsequent acceleration of incarceration rates associated with intensified crime control and drug policies after 1980. Such work is especially prescient for its ability to develop and emphasize such connections across protest and criminal justice domains, while also highlighting the longer-run disjoint consequences of state repression campaigns.

This line of work, while attentive to the imposition of state repression, also seeks to understand more broadly how such struggles intersect with race to shape a range of social movement outcomes. As with much of the research reviewed in this chapter, this area of the literature primarily engages race as a byproduct of movement cases, with the civil rights movement taking center stage. McAdam (1988), for instance, adopts a micro-longitudinal approach to focus on the biographical consequences of civil rights activism. At the community level, Andrews (1997, 2001; see also Andrews and Gaby 2015) demonstrates both the short- and longer-run impacts of local civil rights struggles across a range of political domains, emphasizing the complex manner in which local movement infrastructures and white resistance strategies relate to the trajectories of these outcomes over time.

Given the interactive nature of that struggle – i.e. between civil rights constituencies and the white resistance movements that emerged in response to shifts in the racial status quo in Mississippi and elsewhere in the US South – Andrews (2002) also shifts perspective to view the formation of private white academy schools as a reaction to federal desegregation mandates. Similarly engaging with civil rights counter-mobilizations, McVeigh and his colleagues have demonstrated how organized vigilantism has broader and enduring effects, showing how KKK presence in southern communities during the 1960s relates to continued elevated rates of violent crime (McVeigh and Cunningham 2012), as well as more pronounced electoral support for Republican candidates (McVeigh et al. 2014). The underlying argument emphasizes the pervasiveness of racial division, which can delegitimize authority, disrupt patterns of informal social control, and serve as a "takeoff issue" that provides a basis for political polarization (see also Baldassarri and Bearman 2007).

Other influential work takes up civil rights cases to directly demonstrate how racial dynamics shape the contingent nature of social movement constructs. For instance, Bell's (1980) now-classic interest convergence model posits that civil rights gains for African Americans are likely to occur when black and white interests at least temporarily align. Consistent with Andrews' (2001) focus on movement infrastructures, Payne's (1995) emphasis on how grassroots organizing traditions can durably affect political cultures points to a consideration of how, both within and across ethnic communities, we might see enduring patterns of mobilization in the face of emerging racialized issues such as immigration.

Addressing directly the racial dimension of contemporary immigration struggles, Brown (2013a, 2013b) demonstrates how racial hostilities can, when framed as such by politicians, contribute to spillover effects associated with various immigrant and welfare policies. Steil and Vasi (2014) show how, when applied to immigrant rights and ethnic division, the impacts of proactive and reactive movements are forged via distinct channels, with strong organizations and sympathetic allies aiding the former and rapid structural changes that could be framed as threats by reactionary forces benefiting the latter. And following a similar logic, Bloom (2015) adopts a practice-oriented perspective to show how such structural opportunities do not automatically confer to groups to aid their across-the-board efforts, but rather serve as resources to be strategically leveraged to shape outcomes associated with particular issue domains that may cross-cut race in complex ways.

Conclusion

In sum, understandings of race and ethnicity – whether developed implicitly through the study of civil rights and other like cases, or explicitly by interrogating political contention as a racialized process – reside at the center of a varied body of work on social movement mobilization and outcomes. In this chapter, we have identified at least two primary ways in which this emphasis has benefited social movement scholarship. We review those here, and conclude by suggesting how, in each case, more explicit interrogation of racialized processes can further the development of the field.

First, attentiveness to grievances associated with racial and ethnic inequity and division has contributed to a more precise understanding of the environments that produce contention. A significant strength of ethnic conflict perspectives in particular has been the ability for research in that tradition to draw out how structural arrangements shape group identities and boundaries, showing how such environments can be conducive to protest and other forms of collective action. At the same time, such approaches have been slower to embrace the social movements literature's emphasis on elaborating the processes through which conducive environments translate into collective struggles. Developing approaches that integrate ethnic conflict theory's nuanced attunement to grievances, threat, and intergroup competition with movement scholarship on collective identity, resource deployment, and repertoires of contention remains a continuing challenge. Such efforts can have considerable payoff, however, in their potential to spur the development of stronger theories of race and conflict, and also modes of interrogation that more robustly explain a broader range of cases. In particular, an integrative approach can provide a coherent foundation for overcoming the longstanding divide associated with explanations of left- and right-wing movements, a critique noted and lamented much more frequently than it is engaged theoretically or empirically.

Second, much of the literature discussed above demonstrates how race and ethnicity impact how activists see themselves, as well as how those self-definitions intersect with the racialized assumptions and reactions of authorities and audiences. A full reckoning of such processes should be responsive both to the construction and attribution of racialized inequity and threat, as well as how related discourses shape – and respond to – interactions (tactical and otherwise) among challengers, authorities, counter-movements, and public audiences. Such an approach should press analysts not only to recognize these players, but also to take seriously their interplay. Such efforts might draw strength from both social movement and ethnic competition perspectives, which – in different ways – attend to repression and authorities' reactive efforts to enable or, often, suppress the gains of challengers.

Along these and other dimensions, we see how future advances and breakthroughs in the social movements field require not only a sharpening of existing frameworks but also a look outward to insights from cognate literatures. Largely through foundational studies of the civil rights movement, race has long resided at the core of social movement theory. This connection, however, should not be viewed as implicit – a pairing of convenience or historical coincidence – but rather as one to be engaged actively as a harbinger of continued advances. Whether as a vehicle to refine ecological and interactive thinking, as we suggest here, or as a lever to expand and deepen our general conceptual toolkit, we expect that future influential work will gain power and purchase from serious attention to how social movements shape, and are shaped by, conceptions of race and ethnicity.

References

Andrews, Kenneth T. 1997. "The Impacts of Social Movements on the Political Process: The Civil Rights Movement and Black Electoral Politics in Mississippi." *American Sociological Review* 62: 800–819.

Andrews, Kenneth T. 2001. "Social Movements and Policy Implementation: The Mississippi Civil Rights Movement and the War on Poverty, 1965–1971." *American Sociological Review* 66: 71–95.

Andrews, Kenneth T. 2002. "Movement-Countermovement Dynamics and the Emergence of New Institutions: The Case of 'White Flight' Schools in Mississippi." *Social Forces* 80: 911–936.

Andrews, Kenneth T. and Sarah Gaby. 2015. "Local Protest and Federal Policy: The Impact of the Civil Rights Movement on the 1964 Civil Rights Act." *Sociological Forum* 30: 509– 527.

Baldassarri, Delia and Peter Bearman. 2007. "Dynamics of Political Polarization." *American Sociological Review* 72(5): 784–811.

Beck, E.M. and Stewart E. Tolnay. 1990. "The Killing Fields of the Deep South: The Market for Cotton and the Lynching of Blacks, 1882–1930." *American Sociological Review* 55(4): 526– 539.

Bell, Derrick A. Jr. 1980. "*Brown v. Board of Education* and the Interest-Convergence Dilemma." *Harvard Law Review* 93: 518–533.

Berbrier, Mitch. 1998. "'Half the Battle': Cultural Resonance, Framing Processes, and Ethnic Affectations in Contemporary White Supremacist Rhetoric." *Social Problems* 45(4): 431–450.

Bernstein, Mary. 1997. "Celebration and Suppression: The Strategic Uses of Identity by the Lesbian and Gay Movement." *American Journal of Sociology* 103: 531–565.

Bernstein, Mary and Marcie de la Cruz. 2009. "'What Are You?': Explaining Identity as a Goal of the Multiracial Hapa Movement." *Social Problems* 56(4): 722–745.

Beyerlein, Kraig and Kenneth T. Andrews. 2008. "Black Voting During the Civil Rights Movement: A Micro-Level Analysis." *Social Forces* 87(1): 65–93.

Blalock, Hubert M. 1960. "A Power Analysis of Racial Discrimination." *Social Forces* 39(1): 53–59.

Blalock, Hubert M. 1967. *Toward a Theory of Minority Group Relations*. New York: John Wiley & Sons.

Blee, Kathleen M. 1991. "Women in the 1920s Ku Klux Klan Movement." *Feminist Studies* 17(1): 57–77.

Blee, Kathleen M. 2002. *Inside Organized Racism: Women in the Hate Movement*. Berkeley: University of California Press.

Bloom, Joshua. 2015. "The Dynamics of Opportunity and Insurgent Practice: How Black Anti-Colonialists Compelled Truman to Advocate Civil Rights." *American Sociological Review* 80(2): 391–415.

Bloom, Joshua and Waldo E. Martin Jr. 2014. *Black Against Empire: The History and Politics of the Black Panther Party*. Berkeley: University of California Press.

Bonacich, Edna. 1972. "A Theory of Ethnic Antagonism: The Split Labor Market." *American Sociological Review* 37(5): 547–559.

Bonilla-Silva, Eduardo. 1997. "Rethinking Racism: Toward a Structural Interpretation." *American Sociological Review* 62(3): 465–480.

Bonilla-Silva, Eduardo. 2006. *Racism Without Racists: Color-Blind Racism and the Persistence of Racial Inequality in the United States*, 2nd edn. New York: Rowman & Littlefield.

Brown, Hana. 2013a. "Racialized Conflicts and Policy Spillover Effects: The Role of Race in the Contemporary U.S. Welfare State." *American Journal of Sociology* 119(2): 394–443.

Brown, Hana. 2013b. "Race, Legality and the Social Policy Consequences of Anti-Immigration Mobilization." *American Sociological Review* 78(2): 290–314.

Calhoun-Brown, Allison. 1996. "African American Churches and Political Mobilization." *Journal of Politics* 58(4): 935–953.

Caren, Neal, Kay Jowers and Sarah Gaby. 2012. "A Social Movement Online Community: Stormfront and the White Nationalist Movement." In *Media, Movements, and Political Change*, vol. 33 of *Research in Social Movements, Conflicts and Change*, edited by Jennifer Earl and Deana A. Rohlinger, 163–193. Bingley: Emerald Group Publishing Limited.

Carson, Clayborne. 1981. *In Struggle: SNCC and the Black Awakening of the 1960s*. Cambridge, MA: Harvard University Press.

Cunningham, David. 2003. "State vs. Social Movement: The FBI's COINTELPRO Against the New Left." In *States, Parties, and Social Movements: Protest and the Dynamics of Institutional Change*, edited by Jack Goldstone, 45–77. New York: Cambridge University Press.

Cunningham, David. 2004. *There's Something Happening Here: The New Left, the Klan, and FBI Counterintelligence*. Berkeley: University of California Press.

Cunningham, David. 2012. "Mobilizing Ethnic Competition." *Theory and Society* 41(5): 505–525.

Cunningham, David. 2013. *Klansville, USA: The Rise and Fall of the Civil Rights-Era Ku Klux Klan*. New York: Oxford University Press.

Davenport, Christian, Sarah A. Soule, and David A. Armstrong II. 2011. "Protesting While Black? The Differential Policing of American Activism, 1960 to 1990." *American Sociological Review* 76(1).

Deloria, Vine, Jr. 1981. "Native Americans: the American Indian Today." *Annals of the American Academy of Political and Social Science* 454: 139–149.

Earl, Jennifer. 2011. "Political Repression: Iron Fists, Velvet Gloves, and Diffuse Control." *Annual Review of Sociology* 37: 261–284.

Earl, Jennifer S. and Sarah A. Soule. 2006. "Seeing Blue: A Police-Centered Explanation of Protest Policing." *Mobilization* 11: 145–164.

Einwohner, Rachel L. 2006. "Identity Work and Collective Action in a Repressive Context: Jewish Resistance on the 'Aryan' Side of the Warsaw Ghetto." *Social Problems* 53(1): 38–56.

Embrick, David G. and Kasey Henricks. 2013. "Discursive Colorlines at Work: How Epithets and Stereotypes Are Racially Unequal." *Symbolic Interaction* 36(2): 197–215.

Ganz, Marshall. 2000. "Resources and Resourcefulness: Strategic Capacity in the Unionization of California Agriculture, 1959–1966." *American Journal of Sociology* 105(4): 1003–1062.

Ganz, Marshall. 2009. *Why David Sometimes Wins: Leadership, Organization, and Strategy in the California Farm Worker Movement.* New York: Oxford University Press.

Ginwright, Shawn A. 2007. "Black Youth Activism and the Role of Critical Social Capital in Black Community Organizations." *American Behavioral Scientist* 51(3): 403–418.

Heredia, Luisa. 2011. "From Prayer to Protest: The Immigrant Rights Movement and the Catholic Church." In *Rallying for Immigrant Rights : The Fight for Inclusion in 21st Century America*, edited by Kim Voss and Irene Bloemraad, 101–122. Berkeley: University of California Press.

Hirschman, Charles. 1983. "America's Melting Pot Reconsidered." *Annual Review of Sociology* 9: 397–423.

Irons, Jenny. 2010. *Reconstituting Whiteness: The Mississippi State Sovereignty Commission.* Nashville, TN: Vanderbilt University Press.

Jenkins, J. Craig and Charles Perrow. 1977. "Insurgency of the Powerless: Farm Worker Movements (1946–1972)." *American Sociological Review* 42(2): 249–268.

Luders, Joseph. 2003. "Countermovements, the State, and the Intensity of Racial Contention in the American South." In *States, Parties, and Social Movements*, edited by Jack A. Goldstone. New York: Cambridge University Press.

Martinez, Lisa M. 2005. "Yes We Can: Latino Participation in Unconventional Politics." *Social Forces* 84(1): 135–155.

Martinez, Lisa M. 2011. "Mobilizing Marchers in the Mile-High City: The Role of Community-Based Organizations." In *Rallying for Immigrant Rights: The Fight for Inclusion in 21st Century America*, edited by Kim Voss and Irene Bloemraad, 123–141. Berkeley: University of California Press.

McAdam, Doug. 1982. *Political Process and the Development of Black Insurgency, 1930–1970.* Chicago: University of Chicago Press.

McAdam, Doug. 1983. "Tactical Innovation and the Pace of Insurgency." *American Sociological Review* 48(6): 735–754.

McAdam, Doug. 1986. "Recruitment to High-Risk Activism: The Case of Freedom Summer." *American Journal of Sociology* 92(1): 64–90.

McAdam, Doug. 1988. *Freedom Summer.* New York: Oxford University Press.

McAdam, Doug, Robert J. Sampson, Simon Weffer, and Heather MacIndoe. 2005. "'There Will Be Fighting in the Streets': The Distorting Lens of Social Movement Theory." *Mobilization* 10(1): 1–18.

McCarthy, John D. and Mayer N. Zald. 1977. "Resource Mobilization and Social Movements: A Partial Theory." *American Journal of Sociology* 82(6): 1212–1241.

McVeigh, Rory. 1999. "Structural Incentives for Conservative Mobilization: Power Devaluation and the Rise of the Ku Klux Klan, 1915–1925." *Social Forces* 77(4): 461–496.

McVeigh, Rory. 2004. "Structured Ignorance and Organized Racism in the United States." *Social Forces* 82(3): 895–936.

McVeigh, Rory. 2009. *The Rise of the Ku Klux Klan: Right Wing Movements and National Politics.* Minneapolis: University of Minnesota Press.

McVeigh, Rory and David Cunningham. 2012. "Enduring Consequences of Failed Right-Wing Activism: Klan Mobilization in the 1960s and Contemporary Crime Rates in Southern Counties." *Social Forces* 90, 3: 843–862.

McVeigh, Rory, David Cunningham, and Justin Farrell. 2014. "Political Polarization as a Social Movement Outcome: 1960s Klan Activism and its Enduring Impact on Political Realignment in Southern Counties, 1960–2000." *American Sociological Review* 79(6): 1144–1171.

Morris, Aldon. 1984. *The Origins of the Civil Rights Movement: Black Communities Organizing for Change*. New York: Free Press.

Nagel, Joane. 1996. *American Indian Ethnic Renewal: Red Power and the Resurgence of Identity and Culture*. New York: Oxford University Press.

Nielsen, François. 1985. "Toward a Theory of Ethnic Solidarity in Modern Societies." *American Sociological Review* 50(2): 133–149.

Oberschall, Anthony. 1973. *Social Conflict and Social Movements*. Englewood Cliffs, NJ: Prentice-Hall.

Oliver, Pamela E. 2008. "Repression and Crime Control: Why Social Movements Scholars Should Pay Attention to Mass Incarceration as a Form of Repression." *Mobilization* 13(1): 1–24.

Olzak, Susan. 1992. *The Dynamics of Ethnic Competition and Conflict*. Palo Alto, CA: Stanford University Press.

Omi, Michael and Howard Winant. 1994. *Racial Formation in the United States: From the 1960s to the 1990s*. New York: Routledge.

Owens, Peter B., David Cunningham, and Geoff Ward. 2015. "Threat, Competition, and Mobilizing Structures: Motivational and Organizational Contingencies of the Civil Rights-Era Ku Klux Klan." *Social Problems* 62(4): 572–604.

Pager, Devah. 2003. "The Mark of a Criminal Record." *American Journal of Sociology* 108(5): 937–975.

Pattillo-McCoy, Mary. 1999. *Black Picket Fences: Privilege and Peril Among the Black Middle Class*. Chicago: University of Chicago Press.

Payne, Charles M. 1995. *I've Got the Light of Freedom: The Organizing Tradition and the Mississippi Freedom Struggle*. Berkeley: University of California Press.

Reger, Jo, Daniel J. Myers, and Rachel L. Einwohner, eds. 2008. *Identity Work in Social Movements*. Minneapolis: University of Minnesota Press.

Robnett, Belinda. 1996. "African-American Women in the Civil Rights Movement, 1954–1965: Gender, Leadership, and Micromobilization." *American Journal of Sociology* 101(6): 1661–1693.

Simi, Pete and Robert Futrell. 2009. "Negotiating White Power Activist Stigma." *Social Problems* 56(1): 89–110.

Simi, Pete and Robert Futrell. 2015. *American Swastika: Inside the White Power Movement's Hidden Spaces of Hate*, 2nd edn. Lanham, MD: Rowman & Littlefield.

Snow, David A., E. Burke Rocheford, Steven K. Worden, and Robert D. Benford. 1986. "Frame Alignment Processes, Micromobilization, and Movement Participation." *American Sociological Review* 51(4): 464–481.

Snow, David A. and Doug McAdam. 2000. "Identity Work Processes in the Context of Social Movements: Clarifying the Identity/Movement Nexus." In *Self, Identity, and Social Movements*, edited by Sheldon Stryker, Timothy Joseph Owens, and Robert W. White. 41–67. Minneapolis: University of Minnesota Press.

Snow, David A., Louis A. Zurcher, and Sheldon Ekland-Olson. 1980. "Social Networks and Social Movements: A Microstructural Approach to Differential Recruitment." *American Sociological Review* 45(5): 787–801.

Steil, Justin Peter and Ion Bogdan Vasi. 2014. "The New Immigration Contestation: Social Movements and Local Immigration Policy Making in the United States, 2000–2011." *American Journal of Sociology* 119(4): 1104–1155.

Steinman, Erich. 2012. "Settler Colonial Power and the American Indian Sovereignty Movement: Forms of Domination, Strategies of Transformation." *American Journal of Sociology* 117(4): 1073–1130.

Tilly, Charles. 1978. *From Mobilization to Revolution*. Reading, MA: Addison Wesley.

Tolnay, Stewart E. and E.M. Beck. 1995. *A Festival of Violence: An Analysis of Southern Lynchings, 1882–1930*. Urbana: University of Illinois Press.

Tolnay, Stewart E., Glenn Deane and E.M. Beck. 1996. "Vicarious Violence: Spatial Effects on Southern Lynchings, 1890–1919." *American Journal of Sociology* 102(3): 788–815.

Van Deburg, William L. 1992. *New Day in Babylon: The Black Power Movement and American Culture, 1965–1975*. Chicago: University of Chicago Press.

Van Dyke, Nella and Sarah A. Soule. 2002. "Structural Social Change and the Mobilizing Effect of Threat: Explaining Levels of Patriot and Militia Organizing in the United States." *Social Problems* 49(4): 497–520.

Yukich, Grace. 2013. "Constructing the Model Immigrant: Movement Strategy and Immigrant Deservingness in the New Sanctuary Movement." *Social Problems* 60(3): 302–320.

32

Bringing the Study of Religion and Social Movements Together: Toward an Analytically Productive Intersection[1]

David A. Snow and Kraig Beyerlein

Introduction

The end of the twentieth century was marked by an obsessive compilation of retrospective lists, which assessed the greatest moments and the most important individuals of the previous hundred years ...Yet in almost all these efforts, religious matters received remarkably short shrift. When religious individuals were highlighted, they were usually those most closely identified with secular political trends. Martin Luther King Jr. is an obvious example. After all, the attitude seemed to be, what religious change in recent years could possibly compete in importance with the secular trends, movements like fascism or communism, feminism or environmentalism? To the contrary, I suggest that it is possibly religious changes that are the most significant, and even the most revolutionary, in the contemporary world. Before too long, the turn-of-the-millennium neglect of religious factors may come to be seen as comically myopic, on par with a review of eighteenth century that managed to miss the French Revolution.

So begins the first chapter of Philip Jenkins' (2002) *The Next Christendom: The Coming of Global Christianity*. But Jenkins is not referring to Christianity in general. Rather, the focus in this book and subsequent ones, such as *The New Faces of Christianity: Believing the Bible in the Global South* (2006), is on the rise and spread of the fastest-growing and arguably most personally gripping and enthusiastic variant of Protestantism – Pentecostalism or what is also referred to as the "renewalist" movement. According to the Pew Research Center's study of Global Christianity:

Pentecostalism, and its related "renewalist" or "spirit-filled" movements, was one of the most influential developments in global Christianity in the 20th century, and it is poised to have an even greater influence in the 21st century. Nowhere is this more evident

The Wiley Blackwell Companion to Social Movements, Second Edition. Edited by David A. Snow, Sarah A. Soule, Hanspeter Kriesi, and Holly J. McCammon.
© 2019 John Wiley & Sons Ltd. Published 2019 by John Wiley & Sons Ltd.

than in the "global South," where Pentecostalism is reshaping the social, political and economic landscape of many countries in Latin America, Africa and Asia.

(Pew Research Center's Forum on Religion and Public Life 2006)

Given the rapid growth and expansion of this movement, coupled with its concentration among the very poor in a world of increasing global inequality, it can be argued that the Pentecostal Movement, and other "spirit-filled" movements, are certainly one of the most potent and durable social movements worldwide over the past half century. Indeed, Jenkins goes so far to suggest that it is "perhaps the most successful social movement of the past century" (2002: 8).

But it is a good bet that you would not have an inkling of this if your scholarly reading was nested in the study of social movements as represented in the United States and Europe. This is partly because the study of social movements as a significant substantive field within the larger profession rarely intersects with the study of religion or religious movements.

Realizing this glaring oversight and consequential hole in the literature on social movements, sociologists of religion Fred Kniss and Gene Burns wrote a chapter on religious movements for the 2004 *Blackwell Companion to Social Movements*. It began by referencing the late Mayer N. Zald's 1981 H. Paul Douglas Lecture to the Religious Research Association. In a published revision of that lecture, Zald and McCarthy noted that "the sociology of religion and the sociology of social movements can be invigorated" through greater "interchange." More concretely but not surprisingly given their major joint contributions to the study of social movements, they argued that "it is clear that the study of social movements from a resource mobilization perspective and the study of the transformation of and within religion have much to offer each other" (Zald and McCarthy 1987: 95). But neither their general nor more focused call for greater interchange between these two areas of scholarly inquiry generated much research or theorizing. As Kniss and Burns put it, Zald's "scholarly call to arms fell on deaf ears" (2004: 694). So Kniss and Burns picked up this call, seeking, in their words, to "update the argument that there are many fertile areas of inquiry at the intersection of religion and social movements" (ibid.: 695). And they did so in a systematic and quite compelling manner, at least from our vantage point. But here we are skating toward the end of the second decade of the twenty-first century with the world awash in religious enthusiasm, much of which manifests itself in social movements, but with little evidence that social movements scholars have heard of, much less paid any attention to, Kniss and Burns' call for scholarly inquiry at the intersection of religion and social movements. Indeed, it appears that Kniss and Burns' call for greater interchange between these areas of inquiry has also fallen on deaf ears. Interestingly, Lindekilde and Kuhle more recently made a similar call for "integrating elements of the sociological study of religion with the sociological study of social movements" (2015: 180). But they did so without acknowledging Kniss and Burns' earlier appeal, thus suggesting the absence of a niche of scholars working at this intersection.

As evidence of this general neglect of a potentially fruitful interchange among scholars of religion and social movements, consider the following: In McAdam, Tarrow, and Tilly's highly-cited *Dynamics of Contention* (2001), there is no mention of religion or religious movements in the index. The same neglect also holds for the most recent edition of della Porta and Diani's text entitled *Social Movements* (2006), as well as for Staggenborg's more recent text bearing the same title (2010). Tarrow's *Power in Movement* (1998) does somewhat better, mentioning both religion and religious movements in the index, with several pages referenced for each, but only in passing. And Tilly and Tarrow's second edition of *Contentious Politics* (2015) indexes religious movements, but again in passing on only four pages of the book. Finally, this glossing of religion and religious movements in the study of social movements can be seen by inspection of the contents of the articles in the field's major national and international journal, *Mobilization*. The first volume of the journal was issued in 1996. From then through volume 20 of 2015, there were 344 articles, but only 11 had something significant to say about religious movements or religion as a variable. That is 3.2% of the articles. How is that possible, given the world we live in today?

To note and highlight the glossing of religion in the study of social movements is not to say that there is not some prior work on the intersection of religion and movements. One line of such work focuses on the role of religion as organizational, ideological, and tactical resources in social movements. Leading the way is Morris' (1984) study of how black churches facilitated the emergence and diffusion of the civil rights movement in the American South. Others include Christian Smith's (1996a) research on the US Central America Peace Movement (see also Nepstad 2004); Kurzman's (2005) examination of the 1979 Iranian Revolution; Munson's (2008) work on the pro-life movement; Wood's (2002) study of faith-based community organizing (see also Warren 2001); Juergensmeyer's *Terror in the Mind of God: The Global Rise of Religious Violence* (2003); Nepstad's (2008) research of the Plowshares movement; Sager's (2012) investigation of how political and religious actors on the right used faith-based initiatives to advance their positions; Bentele et al.'s (2013) research on battles over religious inclusion laws; and Beyerlein, Soule, and Martin's (2015) analysis of the impact of religion on police presence at protest events. Another line of scholarship at the intersection of religion and social movements draws on either insights from the social movement literature to explain mobilization of and conflict within religious groups, or on religious revivals and movements to question and refine social movement theorization. Examples here include Stark's (1996) *The Rise of Christianity*; Smith's (1991) work on Liberation theology; Wilde's study of the Vatican II Council (2007); Young's (2006) analysis of the association of evangelical-based confessional protests with the rise of national movements in the US in the 1830s; Bruce's (2011) work on *Voice of the Faithful*; and Davis and Robinson's book entitled, *Claiming Society for God: Religious Movements & Social Welfare* (2012), wherein they show how four former or current movements build grassroots networks of religious-based social service agencies, hospitals, schools, and businesses while propagating their own brand of religious faith at the local level. But as illuminating and insightful as these studies may be in illustrating the religion/social movements intersection, this work, with an exception or two, has yet to figure significantly in social movement theorizing and associated research.

To be fair to social movement scholars, it is noteworthy that students of religious movements and so-called cults also often ignore or side-step the social movements literature. In the second edition to their book entitled, *Cults and New Religions*, for example, Cowan and Bromley (2015) neither index social movements nor include social movement scholars in their references, and the same gloss holds for Ingersoll's analysis of the Christian Reconstructionist movement (2015).

For all practical purposes, then, scholarship on social movements and on religious movements appear to be sequestered on two ships in close proximity but which pass each other on a dark, foggy night, with only a vague sense of each other's existence. Work in one domain rarely cites work in the other, and when they do, whether one-way or reciprocal, the conversation is rarely used to extend or refine existing work conceptually or theoretically.

In light of these observations, two sets of questions emerge. First, what accounts for this gloss, this failure to acknowledge the mutual existence of these separate spheres of knowledge and associated practitioners? And, second, what difference does it make if the two spheres of inquiry pass each other like ships in the night? What is lost analytically or, conversely, what might be gained by increasing the theoretical and empirical overlap between the two areas? Because of space limitations and the importance of the second question in establishing productive connections between the two areas of inquiry, we focus on the second question in the remainder of the chapter.[2]

Suggested Theoretical Intersections

How might the boundary between study of religious movements and other social movements be removed, or at least made more permeable? And, relatedly, what is gained by doing so? Instead of two fields existing in isolation, what can we learn by shifting scholarly attention to how these fields intersect and can speak to one another? Here we offer four provisional suggestions as to what is possible.

First, we need to reconsider not just the analytic and theoretic utility of splitting religious movements from social movements, but also the empirical basis for doing so. Much of what we do as researchers and theoreticians is predicated on some degree of lumping and splitting (Zerubavel 1991, 1996). It is a necessary step in the research and analytic process, but we should be clear about the criteria used for lumping and splitting. So what really are the key differences between religious movements and social movements? If we conceptualize social movements as collectivities acting with some degree of organization and continuity, partly or totally outside of institutional or organizational channels, for the purpose of challenging extant systems of authority, or resisting change in such systems, in the organization, society, culture, or world system in which they are embedded (Snow 2004; Snow and Soule 2010), then clearly, from a set-theoretic standpoint, religious movements are a subset of social movements rather than a different set of movements. This holds, we contend, whether we consider religious movements operating within the larger sociocultural context, as with the Pentecostal or Renewalist movement, or within a particular institutional context, as with the women's ordination movement (Chaves 1997; Katzenstein 1998).

But even then, how do we classify some movements as instances or cases specifically of religious movements and not also political movements? To illustrate the difficulty, consider early Christianity. Was it really just a religious movement? Arguably not, as Christianity's origins and evolving character are not understandable apart from the political context of the times. In fact, it is difficult to understand the early Christian movement as just a religious movement as it blended both religious and political themes. As Resa Aslan writes in his (2013) widely read book, *The Zealot: The Life and Times of Jesus of Nazareth*:

> In the end, there are only two hard historical facts about Jesus of Nazareth upon which we can confidently rely: the first is that Jesus was a Jew who led a popular Jewish movement in Palestine in the beginning of the first century C.E.; the second is that Rome crucified him for doing so. By themselves these two facts cannot provide a complete portrait of the life of a man who lived two thousand years ago. But when combined with all we know about the tumultuous era in which Jesus lived – and thanks to the Romans, we know a great deal – these two facts can help paint a picture of Jesus of Nazareth that may be more historically accurate than the one painted in the gospels. Indeed, the Jesus that emerges from this historical exercise [is of] a zealous revolutionary swept up, as all Jews of the era were, in the religious and political turmoil of first-century Palestine .... (xxviii)

Similarly, Christianity's widespread diffusion in the early fourth century cannot be fully understood apart from the conversion of Constantine and his melding of the church and empire and the cross and sword (Carroll 2001). The same can also be said of Islam and its various associated movements (Armajani 2012; Rashid 2002). And how do we get a firm handle on politics today in the United States without considering the movement-like rumblings of Christian renewalists and evangelicals? And the same question can be asked about the recent wave of revolutionary movements and protests that have jarred significant portions of the Middle East. For example, as Talal Asad, a noted scholar of the relationship between religion and secularity, noted upon returning from Cairo, where he was conducting fieldwork during Arab Spring:

> My own work has questioned the mutually exclusive categorization of the secular (read political) and the religious, and I think there is lots of evidence, empirical and analytic, to show that the way in which secularity has been thought of conventionally won't do to understand all that has occurred in recent history. Just recently, I saw scenes on *Democracy Now!* of people carrying placards with slogans for the camera, in Arabic, which said, "We insist on the trial of such and such," but which started off with "*Allahu akbar!*" These utterances were not seen as inconsistent. I saw this myself in Tahrir Square.
>
> (Schneider 2011)

Although some movements seem to be easily lumped into the religious-movement set, such as the Moonies, Hare Krishna, or the Children of God, the above discussion makes clear that coding a movement as religious is not a simple task, as there are many movements that appear to be neither purely religious movements nor purely political movements. Perhaps the best example today is ISIS, in that it contains both religious and political elements and cannot be understood apart from their intersection. It arose in the vacuum created by two failed-states (Iraq and Syria), proclaimed the establishment of a new kind of state, albeit a religiously inspired caliphate, and organized itself politically. But generally everything it has done was/is theologically rationalized and justified, including the flying of a black flag, its beheadings, the mass killing of its captured infidels, and the sexual enslavement and rape of its conquered female victims, particularly if they have practiced a religion other than its version of Sunni Islam (Callimachi 2015; McCants 2015; Warrick 2016; Wood 2015). So it could be argued that ISIS is employing religion instrumentally, as a resource. However, several observers have argued quite persuasively that ISIS is a deeply religious, millenarian movement with an apocalyptic, end-of-times eschatology with the view that the final days are impending rather than 1000 years hence (McCants 2015; Wood 2015).

What difference does it make how we analytically classify ISIS or early Christianity? By classifying both as purely religious movements, we risk sealing them off from close inspection and analysis by social movement scholars. And, in doing so, we are unwittingly undermining and curtailing our understanding of social movements. Think of how much empirically richer and theoretically refined our understanding of social movements would be if the post-1960s study of social movements had not been limited to those collective actions occurring primarily since the development of the nation state.[3] What has been missed? A lot, in our view, since most of human history and associated collective action precedes the rise of the modern nation state.

Second, so, while softening the boundaries between religious and social movements in the process of reexamining their similarities and differences, let us extend our empirical and analytical gaze back into history prior to the evolution and flowering of nation-states. There are probably countless examples of movements that would serve as useful cases for extending and/or refining our theorizing about social movements. For illustrative purposes, however, let us briefly consider the movement associated with the establishment of the 27 books of the New Testament as the canonized basis of Christianity. Whatever one believes about the New Testament's "sacred" status, there is little, if any, question regarding its contested and politicized character (Barnstone and Meyer 2008; Bauer 1971 [1934]; Ehrman 2003; Pagels 1989 [1979], 2003, 2012). Early on, during the first several centuries after the birth of the historical Christ, and well into the fifth century, there was no single, "orthodox" or canonized Christianity. Rather, there were numerous, competing Christianities, or Christian movements, with different interpretations of Christ's nature (e.g. divine versus human versus both or a fusion of the two natures) and teachings, scattered throughout early Christendom (Bauer 1971 [1934]; Ehrman 2003; Jenkins 2010; Pagels 1989 [1979]).

The process establishing Christian orthodoxy rests, according to early Christian scholar Bart Ehrman, as much on "struggles over power" as on theological differences (Bauer 1971 [1934]; Ehrman 2003: 175). A number of noteworthy periods in this canonization process highlight the conflict and power dynamics in which it was embedded (Ehrman 2003; Jenkins 2010; Pagels 1989 [1979]). Among them is the one keyed to the Roman Christian community and its belief in the dual nature of Christ and the church's hierarchical structure of bishops, priests, and deacons, "who understood themselves to be the guardians of the only 'true faith'" (Pagels 1989 [1979]: xxiii). This critically-noteworthy period occurred in the middle of the second century when some 52 texts now known as the *Gnostic Gospels*, and others like them, were denounced as heretical by Catholic bishops, perhaps most importantly Irenaeus, the Bishop of Lyons and author of a five-volume harangue entitled *The Destruction and Overthrow of Falsely So-Called Knowledge*. The result was that such denigrated texts were banned, destroyed or hidden, as was the case with the

Gnostic Gospels, which were discovered some 1600 years later (in 1945) buried in the cliffs of Nag Hammadi in Upper Egypt.

This, along with the banning and criminalizing of other "heretical" texts, represented an exclusionary step in establishing and limiting the New Testament canon and what could be included in the emerging sanctified Christian library. While conflicts over the correct or orthodox teachings and practices of early Christianity involved much saber-rattling and some associated bloodshed, it is also interesting to note that these doctrinal disputes were waged mainly with words, thus constituting framing wars of sorts. As Ehrman writes in *Lost Christianities*:

> The battle for converts was, in some ways, the battle over texts, and the proto-orthodox party won the former battle by winning the latter. One of the results was the canonization of the twenty-seven books that we now call the New Testament.
>
> (2003: 180)

This dynamic intersection of religion and politics and its relevance to social movements is also illustrated equally poignantly in the *Book of Revelation*, the last and most disturbing book of the New Testament.[4] Although the book has been used by movements across the centuries and across the globe to forecast the end of time and the character of the world's cataclysmic collapse, it was not written with that wider, historic appeal in mind. Rather, as Elaine Pagels, a scholar of early Christianity, argues, John (she is not referring to John of the Gospels but a different John – John of the island of Patmos) wrote the book with two contemporaneous battles in mind: one "against the Romans," and one against "God's people who had accommodated" the Romans and became "accomplices in evil" (Pagels 2012: 35; see also Kirsch 2006). As Pagels writes:

> [T]o John's dismay, the majority of Jews, and later Jesus' Gentile followers, as well, would continue to "follow the beast and to flirt with the whore called Babylon," that is with Rome and its culture. Instead of sharing John's vision of the imminent destruction of the world and preparing for its end, many other followers of Jesus sought ways to live in that world, negotiating compromises with Rome's absolutist government as they sought to sort out, in Jesus' words, what "belongs to Caesar" and what "to God."
>
> (Pagels 2012: 34–35)

Additionally, John is said to have been competing with other prophets with other warnings of revelations, and "was angry that some of his bearers were also listening to them and heeding their messages" (ibid.: 39, 44).

Thus, John was working on a number of fronts simultaneously, but with the Romans consuming most of his attention and wrath. It is for this reason that Pagels contends that "what John did in the Book of Revelation … was create *anti-Roman propaganda* (ibid.: 16, italics in original). He was trying to strengthen the resolve of Jesus' followers shortly after Jerusalem had been destroyed and all seemed hopeless. But his harangues and negative "othering" were done indirectly – that is, his charges and cryptic images and visions were in coded language – because public antagonism of the Romans was dangerous and could invite reprisal. For example, the famed number 666, long read as the mark or digits of the devil, was the name of the hated and erratic Roman Emperor Nero spelled out in Jewish numerology. In sum, Pagels argues that *Revelation* can be read as an anti-Roman tract. In some respects, then, it might be argued that John intended *Revelation* to function for the followers of Jesus much as Marx and Lenin intended their Communist Manifesto to function for the working class: a call to mobilization. As well, *Revelation*, when articulated with contemporary events, has been a source of end-times movement mobilization ever since.[5]

What these historical analyses point to is the potential empirical and analytical utility for students of social movements of pulling back the curtain of the nation-state to examine the rise, course, and character of social movements throughout human history. A careful reading of Montefiore's (2011) 600+-page biography of Jerusalem suggests that if social movement scholars did nothing more than zero in on social movement-like activity in and around Jerusalem from the time of David to the present, they would unearth a treasure trove of materials for inspection and analysis that might well lead to important theoretical extensions and refinements.

A *third* line of research and theorization that would benefit social movement scholars concerns the conditions facilitating the emergence and decline of religious enthusiasm. When does religion become a social force rather than just a variable in some theorized regression model? What conditions account for the transformation of religion from a variable exhibiting some influence on the phenomenon being investigated into a dynamic social force? Or, to borrow the language of Ronald A. Knox, a Catholic chaplain at Oxford in the 1930s and a translator of both the Old and New Testaments, what accounts for the rise and fall of waves of religious enthusiasm, or what Lindekilde and Kuhle (2015) have more recently called "religious revivalism"?

We know that social movements cluster in time and space, with this clustering conceptualized in terms of cycles (Tarrow 1994) and/or waves (Koopmans 2004), and we know this clustering occurs across all kinds of movements, whether predominantly political or religious. Knox provides a detailed historical account of such clustering in his examination of religious movements occurring in the seventeenth and eighteenth centuries in the wake of the Protestant Reformation. He titles his book *Enthusiasm* (1950), in order to capture the course and character of the movements spawned during this era and the role of their enthusiastic leaders. If Knox were alive and writing today, it is likely that he would be joined by other scholars noting that we are in the midst of another era or cycle of religious enthusiasm, this one characterized in part by the retrieval and accenting of what the adherents perceive to be the "fundamentals" of their faith (Armstrong 2001; Aslan 2010; Marty and Appleby 2004). "One of the most startling developments of the late twentieth century," writes Karen Armstrong, one of the foremost contemporary writers on religion, "has been the emergence within every major religious tradition of a militant piety popularly known as 'fundamentalism'" (2001: xi).

Identifying and lumping together various movements under the canopy of fundamentalism can understandably generate a bit of controversy, particularly "when used outside of the Protestant tradition" (Ruthven 2016), but it may be easier to gain conceptual clarity on this lumping than it is to identify in a compelling manner the set of conditions that give rise to this fundamentalist variant of religious enthusiasm or to religious revivalism more broadly. The problem is not a shortage of explanations;

there are a number of competing yet overlapping ones ranging from economic imperialism to cultural imperialism, from various disruptions associated with globalization processes to the strains of late capitalism. The problem is that we do not have a good sense of whether these processes work independently or in conjunction with each other in different combinations in different contexts. Also, these are very macro processes which do not hone in on the ground where religious enthusiasm plays out. So there is much to be learned here by both scholars of religion and scholars of social movements, with both being beneficiaries of their respective inquiries.

Here we suggest one line of theorizing grounded in identity theory and keyed to the concept of collective identities. By collective identities, we refer to national identities, racial and ethnic identities, religious identities, organizational identities, to any kind of group-based identity for which there is a "shared sense of 'one-ness' or 'we-ness' anchored in real or imagined attributes and experiences among those who comprise the collectivity and in relation or contrast to one or more actual or imagined sets of 'others'" (Snow and Corrigall-Brown 2015: 175, and Chapter 24 by Flesher Fominaya, in this volume). The core proposition is that in the modern, globalizing world there are numerous collective identities at play, and they are arrayed, just like our individual, role-based identities, in what Stryker (1980) called a salience hierarchy. If so, this means that the bases for our various collective identities do not disappear as secularization theorists once argued in reference to religion.[6] Instead, it means that some collective identities may be fallow, layered over by other more salient identities, much in the same way as Taylor (1989) argued about abeyance organizations and structures. However, when the dominant and relatively salient collective identities, such as nationality or ethnicity, are peeled or eroded away, then a submerged collective identity may surface or rise in salience. Such is the case, we conjecture, with the enthusiastic resurgence of religion today, as illustrated by the flourishing of Pentecostalism, particularly in the Global South (Jenkins 2002, 2006). Moreover, it is arguable that religion constitutes a kind of essentialist identity that provides the fall back or default resource for collective identity when other identities have lost their salience and basis for a sense of collective coherence due to exogenous factors, like globalization and its tag-team partner, cultural imperialism, or indigenous factors like state breakdown and the sometimes resultant prospect of becoming a failed state. Isn't this what has happened in Syria and Iraq with the rise and spread of ISIS?

The *fourth* line of research and theorization we suggest entails examination of variation in the strategies religiously enthusiastic movements pursue in relation to the state, regime, empire, or society in which they are embedded. Some religiously-based movements pursue a path of strategic accommodation, which Snow (1979: 30) has conceptualized as a form of "dramatic ingratiation" involving a concerted effort to gain the favor or good will of authorities by "fostering the impression that [the groups'] values, aims, and/or conduct are in conformity with, or at least not incongruent with, certain values, traditions, and normative standards within the ambient society." Perhaps the most historically famous example of such strategic accommodation is found in Mark 12:17 when Jesus reportedly said, in response to questions about paying taxes to Caesar, "Render unto Caesar the things that are Caesar's, and to God the things that are God's." A much more recent example of strategic accommodation via dramatic ingratiation is found in some of the former public practices and behaviors of the exported/imported Japanese-based Buddhist movement formerly called Nichiren Shoshu of America (Snow 1979), and now known as Sokagakkai International and firmly institutionalized in the United States and elsewhere.

For other movements, the strategic choice appears to be violence, as John, the author of *The Book Revelation,* seems to be suggesting in virulent opposition not only to the Romans, but also to the Jews and Gentiles he abhorred for their accommodation. More recent examples of this violent strategy are recounted by Hall (2000) in his examination of the cases of Jonestown, the Branch Davidians in Waco, Aum Shinrikyo in Japan, the Solar Temple, and Heaven's Gate, by Juergensmeyer's (2003) accounting of the rise of religious terrorism in today's world, and by a spate of work on ISIS (Callimachi 2015; McCants 2015; Stern and Berger 2015).

The principal strategy for other religious enthusiasts does not entail violence or terrorism but, as Davis and Robinson (2012: 1) contend in *Claiming Society for God,* it involves "a patient, beneath-the-radar takeover of civil society that [they] call 'bypassing the state.'" More concretely, it involves the grassroots construction and maintenance of "vast networks of alternative religious, cultural, and economic institutions" without challenging the state directly (ibid.: 31). Their illustrative cases include the Muslim Brotherhood in Egypt, Shaz in Israel, Comunione e Liberazione in Italy, and the Salvation Army in the United States.

A fourth strategy pursued by some movements in relation to the embedding state or authority structure is neither attacking it directly nor indirectly, but exiting its sphere of control, or at least attempting to do so. Illustrations range from communal movements (Berger 1981; Kanter 1972), to separatist and secessionist movements, such as the Christian Reconstructionists (Ingersoll 2015), to some religious sects such as the Amish, to perhaps mass suicide as the ultimate form of exit, as purportedly occurred in Masada around 73 AD and among the Heaven's Gate adherents in San Diego in March 1997 (Hall 2000). This exit strategy is suggested in Hirschman's *Exit, Voice, and Loyalty* (1970), but it is a strategy that has received comparatively little attention from social movement scholars because of more general interest in direct challenges to the state or other authority structures.[7]

The point here is not to belabor these alternative strategies but, rather, to direct attention to the conditions that account for their selection and execution and their likely sequencing, since they are clearly not mutually exclusive. For example, Davis and Robinson's (2012) observations about the bypassing strategy of the Muslim Brotherhood may hold true at some points in time and in some places but clearly not across the lifespan of the Brotherhood, which has also engaged in violence strategically (see Kandil 2016). The same can be observed with Hamas and Hezbollah. Just as we should explore the conditions associated with selection of one strategy over another, we also want to know the conditions under which these strategies are blended and sequenced.

Conclusion

In sum, we have argued for breaking down the boundaries between the study of social movements and religion, particularly religious movements, and proposed to increase the interchange between these spheres of inquiry. One way to think about this intersection is in terms of a Venn diagram, wherein the overarching, outer circle is for social movements in general, with different kinds of movements – including not only political and religious movements but also identity-based and self-help or therapeutic movements – represented by sometimes independent and other times overlapping circles within. That movements of different kinds overlap on occasion is hardly surprising in light of research on coalitions and multi-organizational fields (see Chapter 14 by Brooker and Meyer, in this volume, and Rucht 2004). But what begs for more penetrating analysis is the extent to which the degree of intersection varies over time and the factors that account for that variation. The important analytic point is that the degree of overlap is itself a dynamic process, but it is one that has not received sufficient analysis, particularly, we contend, in the case of religious and political movements.

We noted at the outset that we are not the first to call for greater intersectionality and cross-fertilization between the two fields (see Kniss and Burns 2004; Zald and McCarthy 1987). But there is good evidence that earlier calls for such mobilization have fallen on deaf ears, so we have picked up the sword, so to speak, by suggesting four avenues for facilitating the interchange while simultaneously addressing some major questions of importance to both areas of inquiry, but particularly the study of social movements. However, we do not think the flow of empirical and analytic edification would be one way, such that social movement scholars would be the only beneficiaries. Rather, we think scholars of religion and religious movements would benefit from accessing the conceptual and theoretical toolkit of social movements' scholars. But our guess is that scholars of social movements might have the most to gain because new troves of movements and associated contextual data would become available. So let's remove our blinders that split aspects of the world into separate spheres, pull back the curtains of history and examine more seriously and persistently than heretofore the intersection between social movements and religion, and particularly religious movements.

Notes

1   This is a significantly revised version of a paper that Snow presented for the Distinguished Social Change & Social Movement Scholar Lecture at Vanderbilt University, Nashville, TN, November 6, 2015.

2   Snow (2015) has elaborated an array of factors which have speculatively impeded the intersection of the study of social movements and religion. They include the social science penchant for "lumping and splitting"; the "opiate of the masses" hangover accenting the conservatizing function of religion; the biographic backgrounds of social movement scholars; the dominance of political opportunity and the contentious politics perspective in the study of social movements, which deflect attention from other institutional spheres; the linkage of the rise of social movements with the rise of the nation-state beginning in the early nineteenth century; and the cultural tendency to give religion a free pass, a kind of free-ride, when discussing and attributing reasons for various social ills/problems. In addition, Smith (1996b) theorizes why social movement scholars have neglected religion as an explanatory factor in collective action and social movements.

3   Here we refer to the Tilly and Tarrow linkage of the social movement as a collective entity with the rise and development of the nation-state beginning in the early nineteenth century (Tarrow 1994; Tilly and Tarrow 2015). As Tarrow wrote in *Power in Movement* (1994: 65):

"It was the expansion and consolidation of the nation state that prodded the social movement into existence, and this was true all over the West, regardless of the degree of state centralizations."

4   Whether the author of the *Book of Revelation* was John the disciple of Jesus or another John is not known with certainty. He is sometimes referred to as John of Patmos because he wrote the book on "the small island of Patmos, off the coast of Turkey" (Pagels 2012: 4), but neither there nor elsewhere is there evidence that he claimed to be John the disciple (see Ehrman 2003: 4; Kirsch 2006: 59). The difficulty of discerning the authorship of apocalyptic texts is not peculiar to the *Book of Revelation*, however, as it was commonplace for the authors of such texts to "conceal their identities behind the names of revered biblical figures," exhibiting a practice called "pseudonymity" (Kirsch 2006: 55).

5   One relatively recent, chilling example of the use of the *Book of Revelation* as a basis for mobilization was its centrality to the visionary claims of David Koresh and his Branch Davidian organization. Prior to his death in the 1993 siege at the Branch Davidian compound in Waco, Texas, Koresh (1995) wrote an exhaustive update consisting of both revision and addendum to the *Book of Revelation*. Foretelling inevitable destruction and his own martyrdom, Koresh incorporated his own fabricated prophecies into those of the *Book of Revelation*. Interestingly, Koresh is the biblical Hebrew name of Cyrus, the pagan messiah from ancient Persia. As one observer of "end-times" eschatology notes, "the fact that the name 'Koresh' first appears in the Bible and then figures in the headlines of the late twentieth century show the remarkable staying power of the messianic idea" (Kirsch 2006: 29), particularly as elaborated in the *Book of Revelation*.

6   The secularization thesis reflects the once popular linear conception of cultural evolution and modernization theory. In relation to religion in general, this linear conception manifested itself in the secularization thesis, arguably captured most starkly in the Death of God movement within Christian theology in the 1960s and memorialized by *Time* magazine with its April 8, 1966, cover story asking, "Is God Dead?"

7   But see Lindekilde and Kuhle (2015), who distinguish between religious revivalism based on "exit" in contrast to revivalism based on "voice." For a more general summary overview of the "exit strategy," see Snow and Soule (2010: 12–15) and Tierney (2013).

References

Armajani, Jon. 2012. *Modern Islamist Movements: History, Religion, and Politics*. Malden, MA: Wiley-Blackwell.

Armstrong, Karen. 2001. *The Battle for God: A History of Fundamentalism*. New York: Ballantine Books.

Aslan, Reza. 2010. *Beyond Fundamentalism: Religious Extremism in the Age of Globalization*. New York: Random House.

Aslan, Reza. 2013. *Zealot: The Life and Times of Jesus of Nazareth*. New York: Random House.

Barnstone, Willis and Marvin Meyer. 2008. *The Gnostics and Their Scriptures*. Boston: Shambhala.

Bauer, Walter. 1971 [1934]. *Orthodoxy and Heresy in Earliest Christianity*. English translation, edited by Robert A. Craft and Gerhard Krodel. Philadelphia, PA: Fortress.

Bentele, Keith, Rebecca Sager, Sarah A. Soule, and Gary Adler, Jr. 2013. "Breaking Down the Wall between Church and State: Adoption of Religious Inclusion Legislation, 1995–2009." *Journal of Church and State* 56: 503–533.

Berger, Bennett M. 1981. *The Survival of a Counterculture: Ideological Work and Everyday Life among Rural Communards*. Berkeley: University of California Press.

Beyerlein, Kraig, Sarah A. Soule, and Nancy Martin. 2015 "Prayers, Protest, and Police: How Religion Influences Police Presence at Collective Action Events in the United States, 1960–1995." *American Sociological Review* 80: 1250–1271.

Bruce, Tricia Coleen. 2011. *Faithful Revolution: How Voice of the Faithful Is Changing the Church*. New York: Oxford University Press.

Callimachi, Rurmini. 2015. "ISIS Enshrines a Theology of Rape." *New York Times*, August 13.

Carroll, James. 2001. *Constantine's Sword: The Church and the Jews*. Boston: Houghton Mifflin.

Chaves, Mark. 1997. *Ordaining Women: Culture and Conflict in Religious Organizations*. Cambridge, MA: Harvard University Press.

Cowan, Douglas E. and David G. Bromley. 2015. *Cults and New Religions: A Brief History*. Oxford: Wiley Blackwell.

Davis, Nancy and Robert V. Robinson. 2012. *Claiming Society for God: Religious Movements & Social Welfare*. Bloomington: Indiana University Press.

della Porta, Donatella and Mario Diani. 2006. *Social Movements: An Introduction*. 2nd edn. Oxford: Blackwell.

Ehrman, Bart D. 2003. *Lost Christianities: The Battles for Scripture and the Faiths We Never Knew*. New York: Oxford.

Hall, John R. 2000. *Apocalypse Observed: Religious Movements and Violence in North America, Europe, and Japan*. London: Routledge.

Hirschman, Albert O. 1970. *Exit, Voice, and Loyalty: Responses to Decline in Firms, Organizations, and States*. Cambridge, MA: Harvard University Press.

Ingersoll, Julie J. 2015. *Building God's Kingdom: Inside the World of Christian Reconstruction*. New York: Oxford University Press.

Jenkins, Philip. 2002. *The Next Christendom: The Coming of Global Christianity*. New York: Oxford University Press.

Jenkins, Philip. 2006. *The New Faces of Christianity: Believing the Bible in the Global South*. New York: Oxford University Press.

Jenkins, Philip. 2010. *Jesus Wars*. New York: HarperCollins.

Juergensmeyer, Mark. 2003. *Terror in the Mind of God: The Global Rise of Religious Violence*. Berkeley: University of California Press.

Kandil, Hazem. 2016. *Inside the Brotherhood*. New York: Polity Press.

Kanter, Rosabeth Moss. 1972. *Commitment and Community: Communes and Utopias in Sociological Perspective*. Cambridge, MA: Harvard University Press.

Katzenstein, Mary Fainsod. 1998. *Faithful and Fearless*. Princeton, NJ: Princeton University Press.

Kirsch, Jonathan. 2006. *A History of the End of the World*. San Francisco, CA: Harper San Francisco.

Kniss, Fred and Gene Burns. 2004. "Religious Movements." In *The Blackwell Companion to Social Movements*, edited by David A. Snow, Sarah A. Soule, and Hanspeter Kriesi, 694–715. Oxford: Blackwell.

Knox, Ronald A. 1950. *Enthusiasm: A Chapter in the History of Religion*. New York: Oxford University Press.

Koopmans, Ruud. 2004. "Protest in Time and Space: The Evolution of Waves of Contention." In *The Blackwell Companion to Social Movements*, edited by David A. Snow, Sarah A. Soule, and Hanspeter Kriesi, 19–46. Oxford: Blackwell.

Koresh, David. 1995. "The Seven Seals of the Book of Revelation," unfinished manuscript. In *Why Waco?*, edited by James D. Tabor and Eugene V. Gallagher, 191–203. Berkeley: University of California Press.

Kurzman, Charles. 2005. *The Unthinkable Revolution in Iran*. Cambridge, MA: Harvard University Press.

Lindekilde, Lasse and Lene Kuhle. 2015. "Religious Revivalism and Social Movements." In *The Oxford Handbook of Social Movements*, edited by Donatella della Porta and Mario Diani, 173–184. Oxford: Oxford University Press.

McAdam, Doug, Sidney Tarrow, and Charles Tilly. 2001. *Dynamics of Contention*. New York: Cambridge University Press.

McCants, William. 2015. *ISIS – The Apocalypse: The History, Strategy, and Doomsday Vision of the Islamic State*. New York: St. Martin's Press.

Marty, Martin E. and R. Scott Appleby, eds. 2004. *Fundamentalisms Comprehended*. Chicago: University of Chicago Press.

Montfiore, Simon Sebag. 2011. *Jerusalem: The Biography*. New York: Alfred A. Knopf.

Morris, Aldon D. 1984. *The Origins of the Civil Rights Movement: Black Communities Organizing for Change*. New York: Free Press.

Munson, Ziad. 2010. *The Making of Pro-Life Activists: How Social Movement Mobilization Works*. Chicago: University of Chicago Press.

Nepstad, Sharon Erikson 2004. *Convictions of the Soul: Religion, Culture, and Agency in the Central America Solidarity Movement*. New York: Oxford University Press.

Nepstad, Sharon Erikson. 2008. *Religion and War Resistance in the Plowshares Movement*. New York: Cambridge University Press.

Pagels, Elaine. 1989 [1979]. *The Gnostic Gospels*. New York: Vintage Books.

Pagels, Elaine. 2003. *Beyond Belief: The Secret Gospel of Thomas*. New York: Random House.

Pagels, Elaine. 2012. *Revelations: Visions, Prophecy, & Politics in the Book of Revelation*. New York: Viking.

Pew Research Center Forum on Religion & Public Life. 2006. "Pentecostal Resource Page." October 5. Available at: http://www.pewforum.org/2006/10/05/pentecostal-resource-page/

Rashid, Ahmed. 2002. *Jihad: The Rise of Militant Islam in Central Asia*. New Haven, CT: Yale University Press.

Rucht, Dieter. 2004. "Movement Allies, Adversaries, and Third Parties." In *The Blackwell Companion to Social Movements*, edited by David A. Snow, Sarah A. Soule, and Hanspeter Kriesi, 197–216. Oxford: Blackwell.

Ruthven, Malise. 2016. "Inside Obedient Islamic Minds." *The New York Review of Books*. April 7: 79–81.

Sager, Rebecca. 2012. *Faith, Politics, and Power: The Politics of Faith-Based Initiatives*. New York: Oxford University Press.

Schneider, Nathan. 2011. "The Suspicious Revolution: An Interview with Talal Asad." Available at: http://blogs.ssrc.org/tif/2011/08/03/the-suspicious-revolution-interview-with-talal-asad/

Smith, Christian. 1991. *The Emergence of Liberation Theology: Radical Religion and Social Movement Theory*. Chicago: University of Chicago Press.

Smith, Christian. 1996a. *Resisting Reagan*. Chicago: University of Chicago Press.

Smith, Christian. 1996b. "Correcting a Curious Neglect, or Bringing Religion Back In." In *Disruptive Religion*, edited by Christian Smith, 1–25. New York: Routledge.

Snow, David A. 1979. "A Dramaturgical Analysis of Movement Accommodation: Building Idiosyncrasy Credit as a Movement Mobilization Strategy." *Symbolic Interaction* 2: 23–44.

Snow, David A. 2004. "Social Movements as Challenges to Authority: Resistance to an Emerging Conceptual Hegemony." In *Authority in Contention, vol. 25 of Research in Social Movements, Conflict, and Change*, edited by Daniel J. Meyers and Daniel M. Cress, 3–25. New York: Elsevier.

Snow, David A. 2015. "Bringing the Study of Religion and Social Movements Together: Toward an Analytically Productive Intersection," Distinguished Social Change & Social Movements Scholar Lecture. Vanderbilt University, November 6.

Snow, David A. and Catherine Corrigall-Brown. 2015. "Collective Identity" In James D. Wright (ed.), *International Encyclopedia of Social and Behavioral Sciences*, 2nd edn, 174–180. Oxford: Elsevier.

Snow, David A. and Sarah A. Soule. 2010. *A Primer on Social Movements*. New York: W. W. Norton.

Staggenborg, Suzanne. 2010. *Social Movements*. New York: Oxford University Press.

Stark, Rodney. 1996. *The Rise of Christianity: A Sociologist Reconsiders History*. Princeton, NJ: Princeton University Press.

Stern, Jessica and J.M. Berger. 2015. *ISIS: Inside the State of Terror*. New York: HarperCollins.

Stryker, Sheldon. 1980. *Symbolic Interactionism: A Social Structural Version*. Menlo Park, CA: Benjamin Cummings.

Tarrow, Sidney. 1994. *Power in Movement: Social Movements, Collective Action and Politics*. New York: Cambridge University Press.

Tarrow, Sidney. 1998. *Power in Movement*. 2nd edn. Cambridge: Cambridge University Press.

Taylor, Verta. 1989. "Social Movement Continuity: The Women's Movement in Abeyance." *American Sociological Review* 54: 761–775.

Tierney, Amber. C. 2013. "System Exiting and Social Movements." In *The Wiley-Blackwell Encyclopedia of Social and Political Movements*, vol. III, edited by David A. Snow, Donatella della Porta, Bert Klandermans, and Doug McAdam, 1310–1312. Oxford: Wiley Blackwell.

Tilly, Charles and Sidney Tarrow. 2015. *Contentious Politics*, 2nd ed. New York: Oxford University Press.

Warren, Mark R. 2001. *Dry Bones Rattling*. Princeton, NJ: Princeton University Press.

Warrick, Joby. 2016. *Black Flags: The Rise of ISIS*. New York: Anchor Books.

Wilde, Melissa. 2007. *Vatican II: A Sociological Analysis of Religious Change*. Princeton, NJ: Princeton University Press.

Wood, Graeme. 2015. "What ISIS Really Wants." *The Atlantic,* March 31, pp. 78–94.

Wood, Richard L. 2002. *Faith in Action*. Chicago: University of Chicago Press.

Young, Michael P. 2006. *Bearing Witness against Sin: The Evangelical Birth of the American Social Movement*. Chicago: University of Chicago Press.

Zald, Mayer N. and John D. McCarthy. 1987. "Religious Groups as Crucibles of Social Movements." In *Social Movements in an Organizational Society: Collected Essays*, edited by Mayer N. Zald and John D. McCarthy, 67–95. New Brunswick, N J: Transaction Books.

Zerubavel, Eviatar. 1991. *The Fine Line: Making Distinctions in Everyday Life*. Oxford: Oxford University Press.

Zerubavel, Eviatar. 1996. "Lumping and Splitting: Notes on Social Classification." *Sociological Forum* 11: 121–133.

33

Human Rights and Social Movements: From the Boomerang Pattern to a Sandwich Effect

Kiyoteru Tsutsui and Jackie Smith

Introduction

Human rights and social movements have long had mutually constitutive relationships with each other. Many social movements have promoted human rights causes domestically and internationally since the late eighteenth century, elevating human rights to a guiding principle in international politics. Collective political mobilizations challenging torture, slavery, discrimination against women, and other repressive practices have played critical roles in expanding "the universe of obligations" of governments across the globe to ensure fundamental rights to every human being. Indeed, most observers point out that social movement engagement was critical in institutionalizing universal human rights principles into international declarations and treaties, despite resistance from powerful states (Gaer 1996; Tsutsui, Whitlinger, and Lim 2012). Once established, international human rights institutions have contributed to the diffusion of human rights ideas the world over, and they have directly and indirectly empowered various local actors. This has furthered collective mobilization around human rights and increased the challenges to both national and international authorities. This growth in human rights claims-making has, in turn, further enhanced the legitimacy of human rights across the globe, inspiring even more social movements (Kaldor 2003).

Curiously, however, social scientists in the United States have been slow to focus serious attention on this critical relationship between social movements and human rights until recently.[1] On the one hand, social movement studies have long neglected the impact of social movements on the rise of human rights in the contemporary world as well as the influence of international human rights institutions on local activism. Focused almost exclusively on domestic factors that shape national-level political changes, social movement scholars failed to recognize the international

The Wiley Blackwell Companion to Social Movements, Second Edition. Edited by David A. Snow, Sarah A. Soule, Hanspeter Kriesi, and Holly J. McCammon.
© 2019 John Wiley & Sons Ltd. Published 2019 by John Wiley & Sons Ltd.

dimensions of social movements and the impact of collective popular challenges on global political dynamics until the late 1990s.

On the other hand, scholarship on human rights has tended to focus more on the impact of global human rights on state practices, seeing social movements, at best, as one of the independent variables that shape policy outcomes. As a result, only a handful of studies on human rights examined the impact of global human rights on social movements until the turn of the twenty-first century.

This cursory review of the literature points to a picture of two ships sailing past each other: social movement scholars overlooked the relationships between social movements and the international human rights regime, and scholars of human rights politics failed to fully recognize the impact of social movements in human rights politics. The vocabulary these scholars typically use is indicative of these tendencies. Social movement scholars are much more likely to discuss specific rights issues such as civil rights and women's rights, those issues that became prominent in domestic politics in the United States. Human rights scholars tend to call social movement actors by different names such as NGOs, civil society actors, and human rights defenders, signaling their focus on broader constituencies that support the principle of human rights and shape policy outcomes. The existence of social movements in itself is not of high relevance to them, and only when activists have an impact on policy outcomes do they pay attention to social movements.

Considering how intertwined these two political concepts are in reality, it is puzzling how long it took for scholars to draw a tight connection between the two. One main reason for this is the timing of the rise of human rights in the contemporary world and that of the development of social movement research.

Human rights became a vocabulary for political mobilization in the post-World War II era. Initially, core international human rights documents such as the Universal Declaration of Human Rights (UDHR), the International Covenant on Civil and Political Rights (ICCPR), and the International Covenant on Economic Social and Cultural Rights (ICESCR) were leveraged for self-determination in independence movements in Asia and Africa and autonomous regions in developed countries. Perhaps this is not surprising, considering that the first article of both the ICCPR and the ICESCR refers to the right of self-determination. The early US civil rights movement also embraced human rights language in its early stages, and activists such as Fannie Lou Hamer used the UDHR in her organizing work. In the late 1940s and early 1950s, the National Association for the Advancement of Colored People (NAACP) and its precursor organization brought the "We Charge Genocide" petition to the United Nations. However, the leaders of the movement soon chose civil rights framing instead, fearing that the language of human rights, with its association with social and economic rights pushed by the Eastern bloc, would doom the movement to failure (Anderson 2003). Thus, in the few decades after the end of World War II, international human rights instruments were used more for developing countries' mobilization for independence, and Cold War dynamics led many social movements in the West to distance themselves from human rights language.

Human rights gained traction for more reform-oriented social movements in the 1970s (Moyn 2010). Many movements have emerged since then to leverage expanding global human rights principles and instruments, making the relationship between human rights and social movements a more viable topic of research. Studies on social movements developed around the same time, since the late 1970s. However, from Charles Tilly's classic work in the late 1970s to the crystallization of the "holy trinity" of political opportunities, resource mobilization, and framing by the early 1990s, their focus has been on domestic political environments. The paradigm case of this scholarship has been the civil rights movement. This influenced the analytical focus of this line of research, delaying attention to the broader influence of human rights on social movements.[2]

Scholars of human rights – particularly those in law and political science, who dominated early scholarship on human rights – focused on policy outcomes and legal decisions, viewing social movements as nothing more than an intervening variable. They did not examine social movements as the main object of their research, thus neglecting the causal connection between global human rights and local activism.

For those reasons, scholarship that explicitly links human rights and social movements developed surprisingly late, in the late 1990s. The next section reviews this literature, followed in the subsequent section by an examination of recent trends and suggestions for productive future directions in these lines of research.

Key Insights in the Research on Human Rights and Social Movements

Studies that focus on the interplay between global human rights and social movements emerged in the late 1990s, when Keck and Sikkink (1998) examined how local activists used international human rights norms and institutions to advance their movements, and Smith, Chatfield, and Pagnucco (1997) studied how transnational social movements leverage human rights in their campaigns for social justice that target international institutions such as the IMF and the World Bank. Since then, many empirical studies have documented: (1) how local activists strategically adopt global human rights ideas and instruments to advance their cause; and (2) how they form transnational coalitions to challenge international authorities. We examine these two types of global-local interface separately.

Local adoption of global human rights and its transformative impact

First, research on how local actors use global human rights institutions for their local goals has identified some recurring factors that correspond to the three key dimensions in social movement studies – political opportunities, resource mobilization, and framing (McAdam, McCarthy, and Zald 1996). First, international human rights forums, such as the UN Human Rights Committee and the European Court of Human Rights, provide disadvantaged groups with new opportunities for claims-making (see Chapter 1 by McAdam and Tarrow, in this volume, on political opportunities), thus enabling boomerang patterns by which repressed local actors go to international forums to gain leverage against their government (Keck and Sikkink 1998). These international forums exert varying levels of pressures on local authorities to address human rights problems, ranging from naming-and-shaming to legally binding decisions. Second, international flows of mobilizing resources reach far corners of the world and facilitate collective action by marginalized populations (see Chapter 4 by Edwards, McCarthy, and Mataic, in this volume, on resources).

These resources include material aid such as foundation grants and Official Development Assistance that typically flow from developed to developing countries. Human resources also play important roles, as activists, journalists, and researchers visit vulnerable communities the world over to offer advice on how to stage effective political mobilization and to expose local human rights violations. Third, symbols and vocabularies that carry international currency can become useful tools in framing movement goals. In their efforts to legitimate movements, activists often draw on international human rights documents and framing used in other successful movements. Such framing efforts often help in publicizing human rights violations and in making the case that the relevant authorities need to correct injustices (see Chapter 22 by Snow, Vliegenthart, and Ketelaars, in this volume, on framing).

In sum, global human rights institutions assist local social movements: (1) by creating new political opportunities at the international level that enable local actors to exert external pressures on local authorities; (2) by increasing international flows of material and human resources for political mobilization; and (3) by providing frames for social movements that appeal to and engage international audiences and local publics (Tsutsui 2006; Tsutsui and Shin 2008). These three dimensions offer a useful framework for analyzing the impact of global factors on local social movements.

There is a fourth dimension that has only recently received attention from scholars in this area, the construction of movement actorhood by global human rights. Because most earlier studies (e.g. Keck and Sikkink 1998; Risse, Ropp, and Sikkink 1999) took as given the activists' perspectives, interests, and goals, they failed to examine how global human rights have the capacity to form and reconstitute local movement actorhood, a subject position through which social movement actors engage in collective mobilization for social change.[3] They typically assumed that social movement actors are bounded entities with clearly defined goals seeking to leverage global opportunities, resources, and vocabularies for their gains. Seeing global human rights simply as a means to pre-defined ends, they overlooked how global human rights can shape movement actorhood itself and circumscribe how actors interpret their social and political world, formulate their approaches, and carry out their concrete actions.[4]

Recent studies have paid more attention to constitutive effects of global human rights on movement actorhood. Merry (2006) is one of the earliest studies to examine the impact of global human rights on local actors' subject position. She argues that women take on a new subjectivity when they invoke international law on women's rights. Rosen and Yoon (2009) also examine the emergence of new subject positions among New York City activists as they incorporated an international women's rights discourse, thereby forging a new counter-hegemonic space. The primary focus of these studies, however, is on negotiations between global law and local cultures and how local actors "vernacularize" or adapt and adopt international ideas, exercising their agency, rather than how the latter transforms the former. Tsutsui (2017) is the first to explicitly theorize the transformative impact of global human rights on local actors. Drawing on the multi-institutional politics approach of Armstrong and Bernstein (2008), he examines how changing understandings about their position in local society and their entitled rights galvanized minority activism in Japan, leading to greater activities and subsequent successes.

These four dimensions of the global-local interplay do not necessarily exhaust how human rights impact social movements, but should be the first step in future studies of this kind. A second line of research on the global-local interplay examines the formation of transnational social movements. These movements challenge international authorities to change their operations and, as such, are distinct from local activism that pursues local goals.

Transnational social movements targeting global authorities

As noted above, much research on social movements in the United States has not been attentive to the ways social movements cross national boundaries or engage in political activities outside the formal jurisdictions of national governments. Thus, until the late 1990s there was little attention to transnational dimensions of social movements (see Chapter 6 by Clifford Bob, in this volume, on transnational contexts). At that time, more social movements were beginning to develop formal organizations and informal connections that crossed national boundaries, and they were encouraged and supported by the proliferation of technologies that facilitated transnational communication and exchange as well as by a series of UN-sponsored Global Conferences on issues such as the environment, human rights, women, and social development. Smith's research documents a rapid proliferation of formally organized transnational social movement organizations (TSMOs) beginning in the late 1980s and continuing until the turn of the twenty-first century (Smith 2008; Smith and Wiest 2012). Noteworthy here is the fact that human rights TSMOs are the most numerous in this population, comprising roughly a third of all TSMOs. Moreover, over time we see growing numbers of TSMOs adopting multi-issue frames that combine human rights claims with, for instance, concerns for environmental protection or the transformation of the global economy. Qualitative research links such shifts to the end of the Cold War and to the expansion of dialogues among activists from the Global North and Global South and from a diverse array of class and social positions (e.g. Moghadam 2012; Rothman and Oliver 1999; Vargas 2003). In addition, experiences in global settings changed activists' analyses of global problems and their understandings of the inter-state system, leading to shifts in organizing strategies and emphases.

Qualitative research further shows that recent decades have brought a dramatic expansion of "translocal" networks of activists who deploy varied strategies of engaging global human rights frameworks in local struggles (see, e.g. Desai 2015). Technological developments that facilitate transnational communication as well as the development and learning of transnational organizing strategies and capacities contribute to the possibilities for local activists to draw from and connect with the broader global network of human rights advocates. Globally, organizations and campaigns have been working to better connect local needs and priorities with global strategies. Thus, the World Social Forum process, which emerged in 2001 as part of the global protests resisting economic globalization, has inspired and helped connect local, national, and regional movements and to connect global analyses with local struggles (see, e.g. Sen 2007; Smith et al. 2011). It is important to note here that these movements do not simply seek to advance their local goals but place their issues in the context of global challenges, and advocate for global solutions to these problems, thus also targeting global institutions.

An important theme that is apparent when considering the ways activists have engaged global human rights discourse and institutions is that there is a more coherent critique of the incompatibilities between global financial institutions, such as the World Trade Organization, the World Bank, and the International Monetary Fund and international human rights. Activists from the Global South especially have been demanding formal recognition and protection of the "right to development," and economic, cultural, and social rights more generally, as they have resisted the abuses stemming from the growing power of transnational corporations and global finance (Pleyers 2011; Smith 2008). More recently, activists have come together across both North and South to demand protection from growing threats to basic human needs such as food, water, and housing (e.g. Harvey 2012; McMichael 2015). As we discuss below, since the 1990s and especially in the 2000s, more activists are coming together to demand "the right to the city," that is, they are challenging conventional notions of citizenship based on national identities and individual property ownership and proposing that the city is the more appropriate unit for their commitment and organizing efforts (Holston 2009).

New Trends and Future Directions

The assumption in much of these studies has been that local actors will receive help from international actors and institutions to achieve their goals. The boomerang pattern, as identified by Keck and Sikkink (1998), symbolizes this dynamic: deprived of means to challenge authorities locally, actors appeal to international society to produce a boomerang effect of international authorities pressuring local power holders for desired changes. Similarly, transnational social movements target powerful international organizations so that international authorities would change their policies, which should subsequently alleviate human rights violations in many localities. It is also important to note that this process is beneficial for local activists to the extent the international institutions are effective and national governments are responsive to international pressures.

Recently, questions about the efficacy of the international human rights regime have intensified, leading some to claim the "twilight" or "endtimes" of human rights (Hopgood 2013; Posner 2014). These observers question the capacity of international human rights institutions to exert real changes in the face of growing opposition by state governments. They also express concerns about global actors' lack of sensitivity to local cultural practices in trying to implement reform. In response to these concerns, two aspects of the interaction between human rights and social movements call for more attention.

Feedback from local activism to global human rights institutions

First, global institutions do not stand on thin air, and they need constant reinforcement by local and other actors. Existing studies tend to take both the national state and international human rights institutions as given, and they treat the global-local interaction as a unidirectional process whereby the global shapes the local. That is, many studies on global human rights examine how, and to what extent, international human rights treaties and organizations impact local politics, seeing the global and national entities as preexisting and self-sustaining, with little need for local actors' contributions. In practice, both national and international institutions are shaped by interactions among diverse actors working at multiple scales. In many cases human rights movements have been the prime movers working to advance both human rights treaties and institutional innovations that improve compliance (Gaer 1996; Sikkink 2011; Smith 2008; Tsutsui, Whitlinger, and Lim 2012). Prior research and experience show that effective implementation of human rights norms requires more than just treaties and implementing bodies. It is essential to also have engaged actors working at local and trans-local scales, who are capable of monitoring human rights practices and holding local and national officials accountable to human rights commitments (Hafner-Burton and Ron 2009; Hafner-Burton and Tsutsui 2005; Simmons 2009; Smith-Cannoy 2012).

From the abolitionist, anti-slavery campaign (Martinez 2012) – arguably the first truly transnational movement for human rights – through the adoption of the Universal Declaration of Human Rights (Glendon 2001), to more recent norms about specific human rights issues such as the Apartheid (Klotz 1995; Soule 2009), torture and forced disappearance (Brysk 1994; Méndez 2011), female genital mutilation (Boyle 2002; Shannon 2012), and discrimination based on descent (Tsutsui 2017), local actors' commitment to problematize and publicize the issues globally and to establish an international understanding about prohibited human rights violations has been the foundation that has sustained the edifice of international human rights institutions. With support from officials of international organizations and sympathetic governments, civil society actors' tireless efforts have reinforced and expanded the international human rights regime. For instance, within the past few decades, we have seen the introduction of new institutional mechanisms – all resulting from movement initiatives – that have strengthened the monitoring and implementation of human rights, including the UN Office of the High Commissioner for Human Rights, the International Criminal Court, the UN Permanent Forum on Indigenous Issues, UN Women, and the reorganized Human Rights Council with a new potentially powerful mechanism called the Universal Periodic Review. Despite persistent challenges, each of these innovations represents a significant step that alters the relative power of states against human rights claims by civil society actors.

Nevertheless, in the current political environment – marked by economic and environmental instability and the rise of right-wing parties and leaders across the world – we are seeing critical challenges to the international human rights architecture. In part, this results from the effects of globalization on reducing the governing capacities of national states and expanding the power of transnational corporations. States are assumed to be the legally accountable parties to international human rights law. However, global economic integration has reduced states' ability to ensure the economic and other human rights of their citizens. At the same time, powerful states like the United States and transnational corporations have gained extraordinary influence over the day-to-day experiences of many people around the world, while being much less directly accountable to existing international human rights treaties. This creates a crisis for human rights institutions as well as for many national states, whose very legitimacy rests upon the premise (and promise) of human rights (Gibney 2008). As Brexit and the new regime in the United States threaten the foundations of multilateralism itself, this institutional crisis is especially problematic. The impressive gains that various local and transnational actors have made in the past few decades are under threat in the current political environment, reminding us of the need for social movement actors to continue to support the international human rights system.

Local initiatives at the municipal level

Second, the limited effectiveness of international human rights institutions at improving local human rights practices has helped fuel the more recent expansion of local initiatives to implement global ideals at the local municipal level. Frustrated by national governments' lack of responsiveness to residents' concerns about economic, social, and cultural as well as political and civil rights, activists have been working to hold local authorities accountable for human rights protections. For their part, cities are finding that neoliberal economic policies have left them with insufficient resources to address growing demands in conventional ways, and municipal authorities have increasingly come together in attempts to respond to these challenges (Barber 2013). Factors such as growing urban populations, inequality, inter-urban competition for investment, and declining national government support for social welfare have made cities the sites of a growing global wave of place-based human rights claims-making. This trend first appeared in the Global South, and in particular in Latin America in the 1990s and has expanded to countries of the Global North during the 2000s (Chueca 2016; Harvey 2012; Holston 2009). In response to the need to maintain local political and social stability, cities are finding it in their interest to champion human rights that national governments do not necessarily support, such as the rights of undocumented residents. In the United States, a national movement for "Sanctuary Cities" has emerged to support local protections for undocumented immigrants, defying federal government efforts to detain and deport non-citizens. The US Conference of Mayors recently endorsed both the International Coalition of Cities Against Racism and the Cities for CEDAW campaign.

The Cities for CEDAW campaign is a locally-based human rights initiative in the United States that seeks to advance international protections for women that have been stalled by the US government's failure to ratify the Convention on the Elimination of All Forms of Discrimination Against Women (CEDAW). This campaign has sought to effectively realize the CEDAW convention by convincing municipal authorities to adopt local CEDAW ordinances. Effectively, this would produce a "bottom-up" ratification process whereby mobilization in local communities produces national compliance with global human rights norms. To date, six cities have formally adopted local CEDAW ordinances, and more than 50 cities are currently working toward this goal.[5]

As activists from different localities have come together in transnational organizational networks and in physical spaces like the World Social Forums, we have seen increasing coherence of what is being called the "right to the city" or the human rights cities movement (Mayer 2012; Oomen et al. 2016). Instead of working to target national governments or international institutions, more human rights activists are mobilizing at local levels to help realize human rights in local communities. Starting with the grounded experiences of urban residents, they are demanding that cities formally recognize and take steps to protect basic rights such as the right to affordable housing, racial justice, clean water, a healthy environment, and living wages. They are engaging with international human rights machinery such as the Inter-American Court of Human Rights, the UN's Universal Periodic Review process, the Convention Against Torture, and the Convention on the Elimination of All Forms of Racial Discrimination.[6] In some cities, residents are forming diverse coalitions to press municipal leaders to make formal commitments to becoming "human rights cities," and, to date, more than 30 such cities exist.[7]

A "human rights city" is a municipality that refers explicitly to the UDHR and other international human rights standards and/or law in their formal charters, policies, statements, and programs. Analysts have observed growing numbers of such cities since 2000 (Grigolo 2011; van den Berg and Oomen 2014). Some human rights cities incorporate a particular set of human rights into their formal governing agenda, such as San Francisco's 1999 ordinance implementing the Convention on the Elimination of Discrimination Against Women or Barcelona's anti-discrimination and immigrant rights programs. Other cities have explicitly designated themselves as human rights cities, indicating a commitment to moving towards the realization of the broad array of human rights. The Human Rights Cities initiative was launched by the Peoples Decade on Human Rights Learning (PDHRE) following the UN Human Rights Conference in Vienna in 1993. The group defined a human rights city as:

> a city or a community where people of good will, in government, in organizations and in institutions, try and let a human rights framework guide the development of the life of the community. Equality and nondiscrimination are basic values. Efforts are made to promote a holistic vision of human rights to overcome fear and impoverishment, a society that provides human security, access to food, clean water, housing, education, healthcare and work at livable wages, sharing these resources with all citizens—not as a gift, but as a realization of human rights.[8]

Key elements of the strategy outlined by PDHRE organizers include extensive efforts at popular education known as "human rights learning" and a commitment to broad popular participation in shaping and monitoring policies, typically through a Human Rights Steering Committee. Organizers are explicit in pointing out that cultural change is essential to advancing human rights, and it is not enough simply to change the laws. PDHRE leader Shulamith Koenig has worked directly with local organizers to help them develop human rights city initiatives, and the group also promotes the initiative at the World Social Forums and in other movement venues, encouraging and providing resources for activists to re-imagine the cities in which they live. Rosario in Argentina became the first human rights city of this kind in 1997.[9]

In addition to local initiatives, there has been growing momentum among local human rights leaders to expand and strengthen horizontal networking across human rights cities in the United States and internationally. For instance, municipal leaders in Europe began meeting in 1998 as part of a conference on "Cities for Human Rights," organized to commemorate the 50th anniversary of the Universal Declaration of Human Rights. This meeting generated a series of bi-annual meetings and the European Charter for Safeguarding Human Rights in the City, which now has over 400 municipal parties.[10] The Forum of Local Authorities convened local authorities alongside the World Social Forum since 2001, debating a draft text of a World Charter of the Right to the City (Oomen and Baumgärtel 2012: 6). In mid-2016, activists working in the US Human Rights Network have formed a National Human Rights Cities Alliance to organize periodic gatherings of human rights city organizers and to document and share best practices and models for implementing local human rights initiatives.[11] And following the electoral success of right-wing candidates in the United States and elsewhere, more analysts and activists are recognizing the significance of cities as sites for human rights mobilization (see, e.g. Baird and Hughes 2016; Barber 2016).

This shift in momentum of human rights organizing from the global to the local levels might be seen as reflecting the limitations and failures of the neoliberal globalization project and its institutions. As national governments have shifted more attention and authority to international economic and political institutions, they have undermined their own authority and redirected it both upward to intergovernmental institutions like the UN and the World Trade Organization, outward to corporations (through privatization), and downward to cities and local regions (Markoff 1999). Meanwhile, economic globalization has contributed to rising inequality and the emergence of urban centers that have fueled the key processes driving global finance and trade, changing both the nature of state authority and its long-term viability under neoliberalism (Sassen 1991, 2014). As national and global institutions have failed to address increasingly urgent global crises, such as climate change, rising inequality, and growing insecurity in regard to access to food and other basic needs, activists in local communities have responded by putting forward new strategies to address such needs.

Conclusion

Our review of international human rights movements shows the dynamic relationships between social movements and formal institutions and between local and global political arenas in the work of advancing human rights. Despite some setbacks and the potentially challenging years ahead, international human rights institutions continue to operate to support local struggles for better human rights practices. The institutional scaffolding is quite strong for many international bodies, and despite some potential trends for de-institutionalization – such as in defections from the International Criminal Court by a few African and Asian countries – the Human Rights Council and many treaty monitoring bodies have been working steadily to promote and protect human rights. The recent research we examined here suggests that we will see a growing collection of locally organized and horizontally networked actors helping constitute a changing global human rights movement that once followed a more international and national organizational arrangement.

Thus, what we see in contemporary society is a shift from a reliance on top-down globally initiated changes for human rights protection to a combination of bottom-up and top-down efforts. On the one hand, global level efforts that seek to generate pressure on national governments continue, even if they are limited largely to naming and shaming and lack enforcement mechanisms. On the other hand, bottom-up mobilizations at local, even municipal levels, focus on translating global norms into local practices, producing more immediate small-scale changes with a view to accumulating these changes across different locales to achieve global-level transformation. In this way a "double-boomerang" pattern continues to be one part of contemporary relationships between human rights and social movements, whereby local agents' appeals to international human rights law both strengthen local leverage and enhance the practical impacts and legitimacy of international human rights law (Kaldor 2003). We believe that what we are witnessing here might be described as a "sandwich effect," whereby global institutions' pressures from above and grassroots mobilization from below combine to increase the pressure on local and national governments, as well as transnational corporations and some intergovernmental organizations, to comply with and advance human rights norms.

The bottom-up mobilizations grew ever stronger because of decades of efforts by international organizations to both define and strengthen the international human rights machinery and to build the capacities and translocal networks of local actors. To that extent, it is also important to recognize the importance of the transformative effects of human rights ideas not only in shaping the international institutional arena but also in constituting movement actorhood. These effects might not be captured in easily measurable ways in quantitative analyses, but they have raised the potential for local actors to challenge authorities at local levels and sustain global efforts for social change. After decades of global ideas and institutions empowering local actors, the local actors have developed new understandings of how local conditions are shaped by global forces, and they have developed broad and deep networks of translocal ties that significantly enhance their capacity to support global human rights institutions and to influence local and national governments.

Notes

1 Our review covers the perspective from US sociology of social movements literature, which differs from that emerging from other national and regional contexts and from other sub-fields, such as world-systems analysis and the sociology of race and ethnicity. In particular, this tradition tends to be US-centric and guilty of "methodological nationalism," if not American exceptionalism. Because social movements tend to cross national and other boundaries and defy researchers' categories of issue-focus, insider/outsider politics, and formal vs. informal organization, prevailing conceptual schemes often obscure the complex ways that people engage in the work of social change. For instance, the social movement literature distinguishes movements such as LGBTQ rights, women's rights, labor rights, anti-poverty, and racial or environmental justice as separate movements, whereas in reality they all advance human rights claims in some form. Many are also tied to varying degrees with regional or global networks, whether or not studies focusing on their national or local activities are able to see those connections. Alongside growing connections and dialogue across the Global North and the Global South in both movements and in the academy, we are seeing a greater appreciation for the ways prevailing epistemologies impact our understandings of the world and especially of the emancipatory movements operating outside hegemonic logics (see Conway 2017; Dalsheim 2017).
2 Partial correctives to this emerged in the late 1990s as Skrentny (1998, 2002), Layton (2000), and McAdam's (1999) revised version of the classic acknowledged the influence of the Cold War politics and human rights language on the civil rights movement.

3   The concept, movement actorhood, has a good deal of affinity with the more frequently used term, identity. Reflecting the primary focus of early social movement research, identity is often used in the context of examination of what level of collective identity is needed for social movements to emerge (for an excellent recent review, see Snow and Corrigall-Brown 2015). This led to research focus on how a shared sense of "we-ness" can be created among relevant actors, what kinds of symbols facilitate this process, what types of collective identities are more likely to enable mobilization and in what contexts, and other questions that focus on movement emergence. While sympathetic to this approach, scholars who examine movement actorhood demonstrate a greater interest in movement goals and strategies and how actors' subject positions guide them, reflecting the multi-institutional politics approach (Armstrong and Bernstein 2008). The use of this term is also a response to the call by Brubaker and Cooper (2000) to move away from "identity" and use more precise terms; identity has been overloaded as an analytical concept because scholars use it to refer to three related but different social processes: (1) identification and categorization; (2) self-understanding and social location; and (3) commonality, con-nectedness, and groupness, and movement actorhood is primarily about the second cate-gory, actors' self-understanding about their place in society (Tsutsui 2017).

4   To be sure, social movement scholars have examined local actors' orientations, motiva-tions, and identities in great detail (Goodwin, Jasper, and Polletta 2001; Polletta 1998; Polletta and Jasper 2001). Such studies, however, largely overlook the impact of global factors, focusing instead on the influence of the state and/or interactions among movement actors.

5   See http://citiesforcedaw.org/

6   The US Human Rights Network is a leading example of a national social movement organization that helps translate international human rights into local settings. It does so by, for instance, helping bring grassroots activists to official international human rights meetings to testify about local conditions and by assembling information from local activists as part of the civil society "shadow reports" filed in international bodies for offi-cial reviews of US compliance with international human rights obligations (see, e.g. http://ushrnetwork.org/).

7   Scholarly research and formal documentation of these activist initiatives are limited, given their dispersion and localized nature. However, Smith has been part of a growing network of activists, human rights lawyers, and scholars working to document and advance new thinking about these local initiatives. Along with students, Smith helped draft the Wikipedia entry on Human Rights Cities, see https://en.wikipedia.org/wiki/Human_Rights_City

8   See http://pdhre.org/achievements-HR-cities-mar-07.pdf

9   For more details about human rights cities, see, e.g. Marks, Modrowski, and Lichem (2008), Oomen, David, and Grigolo (2016), and Smith, (forthcoming).

10 See http://www.uclg-cisdp.org/en/right-to-the-city/european-charter

11 See http://www.ushrnetwork.org/our-work/project/national-human-rights-city-network

References

Anderson, Carol. 2003. *Eyes Off the Prize: African-Americans and the Struggle for Human Rights, 1948–1954*. New York: Cambridge University Press.

Armstrong, Elizabeth A. and Mary Bernstein. 2008. "Culture, Power, and Institutions: A Multi-Institutional Politics Approach to Social Movements." *Sociological Theory* 26: 74–99.

Baird, Kate Shea and Steve Hughes. 2016. "America Needs a Network of Rebel Cities to Stand up to Trump." *In These Times*. Available at: http://inthesetimes.com/article/19678/america-needs-a-network-of-rebel-cities-to-stand-up-to-trump (accessed December 15, 2016).

Barber, Benjamin R. 2013. *If Mayors Ruled the World: Dysfunctional Nations, Rising Cities*. New Haven, CT: Yale University Press.

Barber, Benjamin. 2016. "Can Cities Counter the Power of President-Elect Donald Trump?" *The Nation*. Available at: https://www.thenation.com/article/can-cities-counter-the-power-of-president-elect-donald-trump/ (accessed: December 15, 2016).

Boyle, Elizabeth. 2002. *Female Genital Cutting: Cultural Conflict in the Global Community*. Baltimore, MD: Johns Hopkins University Press.

Brubaker, Rogers and Frederick Cooper. 2000. "Beyond 'Identity.'" *Theory and Society* 29: 1–47.

Brysk, Allison. 1994. *The Politics of Human Rights in Argentina: Protest, Change, and Democratization*. Stanford, CA: Stanford University Press.

Chueca, Eva Garcia. 2016. "Human Rights in the City and the Right to the City: Two Different Paradigms Confronting Urbanisation." In *Global Urban Justice: The Rise of Human Rights Cities*, edited by Barbara Oomen, Martha F. Davis and Michele Grigolo, 103–120. New York: Cambridge University Press.

Conway, Janet. 2017. "Modernity and the Study of Social Movements: Do We Need a Paradigm Shift?" In *Social Movements and World-System Transformation*, edited by Jackie Smith, Michael Goodhart, Patrick Manning, and John Markoff, 17–34. New York: Routledge.

Dalsheim, Joyce. 2017. "Other Moral Orders: Epistemology & Resistance in Israel/Palestine." In *Social Movements and World-System Transformation*, edited by Jackie Smith, Michael Goodhart, Patrick Manning, and John Markoff, 35–53. New York: Routledge.

Desai, Manisha. 2015. *Subaltern Movements in India: Gendered Geographies of Struggle Against Neoliberal Development*. New York: Routledge.

Gaer, Felice D. 1996. "Reality Check: Human Rights NGOs Confront Governments at the UN." In *NGOs, the UN, and Global Governance*, edited by Thomas G. Weiss and Leon Gordenker, 51–66. Boulder, CO: Lynne Rienner.

Gibney, Mark. 2008. *International Human Rights Law: Returning to Universal Principles*. Boulder, CO: Rowman & Littlefield.

Glendon, Marry Ann. 2001. *A World Made New: Eleanor Roosevelt and the Universal Declaration of Human Rights*. New York: Random House.

Goodwin, Jeff, James M. Jasper, and Francesca Polletta, eds. 2001. *Passionate Politics: Emotions in Social Movements*. Chicago: University of Chicago Press.

Grigolo, Michele. 2011. "Incorporating Cities into the EU Anti-Discrimination Policy: Between Race Discrimination and Migrant Rights." *Ethnic and Racial Studies* 34(10): 1751–1769. doi: 10.1080/01419870.2010.538422.

Hafner-Burton, Emilie and James Ron. 2009. "Seeing Double: Human Rights Impact Through Qualitative and Quantitative Eyes?" *World Politics* 61: 360–401.

Hafner-Burton, Emilie and Kiyoteru Tsutsui. 2005. "Human Rights in a Globalizing World: The Paradox of Empty Promises." *American Journal of Sociology* 110: 1373–1411.

Harvey, David. 2012. *Rebel Cities: From the Right to the City to the Urban Revolution*. New York: Verso.

Holston, James. 2009. "Insurgent Citizenship in an Era of Global Urban Peripheries." *City and Society* 21(2): 245–267. doi: 10.1111/j.1548-744X.2009.01024.x.

Hopgood, Stephen. 2013. *The Endtimes of Human Rights*. Ithaca, NY: Cornell University Press.

Kaldor, Mary. 2003. *Global Civil Society: An Answer to War*. Cambridge: Polity.

Keck, Margaret and Kathryn Sikkink. 1998. *Activists Beyond Borders*. Ithaca, NY: Cornell University Press.

Klotz, Audie. 1995. *Norms in International Relations: The Struggle against Apartheid*. Ithaca, NY: Cornell Universtiy Press.

Layton, Azza Salama. 2000. *International Politics and Civil Rights Policies in the United States, 1941–1960*. New York: Cambridge University Press.

Markoff, John. 1999. "Globalization and the Future of Democracy." *Journal of World-Systems Research* 5(2): 242–262. Available at: http://www.jwsr.org/wp-content/uploads/2013/05/Markoff-v5n2.pdf

Marks, Stephen P., Kathleen A. Modrowski, and Walther Lichem. 2008. *Human Rights Cities: Civic Engagement for Societal Development*. Available at: http://www.pdhre.org/Human_Rights_Cities_Book.pdf: People's Movement for Human Rights Learning & UN Habitat.

Martinez, Jenny S. 2012. *The Slave Trade and the Origins of International Human Rights Law*. New York: Oxford University Press.

Mayer, Margit. 2012. "The 'Right to the City' in Urban Social Movements." In *Cities for People Not for Profit: Critical Urban Theory and the Right to the City*, edited by Neil Brenner, Peter Marcuse and Margit Mayer, 63–85. New York: Routledge.

McAdam, Doug. 1999. *Political Process and the Development of Black Insurgency, 1930–1970*. 2nd edn. Chicago: University of Chicago Press.

McAdam, Doug, John D. McCarthy, and Mayer N. Zald, eds. 1996. *Comparative Perspectives on Social Movements: Political Opportunities, Mobilizing Structures, and Cultural Framings*. New York: Cambridge University Press.

McMichael, Philip. 2015. "The Land Question in the Food Sovereignty Project." *Globalizations* 12(4): 434–451. doi: http://dx.doi.org/10.1080/14747731.2014.971615.

Méndez, Juan E. 2011. *Taking a Stand: The Evolution of Human Rights*. New York: Palgrave Macmillan.

Merry, Sally Engle. 2006. *Human Rights and Gender Violence: Translating International Law into Local Justice*. Chicago: University Of Chicago Press.

Moghadam, Valentine. 2012. *Globalization and Social Movements: Islamism, Feminism and the Global Justice Movement*, 2nd edn. Boulder, CO: Rowman & Littlefield.

Moyn, Samuel. 2010. *The Last Utopia: Human Rights in History*. Cambridge, MA: Belknap Press of Harvard University Press,

Oomen, B. and M. Baumgärtel. 2012. "Human Rights Cities." In *The Sage Handbook of Human Rights*, edited by Anja Mihr and Mark Gibney, 709–729. Available at: http://www.researchgate.net/publication/277775662_Human_Rights_Cities: Sage

Oomen, Barbara, Martha F. Davis, and Michele Grigolo, eds. 2016. *Global Urban Justice: The Rise of Human Rights Cities*. New York: Cambridge University Press.

Pleyers, Geoffrey. 2011. *Alter-Globalization: Becoming Actors in the Global Age*. Malden, MA: Polity Press.

Polletta, Francesca. 1998. "It was Like a Fever… Narrative and Identity in Social Protest." *Social Problems* 45: 137–159.

Polletta, Francesca and James M. Jasper. 2001. "Collective Identity and Social Movements." *Annual Review of Sociology* 27: 283–305.

Posner, Eric A. 2014. *The Twilight of Human Rights Law*. New York: Oxford University Press.

Risse, Thomas, Stephen C. Ropp, and Kathryn Sikkink, eds. 1999. *The Power of Human Rights: International Norms and Domestic Change*. New York: Cambridge University Press.

Rosen, Mihaela Serban, and Diana H. Yoon. 2009. "'Bringing Coals to Newcastle'? Human Rights, Civil Rights and Social Movements in New York City." *Global Networks* 9: 507–528.

Rothman, Franklin Daniel and Pamela E. Oliver. 1999. "From Local to Global: The Anti-Dam Movement in Southern Brazil 1979–1992." *Mobilization: An International Journal* 4(1): 41–57.

Sassen, Saskia. 1991. *The Global City: New York, London, Tokyo*. Princeton, NJ: Princeton University Press.

Sassen, Saskia. 2014. "Expelled: Humans in Capitalism's Deepening Crisis." *Journal of World-Systems Research* 19(2): 198–201. doi: http://dx.doi.org/10.5195/jwsr.2013.495.

Sen, Jai. 2007. "The World Social Forum as an Emergent Learning Process." *Futures* 39: 507–522.

Shannon, Kelly J. 2012. "The Right to Bodily Integrity: Women's Rights as Human Rights and the International Movement to End Female Genital Mutilation, 1970s–1990s." In *The Human Rights Revolution: An International History*, edited by Akira Iriye, Petra Goedde, and William I. Hitchcock, 285–310. New York: Oxford University Press.

Sikkink, Kathryn. 2011. *The Justice Cascade: How Human Rights Prosecutions Are Changing World Politics*. New York: W.W. Norton & Company.

Simmons, Beth A. 2009. *Mobilizing for Human Rights: International Law in Domestic Politics*. New York: Cambridge University Press.

Skrentny, John D. 1998. "The Effect of the Cold War on African-American Civil Rights, 1945–1968." *Theory and Society* 27: 237–285.

Skrentny, John D. 2002. *The Minority Rights Revolution*. Cambridge, MA: Harvard University Press.

Smith, Jackie. 2008. *Social Movements for Global Democracy*. Baltimore, MD: Johns Hopkins University Press.

Smith, Jackie. forthcoming. "Responding to Globalization and Urban Conflict: Human Rights City Initiatives." *Studies in Social Justice*.

Smith, Jackie, Scott Byrd, Ellen Reese, and Elizabeth Smythe, eds. 2011. *Handbook of World Social Forum Activism*. Boulder, CO: Paradigm Publishers.

Smith, Jackie, Charles Chatfield, and Ron Pagnucco, eds. 1997. *Transnational Social Movements and Global Politics: Solidarity Beyond the State*. Syracuse, NY: Syracuse University Press.

Smith, Jackie and Dawn Wiest. 2012. *Social Movements in the World-System: The Politics of Crisis and Transformation*. New York: Russell Sage Foundation.

Smith-Cannoy, Heather. 2012. *Insincere Commitments: Human Rights Treaties, Abusive States, and Citizen Activism*. Washington, DC: Georgetown University Press.

Snow, David A. and Catherine Corrigall-Brown. 2015. "Collective Identity." In *International Encyclopedia of the Social and Behavioral Sciences*, edited by James D. Wright, 174–180. Oxford: Elsevier.

Soule, Sarah A. 2009. *Contention and Corporate Social Responsibility*. New York: Cambridge University Press.

Tsutsui, Kiyoteru. 2006. "Redressing Past Human Rights Violations: Global Dimensions of Contemporary Social Movements." *Social Forces* 85: 331–354.

Tsutsui, Kiyoteru. 2017. "Human Rights and Minority Activism in Japan: Transformation of Movement Actorhood and Local-Global Feedback Loop." *American Journal of Sociology* 122(4): 1050–1103.

Tsutsui, Kiyoteru, and Hwa Ji Shin. 2008. "Global Norms, Local Activism, and Social Movement Outcomes: Global Human Rights and Resident Koreans in Japan." *Social Problems* 55: 391–418.

Tsutsui, Kiyoteru, Claire Whitlinger, and Alwyn Lim. 2012. "International Human Rights Law and Social Movements: States' Resistance and Civil Society's Insistence." *Annual Review of Law and Social Science* 8: 367–396.

van den Berg, Esther and Barbara Oomen. 2014. "Towards a Decentralization of Human Rights: The Rise of Human Rights Cities." In *The Future of Human Rights in an Urban World: Exploring Opportunities, Threats and Challenges*, edited by Thijs van Lindert and Doutje Lettinga, 11–16. Available at: https://www.amnesty.nl/content/uploads/2016/12/the_future_of_human_rights_in_an_urban_world_0.pdf: Amnesty International –Netherlands (accessed January 21, 2018).

Vargas, Virginia. 2003. "Feminism, Globalization and the Global Justice and Solidarity Movement." *Cultural Studies* 17(6): 905–920.

34

Globalization and Social Movements

Massimiliano Andretta, Donatella della Porta,
and Clare Saunders[1]

Introduction

The issue of how globalization affects social movements and vice versa is very complex
and heavily debated in social movement research. Given that globalization takes place
within economic, political and cultural spheres of human action, we organize our chapter
by focusing on these three spheres separately. Since movements that operate across the
entire globe are rare phenomena, we refer mainly in this chapter to transnational rather
than global movements. Transnational movements are movements with operations in
more than one country at any particular time. They consist of informal networks and
formal federated organizations with national chapters. Our primary emphasis in this
chapter is on how globalization affects movements and how transnational movements,
in turn, emerge and react. In what follows, we will address the socio-economic, political
and cultural dimensions of globalization and transnational movements.

Global Capitalism and Social Movements

Several recent social movements have addressed the developments of global capitalism,
in particular, neoliberal policies of privatization of social services, the deregulation of
markets, and austerity policies. Social movement scholars have developed a useful set
of concepts and theories to understand social movements in core capitalist countries
with developed welfare states. This kit is, however, insufficient to make sense of contentious politics around the globe since the 2000s, especially of the transnational
dimensions of contemporary anti-austerity protests. Such protests have brought fresh
attention to the links between capitalist developments and movements. In order to
properly understand the scaling of identities, the organizational structures, and
framing of transnational movements, attention needs to be given to changes in global

The Wiley Blackwell Companion to Social Movements, Second Edition. Edited by David A. Snow,
Sarah A. Soule, Hanspeter Kriesi, and Holly J. McCammon.
© 2019 John Wiley & Sons Ltd. Published 2019 by John Wiley & Sons Ltd.

capitalism. Marxist, neo-Marxist, or post-Marxist theories are particularly useful for drawing attention to the ways in which capitalism has developed.

The World Systems Approach

Some time ago, the *world system approach* (Wallerstein 1990) theorized anti-systemic movements, pointing at internal differences within capitalism – in particular, between capitalism at the core, the semi-periphery, and the periphery. This approach, which has historically had more influence in research on labor than on other social movements, considered that it was anti-systemic movements' task to resist greedy capitalism. As Immanuel Wallerstein noted, "to be anti-systemic is to argue that neither liberty nor equality is possible under the existing system and that both are possible only in a transformed world" (1990: 36). In this vision, capitalist oppression is expected to result in the revolt of the oppressed, but with different dynamics at the core, the semi-periphery, and the periphery. Although the world has changed considerably since the theory was introduced, it can be applied to the new/emergent position of countries in the global system, with China considered by some scholars as a new hegemon.

The world system approach generates the expectation that protests and movements will result because the economically oppressed will rebel. While this approach was criticized for being too structural and for underplaying the political conditions under which these movements emerge, what remains useful is the attention given to the ways in which specific characteristics of hegemonic capitalism influence the socio-economic conditions at the core, the semi-periphery, and the periphery (Arrighi, Hopkins, and Wallerstein 1989). So, in Latin America, movements developed to target the form of neoliberalism existing in the semi-periphery with different timing and intensity than those taking place in western democracies, which are developing and targeting conditions in the economic core (Wallerstein 2010: 141). The prediction that capitalist expansion produces resistance, first of all on labor conditions, appears to be confirmed by research addressing the emergence and development of labor conflicts, including in the BRICS countries (that is, Brazil, Russia, India, China, and South Africa) (Silver 2003; Zajak 2016).

Multitudes in the empire

Some expectations about the territorial expansion of capitalism at the global level and its effects on movement mobilizations emerged recently within the debate on the *empire*, as a new capitalist formation. In particular, Hardt and Negri (2000) singled out in the "multitude" the new anti-capitalist subject, which they see as an emerging global opposition. In their analysis, the empire represents a step forward in the evolution of Foucault's bio-political power which is now attributed to international organizations such as the UN or the IMF, and even more to huge transnational corporations. With the precariousness of labor, capitalist exploitation has expanded beyond the factory and now involves significant movement of people from the countryside into global cities. Through this expansion the empire produces its own opposition as the "imperial power can no longer discipline the power of the multitude; it can only impose control over their general social and productive capacities" (ibid.: 211). In this vision, exploitation in the empire would produce rebellion, but in this case on a global scale. The proletariat would now include all those exploited by and subject to capitalist domination, that is, the multitudes (ibid.: 53).

Reflections on the multitudes contribute to social movement research by giving attention to the ways in which contradictions in social and political systems interact in a global context. Massive expulsions of people produced by climate change, wars, or land acquisition of large corporations (Sassen 2013) produce various forms of everyday resistance to exploitation, for example, of the type that Asef Bayat (2010) has defined as non-movements. Similarly, the revolts during the Arab Spring involved pauperized groups in global cities (della Porta 2014) and asylum seekers in Europe, and "illegal" migrants in the USA have made claims for their rights.

Neoliberalism and global conflicts

When analysing transnational social movements in the new millennium, one has to consider also significant transformations in global capitalist formations. Social movements within neoliberalism are affected by transformations in relations between the state and market. In so-called Fordist societies, Keynesian forms of state intervention were used to overcome periodic crises through fiscal and monetary policies, with an expansion in public expenditure. Welfare policies have been able to reduce social inequalities and buffer the effects of market dynamics. Theorization about new social movements mainly referred to the consolidation of a specific (and quite exceptional) moment in the relations between the state and the market in advanced democracies. New social movements were indeed considered to be stronger in countries in which the class cleavage was pacified, leaving space for the emergence of new cleavages (Kriesi et al. 1995). For scholars like Alain Touraine (1985) and Alberto Melucci (1996), the industrial society and its main conflicts around material productions were eclipsed by the development of new conflicts around immaterial forms of property. Since the 1980s, the rapid decline of Fordism was, however, reflected in a re-emergence of conflicts on economic issues, addressing the increasing social inequalities and the retrenchment of the welfare state (Hutter 2014).

In different forms, social movements have networked at the transnational level, finding expression especially within the Global Justice Movement (see below). Such networks have facilitated the bridging of concerns from "old" and "new" movements within broad and heterogeneous coalitions within which anti-neoliberalism worked as a master frame (della Porta et al. 2006; Smith et al. 2007). While the Global Justice Movement has been the expression of transnational protests in the rampant years of neoliberalism, the wave of anti-austerity movements in the 2010s were reacting to the crisis of neoliberalism. This wave of protest began with the pots-and-pans revolt in Iceland in 2008 (Júlíusson and Helgason 2013), followed by large Occupy protests that spread from the Arab Spring to Southern Europe and then to the USA in 2011, and to Turkey and Brazil in 2013. Increasing inequalities, aggravated by austerity economic policies, were opposed by movements stigmatizing the move toward the free market and away from social protection (della Porta 2015, 2017a).

The social composition of this wave of protests reflected changes in global capitalism, mobilizing broad coalitions of people who had been hit particularly hard by the global recession: from young people in precarious positions in the labor market (who defined themselves as the "generation without a future") to retired people hit by cut in pensions and in social services, and also those employed in the public sector and blue-collar employees, who had suffered declining labor protection, in the context of the increasing liberalization of the labor market.

Some characteristics of this latter wave of protests resemble those singled out by Karl Polanyi in his influential analysis of the liberalism in the nineteenth century (Polanyi 1957 [1944]). In *The Great Transformation*, Polanyi identified a *double movement* in capitalist development, with movement toward the free market balanced by counter-movements for social protection. Building upon Polanyi, Burawoy (2015: 16) singled out a sequence of three successive counter-movements at the global level, respectively for labor rights, social rights, and human rights. As he notes, "If these movements were globally connected, it was their national framing that drove their distinctive momentum. They may share underlying economic causes but their expression is shaped by the terms and structure of national politics." As in Polanyi's counter-movements, in the second great transformation related to neoliberalism, several movements emerged with a focus on the defense of the rights to housing, health, education, and jobs. These rights developed in the 1960s and 1970s in the First World in social democracies and in developing states, and in the Second World in socialist regimes. In this sense, these movements are to a certain extent backward-looking, aiming at a re-establishment of old rights that are seen as being challenged by neoliberalism (della Porta et al. 2017). At the same time, however, these movements face the important challenge of building a transnational coalition of social groups that are being damaged by different aspects of neoliberalism and its crisis.

With reference to the recent global dynamics in capitalism, Harvey (2003) pointed to the development, together with forms of accumulation by production, of forms of accumulation by "accumulation by dispossession."

> As in the case of labour supply, capitalism always requires a fund of assets outside of itself if it is to confront and circumvent pressures of over-accumulation. If those assets, such as empty land or new raw material sources, do not lie to hand, then capitalism must somehow produce them.
>
> (ibid.: 143)

Neoliberalism results in the privatization and downsizing of public services, while liberalization and deregulation favor the growth of financial capitalism at the cost of production. In different ways in different geopolitical areas, social movements have appeared bifurcated between mobilizations around production (such as factory protests against capitalist expansion), and mobilization around accumulation by dispossession (e.g. protest against a re-commodification of previously de-commodified goods, such as social services). While in the former, "the exploitation of wage labour and conditions defining the social wage are the central issues," the latter include

> resistance to classic forms of primitive accumulation (such as displacement of peasant populations from the land); to the brutal withdrawal of the state from all social obligations (except surveillance and policing); to practices destructive of cultures, histories, and environments; and to the "confiscatory" deflations and inflations wrought by the contemporary forms of finance capital in alliance with the state.
>
> (Harvey 2005: 203)

The very over-exploitative logic of accumulation by dispossession is expected to impact the forms of collective mobilization, both in waves of protest against the flexibilization of the labor market and in protests in defense of public services, such as health or housing, which have been central in the anti-austerity movements in Europe and beyond (della Porta et al. 2017).

The construction of social coalitions among different social groups certainly requires the development of new protest strategies and new identities. To this end, the so-called "movements of the squares" which have mobilized world-wide have developed innovative, participatory, and deliberative conceptions and practices of democracy (della Porta 2013). In Tahrir Square in Cairo, Puerta del Sol in Madrid, Syntagma Square in Athens, Zuccotti Park in New York, Taksim Square in Istanbul,

> a prefigurative politics took priority, imagining what education, family, welfare, and banking might look like in a "really" democratic world. This participatory democracy embraced a new political language of accountability suspicious of all inherited institutions and ideologies, and even of leadership itself.
>
> (Burawoy 2015)

Besides prefiguration, protests against neoliberalism and its crisis, in Latin America as well as in Southern Europe, have produced a wave of movement parties which have been extremely (and surprisingly) successful (della Porta et al. 2017; Roberts 2015).

Contrary to the expectation that *movements of crisis*, sparked by unemployment, food shortages, and dislocations, are short-lived, small, violent and unsuccessful (Kerbo 1982), anti-austerity protests have instead often been long-lasting, huge, peaceful, and successful. A noticeable difference with the Global Justice Movement, which addressed neoliberalism in its rampant years, is the anti-austerity protests' stronger focus on issues of national sovereignty. Transnational campaigns against neoliberalism in crisis are emerging, for example, in Europe with the Blockupy protests against the European Central Bank or the first European Strike against Austerity. But transnational coordination seems rather different given the different timing and intensity of economic recession (della Porta 2017a, 2017b).

All the transformations in global capitalism that we discuss clearly have an effect on the forms of protest that have emerged and developed at different geographic levels. Economic structures are, however, to be considered in their links with the political and cultural developments at global level.

Social Movements and Political Globalization

A global political environment: between threats and opportunities

The globalization process also implies the set-up of political tools to regulate and reproduce this social structure through, among others, the proliferation of international governmental Organizations (IGOs) and non-governmental organizations (NGOs) (Boli and Thomas 1999). From this perspective, the international system based on the nation state seems to be mutating into a political system composed of overlapping multi-level authorities with scant democratic legitimacy (Held and McGrew 2000: 27). The emerging global political environment filters the different ways social movements frame economic or financial globalization and the ways they mobilize.

From World War II onwards, there has been growth in the number of IGOs, both with a worldwide scope of action (like the United Nations) and a regional one (like the EU, but also the Mercosur in Latin America and NAFTA in North America). They often have military power (like the North Atlantic Treaty Organization (NATO) or the now defunct Warsaw Pact) or economic objectives (like the International Monetary Fund, the World Bank, or the World Trade Organization). The scope of changes in international governance can be seen in the growth of IGOs, which rose from 37 to 309 between 1909 and 1988 (Princen and Finger 1994: 1).

IGOs have been at once tools for economic globalization through policies liberalizing trade and the movement of capital, and expressions of an attempt to govern processes that can no longer be handled at a national level. If opposition has arisen to the neoliberal policies of the so-called international financial institutions, which wield strong coercive power through the threat of economic sanctions and conditionalities on international credit, some international institutions have started to pressure national governments to enhance democracy and human rights and promote peace (Pevehouse and Russett 2006; Risse, Ropp, and Sikkink 1999). In this sense, the global political environment produces a complex system of interactions which might either help or threaten social movement concerns.

Likewise, the manifest "deficit of democracy" of many of these international governmental organizations, especially in international negotiation processes, has opened the window for non-governmental organizations (the more formal organizations within social movements) to discuss and evaluate the decisions of these international government groups. This, in turn, produces a complex environment of interactions that spreads, through diffusion and pressure, norms, frames and visions of democracy and human, social, and environmental rights, while creating transnational networks that could be activated in specific protest campaigns (Keck and Sikkink 1998). In sum, the globalization of politics created a complex environment in which different patterns of interactions between international governmental organizations, states, and social movement organizations are possible, ranging from cooperative to overtly conflictual.

Global politics and social movement mobilization

If social movements, conceived as particular patterns of network interactions challenging dominant codes (Melucci 1996), have traditionally mobilized on domestic issues, they are increasingly focused on transnational politics, and are contributing to the creation of transnational public opinion, restructuring network relations on a transnational scale, infusing global politics into domestic dynamics, and interacting with transnational NGOs, IGOs, international institutions, and negotiations.

By drawing on, and re-elaborating, a typology of contention based on work by Imig and Tarrow (2001: 17) concerning European mobilizations, we can isolate four types of social movement mobilizations dealing with global politics (Table 34.1). We now briefly discuss each type.

Table 34.1   Typology of social movements mobilizations engaging in global politics

Level of coordination	Target level	
	Transnational	Domestic
Transnational	Collective transnational	Cooperative transnational
Domestic	Rooted cosmopolitan	Domesticated

The best example of *collective transnational mobilization* dealing with global politics is certainly the Global Justice Movement (della Porta et al. 2006). After Seattle, ever more frequent mention was made of a global movement, built upon networks of networks based on multiple identities and organizational formats: ranging from environmental organizations to religiously-based NGOs and associations; from traditional leftist groups to anarchist and anti-capitalist movements.

Although the majority of demonstrators against the World Trade Organization in Seattle in 1999 were North American, the international nature of demonstrations is confirmed by the parallel initiatives organized in more than a hundred cities in the world's North and South for the "Global Action Day." In the early 2000s, every international summit of any importance was accompanied by counter-summits and protest demonstrations that often got wider press coverage than the official agenda. The number of counter-summits and transnational protests continued to rise in 2002 and 2003 (Pianta and Silva 2003), while the threat of an armed conflict in Iraq led to an additional wave of demonstrations. The movement organized not only transnational protests and counter-summits, but also its own global events. "Another Possible Globalization" was discussed at the World Social Forums (WSF) in Porto Alegre (Schönleitner 2003). In thousands of seminars and meetings, proposals of a more or less realistic and original consistency were hammered out for a bottom-up globalization; alternative politics and policies were debated, and some of them were already tested (including the "participatory budgets" which, among others in Porto Alegre, involve citizens in public decision-making). From 2002 onwards, especially, the experience of the Social Forums as a place to meet and engage in debate has been extended to local and macro-regional levels (della Porta et al. 2006).

The complexity of such collective transnational mobilizations brought forth different ideas about how to reconfigure global politics in a more democratic fashion. Although some networks were engaged in bringing the "state back in," the dominant frame of the movement pointed to the building of a cosmopolitan democracy with different levels of governance interacting with each other and all levels involving civil society actors and citizens in a deliberative discussion on the decisions to be taken (della Porta 2009).

In *cooperative transnational mobilizations*, social movements coordinate transnationally but their main targets are domestic. One glaring example of such mobilizations is the coordinated anti-war global day of protest against the Iraqi invasion by the USA and its allies (the so-called "coalition of the willing") under the Bush administration and following the terrorist attack on the USA in 2001 September 11. The global day against the war was coordinated within the Global Justice Movement WSF, but the protests were nationally organized by domestic social movements in hundreds of cities, involving millions of people worldwide (Walgrave and Rucht 2010).

Paradoxically, the biggest event coordinated by the Global Justice Movement was also its point of decline: the peace movement that mobilized beginning in February 2003 started to follow domestic logics and absorbed the energy of the original movement, bringing about a gradual abandonment of the issue related to neoliberalism, and the dismantling of transnational infrastructures (Andretta and Chelotti 2010; Hadden and Tarrow 2007).

Other kinds of cooperative transnational mobilizations can be found in support of weak domestic groups facing closed states. Especially on the issues of human rights, environmental threats, and women rights, in the world periphery (Latin America, Africa, and Asia), domestic social movements have been trying to change their governments' behavior and policies by making connections with transnational advocacy groups, which in turn push democratic governments and IGOs to pressure those states. This is what Keck and Sikkink (1998) called the "boomerang effect."

Finally, some sort of cooperative transnational mobilizations have supported the so-called Arab Spring: especially through the role of social media, domestic groups in the Middle East have interacted with each other by sharing ideas, tactics, and frames, as well with the West to gain support (Howard and Hussain 2011).

We derive the locution "*rooted cosmopolitan*" from Tarrow (2005), who refers to citizens who draw on local resources and settings but get involved in transnational mobilizations. We adapt the application of the concept here to refer to mobilizations that are domestically based, though influenced by some sort of transnational diffusion of tactics, ideas, and organization, and which target transnational institutions and actors. Examples are the Occupy movement which spread from the USA to Europe targeting financial institutions (Uitermark and Nicholls 2012), the Indignados movement in Spain (Castaneda 2012) targeting the World Bank, the IMF and the EU, and citizens mobilizing through political forms of consumerism, often supported by national and local consumerist organizations, which promote boycotting to put pressure on transnational corporations accused of unfair behavior, or to criticize the global market of food production and distribution (Micheletti and McFarland 2009). Those mobilizations are "cosmopolitan" because their main concerns are related to global issues, and they are "rooted" because they draw on domestic, local, and even individual resources and networks.

The most spectacular financial crisis in recent world history seems to have produced fragmented and nationally based mobilizations dealing with the same issues known as *domesticated mobilizations*. These mobilizations domesticate global politics, in terms of level of coordination, network building, and defining relevant targets. Certainly domestic and local protests against neoliberalism, which targeted national and local institutions and actors, were already dominant in the Global South: in Africa (Dwyer and Zeilig 2012); in Asia (Broadbent and Brockman 2011); and Latin America (Almeida 2014). The domestication of global politics through local and domestic mass mobilization has even led to a "theory of local opposition to globalization" (ibid.). The social costs of global transformations have been intensified by the recent economic crisis (Tamamović 2015). A study of the most affected European countries has shown that the type of domestic anti-austerity movement and its impact on domestic politics depended on the intensity of the economic crisis, and the consequent rigidity of the austerity policies, mediated by specific political opportunities and national social movement traditions (della Porta et al. 2017).

In domesticated mobilizations, national and local institutions are targeted for different reasons: on one hand, they are considered blind implementers of decisions made elsewhere; on the other, they are accused of making democratic representation an empty promise, as the voice of affected interests and citizens is systematically excluded by the decision-making processes and in some cases also by the public debate in mainstream media.

Global Social Movements and Culture

For Jasper (2010: 60) culture "consists of shared mental worlds and their perceived embodiments." A contrasting definition considers culture to refer to the things that people (in our case, activists) share (Lofland 1995; see also Swidler 1986). Thus, movements can be thought of as cultural in two ways: through the actions that activists take as carriers of culture *and* as challengers of mainstream cultural norms (see Chapter 3 by Jasper and Polletta, in this volume). First, thinking of social movements as a global cultural phenomenon in themselves draws attention to the way movements organize, define problems, and craft repertoires. In this sense, transnational movements carry cultures which diffuse across nations. Second, transnational movements pose a direct challenge to dominant cultural norms such as economic growth, consumerist culture, and bias against ethnic minorities across multiple nations. We introduce these two facets of culture in transnational movements in turn. The first is associated with transnational networks and diffused behaviors, whereas the second is associated with global targets. Both are a reaction not only to the global homogenization of culture, but also to the economic and political trends we identify above. Both types of culture are mutually co-constituted by each other and by the economic and political arenas.

Culture across global movements

Movement tactics, ideas, and organizational forms diffuse across countries (see Chapter 13 by Soule and Roggeband, in this volume). Evidence of the diffusion of tactics, ideas, and organizational forms provides scholars with one means of assessing the extent of a common culture among movements across the globe. Here we discuss examples of diffusion across very different types of nations in terms of political regimes, domestic economies, and local cultures.

Until relatively recently, the diffusion of culture across social movements from one country to others was largely assumed to originate in the Western developed world (Chabbot and Duyvendak 2002). This way of thinking about diffusion was challenged by the reality of global activism in two main ways: by the diffusion of movement tactics and ideas *to* rather than from the West; and by social movement organizations (SMOs) from across the globe organizing *together* in dialogue within face-to-face global forums (e.g. the World Social Forum) and on the Internet.

The Occupy movement provides an illustration of *tactical diffusion* and also challenges the dominant idea that diffusion originates in the West. While the origins of the global Occupy movement are diverse, common to most accounts of its genealogy is its inspiration in the Arab Spring, particularly the Tahrir Square occupations

(Kerton 2012). Spreading to Southern Europe in May and to the USA in September 2011, when protesters "occupied" Zuccotti Park, Manhattan (Chomsky 2012; Gitlin 2012; Graeber 2013), the protest went on to inspire similar protests in more than 700 cities around the world (Roth, Saunders, and Olcese 2014).

The Zapatistas provide an example of how movement *ideas have diffused* from the South to the West. The Zapatista army, a Chiapas-based (south Mexico) insurgent group, has been instrumental in the spread of arguments against neoliberalism across the world (Ramirez et al. 2008). Zapatistas have been especially concerned about social justice. Their struggle came to global attention when, in 1994, the Zapatistas engaged in an armed "war" against the Mexican government. The coup failed and the group more recently has turned its attention toward sharing its critique of neoliberalism with the world. Its ideas spread to Europe from 1994 onwards, as a result of European activists' attendance at Intercontinental Encuentros Against Neoliberalism and for Humanity conferences held in Chiapas, Mexico, in 1996 and Spain in 1997 and a 16-day tour with the Zapatistas from Chiapas to Mexico City in Spring 2001 (Chesters and Welsh 2006). The Encuentro – a gathering of activists – is a Latin American means of organizing activism. It motivated the WSF which manifests as an event using democratic innovations from movements across the globe, particularly, consensus decision-making with spokes and hubs.

Diffusion of social movement culture is facilitated not only by organizational structures (including the Internet), but also by the cultural status of items being diffused (Strang and Soule 1998). For example, a movement tactic, idea, or organizational form is only going to diffuse around the globe if it is able to generate cultural resonance in multiple countries. Thus, it is important to discuss the "meaning work" of movements. Movement entrepreneurs select cultural symbols that will appeal to their target audience (Snow et al. 1986). Feminist movements, for example, reach out across national borders by drawing on the cultural concept of "sisterhood" (Rupp and Taylor 1999). Similarly, Carroll and Ratner find that activists and organizations that possess a "political economy master frame" – in which "power is viewed as systemic, institutional, structural and materially grounded, for instance, in wealth" (1996: 609) are most likely to be involved in cross-movement and presumably cross-national activity.

Challenging global cultural norms

Mass culture is often conceived as hegemony of the ruling class, which dupes everyday publics into compliance (Adorno and Horkheimer 1997 [1944]). Thus, to change the global neoliberal system requires challenging cultural hegemony. In this line, Flesher Fominaya writes about cultural resistance as "movement culture consciously created for political resistance" (2014: 82). Transnational movements do this in multiple ways, but we only have the space in this chapter to focus on some key ways in which activists have resisted globalized consumer culture.

Although they have precedents as far back as boycotts of sugar from slavery plantations in the eighteenth century, transnational anti-consumerist movements have more recently been motivated by Naomi Klein's (2001) seminal *No Logo*. This book has become a cultural icon, even "a cultural manifesto for the critics of unfettered capitalism worldwide."[2] Anti-consumerist actions include buying nothing, buying only good things, avoiding the purchase of ethically or environmentally dubious products, changing the meanings of adverts, and stealing from unethical corporations.

Adbusters' International Buy Nothing Day draws attention away from the consumerism that supports the current economic system (Boivie 2003; Rumbo 2002). Other buy nothing movements include intentional communities that retract entirely from consumerist society and engage in self-sufficiency (Trainer 2000) and grow-your-own food movements. La Via Campesina, founded in 1993, supports small and medium-sized farmers, the landless, and agricultural workers (Martinez-Alier 2011). Its cultural resistance work pushes for everyone's right to food from small-scale agriculture. One consequence is a glocal (i.e. in many localities across the globe) food resurgence (Starr 2010). The purchase of ethically sound products, that we mentioned earlier, is on the rise as a form of global resistance (Stolle and Michelleti 2015). In particular, it is a hot topic in relation to fashion. No Sweat campaigns have been raising awareness of sweatshop labour since the 1990s (Ross 1997). Fashion Revolution has recently been using the Internet technology of "hauling," to reveal "the labour behind the label."

Subvertising involves subverting the messages of advertisements to reveal unpleasant truths about brands and to challenge globally homogenizing culture. In the words of Holt (2002: 86), the emphasis is on "peeling away the brand veneer." Subvertising specialists The Yes Men have taken subvertising to its limits. Since the early 2000s, their spoof World Economic Forum website (http://www.we-forum.org/en/index.shtml) has led to multiple invitations to transnational economic and corporate events at which they masquerade as official representatives of international financial organizations and corporations. One stunt involved one of them pretending to be a spokesman for Dow Chemicals (the owners of Union Carbide) and admitting full responsibility for the Bhopal pollution catastrophe on BBC news (Carducci 2006).

Ethical shoplifting has a long tradition in the environmental movement. Wall (2002), for example, reports on how Earth First! activists stole illegally harvested timber from a warehouse. A new ethos around stealing has been developed by Yo Mango, which claims to be a political network of shoplifters. The term Yo Mango literally translates as "I steal." Goods are appropriated from supermarkets and re-appropriated for community enjoyment. Yo Mango creates its own parodies of consumer culture through stickers and slogans such as 'Happy Shoplifter' (Flesher Fominaya 2014: 108–109).

There are points of critique for all these forms of cultural resistance. Lasn (1999) refers to "meme wars" which involve mainstream culture counteracting or absorbing memes of resistance activists. An unintended consequence of cultural resistance is that it provides the mainstream with inspiration for re-branding. Moore (2004), for example, found that it was after the punk movement had gained popularity that it became possible to purchase ready-ripped jeans with safety pins. Attempts to reclaim culture remain thwarted by the financial and political power of corporations. Intentional communities run the risk of isolating themselves from broader communities (Connelly et al. 2012). This is not to suggest, however, that cultural resistance is entirely fruitless. Millions have become empowered through acts of cultural resistance. Diffusion of movement culture (tactics, ideas, and organizational structures) allows the ripples of the effects to be felt globally.

Conclusion

Our discussion of globalization and social movements has revealed the complexity of the processes of globalization and the multiple ways in which they affect and are affected by social movements. Many strands of scholarship have been used to explain the rise and fall of global social movements. As we have noted, the field is rich with contributions from political theory, political economy, sociology, and cultural studies. Much progress has been made in adapting old theories to suit new situations, but there is still a need to merge different theories to provide a coherent analytical framework to understand the socio-political context of global movements, their actions, and the outcomes that they have. This is a difficult challenge for scholars in the context of globalization processes, the effects of which vary over time and from place to place.

Indeed, while the Global Justice Movement had spread the impression of a growing trend towards a globalization of contentious politics, the anti-austerity protests appeared as a turning point testifying to (or even pushing for) a return of power to the domestic level. A cross-time comparison of the moment of globalization or domestication of protest will certainly help us understand the conditions and mechanisms for the two processes.

Additionally, if we look at the challenge of transnational protests in constructing not only the image of a common enemy but also a cosmopolitan self, we can see two contrasting paths emerging, On the one hand, the concept of the multitude points to the potential for the multitudes to revolt, even without prior development of common identities and solidarities. On the other, however, these protests are seen as addressing the need of the constitution of a new (post-national) concept of citizenship (Gerbaudo 2016).

Although the role of the technological revolution in both globalization processes and social movement coordination is not made explicit in our discussion, we do not deny its importance. Other future research might consider how the Internet, vis-à-vis face-to-face interaction, facilitates interactions between institutions and movements, and between and across movements across the world. An integrated economic, political and cultural multitudes perspective could be a useful approach to understanding the impacts of on-line media on movements.

Notes

1   As some assessment process requires formal attribution, we declare that Donatella della Porta is responsible for the section on "Global Capitalism and Social Movements," Massimiliano Andretta for "Social Movements and Political Globalization," and Clare Saunders for "Global Social Movements and Culture" and "Conclusion."

2   See http://www.naomiklein.org/no-logo

References

Adorno, Theodor, W. and Max Horkheimer. 1997 [1944]. *Dialectic of Enlightenment*. London: Verso.

Almeida Paul. 2014. *Mobilizing Democracy: Globalization and Citizen Protest*. Baltimore, MD: Johns Hopkins University Press.

Andretta, Massimiliano and Nicola Chelotti. 2010. "The G8 in Italy between Politics and Protest: A Case of Success?" In *Italian Politics: Managing Uncertainty*, edited by Marco Giuliani and Erick Jones, 130–148. Oxford: Berghahn Books.

Arrighi, Giovanni, Terence K. Hopkins, and Immanuel Wallerstein. 1989. *Anti-Systemic Movements*. London: Verso.

Bayat, Asef. 2010. *Life as Politics: How Ordinary People Change the Middle East*. Stanford, CA: Stanford University Press.

Boivie, Illana. 2003. "Buy Nothing, Improve Everything." *The Humanist* 63(3): 7–9.

Boli, John and George M. Thomas. 1999. *Constructing the World Culture: International Nongovernmental Organizations since 1875*. Stanford, CA: Stanford University Press.

Broadbent, Jeffrey and Vicky Brockman, eds. 2011. *East-Asian Social Movements: Power, Protest and Change in a Dynamic Region*. New York: Springer.

Burawoy, Michael. 2015. "Facing an Unequal World." *Current Sociology* 63(1): 5–34.

Carducci, Vince. 2006. "Culture Jamming: A Sociological Perspective." *Journal of Consumer Culture* 6(1): 116–138.

Carroll, William K. and Robert S. Ratner. 1996. "Master Framing and Cross-Movement Networking in Contemporary Social Movements." *The Sociological Quarterly* 37(4): 601–625.

Castaneda Ernesto. 2012. "The Indignados of Spain: A Precedent to Occupy Wall Street." *Social Movement Studies* 11(3–4): 309–319.

Chabot, Sean and Jan Willem Duyvendak. 2002. "Globalization and Transnational Diffusion Between Social Movements: Essentialist Diffusionism and Beyond." *Theory and Society* 31: 697–740.

Chesters, Graeme and Ian Welsh. 2006. *Complexity and Social Movements: Multitudes at the Edge of Chaos*. London: Routledge.

Chomsky, Noam. 2012. *Occupy*, London: Penguin.

Connelly, James, Graham Smith, David Benson, and Clare Saunders. 2012. *Environmental Politics: From Theory to Practice*, 3rd edn. New York: Routledge.

della Porta, Donatella. 2009 "Democracy in Movement: Some Conclusions." In *Democracy in Social Movements*, edited by Donatella della Porta, 262–274. Basingstoke: Palgrave Macmillan.

della Porta, Donatella. 2013. *Can Democracy Be Saved?* Cambridge: Polity.

della Porta, Donatella, 2014. *Mobilizing for Democracy*. Oxford: Oxford University Press.

della Porta, Donatella. 2015. *Anti-Austerity Protests in the Crisis of Late Neoliberalism*. Cambridge: Polity.

della Porta, Donatella. 2017a. "Neoliberalism and Its Discontents: An Introduction." In *Late Neoliberalism and its Discontents in the Economic Crisis*, edited by Donatella della Porta, Massimiliano Andretta, Tiago Fernandes, Eduardo Romanos, Francis O'Connor, and Markos Vogiatzoglou. London: Palgrave.

della Porta, Donatella. 2017b. *Riding the Wave*. Amsterdam: Amsterdam University Press.

della Porta, Donatella, Massimiliano Andretta, Lorenzo Mosca, and Herbert Reiter. 2006. *Globalization from Below: Transnational Activists and Protest Networks*. Minneapolis: University of Minnesota Press.

della Porta, Donatella, Joseba Fernandez, Hara Kouki, and Lorenzo Mosca. 2017. *Movement Parties*. Cambridge: Polity.

Dwyer, Peter and Louis Zeilig. 2012. *African Struggles Today: Social Movements since Independence*. Chicago: Haymarket Books.

Flesher Fominaya, Cristina. 2014. *Social Movements and Globalization: How Protests, Occupations and Uprisings Are Changing the World*. Basingstoke: Palgrave Macmillan.

Gerbaudo, Paolo. 2016. *The Mask and the Flag*. London: Hurst.

Gitlin, Todd. 2012. *Occupy Nation: The Roots, the Spirit, and the Promise of Occupy Wall Street*. New York: HarperCollins.

Graeber, David. 2013. *The Democracy Project: A History. A Crisis. A Movement*. London: Allen Lane.

Hadden Jennifer and Sidney Tarrow. 2007. "Spillout or Spillover? The Global Justice Movement in the United States after 9/11." *Mobilization* 4: 195–213.

Hardt, Michael and Antonio Negri. 2000. *Empire*. Cambridge, MA: Harvard University Press.

Harvey, David. 2003. *New Imperialism*. Oxford: Oxford University Press.

Harvey, David. 2005. *A Brief History of Neoliberalism*. Oxford: Oxford University Press.

Held, David and Anthony McGrew. 2000. *The Global Transformation Reader: An Introduction to the Globalization Debate*. Cambridge: Polity.

Holt, Douglas B. 2002. "Why Do Brands Cause Trouble? A Dialectical Theory of Consumer Culture and Branding." *Journal of Consumer Research* 29(1): 70–90.

Howard Philip N. and Muzammil M. Hussain. 2011. "The Role of Digital Media." *Journal of Democracy* 22(3): 35–48.

Hutter, Swen. 2014. *Protesting Economics and Culture in Western Europe: New Cleavages in Left and Right Politics*. Minneapolis: University of Minnesota Press.

Imig, Doug and Sidney Tarrow. 2001. "Studying Contention in an Emerging Polity." In *Contentious Europeans: Protest and Politics in an Emerging Polity*, edited by Doug Imig and Sidney Tarrow, 3–26. Lanham, MD: Rowman & Littlefield.

Jasper, James M. 2010. "Cultural Approaches in the Sociology of Social Movements." In *Handbook of Social Movements Across Disciplines*, edited by Bert Klandermans and Conny Roggeband, 59–110. New York: Springer.

Júlíusson, Árni Daníel and Magnús Sveinn Helgason. 2013. "Roots of the Saucepan Revolution in Iceland." In Understanding European *Movements: New Social Movements, Global Justice Struggles, Anti-Austerity Protest*, edited by Cristina Flesher Fominaya and Laurence Cox, 189–202. London: Routledge

Keck, Margaret E. and Kathryn Sikkink. 1998. *Activists Beyond Borders: Advocacy Groups in International Politics*. Ithaca, NY: Cornell University Press.

Kerbo, Harold R. 1982. "Movements of 'Crisis' and Movements of 'Affluence': A Critique of Deprivation and Resource Mobilization Theory" *Journal of Conflict Resolution* 26. 645–63.

Kerton, Sarah. 2012. "Tahrir, Here? The Influence of the Arab Uprisings on the Emergence of Occupy." *Social Movement Studies* 11(3–4): 302–308.

Klein, Naomi. 2001. *No Logo*, London: Fourth Estate.

Kriesi, Hanspeter, Ruud Koopmans, Jan Willem Duyvendak, and Marco Giugni. 1995. *The Politics of New Social Movements in Western Europe*. Minneapolis: University of Minnesota Press.

Lasn, Kalle. 1999. *Culture Jam: The Uncooling of America*. New York: Eagle Brook.

Lofland, John. 1995. "Charting Degrees of Movement Culture." In *Social Movements and Culture*, edited by Hank Johnston and Bert Klandermans, 188–216. Minneapolis: University of Minnesota Press.

Martinez-Alier, Joan. 2011. "The EROI of Agriculture and its Use by Via Campasina." *The Journal of Peasant Studies* 38(1): 145–160.

Melucci, Alberto. 1996. *Challenging Codes*. Cambridge: Cambridge University Press.

Micheletti, Michele and Andrew McFarland, eds. 2009. *Creative Participation: Responsibility-Taking in the Political World*. Boulder, CO: Paradigm.

Moore, Ryan. 2004. "Postmodernism and Punk Subculture: Cultures of Authenticity and Deconstruction." *The Communication Review* 7(3): 305–327.

Pevehouse, Jon and Bruce Russett. 2006. "Democratic International Governmental Organizations Promote Peace." *International Organization* 60(4): 969–1000.

Pianta, Mario and Federico Silva. 2003. *Globalisers from Below. A Server on Global Civil Society Organisations*. GLOBI Research Report.

Polanyi, Karl. 1957 [1944]. *The Great Transformation: The Political and Economic Origins of Our Time*. London: Beacon Press.

Princen, Thomas and Matthias Finger. 1994. "Introduction." In *Environmental NGOs in World Politics: Linking the Local and the Global*, edited by Thomas Princen and Matthias Finger, 1–25. London: Routledge.

Ramírez, Gloria Muñoz, Laura Carlsen, and Alejandro Reyes Arias. 2008. *The Fire and the Word: A History of the Zapatista Movement*. San Francisco: City Lights Publishers.

Risse Thomas, Stephen C. Ropp, and Kathryn Sikkink, eds. 1999. *The Power of Human Rights*. Cambridge: Cambridge University Press.

Roberts, Kenneth. 2015. *Changing Course in Latin America*. Cambridge: Cambridge University Press.

Ross, Andrew. 1997. *After the Year of the Sweatshop*, London: Verso.

Roth, Silke, Clare Saunders, and Cristiana Olcese. 2014. 'Occupy as a Free Space: Mobilization Processes and Outcomes." *Sociological Research Online*, 19(1). Available at: http://www.socresonline.org.uk/19/1/1.html. doi: 10.5153/sro.3201.

Rumbo, Joseph D. 2002. "Consumer Resistance in a World of Advertising Clutter: The Case of Adbusters." *Psychology and Marketing* 19(2): 127–148.

Rupp, Leila J. and Verta Taylor. 1999. "Forging Feminist Identity in an International Movement: A Collective Identity Approach to Twentieth-Century Feminism." *Signs* 24(2): 363–386.

Sassen, Saskia. 2013. *Expulsions*. Cambridge: Cambridge University Press.

Schönleitner, Gunther. 2003. "World Social Forum: Making Another World Possible?" In *Globalizing Civic Engagement: Civil Society and Transnational Action*, edited by John Clark, 109–126. London: Earthscan.

Silver, Beverly. 2003. *The Forces of Labour*. Cambridge: Cambridge University Press.

Smith, Jackie, Marina Karides, Marc Becker, et al. 2007. *The World Social Forums and the Challenge of Global Democracy*. Boulder, Co: Paradigm Publishers.

Snow, David A., E. Burke Rochford Jr, Steven K. Worden, and Robert D. Benford. 1986. "Frame Alignment Processes, Micromobilization and Movement Participation." *American Sociological Review* 51: 456–481.

Starr, Amory. 2010. "Local Food: A Social Movement?" *Cultural Studies Critical Methodologies* 10(6): 479–490.

Stolle, Dietland and Michelle Michelleti. 2015. *Political Consumerism: Global Responsibility in Action*. Cambridge: Cambridge University Press.

Strang, David and Sarah A. Soule. 1998. "Diffusion in Organizations and Social Movements: From Hybrid Corn to Poison Pills." *Annual Review of Sociology* 24: 265–290.

Swidler, Anne. 1986. "Culture in Action: Symbols and Strategies." *American Sociological Review*, 51(2): 273–286.

Tamamovic', Aleksandra Ivanković, ed. 2015. *The Impact of the Crisis on Fundamental Rights Across Member States of the EU: Comparative Analysis*. Report commissioned by the LIBE Committee, European Parliament. Available at: http://www.europarl.europa.eu/RegData/etudes/STUD/2015/510021/IPOL_STU%282015%29510021_EN.pdf

Tarrow, Sidney. 2005. *The New Transnational Activism*. Cambridge: Cambridge University Press.

Touraine, Alain. 1985. "An Introduction to the Study of Social Movements." *Social Research* 52: 749–788.

Trainer, Ted. 2000. "Where Are We, Where Do We Want to Be, How Do We Get There?" *Democracy and Nature* 6(2): 267–286.

Uitermark, Justus and Walter Nicholls. 2012. "How Local Networks Shape a Global Movement: Comparing Occupy in Amsterdam and Los Angeles." *Social Movement Studies* 11(3–4): 295–301.

Walgrave, Stephan and Dieter Rucht, eds. 2010. *The World Says No to War*. Minneapolis: University of Minnesota Press.

Wall, Derek. 2002. "Snowballs, Elves and Skimmingtons? Genealogies of Environmental Direct Action." In *Direct Action in British Environmentalism*, edited by Ben Seel, Matthew Paterson, and Brian Doherty, 79–92. London: Routledge.

Wallerstein, Immanuel. 1990. "Antisystemic Movements: History and Dilemma." In *Transforming the Revolution*, edited by Samir Amin, Giovanni Arrighi, André Gunder Frank, and Immanuel Wallerstein. New York: Monthly Review Press.

Wallerstein, Immanuel. 2010. "Structural Crises." *New Left Review* 62: 133–142.

Zajak, Sabrina. 2016. *Transnational Activism, Global Labor Governance, and China*. London: Palgrave.

35

Political Extremism and Social Movements

Robert Futrell, Pete Simi, and Anna E. Tan

Introduction

Our task in this chapter is to discuss research on political extremism and the relationship between extremism and social movements. This is a complicated matter. In some respects, all social movements represent political extremism. Social movements typically originate outside established institutions and seek recognition in ways that challenge existing codes, practices, power relations, and authorities (McAdam, Tarrow, and Tilly 2003; Melucci 1996; Snow 2004). Without routine access to power holders, movements resort to extreme or "extraordinary means" (Tilly 1978) to express their grievances. These challenges always carry the potential to disrupt systems that support established interests and, in that sense, may be considered extreme reactions by those in power.

But, our field has highlighted left-leaning progressive movements, while other forms of collective action that advocate violence, terror, hatred, and intolerance have gone understudied and undertheorized. The imbalance toward left reformist activism in social movement studies has implications for what we know about movements as a general phenomenon and extremist activism specifically. In fact, we find it quite difficult to fundamentally distinguish between an "extremist movement" and other movement types. We see extremism largely as a politicized term that obscures commonalities between routine movements and movements that embrace highly marginalized ideologies and actions. Though our field's theories and concepts primarily reflect research on more mainstream movements, many of the same dynamics apply to extremist activism. In short, we do not see extremism as a fundamentally different unit of analysis that requires fundamentally new or distinct theories and concepts. At this point, a thorough understanding of extremism requires additional empirical scrutiny and more nuanced analyses to explain how political groups respond to different pressures, constraints, and opportunities.

The Wiley Blackwell Companion to Social Movements, Second Edition. Edited by David A. Snow, Sarah A. Soule, Hanspeter Kriesi, and Holly J. McCammon.
© 2019 John Wiley & Sons Ltd. Published 2019 by John Wiley & Sons Ltd.

In what follows, we briefly discuss in more depth the complications involved in defining "extremism" and "extremist movements." Then we address some of the qualities of extremist movements using broadly established concepts in the social movements field. We end with important questions that remain for scholars to pursue to establish more robust insights about extremist political action.

Conceptualizing Extremism

Social movement researchers have relegated extremism, especially right-wing activism, to a relatively small corner of the field, in part because they are too "awkward" (Blee 2006; Polletta 2011) or "distasteful" (Esseveld and Eyerman 1992) to study. This disinterest reveals something about the political nature of social movements research, in particular, how some movements are politicized as extreme or radical in a pejorative, moralizing sense.[1] As Polletta (2011) observes, the distinctions between reformist movements, interest groups, terrorist networks, unions, nongovernmental organizations "often reflect the idiosyncrasies of how subfields have developed rather than anything intrinsic to the phenomena themselves." That said, we have to draw some conceptual lines somewhere. The question is, where?

The line between reformist and extremist movements is unclear. Perhaps under the right conditions, all movements have the capacity to develop more drastic ideas and strategies (McCauley and Moskalenko 2011). We see this, for instance, in the way that environmentalism's broad umbrella covers groups from the reformist-minded Natural Resources Defense Council, to the direct action campaigns of Greenpeace International, to the Earth Liberation Front's (ELF) "covert sabotage and guerilla eco-warfare." These groups are connected by ideals about environmental protection and some activists may have allegiances across the groups, even though their specific ideological principles and the tactics they advocate differ wildly. Such connections between extreme and moderate factions make it difficult to draw the line between what is and is not extremism.

As Sotlar (2004) explains, extremism is more a political term than a precise scientific concept. Extremism connotes views and practices on the right or left of the political spectrum that lie far outside mainstream societal attitudes and usually draw broadly negative reactions. Among researchers, extremism typically refers to groups and ideologies that are not aligned with state norms, reject pluralist governance, oppose the existing social order, and condone some form of violence for their cause. Like social movement scholars generally, many analysts studying extremism make an additional distinction between those who embrace extremist ideologies and those who take violent extremist action. Most people who are sympathetic to, or even hold deeply extremist views, never engage in political violence. Even among those who do take extreme political acts, not all are "ideologues or deep believers in a nuanced, extremist doctrine" (Borum 2011: 9; also McCauley and Moskalenko 2011). That said, extremist culture can inspire extreme acts and offers a repertoire of tactics for activists to use. In the right context, such as when political opportunities emerge (della Porta 1995, 2008; Snow and Byrd 2007), threats appear eminent (Ivarsflaten 2008; McVeigh 2009; Van Dyke and Soule 2002; Wright 2007), groups feel disenfranchised (Aho 1990; Dobratz and Shanks-Meile 1997) and frustrations set in (McCauley and Moskalenko 2011), then political groups may turn to the sorts of rhetoric and violence that define extremism.

Mobilization

Questions about who participates in collective action, how they participate, and why, have long driven social movement researchers. Answers to these mobilization questions highlight the formal and informal collective ways that people engage one another to define problems, encourage action, and organize that action into sustained collective efforts. Extremist movements display various similarities to the meso-level groups, organizations, and informal networks of more moderate movements. In this section, we discuss research insights on how people become involved in extremist groups, extremist organization and social networks, and the how extremists use the Internet as a mobilization tool.

Extremist radicalization

Both researchers and the public alike seem perpetually curious (and worried) about those who hold extreme political attitudes and engage in extremist actions. Researchers have come to see an individual's steps into extremism, typically termed radicalization, as a slow gradual process, full of fits and starts, rather than a singular, linear trajectory driven solely by "extremist personality" traits or simplistic ideological commitment. McCauley and Moskalenko (2011: 4) argue that, under the right circumstances, anyone may become a radical. Increasingly, that process looks like a "puzzle" that requires "a multifactorial and contextualized approach to understanding how ordinary individuals transform" into extremists (Hafez and Mullins 2015: 958; see also Borum 2011; Cross and Snow 2011).

It is a far-fetched notion that researchers will find the "extremist personality profile" and demographic patterns to understand extremism (Hafez and Mullins 2015). Radicalization-as-process arguments are also problematic because process implies an orderly sequence of steps or phases toward mobilization (ibid.). As Hafez and Mullins (ibid.: 959) observe, "the absence of a clear pattern or pathway to radicalization is precisely what is frustrating scholars and intelligence analysts alike. Reality is far too complex for a single, parsimonious explanation." They instead identify four factors quite common to all social movements – personal and collective grievances, political and religious ideologies, networks and interpersonal ties, and enabling environments and support structures – that work together to produce radicalization. Grievances, such as disenchantment, discrimination, and exclusion are "the landscape that frames the proximate causes of radicalization" but do not directly cause extremist mobilization (ibid.: 962). Likewise, ideology provides stories, encouragements, and rationales for extremists, but "like grievances, their place in the radicalization puzzle is not always at the center" (ibid.: 966). Social networks are critical to radicalization as they offer blocs of similar people, with some degree of preexisting familiarity, trust, and solidarity. Strong ties increase an individual's cohesion with the group and decrease the likelihood of defection, even as extremist activity ramps up.

Research also points to "enabling environments and support structures," such as websites, social media, and indigenous spaces to meet, commiserate, and plan actions. These structures both nourish established networks and also allow for "seekers and searchers" (Snow and Soule 2010: 119) to connect and feel part of a movement. A recent line of research focuses on the influence of non-ideological risk factors such as childhood trauma and adolescent misconduct in the lives of individuals who become violent extremists (Simi, Sporer, and Bubolz 2016). More specifically, Simi, Sporer, and Bubolz (2016) found that violence and other forms of anti-social behavior *preceded* extremist involvement while the group context of extremism provides a variety of social functions such as protection, shelter, and emotional support. While these are the puzzle pieces, we do not yet know exactly how the pieces fit together. "Each piece of the puzzle can come in a different representation just like similarly structured jigsaw puzzles could reveal diverse images once their pieces are interconnected" (Hafez and Mullins 2015: 959).

Most scholars distinguish between adherence to extremist political ideas and engagement in extremist political action.[2] The pyramid model of radicalization (McCauley and Moskalenko 2008) suggests that the majority of those who profess a belief in extremist ideas never take violent extremist action. Sympathizers who constitute the extremist base may agree with extremist goals, but do not demonstrate the degree of belief, feeling, and behaviors associated with increased radicalization, such as violence. A key question is "How do people move from embracing extremist views to engaging in extremist action?" (ibid.)

McCauley and Moskalenko (2008, 2011) demonstrate radicalization's complexities by highlighting 12 radicalization mechanisms at three levels: individual, group, and mass society. Individual mechanisms range from personal victimization to seeking the risk and status that come with involvement in an outlaw group. Group level radicalization includes such circumstances as when group members influence each other to adopt increasingly radical views or groups in political competition with other groups turn to radical tactics. Mass radicalization may occur when extremist groups provoke governments into overreactions that draw new members to support their cause, when people begin to see an enemy as inhuman and distaste turns to hatred, and when groups use martyrs to radicalize new adherents for the cause. These mechanisms do not operate alone. Multiple mechanisms typically interact and reinforce one another. As McCauley and Moskalenko (2011: 214) explain, "Individual mechanisms do not disappear when an individual joins a group and group mechanisms do not disappear when a group participates in some larger organisation or mass public." These mechanisms are also not limited to a particular cultural milieu.

Despite its many strengths, Gartenstein-Ross (2012) points out that this model "shares a blind spot with the preponderance of Western scholarship: an unwillingness to take religious ideology seriously as a mechanism of radicalization." Indeed, McCauley and Moskalenko (2011: 5) reject the "bad ideology" argument as "both too simple and too general to be useful for understanding radicalization." But, as Gartenstein-Ross argues, discounting religious ideology as a radicalization mechanism rests on a tenuous assumption that needs more empirical investigation (see Chapter 32 by Snow and Beyerlein, in this volume). It is clear that many people identify with extremist ideas while also avoiding extremist action. But it is also reasonable to think that "violent action is more likely to spring from ideas when the inescapable conclusion of the ideas is that violence is [justified] and necessary" (Gartenstein-Ross 2012). As Simi and Futrell (2015: xiv) point out, "when extremist ideology endures, so does the potential for extremist action." Too easily dismissing ideology as a force in extremist mobilization risks ignoring important questions about the role of ideas in the different routes to radical action.

Organization and Networks

Extremists face myriad difficulties organizing and sustaining activist networks. The most radical exist on society's margins and many are reticent to openly announce to the world who they are and what they seek. The stigma they bear and repression they face constrain their capacity to organize. Many persist in "submerged networks" (Melucci 1989, 1996), although some align with fairly public movement spokespersons and organizations. These complications lead some to interpret extremist activism as disorganized and ineffective. Yet, emphasizing extremism's disorganized aspects can obscure "its strategic, structured, and persistent dimensions" (Simi and Futrell 2015: 11; see also Blee 2002).

Extremists tend to be linked through fluid, transitory, and informal networks anchored in hidden spaces where they meet and support one another. These movement spaces require deliberate and calculated organization to create and sustain over time. Within these spaces, extremists create, share, and maintain collective identity, ideological convictions, and emotional connections that ground their activism (Futrell and Simi 2004). They also use these spaces to appraise their mobilization capacity, as well as prepare for and plan responses to repression they may face.

Clandestine movement spaces offer solace from the constant stigma faced by those on society's political, economic, and ideological margins. By definition, political extremism represents fringe ideas and actions that draw ire and repression from mainstream society. "The more stigmatized they are, the more costly it is to join" (Klandermans and Mayer 2006: 73). Some members escape by physically moving to underpopulated places to be left alone, even walling themselves off into private communities (Simi and Futrell 2015). But most extremists are constantly surrounded by those who vilify their beliefs. They live in the midst of those who oppose their political goals (Simi and Futrell 2009). They often hide their extremism day-to-day in an attempt to avoid the inevitable conflict that would come if they were to speak publicly about their beliefs. But, as Klandermans and Mayer (2006) explain, extremists are not likely to abandon their fellow activists because others denounce their beliefs, but instead respond to their stigma by more deeply committing to their cause. In this way, extremist stigma is "a resource for the movement, helping it to hold together" (ibid.: 73). Extremists' free spaces provide the organizational opportunities, including a "reservoir of experienced activists, ready-made action repertoires, and ideological interpretation frames on which to lean" (ibid.). Under these conditions, "radicalization and recruitment are local and highly personal tasks, involving interpersonal ties, bonds of solidarity, and trust" (Hafez and Mullins 2015: 964). The more diversified, available, and tightly-bounded the free spaces, the more likely activists will sustain their connections with other extremists and their commitment to the cause (Futrell and Simi 2004).

Despite the challenges, extremists across the political spectrum maintain "above-ground" organizations that engage in some aspects of institutional politics. Several European right-wing extremist groups support political parties that participate in state and national parliaments, such as France's *Front National*, Germany's National Democratic Party, Italy's *Alleanza Nazionale*, Austria's Freedom Party, and the Flemish *Vlaams Blok*. In the USA, several white power leaders publicly represent the Ku Klux Klan, Neo-Nazi, and Christian Identity groups. Militant jihadist groups follow public pronouncements of radical Islamic leaders, as illustrated in the case of the Islamic State of Iraq and Syria (ISIS), which controlled for a time large swaths of territory in Iraq and Syria and claimed a new caliphate. Left-wing groups such as the Animal Liberation Front (ALF), People for the Ethical Treatment of Animals (PETA), and the Earth Liberation Front (ELF), support a cadre of high-profile leaders, who elaborate ideological positions and provide legitimacy for their cause. Non-profit organizations, press officers, authors, university professors, and others offer moral, strategic, and financial support to underground activists (Liddick 2013). Yet, these public leaders struggle to mobilize activists as they walk a fine line legitimizing their opposition to issues that many people may support in principle, such as opposing wanton animal abuse and ecological destruction, while also representing extremist actions that compromise their legitimacy.

Internet activism

Extremists use the Internet as a powerful tool for organizing and sustaining their cause. Prior to the advent of the Internet, extremists' efforts to spread their message, recruit new members, and plan their actions were limited to relatively small audiences (Stern 1999). Today, cyberspace offers clandestine groups around the world a relatively safe, anonymous, easy way to disseminate information to broad audiences, coordinate their activities, and maintain social networks. Political extremists maintain websites in most of the world's regions accessible through Google and other similar search engines. However, the "dark net," which is accessible only through specialized software and offers complete anonymity, appears to harbor the most militant sites (Bartlett 2015; Mantel 2009).

The Internet is an efficient low-cost way for movements to distribute information about their causes (Earl and Kimport 2013; see Chapter 16 by Earl, in this volume). Many extremist websites offer users access to ideological writings and speeches, narratives about movement heroes, and other propaganda materials. Users can often download training manuals that discuss how to organize extremist cells, cultivate new recruits, avoid police surveillance, hack websites, build bombs, use weapons, and plot assassinations (Hale 2012). Some websites provide ongoing reports of "movement victories" in the form of rallies, marches, riots, and violence against their enemies. ISIS has notoriously used YouTube to publicize its executions in the name of jihad. Other sites provide access to extremist lifestyles, including accoutrements of the groups such as clothing, jewelry, flags, and other movement symbols, available for everyone from the most committed activist to the merely curious.

Extremists also leverage social networking technologies, such as web forums, blogs, wikis, digital games, Second Life, Twitter, YouTube and Facebook, where their posts celebrate violence and users seek to recruit new members (Hale 2012; Mantel 2009). These mechanisms allow users to upload content and engage in sustained interaction with other like-minded adherents, reach large numbers of people, and create "echo chambers" to reinforce extremist ideas (De Koster and Houtman 2008; Stevens and Neumann, 2009). Extremists' online interactions often bring them into a subculture full of coded language and exclusive symbolism, which can enhance users' sense of fellow-feeling (Bjelopera 2011; Hale 2012; Simi and Futrell 2006, 2015). Sageman (2008: 41) goes farther, arguing that "face to face radicalisation has been replaced by online radicalisation." Most studies, however, underscore the complementary nature of online and face-to-face networking (Pantucci 2011; Schmidle 2009; Simi and Futrell 2006; Stevens and Neumann 2009).

ISIS' web presence offers a sense of what relatively resource-rich extremists can do online. The movement has pursued a "state-of-the-art digital propaganda campaign" run by savvy graphic designers, marketers, and information technology experts (Carty 2015). Its primary Twitter account posts official announcements, while regional accounts offer live feeds that show ground-level activities in the provinces they control (Kingsley 2014). These activities include field operations, humanitarian community work, and mundane pursuits to paint them as "regular folks, just like the viewers, but on a political mission" (Carty 2015: 116). The group also manipulates Twitter hashtags to ensure that they trend in popularity, creating the impression that they have more followers than they actually do (Carty 2015; Kingsley 2014). Extremists link their tweets via hashtags to popular cultural events and non-political subjects to create "cross-talk" and spread their message beyond the already committed (Carty 2015; Graham 2016; Marszal 2014). ISIS also released a "Hollywood-caliber" feature-length film on YouTube, which paints the extremist group as "a dominant and invincible force" (Carty 2015; Kingsley 2014). Additionally, the group attempts to overcome language barriers (Mantel 2009) by translating their primary Arabic language into English for western audiences.

Castells (2005) observes that "the network society is a hyper social society, not a society of isolation" (see also Carty 2015; Earl and Kimport 2013). Extremists use the web to build expansive cyber-communities where they create and preserve their ideas and sustain virtual solidarity. Importantly, extremists also use their online activity to organize and extend their real-world activism within their locales and far beyond (Simi and Futrell 2006, 2015). Around the globe, extremist actions occur mainly at local levels, but they are adapting to the transnational nature of politics and their causes (Caiania and Krölla 2015). Extremists use the myriad virtual outlets as key mobilization resources to reach adherents and cultivate new ones beyond their locales and borders. von Merring and McCarthy (2013) note that international networking among extremists is on the rise, and formal international cooperation among right-wing extremists may indeed be on the horizon, especially in Europe. Globalization and the rise of Islamophobia have provided renewed motivation for transnational cooperation and an increase in populist movements, while the Internet offers the medium through which to connect (ibid.). The web "may act as a 'force' multiplier' for these types of groups, by enhancing [their communicative] power ... and allowing them to 'push above their weight'" (Caiania and Krölla 2015: 343).

Context and Strategy

There has been considerable effort among social movement scholars to study how movements come to embrace certain types of strategies and tactics, how these change over time, and how the use of strategies and tactics impact the effectiveness of movement mobilization (McAdam, McCarthy, and Zald 1996; Meyer 2007; Tilly 1978, 1986). Tilly's focus on a "repertoire of contention" described how movements adopt a "whole set of means … for making claims of different types on different individuals" (1986: 2). While strategies refer to a general overall plan, tactics include the specific methods or techniques actors use to achieve movement goals including the expression of discontent related to particular grievances. The focus on movement strategies and tactics is especially relevant for thinking about how extremism relates to social movements. In this section, we consider how extremism can, in some cases, be a response to political repression and the structure of political opportunities. We then discuss the emergence of strategies linked to more extreme tactics (e.g. vandalism, sabotage, personal assaults, and mass casualty violence such as shooting rampages and bombings).

Strategies and tactics typically change over a movement's life course (Whittier 1997). A more moderate movement may shift toward extremism as the movement redefines itself from "peaceful" to "antagonistic" (Wright 2007). By the same token, a movement that employs more extreme measures may moderate over time as members either seek mainstream legitimacy or leave the movement all together (Jenkins and Eckert 1986). Despite the conventional wisdom that terrorist organizations or individual members rarely moderate, quite the opposite is actually the case (Horgan 2009; LaFree and Miller 2008).

But even within the same historical moment, a movement may employ extreme tactics in one situation and moderate tactics in another. Extreme tactics are not all-encompassing nor totalizing in any simplistic fashion. As Tilly (2004) reminds us, too often we lose sight of the contextual circumstances related to when and how social movement actors come to rely on tactics that can be described as extreme. We should be cautious about ascribing labels like "extreme movement" lest we forget that all movements can be defined as such, depending on the circumstances. Maybe more importantly, Tilly also reminds us that legitimate state actors use extreme tactics that quite clearly meet standard definitions of terrorism. In fact, the vast majority of large-scale acts of violence are committed by nation-states rather than non-governmental organizations (Gurr 2015 [1970]). We now turn to the larger context critical to the formation of extreme strategies and tactics.

Political repression and violence

Extremism can be a by-product of the political context. In treacherous political environments secretive movements that work underground and exercise strong internal discipline have a competitive advantage over organizations that are open, loosely organized, and less hierarchical. To operate successfully in such circumstances a movement often adopts a radical ideology, uses violence as a strategy, and deals harshly with internal dissent. Movements that do not are more easily suppressed, clearing the field for organizations with a more radical and authoritarian cast.

Social movements, by definition, are working against a more powerful system that often has the means to use violence both legitimately and illegitimately (Melucci 1996; Snow 2004; Tilly 1978). In repressive states where political elites dominate by force, actors may have little choice but to respond by using violence. In settings characterized by government "death squads," such as El Salvador in the 1980s (Almeida 2008) or Apartheid South Africa (Seidman 2001), it is unclear whether dissidents' violent tactics would be considered extreme. As such, the specific tactics employed will depend, in part, on the type of opportunities available within a given context. More specifically, Almeida (2008) analyzed waves of protest over eight decades in El Salvador, and found that a shift to state-sponsored repression pushed democratic movements into revolutionary and violent forms of resistance. Similarly, White (1989) and Bosi (2006) both argued that the turn to violence of the Irish Republican Army was more a response to government repression than an expression of the intensity of group grievances.

This approach to explaining the features of social movements views tactical orientations as a response, in part, to the structure of political opportunities. In this sense, extremism is relational and what is considered extreme varies according to political context. In contexts where actors face repressive environments, violent tactics may simply be understood as "self-defense" as was the case with a number of organizations that represented the US black nationalist movement during the 1960s and 1970s (e.g. the Black Panther Party for Self-Defense) (Bloom and Martin 2013). To a large extent the perception of whether tactics are extreme hinge on whether these tactics are viewed as justified.

One area that is especially relevant to evaluating the relationship between social movements and extremism involves the policing of protest. The subfield underscores the importance of how movements interact with authorities and the public more broadly (della Porta and Reiter 1998; Earl 2003; Earl and Soule 2006; Earl, Soule, and McCarthy 2003). Earl (2003), in particular, points out important distinctions in terms of how different types of repression are likely to result in different outcomes in terms of movement mobilization.

Internal organizational dynamics and extremism

Although we see political context as one of the primary external conditioning forces shaping the development of extreme strategies and tactics, the next section outlines different types of internal movement dynamics where extremism is more likely to emerge. Extreme tactics may be highly visible such as a suicide bombing, but the planning of an extreme tactic often involves a series of much less visible or underground dimensions. In turn, underground spaces provide activists opportunities to build strong affective ties to each other that facilitate shifts in interpretive frames consistent with extremism (della Porta and Diani 2006).

Movement organizations may begin by using relatively normative tactics such as rallies, marches, and leafleting, but shift over time as activists come to perceive moderate tactics as ineffective. The transition to more extreme tactics may reflect a type of "learning curve" (Mead 1938) involving a cognitive reorientation where activists begin to consider violence as a necessary mobilization tactic (della Porta 1995). All movements incorporate some degree of secretive and hidden operations, but delineating the extent a movement operates in an underground fashion offers an important indicator of extremism. Broadly speaking, movements that rely on clandestine, underground tactics can be considered more extreme than open, transparent movements that primarily exist above ground. Previous studies have viewed the transition underground as reflecting a "cycle of protest" (Zwerman, Steinoff, and della Porta 2000) that combines the internal dynamics of the group, such as solidarity commitments and affective ties among members. Moving underground is both an individual and group decision that can be considered an individual and organizational turning point. Once a group commits to moving underground, certain tactics become preferred or consistent with the logic of underground mobilization. For example, during the 1960s the Student for Democratic Society (SDS) emerged as a left-wing nonviolent student-led movement organization promoting anti-war, anti-racism, and various progressive issues more generally (Sale 1974). In 1970, a small SDS splinter group formed the revolutionary faction, Weather Underground, which turned toward violent tactics, including a bombing campaign (Berger 2006; Rudd 2009).

But underground organization does not occur in vacuum. The emergence of highly clandestine operations are typically part of a larger movement culture and context. The term radical flank was originally introduced by Freeman (1975) to describe how more revolutionary groups generated both positive and negative effects for the more moderate sectors of the movement (see also Haines 1988). In some cases, splinters from an existing organization form as off-shoots or factions committed to more radical, direct action involving violence (Jenkins 1983; Marullo 1996; White 2010). In other cases, an entire movement group may shift toward radical tactics. The latter is illustrated by the recent evolution of the Nigerian-based Boko Haram. Led by Muhammad Yusef between 2002 and 2009, Boko Haram was relatively moderate, engaging only in low-level conflict with police and civilians opposed to their mission (Meehan and Speier 2011). Police repression increased in 2009, Yusef was killed, and Abubakar Shekau assumed leadership. Under Shekau, Boko Haram has become one of the world's most violent extremist organizations (Agbiboa 2013; Sani 2011; START 2013).

State repression is one type of organizational push that may encourage movements to adopt strategies and tactics aimed at undermining suppression. Many of these tactics are focused on promoting decentralized organizational principles. For example, leaderless resistance (LR) was originally formed as an anti-communist strategy in the 1960s aimed at the Soviet Union and Soviet Bloc countries to support Central Intelligence Agency (CIA) efforts (Michael 2012). More recently, the US and European far right have adopted LR. In 1992, white supremacist Louis Beam wrote an essay suggesting that previously unsuccessful far-right efforts were due to flawed tactics such as highly visible organizations, leaders, and members (Beam 1992). Left-wing and jihadi movements have also embraced LR to avoid detection while planning and executing violent plots. Far-right ideologues also promote "lone wolf terrorism" that encourages unaffiliated individual activists to attack without warning and conceal ties to any organization, movement, or other members (Michael 2012; Simon 2013). Most recently, ISIS released communiques directing adherents to pursue lone wolf attacks (Engel 2016: 2). Lone wolf activism relies on emulation and inspiration, creating ambiguity between violent plots directed by extremist leaders and purely individual acts.

The matter of assessing the relationship between extremism and movement tactics is complicated by several factors. Social movement actors may use certain terms in public to describe their tactics while using different terms behind closed doors. Left-wing actors are careful to avoid terms suggesting violence preferring terms like "direct action" (della Porta and Reiter 1998). Segments of the far right, however, often use terms that celebrate violence in music lyrics, group names, and various other slogans and movement imagery (Futrell, Simi, and Gottschalk 2006; Simi and Futrell 2015). At the same time, when individuals or small cells commit violent action, recognized leaders and organizations are reluctant to "take credit" and often careful about distancing themselves from these incidents to avoid legal and public relations problems (Simi and Futrell 2015). In contrast, various radical jihadi organizations like al-Qaeda and ISIS often claim responsibility for violent attacks as a means of bolstering their credibility and improving fundraising capacity (Ligon, Harms, and Derrick 2015).

Conclusion

We conclude with some questions about the relationship between extremism and social movements that need further study. Conceptual ambiguity remains a major obstacle to understanding extremism. We need to continue refining definitions so that they can be applied consistently across different groups and ideological orientations, no matter how awkward or distasteful they may be to study. At the same time, scholars should continue to consider any distinctive qualities that may characterize extremist efforts across ideological orientations. Researchers should also continue to study the relationship between violence and extremist ideas. In particular, under what conditions do extremist ideas produce extremist action, and precisely when do those who are not deeply committed to extremist ideas engage in extremist action?

As researchers continue to parse the relative importance of ideology to extremist movements, they should pay particular attention to religion's role (Gartenstein-Ross 2012; see Chapter 32 by Snow and Beyerlein, in this volume). Assessing the importance of religion, however, is very complicated. For example, some discourse suggests that the entire Muslim religion is inherently prone to violence or, alternatively, that religion has virtually nothing to do with extremist movements like ISIS or al-Qaeda. The first perspective clearly overgeneralizes from a relatively small number of extremists to a much larger global religious community. And, even in violent jihadist networks, ideological prescriptions vary (Snow and Byrd 2007). Hafez (2007) notices at least three distinct narratives of martyrdom within recruitment materials for jihadist suicide terrorism, rather than any single unified ideology. The latter perspective suggests that Islamic extremists are not "real" religious adherents, which can discourage important questions about how extremist movements interpret religious doctrine and use religion as a mobilizing resource.

Islam is certainly not the only religion that influences social movements and extremism. Christianity plays an important role among violent anti-abortionists (e.g. the Army of God) and the Christian Right more broadly. Segments of the US white supremacist movement have also mobilized around Biblical doctrine. Most notably, Christian Identity, which involves a radical reinterpretation of the Bible, argues that Aryans are "God's chosen people," Jewish people are the literal descendants of Satan, and "nonwhites" are not fully human (Aho 1990; Barkun 1994).

Such perspectives point out the nuance needed to understand extremist ideational work. Multiple and, sometimes competing, extremist narratives suggest a very complex process where certain individuals embrace particular beliefs and not others. Scholarship has long established that insurgents engage in a wide range of rhetorical activities to mobilize constituents. The framing perspective (Benford and Snow 2000; Snow 2004; Snow et al. 1986), in particular, has been useful in analyzing the signifying work or meaning construction by movements and their adversaries. More use of framing concepts to understand ideational processes among extremist groups could shed additional light on how shifts and changes in extremists' discursive activities affect mobilization strategies.

We also need comparative studies to examine similarities and differences along a number of dimensions. For instance, what commonalities and distinction are there between right-wing and left-wing radicals? Why does it seem that extremist movements are more effective than moderate movements in using social media and other information communication technologies to spread their ideas and mobilize adherents? Comparative work could also shed light on differences and similarities in mobilization patterns under different governmental regimes and political cultures. In all, we think paying further attention to extremism is warranted as this area provides important details about the character of politics, culture, activism, and society more broadly.

Notes

1   We do not make hard distinctions between the terms extremism and radicalism. From a conceptual standpoint we see them as largely interchangeable terms. Writers often use one of the terms to define the other. For instance, if Cross and Snow (2011) define radicals and radicalism as the people and "the practice of … extreme movement activity," then one can also define extremists and extremism as those who embrace and practice radical activism. Researchers will also use radicalization to refer to the process through which people come to embrace extremist ideology and tactics, though admittedly "extremization" has not caught on as a term for those who take on radical ideas and actions.

2   This distinction between belief and engagement is commonplace in most social movements (see, e.g. Klandermans and Oegema 1987 and Oegema and Klandermans 1994). One question that deserves further attention is whether there is less slippage between belief and engagement among the most extreme groups because they may be more exclusive and tightly bounded.

References

Agbiboa, Daniel. 2013. "The Ongoing Campaign of Terror in Nigeria: Boko Haram versus the State." *Stability, International Journal of Security and Development* 2:3. Available at: http://www.stabilityjournal.org/articles/10.5334/sta.cl/

Aho, James. 1990. *The Politics of Righteousness: Idaho Christian Patriotism*. Seattle, WA: University of Washington Press.

Almeida, Paul. 2008. *Waves of Protest: Popular Struggle in El Salvador, 1925–2005*. Minneapolis: University of Minnesota Press.

Barkun, Michael 1994. *Religion and the Racist Right: The Origins of the Christian Identity Movement*. Chapel Hill: University of North Carolina Press.

Bartlett, Jamie. 2015. *The Dark Net: Inside the Digital Underworld*. London: William Heinemann.

Beam, Louis. 1992. "Leaderless Resistance." *The Seditionist* February, issue 12. Available at: http://www.louisbeam.com/leaderless.htm

Benford, Robert D. and David A. Snow. 1992. "Master Frames and Cycles of Protest." In *Frontiers in Social Movement Theory*, edited by Aldon D. Morris and Carol McClurg Mueller, 133–155. New Haven, CT: Yale University Press.

Benford, Robert and David A. Snow. 2000. "Framing Processes and Social Movements: An Overview and Assessment." *Annual Review of Sociology* 26: 611–639.

Berger, Dan. 2006. *Struggle Within: Prisons, Political Prisoners, and Mass Movements in the United States*. Oakland, CA: PM Press.

Bjelopera, Jerome P. 2011. "American Jihadist Terrorism: Combating a Complex Threat." *Congressional Research Service Report for Congress*, Washington, DC: Congress Research Service.

Blee, Kathleen. 2002. *Inside Organized Racism: Women in the Hate Movement*. Berkeley: University of California Press.

Blee, Kathleen. 2006. "Can We Learn from Racists?" *Mobilization: An International Quarterly* 11(4): 479–482.

Bloom, Joshua and Waldo Martin. 2013. *Black against Empire: The History and Politics of the Black Panther Party*. Berkeley: University of California Press.

Borum, Randy. 2011. "Radicalization into Violent Extremism I: A Review of Social Science Theories." *Journal of Strategic Security* 4: 7–36.

Bosi, Lorenzo. 2006. "The Dynamic of Social Movement Development: Northern Ireland's Civil Rights Movement in the 1960s." *Mobilization* 11: 81–100.

Caiania, Manuela and Patricia Krölla. 2015. "The Transnationalization of the Extreme Right and the Use of the Internet." *International Journal of Comparative and Applied Criminal Justice* 39: 331–351.

Carty, Victoria. 2015. *Social Movements and New Technology*. Boulder, CO: Westview Press.

Castells, Manual. 2005. "The Network Society: From Knowledge to Policy." In *The Network Society: From Knowledge to Policy*, edited by Manuel Castells and Gustavo Cardoso. Washington, DC: Johns Hopkins Center for Transatlantic Relations.

Cross, Remy and David A. Snow. 2011. "Radicalism within the Context of Social Movements: Processes and Types." *Journal of Strategic Security* 4: 115–130.

De Koster, Willem and Dick Houtman. 2008. "'Stormfront Is Like a Second Home to Me': On Virtual Community Formation by Right-Wing Extremists." *Information, Communication & Society* 11: 1153–1175.

della Porta, Donatella. 1995. *Social Movements, Political Violence, and the State: A Comparative Analysis of Italy and Germany*. Cambridge: Cambridge University Press.

della Porta, Donatella. 2008. "Research on Social Movements and Political Violence." *Qualitative Sociology* 31(3): 221–230.

della Porta, Donatella and Mario Diani. 2006. *Social Movements: An Introduction*. Hoboken, NJ: Wiley.

della Porta, Donatella and Herbert Reiter. 1998. *Policing Protest: The Control of Mass Demonstration in Western Democracies*. Minneapolis: University of Minnesota Press.

Dobratz, Betty A. and Stephanie L. Shanks-Meile. 1997. *The White Separatist Movement in the United States: "White Power, White Pride!"* Baltimore, MD: Johns Hopkins University Press.

Earl, Jennifer. 2003. "Tanks, Tear Gas and Taxes: Toward a Theory of Movement Repression." *Sociological Theory* 21: 44–68.

Earl, Jennifer and Katrina Kimport. 2013. *Digitally Enabled Social Change: Activism in the Internet Age.* Cambridge, MA: MIT Press

Earl, Jennifer and Sarah A. Soule. 2006. "Seeing Blue: A Police-Centered Explanation of Protest Policing." *Mobilization* 11: 145–164.

Earl, Jennifer, Sarah A. Soule, and John D. McCarthy. 2003. "Protest Under Fire? Explaining Protest Policing." *American Sociological Review* 68: 581–606.

Engel, Pamela. 2016. "There's a Key Difference between Orlando Attack and Past ISIS-Claimed Massacres." *Business Insider*. Available at: http://www.businessinsider.com/isis-statement-orlando-shooting-attack-2016-6

Esseveld, Johanna and Ron Eyerman. 1992. "Which Side Are You On? Reflections on Methodological Issues in the Study of 'Distasteful' Social Movements." In *Studying Collective Action*, edited by Mario Diani and Ron Eyerman, 216–237. London: Sage.

Freeman, Jo. 1975. *The Politics of Women's Liberation: A Case Study of an Emerging Social Movement and Its Relation to the Policy Process.* Reading, MA: Addison-Wesley Longman Limited.

Futrell, Robert and Pete Simi. 2004. "Free Space, Collective Identity, and the Persistence of U.S. White Power Activism." *Social Problems* 51(1): 16–42.

Futrell, Robert, Pete Simi, and Simon Gottschalk. 2006. "Understanding Music in Movements: The White Power Music Scene." *The Sociological Quarterly* 47(2): 275–304.

Gartenstein-Ross, David. 2012. "A Blind Spot (Review of *Friction: How Radicalization Happens to Them and Us*)." Available at: http://www.daveedgr.com/news/friction-how-radicalization-happens-to-them-and-us/

Graham, Roderick. 2016. "Inter-ideological Mingling. White Extremist Ideology Entering the Mainstream on Twitter." *Sociological Spectrum* 36: 1–13.

Gurr, Ted. 2015 [1970]. *Why Men Rebel.* London: Routledge.

Hafez, Mohammed. 2007. *Suicide Bombers in Iraq: The Strategy and Ideology of Martyrdom.* Washington, DC: United States Institute of Peace.

Hafez, Mohammed and Creighton Mullins. 2015. "The Radicalization Puzzle: A Theoretical Synthesis of Empirical Approaches to Homegrown Extremism." *Studies in Conflict & Terrorism* 38: 958–975.

Haines, Herbert H. 1988. *Black Radicals and the Civil Rights Mainstream, 1954–1970.* Knoxville: University of Tennessee Press.

Hale, Chris W. 2012. "Extremism on the World Wide Web: A Research Review." *Criminal Justice Studies* 25: 343–356.

Horgan, John. 2009. *Walking Away from Terrorism: Accounts of Disengagement from Radical Extremist Movements.* New York: Routledge.

Ivarsflaten, Elisabeth. 2008. "What Unites Right-Wing Populists in Western Europe? Re-Examining Grievance Mobilization Models in Seven Successful Cases." *Comparative Political Studies* 41(1): 3–23.

Jenkins, Craig. 1983. "Resource Mobilization Theory and the Study of Social Movements." *Annual Review of Sociology* 9: 527–553.

Jenkins, J. Craig and Craig M. Eckert. 1986. "Channeling Black Insurgency: Elite Patronage and the Development of the Civil Rights Movement." *American Sociological Review* 51: 812–830.

Kingsley, Patrick. 2014. "Who Is Behind ISIS's Terrifying Online Propaganda Operation?" *The Guardian*, June 23. Available at: https://www.theguardian.com/world/2014/jun/23/who-behind-isis-propaganda-operation-iraq (accessed June 9, 2016).

Klandermans, Bert and Nonna Mayer. 2006. *Extreme Right Activists in Europe: Through the Magnifying Glass*. New York: Routledge.

Klandermans, Bert and Dirk Oegema. 1987. "Potentials, Networks, Motivations, and Barriers: Steps Towards Participation in Social Movements." *American Sociological Review* 52(4): 519–531.

LaFree, Gary and Erin Miller. 2008. "Desistance from Terrorism: What Can We Learn from Criminology?" *Dynamics of Asymmetric Conflict* 1: 203–230.

Liddick, Donald R. 2013. "The Radical Environmental and Animal Liberation Movements." In *Extremism in America*, edited by George Michael, 249–273. Gainesville: University Press of Florida.

Ligon, Gina, McKenzie Harms, and Douglas Derrick. 2015. "Lethal Brands: How VEOs Build Reputations." *Journal of Strategic Security* 8: 27–42.

Mantel, Barbara. 2009. "Terrorism and the Internet." *CQ Researcher*, 129–153.

Marszal, Andrew. 2014. "How ISIS Used Twitter and the World Cup to Spread its Terror." *The Telegraph*. Available at: http://www.telegraph.co.uk/news/worldnews/middleeast/iraq/10923046/How-Isis-used-Twitter-and-the-World-Cup-to-spread-its-terror.html (accessed June 9. 2016).

Marullo, Sam. 1996. "Frame Changes and Social Movement Contraction: U.S. Peace Movement Framing After the Cold War." *Sociological Inquiry* 66: 1–28.

McAdam, D. 2010. *Political Process and the Development of Black Insurgency, 1930–1970*. Chicago: University of Chicago Press.

McAdam, Doug, John D. McCarthy, and Mayer N. Zald. 1996. *Comparative Perspectives on Social Movements: Political Opportunities, Mobilizing Structures, and Cultural Framings*. Cambridge: Cambridge University Press.

McAdam, Doug, Sidney Tarrow, and Charles Tilly. 2003. *Dynamics of Contention*. Cambridge: Cambridge University Press.

McCauley, Clark R. and Sophia Moskalenko. 2008. "Mechanisms of Political Radicalization: Pathways Toward Terrorism." *Terrorism and Political Violence* 20: 415–433.

McCauley, Clark R. and Sophia Moskalenko. 2011. *Friction: How Radicalization Happens to Them and Us*. New York: Oxford University Press.

McVeigh, Rory. 2009. *The Rise of the Ku Klux Klan: Right-Wing Movements and National Politics*. Minneapolis: University of Minnesota Press

Mead, George Herbert. 1938. *The Philosophy of the Act*. Chicago: University of Chicago Press.

Meehan, Patrick and Jackie Speier. 2011. *Boko Haram: Emerging Threat to the U.S. Homeland*. Report from the U.S. House of Representatives Committee on Homeland Security, sub-committee on Counterterrorism and Intelligence [released November 30, 2011].

Melucci, Alberto. 1989. *Nomads of the Present*. London: Hutchinson Radius

Melucci, Alberto. 1996. *Challenging Codes: Collective Action in the Information Age*. New York: Cambridge University Press.

Meyer, David S. 2007. *The Politics of Protest: Social Movements in America*. Oxford: Oxford University Press.

Michael, George. 2012. *Lone Wolf Terror and the Rise of Leaderless Resistance*. Nashville, TN: Vanderbilt University Press.

Oegema, Dirk and Bert Klandermans 1994. "Why Social Movement Sympathizers Don't Participate: Erosion and Nonconversion of Support." *American Sociological Review* 59(5): 703–722.

Pantucci, Raffaello. 2011. "A Typology of Lone Wolves: Preliminary Analysis of Lone Islamist Terrorists." In *Developments in Radicalisation and Political Violence*, Kings College, London: International Centre for the Study of Radicalisation and Political Violence. Available at: http://www.trackingterrorism.org/sites/default/files/chatter/1302002992ICSRPaper_ ATypologyofLoneWolves_Pantucci.pdf (accessed June 8, 2016).

Polletta, Francesca. 2011. "Mobilization Forum: Awkward Movements." *Mobilization: An International Journal* 11: 475–478.

Rudd, Mark. 2009. *Underground: My Life with the SDS and the Weathermen*. New York: William Morrow.

Sageman, Marc. 2008. *Leaderless Jihad Terror Networks in the Twenty-First Century*. Philadelphia, PA: University of Pennsylvania Press.

Sale, Kirkpatrick. 1974. *SDS*. New York: Vintage Books.

Sani, Shehu. 2011. "Boko Haram: History, Ideas, and Revolt." *Vanguard Special Report*. Available at: http://www.vanguardngr.com/2011/07/boko-haram-history-ideas-and-revolt-4/ (accessed March 4, 2014).

Schmidle, Robert E. 2009. "Positioning Theory and Terrorist Networks." *Journal for the Theory of Social Behaviour* 40: 65–78.

Seidman, Gay. 2001. "Guerillas in Their Midst: Armed Struggle in the South African Anti-Apartheid Movement." *Mobilization* 6: 111–127.

Simi, Pete and Robert Futrell. 2006. "Cyberculture and the Endurance of White Power Activism." *Journal of Political and Military Sociology* 34: 115–142.

Simi, Pete and Robert Futrell. 2009. "Negotiating White Power Activist Stigma." *Social Problems* 56(1): 89–110.

Simi, Pete and Robert Futrell. 2015. *American Swastika: Inside the White Power Movement's Hidden Spaces of Hate*. Lanham, MD: Rowman & Littlefield Publishers.

Simi, Pete, Karyn Sporer, and Bryan Bubolz. 2016. "Narratives of Childhood Adversity and Adolescent Misconduct as Precursors to Violent Extremism: A Life Course Criminological Approach." *Journal of Research in Crime and Delinquency* 53(4): 536–563. doi: 10.1177/0022427815627312.

Simon, Jeffrey. 2013. *Lone Wolf Terrorism: Understanding the Growing Threat*. Washington, DC: IOS Press.

Snow, David. A. 2004. "Social Movements as Challenges to Authority: Resistance to an Emerging Conceptual Hegemony." In *Authority in Contention: Research in Social Movements, Conflict, and Change*, edited by Daniel J. Meyers and Daniel M. Cress. vol. 25, 3–25. New York: Elsevier.

Snow, David A. and Scott Byrd. 2007. "Ideology, Framing Processes, and Islamic Terrorist Movements." *Mobilization: An International Quarterly* 12: 119–136.

Snow, David A., E. Burke Rochford, Steven Worden, and Robert D. Benford. 1986. "Frame Alignment Processes, Micromobilization, and Movement Participation." *American Sociological Review* 51: 464–481.

Snow, David A. and Sarah A. Soule. 2010. *A Primer on Social Movements*. New York: W. W. Norton.

Sotlar, A. 2004. "Some Problems with a Definition and Perception of Extremism within a Society." In *Policing in Central and Eastern Europe: Dilemmas of Contemporary Criminal Justice*, edited by Gorazd Mesko, Milan Pagon, and Bojan Dobovsek, 703–707. Available at: https://www.ncjrs.gov/pdffiles1/nij/Mesko/208033.pdf

START. 2013. Global Terrorism Database. *Study of Terrorism and Responses to Terrorism*. Available at: http://www.start.umd.edu/gtd/ (accessed March 4, 2014).

Stern, Kenneth S. 1999. *Hate and the Internet*. New York: American Jewish Committee.

Stevens, Tim and Peter R. Neumann. 2009. *Countering Online Radicalisation: A Strategy for Action*. Kings College, London: International Centre for the Study of Radicalisation and Political Violence.

Tilly, Charles. 1978. *From Mobilization to Revolution*. Reading, MA: Addison-Wesley.

Tilly, Charles. 1986. *The Contentious French*. Oxford: Oxford University Press.

Tilly, Charles. 2004. *Social Movements, 1768–2004*. New York: Routledge.

Van Dyke, Nella, and Sarah A. Soule. 2002. "Structural Social Change and the Mobilizing Effect of Threat: Explaining Levels of Patriot and Militia Organizing in the United States." *Social Problems* 49: 497–520.

von Merring, Sabine and Timothy Wynn McCarthy. 2013. "Introduction." In *Right Wing Radicalism Today: Perspectives from Europe and the U.S.*, edited by Sabine von Merring and Timothy Wynn McCarthy, 1–12. New York: Routledge.

White, Robert. 1989. "From Peaceful Protest to Guerrilla War: Micro-Mobilization of the Provisional Irish Republican Army." *American Journal of Sociology* 94: 1277–1302.

White, Robert. 2010. "Structural Identity Theory and the Post-Recruitment Activism of Irish Republicans: Persistence, Disengagement, Splits and Dissidents in Social Movement Organizations." *Social Problems* 57: 341–370.

Whittier, Nancy. 1997. "Political Generations, Micro-cohorts, and the Transformation of Social Movements." *American Sociological Review* 62: 760–78.

Wright, Stuart A. 2007. *Patriots, Politics, and the Oklahoma City Bombing*. New York: Cambridge University Press.

Zwerman, Gilda, Patricia Steinoff, and Donatella della Porta. 2000. "Disappearing Social Movements: Clandestinity in the Cycle of New Left Protest in the U.S., Japan, Germany, and Italy." *Mobilization* 5: 85–104.

36

Nationalism, Nationalist Movements, and Social Movement Theory

HANK JOHNSTON

Introduction

In its broadest conceptualization, nationalism is an *idée-force* that has shaped the modern world, akin to other universal principles such as democracy, human rights, and socialism. Yet national identity is often overlaid upon these other ideas, as well as merged with political ideologies such as Leninism, Fascism, Maoism, and various religions (Roman Catholicism in Northern Ireland, Buddhism in Tibet, Islam in Chechnya) – and secularism too (i.e. the French Revolution and the Mexican Revolution). In different raiment, nationalism is the foundational principle of the modern state and contemporary national state system. For these two reasons, the plasticity of its mobilizing potential and the fact that it resides at the intersection of the state and society, nationalism should be an analytical concept of great importance to social movement researchers. Most obviously, it motivates some of the most destabilizing and violent manifestations of all forms of collective actions, especially outside of the democratic West.

Following Benedict Anderson (1991), nationalism is the articulation of an imagined national community, which was made possible by technologies and artifacts of a market culture in Europe: improved communication, roads, canals, national languages, large printing presses, and daily newspapers. Anderson holds that the "revolutionary vernacularizing thrust of capitalism" helped transcend local regional identifications and weakened tribal and feudal loyalties. National cultures and identities were solidified by the unifying symbolic work of politicians and intellectuals, such as promoting traditions, revising history, and recounting myths of origin (Connor 1978). Thus, European territorial aggregations based on the Treaty of Westphalia in 1648 were defined culturally and unified as never before, creating state organizations that, as other scholars have pointed out, were more conducive to war-making, trade, and defense of frontiers than archaic state forms (Mann 1993;

The Wiley Blackwell Companion to Social Movements, Second Edition. Edited by David A. Snow, Sarah A. Soule, Hanspeter Kriesi, and Holly J. McCammon.
© 2019 John Wiley & Sons Ltd. Published 2019 by John Wiley & Sons Ltd.

Tilly 1992). Numerous historians of nationalism have traced this association of a dominant national culture with the modern state (Gellner 1983; Hayes 1958, 1966; Kohn 1955; Smith 1986), noting links to the American Revolution, the French Revolution and, later, the reaction of Central European states to Napoleon's drive to create an empire. A fundamental theme in these studies was the relation of nationalism to the Enlightenment's notions of popular sovereignty, the principle that the authority to rule emanates from the people rather than being hereditary or divinely bestowed. In this way, articulating a narrative of the "nation" and all its meanings became a discursive tool of the ascendant bourgeois political class to legitimate their authority and dismiss the *ancien régime*.

Popular sovereignty plus nationalism equals a fundamental state-building dilemma that appeared in the nineteenth century and persists to this day, and which can be summed up in the question: Who precisely belongs to the nation? By defining a nation one way, one also draws a boundary line that categorizes others as nonnationals. These boundaries often exclude some citizens – minority ethnics – who reside within the national state, and for whom full rights are denied. It is not by chance, therefore, that shortly after new visions of the centralized national state diffused throughout Europe, encouraged by the French Revolution and the Napoleonic Wars, that the first wave of nationalist movements mobilized in 1848 against more traditional state forms such as the Hapsburg Empire (Hroch 1985). Reasons for this were that the *anciens régimes* did not reflect the ethnic-national identities of the people within their borders. State elites were, in a sense, foreign rulers who demanded taxes but limited the rights and representation of minority-national groups. Regional national identities, often based on linguistic patterns, were encouraged by local cultural and political elites as a means to pursue their own interests against those of empire. A defining characteristic of most nationalist movements is a link between a collective national identity and claims of territorial sovereignty (Hechter 2000).

Similar processes were at work one hundred years later as indigenous elites animated anticolonial movements in Asia and Africa against foreign rule (Strang 1992). Connor's juxtaposition of *nation building* and *nation destroying* (1972) captures this paradox, namely that building state legitimacy on defining a "nation" almost inevitably brings with it the exclusion of minority nationalities – immigrants and regional cultures – residing within the territory. It is generally accepted in the social sciences that "nation" does not refer to a state, as in member states of the United Nations, but rather to a large community of people with a common identity, of which a shared language, cultural patterns, and religion are usually the most basic elements.

Other elements of a nation include attachment to a territory or region, common history, shared traditions, rituals, myths, and uniting symbols, such as flags, anthems, and images. As such, nations refer to a people or an ethnic group, and are to be distinguished from the institutional political order of the state (Smith 1979). Thus, the common term "nation state" is technically incorrect in most instances because the vast majority of modern states are composed of several distinct ethnic-national groups. In many contemporary states, it is common that one ethnic-national group dominates political and economic institutions, which relegates other national groups to minority status (Connor 1978), raising the specter of deep and strong grievances based on Tilly's (1978) powerfully mobilizing catnet structures and giving rise to minority nationalist movements. Such movements should be considered as significant phenomena in the field of contentious politics.

The attentive reader will notice several different goals and dimensions of nationalism in our discussion so far. Brubaker (1992) has identified the three basic categories: (1) There are nationalisms of established states, which often have the timbre of jingoistic patriotism. This platform typically reflects the strategic attempts by political elites and entrepreneurs to fortify the national identity and garner electoral support for themselves and their programs, including mobilizing for war. This is a form of nationalism that enjoys institutional resources and support, such as the official patriotic youth movement Nashi that promotes state-sponsored Russian nationalism. State-facilitated nationalisms are often players in the field of minority-nationalist contention and boundary definition insofar as they represent powerful forces that stand against minority nationalist claims. (2) More central to social movement research are nationalisms of ethnic minorities within existing states who pursue territorial claims and/or civil and political rights. These include movements of separatism and of increased sovereignty and autonomy that are territorially delimited. The African-American civil rights movement in the USA was not a nationalist movement in this sense (although a Black-cultural nationalist wing emerged) because its political and civil rights claims were not directed toward any kind of territorial sovereignty. Finally, (3) there are the state-building nationalisms typical of the national liberation movements of the post-war period, when nationalist leaders sought to unify an ethnically diverse populace under the banner of a new and transcendent national identity. (4) Olzak (2013) adds a fourth category to Brubaker's that describes less-organized uprisings directed against target ethnic populations, which often take the form of mob violence. These would include, on the one hand, the manifestations of minority-nationalist anger against the majority, as in the Uyghur violence against Han Chinese in Urumqui in 2009, and in Osh, Uzbekistan, where Kyrgyz violence against Uzbeks left over 400 dead in 2010. On the other hand, there are episodes of majority violence – sometimes officially sanctioned – against ethnic minority groups, as in the current campaign against the Rohingya minority in western Rakhine state, Myanmar. These violent outbursts sometimes descend into broader campaigns of genocide and ethnic cleansing with the support of the state.

State-Facilitated Nationalisms

The first category of state nationalism recognizes the syncretism between the modern state and the definition of a people. The lesson that framing governance in terms of the nation and people imparts legitimacy was quickly learned by political elites vying for popular support in emerging European states (Duara 1996). Official nationalism can be seen in Russia today as a means of generating popular support for the state in the face of Western sanctions. It is used by the regime of General Abdel Fattah el-Sisi in Egypt to justify the curtailment of democratic liberties and legitimize his repressive policies of social control. Official nationalism often takes a militaristic color, as in fascist Italy, Germany, and Japan in the last century. It is not uncommon that elements of racism motivate popular support via notions of national traits and superiority. Manifestations of state nationalism often attract the attention of political scientists because they are articulated by the ruling parties, but – it is fair to say – are less studied by social movement researchers because of their institutional grounding. On the other hand, extremist right-wing nationalist groups and their contemporary permutations (the Tea Party, for example), often mobilizing in the liberal democracies of the West, fall fully within the field's scope of research and have been frequently studied (Skocpol and Williamson 2011; Van Dyke and Meyer 2014). Xenophobic movements of the majority often target minority groups residing within state boundaries as objects of denigration and exclusion. When minority nationalisms lead to secessionist movements and insurgencies, the interest of social movement researchers regretfully seems to fade, relinquishing attention to specialists in international relations and collective violence.

State-Destroying Nationalisms

Regarding Brubaker's second category, nationalist movements often seek to break away from the ruling state system and establish new, independent states based on the minority national identity. The illegitimacy and vulnerability of the majority-group governance are important factors in the opening of political opportunities for the mobilization of secessionist movements. Where states are weak, secessionist movements are more likely to be successful. According to Tarrow, Tilly, and McAdam, the drive for new states began early in the establishment of the European state system:

> First by generating resistance and demands for political autonomy on the part of culturally distinctive populations living within the perimeters of a nationalizing state. Second, by proselytizing among culturally related citizens of neighboring states—or at least providing support for their aspirations. Third, by providing clear, advantageous models of statehood for the envious gaze of would-be leaders of stateless would-be nations.
>
> (2001: 233)

Secessionist goals are common where the minority nationalist community is large, regionally concentrated, and the state is seen as politically unresponsive and repressive of minority national rights (such as linguistic rights, as in Catalonia and Quebec in the 1970s).

State boundaries fluctuate with wars and treaties, sometimes carving up a territory such that a region where an ethnolinguistic group resides is ceded to an adjacent state made up of a different national group. When this occurs, especially when there is a strong historical memory of territory lost, irredentism (or revanchism, a synonym) is a common subtype of secessionist ideology. Irredentism is when a national minority seeks to reattach to the adjacent state or reclaim an old state boundary often aided by neighboring states, or by groups and organizations within it, as in the case of support from the Republic of Ireland flowing to Sinn Féin in Northern Ireland. The Palestinian movement is an irredentist nationalism in that it seeks to reclaim territory that was lost when the state of Israel was created in 1948 and later in the Six Days War of June 1967 (Alimi 2007; Robinson 1997).

The nationalist movements in the former Soviet republics were secessionist, although most started – under constrained political opportunities – as movements demanding more democratic freedoms. While the Tibetan nationalist movement currently assumes a diffuse and clandestine form that only occasionally breaks the surface of public life, many of its proponents do not seek to accommodate to Chinese rule but rather resist it and ultimately seek succession from it. Because secessionist movements threaten the integrity of the state and the depletion of its territory and resources, they are almost always violently opposed by the state. China is made up of over 25 large national groups (over 500,000 members) and many more small ones. The communist regime has crushed Tibetan and Uyghur nationalist protests when they occurred, unwilling to entertain any challenges to Han Chinese ethnic dominance. Folkloric expressions such as dance and music festivals may be permitted, but political mobilization is not.

The same logic operates in contemporary Russia, which is a patchwork of over a hundred national minorities, of which six have populations over a million. One of these, the Chechens, mobilized a strong nationalist movement in the early 1990s, which Russia deemed a threat to its territorial integrity (Johnston 2008). Russia invaded Chechen territory to squelch secessionist claims, and for years, the Chechens fought vastly superior Russian forces to a stalemate, twice forcing Russian withdrawals and winning de facto independence. Yet allowing one rebellion to succeed would establish an unwanted precedent, and this was a road down which Moscow was unwilling to travel. Ultimately, the Russian army crushed the Chechen insurgency and reincorporated the war-torn region into the Russian federation. Although estimates vary, a conservative figure for civilian deaths in the two Chechen wars is 200,000. Secessionist wars have been among the great tragedies of the last century (Gurr 2000). The nationalist claims of the Ibo people of Nigeria in great part precipitated the Nigerian civil war, 1967–1970, which claimed over two million lives. The secessionist war of East Pakistan in 1971 led to the creation of Bangladesh and caused the death of an estimated three million. In 1992–1995, the Bosnian war fueled the ethnic cleansing and genocide in which close to 100,000 are thought to have died, and 2.2 million were forced to flee from their homes.

National Liberation Movements

Movements for independence by colonized peoples parallel secessionist movements in that they too mobilize against ethnically (racially) based subordination. Anticolonial nationalist movements were common in the post-war period of the twentieth century as European powers, weakened by World War II, were challenged by national liberation fronts in Asia and Africa. Because colonial societies in Africa and Asia were often segmented and/or tribal, anticolonial nationalism was a powerful unifying ideology. As nationalist liberation movements gathered strength, they sometimes could gain the peaceful acquiescence of the colonial power to withdraw and grant independence. In other instances, long wars of independence had to be fought, as in Indochina, Algeria, and Angola.

The model of state-seeking nationalisms was attractive to leaders of nationalist movements of independence in Asian and Africa (and before that in Latin America during the nineteenth century). In Burma and Malaya, nationalist movements mobilized against British colonial rule. Ho Chi Minh blended nationalism and Marxism in the movement against the French. In India, Gandhi transformed the Indian National Congress into a mass-based movement of national resistance against the British, culminating in Indian independence in 1947. Hechter (2000) notes that it is common that colonial rule involved the best and the brightest of the local population in colonial administration, and that the weakening of colonial rule often led to the politicization of local elites in the two directions mentioned above, either as leaders of nation-building movements or as leaders of local ethnic groups who resist state-building by the new majority. Ethnically distinct groups, whose identities were given shape by colonial administrations, see their opportunities limited in new states. In such cases, it is common that former colonially trained local administrators are leaders in congealing minority-national claims in newly independent states.

National identity, collective identity, and social psychology

The historiography of nationalism studies identifies a period when assumptions of political, economic, and social development guided by nation-building perspectives pointed to the inevitable erosion of minority-national and regional identities in modern states (Deutsch 1953; Lipset and Rokkan 1967). The idea was that old local and tribal identifications were residues of the past and will or should be replaced by a broader legitimizing conception of citizenship-based patriotic identification with the state and nation. Notice how this perspective proposes an official, state-facilitated, broad national identity, usually based on majority-group ethnicity that elides recognition that minority-national ethnic groups may be reluctant to participate in the project. This tension was common among the new states being formed out of former colonies in Africa and Asia in the postwar period. The political instability of these states, plus the appearance of minority nationalisms in Europe as it recovered from World War II, led scholars to ponder the "primordial" foundation of communal identities as something that is not easily replaced by broader categories of nonethnic definitions of civic citizenship.

Geertz (1963) used the term "primordial" to suggest that tribal and minority-ethnic identifications were so basic that they must be accommodated in building new states. Connor (1972) suggested that a primordial quality to ethnic identification explained the resurgence of Western minority nationalist movements in the 1960s – in Quebec, Scotland, Wales, the Basque region, to name a few. Even today, studies of civil wars and collective violence often take national identity as basic and immutable, rather that seeing it as a social construction emergent from diverse social forces (James 1999; Trevor-Roper 1983). Social psychological experiments also frequently reflect unrecognized biases of taking ethnic and racial categories as givens (Reicher and Hopkins 2001a). From these unconscious assumptions of difference, it is a short step to formulations of primordialism that draw upon vague biological and racial references. These are today widely rejected by the social sciences, even though in the popular press references to national essence are invoked frequently, say, regarding Israel-Palestine, Serbia-Kosovo, or Kurdistan-Turkey (Chandra 2012).

It is entirely plausible that, if there is any truth in the term "primordial," it lies in the intersection of fundamental cognitive processes with the imprints of early socialization rather than in biology (Johnston 1985). I have in mind that ethnic ties are primary or primordial in ways that parallel the fundamental identifications with immediate family and extended kin – composing a basic dimension of social identity derived from early socialization in the language spoken at home, among friends and family – that form influential templates but not immutable ones (Johnston 2008), powerful in shaping behavior under the right conditions but not determined in terms of content. Although primordialism is widely dismissed today in favor of the nation as an imagined community, socially constructed over time, it makes sense that constructivist perspectives should not completely deny the social-psychological and cognitive depth of ethnic-national identities, and that there are strong human tendencies to identify that way, especially given the emotions and intensity that nationalism can invoke. Let us see what a nuanced approach to the collective identity of nationalist movements might look like – one that melds findings of constructivism with empirical findings in social psychology about identity, categorization, and social cognition, and one that helps explain the passion and emotion that nationalist identity evokes.

Prior to World War II, the social psychology of intergroup relations often focused on the measurement of ethnic and racial differences, thereby "legitimizing the ideas of class, national, and, in particular, racial hierarchies" (Reicher and Hopkins 2001a: 384). After the war, important research in social psychology explored ethnic and racial prejudice, stereotyping, identities, and categorization processes, with the normative goal of reducing prejudice and ethnic/racial discrimination. Allport's (1954) *The Nature of Prejudice* was a significant early contribution in this corpus. Especially relevant were studies that shed light on how ethnocentrism, conformity, and stereotyping help construct, confirm, and intensify national identification. Sherif and colleagues' schoolboy exercise at Robbers Cave camp (1961) showed how the unequal distribution of scarce resources among temporary (but strongly ethnocentric) social groups can lead to intergroup conflict. As a whole, these studies pointed to several fundamental social psychological and cognitive processes that lie at the base of social identification. For scholars of nationalism, they help drive its articulation at a micro-analytical level, and raise research questions regarding how these processes are shaped by structural and leadership factors at the macro level. This micro-macro intersection also raises plausible hypotheses about both the strength of national identity and the limits to its transcendence, say, forging multiethnic conceptions of citizenship or pan-movements of identification, such as pan-African, pan-Arab, and pan-European identities.

There is a large literature in social psychology relevant to national identity, which does not often find its way to the field of contentious politics. One strand of research explores the layering and contextualization of different aspects of identity, and how they affect action (Tajfel 1981; Tajfel and Turner 1979; Turner 1982). Known as the social identity perspective, Tajfel, Turner, and colleagues have proposed a structure of the self that is characterized by two basic dimensions. First and foundational is personal identity, a focus more typical of psychology, which captures the individual level of development and continuity of being oneself (Erikson 1968). Second, social-identity research has specifically explored those aspects of identity that derive from group membership and its basis in drawing in-group and out-group distinctions. Depending on social context and behavior, different social identities will come to the foreground and others will lie dormant. Structural relations will privilege some identities over others and impart a degree of identity stability. They also will politicize them when group interests come into conflict (Simon and Klandermans 2001). This politicization is partly driven and intensified by processes that social psychological research has linked with social identity: conformity, ethnocentrism, in-group and out-group stereotyping, homogeneity biases, and favoritism (Fiske 2000; Oakes, Haslam, and Reynolds 1994; Turner et al. 1987).

Ethnocentrism contributes to high valuation of one's own group and characteristics (Tajfel 1981). Also, there is a large body of social psychological research in the social cognition perspective that sees several tendencies relevant to nationalism as products of basic cognitive processes. Complex intergroup realities are processed and categorized to make them understandable, even when perception is faulty, unreliable, or limited. These are fundamental processes in how people think, define themselves, and define the groups they belong to. Thus, it is not uncommon that nationalist movements draw upon these responses among members in ways that may lead to radicalism and violence. If the school boys at the Robbers Cave camp (Sherif et al. 1961), acting on a collective identity only two weeks old, attacked their opponents over an unjust distribution of prizes, how much more potential for violence resides in the coalescence of forces when the stakes are higher? To this, in the real world, one must add the accelerating and intensifying effect of political entrepreneurs creating national narratives of past greatness, present grievances, and future triumphs to mobilize support. Reicher and Hopkins (2001b) have elaborated an approach to nationalism based on social categorization mechanisms. They emphasize how the cognitive tendencies of ethnocentrism and stereotyping that animate nationalism are powerful but highly contextual. Thus, these social psychological tendencies are susceptible to different narrative definitions as strategically mobilized by political elites, all drawing on a metanarrative of the nation. Their analysis of narratives of Scottish nationalism shows how different political entrepreneurs activate nationalist identifications that are both compelling and contextual.

Applied to nationalist movements, these processes can impart intensity to national identification that, in most other kinds of social movements, is found among only the most committed activists. Explorations of emotional dimensions of mobilization, which have threaded through social movement theory for the past 20 years, suggest that national pride and resentment of collective subordination are powerful motivators for collective action (Flam 2015; Goodwin, Jasper, and Polletta 2001). Reflexive emotions, that is, those emotions that have a physiological and automatic basis (Goodwin, Jasper, and Polletta 2004), can transform persistent national resentment and shared affective bonds into intense episodes of conflict. While interethnic violence sometimes occurs outside the context of nationalist movements, many of same emotions are present when movement groups take up arms or invade an ethnic neighborhood. The genocide in Rwanda was not part of a nationalist movement, but the ethnic cleansing in Sarajevo was. In a related vein, the genocide in Darfur represents a case where the state mobilized nationalist sentiments of the Arab majority in the north to oppose a regional ethnic-national minority's claims of political autonomy in the south. Because modern states claim a monopoly on the means of violence, when they invoke majority national identities as justifications for mobilization, it is common that emotions can precipitate a violent turn. In response, regional nationalist movements often take up arms to defend themselves, especially when there is a compelling territorial basis to their claims. The volatility of nationalist identity and the emotions associated with it produce a strong correlation between nationalist violence and the demagoguery and manipulation by nationalist leaders.

Structural factors in nationalist mobilization

The microsociological basis of national identity and its emotional underpinnings do not by themselves lead to mobilization. Research in sociology and political science has sought to identify the array of meso- and macro-level factors that bring salience to nationalist identities and make them relevant for political mobilization. Indeed, this level of analysis has driven theoretical work for the past 50 years since the resurgence of social-scientific interest in minority-ethnic nationalisms as a counterpoint to nation-building perspectives (Almond and Coleman 1960; Apter 1967; Connor 1972; Geertz 1963). In the empirical world one encounters nationalist parties that compete in democratic political arenas such as in Scotland, Quebec, and Catalonia, minority-nationalist violence as with the Basque ETA in Spain or the Kurdish PKK in Turkey, national liberation movements characteristic of postcolonial struggles in Africa and Asia, unobtrusive but simmering nationalist sentiments, such as in Tibet, Dagestan, or Xinjiang, and irredentist nationalisms as with the Albanian Kosovars in Serbia and Armenians in Nagorno-Karabakh. Movements in all these categories pose challenges to the integrity of the state, but take many different forms regarding goals, strategies, and tactics, and mobilization structures. Given this array of manifestations, the study of nationalist movements is squarely situated in the field of contentious politics, writ large (McAdam, Tarrow, and Tilly 2001: Chapter 8). Recognizing the varieties of state governance and economic development, especially regarding labor markets and the cultural division of labor – theoretical explanations give meso- and macro-level variables and mechanisms different weights and combinations. The task is to systematize our thinking about how patterns of ethnic-based inequalities and subordination in different state systems might lead to different permutations of nationalist mobilization.

Party Nationalism in Democratic States

The openness of state institutions – for example, when ethnic minorities enjoy legal protection and access to open channels of political representation – influences the trajectory and strategies of nationalist movements. In democratic states, it is common that nationalist movements pursue political party mobilization, plebiscites about regional autonomy, and cultural promotion. Movements here are composed of party organizations, NGOs that promote the minority language and culture, and culturally themed citizen groups that freely operate. National identification may be strong among many citizens, but the availability of civil liberties and institutional political channels tends to undercut the attractiveness of nationalist movements as the main vehicle of interest articulation, paralleling a political opportunity explanation of protest (Eisinger 1973). However, Wilkinson (2004) has found that the embedded presence of ethnic-based parties can sometimes have the opposite effect of increasing the volatility of nationalist politics, as in his study of India.

In democracies, citizens balance a complex array of interests, claims, grievances, and identities, as the pluralist model of cross-cutting political allegiances would predict. Because of this, and because a territorial basis for minority nationalist identity is mostly absent, nationalist movements in the United States are few and relatively weak. There were strands of Black, Chicano, and American Indian nationalism in the 1960s and 1970s, but these were represented by relatively small groups pursuing cultural and/or extreme political demands within broader ethnic-based movements for civil rights and economic opportunities. In other developed democracies of the West, when territoriality is added to the mix, nationalist movements may become potent political forces, such as in Quebec, Scotland, Catalonia, and Euzkadi, but primarily driven by institutional political contention. State responsiveness to less extreme demands, as exemplified by widespread linguistic accommodation or the creation of regional political institutions, as in Canada and the UK, means that more extreme groups pursuing full political independence, are marginalized, rejected by most citizens in favor of the benefits of remaining within the existing state. Smaller nationalist movements in Western democracies, such as Welsh, Breton, Lombard, South Tyrolean, Corsican, and Sami, are weak for several reasons. Citizens with strong and animating national identities are few. The benefits that derive from state membership, especially when its policies encourage ethnic pluralism and affirmative action, may be considerable. Also, overall levels of ethnic discrimination may be relatively low, and economic opportunities – while perhaps not abundant in an affirmative-action sense – may be widely available within the existing state.

Labor Market Inequalities and Ethnic Competition

If parties are key mobilizing structures of minority nationalism in democracies, the necessary causal question is, what gives rise to them? What drives the clustering of interests along minority-nationalist definitions rather that other configurations available in open polities, such as class, values, gender, or policy issues? An early insight among sociologists of minority nationalisms was that labor market inequalities play a key role. Notably, these studies were in Western societies, where one might expect the homogenizing effects of industrialization, urbanization, media, and market to mitigate their salience. Hechter's thesis of internal colonialism (1975) was predicated upon his analysis of "Celtic fringe" in the United Kingdom. He applied dependency-theory concepts of core and peripheral regions and the exploitation of the former by the latter to patterns of unequal industrialization in Britain, showing how the English industrial center diverted wealth and resources from Scotland, Wales, and Ireland. The result was a "cultural division of labor," akin to Bonachich's (1972) notion of a "split labor market" along ethnic lines. In the Celtic regions, it was the English who were the majority ethnic group that dominated positions in enterprise, higher-level management, and administration, relegating minority ethnics in each region to subordinate employment and creating overlapping class and ethnic cleavages. The translation of these structural relations to contentious politics was accomplished primarily by regional politicians and cultural entrepreneurs. They emphasized the distinctiveness of minority cultures, which had been fading for some time, as a key element in the strategy of nationalist political mobilization. Thus, the

Scottish Nationalist Party, Plaid Cymru in Wales, and Irish nationalism all have roots that date back to English "internal colonial" development of the British Isles. The resurgence of modern minority nationalist parties rests on the hyper-accentuation of fading regional cultures to make claims against core-imposed labor market inequities. Diez-Medrano (1994) concluded that the cultural division of labor mechanisms shaped voting patterns in the Basque country after Spain's transition to democracy. Mettam and Williams (1998) examined employment patterns from the Estonian Soviet Republic – that is, before Estonia's independence – to propose that a cultural division of labor contributed to Estonian nationalist identity.

Another theoretical approach related to labor markets is the ethnic competition model, which emphasizes the articulation of ethnic boundaries through increasing contact. Among its proponents, Olzak (1983, 1992) and Nagel and Olzak (1982) suggested that economic development and modernization brought ethnic groups into sustained competition for resources, most notably for jobs, and this increased ethnic conflict. Their model held that ethnic competition increases within labor markets – rather than the stratification of labor markets *à la* internal colonialism. While ethnic competition can take many forms, of which a nationalist movement is just one manifestation, several of the main proponents of this view were well versed in the social movement literature, and the mobilization of minority nationalist parties was never far from the perspective's agenda. Many of the studies that probed the ethnic-competition perspective employed the analysis of voting data as the methodology of choice: Nielsen (1980) regarding support for the Flemish nationalist party, Ragin (1979), regarding Welsh nationalism; Diez-Medrano (1994) in the Basque country; Olzak (1982) regarding Québécois nationalism.

As the ethnic-competition model was being developed, a focus on resources and organization guided much social movement research in North America. The competition model drew upon resource mobilization insights to explain why some groups mobilize along ethnic lines. It followed McCarthy and Zald's (1977) paradigmatic observation that, rather than mitigating collective grievances, prosperity increases mobilization because more resources become available to facilitate collective action. The ethnic competition model combined this logic with evidence of increasing labor-market competition to explain several minority-nationalist parties in the most advanced societies of Europe and North America, as well as ethnic mobilizations that were not territorially based, such as the Black civil rights movement, the Chicano movement, and the American Indian movement. Sharpening ethnic boundaries was a powerful tool of politicians to strengthen participation in regionalist parties. Barth's (1969) insights on ethnic boundaries provided the conceptual justification for resource mobilization concepts based on a social constructionist approach to ethnic identities. For participants of a nationalist movement, stressing one's minority-nationalist identity imparted a collective basis to perceived injustices. For political and cultural elites, articulating, for example, Scottish, Breton, Welsh, or Lombard identities – which, according to modernization theory, would have been in retreat for decades – was a political strategy to mobilize a nationalist political base. In this sense, minority-national identities were intentionally constructed as an "interpretative resource" for mobilization, as opposed to being "primordially" dormant and awaiting activation in the Geertzian sense (1963). Analytically, a focus on the social construction of ethnic boundaries allowed for aggregation of organizational and material resources to wage political battle for nationalist parties.

Conclusion: Nationalist Movements in the New Millennium

I conclude by pointing out that a considerable body of research presents evidence for labor market factors giving rise to politicized ethnicity. Hechter and Okamoto (2001: 197) suggest that empirical support for both the internal colonial and ethnic competition models may be explained by variations in levels and focus of analysis: internal colonialism can explain persistent ethnic segmentation; ethnic competition processes explain timing and mobilization. Both models recognize the role of political entrepreneurs who "play the ethnic card" in minority-nationalist mobilization. This is an observation that also applies to the recent rise of right-wing populism in European and North American democracies. In the United States, Trump's 2016 presidential campaign appeals to white-working-class fears of job loss and articulates anti-immigrant xenophobia. This is the other side of minority nationalist mobilization, namely, jingoistic, majority-group nationalism that taps the social-psychological and emotional elements of threatened group identity. While labor market competition remains a factor in Trumpism and the Independence Party in the UK, anti-immigration and anti-Muslim themes in rightist platforms indicate other mechanisms of ethnic boundary-making than just demagoguery by political entrepreneurship. Also, both the internal-colonial and ethnic-competition models are linked to theories that recent research has transcended and/or elaborated in new directions. Internal-colonial concepts were based on dependency-theory and world-system analysis of the 1970s. The ethnic competition model was based on resource mobilization concepts of the 1980s. While resource-mobilization insights include some enduring findings in the field of social movement research, recent theoretical work has moved into new areas that hold promise for deepening our understanding of the complexity of nationalist mobilization in the new millennium.

Notably Wimmer's (2013) analysis of ethnic boundary-making charts a course that reflects several strands of social movement research that are more current, specifically reflecting an interest in identifying generalizable processes and mechanisms of contentious politics. His aim is to chart a research program based on a dynamic approach to boundaries. For social movement scholars, this process-and-mechanism focus will ring familiar as a theme of the dynamics of contention perspective (McAdam, Tarrow, and Tilly 2001; see also McAdam and Tarrow 2011), but Wimmer applies it to how ethnic boundaries change and/or become solidified. Moreover, his analysis draws upon two additional – and even more recent – theoretical threads that bring contentious politics to the foreground of the boundary-making process.

Wimmer articulates a Bourdieusian field theory approach to understand how social actors are relationally situated in ways that shape their strategic choices and power. Field theory directs attention to the opportunities and constraints of defining identity boundaries, and on the dynamic ways that these play out. The implications for movement research are apparent regarding conceptualizing the strategic interaction of civic and state actors in the field of play (see Fligstein and McAdam 2012; McAdam and Boudet 2012). The interplay between the state and challenging nationalist actors becomes the defining element of the mobilization field. Wimmer also draws on network theory to chart how field positions provide access to resources, including symbolic ones, to wage battles over boundaries and impart to them historical stability.

Here too, the network perspective on ethnic boundaries parallels recent developments in social movement analysis, especially Mische's (2008) work on cultural domains and the strategic use of symbolic resources in activist networks (see also Diani 2015; Diani and Mische 2015). Wimmer's aim is to identify the mechanisms of boundary change that the ethnic competition model left implicit by taking for granted extreme social constructionism, an assumption that failed to see the network and field-derived ways that ethnic definitions are guided and shaped.

A field perspective on nationalist movements identifies processes that suggest a fine-grained complexity of players on both the movement's and the state's side of the turf. Simple dichotomies of minority versus majority identities, and of a challenging nationalist movement versus the majority state, miss a great deal of detail. There is a body of research that indicates that boundary-making and boundary-enforcing start with the "quotidian disruption" (Snow et al. 1998) characteristic of minority-ethnic life. The focus here is not on majority political elites and policy-makers, but local police and petty bureaucrats who enforce discriminatory policies every day. Even prejudice from neighbors add a personalized layer to those policies by tone of voice, small insults, and, generally, making life difficult for nationalist minorities. These observations mean that a more empirically accurate conceptualization of the field of nationalist movement contention must move beyond a simple challenger-state dichotomy to incorporate the complex networks of interaction among different levels of state organization and the movement groups, organizations, and central actors.

Finally, in addition to microsociological processes of boundary-making, a body of research has emerged that points to additional players in the field of play at the most macro-level. Nationalist movements mobilize in state systems, which in turn are embedded in the expanding system of global economic integration and international regimes of human rights, indigenous rights, and rights of self-determination (Olzak 2006). As globalization spreads a world culture that values human rights and civil liberties, nationalist claims are fostered by networks of activists in non-governmental organizations that promote the discourse of minority-national self-determination and justice. The availability of global-level channels of claim-making through NGO pressure on states opens political opportunities and encourages nationalist movements, not only in developed states but also less developed ones. We conclude, therefore, by observing that there are not only new players in the boundary-making field of ethnic contention, but they are also operative at the micro- and macro-levels of analysis.

References

Alimi, Eitan Y. 2007. *Israeli Politics and the First Palestinian Intifada*. New York: Routledge.

Allport, Gordon W. 1954. *The Nature of Prejudice*. Reading, MA: Addison-Wesley.

Almond, Gabriel, and James Coleman. 1960. *The Politics of Developing Areas*. Princeton, NJ: Princeton University Press.

Anderson, Benedict. 1991. *Imagined Communities*. Rev. edn. London: Verso.

Apter, David. 1967. *The Politics of Modernization*. Chicago: University of Chicago Press.

Barth, Fredrick. 1969. *Ethnic Groups and Boundaries*. Los Angeles: Sage.

Bonachich, Edna. 1972. "A Theory of Ethnic Antagonism: The Split Labor Market." *American Sociological Review* 37: 547–559.

Brubaker, W. Rogers. 1992. "Citizenship Struggles in Soviet Successor States." *International Migration Review* 26(2): 269–291.

Chandra, Kanchan. 2012. *Constructivist Theories of Ethnic Politics*. New York: Oxford University Press.

Connor, Walker. 1972. "Nation Building or Nation Destroying." *World Politics* 24: 319–335.

Connor, Walker. 1978. "A Nation is a Nation, Is a State, is an Ethnic Group, is a…" *Ethnic and Racial Studies* 1: 377–400.

Deutsch, Karl. 1953. *Nationalism and Social Communication*. Cambridge, MA: MIT Press.

Diani, Mario. 2015. *The Cement of Civil Society: Studying Networks in Localities*. New York: Cambridge University Press.

Diani, Mario and Anne Mische. 2015. "Network Approaches and Social Movements." In *The Oxford Handbook of Social Movements*, edited by Donatella della Porta and Mario Diani, 306–325. Oxford: Oxford University Press.

Diez-Medrano, Juan. 1994. "The Effects of Ethnic Segregation and Ethnic Competition of Political Mobilization in the Basque Country, 1988." *American Sociological Review* 59: 873–889.

Duara, Prasenjit. 1996. "Historicizing National Identity, or Who Imagines What and When." In *Becoming National*, edited by Geoff Eley and Ronald Grigor Suny, 151–178. New York: Oxford University Press.

Eisinger, Peter. 1973. "The Conditions of Protest Behavior in American Cities." *American Political Science Review* 67: 11–28.

Erikson, Erik. 1968. *Identity: Youth and Crisis*. New York: W. W. Norton.

Fiske, Susan T. 2000. "Stereotyping, Prejudice, and Discrimination at the Seam between the Centuries: Evolution, Culture, Mind, and Brain." *European Journal of Social Psychology* 30: 299–322.

Flam, Helena. 2015. "Micromobilization and Emotions." In *The Oxford Handbook of Social Movements*, edited by Donatella della Porta and Mario Diani, 264–276. Oxford: Oxford University Press.

Fligstein, Neil and Doug McAdam. 2012. *A Theory of Fields*. New York: Oxford University Press.

Geertz, Clifford. 1963. "The Integrative Revolution: Primordial Sentiments and Civic Politics in New States." In *Old Societies New Societies*, edited by Clifford Geertz, 105–157. New York: The Free Press.

Gellner, Ernst. 1983. *Nations and Nationalism*. Oxford: Blackwell.

Goodwin, Jeff, James M. Jasper, and Francesca Polletta. 2001. *Passionate Politics: Emotions and Social Movements*. Chicago: University of Chicago Press.

Goodwin, Jeff, James M. Jasper, and Francesca Polletta. 2004. "Emotional Dimensions of Social Movements." In *The Blackwell Companion to Social Movements*, edited by David A. Snow, Sarah A. Soule, and Hanspeter Kriesi, 413–432. London: Blackwell.

Gurr, Ted Robert. 2000. *Peoples Versus States: Minorities at Risk in the New Century*. Washington, DC: United States Institute of Peace.

Hayes, Carleton J. H. 1958. The *Historical Evolution of Modern Nationalism*. New York: Russel and Russel.

Hayes, Carleton J. H. 1966. *Essays on Nationalism*. New York: Macmillan.

Hechter, Michael. 1975. *Internal Colonialism*. London: Routledge.

Hechter, Michael. 2000. *Containing Nationalism*. New York: Oxford University Press.

Hechter, Michael and Dina Okamoto. 2001. "Political Consequences of Minority Group Formation." *Annual Review of Political Science* 4: 189–215.

Hroch, Miroslav. 1985. *The Social Preconditions of National Revival in Europe*. New York: Cambridge University Press.

James, Simon. 1999. *The Atlantic Celts*. Madison, WI: University of Wisconsin Press.

Johnston, Hank. 1985. "Catalan Ethnic Mobilization: Some 'Primordial' Revisions of the Ethnic Competition Model." *Current Perspectives in Social Theory* 6: 129–147.

Johnston, Hank. 2008. "Ritual, Strategy, and Deep Culture in the Chechen National Movement." *Critical Studies on Terrorism* 1: 321–342.

Kohn, Hans. 1955. *Nations and Nationalism*. New York: D. Van Nostrand.

Lipset, Seymour Martin and Stein Rokkan. 1967. *Party Systems and Voter Alignments*. New York: Free Press.

Mann, Michael. 1993. *The Sources of Social Power: The Rise of Classes and Nation States, 1716–1914*. New York: Cambridge University Press.

McAdam, Doug and Hillary Boudet. 2012. *Putting Social Movements in their Place*. New York: Cambridge University Press.

McAdam, Doug and Sidney Tarrow. 2011. "Dynamics of Contention Ten Years On: A Special of Mobilization." *Mobilization: An International Quarterly* 16(1): 1–10.

McAdam, Doug, Sidney Tarrow, and Charles Tilly. 2001. *Dynamics of Contention*. New York: Cambridge University Press.

McCarthy, John D. and Mayer N. Zald. 1977. "Resource Mobilization and Social Movements: A Partial Theory." *American Journal of Sociology* 82: 1212–1241.

Mettam, Colin W. and Stephan Wyn Williams. 1998. "Internal Colonialism and Cultural Divisions of Labour in the Soviet Republic of Estonia." *Nations and Nationalism* 4: 363–388.

Mische, Anne. 2008. *Partisan Publics*. Princeton, NJ: Princeton University Press.

Nagel, Joanne and Suzanne Olzak. 1982. "Ethnic Mobilization in New and Old States: An Extension of the Ethnic Competition Model." *Social Problems* 30: 127–143.

Nielsen, Francois. 1980. "The Flemish Movement in Belgium after World War II: A Dynamic Analysis." *American Sociological Review* 45(1): 253–275.

Oakes, Penelope J., S. Alexander Haslam, and Katherine J. Reynolds. 1994. "Social Categorization and Social Context: Is Stereotype Change a Matter of Information or of Meaning?" In *Social Identity and Social Cognition*, edited by Dominic Abrams and Michael A. Hogg, 55–79. Oxford: Blackwell.

Olzak, Suzanne. 1982. "Ethnic Mobilization in Quebec." *Racial and Ethnic Studies* 5(3): 253–275.

Olzak, Suzanne. 1983. "Contemporary Ethnic Mobilization." *Annual Review of Sociology* 9: 355–374.

Olzak, Suzanne. 1992. *The Dynamics of Ethnic Competition and Conflict*. Stanford, CA: Stanford University Press.

Olzak, Suzanne. 2006. *The Global Dynamics of Racial and Ethnic Mobilization*. Stanford, CA: Stanford University Press.

Olzak, Susan. 2013. "Competition Theory of Ethnic/Racial Conflict and Protest." In *The Wiley-Blackwell Encyclopedia of Social and Political Movements*, edited by David A. Snow, Donatella della Porta, Bert Klandermans, and Doug McAdm, 240–243. Malden, MA: Blackwell.

Ragin, Charles C. 1979. "Ethnic Political Nationalism: The Welch Case." *American Sociological Review* 44(4): 619–635.

Reicher, Stephen and Nick Hopkins. 2001a. "Psychology and the End of History: A Critique and a Proposal for the Psychology of Social Categorization." *Political Psychology* 22(2): 383–407.

Reicher, Stephen and Nick Hopkins. 2001b. *Self and Nation: Categorization, Contestation, and Mobilization*. London: Sage.

Robinson. Glen E. 1997. *Building a Palestinian State: The Incomplete Revolution*. Bloomington: Indiana University Press.

Sherif, Muzafer, O.J. Harvey, B. Jack White, William R. Hood, and Carolyn R. Sherif. 1961. *Intergroup Conflict and Cooperation: The Robbers Cave Experiment*. Norman: University of Oklahoma Press.

Simon, Bernd and Bert Klandermans. 2001. "Politicized Collective Identity." *American Psychologist* 56: 319–331.

Skocpol, Theda and Vanessa Williamson. 2011. *The Tea Party and the Remaking of Republican Conservativism*. New York: Oxford University Press.

Smith, Anthony. 1979. *Nationalism in the Twentieth Century*. Canberra: ANU Press.

Smith, Anthony. 1982. *Ethnicity and Nationalism*. New York: E.J. Brill.

Smith, Anthony. 1986. *The Ethnic Origins of Nations*. Oxford: Blackwell.

Snow, David A., Daniel Cress, Liam Downey, and Andrew Jones. 1998. "Disrupting the Quotidian: Reconceptualizing the Relationship between Breakdown and the Emergence of Collective Action." *Mobilization* 3(1): 1–22.

Strang, David. 1992. "The Inner Incompatibility of Empire and Nation: Popular Sovereignty and Decolonization." *Sociological Perspectives* 35: 367–384.

Tajfel, Henri. 1981. *Human Groups and Social Categories*. New York: Cambridge University Press.

Tajfel, Henri and John C. Turner. 1979. "An Integrative Theory of Intergroup Conflict." In *The Social Psychology of Intergroup Relations*, edited by William G. Austin and Stephen Worchel, 22–97. Monterey, CA: Brooks-Cole.

Tarrow, Sidney, Charles Tilly, and Doug McAdam. 2001. *Dynamics of Contention*. New York: Cambridge University Press.

Tilly, Charles. 1978. *From Mobilization to Revolution*. Reading, MA: Addison-Wesley.

Tilly, Charles. 1992. *Coercion, Capital, and European States*. Malden, MA: Blackwell.

Trevor-Roper, Hugh. 1983. "The Invention of Tradition: The Highland Tradition of Scotland." In *The Invention of Tradition*, edited by Terence O. Ranger and Eric Hobsbawm, 15–41. Cambridge: Cambridge University Press.

Turner, John C. 1982. "Towards a Cognitive Redefinition of the Social Group." In *Social Identity and Intergroup Relations*, edited by Henri Tajfel, 15–39. Cambridge: Cambridge University Press.

Turner, John C., Michael A. Hogg, Pelenope J. Oakes, Stephen D. Reicher, and Margaret S. Wetherell. 1987. *Rediscovering the Social Group: A Self-Categorization Theory*. Oxford: Blackwell.

Van Dyke, Nella and David S. Meyer. 2014. *Understanding the Tea Party Movement*. Farnham: Ashgate.

Wilkinson, Steven I. 2004. *Votes and Violence: Electoral Competition and Ethnic Riots in India*. New York: Cambridge University Press.

Wimmer, Andreas. 2013. *Ethnic Boundary Making: Institutions, Power, and Networks*. New York: Oxford University Press.

37

War, Peace, and Social Movements[1]

David S. Meyer and Sidney Tarrow

Introduction

War is awful. One of the enduring mysteries of human life is the capacity of leaders to get young men to risk their lives to take up arms against other groups, and persuade the populace to pay for it. As the mechanics of war-making became more destructive and the societies that waged war became more complex, states have had to work harder and harder to build support for war. Sometimes, nationalist movements urged governments to make war, but at others, citizens resisted their governments' plans to go to war. Mostly, these efforts failed, but, at times, they succeeded in stopping the rush to war. Occasionally, as in Russia in 1917, popular movements brought down states in the midst of war, while, in others – as in Italy in 1922 – they brought states down in war's wake (Tarrow 2015: Chapter 4). In this chapter, we discuss the historical link between war-making, state-building and contention over war and the efforts of citizens to oppose war-making.

Our highly synthetic effort will explore three paradoxes regarding the relationship among war, states, and peace movements: First, the mobilization of material resources to make war costs money, and this leads to extraction from citizens who often resist (Tilly 1992). But, second, in order to gain support for war, states try to increase their legitimacy, which can lead to both democratization and to greater social benefits (Mann 1988: 136) that, paradoxically, provide the space and resources for citizens to organize oppositional movements. The third paradox is that peace movements are seldom strong enough to end wars on their own and become dependent on other movements and parties. This helps to increase their reach beyond their pacifist cores, but frequently produces internal conflicts and ensnares them in ordinary politics.

We begin with the shift from the blurred boundaries between war and political contention in early European states to the "Westphalian state" in which sharp lines

The Wiley Blackwell Companion to Social Movements, Second Edition. Edited by David A. Snow, Sarah A. Soule, Hanspeter Kriesi, and Holly J. McCammon.
© 2019 John Wiley & Sons Ltd. Published 2019 by John Wiley & Sons Ltd.

developed between war and domestic contention. From there, we move to contemporary states and to the admixture of nationalism and democracy as these states go to war and seek legitimation from their citizens, who often resist. In the second section, we shift our focus to such antiwar movements, which have a long history in the lives of democracies. Here, we focus mainly on the development of peace movements in the United States, tracing the roots of opposition in pacifism and religious traditions, and the connections among peace movements and other movements and parties.

We turn, finally, to the opposition to the War in Iraq after the turn of the new century. A crucial dilemma connect the three parts of the chapter: modern warfare depends on citizen support, at least passively, but in buying consent, modern states have provided citizens both the motivation and capacity to oppose their governments.

The Sociology of War and Movements

Max Weber (2013 [1922]) famously saw war-making as a vital function of states, but he also recognized that citizens would be reticent about donating their money and risking their lives for war. States promote support for war-making in several ways: through coercion; by mobilizing emotion through nationalism; and by providing the benefits of citizenship. Citizens contribute not only financial and human resources to war-making states but also the infrastructure that war-making requires (Mann 1988; Tarrow 2015).

In the modern era, this exchange between citizens and their states reveals our first paradox: even as it was extracting resources to fight its wars, the modern state developed civilian control of all bureaucratic institutions, including the military, confining both the state and the citizens ostensibly served (and governed) by it (Tilly 1992). The paradox is that the war-making/state-building/extractive cycle ultimately led to protection, production, and citizenship which, in turn, provided citizens with the opportunities and the tools to contest the very war-making that had produced their rights as citizens.

The first sociologists to train their sights on the military emphasized the development of a bureaucratic institution, staffed by professionals who served the state (see Huntington 1957; Janowitz 1960). The field of military sociology developed largely independently of the study of war, which was most taken up by scholars of international relations. A few sociologists, like Mann (1988), Tilly, and Williams (2003) put war at the center of their research, but paid little attention to the relationships among war, citizenship, and movements. But movements against war and its exactions were the indirect result of the growth in state-building that initially grew out of the needs of war-making and the state-building/extraction cycle that it produced.

Part of the reason for the neglect of the relations between war and movements among movement scholars is that – unlike peace – war comes in so many varieties that it is difficult to generalize about its relationship to movements. Mann (1988) divided wars historically, ranging from the "limited wars" of the early modern period (1648–1914), to the "citizen warfare" of the period between World War I and the end of World War II, to what he called "the nuclear age" (ibid.: 166–178). At the time, Mann could not have realized how globalization and internationalization – which he studied later (Mann 2012, 2013) – would produce a new phase: mixtures of conventional and unconventional warfare between states and transnational social movements.

A more structural classification of wars came from international relations specialists, who divided wars into "interstate," "extra-state," and "civil." War evolved from conflicts fought by professionals at a distance from social life to total war between states which engaged civilian populations at home. The largest share of contemporary wars are fought by major powers against insurgents who challenge not only the hegemony of these powers as well as local authorities, but, sometimes – as in the case of ISIS – the state system itself. While the contemporary templates for conducting and studying wars emphasize interstate wars, contemporary civil wars are just as ferocious, and have produced the largest growth of casualties and deaths in the post-1945 period (Sarkees and Wayman 2010). Indeed, the major military phenomena of the early twenty-first century involve transnational movements against states. These "new wars" (Kaldor 2012), which have mushroomed since the 1990s, are less formal than interstate wars, involve ideologically-committed combatants, combine military with political warfare, and – because they are so difficult to suppress – drag on for years, if not for decades (Crane and Reisner 2011; Hironaka 2005).

Although these "new wars" have expanded the role of movements in military conflicts, they are not alone. In each period of history we find intimate relations among war-making, state-building, and social movements. In early modern European history, the very distinction between war and domestic contention was impossible to make. The reason, of course, is that dynastic states had porous boundaries, their domains were often scattered over wide territories, and rulers were constantly under challenge from within and outside of their own borders. States had limited despotic and infrastructural powers (Mann 1988: 7–19) and operating far from rulers' seats of power increased local vulnerabilities. Until the development of gunpowder, "the capacity of armies to kill did not greatly increase through much of recorded history" (ibid.: 133).

This limit meant that – apart from those poor souls who found themselves impressed in their lords' armies and the mercenary soldiers for whom war was a way of life — ordinary subjects felt the pressure of war mainly when their towns were besieged, their farms sacked, their houses taken over to billet soldiers, and they suffered taxes to pay for their rulers' wars. War-making could produce popular resistance (Finer 1975; Tilly 1990), but usually for only as long as hostilities continued. It was only when dynastic conflicts merged with conflicts between religious movements that European wars became more general – and more savage.

More familiar movement activists first appeared in the wars of religion (Walzer 1971), mainly during the religious wars from 1524 to 1648. In Britain, for example, Catholic activists fought the Reformation hiding in "priest's holes" in noble Catholic households, while Protestants blended ideological fervor with military ardor in Cromwell's "New Model Army." As Hall (2009) writes, "In Great Britain and more widely, the Protestant Reformation was an international movement that inspired and gained strength from the contentious politics within societies."

With the founding of the "Westphalian" state system, writes Hall (ibid.: 106), "whatever the specific rapprochement between state, Reformation, and Catholicism, there was one general outcome." Conflict between religious movements became "contained" within states: states took over from the Catholic Church and contending Protestant confessions the "religious" function of determining the boundaries of acceptable doctrine and practice. In establishing the principle that the religion of the ruler would henceforth determine the religion of the realm, the Treaty of Westphalia had the unintended effect of confining social and religious conflict within state boundaries, thus creating the modern distinction between domestic contention and interstate conflicts.

This did not reduce the amount of social and religious conflict, but it did drive ideological conflict within state borders, where it gave rise to newly-nationalized social and political movements. From the late eighteenth century onward, insurgent movements and the states they created urged citizens to go to war on behalf of ideology as well as interests. The results, in the French and American Revolutions, included the invention of the citizen army (Kestnbaum 2002). In the longer run, states began to use the modern instruments of the mass media, propaganda and the educational system to gain and to maintain support for their conflicts. Ultimately, this led to what Mosse (1975) called "the nationalization of the masses" and to mass support for expanding states.

As the costs of war – both human and financial – rose, states began to allocate resources to citizens as incentives for loyalty and military service. Women's suffrage, mothers' and widows' pensions, the vote for 18-year-olds, and the GI Bill of Rights can all be seen as results of the exchange between states and their citizens in war's wake. War – and the legitimation of war through the creation of citizenship – helped to produce the modern welfare state (Tilly 1990).

In the meantime, war-making was becoming industrialized, extending its domestic reach even further. The industrialization of war increased the lethality of conflict and the size of armies; it also led states to forge close ties with war industries and to invest heavily in research and development (Thorpe 2014; Weiss 2014). This led to tight links between political and economic elites, but it also implicated the whole population in military production and helped to lead to mass mobilization using all the instruments of the state (Mann 1988: 134–135). In World War I, with the exception of Italy, the previously pacifist European working-class movements turned on a dime and supported the voting of war credits. Much earlier, in America, out-going President George Washington (1796) warned his countrymen about exactly these dangers, resulting from political entanglements abroad and the economic and political burdens of supporting a large military domestically. But war was hard to resist. No sooner had the new nation approved the federal Constitution than it became entangled in domestic quarrels brought on by the distant war between France and Britain, and actually passed "Alien and Sedition" Acts to suppress domestic dissent (Stone 2004: Chapter 2). This was but the first of many "ratchet effects," when rulers passed draconian policies in attempting to suppress domestic antiwar movements.

Military sociologists, both in and out of uniform, found that neither ideology nor fear kept soldiers engaged at the front line as effectively as loyalty to their comrades (Shils and Janowitz 1948; Wong et al. 2003). Meanwhile, for those farther from the front, claiming to fight wars in the name of rights and freedoms could invigorate patriotic fervor and support, but it could also lead to demands for reform and even, at times, to revolution. Again, there is a paradox: preparations for war can build domestic infrastructure and, ultimately, democracy, which can undermine the capacity for war-making.

Wars often lead to the demand for new rights: The American Civil War was begun to preserve the union, but Lincoln eventually embraced the Abolitionists' demand to use it to free the slaves. World War I was fought over territory and domination but it also satisfied the demands of the Suffragettes for votes for women in Britain and the United States, and brought a revolution to Russia. World War II came closest to a war to oppose tyranny than any modern war and led to the welfare state in Europe and to the GI Bill of Rights in the United States (Altschuler and Blumin 2009; Mettler 2004). As for the Vietnam War, to which we return below, it led to the vote for 18-year-olds and to the civil liberties movement of the 1970s (Stone 2004).

As these brief examples suggest, the relationship between war and social movements takes various forms:

1. *Domestic political contention often leads to war.* Political conflict led to civil war in revolutionary France, when the Jacobin faction of the Republican coalition launched a "reign of terror and virtue" against its political opponents, and fought a civil war against Catholic counter-revolutionaries in the West, where opposition to the nationalization of the church and refusal to serve in the army threatened the revolution (Tilly 1964).

2. *Movements can put pressure on states to go to war to achieve their political objectives.* This was evident in the lead-up to the American Civil War, as anti-slavery advocates both within and outside the Republican Party advanced the theory that although slavery was protected by the Constitution in the southern states, freedom was national, and the duty of good patriots was to surround the slaveholder by "a wall of anti-slavery fire" (Oakes 2012).

3. *Social movement support can endow governments with a military capacity that they would lack if they had to depend only on conscript armies.* The French *levée en masse* of 1792 was launched with a campaign to convince volunteers that they were fighting for *la patrie*, instead of expanding the power of a distant government.

4. *War can empower a social movement, often leading to reform and sometimes to revolution.* By freeing the slaves, the American Civil War led to the passage of the Thirteenth Amendment and, with much delay, to citizenship for African-Americans, and to the germ of America's welfare state by according pensions to widows and veterans (Skocpol 1992).

5. *War leads to an increase in international contacts and indirectly to the rise of transnational movements.* World War I so weakened the Tsarist monarchy that it crumbled rapidly in February and October, 1917, and lit a flame across Europe.

6. *Mobilization for war can stimulate peace movements as well as related claims for democratization.* From the anti-tax riots in France in the eighteenth century to the anti-Vietnam War movement in America, wars both put strains on domestic actors and triggered resistance to war-making.

This takes us to the second part of our effort: on peace movements.

Peace Movements

Although the development of powerful states that could extract substantial resources and fight long and destructive wars unleashed challenging movements addressing a wide range of issues, peace movements provide a particularly interesting window to see these dynamics. Activism for peace has virtually always been tied up with a range of other issues (e.g. abolition, suffrage, socialism), and has often included a transnational component, as crusaders have tried to forge alternative ties with potential enemies (DeBenedetti 1980; Rupp 1997). Peace activism has also included both reluctance to engage in particular wars and principled opposition to war and violence altogether.

In Europe, socialism animated and united unsuccessful opposition to World War I. In the wake of that particularly destructive war, pacifist campaigns grew with narrower visions of justice. For example, the United Kingdom's Peace Pledge Union set resistance to war as an absolute value that trumped all other concerns – including the rise of fascism (Ceadel 2000). After World War II, both states and activists worked to set up international accords to reduce the likelihood of war, particularly the new horror of nuclear weapons. Since the middle of the twentieth century, peace movements have crested and waned globally in response to actual wars and to the perceived threats of nuclear weapons, frequently intersecting with other movements. Opposition to America's war in Vietnam, followed by the "new social movements" of the 1970s and 1980s, brought thousands of members of the new middle classes into the streets against war-making (Klandermans 1991). The peace movement was one of the main sources of a new cleavage in European politics – "left-libertarians" against traditional conservatives (Kitschelt 1994).

Opposition to war in America has as long a history as American participation in wars, including both principled objections to war and personal commitments to avoid the risks and costs of military service. From Quakers who tried to negotiate a neutral course in the American Revolution (DeBenedetti 1980), to Irish Catholic immigrants in New York City who staged riots in resistance to the Civil War draft during the Civil War, interest and principle uneasily coexisted within diverse movements. Rioters tore up streetcar tracks, cut telegraph lines, and looted stores; some beat and even hung black people unfortunate enough to be caught up in the enthusiasms of resistance (Meyer 2015: 101–102). Mobilizing a citizen army in a civil war was a difficult struggle, especially when the citizens could see their wealthier countrymen buying their own safety by hiring replacements.

In the twentieth century, as the prospect for war increased, core peace activists were joined by socialists, isolationists, and universalists who were unconvinced by the patriotic drumbeat. On the other side were nationalists, imperialists, and those who thought of war-making as an outlet for "manly courage" – like future president Theodore Roosevelt, who led a brigade of "Rough Riders" into battle in Cuba in the Spanish-American War. Peace movements crested and receded in concert with American military engagement.

This pattern changed drastically with World War II. After the Japanese attack on Pearl Harbor, American participation in World War II was far less unpopular than previous wars. For the first time, the government offered alternative service to conscientious objectors, but there were few of these, as the mass of the population rallied behind a popular President and a country that had been severely wounded by the Great Depression and by the Japanese "sneak attack" on Pearl Harbor.

At war's end, with the introduction of nuclear weapons into world politics, the options for both the nation and for peace movements changed dramatically (Boyer 1985; Wittner 1984). Widespread horror and fear of nuclear weapons were episodically supplanted by a fear of Communism in general, and the Soviet Union in particular. America committed itself to becoming an ongoing presence in world politics. This led to a network of international military alliances, to a decades-long Cold War with the Soviet Union, to broad financial investment in both Europe and the United States, a nuclear arms race, and to a shift in opportunities for social movements.

By the mid-1950s, fear of nuclear holocaust produced a growing peace movement in both Europe and America, first, against nuclear arms and then against war in general (Chatfield and Kleidman 1992; Rochon 1988; Wittner 1984). But what was the composition of these movements, and how did they relate to contentious politics in general? It is difficult, and ultimately counterproductive, to draw sharp lines between the peace movement and other significant movements – either in Europe or in America: A relatively small core of organizations maintained opposition to aggressive foreign and military policies and nuclear weapons, but the movement also drew on activists from civil rights, the women's and environmental movements, and from the left wing of the parties of the Left.

For example, the pacifist Fellowship of Reconciliation staged Freedom Rides on behalf of civil rights, and Catholic Workers who staged civil disobedience against nuclear weapons also worked to highlight and combat poverty and economic injustice (Wittner 1984). When issues of war and peace were salient, often the result of external events in conjunction with successful organizing, activists gathered around antiwar and antinuclear claims. When those issues seemed less urgent or less promising, activists turned to other issues.

In the 1950s, when radioactive fallout from nuclear tests appeared in the atmosphere, the peace movement swelled, uniting a broad range of activists and organizations (notably: the Committee for Nonviolent Action and the Committee for a SANE Nuclear Policy and the British Campaign for Nuclear Disarmament, which introduced the peace symbol into popular iconography). These organizations employed a broad spectrum of contentious actions, including civil disobedience, public demonstrations, political education efforts, and lobbying (Katz 1987). But after the nuclear powers signed a treaty banning atmospheric testing in 1963, reflecting their hybrid commitments, many peace activists on both continents turned to more pressing domestic issues.

The resolution to the test ban campaign provides a key for understanding the ongoing dynamics of challenge and response on issues of war and peace in postwar America. In contrast to the admonition contained in his (1961) farewell address, Eisenhower, like his immediate predecessor and successor, presided over increased investment in nuclear weapons, in greater military engagement abroad, and in increased spending on domestic policies, including civilian infrastructure. Surprisingly often, domestic political reforms, including the interstate highway system, a dramatic expansion of post-secondary education, and federal support of civil rights reforms, were justified in terms of prevailing in the Cold War (Dudziak 2000).

In both Europe and America, peace activists used the most immediate, salient, and threatening aspects of an aggressive military posture to lodge broader claims against militarism. Thus, activists vigorously resisted crisis relocation plans, refusing to relocate underground or leave cities – even for practice. They focused on atmospheric fallout to talk about the costs and dangers of nuclear weapons (Divine 1978). Authorities managed to tamp down the movement by reducing the visibility and threat of their military ambitions without scaling back those ambitions. As an example, an agreement about ending atmospheric testing – and radioactive fallout – was accompanied by an increase in testing underground; civil defense and population relocation drills gradually disappeared. Although committed pacifists still had many grievances with the policies, they were unable to mobilize the same extent of support and visibility they had earlier enjoyed (Meyer 1993a, 1993b).

At the same time, the government recognized and institutionalized popular concerns about war and peace, redefining them in the process. In 1963, President Kennedy established the Arms Control and Disarmament Agency (ACDA), explicitly concerned with reducing the likelihood, potential damage, and costs of war. Committed to manage rather than end the arms race, ACDA typically housed both political appointees and civil servants who expressed a range of views about how to deal with the Soviet Union and the nuclear arms race; importantly, it also represented a source of information and influence for advocates both inside and outside government (Meyer 1990). ACDA also represented a more or less constant attempt at international arms control based on negotiations. Because challengers mobilize most effectively when large numbers of people believe that there is a tractable problem not being managed by government, the establishment of negotiations and government agencies like ACDA worked to ameliorate extra-institutional concerns and mobilization – most of the time.

An effective domestic truce on nuclear weapons led experienced and trained activists and their organizations to look beyond peace and war at other issues. As the urgency of antinuclear activism receded, would-be activists "spilled out" into other causes (Hadden and Tarrow 2007), particularly into the dramatic and very urgent civil rights movement, which was ready to accommodate them. Campus-based chapters of SANE became the infrastructure for the new Students for a Democratic Society (SDS), and sent activists to the South to work in the civil rights movement, when the nuclear issue was somewhat less pressing (Miller 1987).

These activists were not alone in connecting domestic and international politics. Ironically, in seeking to build support for his own initiatives on civil rights, President Lyndon Johnson linked progress at home to the global struggle against Communism. Speaking before Congress on behalf of the Voting Rights Act, Johnson (1965) likened the struggle of the brave civil rights activists facing segregationist violence in Selma to the struggles of American soldiers in battle around the world – including in Vietnam. Johnson, like many of his predecessors, saw forceful federal government action at home as consonant with a strong military serving America's ambitions abroad.

Just one month later, however, SDS sponsored the first national march against the war in Vietnam, antagonizing Johnson, while sparking the antiwar movement. Till that point, SDS had been a rather small organization with a broad and ambitious agenda. But by moving first against the war, it attracted large numbers of college students across the country to flood into campus-based chapters of the group.

War, and the movement against the war, helped to radicalize a generation of young Americans.

Although it is often easy for most citizens to ignore nuclear weapons and preparations for war, this was much less the case with respect to the deployment of troops in combat abroad, particularly when those troops were conscripts. America's increased participation in the war in Vietnam, sustained by the military draft, provoked the reemergence of the peace movement, and it was a movement that was larger and more volatile than prior peace movements. Partly, this reflected the understandable reluctance of young men to abandon their routines and go into battle far from home. But, as with New York's civil war riots a century earlier, resisting going to war didn't require deep political commitments or sophisticated analysis, and it could be extremely disruptive. What was new, compared to past mobilizations, was that in the 1960s a great many of these young men were college students, and the campuses, many with existing SANE or SDS chapters, were places in which to organize. Activists who had worked in movements for free speech, civil rights, and against nuclear weapons, flooded into the antiwar movement (DeBenedetti 1990; Zaroulis and Sullivan 1984), carrying a range of concerns. Some saw the war as a misuse of resources, others saw it as an expression of imperialism, while still others used opposition to the war to lodge broader claims against the United States particularly, and against capitalism in general. Opposition to the draft was the focal point that brought together these different perspectives.

For a time, despite considerable individual and organizational overlap, authorities and many activists treated the antiwar and civil rights movement as separate entities. Civil rights leaders were reluctant to challenge Johnson on peace issues, and to muddy the moral clarity and organizational discipline of their movement. By 1967, however, opposition to the war had become unavoidable for many activists, most notably for Martin Luther King. In a controversial speech at the Riverside Church in New York, King linked the cause of civil rights with the war, which he saw as a sinkhole for the resources needed to build a just society at home, announcing:

> America would never invest the necessary funds or energies in rehabilitation of its poor so long as adventures like Vietnam continued to draw men and skills and money like some demonic, destructive suction tube. So I was increasingly compelled to see the war as an enemy of the poor and to attack it as such.
>
> (King 1967)

The antiwar movement mobilized mass demonstrations, civil disobedience campaigns, and engaged in electoral campaigns, mostly within the Democratic Party. In 1968, the movement animated challenges to President Lyndon Johnson's reelection, ultimately pressuring him to withdraw from the race. Antiwar activists continued to organize and mobilize, turning up in large numbers at the Democratic National Convention. Denied access to the convention floor, they protested outdoors, facing arrests and police violence as the Party awarded its presidential nomination to Johnson's vice-president, Hubert Humphrey (Farber 1988).

Although Humphrey tried to position himself against the war, his opponent, Richard Nixon, promised to end the war with a secret plan that involved executing – or at least threatening – an escalating military engagement, potentially including the use of nuclear weapons. Nixon defeated Humphrey, and American engagement spread to Cambodia. But the Nixon administration responded to the movement in other ways, reworking the Selective Service system and then ending the draft altogether. The administration also presided over the ratification of the Twenty-sixth Amendment to the Constitution, which lowered the voting age to 18. Both moves had the effect of reducing the salience of some grievances about the war without stopping the fighting. Even as mobilized opposition diminished, the war continued.

After the war, political leaders were reluctant to risk the public unrest associated with extended military commitments abroad. In the 1980s, this posture was codified into a doctrine first articulated by Caspar Weinberger, Secretary of Defense under Ronald Reagan. The Weinberger Doctrine rejected not only sustained military engagement abroad, but even shorter deployments, unless the military could be confident of both public support and a quick victory.

In the 1980s, a new element could be discerned in the international peace movement: growing links between American and European peace activists. This quasi-alliance emerged in the conflicts over the Reagan arms buildup and the president's plan to emplace medium-range nuclear weapons in Europe. But the same wave of protests revealed gaps between the two continents, with most European activists seeking a total ban on nuclear weapons and the American branch of the movement cohering around a proposal to stop the growth of nuclear armaments (Rochon 1988).

Between 1975 and 2003, the United States sometimes went into combat internationally, but for limited periods with limited objectives, as the so-called Weinberger/Powell doctrine prescribed. These efforts sometimes provoked protest, but usually only for brief periods, and never with the vigor and volatility of the Vietnam era movement. Similarly, while there was some mobilization against the initial post-9/11 military deployment in Afghanistan, it did not capture the public's imagination or find its way into mainstream policy discourse (LaFeber 2009).

Not so with the American wars of the early twenty-first century. The long lead-up to the 2003 invasion of Iraq offered both provocation and opportunity for the reemergence of the American peace movement. In concert with millions of activists abroad (Walgrave and Rucht 2010), and sometimes with their governments, American peace activists rejected both the costs and the wisdom of the mission. The success of the Bush administration's campaign to sell the war to its allies and the American public, predicated on inaccurate claims about Iraqi capabilities, was short-lived, although the deployment was surely not and led indirectly to the next decade of chaos and civil strife in both the Middle East and North Africa.

Again, the peace movement could not be understood in isolation from contentious politics in general. Activists mobilized an unprecedented global campaign to prevent the invasion, as traditional peace groups were joined by a broad range of organizations with diverse grievances against the Bush administration (Heaney and Rojas 2015; Meyer and Corrigall-Brown 2005). At both the grassroots and national levels, peace activists successfully mobilized a broad repertoire of tactics against the war. They drew on the repertoire of contention that had evolved since the 1960s in major social movements in America (Tilly and Tarrow 2015).

After an initial pause, the movement reemerged strongly as news of schism and unrest flowed from Iraq. Activists seized on the news of grotesque mistreatment of prisoners in the Abu Ghraib prison in Iraq, and in the American prison at Guantanamo Bay. But President Bush presided over the extended war while working to make it harder to mobilize opposition. Each time an election approached, administration spokespersons, like Homeland Security Secretary Tom Ridge, were urged to announce a red alert (Tarrow 2015: 268).

This is where the "new" nature of twenty-first-century conflicts come into play. In traditional interstate wars, there is a defined enemy, a territorially-delimited "front," and a conventional spectrum of war-making tools. But in the post-9/11 world, conflict bridged conventional and unconventional means, the "enemy" was territorially unlimited, and combined the passion of a movement with the tools of modern warfare. This made war-making a frustrating and dispersed enterprise but it also provided the administration with an unusual armament of political tools. Constantly invoking the threat of terrorism, the Bush administration emphasized the ominous, proximate, and widespread threat to America. Deploying a small all-volunteer military meant that the human toll of the war was concentrated within a rather narrow sliver of the American public, even as those service people and their families paid heavy costs – and generated their own antiwar campaigns (Leitz 2014). And following well-established precedent, the war was funded through deficit spending, and the administration was disturbingly effective at concealing its true financial costs (Blimes and Stiglitz 2008).

After a dramatic wave of mobilization, fed by activists from the global justice movement as well as from the traditional peace movement (Hadden and Tarrow 2007), much of the antiwar movement turned away from street protests to contest the Bush administration's policies through elections in 2004 and 2006. In 2008, Senator Hillary Clinton's initial vote to authorize the invasion of Iraq was a critical issue that undermined her support within the Democratic Party, and helped Senator Barack Obama – who campaigned on an antiwar platform – to win first the Democratic nomination and then the presidency.

The wars in Afghanistan and Iraq didn't end when Barack Obama took office. Indeed, as he promised, he initially channeled more resources in the Afghanistan war, albeit without notable success. Nonetheless, activists who had worked hard for his election – many of them self-identified Democrats – were willing to give the new president slack in dealing with complicated foreign policy problems. Demonstrations against the wars in Iraq and Afghanistan continued, but they were smaller and mainly limited to major population centers, and espoused rhetoric more skewed to radical critiques than in the past.

Heaney and Rojas (2015), by surveying activists at those demonstrations, were able to understand why: the "party in the street" was broad but fickle; self-identified Democrats were no longer coming out to demonstrate in large numbers against a Democratic President. This continued throughout Obama's mandate, even as he ramped up the use of drones outside the battlefield and began offensive actions against the Islamic State, all the while refusing to admit that he had put American "boots on the ground." Obama's foreign and military policies, whatever their merits globally, were able to manage and contain the domestic opposition.

Conclusion

This leads us to a few general conclusions – and to a question – about the development of peace and antiwar movements in America.

First, although a dedicated core of activists with moral or political commitments to peace are virtually always trying to organize on behalf of their concerns, they must reach beyond this core in order to have an impact. Historically, the peace movement swells and contracts like the bellows of an accordion depending upon circumstance. Large-scale peace and antiwar campaigns develop when the costs and consequences of war and the preparations for war become salient, often a function of policy, political alignments, and politics. When the government responds strategically to activist movements, it splits the core from a broader array of organizations and a mass public.

Second, the fine lines that scholars tend to draw between peace activism and activism on behalf of other social causes do not serve our understanding very well. Depending on the political context, activists move among movement concerns, concentrating on the issues that appear most urgent or promising. The peace movement has always been a "hybrid" movement, benefiting from alliances in times of threat of military involvement, and retreating into a militant core in times of relative peace.

Third, the United States has paradoxically assured support for a global military presence by building institutions both inside and outside government that bolster the infrastructure on which social movements can draw (Tarrow 2015: Chapter 9). Under Eisenhower, the massive expansion of post-secondary education afforded young people both the space to consider politics and policy, and a place where they could meet like-minded youth. Under Kennedy, the establishment of the Arms Control and Disarmament Agency provided an institutional site for some movement concerns and a source of information and legitimacy for later organizing.

Fourth, peace activists continue to confront an American paradox. Activism abroad has often been accompanied by the expansion of domestic rights and the expansion of the welfare state. But opponents of an activist American state in foreign and military affairs also frequently oppose its activist domestic ambitions. Those concerned with peace and social welfare must find a way to support state action at home while emphasizing its limits abroad.

Finally, we end with a big question. Most peace movements in American history targeted wars that were finite, had discrete beginnings and ends and, even when they did not, were aimed at a single geo-political entity, like the Soviet Union. That determined – or at least conditioned – their strategies, their composition, and their outcomes. But the wars of the early twenty-first century have been diffused across the globe, have had no distinct beginnings and ends (although 9/11 appeared to many to be a "critical juncture"), and are aimed at a wide range of enemies that have the characteristics of a movement, rather than a state. How this transformation of war has affected the military posture of major states, and how this, in turn, affects the nature and prospects for the peace movement are the next big questions in the study of war, peace, and social movements.

Note

1 We dedicate this chapter to the memory of our colleague at Cornell and at Irvine, Robin Williams.

References

Altschuler, Glenn and Start Blumin. 2009. *The GI Bill: A New Deal for Veterans*. New York: Oxford University Press.

Blimes, Linda J. and Joseph E. Stiglitz 2008. *The Three Trillion Dollar War: The True Cost of the Iraq Conflict*. New York: W.W. Norton.

Boyer, Paul. 1985. *By the Bomb's Early Light: American Thought and Culture at the Dawn of the Atomic Age*. Chapel Hill: University of North Carolina Press.

Ceadel, Martin. 2000. *Semi-Detached Idealists: The British Peace Movement and International Relations, 1854–1945*. Oxford: Oxford University Press.

Chatfield, Charles and Robert Kleidman. 1992. *The American Peace Movement: Ideals and Activism*. Boston: Twayne.

Crane, David M. and Daniel Reisner. 2011. "Status and Liabilities of Nonstate Actors Engaged in Hostilities." In *New Battlefields, Old Laws; Critical Debates on Asymmetric Warfare*, edited by William C. Banks, 67–84. New York: Columbia University Press.

DeBenedetti, Charles. 1980. *The Peace Reform in American History*. Bloomington: Indiana University Press.

DeBenedetti, Charles. 1990. *An American Ordeal: The Antiwar Movement of the Vietnam Era*. Syracuse, NY: Syracuse University Press.

Divine, Robert A. 1978. *Blowing on the Wind: The Nuclear Test Ban Debate, 1954–1960*. New York: Oxford University Press.

Dudziak, Mary E. 2000. *Cold War Civil Rights*. Princeton, NJ: Princeton University Press.

Eisenhower, Dwight David. 1961. "Farewell Address." Yale Law School, Lillian Goldman Library. Avalon Project. Available at: http://avalon.law.yale.edu/20th_century/eisenhower001.asp (accessed May 3, 2016).

Farber, David. 1988. *Chicago '68*. Chicago: University of Chicago Press.

Finer, Samuel E. 1975. "State- and Nation-Building in Europe: The Role of the Military." In *The Formation of National States in Western Europe*, edited by Charles Tilly, 84–163. Princeton, NJ: Princeton University Press.

Hadden, Jennifer and Sidney Tarrow. 2007. "Spillover or Spillout? The Global Justice Movement in the United States after 9/11." *Mobilization: An International Quarterly* 12(4): 359–376.

Hall, John R. 2009. *Apocalypse: From Antiquity to the Empire of Modernity*. Cambridge: Polity.

Heaney, Michael T. and Fabio Rojas. 2015. *Party in the Street: The Antiwar Movement and the Democratic Party after 9/11*. New York: Cambridge University Press.

Hironaka, Ann. 2005. *Neverending Wars: The International Community, Weak States, and the Perpetuation of Civil War*. Cambridge, MA: Harvard University Press.

Huntington, Samuel P. 1957. *The Soldier and the State*. Cambridge, MA: Belknap Press.

Janowitz, Morris. 1960. *The Professional Soldier*. Glencoe, IL: The Free Press.

Johnson, Lyndon Baines. 1965. "Speech before Congress on Voting Rights." May 15. Available at: http://millercenter.org/president/speeches/speech-3386 (accessed May 4, 2016).

Kaldor, Mary. 2012. *New and Old Wars: Organized Violence in a Global Era*. Stanford, CA: Stanford University Press.

Katz, Milton. 1987. *Ban the Bomb*. New York: Praeger.

Kestnbaum, Meyer. 2002. "Citizen-Soldiers, National Service and the Mass Army: The Birth of Conscription in Revolutionary Europe and North America." *Armed Forces and Society* 20: 117–44.

King, Martin Luther, Jr. 1967. "Beyond Vietnam." New York, April 4. Available at: http://kingencyclopedia.stanford.edu/encyclopedia/documentsentry/doc_beyond_vietnam/ (accessed May 6, 2016).

Kitschelt, Herbert. 1994. *The Transformation of European Social Democracy*. Cambridge: Cambridge University Press.

Klandermans, Bert, ed. 1991. *International Social Movement Research: Peace Movements in Western Europe and the United States*. Greenwich, CT: JAI Press.

LaFeber, Walter. 2009. "The Rise and Fall of Colin Powell and the Powell Doctrine." *Political Science Quarterly* 124(1): 71–93.

Leitz, Lisa. 2014. *Fighting for Peace: Veterans and Military Families in the Anti-Iraq War Movement*. Minneapolis: University of Minnesota Press.

Mann, Michael. 1988. *States, War and Capitalism: Studies in Political Sociology*. Oxford: Blackwell.

Mann, Michael. 2012. *The Sources of Social Power, vol. III: Global Empires and Revolution*. Cambridge: Cambridge University Press.

Mann, Michael. 2013. *The Sources of Social Power, vol. IV: Globalizations, 1945–2011*. Cambridge: Cambridge University Press.

Mettler, Suzanne. 2004. *Soldiers to Citizens: The G.I. Bill and the Making of the Greatest Generation*. Oxford: Oxford University Press.

Meyer, David S. 1990. *A Winter of Discontent: The Nuclear Freeze and American Politics*. New York: Praeger.

Meyer, David S. 1993a. "Protest Cycles and Political Process: American Peace Movements in the Nuclear Age." *Political Research Quarterly* 46(3): 451–479.

Meyer, David S. 1993b. "Peace Protest and Policy: Explaining the Rise and Decline of Antinuclear\ Movements in Postwar America." *Policy Studies Journal* 21: 35–51.

Meyer, David S. 2015. *The Politics of Protest: Social Movements in America*. New York: Oxford University Press.

Meyer, David S. and Catherine Corrigall-Brown. 2005. "Coalitions and Political Context: US Movements against Wars in Iraq." *Mobilization: An International Quarterly* 10: 327–344.

Miller, James. 1987. *Democracy Is in the Streets*. New York: Touchstone.

Mosse, George. 1975. *The Nationalization of the Masses: Political Symbolism and Mass Movements in Germany from the Napoleonic Wars through the Third Reich*. New York: Fertig.

Oakes, James. 2012. *Freedom National: The Destruction of Slavery in the United States, 1861–1985*. New York: W.W. Norton.

Rochon, Thomas R. 1988. *Mobilizing for Peace*. Princeton, NJ: Princeton University Press.

Rupp, Leila J. 1997. *Worlds of Women: The Making of an International Women's Movement*. Princeton, NJ: Princeton University Press.

Sarkees, Meredith and Frank Whelon Wayman. 2010. *Resort to War: A Data Guide to Inter-State, Extra-State, Intra-State and Non-State Wars, 1816–2007*. Washington, DC: CQ Press.

Shils, Edward A. and Morris Janowitz. 1948. "Cohesion and Disintegration in the Wehrmacht in World War II." *Public Opinion Quarterly* 12: 280–315.

Skocpol, Theda. 1992. *Protecting Soldiers and Mothers: The Political Origins of Social Policy in the United States*. Cambridge, MA: Harvard University Press.

Stone, Geoffrey R. 2004. *Perilous Times: Free Speech in Wartime*. New York: Norton.

Tarrow, Sidney. 2015. *War, States, and Contention*. Ithaca, NY: Cornell University Press.

Thorpe, Rebecca. 2014. *The American Warfare State: The Domestic Politics of Military Spending*. Chicago: University of Chicago Press.

Tilly, Charles. 1964. *The Vendée*. Cambridge, MA: Harvard University Press.

Tilly, Charles. 1990. *Coercion, Capital, and European States, AD 990–1992*. Cambridge, MA: Blackwell.

Tilly, Charles. 1992. "Where Do Rights Come from?" In *Contributions to the Comparative Study of Development*, edited by Lars Mjøset, 9–37. Oslo: Institute for Social Research.

Tilly, Charles and Sidney Tarrow. 2015. *Contentious Politics*. Oxford: Oxford University Press.

Walgrave, Stefaan and Dieter Rucht, eds. 2010. *The World Says No to War: Demonstrations against the War on Iraq*. Minneapolis: University of Minnesota Press.

Walzer, Michael. 1971. *Revolution of the Saints. A Study in the Origins of Radical Politics*. New York: Atheneum.

Washington, George. 1796. "Farewell Address." Yale Law School, Lillian Goldman Library. Avalon Project. Available at: http://avalon.law.yale.edu/18th_century/washing.asp (accessed May 3, 2016).

Weber, Max. 2013 [1922]. *Economy and Society*. Edited by Guenther Roth and Claus Wittich. Berkeley: University of California Press.

Weiss, Linda. 2014. *America, Inc? Innovation and Enterprise in the National Security State*. Ithaca, NY: Cornell University Press.

Williams, Robin M. 2003. *The Wars Within: Peoples and States in Conflict*. Ithaca, NY: Cornell University Press.

Wittner, Lawrence. 1984. *Rebels against War: The American Peace Movement, 1933–1983*. Philadelphia, PA: Temple University Press.

Wong, Leonard, Thomas A. Kolditz, Raymond A. Millen, and Terrence M. Potter. 2003. "*Why They Fight: Combat Motivation in the Iraq War*." Carlisle, PA: US Army War College, Strategic Studies Institute.

Zaroulis, Nancy and Gerald Sullivan. 1984. *Who Spoke up? American Protest against the War in Vietnam, 1963–1975*. New York: Doubleday.

38

Authoritarian Regimes and Social Movements

Xi Chen and Dana M. Moss[1]

Introduction

All governments possess many of the same characteristics and do many of the same things, but it is also true that to demur under one regime is not the same as demurring under another (Linz 2000). By definition, democracies uphold a meaningful degree of political pluralism, competition, and rights, while non-democracies do not. As a result, polity members who object to some hardship or policy in places such as Russia, China, Saudi Arabia, Iran, and Jordan typically take different risks and incur different costs for their dissent than do those in Brazil, India, Japan, Canada, the USA, and the UK. And yet, despite these risks, social movements are a normal feature of socio-political life in authoritarian states and have the potential to challenge illiberal systems of governance. They can also induce a range of significant outcomes, from policy concessions to democratization, and from violent repression to civil war. For these reasons, understanding the relationship between authoritarian regimes and movements is vital to understanding social conflict and change more broadly.

Theorizing the effects of regime type on mobilization has long been the purview of political process/opportunity theorists who analyze the effects of contextual conditions and changes therein on the emergence, dynamics, and outcomes of protest and social movements. This paradigm asserts that a regime's degree of liberalization and its propensity and capacity to repress, among other factors, shape the character of collective action (Kriesi 2005; McAdam 1996; McAdam, Tarrow, and Tilly 2001). Because authoritarian regimes are "closed" to dissent, scholars have logically argued that subordinate groups have little chance to engage in forms of protest other than through covert resistance or open revolt. James Scott's (1985: xv) hallmark work on the "weapons of the weak," for example, argues that subordinate classes throughout history have seldom been afforded the luxury of open and organized political activity because it was "dangerous, if not suicidal." Scott's formative writings draw a sharp

The Wiley Blackwell Companion to Social Movements, Second Edition. Edited by David A. Snow, Sarah A. Soule, Hanspeter Kriesi, and Holly J. McCammon.
© 2019 John Wiley & Sons Ltd. Published 2019 by John Wiley & Sons Ltd.

distinction between normal periods when powerless people engage in everyday forms of resistance, such as foot-dragging and stealing, and extraordinary conditions when the aggrieved launch collective rebellions.

In keeping with this perspective, theories of regimes' effects on social movements have largely assumed, explicitly or implicitly, that the regular use of the modern protest repertoire – defined by Charles Tilly as moderate, public claims-making using symbolic demonstrations of worthiness, unity, numbers, and commitment, or "WUNC" – is foreclosed to dissenters in authoritarian states. At the same time, however, research on contentious politics also "contains built-in affinities with relatively democratic social movement politics" and has fared poorly as a guide to understanding mobilization in other contexts (McAdam, Tarrow, and Tilly 2001: 18). In order to address this shortcoming, a growing field of research is yielding important findings that not only call for a reevaluation of expectations about mobilization under authoritarianism, but also enrich our understanding of social movements and contentious politics in general.

Several empirical observations have begun to reshape theories of contentious politics in authoritarian states in fundamental ways. First, scholars have become increasingly attuned to the variety of non-democratic regime types and changes in the practice of authoritarian rule in recent decades. In the post-Cold War era, the number of authoritarian regimes incorporating democratic practices into their governing strategies has increased dramatically. Liberalization, once viewed as the first step toward a regime's transition to democracy (Przeworski 1991), has instead become a common feature of authoritarianism. Protests can also fulfill important functions for elites and perpetuate regime legitimacy and longevity, rather than signifying a crisis that foments regime destabilization or decline. Second, incidents of protest and social movement organizing have become relatively *routinized* features of social life in authoritarian states. Rather than emerging above-ground as radical and riotous, movements often exhibit the characteristics of the modern WUNC variety. As a result, researchers are increasingly finding that changes in authoritarian systems have created new patterns of popular contention that warrant systematic attention.

Building on these insights, this chapter describes correctives to conceptualizations of authoritarian systems as *monolithic*, as uniformly *violent* and *closed*, as *cohesive* in their responses, and as *insular* in their repressive dynamics. First, we unpack the term "authoritarian" to discuss a fuller range of non-democratic regime types. Second, we illustrate variation in state authorities' repressive tactics and in their propensities to repress. Third, we demonstrate that activists' access to regime officials and their opportunities for bargaining vary across non-democratic contexts. Fourth, we explain that rather than exhibiting cohesion, regimes are comprised of varying levels of powerholders and elites who mobilize protests during periods of intra-regime competition. And, finally, we demonstrate that authoritarian repression is often transnational in scope and effect. We conclude with suggestions for further research along these key lines of inquiry.

Understanding Authoritarianism and its Iterations

Although regimes are typically characterized as democratic or authoritarian, Max Weber reminded us that it "is very exceptional" for regimes to belong to "only to one or another of these pure types" (1978: 262). Researchers have increasingly recognized that most regimes fall into a "gray zone" between ideal types (Carothers 2002) and that "[d]ifferent kinds of authoritarianism differ from each other as much as they differ from democracy" (Geddes 1999: 121). As a result, scholars have produced a dizzying array of competing terms with overlapping definitions, rendering simple categorizations elusive (Zhao 2001). Because differences among authoritarian regimes matter for understanding the dynamics of contention and variations therein, we provide a basic but non-exhaustive overview of several common terms and their definitions below.

Two of the most notable ideal types are that of *totalitarianism*, which refers to regimes that strive to subordinate all aspects of the individual and society to the state, and *sultanism* (Chehabi and Linz 1998) or *personalistic* regimes, defined as when "traditional domination develops an administration and a military force which are purely personal instruments of the master" (Weber 1978: 231). Both regime types take an iron-fisted approach to dissent in accordance with leaders' strategic and ideological intolerances for criticism and deploy collective punishment as a "solution" to rebellion (Byman 2016; Moore 1978). Totalitarian regimes are distinct in that they require mass participation in state-sponsored movements to enforce party loyalty to a grand ideological scheme. Overall, oppositional action is forced underground and into "unobtrusive" forms of resistance due to ruthless persecution (Johnston and Mueller 2001).

Authoritarianism is often used interchangeably with *dictatorship* and *autocracy* to refer to non-democracies in general, but authoritarianism is also considered to be a key subtype of non-democracies. Linz (2000) argues that authoritarianism is a liberalized form of totalitarianism that lacks mass mobilization of the populace on behalf of a single party, while Levitsky and Way (2010) define "full" authoritarian regimes as those that preclude opportunities for challengers to compete legally for executive power. In these cases, some limited sub-national political pluralism is permitted, but civil liberties are so systematically violated that opposition groups and social movements lack minimal protections. In either case, authoritarianism is understood as a state system that is highly punitive of dissent and lacking a meaningful degree of political competition.

Newer conceptualizations reflect changes in the form and practice of authoritarian rule in the post-Cold War period, with important implications for mobilization. *Electoral authoritarianism* and *hybrid regimes*, such as Vladimir Putin's regime in Russia and Hugo Chavez's regime in Venezuela, are more liberal than full authoritarian regimes because they permit some meaningful electoral competition and civic organizing (Diamond 2002; Schedler 2013). However, hybrids also heavily skew the outcomes of institutional competition in favor of incumbents. Hybridization has also signified a change in the forms that protest takes; for example, Robertson (2010) finds that hybrid regimes are also likely to exhibit "hybrid protest," including both symbolic demonstrations common to democracies and direct actions such as strikes. A variant of the hybrid is *competitive authoritarianism* (Levitsky and Way 2010), which permits competition between groups for executive power, but wherein elections are unfree and unfair. Polity members may organize and protest to some degree under each of these types, but their movements remain at significant risk of persecution.

Lastly, the term *liberalized authoritarianism* is derived by Moss (2014) to refer to authoritarian regimes that do not permit any contestation for executive power, but

whose authorities nevertheless exhibit a relatively expanded tolerance for mobilization and protest activity in comparison with years past. These regimes seek to avoid
violent confrontation with protesters for fear of inciting a backlash and negative
international attention. As a result, officials formally and informally manage dissent
by bargaining with activists so long as protesters do not violate political taboos by
calling for revolution and democracy (Chen 2012; Lee and Zhang 2013; Su and He
2010). So although activists face harassment and repression, the willingness of officials to accommodate some protests can enable activists to gain concessions without
producing mass disruptions; Moss (2014) calls this dynamic "contained escalation."

The evolving character of contemporary authoritarian regimes has had a number
of effects. While reforms are used by elites to legitimize their power and stabilize
their rule, they also increase opportunities for social movements to capitalize on
regimes' discursive commitments to reform and democracy. Such opportunities mean
that people begin to talk less and walk more (Johnston 2004), and elites' failures to
live up to their promises can spark destabilizing protests that produce defections and
executive turnover (Almeida 2003; Trejo 2012), as in the case of Ukraine's Orange
Revolution in 2004. At the same time, regimes adapt to these threats in a number of
ways, as when elites "manage" the streets by sponsoring loyalist movements
(Robertson 2007, 2010). For this reason, the emergence of protests in authoritarian
states can destabilize regimes under certain conditions, but does not necessarily
herald democratization or signify the functioning of an independent civil society.

Variation in Regime Repression and Propensities for Violence

In addition to bringing attention to variation among non-democratic regimes
types, scholars of mobilization have also refined understandings as to how and
why non-democratic regimes repress their critics. While democracy has been shown
to decrease violent retribution by state actors against their citizens (e.g. Davenport
2007; De Mesquita et al. 2005; Keith 2002), authoritarian regimes are far from
uniformly violent against their subjects. As we discuss above, many allow for
certain forms of collective action to occur, albeit within strict limits, thus giving
activists a *relatively* safe venue within which to propose reforms and participate in
lower-level decision-making processes. Single-party authoritarian governments,
for example, have been shown to exhibit reduced degrees of violent state repression in comparison with military dictatorships and sultanistic regimes because
"they provide some venue within which discussion/aspirations/activism can take
place" (Davenport 2007: 500). This produces a "tyrannical peace" that makes
violent repression less likely.

Many authoritarian regimes also refrain from using an annihilative approach
because violence risks provoking a backlash and fueling insurgencies.[2] While regimes
can sometimes win – at least in the short term – through overwhelming and indiscriminate force (Byman 2016), mass killings also risk fueling movement participation
and radicalization, damaging international regime legitimacy, and undermining
domestic control. Regimes often destabilize themselves, therefore, when they refuse
to negotiate with protesters who then come to see "no other way out" but to fight
back (Goodwin 2001). State officials sensitive to the threats posed by backlash

(Hess and Martin 2006), therefore, sometimes show a meaningful degree of restraint when faced with certain types of protests.

Externally-derived pressures have also created a more favorable environment for popular contention by encouraging regimes to respond with restraint. Officials typically seek to avoid being "named and shamed" by other states and multilateral institutions and to incur sanctions for the violent repression of protest, and therefore modify their repressive tactics in response (Hafner-Burton and Tsutsui 2007; Keck and Sikkink 1998; Roessler 2005; Ron 1997). Post-1989 reforms in the Chinese case have demonstrated that authorities wish to avoid another embarrassing Tiananmen-scenario, and have enacted policies intended to deescalate, rather than crush, protests by those constituencies they claim to protect (Chen 2012; Su and He 2010). This does not necessarily mean that regimes are less cruel, however. Instead, leaders may change tactics simply to avoid international sanction without exhibiting leniency toward dissent (Ron 2000).

In addition to their varying propensity to repress movements, authoritarian regimes also use a range of tactics to monitor, undermine, or neutralize their opponents (Tilly 2006). Methods include less intrusive, "softer" tactics such as surveillance, censorship, legal persecution, resource deprivation, "disattention," or the selective neglect of claims-making by social movements (Moss 2014; see also Bishara 2015 on "ignoring"). Regimes also censor the Internet and social media, which have played an increasingly important role in popular mobilization in recent years (King, Pan, and Roberts 2013). Non-violent tactics such as these are often more effective than violence in undermining movements because they chip away at movements' resources and participation while simultaneously enabling regimes to maintain "a veneer of liberalism" (Moss 2014: 263). Regimes also subcontract repression to other actors by inciting or sponsoring loyalist movements to enact violent repression on their behalf. Because imposing martial law, banning opposition activity outright, and cracking down on movements can be a high-cost strategy, incumbents may instead opt to orchestrate retribution that is "carried out by non-state actors, such as vigilantes, paramilitaries, and militias" (Roessler 2005: 209). Local officials in China routinely delegate repression to thugs and other non-state actors against collective actors mobilizing on behalf a variety of issues, such as land expropriation, house demolition, industrial restructuring, urban management, and petitioning control (Chen 2017). Such informal repressive tactics are a key factor enabling the survival of post-Cold War autocracies (Kirschke 2000; Levitsky and Way 2010) because they enable regimes to avoid confronting protesters directly and to skirt blame for ensuing abuses, harassment, and victimization. As such, regimes' nuanced responses to protest emphasize the importance of disaggregating state responses in non-democratic contexts.

In addition to using different methods to undermine mobilization, it is important to note that authoritarian regimes do not typically rely on *either* a softer or harder approach. Instead, they deploy carrot and stick measures simultaneously, adapting on-the-fly to test what will "work" to clear protesters off the streets (Rasler 1996). During the onset of the Syrian uprising in March 2011, for example, the regime of Bashar al-Assad made concessions by ending its decades-long emergency law and lifted the ban on social media while also deploying security forces to detain and kill protesters. Moreover, authoritarian regimes take varied approaches toward different types of groups and claims. For example, the Chinese government in the reform era has been relatively lenient toward localized and economically-driven protests while taking iron-fisted measures against broader religious and political movements, such as the student movement in 1989 and the Falungong movement in 1999 (Perry 2002). In addition, not all groups and institutions within a state's security apparatus react in a cohesive or orchestrated fashion to protest. During Egypt's revolutionary uprising in January and February of 2011, the police and *baltagiyyah*, plain-clothed policemen and paid thugs, attacked protesters in Tahrir Square as members of the military watched on the sidelines. As a result, the disaggregation of regime tactics and perpetrators is necessary for understanding cycles of contention.

Variation in Institutional Access and Regime Responsiveness

It is commonly thought that challengers have no choice but to storm the citadel walls to contest their oppression and marginalization in authoritarian states. However, regime leaders are often aware of the danger of being isolated from society, and therefore foster grievance-airing and conflict resolution in specific ways. Indeed, some regimes exhibit a relatively high degree of responsiveness and sophisticated strategies for managing institutional access that challenge the notion of challengers as outsiders. In the German Democratic Republic, for example, individual claims-making became routinized, with thousands of written grievances reaching authorities each year (Straughn 2005: 1604); receiving agents were then required to give a written response within a specified period of time. Some contemporary Arab monarchies in the Middle East also maintain a form of "desert democracy" wherein rulers routinely carry out political consultation with elites and ordinary people (Herb 1999), and in China, the state developed the *xinfang* (letters and visits) system to manage citizen complaints and petitions.

At the same time, regime responsiveness under authoritarianism is obtained in a different way than in democracies, and such forms of access or "institutional absorption" (Lee and Zhang 2013) do not prevent subordinate groups from resorting to protests. In fact, such systems may provide citizens with incentives to stage certain forms of collective demonstrations. This is mainly because even when regimes install institutions to facilitate citizens' claims-making, the responsiveness to moderate and lawful participation is usually very low. To elicit adequate responses from authoritarian regimes, citizens often need to stage collective actions with "troublemaking" tactics (Chen 2012). Although such collective protests are usually local, low-intensity, and limited in their claims, they still face the risk of repression, and it is often unclear how far participants can push their complaints and demands. For example, Straughn (2005: 1605) points out that under state socialism's system of ideological orthodoxy and repression of critical speech, the boundary between consent and dissent was far more ambiguous than in liberal democracies. As a result, ordinary citizens and activists who test the responsiveness of authoritarian states risk being perceived as troublemakers (Fitzpatrick 1996) and incurring repression.

Regime responsiveness and accommodation may also do more to contribute to authoritarian stability than signify the nascent stages of democratization. When citizens appropriate available channels to articulate their interests to officials via contentious bargaining, this can temper and placate aggrieved populations, thus making collective actors less likely to resort to overtly disruptive tactics, criticize central authorities, or challenge the overall legitimacy of the regime itself. If the state treats the grievances of its opponents as reasonable and allows them means of protest, then the opposition is likely to organize itself within existing institutional boundaries as a social or reform movement (Goldstone and Useem 1999: 994). As a result, their claims and tactics will be "contained" (Moss 2014). If not, however, officials can stoke outrage, inciting expanded protests and radicalization.

Authoritarian regimes may also maintain stability by accommodating civil society organizations. Oxhorn (1995) has shown how the military regime in Chile generated an array of democratic and participatory structures among the rural poor, and Wickham's (2004) study of the Wasat movement in Egypt suggests that opportunities for formal partisan participation served as an inducement to Wasat activists to maintain moderate aims.[3] Many civil society organizations in China, such as underground labor organizations, similarly adjusted their strategies to the political environment. Rather than organizing collective protests, they focused on coaching citizens to make individual rights claims (Fu 2016).

Authoritarian states also actively sponsor government-organized non-government organizations (GONGOs) as a means to manage dissent, thereby creating a distinct "organizational ecology" (Robertson 2010). Rather than resembling totalitarian-like organizations that support the ruling regime or party, these organizations instead mimic independent non-governmental organizations, often for the purposes of charity and development. Such organizations typically receive a disproportionate amount of state support and are treated as more legitimate than their independent counterparts. As such, they can also enable participants to talk back to the state and advocate for concessions even though they are not transgressive (Moss 2014). This suggests that while managing organizational ecology is an important strategy for authoritarian regimes to control social movements, they do not automatically or easily coopt their critics through these mechanisms.

Authoritarian Power-Sharing, Elite Divisions, and Protest

In authoritarian contexts, popular contention is shaped not only by the relationship between ruling elites and subordinate groups, but also by the relationships operative *among* ruling elites and their power-sharing arrangements (Kandil 2016; Slater 2010). Power-sharing in authoritarian systems, which have increasingly come to include elections, are a critical component of authoritarian politics that determine regime durability (Svolik 2012) and shape a regime's responses to dissent. Cleavages between elites, including between executive authorities and the various groups comprising the security apparatus, can create opportunities for mobilization (McAdam 1996; Tilly and Tarrow 2007) both "from above" and "from below." For this reason, rather than characterizing authoritarian regimes as cohesive, many scholars are now usefully analyzing how regime members share and compete for power and theorizing how these dynamics shape popular contention.

As we reference above, some scholars have uncovered a correlation between electoral competition in authoritarian states and heightened levels of protest, suggesting that even when elections are strictly controlled and implemented in order to legitimize authoritarianism, they nevertheless present opportunities for movements to contest the terms and outcomes of power-sharing. Elections are particularly conducive to protest movements in hybrid regimes where elections are competitive but often suffer from irregularities. Many competitive authoritarian regimes witness "an upsurge in mass participation, not just in elections, but also in the streets before and sometimes after the elections" in support of particular candidates and parties and in protest over dubious electoral outcomes (Bunce and Wolchik 2006: 5).

On the other hand, in authoritarian regimes that lack elections, power struggles may stimulate popular movements for different reasons, suggesting that elites incite movements and protest as bargaining mechanisms to resolve intra-elite disputes. In discussing the student movement in China in 1989, for example, McAdam et al. (2001: 209) argue:

> Why would party elites risk mobilizing the masses in the first place? Ironically, how the [Chinese Communist Party] exercises its monopoly on power constrains strategic action by Party elite. Lacking any independent political institutions (e.g. free elections, an autonomous judiciary, or independent trade unions), the Party actually has few vehicles available for resolving internal factional conflicts. The extraordinary control that Party elites enjoy over most sectors of Chinese society makes orchestrated mass struggle a logical response to the problem.

In addition to intra-elite competition at the national level, relations among state elites at different levels may also provide dynamics for popular contention (Kandil 2016). The operation of "fragmented authoritarianism" in China is a case in point (Mertha 2009). On the one hand, the central government heavily relies on citizen complaints and petitions to monitor local officials (Chen 2012; Lorentzen 2013). On the other, divergent agendas and attitudes between officials provide incentives and resources for ordinary Chinese to lodge their complaints and stage collective protests (Cai 2010; Chen 2012; Lee 2007; O'Brien and Li 2006). Protests staged by Chinese peasants against excessive taxes, fees, and other burdens imposed by local governments, which were common in the 1990s across China, were strongly encouraged by the central government and official media. Deeply concerned about the potential of peasants' protests to destabilize the regime, central authorities often exert strong pressure on local officials for burden reduction, thus providing legitimacy and protection for protesters. Local elites in Russia also use protests as a means to gain leverage against central authorities. When regional leaders have poor political relations with the center, they often have few bargaining resources other than to mobilize workers to pressure the center for resources and assistance. In this way, local authorities use protest movements and labor strikes as a means to exert pressure on central authorities to reallocate attention and resources (Robertson 2007: 783).

Authoritarian Regimes and Transnational Dynamics of Contention

While official boundaries demarcate the reach of governing authorities in important ways, the dynamics of contention between authoritarian regimes and social movements are not strictly contained by state borders. In contrast to the "closed polity" approach (Gleditsch 2007) of regime and social movement studies that analyze authoritarianism as an insular phenomenon, authoritarianism's effects on dissent are instead transnational in cause, character, and consequence.

As research on globalization and cross-national mobilization demonstrates, transnational social movements play an important role in contesting authoritarian policies and practices. Lacking recourse against state repression, social movements in authoritarian states often rely on outside allies to "name and shame" regime practices and lobby states and international organizations to intervene on their behalf (Hafner-Burton and Tsutsui 2007). Allied movements and organizations mobilizing from within democratic states can provide critical assistance to anti-authoritarian movements and repressed populations, channeling resources to besieged movements and publicizing regime atrocities that violate international norms and laws (Keck and Sikkink 1998). In this way, transnational advocacy networks may mitigate repression, but only when autocrats are sensitive to criticism and/or seek to avoid censure and sanctions by other states, as we discuss above.

Mobilization in authoritarian states is also an increasingly globalized phenomenon, as activists use technologies and communications to disseminate information and expose regime abuses to international audiences. The political opportunities afforded by the internationalization of dissent make it increasingly difficult for regimes to quash movements in the dark (Tarrow 2005). The documentation of the Arab Spring revolutions of 2011 by social media users on the ground, for example, helped anti-regime movements overcome media blackouts, refute regime propaganda, and gain internal and external support. The documentation of regime atrocities by everyday citizens armed with digital recording devices has also granted movements leverage in pushing for sanctions against autocrats in conjunction with international institutions such as the United Nations and the International Criminal Court.

However, even when social movements successfully externalize their grievances, claims, and demands, activists may nevertheless be subjected to retaliation for their efforts without the decisive, protectionist interventions by external actors. Otherwise, when members of social movements take heightened risks to attract the support of external allies, they may incur significant repression that their movement allies overseas are helpless to prevent (Bob 2002). In addition, the very technologies that anti-authoritarian movements use to publicize grievances and facilitate mobilization, such as Facebook and YouTube, can afford greater opportunities for regimes to identify, surveil, and punish dissenters (Gunitsky 2015).

Relatedly, authoritarian regime repression against dissidents is not a contained dynamic. Instead, regimes import tools and methods of repression from their authoritarian allies and democratic governments alike, as well as from for-profit entitles based across the globe. And because social movements are often transnational in character, states also work together to repress transnational movements, from communist (Miller 1981) to Islamist movements. As Moss (2016) notes, "[s]uch collaborations include military interventions against pro-democracy movements, such as the repression of Bahraini protesters by Saudi military forces in 2011, extradition agreements, rendition programs, and resource transfers of weapons and spyware" (see also Blanton 1999; Gordon 1987).

Authoritarian repression also foments transnational activism through migration (Quinsaat 2013). Activists facing repression are often pushed across borders, producing exile and émigré activist networks. Migration out of illiberal states can therefore provide critical opportunities for the mobilization of "long-distance nationalists" who challenge regimes from afar, mobilize resources on behalf of their compatriots at home, incite mobilization online, and support insurrections – all without suffering the direct consequences of their actions (Anderson 1998). Movements can thus "exit" and gain a new "voice" upon resettlement in friendly states (Hirschman 1978).

At the same time, not all emigrants are free to mobilize after resettling abroad because some authoritarian regimes engage in what Moss (2016) calls "transnational repression," punishing their emigrants overseas in direct and indirect ways. Regimes can deter mobilization among diasporas by threatening to permanently exile emigrants for speaking out from abroad and by holding their family members hostage in the home country. Regimes also police the politics of their émigrés through surveillance by pro-regime agents and informants. For these reasons, the threats posed by transnational repression can have widespread deterrent effects on public anti-regime mobilization among diaspora communities (ibid.). North African regimes, for example, have worked to control and intimidate their citizens abroad through the establishment of associations, or *amicales*, which facilitated surveillance and policed loyalty among the diaspora (Brand 2006); they also partnered with European governments to repress the mobilization of migrant labor movements (Miller 1981). While not all non-democratic regimes encroach upon their diasporas to the same degree, regimes lying at the "full" authoritarian and totalitarian end of the non-democratic spectrum are likely to view dissent abroad as egregious for both ideological and practical reasons. The ways in which authoritarianism in migrants' home countries impacts their mobilization processes abroad are a dynamic warranting further scrutiny.

Conclusion

The study of collective action under and against authoritarianism remains a pressing topic of inquiry because the conditions under which collective actors contest non-democratic authorities have implications for understanding collective action, regime change, and conflict. Recent studies have made significant advances by refining characterizations of authoritarian regimes as monolithic, uniformly violent, closed, cohesive, and insular. Instead, authoritarian regimes vary in character, use a range of tactics to manage and repress collective action, exhibit varying degrees and mechanisms of responsiveness, are comprised of competing elites, and exhibit transnational dynamics of contention and repression.

These theoretical and empirical advances should be further appreciated in light of the fact that scholars face a distinct set of challenges in pursuing research on the subject. Scholars who live in non-democratic states are often constrained from writing directly on authoritarianism and protest due to repression; those who reside in democratic states but maintain citizenship in authoritarian countries-of-origin may be forced to self-censor in order to maintain access to and protect their family members in the home country. As a result, many researchers who are best positioned to analyze state-society relations in these contexts face significant constraints in doing so. Additionally, for scholars based in democratic states, the costs of internationally-based fieldwork are high, and they confront barriers to data collection that include regime oversight and censorship, access to dissidents, and the fear barrier of the wider populace (e.g. Wedeen 2015 [1999]). Scholars who tackle delicate subjects during periods of regime consolidation and authoritarian retrenchment assume personal risks as well.[4]

With these challenges in mind, we propose several lines of inquiry that require further analysis. First, although we lacked the space to systematically address it here, the question of how social movements facilitate freer and fairer systems of governance is an important topic at the heart of social science research (Adler and Webster 1995; Bermeo 1997; Collier 1999; Collier and Mahoney 1997; Posusney 2004). A range of variables have been shown to make it more likely that movements will successfully challenge and overthrow dictatorships, including the degree of elite and military cohesion (Slater 2010), demographic changes, the "tidal" forces of nationalism (Beissinger 2002), and information cascades (Kuran 1991; Lohmann 1994). As scholars continue to pursue explanations of anti-authoritarian movement success and democratization, we suggest that rather than working to pinpoint a single variable or formula that "works" in every case, scholars would do well to demonstrate how different causal combinations operate across similar types of insurrections (e.g. Goodwin 2001; Slater 2010) and vary, depending on the time frame and protest wave under scrutiny.

A related but understudied question is how anti-authoritarian social movements paradoxically reconstitute the very systems that they seek to overthrow, both internally and as victors in revolutionary state takeovers. Communist movement success in overthrowing "traditional" authoritarian systems in Russia, China, and Cambodia, for example, led to mass killings, extreme repression, and non-democratic systems of power that persist in different forms to this day. This reflects the importance of rethinking assumptions that social movement mobilization is inherently liberalizing since movements can foment fascism, nationalism, communism, religious extremism, and its various iterations, such as Ba'athism in Syria and Iraq. Far more research is needed to understand how and why movements professing egalitarian principles and the rights of the marginalized engage in their own sets of repressions and reconstitute the illiberalism that they claim to displace.

We also suggest that scholars continue to problematize the traditionally sharp distinction drawn between regime members and their challengers. Not only do authoritarian regimes commonly rely on popular participation and acquiescence to conduct repression, but high-level authorities rely on subordinate members of the populace to stock their security apparatuses and to commit acts of violence on their behalf. As a result, regime elites not only have to be concerned with managing the streets, but also how to maintain the allegiance of their rank-and-file, especially during periods when subordinates are ordered to turn their guns on fellow citizens and members of their own communities. The dynamics of loyalty and dissent among the various members of the state security apparatus and how this is shaped by ethnicity, race, religion, and regionalism remain a pressing topic of inquiry because the extent to which regimes exhibit cohesive counter-mobilization greatly influences the evolution of protest movements and violent conflict (Kandil 2016; Slater 2010). This also requires attending to how regimes build and manage security apparatuses – and in turn, how these apparatuses manage and repress one another – which has been largely neglected in the study of state-society relations and repression to date.

Lastly, we suggest that scholars use studies of mobilization in authoritarian states to better understand the dynamics of repression in other contexts, including those in liberal Western states. While most studies treat authoritarianism as a national-level regime characteristic, authoritarianism can operate at different levels, including in the supra-national, national, and sub-national arenas; democratic states also sometimes act in an authoritarian fashion inside and outside of their borders, as in the case of racial/ethnic-apartheid regimes (e.g. Ron 2000; White 1989). Additionally, authoritarianism is not confined to political institutions, but can also characterize social, cultural, and corporate entities. The repression and management of workforces and unions in US history (e.g. Fantasia 1988; Stepan-Norris and Zeitlin 1996), for example, mirror many of the tactics used by authoritarian states to manage opposition movements. We therefore expect that the effects of repression on protest and mobilization across contexts will be similar and therefore warrant cross-case and multilevel comparisons. In this way, studies of mobilization in authoritarian and democratic states can better inform one another and refine the pervasive belief that the emergence of collective dissent in non-democracies is exceptional.

Notes

1   The authors contributed equally to this chapter.
2   See Einwohner (2003), Einwohner and Maher (2011), Goldstone and Tilly (2001), Maher (2010), and Rasler (1996) on backlash and the escalation of collective resistance.
3   See also Clarke (2011) on how Egypt's authoritarianism can foment social movement coalitions.
4   This occurred in the extreme but not unprecedented case of Giulio Regeni, a 28-year-old Italian graduate student researching Egypt's trade unions, who was tortured and murdered extrajudicially by state security agents in Cairo in 2016 (Spencer 2016).

References

Adler, Glenn and Eddie Webster. 1995. "Challenging Transition Theory: The Labor Movement, Radical Reform, and Transition to Democracy in South Africa." *Politics and Society* 23(1): 75–106.

Almeida, Paul D. 2003. "Opportunity Organizations and Threat-Induced Contention: Protest Waves in Authoritarian Settings." *American Journal of Sociology* 109: 345–400.

Anderson, Benedict. 1998. *The Spectre of Comparisons: Nationalism, Southeast Asia, and the World*. New York: Verso.

Beissinger, Mark R. 2002. *Nationalist Mobilization and the Collapse of the Soviet State: A Tidal Approach to the Study of Nationalism*. New York: Cambridge University Press.

Bermeo, Nancy. 1997. "Myths of Moderation: Confrontation and Conflict during Democratic Transitions." *Comparative Politics* 29: 305–22.

Bishara, Dina. 2015. "The Politics of Ignoring: Protest Dynamics in Late Mubarak Egypt." *Perspectives on Politics* 13: 958–975.

Blanton, Shannon. 1999. "Instruments of Security or Tools of Repression? Arms Imports and Human Rights Conditions in Developing Countries." *Journal of Peace Research* 36: 233–244.

Bob, Clifford. 2002. "Political Process Theory and Transnational Movements: Dialectics of Protest among Nigeria's Ogoni Minority." *Social Problems* 49: 395–415.

Brand, Laurie A. 2006. *Citizens Abroad: Emigration and the State in the Middle East and North Africa*. New York: Cambridge University Press.

Bunce, Valerie and Sharon L. Wolchik. 2006. "Favorable Conditions and Electoral Revolutions." *Journal of Democracy* 17: 5–18.

Byman, Daniel. 2016. "'Death Solves All Problems': The Authoritarian Model of Counterinsurgency." *Journal of Strategic Studies* 39: 62–93.

Cai, Yongshun. 2010. *Collective Resistance in China: Why Popular Protests Succeed or Fail*. Stanford, CA: Stanford University Press.

Carothers, Thomas. 2002. "The End of the Transition Paradigm" *Journal of Democracy* 13: 5–21.

Chehabi, Houchang E. and Juan J. Linz. 1998. *Sultanistic Regimes*. Baltimore, MD: Johns Hopkins University Press.

Chen, Xi. 2012. *Social Protest and Contentious Authoritarianism in China*. New York: Cambridge University Press.

Chen, Xi. 2017. "Origins of Informal Coercion in China." *Politics and Society* 45(1): 67–89.

Clarke, Killian. 2011. "Saying 'Enough': Authoritarianism and Egypt's Kefaya Movement." *Mobilization: An International Quarterly* 16: 397–416.

Collier, Ruth Berins. 1999. *Paths toward Democracy: The Working Class and Elites in Western Europe and South America*. New York: Cambridge University Press.

Collier, Ruth Berins and James Mahoney. 1997. "Adding Collective Actors to Collective Outcomes: Labor and Recent Democratization in South America and Southern Europe." *Comparative Politics* 29: 285–303.

Davenport, Christian. 2007. "State Repression and the Tyrannical Peace." *Journal of Peace Research* 44: 485–504.

De Mesquita, Bruce Bueno, Feryal Marie Cherif, George W. Downs, and Alastair Smith. 2005. "Thinking Inside the Box: A Closer Look at Democracy and Human Rights." *International Studies Quarterly* 49: 439–458.

Diamond, Larry Jay. 2002. "Thinking About Hybrid Regimes." *Journal of Democracy* 13: 21–35.

Einwohner, Rachel L. 2003. "Opportunity, Honor, and Action in the Warsaw Ghetto Uprising of 1943." *American Journal of Sociology* 109: 650–675.

Einwohner, Rachel L. and Thomas Maher. 2011. "Threat Assessment and Collective-Action Emergence: Death-Camp and Ghetto Resistance during the Holocaust." *Mobilization: An International Quarterly* 16: 127–146.

Fantasia, Rick. 1988. *Cultures of Solidarity: Consciousness, Action and Contemporary American Workers*. Berkeley: University of California Press.

Fitzpatrick, Sheila. 1996. "Supplicants and Citizens: Public Letter-Writing in Soviet Russia in the 1930s." *Slavic Review* 55: 78–105.

Fu, Diana. 2016. "Disguised Collective Action in China." *Comparative Political Studies*, 50(4): 499–527.

Geddes, Barbara. 1999. "What Do We Know About Democratization After Twenty Years?" *Annual Review of Political Science* 2: 115–144.

Gleditsch, Kristian Skrede. 2007. "Transnational Dimensions of Civil War." *Journal of Peace Research* 44: 293–309.

Goldstone, Jack A. and Charles Tilly. 2001. "Threat (and Opportunity): Popular Action and State Response in the Dynamics of Contentious Action." In *Silence and Voice in the Study of Contentious Politics*, edited by Ronald R. Aminzade, Jack A. Goldstone, Doug McAdam, et al., 179–194. New York: Cambridge University Press.

Goldstone, Jack A. and Bert Useem. 1999. "Prison Riots as Microrevolutions: An Extension of State-Centered Theories of Revolution." *American Journal of Sociology* 104: 985–1029.

Goodwin, Jeff. 2001. *No Other Way Out: State and Revolutionary Movements, 1945–1991.* New York: Cambridge University Press.

Gordon, Paul. 1987. "The Killing Machine: Britain and the International Repression Trade." *Race & Class* 29: 31–52.

Gunitsky, Seva. 2015. "Corrupting the Cyber-Commons: Social Media as a Tool of Autocratic Stability." *Perspectives on Politics* 13: 42–54.

Hafner-Burton, Emilie and Kiyoteru Tsutsui. 2007. "Justice Lost! The Failure of International Human Rights Law to Matter Where Needed Most." *Journal of Peace Research* 44: 407–425.

Herb, Michael. 1999. *All in the Family: Absolutism, Revolution, and Democracy in the Middle Eastern Monarchies.* Albany, NY: State University of New York Press.

Hess, David and Brian Martin. 2006. "Repression, Backfire, and the Theory of Transformative Events." *Mobilization: An International Quarterly*, 11: 249–267.

Hirschman, Albert. 1978. "Exit, Voice, and the State." *World Politics*, 31: 90–107.

Johnston, Hank. 2004. "Talking the Walk: Speech Acts and Resistance in Authoritarian Regimes." In *Repression and Mobilization*, edited by Christian Davenport, Hank Johnston, and Carol Mueller, 108–137. Minneapolis: University of Minnesota Press.

Johnston, Hank and Carol Mueller. 2001. "Unobtrusive Practices of Contention in Leninist Regimes." *Sociological Perspectives* 44: 351–375.

Kandil, Hazem. 2016. *The Power Triangle: Military, Security, and Politics in Regime Change.* Oxford: Oxford University Press.

Keck, Margaret E. and Kathryn Sikkink. 1998. *Activists Beyond Borders.* Ithaca, NY: Cornell University Press.

Keith, Linda Camp. 2002. "Constitutional Provisions for Individual Human Rights (1977–1996): Are They More than Mere 'Window Dressing?'" *Political Research Quarterly* 55: 111–143.

King, Gary, Jennifer Pan, and Margaret E. Roberts. 2013. "How Censorship in China Allows Government Criticism but Silences Collective Expression." *American Political Science Review* 107: 326–343.

Kirschke, Linda. 2000. "Informal Repression, Zero-Sum Politics and Late Third World Transition." *Journal of Modern African Studies* 38: 383–405.

Kriesi, Hanspeter. 2005. "Political Context and Opportunity." In *The Blackwell Companion to Social Movements*, edited by David A. Snow, Sarah A. Soule, and Hanspeter Kriesi, 67–90. Oxford: Blackwell.

Kuran, Timur. 1991. "Now Out of Never: The Element of Surprise in the East European Revolution of 1989." *World Politics* 44: 7–48.

Lee, Ching Kwan. 2007. *Against the Law: Labor Protests in China's Rustbelt and Sunbelt.* Berkeley: University of California Press.

Lee, Ching Kwan and Yonghong Zhang. 2013. "The Power of Instability: Unraveling the Microfoundations of Bargained Authoritarianism in China." *American Journal of Sociology* 118: 1475–1508.

Levitsky, Steven and Lucan A. Way. 2010. *Competitive Authoritarianism: Hybrid Regimes After the Cold War.* New York: Cambridge University Press.

Linz, Juan J. 2000. *Totalitarian and Authoritarian Regimes.* Boulder, CO: Lynne Rienner Publishers.

Lohmann, Susanne. 1994. "The Dynamics of Informational Cascades: The Monday Demonstrations in Leipzig, East Germany, 1989–91." *World Politics* 47: 42–101.

Lorentzen, Peter L. 2013. "Regularizing Rioting: Permitting Public Protest in an Authoritarian Regime." *Quarterly Journal of Political Science* 8: 127–158.

Maher, Thomas. 2010. "Threat, Resistance, and Collective Action: The Cases of Sobibor, Treblinka, and Auschwitz." *American Sociological Review* 75: 252–272.

McAdam, Doug. 1996. "Political Opportunities: Conceptual Origins, Current Problems, Future Directions." In *Comparative Perspectives on Social Movements*, edited by Doug McAdam, John D. McCarthy, and Mayer N. Zald, 23–40. New York: Cambridge University Press.

McAdam, Doug, Sidney Tarrow, and Charles Tilly. 2001. *Dynamics of Contention*. New York: Cambridge University Press.

Mertha, Andrew. 2009. "'Fragmented Authoritarianism 2.0': Political Pluralization in the Chinese Policy Process." *The China Quarterly* 200: 995–1012.

Miller, Mark. 1981. *Foreign Workers in Western Europe: An Emerging Political Force*. New York: Praeger.

Moore, Barrington, Jr. 1978. *Injustice: The Social Bases of Obedience and Revolt*. White Plains, NY: M.E. Sharpe.

Moss, Dana M. 2014. "Repression, Response, and Contained Escalation under 'Liberalized' Authoritarianism in Jordan." *Mobilization: An International Quarterly* 19: 261–286.

Moss, Dana M. 2016. "Transnational Repression, Diaspora Mobilization, and the Case of the Arab Spring." *Social Problems* 63(4): 480–498.

O'Brien, Kevin and Lianjiang Li. 2006. *Rightful Resistance in Rural China*. New York: Cambridge University Press.

Oxhorn, Philip. 1995. *Organizing Civil Society: The Popular Sectors and the Struggle for Democracy in Chile*. University Park, PA: The Pennsylvania State University Press.

Perry, Elizabeth. 2002. *Challenging the Mandate of Heaven: Social Protest and State Power in China*. Armonk, NY: M.E. Sharpe.

Posusney, Marsha P. 2004. "Enduring Authoritarianism: Middle East Lessons for Comparative Theory." *Comparative Politics* 36(2): 127–138.

Przeworski, Adam. 1991. *Democracy and the Market: Political and Economic Reforms in Eastern Europe and Latin America*. Cambridge: Cambridge University Press.

Quinsaat, Sharon Madriaga. 2013. "Migrant Mobilization for Homeland Politics: A Social Movement Approach." *Sociology Compass* 7: 952–964.

Rasler, Karen. 1996. "Concessions, Repression, and Political Protest in the Iranian Revolution." *American Sociological Review* 61: 132–152.

Robertson, Graeme B. 2007. "Strikes and Labor Organization in Hybrid Regimes." *American Political Science Review* 101: 781–798.

Robertson, Graeme B. 2010. *The Politics of Protest in Hybrid Regimes: Managing Dissent in Post-Communist Russia*. New York: Cambridge University Press.

Roessler, Philip G. 2005. "Donor-Induced Democratization and the Privatization of State Violence in Kenya and Rwanda." *Comparative Politics* 37: 207–225.

Ron, James. 1997. "Varying Methods of State Violence." *International Organization* 51: 275–300.

Ron, James. 2000. "Savage Restraint: Israel, Palestine and the Dialectics of Legal Repression." *Social Problems* 47: 445–472.

Schedler, Andreas. 2013. *The Politics of Uncertainty: Sustaining and Subverting Electoral Authoritarianism*. New York: Oxford University Press.

Scott, James. 1985. *Weapons of the Weak*. New Haven, CT: Yale University Press.

Slater, Dan. 2010. *Ordering Power: Contentious Politics and Authoritarian Leviathans in Southeast Asia*. New York: Cambridge University Press.

Spencer, Richard. 2016. "New Claims that Murdered Cambridge Student Giulio Regeni Was Arrested by Egyptian Police." *The Telegraph*, 21 April. Available at: http://www.telegraph. co.uk/news/2016/04/21/new-claims-that-murdered-cambridge-student-giulio-regeni-was-arr/

Stepan-Norris, Judith and Maurice Zeitlin. 1996. *Talking Union*. Chicago: University of Illinois Press.

Straughn, Jeremy Brooke. 2005. "'Taking the State at Its Word': The Arts of Consentful Contention in the German Democratic Republic." *American Journal of Sociology* 110: 1598–1650.

Su, Yang and Xin He. 2010. "Street as Courtroom: State Accommodation of Labor Protest in South China." *Law and Society Review* 44: 157–184.

Svolik, Milan. 2012. *The Politics of Authoritarian Rule*. New York: Cambridge University Press.

Tarrow, Sidney. 2005. *The New Transnational Activism*. New York: Cambridge University Press.

Tilly, Charles. 2006. *Regimes and Repertoires*. Chicago: University of Chicago Press.

Tilly, Charles and Sidney Tarrow. 2007. *Contentious Politics*. Boulder, CO: Paradigm Publishers.

Trejo, Guillermo. 2012. *Popular Movements in Autocracies: Religion, Repression, and Indigenous Collective Action in Mexico*. New York: Cambridge University Press.

Weber, Max. 1978. *Economy and Society: An Outline of Interpretive Sociology*. Berkeley: University of California Press.

Wedeen, Lisa. 2015 [1999]. *Ambiguities of Domination: Politics, Rhetoric, and Symbols in Contemporary Syria*. Chicago: University of Chicago Press.

White, Robert W. 1989. "From Peaceful Protest to Guerrilla War: Micromobilization of the Provisional Irish Republican Army." *American Journal of Sociology* 94: 1277–1302.

Wickham, Carrie Rosefsky. 2004. "The Path to Moderation: Strategy and Learning in the Formation of Egypt's Wasat Party." *Comparative Politics* 36: 205–228.

Zhao, Dingxin. 2001. *The Power of Tiananmen: State-Society Relations and the 1989 Beijing Student Movement*. Chicago: University of Chicago Press.

39

Revolution and Social Movements

Jack A. Goldstone and Daniel P. Ritter

Introduction

For most of the twentieth century, revolutions and social movements were treated as entirely different phenomena, examined by different scholars, using different approaches. Revolutions were analyzed as macro-social events, caused by great historical forces – modernization, the rise of new classes, transformative ideologies, or changing international orders that placed pressures on vulnerable regimes. In revolutions, the leading actors' goal was to replace the government and to transform the political and/or socio-economic order in society, and they operated through civil or guerilla wars and massive urban insurrections. They arose only in authoritarian regimes (monarchies or military dictatorships) and involved violent attacks on elites and rulers.

Social movements, by contrast, were analyzed as meso- or micro-level events, caused by particular, voluntarily-formed groups mobilizing for relatively narrow purposes related almost exclusively to that group's interests. Their goal was never to replace the government or to transform the entire political order, but to advance their group's agenda either in regard to inclusion in the existing political and social order or to modify specific policies of the existing government (McCarthy and Zald 1977). Social movements might in some cases use limited violence, but for the most part they operated through peaceful means: strikes, boycotts, sit-ins, demonstrations, marches, and occupations. They arose only in at least partially liberal societies where citizens had the rights of speech and assembly, and were able to use those rights to protest to gain attention and influence the government's actions.

Today, these descriptions seem a bit like caricatures. In the last 30 years, we have seen a succession of "color revolutions" (sometimes referred to as nonviolent or unarmed revolutions) that overturned governments not by civil or guerilla war or by violent urban insurrections, but by using the predominantly peaceful repertoire of

The Wiley Blackwell Companion to Social Movements, Second Edition. Edited by David A. Snow, Sarah A. Soule, Hanspeter Kriesi, and Holly J. McCammon.
© 2019 John Wiley & Sons Ltd. Published 2019 by John Wiley & Sons Ltd.

social movements – demonstrations, marches, strikes, and occupations. These included the Philippines' "People Power" revolution of 1986, the anti-communist revolutions in Eastern Europe and the Soviet Union in 1989–1991, Serbia's "Bulldozer Revolution" in 2000, the "Orange Revolution" in Ukraine in 2004, and, most recently, the fall of the authoritarian regimes of Zine al-Abidine Ben Ali in Tunisia and Hosni Mubarak in Egypt in 2011 (Lawson 2015b). We have also come to understand that many of the historical "great revolutions" – the Puritan Revolution in seventeenth-century England, the French Revolution of the eighteenth century, and the even the Russian Revolution of 1917 – began with social movement campaigns for political reforms, including pamphleteering, peaceful mobilization into clubs or political parties, and reform programs in law courts and national assemblies (Parliament, the Estates-General, and the Duma). These only gradually led to civil wars and efforts to create new political and social orders. These outcomes evolved in response to state actions, international pressures, and factional struggles among reformers, which empowered radicals and led to wider mobilization and more extreme, violent conflicts, most of which had not been anticipated just a few years before (Goldstone 2003).

The line between social movements and revolutions has thus blurred, both in theory and in recent events. Since the late 1990s, the contentious politics approach has therefore treated revolutions and social movements as similar in many ways. McAdam, Tarrow, and Tilly (2001), Goldstone (1998), and Aminzade, Goldstone, and Perry (2003) have identified a variety of mechanisms that appeared in both social movements and revolutions. They consider both kinds of events to share a number of common causal features but to differ in their trajectories and outcomes, due to factors that develop in the course of contention between movement actors and their targets.

Yet they still treated social movements and revolutions separately; as do most scholars in these fields. Moreover, scholars in sociology and political science still struggle to unify approaches to collective action that stress agency and voluntarism with approaches that focus on structural determination of events (Mahoney and Snyder 1999; Ritter 2015). Moreover, studies of social movements and revolutions are both still seeking the best way to incorporate culture and emotions into their analysis (Foran 2005; Goodwin and Jasper 1999; Goodwin, Jasper, and Polletta 2001).

In this chapter, we do not wish to deny the differences between revolutions and social movements. It remains true that social movements are more common in democratic and semi-authoritarian regimes than in full dictatorships; that guerilla warfare is a tactic of revolutionary movements but not social movements (although terrorism is used by both); that revolutions commonly produce civil wars but social movements generally do not (although they can, as with the anti-slavery movement in the nineteenth-century United States), and that the outcomes of social movements are generally (although by no means always) less transformative than the outcomes of revolutions.

Yet we will focus here on the overlaps and similarities between social movements and revolutions, and particularly on the issue of how some social movements morph into revolutionary efforts to change regimes. We shall discuss how the theories and research approaches developed for each field can also prove valuable for the other.

Origins of Revolutions and Social Movements

Both social movements and revolutions often begin with a tension between the actions or policies of the existing government and what some actors see as what is just or necessary. Charles Tilly (1978) referred to mobilization on these terms as little more than the logical continuation of the everyday struggle for resources. The actors may be elites within or outside the government, or peasants, workers, professionals, intellectuals, or soldiers. These actors may make efforts to try to resolve this tension through normal institutional politics or legal actions. But whether because such efforts fail, or because they deemed such efforts as closed to them (Goodwin 2001), these actors try to enlist supporters to participate in alternative methods to change government policies or personnel. If they are able to mobilize supporters to act, then what McAdam, Tarrow, and Tilly (2001) would call an episode of "contentious politics" has begun.

To be sure, in some cases the source of tension is not the government per se. For example, ecological and environmental movements may target loggers or fishermen whose actions are endangering animals; anti-nuclear movements may target utilities who operate nuclear power stations; and anti-abortion protestors may target doctors or facilities that perform abortions. Yet in each case the larger goal of the movement is to force the government to act to change or constrain the actions of the immediate targets. In this sense, revolutions and social movements alike are in one way or another, either explicitly or implicitly, directed at the state.

There has been considerable debate on what factors prompt social movement and revolutionary mobilization. This has sometimes been put in terms of whether the motivation is economic "greed" (the desire for greater resources, material advantages or benefits) or cultural/political "grievances" (rebelling against ethnic or other identity discrimination, cultural opposition or political exclusion) (see Collier and Hoeffler 2002). Yet it is now widely recognized that this dichotomy is too simplistic, and even misleading (Keen 2008). Economic deprivation generally does not by itself produce political mobilization; what matters is whether such deprivation is seen as unjust and whether government is seen to be either culpable or capable of rectifying that deprivation (Goodwin 2001). Moreover, issues of unjust deprivation raise questions of whether identity or cultural differences or political exclusion lie behind the deprivation of any particular set of actors; thus the two motivations become inextricably bound together.

To take just a few examples, Elisabeth Wood's (2003) study of revolutionary mobilization in El Salvador showed how peasants who felt they had been deprived of land rights mobilized and joined an insurgency not mainly because they thought they would gain economically, but because they felt a need to regain agency and meaningful identity from those who had undermined their local society. In addition, the US anti-slavery movement of the nineteenth century and the alcohol prohibition movement of the twentieth century arose not because movement actors felt themselves to be economically deprived or stood to benefit materially if they succeeded, nor because they felt themselves to be victims of discrimination or exclusion. Rather, these actors mobilized because they felt it was morally unjust for *others* to profit from slavery or sale of alcohol (Young 2006). Issues of *justice* – whether defined in terms of economic fairness, political rights, identity issues, or cultural expression – thus are central to the motivation for social movements and revolutions (Moore 1978).

It is also very clear that different actors *within the same* social or revolutionary movement act for different reasons. Elites may be concerned about what they see as social or political injustice or exclusion in regard to *their* interests, while popular groups may be more concerned with economic issues. Or the reverse may be true, with elites seeking material gains whipping up popular support by appealing to ideals of cultural, religious, or ethnic identity and asserting themselves as champions of an ideal. As Eric Selbin (2010) has shown, revolutionary elites rarely can gain support unless they attach their struggle to a folk-narrative of identity, injustice, and rectification that resonates with popular culture. Social movement scholars have discussed the same phenomenon as building "injustice frames" that encourage a variety of actors to share a sense of injustice and outrage over actions or issues at the core of a movement (Gamson 2013; Snow et al. 1986).

Pointing to specific economic, political, or other grievances is thus not a sound basis for explaining revolutions or social movements. Rising prices, land seizures, low wages, ethnic discrimination, political exclusion, or other factors are generally quite widespread and long-lasting, yet movements to change them are rare and often transient. This is because mobilization around any issue, for social movements or revolutions, requires that economic, political, identity, or cultural issues become defined as matters of injustice, where governments can be held culpable and capable of change. Studies of both revolutions and social movements thus require an attempt to describe the framing or cultural narrative that gives meaning to participants' actions. Otherwise their origins cannot be understood.

Processes of Mobilization

Anger and distress over unjust deprivation or exclusion may be necessary for social movements and revolutions to be possible, but they are far from sufficient. If people feel isolated and helpless in their distress, they may turn to self-destructive behavior, depression, or local episodes of violence.

For a social movement or revolutionary movement to gather force, there must also be channels for people to share their feelings and become part of a larger group of like-minded people; and moreover to believe that acting as part of that group can be a meaningful way to gain attention to their needs. Something must therefore link actors into larger networks or groups (Gould 1993).

This linking can be done through a vanguard party or guerilla movement, as in the classic revolutionary strategies of V.I. Lenin and Mao Zedong. It can also be developed through neighborhood social networks, as was common in the cities of nineteenth-century Europe (Gould 1995), or through workers' unions or peasant villages' local leadership (Skocpol 1979). Often, religious organizations have been the nucleus for organizing social and revolutionary movements, having played a key role in social movements from the Abolitionist and Temperance movements (Young 2006) to the Tea Party in America (Skocpol and Williamson 2012), and in revolutions from the Puritan Revolution of seventeenth-century England to the Solidarity movement in Poland (Osa 2003) and the Islamic Revolution of 1979 in Iran (Kurzman 2004).

In recent years, it has been popular to suggest that the virtual networks of social media can be an effective tool in recruiting and mobilizing people for social movements or revolution (see Chapter 16 by Earl, in this volume, on technology and social media). This has no doubt been true, as social media did play a critical role in the early phases of organization and tactical execution during many of the Arab uprisings of 2011, and continues to play a key role in gaining adherents for the Islamic State (Berger and Morgan 2015; Brym et al. 2014; Ritter and Trechsel 2014). Yet this scholarship also finds that social media, while effective in conveying information and sharing feelings, are not by themselves sufficient to motivate people to undertake high-risk activism or to sustain concerted protest (Wolfsfeld, Segev, and Sheafer 2013). Such actions depend on the reinforcement provided by participation in shared activities, gaining common experiences, and sharing the burdens and rewards of protest actions. Scholars have also suggested that an important function of social media is its capacity to transmit the revolution or movement to concerned audiences and third parties not directly involved in the struggle, but potentially crucial to their outcomes (Ritter and Trechsel 2014).

Mobilization for both social movements and revolutions is subject to what Mancur Olson (1971) dubbed the collective action problem. That is, it is tempting for potential participants in movements or revolutions to let others do the hard work of organizing, demonstrating, protesting, and taking risks or expending time and resources, because if change is achieved, even those who did not actively participate will still enjoy the benefits. Scholars have since broken down the collective action problem into a series of discrete organizational problems, and outlined methods of solving them (Heckathorn 1996; Lichbach 1998). These mainly involve providing incentives for participation (which may be psychological or material, taking the form of providing help and support to movement supporters), providing powerful narratives and symbols that evoke an emotional response and feelings of loyalty or obligation or moral necessity, and providing leadership that inspires followers through effective organization and plans for success (Selbin 1998, 2010).

Leadership structure is especially important, as for both social movements and revolutions it is necessary to have leaders who can provide a compelling vision, and also who can organize actions, schedules, and responses to state counter-actions in effective ways (Aminzade, Goldstone, and Perry 2003; Goldstone 2001; Selbin 1998). In particular, having a leadership structure that bridges the space between top leaders and the rank and file through a strong set of local and intermediate leaders is vital for sustained and effective mobilization (Robnett 1996).

One major difference between social movements and revolutions is that social movements can sometimes be effective even from a very narrow or local base. For example, most social movements focus on a particular issue or the interests of a particular group, and need to mobilize only members of that group or those concerned with that issue. If they are then successful in gaining the attention of government officials, and sufficient sympathy and support (or at least non-opposition) from the general public, they may succeed without wider mobilization. However, revolutions almost invariably need to build broader alignments or coalitions that not only unite elites and popular groups in pursuit of change, but that also bridge different groups of actors (Chenoweth and Stephan 2011; Nepstad 2011). For example, most revolutions in early modern Europe were carried forward not by urban protest alone, nor by peasant uprisings alone, but by the combination of rural and urban upheavals (Goldstone 2016). Even in the Arab Revolutions of 2010–2011, it is clear that successful mass mobilization depended on drawing in a variety of urban professionals, supporters in the military, factory workers, rural villagers, government officials, religious groups, and university students (Goldstone 2011).

Yet the same kind of broad coalition building is also vital to national-level social movements, and particularly those whose goals affect the lives of a great many people. Thus, the US civil rights movement could not have succeeded without support from black professionals and unskilled workers in the South but also black factory workers in the North and white civil rights activists and supporters in the courts and legal profession, the universities, and state and national governments (McAdam 1982, 1990).

Elites play a pivotal role in articulating injustice frames, disseminating narratives and symbols to promote mobilization, and organizing coalitions of actors from varied walks of life and from grass-roots to regional and national levels to pursue a course of movement or revolutionary activity. Without elite leadership and support it is almost impossible for large-scale social movements or revolutionary movements to succeed (Goldstone 2016; Kim and Bearman 1997; McAdam, McCarthy, and Zald 1996; Skocpol 1979). Yet this begs the question – why should elites, who benefit from existing social relations, undertake to lead social movements or revolutions?

Elites as Pivots

In any society, elite unity is usually fragile and only secured by the actions of a regime that actively seeks to unite and reward diverse elite groups. Thus elite unity can easily fracture: a shortage of elite positions, due to economic or demographic change or competition from newly arrived or upwardly mobile groups can lead to intra-elite factionalism (Goldstone 2016). Defeat in war or economic crisis can lead some elites to decide the government can no longer be effective (Skocpol 1979). Governments may turn against certain religious groups or exclude others, seeking to strengthen central control or the power of one particular group; but this forfeits the loyalty of those elites who lose out. Finally, elites from subordinate or partially excluded groups may have gone along with the government while eking out their own progress within the system, but they may decide when confident enough that it is time to seek action on behalf of the injustices faced by their entire group. Even police and military officers may turn against the government, if they believe the government is no longer serving the nation's interest or is turning too strongly against their own status and goals (Barany 2016).

Elite dissension is thus one of the pivots on which social movements and revolutions turn. Yet elites themselves are never wholly in control of the processes of opposition that they begin. Indeed, one of the mechanisms by which social movements turn into revolutions is through the expansion and radicalization of what elites may have believed was simply a reform movement to seek change or rectification of problems within the existing order.

One of the most striking cases is the collapse of communist regimes in Eastern Europe and the Soviet Union in 1989–1991. Through most of the twentieth century,

Communist Party leaders were willing to ruthlessly defend their regimes against popular opposition and troublesome intellectuals, from Stalin's purges and *gulags* to the violent repression of protests in Hungary in 1956 and in Czechoslovakia in 1968. But by the late 1970s, the weakness of the Soviet model, both militarily and economically, was becoming apparent even to communist elites. The declining growth rates, the inability to produce the desired consumer goods, failures to innovate to keep pace with western technology, and growing corruption and the yawning gap between the coddled elites and struggling masses left even Communist Party leaders believing that major reforms were needed to preserve their system. The selection of Mikhail Gorbachev to lead the Soviet Union, and his reform programs of *glasnost* "openness" and *perestroika* "restructuring," aimed to restore strength and flexibility to Communist Party rule (Aslund 1991).

Yet this reform movement created a challenge even for party leaders – many of whom had lost confidence in the legitimacy and effectiveness of the communist system (Sharman 2003). They could either try to rebuild communist rule in the face of Gorbachev's exposure of widespread corruption and incompetence; or they could join the critique of communist rule and reposition themselves as leaders of emerging nationalist movements in their own provinces. Many chose the latter, and supported large demonstrations to manifest nationalist solidarity. When some elements in the military sought to end Gorbachev's reforms by staging a coup, other elements in the military refused to go along, while civilians defended the Moscow Parliament building and other key installations against the coup. What followed was a mass defection from the Communist Party, leaving Gorbachev without allies and producing a series of mainly peaceful secessionist movements that led to the disintegration of the Soviet Union and its replacement by a set of national states – not an outcome that was sought or even imagined when Gorbachev began his reforms (Dunlop 1993).

Another case of gradual movement toward revolution is beautifully shown in Markoff's (1996) study of the French Revolution. Markoff showed how the professional and bureaucratic elites who had acted to challenge the monarchy's system of taxation and aristocratic privileges were shocked by the scale of the popular urban and rural protests that ensued. While the popular grievances were mainly about concrete economic issues, such as land shortages and high rents, low wages and high food prices, or excessive local taxes, the elites interpreted the actions of peasants and workers as requiring the dismantling of feudal legal and social institutions. They therefore, in response to every wave of popular unrest, undertook increasingly radical and revolutionary actions. Meanwhile, their radical attacks on church and monarchy provoked counter-movements and international conflicts, which in turn further militarized and revolutionized the actions of the elites. By the early 1790s, the revolutionary leadership was undertaking actions to abolish the monarchy and change France's entire system of governance in ways that had not been expected just a few years before.

In sum, although elites play an absolutely vital role in catalyzing, leading, and organizing social and revolutionary movements, it would be a mistake to see them as fully in control of such movements. In fact, elites have to play a many-sided role, answering to the popular demands and actions that they set in motion, but also reacting to the responses of states and the challenges and opportunities created by key events.

States, Events, and Opportunity Structures

Both the state-centered theory of revolutions (Goldstone 2014; Goodwin 2001) and the political process model of social movements (McAdam 1982; McAdam, McCarthy, and Zald 1996; Tarrow 2011) with their emphasis on political opportunity structures, emphasize that movements cannot grow and succeed unless they are able to take advantage of weaknesses in the ability of states to respond.

Any social movement seeking change or reform, as well as any revolutionary effort, faces forces that seek to defend the status quo – and those are usually forces that have the power of the state and its coercive capacities on their side. As a result, most protests fail to spread, most social movements have to compromise or be patient, and most revolutionary efforts fail. Only where states are disinclined, impeded, or unable to contain or crush the opposition can movements, revolutionary or otherwise, grow.

Scholars have identified a variety of factors that can impose and convey state weakness: a fiscal crisis; defeat in war; elite defections; constraints from, or shifts in, external support for the regime; or events that lay bare state incompetence (such as the Chernobyl power plant accident in the USSR). Sometimes long-term trends in population age, urbanization, or economic/technological change gradually shift the balance of power and resources between a state and other groups. Then a single sudden event or series of events – such as a burst of ruinous inflation or the failure to contain a series of demonstrations – can trigger a cycle in which movement groups act, find less state opposition than they expected, and then protests cascade and grow (Lohmann 1994; Ritter 2012). For social movements as well, both long-term trends and sudden events are capable of generating waves of mobilization (Sewell 2003).

Although states would seem to be in a commanding position, with superior information, forces, and organization, this is not always the case. State leaders may *not* know accurately how their actions are viewed by the populace (indeed the latter may conceal their hatred for the regime until the government's weaknesses are exposed; Kuran 1995). Elites or the military may be ready to defect or stand aside, leaving a ruler isolated and unable to defend him or herself. Rulers may be so over-confident as to think their continued rule is inevitable and not in need of a vigorous offense; or they may (wrongly) think that only a small opposition exists and that crushing it visibly and dramatically will end the threat. In order to defeat an opposition movement, the state must be able to succeed in a series of tasks: accurately *identify* the main opposition actors; *isolate* them from the broader public and potential supporters; *repress* them in a proportionate and targeted way that will not anger the broader public or create additional supporters, and *win support* for these actions from other actors in society (Goldstone and Tilly 2003). Any events or conditions that disrupt these processes will enable anti-state movements to grow.

Although it has long been a goal of social scientists to predict the onset and outcome of revolutions and social movements, the facts that movement trajectories can be affected by sudden events, that elite and popular preferences are often concealed, and that the relationships among revolutionary leaders, their followers, and states are dynamic and complex – with oftentimes no actor by themselves fully informed nor in control of outcomes – make this difficult (Kurzman 2004). What one can say is that social movements are more likely to attain success in times of crisis that distract or limit the capacity of governments (della Porta 2014; Goldstone 1980), and that revolutions are more likely to arise and succeed where long-term factors have created deep elite divisions and fiscal or military weakness in the state (Goldstone 2014). Yet the details of how social movements and potentially revolutionary situations evolve have to be followed through a contingent process of opposition and state moves and responses.

Dynamics of Repression and Radicalization

When a social movement aiming to change the status quo first appears, state leaders have to choose how to respond. If the demands are minor, can they simply be granted with concessions? A confident state may say yes, but an anxious leader may refuse any concessions because that might encourage other groups and indicate state weakness.

   If concessions are not granted, should the state just wait for the movement to fade away? That depends on assessing its strength. If movement leaders are able to sustain a campaign of protests, marches, demonstrations, boycotts, and other disruptive actions, the state may feel it must respond, either with concessions or repression.

   Movement leaders need to make their own assessments. If the actions they choose are too extreme, they may alienate the broader public and provoke vigorous repression from the state; if the actions are too weak, they may simply pass without any effect. Ideally, the protest movement's actions will win supporters by calling attention to an injustice, create enough disruption to motivate the state to respond, and indicate enough strength to continue the movement struggle (Nepstad 2011; Schock 2005).

   Both social movements and revolutionary movements can choose their actions from a similar menu: peaceful actions include marches, demonstrations, petitions (presented by a massed group), boycotts, strikes, occupations of central or symbolic spaces, media campaigns ("pamphlet wars" in the early days of print, now TV/radio/ social media), "sit-ins," vigils, fund-raisers, and burning effigies (Sharp 1973). More aggressive actions range from harassing officials to arson; sabotage; kidnapping (most famously in the USA, the newspaper heiress Patty Hearst); attacks on farms, factories, or police stations or other government offices; bombing and other terrorist tactics (including spreading poisons as with Aum Shinrikyo in Japan); and finally guerilla warfare and all-out civil war.

   Authorities can also choose from a range of actions, including ignoring the protest group, arresting leaders, mass arrests of supporters, use of non-lethal force (tear gas, rubber bullets) and use of lethal force (firing into crowds or using airpower or other military weapons against the movement). When the government acts to contain or discourage the movement (Moss 2014), it risks using too little force or too much. Too little force will not discourage protest and it may grow. Too much force – that is, a disproportionate response, such as killing unarmed students – may reduce the legitimacy of the government and lead to elite defections or greater popular support for the opposition group (Ginkel and Smith 1999). Indeed, the indiscriminate use of force, which puts innocents in danger and punishes those who do not support the movement as much as those who do, is the most damaging to the regime and likely to reduce its support (Machain, Moran, and Regan 2011; Martin 2006).

Use of repressive force is most effective against social and revolutionary movements when the actors identified with the movement are a distinct group and are not supported or seen as justified by the great bulk of the population. Such groups can be harshly repressed with few repercussions for the regime. However, if the actors in the movement are fairly representative of the broader society, and if they have popular sympathy, government use of force is likely to undermine rather than strengthen the regime.

Such processes underlie the escalation of social movements into more radical or even revolutionary efforts. When the regime is seen as unjustly repressing innocent or representative members of the population, emotions may turn more widely against the regime. Demands may then escalate for regime change rather than just shifts in policy. For instance, the Egyptian government enjoyed considerable success in its armed pursuit of Islamists during the 1990s. While the campaign was not an outright success, the authoritarian regime's war on what was widely perceived to be a terrorist group did meet with considerable popular approval. On the other hand, the very same government faced a much harder task when it sought to stamp out the Muslim Brotherhood in the early 2000s. Unlike the violent Islamists of the 1990s, the Brotherhood had cleverly adopted a constitutional rhetoric and undertook the provision of useful public services that elicited additional support from society at large, and put pressure on the government to treat the group with restraint (Ritter 2015). Suppression of Brotherhood-linked candidates in the 2005 election, and acts of violence against youth who opposed the regime, broadened support for protest and fed the revolutionary mobilization of 2010.

In recent decades, revolutionary movements have come to operate more like social movements, eschewing more violent tactics and relying on peaceful mass mobilization. This has proven especially effective where regimes are constrained in their response to protest by alliances or dependence on other states who insist on respect for human rights or who support democratic institutions (Ritter 2015). Large marches or occupations that manifest national-level civil resistance, especially if accompanied by significant elite defections, can leave the ruler with no choice but to resign or flee. Some scholars have argued that since the 1970s such conditions have spread, making nonviolent mobilization a more effective way of changing regimes than violent actions (Chenoweth and Stephan 2011; Nepstad 2011).

Outcomes

The strategies and tactics employed by contemporary activists and revolutionaries represent one of the clearest areas of convergence between social movements and revolutions over the past four decades. While recent scholarship has shown that the use of civil resistance is twice as likely to lead to movement success as are violent tactics, it still remains painfully clear that nonviolent tactics are far from always effective. At best, we might expect movements and revolutions to accomplish their goals, whatever they might be, in roughly half of the occasions during which civil resistance tactics are employed (Chenoweth and Stephan 2011). One of the most pertinent questions in social movement and revolution research alike thus becomes "Which factors determine movement/revolution outcomes?"

Until well into the 1960s, violence remained an obvious dimension of most definitions of revolutions (Arendt 1963; Johnson 1966). However, starting with the Iranian Revolution of 1977–1979, revolutions have increasingly come to resemble social movements in the sense that violence is often eschewed, notwithstanding the maximalist aims and considerable challenges faced by revolutionaries. As a result, no longer are revolutions per definition violent ordeals, but instead frequently take the shape of enormous social movements, employing protests, demonstrations, and other forms of civil resistance as their methods of choice (see Chapter 19 by Schock and Demetriou, in this volume, for a discussion of violence vs. nonviolence as strategic alternatives).

At the level of human agents, we might therefore argue that the guerilla warriors and revolutionary vanguard parties of the past have been replaced in revolutionary episodes by civic protesters and peaceful activists. Importantly, this has meant that the contemporary revolutionary's participation is constrained neither by the individual's gender nor his or her age, a fact that some scholars have embraced as a vital part of their explanation as to why nonviolent movements have a relatively high success rate. Since civil resistance campaigns do not "discriminate" against particular categories of people, such movements enjoy what Chenoweth and Stephan (2011) refer to as a "participation advantage," which in turn increases their chances of success as size of protests are seen as central to the eventual outcome.

Others have argued even more directly for an explicit link between contemporary, unarmed revolutions and social movements. For instance, Schock (2005) has suggested that a nonviolent revolutionary movement's ability to exploit political opportunities, to frame their struggle in a manner conducive to third party support, and to mobilize resources goes a long way toward explaining its success. In social movement language, Schock explored how well the political process model helps us understand the outcomes of unarmed insurrections. While he found that social movement theories can indeed contribute to a fuller understanding of civil resistance, he simultaneously argued that such an understanding must be complemented by attention to activists' strategic choices.

A heavy focus on the strategies and tactics employed by activists is perhaps the most distinguishing feature of research on civil resistance. Ever since Gene Sharp (1973) introduced social scientists to the theories of Mohandas Gandhi, scholars have repeatedly reasserted Sharp's claim that the path to nonviolent success goes through careful strategic planning. Although this line of reasoning has become dominant in the literature, some scholars have sought to challenge the heavily voluntaristic view that political contexts – domestic and international alike – matter only tangentially to the outcome of revolutionary movements.

For one, Nepstad (2011) has pointed out that activists' choices, while important, only tell one half of the story. How the military and other security forces behave is equally important, and Nepstad skillfully shows how the action of the activists and the military are shaped by their interactions with one another on the revolutionary battlefield. In this manner, Nepstad manages to remain focused on the intentions and actions of the activists, without losing track of the larger structural context.

Although nonviolent activists may be more likely than violent ones to discourage armed personnel from violently repressing a revolutionary movement, the preexisting relationship between the agents of repression and the regime itself matters greatly.

More recently, an emerging generation of scholars have sought to explore contemporary revolutionary movements from a more structural perspective (Beck 2015; Lawson 2005, 2015a; Ritter 2015). Lawson (2005) has argued that rather than any inherent power resident in peaceful tactics of contention, contemporary, "negotiated" revolutions occur when old elites can no longer rule and their formerly obedient subjects will no longer accept the existing power relations. Lawson also points to the international contexts of revolutionary episodes, arguing that without careful attention to the global conditions in which challengers rise against their leaders, no thorough understanding of revolutionary change can be accomplished.

Similarly, Ritter (2015) examined six revolutionary movements in the Middle East and North Africa that either ousted national leaders in predominantly unarmed fashion or saw initially nonviolent activists violently repressed by their rulers, thus causing their struggles to degenerate into civil wars or simply result in failure. Ritter found that unarmed revolutions resulted not primarily from the tactical shrewdness of would-be revolutionaries, but rather from a particular form of constraint emanating from authoritarian leaders' international relations with Western powers. Since the leaders of pre-revolution Iran, Tunisia, and Egypt were rhetorically committed to the core values of their foreign patrons, dealing with nonviolent protests on a mass scale represented a particularly complex challenge.

Ritter thus argued that because civil resistance is in fact little more than human rights in action – especially the rights to peaceful assembly and free speech – authoritarian leaders aligned with the West were held hostage by the liberal discourse they had voluntarily embraced in order to justify foreign patronage. In that type of rhetorical context, what Ritter calls an "iron cage of liberalism," nonviolent tactics became highly potent. Conversely, in countries either hostile or more neutrally positioned toward the democratic world – in this case, revolutionary Iran, Libya, and Syria – the protesters' nonviolent tactics were less effective as they represented the concretization of alien values. More importantly, unconstrained by crucial international relations (or even, as in Syria, supported by Russian arms and encouragement), the three governments responded to peaceful protesters with systematic, brutal repression that either caused the movements to collapse or transform into violent struggles against the state (Ritter 2015).

Conclusion: Paradoxes of Movement-Revolution Convergence

While more research is necessary in order to more fully understand the causes of success and failure in episodes of revolutionary and social movements, there appears to be an interesting paradox at play here. How come that nonviolent protesters seemed to reap greater success against authoritarian regimes in the Middle East and North Africa in the 2010s than similar challenges – like the Occupy and Indignados movements – achieved against democratic states in Europe and the United States? Should we not expect Western democracies to be more vulnerable in the face of explicitly democratic forms of anti-systemic challenges than are authoritarian leaders with a reputation of human rights abuse?

The paradox might be explained by the fact that the nonviolent forms of protests that have come to exemplify political struggles in the West – and increasingly around the world – lose their competitive advantage when faced with an explicitly and genuinely democratic opponent. The very fact that peaceful protest is permitted in democratic settings seems to result in movement impotence as democratic states can sit back and wait – either for the movement to go away, which automatically solves the issue, or turns violent and destructive, which then justifies its repression.

This contradiction might help explain the efficacy of civil resistance in semi-authoritarian settings, and it might also help explain why contemporary revolutions seem to be producing less "revolutionary" outcomes than their historical predecessors. While nonviolent, movement-type tactics might be effective in producing regime change, they seem to be much less well suited for generating radical social change. Indeed, with the exception of the first unarmed revolution of the past four decades, that of Iran in 1977–1979, one would be hard-pressed to find nonviolent revolutionary struggle that has produced anything other than a neoliberal democracy of shifting quality. As Goldstone (2014) has pointed out, the usual outcome for "color" revolutions is a weak and often unstable form of populist democratic regime. In other words, it seems that civil resistance trades fundamental social change for more superficial political change.

We might therefore close by suggesting that social movements are becoming less effective in the developed world. The traditional carrier organizations for movements – unions, neighborhood associations, and voluntary associations of all types – may be getting weaker as social capital is strained by the forces of local and international migration, income polarization, and the segmentation of popular media (Putnam 2001). Only movements that have joined or even become political parties seem to be effective in challenging the status quo. At the same time, revolutions in semi-authoritarian countries are increasingly resembling the social movements that are now on the wane in the democratic world. Yet as they do so, becoming what we would like to call "revolution by social movement," they are becoming less transformative. More research will be necessary to confirm these trends; but it appears that social movements and revolutions are drawing closer in the real world, as well as in sociological and political theory.

References

Aminzade, Ronald R., Jack A. Goldstone, Doug McAdam, et al. 2003a. *Silence and Voice in the Study of Contentious Politics*. Cambridge: Cambridge University Press.

Aminzade, Ronald R., Jack A. Goldstone and Elizabeth J. Perry. 2003b. "Leadership Dynamics and Dynamics of Contention." In *Silence and Voice in the Study of Contentious Politics*, edited by Ronald R. Aminzade, Jack A. Goldstone, Doug McAdam, et al., 126–154. Cambridge: Cambridge University Press.

Arendt, Hannah. 1963. *On Revolution*. New York: Viking Press.

Aslund, Anders. 1991. *Gorbachev's Struggle for Economic Reform*. Updated and expanded edition. Ithaca, NY: Cornell University Press.

Barany, Zoltan. 2016. *How Armies Respond to Revolutions and Why*. Princeton, NJ: Princeton University Press.

Beck, Colin. 2015. *Radicals, Revolutionaries, and Terrorists*. Cambridge: Polity.

Berger, J.M. and Jonathan Morgan. 2015. *The ISIS Twitter Census: Defining and Describing the Population of ISIS Supporters on Twitter*. Washington, DC: The Brookings Institution.

Brym, Robert, Melissa Godbout, Andreas Hoffbauer, Gabe Menard, and Tony Huiquan Zhang. 2014. "Social Media in the 2011 Egyptian Uprising." *British Journal of Sociology* 65: 266–292.

Chenoweth, Erica and Maria Stephan. 2011. *Why Civil Resistance Works*. New York: Columbia University Press.

Collier, Paul and Anke Hoeffler. 2002. "Greed and Grievance in Civil War." Policy Research Working Paper 2355. Washington, DC: The World Bank.

della Porta, Donatella. 2014. *Mobilizing for Democracy: Comparing 1989 and 2011*. Oxford: Oxford University Press.

Dunlop, John B. 1993. *The Rise of Russia and the Fall of the Soviet Empire*. Princeton, NJ: Princeton University Press.

Foran, John. 2005. *Taking Power: On the Origins of Third World Revolutions*. New York: Cambridge University Press.

Gamson, William A. 2013. "Injustice Frames." In *The Wiley-Blackwell Encyclopedia of Social and Political Movements*, edited by David A. Snow, Donatella della Porta, Bert Klandermans and Doug McAdam, 607–608. New York: Wiley.

Ginkel, John and Alastair Smith. 1999. "So You Say You Want a Revolution? A Game Theoretic Explanation of Revolution in Repressive Regimes." *Journal of Conflict Resolution* 43: 291–316.

Goldstone, Jack A. 1980. "The Weakness of Organization." *American Journal of Sociology* 85: 1017–1042.

Goldstone, Jack A. 1998. "Social Movements or Revolutions? On the Evolution and Outcomes of Collective Action." In *From Contention to Democracy*, edited by Marco Guigni, Doug McAdam, and Charles Tilly, 125–145. Lanham, MD: Rowman & Littlefield.

Goldstone, Jack A. 2001. "Toward a Fourth Generation of Revolutionary Theory." *Annual Review of Political Science* 4: 139–1387.

Goldstone, Jack A. 2003. "Comparative Historical Analysis and Knowledge Accumulation in the Study of Revolutions." In *Comparative Historical Analysis in the Social Sciences*, edited by James Mahoney and Dietrich Rueschemeyer, 41–90. Cambridge: Cambridge University Press.

Goldstone, Jack A. 2011. "Cross-Class Coalitions and the Making of the Arab Revolts of 2011." *Swiss Political Science Review* 17: 457–462.

Goldstone, Jack A. 2014. *Revolutions: A Very Short Introduction*. New York: Oxford University Press.

Goldstone, Jack A. 2016. *Revolution and Rebellion in the Early Modern World* (25th Anniversary Edition). New York: Routledge.

Goldstone, Jack A. and Charles Tilly. 2003. "Threat (and Opportunity): Popular Action and State Response in the Dynamics of Contentious Action. In *Silence and Voice in the Study of Contentious Politics*, edited by Ronald R. Aminzade, Jack A. Goldstone, Doug McAdam, et al., 179–195. Cambridge: Cambridge University Press.

Goodwin, Jeff. 2001. *No Other Way Out: States and Revolutionary Movements 1945–1991*. Cambridge: Cambridge University Press.

Goodwin, Jeff and James M. Jasper. 1999. "Caught in a Winding, Snarling Vine: The Structural Bias of Political Process Theory." *Sociological Forum* 14: 27–54.

Goodwin, Jeff, James M. Jasper, and Francesca Polletta, eds. 2001. *Passionate Politics: Emotions and Social Movements*. Chicago: University of Chicago Press.

Gould, Roger. 1993. "Collective Action and Network Structure." *American Sociological Review* 58: 182–196.

Gould, Roger. 1995. *Insurgent Identities: Class, Community and Protest in Paris from 1848 to the Commune*. Chicago: University of Chicago Press.

Heckathorn, Douglas D. 1996. "The Dynamics and Dilemmas of Collective Action." *American Sociological Review* 61: 250–277.

Johnson, Chalmers. 1966. *Revolutionary Change*. Boston: Little, Brown and Company.

Keen, David J. 2008. *Complex Emergencies*. New York: Wiley.

Kim, Hyojoung and Peter S. Bearman. 1997. "The Structure and Dynamics of Movement Participation." *American Sociological Review* 62: 70–93.

Kuran, Timur. 1995. *Private Truth, Public Lies*. Cambridge, MA: Harvard University Press.

Kurzman, Charles. 2004. *The Unthinkable Revolution in Iran*. Cambridge, MA: Harvard University Press.

Lawson, George. 2005. *Negotiated Revolutions: The Czech Republic, South Africa, and Chile*. Aldershot: Ashgate.

Lawson, George. 2015a. "Revolutions and the International." *Theory and Society* 44(4): 299–319.

Lawson, George. 2015b. "Revolution, Nonviolence, and the Arab Uprisings." *Mobilization* 20(4): 453–470.

Lichbach, Mark Irving. 1998. *The Rebel's Dilemma*. Ann Arbor: University of Michigan Press.

Lohmann, Susanne. 1994. "The Dynamics of Informational Cascades: The Monday Demonstrations in Leipzig, Germany, 1989–91." *World Politics* 47: 42–101.

Machain, Carla Martinez, T. Clifton Morgan, and Patrick M. Regan. 2011. "Deterring Rebellion." *Foreign Policy Analysis* 7: 295–316.

Mahoney, James and Richard Snyder. 1999. "Rethinking Agency and Structure in the Study of Regime Change." *Studies in Comparative International Development* 34: 3–32.

Markoff, John. 1996. *The Abolition of Feudalism*. University Park, PA: Penn State University Press.

Martin, Brian. 2006. *Justice Ignited: The Dynamics of Backfire*. Lanham, MD: Rowman & Littlefield.

McAdam, Doug. 1982. *Political Process and the Development of Black Insurgency, 1930–1970*. Chicago: University of Chicago Press.

McAdam, Doug. 1990. *Freedom Summer*. Oxford: Oxford University Press.

McAdam, Doug, John D. McCarthy, and Mayer N. Zald. 1996. *Comparative Perspectives on Social Movements: Political Opportunities, Mobilizing Structures, and Cultural Framings*. Cambridge: Cambridge University Press.

McAdam, Doug, Sidney Tarrow, and Charles Tilly. 2001. *Dynamics of Contention*. Cambridge: Cambridge University Press.

McCarthy, John D. and Meyer N. Zald. 1977. "Resource Mobilization and Social Movements: A Partial Theory." *American Journal of Sociology* 81: 1212–1241.

Moore, Barrington Jr. 1978. *Injustice: The Social Basis of Obedience and Revolt*. New York: Routledge.

Moss, Dana. 2014. "Repression, Response, and Contained Escalation Under 'Liberalized' Authoritarianism in Jordan." *Mobilization* 19: 261–286.

Nepstad, Sharon. 2011. *Nonviolent Revolutions*. New York: Oxford University Press.

Olson, Mancur. 1971. *The Logic of Collective Action: Public Goods and the Theory of Groups*. Cambridge, MA: Harvard University Press.

Osa, Maryjane. 2003. *Solidarity and Contention: Networks of Polish Opposition*. Minneapolis: University of Minnesota Press.

Putnam, Robert D. 2001. *Bowling Alone*. New York: Simon & Schuster.

Ritter, Daniel P. 2012. "Inside the Iron Cage of Liberalism: International Contexts and Nonviolent Success in the Iranian Revolution." *Research in Social Movements, Conflicts and Change* 34: 95–121.

Ritter, Daniel P. 2015. *The Iron Cage of Liberalism: International Politics and Unarmed Revolutions in the Middle East and North Africa*. Oxford: Oxford University Press.

Ritter, Daniel P. and Alexander H. Trechsel. 2014. "Revolutionary Cells: On the Role of Texts, Tweets, and Status Updates in Nonviolent Revolutions." In *The Internet and Democracy in Global Perspective: Voters, Candidates, Parties, and Social Movements*, edited by Bernard Grofman, Alexander H. Trechsel and Mark Franklin, 111–128. New York: Springer.

Robnett, Belinda. 1996. "African-American Women in the Civil Rights Movement, 1954–1965: Gender, Leadership and Micromobilization." *American Journal of Sociology* 101: 1661–1693.

Schock, Kurt. 2005. *Unarmed Insurrections: People Power Movements in Nondemocracies*. Minneapolis: University of Minnesota Press.

Selbin, Eric. 1998. *Modern Latin American Revolutions*. Boulder, CO: Westview Press.

Selbin, Eric. 2010. *Revolution, Rebellion, Resistance: The Power of Story*. London: Zed.

Sewell, William H. Jr. 2003. "It's about Time: Temporality in the Study of Social Movements and Revolutions." In *Silence and Voice in the Study of Contentious Politics*, edited by Ronald R. Aminzade, Jack A. Goldstone, Doug McAdam, et al., 89–125. Cambridge: Cambridge University Press.

Sharman, J.C. 2003. "Culture, Strategy, and State-Centered Explanations of Revolution, 1789 and 1989." *Social Science History* 27: 1–24.

Sharp, Gene. 1973. *The Politics of Nonviolent Action* (3 vols). Boston: Extending Horizons.

Skocpol, Theda. 1979. *States and Social Revolutions*. Cambridge: Cambridge University Press.

Skocpol, Theda and Vanessa Williamson. 2012. *The Tea Party and the Remaking of Republican Conservatism*. New York: Oxford University Press.

Snow, David A., E. Burke Rochford, Jr., Steven K. Worden and Robert D. Benford. 1986. "Frame Alignment Processes, Micromobilization, and Movement Participation." *American Sociological Review* 51: 464–481.

Tarrow, Sidney. 2011. *Power in Movement*, 3rd ed. Cambridge: Cambridge University Press.

Tilly, Charles. 1978. *From Mobilization to Revolution*. Reading, MA: Addison-Wesley.

Wolfsfeld, Gadi, Elag Segev and Tamir Sheafer. 2013. "Social Media and the Arab Spring: Politics Comes First." *International Journal of Press/Politics* 18: 115–137.

Wood, Elisabeth Jean. 2003. *Insurgent Collective Action and Civil War in El Salvador*. Cambridge: Cambridge University Press.

Young, Michael P. 2006. *Bearing Witness Against Sin: The Evangelical Birth of the American Social Movement*. Chicago: University of Chicago Press.

40

Terrorism and Social Movements

COLIN J. BECK AND ERIC W. SCHOON

Introduction

Over the past 25 years, research on the causes, dynamics, and consequences of terrorism has largely evolved parallel to research on social movements and collective action. In spite of attempts to situate movements like the 1960s civil rights movement and terrorist groups like Italy's Red Brigade within the same theoretical space (McAdam, Tarrow, and Tilly 2001), and work highlighting the contributions of social movement theory to the study of terrorism (Beck 2008; Bosi and Giugni 2012; Gunning 2009), dialogue between the literatures on terrorism and social movements has been slow and fragmented. Yet, recent research on terrorism that integrates concepts from the literatures on social movements and collective action demonstrates the utility of bridging this gap (Alimi, Demetriou, and Bosi 2015; Beck 2015; Goodwin 2006; Kurzman 2011; Olzak 2016; Schoon 2015; Wiktorowicz 2005).

Rather than articulate, once again, the utility of social movement theory for the terrorism researcher, here we flip the appeal on its head. We argue that the theoretical poverty of terrorism studies provides an opportunity for the social movements' scholar. Were researchers to take terrorism seriously as a case of mobilization, both subfields would benefit. This places sociologists in an unfamiliar position. Instead of setting up camp alongside the road and waiting for a distant empire to require tribute, as Abbott (2001) has it, sociologists of movements have the chance to make another field a tributary. This chapter provides a map for this effort.

Specifically, we outline several central questions in current research on terrorism. First, how should terrorism be defined? Second, why do individuals and organizations turn to terrorism? Next, what conditions impact the levels and types of violence caused by actors engaged in terrorism? Fourth, what is distinct about terrorist organizations and how they grow, expand, and evolve? Finally, how do social context and relationships shape the behaviors of organizations engaged in terrorism?

The Wiley Blackwell Companion to Social Movements, Second Edition. Edited by David A. Snow, Sarah A. Soule, Hanspeter Kriesi, and Holly J. McCammon.
© 2019 John Wiley & Sons Ltd. Published 2019 by John Wiley & Sons Ltd.

Addressing each of these questions in turn, this chapter proceeds by reviewing relevant contemporary research on terrorism and then discusses how scholarship on social movements and collective action can contribute, or already has, to seemingly intractable challenges. We conclude by detailing specific intersections between research on terrorism and scholarship on social movements that may provide new answers to these long-standing questions.

Defining Terrorism and Terrorists

While building a cumulative body of research on any topic requires some shared understanding of the thing being studied, scholars have yet to arrive at a conclusive definition of terrorism. As early as the 1980s, Schmid and Jongman (1988) identified 109 different definitions of terrorism that had as many as 22 elements in common. This has "resulted in an elusive pursuit for a single definition of terrorism that appears to be unattainable and potentially counterproductive" (Young and Findley 2011: 414). Many political scientists and sociologists have weighed in, emphasizing motivations, outcomes, symbolism, intensity, targets, asymmetry and so on (Crenshaw 1981; Enders and Sandler 2002; Hoffman 1998; Lizardo 2008; Tilly 2004; Young and Findley 2011). However, attempts to offer precise, clearly specified definitions are often criticized as overly-narrow, whereas broader definitions fail to provide analytic clarity, leading to "the road of obscurantism" (Gibbs 1989: 329).

The process of legally identifying terrorist groups is similarly inconsistent (Perry 2003). For example, in their analysis of formal terrorism designations by the United States, the United Kingdom, and the European Union, Beck and Miner (2013) find that the institutional designation of terrorism hinges on specific markers, such as targeting aviation or having an Islamic ideological foundation. Extending the idea that terrorist designation is contingent on specific group-level markers, Chou (2015) finds that the more a violent organization exhibits state-like features (i.e., effective, representative, and secular), the less likely they are to be designated a terrorist organization.

In an attempt to productively address these definitional inconsistencies, Young and Findley (2011) suggest that scholars embrace the diversity in definitions of terrorism. Highlighting the growth of databases that record various acts of political violence, they recommend establishing a firm minimal definition, then working to identify empirical regularities among recorded terrorist events to develop basic typologies that would allow researchers to better account for variation. However, Young and Findley's focus on inductive analysis does not culminate in a proposed definition. Nor does it provide a clear way to assess the definitions offered by others.

We contend that a more fruitful approach for moving beyond the definitional debate can emerge from the literature on social movements. By placing terrorism within the theoretical spectrum of other phenomena widely studied by scholars of social movements, researchers can eschew problematic efforts to define a heterogeneous class of activities within a homogeneously bounded definition, and instead situate it within the broader study of contentious politics (e.g. Alimi et al. 2015; Beck 2015; McAdam et al. 2001). In essence, this involves a wholesale shift away from attempting to establish a single, all-encompassing definition of terrorism.

Instead, a focus on the scope conditions for the study of terrorism would delimit the universe of comparable phenomena. As such, researchers should study terrorism as a repertoire of contention, terrorism as a tactic, terrorism as an organizational attribute, terrorism as a category of violence, and so forth. To some extent, this is the strategy already employed by social movements scholars when they consider the phenomenon (Alimi et al. 2015; Beck 2015; della Porta 1995, Goodwin 2006; Olzak 2016; Tilly 2004). Building on this work may help articulate a more systematic agenda for the study of terrorism and provide entrée for broader comparative research. The distinct advantage of this approach lies in the theoretical bridge between terrorism and other types of political behavior. This accounts for the diversity of definitions and provides a foundation for more nuanced interrogation of terrorism.

Radicalization of Individuals and Groups

A key issue in terrorism studies is how an individual, organization, or movement turns to terrorism. In essence, the question is radicalization. Under what conditions do individuals and groups radicalize? What processes make violence a more likely strategy? Can these processes be interrupted in some fashion? We draw a distinction here, not always explicit in the research, between the radicalization of individuals and the radicalization of groups. While there may be commonalities between the two, social movement research suggests that scholars should examine them differently.

Dynamics of individual radicalization

An increasingly critical question in research on terrorism is how we evaluate the motives of individuals, who are inspired by a larger terrorist organization, versus actors, who are directed by those organizations. A common approach is to find similar conditions motivating independent actors who engage in terrorism (e.g. Bakker and de Graaf 2011; Moskalenko and McCauley 2011; Phillips 2015; Spaaij 2010). While some researchers have drawn comparisons between non-organizational ideological violence versus organizations involved in terrorism, these efforts have largely focused on differences in activity (i.e. lethality) rather than differences in motivation (Phillips 2015). Instead, the majority of research in this area has typically compared independent terrorists with perpetrators of other types of violent crime and non-violent participants in extremist groups to understand how individual-level characteristics differ.

For example, in their study of right-wing extremist terrorism, Gruenewald, Chermak and Freilich (2013) find that violent "loners" are more likely to live alone than others with far-right ideologies, are more likely to have a history of mental illness, and were actually less involved in right-wing movement activities – such as attending protests – than other far-rightists. However, a report by the International Centre for Counter-Terrorism in The Hague, the Netherlands, highlights that, in spite of often being uninvolved in broader movement activities, independent terrorists are ideologically active and "often distribute their ideas and manifestos to the outside world" (Bakker and De Graaf 2010: 4). Consistent with this finding, Berntzen and Sandberg show that the ideological motivations espoused by lone wolf terrorists should be seen as "acting from rhetoric embedded in larger social movements" (2014: 1).

This research on independent actors suggests points of intervention for the social movements scholar via the literature on networks and framing. Regarding the role of networks, researchers have shown that people are more likely to join a movement if they have or forge network ties with other activists (McAdam 1988; Munson 2010; Snow, Zurcher, and Ekland-Olson 1980). This is also the case for movements that employ terrorism. For instance, Wiktorowicz (2005) documents how an Islamist organization makes use of personal contacts to socialize into increasing acceptance of violence as a political tool. This suggests that basic social movements research on recruitment and joining could further illuminate the process for radical organizations. Further, Abrahms (2008) argues that individual terrorists develop emotional ties and solidarity with a group that explain seemingly irrational uses of violence. della Porta (1995) notes a similar process among members of small 1970s radical organizations. By contrast, independent actors – especially right-wing terrorists in the United States (Gruenewald et al. 2013) – appear often to have some relationship to broader movement networks. However, existing evidence suggests that they may not be deeply embedded or hyper-active in these networks. Instead, individual actors appear to be ideologically extreme but moderately involved. These findings parallel the social movements literature on identity in activism that sees solidarity and identification with a group both as a resource for mobilization and a goal of some mobilization efforts (e.g. Bernstein 1997; Polletta 1998).

With the advent of independent, individual terrorist violence, attention has turned to the media and Internet presence of radical groups, highlighting the productive potential of examining the role of online networks. Lewis, Gray, and Meierhenrich (2014) provide an example of this type of research with their examination of the network structure of online activism in general. Consistent with the idea that many actors may sympathize with a movement but few will become actively involved, they find more than 200 000 "weak components" wherein all members could directly or indirectly reach one another but were fully disconnected from all other components. Within each of these components, the probability of participation beyond initially "liking" the page was higher for those who joined a Facebook group without being recruited, with the networks centering around a small number of highly active participants. The possibility that a similar dynamic exists for radical activism could be fruitfully explored.

Another way of understanding individual radicalization is through analyses of framing. From a social movements perspective, media – whether social or not – are analyzable from a framing perspective (Benford and Snow 2000). Radical appeals often involve frame alignment and bridging processes, and frame articulation and elaboration are one way to motivate violent behavior (Snow and Byrd 2007). Given the growing interest in content analysis of social media posts and discussions, it is striking that frame analysis has not been commonly employed. In our view, there are whole dissertations waiting to be written from this perspective.

Dynamics of group radicalization

Terrorism researchers have long considered when and why groups turn to terrorism to achieve political aims. These researchers, similar to those who study social movements, have mostly discarded economic grievances and relative deprivation as an explanation of terrorism (Krueger and Maleckova 2003; Piazza 2006). Attention, instead, focuses on group-level decisions to employ terrorism, often with a presumption of rational actors (Bloom 2005; Kydd and Walter 2006; Pape 2005). Carter (2016) notes that violent tactics are carefully selected in an attempt to shape state responses, providing evidence that terrorism is used instead of guerilla tactics when groups aim to avoid forceful state responses. Similarly, Findley and Young (2015) argue that terrorism is used to spoil peace agreements during civil war, providing a power position to otherwise weaker actors. Addressing the paradox of why actors use terrorism even when it is counterproductive, Kalyvas (2004) argues that the choice to engage in indiscriminate violence is typically driven by the fact that it is cheaper than selective violence. While rational action is an underlying assumption in existing explanations of the decision to employ terrorism, researchers usually indicate that it is bounded (e.g. Simon 1991; see also Carter 2016).

A movements counterpoint to this research lies in theories of protest cycles (Tarrow 1989). della Porta (1995) argues that radical left-wing violence in Europe was part and parcel of the 1960s–1970s protest cycle. Relatedly, terrorism could be seen as a case of tactical innovation (McAdam 1983). New tactics, or activation of old ones, create an advantage for its user as elites and states do not have the capability to counter them as readily. Turning from common political actions to terrorism may thus create a tactical opportunity for an organization in the short run.

Terrorism may also represent a special case of the repression-protest paradox. Violence and radicalization are one possible outcome of repression as moderates leave a movement and opportunities for nonviolent engagement are decreased (Beck 2015; della Porta 1995; Piazza 2006; Shellman, Levey, and Young 2013). This is a common finding among terrorism researchers, even as they fail to make the theoretical connection. It seems likely, that in some cases, terrorism is a case of there being "no other way out" of a political dilemma, just as it is for some revolutions (Goodwin 2001).

Intensity and Targets of Violence

Consistent with the centrality of violence to our understanding of terrorism, a growing body of research has sought to understand what factors influence both the intensity of violence used by terrorists and the targets they choose (Asal and Phillips 2015; Asal and Rethemeyer 2008; Berman 2009; Cronin 2009; Kydd and Walter 2006; Olzak 2016; Sandler 2014; Valentino 2014). While research examining definitions of terrorism and the dynamics of radicalization have necessarily relied more on small-N and qualitative research (see Young and Findley 2011), research on lethality and target choice is dominated by large-N statistical analyses that rely on the growing corpus of terrorism data.

As Olzak (2016) highlights, research to date has found a variety of factors that appear to influence terrorist groups' levels of lethality, ranging from an organization's rivalries to their network position. However, the most consistent finding in the literature to date is that religious or ethnic ideologies are associated with higher levels of violence (Asal and Rethemeyer 2008; Berman 2009; Piazza 2009). These findings are typically explained via one of two causal mechanisms. Following economic club models, the first mechanism assumes that religious and ethnic groups are better able to establish insular communities that increase members' commitment and willingness to use violence (Berman 2009; Berman and Laitin 2008). The second assumes that religious and ethnic groups are more successful at defining themselves in opposition to a coherent and inferior "other," making extreme violence less problematic in the eyes of individual perpetrators (see Asal and Rethemeyer 2008). In each case, the underlying assumption is that organizational ideologies are drivers of commitment, and commitment in turn increases capacity and decreases risks associated with inflicting physical damage.

In an excellent example of the kind of interdisciplinary work that we advocate here, Susan Olzak (2016) builds on social movements research and organizational theory to challenge and advance these existing explanations. She argues that being able to easily associate an organization with a single, recognizable belief structure will enhance the organization's appeal to their audience. This appeal fosters greater legitimacy, better matching between adherents and organizations, and lower coordination costs, all of which positively influence lethality and longevity. Yet Schoon (2014, 2015) argues that it is easier to identify illegitimacy than it is legitimacy. Illegitimacy can come with specific strategic benefits in light of the social constraints associated with legitimate norms. From this perspective, organizational illegitimacy is as important a problem for exploration as that of legitimation processes.

Contrary to the focus on organizational features highlighted in the literature on lethality, other scholars have emphasized the importance of a violent organizations' target in shaping their broader strategies. Kydd and Walter (2006) argue that features of a targeted government (e.g. power, resolve, trustworthiness) shape the extent to which a government can or will grant concessions to an organization. They also argue that the choice of target (i.e. the World Trade Center in 2001 vs. the bombing of the *USS Cole* in 2000) is shaped by an organization's goals and audience. Beck (2015) goes so far as to suggest that regime type by itself predicts the type of political violence and contention that is most likely. Young and Findley (2011) also highlight that differences in target reflect an organization's operational capacity.

Toward a configurational approach

While target choice and the determinants of lethality have largely been treated as parallel but distinct questions in research on terrorism, research by social movements scholars suggests that these concerns may be causally connected. In their research on violence in collective action, Martin and colleagues (2009) show that a linear relationship between the composition of a protest and the escalation of violence cannot be assumed. Instead, different compositions of protest have variable effects when violence is disaggregated into attacks on authorities, attacks on civilians, public property damage and private property damage. This has implications for linking organizational composition, target choice, and lethality and suggests a more complex configurational logic than is typically recognized in existing research on terrorism.

This is a dynamic that social movement scholars know well. Tactics do not occur in a vacuum, and can be determined by the target of contention. For instance, mobilizing public opinion takes a different form than targeting elites (Burstein and Linton 2002; McCarthy and Zald 1977). In fact, targets are often implicitly bundled with particular repertoires: boycotts may be effective against corporations but are senseless against governments (King 2008). Tactics are also dependent on organizational form (Staggenborg 1988) and groups may acquire preferences for particular strategies and actions (Jasper 1997), what Lichterman and Eliasoph (2014; Eliasoph and Lichterman 2003) term group styles. The key point here is that discussion of tactical choice and effects in terrorism studies could be on much firmer footing if it incorporated the long-standing insights of social movements research.

Organizational Expansion and Operational Diversification

A growing body of scholarship has sought to understand the organizational expansion and operational diversification of groups that engage in terrorism. The United States Government's list of Foreign Terrorist Organizations includes organizations that support legal political parties, publish newspapers, run TV stations, provide a variety of social services (such as healthcare and educational programs), produce/refine/sell drugs, and traffic or sell cigarettes, antiquities, oil, weapons, and people, among other things (Felbab-Brown 2010; Greenland et al. 2016; Mampilly 2011; Marcus 2007; Williams and Felbab-Brown 2012). These illicit activities represent only a fraction of the observed operations of violent groups. The diversity challenges widespread assumptions in research on terrorism.

The crime-terror nexus

Early studies of terrorism tended to focus primarily on violent organizations that claimed to represent some sort of higher cause (Hoffman 1998; see also Wang 2010). These organizations were supposedly motivated by the need to "right an injustice or redress a grievance" (Asal, Milward, and Schoon 2015: 112; see also Abadinsky 1994; Morselli, Giguère, and Petit 2007). Yet, the end of the Cold War significantly curtailed state funding for violent non-state actors, and a growing number of violent organizations began participating in criminal operations to finance their activities (Makarenko 2004). This evolution challenged the ideal-typical separation between ideologically-driven terrorist organizations and "greed"-driven rebel groups, as conceptualized in the literature on economic motivations for civil war (e.g. Collier and Hoeffler 1998; Metz 1993; Snow 1996). Terrorism researchers treated criminal activity as purely profit-driven and non-ideological (Cilluffo 2000; Hejnova 2010). Consequently, ideologically-driven organizations' decisions to participate in crime presented a paradox for research attempting to distinguish terrorist organizations from other types of covert and illegal groups (for a review, see Asal et al. 2015).

As a growing number of organizations collect an increasingly large proportion of their resources from criminal activities, a body of scholarship has emerged examining the nexus between crime and terrorism (Hutchinson and O'Malley 2007; Wang 2010). Dominated by small-N analyses, this research worked to conceptualize the variable relationships between criminal organizations and terrorist organizations, and develop theoretical frameworks to help distinguish between these two realms of activity. Makarenko (2004) reviews existing literature on organizations involved in both activities in an attempt to map the continuum between crime and terrorism. She argues that "organised crime and terrorism exist on the same plane, and thus are theoretically capable of converging at a central point" (ibid.: 131). She develops a typology for situating the different types of intersection between crime and terrorism, condensing the various points on the continuum from pure-crime to pure-terrorism into distinct categories.

Subsequent scholarship has directed more attention to institutional and organizational dynamics that might shape the way crime and terrorism intersect. Morselli and colleagues (2007) highlight the tradeoff between efficiency and security, arguing that criminal networks need to prioritize efficiency, as their primary goal is to increase profit, whereas terrorist organizations' ideological focus results in an attempt to prioritize security and secrecy. Consistent with earlier research that highlights differences between networks in public management versus the utility of networks in covert and illegal activities (Arquilla and Ronfeldt 2001; Raab and Milward 2003), Morselli et al. (2007) compare network data on a criminal enterprise and a terrorist organization. They show how these distinct organizational imperatives result in divergent relational structures among actors in each type of group. These findings add nuance to Dishman's (2005) assertion that the increasingly networked structure of terrorist organizations undermines the capacity for a central authority to manage operational activities, thereby increasing the risk that cells in a violent network will pursue other activities on their own initiative. Following from these initial theoretical developments, subsequent research has examined organizational features that shape participation in crime, showing, for example, that ethnopolitical groups and groups with large numbers of alliances are more likely to participate in crime (Asal et al. 2015).

For the social movements scholar, a key way of thinking about the crime-terror nexus can come from the resource mobilization tradition (McCarthy and Zald 1977). Terrorist groups are, after all, organizations. In our view, the expansion of activities into non-terrorism realms is a case of the organizational imperative. Once established, organizations seek persistence, and the resources that black market activities and kidnapping for ransom allow a group to continue even when the chances of political success are diminished. It could also be useful to consider terrorism as akin to a social movement sector comprising multiple social movement industries (Zald and McCarthy 1980). A terrorism movement sector could easily be said to comprise industries of political violence, illicit businesses, ransoming, etc. Notably, Gambetta (1996) concludes that there is a similar dynamic among criminal mafias in Italy. From this perspective, the diversity of groups and organizational activities is not a surprise, but rather to be expected.

Violent non-state actors as civil society organizations

Beyond a particular focus on crime, other scholars have sought to make sense of violent organizations' provision of social services and other public goods. This is a long-standing feature of work on religious terrorist organizations (e.g. Wickham 2002; Wiktorowicz 2004). For example, Davis and Robinson (2012) argue that religious groups attempt to bypass the state and take over civil society to build their power. This allows an organization to avoid direct confrontations with state power and create a mobilizing base of supporters. Researchers on the variety of Islamic activism have thus noted that the success of this strategy is dependent on the power and legitimacy of the state itself (Beck 2009; Moaddel 2002; Schwedler 2006; Starrett 1998).

Secular organizations also try to provide public goods as a way to enhance their legitimacy and act as de facto states to a population (see Mampilly 2011). Adopting an explicitly rational-choice framework, Berman and Laitin (2008) argue that the creation of economic "clubs" through the provision of local public goods helps groups weed out potential defectors and increase their capacity. As discussed above, this has been associated with higher degrees of lethality and longevity (see Olzak 2016).

Felbab-Brown (2010) also argues that service provision and community involvement contribute to the cultivation of political capital among local populations (see also Marcus 2007). Through detailed comparisons of the Revolutionary Armed Forces of Colombia (FARC), the Taliban in Afghanistan, and the Shining Path in Peru, she demonstrates how, under certain local economic and social conditions, participation in the illicit drug economy can help violent organizations to cultivate or maintain local economic opportunities and provide much-needed local resources. This, in turn, helps them build legitimacy.

As outlined above, resource mobilization theory would expect such organizational expansion and goal evolution. A second movements approach to thinking about diversity in terrorist group activities is to consider the difference between initiator and spin-off movements (see McAdam 1995). Initiating movements tend to have a structural advantage, while spin-offs are more likely to see failure. Such failure, as in protest cycles research, lends itself to diversification strategies as the collective group struggles to maintain its purpose. Operational changes here may be similar to abeyance structures for movements (Taylor 1989). While terrorism researchers have considered how and why groups split off from one another (Cronin 2009), a social movements perspective would view these transformations as natural evolutions of contentious organizations.

Interactional Dynamic with Actors and Contexts

A growing body of research on terrorism has turned attention to how terrorist activities and patterns of behavior are shaped by the interactional dynamics between actors and their social context. By focusing on the relationships between actors and their contexts, these efforts help to specify important scope conditions for theories seeking to explain terrorist violence, thereby providing a foundation for improved case comparison and theory development.

In her book, *Dying to Kill*, Bloom (2005) argues that the decision for terrorist organizations to use suicide missions is not reflective of particular ideologies or ideological goals, and is instead shaped by a process of competitive outbidding in an effort to appeal to local actors. As mentioned above, Kydd and Walter (2006) apply this type of conjunctural logic to the study of terrorist strategies. They argue that terrorist violence is "a form of costly signaling" (ibid.: 5), and that the type of activities that groups using terrorism will engage in are shaped by the target they are signaling (i.e., an external enemy versus a local population) and what needs to be signaled (i.e., power, resolve, trustworthiness). Similarly, in her work on the link between terrorism and democracy, Chenoweth (2013) tackles the assumption that democracy is the ultimate bulwark against terrorism. Using historical data, she shows that terrorism was more common in democracies than authoritarian regimes by the end of the twentieth century. In addition, democracies do not generally have high levels of chronic terrorism unless they engaged in military intervention or occupation (see also Pape 2005), or are poor and experiencing territorial conflicts. Moreover, moderately wealthy and transitioning democracies are at higher risk of domestic terrorism.

From a movements perspective, these findings are not surprising. Regime type and social context affect the various political opportunities available to any political group, and so it is self-evident that differing contexts would lead to differing strategies, terrorism among them. As we discussed above, curbed opportunities for political participation may make political violence the only option for some groups. And democracies themselves may be particularly vulnerable to the theatrical dimensions of symbolic violence (see Juergensmeyer 2001).

Terrorism researchers also have not yet caught up to the insights of relational sociology, where the dyad is considered the fundamental analytical unit. Alimi, Demetriou, and Bosi (2014) draw on the dynamics of contention paradigm (McAdam, Tarrow, and Tilly 2001) to theorize the interactional aspects of terrorism. Using case studies on the Red Brigades, the Cypriot independence movement, and al-Qaeda, Alimi et al. argue that relational mechanisms govern radicalization. Interactional partners for militant groups can vary, ranging from within a movement, counter-movements, and the state. The key point is that the use of violence does not occur in a vacuum but within the social context that the group is located.

More broadly, it could be useful to think of terrorism as part of a strategic action field (Fligstein and McAdam 2012). From this view, terrorist organizations usually would be challengers to incumbents who have the support of a governance unit that enforces norms of political participation. Rather than focus on the rationality or irrationality of the use of terrorism, the researcher could analyze the "social skill" that lies behind the strategic calculations of militants. This would bring in considerations of information resources and leadership (see Ganz 2000). Causes of terrorism could be due to exogenous shocks that rupture the field, but terrorism itself might be such a shock that creates a new episode of contention, as in the events following September 11th. And instead of looking at how different groups end, the researcher would examine the "settlements" of episodes of contention. This is a subtle distinction, but a noteworthy one. Terrorism might persist but be incorporated into the routine expectations of a newly stable field, much as we see with what military strategists call the "Long War" against contemporary international terrorism.

The point here is that social movement theory has much more nuanced and more sophisticated ways of thinking about the interactional dynamics of terrorism than what is currently found in terrorism studies. And in this poverty lies great opportunity for a more robust theory of terrorism.

Conclusion

In this brief review, we have highlighted five different areas of current terrorism research in which we believe the social movements scholar could fruitfully intervene. This is not novel. Others have suggested for some time that the study of terrorism would benefit from a large dose of movement theory (Beck 2008; Bosi and Giugni 2012; Gunning 2009). But we make a different appeal here. Rather than see social movement theory be cursorily appropriated by terrorism researchers, we think that social movements scholars should appropriate terrorism research. Our argument is simple – terrorism is a type of social movement activity. And it should be analyzed as such.

To summarize our observations, we suggest that a social movement view of terrorism could do the following:

1. Redefine terrorism as one form of contentious politics, moving past the definitional debates of the field.
2. Analyze individual radicalization as a case of activist social network recruitment, biographical availability, and identity formation.
3. Consider terrorist propaganda and social media use through the lens of framing.
4. Place group-level radicalization within the wider context of political activity, including tactical innovation, protest cycles, and the repression-protest paradox.
5. Treat the lethality of terrorist groups and tactics as a product of organizational characteristics and repertoires of contention.
6. See organizational growth and diversification as a case of resource mobilization dynamics.
7. Emphasize the relational aspects of terrorist actors with other actors and the environment, including political opportunities and the terrorism strategic action field.

We view these suggestions merely as a starting point for a serious social movements exploration of terrorism. Yet the question remains, why would a social movements scholar want to take terrorism seriously? Of course, we could point to the lives lost and altered, the amount of public and government attention, the billions of dollars spent in its prevention, and so on, that all create terrorism as a pressing contemporary social problem. But we think a sustained study of terrorism is useful on purely intellectual grounds, as well.

Social movements researchers have long recognized that our field is potentially limited by its ideal-typical model of 1960s equality movements (McAdam et al. 2005). And some have lamented the lack of research outside of contemporary western democracies (Johnston 2006). In our view, terrorism provides a necessary antidote to these limitations and an opportunity. Terrorist groups are not mass-based movements that seek to influence elites and democratic governments on behalf of a marginalized population. In fact, activism in a truly repressive setting may often turn toward political violence. Many, and many of the most prominent, terrorist organizations develop in non-western settings. One of the solutions to the field's blind spots, then, should entail a focused consideration of terrorism.

Social movements scholar also need not fret about their ability to conduct empirical studies of terrorism. The extant toolkit of social movement studies already provides the necessary skills. We are skilled at analyzing large-scale event data, case studies, organizational dynamics, and undertaking content analysis.

In short, the continued relevance of terrorism in terms of attention, policy formation, and grant-making suggests that we should not miss this opportunity. Terrorists are activists. Terrorism is contention. It is time for social movements scholars to research and theorize accordingly.

References

Abadinsky, Howard. 1994. *Organized Crime*. New York: Nelson-Hall.

Abbott, Andrew. 2001. *Chaos of Disciplines*. Chicago: University of Chicago Press.

Abrahms, Max. 2008. "What Terrorists Really Want: Terrorist Motives and Counterterrorism Strategy." *International Security* 32(4): 78–105.

Alimi, Eitan Y., Chares Demetriou, and Lorenzo Bosi. 2015. *The Dynamics of Radicalization: A Relational and Comparative Perspective*. Oxford: Oxford University Press.

Arquilla, John and David Ronfeldt. 2001. "Networks and Netwars." Available at: https://www.rand.org/pubs/monograph_reports/MR1382.html (accessed April 10, 2017).

Asal, Victor, H. Brinton Milward, and Eric W. Schoon. 2015. "When Terrorists Go Bad: Analyzing Terrorist Organizations' Involvement in Drug Smuggling." *International Studies Quarterly* 59(1): 112–123.

Asal, Victor and Brian J. Phillips. 2015. "What Explains Ethnic Organizational Violence? Evidence from Eastern Europe and Russia." *Conflict Management and Peace Science* 738894215614504.

Asal, Victor and R. Karl Rethemeyer. 2008. "The Nature of the Beast: Organizational Structures and the Lethality of Terrorist Attacks." *The Journal of Politics* 70(2): 437–449.

Bakker, Edwin and Beatrice de Graaf. 2010. "Lone Wolves." Available at: http://www.icct.nl/download/file/ICCT-Bakker-deGraaf-EM-Paper-Lone-Wolves.pdf (accessed April 10, 2017).

Bakker, Edwin and Beatrice de Graaf. 2011. "Preventing Lone Wolf Terrorism: Some CT Approaches Addressed." *Perspectives on Terrorism* 5(5–6). Available at: http://www.terrorismanalysts.com/pt/index.php/pot/article/view/preventing-lone-wolf (accessed April 10, 2017).

Beck, Colin J. 2008. "The Contribution of Social Movement Theory to Understanding Terrorism." *Sociology Compass* 2(5): 1565–1581.

Beck, Colin J. 2009. "State Building as a Source of Islamic Political Organization." *Sociological Forum* 24(2): 337–356.

Beck, Colin J. 2015. *Radicals, Revolutionaries, and Terrorists*. Cambridge: Polity.

Beck, Colin J. and Emily Miner. 2013. "Who Gets Designated a Terrorist and Why?" *Social Forces* 91(3): 837–872.

Benford, Robert D. and David A. Snow. 2000. "Framing Processes and Social Movements: An Overview and Assessment." *Annual Review of Sociology* 26(1): 611–639.

Berman, Eli. 2009. *Radical, Religious, and Violent*. Cambridge, MA: MIT Press.

Berman, Eli and David D. Laitin. 2008. "Religion, Terrorism and Public Goods: Testing the Club Model." *Journal of Public Economics* 92(10): 1942–1967.

Bernstein, Mary. 1997. "Celebration and Supression: The Strategic Uses of Identity by the Lesbian and Gay Movement." *American Journal of Sociology* 103(3): 531–565.

Berntzen, Lars Erik and Sveinung Sandberg. 2014. "The Collective Nature of Lone Wolf Terrorism: Anders Behring Breivik and the Anti-Islamic Social Movement." *Terrorism and Political Violence* 26(5): 759–779.

Bloom, Mia. 2005. *Dying to Kill: The Allure of Suicide Terror*. New York: Columbia University Press.

Bosi, Lorenzo and Marco Giugni. 2012. "The Study of the Consequences of Armed Groups: Lessons from the Social Movement Literature." *Mobilization: An International Quarterly* 17(1): 85–98.

Burstein, Paul and April Linton. 2002. "The Impact of Political Parties, Interest Groups, and Social Movement Organizations on Public Policy: Some Recent Evidence and Theoretical Concerns." *Social Forces* 81(2): 380–408.

Carter, David B. 2016. "Provocation and the Strategy of Terrorist and Guerrilla Attacks." *International Organization* 70(1): 133–173.

Chenoweth, Erica. 2013. "Terrorism and Democracy." *Annual Review of Political Science* 16(1): 355–378.

Chou, Winston. 2015. "Seen Like a State: How Illegitimacy Shapes Terrorism Designation." *Social Forces* sov083.

Cilluffo, Frank. 2000. "The Threat Posed from the Convergence of Organized Crime, Drug Trafficking, and Terrorism." Testimony of the Deputy Director, Global Organized Crime Program, Director, Counterterrorism Task Force, Center for Strategic and International Studies, Washington (DC). to the US House Committee on the Judiciary Subcommittee on Crime. Available at: http://csis-prod.s3.amazonaws.com/s3fs-public/legacy_files/files/attachments/ts001213_cilluffo.pdf (accessed April 10, 2017).

Collier, Paul and Anke Hoeffler. 1998. "On Economic Causes of Civil War." *Oxford Economic Papers* 50(4): 563–573.

Crenshaw, Martha. 1981. "The Causes of Terrorism." *Comparative Politics* 13(4): 379–399.

Cronin, Audrey Kurth. 2009. *How Terrorism Ends: Understanding the Decline and Demise of Terrorist Campaigns*. Princeton, NJ: Princeton University Press.

Davis, Nancy J. and Robert V. Robinson. 2012. *Claiming Society for God: Religious Movements and Social Welfare*. Bloomington: Indiana University Press.

della Porta, Donatella. 1995. *Social Movements, Political Violence, and the State: A Comparative Analysis of Italy and Germany*. Cambridge: Cambridge University Press.

Dishman, Chris. 2005. "The Leaderless Nexus: When Crime and Terror Converge." *Studies in Conflict & Terrorism* 28(3): 237–252.

Eliasoph, Nina and Paul Lichterman. 2003. "Culture in Interaction." *American Journal of Sociology* 108(4): 735–794.

Enders, Walter and Todd Sandler. 2002. "Patterns of Transnational Terrorism, 1970–1999: Alternative Time-Series Estimates." *International Studies Quarterly* 46(2): 145–165.

Felbab-Brown, Vanda. 2010. *Shooting Up*. Washington, DC: Brookings Institution Press. Available at: https://www.brookings.edu/book/shooting-up/ (accessed April 10, 2017).

Findley, Michael G. and Joseph K. Young. 2015. "Terrorism, Spoiling, and the Resolution of Civil Wars." *The Journal of Politics* 77(4): 1115–1128.

Fligstein, Neil and Doug McAdam. 2012. *A Theory of Fields*. Oxford: Oxford University Press.

Gambetta, Diego. 1996. *The Sicilian Mafia: The Business of Private Protection*. Cambridge. MA: Harvard University Press.

Ganz, Marshall. 2000. "Resources and Resourcefulness: Strategic Capacity in the Unionization of California Agriculture, 1959–1966." *American Journal of Sociology* 105(4): 1003–1062.

Gibbs, Jack P. 1989. "Conceptualization of Terrorism." *American Sociological Review* 54(3): 329–340.

Goodwin, Jeff. 2001. *No Other Way Out: States and Revolutionary Movements, 1945–1991*. New York: Cambridge University Press.

Goodwin, Jeff. 2006. "A Theory of Categorical Terrorism." *Social Forces* 84(4): 2027–2046.

Greenland, Fiona, James V. Marrone, Oya Topcuoglu, and Tasha Vorderstrasse. 2016. *Evaluating the Illicit Antiquities Trade*. Chicago: University of Chicago.

Gruenewald, Jeff, Steven Chermak, and Joshua D. Freilich. 2013. "Distinguishing 'Loner' Attacks from Other Domestic Extremist Violence." *Criminology & Public Policy* 12(1): 65–91.

Gunning, Jeroen. 2009. "Social Movement Theory and the Study of Terrorism." *Critical Terrorism Studies: A New Research Agenda*. Available at: http://www.academia.edu/5109117/Social_Movement_Theory_and_the_Study_of_Terrorism

Hejnova, Petra. 2010. "Beyond Dark and Bright: Towards a More Holistic Understanding of Inter-Group Networks." *Public Administration* 88(3): 741–763.

Hoffman, Bruce. 1998. *Inside Terrorism*. New York: Columbia University Press.

Hutchinson, Steven and Pat O'Malley. 2007. "A Crime–Terror Nexus? Thinking on Some of the Links between Terrorism and Criminality." *Studies in Conflict & Terrorism* 30(12): 1095–1107.

Jasper, James M. 1997. *The Art of Moral Protest: Culture, Biography, and Creativity in Social Movements*. Chicago: University of Chicago Press.

Johnston, Hank. 2006. "'Let's Get Small': The Dynamics of (Small) Contention in Repressive States." *Mobilization: An International Journal* 11(2): 195–212.

Juergensmeyer, Mark. 2001. *Terror in the Mind of God: The Global Rise of Religious Violence*. Berkeley: University of California Press.

Kalyvas, Stathis N. 2004. "The Paradox of Terrorism in Civil War." *The Journal of Ethics* 8(1): 97–138.

King, Brayden G. 2008. "A Political Mediation Model of Corporate Response to Social Movement Activism." *Administrative Science Quarterly* 53(3): 395 421.

Krueger, Alan B. and Jitka Maleckova. 2003. "Education, Poverty and Terrorism: Is There a Causal Connection?" *Journal of Economic Perspectives* 17(4): 119–144.

Kurzman, Charles. 2011. *The Missing Martyrs: Why There Are So Few Muslim Terrorists*. New York: Oxford University Press.

Kydd, Andrew H. and Barbara F. Walter. 2006. "The Strategies of Terrorism." *International Security* 31(1): 49–80.

Lewis, Kevin, Kurt Gray, and Jens Meierhenrich. 2014. "The Structure of Online Activism." *Sociological Science* 1: 1–9.

Lichterman, Paul and Nina Eliasoph. 2014. "Civic Action." *American Journal of Sociology* 120(3): 798–863.

Lizardo, Omar. 2008. "Defining and Theorizing Terrorism: A Global Actor-Centered Approach." *Journal of World-Systems Research* 14(2): 91.

Makarenko, Tamara. 2004. "The Crime-Terror Continuum: Tracing the Interplay between Transnational Organised Crime and Terrorism." *Global Crime* 6(1): 129–145.

Mampilly, Zachariah Cherian. 2011. *Rebel Rulers: Insurgent Governance and Civilian Life during War*. Ithaca, NY: Cornell University Press.

Marcus, Aliza. 2007. *Blood and Belief*. New York: New York University Press.

Martin, Andrew W., John D. McCarthy, and Clark McPhail. 2009. "Why Targets Matter: Toward a More Inclusive Model of Collective Violence." *American Sociological Review* 74(5): 821–841.

McAdam, Doug. 1983. "Tactical Innovation and the Pace of Insurgency." *American Sociological Review* 48(6): 735–754.

McAdam, Doug. 1988. *Freedom Summer*. New York: Oxford University Press.

McAdam, Doug. 1995. "'Initiator' and 'Spin-Off' Movements: Diffusion Processes in Protest Cycles." In *Repertoires and Cycles of Collective Action*, edited by Mark Traugott, 217–239. Durham, NC: Duke University Press.

McAdam, Doug, Robert J. Sampson, Simon Weffer, and Heather MacIndoe. 2005. "'There Will Be Fighting in the Streets': The Distorting Lens of Social Movement Theory." *Mobilization: An International Quarterly* 10(1): 1–18.

McAdam, Doug, Sidney Tarrow, and Charles Tilly. 2001. *Dynamics of Contention*. New York: Cambridge University Press.

McCarthy, John D. and Mayer N. Zald. 1977. "Resource Mobilization and Social Movements: A Partial Theory." *The American Journal of Sociology* 82(6): 1212–1241.

Metz, Steven. 1993. *The Future of Insurgency*. Carlisle, PA: Strategic Studies Institute, US Army War College.

Moaddel, Mansoor. 2002. *Jordanian Exceptionalism: A Comparative Analysis of State-Religion Relationships in Egypt, Iran, Jordan, and Syria*. Basingstoke: Palgrave Macmillan.

Morselli, Carlo, Cynthia Giguère, and Katia Petit. 2007. "The Efficiency/Security Trade-off in Criminal Networks." *Social Networks* 29(1): 143–153.

Moskalenko, Sophia and Clark McCauley. 2011. "The Psychology of Lone-Wolf Terrorism." *Counselling Psychology Quarterly* 24(2): 115–126.

Munson, Ziad W. 2010. *The Making of Pro-Life Activists: How Social Movement Mobilization Works*. Chicago: University of Chicago Press.

Olzak, Susan. 2016. "The Effect of Category Spanning on the Lethality and Longevity of Terrorist Organizations." *Social Forces* 95(2): 559–584.

Pape, Robert A. 2005. *Dying to Win: The Strategic Logic of Suicide Terrorism*. New York: Random House.

Perry, Nicholas J. 2003. "The Numerous Federal Legal Definitions of Terrorism: The Problem of Too Many Grails." *Journal of Legislation* 30: 249–274.

Phillips, Brian J. 2015. "Deadlier in the U.S.? On Lone Wolves, Terrorist Groups, and Attack Lethality." *Terrorism and Political Violence*. Available at: https://ssrn.com/abstract=2608771

Piazza, James A. 2006. "Rooted in Poverty: Terrorism, Poor Economic Development, and Social Cleavages." *Terrorism and Political Violence* 18: 159–177.

Piazza, James A. 2009. "Is Islamist Terrorism More Dangerous?: An Empirical Study of Group Ideology, Organization, and Goal Structure." *Terrorism and Political Violence* 21(1): 62–88.

Polletta, Francesca. 1998. "'It Was like a Fever...' Narrative and Identity in Social Protest." *Social Problems* 45(2): 137–159.

Raab, Jörg and H.Brinton Milward. 2003. "Dark Networks as Problems." *Journal of Public Administration Research and Theory* 13(4): 413–439.

Sandler, Todd. 2014. "The Analytical Study of Terrorism: Taking Stock." *Journal of Peace Research* 51(2): 257–271.

Schmid, Alex Peter and Albert J. Jongman. 1988. *Political Terrorism: A New Guide to Actors, Authors, Concepts, Data Bases, Theories and Literature*. Amsterdam: North-Holland Publishing Company.

Schoon, Eric W. 2014. "The Asymmetry of Legitimacy: Analyzing the Legitimation of Violence in 30 Cases of Insurgent Revolution." *Social Forces* 93(2): 779–801.

Schoon, Eric W. 2015. "The Paradox of Legitimacy: Resilience, Successes, and the Multiple Identities of the Kurdistan Workers' Party in Turkey." *Social Problems* 62(2): 266–285.

Schwedler, Jillian. 2006. *Faith in Moderation: Islamist Parties in Jordan and Yemen*. New York: Cambridge University Press.

Shellman, Stephen M., Brian P. Levey, and Joseph K. Young. 2013. "Shifting Sands Explaining and Predicting Phase Shifts by Dissident Organizations." *Journal of Peace Research* 50(3): 319–336.

Simon, Herbert A. 1991. "Bounded Rationality and Organizational Learning." *Organization Science* 2(1): 125–134.

Snow, David A. and Scott C. Byrd. 2007. "Ideology, Framing Processes, and Islamic Terrorist Movements." *Mobilization: An International Journal* 12(2): 119–136.

Snow, David A., Louis A. Zurcher, Jr., and Sheldon Ekland-Olson. 1980. "Social Networks and Social Movements: A Microstructural Approach to Differential Recruitment." *American Sociological Review* 45(5): 787–801.

Snow, Donald M. 1996. *Uncivil Wars: International Security and the New Internal Conflicts*. Boulder, CO: Lynne Rienner Publishers.

Spaaij, Ramón. 2010. "The Enigma of Lone Wolf Terrorism: An Assessment." *Studies in Conflict & Terrorism* 33(9): 854–870.

Staggenborg, Suzanne. 1988. "The Consequences of Professionalization and Formalization in the Pro-Choice Movement." *American Sociological Review* 53(4): 585–605.

Starrett, Gregory. 1998. *Putting Islam to Work: Education, Politics, and Religious Transformation in Egypt*. Berkeley: University of California Press.

Tarrow, Sidney G. 1989. *Democracy and Disorder: Protest and Politics in Italy, 1965– 1975*. New York: Oxford University Press.

Taylor, Verta. 1989. "Social Movement Continuity: The Women's Movement in Abeyance." *American Sociological Review* 54(5): 761–775.

Tilly, Charles. 2004. "Terror, Terrorism, Terrorists." *Sociological Theory* 22(1): 5–13.

Valentino, Benjamin A. 2014. "Why We Kill: The Political Science of Political Violence against Civilians." *Annual Review of Political Science* 17(1): 89–103.

Wang, Peng. 2010. "The Crime-Terror Nexus: Transformation, Alliance, Convergence." *Asian Social Science* 6(6): 11.

Wickham, Carrie Rosefsky. 2002. *Mobilizing Islam: Religion, Activism, and Political Change in Egypt*. New York: Columbia University Press.

Wiktorowicz, Quintan, ed. 2004. *Islamic Activism: A Social Movement Theory Approach*. Bloomington: Indiana University Press.

Wiktorowicz, Quintan. 2005. *Radical Islam Rising: Muslim Extremism in the West*. Lanham, MD: Rowman & Littlefield Publishers.

Williams, Phil and Vanda Felbab-Brown. 2012. *Drug Trafficking, Violence, and Instability*. DTIC Document. Available at: http://oai.dtic.mil/oai/oai?verb=getRecord&metadataPrefix= html&identifier=ADA560718 (accessed April 10, 2017).

Young, Joseph K. and Michael G. Findley. 2011. "Promise and Pitfalls of Terrorism Research." *International Studies Review* 13(3): 411–431.

Zald, Mayer N. and John D. McCarthy. 1980. "Social Movement Industries: Competition and Cooperation among Movement Organizations." Available at: https://deepblue.lib.umich. edu/handle/2027.42/50975 (accessed April 3, 2017).

Index

References to Notes contain the letter 'n', followed by the number of the note.

The Wiley Blackwell Companion to Social Movements, Second Edition. Edited by David A. Snow,
Sarah A. Soule, Hanspeter Kriesi, and Holly J. McCammon.
© 2019 John Wiley & Sons Ltd. Published 2019 by John Wiley & Sons Ltd.